Middle East

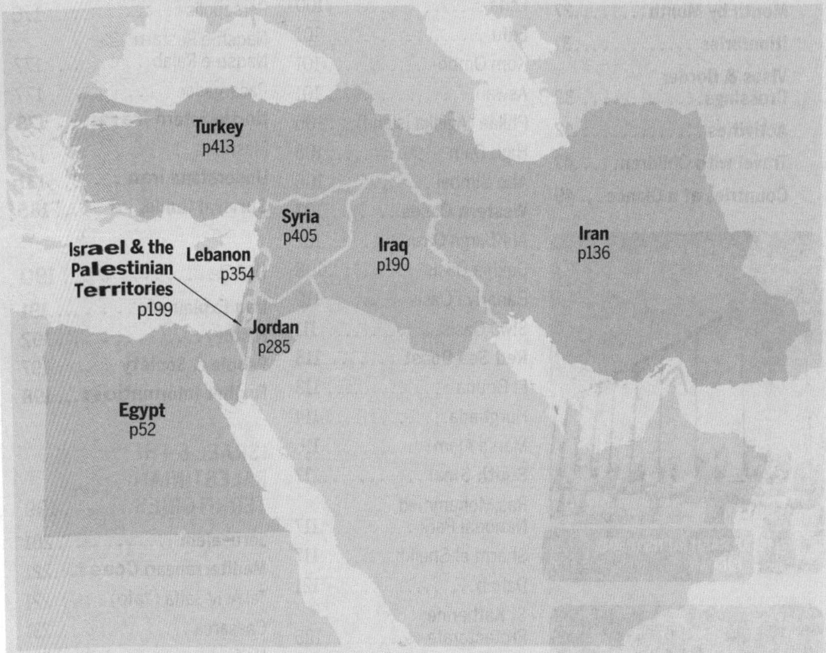

Anthony Ham, Paul Clammer, Orlando Crowcroft, Mark Elliott, Anita Isalska, Jessica Lee, Virginia Maxwell, Simon Richmond, Daniel Robinson, Anthony Sattin, Dan Savery Raz, Andy Symington, Jenny Walker, Steve Waters

PLAN YOUR TRIP

Welcome to the Middle East 6
Middle East Map....8
The Middle East's Top 21....10
Need to Know 20
What's New 22
If You Like... 23
Month by Month....27
Itineraries 31
Visas & Border Crossings.... 38
Activities 42
Travel with Children....47
Countries at a Glance...49

LKPRO/SHUTTERSTOCK ©

JERASH RUINS (P301), JORDAN

KYLIE NICHOLSON/SHUTTERSTOCK ©

ST KATHERINE'S MONASTERY (P125), EGYPT

ON THE ROAD

EGYPT.... 52
Cairo.... 53
Saqqara, Memphis & Dahshur 77
Mediterranean Coast... 80
Alexandria 80
Nile Valley 86
Luxor 86
Esna 100
Edfu 101
Kom Ombo 101
Aswan.... 101
Philae (Agilika Island)....106
High Dam....106
Abu Simbel 106
Western Oases 107
Al Kharga Oasis 107
Dakhla Oasis....108
Bahariya Oasis 110
Siwa Oasis....111
Red Sea Coast 113
El Gouna 113
Hurghada.... 114
Marsa Alam.... 116
South Sinai 117
Ras Mohammed National Park 117
Sharm el-Sheikh....117
Dahab.... 121
St Katherine Protectorate 125
Nuweiba.... 125
Taba 128
Understand Egypt 129
Survival Guide....131

IRAN.... 136
Tehran.... 137
Western Iran 149
Tabriz 149
Kandovan....153
Qazvin 153
Alamut Valley 155
Central Iran.... 156
Kashan....156
Esfahan 158
Yazd 164
Shiraz.... 170
Persepolis 175
Naqsh-e Rostam & Naqsh-e Rajab 177
Pasargadae 177
Northeastern Iran.... 178
Mashhad 178
Understand Iran 181
Survival Guide.... 185

IRAQ 190
Iraq Explained....191
History 192
People & Society 197
Further Information... 198

ISRAEL & THE PALESTINIAN TERRITORIES 199
Jerusalem 201
Mediterranean Coast...221
Tel Aviv-Jaffa (Yafo) 221
Caesarea 231
Haifa.... 231
Akko 236
Lower Galilee & Sea of Galilee 238
Nazareth 238
Tiberias 240
Sea of Galilee 242
Beit She'an 243
Upper Galilee & Golan Heights....244

Contents

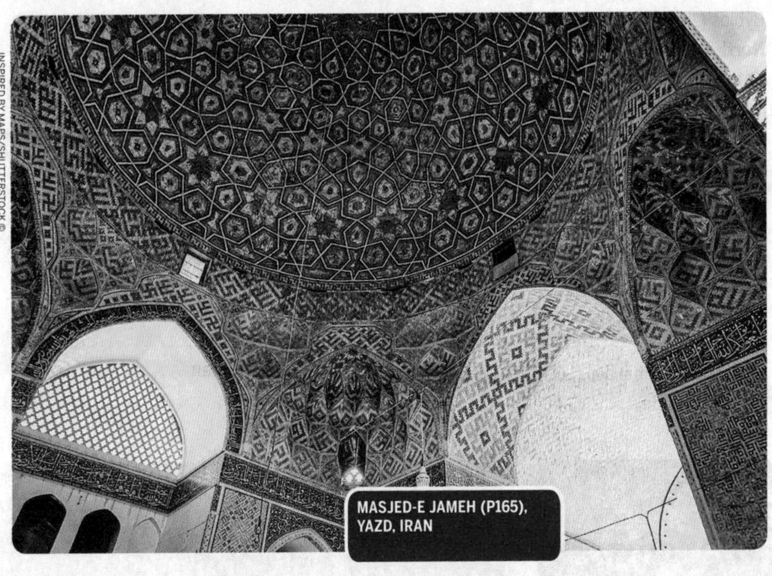
INSPIRED BY MAPS/SHUTTERSTOCK ©

MASJED-E JAMEH (P165), YAZD, IRAN

Tsfat (Safed) 244
Golan Heights 247
Dead Sea 249
Ein Gedi 249
Masada 250
Ein Bokek 251
The Negev 251
Mitzpe Ramon 251
Eilat 252
West Bank 256
Ramallah 256
Jericho & Around 259
Bethlehem 261
Nablus 264
Jenin 265
Gaza Strip 266
Understand Israel & the Palestinian Territories 267
Survival Guide 275

JORDAN 285

Amman 288
Jerash & the North 300
Jerash 301
Ajloun 304
Ajloun Forest Reserve 305
Irbid 306
Umm Qais (Gadara) 306
Dead Sea & the West 307
Bethany-Beyond-the-Jordan (Al-Maghtas) 307
Dead Sea 308
Mujib Biosphere Reserve 310
Azraq & the East 310
Hallabat 310
Azraq 311
Around Azraq 312
Madaba & the King's Highway 313
Madaba 313
Mt Nebo 316
Machaerus (Mukawir) 316
Karak 317
Tafila 318
Dana Biosphere Reserve 318
Shobak 320
Petra & the South 320
Petra & Wadi Musa 320
Wadi Rum 333
Aqaba 337
Understand Jordan 343
Survival Guide 347

LEBANON 354

Beirut 356
Central Lebanon 372
Jeita Grotto 372

ON THE ROAD

Byblos (Jbail) 373
North Lebanon 375
Batroun 375
Tripoli (Trablous) 377
The Qadisha Valley...... 380
South Lebanon 382
Sidon (Saida) 382
Tyre (Sour) 385
Chouf Mountains 387
Deir Al Qamar 388
Bekaa Valley 389
Baalbek 390
Understand Lebanon... 392
Survival Guide........ 401

SYRIA............. 405
Syria Explained....... 406
History 407
People & Society 410
Further Information... 412

TURKEY 413
İstanbul 416
Aegean Coast 436
Çanakkale 436
Troy................. 440
Eceabat 440
Gallipoli Peninsula 441
Bursa 442
Bergama (Pergamum)... 443
İzmır 444
Selçuk................ 446
Ephesus 449
Kuşadası 451
Pamukkale.............. 452
Bodrum Town 453
Marmaris 456
Mediterranean Coast 458
Fethiye 458
Patara................ 460
Kalkan 461
Kaş 461

ANTON BELO/SHUTTERSTOCK ©
GIZA (P60), EGYPT

COZY NOOK/SHUTTERSTOCK ©
DEAD SEA (P308), JORDAN

S-F/SHUTTERSTOCK ©
CAPPADOCIA (P475), TURKEY

Contents

Olympos & Çıralı 463
Antalya. 463
Side. 467
Alanya 468
Central Anatolia 469
Ankara 469
Safranbolu. 472
Konya 473
Cappadocia 475
Göreme 476
Avanos 478
Ürgüp 478
Kayseri 479
Black Sea Coast & Northeastern Anatolia 480
Trabzon. 480
Erzurum 482
Kars 484
Doğubayazıt 485
Understand Turkey 486
Survival Guide. 488

UNDERSTAND

The Middle East Today 494
History 496
Religion 526
Architecture 531
Middle Eastern Cuisine 536
The Arts 543
Landscape & Environment 552

SURVIVAL GUIDE

Traveller Etiquette 558
Safe Travel 560
Women Travellers 562
Directory A–Z 564
Transport 571
Health 577
Language 582
Index 594
Map Legend 605

SPECIAL FEATURES

The Pyramids of Giza . . . 62
Luxor's West Bank 92
St Katherine's Monastery 126
Temple Mount/ Al Haram Ash Sharif . . . 210
Petra 322
Aya Sofya. 418
Topkapı Palace 424

Welcome to the Middle East

The Middle East is a grand epic, a cradle of civilisations and a beautiful, complicated land that's home to some of the planet's most hospitable people.

History Writ Large

In the Middle East, history is not something you read about in books. Here, it's a story written on the stones that litter the region, from the flagstones of old Roman roads to the building blocks of Ancient Egypt, and the delicately carved tombs and temples from Petra to Persepolis. This is where humankind first built cities and learned to write, and it was from here that Judaism, Christianity and Islam all arose. Wherever you find yourself, the past is always present because here, perhaps more than anywhere else on earth, history is the heart and soul of the land.

Home of Hospitality

At some point on your visit to the Middle East, you'll be sitting in a coffeehouse or looking lost in a labyrinth of narrow lanes when someone will strike up a conversation and, within minutes, invite you home to meet their family and share a meal. Or someone will simply approach and say with unmistakable warmth, 'Welcome'. These spontaneous, disarming and utterly genuine words of welcome can occur anywhere across the region. And when they do, they can suddenly (and forever) change the way you see the Middle East.

Cities

The Middle East's cities read like a roll-call of historical heavyweights: Jerusalem, Beirut, Cairo, İstanbul, Esfahan... Aside from ranking among the oldest continuously inhabited cities on earth, these ancient-modern metropolises are places to take the pulse of a region. It is in the Middle East's cities, too, that you find the stirring, aspirational architecture that so distinguishes the three great monotheistic faiths. There they sit alongside the more secular charms of bazaars and coffee shops that seem to embody all the mystery and storytelling magic of a land that gave us *The Thousand and One Nights.*

Wilderness

Beyond city limits, the Middle East is a land of mighty rivers (the Nile, Euphrates), even mightier deserts (the Sahara and peerless Wadi Rum) and green landscapes of exceptional beauty. Exploring these wilderness areas – from snow-capped summits in Turkey, Iran and Lebanon to the kaleidoscopic waters of the Red Sea – lies at the heart of the region's appeal. The message is simple: forget the clichés that masquerade as Middle Eastern truth – a visit here is one of the most varied and soulful travel experiences on earth.

JOHN WALKER/SHUTTERSTOCK ©

Why I Love the Middle East

By Anthony Ham, Writer

I first fell for the Middle East in Damascus. Here was a city of storytellers, of warm and welcoming people, of history brought alive at every turn. Ten years later (a decade in which I had marvelled at the peerless beauty of Esfahan and struck out into the Sahara at Siwa, among many Middle Eastern journeys), I returned to Damascus and fell in love all over again. War has since engulfed the country, but Damascus, and the Middle East, has seen it all before. And nowhere else on earth have I encountered such warmth from ordinary people.

For more about our writers, see p608

Above: Petra's Siq (p321), Jordan

Middle East

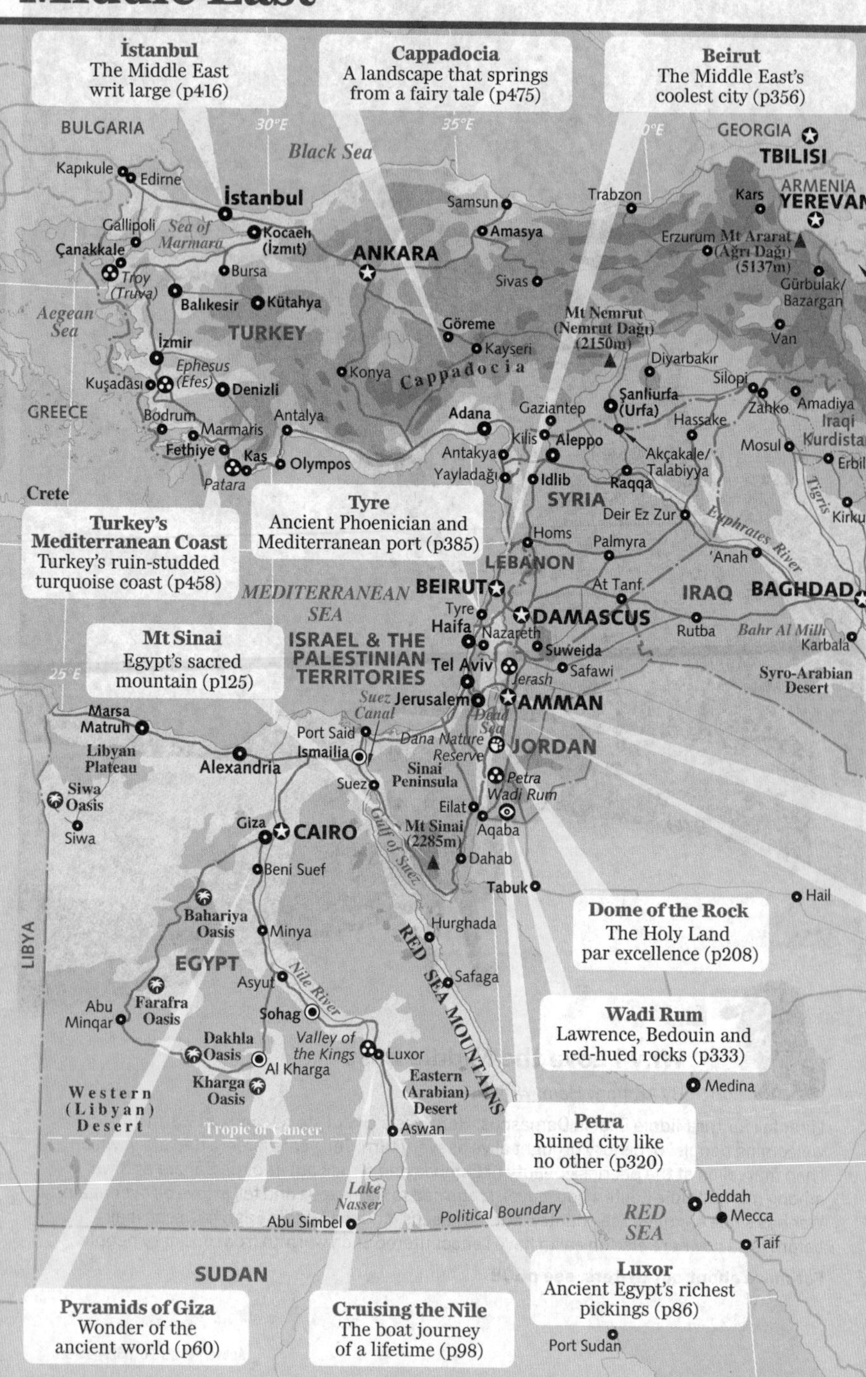

İstanbul
The Middle East writ large (p416)
Cappadocia
A landscape that springs from a fairy tale (p475)
Beirut
The Middle East's coolest city (p356)
Turkey's Mediterranean Coast
Turkey's ruin-studded turquoise coast (p458)
Tyre
Ancient Phoenician and Mediterranean port (p385)
Mt Sinai
Egypt's sacred mountain (p125)
Dome of the Rock
The Holy Land par excellence (p208)
Wadi Rum
Lawrence, Bedouin and red-hued rocks (p333)
Petra
Ruined city like no other (p320)
Luxor
Ancient Egypt's richest pickings (p86)
Pyramids of Giza
Wonder of the ancient world (p60)
Cruising the Nile
The boat journey of a lifetime (p98)
BULGARIA
GEORGIA
TBILISI
ARMENIA
YEREVAN
Black Sea
Kapıkule
Edirne
İstanbul
Kocaeli (İzmit)
Gallipoli
Sea of Marmara
Çanakkale
Troy (Truva)
Bursa
ANKARA
Samsun
Amasya
Trabzon
Kars
Erzurum
Mt Ararat (Ağrı Dağı) (5137m)
Gürbulak/Bazargan
Sivas
Balıkesir
Kütahya
Aegean Sea
TURKEY
İzmir
Ephesus (Efes)
Kuşadası
Denizli
Göreme
Kayseri
Konya
Cappadocia
Mt Nemrut (Nemrut Dağı) (2150m)
Van
Diyarbakır
Silopi
Zahko
Amadiya
Iraqi Kurdistan
GREECE
Bodrum
Marmaris
Antalya
Fethiye
Kaş
Patara
Olympos
Adana
Gaziantep
Şanlıurfa (Urfa)
Hassake
Kilis
Aleppo
Antakya
Yayladağı
Idlib
Akçakale/Talabiyya
Raqqa
Mosul
Erbil
Crete
SYRIA
Deir Ez Zur
Euphrates River
Tigris
Kirkuk
Homs
Palmyra
'Anah
LEBANON
BEIRUT
At Tanf
IRAQ
BAGHDAD
MEDITERRANEAN SEA
Tyre
Haifa
Nazareth
DAMASCUS
Rutba
Bahr Al Milh
Karbala
ISRAEL & THE PALESTINIAN TERRITORIES
Suweida
Tel Aviv
Safawi
Jerash
Syro-Arabian Desert
Jerusalem
AMMAN
Suez Canal
Dead Sea
Marsa Matruh
Port Said
Dana Nature Reserve
JORDAN
Libyan Plateau
Alexandria
Ismailia
Sinai Peninsula
Siwa Oasis
Suez
Petra
Wadi Rum
Eilat
Aqaba
Siwa
Giza
CAIRO
Gulf of Suez
Mt Sinai (2285m)
Dahab
Beni Suef
Tabuk
Hail
Bahariya Oasis
Minya
Hurghada
LIBYA
EGYPT
RED SEA MOUNTAINS
Safaga
Asyut
Nile River
Abu Minqar
Farafra Oasis
Sohag
Dakhla Oasis
Valley of the Kings
Luxor
Al Kharga
Medina
Kharga Oasis
Eastern (Arabian) Desert
Western (Libyan) Desert
Tropic of Cancer
Aswan
Lake Nasser
Political Boundary
Abu Simbel
Jeddah
Mecca
RED SEA
Taif
SUDAN
Port Sudan
30°E
35°E
40°E
25°E

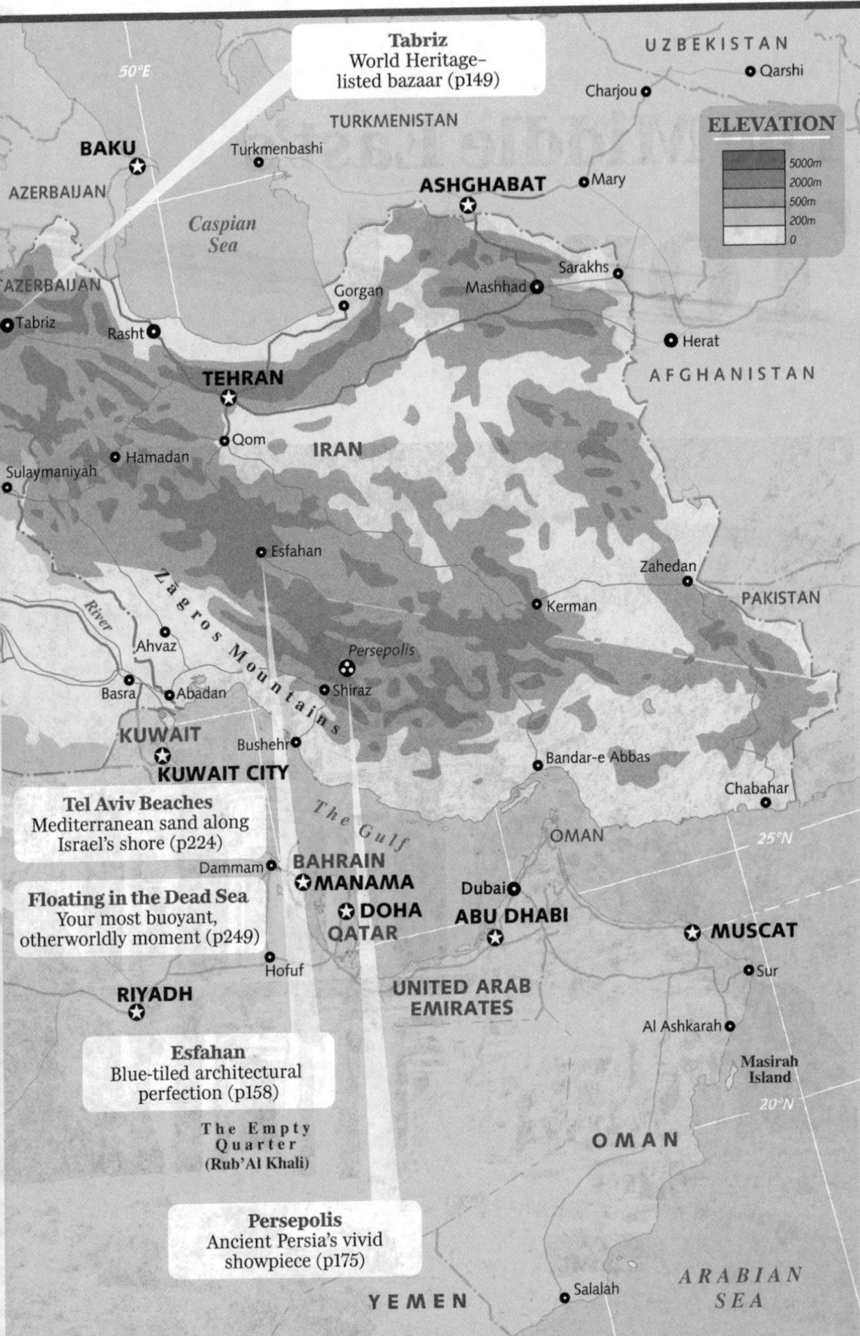
0 300 km
0 180 miles
Tabriz
World Heritage-listed bazaar (p149)
UZBEKISTAN
Qarshi
Charjou
TURKMENISTAN
ELEVATION
5000m
2000m
500m
200m
0
50°E
BAKU
Turkmenbashi
AZERBAIJAN
ASHGHABAT
Mary
Caspian Sea
Sarakhs
AZERBAIJAN
Gorgan
Mashhad
Tabriz
Rasht
Herat
TEHRAN
AFGHANISTAN
Qom
Hamadan
IRAN
Sulaymaniyah
Esfahan
Zahedan
Zagros Mountains
River
Kerman
PAKISTAN
Ahvaz
Persepolis
Basra
Abadan
Shiraz
KUWAIT
Bushehr
KUWAIT CITY
Bandar-e Abbas
Chabahar
Tel Aviv Beaches
Mediterranean sand along Israel's shore (p224)
The Gulf
OMAN
25°N
Dammam
BAHRAIN
MANAMA
Dubai
Floating in the Dead Sea
Your most buoyant, otherworldly moment (p249)
DOHA
ABU DHABI
QATAR
MUSCAT
Hofuf
Sur
UNITED ARAB EMIRATES
RIYADH
Al Ashkarah
Esfahan
Blue-tiled architectural perfection (p158)
Masirah Island
20°N
The Empty Quarter
(Rub'Al Khali)
OMAN
Persepolis
Ancient Persia's vivid showpiece (p175)
ARABIAN SEA
Salalah
YEMEN
15°N

The Middle East's Top 21

Petra, Jordan

1 The ancient Nabataean city of Petra (p320) is one of the Middle East's most treasured attractions, and it's a place utterly unlike anywhere else on earth. Entering through the impossibly narrow canyon feels like discovering a hidden treasure, and when the sun sets over the honeycombed landscape of tombs, carved facades and pillars all hewn from the rose-red sandstone cliffs, it's a hard-hearted visitor who's left unaffected by its magic. Allow a couple of days to do the site justice and to visit the main monuments at optimum times of the day. Below left: Monastery (p326)

Pyramids of Giza, Egypt

2 Towering over both the urban sprawl of Cairo and the desert plains beyond, the Pyramids of Giza (p60) and the Sphinx are at the top of every traveller's itinerary. Yes, you'll have to fend off hordes of people pushing horse rides and Bedouin headdresses to enjoy this ancient funerary complex, but your persistence will be rewarded with one of the region's signature experiences – no trip to Egypt is complete without a photo of you in front of the last surviving ancient wonder of the world. Below: Sphinx (p61)

TENKL/SHUTTERSTOCK ©

2

ANTON BELO/SHUTTERSTOCK ©

3

BIBIANA CASTAGNA/SHUTTERSTOCK ©

4

EFESENKO/SHUTTERSTOCK ©

Dome of the Rock, Israel & the Palestinian Territories

3 Few places on earth excite emotions to quite the same extent as Jerusalem's Dome of the Rock (p208), a gold-plated mosque of singular beauty. Sacred to Muslims, Jews and Christians alike – it was said to be here that Abraham showed his readiness to sacrifice his son to God, and from here that Mohammed ascended to heaven – it's an epicentre of religious convergence and conflict. But after a visit, it's usually the unmistakable spiritual dimension that lives longest in the memory.

Esfahan, Iran

4 There are few more beautiful places on the planet than Esfahan's (p158) bejewelled core. The city's blue-tiled mosques, intricate and exquisite, share the city centre with refined pleasure palaces and elegant arched bridges, all within sight of expansive gardens, tree-lined boulevards and a central square that brims with life. Tea houses, hidden away beneath the arches and throughout the splendid bazaar, are another wonderful entry point into this most beguiling of cities. It's easily Iran's most beautiful urban core, and possibly one of the most beautiful on earth.

Cruising the Nile, Egypt

5 The Nile is Egypt's lifeline, an artery that feeds the entire country, from south to north. Only by setting adrift on it can you appreciate its importance and its beauty, and more practically, only by boat, preferably a wind-propelled felucca (p106), can you see some archaeological sites as they were meant to be seen – from the waters of the Nile. Sailing is the slowest and most relaxing way to go, but even from the deck of a multistorey floating hotel, you'll still glimpse the magic.

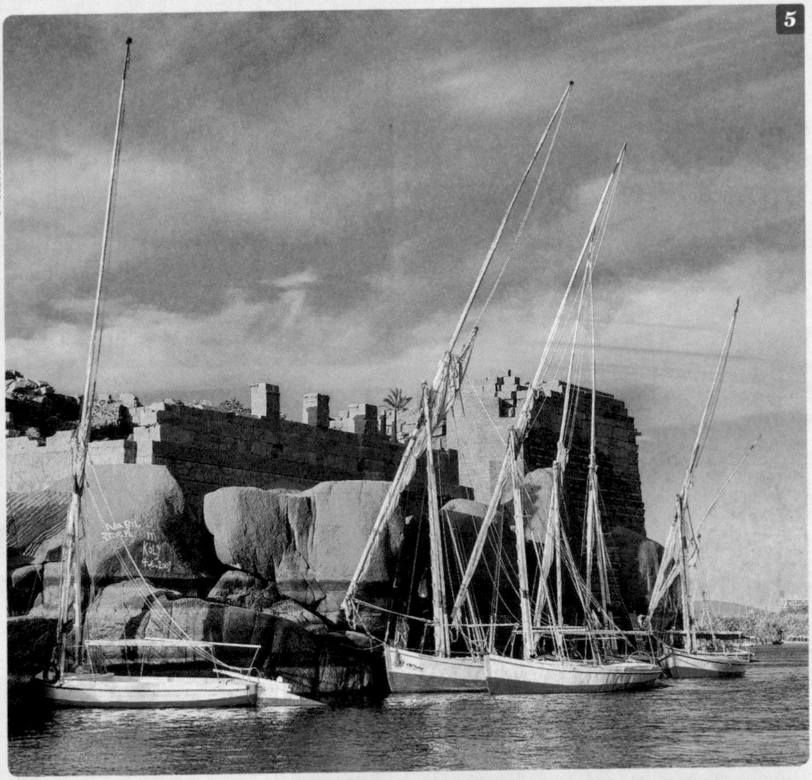

5

Wadi Rum, Jordan

6 It wasn't just the sublime vista of Wadi Rum (p333) – with its burnished sandstone cliffs and fire-coloured dunes – that impressed Lawrence of Arabia as he rode on camel-back through the land of the Bedouin. He was also impressed by the stoicism of the people who endured unimaginable hardships associated with a life in the desert. Today, it's possible to get a glimpse of that traditional way of life, albeit with a few more creature comforts, by staying in one of the Bedouin camps scattered across this glorious desert wilderness.

6

ENRICO LUZI/SHUTTERSTOCK ©

EFESENKO/SHUTTERSTOCK ©

DIEGO FIORE/SHUTTERSTOCK ©

Cappadocia, Turkey

7 Cappadocia (p475) was Mother Nature in her surrealism phase. This lunarscape of wacky rock, sculpted by wind and rain, could have been ripped right off the pages of a geological fantasy. Humans have also left their mark, honeycombing the hillsides with cave dwellings and underground cities, and hollowing out Byzantine churches decorated with vibrant frescoes. Today troglodyte living has been shaken up for the 21st century with hot-air ballooning from above, trail-hiking on the ground and seriously cool cave hotels down below.

Persepolis, Iran

8 The Middle East may be strewn with landmarks left by the ancients, but few carry the raw, emotional power of Persepolis (p175). It's the combination of scale (monumental staircases dominate), detail (the bas-reliefs are extraordinary) and setting (the site rises from the sands against a backdrop of pretty hills) that gives this Unesco site its appeal. Begun by Darius the Great at the height of the Achaemenid Empire's powers in the 6th century BC, it's one of the region's most memorable ruined cities. Top right: Apadana Palace (p175)

Beirut, Lebanon

9 Few cities have the cachet of Beirut (p356), and few have fought so hard for it. Battle-scarred yet ever-buoyant, the city rises magnificently to the challenge of balancing the cultures of the West and the Middle East. Beirut is both the sophisticated and hedonistic place that once partied under the sobriquet of the 'Paris of the Middle East', and a demographically diverse city that's rife with contrasts. Never is this more true than at sunset along the waterfront Corniche, where mini-skirted rollerbladers dodge conservative Shiite families enjoying a cool sea breeze.

İstanbul, Turkey

10 In İstanbul (p416), you can board a commuter ferry to flit between continents and be rewarded at sunset with the city's most magical sight, when the tapering minarets of the Old City are thrown into relief against a dusky pink sky. Elsewhere, history resonates with profound force amid the Ottoman and Byzantine glories of the Blue Mosque, Aya Sofya and Topkapı Palace. Such is İstanbul, a collision of continents and a glorious accumulation of civilisations. Little wonder, then, that locals call their city the greatest in the world.
Below: Süleymaniye Mosque (p417)

Luxor, Egypt

11 With the greatest concentration of ancient Egyptian monuments anywhere in Egypt, Luxor (p86) repays time. You can spend days or weeks around this town, walking through the columned halls of the great temples on the east bank of the Nile, such as the Ramesseum, or climbing down into the tombs of pharaohs in the Valley of the Kings on the west bank. Just watching the sun rise over the Nile or set behind the Theban hills are two of Egypt's most unforgettable moments.

10

11

Mediterranean Coast, Turkey

12 Long before the beachgoers discovered Turkey's Mediterranean coast (p458), the Empire builders descended in their droves, leaving the remnants of once-grand cities in their wake. Backed by rugged cliffs that tumble down to a turquoise sea, this famed sun-and-sand destination is a whole lot more than its resorts. Quaint villages snuggle into hillsides, ruins lay scattered across craggy mountain slopes and, down below where the thick forest meets the shore, those white strips of beach beckon all who visit.

Mt Sinai, Egypt

13 It may not be the highest of Sinai's craggy peaks, but Mt Sinai (p125) is the peninsula's most sacred. A place of pilgrimage for Jews, Christians and Muslims alike, the summit affords the magnificent spectacle of light washing over the sea of surrounding mountaintops. Down below, tucked into the mountain's base, is St Katherine's Monastery. Its sturdy Byzantine fortifications are built over the spot where Moses is believed to have witnessed the burning bush. Watching the sunrise from the summit is one of life's great travel moments. Bottom: St Katherine's Monastery (p125)

12

COLORMAKER/SHUTTERSTOCK ©

13

KYLIE NICHOLSON/SHUTTERSTOCK ©

ASHER DAVIDSON/SHUTTERSTOCK ©

KVITKA FABIAN/SHUTTERSTOCK ©

DMYTRO SURKOV/SHUTTERSTOCK ©

Red Sea Diving, Egypt

14 Egypt's Red Sea coastlines (p113) are the doorstep to a wonderland that hides below the surface. Whether you're a seasoned diving pro or a first-timer, Egypt's underwater world of coral cliffs, colourful fish and spookily beautiful wrecks is staggering. Bring out your inner Jacques Cousteau by exploring the enigmatic wreck of WWII cargo ship the *Thistlegorm*, a fascinating museum spread across the seabed and one of the world's best wreck dives. Even if diving isn't your thing, it's easy to snorkel and see this beautiful underwater world.

Tel Aviv-Jaffa, Israel & the Palestinian Territories

15 Just over 100 years ago, Tel Aviv (p221) was little more than sand dunes. Nowadays it's a cool and cosmopolitan Mediterranean city bursting with bars, bistros and boutiques, strung out along beaches where sunbathers bronze their bodies, while the more athletic swim, surf and play *matkot* (beach racquetball). Each beach along the coast of Tel Aviv has its own personality, all set against a deep blue backdrop. And not far away, there's sure to be an innovative restaurant, lounge bar or boutique hotel.

Floating in the Dead Sea, Jordan

16 Floating in the Dead Sea (p308) is one of the world's great natural experiences. Floating is the right word for it: thanks to an eye-stingingly high salt content, it is virtually impossible to swim in the viscous waters of a sea that is 1000ft lower than sea level. The experience is usually accompanied by a mud bath, a bake in the sun and a health-giving spa treatment at one of the modern pleasure palaces lined up along the Dead Sea's shores.

Tabriz Bazaar, Iran

17 The sensory overload that comes from visiting a Middle Eastern souq is nowhere more memorable than in the main market (p149) of Tabriz. Restored to its former glory, this thousand-year-old souq, a Unesco World Heritage site, covers 7 sq km and is a true labyrinth of alleyways, vaulted ceilings and glorious domed halls. Each corner of the bazaar has its speciality, but wander to get lost, follow the enticing smells and explore without hurrying through this world where tourists are rarely seen.

Roman Ruins of Jerash, Jordan

18 For a country so small, Jordan punches well above its weight in world-class monuments, boasting some of the finest Roman ruins outside Rome. Most countries would be pleased to have attractions like the Citadel or the Roman Theatre in Amman, but these pale into insignificance compared with the superbly preserved ruins at Jerash (p301), one of the best places in the Middle East to see the glories of the Ancients. Visit during the Jerash Festival when live performances help to bring this ancient outpost of Rome alive.

17

18

ROBERTO RODRIGUEZ REYES/SHUTTERSTOCK ©

LOES KIEBOOM/SHUTTERSTOCK ©

ANDREW V MARCUS/SHUTTERSTOCK ©

Yazd, Iran

19 Few places have adapted to their environment as well as Iran's desert city of Yazd (p164). It's a gem of winding lanes, blue-tiled domes, soaring minarets, covered bazaars, and fine old courtyard homes topped by *badgirs* (wind towers) and watered by ingenious *qanats* (underground water channels). Several of these homes have been restored and converted into marvellously evocative traditional hotels. Many travellers declare Yazd to be their favourite city in Iran, and it's not difficult to see why, combining as it does a whiff of magic on the cusp of the desert. Above: Masjed-e Jameh (p165)

Tyre, Lebanon

20 Steeped in history and once famous across the ancient world for its dye, enchanting Tyre (p385) is a major Lebanese drawcard and very much a tourist destination on the upswing. Down here in the old Phoenician heartland, major complexes of Roman ruins include a sizeable cemetery, a circus and a beautifully preserved main thoroughfare in a picturesque coastal setting. The old town and fishing harbour ooze character, and you may be lucky enough to swim with turtles in Lebanon's cleanest, clearest water. Top right: Al Bass Archaeological Site (p385)

Ramallah, Israel & the Palestinian Territories

21 Ramallah (p256), in the West Bank, is a fine place to take the pulse of Palestinian life. It's a city that struggles daily with the area's status as a not-quite Palestinian state, but does so with remarkable energy. Proudly Palestinian, it's home to cafes, bars and even a fine brewery, and is a reminder that Palestinians are getting on with life with a real buzz even as the politicians are unable to forge a lasting peace. Ramallah also makes the perfect base for visiting Bethlehem, the place believed to be Christ's birth.

Need to Know

For more information, see Survival Guide (p557)

Currency

Egypt: Egyptian pound (LE)
Iran: Iranian rial (IR)
Iraq: Iraqi dinar (ID)
Israel: new Israeli shekel (NIS)
Jordan: Jordanian dinar (JD)
Lebanon: Lebanese lira (LL)
Syria: Syrian pound (S£)
Turkey: Turkish lira (₺)

Languages

Arabic, Farsi, Hebrew and Turkish; English and French widely spoken.

Visas

Most visas available on arrival; an Israeli stamp will mean no entry to Iran or Lebanon.

Money

ATMs and credit-card use are widespread. US dollars are universally accepted, followed by euros and British pounds. Cash is king in Iran.

Mobile Phones

Local SIM cards are widely available. Mobile coverage is widespread, but patchy in some areas.

When to Go

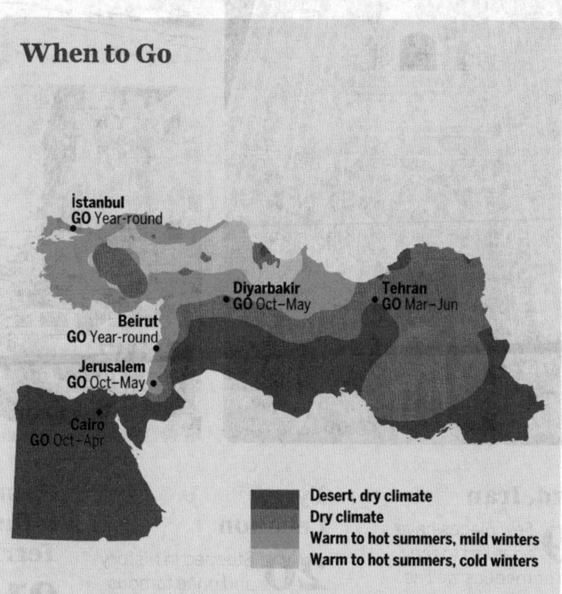

High Season (Jun–Aug)

➡ Mediterranean beaches and Turkish sites extremely crowded in summer.

➡ Religious holidays represent mini high seasons.

➡ Prices sky high and transport crowded; book accommodation well in advance.

Shoulder (Mar–May & Sep–Nov)

➡ Religious festivals aside, spring and autumn represent shoulder seasons in most countries.

➡ Weather often agreeable and crowds generally smaller.

➡ In Iran, prices are highest and crowds biggest during No Ruz (21 March to 3 April).

Low Season (Dec–Feb)

➡ Egypt's Nile Valley and desert regions can be unbearably hot from June to August.

➡ Turkey's Mediterranean and Aegean beaches are almost deserted in winter.

➡ The Christmas–New Year period is high season in many countries.

Useful Websites

Al Bab (www.al-bab.com) Portal covering the entire Arab world.

Al Jazeera (www.aljazeera.com/topics/regions/middleeast.html) CNN of the Arab world.

BBC News (www.bbc.com/news/world/middle_east) Comprehensive news on the region.

Bible Places (www.bibleplaces.com) Biblical sites from across the region.

Haaretz (www.haaretz.com) News from an Israeli perspective.

International Crisis Group (www.crisisgroup.org) In-depth reports on the region's pressure points and recent history.

Lonely Planet (www.lonelyplanet.com/middle-east) Destination information, hotel bookings, traveller forums and more.

Important Numbers

Phone number for the police by country:

Egypt	☎ 126
Iran	☎ 110
Israel & the Palestinian Territories	☎ 100
Jordan	☎ 911
Lebanon	☎ 112
Turkey	☎ 155

Exchange Rates

See p567 for exchange-rate table. For current exchange rates see www.xe.com.

Opening Hours

➡ With a few exceptions, the working week runs from Sunday to Thursday, so the end-of-week holiday is Friday. In Israel and the Palestinian Territories, it's Saturday (Shabbat), while in Lebanon and Turkey, it's Sunday. In countries where Friday is the holiday, many embassies and offices are also closed on Thursday, although in areas where there are lots of tourists, many private businesses and shops are open on Thursday and many shops will reopen in the evening on Friday.

➡ It's worth remembering that shops and businesses may have different opening hours for different times of the year – they tend to work shorter hours in winter and open earlier in summer to allow for a longer lunchtime siesta. During Ramadan (the month-long fast for Muslims), almost everything shuts down in the afternoon.

Arriving in the Middle East

Cairo International Airport, Egypt Prearrange taxi pickup (LE175 to LE200) or bargain on arrival (LE120); one hour to centre. Buses LE5; up to two hours to centre.

Ben Gurion International Airport, Tel Aviv, Israel A taxi costs 160NIS to 200NIS to Tel Aviv, while a train to Tel Aviv costs 14NIS.

İstanbul Atatürk International Airport, Turkey Havataş (Havaş) airport buses run to Taksim Meydanı every 30 minutes (₺12, one hour); a taxi to Sultanahmet/Taksim Meydanı costs ₺50/60. New airport due to open 2018.

Queen Alia International Airport, Amman, Jordan Airport Express bus (JD3.25, 45 minutes) runs hourly to the North Bus Station. A taxi costs JD18 to JD22 from the airport.

Getting Around

Getting around requires careful planning to circumvent the roadblocks (Syria, Iraq and, possibly, Israel if you want to avoid an Israeli stamp in your passport). The Middle East has a reasonable transport network, although distances are long and standards vary from country to country.

Air Decent air connections between most countries, allowing you to hop over the war zones. Only Turkey, Jordan and Egypt have flights to/from Israel.

Train Turkey, Israel, Iran and Egypt have domestic train networks; there are no cross-border train services.

Bus Extensive domestic and international bus services.

Ferry Connects Jordan with Egypt.

Car Road conditions are generally good but poor driving and speeding can be a problem; consider paying extra for a local driver.

For much more on **getting around**, see p572

What's New

Beirut Museums

The marvellous new MIM museum and the recently reopened basement space of the National Museum add a whole new dimension to the city's already considerable cultural offerings. (p357)

Cairo Museums

The Museum of Islamic Art (p60) is open again and is a brilliantly curated collection. Elsewhere in the city, Manial Palace (p57) has finally opened after 10 years of restoration.

Saida

This traditional Sunni town south of Beirut is making an effort to attract more visitors, with the atmospheric souq and bijou sea castle spruced up, and a major reconstruction under way on the land castle. (p382)

Sinai Trail

This 12-day hike across the Sinai is run by three Bedouin tribes. It's wonderful to explore the stunning landscape and spend quality time with the locals. (p125)

Jordan Trail

It is now possible to hike the Jordan Trail from the country's far north to the Red Sea. One particularly memorable stretch is the five-day hike from Dana Biosphere Reserve to Petra. (p305)

Tel Aviv

Israel's brashest city has been that way for a while, but things are ramping up in numerous cool ways – global cuisines, the explosion in wi-fi connectivity and boutique everything from hotels to burger bars. (p221)

Ephesus

Plans have been approved to dredge a canal from the ancient harbour of Ephesus (Efes) to the Aegean, allowing visitors to arrive by boat and restoring the city's original identity as a port. (p449)

Baraka, Umm Qais

An amazing Jordanian community tourism project, with a B&B, local guiding, cooking classes, beekeeping, basket-weaving, mountain biking, camping and wild food foraging options. (p307)

Wild Oryx Safaris

One of the Middle East's best wildlife experiences, newly minted safaris take you out in search of wild Arabian oryx that have been rescued from extinction at Shaumari Wildlife Reserve. (p311)

Persian Food Tours

Get a hands-on experience of making a delicious Iranian meal at this expertly run Tehran cooking class. (p141)

İstanbul Regeneration

The Balat neighbourhood on the Golden Horn is being revitalised; Tophane has become a design precinct; and on İstanbul's Asian side, once-dishevelled Yeldeğirmeni has gained cultural cred. (p416)

Esfahan Music Museum

Esfahan's fab new music museum combines historical interest (displays of old instruments) with live folk performances. (p159)

For more recommendations and reviews, see lonelyplanet.com/middle-east

If You Like...

Ancient Cities

The cradle of civilisation, the crossroads of ancient empires...whatever true cliché you want to use to describe the region, the Middle East has ruins in abundance.

Petra, Jordan Extraordinary tombs hewn from the rock by the Nabataeans. (p320)

Luxor, Egypt Ancient Egypt in all its glory, from the Temple of Karnak to the west bank temples. (p86)

Ephesus, Turkey An astonishing theatre and some wonderfully preserved temples. (p449)

Persepolis, Iran The showpiece landmark from pre-Islamic Persia, famous for its bas-reliefs. (p175)

Caesarea, Israel An aqueduct, an amphitheatre and other Roman ruins spread out along the Mediterranean Coast. (p231)

Jerash, Jordan Temples, arches, a distinctive oval plaza and an outstanding colonnaded way in Jordan's north. (p301)

Temple of Echmoun, Lebanon Unusually intact outpost of Phoenician culture in southern Lebanon. (p384)

Deserts & Oases

It was from the desert that the great monotheistic faiths emerged, and the Middle East is still home to some of the most beautiful and soulful desert landscapes on earth.

Wadi Rum, Jordan Exceptional rock formations, extraordinary colours, Bedouin companions and echoes of TE Lawrence. (p333)

Western Desert, Egypt Remote oasis towns and gateways to the Sahara's White and Black Deserts. (p107)

Ein Gedi, Israel Two spring-fed canyon oases are home to a profusion of plant and animal life. (p249)

Eastern Desert, Jordan The eastern wastes are home to a surprising collection of castles and wildlife sanctuaries. (p310)

Sinai Coast, Egypt The southern peninsula remains one of the Middle East's finest coastal playgrounds with a fascinating hinterland. (p117)

Mosques

Mosques stand at the very heart of Middle Eastern life. In many cases, the architecture speaks to the aesthetic aspirations of a people, with symmetrical forms and exquisite decorative features.

Dome of the Rock, Jerusalem Not technically a mosque, but rather a shrine, and one of Islam's holiest sites, with a graceful octagonal plan, gorgeous mosaic tiles and a gleaming gold dome. (p208)

Blue Mosque, İstanbul The personification of Islamic architectural grace and perfect proportions. (p416)

Masjed-e Jameh, Esfahan One of the high points of Persian Islamic architecture, both in scale and exquisite detail. (p158)

Masjed-e Shah, Esfahan Utterly magnificent blue-tiled mosque in the heart of the city. (p158)

Süleymaniye Mosque, İstanbul The pinnacle of 16th-century Ottoman mosque design and İstanbul's grandest. (p417)

Al Azhar Mosque, Cairo One of the oldest mosques in Egypt and the world's oldest surviving university. (p60)

Masjed-e Nasir Al Molk, Shiraz Stunning example of Iranian mosque architecture. (p170)

Souqs & Bazaars

The souqs and bazaars that snake through so many Middle Eastern towns provide many visitors with their most memorable experiences of the region.

Khan Al Khalili, Cairo The city's Byzantine-era bazaar is a tourist cliché, but with very good reason. (p57)

Jerusalem All the world's a bazaar in the Old City. (p201)

Bethlehem Busy and colourful souq in the town of Jesus's birth. (p261)

Tabriz Bazaar, **Iran** Wonderful example of the historic Persian bazaar. (p149)

Grand Bazaar, **İstanbul** The quintessential Turkish marketplace with carpets and controlled chaos. (p417)

Bazar-e Bozorg, **Esfahan** Fabulous covered market that fans out across the city from its splendid monumental core. (p158)

Saida Small but hugely atmospheric seaside souq in Lebanon. (p382)

Castles & Fortresses

During the Crusades in particular, seemingly every conceivable hilltop was colonised by a defensive fortress. Many remain, in some cases beautifully preserved.

Karak, **Jordan** The most intact of Jordan's Crusader castles. (p317)

Shobak, **Jordan** Less well-preserved than Karak, but its equal in drama and beauty. (p320)

İshak Paşa Palace, **Turkey** Like the evocation of an Arabian fairy tale in Doğubayazıt in eastern Turkey. (p486)

Nimrod Fortress, **Israel** The best-preserved Crusader-era bastion in the Israel-controlled territory of Golan Heights. (p248)

Fortress of Shali, **Egypt** Melting mudbrick fortress rising from the Siwa Saharan oasis. (p111)

Desert Castles, **Jordan** Seventh- and 8th-century desert retreats in evocative desert locations. (p312)

Byblos, **Lebanon** Crusader-era fortress by the Mediterranean in one of Lebanon's oldest settlements. (p373)

Top: Bazar-e Bozorg (p158), Esfahan, Iran

Bottom: Tyre (p385), Lebanon

Biblical Landmarks

The Bible – and the Torah and the Quran – live and breathe in the cities and soil of the Middle East, particularly the Levantine arc.

Jerusalem, Israel From Al Haram Ash Sharif/Temple Mount to the Church of the Holy Sepulchre, Jerusalem is the Bible writ large. (p201)

Bethlehem, Palestinian Territories The Church of the Nativity stands on the site where Jesus is believed to have been born. (p261)

Mt Sinai, Egypt Said to be where Moses received the Ten Commandments from God atop the summit. (p125)

Bethany-Beyond-the-Jordan, Jordan Site where Jesus was baptised. (p308)

Machaerus, Jordan Herod the Great's castle, where John the Baptist was martyred. (p317)

Mt Nebo, Jordan Where Moses looked out over the Promised Land, now within sight of Jerusalem. (p316)

Beaches

The Middle East has some superb places to lay out your towel. You're most likely to feel comfortable doing so in Turkey, Israel and some parts of Egypt.

Çıralı, Turkey Right alongside that old traveller favourite hangout of Olympos. (p463)

Patara, Turkey Twenty kilometres of unbroken and largely unspoiled sand. (p460)

Nuweiba, Egypt One of the quieter Egyptian Red Sea shores with plenty to do or lovely beaches on which to do nothing. (p125)

Dahab, Egypt Yes, it's a scene, but the location is dramatic. (p121)

Tel Aviv, Israel Long stretches of soft sand, with all the amenities of Israel's liveliest city right nearby. (p221)

Coral Beach Nature Reserve, Israel Eilat's best beach is ideal for snorkellers. (p253)

Dead Sea, Jordan Float (because swimming is near impossible) in the buoyant salt sea. (p249)

Berenice Beach, Jordan Learn to dive on Jordan's laid-back southern coast. (p340)

Tyre, Lebanon Crystal-clear waters on Lebanon's best beaches within sight of Roman ruins. (p385)

Diving & Snorkelling

The Red Sea could be the finest place to dive and snorkel on earth, with varied underwater topography in one of the richest and most varied marine ecosystems you'll find.

Sharm El Sheikh, Egypt Base for the *Thistlegorm*, a sunken WWII cargo ship that ranks among the world's best wreck dives. (p117)

Dahab, Egypt A place of Middle Eastern snorkelling legend and home to the famous Blue Hole. (p121)

Ras Mohammed National Park, Egypt A national marine park teeming with more fish life than you can poke a regulator at. (p117)

Aqaba, Jordan Jordan's wedge of the Red Sea has hundreds of coral species and around 1000 fish species. (p337)

Marsa Alam, Egypt A remote and virgin reef offshore and the perfect place for shark spotting. (p116)

Eilat, Israel Israel's best snorkelling, plus a chance to commune with fish without getting wet. (p252)

Hiking

The Middle East is a top hiking destination, with Jordan and Israel in particular offering rewarding trails from short day-hikes to longer, multiday expeditions.

Jordan Trail Hike the length of Jordan, or walk the brilliant five-day chunk from Dana Biosphere Reserve to Petra. (p305)

Lycian Way, Turkey One of the world's most beautiful walks, along the Mediterranean rim from Fethiye to Antalya. (p460)

Dana Biosphere Reserve, Jordan Trek through one of the Middle East's most intact (and most beautiful) ecosystems. (p318)

Makhtesh Ramon, Israel Hike through this vast desert crater, famous for its multicoloured sandstone. (p252)

En Avdat National Park, Israel Trek through canyons and pools in the wonderful Negev Desert. (p252)

Urban Vibes

The Middle East is not just about religion, old stones and history lessons at every turn. The region's cities are vibrant, exciting places racing headlong towards the future.

Beirut, Lebanon One of the most resilient cities on earth, Beirut can be sassy and sophisticated in equal measure. (p356)

Jaffa (p224), Tel Aviv, Israel & the Palestinian Territories

Tel Aviv, Israel Jerusalem's alter ego is dynamic, secular, international and more than a little hedonistic. (p221)

Amman, Jordan Jordan's capital has some of the most enduring oases of urban cool in the region. (p288)

Alexandria, Egypt A culturally rich city as much Mediterranean as Egyptian. (p80)

İstanbul, Turkey One of the greatest cities on earth, European, Middle Eastern and Turkish all at once. (p416)

Tehran, Iran A fascinating city where old and new, secular and Islamic clash with often dynamic results. (p137)

Wildlife

Vestiges of the region's wildlife somehow survive, and ecotourism projects and wildlife reserves now protect some of the Middle East's most charismatic fauna.

Ras Mohammed National Park, Egypt One of the Red Sea's few protected areas teems with marine life. (p117)

Shaumari Wildlife Reserve, Jordan Take a safari to see wild Arabian oryx in this ground-breaking reserve. (p311)

Mujib Biosphere Reserve, Jordan An enclosure for the Nubian ibex and the chance to see caracal. (p310)

Shouf Biosphere Reserve, Lebanon If you're (extremely) lucky, you might see wolves, wild cats, ibex and gazelle. (p388)

Hammams

The hammam (hamam in Turkey and Iran) is a wonderful sensual indulgence. You'll never forget the robust massage on tiled slabs, sweltering steam-room sessions and scalding tea.

Ayasofya Hürrem Sultan Hamamı, İstanbul İstanbul's most beautiful hamam after a stunning recent restoration. (p423)

Al Pasha Turkish Bath, Jordan A rare outpost of tradition in the modern Jordanian capital, Amman, with the full treatment. (p291)

Hammam Al Shifa, Palestinian Territories This local place has a hot room, a sauna and a steam room. (p264)

Month by Month

TOP EVENTS

Nevruz (No Ruz), March

Cappadox Festival, May

İstanbul Music Festival, June

Jerash Festival, July

Beirut International Film Festival, October

January

Much of the region, including desert regions at night, can be bitterly cold and there can be snow on the high peaks from Lebanon to Iran. Egypt and the Red Sea have relatively balmy temperatures.

Christmas (Orthodox)

Orthodox Christians commemorate the birth of Jesus (it's celebrated by Eastern Orthodox churches on 6 and 7 January and by Armenians in the Holy Land on 18 and 19 January). Important among Christian communities in Lebanon, Egypt and Syria.

February

The winter chill continues throughout much of the region, though it's the perfect time of year in the south. Egypt's beaches and Nile Valley can be busy, while Turkish and Iranian mountain roads may be impassable.

March

In Egypt sandstorms can darken the horizon, but hillsides and valleys in the Levant, Turkey and Iran are green; it's a great time for hiking. Low-season room prices in most areas, except Iran during No Ruz.

D-Caf

Downtown Cairo's contemporary arts festival is international, multidisciplinary and great fun. It's also a wonderful way to see the often dilapidated venues in the city centre.

Nevruz (No Ruz)

Kurds and Alevis in Turkey and Iran (where it's called No Ruz) celebrate the ancient Middle Eastern spring festival on 21 March with much jumping over bonfires, huge parties and general jollity. Banned in Turkey until 2005, Nevruz is now an official holiday.

Purim

Purim celebrates the foiling of a plot to wipe out the Jews of ancient Persia. Children and adults put on costumes for an evening of revelry in Israel's streets.

İzmir European Jazz Festival

This jazz festival fills the Aegean city with a high-profile line-up of European and local performers. Gigs, workshops, seminars and a garden party make this a lively time for jazz lovers to visit.

April

Although a shoulder season, April is a wonderful time to visit: the wildflowers are in bloom in the Levant, tourist numbers in Egypt drop off and there's good beach weather in southwest Turkey.

ANZAC Day

On 25 April the WWI battles for the Dardanelles are commemorated and the Allied soldiers remembered. Antipodean pilgrims sleep at Anzac Cove before the dawn services.

Easter

During Holy Week, Catholic pilgrims throng Jerusalem's Via Dolorosa and the Church of the Holy Sepulchre, and many Protestants gather at the Garden Tomb. Dates for Orthodox celebrations differ slightly.

Fajr International Film Festival

Features Iranian and international films and red-carpet events in more than 20 cinemas across Tehran. It has been held in February in previous years, so check the website for details. (p185)

Holocaust Memorial Day

Yom HaSho'ah is a solemn remembrance of the six million Jews, including 1.5 million children, who died in the Holocaust. Places of entertainment are closed. At 10am sirens sound and Israelis stand silently at attention. It takes place in April or March.

Passover

Known as Pesach, this week-long festival celebrates the liberation of the Israelites from slavery in Egypt with ritual family dinners and Shabbat-like closures on the first and seventh days. Lots of Israelis go on holiday, so it's high season in Israel.

İstanbul Film Festival

For a filmic fortnight, cinemas around İstanbul host a packed program of Turkish and international films and events. An excellent crash course in Turkish cinema, but book ahead.

May

Peak tourist season begins in the Levant with warm weather on the way. High-season prices in coastal areas are yet to kick in, but it's good beach weather from the Red Sea to the Mediterranean.

Cappadox Festival

Cappadocia's three-day arts festival merges music, nature walks, art exhibitions, yoga and gastronomy into an extravaganza of Turkish contemporary culture, highlighting the area's natural beauty.

Ramadan (Ramazan)

During the Ramadan fasting month (called Ramazan in Iran), offices may have shorter hours, and restaurants may close during daylight hours. Foodies will love this time; ambitious sightseers may be frustrated. It begins in May in 2019, and in April in 2020 and 2021.

Uluslararasi Bursa Festivali

The city's 2½-week music and dance jamboree, features diverse regional and world music, plus an international headliner or two. Begins in mid-May.

June

You'll encounter long days and warm weather all across the region. The tourist high season draws large crowds and higher room prices in many areas. It can be unbearably hot in Egypt by the end of the month.

Dance with the Sufis

In Luxor, in the third week of the Islamic month of Sha'aban, the Sufi festival of Moulid of Abu Al Haggag offers a taste of rural religious tradition. Several smaller villages have *moulids* around the same time.

Gay Pride in Tel Aviv

Tel Aviv is bedecked with rainbow flags for Israel's biggest and most colourful gay and lesbian extravaganza.

Israel Festival

Four weeks of music, theatre and dance performances (some of them free) in and around Jerusalem add a real spring to the step of the city in early summer. Check out www.israel-festival.org.il for dates and programs.

İstanbul Music Festival

Probably Turkey's most important arts festival, featuring performances of opera, dance, orchestral concerts and chamber recitals. The action takes place at venues such as Aya İrini, the Byzantine church in the Topkapı Palace grounds.

July

A great time for festivals, but the weather can be unpleasantly hot in most areas. It is, however, high season along Turkey's Aegean and Mediterranean coasts.

Beiteddine Festival

Lebanon's full program of summer events continues with this terrific arts festival with music, dance and theatre held in the beautiful courtyard of the Beiteddine Palace. It usually spills over into August. (p387)

Byblos International Festival

Lebanon kicks off the Levantine summer with pop,

SENDERISTAS/SHUTTERSTOCK ©

CHAMELEONSEYE/SHUTTERSTOCK ©

Top: Orthodox Christmas mass, Egypt
Bottom: Statue at Red Sea Jazz festival, Eilat, Israel & the Palestinian Territories

classic, opera and world-music performances, many of which are staged among the ruins of Byblos' ancient harbour. It can start in late June and continue on into August. (p374)

Jerash Festival

Hosted within world-class ruins, Jordan's much-loved Jerash Festival of Culture & Arts brings ancient Jerash to life with plays, poetry recitals, opera and concerts. Held annually since 1981, the festival takes place over 17 days from mid-July to mid-August. (p301)

August

The heat takes its toll everywhere; in Iran desert temperatures can hit 50°C, and unless you're by the beach in Turkey, it's a month to avoid. High-season rates (and overbooking) apply in many coastal areas.

Distant Heat

Build up a sweat at Jordan's annual dance in the desert. This all-nighter takes place in Wadi Rum and features top international electronic-dance-music artists.

Red Sea Jazz

Eilat in August gives you the chance to combine long days by the water with some terrific jazz. Taking place in the last week of August, it draws international acts.

September

Two of the most important Jewish holidays make for mini high seasons in Israel. Elsewhere, temperatures

are starting to fall (only slightly in Egypt) and high-season crowds and prices start to ebb in Turkey. A good month to hike in Iran.

Ashura

Ashura marks the martyrdom of Imam Hossein and is the most intense date on the Shiite Muslim calendar. It's celebrated with religious theatre and parades in which men self-flagellate. Falls in September in 2019, and August in 2020 and 2021.

Aspendos Opera & Ballet Festival

The acclaimed Aspendos Opera & Ballet Festival takes place in this atmospheric Roman theatre near Antalya (June or late August and September).

Rosh Hashanah

The Jewish New Year causes Shabbat-like closures that last for two days. Some Israelis go on holiday, so accommodation is scarce and room prices rise. Unless you're here for the ambience or for religious reasons, avoid this one.

Yom Kippur

The Jewish Day of Atonement is a solemn day of reflection and fasting – and cycling on the empty roads. In Jewish areas, all businesses shut and transportation (including by private car) completely ceases.

İstanbul Biennial

İstanbul's major visual-arts shindig, considered to be one of the world's most prestigious biennials, takes place from mid-September to mid-November in odd-numbered years. Venues around town host the internationally curated event.

October

As the summer heat finally breaks, Egypt comes back into play and the crowds have tapered off in Turkey. Elsewhere, it's a pleasant month with mild temperatures, although rain is possible.

Akbank Jazz Festival

From late September to mid-October, İstanbul celebrates its love of jazz with this eclectic line-up of local and international performers.

Beirut International Film Festival

Beirut's contribution to the cinematic calendar is an increasingly high-profile film festival with a growing reputation as one of the best in the Middle East. (p362)

International Antalya Film Festival

In early October, Turkey's foremost film event features screenings, a parade of stars and the obligatory controversy. At the award ceremony in Aspendos, the Golden Orange, nicknamed the Turkish Oscar, is awarded to film-makers.

Sukkot

The week-long Feast of the Tabernacles holiday recollects the Israelites' 40 years of wandering in the desert. The first and seventh day are Shabbat-like public holidays.

November

Surprisingly chilly weather and smallish crowds even at the more popular sights. The possibility of rain (or snow in Iran) may deter hikers, but Saharan expeditions in Egypt are again possible after the summer break.

Cairo International Film Festival

From the last weekend in November into December, this 10-day event shows recent films from all over the world.

Prophet's Birthday

Moulid Al Nabi is a region-wide celebration with sweets and new clothes for kids and general merriment in all Muslim areas. Falls in November in 2019, and October in 2020 and 2021.

December

The Middle East's winter begins in earnest, and low-season prices apply in most areas, except in Christian areas at Christmas, at ski resorts and in Egypt where Europeans flood in search of winter sun.

Christmas

Midnight Catholic Mass is celebrated in the Church of the Nativity in Bethlehem. Christmas is a public holiday in the West Bank but not in many other areas. Orthodox Christians must wait until early January for their Christmas.

Hanukkah

The Jewish Festival of Lights celebrates the rededication of the Temple after the Maccabean revolt. Families light candles over eight nights using a nine-branched candelabra.

Itineraries

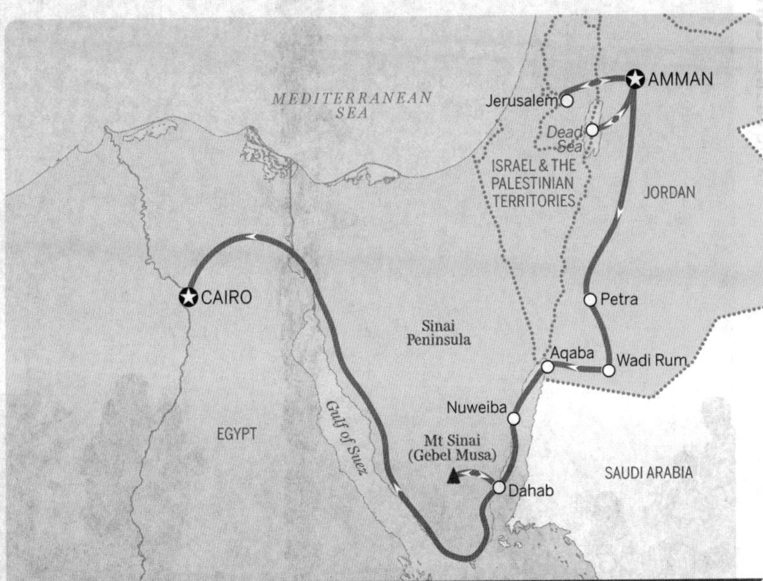

Amman to Cairo

This journey represents a shorter version of the old İstanbul-to-Cairo traveller favourite (no longer possible because of the war in Syria) and includes some of the Middle East's premier attractions.

Your journey starts in **Amman**, a cosmopolitan city with Roman ruins and brilliant restaurants. After visit to the **Dead Sea** (an easy day trip from the capital), detour to **Jerusalem**, the Middle East's spiritual heart. Returning to Jordan, spend some time exploring fabulous **Petra**, the Middle East's most beguiling ancient city. Further south, Petra's rival to the title of Jordan's most spectacular site is **Wadi Rum**, a soulful red-hued desert landscape that rewards those who spend a couple of days exploring. From here, leave Jordan behind and cross the Red Sea at **Aqaba** to **Nuweiba** in Egypt. Where you go from here depends on the prevailing security situation, with much of the Sinai Peninsula considered risky at the time of research. Assuming all is well, continue on from Nuweiba to **Dahab**, for Red Sea snorkelling and an excursion to catch sunrise from atop **Mt Sinai**. From Dahab (or from Nuweiba if security is uncertain) make for clamorous, attraction-rich **Cairo**.

BRAZEN SERPENT MONUMENT ATOP MT NEBO BY ITALIAN ARTIST GIOVANNI FANTONI: JORDAN PIX/GETTY IMAGES ©

JAVIER CRESPO/SHUTTERSTOCK ©

Above: Bronze sculpture at Memorial Viewpoint (p316), Mt Nebo, Jordan

Left: Grotto of the Nativity (p261), Bethlehem, Israel & the Palestinian Territories

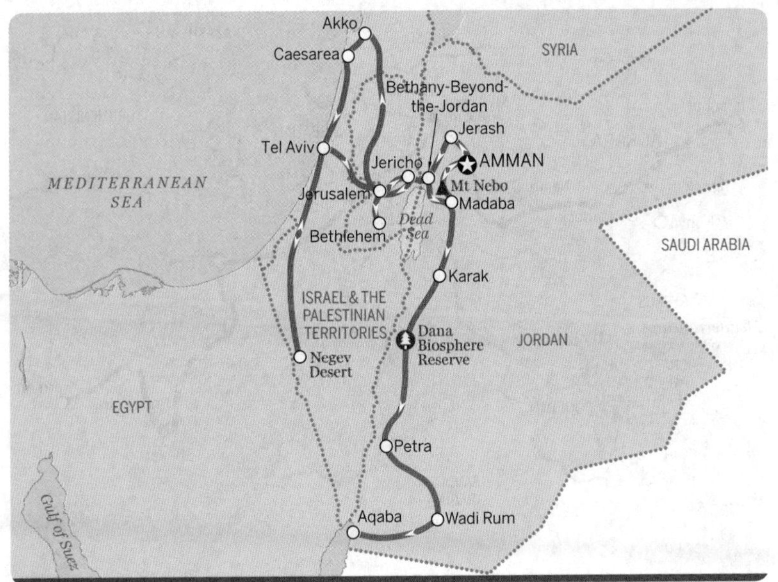

The Middle East's Heartland

Welcome to the Middle Eastern heartland for a trip through the best that Jordan and Israel and the Palestinian Territories have to offer. Although distances can be small, there's a lot to pack in. Most of this trip is best accomplished using public transport.

Amman may lack the cachet of other Middle Eastern cities, but most travellers end up staying longer than planned. From here, it's easy to make side trips to many of Jordan's must-see destinations; the echoes of Moses at **Mt Nebo** and the mosaics of **Madaba** deserve your time. When you're ready to move on, head to **Jerash**, a quiet yet rewarding ancient site with a wonderful colonnaded way running through its heart. Travelling south, **Bethany-Beyond-the-Jordan**, the place where Christ was baptised, resonates strongly with pilgrims, while floating in the buoyant waters of the **Dead Sea** is a signature Middle Eastern experience.

Across the Jordan River, roiling **Jerusalem** is the starting point of so much Middle Eastern history. From Jerusalem, make for the biblical towns of **Bethlehem** and **Jericho**. In Israel's north, timeless **Akko** and the world-class ruins of **Caesarea** are worth as much time as you can give them. On your way back, don't miss **Tel Aviv**, a lively place to let your hair down and discover the hedonistic side of Israeli life. Its antithesis, the **Negev desert**, is a wilderness area that you simply don't expect to find in this ever-crowded corner of the earth.

Crossing back into Jordan, the Crusader castle of **Karak** and the spectacular scenery of **Dana Biosphere Reserve** shouldn't be missed, while **Petra** is an astonishing place, where reality outstrips even the most lofty expectations. If time allows, spend at least a couple of days here, so you can savour the main tombs as well as visit the site's more outlying areas. The same applies to **Wadi Rum** – you could get a taste of this soulful place in a day, but you'll gain a deeper understanding of its gravitas if you sleep out under the stars for at least one night. The laid-back Red Sea port of **Aqaba**, with world-class diving and snorkelling, provides the perfect place to rest at journey's end.

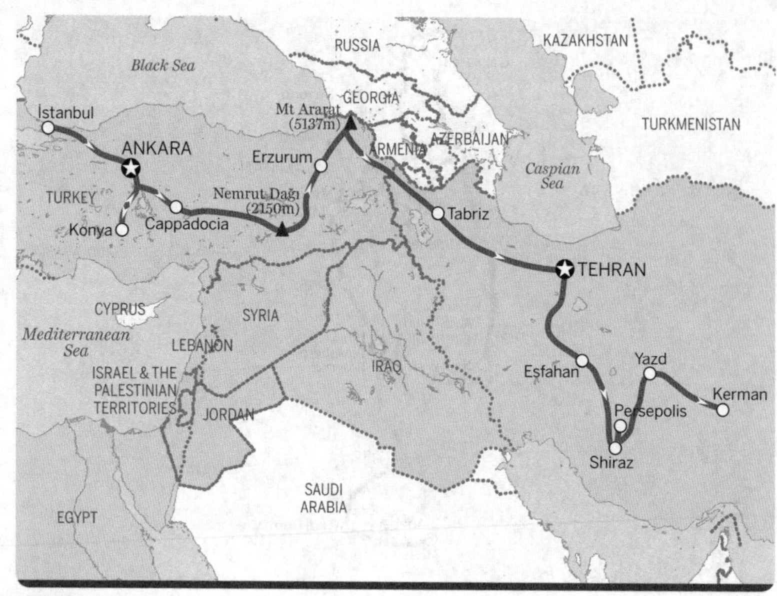

Modern Turkey, Ancient Persia

From marvellous İstanbul to the fascinating cities of central Iran, this itinerary takes you from the Middle East's most Western-oriented corner to its least. Neither, however, conforms to stereotypes and the journey between the two is like traversing the region's complicated soul. Allow two weeks for each country.

İstanbul is at once a destination in its own right and the starting point of so many Turkish journeys. After a few days, make for **Ankara**, the country's underrated capital and then take a detour to conservative but welcoming **Konya**, the spiritual home of the Sufis. Perhaps returning via Ankara, make for the otherworldly landscapes of **Cappadocia** that seem to have sprung from a wonderfully childlike imagination. Linger as long as you can here – it's a landscape that really gets under your skin the longer you stay. When you can finally tear yourself away, begin the long journey east to the brooding statues of **Nemrut Dağı**, surely one of Turkey's most thought-provoking sights. By the time you reach **Erzurum**, you'll have left the last remnants of tourist Turkey, and your reward in this eastern city is a fine open-air gallery of Seljuk and Mongol-era monuments. Consider climbing **Mt Ararat** (although you need to plan well in advance to do so), before crossing the border into Iran.

Your first stop in Iran should be **Tabriz**, not least because its bazaar is one of the finest, most evocative of all Middle Eastern markets. Spend a day or two in **Tehran**, itself home to an overwhelming market as well as fine museums. But after a couple of days, stop resisting the temptation and head on to **Esfahan**, one of the Middle East's most beautiful, most bejewelled cities (at least in the centre), with its utterly exquisite gardens, arched bridges and tiled mosques. **Shiraz** is a cultured, appealing city, not to mention the gateway to **Persepolis**, that towering monument to all that was good about Ancient Persia. Continue to **Yazd** and check into an atmospheric traditional hotel in the old town. Spend two days exploring the old city, visit the Zoroastrian Towers of Silence and perhaps take a trek into the desert. Finish up in **Kerman**, from where you can take a tour to the remarkable 'sand castles' of the Kaluts.

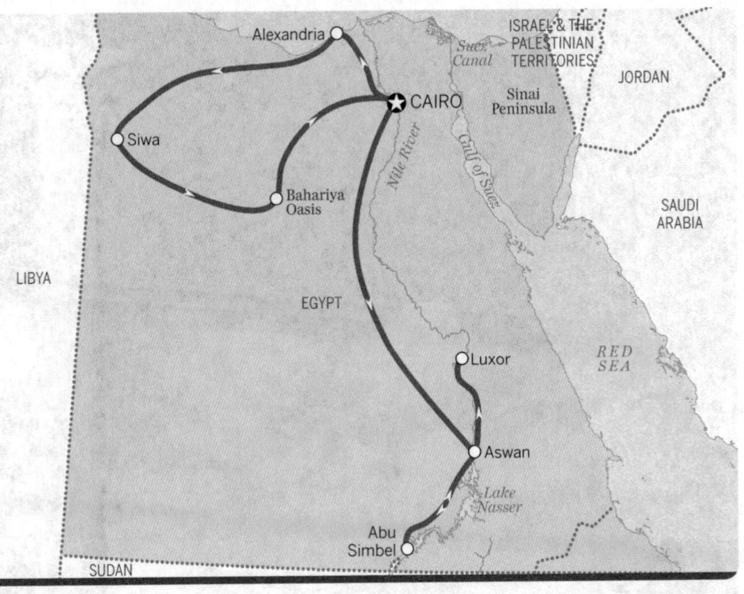

Land of the Pharaohs

There's so much to see in Egypt that it deserves its own itinerary. Count on a week for Cairo and Alexandria, a week for the Western Oases, and another week for the country's south.

So many Egyptian journeys revolve around **Cairo**, and you'll return here again and again. Apart from being the Middle East's largest and most clamorous metropolis, Cairo is also home to the iconic Pyramids of Giza, the Egyptian Museum and a wonderful coffeehouse culture. After Cairo, head north to **Alexandria**, Egypt's sophisticated and quintessentially Mediterranean city. It feels like nowhere else in the country, and a combination of terrific museums and great food gives you further reason to visit. A *really* long journey west is worth it for your first sight of **Siwa**, one of the Sahara's great oasis outposts and home to an ancient temple in the sands. It's the sort of place where you can stand on the outskirts of the village, just as Alexander the Great did, and contemplate eternity. Dusty desert trails lead to the **Bahariya Oasis**; you'll need to rent a private 4WD to reach Bahariya, but why not make it part of a deep desert expedition from Bahariya into the White and Black Deserts.

It's back to Cairo to enjoy the pleasures of civilisation for a day or two before jumping on a train south to **Aswan**, one of Africa's loveliest riverside spots. There's a monastery and museum to anchor your explorations of the city, but its real charm is its proximity to the Nile. Take the detour south into Nubia to **Abu Simbel**, one of Egypt's most extraordinary temples, then from Aswan sail slowly up the Nile aboard a felucca, savouring the slow rhythms of life along this, the world's longest river, all the way to **Luxor**, home to the richest collection of Pharaonic sites in the country. Here you'll find so much of what drew you to Egypt in the first place, including the Temples of Karnak, the Valley of the Kings and the Valley of the Queens.

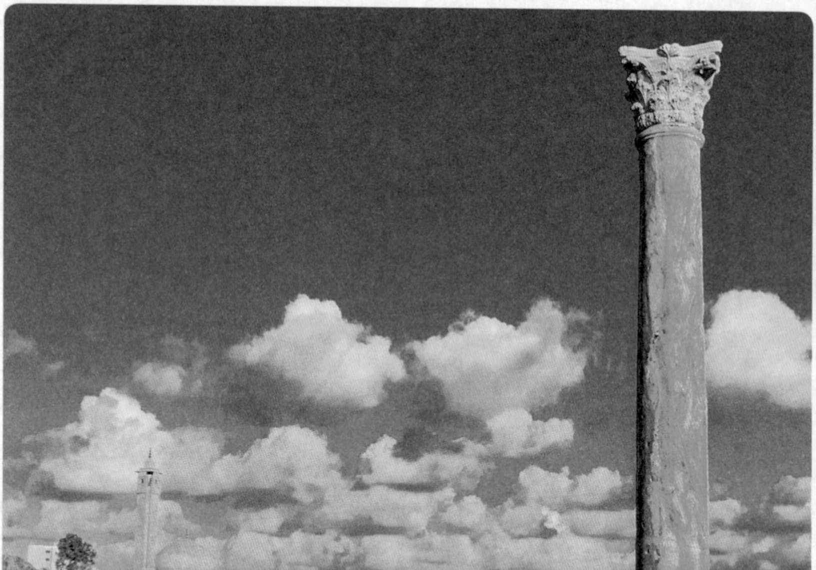

DIEGO FIORE/SHUTTERSTOCK ©

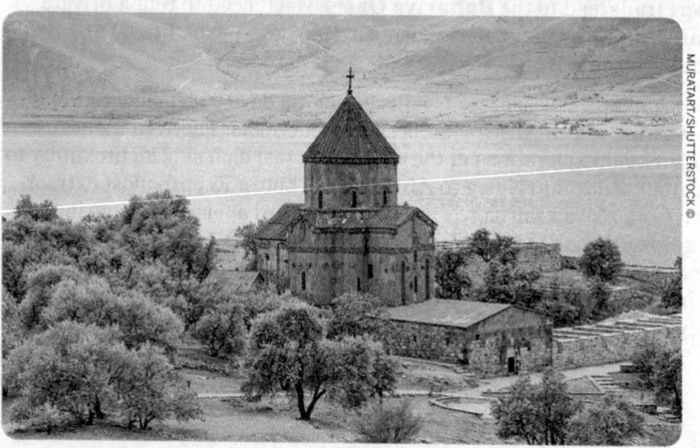

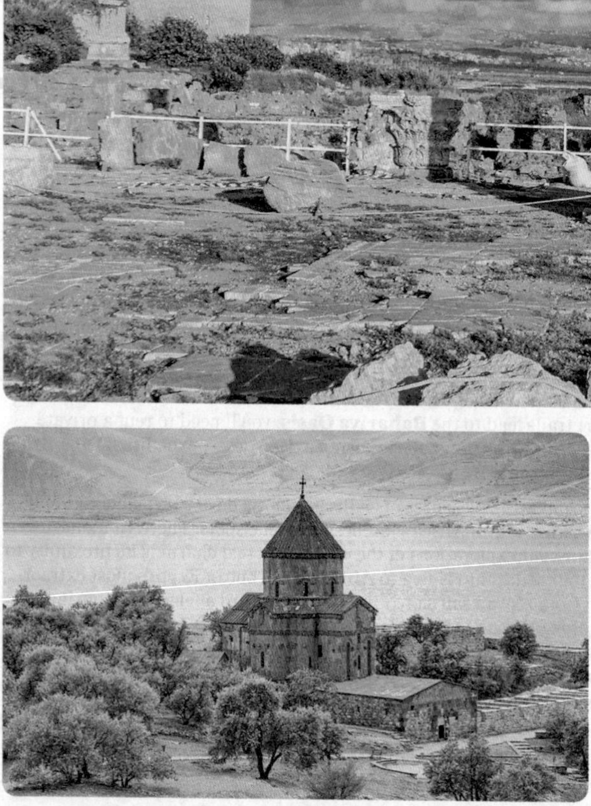

MURATART/SHUTTERSTOCK ©

Above: Tyre (p385), Lebanon

Left: Armenian church, Van, Turkey

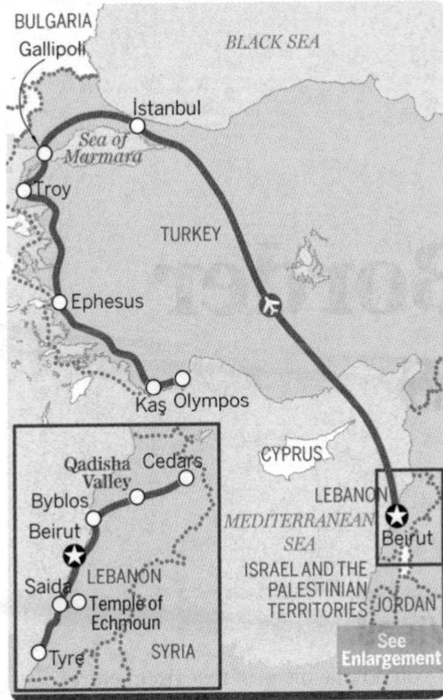

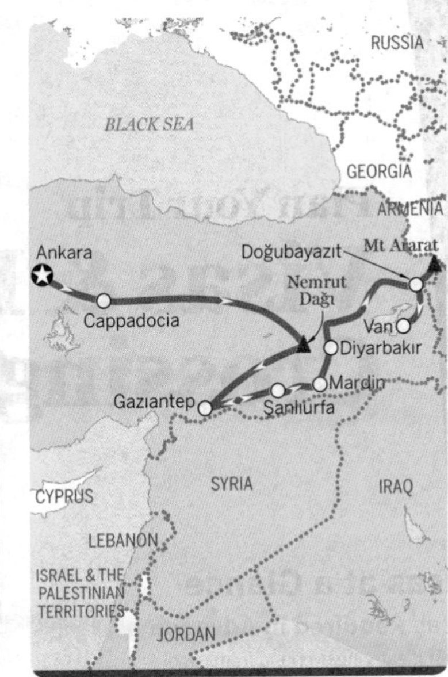

3 WEEKS A Mediterranean Loop

For this Mediterranean sojourn, count on a week to 10 days in Lebanon and two weeks in Turkey.

Begin in **Beirut**, a glamorous metropolis, the Middle East in complicated microcosm and filled with Mediterranean *joie de vivre.* If it's safe, head south to the Phoenician heartland – **Saida**, the **Temple of Echmoun** and **Tyre**. Next, head north to the pretty fishing port of **Byblos** and then finish up with some hiking through the **Qadisha Valley**, finally putting on your skis at the **Cedars**.

From Beirut, fly to **İstanbul** for a few days in that most glorious of cities. Three days should give you a taste before you move on to visit **Gallipoli**, with its poignant echoes of WWI, and **Troy**, where altogether more ancient battles took place. Work your way around the coast, pausing at the mighty ruins of **Ephesus**, which rank among the Middle East's most imposing, and lingering in the delightful Mediterranean villages of **Kaş** or **Olympos** where you'll wonder why life can't always be like this.

3 WEEKS Among the Kurds

The Kurdish homeland spans Turkey, Syria, Iran and Iraq, although Syria and Iraq are off limits, and expressions of Kurdish identity are rare in Iran. Fortunately, journeying through Turkey's east and southeast provides numerous opportunities for experiencing Kurdish culture. Count on three weeks, although you could do it in two.

Begin in **Ankara**, where you'll find a splendid museum and a fine citadel. On your way southeast into the Kurdish heartland, stop in **Cappadocia** and **Nemrut Dağı** before exploring the rarely visited but always fascinating cities of **Gaziantep** and **Şanlıurfa**. Nearby **Mardin** combines a beautiful setting with equally beautiful architecture and a fascinating cultural mix. By the time you reach **Diyarbakır**, with its intriguing architecture, you're deep in Kurdish territory. Head for **Doğubayazıt**, one of eastern Turkey's most extraordinary sights, with a legendary castle and stunning views of **Mt Ararat**; the mountain could not be climbed at time of research, although most travellers content themselves with not-so-distant views from the town anyway. Further south, **Van** is home to the lovely Armenian church on Akdamar Island.

Plan Your Trip

Visas & Border Crossings

Visas at a Glance

Visas Required in Advance

Egypt If entering overland from Israel

Jordan If you need a multiple-entry visa

Turkey Purchase online before travel

Iran Safest option is to obtain in advance

Visas Available on Arrival

Egypt Except if crossing from Israel

Israel and the Palestinian Territories

Jordan Single-entry visas except if first entry on King Hussein/Allenby Bridge

Lebanon

Iran Possibly available at Iranian international airports but there's a risk of rejection – it's best to obtain in advance

Israeli Passport Stamps

OK for entry to: Egypt, Jordan, Turkey

Will be denied entry to: Iran and Lebanon (also Iraq and Syria when they're considered safe to visit)

Visas

If you do one piece of research before setting out on your trip, it should be to familiarise yourself with the requirements for obtaining visas for the countries that you intend to visit. For the unwary, it can be a minefield. For the well informed, it shouldn't pose too many difficulties.

The major issue arises if you plan to visit Israel and the Palestinian Territories. If you do, then you may need to think carefully about the order you visit the countries of the Middle East, or prepare for a little sleight of hand to ensure there is no trace of you having visited Israel and therefore avoid limiting the other countries that you're able visit.

Egypt

Most Egyptian tourist visas can be obtained on arrival. It couldn't be easier if you're arriving by air, while those travelling from Jordan can obtain a visa at the port in Aqaba before boarding the ferry. Visa fees vary by nationality and can usually be paid in Egyptian pounds, US dollars, UK pounds or euros. Visas granted on arrival allow you to stay in Egypt for one month.

The only exception to these general rules is if you plan to enter Egypt from Israel via the Taba border crossing. In this case, we recommend that you apply for your Egyptian visa in advance in Tel Aviv or Eilat. If you just turn up at this border

BANNED: ISRAELI PASSPORT STAMPS

Arab countries have widely varying policies on admitting travellers whose passports show evidence of a visit to Israel. Jordan and Egypt, with which Israel has peace treaties, have no problem at all, and the same goes for Tunisia, Morocco and many of the Gulf emirates (but not Saudi Arabia).

If there's any chance you'll be heading to Arab or Muslim countries during the life of your passport, your best bet is to make sure that it shows no indication that you've been to Israel. Fortunately, Israeli passport inspectors no longer stamp tourists' passports and instead issue a small loose-leaf entry card to serve as proof of lawful entry. Keep this with you at all times until you leave Israel.

Unfortunately, Egyptian and Jordanian officials are not so obliging about their own stamps, even though having a stamp from one of those countries' land crossings to Israel or the West Bank can be no less 'incriminating' than having an Israeli one. This is especially true of Lebanon and Iran, which have been known to put travellers on the next plane out if they find even the slightest evidence of travel to Israel. Such evidence can include a longer stay in Jordan or Egypt than is allowed under that country's visa rules with no evidence of a visa extension.

Some countries, including the United States, allow their citizens to carry more than one passport, but it can still be difficult to make this work without leaving unexplained gaps in the entry/exit paper trail.

crossing without a visa in your passport, your visa must be guaranteed by an Egyptian travel agency – more trouble than it's worth.

Iran

Iranian visas can be a pain to organise. The process is slow (start at least two months before you plan to travel) and somewhat unpredictable, and rules can change without warning. But the vast majority of people do get a visa within two or three weeks. Note that all applications stall over the No Ruz holiday period; submit before 8 March to be sure.

There are three kinds of visas:

Tourist visa Issued for up to 30 days and extendable. Must be obtained before coming to Iran from Iranian embassy or consulate and valid to enter for 90 days from the issue date. The surest option. American and UK citizens are required to be part of a tour group or have an Iranian 'sponsor' in order to obtain a visa.

Tourist visa on arrival (VOA) Issued for 30 days on arrival at any Iranian international airport. Convenient but risky, as you may be denied entry.

Transit visa Issued for five to seven days, this is a last resort. You must enter and exit via different countries, and have a visa or a ticket to an onward country. Not available to US passport holders.

Iraq

Iraq is not considered safe at the time of writing.

Israel & the Palestinian Territories

Tourist visas are issued to nationals of most Western countries at airports and land border crossings. Although most visas are for three-month periods, travellers arriving overland from Egypt or Jordan are sometimes given two-week or one-month visas. Some visas may also come with restrictions relating to travel inside the Palestinian Territories.

Jordan

Visas, required by all visitors, are available on arrival (JD40 for most nationalities) at international airports and most of Jordan's land borders. It makes sense for most travellers to buy a Jordan Pass (www.jordanpass.jo) online before entering the country: this waives the cost of a visa in addition to giving free access to many sites in Jordan, including Petra.

It's not possible to get a visa on arrival at King Hussein Bridge or at Wadi Araba. Check the latest status of Jordan's border crossings on the Jordan Tourism Board website (www.international.visitjordan.com/GeneralInformation/EntryintoJordan.aspx).

Lebanon

Free one-month single-entry tourist visas are available at Beirut's airport for many nationalities.

Syria

It is currently not safe to visit Syria.

Turkey

If you come from Denmark, Finland, France, Germany, Israel, Italy, Japan, New Zealand, Sweden or Switzerland, you don't need a Turkish visa for stays of up to 90 days.

For most other nationalities, three-month, multiple-entry tourist visas must be purchased online at www.evisa.gov.tr/en prior to arrival. Payment can be made by credit card and fees range from US$15 to US$80 depending on nationality. You then print out the visa and present it on arrival in Turkey. Apply at least two days before you plan to travel.

Many Western nationals can obtain a visa on arrival in Turkey, but this is not recommended as travellers have reported extra charges and bad experiences with the customs officials. Cash cannot be used.

Border Crossings

Border crossings in the Middle East can be slow, and it can take hours to pass through immigration and customs formalities, especially if you bring your own car. Showing patience, politeness and good humour *may* speed up the process.

If travelling overland to or from the Middle East, you can approach the region from Africa, the Caucasus, Iran or Europe.

Egypt

The two land border crossings between Egypt and Sudan reopened in 2014 and a number of Sudanese bus companies now operate Aswan–Wadi Halfa–Khartoum services.

If travelling to Sudan, you need to purchase your Sudanese visa beforehand in either Cairo or Aswan. Travelling north from Sudan into Egypt, Egyptian visas are issued at the border. Egyptian departure tax is LE50.

Travel to Libya is currently unsafe.

Iran

Iran's borders with Afghanistan and Pakistan were unsafe and off limits at the time of writing.

Armenia

The border between Iran and Armenia is only 35km long, with one crossing point in Iran at Norduz. Armenian visas are issued at the border, though sometimes the bus leaves before you have your visa! Apart from that, it's pretty smooth.

Azerbaijan

The Azeri border has at least three recognised crossings. You can cross between Astara (Azerbaijan) and Astara (Iran), and Culfa (Azerbaijan) and Jolfa (Iran), the latter leading to the exclave of Nakhchivan, from where you cannot enter Armenia and must fly to get to Baku. The third option, good if you want to go to Jolfa from Baku, is at Bilesuva, the border used by Baku–Nakhchivan buses and plenty of Azeris on their way to Tabriz. Visas are not issued at any of these land borders.

Direct buses between Tehran and Baku, via Astara, are available but are not such a good idea because you'll probably get stuck waiting for hours at the airport. Taking one bus to the border, crossing as a pedestrian and finding another bus is much easier.

A train line was meant to open from Baku to Rasht in 2018, but don't hold your breath.

Turkmenistan

There are three border posts open to foreigners along this 1206km-long frontier. From west to east, there is inconvenient and little-used Incheh Borun/Gyzyl-Etrek, Bajgiran crossing linking Mashhad and the Turkmen capital Ashgabat, and Sarakhs and Saraghs for those heading east; the area around the latter should be visited with caution. You must change transport at all three crossings.

The new train line from near Gorgan crossing at Gyzyl-Etrek has officially opened, but there were no passenger services at the time of writing.

The paperwork and organisation involved in travelling to Turkmenistan is a hassle; Stantours (www.stantours.com) seems to be the best at making it all go (relatively) smoothly.

MIDDLE EAST BORDER CROSSINGS AT A GLANCE

TO/FROM	FROM/TO	BORDER CROSSINGS
Egypt	Israel & the Palestinian Territories	Taba
Egypt	Jordan	Connected by ferry; entry points at Nuweiba & Aqaba
Jordan	Israel & the Palestinian Territories	Crossings at: King Hussein Bridge/Allenby Bridge (close to Jerusalem), Jordan River Bridge/Sheikh Hussein Bridge (close to Beit She'an/Irbid), Wadi Arabia/Yitzhak Rabin (close to Eilat/Aqaba)
Turkey	Iran	Crossings at Gürbulak-Bazargan, near Doğubayazıt (Turkey) and Şahabat (Iran); and the Esendere-Sero border southeast of Van (Turkey)

Turkey

Bulgaria

It's fairly easy to get to İstanbul by direct bus from many points in Europe via Bulgaria. Several Turkish bus lines offer reliable and quite comfortable services between İstanbul and Germany, Italy, Austria and Greece. Because of infrastructure upgrades, the only train service in operation at the time of writing was between İstanbul and Bucharest.

There are three border crossings between Bulgaria and Turkey. The main border crossing is the busy Kapitan-Andreevo/Kapıkule, 18km west of Edirne on the E5. The closest town on the Bulgarian side is Svilengrad, some 10km from the border. This crossing is open 24 hours daily.

There's a second crossing at Lesovo-Hamzabeyli, some 25km north of Edirne; it's a quieter option during the busy summer months than Kapitan-Andreevo/Kapıkule, but takes a little longer to get to, and there's no public transport.

The third crossing is at Malko Târnovo-Kırıkkale, some 70km northeast of Edirne and 92km south of Burgas.

Georgia

The main border crossing is at Sarp on the Black Sea coast, between Hopa (Turkey) and Batum (Georgia). You can also cross inland at the Türkgözü border crossing near Posof, north of Kars (Turkey) and southwest of Akhaltsikhe (Georgia). The Sarp border crossing is open 24 hours a day; Türkgözü is open from 8am to 8pm, although in winter you might want to double check that it's open at all.

Greece

At least six weekly buses travel from Athens' Peloponnese train station to İstanbul. You can also pick up the bus in Thessaloniki and at Alexandroupolis. Alternatively, you can make your own way to Alexandroupolis and take a service from the intercity bus station to the border town of Kipi, but remember that you can't walk across the border, so it's better to take a bus to İpsala (5km east beyond the border) or Keşan (30km east beyond the border), from where there are many buses to the capital.

There were no train services operating between Greece and Turkey at the time of writing because of infrastructure work. For updates, see the websites of Turkish State Railways (www.tcdd.gov.tr) or the Hellenic Railways Organisation (www.ose.gr).

Plan Your Trip
Activities

Top Activities

Best Desert Safaris
Wadi Rum, Jordan; October–May

Best Diving & Snorkelling
Red Sea, Egypt and Jordan; year-round

Best Hiking
Jordan Trail, Dana Biosphere Reserve to Petra; March–May and September–November

Best Sailing
Felucca trip, Aswan to Luxor; year-round

Best Skiing
The Cedars, Lebanon; December–April

Best Sea Kayaking
Kaş, Turkey; May–September

Best Archaeological Digs
For details on archaeological digs in Israel that welcome paying volunteers, try the Biblical Archaeology Society (www.digs.bib-arch.org/digs) or the Hebrew University of Jerusalem (www.archaeology.huji.ac.il/news/excavations.asp).

Best Hot-Air Ballooning
Cappadocia, Turkey and Luxor, Egypt

Best Canyoning
Mujib Biosphere Reserve, Jordan

Planning Your Trip

When to Go

The Middle East is an excellent year-round activities destination, although some activities will require planning to make sure you're here at the right time.

Summer (especially from June to September) is the ideal time to enjoy diving, snorkelling and other water sports.

The rest of the year is likely to be better for most other activities. From June to September, and especially in July and August, desert expeditions in the Sahara and Wadi Rum may be too hot for comfort (and, particularly in the case of the Sahara, may even be impossible). The best time to be in the desert also happens to be your best bet for finding snow in Lebanon and Iran: December to March is the best period if you're here to go snow skiing.

Hiking is possible year-round, although punishing daytime temperatures mean you should avoid the middle of the day if hiking in summer. The most comfortable hiking conditions are September to November and March to May.

What to Take

There are few requirements for most activities and those operators who organise activities (such as diving and snorkelling) will provide the necessary equipment. Bicycles and mountain bikes can be rented in the Middle East, but serious cyclists may want to bring their own bicycles and spare parts. Most hikers head out onto the trail under their own steam, but even those who plan on joining an organised hike in the region with a guide will usually need to bring their own equipment.

Getting Active

From deep-desert safaris in the Sahara to snow-skiing in Lebanon, from hiking the high valleys of central Jordan to diving and snorkelling the Red Sea, there aren't too many activities that you *can't* do in the Middle East.

Cycling & Mountain Biking

The Middle East offers some fantastic, if largely undeveloped, opportunities for cyclists. Unlike in Europe, you're likely to have many of the trails to yourself. However, the heat can be a killer (avoid June to September), and you'll need to be pretty self-sufficient, as spare parts can be extremely scarce. One of the highlights of travelling in this way is that locals in more out-of-the-way places will wonder what on earth you're doing – an ideal way to break the ice and meet new friends.

In Israel, many cycling trails go through forests managed by the Jewish National Fund (www.kkl.org.il); click 'Cycling Routes' on its website. Shvil Net (www.shvilnet.co.il) publishes Hebrew-language cycling guides that include detailed topographical maps. The Arava region in Israel is popular for mountain biking, while mountain biking also has great potential in Jordan, but there's very little in the way of organised expeditions.

In Iran, Esfahan to Yazd is an increasingly popular route for European cyclists. Consider avoiding the main highways and taking the secondary routes, which are much better suited to cycle touring. Cycling traffic is light and few locals ride, but a steady stream of overlanders brave the traffic en route between Europe and Asia. We're not sure we'd be going any further east than central Iran right now, but that has more to do with the security situation than it does with cycling conditions.

HIKING: PERSONAL EQUIPMENT CHECKLIST

- Sturdy hiking boots
- A high-quality sleeping bag – from October to March overnight temperatures can plummet in desert areas
- Warm clothing, including a jacket, jumper (sweater) or anorak (windbreaker)
- A sturdy but lightweight tent
- Mosquito repellent
- A lightweight stove
- Trousers for walking, preferably made from breathable waterproof (and windproof) material such as Gore-Tex
- An air-filled sleeping pad
- Swiss Army knife
- Torch (flashlight) or headlamp, with extra batteries

Desert Safaris

An expedition into the deserts of the Middle East will rank among your most memorable experiences of the region – the solitude, the gravitas of an empty landscape, the interplay of light and shadow on the sands. Various kinds of desert expeditions are possible, although they represent very different experiences. Camel trekking is environmentally friendly and slows you down to the pace of the deserts' traditional Bedouin inhabitants, but you'll be restricted to a fairly small corner of the desert. Travelling by 4WD allows you to cover greater distances but is usually more expensive.

Where to Go on a Desert Safari

Wadi Rum (p333) in Jordan has many calling cards: the orange sand, the improbable rocky mountains, the soulful Bedouin inhabitants who are the ideal companions around a desert campfire, and the haunting echoes of TE Lawrence. When you add to this the ease of getting here and exploring – it's accessible from major travel routes and is compact enough to visit within short time frames – and the professional operators that run expeditions here, it's hardly surprising that Wadi Rum is the desert experience that travellers to the Middle East love most. Everything is possible here, from afternoon camel treks to 4WD safaris and hikes lasting several days.

Other deserts where expeditions are possible include Egypt's Western Oases, for 4WD safaris into the Sahara from Bahariya

Oasis (p110) and Siwa Oasis (p111). If the security situation permits, Egypt's Sinai Peninsula (p117) is good for overnight, two- or three-day camel treks.

Israel is another possibility, with the Negev Desert (p251) a wonderful place to explore, as are the wild wadis and untamed mountains around the southern end of the Dead Sea (p308) on the Israeli side of the border.

Diving & Snorkelling

The Red Sea is one of the world's premier diving sites. Snorkellers heading out for the first time will be blown away by this dazzling underwater world of colourful coral and fish life, extensive reef systems and the occasional shipwreck. For experienced divers, there are plenty of sites to escape the wide-eyed newbies and see underwater landscapes that are both challenging and exceptionally beautiful.

Most dive centres offer every possible kind of dive course. The average open-water certification course for beginners, either with CMAS, PADI or NAUI, takes about five days and usually includes several dives. The total cost starts from around US$300; prices depend on the operator and location. A day's diving (two dives), including equipment and air fills, costs US$75 to US$150.

An introductory dive is around US$80. Full equipment can be hired for about US$30 per day.

BEST LONG-DISTANCE HIKES

Lycian Way (p460) Fethiye to Antalya along Turkey's Mediterranean coast.

Jordan Trail (p305) Jordan north to south.

Israel National Trail (Shvil Yisra'el) Travel 940km through Israel's most-scenic areas.

Nativity Trail It's 160km from Nazareth to Bethlehem.

Abraham Path Planned trans–Middle Eastern trail is operational from Nabus via Jericho to Hebron.

Lebanon Mountain Trail Runs along Lebanon's rocky spine.

The best bases for diving and snorkelling are in Sharm El Sheikh (p117), Dahab (p121), Nuweiba (p125) or Hurghada (p114) in Egypt; Aqaba (p337) in Jordan; and Eilat (p253) in Israel.

Snorkelling and scuba diving is also possible at many points along Turkey's Mediterranean coast, such as in Marmaris (p456), for example, although what's on offer doesn't come close to the Red Sea.

For something a little different, try diving or snorkelling in the Gulf from Iran. **Kish Diving Center** (☎0912 854 3246; www.kishdiving.com; ⏰7am-6pm) is a good operator.

Hiking

Hiking is one of the most rewarding activities in the Middle East, with memorable trails in Iran, Israel, Jordan, Lebanon and Turkey. Day hikes are possible everywhere, but there are some intriguing longer-haul options as well.

Iran

Solo trekking is possible, but taking a guide is a good idea as much for translation skills along the route as the actual navigation. In remote regions, especially near borders, you may stumble across military/police/security areas; an Iranian guide or a few phrases of Farsi should hopefully smooth over any misunderstandings.

One and two-day walks are possible in many areas, particularly the northwest and around Tehran. For Tehran, nearby Darband (p145) is a good start. Further afield, Kelardasht and Masuleh make good launch pads for mountain walks. Day and overnight desert treks can be easily arranged from Yazd (p164).

But perhaps the most popular and rewarding route (in spring and summer) is through the historic Alamut Valley (p155), once home to the Assassins, including a trek taking you across the Alborz Mountains and down to the Caspian.

Israel & the Palestinian Territories

With almost 10,000km of marked trails, Israel has some fabulous trekking possibilities, from the alpine slopes of Mt Hermon to the desert wadis of the Negev. In the Negev Desert, two spots stand out: Makhtesh Ramon (p252), the Middle East's largest crater, and En Avdat National Park (p252), where you can trek through canyons and pools. The Upper Galilee (p244) and Golan Heights (p247) are also excellent.

HERACLES KRITIKOS/SHUTTERSTOCK ©

Patara (p460), Turkey

At many national parks and nature reserves (www.parks.org.il), basic walking maps with English text are handed out when you pay your admission fee. The website www.tiuli.com, run by Lametayel, Israel's largest camping equipment store, has details in English on the hiking options around the country (the Hebrew website is much more extensive).

Jordan

Jordan is perhaps the Middle East's premier trekking destination, most notably in the spectacular landscapes of Wadi Rum (p333), Dana Biosphere Reserve (p318), Wadi Mujib (p317) and Petra (p320). The long-haul Jordan Trail (p305) runs from the northern Jordanian border to the Red Sea in the south. Our favourite stretch runs from Dana Biosphere Reserve to Petra (five days).

Lebanon

In Lebanon, the Qadisha Valley (p381) offers the pick of the hiking possibilities as you trek from one monastery to the next, although security can be an issue – ask locally before setting out.

Turkey

Some fine trails pass through the mountains of Cappadocia (p475), and Mt Ararat (p485) (5137m) near Doğubayazıt. But our pick of the long-distance walks is the Lycian Way (p460), a stunning, world-class coastal walk between Fethiye to Antalya on the Mediterranean coast.

Horse Riding

The rocky trails of the Middle East lend themselves to exploration by horseback. There aren't many operators out here, least of all ones whom we recommend, but it is possible to visit some of the region's iconic attractions in this way. These include the following:

- Wadi Rum (p336), Jordan
- West Bank tombs (p87), Luxor, Egypt
- Pyramids of Giza (p60), Cairo, Egypt
- Makhtesh Ramon (p252), Israel

Sailing & Boat Trips

From the Nile to the Mediterranean, cruising the waters is a wonderfully laid-back way to travel.

Egypt

Drifting down the Nile aboard a felucca (traditional sailing boat) is one of the quintessential Middle Eastern experiences. Although trips are possible elsewhere, most take place between Aswan and Luxor (p103) and possibilities range from day trips to five-day expeditions with stops at some lesser-visited riverside temples en route. Cairo (p53) is also possible for sunset trips.

Turkey

With its whitewashed villages, idyllic ports and mountainous backdrop, Turkey's Mediterranean and Aegean coasts are ideal for yacht cruising, especially given its proximity to the Greek islands.

The most romantic option is to sail along the coast in a *gület* (traditional wooden yacht). The most popular excursion is a four-day, three-night trip from Fethiye to Kale. Other possibilities include everything from day trips to two-week luxury charters and you can hire crewless bareboats or flotilla boats, or take a cabin on a boat hired by an agency. Ask anywhere near the docks for details; the following towns have the largest number of options: Kuşadası (p451), Bodrum (p453), Fethiye (p458) and Marmaris (p456).

Skiing

'Snow sports in the Middle East' probably sounds like it belongs in the tall-tales-told-to-gullible-travellers category, but not if you're Lebanese, Iranian or Turkish. The skiing can be excellent, if highly localised.

Iran

There are more than 20 functioning ski fields in Iran. The season is long, the snow is often powdery and untracked and, compared with Western fields, skiing in Iran is a bargain.

All the resorts have lodges, chalets and hotels, which charge from about US$50 to US$150 for a room. Ski lifts cost as little as US$10 a day. You can hire skis, poles and boots, but not clothes, at the resorts. Visit the very helpful www.skifed.ir for details on all of the slopes.

The season in the Alborz Mountains (p144) (where most slopes are located) starts as early as November and lasts until just after No Ruz (late March). There is good downhill skiing available near Tabriz and ski resorts can be found at Hamadan and Bijar. Skiing is also possible in the Zagros Mountains.

Lebanon

In the 1970s Beirut was famous for the fact that you could swim in the Mediterranean waters of the Lebanese capital in the morning, then ski on the slopes of Jebel Makmel, northeast of Beirut, in the afternoon. No sooner had the guns of civil war fallen silent than the Lebanese once again reclaimed the slopes from the militias, and their infectious optimism has seen the ski resorts going from strength to strength.

The Cedars (p382) is Lebanon's premier ski resort. The ski season takes place here from around December to April, depending on snow conditions. Equipment can be rented from a number of small ski shops at the base of the lifts.

For more on skiing in Lebanon, check out www.skileb.com.

Turkey

Close to İstanbul, Uludağ National Park (p442), centred on the Great Mountain (2543m), is Turkey's most popular ski resort. The season runs from December to April in most years.

Water Sports

Any Red Sea resort worth its salt will let you indulge your passion for water sports from windsurfing to waterskiing. Many of Turkey's Mediterranean beach resorts also offer ample opportunities for waterskiing, windsurfing, tandem paragliding or parasailing. More specifically, important water-sports locations include the following:

- Eilat (p252), in Israel, is arguably the Middle East's water-sports capital, with waterskiing, parasailing and a host of other thrills on offer.
- Moon Beach, at Sharm El Sheikh (p117), is Egypt's best windsurfing spot.
- Hurghada (p114) in Egypt is good for kitesurfing.
- Aqaba (p337) in Jordan offers a good range of sports.
- Kaş (p461) in Turkey is the region's best spot for sea kayaking.

Plan Your Trip

Travel with Children

We have a simple message for those of you considering travelling with your children to the Middle East: go for it. If you don't believe us, look around – you won't see many families of travellers, but the ones you do see will probably be having a pretty good time.

Middle East for Kids

Health & Safety

All travellers with children should know how to treat minor ailments and when to seek medical treatment. Make sure the children are up to date with routine vaccinations, and discuss possible travel vaccines well before departure as some vaccines are not suitable for children aged under one year.

On the all-important question of security, there are plenty of places in the Middle East that are extremely safe, and any place that's safe for you to visit will generally be safe for your children.

Public transport is rarely easy with children: car sickness is a problem, they'll usually end up on your lap, functional seat belts are rare, even in taxis, and accidents are common.

For more on health while travelling, see p577.

Eating Out

It's common for locals to eat out as a family. As a result, waiters are welcoming, or at least accepting of children. Best of all, the region's cuisine is generally child-friendly, being simple and varied, although you should always make sure the meat is well cooked. On the downside, Middle Eastern ice creams may be too much of a risk for tender young stomachs and, although some places have

Best Regions for Kids

Turkey

For the most part, travelling in Turkey is no different from anywhere else in Europe. The beach resorts of the Aegean and Mediterranean probably hold the greatest appeal, but don't forget the fairy-chimney landscape of Cappadocia. Public transport and road infrastructure is generally excellent, although distances between destinations can be long.

Jordan & Israel & the Palestinian Territories

Israel & the Palestinian Territories has terrific beaches, while Jordan boasts fabulous castles, camel trekking and the chance to float in the Dead Sea. An additional plus to travelling in these two compact places is the short distances to get anywhere, while standards of food hygiene are relatively high.

Egypt

Despite large distances, train rides and sailing boats down the Nile go some way towards compensating. Throw in beaches, Red Sea snorkelling and *Tintin & the Pharaohs* come to life, and kids could easily fall in love with the country.

high chairs, they're in the minority. Kids' menus are rare except in Western-style hotel restaurants in larger cities.

Beach Holidays

The beaches of the Middle East are ideal for families and factoring in some beach time to go with the region's more adult attractions can be an extremely wise move. The safest and most easily accessible place to begin is Turkey's Mediterranean coast. Egypt, Jordan and Israel & the Palestinian Territories all have excellent beaches, many of which have a range of activities on offer, from boat rides to diving and snorkelling.

Culture

Unlike any vaguely news-savvy adult, most children have yet to have their perceptions of the Middle East distorted by stereotypes. Discovering for themselves just how friendly the people of the Middle East can be is a lesson that will last a lifetime. More than that, your own chances of meeting locals (especially local families) is greatly enhanced if you're travelling as a family.

Children's Highlights

Temples & Castles

Temple of Karnak (p87) A sound-and-light show that's a great alternative to history books.

Petra (p320) If they've seen *Indiana Jones*, watch them go wide-eyed with recognition.

Karak (p317) **& Shobak** (p320) Jordanian castles filled with legends of knights and damsels in distress.

Cappadocia (p475) Fairy-tale landscape made for a child's fertile imagination.

Cities

Jerusalem (p201) Child-friendly activities; brings Sunday school lessons to life.

Esfahan (p158) Welcoming open spaces with plenty of families enjoying them.

İstanbul (p416) Make geography interesting by visiting two continents in one day.

Beaches & Activities

Snorkelling the Red Sea (p253) A whole new world to make Nemo look tame.

Spending time on Turkey's beaches (p458) Gentle waters and family-friendly facilities.

Sailing a felucca up the Nile from Aswan to Luxor (p106) An unforgettable journey.

Floating in the Dead Sea (p249) Yes, even Dad floats!

Riding a camel through Wadi Rum (p333) Be Lawrence of Arabia for a day.

Horse riding in Luxor (p95) An original way to experience West Bank temples.

Planning

Accommodation

Your chances of finding what you need (such as cots) increase the more you're willing to pay. And you'll almost certainly want something with a private bathroom and hot water, thereby precluding most budget accommodation. Hygiene standards at many budget establishments can also be poor.

Children under two years usually stay for free in most hotels. There's often a supplementary charge for squeezing in extra beds. Large family rooms or adjoining rooms with connecting doors are occasionally available.

What to Bring

Disposable nappies (diapers), powdered milk, formula and bottled water are widely available throughout the region in most large supermarkets, although don't expect to find your favourite brands; stock up in larger towns as some items won't be available elsewhere.

If you'll be travelling by taxi or minibus, you may consider bringing a child's seatbelt adjuster and/or a car seat; very few vehicles have the latter.

Other useful items to bring include child-friendly insect repellent and a blanket to spread out to use as a makeshift nappy-changing area.

When to Go

The best times to visit the Middle East are in autumn (September to November) or spring (March to May). Travel is certainly possible at other times, but winter (December to February) can be bitterly cold in the evenings and rain can be frequent. And unless you'll be spending all of your time in the water, avoid travel in the summer (especially in July and August) as the extreme heat can be uncomfortable and energy sapping.

Countries at a Glance

Every country in the region promises stirring historical landmarks and provides attractions worth anchoring your visit around. A choice of spectacular landscapes could similarly determine your route through the region, with Turkey, Jordan and Egypt the highlights. If Red Sea diving and snorkelling appeal, it has to be Egypt (and, to a lesser extent, Jordan and Israel), while camel trekking is possible in both Jordan and Egypt. Turkey has the most beautiful beaches, while travellers for whom food is the main event will want to spend most of their time in Turkey and Lebanon.

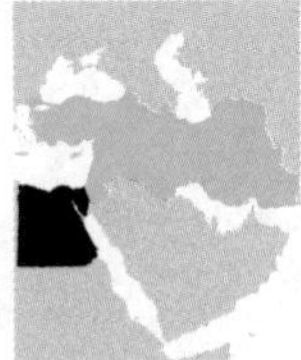

Egypt

Ruins
Diving
Landscapes

The country's Nile Valley is an extraordinary open-air museum to Egypt's glorious past, while the waters off Egypt's Red Sea coast rank among the world's premier diving and snorkelling destinations. Elsewhere, Egypt's landscapes possess stark, desert beauty.

p52

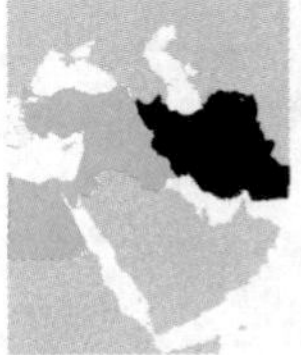

Iran

History
Architecture
Cities

Iran is a friendly, hospitable country with some of the Middle East's most decorated mosques and other religious architecture, the magnificent ruins of Persepolis and engaging, bazaar-filled cities such as Shiraz, Yazd and Esfahan.

p136

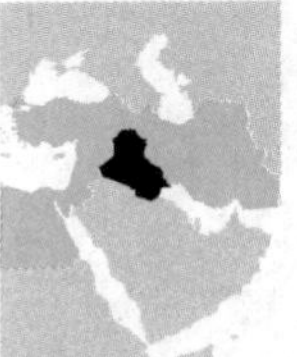

Iraq

Inaccessible

Were it not seriously dangerous to visit Iraq, its appeal would be considerable. Attractions range from ancient ruined cities (many of which were seriously damaged by so-called Islamic State) in the country's Sunni heartland and the storied city of Baghdad to the vibrant Kurdish culture and soaring mountains of the north.

p190

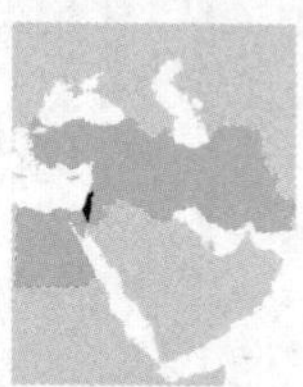

Israel & the Palestinian Territories

History
Cities
Activities

Sacred ground to the three great monotheistic faiths, Israel and the Palestinian Territories are modern countries grafted onto a deeply spiritual land. Visit peerless Jerusalem, cool Tel Aviv and vibrant Ramallah.

p199

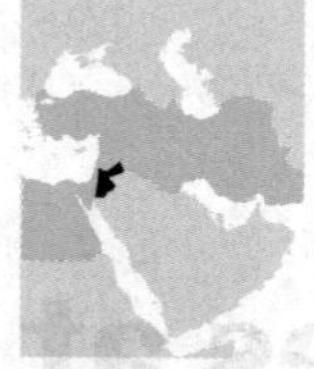

Jordan

Ruins
Landscapes
Activities

In the heart of a tough neighbourhood, Jordan is a travellers' oasis, home to an extraordinary ancient city (Petra), the region's best desert scenery (Wadi Rum) and splendid snorkelling offshore from Jordan's sliver of Red Sea coast.

p285

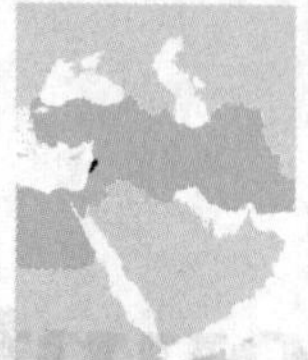

Lebanon

Ruins
Landscapes
Food

From Phoenician remnants to the fantastic Roman ruins at Tyre, from a rugged Mediterranean coast to the interior's snow-capped mountains, Lebanon packs a lot into a very small area. Beirut in particular is a world-class culinary destination.

p354

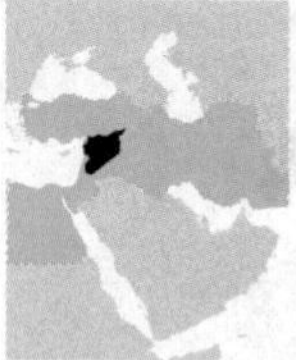

Syria

Inaccessible

Before the war, Syria was a traveller favourite of ancient cities, astonishing ruins, exceptional food and hospitable locals. While conflict ravages most of the country and the country is extremely dangerous to visit, a disrupted version of everyday life continues.

p405

Turkey

Cities
Beaches
Ruins

Turkey is where the Middle East meets Europe, literally so in İstanbul, one of the most beautiful cities on earth. Elsewhere, expect first-rate attractions including breathtaking Cappadocia, an exquisite turquoise-hued coast, Roman Ephesus and soulful Mt Nemrut.

p413

On the Road

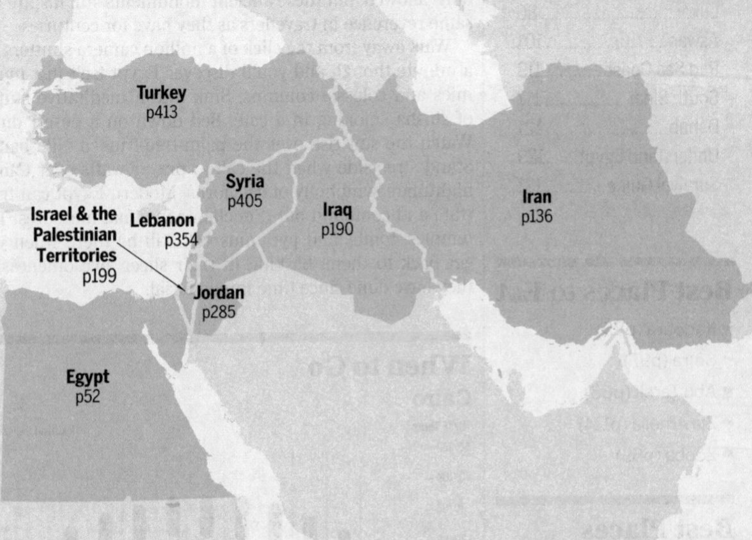
Turkey
p413
Syria
p405
Israel & the Palestinian Territories
p199
Lebanon
p354
Iraq
p190
Iran
p136
Jordan
p285
Egypt
p52

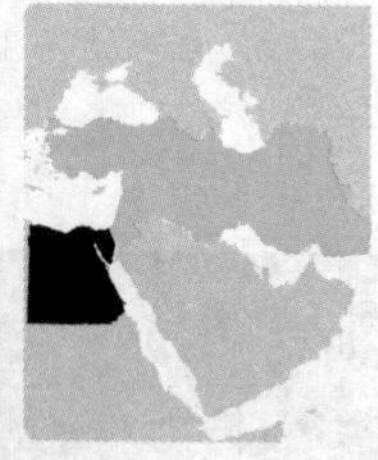

Egypt

Includes ➡

Cairo........................... 53
Mediterranean Coast... 80
Alexandria.................... 80
Nile Valley.................... 86
Luxor 86
Aswan.......................... 101
Red Sea Coast............ 113
South Sinai 117
Dahab.......................... 121
Understand Egypt....... 129
Survival Guide............ 131

Best Places to Eat

- Kadoura (p85)
- Sofra (p97)
- Abu Tarek (p68)
- Zia Amelia (p114)
- Zööba (p69)

Best Places to Stay

- Hotel Longchamps (p65)
- Beit Sabée (p97)
- Oberoi Sahl Hasheesh (p115)
- Albabinshal Heritage Hotel (p112)
- Eskaleh (p107)

Why Go?

Herodotus let the cat out of the bag in the 5th century BC, leaving the door open for over a millennium of conquerors and adventurers to gawp, graffiti and pilfer Egypt's mammoth racks of Pharaonic rubble. Today it may be 'gawping only' allowed, but these ancient monuments still inspire the same reverence in travellers as they have for centuries.

Walk away from the click of a million camera shutters for a minute though and you'll discover Egypt isn't just mummies and colossal columns. Sink into a meditative stupor of shisha smoking in a cafe. Bed down on a desert dune. Watch the sun rise over the palm-tree-fringed Nile banks. Stand streetside when the call to prayer wafts over Cairo's nightmare symphony of car horns. Modern Egypt can frustrate and confound but it enchants in equal measures. The temples, tombs and pyramids will still be there when you get back to them, basking in their sheer awesomeness as they have done since time immemorial.

When to Go

Cairo

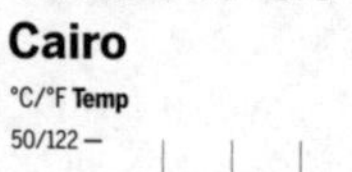

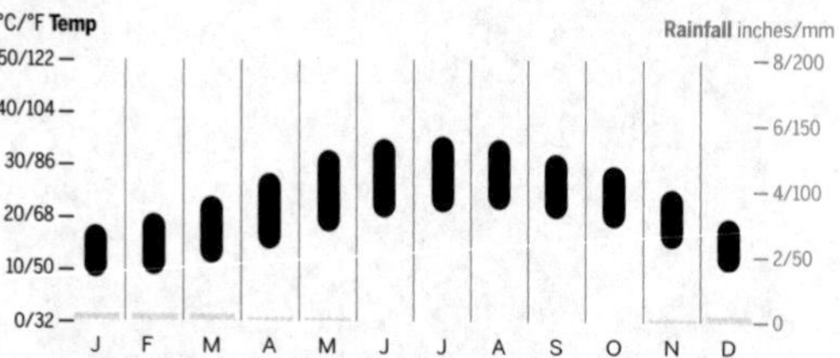

Nov-Feb Egypt's 'winter' is largely sunny and warm; ideal for desert adventures and temple exploring.

Jul-Aug Summer's furnace sizzles but underwater conditions are perfect for Red Sea diving.

Oct Autumn's painterly light makes a Nile journey a photographer's dream.

CAIRO القاهرة

☎02 / POP 22 MILLION

Cairo is chaos at its most magnificent, infuriating and beautiful. This mega-city's constant buzz is a product of its 22-or-so million inhabitants simultaneously crushing Cairo's infrastructure under their collective weight and lifting its spirits up with their exceptional humour. Your nerves will jangle, your snot will run black from the smog and touts will hound you at every turn, but it's a small price to pay to tap into the energy of the place Egyptians call Umm Ad Dunya – the Mother of the World.

Blow your nose, crack a joke and look through the dirt to see the city's true colours. If you love Cairo, it will definitely love you back.

History

Cairo is not ancient, though the presence of the Pyramids leads many to believe otherwise. Its foundations were laid in AD 969 by the early Islamic Fatimid dynasty. Under the rule of subsequent dynasties, Cairo swelled and burst its walls, but at heart it remained a medieval city for 900 years.

It wasn't until the mid-19th century that Cairo started to change in any significant way. The site of modern downtown Cairo, west of what is now Midan Opera, was then a swampy plain subject to the annual flooding of the Nile. In 1863, when the French-educated Ismail Pasha came to power, he was determined to upgrade the image of his capital, which he believed could only be done by starting afresh. For 10 years the former marsh became one vast building site as Ismail invited architects from Belgium, France and Italy to create a brand-new European-style district, which earned the nickname 'Paris on the Nile'. This building boom has continued until the present day, if with somewhat less aesthetic cohesion, with the city's boundaries constantly expanding into the surrounding desert.

NEED TO KNOW

Capital Cairo

Country code ☎20

Language Arabic

Official name Arab Republic of Egypt

Population 93.3 million

Currency Egyptian pound (LE)

Mobile phones Egypt's GSM network has thorough coverage

Visas Single-entry, 30-day tourist visas cost US$25. Many nationalities can purchase e-visas online at www.egyptvisa.com.

Exchange Rates

Australia	A$1	LE13.79
Euro zone	€1	LE20.69
Israel & the Palestinian Territories	1NIS	LE5.70
Jordan	JD1	LE24.62
UK	£1	LE23.29
USA	US$1	LE17.60

For current exchange rates see www.xe.com.

Resources

Egypt Tourism (www.egypt.travel) Official tourism site with trip-planning tools.

Daily News Egypt (www.dailynewsegypt.com) Independent English newspaper.

Mada Masr (www.madamasr.com) Independent progressive online reporting in English.

Egypt Independent (www.egyptindependent.com) Respected online news.

Lonely Planet (www.lonelyplanet.com/egypt) Destination information, hotel bookings and traveller forum.

Sights

Downtown

★**Egyptian Museum** MUSEUM

(Map p66; ☎2579 6948; Midan Tahrir; adult/student LE120/60, after 5.30pm Sun & Thu LE180/90, Royal Mummies Room LE150/75, camera LE50; 9am-7pm Mon-Wed, to 9pm Sun & Thu, to 4pm Fri & Sat; Ⓜ Sadat) One of the world's most important collections of ancient artefacts, the Egyptian Museum takes pride of place in Downtown Cairo, on the north side of Midan Tahrir. Inside the great domed, oddly pinkish building, the glittering treasures of Tutankhamun and other great pharaohs

Egypt Highlights

1 **Pyramids of Giza** (p60) Coming face to face with one of the world's great wonders.

2 **Cairo** (p53) Overloading on mosques, mausoleums, museums and ancient churches.

3 **Abu Simbel** (p106) Sensing the vanity of Ramses II amid his most spectacular temple complex.

4 **Luxor** (p86) Putting on your explorer hat within this mind-boggling cache of tombs and temples.

5 **Siwa** (p111) Hitting the end of the road to revel in the far-from-anywhere vibe and delve into Siwan culture.

6 **Ras Mohammed National Park** (p117) Diving into an underwater fantasia of coral mountains and flitting fish.

7 **Aswan** (p101) Taking a time-out to appreciate the panoramas before sailing on the waters of history on your own Nile journey.

8 **White Desert National Park** (p110) Gaping in awe at this geological wonderland.

9 **Alexandria** (p80) Soaking up the last drops of 19th-century grandeur while strolling the Corniche.

10 **Dahab** (p123) Snorkelling the Lighthouse Reef and then relaxing with a beer and shisha in this backpacker vortex.

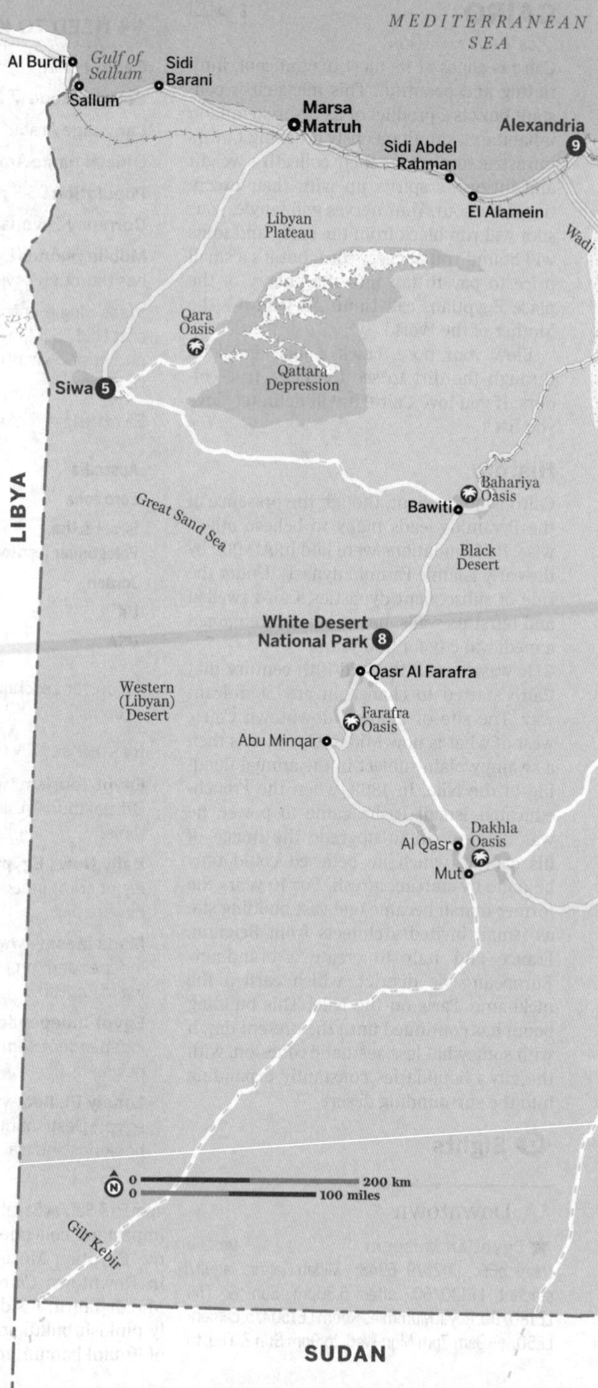

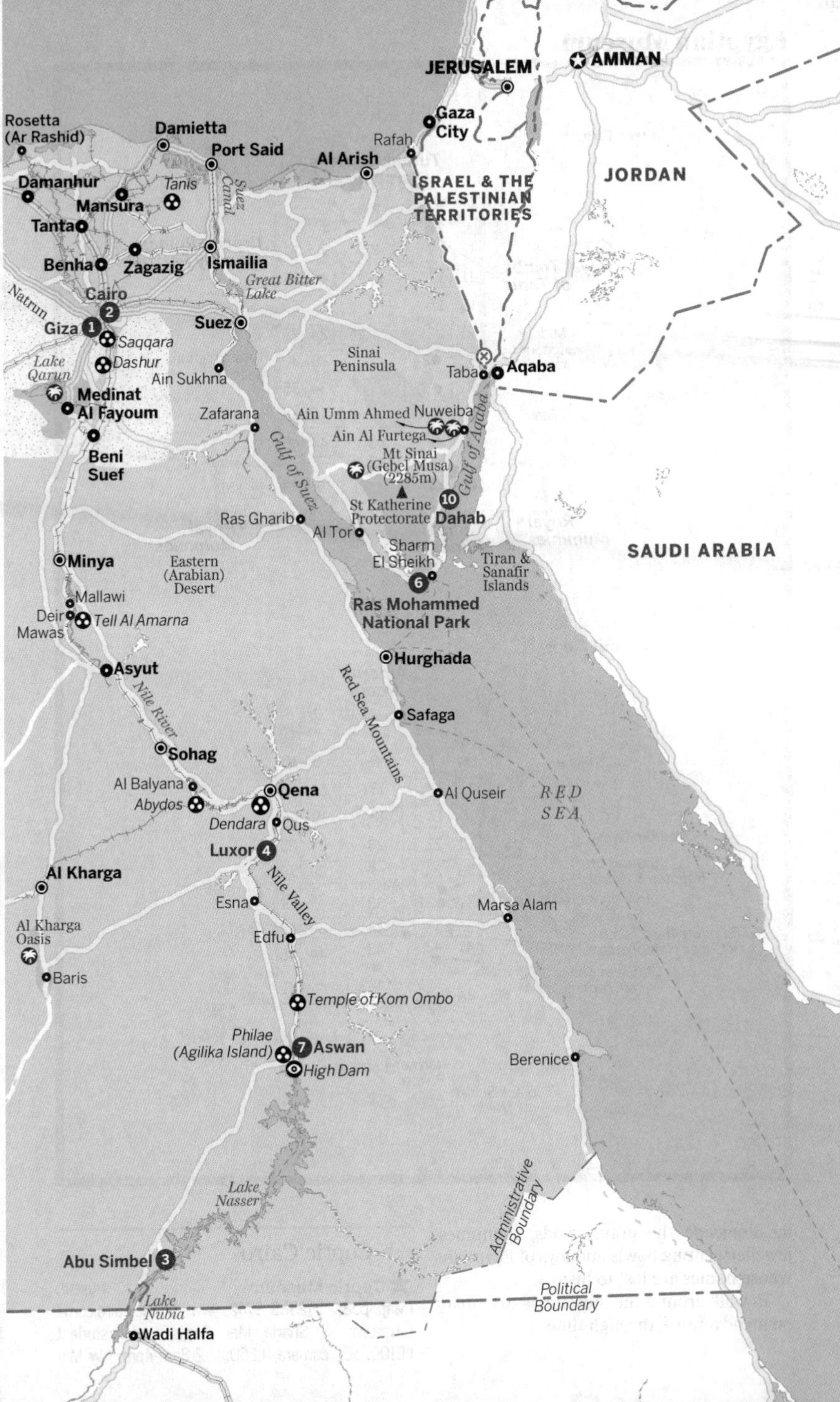

JERUSALEM
AMMAN
Gaza City
Rafah
Rosetta (Ar Rashid)
Damietta
Port Said
Al Arish
ISRAEL & THE PALESTINIAN TERRITORIES
JORDAN
Damanhur
Tanis
Suez Canal
Mansura
Tanta
Benha
Zagazig
Ismailia
Great Bitter Lake
Natrun
Cairo
Giza
Suez
Saqqara
Dashur
Lake Qarun
Sinai Peninsula
Taba
Aqaba
Ain Sukhna
Medinat Al Fayoum
Zafarana
Ain Umm Ahmed
Nuweiba
Ain Al Furtega
Beni Suef
Gulf of Suez
Mt Sinai (Gebel Musa) (2285m)
Gulf of Aqaba
St Katherine Protectorate
Dahab
Ras Gharib
Al Tor
Sharm El Sheikh
Tiran & Sanafir Islands
SAUDI ARABIA
Minya
Eastern (Arabian) Desert
Mallawi
Deir Mawas
Tell Al Amarna
Ras Mohammed National Park
Hurghada
Asyut
Red Sea Mountains
Nile River
Safaga
Sohag
Al Balyana
Qena
Al Quseir
RED SEA
Abydos
Dendara
Qus
Luxor
Nile Valley
Al Kharga
Esna
Marsa Alam
Al Kharga Oasis
Edfu
Baris
Temple of Kom Ombo
Philae (Agilika Island)
Aswan
High Dam
Berenice
Lake Nasser
Administrative Boundary
Abu Simbel
Lake Nubia
Political Boundary
Wadi Halfa

Egyptian Museum

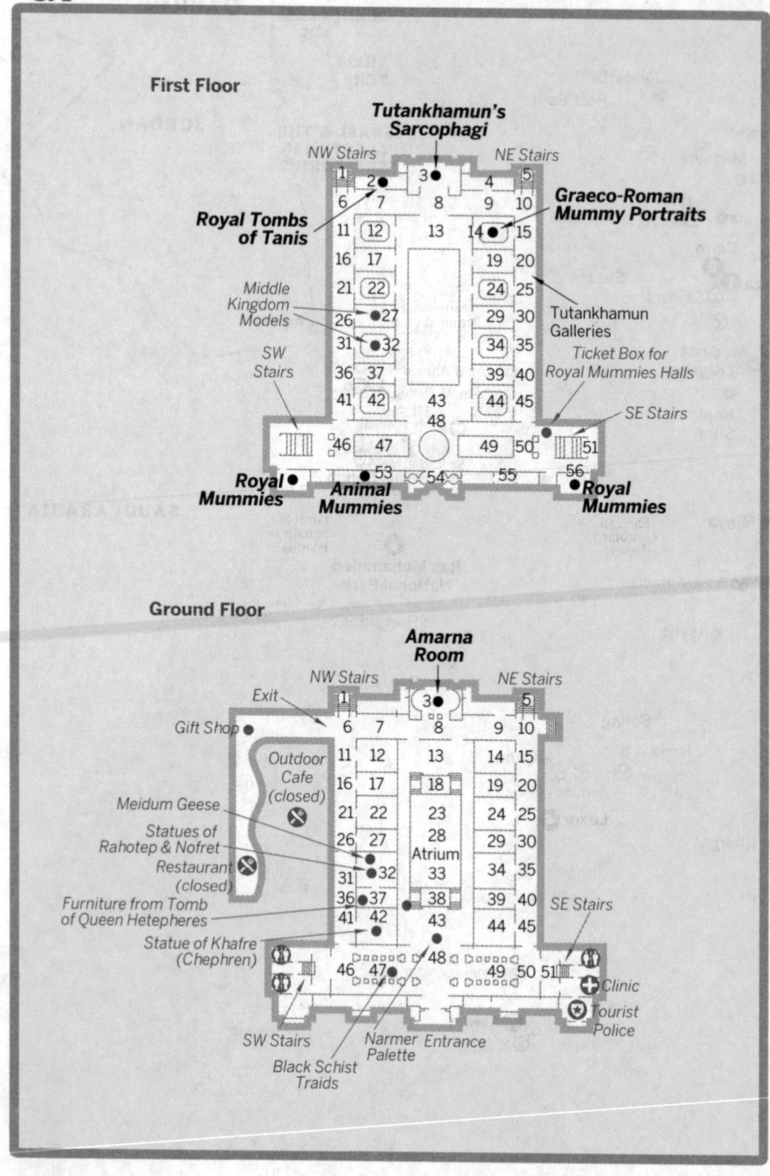

lie alongside the grave goods, mummies, jewellery, eating bowls and toys of Egyptians whose names are lost to history.

To walk around the museum is to embark on an adventure through time.

Coptic Cairo

★Coptic Museum MUSEUM

(Map p58; ☎2363 9742; www.coptic-cairo.com/museum; 3 Sharia Mar Girgis; adult/student LE100/50, camera LE50; ⏲8am-4pm; Ⓜ Mar

Girgis) This museum, founded in 1908, houses Coptic art from the earliest days of Christianity in Egypt right through to early Islam. It is a beautiful place, as much for the elaborate woodcarving in all the galleries as for the treasures they contain. These include sculpture that shows obvious continuity from the Ptolemaic period, rich textiles and whole walls of monastery frescoes. Allow at least a couple of hours to explore the 1200 or so pieces on display.

Hanging Church CHURCH

(Al Kineesa Al Mu'allaqa; Map p58; www.coptic-cairo.com; Sharia Mar Girgis; donations welcome; 8am-4pm, Coptic Mass 8-11am Wed & Fri, 9-11am Sun; M Mar Girgis) FREE Just south of the Coptic Museum on Sharia Mar Girgis (the main road parallel with the metro), a stone facade inscribed with Coptic and Arabic marks the entrance to the 9th-century (some say 7th) Hanging Church, so named because it is suspended over the Water Gate of Roman Babylon. With its three barrel-vaulted, wood-roofed aisles, the interior of the church feels like an upturned ark, resting on 13 elegant pillars representing Christ and his apostles.

Church of St Sergius & Bacchus CHURCH

(Abu Sarga; Map p58; www.coptic-cairo.com/oldcairo/church/sarga/sarga.html; off Sharia Haret Al Kidees Girgis; donations welcome; 8am-4pm; M Mar Girgis) FREE This is the oldest church inside Coptic Cairo's walls, built in the 11th century with 4th-century pillars. It honours the Roman soldiers Sergius and Bacchus, who were martyred in Syria for their Christian faith in AD 296. It is built over a cave where Joseph, Mary and the infant Jesus are said to have taken shelter after fleeing to Egypt to escape persecution from King Herod of Judea, who had embarked upon a 'massacre of the first born'.

Gezira & Roda Islands

Cairo Tower MONUMENT

(Burg Misr; Map p74; 2735-7187; www.cairotower.net; Sharia Hadayek Al Zuhreya, Gezira; adult/child under 6yr LE70/free; 8am-midnight, to 1am summer; M Opera) This 187m-high tower is the city's most famous landmark after the Pyramids. Built in 1961, the structure, which resembles a stylised lotus plant with its latticework casing, was a thumb to the nose at the Americans, who had given Nasser the money used for its construction to buy US arms. The 360-degree views across the city from the top are clearest in the late morning, after the haze burns off, or late afternoon, when you can often spy the Pyramids.

★ Manial Palace MUSEUM

(Mathaf Al Manial, Palace-Museum of Mohammed Ali; Map p74; 2368 7495; 1 Sharia Al Saray, Roda; adult/student LE100/50; 9am-4pm; M Sayyida Zeinab) After a years'-long restoration period, this palace complex, built by the uncle of King Farouk, Prince Mohammed Ali, in the early 20th century, has once again thrown open its doors to the public as a quirky museum. Its interiors and architecture are a fascinating merging of Ottoman, Moorish, Persian and European rococo styles, while the gardens (still closed to the public at the time of research) are planted with rare tropical plants collected by the prince.

Islamic Cairo

★ Khan Al Khalili MARKET

(Map p70; off Sharia Al Azhar & Al Gamaliyya) The skinny lanes of Khan Al Khalili are basically a medieval-style mall. This agglomeration of shops stock everything from soap powder to semiprecious stones, not to mention tacky

HIGHLIGHTS OF THE EGYPTIAN MUSEUM

Tutankhamun Galleries (1st fl) King Tut's treasures occupy a large chunk of the museum's upper floor. Go first to Room 3 to see his sarcophagi while the crowds are light.

Old Kingdom Rooms (Ground fl, Rooms 42, 37 & 32) Look out for the statue of well-muscled Khafre – you may also recognise him from the Sphinx.

Royal Tombs of Tanis (1st fl, Room 2) This room of gem-encrusted gold jewellery was found at the largest ruined city in the Nile Delta.

Graeco-Roman Mummy Portraits (1st fl, Room 14) These wood panel portraits were placed over the faces of embalmed dead, staring up in vividly realistic style.

Middle Kingdom Models (1st fl, Rooms 32 & 27) Get a picture of common life in ancient Egypt, depicted in miniature dioramas made to accompany the pharaoh to the other world.

Royal Mummies Halls (1st fl, Rooms 56 & 46) Visit these around lunch or near closing time to avoid the crowds.

Cairo

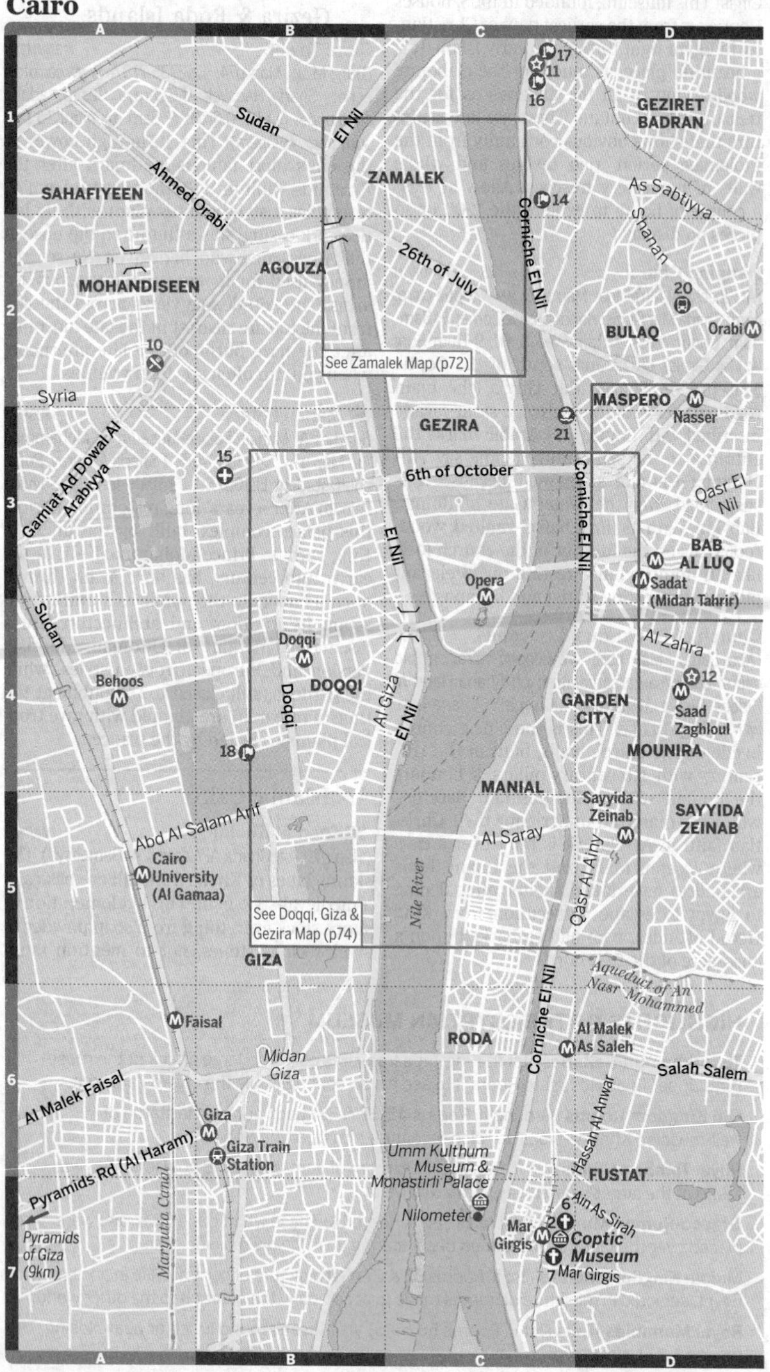

SAHAFIYEEN
MOHANDISEEN
AGOUZA
ZAMALEK
GEZIRET BADRAN
BULAQ
MASPERO
GEZIRA
BAB AL LUQ
DOQQI
GARDEN CITY
MOUNIRA
MANIAL
SAYYIDA ZEINAB
GIZA
RODA
FUSTAT
Sudan
Ahmed Orabi
El Nil
26th of July
Corniche El Nil
As Sabtiyya
Shanan
Syria
Gamiat Ad Dowal Al Arabiyya
6th of October
Qasr El Nil
Opera
Nasser
Orabi
Sadat (Midan Tahrir)
Al Zahra
Doqqi
Behoos
Al Giza
Saad Zaghloul
Abd Al Salam Arif
Al Saray
Sayyida Zeinab
Qasr Al Ainy
Cairo University (Al Gamaa)
Nile River
Aqueduct of An Nasr Mohammed
Faisal
Midan Giza
Al Malek As Saleh
Salah Salem
Al Malek Faisal
Hassan Al Anwar
Giza
Giza Train Station
Pyramids Rd (Al Haram)
Umm Kulthum Museum & Monastirli Palace
Nilometer
Maryutia Canal
Pyramids of Giza (9km)
Mar Girgis
Coptic Museum
Ain As Sirah
See Zamalek Map (p72)
See Doqqi, Giza & Gezira Map (p74)

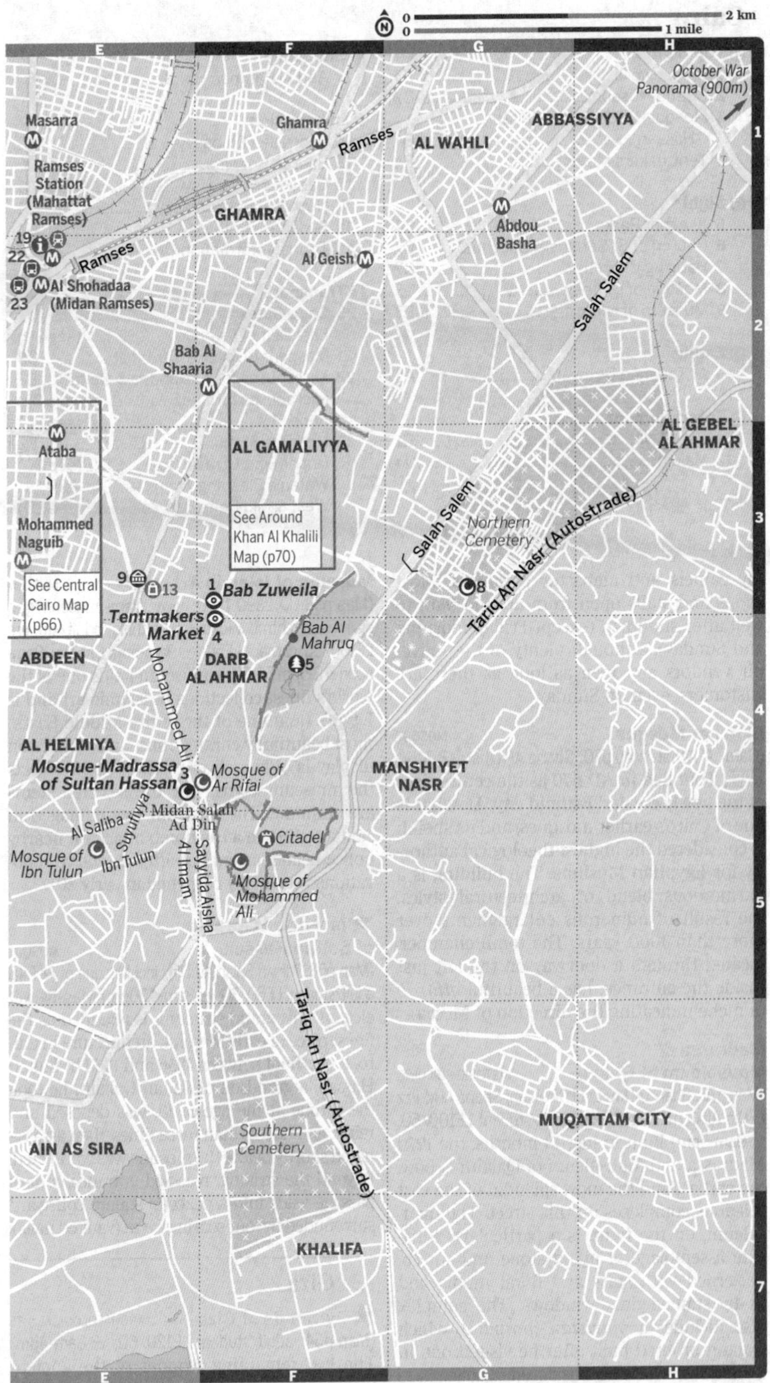
0 2 km
0 1 mile
E
F
G
H
October War Panorama (900m)
Masarra
Ghamra
Ramses
AL WAHLI
ABBASSIYYA
Ramses Station (Mahattat Ramses)
GHAMRA
Abdou Basha
19
22
23
Ramses
Al Geish
Al Shohadaa (Midan Ramses)
Salah Salem
Bab Al Shaaria
Ataba
AL GAMALIYYA
AL GEBEL AL AHMAR
Mohammed Naguib
See Around Khan Al Khalili Map (p70)
Salah Salem
Northern Cemetery
Tariq An Nasr (Autostrade)
See Central Cairo Map (p66)
9
13
1
Bab Zuweila
8
Tentmakers Market
4
Bab Al Mahruq
ABDEEN
DARB AL AHMAR
5
Mohammed Ali
AL HELMIYA
Mosque-Madrassa of Sultan Hassan
3
Mosque of Ar Rifai
MANSHIYET NASR
Midan Salah Ad Din
Al Saliba
Suyufiyya
Citadel
Mosque of Ibn Tulun
Ibn Tulun
Al Imam
Sayyida Aisha
Mosque of Mohammed Ali
Tariq An Nasr (Autostrade)
MUQATTAM CITY
Southern Cemetery
AIN AS SIRA
KHALIFA
1
2
3
4
5
6
7

Cairo

Top Sights
1 Bab Zuweila ... F3
2 Coptic Museum ... C7
3 Mosque-Madrassa of Sultan Hassan ... E4
4 Tentmakers Market ... F4

Sights
5 Al Azhar Park ... F4
6 Church of St Sergius & Bacchus ... C7
7 Hanging Church ... C7
8 Mosque of Qaitbey ... G3
9 Museum of Islamic Art ... E3

Eating
10 At Tabei Ad Dumyati ... A2

Entertainment
11 Bab El Nil ... C1
12 Makan ... D4

Shopping
13 Abd Al Rahman Harraz ... E3

Information
14 Australian Embassy ... C1
15 Badran Hospital ... B3
16 Canadian Embassy ... C1
17 New Zealand Embassy ... C1
18 Sudanese Embassy ... B4
19 Tourist Information Office ... E2

Transport
20 Cairo Gateway ... D2
East Delta Travel Co ... (see 20)
21 Maspero River Bus Terminal ... C3
22 Microbuses for Alexandria & Delta ... E2
Microbuses for Suez ... (see 23)
Super Jet ... (see 20)
23 Ulali Bus Station ... E2
Upper Egypt Travel Co ... (see 20)
Watania Sleeping Train ... (see 19)
West & Mid Delta Bus Co ... (see 20)

toy camels and alabaster pyramids. Most shops and stalls open from around 9am to well after sundown (except Friday morning and Sunday), although plenty of the souvenir vendors are open as long as there are customers, even on Sunday.

Al Azhar Mosque MOSQUE
(Gami' Al Azhar; Map p70; Sharia Al Azhar; 24hr) FREE Founded in AD 970 as the centrepiece of the newly created Fatimid city, Al Azhar is one of Cairo's earlier mosques, and its sheikh is considered the highest theological authority for Egyptian Muslims. The building is a harmonious blend of architectural styles, the result of numerous enlargements over more than 1000 years. The tomb chamber, located through a doorway on the left just inside the entrance, has a beautiful *mihrab* (a niche indicating the direction of Mecca).

Madrassa & Mausoleum of Qalaun HISTORIC BUILDING
(Map p70; Sharia Al Muizz Li Din Allah; Sharia Al Muizz Li Din Allah multisite ticket adult/student LE100/50; 9am-5pm) Built in just 13 months, the 1279 Madrassa and Mausoleum of Qalaun is both the earliest and the most splendid of the vast religious complexes on this street. The mausoleum, on the right, is a particularly intricate assemblage of inlaid stone and stucco, patterned with stars and floral motifs and lit by stained-glass windows. The complex also includes a *maristan* (hospital), which Qalaun ordered built after he visited one in Damascus, where he was cured of colic.

Museum of Islamic Art MUSEUM
(Map p58; 2390 1520; www.islamicmuseum.gov.eg/museum.html; Midan Bab Al Khalq; adult/student LE100/50, camera LE50; 9am-5pm Sat-Thu, 9am-noon & 2-5pm Fri) This museum holds one of the world's finest collections of Islamic art and is Egypt's (and one of the entire Middle East's) most beautifully curated museums. What's on display is only a sliver of the 80,000 objects the museum owns, but the selected items are stunning. The museum was damaged in January 2014 in a car-bomb attack on nearby police headquarters but after extensive renovations was finally reopened in early 2017.

★ **Mosque-Madrassa of Sultan Hassan** MOSQUE
(Map p58; Midan Salah Ad Din; incl Mosque of Ar Rifai adult/student LE60/30; 8am-4.30pm) Massive yet elegant, this grand structure is regarded as the finest piece of early Mamluk architecture in Cairo. It was built between 1356 and 1363 by Sultan Hassan, a grandson of Sultan Qalaun; he took the throne at the age of 13, was deposed and reinstated no less than three times, then assassinated shortly before the mosque was completed. Beyond the striking, recessed entrance, a dark passage leads into a peaceful square courtyard surrounded by four soaring *iwan* (vaulted halls).

Giza

★ **Pyramids of Giza** ARCHAEOLOGICAL SITE
(Map p64; adult/student LE120/60; 8am-4pm) The last remaining wonder of the ancient world; for nearly 4000 years, the extraordi-

nary shape, impeccable geometry and sheer bulk of the Giza Pyramids have invited the obvious questions: 'How were they built, and why?' Centuries of research have given us parts of the answer. Built as massive tombs on the orders of the pharaohs, they were constructed by teams of workers tens-of-thousands strong. Today they stand as an awe-inspiring tribute to the might, organisation and achievements of ancient Egypt.

➡ **Great Pyramid of Khufu**

(Great Pyramid of Cheops; Map p64; interior adult/student LE300/150; ⏲8am-noon & 1-4pm) The oldest pyramid in Giza and the largest in Egypt, Khufu's Great Pyramid stood 146m high when it was completed around 2570 BC. After 46 windy centuries, its height has been reduced by 9m. There isn't much to see inside the pyramid, but the experience of climbing through the ancient structure is unforgettable – though impossible if you suffer the tiniest degree of claustrophobia. The elderly and unfit should not attempt the climb, as it is very steep.

➡ **Cheops Boat Museum**

(Map p64; adult/student LE80/40, camera LE50; ⏲9am-4pm) Immediately south of the Great Pyramid is this fascinating museum with exactly one object on display: one of Cheops' five solar *barques* (boats), buried near his pyramid, and unearthed in 1954. This huge stunning ancient wood vessel, possibly the oldest boat in existence, was carefully restored from 1200 pieces of Lebanese cedar and encased in this museum to protect it from the elements. Visitors to the museum must help this process by donning protective footwear to keep sand out.

➡ **Pyramid of Khafre**

(Pyramid of Chephren; Map p64; adult/student LE60/30; ⏲8am-4pm) Khafre, the second pyramid, seems larger than that of Khafre's father, Khufu. At just 136m high, it's not taller, but it stands on higher ground and its peak is still capped with the original polished limestone casing. Originally all three pyramids were totally encased in this smooth white stone, which would have made them gleam in the sun. Over the centuries, this casing has been stripped for use in palaces and mosques, exposing the softer inner-core stones to the elements.

➡ **Pyramid of Menkaure**

(Pyramid of Mycerinus; Map p64; adult/student LE60/30; ⏲8am-4pm) At 62m (originally 66.5m), this pyramid is the smallest of the trio, only about one-tenth the bulk of the Great Pyramid. The pharaoh Menkaure died before the structure was finished – around the bottom are several courses of granite facing that were never properly smoothed. Inside, you descend into three distinct levels – the largest surprisingly vast – and you can peer into the main tomb.

➡ **Sphinx**

(Map p64) Known in Arabic as Abu Al Hol (Father of Terror), this sculpture of a man with the haunches of a lion was dubbed the Sphinx by the ancient Greeks because it resembled their mythical winged monster who set riddles and killed anyone unable to answer them. A geological survey has shown that it was most likely carved from the bedrock at the bottom of the causeway during Khafre's reign, so it probably portrays his features.

PYRAMIDS PRACTICALITIES

Entrance & Tickets

The main entrance (Map p64) is at the end of Pyramids Rd (Sharia Al Haram), though if you come on a tour bus, you may enter through the gate (Map p64) below the Sphinx, in the village of Nazlet As Samaan.

Additional tickets are required for the Cheops Boat Museum, the **Tomb of Meresankh III** (Map p64; adult/student LE50/25), and the pyramid interiors. The Great Pyramid is always open, along with one of the other two (they alternate every year or so). Pyramid interior and Tomb of Meresankh III tickets can only be purchased at the main entrance ticket office.

Getting There & Away

The most efficient traffic-beating way to reach the Pyramids is to go via metro to Giza (LE2), then by taxi (about LE20), microbus (LE5) or bus (LE2.50). Microbuses cluster at the bottom of the west-side stairs from the metro (drivers are yelling 'Haram'). Buses stop on the north side of Pyramids Rd, just west of the metro underpass. Look out for 355 or 357 (Map p64), which terminate about 250m from the site entrance.

The Pyramids of Giza

TACKLING THE SITE

Constructed more than 4000 years ago, the Pyramids are the last remaining wonder of the ancient world. The giant structures – the ❶ **Great Pyramid of Khufu**, the smaller ❷ **Pyramid of Khafre** and the ❸ **Pyramid of Menkaure** – deservedly sit at the top of many travellers' to-do lists. But the site is challenging to explore, with everything, including the smaller ❹ **Queens' Pyramids** and assorted tombs such as the ❺ **Tomb of Senegemib-Inti**, spread out in the desert under the hot sun. And it all looks, at first glance, a bit smaller than you might have thought.

It helps to imagine them as they were: originally, the Pyramids gleamed in the sun, covered in a smooth white limestone casing. These enormous mausoleums, each devoted to a single pharaoh, were part of larger complexes. At the east base of each was a 'funerary temple', where the pharaoh was worshipped after his demise, with daily rounds of offerings to sustain his soul. In the ground around the pyramids, wooden boats – so-called solar barques – were buried with more supplies to transport the pharaoh's soul to the afterlife (one of these has been reconstructed and sits in the ❻ **Cheops Boat Museum**). From each funerary temple, a long stone-paved causeway extended down the hill.

At the base of the plateau, a lake covered the land where the village of Nazlet As Samaan is now – this was fed by a canal and enlarged with flood waters each year. At the end of each causeway, a 'valley temple' stood at the water's edge to greet visitors. Next to Khafre's valley temple, the lion-bodied ❼ **Sphinx** stands guard.

So much about the Pyramids remains mysterious – including the whereabouts of the bodies of the pharaohs themselves. But there's still plenty for visitors to see. Here we show you both the big picture and the little details to look out for, starting with the ❽ **ticket booth and entrance**.

ATDIGIT/SHUTTERSTOCK ©

Pyramid of Khafre
Khufu's son built this pyramid, which has some surviving limestone casing at the top. Scattered around the base are enormous granite stones that once added a snappy black stripe to the lowest level of the structure.

The Sphinx
This human-headed beast, thought to be a portrait of Khafre, guards the base of the plateau. The entrance is only through Khafre's valley temple. Come early or late in the day to avoid the long queue.

GURGEN BAKHSHETYAN/SHUTTERSTOCK ©

AMR HASSANEIN/SHUTTERSTOCK ©

Pyramid of Menkaure (Mycerinus)
This pyramid opens alternately with the Pyramid of Khafre. The gash in the exterior is the folly of Sultan Al Aziz Uthman, who tried to dismantle the pyramid in 1196.

Cheops Boat Museum
Preserved in its own modern tomb, this 4500-year-old cedar barge was dug up from in front of the Great Pyramid and reassembled by expert craftspeople like a 1224-piece jigsaw puzzle.

JEFF SCHULTES/SHUTTERSTOCK ©

Tomb of Senegemib-Inti
The Giza Plateau is dotted with small tombs like this one. Opening schedules vary each year. Duck inside to look for delicate wall carvings and enjoy a bit of shade.

Ticket Booth & Entrance
Tickets, marked with a hologram sticker, are bought here or at the Sphinx entrance. All other options are counterfeit. This is the only entrance where you can also purchase secondary tickets for the pyramid interiors. Clean bathrooms are in a building just to the east.

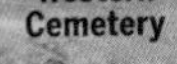

Western Cemetery

Khafre's Funerary Temple

3 2 6 1 5 8 4

Great Pyramid of Khufu (Cheops)
Clamber inside the corridors to marvel at the precision engineering of the seamless stone blocks, each weighing 2.5 tonnes. Pause to consider the full weight of 2.3 million of them.

Queens' Pyramids
These smaller piles were built as the tombs of Khufu's sister, mother and wife. They're in bad shape, but some show the original limestone casing at the base – feel how smoothly the stones are fitted.

MICHAEL MILLARD/SHUTTERSTOCK ©

NICK BRUNDLE PHOTOGRAPHY/GETTY IMAGES ©

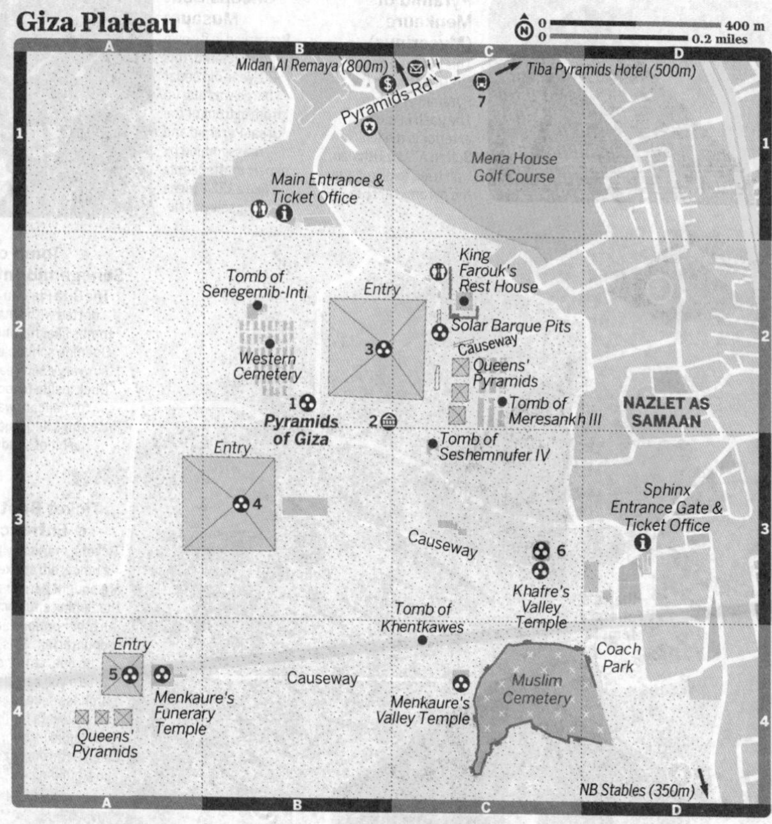

Giza Plateau

Top Sights

1 Pyramids of Giza B2

Sights

2 Cheops Boat Museum B2
3 Great Pyramid of Khufu B2
4 Pyramid of Khafre B3
5 Pyramid of Menkaure A4
6 Sphinx C3

Transport

7 355/357 Bus Stop C1

Tours

Backpacker Concierge TOURS

(☎010-6350-7118; www.backpackerconcierge.com) This boutique travel agency dishes up tailor-made itineraries with a cultural and environmentally responsible focus. Its excellent guides and drivers for day tours in and around Cairo will never take you on unscheduled shopping stops, and it can also put together custom trips with a more adventurous twist.

Manal Helmy TOURS

(☎012-2313-9045; noula.helmy@gmail.com; guiding fee per day US$100) Excellent female guide for the Pyramids and the Egyptian Museum.

Real Egypt TOURS

(☎011-0002-2242; www.realegypt.net) Samir Abbass and his team get consistently recommended by travellers for their tailor-made tours. Can arrange both Cairo day tours as well as longer Egypt itineraries.

Sleeping

Downtown

★ **Pension Roma** PENSION $

(Map p66; ☎2391-1088; www.pensionroma.com.eg; 4th fl, 169 Sharia Mohammed Farid; d LE250-320, tr LE325-420, with shared bathroom s LE125-180, d LE195-273, tr LE275-370; ❄📶) Run by a French-Egyptian woman with impeccable standards, the Roma brings dignity, even elegance, to the budget scene. The towering ceilings, antique furniture and filmy white curtains create a feeling of timeless calm while everything's kept neat as a pin. Most rooms share toilets, though many have showers. Rooms in the new extension have bathrooms and air-con.

Bella Luna Hotel HOSTEL $
(Map p66; ☎2393-8139; www.hotellunacairo.com; 3rd fl, 27 Sharia Talaat Harb; s/d/tr/q US$20/32/38/45; ❄📶) Modern, backpacker-friendly Bella Luna offers great value for money with bright and large simply furnished rooms, all with bathrooms that come with piping hot water. In the cleanliness stakes for Downtown's budget hotels, this place really stands out. Small comforts missing elsewhere (bedside lamps and bathmats) are also provided. The (signed) entry is down an alleyway between two watch shops.

Museum House Hotel HOSTEL $
(Map p66; ☎02-2574-6672, 010-9108-8968; museumhousehotel@gmail.com; 2 Sharia Champollion; s/d/tr LE350/450/550, d/tr with shared bathroom LE350/450; ❄📶) With only nine rooms, this is an intimate choice in a prime position just off Midan Tahrir. There's a cheery blue-and-white theme running throughout with pot plants adding a cosy home-away-from-home feel. Rooms are simple but clean, with good bathrooms, and management are super helpful.

★ **Golden Hotel** HOTEL $$
(Map p66; ☎2390-3815; www.goldenhotelegypt.com; 13 Sharia Talaat Harb; s/d $30/40, new wing $40/50; ❄📶) A serious step-up in room quality for Downtown, Golden's fresh, modern rooms are tiny but come with contemporary bathrooms and good facilities: fridge, satellite TVs, and (miracles never cease) a decent amount of powerpoints. Splash an extra US$10 to grab a recently refurbished rooms in the new wing for way more space and funky burnt-orange walls with stone accents.

City View Hotel HOTEL $$
(Map p66; ☎2773-5980; www.cityview-hotel.com; 1 Sharia Al Bustan; s/d US$40/50; ❄📶) Just a step from the madness of Midan Tahrir, City View is a well-run place with friendly, helpful management and views across to the Egyptian Museum. Rooms are cosy and come with good facilities of mini-fridge, satellite TV and balcony, though the frou-frou drapes and soft furnishings are straight out of grandma's house.

Windsor Hotel HISTORIC HOTEL $$
(Map p66; ☎2591-5810; www.windsorcairo.com; 19 Sharia Alfy; s US$46-62, d US$58-74, s/d with shower & hand basin US$37/46; ❄📶) Ride the hand-cranked elevator up to rooms that ooze old-timer charm with dark furniture and scuffed wood floors (room 25 is our favourite). The air-con is noisy, and management is prone to adding surprise extra charges, but the faded romance of the place – including the restaurant where the dinner bell chimes every evening at 7.30pm – is nostalgia-buff heaven.

★ **Steigenberger Hotel El Tahrir** HOTEL $$$
(Map p66; ☎2575-0777; www.eltahrir.steigenberger.com; 2 Sharia Qasr El Nil; r from US$116; ❄📶🏊) This sophisticated customer has been shaking up the Downtown hotel scene since it opened in early 2017. From the vast, modern minimalist lobby with casual bar to the spacious, contemporary styled rooms, the Steigenberger is a soothing oasis right in the heart of the city. Service here is stellar, and it's also excellent value in comparison to other top-end options.

Zamalek & Gezira

★ **Hotel Longchamps** BOUTIQUE HOTEL $$
(Map p72; ☎2735-2311; www.hotellongchamps.com; 5th fl, 21 Sharia Ismail Mohammed, Zamalek; r US$84-96; ❄📶) Hotel Longchamps is a favourite of returning visitors to Cairo. The comfortable, stylish rooms are spacious, well maintained and come with full mod-cons of a flat-screen TV, a minibar, and, lo and behold, kettles (a rarity in Egypt). Bathrooms are generously sized and modern. The greenery-covered, peaceful rear balcony, where guests gather to chat at sunset, is a major bonus.

DON'T MISS

CAIRO UPON THE NILE

One of the most pleasant things to do on a warm day is to go out on a felucca, Egypt's ancient broad-sail boat, with a supply of beer and a small picnic, just as sunset approaches. The **Dok Dok Landing Stage** (Map p74; Corniche El Nil) is the best spot for hiring one because it's near a wider spot in the river. Subject to haggling, a boat and captain should cost between LE70 and LE100 per hour; your captain will appreciate additional baksheesh.

Central Cairo

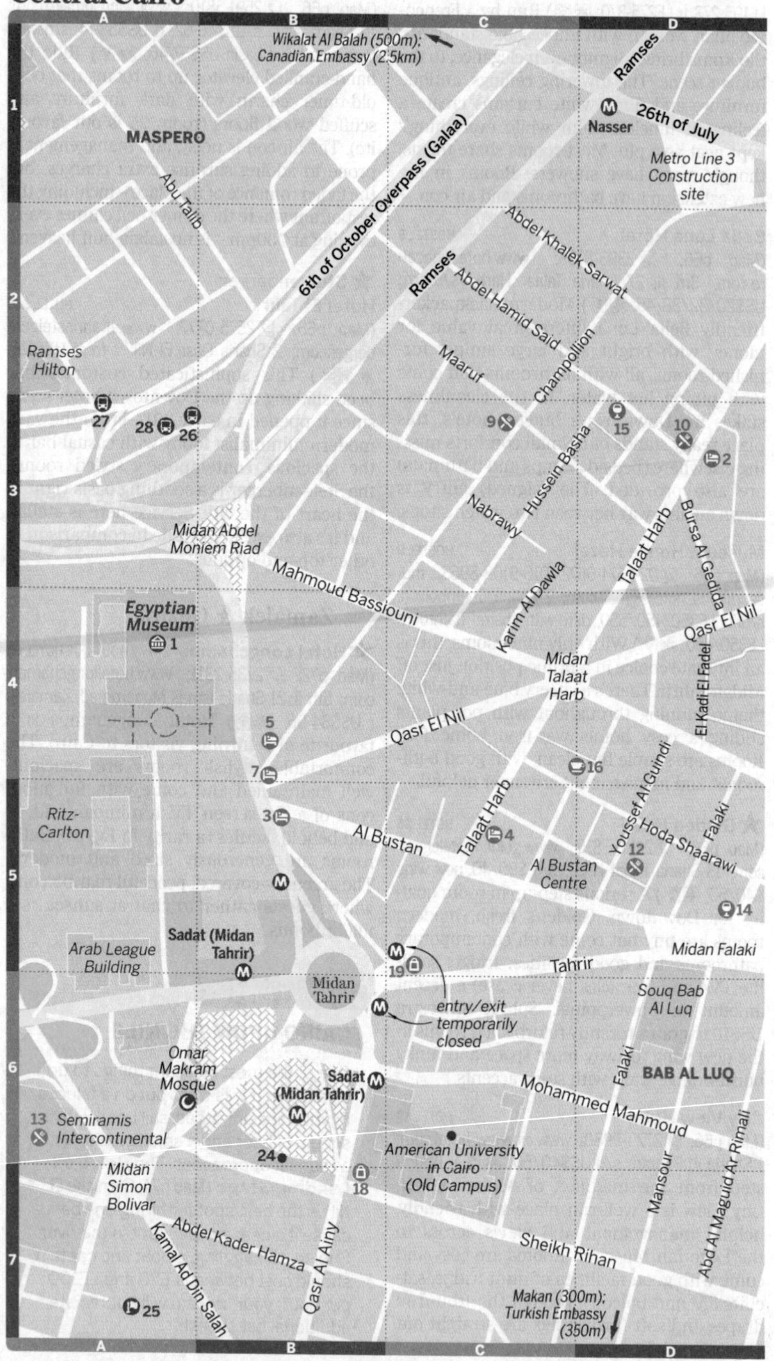

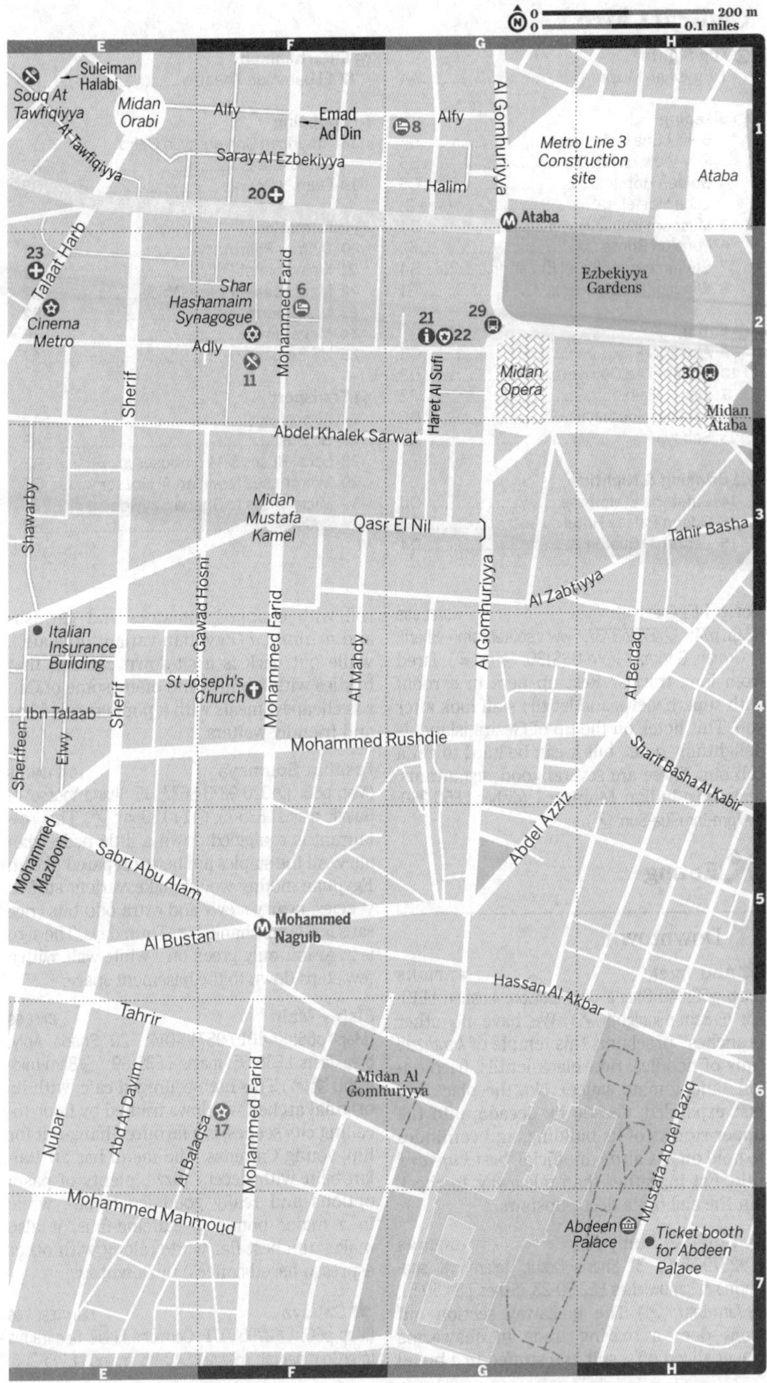
0 200 m
0 0.1 miles
E
F
G
H
1
2
3
4
5
6
7
Souq At Tawfiqiyya
Suleiman Halabi
Midan Orabi
At Tawfiqiyya
Alfy
Emad Ad Din
8
Alfy
Al Gomhuriyya
Metro Line 3 Construction site
Ataba
Saray Al Ezbekiyya
Halim
20
Ataba
Talaat Harb
23
Cinema Metro
Shar Hashamaim Synagogue
Mohammed Farid
6
21
29
22
Ezbekiyya Gardens
Adly
11
Sherif
Haret Al Sufi
Midan Opera
30
Midan Ataba
Abdel Khalek Sarwat
Shawarby
Midan Mustafa Kamel
Qasr El Nil
Tahir Basha
Gawad Hosni
Al Zabtiyya
Italian Insurance Building
St Joseph's Church
Al Mahdy
Al Beidaq
Ibn Talaab
Sherifeen
Elwy
Mohammed Rushdie
Sharif Basha Al Kabir
Abdel Azziz
Mohammed Mazloom
Sabri Abu Alam
Mohammed Naguib
Al Bustan
Hassan Al Akbar
Tahrir
Midan Al Gomhuriyya
Nubar
Abd Al Dayim
Al Balaqsa
17
Mustafa Abdel Raziq
Mohammed Mahmoud
Abdeen Palace
Ticket booth for Abdeen Palace

Central Cairo

Top Sights
1 Egyptian Museum A4

Sleeping
2 Bella Luna Hotel D3
3 City View Hotel B5
4 Golden Hotel C5
Luna Hostel .... (see 2)
5 Museum House Hotel B4
6 Pension Roma F2
7 Steigenberger Hotel El Tahrir B4
8 Windsor Hotel G1

Eating
9 Abu Tarek C3
10 At Tabei Ad Dumyati D3
11 Eish + Malh F2
12 Fasahat Soumaya D5
13 Sabaya A6

Drinking & Nightlife
14 Cafeteria El Horreya D5
15 Odeon Palace Hotel D3
16 Zahret Al Bustan D4

Entertainment
17 El Dammah Theatre F6

Shopping
18 American University in Cairo Bookshop B7
19 Oum El Dounia C5

Information
20 Delmar Pharmacy F1
21 Main Tourist Office G2
22 Main Tourist Police Office G2
23 Misr Pharmacy E2
24 Mogamma B6
25 US Embassy A7

Transport
26 Airport Bus A3
27 Go Bus A3
28 Local Buses & Microbuses A3
29 Microbuses to Midan Al Hussein G2
30 Microbuses to Sharia Sayyida Aisha H2

Sofitel El Gezirah HOTEL $$$
(Map p74; ☎2737-3737; www.sofitel.com; Sharia Al Orman, Gezira; r from US$130;) Tired from long travels? Rest up here in a room with superb views and let the staff look after you. This hotel, on the tip of Gezira island, is delightfully quiet, but it can be hard to get a cab out. There are several good restaurants, including Indian **Manipuri** (dishes LE50-280; 7pm-1am Tue-Sun;).

Eating

Downtown

★ **Abu Tarek** EGYPTIAN $
(Map p66; 40 Sharia Champollion; kushari LE10-25; 8am-midnight;) 'We have no other branches!' proclaims this temple of *kushari* (mix of noodles, rice, black lentils, fried onions and tomato sauce). No, the place has just expanded, decade by decade, into the upper storeys of its building, and continues to hold on to Cairo's unofficial 'best *kushari*' title. Eat in, rather than takeaway, to check out the elaborate decor upstairs.

At Tabei Ad Dumyati EGYPTIAN $
(☎2579-7533; 31 Sharia Orabi; ta'amiyya, shawarma & sandwiches LE2.50-23, dishes LE4.50-51; 7am-1am;) The takeaway section out front does a roaring trade in shawarma (meat sliced off a spit and stuffed in a bread roll with chopped tomatoes and garnish) and *ta'amiyya* (Egyptian variant of falafel), while out back is a sit-down canteen that bustles with families and offers some of Cairo's cheapest meals with a popular salad bar and friendly waiters.

Fasahat Soumaya EGYPTIAN $$
(Map p66; ☎020-9873-8637; 15 Sharia Youssef Al Guindi; mains LE35-75; 1-10.30pm;) This restaurant is squiggled down a little pedestrian alley. All the staples are here, prepared like an Egyptian mother would make: various stuffed veggies, hearty stews and extra odd bits (rice sausage, lamb shanks) on Thursdays. The sign is in Arabic only, green on a white wall, with a few steps down to the basement space.

Eish + Malh CAFE $$
(Map p66; ☎010-9874-4014; 20 Sharia Adly; breakfasts LE35-65, mains LE39-89; 8am-midnight;) This high-ceilinged cafe, with its original arched windows framed by floor-to-ceiling city scenes, is a favoured hang-out for hip, young Cairenes. The menu has an Italian bent with decent pizza, plenty of pasta options and really good ice cream, while in a major bonus to caffeine-fans, it also makes the best flat white (along with other espresso-based coffees) in Downtown.

★ **Sabaya** LEBANESE $$$
(Map p66; ☎2795-7171; Corniche El Nil, Semiramis InterContinental; mezze LE40-95, mains LE145-265;

(⌚1pm-1am) Delicious Lebanese food in a sumptuous but relaxed atmosphere. There's plenty of grilled meat mains, but the mezze here is the real star of the show. Order old favourites hummus and *sambousek* (stuffed pastry triangles), some salads, chicken livers doused in pomegranate molasses and *bel kawarma* (mashed potato doused in lamb's fat), and you've got yourself a real Levantine feast.

Zamalek

★Zööba EGYPTIAN $

(Map p72; ☎16082; www.facebook.com/ZoobaEats; Sharia 26th of July; dishes LE3-36; ⌚8am-1am; 🅩) Egyptian street food gets a modern makeover. Zööba has taken the country's classic cheap eats and given them contemporary twists. Whole-grain *kushari* (mix of noodles, rice, black lentils, fried onions and tomato sauce), beetroot *baladi* bread, pickled lemon and spicy pepper *ta'amiyya* sandwiches and some seriously good salads and shawarma. Eat in at the zinc-clad table amid the most eclectic of decors or take out – this is ideal picnic fodder.

O's Pasta ITALIAN $$

(Map p72; ☎2739-5609; www.facebook.com/ospasta; 159 Sharia 26th of July; mains LE68-155; ⌚4pm-midnight; 🅩) A few years ago, Cairo was a-tizz with new sushi joints; now all the newbie restaurants are Italian and O's Pasta is our pick of the bunch. Squeeze – and we mean squeeze, there's only five tables – into the blue-and-green room to munch on Red Sea calamari pasta doused in spinach and cream sauce, or pecan-basil pesto chicken pasta.

Abou El Sid EGYPTIAN $$

(Map p72; ☎2735-9640; www.abouelsid.com; 157 Sharia 26th of July; mezze LE19-58, mains LE56-120; ⌚noon-1am) Cairo's first hipster Egyptian restaurant (and now a national franchise), Abou El Sid is as popular with tourists as it is with upper-class natives. You can get better *molokhiyya* (garlicky leaf soup, speciality of Egypt) elsewhere, but here you wash it down with a wine or beer and lounge on kitschy gilt 'Louis Farouk' furniture.

Islamic Cairo

Khan El Khalili Restaurant & Mahfouz Coffee Shop EGYPTIAN $$

(Map p70; ☎2590-3788; 5 Sikket Al Badistan; sandwiches & mains LE40-70; ⌚noon-3am; ❄📶) The tranquil Moorish-style interior of this cafe-restaurant, with its strong air-con and tarboosh-hatted waiters, is a popular haven from the khan's bustle. Although geared to capture tourist trade, the food is decent, particularly the *hawashi* (meat patty) and spiced *baladi* sausage sandwiches, and their version of Egypt's bread-based dessert, *umm ali*. The juices are also excellent.

Farahat EGYPTIAN $$

(Map p70; 126a Sharia Al Azhar; pigeons LE55-60; ⌚noon-4am) In an alley off Sharia Al Azhar, this place is legendary for its pigeon, available stuffed or grilled. It doesn't look like much – just plastic chairs outside – but once you start nibbling the succulent, spiced birds, you'll believe the hype.

Drinking & Nightlife

Downtown

Cafeteria El Horreya BAR

(Map p66; ☎02-2392-0397; Midan Falaki; ⌚2pm-1am) El Horreya has long been a living room for locals, artists and foreign residents, with tea, coffee and cold Stella beer on offer. It's not as dusty and dilapidated as it once was, but still oozes vintage Cairo atmosphere. Beer's only served on the right-hand side of the room (without the chessboards).

Zahret Al Bustan COFFEE

(Map p66; Sharia Talaat Harb; ⌚8am-2am) This traditional *ahwa* (coffeehouse) is a bit of an

LOCAL KNOWLEDGE

BELLY-DANCING SHOWS

The best dancers perform at Cairo's five-star hotels, usually to an adoring crowd of wealthy Gulf Arabs. Shows typically begin around 10pm, although the star might not take to the stage until midnight or later. Admission is steep. **Bab El Nil** (Map p58; ☎02-2461-9494; www.fairmont.com/nile-city-cairo/dining/bab-el-nil; Nile City Towers, 2005b Corniche El Nil, Fairmont Nile City Hotel; minimum per person LE1000-1200; ⌚shows 10pm-1am) is one of the classier venues to take in a show.

A less-overpriced alternative is the Nile boat evening cruise belly-dancing shows. Be aware that the crooning lounge-singer style warm up acts on these boats can be hilariously dire. One of the best Nile cruisers is the **Nile Maxim** (Map p72; ☎2738-8888, 012-2241-9500; www.maximrestaurants.com; Sharia Saray Al Gezira, Zamalek; show & dinner LE480-730; ⌚sailings at 8.30pm & 10.30pm).

Around Khan Al Khalili

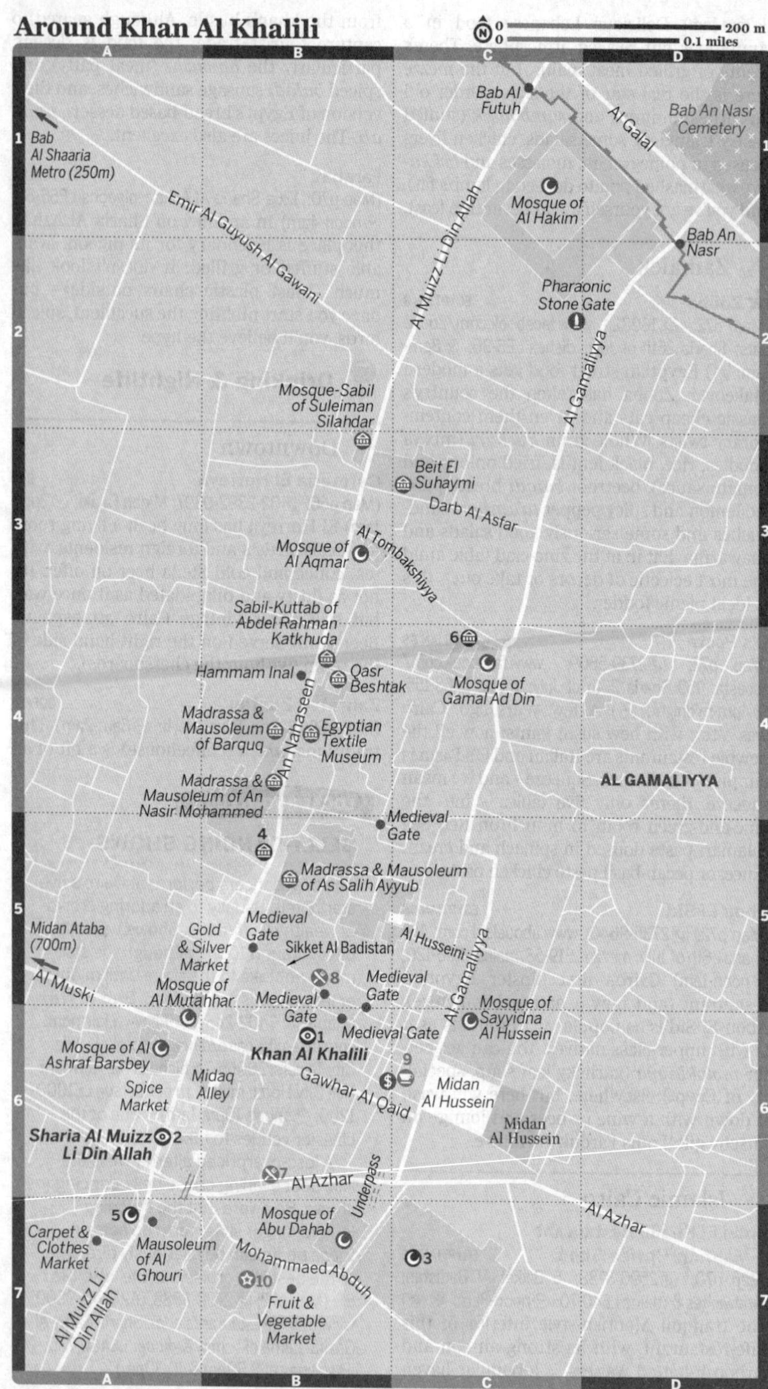

Around Khan Al Khalili

Top Sights
1 Khan Al Khalili ... B6
2 Sharia Al Muizz Li Din Allah ... A6

Sights
3 Al Azhar Mosque ... C7
4 Madrassa & Mausoleum of Qalaun ... B5
5 Mosque-Madrassa of Al Ghouri ... A7
6 Wikala Al Bazara ... C4

Eating
7 Farahat ... B6
8 Khan El Khalili Restaurant & Mahfouz Coffee Shop ... B5

Drinking & Nightlife
9 Fishawi's ... C6

Entertainment
10 Al Tannoura Egyptian Heritage Dance Troupe ... B7

intellectuals' and artists' haunt, though also firmly on many backpackers' lists, so be alert to scam artists. It's in the lane just behind Café Riche.

Odeon Palace Hotel ROOFTOP BAR
(Map p66; ☎02-2577-6637; www.hodeon.com; 6 Sharia Abdel Hamid Said; ⏲24hr) Its fake turf singed from shisha coals, this slightly dilapidated rooftop bar is favoured by Cairo's heavy-drinking theatre and cinema clique, and is a great place to watch the sun go down (or even better, come up).

Zamalek

Sequoia LOUNGE
(☎2576-8086; www.sequoiaonline.net; 53 Sharia Abu Al Feda; ⏲1pm-1am) At the very northern tip of Zamalek, this sprawling Nileside lounge is a swank scene, with low cushions for nursing a shisha while downing a few beers or sipping a cocktail. The chargrilled mains don't tend to live up to the great setting so snack on a range of mezze instead. There's a LE200 minimum fee.

Islamic Cairo

★**Fishawi's** COFFEE
(Map p70; Khan Al Khalili; ⏲24hr, during Ramadan 5pm-3am) Probably the oldest *ahwa* in the city, certainly the most celebrated; Fishawi's has been a great place to watch the world go by since 1773. It's all clouded mirrors and copper tabletops that ooze old-world ambience. Although swamped by foreign tourists and equally wide-eyed out-of-town Egyptians, it is a regular *ahwa,* serving tea and shisha to stallholders and shoppers alike.

☆ Entertainment

Makan TRADITIONAL MUSIC
(Map p58; ☎2792-0878; http://egyptmusic.org; 1 Sharia Saad Zaghloul, Mounira; concert tickets LE40; ⏲concerts Tue & Wed; Ⓜ Saad Zaghloul) The Egyptian Centre for Culture & Art runs this intimate space dedicated to folk music. Don't miss the traditional women's *zar,* a sort of musical trance and healing ritual on Wednesday nights (doors open at 8.30pm). Tuesday evening has various performances of folk music, often an Egyptian-Sudanese jam session (doors open at 7.30pm).

El Dammah Theatre TRADITIONAL MUSIC
(Map p66; ☎2392-6768; www.el-mastaba.org; 30a Sharia Al Balaqsa, Abdeen, Downtown; tickets LE30; ⏲doors open 8pm, concerts 9.30pm) Regular Thursday, Friday and Saturday shows by musical ensembles such as Rango, a trance-y Sudanese folk group, and the El Tanboura Band, playing *simsimiyya,* a musical style from the Suez Canal region, as well as other folk bands from Egypt (check the website for listings).

Al Tannoura Egyptian Heritage Dance Troupe DANCE
(Map p70; ☎2512 1735; Wikala of Al Ghouri, Sharia Mohammed Abduh, Islamic Cairo; show LE30; ⏲performances 7.30pm Mon, Wed & Sat) Egypt's only Sufi dance troupe – more raucous and colourful than the better known white-clad Turkish dervishes – puts on a mesmerising performance three times weekly at the Wikala of Al Ghouri just off Sharia Al Azhar. It's a great opportunity to see one of the medieval spaces in use; arrive about an hour ahead to secure a seat.

Shopping

★**American University in Cairo Bookshop** BOOKS
(Map p66; ☎2797-5929; www.aucpress.com; Sharia Sheikh Rihan, Downtown; ⏲10am-6pm Sat-Thu; Ⓜ Sadat) The best English-language bookshop in Egypt, with a huge selection of material on the politics, sociology and history of Cairo, Egypt and the wider Middle East, as well as other more general nonfiction titles. There are plenty of guidebooks and maps, and a decent fiction section. This is also a great place to find titles by Arab writers in translation.

Zamalek

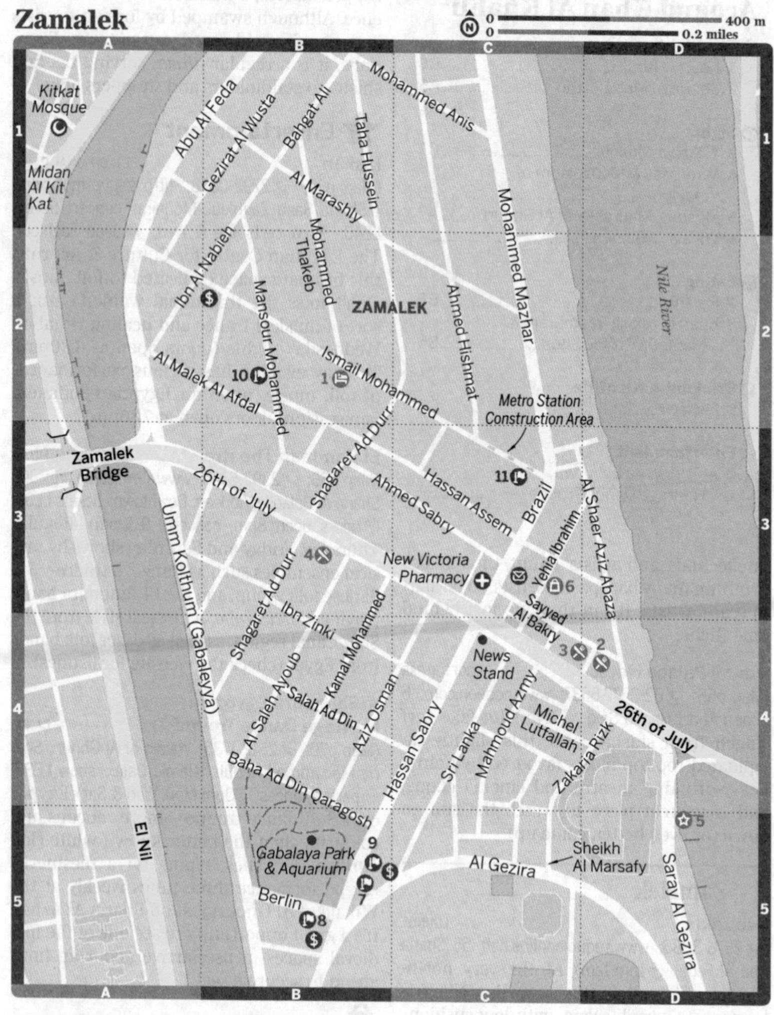

Zamalek

Sleeping

1 Hotel Longchamps B2

Eating

2 Abou El Sid D4
3 O's Pasta C4
4 Zööba B3

Entertainment

5 Nile Maxim D5

Shopping

6 Fair Trade Egypt C3

Information

7 Dutch Embassy B5
8 German Embassy B5
9 Irish Embassy B5
10 Lebanese Embassy B2
11 Spanish Embassy C3

★**Oum El Dounia** ARTS & CRAFTS
(Map p66; ☎2393-8273; 1st fl, 3 Sharia Talaat Harb, Downtown; ⏲10am-9pm) At a great central location, Oum El Dounia sells an exceptionally tasteful and good-value selection of locally made crafts. These include glassware, ceramics, jewellery, cotton clothes made in Akhmim, and other interesting trinkets. Illustrated postcards by cartoonist Golo make a nice change. One room is dedicated to books on Egypt in French.

Fair Trade Egypt ARTS & CRAFTS
(Map p72; ☎2736-5123; 1st fl, 27 Sharia Yehia Ibrahim, Zamalek; ⏲10am-8pm) Crafts sold here are produced in income-generating projects throughout the country. Items for sale include Bedouin rugs, hand-woven cotton, pottery from Al Fayoum and beaded jewellery from Aswan. The cotton bedspreads and shawls are particularly lovely, and prices are very reasonable.

Information

DANGERS & ANNOYANCES

Cairo is a pretty safe city, with crime rates likely much lower than where you're visiting from.

- For female visitors, sexual harassment continues to be a problem.
- Pickpockets and bag-snatchers are rare but do sometimes operate in crowded spots such as Khan Al Khalili, the metro and buses.
- Touts operate around Midan Tahrir and Midan Talaat Harb. Be wary of anyone who approaches you in these areas.
- If anything does get stolen, go straight to the tourist police rather than the normal police.

Main Tourist Police Office (Map p66; ☎126, 2395-9116; Sharia Adly, Downtown; ⏲9am-2pm) On the 1st floor of a building in the alley just left of the main tourist office in Downtown.

Tourist Police (Map p64; ☎126; Pyramids Rd, Giza; ⏲8am-5pm) Across from the Mena House Hotel.

MEDICAL SERVICES

As Salam International Hospital (☎2524-0250, emergency 19885; www.assih.com; Corniche El Nil, Ma'adi; ⏲24hr)

Badran Hospital (Map p58; ☎3337-8823; 3 Sharia Al Ahrar, Doqqi; ⏲24hr)

MONEY

ATMs are numerous, except in Islamic Cairo – the most convenient machine here is below El Hussein hotel in Khan Al Khalili.

LOCAL KNOWLEDGE

CAIRO CRAFTS: WHAT & WHERE

These are the best districts for certain goods.

Gold & silver Head to the gold district on the west end of Khan Al Khalili (p57).

Backgammon & shisha pipes Shops that stock *ahwas* line **Sharia Al Muizz Li Din Allah** (Map p70; Islamic Cairo) around Bein Al Qasreen. Another set of shisha dealers are just east and west of **Bab Zuweila** (Map p58; Sharia Al Muizz Li Din Allah, Islamic Cairo; adult/student LE30/15; ⏲8.30am-5pm).

Appliqué Best buys are at the **Tentmakers Market** (Map p58; Sharia Al Khayamiyya, Islamic Cairo; ⏲9am-6pm Mon-Sat), south of Bab Zuweila.

Carpets The carpet bazaar south of the **Mosque-Madrassa of Al Ghouri** (Map p70; Sharia Al Muizz Li Din Allah, Islamic Cairo; ⏲9am-5pm) FREE has imports; flat-weave Bedouin rugs are the only local style.

Spices Most dealers in the khan are more trouble than they're worth. Try **Abd Al Rahman Harraz** (Map p58; ☎2512-6349; 1 Midan Bab Al Khalq; ⏲10am-10pm) or shops around Midan Falaki.

Perfume In addition to the southwest corner of Khan Al Khalili, try shops around Midan Falaki.

Inlay Artisans in Darb Al Ahmar sell out of their workshops.

Muski glass Available everywhere, but interesting to see the glassblowing studios in the district north of **Bab Al Futuh** (Gate of Conquests; Map p70; Sharia Al Muizz Li Din Allah, Islamic Cairo).

Doqqi, Giza & Gezira

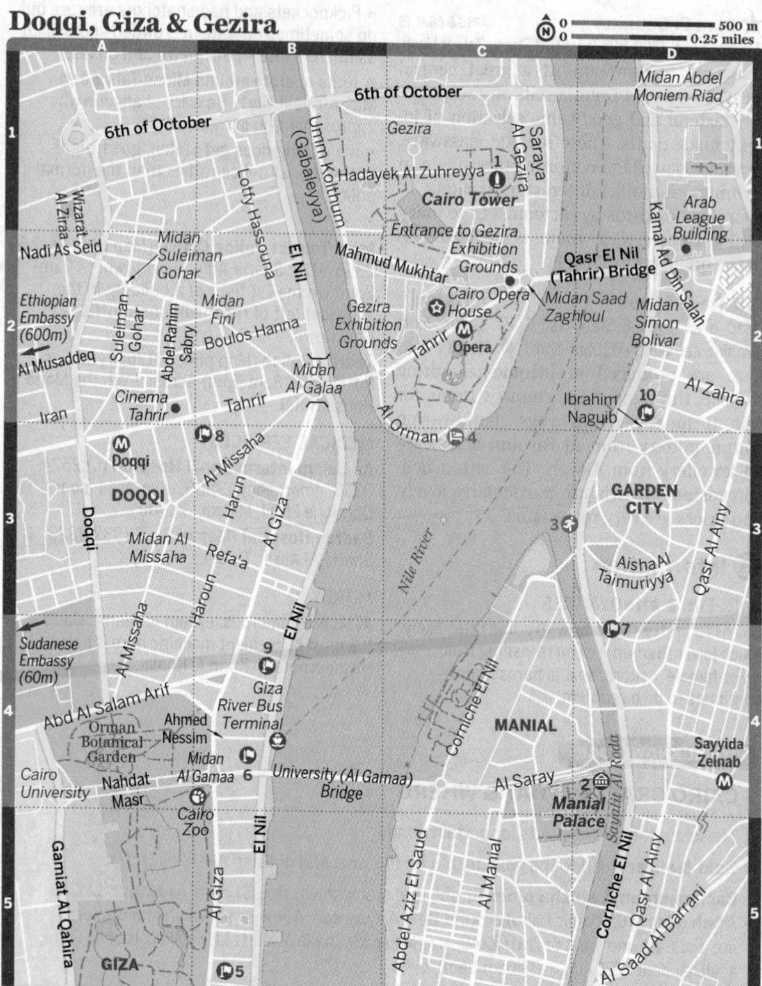

TOURIST INFORMATION

Main Tourist Office (Ministry of Tourism; Map p66; ☎2391-3454; 5 Sharia Adly, Downtown; ⏰9am-6pm)

Tourist Information Office (Ramses Train Station, Midan Ramses, Downtown; ⏰9am-7pm) Inside the train station. The most helpful office.

ℹ Getting There & Away

AIR

Cairo International Airport (☎flight info phoning from landline 0900 77777, flight info phoning from mobile 27777; www.cairo-airport.com; 📶) is 20km northeast of the city centre. There are ATMs in all terminal arrival halls.

Terminal 1 Services most international airlines.

Terminal 2 Partially reopened after a long renovation and now servicing several international airlines.

Terminal 3 EgyptAir's hub and home to all services for other Star Alliance international airlines. The terminal is 2km south of T1.

A free shuttle (service every 30 minutes) connects the terminals.

Doqqi, Giza & Gezira

Top Sights
1 Cairo Tower........C1
2 Manial Palace........D4

Activities, Courses & Tours
3 Dok Dok Landing Stage........C3

Sleeping
4 Sofitel El Gezirah........C3

Eating
Manipuri........(see 4)

Information
5 French Embassy........B5
6 Israeli Embassy........B4
7 Italian Embassy........D4
8 Jordanian Embassy........B3
9 Saudi Arabian Embassy........B4
10 UK Embassy........D2

BUS

Main Bus Station

The main bus station is **Cairo Gateway** (Turgoman Garage; Map p58; Sharia Al Gisr, Bulaq; M Orabi), 400m west of the Orabi metro stop – or pay LE5 or so for a taxi from Tahrir or Sharia Talaat Harb.

Tickets are sold at different windows according to company and destination.

East Delta Travel Co (Map p58; 2419-8533), for Suez and Sinai, and **Super Jet** (Map p58; 02-3572-5032, 2290-9017), for Hurghada, Luxor and Sharm El Sheikh, are to the right.

West & Mid Delta Bus Co (Map p58; 2432-0049; http://westmidbus-eg.com), for Alexandria, Marsa Matruh and Siwa, and **Upper Egypt Travel Co** (Map p58; 2576-0261; Cairo Gateway, Sharia Al Gisr, Bulaq), for Western Desert oases and Luxor, are to the left. (Note that the train is better for Alexandria and Luxor).

Go Bus

Go Bus (Map p66; 19567; www.gobus-eg.com; Midan Abdel Moniem Riad, Downtown) runs regular services to Alexandria, Dahab, El Gouna, Hurghada, Luxor, Marsa Alam and Sharm El Sheikh. Tickets can be booked online.

Buses come in a baffling array of service classes with the higher-priced 'Elite' buses offering bigger seats, wi-fi and a free snack. The 'deluxe' services are pretty much on par with Super Jet and East Delta buses.

Sample ticket prices:

Dahab Economic/Deluxe/Elite LE145/175/330

Hurghada Economic/Deluxe/Elite LE115/140/275

Sharm El Sheikh Economic/Deluxe/Elite LE125/140/275

Services depart/arrive from the Tahrir office on Midan Abdel Moniem Riad (behind the Egyptian Museum, opposite the Ramses Hilton).

MICROBUS

You can get a seat in a microbus to most destinations, including Alexandria, destinations in the Delta, and Suez, from the blocks between Ramses Station and Midan Ulali.

TRAIN

Trains to Alexandria, Upper Egypt and major towns in the Delta are the most efficient and comfortable.

Ramses Station (Mahattat Ramses; 2575 3555; Midan Ramses, Downtown; M Al Shohadaa) is Cairo's main train station. It has a left luggage office, a post office, ATMs and a helpful information office with English-speakers on hand.

Alexandria

There are two classes of trains. Special class makes fewer stops than the Spanish ones.

In both, a first-class *(ula)* ticket gets you a roomier assigned seat and usually a much cleaner bathroom.

Luxor & Aswan

Tourists used to be restricted to travelling on the privately run sleeper train to Luxor and Aswan, but are now allowed to travel on any of the normal, much cheaper seater-only day and night services.

There are two different categories of seater trains (Spanish, and the more expensive Special) which both offer 1st- and 2nd-class air-con seating. There is no difference in journey time. The Special service is just newer rolling stock with slightly bigger seats.

The 8am departure is the most scenic option.

The **Watania Sleeping Train** (02-3748-9488; www.wataniasleepingtrains.com; Ramses Train Station, Midan Ramses, Downtown Cairo; 9am-8pm) has a separate ticket office within Ramses Station.

Getting Around

TO/FROM AIRPORT

For a smooth arrival, arrange an airport pick-up through your hotel.

Bus

Air-con buses (Map p66) 400 and 500 (LE2.50, plus LE2 per large luggage item, one to two hours) run at 20-minute intervals between Midan Abdel Moniem Riad (behind the Egyptian Museum) in central Cairo and the airport bus station.

A free shuttle connects air terminals and the airport bus station.

Taxi

Metered taxis are rarely seen at Cairo Airport so you'll need to negotiate with one of the mob of drivers clustered around the exit. Most drivers charge LE120 to Downtown.

BUS

Cairo is thoroughly served by a network of lumbering sardine-cans-on-wheels but visitors will find only a few uses for them. You can travel more efficiently by metro and/or taxi. Signs are in Arabic only, so you'll have to know your numerals. Fares cost between LE1.50 and LE2.50.

Major bus hubs are **Midan Abdel Moniem Riad** (Map p66), behind the Egyptian Museum, and Midan Ataba.

METRO

The metro (www.cairometro.gov.eg) is blissfully efficient, inexpensive and, outside rush hours (7am to 9am and 3pm to 6pm), not too crowded.

Metro stations have signs with a big red 'M' in a blue star. Tickets cost LE2 to any stop. Trains run every five minutes or so from around 6am until 11.30pm.

Two carriages in the centre of each train are reserved for women.

MICROBUS

Private microbuses (*meekrobas*) can be difficult to use at first as destinations aren't marked. But they're quite useful for major routes: from the Giza metro to the main gate of the Pyramids; and from Midan Ataba to **Sharia Sayyida Aisha** (Map p66) for the Citadel, and to **Midan Al Hussein** (Map p66) for Islamic Cairo.

Fares vary according to distance, from LE2 to LE5.

RIVER BUS

It's of limited utility, but it's scenic; the river bus runs from the Corniche near Downtown Cairo to **Giza** (Map p74), by the zoo and Cairo University. The Downtown **terminal** (Map p58) is located at Maspero. Boats depart every 15 minutes. The trip takes 30 minutes and the fare is LE1.50.

TAXI

For hailing off the street, the whole Cairo cab experience has been transformed by new white taxis with meters and even, on occasion, air-con. Older unmetered, black-and-white taxis still ply the streets as well.

Meter rates start at LE2.50. Hiring a taxi for a longer period runs from LE30 to LE40 per hour, depending on your bargaining skills; LE350 to LE400 for a full day is typical.

If you prefer not to hail off the street, both Uber and Middle East–based Careem (www.careem.com/cairo) operate taxi services in Cairo.

MAJOR BUSES FROM CAIRO GATEWAY

DESTINATION	COMPANY	PRICE	DURATION	TIMES
Al Kharga	Upper Egypt Travel	LE150	8-10hr	9.30pm & 10.30pm
Alexandria	West & Mid Delta	LE55	3hr	hourly 5am-12.05am
Bahariya (Bawiti)	Upper Egypt Travel	LE100	4-5hr	7.30am & 6pm
Dahab	East Delta	LE140	9hr	8am, 1.30pm, 7.30pm & 11pm
Dakhla	Upper Egypt Travel	LE120	8-10hr	7.30am & 6pm
Hurghada	Super Jet	LE120	6hr	7.30am, 12.30pm & 11pm
	Upper Egypt Travel	LE120	6-7hr	1.30pm, 6.30pm & midnight
Luxor	Super Jet	LE150	11hr	1.30pm, 5.30pm & 11.30pm
	Upper Egypt Travel	LE150	11hr	9pm
Sharm El Sheikh	East Delta	LE120	7hr	6.30am, 8am, 1.30pm, 4.30pm, 7.30pm, 11pm & 1am
	Super Jet	LE125	7hr	7.30am, 1.15pm, 6.15pm & 11.30pm
Siwa	West & Mid Delta	LE150	11hr	11.45pm Sat, Mon & Thu
St Katherine	East Delta	LE90	7hr	11am

MAJOR TRAINS FROM CAIRO

Prices are for a 1st-class air-con seat, unless otherwise noted.

DESTINATION	PRICE	DURATION	TIMES
Alexandria (direct)	LE70-100	2½hr	8am, 9am, 11am, 2pm, 3pm, 6pm, 7pm & 10.30pm
Alexandria (stopping)	LE50	3-3½hr	6am, 8.10am, 10am, noon, 1pm, 2.20pm, 3.10pm, 4pm, 5.10pm, 8.15pm & 9pm
Luxor/Aswan (Spanish)	LE109/135	10½hr/14hr	noon, 7pm, 8pm & 10pm
Luxor/Aswan (Special)	LE200/240	10½hr/14hr	8am, 10am, 5.30pm, 9pm & 11pm
Luxor/Aswan (Watania Sleeper)	2-/1-berth cabin US$80/110	9½hr/13hr	Train 84: 8pm (Giza only departure) Train 86: 8.15pm (Ramses) & 8.30pm (Giza)

SAQQARA, MEMPHIS & DAHSHUR سقارة ممفس&

Although most tourists associate Egypt with the Pyramids of Giza, there are known to be at least 118 ancient pyramids scattered around the country, with more being discovered every few years or so. The majority of these monuments are spread out along the desert between the Giza Plateau and the semi-oasis of Al Fayoum. They include the must-see Step Pyramid of Zoser at Saqqara and the Red Pyramid and Bent Pyramid of Dahshur. These three pyramids represent the formative steps of architecture that reached fruition in the Great Pyramid of Khufu (Cheops).

Sights

★Saqqara ARCHAEOLOGICAL SITE

(adult/student LE120/60, parking LE2; 8am-4pm, to 3pm during Ramadan) Covering a 7km stretch of the Western Desert, Saqqara, the huge cemetery of ancient Memphis, was an active burial ground for more than 3500 years and is Egypt's largest archaeological site. The necropolis is situated high above the Nile Valley's cultivation area, and is the final resting place for deceased pharaohs and their families, administrators, generals and sacred animals. The name Saqqara is most likely derived from Sokar, the Memphite god of the dead.

Old Kingdom pharaohs were buried within Saqqara's 11 major pyramids, while their subjects were buried in the hundreds of smaller tombs. Most of Saqqara, except for the Step Pyramid, was buried in sand until the mid-19th century, when the great French Egyptologist Auguste Mariette uncovered the **Serapeum**. Since then, it has been a gradual process of rediscovery: the Step Pyramid's massive funerary complex was not exposed until 1924, and it is in a constant state of restoration. French architect Jean-Philippe Lauer, who began work here in 1926, was involved in the project for an incredible 75 years until his death in 2001. More recently, there has been a string of new discoveries, including a whole slew of mummies and even a new pyramid.

If you keep up a good pace, you can see the high points of Saqqara in about half a day. Start with a quick visit to the **Imhotep Museum**, to get the lay of the land. Head for Zoser's funerary complex, entering through the hypostyle hall, and gaze on the **Step Pyramid**, the world's oldest pyramid. Walk south towards the Causeway of Unas then drive to the **Pyramid of Teti** to see some of the famous Pyramid Texts inside. Afterwards, pop into the nearby **Tomb of Kagemni** before ending with the most wonderful tomb of all, the **Mastaba of Ti**, with its fascinating reliefs of daily life.

Dahshur ARCHAEOLOGICAL SITE

(adult/student LE60/30, parking LE2; 8am-4pm, to 3pm during Ramadan) About 10km south of Saqqara. lies this impressive 3.5km-long field of 4th- and 12th-dynasty pyramids. Although there were originally 11 pyramids here, only the two Old Kingdom ones remain intact. Pharaoh Sneferu (2613–2589 BC), father of Khufu, built Egypt's first true pyramid here, the **Red Pyramid** (North Pyramid), as well as an earlier version, the **Bent Pyramid**. These two striking pyramids are the same height, and together are also the third-largest pyramids in Egypt after the two largest at Giza.

Mit Rahina MUSEUM

(Memphis; adult/student LE60/30, parking LE5; 8am-4pm, to 3pm during Ramadan) The only remaining evidence of Memphis is this noteworthy open-air museum, built around a magnificent fallen colossal limestone **statue of Ramses II**. Its position on its back

ANTON BELO/SHUTTERSTOCK ©

KRISTINA VACKOVA/SHUTTERSTOCK ©

1. Giza, Cairo (p60)
Be awed by the last remaining wonder of the ancient world.

2. Ras Mohammed National Park (p117)
Dive the Red Sea and marvel at some of the world's most spectacular coral-reef ecosystems.

3. Karnak, Luxor (p87)
Explore this extraordinary complex of sanctuaries, kiosks, pylons and obelisks.

4. Aswan (p101)
Sail along the Nile aboard a felucca, savouring the slow rhythms of life.

ANTON_IVANOV/SHUTTERSTOCK ©

3

gives a great opportunity to inspect the carving up close – even the pharaoh's nipples are very precise. Its twin is the statue that stood in Midan Ramses in Cairo until 2006 that was moved to stand guard by the Grand Egyptian Museum construction site.

Getting There & Away

Because of extremely limited public transport options, this area is typically visited as part of an organised tour, or with a private taxi from Cairo hired for the day (LE350 to LE450, plus parking at each site).

MEDITERRANEAN COAST

Alexandria الإسكندرية

03

Founded in 331 BC by 25-year-old Alexander the Great, Alexandria (Al Iskendariyya) is the stuff of legend. Its towering Pharos lighthouse, marking the ancient harbour's entrance, was one of the Seven Wonders of the World, and its Great Library was considered the archive of ancient knowledge. Alas, fate dealt the city a spate of cruel blows and there are few visible remains of the glorious past.

The 19th century kick-started a cosmopolitan makeover and renaissance when Alexandria became one of the Mediterranean's key commercial hubs. This revival was cut short in the 1950s by President Nasser's nationalism. Today the grand modern library of Alexandria sits amid faded remnants of the once-grand seafront Corniche, as a symbol of the city's latest incarnation as Egypt's cultural capital.

Sights

★Bibliotheca Alexandrina MUSEUM
(Map p82; 03-483-9999; www.bibalex.org; Al Corniche, Shatby; adult/student LE70/35; 11am-7pm Sun-Thu, noon-4pm Sat) Alexandria's ancient library was one of the greatest of all classical institutions, and while replacing it might seem a Herculean task, the new Bibliotheca Alexandrina manages this with aplomb. Opened in 2002, this impressive piece of modern architecture is a deliberate attempt to rekindle the brilliance of the original centre of learning and culture. The complex has become one of Egypt's major cultural venues and a stage for numerous international performers, and is home to a collection of brilliant museums.

➡ Antiquities Museum
(http://antiquities.bibalex.org; adult/student LE50/25; 9am-6.30pm Sun-Thu, noon-3.45pm Sat) The Antiquities Museum at the Bibliotheca Alexandrina has a well-curated exhibition of artefacts that romp from the Pharaonic, through the Greek and Roman periods, and into the Byzantine and Islamic eras. The artefacts are well labelled in English and Arabic, and give an interesting insight in the city's Pharaonic and Graeco-Roman past, and the transition between the two periods. The collection includes underwater antiquities from the Eastern Harbour and the Bay of Aboukir.

➡ Manuscript Museum
(adult/student LE30/15; 11am-7pm Sun-Thu, noon-4pm Sat) The Manuscript Museum at the Bibliotheca Alexandrina hosts a wonderfully displayed collection of ancient texts, antiquarian books and maps, including a copy of a fragment of the only surviving papyrus scroll from Alexandria's ancient library. Most of the manuscripts are written in beautiful Arabic calligraphy.

WORTH A TRIP

EL ALAMEIN

This small coastal outpost is famed for the decisive victory won here by the Allies during WWII. More than 80,000 soldiers were killed or wounded in the series of desert battles fought nearby, which helped cement Allied control of North Africa. The **War Museum** (LE50; 9am-4pm Sat-Thu, 9am-noon & 1-4pm Fri) provides an excellent introduction to the Battle of El Alamein. One kilometre to the east are the thousands of graves in the **Commonwealth War Cemetery** (9am-2.30pm). The **German War Memorial** is based in a sandstone building 7km to the west along the highway. The **Italian Memorial**, with a small but interesting museum, is a further 4km west.

The easiest way to get here is to hire a taxi from Alexandria. Expect to pay between LE500 and LE600 return to the War Museum, including ferrying you between the cemeteries.

DON'T MISS

ALEXANDRIA CAFE CULTURE

Ever since the early 1900s, Alexandria's culture has revolved around cafes. Many of these old haunts remain and even though the food and drink in many aren't up to scratch, they are definitely worth a visit, to experience them as living relics of times past and to catch a glimpse of their grand decor.

Delices (Map p84; 03-486-1432; www.delicesgroup.com; 46 Sharia Saad Zaghloul; 8am-11pm;) This old tea room has been in business since 1922 and is *the* place to come for tea and cake. It was a favourite haunt of Allied soldiers during WWII.

Sofianopoulos Coffee Store (Map p84; 03-593-0000; www.facebook.com/Sofianopoulo-for-Import-Coffee-Stores-189063451160251; 21 Sharia Saad Zaghloul; 8am-10pm) Dominated by huge silver coffee grinders and the faintly herbal aroma of roasted java, it's caffeine heaven.

Trianon (Map p84; 03-486-0986; 56 Midan Saad Zaghloul; continental breakfast LE48, mains LE35-110; 9am-midnight;) Stop here to admire the 1930s grandeur of its sensational ornate ceiling and faded but still glorious wall panels.

Athineos (Map p84; 03-486-8131; 21 Midan Saad Zaghloul) The cafe part still has some of its original 1940s fittings but most of it has had a painful revamp.

Brazilian Coffeestore (Map p84; 03-486-5059; www.facebook.com/Brazilian.coffee.stores; 44 Sharia Saad Zaghloul; 7.30am-10pm) This coffee store from 1929 has been revamped but retains its old-world atmosphere.

★ **Alexandria National Museum** MUSEUM
(Map p82; 03-483-5519; 110 Sharia Tariq Al Horreyya; adult/student LE80/40; 9am-4.30pm) This excellent museum sets a high benchmark with its summary of Alexandria's past. Housed in a beautifully restored Italianate villa, the small but thoughtfully selected and well-labelled collection does a sterling job of relating the city's history from antiquity until the modern period. Look out especially for the beautiful tanagra – terracotta statues of Greek women – and the discoveries found underwater in the Mediterranean.

Kom Al Dikka ARCHAEOLOGICAL SITE
(Map p82; Sharia Ismail Mahana; adult/student LE80/40; 9am-4.30pm) Kom Al Dikka was a well-off residential area in Graeco-Roman times, with lovely villas, bath houses and a theatre. The area was known at the time as the Park of Pan, a pleasure garden where citizens of Alexandria could indulge in various lazy pursuits. Although the ruins aren't terribly impressive in scale, they remain a superbly preserved ode to the days of the centurion and include the 13 white-marble terraces of the only Roman amphitheatre found in Egypt.

Catacombs of Kom Ash Shuqqafa ARCHAEOLOGICAL SITE
(Carmous; adult/student LE60/30; 9am-4.30pm) Discovered accidentally in 1900 when a donkey disappeared through the ground, these catacombs are the largest-known Roman burial site in Egypt and one of the last major works of construction dedicated to the religion of ancient Egypt. Demonstrating Alexandria's hallmark fusion of Pharaonic and Greek styles, the architects used a Graeco-Roman approach. The catacombs consist of three tiers of tombs and chambers cut into bedrock to a depth of 35m (the bottom level is flooded and inaccessible).

Sleeping

Hotel Union HOTEL $
(Map p84; 03-480-7312; 5th fl, 164 Al Corniche; s/d LE175/195, with sea view LE200/250;) Get a seafront room and princely views of the Med from the balcony are yours for a pauper's budget. Alexandria's safest, most solid budget option is always bustling with a mix of Egyptian holidaymakers and foreign travellers. The simple rooms are decently maintained and clean, and the staff is a cheerful lot even if the service can be hilariously haphazard.

Triomphe Hotel HOTEL $
(Map p84; 03-480-7585; www.triomphehotel.com; 3rd fl, 26 Sharia Al Ghorfa Al Togareyya; d/tr LE200/250, s/d with shared bathroom LE110/160;) The homely Triomphe has a leafy lobby that feels like you've wandered into someone's living room. Spacious rooms cling to shreds of former elegance, with high ceilings and dark-wood furniture, though some are ageing more gracefully than others. It's worth

Central Alexandria

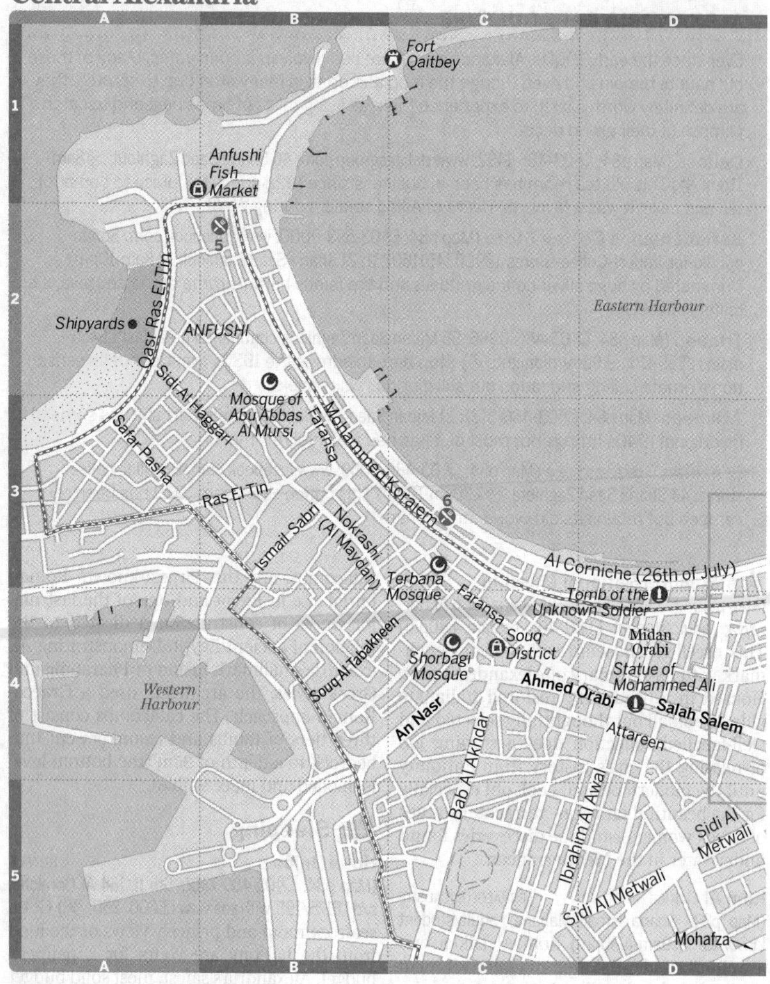

Central Alexandria

Top Sights

1 Alexandria National Museum G3
2 Bibliotheca Alexandrina G2

Sights

Antiquities Museum .... (see 2)
3 Kom Al Dikka F5
Manuscript Museum .... (see 2)
Planetarium .... (see 2)
4 World of Shadi Abdel Salam G2

Eating

5 Kadoura B2
6 Kadoura C3

Drinking & Nightlife

7 Selsela Cafe G1

Transport

8 Servees & Microbuses to Aboukir F5
9 Servees to Cairo F5

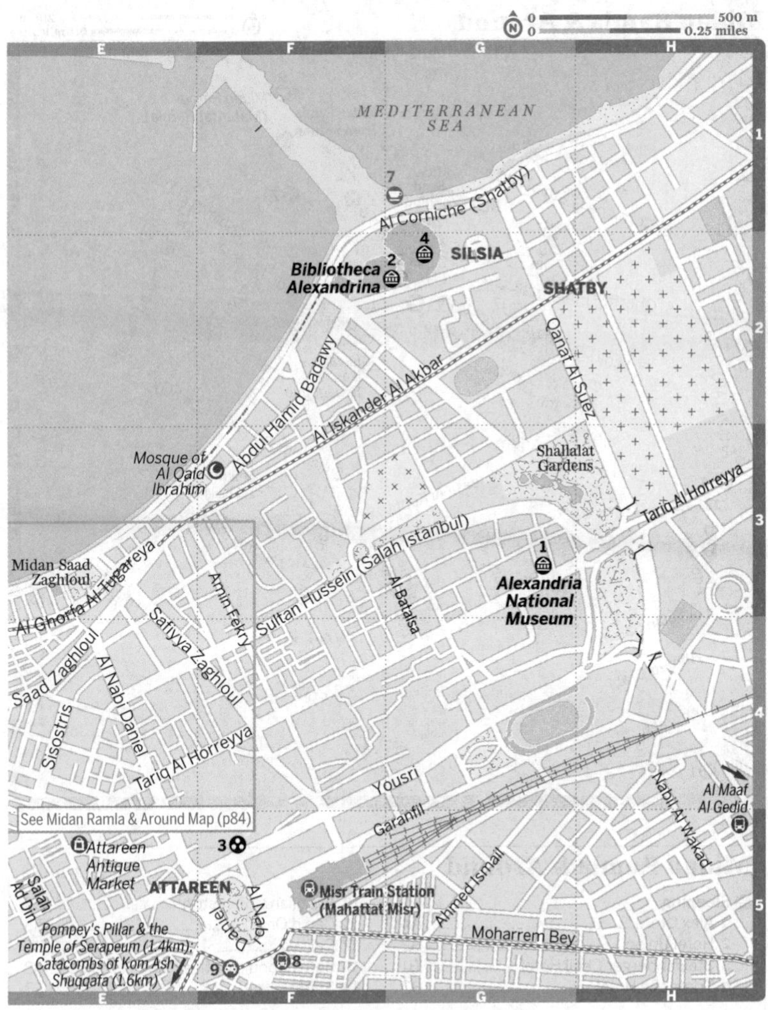

paying extra for the en-suite doubles (which have balconies) even if you're travelling solo.

Alex Otel HOTEL **$$**

(Alexander the Great Hotel; Map p84; ☎012-2560-3476, 03-487-0081; www.facebook.com/alexhotel2014; 5 Sharia Oskofia; s/d/tr LE500/750/900; 📶) In a quiet spot beside St Katherine School, the Alex might not have grand harbour views, but its squeaky-clean rooms are a breath of fresh air. Here you get bright and breezy contemporary style thanks to lashings of white paint, Islamic-design art prints on the walls, new furniture, modern bathrooms and even in-room kettles.

★ Steigenberger Cecil Hotel HISTORIC HOTEL **$$$**

(Map p84; ☎03-487-7173; www.steigenberger.com; 16 Midan Saad Zaghloul; s/d/tr US$137/152/168, s/d with sea view US$152/165; 📶) The historic Cecil Hotel is a true Alexandria legend, though a series of refits over the years have unfortunately erased most of the days-gone-by lustre from when Winston Churchill and writer Lawrence Durrell propped up the famous bar here. Rooms are elegantly attired in red and cream, and seafront ones have sweeping views over the Eastern Harbour.

Midan Ramla & Around

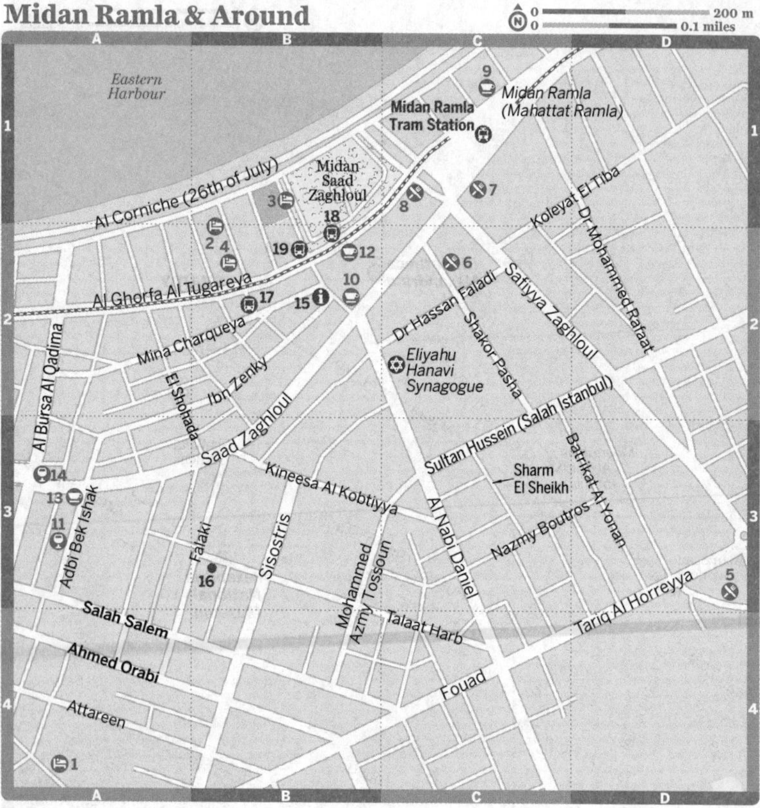

Midan Ramla & Around

Sleeping

1	Alex Otel	A4
2	Hotel Union	B2
3	Steigenberger Cecil Hotel	B1
4	Triomphe Hotel	B2

Eating

5	Abou El Sid	D3
6	Mohammed Ahmed	C2
7	Taverna	C1
8	Trianon	C1

Drinking & Nightlife

9	Athineos	C1
10	Brazilian Coffeestore	B2
11	Cap d'Or	A3
12	Delices	B2
13	Sofianopoulo Coffee Store	A3
14	Spitfire	A3

Information

15	Main Tourist Office	B2
16	Passport Office	B3

Transport

17	Go Bus Ticket Office	B2
18	No 1 Minibus to Sidi Gaber	B2
19	West & Mid Delta Bus Co	B2

Eating

★ Mohammed Ahmed EGYPTIAN $
(Map p84; ☎03-487-3576; 17 Sharia Shakor Pasha, off Sharia Saad Zaghloul; dishes LE2-12; ⊙noon-midnight; 🅔) The perfect lunch stop to scoff *fuul* (fava bean paste) and falafel. Mohammed Ahmed is the undisputed king of spectacularly good and cheap Egyptian standards. Select your *fuul* (we recommend *iskandarani*, mashed up with lots of lime juice and spices), add some falafel, choose a few salads and let the feasting begin.

Taverna EGYPTIAN $

(Map p84; ☎03-487-8591; 1 Midan Saad Zaghloul; mains LE12-48; ⊙noon-4am; ✎) This bustling joint serves some of the best shawarma in town plus excellent hand-thrown sweet or savoury *fiteer* (Egyptian flaky 'pizza'). Can't choose? Order the shawarma *fiteer* for an Egyptian fast-food double-up. Don't miss watching the *fiteer* chef showing off his craft. Eat in or takeaway.

★**Kadoura** SEAFOOD $$

(Map p82; ☎03-480-0405; 33 Sharia Bairam At Tonsi; mains LE70-190; ⊙11.30am-2pm) Pronounced 'Adora', this is one of Alexandria's most authentic fish restaurants, with food served at simple tables in a narrow street. Pick your fish (priced per kilo) from a huge ice-packed selection, usually including sea bass, red and grey mullet, bluefish, sole, squid, crab and prawns. A selection of mezze is served with all orders (don't hope for a menu).

Abou El Sid EGYPTIAN $$

(Map p84; ☎03-392-9609; 39 Sharia Tariq Al Horreyya; mains LE56-125; ⊙1pm-1am) This swish restaurant has kept much of the old setting of cafe Pastroudis, a famous literary haunt, adding the wonderful art of Chant Avenissian and an excellent menu of Egyptian classics, including mezze, stuffed pigeon, a seafood stew and a delicious *molokhiyya* with rabbit or chicken. Alcohol is served. Book ahead.

Drinking & Nightlife

★**Cap d'Or** BAR

(Map p84; ☎03-487-5177; 4 Sharia Adib Bek Ishak; mains LE30-60; ⊙10am-3am) The Cap d'Or, just off Sharia Saad Zaghloul, is one of the only surviving typical Alexandrian bars. With beer flowing generously, stained-glass windows, a long marble-topped bar, plenty of memorabilia decorating the walls and crackling tapes of old French *chanson* (a type of traditional folk music) or Egyptian hits, it feels like a throwback to Alexandria's cosmopolitan past.

Selsela Cafe CAFE

(Map p82; Al Corniche, Shatby Beach; ⊙approx 10am-late) At this fantastic cafe across from the Bibliotheca Alexandrina you can sip tea and smoke shisha to the sound of waves rolling in, and smell sea air instead of petrol fumes (yay). Directly on the water, it has palm-frond-shaded tables replete with twinkling coloured lights, set on a small curving beach where you can hardly hear the traffic.

Spitfire BAR

(Map p84; ☎012-7728-2791; 7 Sharia L'Ancienne Bourse; ⊙2pm-1.30am Mon-Sat) One of the best bars in town, Spitfire is a dimly lit but friendly place with a bit of a rough-and-ready feel, just north of Sharia Saad Zaghloul. Walls are plastered with shipping-line stickers, rock-and-roll memorabilia and photos of drunk regulars. It's a great place for a fun evening out with a mixed clientele of locals, foreign residents and passers-through.

Information

There is no shortage of banks and ATMs in central Alexandria, particularly on Sharia Salah Salem and Sharia Talaat Harb.

Main Tourist Office (Map p84; ☎03-485-1556; Midan Saad Zaghloul; ⊙8.30am-3pm) Hands out a good brochure (with map) of Alexandria sights and has friendly staff.

Getting There & Away

AIR

Burg Al Arab Airport (☎03-459-1484; http://borg-el-arab.airport-authority.com), about 45km southwest of Alexandria, handles all flights in and out of the city.

BUS

The city's main bus station is **Al Moaf Al Gedid Bus Station** (p86), several kilometres south of Midan Saad Zaghloul. To get there, either catch a microbus (LE2) from Misr Train Station or grab a taxi (LE35) from the city centre.

MAJOR BUSES FROM ALEXANDRIA

DESTINATION	PRICE	DURATION	TIME (COMPANY)
Cairo	LE50-65	2½-3hr	hourly 5am-11pm (West & Mid Delta, Super Jet); seven daily (Go Bus)
Hurghada	LE115-150	9hr	9am & 6.30pm (West & Mid Delta); 10pm (Super Jet); 8am & midnight (Go Bus)
Marsa Matruh	LE50	4hr	hourly 6am-10pm (West & Mid Delta); five daily Jun-Sep (Super Jet)
Sharm El Sheikh	LE130-150	8-10hr	9pm (West & Mid Delta); 11pm (Go Bus)
Siwa	LE75	9hr	8.30am, 11am & 10pm (West & Mid Delta)

MAJOR TRAINS FROM MISR TRAIN STATION

Ticket prices are for seats in air-con 1st-class.

DESTINATION	PRICE	DURATION	TIMES
Aswan	LE270	17hr	4.45pm
Cairo (direct)	LE70-100	2½hr	7am, 8am, noon, 2pm, 3pm, 4.45pm, 6pm, 7pm, 8pm & 10pm
Cairo (stopping)	LE60	3-3½hr	6am, 8.15am, 10am, 1pm, 3.30pm, 8.10pm & 9.30pm
Luxor	LE160	15hr	4.45pm & 10pm

The main companies operating from Al Moaf Al Gedid are **West & Mid Delta Bus Co** (Map p84; ☎03-480-9685; Midan Saad Zaghloul; ⌚9am-7pm) and **Super Jet** (☎03-546-7999; 374 Tareq El Horreya; ⌚8am-10pm); both have central-city booking offices, though Super Jet's is inconveniently located in Sidi Gaber.

Go Bus services leave from a separate terminal close by Al Moaf Al Gedid. Their ticket booking **office** (Escort Tourism; Map p84; Sharia Mohammed Talaat Noeman, Mahattet Raml) is near Midan Saad Zaghloul.

MICROBUS

Microbuses for **Aboukir** (Map p82), and servees (service taxis) for **Cairo** (Map p82), depart from outside Misr Train Station; all others leave from **Al Moaf Al Gedid Bus Station** (New Garage; Moharrem Bey). Fares cost around LE50 to Cairo or Marsa Matruh.

TRAIN

There are two train stations in Alexandria. The main terminal is **Misr Train Station** (Mahattat Misr; ☎03-426-3207; https://enr.gov.eg; Sharia Al Nabi Daniel), about 1km south of Midan Ramla. **Sidi Gaber Train Station** (Mahattat Sidi Gaber; ☎03-426-3953) serves the eastern suburbs. Trains from Cairo stop at Sidi Gaber first and most locals get off here, but if you're going to the city centre around Midan Saad Zaghloul, make sure you stay on until Misr Train Station.

At Misr Train Station, 1st- and 2nd-class tickets to Cairo are sold at the ticket office along platform 1.

ℹ Getting Around

MICROBUS

Microbuses zoom along the Corniche. There are no set stops, so when one passes, wave and shout your destination; if it's heading that way, it will stop to pick you up. It costs anywhere from LE1 to LE2 for a short trip.

Microbuses to **Sidi Gaber** (Map p84) start at Midan Saad Zaghloul.

TAXI

There are no working taxi meters in Alexandria. Some sample fares are: Midan Ramla to Misr Train Station, LE10 to LE15; Midan Saad Zaghloul to Fort Qaitbey, LE15; Midan Saad Zaghloul to the Bibliotheca Alexandrina, LE10 to LE15.

TRAM

Alexandria's clackety old trams are fun to ride, but unbearably slow. The central tram station, Mahattat Ramla, is at Midan Ramla; from here lime-yellow-coloured trams go west and blue-coloured ones travel east.

Tram 14 goes to Misr Train Station; tram 15 goes through Anfushi; trams 1 and 25 go to Sidi Gaber Train Station. Fares range from 50pt to LE2.

NILE VALLEY وادي النيل

Luxor الأقصر

☎095 / POP 1,088,900

Luxor is often called the world's greatest open-air museum, but that comes nowhere near describing this extraordinary place. Nothing in the world compares to the scale and grandeur of the monuments that have survived from ancient Thebes.

The setting is breathtakingly beautiful, the Nile flowing between the modern city and west-bank necropolis, backed by the enigmatic Theban escarpment. Scattered across the landscape is an embarrassment of riches, from the temples of Karnak and Luxor in the east to the many tombs and temples on the west bank.

History

Thebes emerged as the main power in Upper Egypt under the 11th- and 12th-dynasty pharaohs. Rising against the northern capital of Heracleopolis, Thebes reunited the country under its political, religious and administrative control. After a period of decline, the Theban princes liberated the country from foreign rule and created the New Kingdom. At the height of their glory and opulence, from 1550 to 1069 BC, all the New Kingdom pharaohs (with the exception of Akhenaten, who moved to Tell al-Amarna) made Thebes their capital. The city had a population of nearly a million, and the architectural activity was astounding.

Sights

East Bank

★Karnak TEMPLE
(☎095-238-0270; Sharia Maabad Al Karnak; adult/student LE120/60, incl open-air museum LE150/75; ⌚6am-6pm; P) Karnak is an extraordinary complex of sanctuaries, kiosks, pylons and obelisks dedicated to the Theban triad but also to the greater glory of pharaohs. The site covers more than 2 sq km; it's large enough to contain about 10 cathedrals. At its heart is the Temple of Amun, the earthly 'home' of the local god. Built, added to, dismantled, restored, enlarged and decorated over nearly 1500 years, Karnak was the most important place of worship in Egypt during the New Kingdom.

The complex is dominated by the great **Temple of Amun-Ra** – one of the world's largest religious complexes – with its famous hypostyle hall, a spectacular forest of giant papyrus-shaped columns. This main structure is surrounded by the houses of Amun's wife Mut and their son Khonsu, two other huge temple complexes on this site. On its southern side, the **Mut Temple Enclosure** (adult/student LE40/20) was once linked to the main temple by an avenue of ram-headed sphinxes. To the north is the Montu Temple Enclosure, which honoured the local Theban war god.

The 3km paved avenue of human-headed sphinxes that once linked the great Temple of Amun at Karnak with Luxor Temple is now again being cleared. Most of what you can see was built by the powerful pharaohs of the 18th to 20th dynasties (1570–1090 BC), who spent fortunes on making their mark in this most sacred of places, which was then called Ipet-Sut, meaning 'The Most Esteemed of Places'. Later pharaohs extended and rebuilt the complex, as did the Ptolemies and early Christians. The further into the complex you venture, the older the structures.

The light is most beautiful in the early morning or later afternoon, and the temple is quieter then, as later in the morning tour buses bring day trippers from Hurghada. It pays to visit more than once, to make sense of the overwhelming jumble of ancient remains.

Luxor Temple TEMPLE
(Map p88; ☎095-237-2408; Corniche An Nil; adult/student LE100/50; ⌚6am-9pm) Largely built by the New Kingdom pharaohs Amenhotep III (1390–1352 BC) and Ramses II (1279–1213 BC), this temple is a strikingly graceful monument in the heart of the modern town. Also known as the Southern Sanctuary, its main function was during the annual Opet celebrations, when the statues of Amun, Mut and Khonsu were brought from Karnak, along the Avenue of Sphinxes, and reunited here during the inundation.

★Luxor Museum MUSEUM
(Map p88; Corniche An Nil; adult/student LE120/60; ⌚9am-2pm & 5-9pm) This wonderful museum has a well-chosen and brilliantly displayed and explained collection of antiquities dating from the end of the Old Kingdom right through to the Mamluk period, mostly gathered from the Theban temples and necropolis. The ticket price puts off many, but don't let that stop you: this is one of the most rewarding sights in Luxor and one of the best museums in Egypt.

West Bank

Colossi of Memnon MONUMENT
(Map p94) FREE The two faceless Colossi of Memnon, originally representing Pharaoh Amenhotep III, rising majestically about 18m from the plain, are the first monuments tourists see when they visit the west bank.

KARNAK SOUND & LIGHT SHOW

Karnak's highly kitsch **sound and light show** (☎02-3385-7320; www.soundandlight.com.eg; LE100, video camera LE35; ⌚shows at 7pm, 8pm & 9pm in winter, at 8pm, 9pm & 10pm in summer) is a 1½-hour Hollywood-style extravaganza that recounts the history of Thebes and the lives of the many pharaohs who built here in honour of Amun, but it is worth a visit particularly for a chance to walk through the beautifully lit temple at night. Shows are cancelled if less than seven people arrive.

The first show is always in English, except for Wednesdays and Sundays, when it is the second.

Luxor – East Bank

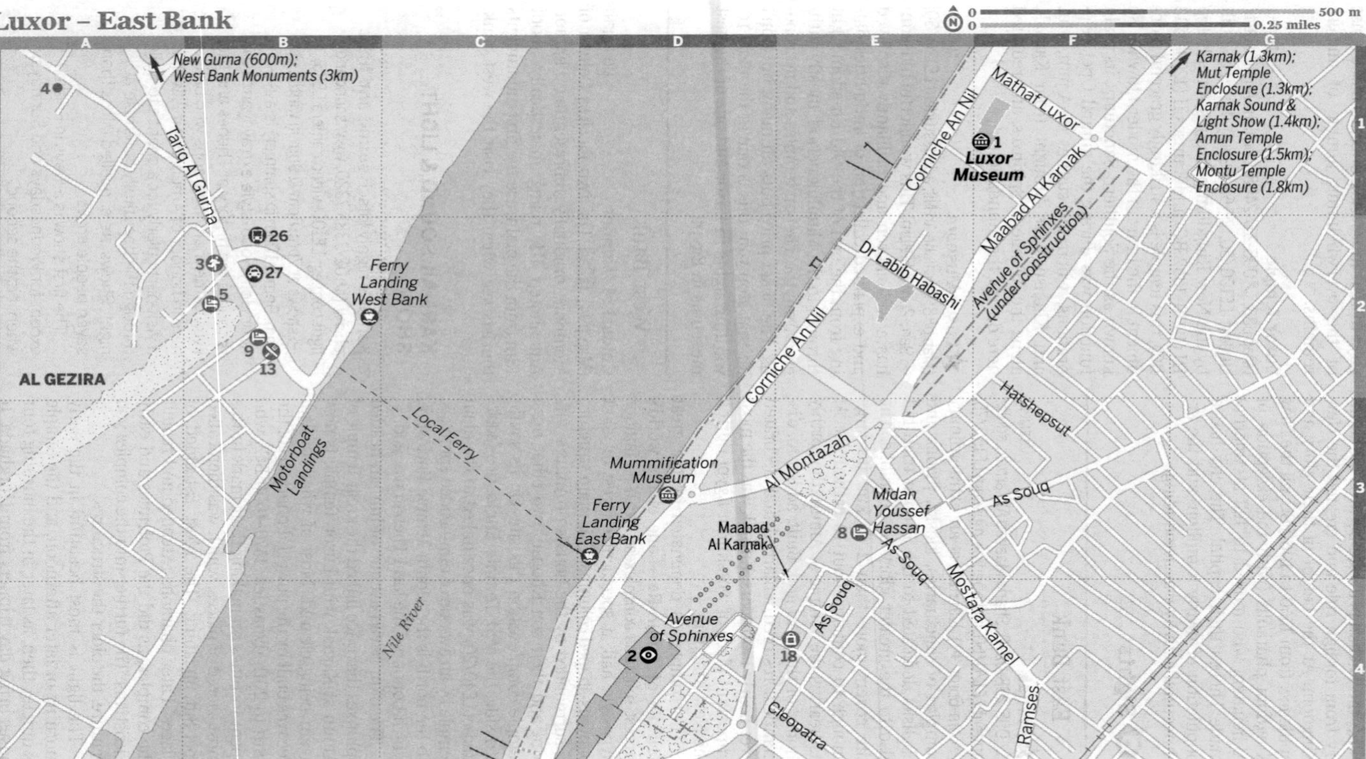

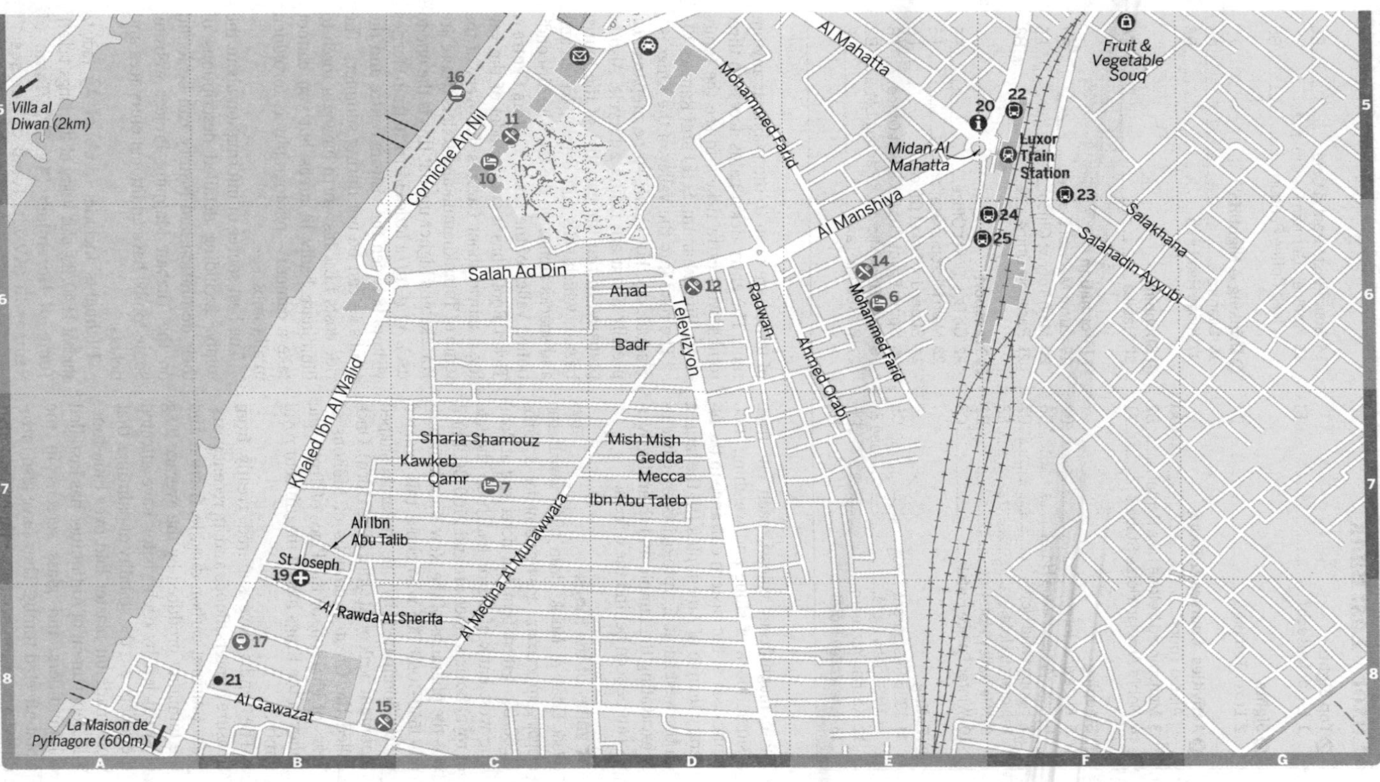
Villa al Diwan (2km)
16
Corniche An Nil
11
10
Al Mahatta
Mohammed Farid
Fruit & Vegetable Souq
20
22
Midan Al Mahatta
Luxor Train Station
23
24
25
Al Manshiya
Salakhana
Salahadin Ayyubi
Salah Ad Din
Ahad
12
14
6
Radwan
Mohammed Farid
Televizyon
Badr
Ahmed Orabi
Khaled Ibn Al Walid
Sharia Shamouz
Kawkeb
Qamr
7
Mish Mish
Gedda
Mecca
Ibn Abu Taleb
Ali Ibn Abu Talib
St Joseph
19
Al Medina Al Munawwara
Al Rawda Al Sherifa
17
21
Al Gawazat
15
La Maison de Pythagore (600m)
A
B
C
D
E
F
G
5
6
7
8

Luxor - East Bank

Top Sights
1 Luxor Museum F1

Sights
2 Luxor Temple D4

Activities, Courses & Tours
Aladin Tours ..... (see 8)
3 Mohammed Setohe Bike Rental B2
4 Nobi's Arabian Horse Stables A1

Sleeping
5 Al Gezira Hotel B2
6 Bob Marley Peace Hotel E6
7 Happy Land Hotel C7
8 Nefertiti Hotel E3
9 Nile Valley Hotel B2
10 Winter Palace Hotel C5

Eating
11 1886 Restaurant C5
As Sahaby Lane ..... (see 8)
12 Koshari Alzaeem D6
13 Nile Valley Hotel B2
14 Sofra Restaurant & Café E6
15 Wenkie's German Ice Cream & Iced Coffee Parlour B8

Drinking & Nightlife
16 Cilantro C5
17 Kings Head Pub B8

Shopping
18 Habiba E4

Information
19 Luxor Medical Centre B7
20 Main Tourist Office E5
21 Passport Office B8

Transport
22 Go Bus Ticket Office F5
23 Main Microbus Station F5
24 Super Jet Ticket Office F6
25 Upper Egypt Bus Co Ticket Office F6
26 West Bank Microbus Parking Lot B2
27 West Bank Taxis B2

These magnificent colossi, each cut from a single block of stone and weighing 1000 tonnes, sat at the eastern entrance to the funerary temple of Amenophis III, the largest on the west bank. Egyptologists are currently excavating the temple and their discoveries can be seen behind the colossi.

★ Valley of the Kings TOMB

(Wadi Biban Al Muluk; Map p94; www.thebanmappingproject.com; adult/student for 3 tombs LE160/80; 6am-5pm, last ticket sold at 4pm) The west bank of Luxor had been the site of royal burials since around 2100 BC, but it was the pharaohs of the New Kingdom period (1550–1069 BC) who chose this isolated valley dominated by the pyramid-shaped mountain peak of Al Qurn (The Horn). Once called the Great Necropolis of Millions of Years of Pharaoh, or the Place of Truth, the Valley of the Kings has 63 magnificent royal tombs.

The tombs have suffered greatly from treasure hunters, floods and, in recent years, mass tourism: carbon dioxide, friction and the humidity produced by the average 2.8g of sweat left by each visitor have affected the reliefs and the stability of paintings that were made on plaster laid over limestone. The Department of Antiquities has installed dehumidifiers and glass screens in the worst-affected tombs. They have also introduced a rotation system: a limited number of tombs are open to the public at any one time. The entry ticket gains access to three tombs, with extra tickets to see the tombs of Ay, Tutankhamun, Seti I and Ramses VI.

The road into the Valley of the Kings is a gradual, dry, hot climb, so be prepared, especially if you are riding a bicycle. Also be prepared to run the gauntlet of the tourist bazaar, which sells soft drinks, ice creams and snacks alongside the tat. The air-conditioned Valley of the Kings Visitors Centre & Ticket Booth has a good model of the valley, a movie about Carter's discovery of the tomb of Tutankhamun and toilets (there are Portakabins higher up, but this is the one to use). A *tuf-tuf* (a little electrical train) ferries visitors between the visitors centre and the tombs (it can be hot during summer). The ride costs LE4. It's worth having a torch to illuminate badly lit areas but you cannot take a camera – photography is forbidden in all tombs.

The best source of information about the tombs, including detailed descriptions of their decoration and history, can be found on the Theban Mapping Project website. Some tombs have additional entry fees and tickets.

Highlights include **Tomb of Ay** (adult/student LE40/20, plus Valley of the Kings ticket), **Tomb of Horemheb (KV 57)**, **Tomb of Ramses III (KV 11)**, **Tomb of Ramses VI**

(KV 9) (adult/student LE80/40, plus Valley of the Kings ticket) and **Tomb of Seti I (KV 17)** (LE1000, plus Valley of the Kings ticket).

★Medinat Habu TEMPLE
(Map p94; adult/student LE40/20; ⏲6am-5pm) Ramses III's magnificent memorial temple of Medinat Habu, fronted by sleepy Kom Lolah village and backed by the Theban mountains, is one of the west bank's most underrated sites. This was one of the first places in Thebes closely associated with the local god Amun. At its height, Medinat Habu contained temples, storage rooms, workshops, administrative buildings, a royal palace and accommodation for priests and officials. It was the centre of the economic life of Thebes for centuries.

Ramesseum TEMPLE
(Map p94; adult/student LE60/30; ⏲6am-5pm) Ramses II called his massive memorial 'the Temple of Millions of Years of User-Maat-Ra'; classical visitors called it the tomb of Ozymandias; and Jean-François Champollion, who deciphered hieroglyphics, called it the Ramesseum. Like other memorial temples it was part of Ramses II's funerary complex. His tomb was built deep in the hills, but his memorial temple was on the edge of the cultivated area on a canal that connected with the Nile and with other memorial temples.

★Tombs of the Nobles TOMB
(Map p94; ⏲6am-5pm) These tombs are some of the best least-visited attractions on the west bank. Nestled in the foothills opposite the Ramesseum are more than 400 tombs belonging to nobles from the 6th dynasty to the Graeco-Roman period. Where royal tombs were decorated with cryptic passages from the Book of the Dead to guide them through the afterlife, the nobles, intent on letting the good life continue after their death, decorated their tombs with wonderfully detailed scenes of their daily lives.

Memorial Temple of Hatshepsut TEMPLE
(Deir Al Bahri; Map p94; adult/student LE80/40; ⏲6am-5pm) At Deir Al Bahri, the eyes first focus on the dramatic rugged limestone cliffs that rise nearly 300m above the desert plain, only to realise that at the foot of all this immense beauty lies a monument even more extraordinary, the dazzling Temple of Hatshepsut. The almost-modern-looking temple blends in beautifully with the cliffs from which it is partly cut – a marriage made in heaven. Most of what you see has been painstakingly reconstructed.

Carter's House & the Replica Tomb of Tutankhamun MUSEUM
(Map p94; adult/student LE50/25; ⏲9am-5pm; P) The domed mud-brick house where Howard Carter lived during his search for Tutankhamun's tomb is surrounded by a garden on what is otherwise a barren slope above the road from Deir Al Bahri to the Valley of the Kings. The house has been restored and decorated with pictures and tools of the excavation. An exact replica of Tutankhamun's burial chamber has been constructed on the edge of the garden along with an exhibition relating to the discovery of the tomb.

Deir Al Medina ARCHAEOLOGICAL SITE
(Monastery of the Town or Workmen's Village; Map p94; adult/student LE80/40; ⏲6am-5pm) This site takes its name from a Ptolemaic temple, later converted to a Coptic monastery – the Monastery of the Town – but the real attraction is the unique **Workmen's Village**. Many of the skilled workers and artists who created tombs in the Valley of the Kings and Valley of the Queens lived and were buried here. Archaeologists have uncovered more than 70 houses in this village and many tombs: the most beautiful are now open to the public.

Valley of the Queens TOMB
(Biban Al Harim; Map p94; adult/student LE80/40; ⏲6am-5pm) At the southern end of the Theban hillside, the Valley of the Queens

DON'T MISS

THE BEST TOMBS

These are the highlight tombs outside of the Valley of the Kings in the Theban necropolis:

Amunherkhepshef (p94)

Nefertari (p94)

Nakht (Map p94; Tombs of the Nobles; adult/student LE60/30; ⏲6am-5pm)

Sennofer (Map p94; Tombs of the Nobles; adult/student LE30/15; ⏲6am-5pm)

Ramose (Map p94; Tombs of the Nobles; adult/student LE40/20; ⏲6am-5pm)

Sennedjem (Deir Al Medina; Map p94; Deir Al Medina adult/student LE80/40; ⏲6am-5pm)

Luxor's West Bank

Sometimes there is no way around the crowds of visitors and hawkers in the Valley of the Kings, but try to go early, before it gets hot. Stop off at the ❶ **Colossi of Memnon** as you pass them, taking a look at the ongoing excavation of the ruins of the Temple of Amenhotep III, whose entrance they once flanked. From the royal tombs, drive around the hillside to visit the massive terraced ❷ **Temple of Hatshepsut**, almost entirely reconstructed but still good to see as it is the best surviving example of classical-style Egyptian architecture in Luxor.

The Theban hillside further to the south is pitted with thousands of tomb openings. The Tombs of the Nobles in what was ❸ **Gurna Village** and the nearby ❹ **Workers' Tombs** at Deir Al Medina are very different in style and construction from the royal burials. In some ways, their views of everyday life are more impressive than the more orthodox scenes on the walls of the royal tombs.

In the afternoon, drop down towards the line between desert and agriculture to see two royal temples. The Ramesseum is dedicated to the memory of Ramses II and contains the upper half of a massive statue of the pharaoh. In midafternoon, when the light starts to soften, head over to ❺ **Medinat Habu**, the temple of Ramses III. The last of the great imperial temples built during the New Kingdom, the temple has retained much of its grandeur, as well as extensive (and often exaggerated) records of the king's reign.

TOP TIPS

- Allow at least one day.
- Tickets for everything except the Valley of the Kings must be bought at the ticket office.
- Bring a hat, sunscreen and plenty of water.
- Photography is not allowed inside the tombs, but there is plenty to see – and photograph – outside.

BLACKMAC / SHUTTERSTOCK ©

Medinat Habu
Original paintwork, applied more than 3000 years ago, can still be seen on lintels and inner columns. Some of this was preserved by the mud-brick houses and chapels of early Christians (since destroyed).

Colossi of Memnon
Although the Greeks called him Memnon, the colossi were built for Pharaoh Amenhotep III, who built the largest of all funerary temples here on the west bank (its ruins are only now being excavated).

DMITRY PETRENKO / SHUTTERSTOCK ©

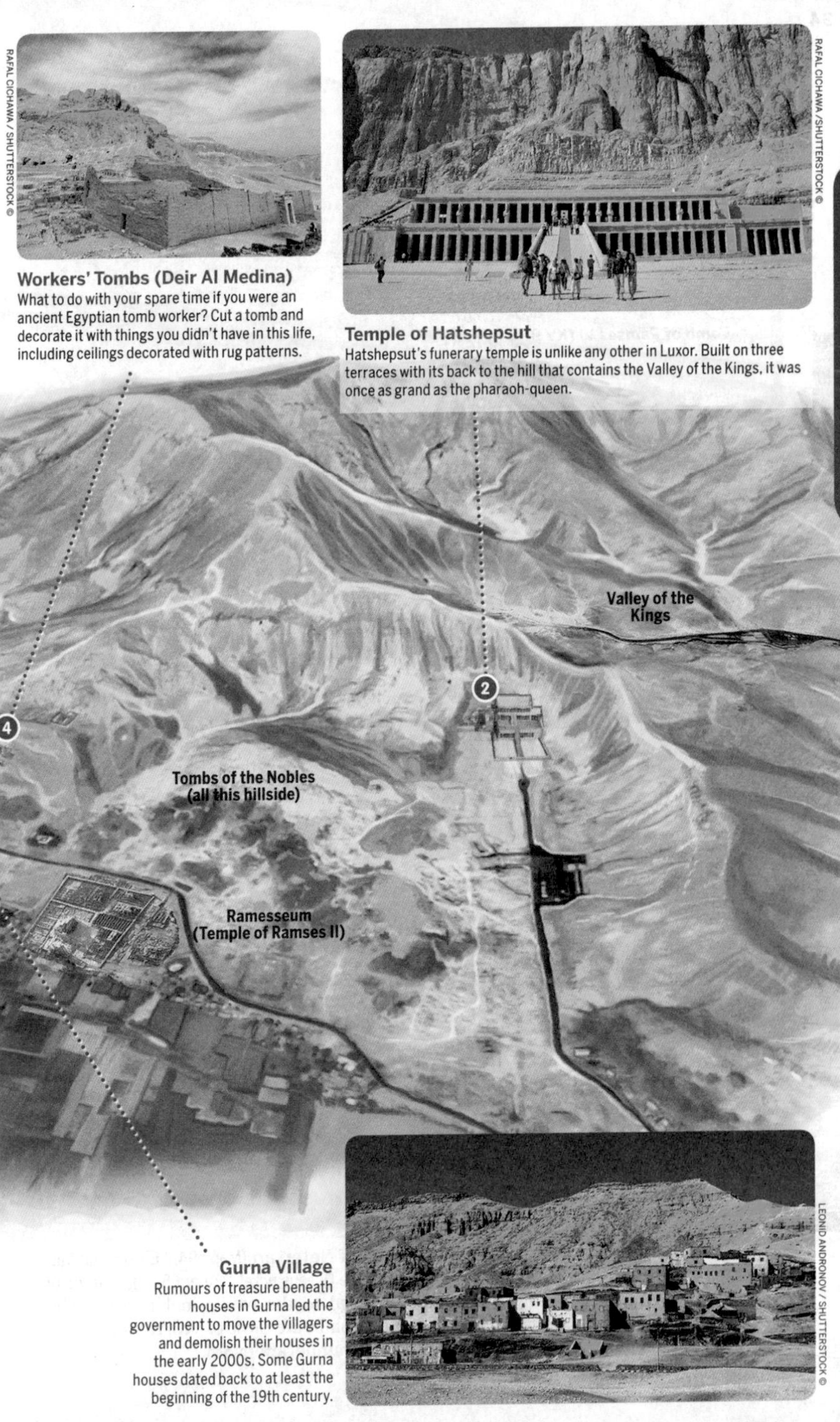

Workers' Tombs (Deir Al Medina)
What to do with your spare time if you were an ancient Egyptian tomb worker? Cut a tomb and decorate it with things you didn't have in this life, including ceilings decorated with rug patterns.

Temple of Hatshepsut
Hatshepsut's funerary temple is unlike any other in Luxor. Built on three terraces with its back to the hill that contains the Valley of the Kings, it was once as grand as the pharaoh-queen.

Gurna Village
Rumours of treasure beneath houses in Gurna led the government to move the villagers and demolish their houses in the early 2000s. Some Gurna houses dated back to at least the beginning of the 19th century.

Luxor – West Bank

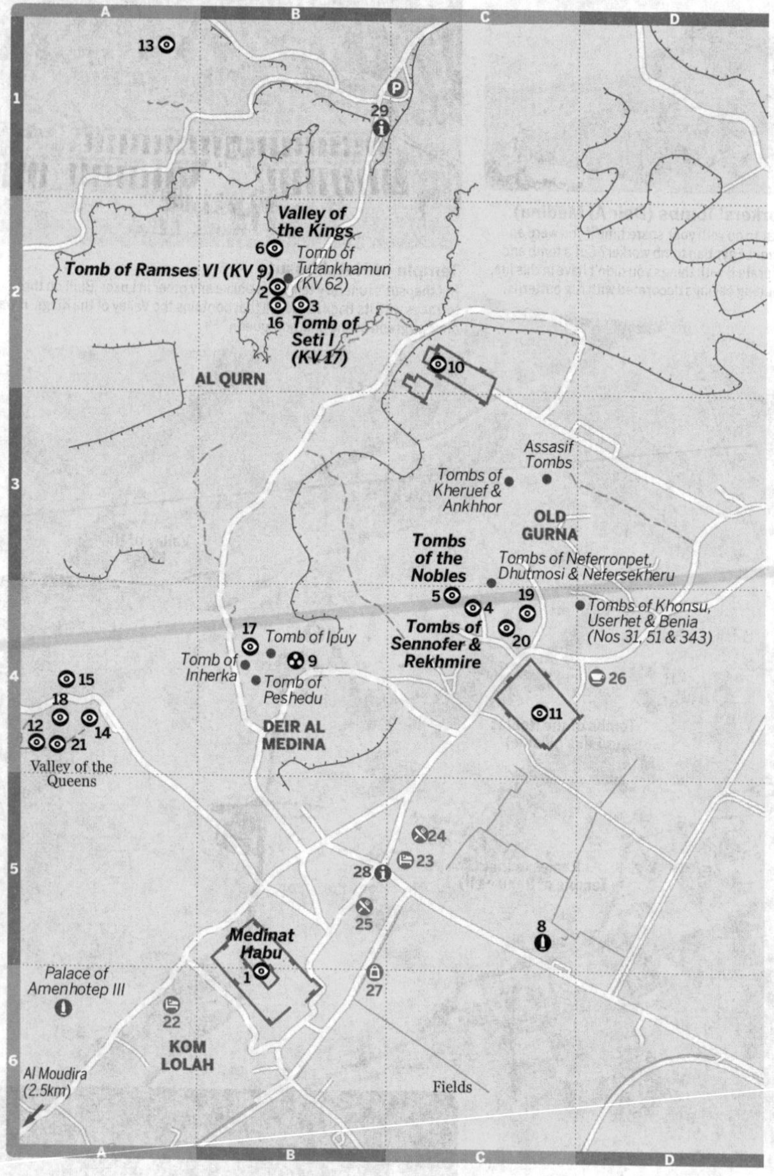

contains at least 75 tombs that belonged to queens of the 19th and 20th dynasties as well as to other members of the royal families, including princesses and the Ramesside princes. Four of the tombs are open for viewing. The most famous of these, the tomb of **Nefertari** (Map p94; LE1000, plus Valley of the Queens ticket; ⏲6am-5pm), was only reopened to the public in late 2016. The other tombs are those of **Titi**, **Khaemwaset** and **Amunherkhepshef**.

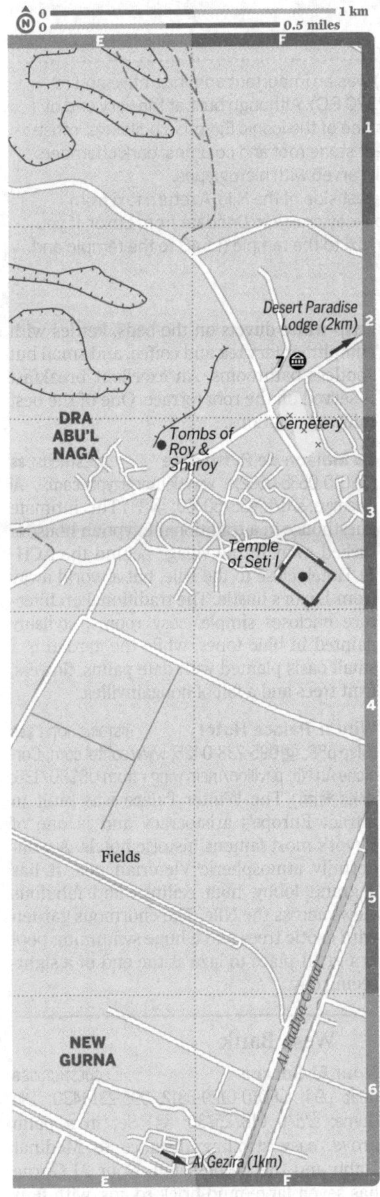

Luxor – West Bank

Top Sights

1 Medinat Habu B6
2 Tomb of Ramses VI (KV 9) B2
3 Tomb of Seti I (KV 17) B2
4 Tombs of Sennofer & Rekhmire C4
5 Tombs of the Nobles C4
6 Valley of the Kings B2

Sights

7 Carter's House & the Replica Tomb of Tutankhamun F2
8 Colossi of Memnon C5
9 Deir Al Medina B4
10 Memorial Temple of Hatshepsut C2
11 Ramesseum C4
12 Tomb of Amunherkhepshef A4
13 Tomb of Ay A1
Tomb of Horemheb (KV 57) ..... (see 2)
14 Tomb of Khaemwaset A4
15 Tomb of Nefertari A4
16 Tomb of Ramses III (KV 11) B2
17 Tomb of Sennedjem B4
18 Tomb of Titi A4
19 Tombs of Menna, Nakht & Amenemope C4
20 Tombs of Ramose, Userhet & Khaemhet C4
21 Valley of the Queens A4

Sleeping

22 Beit Sabée A6
23 Nour El Gourna C5

Eating

24 Marsam Restaurant C5
25 Restaurant Mohammed B5

Drinking & Nightlife

26 Ramesseum Rest House D4

Shopping

27 Caravanserai B6

Information

28 Antiquities Inspectorate Ticket Office B5
29 Valley of the Kings Visitors Centre & Ticket Booth B1

Activities & Tours

★**Nobi's Arabian Horse Stables** HORSE RIDING
(Map p88; 095-231-0024, 010-0504-8558; www.luxorstables.com; camel or horse with helmet per hour approx LE50, donkey LE40; 7am-sunset)

Excellent horses can be found at Nobi's Arabian Horse Stables, which also provides riding hats, English saddles and insurance. Nobi also has 25 camels and as many donkeys, and organises longer horse-riding and camping trips into the desert, or a week from Luxor to Kom Ombo along the West Bank. Call ahead and they will collect you from your hotel.

WORTH A TRIP

DENDARA

Dendara (adult/student LE80/40; 7am-6pm) was an important administrative and religious centre as early as the 6th dynasty (c 2320 BC). Although built at the very end of the Pharaonic period, the Temple of Hathor is one of the iconic Egyptian buildings, mostly because it remains largely intact, with a great stone roof and columns, dark chambers, underground crypts and twisting stairways, all carved with hieroglyphs.

Dendara is 4km southwest of Qena on the west side of the Nile. A return taxi from Luxor will cost you about LE200. There is also a day cruise to Dendara from Luxor. If you arrive in Qena by train, you will need to take a taxi to the temple (LE40 to the temple and back, with some waiting time).

Aladin Tours CULTURAL
(Map p88; 010-0601-6132, 095-237-2386; www.nefertitihotel.com/tours; Nefertiti Hotel, Sharia As Sahaby; 10am-6pm) This very helpful travel agency, run by the young, energetic Aladin, organises sightseeing tours in Luxor and around as well as in the Western Desert, plus boat trips and ferry tickets to Sinai.

Sleeping

East Bank

★**Bob Marley Peace Hotel** HOSTEL $
(Boomerang; Map p88; 095-228-0981; www.peacehotelluxor.com; Sharia Mohammed Farid; dm from LE50, s/d with shared bathroom LE140/250;) The east bank's best-run budget digs, the Bob Marley Peace Hotel (also known as the Boomerang) offers great facilities on a backpacker budget. Rooms and dorm are squeaky clean (private rooms with en suite are surprisingly spacious), breakfast is big and there's a cushion-scattered roof terrace, tour booking, free wi-fi and an easy walk with a pack from Luxor Train Station.

Happy Land Hotel HOSTEL $
(Map p88; 010-0186-4922; www.facebook.com/msht12345; Sharia Qamr; s/d LE85/90, with shared bathroom LE75/80;) The Happy Land, a backpackers' favourite, offers clean rooms and bathrooms, plus friendly service, a copious breakfast with fruit and cornflakes and a rooftop terrace. Competition among Luxor's budget hotels is fierce, and the Happy Land does OK.

★**Nefertiti Hotel** HOTEL $$
(Map p88; 095-237-2386; www.nefertitihotel.com; Sharia As Sahabi, btwn Sharia Maabad Al Karnak & Sharia As Souq; s/d/tr/f US$22/30/36/40;) Aladin As Sahabi runs his family's hotel with care and passion. No wonder this hotel is popular with our readers: simple but scrupulously clean rooms come with crisp white duvets on the beds, kettles with complimentary tea and coffee, and small but spotless bathrooms. An excellent breakfast is served on the roof terrace. One of the best midrange options.

La Maison de Pythagore GUESTHOUSE $$
(010-0535-0532; www.louxor-egypte.com; Al Awamiya; s/d/tr €35/50/60;) This intimate guesthouse in a traditional Egyptian house is tucked away in the village behind the ACHTI Hotel, close to the Nile, but a world away from Luxor's hustle. The traditional architecture encloses simple, cosy rooms, stylishly painted in blue tones, while the garden is a small oasis planted with date palms, flowers, fruit trees and a fall of bougainvillea.

Winter Palace Hotel HISTORIC HOTEL $$$
(Map p88; 095-238-0425; www.sofitel.com; Corniche An Nil; pavillon/main wing r from US$80/136;) The Winter Palace was built to attract Europe's aristocracy and is one of Egypt's most famous historic hotels. A wonderfully atmospheric Victorian pile, it has a grand lobby, high ceilings and fabulous views across the Nile. The enormous garden with exotic trees and a huge swimming pool is a great place to laze at the end of a sightseeing day.

West Bank

Nour El Gourna GUESTHOUSE $
(Map p94; 010-0129-5812, 095-231-1430; Old Gurna; s/d/tr €18/25/30;) Set in a palm grove, easy strolling distance to Medinat Habu and the Ramesseum, Nour Al Gurna has seven large mud-brick rooms, with fans (some with air-con), mosquito nets, small stereos, locally made furniture, tiled bathrooms and traditional palm-thatch ceilings. Romantic and original, with friendly management, this is a tranquil and intimate guesthouse, conveniently located for visiting the west bank's monuments.

Al Gezira Hotel HOTEL $

(Map p88; ☎095-231-0034; www.el-gezira.com; Gezira Al Bayrat; s/d/tr €15/20/25, half board extra €6 per person;) This hotel, in a modern building, is very much a home away from home – literally so for quite a few archaeologists during the winter season. The charming owners make everyone feel welcome and the 11 homey rooms, overlooking the lake or a dried-up branch of the Nile, are well maintained and pristinely clean.

★ **Beit Sabée** BOUTIQUE HOTEL $$

(Map p94; ☎011-1837-5604; www.nourelnil.com/guesthouse; Bairat; d €40-100;) This is a great reinvention of a traditional-style, two-storey, mud-brick house: Beit Sabée has appeared in design magazines for its cool use of local colours and furnishings with a twist. Near the farms behind Medinat Habu, it offers effortlessly chic rooms, a closer contact with rural Egypt and fabulous views of the desert and Medinat Habu from the rooftop.

Nile Valley Hotel HOTEL $$

(Map p88; ☎095-231-1477, 012-2796-4473; www.nilevalley.nl; Al Gezira; s €22-30, d €27-35, f €35-50;) A delightful Dutch-Egyptian hotel in a modern block near the ferry landing. Rooms in both the cheaper old wing and the new wing are light-filled and come with good facilities (air-con, satellite TV, fridge). The rooftop **bar-restaurant** (Map p88; ☎095-231-1477; www.facebook.com/pg/Nilevalleyhotel; meals LE40-80; ⏰8am-11pm) has fantastic views over the Nile to Luxor Temple, while the garden has a pool (and children's pool) for after-temple cooling off.

★ **Al Moudira** HOTEL $$$

(☎095-255-1440, 012-2392-8332; www.moudira.com; Daba'iyya; s/d from €150/180;) Al Moudira is a luxury hotel of a stylish individuality. A fantasy of pointed arches and soaring domes set amid lush gardens and birdsong, the hotel is charming and peaceful. The huge rooms are grouped around a series of verdant courtyards. There is a tranquil restaurant and vibrant bar, a large pool and hammam, all run by friendly staff.

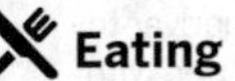

Eating

East Bank

★ **Wenkie's German Ice Cream & Iced Coffee Parlour** ICE CREAM $

(Map p88; ☎012-8894-7380; www.facebook.com/wenkies; Sharia Al Gawazat, opposite the Nile Palace; small/large scoop LE3/5; ⏰2-8pm Sat-Thu) For people who only opened up shop in 2014, Ernst and Babette Wenk have quickly become legends, serving the finest, most delicious ice cream in Luxor. Using organic buffalo milk and fresh fruit, they make and sell ices and sorbets with distinctly local flavours (think hibiscus, mango and doum palm).

Koshari Alzaeem EGYPTIAN $

(Map p88; Sharia Al Masaken Al Shaabeya; dishes LE5-15; ⏰24hr) Probably the best *kushari* in town. The few tables tend to fill up fast. There is a second branch near Midan Youssef Hassan.

★ **Sofra Restaurant & Café** EGYPTIAN $$

(Map p88; ☎095-235-9752; www.sofra.com.eg; 90 Sharia Mohammed Farid; mezze LE16-25, mains LE45-85; ⏰11am-midnight) Sofra remains our favourite restaurant in downtown Luxor. Both the intimate salons and the spacious rooftop terrace are stylishly decorated, sprinkled with antique furniture, chandeliers and original tilework. The menu features excellent mezze and well-executed

TACKLING THE WEST BANK

- The **Antiquities Inspectorate ticket office** (Map p94; main road, 3km inland from ferry landing; ⏰6am-5pm) sells tickets to most sites except for the Temple at Deir Al Bahri, the Assasif Tombs (available at Deir Al Bahri ticket office), the Valley of the Kings and the Valley of the Queens.
- All sites are officially open from 6am to 5pm.
- Photography is not permitted in any tombs.
- Bring plenty of water, a sun hat, sunglasses and sunscreen. Small change for baksheesh is much needed; guardians rely on tips to augment their pathetic salaries.
- Early morning visits are ideal, but that is unfortunately when most tour groups visit the Memorial Temple of Hatshepsut or the Valley of the Kings so try to leave these two to the afternoon.
- Tickets are valid only for the day of purchase, and no refunds are given.

DON'T MISS

FELUCCA SIGHTSEEING

As elsewhere in Egypt, the nicest place to be late afternoon is on the Nile. Expect to pay LE50 to LE100 per boat per hour.

A popular felucca trip is upriver to Banana Island, a tiny isle dotted with palms about 5km from Luxor. The trip takes two to three hours. Plan it in such a way that you're on your way back in time to watch a brilliant Nile sunset from the boat.

traditional Egyptian classics such as stuffed pigeon and excellent duck. With friendly staff and shisha to finish, the place is a treat.

As Sahaby Lane EGYPTIAN $$
(Map p88; ☎095-236-5509; www.nefertitihotel.com/sahabi.htm; Sharia As Sahaby, off Sharia As Souq; dishes LE13-150; ⏲9am-11.30pm) This easy-going restaurant takes over the alleyway running between the souq and the street to the Karnak temples, adjoining the Nefertiti Hotel. Fresh, well-prepared Egyptian standards like *fiteer* and *tagen* (stew cooked in a deep clay pot) are served alongside good pizzas and salads, as well as more adventurous dishes such as camel with couscous.

Gerda's Garden EGYPTIAN, EUROPEAN $$
(☎012-2534-8326, 095-235-8688; opp Hilton Luxor, New Karnak; dishes LE15-45; ⏲6.30-11pm) Gerda is one half of a German-Egyptian couple whose restaurant has built a strong following with European residents and regular visitors to Luxor. The decor is homely provincial European bistro, but the menu features both Egyptian specials (kebab and delicious grilled pigeon) and very European comfort food for those slightly homesick, such as goulash and potato salad.

1886 Restaurant MEDITERRANEAN $$$
(Map p88; ☎095-238-0425; www.sofitel.com; Winter Palace Hotel, Corniche An Nil; mains LE160-310; ⏲7-11pm) The 1886 is the fanciest restaurant in the town centre, serving inventive Mediterranean-French food and a few Egyptian dishes with a twist, all in a grand old-style dining room. The waiters are in formal attire and guests are expected to dress for the occasion – men wear a tie and/or jacket (some are available for borrowing). A grand evening out!

West Bank

Marsam Restaurant EGYPTIAN $
(Sheikh Ali's; Map p94; www.marsamluxor.com; West Bank, near the Ramesseum; mains LE50-100) A lovely place to stop for for dinner on a warm evening or for lunch while seeing the west-bank sights – you can sit in the courtyard under the huge trees and look out at the backs of the Colossi of Memnon. Either way food is simple, mostly Egyptian and very good. Service is friendly and can be slow. Alcohol served.

Restaurant Mohammed EGYPTIAN $$
(Map p94; ☎012-0325-1307, 095-231-1014; Kom Lolah; mains LE40-80; ⏲approx 10am-late) Mohammed's is an old-time Luxor throwback, a simple, family-run restaurant attached to the owner's mud-brick house, where charming Mohammed Abdel Lahi serves with his son Azab, while his wife cooks. The small menu includes meat grills, delicious chicken and duck as well as stuffed pigeon, a local speciality. Stella beer and Egyptian wine are usually available.

Al Moudira MEDITERRANEAN $$
(☎012-0325-1307; Daba'iyya; mains LE75-110; ⏲8am-midnight) Al Moudira has the most flamboyant decor and most sophisticated (and expensive) food on the west bank. Come at lunch for great salads and grills, or at night for a more elaborate menu, which changes daily, of delicious Mediterranean-Lebanese cuisine. This is a great place for a romantic dinner in the courtyard, or by the fire in the winter. Reserve ahead.

Drinking & Nightlife

Kings Head Pub PUB
(Map p88; ☎010-6510-2133; www.facebook.com/KingsHeadPubAndRestaurant; Sharia Khaled Ibn Al Walid; ⏲noon-late) A relaxed and perennially popular place to have a beer, shoot pool and watch sports on a big screen, the Kings Head tries to capture the atmosphere of an English pub without being twee. The laidback atmosphere also means that women can come here without being harassed. At the time of writing, it had been up for sale for a long time.

Cilantro CAFE
(Map p88; lower level, Corniche An Nil; ⏲10am-8pm) A pleasant, popular outdoor cafe, right on the Nile, in front of the Winter Palace Ho-

tel. The former Metropolitan is now part of the Egyptian coffee chain Cilantro, serving dull though usually reliable snacks and good coffee. Away from the hassle of the corniche, right by the waterline, it's a good place to while away a moment.

Ramesseum Rest House CAFE
(Map p94; ☎010-0945-0789; beside the Ramesseum, Gurna; ⏲7am-1am) One of the oldest cafe-restaurants on the west bank, come to this friendly, laid-back place to relax after temple viewings. In addition to the usual mineral water and soft drinks, beer and sometimes wine are available. They also serve simple food – grilled chicken, omelettes and salads.

Shopping

★Caravanserai ARTS & CRAFTS
(Map p94; ☎012-2327-8771; www.caravanserailuxor.com; Kom Lolah; ⏲8am-10pm) This delightful treasure trove of Egyptian crafts, near Medinat Habu on the west bank, is run by friendly Khairy and his family. Inside you'll find beautiful pottery from the Western Oases, Siwan embroideries, a colourful selection of handwoven scarves, amazing appliqué bags and many other crafts that can be found almost nowhere else in Egypt. All at highly reasonable prices.

Habiba ARTS & CRAFTS
(Map p88; ☎010-0124-2026; www.habibagallery.com; Sharia Andrawes Pasha, off Sharia As Souq; ⏲10am-10pm) Run by an Australian woman who promotes the best of Egyptian crafts, Habiba sells an ever-expanding selection of top quality Bedouin embroidery, jewellery, leatherwork, wonderful Siwan scarves, cotton embroidered scarves from Sohag, the best Egyptian cotton towels (usually only for export), mirrors, Aswan baskets and much more – all at fixed prices. New lines include locally made shea-butter products.

Information

DANGERS & ANNOYANCES

- Business has been so slow recently that Luxor's once notorious hasslers seem to have lost heart, though you will still be offered feluccas and motorboats on the corniche and a range of tat as you walk through the souq and the entrance to the Valley of the Kings.
- Some *calèche* (horse-drawn carriage) drivers can be persistent, pushed by the need to feed their horses, many quite malnourished.
- You may also be propositioned or offered sex – offers you should ignore. All this hassle is a sign of the desperate financial situation that Egypt, and particularly Luxor, is in.

MEDICAL SERVICES

Dr Ihab Rizk (☎095-238-2525, 012-2216-0846) English-speaking cardiologist, who will come to your hotel; on the east bank.

Luxor Medical Centre (Map p88; ☎095-228-4092, 010-2004-7091; www.luxormedicalcenter.com; Villa Kamal, Sharia St Joseph; ⏲24hr)

MONEY

There is no shortage of ATMs on the east bank. There are now a couple of ATMs on the west bank, but it is best not to count on them working.

TOURIST INFORMATION

Main Tourist Office (Map p88; ☎095-237-3294, 095-237-2215; Midan Al Mahatta; ⏲9am-8pm) Very helpful and well-informed, opposite the train station.

Getting There & Away

AIR

Luxor Airport (☎095-232-4455) is 7km east of central Luxor. EgyptAir (www.egyptair.com) operates regular flights to Cairo from LE730.

BUS

Upper Egypt Bus Co (Map p88; ☎095-232-3218, 095-237-2118; Midan Al Mahatta; ⏲7am-10pm) and **Super Jet** (Map p88; ☎095-236-7732; Midan Al Mahatta; ⏲8am-10pm)

MAJOR BUSES FROM LUXOR

DESTINATION	PRICE	DURATION	TIME/COMPANY
Cairo	LE150-275	10-12hr	10pm (Upper Egypt); 9am, 1pm & 10.15pm (Super Jet); 1pm, 9.30pm, 11.45pm, 12.30am (Go Bus)
Dahab	LE210	18hr	5pm (Upper Egypt)
Hurghada	LE50-90	4-5hr	7am & 8.30pm (Upper Egypt); 8.30am & 7pm (Super Jet); 8am & 3.30pm (Go Bus)
Sharm El Sheikh	LE175	14hr	5pm (Upper Egypt)

TRAINS FROM LUXOR

Prices are for a 1st-class air-con seat. All trains south to Aswan stop at Esna, Edfu and Kom Ombo. All trains north to Cairo stop at Qena (for Dendara), Balyana (for Abydos) and Asyut (for the Western Desert).

DESTINATION	PRICE	DURATION	TIME
Aswan	Spanish/Special LE53/94	3hr	4.30am, 7.35am, 9.45am & 10.35pm (Spanish); 2.50am, 6.20am, 6.45am, 8.15am, 6.25pm, & 7.40pm (Special)
Cairo	Spanish/Special LE114/203	10hr	1.15am, 10.55am, 8pm & 11.35pm (Spanish); 9.10am, 12.30pm, 2pm, 6.20pm, 7.10pm, 9.10pm & 11.59pm (Special)
Cairo (Watania Sleeping Train)	1-/2-bed berth US$120/100	9hr	8.10pm

have ticket offices just south of the train station. The **Go Bus office** (Map p88; ☎010-0779-1286; www.gobus-eg.com; Sharia Ramses) is just to the north. Most bus services leave from outside of the respective ticket office; check when booking. A taxi from downtown Luxor to the bus offices costs between LE25 and LE35.

MICROBUS

Due to current security concerns, foreigners are not currently allowed to use microbuses between towns in the Nile Valley region.

TRAIN

Special services have newer rolling stock and slightly bigger seats than Spanish services. **Luxor Station** (☎095-237-2018; Midan Al Mahatta) has a tourist office. All train tickets are best bought in advance; if you buy your ticket on the train there is a surcharge of LE6.

The **Watania Sleeping Train** (www.watania sleepingtrains.com) has a ticket booking office inside the station.

Getting Around

TO/FROM THE AIRPORT

There is no bus between the airport and the town and no official price for taxis from Luxor airport into town, so the drivers set their prices, often at about LE100 or more. If you want peace of mind, ask your accommodation to arrange your transfer.

BICYCLE

Many hotels rent out bikes. Prices vary, as does the quality of bikes. Pick one up for LE25 a day from the excellent **Mohamed Setouhy** (Gezira Bike Rental; Map p88; ☎010-0223-9710; LE25 per day; ⏰7am-7pm) on the west bank.

FERRY

Most tourists on organised tours cross to the west bank by bus or taxi via the bridge, about 8km south of town. But the river remains the quickest way to go. The *baladi* (municipal) ferry costs LE2 for foreigners and runs between the **dock** (Map p88) in front of Luxor Temple and the **dock** (Map p88) fronting Gezira village on the west bank.

MICROBUS

To Karnak, take a microbus from the **main microbus station** (Map p88) directly behind Luxor Train Station, or from behind Luxor Temple, for LE1.

The west bank's microbuses operate until around 10pm (LE1 per ride). They run back and forth between the villages so you can always flag one down on your way to one of the sites, although you will have to walk from the main road to the entrance which, in the case of the Valley of the Kings or Queens, is quite far. The **microbus lot** (Map p88) is close to the ferry landing. All microbuses heading to Gurna can drop you at the main ticket office.

TAXI

Passengers have to bargain hard for trips. A short trip around town is likely to cost at least LE20. Taxis can also be hired for day trips around the west bank; expect to pay LE200 to LE300. The **West Bank Taxis stand** (Map p88) is just inland from the public ferry landing.

Esna إسنا

Most visitors come to Esna, 64km south of Luxor on the west bank of the Nile, for the **Temple of Khnum** (adult/student LE50/25; ⏰8am-4.30pm), dedicated to the ram-headed creator god who fashioned humankind on his potter's wheel. Temple construction was begun by Ptolemy VI Philometor (180–145 BC). The Romans added the hypostyle hall, the only part of the temple that is excavated and can be visited today with well preserved carvings from as late as the 3rd century AD.

The simplest way to visit the temple, is by taxi from Luxor. The train station is on the opposite (east) bank of the Nile, away from the town centre, but **kabouts** (pickup trucks) shuttle between the two.

Edfu إدفو

Built on a rise above the broad river valley, the **Temple of Horus** (adult/student LE100/50; 8am-5pm) at Edfu, having escaped destruction from Nile floods, is the most completely preserved Egyptian temple. One of the last ancient attempts at building on a grand scale, the temple dominates this west-bank town, 53km south of Esna. Its well-preserved reliefs have provided archaeologists with much valuable information about temple rituals and the power of the priesthood. Walking through the large, gloomy chambers, visitors are sometimes overwhelmed by a sense of awe at the mysteries of ancient Egypt.

A half-day trip to Edfu and Esna from Luxor costs around LE500.

Edfu train station is on the east bank of the Nile, about 4km from town. To get to the town, you must first take a *kabout* (pick-up truck) from the train station to the bridge, then another into town. Each costs 50pt.

Kom Ombo كوم أمبو

Standing on a promontory at a bend in the Nile, where in ancient times sacred crocodiles basked in the sun on the riverbank, is the **Temple of Kom Ombo** (adult/student LE80/40; 8am-5pm), one of the Nile Valley's most beautifully sited temples. Unique in Egypt, it is dedicated to two gods; the local crocodile god Sobek, and Haroeris (from har-wer), meaning Horus the Elder.

Beside the complex is the the new **Crocodile Museum**. It's well worth a visit for its beautiful collection of mummified crocodiles and ancient carvings, which is well lit and well explained.

The train station is 3.5km from the temple. A taxi from the station should cost around LE40 return.

Hiring a driver from Luxor for a day trip taking in both Edfu and Kom Ombo, either returning to Luxor or moving on to Aswan will cost LE900 to LE1200. A private taxi from Aswan will cost from LE400 to LE500.

Aswan أسوان

097 / POP 312,000

On the northern end of the First Cataract, marking ancient Egypt's southern frontier, Aswan has always been of great strategic importance. The river is wide, languorous and beautiful here, flowing gently down from Lake Nasser around dramatic black-granite boulders and palm-studded islands. This is the perfect place to linger for a few days and recover from the rigours of travelling and temple-viewing.

Sights

★Nubia Museum MUSEUM
(Map p102; Sharia Al Fanadeq; adult/student LE100/50; 9am-1pm & 4-9pm winter, 6-10pm summer) The little-visited Nubia Museum, opposite Basma Hotel, is a treat, a showcase of the history, art and culture of Nubia. Established in 1997 in cooperation with Unesco, the museum is a reminder of what was lost beneath Lake Nasser. Exhibits are beautifully displayed in huge halls, where clearly written explanations take you from 4500 BC through to the present day.

Unfinished Obelisk ARCHAEOLOGICAL SITE
(Map p102; Sharia Al Haddadeen; adult/student LE60/30; 8am-5pm) Aswan was the source of ancient Egypt's finest granite, used to make statues and embellish temples, pyramids and obelisks. The large unfinished obelisk in the Northern Quarries has provided valuable insight into how these monuments were created, although the full construction process is still not entirely clear. Three sides of the shaft, nearly 42m long, were completed except for the inscriptions. At 1168

DON'T MISS

THE UNOFFICIAL NUBIAN MUSEUM

Animalia (Map p102; 097-231-4152, 010-0300-5672; Main St, Siou, Elephantine Island; LE20, incl guided tour; 8am-7pm) is a small but charming museum run by Mohamed Sobhi, a Nubian guide, and his family, who have dedicated part of their large house to the traditions, flora, fauna and history of Nubia. It has a collection of stuffed animals endemic to Nubia, samples of sedimentary rocks and great pictures of Nubia before it was flooded by Lake Nasser.

Aswan

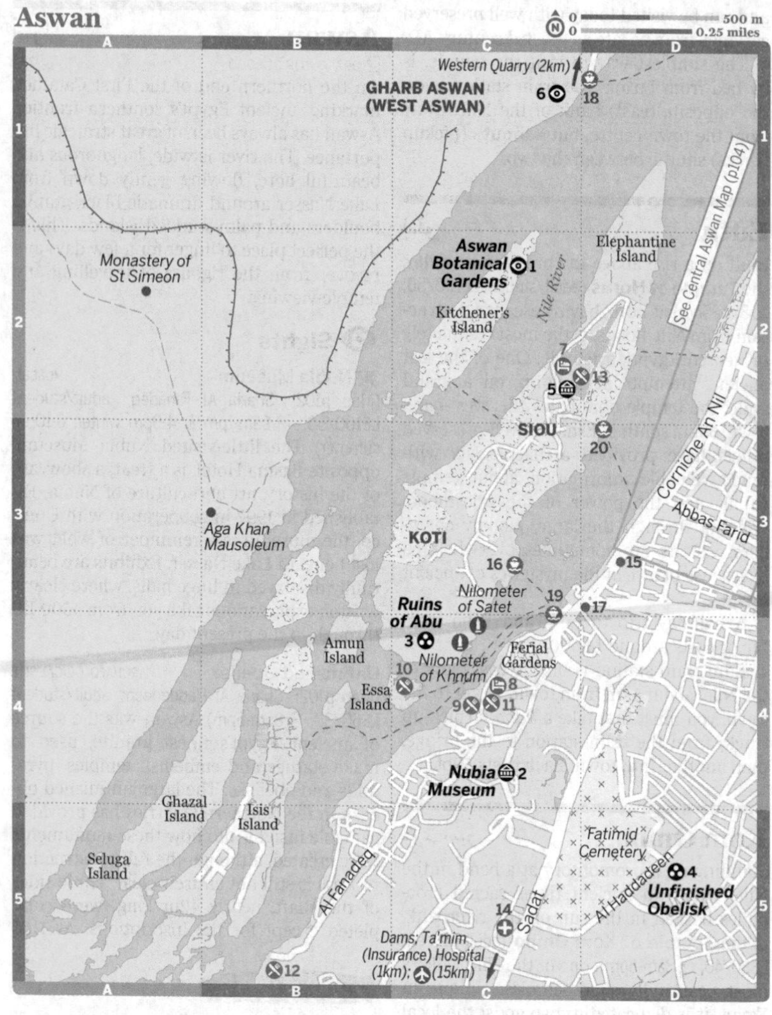

tonnes, the completed obelisk would have been the single heaviest piece of stone the Egyptians ever fashioned.

★Ruins of Abu ARCHAEOLOGICAL SITE

(Map p102; Elephantine Island; adult/student LE35/15; ⏲8am-5pm) The evocative ruins of ancient Abu and the Aswan Museum (partially closed for renovation) lie at Elephantine Island's southern tip. Numbered plaques and reconstructed buildings mark the island's long history from around 3000 BC to the 14th century AD. The largest structure on-site is the partially reconstructed Temple of Khnum (plaque numbers 6, 12 and 13). Built in honour of the god of inundation during the Old Kingdom, it was used for more than 1500 years before being extensively rebuilt in Ptolemaic times.

Tombs of the Nobles TOMB

(Map p102; West Bank; adult/student LE60/30; ⏲8am-4pm) The high cliffs opposite Aswan, just north of Kitchener's Island, are honeycombed with the tombs of the governors, the Keepers of the Gate of the South, and other dignitaries of ancient Elephantine Island. The tombs, known as the Tombs of the Nobles, are still being excavated: sig-

Aswan

Top Sights
1 Aswan Botanical Gardens....C2
2 Nubia Museum....C4
3 Ruins of Abu....C4
4 Unfinished Obelisk....D5

Sights
5 Animalia....C2
6 Tombs of the Nobles....C1

Sleeping
7 Baaba Dool....C2
8 Sofitel Old Cataract Hotel & Spa....C4

Eating
9 1902 Restaurant....C4
10 Ad Dukka....C4
11 Kebabgy....C4
12 Nubian House Restaurant....B5
13 Panorama Restaurant & Bar....D2

Information
14 Aswan Military Hospital....C5
15 Passport Office....D3

Transport
16 Aswan Museum Ferry Dock....C3
17 EgyptAir Office....D3
18 Ferry Landing on Gharb Aswan....D1
19 Ferry Landing to Koti....C3
20 Ferry on Siou....D3

nificant finds were made in 2014 and 2017. Six decorated tombs are currently open to the public.

Activities

The Nile looks fabulous and magical at Aswan, and few things are more relaxing than hiring a felucca before sunset and sailing between the islands, the desert and the huge black boulders. On days when cruise boats dock together in town, hundreds of feluccas circle the islands, so it's a good time to take a felucca a bit further out towards Seheyl Island.

Tours

Small hotels and travel agencies arrange day tours of the area's major sights. Half-day guided tours usually include the Temple of Isis at Philae, the Unfinished Obelisk and the High Dam, and start at LE400 (per person with three to five people), including admission to all sites.

All travel agencies and most hotels in Aswan offer trips to Abu Simbel, but watch out for huge price differences, and check that the bus is comfortable and has air-con. Thomas Cook charges about LE1000 per person, including admission fees and guide. By contrast, budget hotels offer tours for about LE500 to LE600 though not including the entrance fee or guide.

Sleeping

Baaba Dool GUESTHOUSE $
(Map p102; 010-0497-2608; Siou, Elephantine Island; r with shared bathroom per person €14) A great place to unwind for a few days. The rooms in this beautiful mud-brick house are painted in Nubian style, decorated with colourful carpets and local crafts, and have superb views over the Nile and the botanical gardens. It's very basic, but it's clean and there are shared hot showers. Mustapha can arrange meals. Book ahead.

Nuba Nile Hotel HOTEL $
(Map p104; 011-4291-2224, 010-0242-2864; www.nubanilehotel.com; Sharia Abtal At Tahrir; s/d/tr/q LE200/230/280/310;) Although its 3-star claim is amusing, to say the least, this friendly, family-run hotel, always bustling with Egyptian holidaymakers, is one of the more reliable of Aswan's budget hotels, conveniently located just north of the train station. The lobby is quite dark, but the rooms are bright and clean. Check the room before you agree, as they vary considerably.

★ **Philae Hotel** HOTEL $$
(Map p104; 011-1901-1995, 097-246-5090; philaehotel@gmail.com; Corniche An Nil; s/d/tr/ste Nile view US$70/80/105/120, s/d/tr city view US$60/70/90;) By far the best midrange hotel in town. The Philae's modern, minimalist-style rooms are decorated in fabrics with Arabic calligraphy and elegant local furnishings. The hotel restaurant serves mainly vegetarian organic food from its own gardens, and at very reasonable prices for the quality (mains from LE75 to LE90). It's no longer a secret, so book ahead.

Happi Hotel HOTEL $$
(Map p104; 010-0003-6522, 097-245-5032; ali.taher.rizk@gmail.com; 10 Sharia Abtal At Tahrir; s/d/tr US$30/45/55, s/d with Nile view US$40/60;) A much needed arrival on the Aswan hotel scene, the Happi Hotel is well

Central Aswan

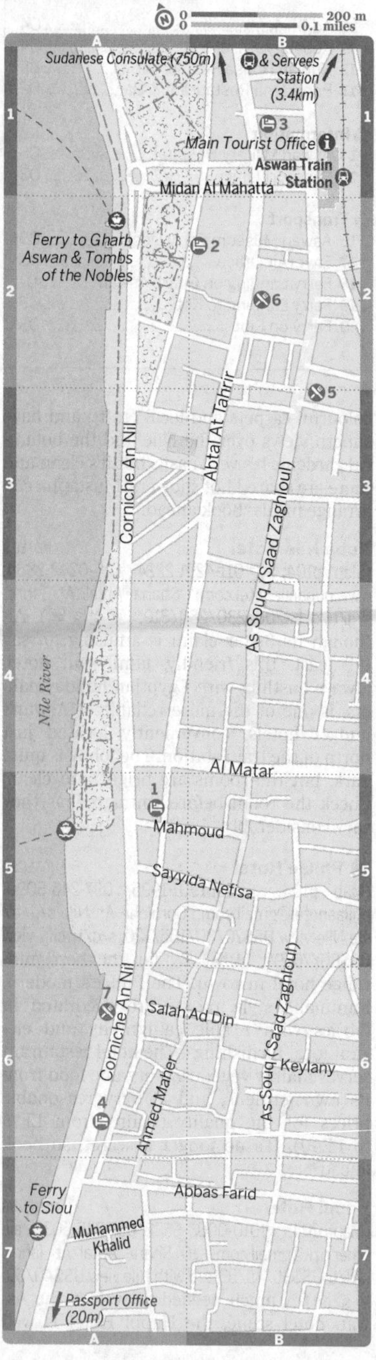

Central Aswan

Sleeping

1 Happi Hotel A5
2 Marhaba Palace Hotel B2
3 Nuba Nile Hotel B1
4 Philae Hotel A6

Eating

5 Al Madina B3
6 Al Makka B2
7 Salah Ad Din A6

run, clean, comfortable and well located, if lacking character. All 65 rooms have TVs, air-con, a mini-bar and wi-fi, and there is a 24-hour cafeteria. The superior rooms are much classier. Friendly management.

Marhaba Palace Hotel HOTEL **$$**
(Map p104; 097-233-0102; www.marhabapalacehotel.omyhotels.club; Corniche An Nil; s/d city view US$35/60, s/d/tr Nile view US$50/70/100;) The homely Marhaba has sparkling clean, cosy rooms with comfortable beds, sumptuous bathrooms (for this price range) and satellite TV. Bright, welcoming and well run, it overlooks a park on the corniche and has two restaurants, friendly staff and a roof terrace with excellent Nile views. Grab a room with a balcony if you can. There is a small swimming pool on the 1st floor.

★ **Sofitel Old Cataract Hotel & Spa** HISTORIC HOTEL **$$$**
(Map p102; 097-231-6000; www.sofitel.com; Sharia Abtal At Tahrir; r from US$225;) The grande dame of Aswan hotels, the Old Cataract is a destination in itself and brings you back to the days of Agatha Christie, who is said to have written part of her novel *Death on the Nile* here (the hotel certainly featured in the movie). The splendid buildings and well-tended gardens command fantastic views of the Nile and the desert.

Eating

Nubian House Restaurant EGYPTIAN **$**
(Map p102; 097-221-0125; Sharia Al Fanadek, south of the Nubian Museum; mains LE30-75; 8am-midnight) The Nubian House was renovated during the spring 2017, and is now more colourful than ever. The Nubian dishes served here are good, but best of all is the view at sunset looking over the First Cataract, and the peace and quiet of the place.

Henna painting is on offer, and sometimes Nubian music.

Salah Ad Din INTERNATIONAL $$
(Map p104; ☎097-231-0361; Corniche An Nil; mains LE35-90; ⊙noon-late) One of the best of the Nileside restaurants, with several terraces and a freezing air-con dining room. The menu has Egyptian, Nubian and international dishes, a notch better than most restaurants in Aswan. The service is efficient and the beers are cold.

There is also a terrace on which to smoke a shisha.

Al Makka EGYPTIAN $$
(Map p104; ☎097-244-0232; Sharia Abtal At Tahrir; dishes LE85-120; ⊙noon-2am) Popular with meat-eating local families, this place is famous for its excellent fresh kebabs and kofta as well as stuffed pigeon. Mains come loaded with bread, salad, tahini, rice and vegetable stew, making it a real feast. Bring your appetite.

Ad Dukka EGYPTIAN $$
(Map p102; ☎012-2216-2379, 097-231-8293; Essa Island; mains LE45-110; ⊙6.30-10pm) This Nubian restaurant, set on an island just beyond Elephantine Island, burnt down and was rebuilt early 2017. It continues to serve excellent Nubian food in large and lavishly decorated portions. It can be a wonderfully atmospheric place to spend an evening as the setting, opposite the Old Cataract Hotel and the ruins of Abu, is spectacular.

To get here, there's a free ferry from the dock opposite the EgyptAir office.

★Panorama Restaurant & Bar INTERNATIONAL $$$
(Map p102; ☎097-230-3455; www.movenpick.com; Mövenpick Resort Aswan, Elephantine Island; mains LE140-290; ⊙noon-11pm) The Panorama is one of the best restaurants in Aswan, even though it is in the Mövenpick's eyesore tower. The food is good, the room elegant and the service friendly and efficient. The real draw, however, is the 360-degree view of Aswan, the river and the desert – spectacular at sunset, glittering at night.

ℹ Information

There are ATMs and exchange booths along the corniche and around Sharia As Souq.

Aswan Military Hospital (Map p102; ☎097-231-7985, 097-231-4739; Sharia Sadat; ⊙24hr)

Main Tourist Office (Map p104; ☎097-231-2811; Midan Al Mahatta; ⊙8am-3pm Sat-Thu)

ℹ Getting There & Away

AIR

Aswan Airport (☎097-348-2440) is located 16km southwest of town. **EgyptAir** (Map p102; ☎097-245-0001; Corniche An Nil; ⊙8am-9pm) has several flights daily to Cairo and three flights per day to Abu Simbel, Sunday to Thursday.

BOAT

Aswan is the most popular starting point for Nile cruises. It's also the best place to arrange an overnight or multiday felucca trip.

BUS

The bus station is 3.5km north of the train station. Services are run by Upper Egypt Bus Co. A taxi there will cost LE60, or it's LE2 in a microbus from downtown.

DESTINATION	PRICE	DURATION	TIME
Abu Simbel	LE50	4hr	8am
Cairo	LE130	14hr	4pm
Hurghada	LE85	7hr	6am, 3pm & 5pm
Marsa Alam	LE50	3hr	5am

Buses to Sudan

Several Sudanese bus companies with offices at Aswan bus station offer services to Khartoum (around LE420) via Wadi Halfa (around LE280). Buses leave early in the morning between 4am and 6am (Saturday to Thursday).

TRAIN

There are 10 trains daily from **Aswan Train Station** (☎097-231-4754; https://enr.gov.eg; Midan Al Mahatta) to Luxor and onward to Cairo. Check train schedules beforehand at Aswan's helpful tourist office as service order does change.

The 5am, 10am, 3pm, 4.35pm, 6pm and 9pm departures use the newer rolling stock VIP 1st class to Luxor (1st/2nd class LE100/70) and Cairo (LE235/135).

The 7am, 4.15pm, 7.45pm, 8pm and 10pm are the normal Spanish service to Luxor (1st/2nd class LE51/30) and Cairo (LE135/70).

All trains stop at Daraw, Kom Ombo, Edfu and Esna.

The **Watania Sleeping Train** (www.watania sleepingtrains.com) departs from Aswan at 7pm daily.

LOCAL KNOWLEDGE

PLANNING A FELUCCA JOURNEY

Most felucca trips begin at Aswan. Trips go to Kom Ombo (two days/one night), Edfu (three days/two nights – the most popular option) or Esna (four days/three nights).

Feluccas are not allowed to sail after 8pm, so most stop at sunset and set up camp on the boat or on shore.

Expect to pay at least LE150 per person per day, including food, and that would be sharing with a boat between six or eight people. On top of this you need to add LE5 to LE10 per person for the captain to arrange the police registration – this needs to be arranged the day before sailing. Do not hand out the whole agreed amount until you get to your destination because there have been several reports of trips being stopped prematurely for a so-called breakdown. If you do have problems, the tourist police or the tourist office should be the first port of call.

Getting Around

FERRY

Two public ferries (LE1) run to Elephantine Island: the ferry (Map p102) departing across from EgyptAir goes to the Aswan Museum (Map p102), while the one (Map p104) across from the Travel Choice office (formerly Thomas Cook) goes to Siou (Map p102). A third public ferry (Map p104) goes from the ferry landing across from the train station to West Aswan (Map p102) and the Tombs of the Nobles for LE1. Foreigners might be expected to pay more than the local ferry fare.

MICROBUS

Microbuses (LE1 to LE2) run along the major roads in Aswan.

TAXI

An all-day taxi tour of some of the sights near Aswan should cost between LE300 and LE400 (excluding entry tickets), depending on distances and number of sights covered. A taxi anywhere within the town costs LE10 to LE20.

Philae (Agilika Island) معبد فيلة

Perched on the island of Philae (fee-*leh*), the **Temple of Isis** (adult/child LE100/50; ⊙7am-4pm Oct-May, to 5pm Jun-Sep) attracted pilgrims for thousands of years and was one of the last pagan temples to operate after the arrival of Christianity. The cult of Isis continued here until at least AD 550.

After the completion of the High Dam, the temple would have entirely disappeared had Unesco not intervened. Between 1972 and 1980, the massive temple complex was disassembled stone by stone. It was then reconstructed 20m higher on nearby Agilika Island, which was landscaped to resemble the original sacred isle of Isis.

The boat landing for the Philae complex is at Shellal, south of the old Aswan Dam. The only easy way to get there is by taxi or organised trip.The return taxi fare is about LE120 to LE150. The return boat trip should not cost more than LE20 per person, plus baksheesh for the boatman, but often costs significantly more. Organised tours usually include the boat fare, sparing you the hassle of haggling.

High Dam السد العالي

Egypt's modern example of construction on a monumental scale, the controversial **Aswan High Dam** (As Sadd Al Ali; adult/child LE30/15; ⊙24hr), 13km south of Aswan, contains 18 times the amount of material used in the Great Pyramid of Khufu and created Lake Nasser, one of the world's largest artificial lakes. Most people visit the High Dam as part of an organised trip to sights south of Aswan.

Abu Simbel أبو سمبل

☎097 / POP 2900

Few tourists linger in the laid-back, quiet town of Abu Simbel, staying no more than the few hours needed to visit the colossal temples for which it is famous. But anyone interested in Lake Nasser and in seeing the temples without the crowds might choose to hang around for a day or two.

Sights

★Temples of Abu Simbel TEMPLE

(adult/student incl guide LE160/80; ⊙6am-5pm Oct-Apr, to 6pm May-Sep) Overlooking Lake Nasser, the Great Temple of Ramses II and the Temple of Hathor, which together make up the Temples of Abu Simbel, are among the most famous and spectacular monuments in Egypt. In a modern marvel of engineering, which matches Ramses II's original construction for sheer audacity, the temple complex was saved from being swallowed by rising waters and lost forever after the building of the High Dam, by being moved lock, stock and barrel to the position it sits upon today.

➡ Great Temple of Ramses II

Carved out of the mountain on the west bank of the Nile between 1274 and 1244 BC, this imposing main temple of the Abu Simbel complex was as much dedicated to the deified Ramses II himself as to Ra-Horakhty, Amun and Ptah. The four colossal statues of the pharaoh, which front the temple, are like gigantic sentinels watching over the incoming traffic from the south, undoubtedly designed as a warning of the strength of the pharaoh.

➡ Temple of Hathor

Next to the Great Temple of Ramses II sits the smaller of Abu Simbel's temples. The Temple of Hathor has a rock-cut facade fronted by six 10m-high standing statues of Ramses and Nefertari, with some of their many children by their side. Nefertari here wears the costume of the goddess Hathor, and is, unusually, portrayed as the same height as her husband (instead of knee-height, as most consorts were depicted).

Sleeping

★Eskaleh GUESTHOUSE $$
(Beit An Nubi; ☎012-2368-0521, 097-340-1288; www.facebook.com/pg/Eskaleh; Sharia Saad Ibn Abu Wakas; d €65; ❄@📶) Part Nubian cultural centre with a library dedicated to Nubian history, part wonderful ecolodge in a traditional mud-brick house, Eskaleh is by far the most interesting place to stay or eat in Abu Simbel. It's also a destination in its own right and a perfect base for a visit to the temples.

Getting There & Away

AIR

EgyptAir has three flights to Aswan from Abu Simbel Airport per day from Sunday to Friday.

BUS

Buses from Abu Simbel to Aswan (LE60, four hours) leave at 6am and 1pm from Wadi El Nil restaurant on the main road.

TOURS

The vast majority of visitors to Abu Simbel come here on an organised tour from Aswan. Budget trips – which basically just include return transport with two hours at the site – start from about LE400. There is no longer a convoy from Aswan to Abu Simbel, but foreigners should travel between 5am and 5pm.

WESTERN OASES

Older than the Pyramids, as sublime as any temple, Egypt's Western Desert is a vast sweep of elemental beauty. The White Desert's shimmering vista of surreal rock formations and the ripple and swell of the Great Sand Sea's mammoth dunes are simply bewitching. Within this intense landscape five oases, shaded by palm plantations and blessed by a plethora of natural hot and cold springs, provide a glimpse of rural Egyptian life.

Dangers & Annoyances

At the time of writing the situation of travelling to the oases was fairly confused, not least in the variety of travel advisories from foreign governments. We recommend that you read the advice of your government before deciding to travel in this region. Currently all excursions into deep desert areas – away from the oases – are banned and foreigners are also not allowed to use microbus transport between oases.

Al Kharga Oasis

الواحات الخارجة

☎092

As the capital of the New Valley Governorate and the closest of the oases to the Nile Valley, Al Kharga is also the most modern and therefore the least exotic. Al Kharga has long stood at the crossroads of vital desert trade routes. This influential location brought it great prosperity, and with the arrival of the Romans, wells were dug, crops cultivated and fortresses built to protect caravan routes.

The new road to Luxor makes it a convenient gateway to the oases, and a smattering of ancient sites here means it's a decent stopover in its own right.

Sights

★Necropolis of Al Bagawat ARCHAEOLOGICAL SITE
(adult/student LE50/25 incl Monastery of Al Kashef; ⏲8.30am-4pm) It may not look like much from afar, but this necropolis is one of the earliest surviving and best-preserved Christian cemeteries in the world. About 1km north of the Temple of Hibis, it's built on the site of an earlier Egyptian necropolis, with most of the 263 mud-brick chapel-tombs appearing to date from the 4th to the 6th centuries AD.

Monastery of Al Kashef RUINS

(Deir Al Kashef; adult/student LE50/25 incl Necropolis of Al Bagawat; 8.30am-4pm) Dominating the cliffs 2km to the north of the Necropolis of Al Bagawat, the ruined Monastery of Al Kashef is strategically placed to overlook what was one of the most important crossroads of the Western Desert – the point where the Darb Al Ghabari from Dakhla crossed the Darb Al Arba'een (Forty Days Rd). The magnificent mud-brick remains date back to the early Christian era. Once five storeys high, much of it has collapsed, but you can see the tops of the arched corridors.

Tours

Mohsen Abd Al Moneem TOURS

(010-0180-6127) Mohsen Abd Al Moneem, from Al Kharga's **tourist office** (010-0180-6127, 092-2792-1206; Midan Nasser; 9am-2pm Sat-Thu), is an tour guide highly recommended by travellers and is a mine of information on the oasis. He can arrange private transport to sights and also to Luxor or Cairo.

Sleeping & Eating

In central Al Kharga, **Wimpy** (Wembe; Midan Basateen; meals LE20-35) serves excellent value Egyptian feasts, and **Pizza Ibn Al Balad** (Midan Sho'ala; pizzas LE20-45; 5pm-late;) has a great menu of *fiteer*.

Kharga Oasis Hotel HOTEL $

(092-2792-1206, 012-6866-6299; Midan Nasser; r LE150, bungalow LE350) This homage to the 1960s' love of concrete blocks is your best bet for bedding down for the night in Al Kharga. The main building sports large rooms with decent beds and bathrooms, but opt for one of the traditionally styled domed bungalows out back, set around a lush palm-filled garden (beware the mosquitoes) for a bit more style.

Qasr Al Bagawat GUESTHOUSE $$

(012-0001-2669, 012-2695-5819; www.qasrelbagawat.com; opposite Necropolis of Al Bagawat; s/d half board €57/66; P) Small and charming eco-lodge with 22 domed mud-brick rooms decorated in local style. There is a hot spring for bathing, a lovely garden for shade and a Bedouin restaurant. The aim of the owners is to let guests completely relax, so no internet or TV in the rooms.

Information

Banque du Caire (off Sharia Gamal Abdel Nasser) Has an ATM.

National Bank of Egypt (Sharia Gamal Abdel Nasser) Across from the museum; has an ATM.

Getting There & Away

BUS

From the **bus station** (092-2792-4587; Sharia Mohammed Farid), Upper Egypt Bus Co operates buses to Cairo (LE120, eight to 10 hours) daily at 9pm and 10pm. There are three services to Asyut (LE30, three to four hours) at 6am, 7am and 9am. The bus heading north to Dakhla Oasis (LE25, three hours) leaves at 2pm.

There's no direct bus service to Luxor.

TAXI

Private taxis can get you to/from Luxor in about three and half hours, using the new highway. This will set you back about LE800. Contact Mohsen Abd Al Moneem at the Al Kharga tourist office to arrange a car for you.

Dakhla Oasis الواحات الداخلة

092

At the centre of Dakhla Oasis lies the town of Mut, now a modern Egyptian town. It has decent facilities and makes the most convenient base for travellers. You will, however, have a richer experience of Dakhla by staying out of town. The slumping mud-brick villages and palmaries, speckled with hot springs, that surround Mut capture the essence of slow-paced oasis life. In particular, Al Qasr is one of the most enchanting places anywhere in the Western Desert.

Sights

One of the must-see sights in the western oases is the extraordinary medieval/Ottoman town of **Al Qasr**, which lies on the edge of lush vegetation at the foot of pink limestone cliffs marking the northern edge of the oasis.

Al Qasr's mud-brick maze of an old town is built on the ancient foundations of a Roman city and is thought to be one of the oldest inhabited areas of the oases. Most of what you can see today dates to the Ottoman period (1516–1798) though its creaky, picturesque labyrinth of narrow, covered streets harks back to its ancient origins. During its heyday, this was probably the capital of the Dakhla Oasis, easily protected by barring the fort's quartered streets.

Deir Al Haggar TEMPLE

(adult/student LE40/20; 8.30am-5pm) This restored sandstone temple is one of the most complete Roman monuments in Dakhla. Dedicated to the Theban triad of Amun, Mut and Khons, as well as Horus (who can be seen with a falcon's head), it was built between the reigns of Nero (AD 54–68) and

Domitian (AD 81–96). Some relief panels are quite well preserved, though most are covered in bird poop.

★ **Qarat Al Muzawwaqa** TOMB
(2km before Deir Al Haggar; adult/student LE40/20; 8am-5pm) These tombs were rediscovered by the Egyptian archaeologist Ahmed Fakri in 1971 and some have since been restored, including the tomb of **Oziri (Petosiris)** and **Badi Baset (Petubastis)**, the only ones open to the public. Featuring spectacular colours and zodiac ceilings, they are particularly interesting for their crossover between Graeco-Roman and Pharaonic styles.

Sleeping & Eating

Central Mut has a decent range of restaurants including **El Forsan Cafe** (092-282-1343; El Forsan Hotel, Sharia Al Wadi; meals LE40-60;), behind the El Forsan Hotel, and **Said Shihad** (Sharia As Sawra Al Khadra; meals LE30-55) for meat-centric meals.

Mut

El Forsan Hotel HOTEL $
(092-2782-1343; Sharia Al Wadi; s/d LE180/250, bungalow without air-con LE120/175;) Ignore the creepy horror-movie corridor as you enter – El Forsan is the best budget deal in town. The place is well kept and even has duvets in the air-con rooms, while out back in the garden are domed, mud-brick (rather worn) bungalows. Friendly manager Zaqaria whips up great breakfasts.

Bedouin Camp & El Dohous Village HOTEL $$
(092-2785-0480, 010-0622-1359; www.dakhlabedouins.com; El Dohous; s/d half board LE250/400; P) El Dohous Village, 3km from Mut centre, has a huge variety of domed and curvy rooms that give off good vibes, all decorated with local crafts. The hilltop restaurant has outstanding views, there are plenty of cushioned chill-out areas strewn about the place and there's a hot spring on site. The friendliness of the staff is just one more reason to stay.

Al Qasr

Al Qasr Hotel HOSTEL $
(092-2787-6013; Main Hwy; r with shared bathroom LE90) This old backpacker favourite sits above a cafe-restaurant on the main highway through Al Qasr. Rooms are as basic as they get, but there's a breezy upstairs communal sitting area where you can play games or relax, and for LE15 you can sleep on a mattress on the roof. Owner Mohamed has a long history of fine hospitality.

★ **Sosal Center for Ethnic Arts and Crafts** GUESTHOUSE $$
(012-2323-2247; www.mervetazmi.com; r per person LE250; P) This lovely villa with five bedrooms is a delightful place to stay for a few days. The house has a kitchen, comfortable living room with a fireplace, and a garden for common use. Next door is a basketry-weaving workshop. The place is self-catering, but breakfast (LE25), lunch (LE85) and dinner (LE95) can be arranged by women from the village nearby.

Desert Lodge BOUTIQUE HOTEL $$$
(092-2772-7061, 02-2690-5240; www.desertlodge.net; s/d/tr half board US$90/150/210; @) This thoughtfully designed, ecofriendly mud-brick fortress of a lodge crowns the hilltop at the eastern edge of Al Qasr, overlooking the old town. Rooms are decorated in minimalist desert style incorporating tranquil pastel blues, pinks and greens. The restaurant is adequate, and there is also a bar, a private hot spring and a painting studio on the desert's edge.

Information

Tourist Office (092-2782-1685, mobile 010-0180-6127; Sharia As Sawra Al Khadra; 8am-3pm) Friendly tourist-office director Omar Ahmad can help with all your oasis queries.

Getting There & Away

From Mut's **bus station** (092-2782-4366; Sharia Al Wadi), Upper Egypt Bus Co runs buses to Cairo (LE115, 10 hours) via Al Kharga Oasis (LE25, two to three hours) and Asyut (LE70, five hours) at 7pm and 7.30pm.

You can also travel to Cairo via Farafra Oasis (LE35, four hours) and Bahariya Oasis (LE60, seven hours) at 8pm.

Getting Around

Most places in Dakhla are linked by pick-ups or microbuses, but working out where they all go requires a degree in astrophysics. Those heading to Al Qasr (LE2.50) depart from Sharia As Sawra Al Khadra. You can take pick-ups to Balat and Bashendi from in front of the hospital for LE2.50. Most others depart from the servees station on Sharia Tamir. A taxi to Al Qasr should cost LE100 with waiting time.

DON'T MISS

WHITE & BLACK DESERTS

Upon first glimpse of the 300-sq-km national park of the **White Desert** (Sahra Al Beida; US$5), you'll feel like Alice through the looking-glass. About 120km south of Bahariya Oasis, on the east side of the road, blinding-white chalk rock spires sprout almost supernaturally from the ground, each frost-coloured lollipop licked into a surreal landscape of familiar and unfamiliar shapes by the dry desert winds. The sand around the outcroppings is littered with quartz and different varieties of deep-black iron pyrites, as well as small fossils. On the west side of the Farafra–Bahariya highway, away from the wind-hewn sculptures, chalk towers called inselbergs burst from the desert floor into a spectacular white canyon. Between them run grand boulevards of sand, like geologic Champs-Élysées.

Further north, about 50km south of Bahariya Oasis, is the **Black Desert** (Sahra Suda). Here, layers of black powder and stones, formed by the erosion of mountains, spread across the peaks and plateaus.

White Desert and Black Desert excursions are easy to arrange in Bahariya. A half-day Black Desert trip costs LE500; a one-night camping trip into the White Desert, including a stop-off at the Black Desert, will cost about LE1600.

Despite the fact that camping in the desert outside the oases is not allowed currently, the tourist police turns a blind eye to safari outfits in Bahariya organising short overnight trips to the White Desert.

Two good Bahariya based tour companies:

White Desert Tours (012-2321-2179; www.whitedeserttours.com; International Hot Spring Hotel) Specialists in desert trips in the Bahariya area.

Eden Garden Tours (010-0071-0707; www.edengardentours.com; Eden Garden Camp; US$50-60 per person per day) Owner Talat is a wonderful guide and passionate about the oases.

Bahariya Oasis الواحات البحرية

02 / POP 35,860

Bahariya is one of the more fetching of the desert circuit oases, and at just 365km from Cairo it's also the most accessible. The oasis' main centre is Bawiti. Away from its dusty, unappealing main road, much of the oasis floor here is covered by sprawling shady date palms and speckled with dozens of natural springs, which beg to be plunged into. The surrounding landscape of rocky, sandy mesas is a grand introduction to the Western Desert's barren beauty.

Sights

Golden Mummies Museum MUSEUM
(Al Mathaf; Sharia Al Mathaf; Bawiti joint site ticket adult/student LE100/50; 8am-4pm) Only 10 of Bahariya's richly decorated cache of 10,000 mummies are exhibited here. While the motifs are formulaic and the work is second-rate, the painted faces show a move away from stylised Pharaonic mummy decoration towards Fayoum portraiture. Underneath the wrappings, the embalmers' work appears to have been sloppy, so these mummies mark the beginning of the end of mummification.

★Ain Gomma SPRING
Ain Gomma is one of the most magnificent springs around. Cool, crystal-clear water gushes into this small pool surrounded by the vast desert expanse, and the funkiest cafe in all of the oases sits beside it. Situated near the town of Al Hayz, you can take a Dakhla-bound bus here, but it's difficult to get back without your own transport. Many safari trips to the White Desert will stop here en route.

Gebel Al Ingleez MOUNTAIN
Clearly visible from the road to Cairo, flat-topped Gebel Al Ingleez, also known as Black Mountain, takes its name from a WWI lookout post. From here Captain Williams, a British officer, monitored the movements of Libyan Senussi tribesmen. But the real reason to come up here is for the fantastic panoramic views, which roll out across the oasis and to the desert beyond.

Sleeping & Eating

In Bawiti **Rashed** (Sharia Misr; meals LE30-45; noon-midnight) and the aptly named **Popular Restaurant** (02-847-2239; Sharia Safaya; set meals LE50-60; 8am-11pm) both serve hearty meals. Popular has beer.

Bawiti

New Oasis Hotel HOTEL $

(☎012-2847-4171; s/d LE150/240, without air-con LE140/180; ❄📶) A study in curvaceous construction, this small, homey hotel has several teardrop-shaped rooms, some with balconies overlooking the expansive palm groves nearby. Inside, the rooms are in good shape, though someone seems to have been a little overzealous with the powder-blue paint. It's one of the nicer budget options in town, located next to El Beshmo spring.

Around Bawiti

★**Eden Garden Camp** HUT $$

(☎010-0071-0707; www.edengardentours.com; hut per person with half board LE220, bungalow per person full board US$35) Located 7km east of Bawiti, in the small, serene oasis of El Jaffara, Eden Garden is a superfriendly place with African-style huts, shaded lounge areas, fresh food and, best of all, two springs just outside its gates: one hot and one cold. Talaat, the owner who conceived the whole place, is a character.

International Hot Spring Hotel HOTEL $$

(☎012-2321-2179, 02-3847-3014; www.whitedeserttours.com; s/d with half board US$50/80; P📶🏊) About 3km outside Bawiti on the road to Cairo, this spa resort has 36 very comfortable rooms and eight chalets, built around a hot spring and set in a delightful garden. There's also a rooftop lounge and a good restaurant, as well as Peter's Bar. The owner Peter Wirth is an old Western Desert hand and organises recommended trips in the area.

Nature Camp BUNGALOW $$

(☎012-2165-3037; naturecamps@hotmail.com; Bir Al Ghaba; r half board per person US$25; P📶🏊) At the foot of Gebel Dist, 17km north of Bawiti, Nature Camp sets new standards for environmentally focused budget accommodation. The peaceful cluster of candlelit and intricately designed thatch huts looks out onto the expansive desert beside its own cold spring. The food is very good (meals LE50) and the owner, Ashraf Lotfe, is a skilled desert hand. The perfect place away from it all.

Information

National Bank of Development (off Sharia Misr; 🕘9am-2pm Sun-Thu) Has an ATM and changes cash.

Tourist Office (☎02-3847-3035, 02-3847-2167; Sharia Misr; 🕘8.30am-2pm Sat-Thu) Run by the friendly Yehia Kandeel, who can also be contacted on 012-2321-6790.

Getting There & Away

From the **bus ticket kiosk** (☎02-3847-3610; Sharia Misr; 🕘9am-1pm & 7-11pm) near the post office, Upper Egypt Bus Co has services to Cairo (LE85, five hours) at 6am, 8am, 10am and 3pm. They are often full, so it's strongly advisable to buy tickets the day before travelling. There are two more Cairo-bound buses that originate in Dakhla and pass through Bawiti around noon and midnight, stopping at the Hilal Coffeehouse (Sharia Misr) at the western end of town.

If you are heading to Farafra (LE30, two hours) and Dakhla (LE50, four to five hours) you can hop on one of the buses headed that way from Cairo. They leave Bahariya around noon from the ticket office.

Siwa Oasis واحة سيوة

☎046 / POP 23,000

Siwa is the stuff of desert daydreams. Just 50km from the Libyan border, this fertile basin brimming with olive trees and palms, on the edge of the Great Sand Sea, epitomises slow-paced oasis life. Set between the shady groves, squat, slouching mud-brick hamlets are connected by winding dirt lanes where trundling donkey carts are still as much a part of the street action as puttering motorbikes and 4WDs. Scattered throughout the oasis are crystal-clear springs, which are a heavenly respite from the harsh heat.

Sights

★**Fortress of Shali** FORTRESS

FREE Central Siwa is dominated by the spectacular organic shapes of the remains of this 13th-century mud-brick fortress. Built from *kershef* (chunks of salt from the lake just outside town, mixed with rock and plastered in local clay), the labyrinth of huddled buildings was originally four or five storeys high and housed hundreds of people. A path leads over the slumping remnants, past the **Old Mosque** with its chimney-shaped minaret, to the top for panoramic views.

Gebel Al Mawta ARCHAEOLOGICAL SITE

(adult/student LE40/20; 🕘9am-5pm) This small hill, at the northern end of Siwa Town, is honeycombed with rock tombs peppered with wall paintings. Its name, Gebel Al Mawta, means 'Mountain of the Dead' and most of the tombs here date back to the 26th dynasty, Ptolemaic and Roman times. Only

1km from the centre of town, the tombs were used by the Siwans as shelters when the Italians bombed the oasis during WWII.

Temple of the Oracle RUINS

(adult/student LE30/15; ⊙9am-5pm) The 26th-dynasty Temple of the Oracle sits in the northwest corner of the ruins of Aghurmi village. Built in the 6th century BC, probably on top of an earlier temple, it was dedicated to Amun (occasionally referred to as Zeus or Jupiter Ammon) and was a powerful symbol of the town's wealth. It is believed Alexander the Great was declared son of Amun in this temple.

Cleopatra's Spring SPRING

(Spring of the Sun) Following the track that leads to the Temple of the Oracle and continuing past the Temple of Umm Ubayd will lead you to Siwa's most famous spring. The crystal-clear water gurgles up into a large stone pool, which is a popular bathing spot for locals and tourists alike. A couple of lovely cafes have comfortable shaded lounging areas and serve soft drinks and delicious snacks; bring your own picnic if you want to hang out for a while.

Tours

Almost all restaurants and hotels in Siwa offer tours in the desert around Siwa Town. Abdu's Restaurant and the Palm Trees Hotel have established a good reputation for their trips. The tourist office is also an excellent place to get help with organising tours.

All desert trips require permits, which cost LE140 per person per day and are usually obtained by your guide from the tourist office. Trip prices vary according to itineraries but the average cost of a car and driver for a full day to visit the sights around Siwa is LE200 to LE300. One of the most popular half-day trips takes you to the cold lake and hot springs at **Bir Wahed**, on the edge of the Great Sand Sea.

Note that due to Libyan smugglers crossing the desert borders, it is currently forbidden to travel much further than Bir Wahed into the desert. Check with the tourist office for updates.

Sleeping

★Al Babinshal Heritage Hotel BOUTIQUE HOTEL $

(☎010-0361-4140; www.facebook.com/Albabinshal-Heritage-Hotel-1242284019179174; Shali; s/d/tr LE285/365/475; 📶) This gorgeous, curvy mud-brick hotel is seamlessly grafted onto, and part of, the Shali fortress with its labyrinthine architecture all built from *kershef* bricks. A maze of tunnels and stairways connects the spacious and cool rooms. Decor is distinctly desert style with date-palm furniture, local textiles and traditional wooden-shuttered windows used in abundance to add to the local vibe.

Palm Trees Hotel HOTEL $

(☎046-460-1703, 012-2104-6652; www.facebook.com/PALM-TREES-816079035146405; Sharia Torrar; s/d LE80/95, with shared bathroom LE50/60, bungalow s/d LE80/120, r with air-con LE120; 📶) If you can handle the mosquitoes (seriously, bring bug-spray), then this popular budget hotel is a lovely place to stay. It has sufficiently tidy rooms boasting screened windows, fans and balconies. The shady garden with date-palm furniture is delightful and the few ground-level bungalows have porches spilling onto the greenery.

★Siwa Relax Retreat HOTEL $$

(☎012-8000-0274; www.facebook.com/SiwaRelaxRetreat; s/d US$65/75, r with shared bathroom US$30; P 📶 🏊) Far away from it all, this place is a dream in which to totally relax for a few days. Built on the edge of the lake, the simple but comfortable rooms are covered in bougainvillea and have floors made of salt crystals. Some have shared bathrooms, others are en suite. There is no electricity, just candles.

Shali Lodge HOTEL $$

(☎010-1118-5820, 046-460-2399; Sharia Subukha; s/d/tr/ste LE385/475/575/650; ⊙Sep-Jun; 📶) This tiny, beautiful hotel, owned by environmentalist Mounir Neamatallah, is nestled in a lush palm grove about 100m from Siwa's main square. The large comfortable rooms have lots of curvaceous mud-brick goodness, exposed palm beams, rock-walled bathrooms and cushioned sitting nooks. Tasteful and quiet, this is how small hotels should be.

Eating

★Abdu's Restaurant INTERNATIONAL $

(☎046-460-1243; Central Market Sq; dishes LE18-50; ⊙8.30am-midnight) Before wi-fi and smartphones, there were places like this – a village hub where people gathered nightly to catch up and swap stories. The longest-running restaurant in town remains the best eating option thanks to its friendly on-the-ball staff and a huge menu of breakfast, pasta, traditional dishes, vegetable stews, couscous, roasted chickens and pizza.

Al Babinshal Restaurant EGYPTIAN $
(☎010-0361-4140; Fortress of Shali; mains LE20-65; ⏰8am-late) On the roof of the hotel of the same name, this might just be the most romantic dining spot in the oases. Moodily lit in the evenings, it's practically attached to the fortress of Shali and has sweeping views over all of Siwa. This is the place in town to try camel-meat stew.

Abo Ayman Restaurant GRILL $
(off Sharia Sadat; meals LE18-40; ⏰11am-midnight) Roasted on a hand-turned spit over coals in an old oil drum, the chickens at Abo Ayman are the juiciest in Siwa. They're well seasoned, and served with salad, tahini and bread. You can sit inside at low tables, but we like the tables outside with street views.

Information

Banque du Caire (Siwa Town; ⏰8.30am-2pm & 5-8pm) Two-hundred metres north from the King Fuad Mosque. The ATM usually works but – just in case – you're better off bringing enough money to Siwa with you. It's a long way to the next bank.

Tourist Office (☎010-0546-1992, 046-460-1338; mahdi_hweiti@yahoo.com; Siwa Town; ⏰9am-2pm Sat-Thu, plus 5-8pm Oct-Apr) Siwa's tourist officer, Mahdi Hweiti, is extremely knowledgeable about the oasis and can help arrange desert safaris or trips to surrounding villages. The office is opposite the bus station.

Getting There & Away

BUS

Siwa's bus stop and ticket office is opposite the tourist police station; when you arrive into town, however, you'll be let off near the central market square. It's sensible to buy your ticket ahead of time as buses are often full.

From the bus stop, West & Middle Delta Bus Co buses depart for Alexandria (LE75, eight hours), via Marsa Matruh (LE40, four hours) at 7am, 10am and 10pm. The 10pm service costs LE10 more. Their direct Siwa–Cairo bus service (LE150, 11 hours) runs on Tuesday, Friday and Sunday at 8pm. Otherwise, get a bus to Alexandria and change there.

MICROBUS

Microbuses going to Marsa Matruh (LE40) leave from the main square near the King Fuad Mosque. They are more frequent and *way* more comfortable than the West & Mid Delta bus, and the same price.

4WD

At the time of writing, due to security concerns, it is not possible to travel to Siwa via the desert road from Bahariya.

Getting Around

Tuk-tuks are numerous. Expect to pay LE50 for two to three hours, or LE20 for a short trip.

Bicycles are one of the best ways to get around and can be rented from most hotels and a number of shops dotted around the town centre. The going rate is LE20 to LE25 per day.

RED SEA COAST
ساحل البحر الأحمر

El Gouna الجونة

☎065 / POP 15,000

El Gouna is a self-contained holiday town and probably the best-run resort in Egypt. Boasting 16 hotels, an 18-hole golf course, plenty of villas, and boutique shopping, restaurants and bars galore, it's about as far removed from Egypt's usual chaotic hustle as you can get. The only local experience you are likely to have is smoking shisha (albeit on a marina terrace overlooking some mighty swanky yachts). But if you're after a place to laze on a beach and do some diving, then you'll definitely enjoy your time here.

Activities

El Gouna is a paradise for water sports. A variety of dive operators and resort activity centres offer a laundry list of activities including sailing, ocean kayaking, fishing, parasailing, jet-skiing, windsurfing, kitesurfing and water-skiing. El Gouna is increasingly used by divers as an alternative base to explore the dive sites around Hurghada.

Sleeping & Eating

★**Captain's Inn** HOTEL $$
(☎065-358-0170; http://captainsinn.elgouna.com; Abu Tig Marina; s/d from US$75/78;) This friendly hotel is a favourite home-away-from-home for divers and kitesurfers in town for thrills on the water rather than fancy rooms. The location, off the main marina, near to restaurants and the beach, is fantastic; the flower-filled courtyard is a great place to relax; and the rooms – decked out in natty blue and white – are light-filled and comfortable.

Mosaique HOTEL $$
(☎065-358-0077; http://mosaique.elgouna.com; Abu Tig Marina; s/d from US$81/84;) We really like Mosaique's bright rooms, with their balconies, comfortable beds and blue-and-white textiles. The location on Abu Tig

Marina makes it easy to go out and explore shops and restaurants, although the extremely tempting heated-pool area may put plans for leaving the hotel on hold. A short walk to the beach, this hotel is popular with families and kitesurfers.

Sheraton Miramar RESORT $$$
(065-354-5606; www.sheratonmiramarresort.com; s/d from US$110/160;) Designed by architect Michael Graves, this mammoth pastel-toned five-star resort is one of the original signature properties of El Gouna. The entire complex is strung along a series of beach-fringed private islands just offshore from town and it's a lovely place to stay if you just want to flop out on the beach.

★ **Zia Amelia** ITALIAN $$
(012-2527-1526; www.facebook.com/ziaameliaelgouna; Kafr El Gouna; mains LE115-150; 1-11pm;) El Gouna's cutest restaurant is rustic done right with a charmingly intimate interior and, weather permitting, an outdoor-dining area shaded by a vine-covered trellis. The menu is home-style Italian with generous portions of lasagne, crisp pizza, homemade pasta and seafood. Leave room for dessert because the tiramisu is decidedly wicked. There's live music most Wednesdays. Booking essential.

Le Garage INTERNATIONAL $$
(012-2741-2100; www.facebook.com/Le-Garage-Gourmet-Burger-El-Gouna-Egypt-1624447677819893; Abu Tig Marina; mains LE80-150; 4pm-midnight;) Flying the flag for the gourmet-burger craze in El Gouna, the 20-selection strong range at Le Garage includes a straight-up burger and varieties such as tandoori chicken, blue cheese with walnuts and grapes, and a burger that's topped with truffles and edible gold leaf. There are a couple of decent veggie options, too.

Information

Information on all aspects of a visit to El Gouna can be found at www.elgouna.com.

Getting There & Away

Go Bus Co (www.gobus-eg.com) runs up to nine services daily to Cairo (LE115 to LE220, six hours). The ticket office and bus stop in El Gouna is on the main plaza in Kafr El Gouna, opposite the tourist information centre.

To Hurghada, buses leave every 20 minutes between 7am and midnight from a bus stop also on the main plaza. Tickets cost LE15.

Hurghada الغردقة

065 / POP 392,540

Plucked from obscurity during the early days of the Red Sea's tourism drive, the fishing village of Hurghada has long since morphed into today's dense band of concrete that marches along the coastline for more than 20km. Still, it's a convenient destination for combining a diving holiday with the Nile Valley sites. Further offshore there is still superb diving aplenty but coral reefs closest to the shore have been degraded by irresponsible reef use. Hurghada's star has largely lost its lustre with package holiday-makers heading to El Gouna instead, while independent travellers prefer to press on to Dahab.

Activities

★ **Jasmin Diving Centre** DIVING
(065-346-0334; www.jasmin-diving.com; Resort Strip, Grand Seas Resort Hostmark; 3-day, 6-dive package €159) This centre, down on the main resort strip, has an excellent reputation and was a founding member of the Hurghada Environmental Protection & Conservation Association (HEPCA).

Subex DIVING
(065-354-7593; www.subex.org; Ad Dahar; 6-dive package €170) This reputable Swiss outfit is known for its professionalism, friendliness and attention to detail.

Sleeping

★ **Luxor Hotel** HOTEL $
(065-354-2877; www.luxorhotel-eg.com; Sharia Mustafa, Ad Dahar; s/d/tr LE120/200/270;) This small hotel on top of Ad Dahar's hill is run by friendly Said and has good-sized, clean rooms all home to drab brown furnishings but with surprisingly good facilities for the price tag, including TV and fridge. If you're solo, upgrade yourself from a single room, as they're a bit poky and dark. Good views from the roof terrace.

Hurghada Marriott Beach Resort RESORT $$
(065-344-4420; www.marriott.com; Resort Strip; r from €80;) Within walking distance of the resort strip's nightlife and restaurants, the well-kept rooms here are spacious and light-filled, and each come with a balcony. Some visitors may be disappointed by the small beach area, but if you want full facilities and the freedom to pick and choose where to eat, it's a great choice.

★**Oberoi Sahl Hasheesh** HOTEL $$$
(☎065-344 0777; www.oberoihotels.com; Hurghada–Safaga Coastal rd, Sahl Hasheesh; ste from €140; P) Peaceful, exclusive and opulent beyond your imagination, the Oberoi sits a good 30-minute drive south from Hurghada and features palatial suites decorated in minimalist Moorish style. Each comes complete with sunken marble baths, private courtyards – some with pools – and panoramic sea views. Justifiably advertised as the most luxurious destination on the Red Sea, the Oberoi is world-class.

Eating & Drinking

Gad EGYPTIAN $
(Sharia Sheraton, Sigala; shawarma LE12-22, mains from LE20, 1kg kofta LE160; 10am-late; P) If you're looking for cheap, filling and tasty Egyptian staples, you can't go wrong with Egypt's favourite fast-food restaurant. The sprawling menu covers soup and salad, falafel and shawarma, *fiteer* and full kebab and kofta meals (sold by the kilo). There's another **branch** (Sharia An Nasr; 10am-late) in Ad Dahar.

★**Star Fish** SEAFOOD $$
(☎065-344-3751; www.facebook.com/starfishredsea; Sharia Sheraton, Sigala; mains from LE60; noon-midnight; P) An extremely popular fish restaurant on the main Sigala drag. You can choose fish from the display, or opt for prawns (grilled, with pasta, or deep-fried) and an excellent fish soup. Or you could go for the blow-out special of soup, lobster, shrimp, fish fillet, calamari and kofta (spiced mincemeat grilled on a skewer), with rice and salad.

White Elephant ASIAN $$
(☎010-0102-5117; Hurghada Marina Promenade, Sigala; mains LE80-130; 4pm-midnight) This is the real deal, Thai food prepared by a Thai chef. So if you want a spicy and zingy Thai feast, let the waiter know you can handle the heat and White Elephant won't scrimp on the spice. *Tom yum* (hot and sour Thai soup) is excellent, as are most dishes with fresh fish from the market.

★**Caribbean Beach Bar** BAR
(Sharia Sheraton, Sigala) If you're looking to chill with a cocktail right next to the sea, this palm-thatched pontoon over the water has a laid-back atmosphere made for lounging. Once the sun has set there's often live music or parties. You have to walk through the Bella Vista Hotel to get here.

Information

El Salam Hospital (☎065-361-5013, 065-361-5012; www.elsalamhospital.com; Corniche; 24hr) Just north of Iberotel Arabella.

Naval Hyperbaric & Emergency Medical Center (☎065-344-9150, 065-354-8450; Corniche) Has a hyperbaric chamber. Near Iberotel Arabella.

Tourist Office (☎065-344-4420; Resort Strip; 8am-8pm Sat-Thu, 2-10pm Fri) Small kiosk in the middle of the resort strip.

Getting There & Away

AIR

Hurghada Airport (☎065-346-2722; Main Hwy), near the resort strip, receives (mostly charter) flights direct from European destinations.

EgyptAir (☎065-346-3035; www.egyptair.com; 8am-8pm Sat-Thu, from 10am Fri) has several daily flights to Cairo. Tickets can be as low as LE718.

BOAT

The high-speed catamaran ferry service between Hurghada and Sharm El Sheikh is operated by **La Pespes** (www.lapespes.com). Boats

BUSES FROM HURGHADA

DESTINATION	PRICE	DURATION	TIMES/COMPANY
Al Quseir	LE20	1½hr	1.30am, 5am, 9.30am & 4pm (Upper Egypt)
Alexandria	LE150-230	9hr	2pm, 4.30pm, 10pm (Go Bus), 2.30pm & 11pm (Super Jet)
Aswan	LE90	7hr	12.30am & 10.30pm (Upper Egypt)
Cairo	LE65-295	6-7hr	20 Go Bus, eight Upper Egypt & five Super Jet departures daily
Luxor	LE50-90	4-5hr	8.30am & 5.30pm (Super Jet), 12.30am & 1.30am (Upper Egypt), 8.15am & 3.30pm (Go Bus)
Marsa Alam	LE50	4hr	2am, 5.30am, 8pm (Upper Egypt)

OFF THE BEATEN TRACK

AL QUSEIR القصير

Far removed from the resort clamour of the rest of the Red Sea coast, the historic city of Al Quseir is a muddle of colourful and creaky coral-block architecture dating from the Ottoman era that sadly is bypassed by most tourists. Al Quseir has a history stretching back to Pharaonic times, when it was the main port for boats heading south to the fabled East African kingdom of Punt.

Ringed in between Sharia Al Gomhurriyya and the waterfront is Al Quseir's old town. It's a twisting labyrinth of alleyways where progress seems happy to hit the snooze button and local life is snail-paced. Within the squiggle of lanes below the **Ottoman fortress** (Sharia Al Gomhurriyya; LE15; ⏲9am-5pm), wind your way past pastel-washed houses, some still boasting original *mashrabiyya* (wooden lattice) window screens and in various states of decay, while looking out for hand-painted hajj decorations and quirkily coloured doors.

Getting There & Away

The bus station is roughly 500m north-west from the old town. Buses run to Cairo (LE100, 10 hours) via Hurghada (LE30, 1½ to two hours), departing at 11am, noon, 9pm and 10.30pm. Buses to Marsa Alam (LE25, two hours) leave at 9am, 2pm, 9pm, 10pm and midnight.

leave at 8am on Sunday, Tuesday and Thursday (adult/child US$40/30, 2½ hours) from Hurghada Tourist Port in Sigala. You must be at the port 1½ hours before departure and have your passport on hand for identification.

Tickets can be purchased in advance from the **La Pespes ticket office** (☎012-1014-2000; www.lapespes.com; Midan Aka, Sharia An Nasr, High Jet Office, Sigala; ⏲10am-10pm).

BUS

Hurghada doesn't have a central bus station. Instead, the major companies, including **Upper Egypt Bus Co** (☎065-354-7582; off Sharia An Nasr, Ad Dahar), **Super Jet** (☎065-355-3499; Sharia An Nasr, Ad Dahar) and **Go Bus** (www.gobus-eg.com; Sharia An Nasr, Ad Dahar), all arrive and depart from their own separate stations, which are strung out along Sharia An Nasr in Ad Dahar. Go Bus has a **ticket booking office** (Sharia Sheraton, Sigala; ⏲10am-10pm) in Sigala.

Getting Around

TO/FROM THE AIRPORT

A taxi to downtown Ad Dahar should cost around LE80, but you'll need to bargain hard.

MICROBUS

Microbuses run from central Ad Dahar, south along the resort strip, and along Sharia An Nasr and other major routes. Rides cost between LE1 and LE3.

TAXI

Taxis from Ad Dahar to the start of the resort strip (around the Marriott hotel) charge about LE40. Expect to pay LE20 travelling from the bus offices to the centre of Ad Dahar, and between LE30 and LE40 to the resort strip.

Marsa Alam مرسى علم

☎065 / POP 6530

In-the-know divers have been heading to Marsa Alam for years, attracted to the seas that offer up some of Egypt's best diving just off the rugged coastline. The long-standing beach camps in this area all arrange dive packages and are specifically set up for those who want to spend most of their time underwater. While the town itself remains a sleepy, nondescript place, the strip of coast to its north and south has been snapped up by eager developers and is now home to a plethora of resorts and half-built hotels.

Sleeping

★**Deep South** CAMPGROUND $
(☎010-0748-7608; http://deepsouthredsea.com; hut/chalet per person €20/30; P) If you're looking to strip it back to the basics of sun, sea and sand, Deep South offers palm-thatch huts and simple, but extravagantly painted chalets, a warm welcome and good food in an exceptionally mellow atmosphere. There are good dive packages too. It's located on a hill across the road from Tondoba Bay, 14km south of Marsa Alam.

★**Marsa Shagra Village** CAMPGROUND $$$
(☎065-338-0021, Cairo office 02-3337-1833; www.redsea-divingsafari.com; Marsa Shagra; s/d

full board tent €65/100, royal tent €70/110, hut €75/110, chalet €95/140; P) This large-scale camp 24km north of Marsa Alam offers a range of accommodation from tent to deluxe chalet, and spectacular snorkelling and diving on the house reef, as well as a full dive centre. Marsa Shagra was one of the first eco-minded places on the Red Sea and, despite the development around it, has stayed true to its sustainable-tourism credentials.

Getting There & Away

AIR

Marsa Alam Airport (065-370-0029; www.portghalib.com/airport; 60km north of Marsa Alam) is 67km north of Marsa Alam along the Al Quseir road. Arrange a transfer in advance with your hotel.

EgyptAir has flights to Cairo four days per week, from LE1525 one way.

BUS

Marsa Alam bus station is just past the T-junction along the Edfu road. Buses to Cairo (LE85 to LE90, 10 to 11 hours) via Al Quseir (LE15, two hours) and Hurghada (LE30 to LE35, 3½ to four hours) depart at 1.30pm and 8.30pm.

SOUTH SINAI

A barren coastline of extraordinary beauty, the Sinai Coast has seen some of history's most significant events of the past several millennia played out against its isolated shores. These days, however, the region is more renowned for its superb coral reefs, unique Bedouin culture and sandy beaches. South Sinai is both nirvana for members of the international diving fraternity and a famous package-tourism escape for Europeans after sun, sand and sea.

Dangers & Annoyances

A spate of tourist kidnappings in 2012 and 2013 along the St Katherine–Sharm El Sheikh road and 2014's Taba tourist bus bombing led most foreign governments to issue cautionary travel advisories (which have yet to be lifted) for the entire South Sinai area. The Sharm El Sheikh metropolitan area is not included in the advisories and is generally considered safe.

Although the potential for a future terrorist attack can never be wholly ruled out, it's important to emphasise that since the 2011 revolution, Dahab has remained one of Egypt's most relaxed destinations and, within the town itself, has experienced no problems, while the Taba border remains the only reliable crossing between Egypt and Israel and overland travellers continue to cross here. There is a high police presence throughout the South Sinai region and checkpoints are common along all main roads as well as at entry points into towns.

Ras Mohammed National Park محمية رأس محمد

About 20km west of Sharm El Sheikh on the road from Al Tor lies the headland of **Ras Mohammed National Park** (€5; 8am-4pm), named by local fishers for a cliff that resembles a man's profile. The waters surrounding the peninsula are considered the jewel in the crown of the Red Sea. The park is visited annually by more than 50,000 visitors, enticed by the prospect of marvelling at some of the world's most spectacular coral-reef ecosystems, including a profusion of coral species and teeming marine life. Most, if not all, of the Red Sea's 1000 species of fish can be seen in the park's waters, including sought-after pelagics, such as hammerheads, manta rays and whale sharks.

Ras Mohammed occupies a total of 480 sq km of land and sea, including the desert in and around the *ras* (headland), Tiran Island, and the shoreline between Sharm El Sheikh harbour and Nabq Protectorate.

Sharm El Sheikh شرم الشيخ

069 / POP 73,000

Purpose-built Sharm El Sheikh occupies a prime position on the southern coast of the Gulf of Aqaba with some of the world's most amazing underwater scenery on its doorstep. The town devotes itself solely to sun-and-sea holidays offering a family-friendly vibe and resort comforts, with world-class diving thrown in.

That said, Sharm isn't everyone's cup of tea. The relentless sprawl of mega-hotels along the coastline here has led to pressing issues of environmental degradation. Since the downing of Metrojet Flight 9268 in 2015, the legions of European holidaymakers who flocked here have petered out because of the lack of direct flights from Europe. Many independent travellers prefer the lower-key town of Dahab.

Sinai

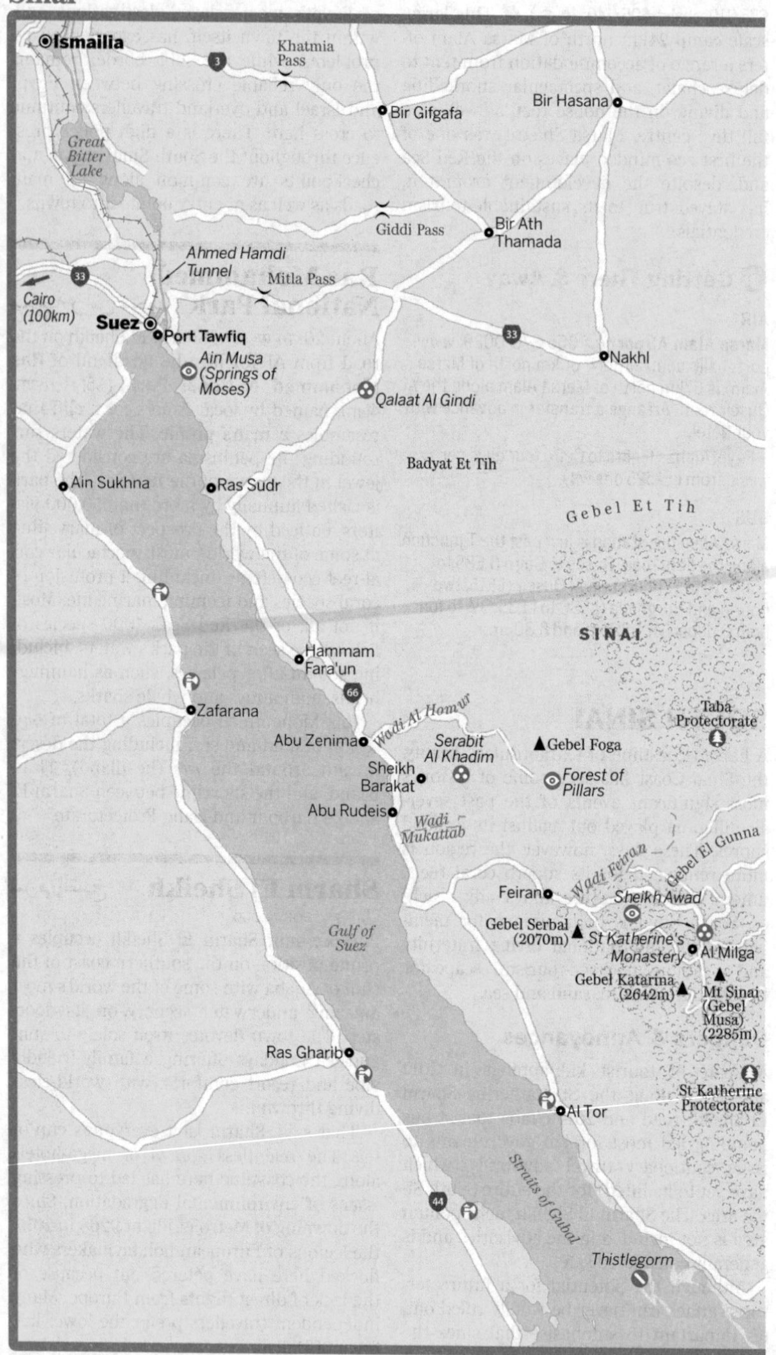
Ismailia
Khatmia Pass
3
Bir Gifgafa
Bir Hasana
Great Bitter Lake
Giddi Pass
Bir Ath Thamada
Ahmed Hamdi Tunnel
Mitla Pass
33
Cairo (100km)
Suez
Port Tawfiq
Nakhl
Ain Musa (Springs of Moses)
Qalaat Al Gindi
Badyat Et Tih
Ain Sukhna
Ras Sudr
Gebel Et Tih
SINAI
Hammam Fara'un
66
Zafarana
Wadi Al Homur
Taba Protectorate
Abu Zenima
Serabit Al Khadim
Gebel Foga
Sheikh Barakat
Forest of Pillars
Abu Rudeis
Wadi Mukattab
Wadi Feiran
Gebel El Gunna
Feiran
Sheikh Awad
Gebel Serbal (2070m)
St Katherine's Monastery
Al Milga
Gulf of Suez
Gebel Katarina (2642m)
Mt Sinai (Gebel Musa) (2285m)
Ras Gharib
St Katherine Protectorate
Al Tor
Straits of Gubal
44
Thistlegorm

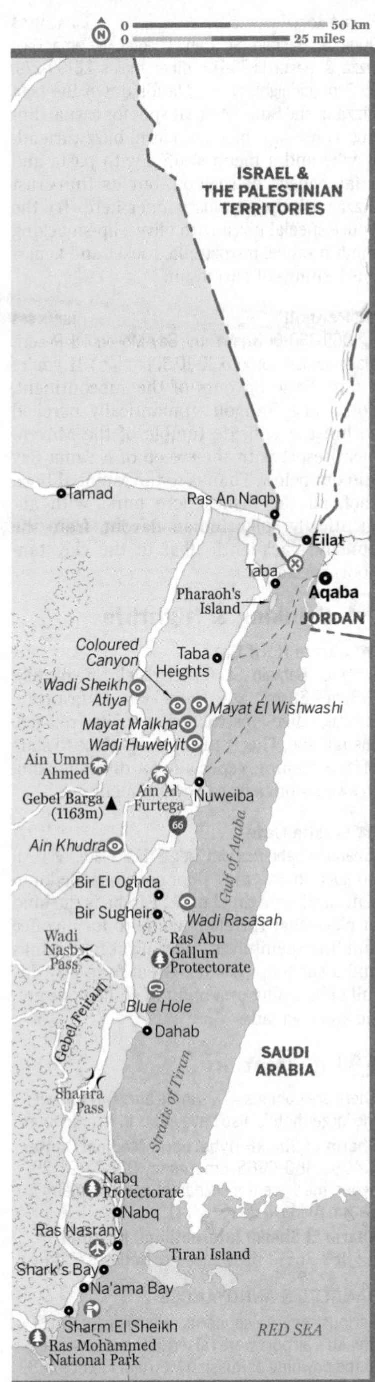

Activities

Camel Dive Club DIVING
(☎069-360-0700; www.cameldive.com; King of Bahrain St, Camel Hotel, Na'ama Bay; PADI discover scuba €80, 1-day 2 dives shore/boat €45/64, snorkelling boat trips €38; ⏰8am-6pm) This highly professional and respected club is owned by Sinai diver Hisham Gabr. As well as being a 5-Star PADI Instructor Development Centre, it is fully fitted out for wheelchair access and holds a PADI Accessibility Award. When booking, look out for the good value accommodation-and-dive packages on the website.

Oonas Dive Club DIVING
(☎069-360-0581; www.oonasdiveclub.com; Na'ama Bay Promenade, Oona's Hotel, Na'ama Bay; PADI discover scuba €72, 1-day 2 dives €63, snorkelling boat trips €35; ⏰8am-6.30pm) Recommended for its friendly and professional instructors, Oonas offers the full gamut of PADI courses as well as live-aboard packages and fun dives. Many people sign up for the good-value one-week dive and hotel packages for €320 (three days' diving), €420 (five days' diving) or €468 (six days' diving).

Sleeping

★Camel Hotel HOTEL $$
(☎069-360-0700; www.cameldive.com; King of Bahrain St, Na'ama Bay; s €36-42, d €42-48, tr €56-63; ❄📶🏊) Attached to the highly reputable dive centre of the same name, Camel Hotel is the smart choice to stay at if diving is your main agenda. Despite being in the heart of Na'ama Bay, the spacious, modern rooms, set around a lovely courtyard pool area, are gloriously quiet (thanks to soundproof windows), so you're guaranteed a good night's sleep.

Oonas Hotel HOTEL $$
(☎069-360-0581; www.oonasdiveclub.com; Na'ama Bay Promenade; s/d/tr/ste €45/64/81/90; ❄📶) The good-size rooms at this friendly combo dive centre and hotel may be a tad plain, but they come with excellent facilities (kettle, fridge and satellite TV) and balconies. The dive centre here comes highly recommended and accommodation is cheaper if booked as part of a dive package. The beach (shared with the neighbouring resort) is a stone's throw away.

Mövenpick Sharm El Sheikh RESORT $$
(☎069-360-0081; www.movenpick.com; Peace Rd, Na'ama Bay; s/d/f US$80/90/135; ❄📶🏊) Dominating Na'ama Bay's northern cliff, this whitewashed hotel terraces majestically down towards the sea like a Sultan's palace. Standard rooms are surprisingly bland and

could do with a revamp, but the breakfast, views and facilities (five private beaches, spa, pool, dive centre and on-site horse stables) are five-star.

Hilton Sharm El Sheikh Fayrouz Resort RESORT $$$
(069-360-0136; www.hilton.com; Peace Rd, Na'ama Bay; s US$80-110, d US$100-139;) It may pale in comparison to the flash-the-cash ostentation of Sharm's newer megahotels, but this family-friendly resort is a low-key, relaxing place in prime position in the middle of Na'ama Bay's promenade. Set amid well-tended gardens of swaying palms and blooming bougainvillea spilling over trellises, the spacious bungalows here have a jaunty blue-and-white theme, big queen-sized beds and well-maintained facilities.

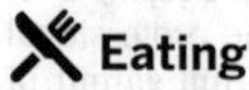

Eating

★**Fares Seafood** SEAFOOD $$
(069-366-3076; City Council St, Hadaba; dishes LE40-300; noon-1am) Always crowded with locals, Fares is a Sharm El Sheikh institution for good-value seafood. Order fish priced by weight or choose from one of the pasta or *tagen* options on the menu. We're pretty partial to the mixed *tagen* of calamari and shrimp. There's another **branch** (069-366-4270; Sharm Al Maya; 11am-1am) at Sharm Old Market.

El Masrien EGYPTIAN $$
(King of Bahrain St, Sharm Old Market, Sharm Al Maya; dishes LE8-80; noon-late;) This old-fashioned restaurant, sprawling over both sides of the road, is our top dining spot in Sharm Old Market. There's a huge range of kebabs but also plenty of gutsy flavoured *tagens* and vegetarian dishes from which you can make a cheap, tasty mezze spread. Egyptian holidaymakers flock here in the evening.

DON'T MISS

TOP DIVES AROUND SHARM

Thistlegorm (Sha'ab Ali) One of the top five wreck dives in the world.

Ras Um Sid The highlight here is a spectacular gorgonian forest along a dramatic drop-off.

Thomas Reef (Straits of Tiran) Plunging walls lined with soft coral, schooling fish and patrolling sharks.

Dunraven This wreck, now encrusted in coral, sank in 1876.

Pomodoro ITALIAN $$
(King of Bahrain St, Camel Hotel, Na'ama Bay; pizza & pasta LE79-119, other mains LE109-279; 11am-midnight;) Hands down the best pizza in the Sinai. A great spot for casual dining, Pomodoro has a modern, buzzy, friendly vibe and a menu stuffed with pasta and a fair whack of seafood, but its thin-crust pizzas are the serious winner here. Try the house special pizza with olives, lip-smacking tomato sauce, mozzarella, rocket and generous lashings of Parmesan.

★**Rangoli** INDIAN $$$
(069-360-0081; Na'ama Bay, Mövenpick Resort; mains LE55-180; 6.30-10.30pm;) If you're a fan of the flavours of the subcontinent, don't miss Rangoli; romantically perched within the cliffside tumble of the Mövenpick Resort with the sweep of Na'ama Bay laid out below. Thanks to the Mumbai-born chef, all the dishes here burst with authentically spicy Indian flavour, from the punchy black-lentil dhal to the clay tandoori specialities.

Drinking & Nightlife

★**Camel Roof Bar** BAR
(King of Bahrain St, Camel Hotel, Na'ama Bay; 3pm-2.30am;) Camel is a favourite among dive instructors for its relaxed, casual vibe. This is the optimal place to start off the evening, especially for divers looking to swap stories from down under.

★**Farsha Cafe** CAFE
(Sharia El Bahr, Ras Um Sid; 11am-late;) All nooks and crannies, floor cushions, Bedouin tents and swinging lamps, Farsha is the kind of place that travellers come to for a coffee and find themselves lingering at four drinks and a shisha pipe later. Great for a lazy day full of lounging or a night of chilled-out music and cocktails.

Information

There are copious ATMs in Na'ama Bay and all the larger hotels also have ATMs in their lobbies.

Sharm El Sheikh Hyberbaric Medical Center (069-360-0865, emergency 012-2212-4292; hyper_med _center@sinainet.com.eg; main Sharm Al Maya Rd; 24hr)

Sharm El Sheikh International Hospital (069-366-0318; Peace Rd, Hadaba; 24hr)

DANGERS & ANNOYANCES

Serious security concerns regarding Sharm El Sheikh's airport were raised in the aftermath of the downing of Russian Metrojet Flight 9268

BUSES FROM SHARM EL SHEIKH

DESTINATION	PRICE	DURATION	TIMES/COMPANY
Alexandria	LE150-260	10hr	9pm (East Delta); 3pm & 11pm (Super Jet); 2pm & 9pm (Go Bus)
Cairo	LE95-240	7hr	9 services daily 7.30am-midnight (East Delta); 6am, 11am, 1pm, 2.30pm, 5.30pm & 11pm (Super Jet); 16 services daily 1.30am-midnight (Go Bus)
Dahab	LE25	1½hr	7am, 8am, 9am, 3pm, 5pm & 9pm (East Delta)
Luxor	LE175	16hr	6pm (East Delta)
Nuweiba	LE50	3½hr	9am (East Delta)
Taba	LE50	4½	9am (East Delta)

As well as the East Delta buses to Dahab, a couple of Go Bus direct Cairo–Dahab services will also pick up passengers from the taxi station. Check with the office for the latest schedule.

in October 2015. A bomb is widely thought to be the cause of the crash. International direct flights into Sharm El Sheikh were suspended afterwards, and many European countries have yet to lift the suspension. Meanwhile, the Egyptian civil aviation authority has been working with a specialist UK security firm to upgrade the airport's security procedures. It's expected that direct international flights into Sharm will resume when the upgrade is completed.

Getting There & Away

AIR

Sharm El Sheikh International Airport (☎069-362-3304; www.sharm-el-sheikh.airport-authority.com; Peace Rd) is Sinai's major travel hub.

Egypt Air (www.egyptair.com) has several flights to and from Cairo per day. Prices fluctuate wildly but fares start from about LE1000.

BOAT

The **La Pespes high-speed catamaran ferry service** (www.lapespes.com; Sharm El Sheikh Marine Port, Sharm Al Maya; adult/child US$40/30; ⏲6pm Sun, Tue & Thu) operates between Sharm El Sheikh and Hurghada three times per week. The journey time takes 2½ hours.

Tickets can be bought from the **ticket office** (☎012-2449-5592, 012-1014-4000; High Jet Office, Peace Rd, Sharm Al Maya; ⏲10am-10pm) near Sharm Old Market.

The ferry sails from Sharm El Sheikh Marine Port. Travellers must be at the port 90 minutes before departure time and have their passport on hand as proof of ID.

BUS

The **East Delta Travel Co bus station** (☎069-366-0660; Sharia Al Rewaysat) is just off Peace Rd behind the Mobil petrol station.

The **taxi station** (☎069-366-1622; Main Rd), just behind the East Delta station, has ticket offices and is the main bus arrival/departure point for Super Jet and Go Bus (www.go-bus.com) services. Go Bus and Super Jet also have a new **ticket office/station** (☎19567; Peace Rd) in Hadaba, near Sharm El Sheikh International Hospital, for passenger pickups and ticket purchasing.

Getting Around

Blue-and-white microbuses regularly ply the stretch between central Na'ama Bay and Sharm El Sheikh. The fare is LE2. Taxis charge a minimum of LE20 between Sharm Old Market and Na'ama Bay. You will need to bargain.

TO/FROM THE AIRPORT

The airport is 10km north of Na'ama Bay at Ras Nasrany. Taxis wait outside the arrivals hall and quote around LE100 to Na'ama Bay. Prepare to bargain hard. Most travellers prefer to skip the taxi debacle completely and prebook an airport transfer with their hotel.

Dahab دهب

☎069 / POP 7500

Low-key, laid-back and low-rise, Dahab is the Middle East's prime beach resort for independent travellers. The startling transformation from dusty Bedouin outpost to spruced-up tourist village is not without its detractors, who reminisce of the days when beach bums dossed in basic huts by the shore. But for all the starry-eyed memories, prosperity has made the town cleaner and more family-friendly, and diving is now a much safer and more organised activity thanks to better regulation of operators. Reeled in by Dahab's mellow ambience, many travellers plan a few nights here and instead stay for weeks.

Dahab

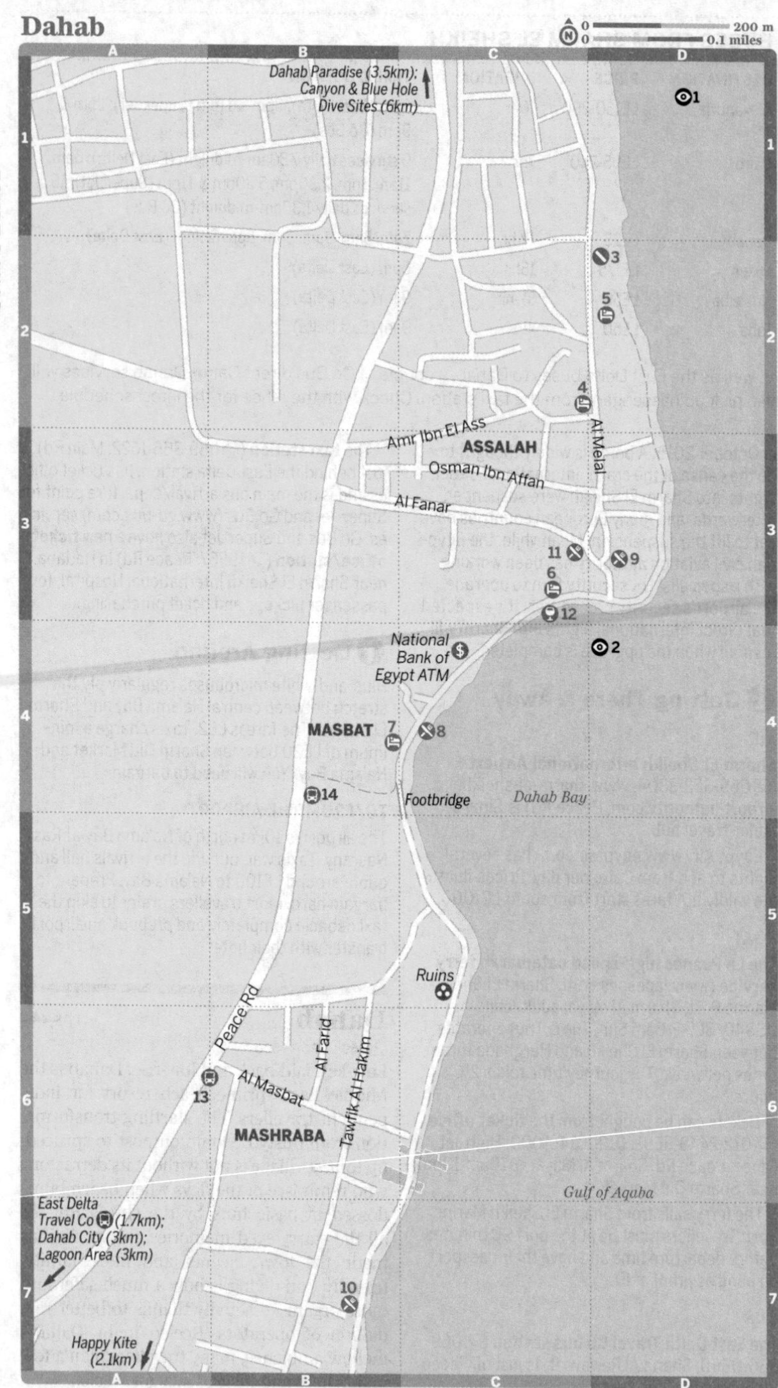
0 200 m
0 0.1 miles
Dahab Paradise (3.5km);
Canyon & Blue Hole
Dive Sites (6km)
Amr Ibn El Ass
ASSALAH
Osman Ibn Affan
Al Fanar
Al Melal
National
Bank of
Egypt ATM
MASBAT
Footbridge
Dahab Bay
Ruins
Peace Rd
Al Farid
Tawfik Al Hakim
Al Masbat
MASHRABA
Gulf of Aqaba
East Delta
Travel Co (1.7km);
Dahab City (3km);
Lagoon Area (3km)
Happy Kite
(2.1km)

Dahab

Sights
1 Eel Garden........D1
2 Lighthouse Reef........D4

Activities, Courses & Tours
3 Dive Urge........D2
Red Sea Relax Dive Centre........(see 6)

Sleeping
4 El Salam Hotel........C2
5 Eldorado........D2
6 Red Sea Relax........C3
7 Seven Heaven........B4

Eating
8 Ali Baba........C4
9 Athanor........D3
10 Lakhbatita........B7
11 Ralph's German Bakery........C3

Drinking & Nightlife
12 Yalla Bar........C3

Transport
13 East Delta Bus Co Ticket Office........A6
14 Go Bus Office........B4

Activities

Snorkelling & Diving

The best reefs for snorkelling are **Lighthouse Reef** and **Eel Garden**, both in Assalah. You can hire snorkelling gear from all the dive centres for about LE25 to LE40 per day. Keep in mind that some of the reefs have unexpected currents – drownings have occurred in Dahab – so keep your wits about you.

Note that despite the intimidating reputation of the **Canyon** and **Blue Hole** dive sites as danger zones for careless divers, the tops of the reefs are teeming with life, making them fine snorkelling destinations when the sea is calm. Most tour companies in town organise half-day Blue Hole snorkelling trips for between LE50 and LE120.

Red Sea Relax Dive Centre DIVING
(069-364-1309; www.red-sea-relax.com; Waterfront Promenade, Masbat; per shore/night dive from US$21/26, PADI discover scuba US$58) Long-standing five-star PADI centre with an excellent reputation. Highly recommended for PADI learn-to-dive courses. AIDA free-diving courses also available.

Dive Urge DIVING
(069-364-0957; www.dive-urge.com; Sharia Al Melal, Assalah; 1 dive €40, PADI discover scuba €85) This five-star PADI centre has commendable environmental credentials: no more than four divers per dive plus litter clean ups are a standard part of their daily diving. The centre and adjoining resort are fully wheelchair accessible.

Tours

This is one of the best places in Sinai to arrange camel safaris into the dramatic mountains lining the coast, especially the spectacular **Ras Abu Gallum Protectorate**. Further afield, the desert area around Nuweiba is home to some of the South Sinai coast's most interesting sights, including the **Coloured Canyon** – jeep safaris to the canyon from Dahab cost between LE300 and LE500 per person.

All the tour operators in Dahab offer tours to Mt Sinai (p125) and St Katherine's Monastery (p125) for about LE180 to LE250 per person.

Sleeping

★**El Salam Hotel** HOTEL $
(069-364-0182; https://elsalamhotel.wordpress.com; Sharia Al Melal, Assalah; s/d/tr US$20/25/35;) This friendly hotel, centred around a garden with traditional-style Bedouin tent chill-out area, offers bright, spacious rooms kitted out with lashings of white and nice little touches such as local appliqué textiles and oriental bedside lamps. If you don't mind being one street back from the shore, it's a great find. Breakfast is US$5 extra.

Seven Heaven HOSTEL $
(069-365-2752, 012-2785-6002; www.7heavenhotel.com; Waterfront Promenade, Masbat; dm LE15, r LE80-120, with air-con LE140;) This all-in-one ramshackle place (combining dive shop and tour office) offers one of the best-value shoestringer deals in town. It has a huge range of rooms, which go up in price as you add in extras; the six-bed dorms, which come with air-con and bathroom, are a bargain. Breakfast not included.

★**Eldorado** BOUTIQUE HOTEL $$
(069-365-2157, 012-2759-3235; www.eldoradodahab.com; Sharia Al Melal, Assalah; s/d €30/50, with shared bathroom €20/35;) This intimate, Italian-owned hotel oozes chic, easy-going beach style. The colourful cabana-type rooms host big beds, painted wood panels and cheerful lemon detailing, plus modern bathrooms and exceptional levels

of brushed-up maintenance. Even better, there's a proper patch of sandy beach out front, which is immaculately cared for and comes complete with beckoning sun loungers and shaded seating.

Red Sea Relax RESORT **$$**
(☎069-365-2604; www.red-sea-relax.com; Waterfront Promenade, Masbat; s/d/tr/f US$38/48/58/78, with shared bathroom dm/d US$6/18;) A small resort tailor-made for divers. Spacious rooms are wrapped around a glistening pool, and are kitted-out with kettles and TVs. Plus there are free water fill-ups, free kayak use, a beckoning rooftop bar and an excellent dive centre. The dormitory means budgeteers get resort facilities for backpacker costs, while dive-centre clients can get their dorm bed for free.

Eating & Drinking

Athanor ITALIAN **$**
(Sharia Al Melal, Assalah; dishes LE18-60; ⏲11am-midnight;) Dahab's best thin-crust pizzas are served up here in the shady garden terrace.

★**Ralph's German Bakery** CAFE **$$**
(Sharia Al Fanar, Masbat; pastries LE7-25, sandwiches & breakfasts LE35-85; ⏲7am-6pm;) Everybody in Dahab ends up at Ralph's at some point. This is Dahab's top stop for breakfast, brunch, and coffee and croissant breaks, and it does a fine line in quiche and apple strudel as well. People who have the willpower to not add a delectable Danish pastry on to their order are doing better than we are.

★**Lakhbatita** ITALIAN **$$**
(Waterfront Promenade, Mashraba; mains LE65-180; ⏲6-11.30pm;) We adore Lakhbatita's eccentric decoration, friendly service and serene ambience, all of which bring a touch of Italian flair to Dahab. The small menu of homemade pasta dishes, many featuring seafood, is a cut above what's served up elsewhere. Try the mushroom ravioli or the garlic and chilli prawns.

Ali Baba INTERNATIONAL **$$**
(Waterfront Promenade, Masbat; mains LE87-193; ⏲10am-late;) This place adds flair to its seafood selection with some inspired menu choices. Great service, comfy sofas to lounge on, stylish lanterns and twinkly fairy lights add to the relaxed seaside ambience. All meals come with a mezze selection to start with. Bring your appetite.

Yalla Bar BAR
(Waterfront Promenade, Masbat; ⏲11am-late;) This hugely popular waterfront bar-restaurant has a winning formula of plenty of comfy seating, including sun loungers out front, friendly staff, cold beer and a decent list of cocktails to keep the punters happy.

Information

There are stand-alone **ATMs** (Waterfront Promenade) scattered along the waterfront.

Getting There & Away

BUS

The **East Delta bus station** (☎069-364-1808) is in Dahab City, well southwest of the centre of the action. East Delta also has a **ticket office** (Peace Rd; ⏲9am-6pm) in Masbat. Buses will pick up passengers from here, but double-check when booking.

The **Go Bus office** (☎19567; www.gobus-eg.com; Peace Rd) is conveniently central; just west of Masbat's footbridge.

TAXI

Local pick-up taxis are no longer allowed to operate outside the Dahab area. Taxis touting for business to Nuweiba (LE200), Sharm El Sheikh airport (LE250) and St Katherine's (LE300 to

BUSES FROM DAHAB

DESTINATION	PRICE	DURATION	TIMES/COMPANY
Cairo	LE115-270	9hr	9am, 12.30pm, 3pm, 7.30pm & 10pm (East Delta); 12.30am, 9am, 1.15pm & 9.30pm (Go Bus)
Luxor	LE210	18hr	4pm (East Delta)
Nuweiba	LE30	1hr	10.30am (East Delta)
Sharm El Sheikh	LE25	1½hr	8am, 9am, 10am, 12.30pm, 3pm, 4pm, 5pm, 7pm, 7.30pm, 9.30pm, 10pm, 10.30pm & 11pm (East Delta)
Taba	LE40	2½hr	10.30am (East Delta)

Note that a couple of the Go Bus Cairo-bound services will also drop off passengers in Sharm El Sheikh. Check at the Go Bus office for the current timings.

LE350) hang out at the East Delta bus station or can be booked through hotels and travel agencies in town.

Getting Around

A variety of variously banged-up pick-ups operate as local taxis. From Masbat to the bus station costs between LE10 and LE15. To get to the Blue Hole independently you can negotiate with any of the pick-up drivers in town (LE100 to LE120 return). Don't forget to arrange a return time.

St Katherine Protectorate
محمية سانت كاترين

069

St Katherine Protectorate (admission LE25) incorporates a 4350-sq-km area of high-altitude desert and protects a wealth of historic sites sacred to the world's three main monotheistic religions. Rising up out of the desert and jutting above the other peaks is the towering 2285m Mt Sinai (Gebel Musa). Tucked into a barren valley at Mt Sinai's foot is the ancient St Katherine's Monastery. Approximately 3.5km from here is the small town of Al Milga, which is also called Katreen and is known as the 'Meeting Place' by local Jabaliyya Bedouin.

Sights

★St Katherine's Monastery MONASTERY
(Cairo 02-2482-8513; www.sinaimonastery.com; 9-11.30am Mon-Thu & Sat, except religious holidays) FREE This ancient monastery traces its founding to about AD 330, when Byzantine empress Helena had a small chapel and a fortified refuge for local hermits built beside what was believed to be the burning bush from which God spoke to Moses. Today St Katherine's is considered one of the oldest continually functioning monastic communities in the world. If the monastery museum is locked, ask at the Church of the Transfiguration for the key.

★Mt Sinai MOUNTAIN
(Gebel Musa; compulsory guide LE175, camel rides one-way LE250) Known locally as Gebel Musa, Mt Sinai is revered by Christians, Muslims and Jews, all of whom believe that God delivered his Ten Commandments to Moses at its summit. The mountain is easy and beautiful to climb, and offers a taste of the magnificence of southern Sinai's high mountain region. For pilgrims, it also offers a moving glimpse into biblical times. All hikers must be accompanied by a local Bedouin guide (hired from the monastery car park).

Sleeping

El Malga Bedouin Camp HOSTEL $
(Sheikh Mousa Camp; 010-0641-3575; www.sheikmousa.com; Al Milga; dm/s/d LE30/125/180, s/d with shared bathroom LE75/120;) Owned by the affable Sheikh Mousa and run by on-the-ball Salah, this is by far the best-run camp in town. The en suite rooms are large and comfortable, while the small, basic rooms and dorms share excellent bathroom facilities with hot water. There's a shaded cushion-strewn terrace to chill out on and good meals are dished up by the kitchen.

Monastery Guesthouse GUESTHOUSE $$
(069-347-0353; www.sinaimonastery.com; St Katherine's Monastery; s/d US$35/60;) This guesthouse right next to St Katherine's Monastery offers well-kept rooms surrounding a pleasant courtyard where a cafe offers filling and tasty meals. Make sure to ask for a mountain-view rather than a courtyard-view room. Note that the guesthouse was temporarily closed during our last visit, so make sure to phone ahead to check it's open and to make a reservation.

Information

Banque Misr (10am-1pm & 5-8pm Sat-Thu) Beside the petrol station; has an ATM and also changes US dollars and euro.

DANGERS & ANNOYANCES

In April 2017, there was a gun attack on a police checkpoint in the St Katherine Protectorate area, which killed one policeman. The police presence around the St Katherine area remains high, with several security checkpoints along the road.

Getting There & Away

The **bus station** (069-347-0250) is just off the main road in Al Milga, behind the mosque. East Delta Travel Co runs one daily bus to Cairo (LE90, seven hours) at 6am via Wadi Feiran and Suez.

Taxis charge around LE300 to LE350 to either Dahab or Sharm El Sheikh.

Nuweiba
نويبع

069 / POP 20,000

Nuweiba these days isn't much of a looker. Stretching over 15km, it lacks a defined centre or cohesive ambience, and functions primarily as a port for the Aqaba-bound ferry to Jordan. Tarabin (Nuweiba's beachfront area) is home to a scattering of low-key beach camps but due to a lack of tourism trade many have been left to go to seed.

St Katherine's Monastery

A HISTORY OF THE MONASTERY

4th Century With hermetic communities congregating in the area, a chapel is established around the site of Moses' miraculous ❶ **Burning Bush**.

6th Century In a show of might, Emperor Justinian adds the monastery ❷ **fortifications** and orders the building of the basilica, which is graced by Byzantine art, including the ❸ **Mosaic of the Transfiguration**.

7th Century The prophet Mohammed signs the ❹ **Ahtiname**, a declaration of his protection of the monastery. When the Arab armies conquer Egypt in AD 641, the monastery is left untouched. Despite the era's tumultuous times, monastery abbot St John Klimakos writes his famed ❺ **Ladder of Divine Ascent** treatise, depicted in the Sacred Sacristy.

9th Century Extraordinary happenings surround the monastery when, according to tradition, a monk discovers the body of St Katherine on a mountain summit.

11th Century To escape the wrath of Fatimid caliph Al Hakim, wily monks build a mosque within the monastery grounds.

15th Century Frequent raids and attacks on the monastery lead the monks to build the ❻ **Ancient Gate** to prevent the ransacking of church treasures and to keep the monastic community safe.

19th Century In 1859 biblical scholar Constantin von Tischendorf borrows 347 pages of the ❼ **Codex Sinaiticus** from the monastery, but fails to get his library books back on time. Greek artisans travel from the island of Tinos in 1871 to help construct the ❽ **bell tower**.

20th Century Renovations inside the monastery reveal 18 more missing parchment leaves from the Codex Sinaiticus, proving that all the secrets hidden within these ancient walls may not yet be revealed.

BADAHOS / SHUTTERSTOCK ©

Fortifications

The formidable walls are 2m thick and 11m high. Justinian sent a Balkan garrison to watch over the newly fortified monastery, and today's local Jabaleyya tribe are said to be their descendents.

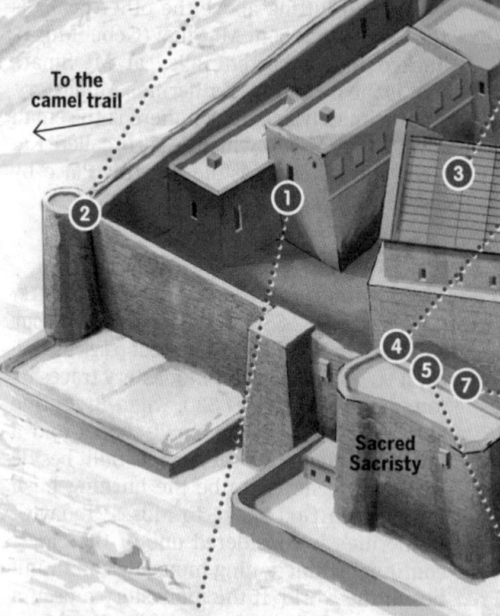

The Burning Bush

This flourishing bramble (the endemic Sinai shrub *Rubus Sanctus*) was transplanted in the 10th century to its present location. Tradition states that cuttings of the plant refuse to grow outside the monastery walls.

PHOTOS BY AVA / SHUTTERSTOCK ©

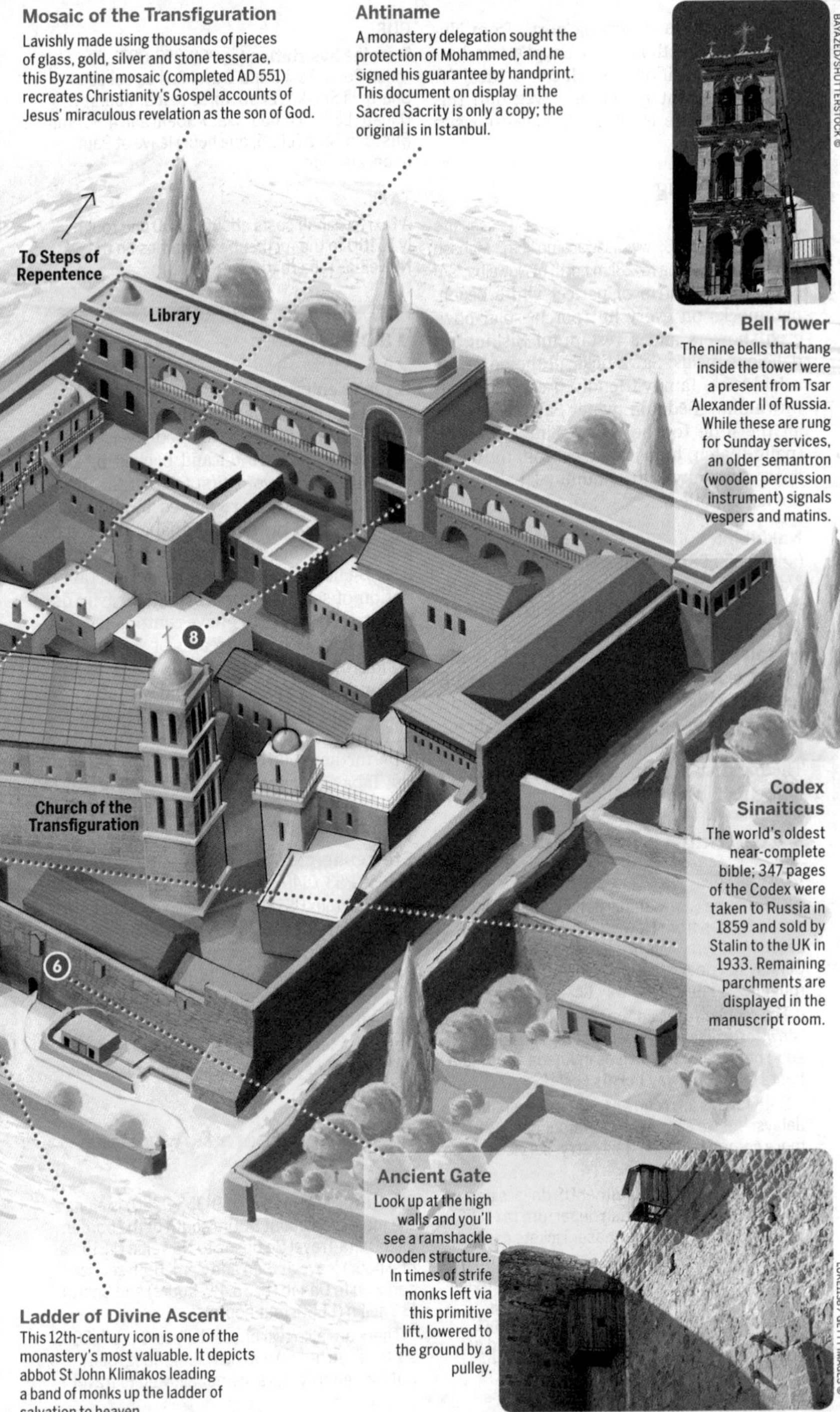

Mosaic of the Transfiguration
Lavishly made using thousands of pieces of glass, gold, silver and stone tesserae, this Byzantine mosaic (completed AD 551) recreates Christianity's Gospel accounts of Jesus' miraculous revelation as the son of God.
Ahtiname
A monastery delegation sought the protection of Mohammed, and he signed his guarantee by handprint. This document on display in the Sacred Sacrity is only a copy; the original is in Istanbul.
BAYAZED/SHUTTERSTOCK ©
To Steps of Repentence
Library
Bell Tower
The nine bells that hang inside the tower were a present from Tsar Alexander II of Russia. While these are rung for Sunday services, an older semantron (wooden percussion instrument) signals vespers and matins.
8
Church of the Transfiguration
Codex Sinaiticus
The world's oldest near-complete bible; 347 pages of the Codex were taken to Russia in 1859 and sold by Stalin to the UK in 1933. Remaining parchments are displayed in the manuscript room.
6
Ancient Gate
Look up at the high walls and you'll see a ramshackle wooden structure. In times of strife monks left via this primitive lift, lowered to the ground by a pulley.
LUKE1138 / GETTY IMAGES ©
Ladder of Divine Ascent
This 12th-century icon is one of the monastery's most valuable. It depicts abbot St John Klimakos leading a band of monks up the ladder of salvation to heaven.

The coastline stretching north from Nuweiba to Taba though, is Egypt's last bastion of the traditional beach camp. Ideal for those who want to seriously veg out, this stretch of shore is all about back-to-basics beach living.

Sleeping

★ Sawa Camp CAMPGROUND $
(☎010-0272-2838; www.sawacamp.com; Mahash area, Nuweiba–Taba rd, 28km north of Nuweiba; s/d hut US$6/8) A strip of perfect white beach, hammocks on every hut porch, solar-powered showers and a restaurant dishing up delicious meals: Sawa ticks all the boxes for a laid-back, family-friendly break all about unwinding. Bedouin owner Salama has got all the little touches right. Simple *hoosha* (palm-thatch) huts just steps from the shore have electricity and communal bathrooms are kept spotless.

Nakhil Inn BOUTIQUE HOTEL $$
(☎069-350-0879; www.nakhil-inn.com; Tarabin; s/d €35/42;) The Nakhil is a cosy compromise for those who want hotel comforts without the crowds. The studio-style wooden cabins exude simple beach chic, while guests can go kayaking, diving, or simply unwind while lazing about in one of the hammocks or palm-thatch roofed cabanas along the immaculately-kept private beach. The big drawcard though is snorkelling the house reef just offshore.

Getting There & Away

BOAT

AB Maritime (www.abmaritime.com.jo) runs two public **ferries** from Nuweiba to Aqaba. The so-called 'fast-ferry' service leaves Nuweiba from Sunday to Friday at (supposedly) 1pm and takes roughly 2½ hours. One-way tickets cost US$100.

The regular ferry, commonly called the 'slow-ferry', leaves Nuweiba at (again, supposedly) noon daily and arrives in Aqaba about four hours later. One-way tickets cost US$90.

Both ferries are renowned for interminable delays, but we cannot stress enough how much more comfortable the 'fast-ferry' service is than its sister regular service.

Tickets can be paid in either US dollars or Egyptian pounds. Egyptian departure tax (LE50) is paid at the time of purchase. Tickets can only be purchased on the day of departure, at the **ferry ticket office** (☎069-352-0427; Nuweiba Port area; ⏲9am-3pm) in a small building near the port. Travellers must be at the port two hours before sailing to buy tickets and get through the shambolic departure formalities in the terminal building.

BUS

From the **bus station** (☎069-352-0371; Nuweiba Port), East Delta Travel Co has buses to Sharm El Sheikh (LE50, three to four hours) via Dahab (LE30, 1½ hours) at 7.30am and 4.30pm. Buses to Taba (LE25, one hour) leave at 9am, noon, and 3pm.

TAXI

A taxi to Dahab costs about LE200 and roughly LE100 to the further beach camps on the Nuweiba–Taba road.

Taba طابا

☎069

If you're entering Egypt overland from Israel and the Palestinian Territories, the scruffy border town of Taba, loomed over by the monolithic Taba Hotel and backed by barren hills, will be your first taste of the Sinai. With its narrow shore lapped by the azure blue waters of the Gulf of Aqaba, this coastline has been bigged-up by developers as the new Sharm El Sheikh for years. A combination of security worries and a heavily destructive flood in 2014 have continued to put the brakes on Taba's dreams of sun-and-fun holidaymaker hordes though.

For fully resort-based holidays Taba provides good beach-break deals. Though for sand-between-your-toes beach-hut bliss, hop a bit further south to the beach camps along the Taba–Nuweiba road.

Sleeping

Steigenberger Taba Hotel RESORT $$
(☎069-353 0140; www.steigenberger.com; Taba Beach; r from US$80;) You can't miss this mammoth resort complex. It towers over Taba's low-rise town. If you've just wandered across the dusty border and want to rest up before moving onward, this is a fine place to relax for a day. Staff are friendly and helpful, classically styled rooms come with all mod-cons and comfy queen-sized beds, and the pool is enormous.

Getting There & Away

BUS

Taba's **bus station** (☎069-353 0250) is along the main road about 800m south of the border. East Delta Travel Co buses to Nuweiba (LE15, one hour) leave at 6am and 3pm. Both services carry on to Dahab (LE35, 2½ hours) and Sharm El Sheikh (LE50, four hours).

There are also two buses daily to Cairo (LE80, six to seven hours) via the Nakhl–Suez road but foreign travellers are not allowed to travel this route due to security issues. For travellers who've crossed the border from Eilat and want to journey directly to Cairo, the only option is to go via Sharm El Sheikh.

CROSSING TO/FROM ISRAEL

The Taba–Eilat border is open 24 hours daily. Just inside the border you'll find an ATM and foreign-exchange booths. Egyptian departure tax is LE75. The Taba side of the border technically only issues the free Sinai-only entry stamp. Purchase a full Egyptian visa online or buy in advance in either Israel or Jordan.

UNDERSTAND EGYPT

Egypt Today

Egypt was long seen as the land of eternity, where nothing ever changed. That image has been shattered by events since 2011, but some things remain: Egypt's location, its huge population and its control of the Suez Canal ensure that it is still a major player in the region. Egyptians seemed united in January 2011 when they forced President Hosni Mubarak from power, but they have been increasingly divided ever since. The Muslim Brotherhood's candidate Mohammed Morsi became Egypt's first democratically elected president in 2012 but within a year millions were back in the streets protesting against his increasingly Islamist agenda. The army intervened to remove him from power and crushed his supporters in months of bloodshed. In June 2014, former army chief Abdel Fattah al-Sisi won the presidential election and has overseen a clampdown on the Muslim Brotherhood and pro-democracy activists. Sisi's rule has struggled to address Egypt's political and economic instability. Old problems of mass poverty, poor education and growing sectarian conflict are all, to some degree, interconnected, and can't be resolved easily. Most Egyptians are significantly worse off than when they rose up against Mubarak and hope the future will bring a more stable and prosperous life.

History

Ancient Egypt

For centuries before 3000 BC, the fertility and regularity of the annual Nile floods supported communities along the Nile valley. These small kingdoms eventually coalesced into two important states, one covering the valley, the other consisting of the Delta itself.

The pharaoh Menes' (Narmer's) unification of these two states in about 3100 BC set the scene for the greatest civilisation of ancient times.

Little is known of the immediate successors of Menes except that, attributed with divine ancestry, they promoted the development of a highly stratified society, patronised the arts and built numerous temples and public works. In the 27th century BC, Egypt's pyramids began to materialise. Ruling from nearby Memphis, the Pharaoh Zoser and his chief architect, Imhotep, built what may have been the first – the Step Pyramid at Saqqara.

For the next three dynasties and 500 years (a period called the Old Kingdom), the power of Egypt's pharaohs, and the size and scale of their pyramids and temples increased dramatically. The immense dimensions of these buildings served as a reminder of the pharaoh's importance and power over his people. The last three pharaohs of the 4th dynasty, Khufu (Cheops), Khafre (Chephren) and Menkaure (Mycerinus), left their legendary mark by commissioning the three Great Pyramids of Giza.

The New Kingdom, its capital at Thebes and later Memphis, represented a renaissance of art and empire in Pharaonic Egypt. For almost 400 years, from the 18th to the 20th dynasties (1550–1069 BC), Egypt was a formidable power in northeast Africa and the eastern Mediterranean. But by the time Ramses III came to power (1184 BC) as the second pharaoh of the 20th dynasty, disunity had again become the norm. Taking advantage of this, the army of Alexander the Great took control of Egypt in the 4th century BC.

Alexander founded a new capital, Alexandria, on the Mediterranean coast, and for the next 300 years the land of the Nile was ruled by a dynasty established by one of the Macedonian's generals, Ptolemy. Romans followed the Ptolemaic dynasty, during which time Christianity took hold. Then came Islam and the Arabs, conquering Egypt in AD 640. In due course, rule by the Ottoman Turks and the Europeans followed (the French under Napoleon, then the British) – shifts of power common to much of the Middle East.

Modern Egypt

Egyptian self-rule was restored through the Revolution of 1952, led by the Free Officers. Colonel Gamal Abdel Nasser, the coalition's leader, was confirmed as president

ESSENTIAL EGYPTIAN DISHES

Fatta Rice and bread soaked in a garlicky-vinegary sauce with lamb or chicken.

Fiteer Flaky pastry stuffed with sweet or savoury ingredients. Often called Egyptian pizza.

Mahshi kurumb Rice- and meat-stuffed cabbage leaves doused with *samna* (clarified butter).

Molokhiyya A viscid jute-leaf soup flavoured with garlic and coriander.

Hamam mahshi Roast pigeon stuffed with *fireek* (green wheat) and rice.

Ta'amiyya Egyptian felafel; made from fava beans instead of chick peas.

in elections in 1956 and successfully faced down Britain, France and Israel to reclaim the Suez Canal. Nasser was unsuccessful, however, in the 1967 war with Israel, and died shortly after of heart failure. Anwar Sadat, his successor, also fought Israel, in 1973. The eventual outcome of the so-called October War was the 1979 Camp David Agreement, which established peace with Israel. In certain quarters, Camp David was viewed as treacherous abandonment of Nasser's pan-Arab principles; it ultimately cost Sadat his life at the hands of an assassin in 1981.

Sadat's murderer was a member of the terrorist organisation Islamic Jihad. Sadat's successor, Hosni Mubarak, reinstated emergency law and cracked down on Islamist groups. For almost three decades, Mubarak managed to control the domestic political situation – and the Muslim Brotherhood. But discontent brewed among the poorer sections of society as the country's economic situation worsened. Frequent attempts were made on the life of the president and his ministers. In 1997, another Islamist group, Gama'a Al Islamiyya, carried out a bloody massacre of 58 holidaymakers and four Egyptians at the Temple of Hatshepsut in Luxor. The massacre crippled the economy and destroyed grassroots support for militant groups.

The Muslim Brotherhood declared a ceasefire the following year and entered the political process. It won the 2012 presidential election, following the overthrow of Mubarak, but its lack of experience in running a government quickly alienated it from the majority of Egyptians, especially when President Morsi pushed through an Islamist constitution without sufficient consultation. Since his overthrow in the summer of 2013, the military has ruled, either directly, or through the election of former field marshal, now president, Sisi.

People

With 93 million people, Egypt has the third-largest population in Africa (after Nigeria and Ethiopia) and is also the most populous country in the Arab world.

The blood of the pharaohs flows in the veins of many Egyptians today, but centuries of invading Libyans, Persians, Greeks, Romans, Arabs and Turks have added to the mix. Some independent indigenous groups persist: the nomadic Bedouin tribes, now for the most part settled in Sinai and Egypt's deserts; the Berbers of Siwa Oasis; and dark-skinned Nubians from the regions south of Aswan that were swallowed up by the High Dam.

About 90% of Egypt's population is Muslim; much of the remainder is Coptic Christian. The two communities have a mixed history, with periodic flare-ups of sectarian violence. Islam permeates most aspects of Egypt's culture, from social norms and mores to laws, but Egypt does not follow Sharia law and Islamic fundamentalism is supported only by a minority.

Arts

Literature

Egypt's literary pride is Naguib Mahfouz (1911–2006), awarded the Nobel Prize in 1988. Alaa Al Aswany is Egypt's most globally well known contemporary writer. His 2002 blockbuster *The Yacoubian Building* is the world's biggest-selling novel in Arabic. Other Internationally recognised names include Ahadaf Soueif, Booker prize shortlisted for her novel *The Map of Love*, and Nawal Al Saadawi, whose nonfiction book *The Hidden Face of Eve* is still banned in Egypt. *Maryam's Maze* by Mansoura Ez Elden and *Taxi* by Khaled Al Khamissi are two of the most prominent works by Egypt's vibrant new generation of writers.

Cinema

Egypt's golden years were the 1940s and 1950s, when Cairo studios turned out more than 100 movies a year, filling cinemas throughout the Arab world with charming musicals that are still classics of regional cinema. Egypt's best-known director is Youssef Chahine (1926–2008), honoured at Cannes in 1997 with a lifetime achievement award. The political upheavals of recent years has seen a revival of Egypt's filmmakers: *The Square*, a documentary about Cairo's Tahrir Square during the anti-Mubarak protests by Jehane Noujaim was nominated for an Oscar in 2014.

Music

Alongside cinema, classical Arabic music peaked in the 1950s, the prime years of iconic diva Umm Kolthum. The country came to a standstill during her weekly live radio broadcast of lovelorn songs, some upwards of an hour long. Contemporary music is more lightweight, in the form of pop stars like Amr Diab, known across the Arab world for catchy choruses and loads of synthesisers. During the 2011 revolution, protest songs filled the air, and hip hop has inspired many working-class performers.

Food & Drink

Egyptian food is an earthy variant of Middle Eastern cuisine – a mix of dishes from Turkish, Levantine, Greek and ancient Egyptian traditions. Compared with its neighbours, Egyptian cuisine might seem to lack refinement and diversity, but the food here is good, honest peasant fare that packs an occasional sensational punch. High points include seafood on the Mediterranean coast, pickled vegetables with loads of garlic, succulent mangoes in summer and fresh dates in autumn, and a dish called *kushari* (a mix of noodles, rice, black lentils, fried onions and tomato sauce) for a carbohydrate load.

SURVIVAL GUIDE

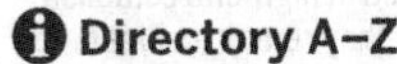

Directory A–Z

ACCOMMODATION

In Cairo, Alexandria, Luxor and Aswan, there are options for all budgets. The Red Sea coast resorts and Sharm El Sheikh are largely dedicated to package tourism. In the Western Desert oases, budget options range from bare-bones operations to very backpacker-friendly.

Rates at all hotels are negotiable in off-peak seasons, generally March to September (November to January on the Mediterranean coast) and especially during the middle of the week.

Many hotels will take US dollars or euros in payment, and some higher-end places even insist on it, though officially taking payment in currencies other than Egyptian pound is illegal. Lower-end hotels are usually cash only, though it's not a given that all upmarket hotels accept credit cards.

CHILDREN

Visiting Egypt with children can be a delight. For them, seeing ancient monuments – or a camel for that matter – up close can be a fantasy made real. For you, the incredibly warm welcome towards young ones can smooth over many small practical hassles.

- Safety standards may make visitors nervous: don't expect car seats (or even seat belts, for that matter) in taxis.
- In resort towns formula is readily available, as are disposable nappies, but these can be hard to find in out-of-the-way places.
- Restaurants everywhere are very welcoming to families. High chairs are often available in better restaurants.
- For infants, you'll want a sling or back carrier – strollers will get you nowhere.

DISCOUNT CARDS

The International Student Identity Card (ISIC) Gives discounts on museum and site entry fees. Some travellers have also been able to get the discount with HI cards and Eurail cards.

EMBASSIES & CONSULATES

Embassies are in Cairo.

Australian Embassy (Map p58; ☎02-2770-6600; www.egypt.embassy.gov.au; 11th fl, World Trade Centre, 1191 Corniche El Nil; ⏰8am-4.15pm Sun-Wed, to 1.30pm Thu)

Canadian Embassy (Map p58; ☎02-2461-2200; www.canadainternational.gc.ca/egypt-egypte; 18th fl, South Tower, Nile City Towers, 2005 Corniche El Nil; ⏰8am-4.30pm Sun-Wed, to 1.30pm Thu)

SLEEPING PRICE RANGES

The following price ranges refer to a double room in high season (November to February). Unless stated otherwise breakfast and taxes are included.

$ less than LE540 (US$30)

$$ LE540–1800 (US$30–100)

$$$ more than LE1800 (US$100)

Dutch Embassy (Map p72; ☎02-2739-5500; http://egypt.nlembassy.org; 18 Sharia Hassan Sabry, Zamalek; ⏰8am-5pm Sun-Thu)

French Embassy (Map p74; ☎02-3567-3200; www.ambafrance-eg.org; 29 Sharia Charles de Gaulle, Giza; ⏰9.30am-5pm Sun-Thu)

German Embassy (Map p72; ☎02-2728-2000; www.kairo.diplo.de; 2 Sharia Berlin, off Sharia Hassan Sabry, Zamalek; ⏰8am-3pm Sun-Thu)

Irish Embassy (Map p72; ☎02-2728-7100; www.dfa.ie/irish-embassy/egypt; 18 Sharia Hassan Sabry, Zamalek; ⏰9am-3pm Sun-Thu)

Israeli Embassy (Map p74; ☎02-2359-7304; http://embassies.gov.il; 6 Sharia Ibn Malek, Giza; ⏰9am-4pm Sun-Thu)

Italian Embassy (Map p74; ☎02-2794-3194; www.ambilcairo.esteri.it; 15 Sharia Abd Al Rahman Fahmy, Garden City; ⏰9am-3.30pm Sun-Thu)

Jordanian Embassy (Map p74; ☎02-3749-9912, 02-3748-5566; 6 Sharia Gohainy, Doqqi; ⏰9am-3pm Mon-Thu)

Lebanese Embassy (Map p72; ☎02-2738-2823; 22 Sharia Mansour Mohammed, Zamalek; ⏰9.30am-12pm Sat-Thu)

New Zealand Embassy (Map p58; ☎02-2461-6000; www.mfat.govt.nz; Level 8, North Tower, Nile City Towers, 2005 Corniche El Nil; ⏰9am-3pm Sun-Thu)

Saudi Arabian Embassy (Map p74; ☎02-3762-5000; http://embassies.mofa.gov.sa; 2 Sharia Al Yaman, Giza; ⏰9am-4pm Sun-Thu)

Spanish Embassy (Map p72; ☎02-2735-6462; www.exteriores.gob.es; 41 Sharia Ismail Mohammed, Zamalek; ⏰8am-3.30pm Sun-Thu)

> ### ℹ PRACTICALITIES
>
> **Alcohol** Available, typically only at tourist spots and higher-end restaurants. Drinking on the street is taboo, as is public drunkenness.
>
> **Electricity** Increasingly unreliable since 2011; everywhere in Egypt suffers regular, usually daily, outages.
>
> **Security** Checkpoints are common on highways and other main roads. Always have your passport easily on hand.
>
> **Smoking** Common in Egypt, including in restaurants and bars. Nonsmoking facilities are rare.
>
> **Water** Tap water in Egypt is not considered safe to drink, with the exception of Cairo where it's drinkable but less than delicious.
>
> **Weights & Measures** Egypt uses the metric system.

Sudanese Embassy (Map p58; ☎02-3748-5648; 3 Sharia Ahmed Ali Al Shatouri, Doqqi; ⏰9am-4pm Sun-Thu)

UK Embassy (Map p74; ☎02-2791-6000; www.ukinegypt.fco.gov.uk; 7 Sharia Ahmed Ragheb, Garden City; ⏰8am-3.30pm Sun-Wed, to 2pm Thu)

US Embassy (Map p66; ☎02-2797-3300; https://eg.usembassy.gov; 5 Sharia Tawfiq Diab, Garden City; ⏰9am-4pm Sun-Thu)

GAY & LESBIAN TRAVELLERS

Egypt is a conservative society that increasingly condemns homosexuality. In late 2017, the Egyptian government launched a large crack-down on the LGBT community, arresting 57 people in a series of raids.

For LGBT travellers the situation is not as bleak. As long as common sense discretion is used and public displays of affection are avoided – the same goes for heterosexual couples – foreign gay or lesbian couples should have no issues. Solo male gay travellers should not use gay dating apps while here, as the police are known to target app users.

MONEY

Change There is a severe shortage of small change, which is invaluable for tips, taxi fares and more. Hoard small bills and always try to break big bills at fancier establishments.

Currency Egyptian pound (LE), *guinay* in Arabic, divided into 100 piastres (pt).

Exchange Rate The government freed the exchange rate in 2016, which led to the Egyptian pound losing half its value against hard currencies.

Notes and Coins 5pt, 10pt and 25pt coins are basically extinct; 50pt notes and coins are also on their way out. LE1 coins are the most commonly used small change, while LE5, LE10, LE20, LE50, LE100 and LE200 notes are commonly used.

ATMs

Cash machines are common, although in some places (in the oases, for instance) you might have to look harder to find one. Then you'll be stuck if there's a technical problem, so load up before going somewhere remote. Some ATMs won't let you withdraw more than LE2000. All Banque du Caire ATMs allow larger withdrawals.

Credit Cards

Major cards are accepted in high-end establishments. In remote areas they remain useless. You may be charged a percentage of the sale in fees (anywhere between 3% and 10%).

Money Changers

Money can be officially changed at Amex and Travel Choice Egypt (formerly Thomas Cook) offices, as well as at commercial banks, foreign exchange (forex) bureaux and some hotels. Rates no longer vary, though some places may charge commission. Don't accept any badly defaced, shabby or torn notes because you'll have difficulty offloading them later.

Tipping

Always keep small change as baksheesh is expected everywhere. When in doubt, tip.

Cafes Leave LE5 to LE10.

Guards at tourist sites LE5 to LE20.

Metered taxis Round off the fare or offer around 5% extra, depending on the ride.

Mosque attendant Leave LE5 to LE10 for shoe covers, more if you climb a minaret or have some guiding.

Restaurants For good service leave 10%; in smart places leave 15%.

OPENING HOURS

The weekend is Friday and Saturday; some businesses close Sunday. During Ramadan, offices, museums and tourist sites keep shorter hours.

Banks 8.30am–2.30pm Sunday–Thursday

Bars and clubs Early evening until 3am, often later (particularly in Cairo)

Cafes 7am–1am

Government offices 8am–2pm Sunday–Thursday; tourist offices are generally open longer

Post offices 8.30am–2pm Saturday–Thursday

Private offices 10am–2pm and 4pm–9pm Saturday–Thursday

Restaurants Noon–midnight

Shops 9am–1pm and 5pm–10pm June–September, 10am–6pm October–May; in Cairo shops generally open 10am–11pm

PUBLIC HOLIDAYS

In addition to the main Islamic holidays, Egypt celebrates the following public holidays.

New Year's Day (1 January) Official national holiday, but many businesses stay open.

Coptic Christmas (7 January) Most government offices and all Coptic businesses close.

January 25 Revolution Day (25 January)

Sham An Nessim (March/April) On the first Monday after Coptic Easter, this tradition with Pharaonic roots is celebrated by all Egyptians, with family picnics. Few businesses close, however.

Sinai Liberation Day (25 April) Celebrating Israel's return of the peninsula in 1982.

May Day (1 May) Labour Day.

Revolution Day (23 July) Date of the 1952 coup, when the Free Officers seized power from the monarchy.

Armed Forces Day (6 October) Celebrates Egyptian successes during the 1973 war with Israel, with some military pomp.

EATING PRICE RANGES

The following price ranges refer to a typical main dish.

$ less than LE50 (US$3)

$$ LE50–150 (US$3–8)

$$$ more than LE150 (US$8)

SAFE TRAVEL

The incidence of crime, violent or otherwise, in Egypt is negligible compared with many Western countries, and you're generally safe walking around day or night. Generally, unwary visitors are parted from their money through scams and hustlers, rather than crime.

Terrorism

There has been a significant rise in terror attacks in Egypt since the downfall of President Morsi in 2013. Almost all have been aimed at security and government targets, with the majority occurring in North Sinai. In November 2017 militants attacked the Al Rawda Mosque in Bir Al Abd in North Sinai, killing 305. North Sinai remains a no-travel region. Cautionary travel advisories remain in place for most of the South Sinai and parts of the Western Desert.

Elsewhere, there has been sporadic militant activity, the most recent being explosions in Coptic churches in Tanta and Alexandria in April 2017 (Palm Sunday) that killed at least 44 people and a gun attack on Christian pilgrims near Minya in May 2017 where 30 people died.

Unsurprisingly, there is a heavy security presence throughout the country, including at tourist sites.

TELEPHONE

To dial an Egyptian number from outside the country, dial your international access code, Egypt's country code and then the number, dropping the first 0 from the area code.

Country code	20
International access code	00
Ambulance	123
Fire	180
Tourist police	126

Mobile Phones

Egypt's GSM network has thorough coverage. SIM cards from any of the three carriers (Vodafone, the largest; Mobinil; Etisalat) cost LE15. You can buy them as well as top-up cards from most kiosks, where you may be asked to show your passport. For pay-as-you-go data service (about LE5 per day or LE50 per month), register at a company phone shop.

TIME

Egypt is two hours ahead of GMT/UTC. Egypt does observe Daylight Saving Time, but the clocks are turned back an hour during Ramadan, if it falls in the summer, to cut the day short for observers

TRAVELLERS WITH DISABILITIES

Egypt for All (012-2657-7774; www.egyptforall.com) Agency specialised in making travel arrangements for mobility impaired visitors, from day trips to complete Egypt tours.

VISAS

Required for most nationalities. Single-entry, 30-day tourist visas cost US$25 and are available online (www.egyptvisa.com) for 41 nationalities. Otherwise, visas can be purchased at airports (and Nuweiba port) on arrival.

Sinai-Only Entry Stamp

If you are entering Egypt through the Sinai (at Sharm El Sheikh Airport or at Taba), and are not leaving the South Sinai area (between Sharm El Sheikh and Taba, including St Katherine's Monastery but not Ras Mohammed National Park), you do not require a visa and can be issued with a free Sinai-only entry stamp, good for a 15-day stay.

Visa Extensions

Visa extensions used to be routine, but are now subject to scrutiny, especially after repeat extensions. Most large cities have passport offices for extensions:

Alexandria (Map p84; 03-482-7873; 2nd fl, 25 Sharia Talaat Harb; 8.30am-2pm Mon-Thu, from 10am Fri, 9am-11am Sat & Sun) Go to counter eight on the 2nd floor.

Aswan (Map p102; 097-231-2238; 1st fl, Police Bldg, Corniche An Nil; 8am-2pm & 6-8pm Sun-Thu)

Cairo (Passport Office; Map p66; Mogamma Bldg, Midan Tahrir; 8am-1.30pm Sat-Wed) Head to the 1st floor, get a form from the hallway table manned by police officers, have your form signed at window 12, then stamps from window 43 and file all back at window 12; next-day pickup is at window 38.

Luxor (Map p88; 095-238-0885; Sharia Khaled Ibn Al Walid; 8am-2pm Sat-Thu)

Getting There & Away

ENTERING EGYPT

If you are entering or leaving Egypt as a tourist through the international airports, procedures are typically speedy, no questions asked. By land or sea, the process is similar, though it is usually slower and more chaotic. E-visas can now be purchased before arrival from the official government site www.egyptvisa.com. Your passport must be valid for at least eight months from your date of entry.

If you are crossing a land border with your own vehicle, prepare for a lengthy spell with immigration and customs officials.

> **PORT TAX**
>
> All Egyptian international ferries charge LE50 port tax per person on top of the ticket price.

AIR

Cairo International Airport (p74) Egypt's main entry point.

Burg Al Arab Airport (p85) Flights from Middle Eastern and North African cities.

Hurghada Airport (p115) Mainly charter international flights.

Luxor Airport (p99) EgyptAir flies direct from London Heathrow.

Marsa Alam Airport (p117) Charter flights from Europe.

Sharm El Sheikh International Airport (p121) Historically an excellent Egypt entry point for travellers looking for low-cost fares but since late 2015's Metrojet Flight 9268 disaster, most direct international services have been suspended.

LAND

The only land border Egypt share with the rest of the Middle East is with Israel and the Palestinian Territories. Egypt also has recently opened land borders with Sudan. Its Amsaad border crossing to Libya is officially open but due to the security situation, travel to Libya is not recommended.

Israel & the Palestinian Territories

Rafah The border crossing to the Gaza Strip opens only intermittently. Foreign travellers cannot cross at this border.

Taba The Taba border is the main entry/exit point between Egypt and Israel. Buy an Egypt e-visa online beforehand as technically only the free Sinai-only entry stamp is issued here. Departure tax from Israel is 101NIS. Departure tax from Egypt is LE75.

SEA

Jordan

AB Maritime (www.abmaritime.com.jo) runs both a daily fast and slow passenger ferry connecting Nuweiba in Egypt and Aqaba in Jordan. Both Egyptian and Jordanian visas are available on arrival.

Saudi Arabia

Ferries run from Hurghada and Safaga to Duba in Saudi Arabia, though they follow erratic schedules. Note that tourist visas are not available for Saudi Arabia, though there is an elusive tourist transit visa, which you must apply for well in advance.

Getting Around

AIR

EgyptAir is the main domestic carrier. Nile Air also flies between Cairo and the main centres, though it has fewer services.

BICYCLE

Cycle tourism is rare because of long distances plus intense heat.

The Cairo-based club **Cycle Egypt** (www.cycle-egypt.com), and its very active Facebook group, is a good starting point for making local contacts and getting advice on shops and gear.

BOAT

No trip to Egypt is complete without a trip down the Nile River. There are plenty of cruise ships plying between Aswan and Luxor, ranging from midrange to five-star luxury experiences. The main centre for organising and beginning multi-day felucca (Egyptian sailing boat) trip is Aswan.

La Pespes (www.lapespes.com) run a high-speed catamaran ferry service three times per week between Sharm El Sheikh and Hurghada.

BUS & MICROBUS

You can get to most places in Egypt on a bus, at a very reasonable price. For many long-distance routes beyond the Nile Valley, it's the best option, and sometimes the only one. Buses aren't necessarily fast, though, and if you're going to or from Cairo, you'll lose at least an hour just in city traffic.

Microbuses (pronounced *meekrobas*) run along most of the same routes as buses. They run on no set schedule – they just wait until they're full. There are certain parts of the country (in the Western Desert, and the Nile Valley) where foreigners are currently not allowed to use microbuses between towns.

CAR & MOTORCYCLE

Driving in Cairo is a crazy affair, and although it's slightly less nerve-racking in other parts of the country, it is more dangerous. Night driving should be completely avoided. That being said, some intrepid readers have reported that self-driving is a wonderful way to leave the tour buses in the dust.

A motorcycle would be a good way to travel around Egypt, but you must bring your own, the red tape is extensive and the risks perhaps greater than in a car. Ask your country's automobile association and Egyptian embassy about regulations.

Petrol and diesel are usually readily available (there are occasional critical shortages) and very cheap. But stations can be scarce outside of Cairo. As a rule, when you see one, fill up.

DOMESTIC FLIGHT FARES

For the best prices when booking domestic flights using EgyptAir's website, change your home location to Egypt. Prices show up in Egyptian pounds, and are often half what the same flight costs when using a home location outside of Egypt.

LOCAL TRANSPORT

Microbus

Microbuses are ubiquitous within Egyptian towns. They run along prescribed routes stopping anywhere along the route on request.

Pick-up Trucks & Tuk-Tuks

Covered pickup trucks are sometimes used within rural areas. To indicate to the driver that you want to get out, pound on the floor with your foot. Tuk-tuks are becoming a popular cheap alternative to taxis, mostly in more rural towns.

Taxi

Even the smallest cities in Egypt have taxis. They're inexpensive and efficient, even if in some cities the cars themselves have seen better days.

Fares In Cairo metered taxis are taking over, but everywhere else, locals know the accepted price and pay it without (much) negotiation. Check with locals for taxi rates, as fares change as petrol prices rise.

Hailing Just step to the roadside, raise your hand and one will likely come screeching to a halt. Tell the driver where you're headed – he may decline the fare if there's bad traffic or it's too far.

Negotiating For short fares, setting a price beforehand backfires, as it reveals you don't know the system. But for long distances agree on a price before getting in.

Paying In unmetered taxis, avoid getting trapped in an argument by getting out first, then handing money through the window.

TRAIN

Along the two main routes (Cairo–Alexandria, and Cairo–Aswan) trains have modern rolling stock and are the preferable mode of transport. Outside of these though, cars are often grubby and battered and you'd have to be very fond of trains to prefer them to a deluxe bus.

For specific schedules, consult the **Egyptian Railways** (https://enr.gov.eg) website, where you can also purchase tickets.

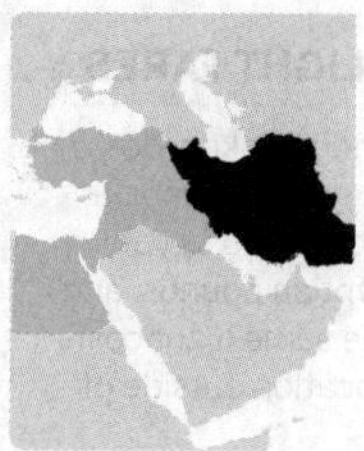

Iran

Includes ➡

Tehran 137
Tabriz 149
Kandovan 153
Qazvin 153
Alamut Valley 155
Kashan 156
Esfahan 158
Yazd 164
Shiraz 170
Persepolis 175
Mashhad 178
Understand Iran 181
Survival Guide 185

Best Places to Eat

- ➡ Shahriar Restaurant (p152)
- ➡ Divan (p145)
- ➡ Dizi (p144)

Best Places to Stay

- ➡ Saraye Ameriha Boutique Hotel (p157)
- ➡ See You In Iran Hostel (p141)
- ➡ Kandovan Laleh Rocky Hotel (p153)
- ➡ Iran Hotel (p161)

Why Go?

Rewarding doesn't begin to cover Iran as a destination. This exceptionally welcoming country has a multifaceted history and rich, artistic culture manifested in myriad ways. Hospitality is a way of life here and chatting with locals over tea or a meal will likely provide your most memorable moments.

Stunning mosques, palaces and ruins from different eras provide architectural wonder, while the shopping culture of the brilliant bazaars adds a colour beyond description. The outdoors, too, is captivating, with baking deserts and soaring mountain ranges providing a spectacular backdrop wherever you gaze.

Good, cheap transport makes getting around easy and Iran is also very safe for travellers. Though Iranian citizens are often subject to government repression, culturally sensitive and respectful foreigners are unlikely to encounter problems. In fact, many travellers rate Iran as their most-memorable-ever travel experience: come and see why.

When to Go

Tehran

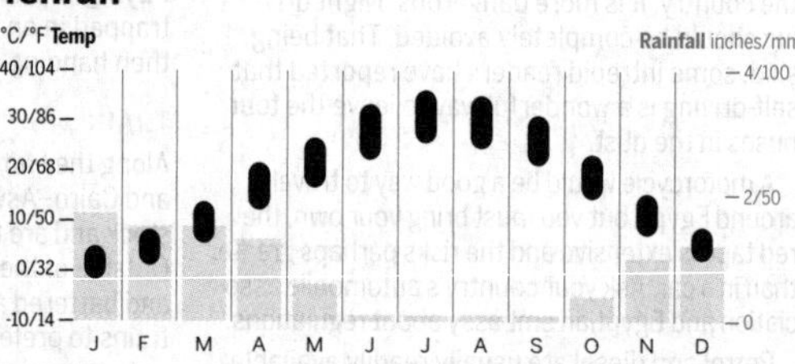

Jan Skiing in the Alborz Mountains near Tehran.

Apr Enjoy mild temperatures and spectacular spring flowers.

Oct It's cooled off in the hot south but serious cold hasn't hit the north.

TEHRAN تهران

☎021 / POP 8.43 MILLION / ELEV 1300M

Hugging the lower slopes of the magnificent, snowcapped Alborz Mountains, Tehran is Iran's most secular and liberal city. Spend time here – as you should – and you'll soon realise that the city is so much more than a chaotic jumble of concrete and crazy traffic blanketed by a miasma of air pollution. This is the nation's dynamic beating heart, the place to get a handle on modern Iran as well as to gain an overview of the country's past in the city's excellent museums.

History

Tehran wasn't particularly significant until it became the 19th-century centre of Qajar Persia and steadily expanded. By 1900 it had grown to 250,000 people, and in the 20th century it became one of the most populous cities on earth.

Sights

★Golestan Palace PALACE

(کاخ گلستان; Map p142; ☎021-3311 3335; www.golestanpalace.ir; Arg Sq; general admission IR150,000, main halls IR150,000, other galleries & halls IR80,000; ⏰9am-5pm; Ⓜ Panzdah-e Khordad) The glories and excesses of the Qajar rulers are played out across this complex of grand buildings decorated with beautifully painted tiles and set around an elegant garden that's worth visiting in its own right. There are separate tickets for nine different sections, which you need to buy at the gate: the ones worth paying extra for are the Main Halls, which includes the spectacular **Mirror Hall**, and the **Negar Khaneh** (Iranian Painting Gallery).

★Grand Bazaar BAZAAR

(بازار بزرگ; Map p142; main entrance Panzdah-e Khordad Ave; ⏰7am-5pm Sat-Wed, to noon Thu; Ⓜ Panzdah-e Khordad) The maze of bustling alleys and the *bazari* (shopkeepers) that fill them make this a fascinating, if somewhat daunting, place to explore. The bazaar's covered stores line more than 10km of lanes and there are several entrances, but you get a great view down a central artery by using the main entrance facing the square Sabzeh Meydan. The warren includes the impressive **Imam Khomeini Mosque**, and the ornately decorated **Imamzadeh Zeid**, a shrine to a descendant of the prophet.

★Treasury of National Jewels MUSEUM

(موزه جواهرات ملی; Map p142; ☎021-6446 3785; www.cbi.ir; Ferdowsi St; IR200,000; ⏰2-4.30pm Sat-Tue; Ⓜ Sa'di) Owned by the Central Bank and accessed through its front doors, the cavernous vault that houses what is commonly known as the 'Jewels Museum' is not to be missed. The Safavid, Qajar and Pahlavi monarchs adorned themselves and their

NEED TO KNOW

Capital Tehran

Country code ☎98

Languages Farsi (Persian), Azari, Arabic, other ethnic languages

Official name Islamic Republic of Iran

Population 82.8 million

Currency Iranian rial (IRR).

Mobile phones Your foreign SIM may not work. Local SIMs easily obtained (p187).

Money Foreign credit and debit cards don't work (p186). *Bring all you need in cash.*

Visas Nearly all need a visa and US, UK and Canadian citizens will need a guide too.

Exchange Rates

Australia	A$1	IRRXX
Euro zone	€1	IRRXX
Turkey	1TKL	IRRXX
UK	£1	IRRXX
USA	US$1	IRRXX

For current exchange rates see www.xe.com.

Time 3½ hours ahead of UTC/GMT. Daylight saving late-March to late-September.

Emergency ☎115 (ambulance), ☎110 (police).

Dress Women must conform to a dress code (p187).

Transport Good network of buses, trains, shuttle taxis and domestic flights (p189).

Connections Direct buses from Turkey, Azerbaijan, Armenia; trains from Turkey. Direct flights from Turkey, Europe, Central Asia and the Persian Gulf.

Alcohol Banned.

Daily Costs Budget hotel double room US$40, restaurant mains US$8, six-hour bus US$10.

Iran Highlights

1 **Esfahan** (p158)
Admiring the enormous square and the stunning buildings that surround it.

2 **Persepolis** (175)
Looking upon the ruined, yet majestic, works of the mighty Achaemenid Kings of Kings.

3 **Alamut Valley** (p155) Hiking the Alborz range in this fabled, utterly picturesque landscape.

4 **Mashhad** (p178)
Watching Shiite Islam in action at the spectacular shrine of Imam Reza.

5 **Yazd** (p165)
Pacing the ancient mud-brick centre of this enchanting desert town.

6 **Tabriz** (p149)
Diving into the sights, sounds and smells of the fabulous bazaar.

7 **Tehran** (p137)
Getting energised by the frantic buzz and browsing the excellent museums.

8 **Shiraz** (p170)
Exploring the poetic history of this liberal town.

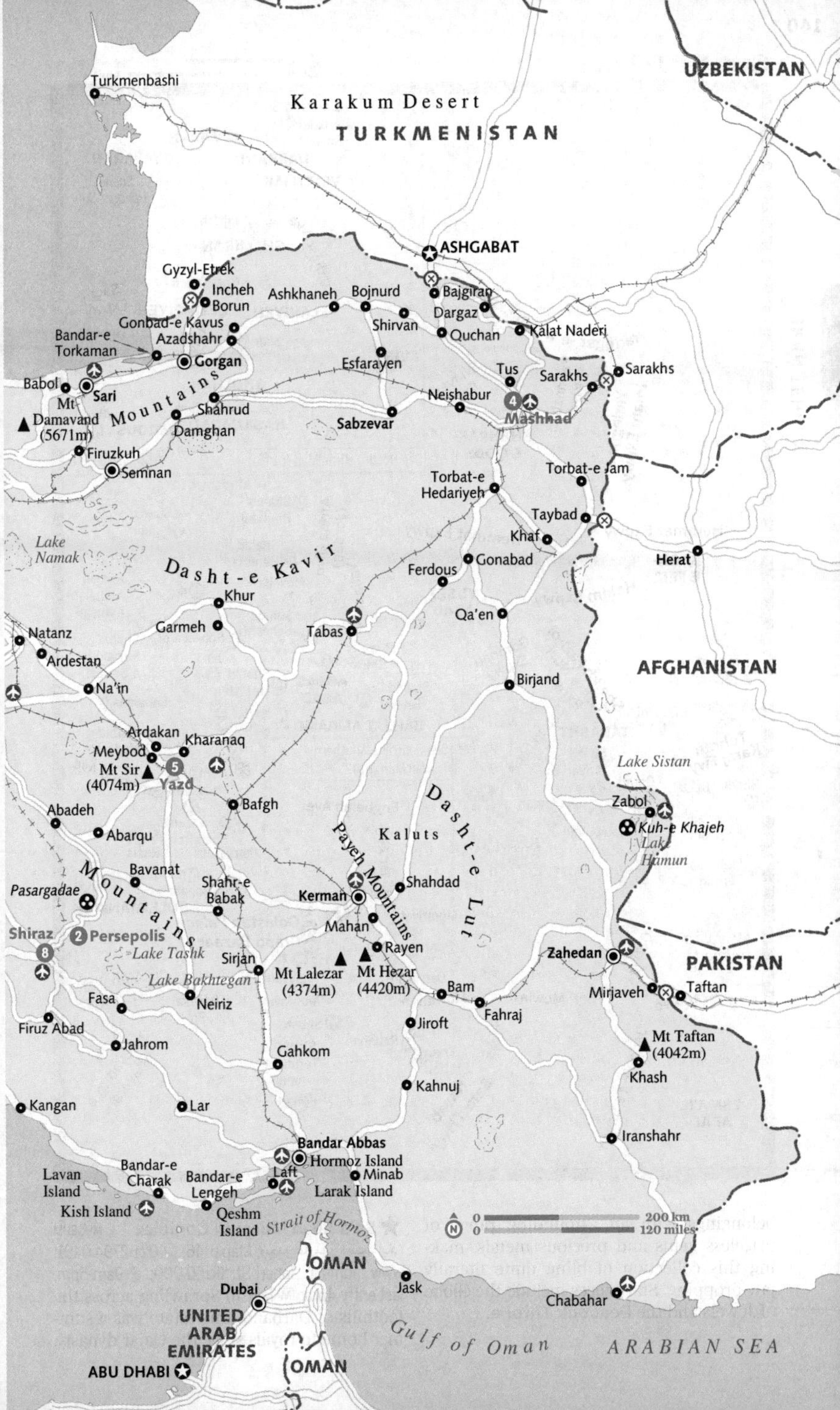
UZBEKISTAN
Turkmenbashi
Karakum Desert
TURKMENISTAN
ASHGABAT
Gyzyl-Etrek
Incheh
Borun
Ashkhaneh
Bojnurd
Bajgiran
Dargaz
Shirvan
Quchan
Kalat Naderi
Gonbad-e Kavus
Azadshahr
Bandar-e
Torkaman
Gorgan
Esfarayen
Tus
Sarakhs
Sarakhs
Babol
Sari
Mt
Damavand
(5671m)
Mountains
Shahrud
Damghan
Sabzevar
Neishabur
4
Mashhad
Firuzkuh
Semnan
Torbat-e
Hedariyeh
Torbat-e Jam
Taybad
Khaf
Lake
Namak
Dasht-e Kavir
Gonabad
Herat
Ferdous
Khur
Qa'en
Garmeh
Tabas
Natanz
Ardestan
AFGHANISTAN
Na'in
Birjand
Ardakan
Kharanaq
Meybod
Mt Sir
(4074m)
5
Yazd
Lake Sistan
Bafgh
Dasht-e Lut
Zabol
Abadeh
Kuh-e Khajeh
Abarqu
Kaluts
Lake
Hamun
Payeh Mountains
Mountains
Bavanat
Shahr-e
Babak
Shahdad
Pasargadae
Kerman
Mahan
Shiraz
2 Persepolis
8
Lake Tashk
Rayen
Zahedan
PAKISTAN
Sirjan
Mt Lalezar
(4374m)
Mt Hezar
(4420m)
Lake Bakhtegan
Bam
Mirjaveh
Taftan
Fasa
Neiriz
Fahraj
Firuz Abad
Jiroft
Jahrom
Mt Taftan
(4042m)
Gahkom
Khash
Kahnuj
Kangan
Lar
Iranshahr
Bandar Abbas
Hormoz Island
Minab
Lavan
Island
Bandar-e
Charak
Bandar-e
Lengeh
Laft
Larak Island
Kish Island
Qeshm
Island
Strait of Hormoz
0
200 km
0
120 miles
N
OMAN
Dubai
Jask
Chabahar
UNITED
ARAB
EMIRATES
Gulf of Oman
ARABIAN SEA
ABU DHABI
OMAN

Greater Tehran

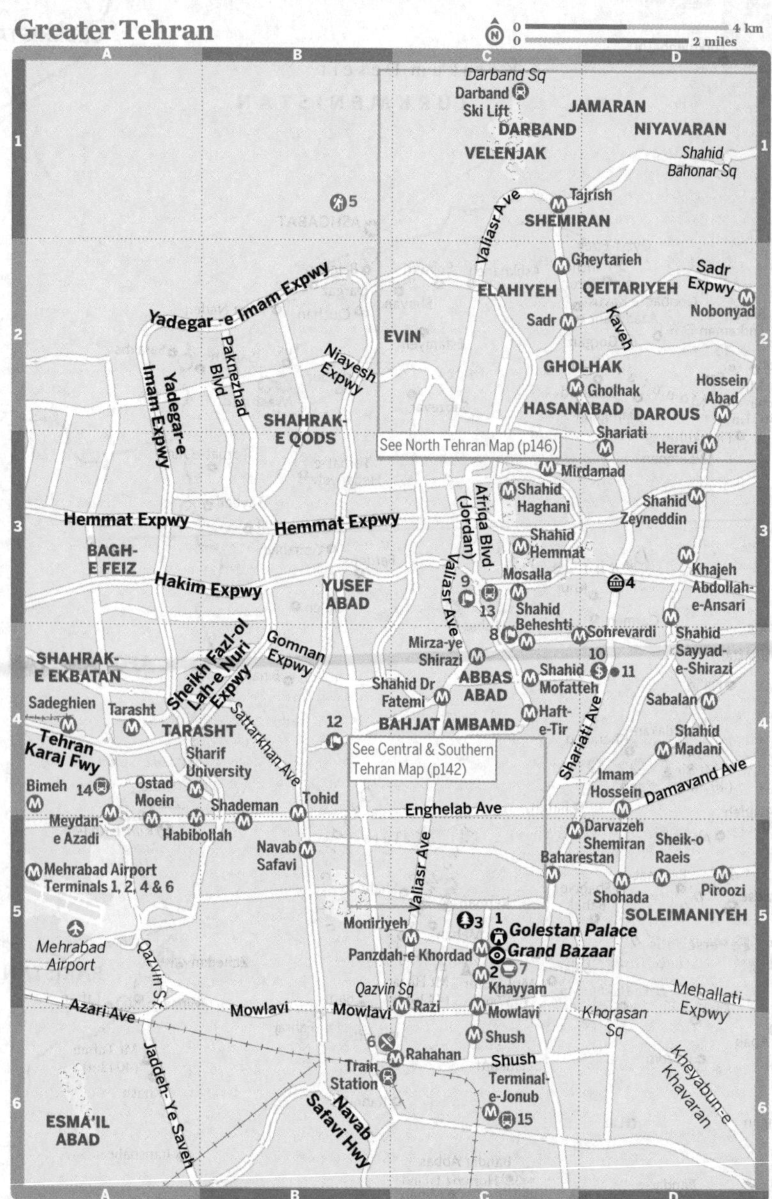

belongings with an astounding range of priceless gems and precious metals, making this collection of bling quite literally jaw-dropping. Star pieces include the Globe of Jewels and the **Peacock Throne**.

★ **Sa'd Abad Museum Complex** MUSEUM
(مجموعه موزه سعد آباد; Map p146; ☎021-2794 0491; www.sadmu.ir; Taheri St; IR150,000; ⏰9am-5pm, last entry 4pm; Ⓜ Tajrish) Sprawling across the foothills of Darband, this estate was a summer home to royals since the Qajar dynasty,

Greater Tehran

Top Sights
1 Golestan Palace....C5
2 Grand Bazaar....C5

Sights
3 Park-e Shahr....C5
4 Reza Abbasi Museum....D3

Activities, Courses & Tours
5 Darakeh....B1

Eating
6 Azari Traditional Teahouse....B6

Drinking & Nightlife
7 Haj Ali Darvish Teahouse....C5

Information
8 Afghan Embassy....C4
9 Australian Embassy....C3
10 Bank Melli....D4
11 Foreign Intelligence Office....D4
12 Pakistani Embassy....B4

Transport
13 Terminal-e Arzhantin....C3
14 Terminal-e Gharb....A4
15 Terminal-e Jonub....C6

although it was the Pahlavis who expanded it to the site you see today. Covering 110 hectares and comprising 18 separate buildings, it will take you a good three hours to see everything. For a glimpse into the luxurious life of the shahs, don't miss the extravagant 54-room **White Palace**, built in the 1930s. The more classical-looking **Green Palace** dates from the end of the Qajar era.

Niyavaran Cultural-Historic Complex MUSEUM
(موزه کاخ نیاوران; Map p146; ☎021-2228 7026; www.niavaranmu.ir; Niyavaran Ave, off Shahid Bahonar Sq; grounds IR15,000; ⊙9am-6pm Apr-Sep, 8am-4pm Oct-Mar; Ⓜ Nobonyad, then taxi) In the Alborz foothills is the palace where Shah Mohammad Reza Pahlavi and his family spent most of the last 10 years of royal rule. It's set in 5 hectares of landscaped gardens and has six separate museums, the best of which is the elegant 1960s **Niyavaran Palace**, with its clean lines, opulent interior and sublime carpets.

Courses

Persian Food Tours COOKING
(www.persianfoodtours.com; per person 2-4 people €80, 5 or more people €65) Tehran-based Matin and Shirin run this superb cooking course that starts with a morning shopping expedition around Tajrish Bazaar then moves on to their beautiful purpose-built kitchen, where four local dishes and a special drink are prepared for a late lunch. It's hands-on, great fun and an ideal way to learn about Iranian cuisine.

Tours

Ali Taheri TOURS
(☎0912 303 0590; www.iran-tehrantourist.com; tours per day US$70) Personable guide Ali and his sons speak excellent English and know Tehran (and much of the rest of the country) well. They have a variety of cars and even a van in which to arrange tours.

Houman Najafi TOURS
(☎0912 202 3017; houman.najafi@gmail.com) Tehran-based Houman conducts tours around Iran. He is well connected with local environmental groups and specialises in arranging a variety of outdoor adventure and nature tours.

Sleeping

There are many budget options on or around noisy Amir Kabir St.

★ **See You In Iran Hostel** HOSTEL $
(Map p142; ☎021-8883 2266; www.seeyouiniran.org; 2 Vahdati-Manesh Dead End, off South Kheradmand St; dm/s/d without bathroom €15/45/80; ❄📶; Ⓜ Haft-e Tir) What started as a Facebook forum for helping travellers in Iran has blossomed into Tehran's first fully-legit hostel. Run by a clued-up, youthful and open-minded team, this place was just opening up when we were in town, but already looks fantastic, with charmingly decorated rooms and super-comfy beds. There's a cafe, a gift shop (stocking colourful craft products made by mehr-o-mah.com, an NGO helping women and children in poverty) and a spacious garden shaded by trees.

Firouzeh Hotel HOTEL $
(Map p142; ☎021-3311 3508; www.firouzehhotel.com; Dowlat Abad Alley, off Amir Kabir St; s/tw without bathroom US$26/38; ❄@📶; Ⓜ Mellat) If ever there was a hotel the atmosphere of which revolved around one man, this is it. Mr Mousavi is the personification of Persian hospitality, and his enthusiasm, useful information and help with travel bookings make an otherwise unremarkable little hotel in

Central & Southern Tehran

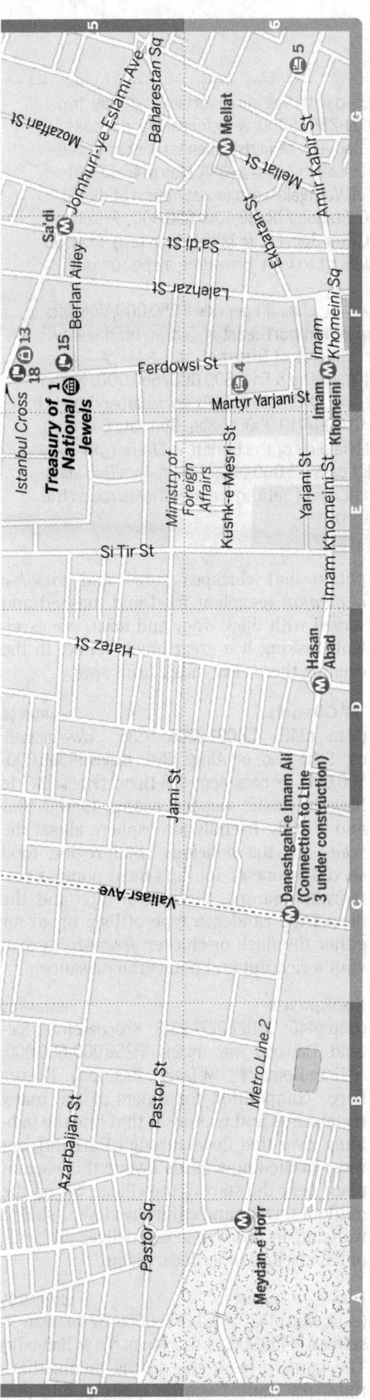

Central & Southern Tehran

Top Sights
1 Treasury of National Jewels F5

Sights
2 Park-e Laleh A2

Sleeping
3 Espinas Khalige Fars Hotel C2
4 Ferdowsi International Grand Hotel F6
5 Firouzeh Hotel G6
6 Howeyzeh Hotel E2
7 Iran Markazi Hotel F4
8 See You In Iran Hostel F1

Eating
9 Dizi E1

Drinking & Nightlife
10 Cake Studio Vorta B3

Shopping
11 Bottejeghe D3
12 Gita Shenasi D3
13 Jomeh Bazaar F5

Information
14 French Embassy D4
15 German Embassy F5
16 Iraqi Embassy C1
17 Italian Embassy D4
18 Turkish Embassy F5
19 UK Embassy F4

an unlovely part of town into a backpacker centre. The small rooms come with cable TV, fridge, and bathrooms with shower and basin; toilets are shared.

Howeyzeh Hotel HOTEL $$
(Map p142; 021-8880 4344; www.korsarhotels.com; 115 Taleghani Ave; s/d US$120/160; P ❄ 📶; M Taleghani) It's worth paying a bit extra for the Howeyzeh's contemporary-styled grey-marble lobby and restaurant area with accents of teal and gold. Rooms don't disappoint either, being equally pleasant, and there's also a spa with Jacuzzi and sauna.

Iran Markazi Hotel HOTEL $$
(Iran Central Hotel; Map p142; 021-3399 6577; www.markazihotel.ir; 419 Lalehzar St; s/tw US$50/70; ❄ 📶; M Sa'di) There's no lift at this small hotel with compact, functional rooms and old-fashioned furnishings. The price is reasonable for the centrally located area, though, and it's on an interesting street lined with spectacular chandelier and light-fitting shops. Bathrooms have Western-style toilets.

WORTH A TRIP

SKIING

Between December and March, Tehran is blessed with five ski resorts within day-trip distance. The easiest to access is **Tochal** (021-2387 5000; www.tochal.org; day pass incl Tochal Telecabin IR650,000; 5am-midnight Dec-Apr; M Tajrish, then taxi), connected directly to northern Tehran via the **Tochal Telecabin** (تله کابین توچال; Map p146; 021-2387 5000; www.tochal.org; Yaddeh-ye Telecabin, off Velenjak Ave; one-way/return Station 2 IR100,000/150,000, Station 5 IR130,000/270,000, Station 7 IR380,000/650,000; from Station 1 8.30am-2pm Sat, Tue & Wed, to 3pm Thu, 7am-3pm Fri; M Tajrish, then taxi). In good weather, even if you're not skiing, Tochal is a delight to visit, providing a spectacular, scenic escape from the city.

The next closest resorts are **Abali** (پیست اسکی آبعلی; chair lift per ride IR150,000, drag lifts per day IR250,000; 8am-6pm Dec-Mar), around 50km northeast of Tehran on the way to Mt Damavand, then the neighbouring resort villages of **Shemshak** (پیست اسکی شمشک; 021-2652 7445; www.skicomplex.ir; lift pass Sat-Wed/Thu & Fri IR600,000/660,000; 8am-3pm late Dec-Apr) and **Darbansar** (پیست اسکی دربندسر; 021-2652 5175; www.darbandsarski.ir; lift pass all day/8am-3pm/4-9pm IR1,200,000/ 940,000/710,000; 8am-9pm late Dec-Mar), 62km north of the city. The largest resort, and the pick of the bunch, is **Dizin** (پیست اسکی دیزین; 0912 818 3454; www.dizinskiresort.com; lift pass IR1,060,000; 8am-4pm Dec-May). It is, however, the furthest away, sitting 125km north of Tehran via the Chalus road (the only route usually possible during the ski season).

Ferdowsi International Grand Hotel HOTEL $$$
(Map p142; 021-6672 7026; www.ferdowsihotel.com; 20 Kushik Mesri St, off Ferdowsi St; s/d from US$143/201; P ❄ @ 🛜 ≋; M Imam Khomeini) This is the only international-standard hotel within an easy walk of the museums, Golestan Palace and bazaar, and as such is popular with tour groups. The quiet, mostly spacious rooms are well equipped and fair value (ask for a renovated room). Service is professional and facilities include a decent size men-only pool, sauna and gym.

Espinas Khalige Fars Hotel HOTEL $$$
(Map p142; 021-8899 6658; www.espinashotels.com; 126 Keshavarz Blvd; r from US$282; P ❄ @ 🛜 ≋; M Meydan-e Valiasr) Polite service marks out the well-located Espinas, where the rooms and suites combine modern comforts with an understated dash of Iranian style in the decor. There's an underground gym, sauna and pool; women may be able to use these facilities before 3pm, otherwise it's men only.

Eating

The wealthy north has international flavours served in designer spaces.

★ **Azari Traditional Teahouse** IRANIAN $
(Map p142; 021 5537 3665; 1 Valiasr Ave; mains IR110,000-150,000; teahouse 6am-midnight, restaurant 11am-5pm & 7-11pm; 🛜; M Rahahan) Just north of the train station, this large and wonderfully atmospheric *chaykhaneh* (teahouse) is justly popular with locals. The *dizi* (lamb, potato and chickpea stew) and *kashk-e bademjan* (eggplant fried and mashed and served with thick whey and mint) are excellent, making it a great lunch venue. In the evening there's live music from 8pm.

★ **Gilaneh** IRANIAN $$
(Map p146; 021-2205 5335; www.gilaneh.co; Saba Blvd, off Afriqa Blvd; mains IR365,000-500,000; noon-4pm & 8-11pm; 🛜; BRT to Niayesh) Rustic wooden beams, glazed tiles and a lively, friendly atmosphere all set the scene for the delicious Gilan-region food served at one of Tehran's most popular restaurants. Sample the mix of dips and the deep fried zander, a type of fish, or go for either the duck or chicken *fesenjan* (a dish with a rich nut and pomegranate sauce).

Koohpayeh IRANIAN $$
(Map p146; 021-2271 2518; Khoopayeh Sq, Sarband, Darband Ave; mains IR250,000-680,000; 11am-11pm; 🛜; M Tajrish, then taxi) There's fierce competition for diners at the many restaurants and teahouses that line the babbling river that flows through Darband, but most in-the-know locals favour this elegant place near the start of the village. Sit on the outdoor terrace and enjoy the view as skilled waitstaff in red waistcoats deliver all kinds of kababs and other local dishes.

Dizi IRANIAN $$
(دیزی; Map p142; 021-8881 0008; 52 Kalantari St; set meal IR450,000; noon-4pm; 🛜; M Haft-e-Tir) The name gives a clue to the menu: that's right, it's Iran's favourite lamb, potato and

chickpea stew. Here they do it damn well, served with all the trimmings including fresh herb salad and a jug of the minty yoghurt drink *dugh*. The staff will show you how to eat it, if in doubt, and take photos of you.

Divan IRANIAN $$$
(Map p146; ☎021-2265 3853; 8th fl, Sam Center, Fereshteh St; mains IR650,000; ⏰noon-4, 7.30-11pm; 📶; 🚌BRT to Mahmoodiyeh) Plush Divan is the pick of several restaurants operated by the Monsoon Group on the 8th floor of the Sam Center. Chic furnishings, including portraits by Iranian artist Fataneh Dadkhah, set the the luxe tone. A tempting menu of traditional Persian dishes with a modern twist delivers both on flavour and presentation.

Drinking & Nightlife

Over the past decade Tehran has developed a modern cafe scene that contrasts with the more traditional teahouses. Meydan-e Valiasr is one of the livelier evening zones, with juice bars, ice-cream kiosks and good cafes.

★ **Sam Cafe** CAFE
(Map p146; ☎021-2265 3842; www.samcafe.ir; 1st fl, Sam Center, Fereshteh St; ⏰9am-10pm; 📶; 🚌BRT to Mahmoodiyeh) A coffee roaster dominates the entrance to the slickest of north Tehran's many fashionable cafes and chief hang-out of the city's privileged. Down your third-wave brew at the long shared table or lounging in a low-slung comfy chair.

Haj Ali Darvish Teahouse TEAHOUSE
(Map p142; ☎021-5581 8672; www.facebook.com/kazemmab; Grand Bazaar; ⏰7am-5pm Sat-Wed, to noon Thu; Ⓜ Panzdah-e Khordad) There's been a teahouse here next to Abdollah Khan Madrassa since 1917, and Haj Kazem's father Ali took over the business in 1962. It's now a stand-up 2m-wide stall rather than a sit-down teahouse, but still worth searching out for its six types of tea (IR20,000), hot chocolate and coffee.

Cake Studio Vorta CAFE
(Map p142; ☎021-6647 5300; 979 Enghelab Ave; ⏰8.30am-10pm Sat-Thu, 3-10pm Fri; 📶; Ⓜ Teatr-e Shahr) Who doesn't love a cupcake? At this cute and buzzy cafe close by Tehran University, they're made well-slathered with butter-cream icing, plus there's several other sweet confections to go with the good coffee and excellent range of herbal and fruit teas.

Shopping

There are carpet stores all over Tehran but nowhere is the experience as memorable, and the price as negotiable, as in the bazaar, with its more than 4000 merchants.

★ **Jomeh Bazaar** MARKET
(جمعه بازار, Friday Market; Map p142; Jomhuri-ye Eslami Ave; ⏰8.30am-2pm Fri; Ⓜ Sa'di) All levels of this car park are transformed every Friday morning when traders from across Iran and Central Asia and members of the general public lay out their stalls to sell whatever they can.

Bottejeghe FASHION & ACCESSORIES
(فروشگاه رخت ایرانی بته جقه; Map p142; www.bottejeghe; 972 Enghelab Ave; ⏰10am-9pm Sat-Thu, 11am-9pm Fri; Ⓜ Teatr-e Shahr) Nailing a trendy Iranian fashion look with attractive shirts, gilets and jackets in cotton, linen and soft wool, Bottejeghe also sells a rainbow selection of scarves and an attractive selection of cushion covers and other local crafts and knick-knacks – all great as gifts.

DON'T MISS

CITY ESCAPES

For those with a desire to see some greenery, the three capital parks (http://parks.tehran.ir), **Park-e Shahr** (پارک شهر; Map p108; cnr Fayazbakhsh & Vahdat-e Eslami Sts; ⏰5am-midnight; Ⓜ Imam Khomeini), **Park-e Laleh** (پارک لاله; Map p142; Keshavarz Blvd; Ⓜ Meydan-e Enghelab Eslami), and **Park-e Mellat** (پارک ملت,; Map p146; Valiasr Ave; 🚌BRT to Niayesh), provide a welcome escape from the in-town traffic chaos. Alternatively, **Park-e Jamshidiyeh** (پارک جمشیدیه; Map p146; ☎021-2228 7793; Shahid Omidvar St; ⏰7am-midnight; Ⓜ Tajrish, then taxi) links the city with the leafy mountain area of Darband. With a ski lift and hiking trails, **Darband** (دربند; Map p146; Ⓜ Tajrish, then taxi) is most popular in the evenings and on Thursdays and Fridays. It's reached from Tajrish Sq, where the road north gives way to a path that winds up a narrow rocky valley, with water cascading down the slope. The trail passes a picturesque succession of teahouses, restaurants and fruit-conserve stalls.

Another pleasant city get-away is the village of **Darakeh** (دراکه; Map p108; Ⓜ Tajrish, then taxi), to the West of Tehran, which offers riverside restaurants and hiking paths.

North Tehran

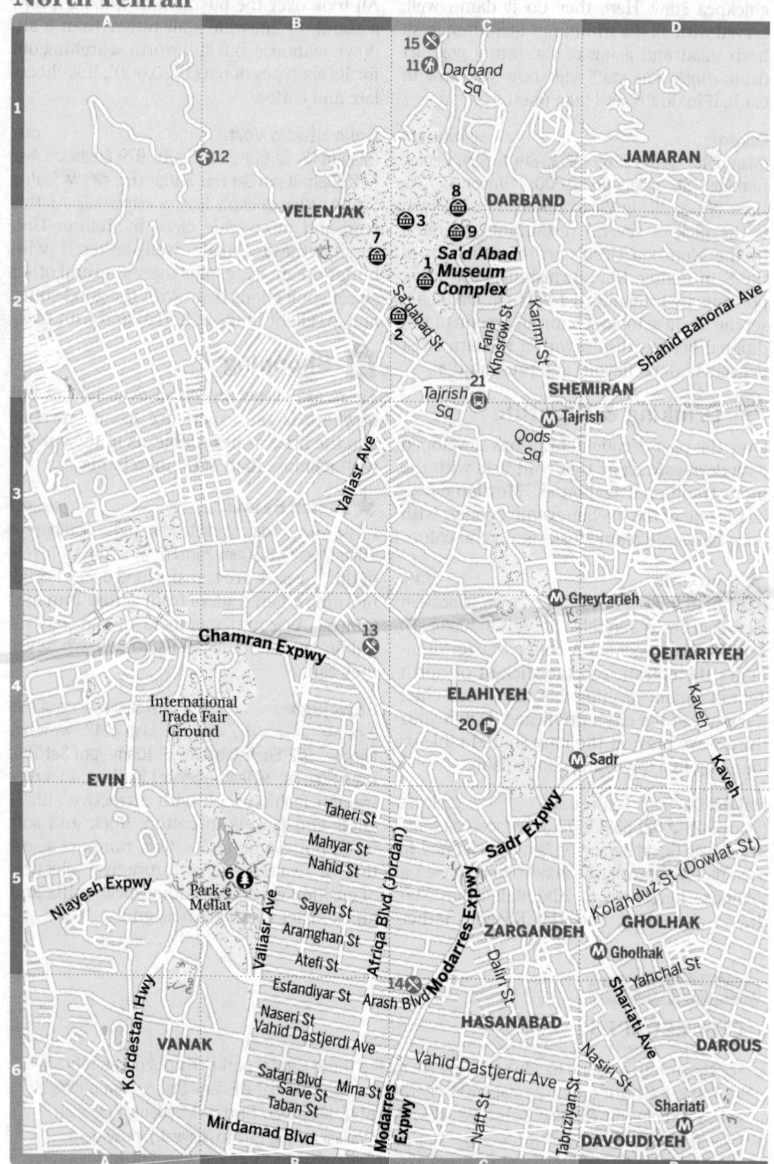

Orientation

The whole city slopes down from the Alborz mountains: if you're walking uphill you're usually going north. Differences between poorer, congested southern Tehran, where the major sights are, and the comparatively glitzy north are plain to see. Valiasr Ave runs 17km from south to north.

Information

Tehran has no tourist information office but you can buy city maps at some newspaper kiosks and **Gita Shenasi** (Map p142; ☎021-6670 3221; www.gitashenasi.com; 20 Ostad Shahriar St; ⌚8am-6.30pm Sat-Wed, to 1pm Thu; Ⓜ Teatr-e Shahr).

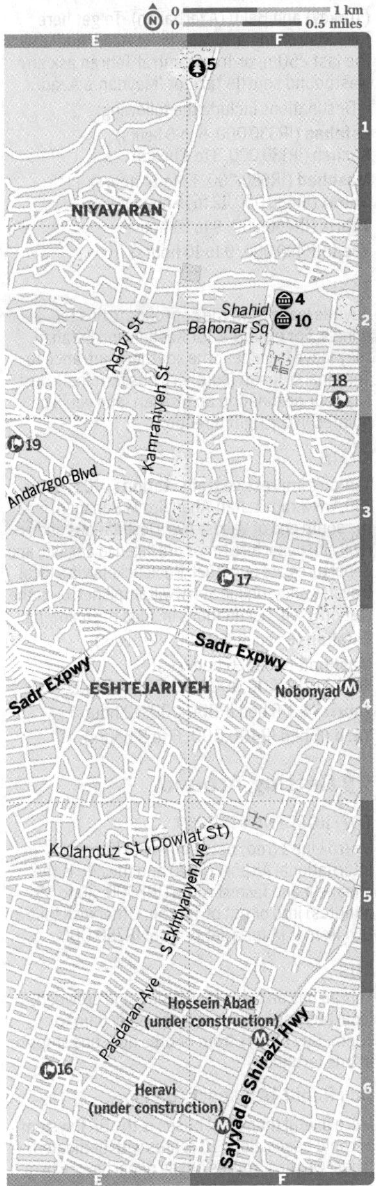

North Tehran

Top Sights
1 Sa'd Abad Museum Complex............C2

Sights
Ahmad Shahi Pavilion..................(see 4)
Automobile Museum....................(see 4)
2 Fine Art Museum..........................C2
Imperial Library Museum.............(see 4)
Jahan-Nama Museum & Gallery..........(see 4)
3 Military Museum.........................C2
4 Niyavaran Cultural-Historic Complex..........F2
5 Park-e Jamshidiyeh........................F1
6 Park-e Mellat...............................B5
7 Royal Automobile Museum..............B2
8 Royal Costume Museum..................C1
9 Royal Tableware Museum...............C2
10 Sahebgharanieh Palace..................F2

Activities, Courses & Tours
11 Darband......................................C1
12 Tochal Telecabin...........................B1

Eating
13 Divan..B4
14 Gilaneh..C6
15 Koohpayeh...................................C1

Drinking & Nightlife
Sam Cafe.....................................(see 13)

Information
16 Azerbaijani Embassy......................E6
17 Dutch Embassy..............................F3
18 New Zealand Embassy....................F2
19 Turkmenistan Embassy...................E3
20 US Interests Section of Swiss Embassy..........C4

Transport
21 Tajrish Bus Station........................C2

DANGERS & ANNOYANCES

Given its chaotic traffic, the most dangerous thing you could possibly do in Tehran is cross the road. Otherwise, Iran's capital is a very safe place for travellers, with low levels of street crime.

EMERGENCY

If your emergency is not life threatening, ask your hotel for the most appropriate hospital or police station.

INTERNET ACCESS

All hotels and many restaurants and cafes offer free wi-fi. For a map showing hot spots, see https://wifispc.com/iran.

MONEY

There are dozens of exchange shops on Ferdosi St south of Ferdosi Sq.

TRAVEL AGENCIES

There are numerous travel agencies throughout the centre.

VISA EXTENSIONS

Try not to extend your visa in Tehran, unless you cannot avoid it – the process tends to get more difficult whenever there is an international-relations issue. If you must, head for the **Foreign Intelligence Office** (Map p142; Soroush St, near Shariati Ave; 8am-1.30pm Sat-Wed, to 11.45am Thu; Shahid Mofatteh, then taxi), go through the gate and get your forms from the building on the left, and make photocopies if necessary. Pay the fee at the **Bank Melli** (Map p142; Shariati Ave) five minutes away down Hamid Alley and across Shariati Ave. Return for security check and, *insh'Allah,* the extension.

Getting There & Away

Every town and city of any size is directly linked to Tehran by bus, and usually by air and train.

AIR

All international services use **Imam Khomeini International Airport** (IKIA, IKA; www.ikia.airport.ir; Imam Khomeini International Airport), 35km south of Tehran.

Mehrabad Airport (Map p142; 021-61021, flight information 199; http://mehrabad.airport.ir; Mehrabad Airport Terminal 1&2), south of Azadi Sq in the west of Tehran, is used for domestic flights. Every day there are flights between here and almost every provincial capital in Iran. **Iran Air** (021-4662 1888; www.iranair.com) flies most routes and is complemented by a number of smaller airlines.

BUS

Tehran has four bus terminals:

Terminal-e Arzhantin (Terminal-e Beyhaghi, Central Terminal; Map p142; 021-8874 2622; http://terminals.tehran.ir; Arzhantin Sq; Mosalla, then taxi) The most central bus terminal; easily accessible by either public transport or taxi. Many VIP services start and finish here.

Terminal-e Shargh (Eastern Terminal; 021-7770 0590; http://terminals.tehran.ir; Damavand Rd; BRT to Tehran Pars) Has buses to Khorasan province and the Caspian region. To get there, take the BRT east from Enghelab Ave, or take a taxi (IR325,000 from central Tehran).

Terminal-e Jonub (Southern Terminal; Map p142; 021-5518 5556; http://terminals.tehran.ir; Abassi St; Terminal-e Jonub) Has buses heading to all points south and southeast. To get here take Metro Line 1 to Terminal-e Jonub then walk about 300m through a tunnel, or grab a taxi heading south.

Terminal-e Gharb (Terminal-e Azadi, Western Terminal; Map p142; 021-4464 6269; http://terminals.tehran.ir; Meydan-e Azadi) Tehran's busiest terminal; caters for the Caspian region and western Iran, as well as international destinations including Ankara and İstanbul (Turkey) and Baku (Azerbaijan). To get here take Metro Line 4 to Meydan-e Azadi and walk the last 250m, or from central Tehran ask any westbound shuttle taxi for 'Meydan-e Azadi'.

Destinations include the following:

Esfahan (IR330,000, 5 to 6 hours)
Kashan (IR180,000, 3 to 4 hours)
Mashhad (IR680,000, 13 to 14 hours)
Shiraz (IR680,000, 12 to 15 hours)
Tabriz (IR460,000, 9 to 10 hours)
Yazd (IR490,000, 9 to 10 hours)

TAXI

Savaris leave from the appropriate bus terminals. For example, for Kashan and Esfahan they leave from near the southern entrance to Terminal-e Jonub (southern bus terminal). Just say your destination and 'savari' and you'll be pointed in the right direction.

TRAIN

Tehran's impressive **train station** (021-5149, 139; www.raja.ir; Rah-Ahan Sq; Rahahan) is at the south end of Valiasr Ave. Destinations and arrival and departure times are listed in English, and departures are punctual. Book tickets via a local travel agency, online at www.iranrail.net, or at the station itself. Destinations include the following:

Esfahan (6 bed IR350,000, 7½ hours)
Mashhad (4 bed/6 bed/seat IR800,000/500,000/400,000, 10 to 12 hours)
Tabriz (4 & 6 bed IR500,000, 12 hours)
Yazd (6 bed IR400,000, 6 to 8 hours)

Getting Around

TO/FROM THE AIRPORT

Metro Line 1 (red) between Imam Khomeini International Airport (IKIA) and the city is the cheapest and fastest route (IR7000, 30 to 55 minutes) into or out of Tehran. Otherwise take a taxi from IKIA for a set price of IR750,000.

BUS

Tehran has an extensive, if slow and crowded, local bus network, running roughly 6am to 10pm. Buy tickets from booths near bus stops or at bus terminals.

Bus Rapid Transport (BRT)

More useful than local buses is the BRT system of rapid buses along 10 routes with dedicated lanes. On most routes buses depart every two or three minutes. Tickets cost IR7000. Two lines are particularly useful to travellers:

Rah-Ahan (train station) to Tajrish Good for hops along Valiasr Ave up to **Tajrish bus station** (Map p146), but the traffic lights and bus bank ups at major stops mean it's less than rapid.

Azadi to Tehran Pars Links the centre of town with Azadi Sq in the west and, most usefully, Terminal-e Shargh (Eastern Bus Terminal).

METRO
The best way to get around is by **Tehran Metro** (http://metro.tehran.ir), which has transformed the way the city moves, cutting journey times by up to an hour on some cross-town trips. At the time of writing five lines were complete and another two under construction.

There are two main ways you can pay for tickets. Magnetic tickets cost single/two-trips IR7000/11,0000 between any two stations on the system. Better value and more convenient are stored value cards, which cost an initial IR50,000 including IR35,000 of travel credit.

TAXI
Motorcycle taxis loiter on major corners all over town and make an adrenalin-inducing way to get across town in a hurry. They cost as much as taxis but take half the time.

Private Taxi
If hailing a taxi, yellow and green cars are typically official private taxis. However, many locals use the app Snapp (https://snapp.ir) to arrange rides. Alternatively, get your hotel to call a **Wireless Taxi** (☎133) or call the **Women's Taxi Company** (☎1814), whose green taxis are for female passengers only. Agree on a price before getting in the vehicle. Most drivers won't go anywhere for less than IR100,000.

Shuttle Taxi
Shuttle taxis ply main thoroughfares between major meydans (squares).

WESTERN IRAN ایران غربی

Tabriz تبریز

☎041 / POP 1.6 MILLION / ELEV 1397M

A fascinating bazaar and the buzz of commerce and mingling ethnicities make this sprawling city a very positive introduction to Iran for overlanders. It had a spell as capital and has proven influential in the country's recent history, playing an important part in the constitutional revolution of the early 20th century and seeing major protests against both the Shah and post-Revolution regime. It can be freezing cold in winter, but the Azari welcome is warm any time of year.

Sights

★Tabriz Bazaar BAZAAR
(بازار تبریز; ⏲roughly 8am-9pm Sat-Thu) The magnificent, labyrinthine, Unesco-listed Tabriz bazaar covers some 7 sq km, with 24 caravanserais (sets of rooms arrranged around a courtyard) and 22 impressive *timches* (domed halls). Construction began over a millennium ago, though much of the fine brick vaulting dates to the 15th century. Hidden behind innocuous shopfronts, the open Ferdosi mall is a good entry point.

Shahriyar House Museum MUSEUM
(☎041-3555 8847; Maqsoudieh Alley, off Tabazan St; IR80,000; ⏲7.30am-7.30pm Sat-Thu, to 1pm Fri) Enter a time warp to late-'70s Tabriz in the preserved house of much-loved poet Ostad Shahriyar (1906–88). Surrounded by his everyday belongings, you almost expect the late poet to wander out of the bedroom. He is buried in the **Poets' Mausoleum**.

Blue Mosque MOSQUE
(Masjed-e Kabud, مسجد کبود; Imam Khomeini St; IR150,000; ⏲8am-5.30pm Sat-Thu) When constructed for ruler Jahan Shah in 1465, the Blue Mosque with its intricate turquoise mosaics was one of the most famous buildings of its era. Unfortunately, it was badly damaged in an earthquake in 1773, leaving only the main *iwan* (entrance hall) and Jahan Shah's tomb intact.

Azarbaijan Museum MUSEUM
(موزه آذربایجان; ☎041-3526 1696; Imam Khomeini St; IR200,000; ⏲8am-5.30pm Tue-Sun) This museum's entrance is a great brick portal with big wooden doors guarded by two stone rams. Ground-floor exhibits include finds from Hasanlu (an Iron Age town that developed into a citadel over 4000 years), a 3000-year-old copper helmet and curious stone 'handbags' from the 3rd millennium BC.

Activities

Mt Sahand TREKKING
(Kamal Dag) Mt Sahand (3707m) is the gigantic volcanic lump south of Tabriz; Kamal is its highest peak. Access is via Sahand Ski Resort, about 60km by road from downtown Tabriz. You should be able to see the summit from the resort: it's 5km and a 900m ascent along a well-defined ridge. BYO taxi.

Tours

Nasser Khan TOURS
(☎0914 116 0149; amicodelmondo@yahoo.com) A legendary polyglot pillar of the tourist-information office, Nasser often takes small groups on people-watching trips and cultural experiences including *zurkhaneh* (traditional body-building gyms).

Sleeping

There are free, well-equipped, guarded campsites near the university and in Elgoli Park.

Central Tabriz

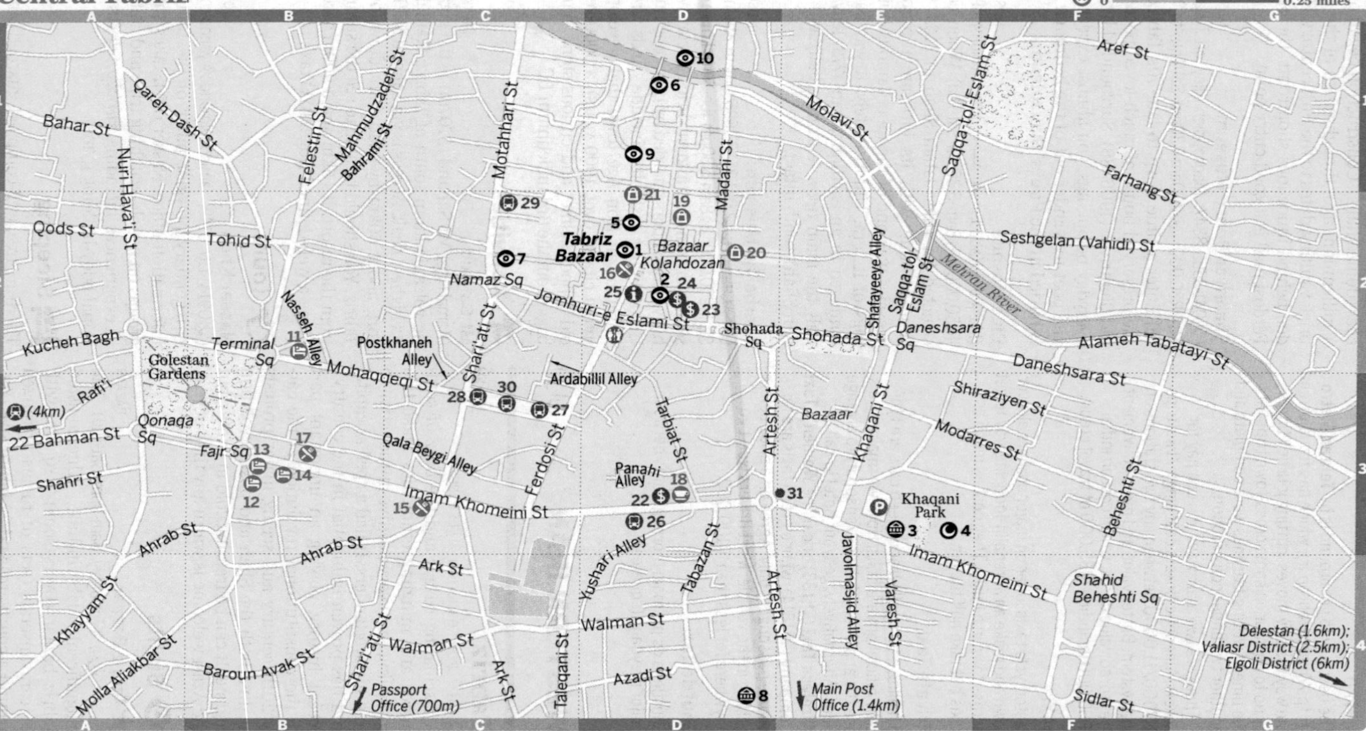

Central Tabriz

Top Sights
1 Tabriz Bazaar..D2

Sights
2 Amir Bazaar..D2
3 Azarbaijan Museum................................E3
4 Blue Mosque..E3
5 Carpet Bazaar..D2
6 Coppersmith Bazaar................................D1
7 Fruit Bazaar..C2
8 Shahriyar House Museum........................D4
9 Spice Bazaar..D1
10 Vegetable Bazaar....................................D1

Activities, Courses & Tours
Nasser Khan....................................(see 25)

Sleeping
11 Darya Guesthouse..................................B2
12 Hotel Sina..B3
13 Morvarid Hotel......................................B3
14 Ramsar Guesthouse................................B3

Eating
15 Emarat Restaurant..................................C3
16 Rahnama Dairy......................................D2
17 Tabriz Modern Restaurant........................B3

Drinking & Nightlife
18 Shahriar Restaurant................................D3

Shopping
19 Kolahdozan Bazaar..................................D2
20 Leather Market......................................D2
21 Small-Knot Carpet Bazaar........................D2

Information
22 Hitvan Hivan..D3
23 Mahmud Abidan Exchange........................D2
24 Ramin Exchange....................................D2
25 Tourist Information Office........................D2

Transport
26 Aram Safar..D3
27 City Bus 110..C3
28 City Bus 111..C3
29 City Bus 115..C2
City Bus 136....................................(see 29)
30 City Bus 160..C3
31 Meydan-e Sa'at......................................E3

Ramsar Guesthouse HOTEL $
(☎041-3551 2417; Imam Khomeini St; s/tw IR690,000/870,000;) Clean, simple rooms come in a range of sizes at this cheerful place. Cheaper rooms without bathroom are also available.

Darya Guesthouse GUESTHOUSE $
(☎041-3554 0008; www.darya-guesthouse.com; Mohaqqeqi St; s/tw/tr IR690,000/870,000/1,210,000;) A favourite budget-traveller's dosser, Darya has a variety of clean, basic, thin-walled rooms. It can be chaotic, but the friendly English-savvy owner pulls it all together. The rooms without bathroom are cheaper still. Don't confuse it with the totally unrelated Darya Hotel.

Hotel Sina HOTEL $$
(☎041-3551 6211; Fajr Sq; s/tw IR1,100,000/1,500,000;) Calm yet central, this relatively plush option has bright corridors with strip carpets over clean tiled floors. Rooms are neat and fully equipped. Enter from Felestin St. Parking is limited.

Morvarid Hotel HOTEL $$
(☎041-3551 3336; www.hotelmorvarid.com; Fajr Sq; s/tw/tr IR860,000/1,200,000/1,500,000;) Right on Fajr Sq, opposite Golestan Gardens, the historic, central Morvarid has been serving travellers for decades, with tidy rooms, dependable bathrooms and smiling service.

Pars Elgoli Hotel HOTEL $$$
(☎041-3380 7820; www.pars-hotels.com; Elgoli Park; s/d/ste US$81/118/217; ; Ⓜ Elgoli) Three convex walls of gleaming blue glass overlook the city's favourite park, 8km from the centre. It has everything you'd expect from a top business hotel, except for alcohol in the minibar beers. The atrium is airy and there's a **revolving restaurant** (meals IR250,000-500,000; ⏰7.30-11pm) on top. It's only a 500m dawdle from the Elgoli metro station.

Eating

Good street-food options include tasty potato-and-boiled-egg wraps.

Emarat Restaurant IRANIAN $
(Shari'ati St; meals IR190,000) Carpeted booths in a wide, airy space, English menus and a plaster waterfall complete with monkeys and goats complement the excellent traditional Iranian food here. Service is friendly.

Talar Bozorg Elgoli IRANIAN $
(☎041-3380 5263; Elgoli Park; meals US$5) Within Elgoli's mock Qajar palace, this busy, unpretentious family restaurant serves *Tabrizi köfte*, a local home-cooking speciality that's like a giant Scotch egg. Order ahead in winter. Weekends are crowded.

Rahnama Dairy SWEETS $
(Ferdosi St; snacks from IR30,000; ⏰7am-9pm Sat-Thu, to 2pm Fri) This simple dairy-cafe at the main bazaar entrance serves unbeatable breakfasts of *must-asal* (yogurt and honey) and *khame-asal* (cream and honeycomb).

Tabriz Modern Restaurant IRANIAN $$
(☎041-3556 3841; Imam Khomeini St; full-service meals IR240,000-400,000; ⊙noon-11pm; 📶) Go the excellent fried trout (IR270,000) at this friendly, rather ornate basement dining hall. Prices include 'full service': salad bar, *mast* (yogurt), soft drink and delicious barley-and-barberry soup. And, of course, there are kababs too.

Drinking & Nightlife

★**Shahriar Restaurant** TEAHOUSE
(Nobar Hammam; ☎041-3554 0057; Imam Khomeini St; chay IR50,000) There are several interesting rooms in this converted subterranean 19th-century bathhouse, though the *qalyan*-wafting *chaykhaneh* (teahouse) is the most exotic. The other, larger room, popular with groups, is a restaurant (meals from IR200,000) with tables and chairs as well as carpeted booths; it does very good *dizi* and kababs.

Radio Cafe CAFE
(☎0914 412 6645; Valiasr; coffee/cake from IR100,000/80,000; ⊙11am-11pm) The coffee's first class and the light meals are very moreish, but it's the red-velvet cake that really draws the crowds at weekends. It's at the western end of Valiasr, past the evil flyover.

Information

CONSULATES

Azerbaijani Consulate (https://evisa.gov.az; Aref St, Valiasr) Citizens of most countries can now get an e-visa (US$23, valid for 30 days) online in three working days.

Turkish Consulate (☎041-3327 1882; http://tebriz.bk.mfa.gov.tr; Homafar Sq, Valiasr; ⊙9.30am-noon Sun-Thu)

MONEY

Hitvan Hivan (Imam Khomeini St; ⊙8am-8pm Sat-Thu), near Tarbiat St, offers quick and easy exchanges.

Mahmud Abidan Exchange (araye Amir, Timche Amirno 11; ⊙9am-6pm Sat-Wed, to 3pm Thu) Good rates and no queue (but no sign).

Ramin Exchange (☎041-3526 2016; ramin.chalani@hotmail.co.uk; 69 Saraie Amir, Passage Farsh; ⊙9am-6pm Sat-Thu) Reliable exchange office with decent rates.

TOURIST INFORMATION

Tourist Information Office (☎041-3524 6235; www.tabriz.ir; Ferdosi St; ⊙9am-2pm & 4-7pm Sat-Thu) Nasser Khan has excellent free maps and is a mine of information on Tabriz and the surrounding area. He'll create bespoke tours to whatever you want to see.

VISA EXTENSIONS

Passport Office (☎041-3477 6666; Saeb St; ⊙8am-1.30pm Sat-Wed, to 11.30pm Thu) Visa extensions currently cost IR375,000. No English is spoken, and they may want you to pay with an Iranian credit card, so you might need to find an agreeable Iranian and pay them back.

Getting There & Away

AIR

İstanbul US$183, daily with **Turkish Airlines** (☎041-1329 6353; www.turkishairlines.com; 57 Nasim St, Valiasr; ⊙9am-5pm Sat-Wed, to 1pm Thu).

Tehran IR1,766,000, almost hourly between 7am and midnight with local airline **ATA** (www.ataair.ir) and at least daily with Caspian, Kish, **Iran Air** (☎041-3655 4002) and **Qeshm** (☎021-4764 0000; www.qeshm-air.com).

Mashhad IR1,880,000, daily with ATA and **Iran Air Tour** (☎021-8931 7711; www.iat.aero), Tuesday and Friday to Sunday with **Meraj** (Ascension; ☎021-63 266; http://merajairlines.ir/en) and Sunday with Iran Air.

Esfahan IR1,9250,000, Monday, Wednesday and Saturday with **Mahan Air** (www.mahan.aero).

BUS & TAXI

Most buses and savaris use the main bus terminal, 3km south of the centre.

Buses go to the following destinations:

Esfahan (IR520,000, 12 hours)
Qazvin (IR290,000, VIP; 6 hours)
Shiraz (IR950,000, 22 hours)
Tehran (IR330,000, VIP; 8 hours)

International Buses

Bus services to Yerevan (Armenia; US$48, 15 hours), and with **Aram Safar** (☎041-3556 0597; Imam Khomeini St) for İstanbul (Turkey; IR1,400,000, 30 hours) and Baku (Azerbaijan; IR800,000IR, 13 to 17 hours) all typically leave around 10pm from outside the relevant ticket offices on Imam Khomeini Ave.

Services sometimes leave from the train-station concourse, so double-check.

TRAIN

Overnight trains to Tehran (12 hours) depart at 4.40pm (from IR442,500) and 6pm (from IR372,500), running via Qazvin. There's also at least one daily train to Mashhad (IR920,000, 24 hours), leaving at 12.25pm, which could be used for Zanjan and Qazvin. The **train station** (☎041-3444 4419; Rahahan Sq) is 4.5km west of Farj Sq. Shuttle taxis and city bus 111 drop off at the junction of Mellat Blvd and 22 Bahman St.

The 8.20am local train to Jolfa (IR25,000, three hours) operates Tuesday, Thursday and Sunday.

The only international train service currently running is Tabriz to Nakhchivan twice a week.

Getting Around

TO/FROM THE AIRPORT

Tabriz International Airport Airport bus 136 runs from Motahhari St every 40 minutes. Taxis (with blue stripe) should cost IR60,000.

BUS

Pre-buy IR10,000 tickets. Useful routes from the major city-bus terminal include bus 160 to the main bus terminal and bus 110 to Valiasr. Several services run the length of 22 Bahman St (for the train station), including bus 111. Buses 136, to the airport, and 115, to the Marand terminal, leave from the western side of the bazaar.

METRO

Metro line 1 is open from Elgoli to Ostad Shahriar and will soon be extended to Sa'at Sq. See http://tabrizmetro.ir/ for updates.

SHUTTLE TAXI

A key route runs along Imam Khomeini St from Fajr Sq to Abresan Crossing (IR20,000) but on returning diverts onto Jomhuri-e Eslami St when passing the bazaar.

Kandovan کندوان

041 / POP 740 / ELEV 1575M

Channelling Turkey's Cappadocia and looking like the cover of a fantasy novel, Kandovan's curious troglodyte cliff dwellings have been carved into eroded volcanic lahar pillars. These cones sit above a newer, lower village, which has spread extensively around their base. Beat the incessant crowds by coming late in the day, when the light is soft and the rocks have a warm glow. The village has an admission fee of IR30,000. The area also has interesting hiking possibilities.

Sleeping & Eating

Non-troglodyte homes in the lower village offer **rooms**; these vary from US$3 to US$25 and differ wildly. Most are summer-only. Eateries cluster along the riverbank.

Jamshid HOMESTAY $

(041-3323 0016; r IR350,000) Has slightly tatty rooms but offers a hot-water shower and indoor squat toilet.

★Kandovan Laleh Rocky Hotel BOUTIQUE HOTEL $$$

(041-3323 0191; http://kandovan.lalehhotels.com; r without/with Jacuzzi US$118/145, ste US$188-252; P) The Laleh's 10 remarkable rooms have been carved out of 'fairy chimney' rock knolls. Inside they're luxurious affairs, with stylish lighting, underfloor heating and (in many) Jacuzzis.

Getting There & Away

Minibuses from central Tabriz run regularly to Osku (IR30,000, 50 minutes) till around 6pm. From Osku to Kandovan (25km) taxis charge US$10 return, plus US$3 per hour of waiting time. Minibuses are extremely rare. A private taxi from Tabriz to Kandovan costs around US$22 return.

Qazvin قزوین

028 / POP 395,000 / ELEV 1301M

Qazvin is a pleasant city with a wonderfully restored caravanserai-turned-arts precinct, some quirky museums and a handful of decent eating options. Famed for carpets and seedless grapes, it was once the capital of all Iran, but for most foreign travellers it's primarily the staging point for excursions to the famous Castles of the Assassins and trekking in the sensational Alamut Valley. The city centre is Azadi Sq, widely known as Sabz Meydan.

Sights

★Sa'd-al Saltaneh Caravanserai BAZAAR

(8am-10pm) This huge, beautifully restored Qajar-era caravanserai is the design centre of Qazvin. The long, vaulted passages house independent artists showcasing exquisitely crafted wares, as well as galleries, coffee shops, restaurants and quiet, hidden courtyards perfect for relaxing.

Anthroplogy Museum MUSEUM

(Qajar Bath; 028-3323 3155; Obeyd-e Zarani St; IR50,000; 8am-6pm) In a beautifully restored subterranean bathhouse dating from the Sassanian period, lifelike mannequins document the cultural traditions of the province.

Activities

Mehdi Babayi HIKING

(0912 682 3228) Mehdi Babayi is an experienced trekking and climbing guide and driver who, despite his advancing years, displays an enviable level of fitness.

Safa Hammam BATHHOUSE

(Molavi St, at Taqavi Alley; bath IR50,000; 7am-7pm Sat-Thu, to 2pm Fri) Safa Hammam is the best known of Qazvin's traditional subterranean bathhouses to remain active. The domed central rest area is attractive.

Tours

All accommodation options can book Alamut Valley tours, best started early in the morning. The **Nakhajir Camping Shop** (028-3222 4551; Ferdosi St; 8am-1pm & 4-9pm Sat-Thu) is good for outdoor supplies.

★**Yousef Shariyat** TOURS
(☎0919 180 7076; yousef.sh.khoo@gmail.com; day trip with 2/3/4 passengers $US60/70/80) Yousef's in-depth knowledge of the Alamut Valley, excellent English, intelligent, eclectic conversation and safe, relaxed driving make him the first choice for guided day trips in the region.

Sleeping

Some English is spoken at the following hotels and staff can organise Alamut trips.

Mosaferkhaneh Abrisham MOSAFERKHANEH $
(Abrisham Guesthouse; ☎028-3357 8181; Molavi St, off Montazeri Sq; tw/tr without bathroom IR610,000/800,000; ❄📶) This friendly guesthouse offers clean, budget-savvy rooms with shared bathrooms above a supermarket.

Taleghani Inn HOSTEL $
(☎028-3322 4239; Khaleqi Alley, off Taleqani St; d IR600,000; 📶) Safe, cheap and central, this renovated guesthouse up an alley (the one past Yas Alley) presents basic, clean rooms.

Alborz Hotel BUSINESS HOTEL $$
(☎028-3323 6631; info@alborzhotel.com; Talegani St; tw US$60; P❄@📶) It's in a great central location, but the clean, comfortable rooms are fairly expensive given that the hallways are worn out and the wi-fi's patchy (it works best in the coffee shop).

Behrouzi Traditional Hotel HISTORIC HOTEL $$$
(Khane Sonatti Behrouzi; Ashgari Lane; s/d/tr $US48/95/145; 📶) You'll never want to leave this exquisitely restored Qajar-era traditional house, right in the centre of the old town. The rooms, graceful yet sumptuous, are arranged around a central courtyard. There's also a fantastic private *hammam*. It's the perfect après-trek reward.

Eating

Sib Restaurant IRANIAN $$
(Sa'd-al Saltaneh caravanserai; meals IR250,000; ⏲11am-10pm) Come to this bright new place in a hidden courtyard towards the back of Sa'd-al Saltaneh caravanserai for the airy ambience and the tasty Persian favourites.

Nemooneh IRANIAN $$
(☎028-3332 8448; cnr Buali & Ferdosi Sts; meals from IR280,000; ⏲noon-3.30pm & 7-10.30pm; ❄) Locals rate this the best feed in Qazvin, and it's hard to argue. The handy picture menu helps visitors explore beyond kababs and try some Iranian specialties, such as *khoresht fesenjan* (chicken and walnut stew) or the succulent butter-fried salmon.

Drinking & Nightlife

★**Negarossaltaneh** CAFE
(34 Vazir Bazaar; coffee & snacks from IR50,000; ⏲10am-10pm Sat-Thu, 5-10pm Fri) Deep within the Sa'd-al Saltaneh caravanserai is this favourite. An English menu reveals heart-starting espressos and lattes, exotic teas and trippy herbal concoctions, deliciously wicked petit fours and even breakfast eggs, all in a relaxing, intimate space.

Cafe Voraza CAFE
(☎028-3333 3001; http://coffeeshopvozara.com/; Khayyam St, cnr Adl Blvd; ⏲10am-late) Locals and tourists alike cram this tiny hole-in-the-wall cafe at the northern end of Khayyam St for its eclectic range of coffees (included iced), cakes and ice creams (the chocolate ice-cream cake is the best!).

Information

Tourist Information (☎028-3335 4708; http://qazvin.ir; Naderi St; ⏲9am-6pm) The helpful staff at this office facing the historic Darbe Khoushk Gate dispense great free maps and useful brochures and are only too happy to design a walking tour taking in all the major sights.

Tourist Information Booth (☎0912 282 9049; www.qazvin.ir; Sa'd-al Saltaneh caravanserai; ⏲theoretically 8am-12.30pm & 5-7pm Sat-Thu) Should you find it open, you might be able to grab a map or two from this office at the Imam St entrance to the Sa'd-al Saltaneh caravanserai.

Getting There & Away

BUS, MINIBUS & TAXI

A number of handy services run from the **main bus terminal** (Darvazeh Sq), which has a **Golden ticket agent** (☎028-3356 1117; www.safartalaei.ir; Main Bus Terminal).

Official Tehran savaris (IR200,000) leave from the front car park. Unofficial ones pick up at Valiasr Sq. Mo'allem Kalayeh savaris (US$10, 1¾ hours) depart from Qarib Kosh (Minudar) Sq, with the gigantic Silk Road monument, 3km east of Valiasr Sq.

TRAIN

The best-timed trains to Tehran (IR50,000, 2½ hours) depart at 8am and 9.56am. Sleeper trains run to Tabriz at 7.53pm (IR352,000, 11 hours) and to Mashhad (IR1,012,000, 14 hours) at 8pm; book them early if you can.

Getting Around

For the bus terminal, change shuttle taxi at Valiasr Sq. From the terminal to Azadi Sq loop around via the bazaar. Dar bast (private hire) anywhere inside the ring road will cost IR50,000.

Alamut Valley الموت

ELEV 1400M

Few places in Iran offer a more tempting invitation to hike, explore and reflect than the fabled Alamut Valley. Beneath soaring Alborz peaks, the inspiring landscapes are delightfully varied and spiced by a fascinating medieval history: the ruined fortresses dotting the valley were home to the feared medieval religious cult of the Assassins.

Taking a tour, or savaris plus taxis, it's possible to visit Alamut Castle (the best of the fortresses) and other attractions in a long day from Qazvin. But it's much more fun to take your time, staying at Gazor Khan and doing some hiking.

Mo'allem Kalayeh & Around معلم كلايه

☎028 / POP 3420 / ELEV 1652M

Sometimes called Alamut town, Mo'allem Kalayeh is the Alamut Valley's one-street district centre. It's a useful transport staging post for the region and has two of the valley's popular sights nearby.

Sights

Andej CANYON

(اندج) The 8km road spur to Andej (elevation 1587m) passes alongside three truly awesome red-rock side canyons, where you can cross the river on a rickety bridge and explore. The turnoff is just northwest of Shahrak, which has a prominent (but not assassin-related) castle ruin. After the canyons, fork left up the hill in Andej village and double back around towards Mo'allem for a magnificent perspective from above.

Evan Lake LAKE

(Ovan Lake; دریاچه اوان; IR50,000) This small mountain lake is accessed via a side road between Razmiyan and Mo'allem. It's a pretty spot with a mountain backdrop, though the views are marred by power lines.

Sleeping

Campground CAMPGROUND $

(Caravanserai) On the right as you first enter Mo'allem Kalayeh you'll see the raised concrete tent sites of this campground.

Haddodi Restaurant APARTMENT $

(☎028-3321 6362, 0936 457 7241; tw IR800,000) Haddodi Restaurant, on the main street 50m east of the eagle statue, offers several twin rooms and a couple of larger apartments. Meals are available but not included in rates.

Getting There & Away

Rare buses and savaris loiter in the town centre, 650m east of the eagle statue. Savaris to Qazvin (IR400,000) are an hour quicker than the dreadfully slow bus (IR100,000, daily except Friday) that departs once feeder buses from outlying villages have arrived. For Gazor Khan, taxi charters cost IR250,000, or IR400,000 including a side trip to Andej. Or take the returning school bus (school days only, IR50,000, 45 minutes) around 11.45am.

Gazor Khan گازرخان

☎028 / ELEV 2062M

The pleasant, unpretentious little cherry-growing village of Gazor Khan goes about its business under the crag-top ruined castle that is the valley's major sight.

OFF THE BEATEN TRACK

TREKKING TOWARDS THE CASPIAN

Crossing the Alborz on foot from the Alamut Valley to the Caspian hinterland is scenically stunning and culturally fascinating. A road now covers the three-day route below but it still makes a good hike.

Start in pretty, canyon-framed **Garmarud**, 18km east of the Gazor Khan turning, then go via picturesque **Pichebon hamlet** and across 3200m **Salambar Pass** beside a small, partly renovated **caravanserai**. It's a slow descent to Salajanbar. Scenic **Maran** is next, then it's another downhill to pretty **Yuj** among flower-filled meadows.

You can camp anywhere, but if you're near a village, always ask permission. Pichebon has especially attractive soft, grassy meadows, and there are homestays in Maran and Yuj. While it's best to bring all your own food, there are simple grocery shops in the villages along the route.

It's worth asking the advice of a tour company such as recommended **Caspian Trek** (Farzin Malaki; ☎0911 291 0700; www.caspiantrek.com) for route advice.

Sights & Activities

Several tempting mountain **hikes** start in Gazor Khan or Khoshkchal village, a steep, 15-minute 4WD ride beyond. Accommodation options can give route advice.

Alamut Castle RUINS
(قلعه الموت; IR150,000; dawn-dusk; P) The region's greatest attraction is the fabled ruin of Alamut Castle, Hasan-e Sabbah's famous fortress. The site is a dramatic crag rising abruptly above Gazor Khan. The access path starts about 700m beyond the village square and requires a steep 25-minute climb via an obvious stairway. The archaeological workings on top are shielded by somewhat unsightly corrugated-metal sheeting, but the phenomenal views from the ramparts are unmissable.

Sleeping

Hotel Farhangian HOTEL $
(028-3377 3446; ste IR600,000) A converted school, the Farhangian has reasonably well-equipped though not luxurious 'suites' with kitchen and bathroom. Get the Qazvin tourist information office (p154) to make a booking for you. There's no English sign, but it's tucked behind the Alamut Research Centre, up a short driveway that heads south from the castle trailhead. Bring your own food.

Getting There & Away

To Qazvin a taxi is likely to cost anything from IR400,000 (2½ hours), or you can take the school bus to Mo'allem Kalayeh (school days only, IR50,000, 45 minutes) and try your luck from there. Both leave from the village square at 7am.

CENTRAL IRAN ایران مرکزی

Kashan

Many travellers opt to bypass Kashan on their journeys between Tehran, Esfahan and Yazd, but this oasis city on the edge of the Dasht-e Kavir is one of Iran's most alluring destinations. It not only boasts a cluster of architectural wonders, an atmospheric covered **bazaar** (بازار; 9am-noon & 4.30-8pm Sat-Thu) and a Unesco-recognised garden, but it also offers some of central Iran's best traditional hotels.

History

During the Seljuk period (AD 1051–1220) Kashan became famous for its textiles, pottery and tiles, reaching high levels of accomplishment in each of these cottage industries. Today the town is more widely known as a major centre for the production of rose water, which is sold at outlets around the main tourist attractions and at dedicated stores in the bazaar.

Sights

Most of Kashan's sights are located in the old quarter, clustered around Alavi St and within walking distance of the bazaar.

★ **Khan-e Boroujerdi** HISTORIC BUILDING
(خانه بروجردی ها; off Alavi St; US$0.50; 8am-sunset) Legend has it that when Sayyed Jafar Natanzi, a samovar merchant known as Boroujerdi, met with carpet merchant Sayyed Jafar Tabatabaei to discuss taking his daughter's hand in marriage, Mr Tabatabaei set one condition: his daughter must be able to live in a home at least as lovely as his own. The result – finished some 18 years later – was the Khan-e Boroujerdi. Made distinctive by its six-sided, domed *badgirs* (wind towers), the house boasts frescoes painted by Kamal al-Molk, the foremost Iranian artist of the time.

The neighbouring **Khan-e Tabatabaei** (خانه طباطبایی; 031-5422 0032; off Alavi St; ,IR350,000; 8am-sunset) is also worth a visit.

★ **Bagh-e Fin** GARDENS
(باغ تاریخی فین, Fin Garden; Amir Kabir Rd; garden IR200,000, museum IR80,000; 9am-sunset) Designed for Shah Abbas I in the 16th century, this delightful garden with its old cedars, spring-fed pools and fountains is renowned as being the very epitome of the Persian garden and its evocation of heaven. Given its influence in the planning of gardens as far afield as India and Spain, Fin Garden, which lies in the suburb of Fin, 9km southwest of central Kashan, has justly earned a place on the Unesco World Heritage list.

Hammam-e Sultan Mir Ahmad HISTORIC BUILDING
(حمام سلطان میراحمد; off Alavi St; IR150,000; 8am-5pm, to 7pm summer) This 500-year-old *hammam* is a superb example of an Iranian bathhouse. A recent restoration has stripped away 17 layers of plaster (note the wall inside the second room) to reveal the original *sarough*, a type of plaster made of milk, egg white, soy flour and lime that is said to be stronger than cement.

Tours

Kashan has several licensed driver-guides who specialise in bringing the old quarter and city environs to life for visitors. Most also cover half-day trips to pretty mountain villages such as famed **Abyaneh**. Their rates, which are largely set by government agencies, tend to be around US$30 for a half-day tour and US$50 for a full-day tour.

★Mostafa Ramezanpoor HISTORY
(☎0913 039 9198; m.ramezanpoor@yahoo.com; half-/full-day tour US$30/50) This excellent licensed guide is a mine of information, not just about his home town of Kashan, but of the entire central region of Iran.

Sleeping

Renovated townhouses and mansions, with stained-glass windows, water features and elaborate plaster work, number among some of Iran's most delightful places to stay and there are options to fit all budgets. Book ahead in high season.

Ehsan Historical Guest House HOTEL $
(☎031-5545 3030; www.ehsanhouse.com; off Fazel-e Navaghi St; d/tr IR2,106,600/2,700,000, without bathroom IR1,500,000/1,800,000; ❄@📶) Rooms come in many shapes in this traditional house, one of the first of its kind in Kashan. Most are arranged around a pretty courtyard with a large decorative pool – a good setting for dinner (meals around IR200,000). The hotel uses profits to help fund its NGO, which promotes the arts and is linked with the neighbouring Taj House Art Gallery.

★Manouchehri House HOTEL $$
(☎031-5524 2617; www.manouchehrihouse.com; 49 7th Emerat Alley, off Sabat Alley & Mohtasham St; d/tr/q from IR2,650,000/3,500,000/4,700,000 ; ❄@📶) Opened in 2011 after a three-year restoration project, this traditional house is a joy to behold with a stunning central courtyard featuring an *iwan* overlooking a huge decorative pool. The hotel has nine comfortable rooms, the amenities are excellent (restaurant, in-house cinema) and the service is exemplary. Book well in advance at this Kashan favourite.

★Saraye Ameriha Boutique Hotel BOUTIQUE HOTEL $$$
(خانه عامری ها; ☎031-5524 0220; www.sarayeameriha.com; Alavi St; s/d/ste US$82/115/180; ⏲9am-6pm; ❄@📶) This is the jewel in the crown of Kashan's accommodation. Set within the most impressive of Kashan's restored mansions, guests dine under a twinkling dome of mirrors, sip tea to the sound of splashing fountains, soak in a tub the size of a fish pond and wake up to coloured light dancing on luxury linen.

KASHANI TEXTILE

Kashan has been an important centre for textile production since the Safavid era and students from Tehran are posted here to study at a dedicated textile **Handicraft Workshop** (Kargahe Sanaye Daste; Alavi St; ⏲8am-2pm Sat-Wed) FREE. It's possible to visit the working looms with their hanging bags weighing down the colourful strands of the warp and the weft. Manouchehri House is contributing to the preservation of age-old skills through their support of local artisans. Nonguests can visit the hotel's shop where it's possible to purchase handwoven silk fabric.

Eating & Drinking

In summer, locals promenade around Fin Rd, pausing for kababs and *chay* in the restaurants near Bagh-e Fin; in winter, people congregate in the covered alleyways of the bazaar and various teahouses lure the shoppers in from the cold.

Abbasi Teahouse & Traditional Restaurant IRANIAN $$
(Khan-e Abbasian, off Alavi St; meals IR200,000; ⏲11am-midnight) Occupying the basement *khadameh* of the Khan-e Abbasian, this family-run restaurant is justly popular with visitors. Traditional seating is arranged around a fountain and the menu features equally traditional dishes, including *dizi*.

★Mirrors Restaurant IRANIAN $$$
(Saraye Ameriha Boutique Hotel Restaurant; ☎031-5524 0220; www.sarayeameriha.com; Alavi St; mains IR450,000; ⏲noon-3.30pm & 7-11pm) It is worth dining in this fabulous little restaurant for the sheer pleasure of sitting in pools of coloured light by day and under a canopy of mirrored stars at night. Ask for the daily stew and relax in the company of Kashanis enjoying a special occasion.

Getting There & Away

BUS

The main **Kashan bus terminal** (off Persian Gulf Blvd) is on the northern edge of the city. Buses from this terminal leave regularly to Tehran (VIP IR160,000, 3½ hours) via Qom (IR100,000, 1¼ hours), to Esfahan (VIP/*mahmooly* IR115,000/80,000, 2½ hours) and to Shiraz (VIP IR450,000, 10 hours).

PERSIAN GARDENS

A group of Iranian gardens, several in Central Iran, are on the World Heritage list as the best existing examples of the classic Persian Garden form. Traditionally conceived to symbolise Paradise, these gardens are divided into four sections symbolising the Zoroastrian elements of sky, earth, water and plants. With fine examples in Kashan, Esfahan and Yazd, the earliest gardens date from the 6th century BC.

The bus from Yazd does not enter Kashan – alight at the highway; taxis (IR80,000) wait at the junction to ferry passengers into town.

Buses depart from the terminal; boarding is also possible at Montazeri Sq (buy a ticket on the bus or purchase in advance).

TRAIN

The **train station** (end of Ayatollah Yasrebi St) is about 2km northeast of the city centre and a taxi into town costs around IR80,000. There are four trains a day between Kashan and Tehran (IR165,000, 3½ hours) between 2pm and 7pm. There are also daily trains to Esfahan (IR220,000, 4½ hours).

Getting Around

A *dar bast* taxi within town usually costs IR100,000. From Kashan bus terminal it costs IR160,000 (IR20,000 extra at night).

Esfahan اصفهان

031 / POP 1,760,000 / ELEV 1571M

Esfahan is Iran's top tourist destination for good reason. Its profusion of tree-lined boulevards, Persian gardens and important Islamic buildings gives it a visual appeal unmatched by any other Iranian city, and the many artisans working here underpin its reputation as a living museum of traditional culture. Walking through the historic bazaar, over the picturesque bridges and across the Unesco-listed central square are sure to be highlights of a holiday.

History

The Buyid period saw an explosion of construction here, then in 1047 the Seljuks made Esfahan their capital. The Mongols put an end to that; it wasn't until the Safavids that Esfahan once again became Iran's premier city. Taking the throne in 1587, Shah Abbas I transformed it into a city worthy of an empire.

Sights

Most sites are within easy walking distance of the main street, tree-lined Chahar Bagh (Four Gardens). Built in 1597 the street was once lined with many palaces and the four gardens after which it is named. Although it's over 5km long, the middle section of the street, called Chahar Bagh Abbasi St, between **Si-o-Seh Pol** (Si-o-Seh Bridge) and Takhti Junction, is close to the bazaar and offers opportunities to stroll along nearby Zayandeh River with its series of historic **bridges** (پلهای زاینده رود).

★Naqsh-e Jahan (Imam) Square SQUARE
(میدان نقش جهان)میدان امام); horse-drawn carriage ride IR80,000, up to 3 people) Hemmed in on four sides by architectural gems and embracing the formal fountains and gardens at its centre, this wondrous space is a spectacle in its own right. It was laid out in 1602 under the reign of the Safavid ruler, Shah Abbas the Great, to signal the importance of Esfahan as a capital of a powerful empire. Cross the square on a clear winter's day and it's a hard heart that isn't entranced by its beauty.

★Masjed-e Shah MOSQUE
(مسجد امام; Masjed-e Imam; Naqsh-e Jahan (Imam) Sq; IR200,000; ⏲9-11.30am & 1-4.15pm Sat-Thu, 1-4.15pm Fri) This elegant mosque, with its iconic blue-tiled mosaics and its perfect proportions, forms a visually stunning monument at the head of Esfahan's main square. Unblemished since its construction 400 years ago, it stands as a monument to the vision of Shah Abbas I and the accomplishments of the Safavid dynasty. The mosque's crowning dome was completed in 1629, the last year of the reign of Shah Abbas.

★Masjed-e Jameh MOSQUE
(مسجد جامع; Allameh Majlesi St; IR200,000; ⏲9-11am & 1.15-4.30pm) The Jameh complex is a veritable museum of Islamic architecture while still functioning as a place of worship. Showcasing the best that nine centuries of artistic and religious endeavour has achieved, from the geometric elegance of the Seljuks to the more florid refinements of the Safavid era, a visit repays time spent examining the details. Covering more than 20,000 sq metres, this is the biggest mosque in Iran.

★Bazar-e Bozorg BAZAAR
(بازار بزرگ; ⏲around 9am-8pm Sat-Thu) One of Iran's most historic and fascinating bazaars, this sprawling covered market links Naqsh-e Jahan (Imam) Sq with the Masjed-e Jameh. At its busiest in the mornings, the bazaar's

arched passageways are topped by a series of small perforated domes, each spilling shafts of light onto the commerce below. While the oldest parts of the bazaar are more than a thousand years old, most of what can be seen today was built during Shah Abbas' ambitious expansions of the early 1600s. The main entrance is via the Qeysarieh Portal at the northern end of Naqsh-e Jahan (Imam) Sq.

Kakh-e Chehel Sotun PALACE

(کاخ چهلستون, Chehel Sotun Palace; Ostandari St; IR200,000; ⊙9am-4pm) Built as a pleasure pavilion and reception hall, using the Achaemenid-inspired *talar* (columnar porch) style, this beautifully proportioned palace is entered via a terrace that perfectly bridges the transition between the Persian love of gardens and interior splendour. The 20 slender, ribbed wooden pillars of the palace rise to a superb wooden ceiling with exquisite inlay work.

Masjed-e Sheikh Lotfollah MOSQUE

(مسجد شيخ لطف الله, Sheikh Lotfollah Mosque; Naqsh-e Jahan (Imam) Sq; IR200,000; ⊙9-11.30am & 1-4pm 22 Sep-21 Mar, 9am-12.30pm & 2-6pm 22 Mar-21 Sep) Punctuating the middle of the arcades that hem Esfahan's largest square, this study in harmonious understatement complements the overwhelming richness of the larger mosque, Masjed-e Shah, at the head of the square. Built between 1602 and 1619 during the reign of Shah Abbas I, it was dedicated to the ruler's father-in-law, Sheikh Lotfollah, a revered Lebanese scholar of Islam who was invited to Esfahan to oversee the king's mosque (now the Masjed-e Shah) and theological school.

Kakh-e Ali Qapu PALACE

(کاخ عالی قاپو, Ali Qapu Palace; Naqsh-e Jahan Sq; admission IR200,000, audio tour IR15,000; ⊙9am-4pm winter, to 6pm summer) Built at the very end of the 16th century as a residence for Shah Abbas I, this six-storey palace also served as a monumental gateway to the royal palaces that lay in the parklands beyond (Ali Qapu means 'Gate of Ali'). Named after Abbas' hero, the Imam Ali, it was built to make an impression, and at six storeys and 38m tall, with its impressive elevated terrace featuring 18 slender columns, it dominates one side of Naqsh-e Jahan (Imam) Sq.

Activities

★Nazhvan Cultural & Recreational Resort PARK

(Nazhvan Park; ☎031-3784 0034; www.nazhvan-park.ir; free park admission, average IR180,000 per attraction; discount for child under 5yr; ⊙8am-sunset) FREE This park on the outskirts of Esfahan encompasses a large complex of attractions that makes a pleasant contrast to Esfahan's intense city experience. The park includes the Birds Garden (IR180,000), the Esfahan Aquarium (IR500,000), a Sea Shell Museum (IR150,000), a Reptile House (IR150,000) and a Butterfly Collection (IR80,000). Each attraction is charged separately and there is no combined ticket.

WORTH A TRIP

JOLFA

The Armenian quarter of Esfahan dates from the time of Shah Abbas I, who transported a colony of Christians from the town of Jolfa (now on Iran's northern border) en masse, and named the village 'New Jolfa'. Abbas sought their skills as merchants, entrepreneurs and artists and he ensured that their religious freedom was respected – albeit at a distance from the city's Islamic centre. At one time over 42,000 Armenian Christians lived here and there are a number of historic churches and museums (including the delightful **Isfahan Music Museum** (☎031-3625 6912; www.isfahanmusicmuseum.com; Mehrdad St (Shahid Ghandi); IR300,000; ⊙9am-1pm & 3.30-9pm)) to explore, crowned by the beautiful **Kelisa-ye Vank** (کلیسای وانک, Vank Cathedral, Church of St Joseph of Arimathea; Kelisa St; IR200,000; ⊙8.30am-5.30pm Sat-Thu, to 12.30pm Fri); this cathedral, with its sumptuously painted interior, continues as a focal point of the Armenian Church in Iran.

There's more to Jolfa than its religious relics, however. With boutiques, cafes (such as **Marseille** (☎031-3628 0252; Kalissa St; coffee IR200,000; ⊙9.30am-2pm & 5-11pm Sat-Thu) and **Sharbat Khan** (Sour Orange Cafe; ☎031-3627 5269; Kalissa St, off Hakim Nezami Ave, opposite Julfa Hotel; ⊙8am-10pm)) and fashionable restaurants (including **Arc A** (☎031-3629 0920; Vank Church Alley, Kalissa St; mains IR450,000; ⊙9am-midnight) and the romantic **Romanos** (☎031-3624 0094; off Jolfa Sq; mains IR250,000; ⊙11am-midnight; 📶) located in an old bathouse), it's easy to spend a day pottering in and around delightful little Jolfa Square enjoying the sophisticated ambience of this tree-lined enclave.

Central Esfahan

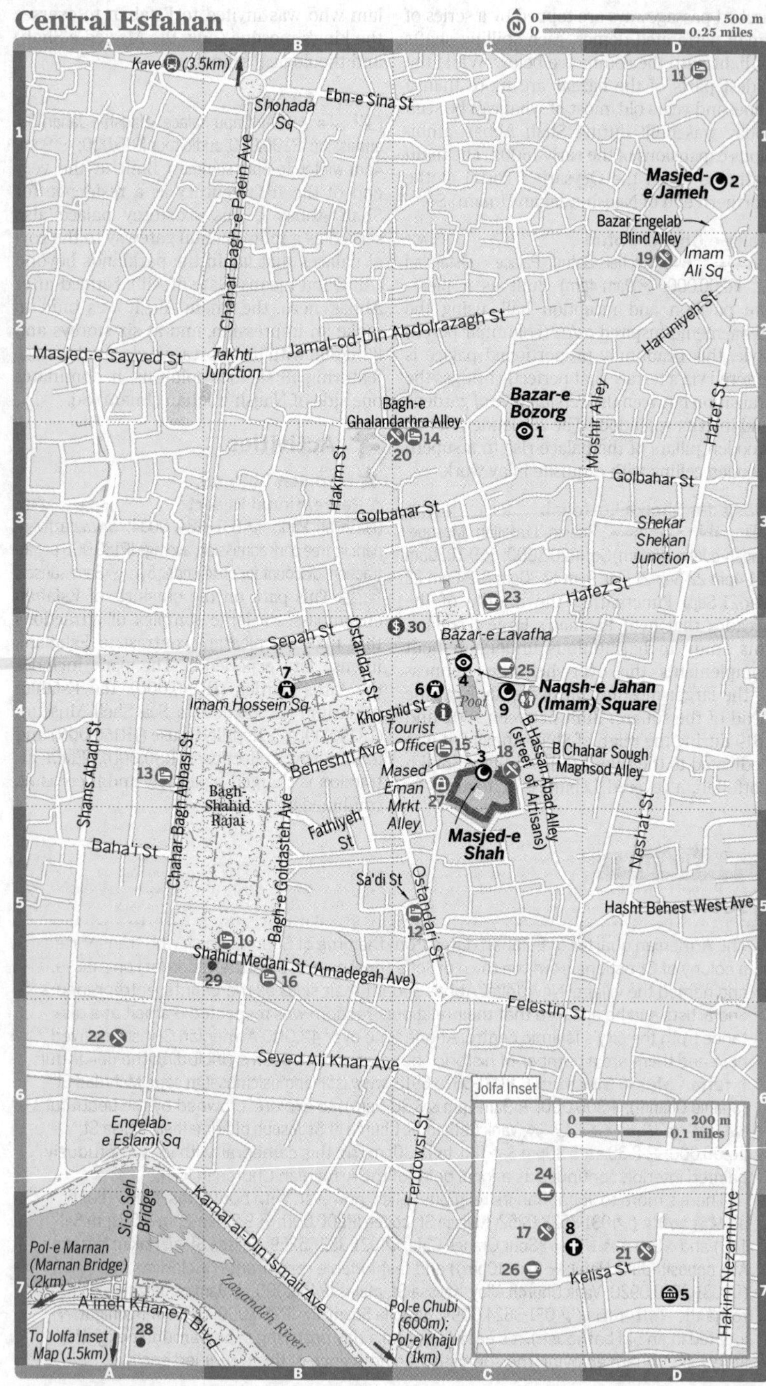

Central Esfahan

Top Sights
1 Bazar-e Bozorg ... C3
2 Masjed-e Jameh ... D1
3 Masjed-e Shah ... C4
4 Naqsh-e Jahan (Imam) Square ... C4

Sights
5 Isfahan Music Museum ... D7
6 Kakh-e Ali Qapu ... C4
7 Kakh-e Chehel Sotun ... B4
8 Kelisa-ye Vank ... C7
9 Masjed-e Sheikh Lotfollah ... C4

Sleeping
10 Abbasi Hotel ... B5
11 Ebnesina Traditional Hotel ... D1
12 Hasht Behesht Apartment Hotel ... C5
13 Iran Hotel ... A4
14 Isfahan Traditional Hotel ... C3
15 Jaam Firouzeh Hotel ... C4
16 Safir Hotel ... B5

Eating
Abbasi Teahouse & Traditional Restaurant ... (see 10)
17 Arc A ... C7
18 Bastani Traditional Restaurant ... C4
Chehel Sotun Restaurant ... (see 10)
19 Haj Mahmood Beryani ... D2
20 Malek Soltan Jarchi Bashi ... C3
21 Romanos ... D7
22 Shahrzad ... A6

Drinking & Nightlife
23 Azadegan Teahouse ... C3
24 Marseille Cafe ... C6
25 Roozegar ... C4
26 Sharbat Khan Bahar Nareng ... C7

Shopping
27 Hossein Fallahi ... C4
Paradise Handicrafts ... (see 6)

Information
28 Donyaye Parvaz Tour & Travel Agency ... A7
29 Iran Travel & Tourism ... B5
30 Jahan-e Arz Money Changer ... C4

Tours

We Go Persia OUTDOORS
(☎0903 209 7700; www.wegopersia.com) Guide and tour operator Mojtaba Salsali knows Esfahan like the back of his hand and revels in uncovering the hidden secrets of the city for his guests.

Maryam Nekoie OUTDOORS
An English teacher with over 10 years of experience in guiding. Specialises in walking tours of Esfahan.

Sleeping

Finding decent and affordable accommodation in Esfahan can be difficult, especially from mid-March until the end of August. Booking ahead is essential at that time and advisable year-round. Low-season discounts of 20% are common.

★Iran Hotel HOTEL $
(☎031-3220 2740; www.iranhotel.biz; Chahar Bagh Abbasi St; s/d/tr/q US$26/42/54/66; ❄📶) On a quiet lane in an excellent location, this modest hotel with its stylish foyer offers comfortable rooms with low beds, Persian rugs and a fridge. The welcoming, helpful, English-speaking management make this a top choice.

★Hasht Behesht Apartment Hotel APARTMENT $$
(☎031-3221 4869; www.hbahotel.com; cnr Ostandari St & Aghili Alley; d/tr/q apt US$54/69/84; ❄📶) It may be a bit short on style, but the centrally located Hasht Behesht, run by a delightful family, is one of the best accommodation options in town, offering clean and well-maintained apartments with comfortable beds, equipped kitchenettes and satellite TV. Enter off Aghili Alley. Transfers from the airport are available and there's a ticket-booking service. Breakfast available for IR200,000.

★Isfahan Traditional Hotel HOTEL $$
(Samaeian Historical House; ☎031-3223 6677; www.ethotel.ir; Bagh-e Ghalandarhra Alley, off Hakim St; s/d/tr IR1,530,000/2,610,000/4,250,000; ❄📶✖) Located in the bazaar near the ancient Masjed-e Hakim (Hakim Mosque), this hotel is set around two courtyards in adjoining Safavid- and Qajar-period homes. The characterful rooms are clean and comfortable, with satellite TV and private modern bathrooms. The cavernous restaurant here is a popular lunch spot with tour groups.

Ebnesina Traditional Hotel TRADITIONAL HOUSE $$
(☎0913 408 2557; hoseinomidzad@gmail.com; off Ebnesina St, behind Masjed-e Jameh; d/tr IR1,950,000/2,550,000) This lovely old house,

IRAN'S NOMADS

Despite 20th-century resettlement programs, there are still about a million people living as nomads in Iran. They are mostly Turkic Qashqa'i and Bakhtiyari, but there are also Kurds, Lors, Baluchis and smaller groups. To visit them it's best to go with a specialist guide from Esfahan or Shiraz.

with a dazzling set of murals in the foyer and copious mirror work, is something of a treat in a city lacking in characterful accommodation. With good views from the rooftop coffee shop (open in summer), the 60 rooms each sport a hand-painted door with roses and paisley patterns. Management is friendly, though not much English is spoken.

Jaam Firouzeh Hotel HOTEL $$
(☎031-3224 5215; www.firouzehhotel.com; Saadi St, off Ostandari St, near Naqsh-e Jahan (Imam) Sq; d/tr US$50/65) If this hotel was any closer to Esfahan's iconic square, guests would be taking up residence in Ali Qapu Palace. Aside from the perfect location, this new hotel offers friendly service, a stylish seating area in the foyer and spotless rooms. A minor downside is the absence of views – the windows are very small and some have no windows at all.

Safir Hotel HOTEL $$
(☎031-3222 2640; www.safirhotel.net; Shahid Medani St; r from US$120; P❄@📶🏊) In an excellent location in the centre of town, the 60 spacious rooms have tiled floors, double-glazed windows and bathrooms with tubs. There's a top-floor restaurant and a smart modern internet cafe in the lobby.

★Abbasi Hotel HOTEL $$$
(☎031-3222 6010; www.abbasihotel.ir; Shahid Medani St; r/deluxe from US$150/200, ste from US$260; P❄@📶🏊) The Abbasi's main building was once the caravanserai of the Madraseh-ye Chahar Bagh; arranged around a huge garden of ponds and towering cedars, and with a view of the madraseh's lovely dome beyond, this is a very special place to stay. Unfortunately, the same can't be said for the characterless new building on the eastern side of the central garden courtyard.

Eating

Specialities include *beryani* (ground mutton wrapped in flat bread), *khoresht-e mast* (a strange concoction of lamb, yoghurt, egg, saffron, sugar and orange peel) and *gaz*, a delicious nougat. Saffron or pistachio ice cream is also a must. Chahar Bagh Abbasi St is wildly popular with locals for fast food.

★Bastani Traditional Restaurant IRANIAN $
(☎031-3220 0374; www.bastanitraditionalrestaurant.ir; Chaharsogh Maghsod Bazar, Naqsh-e Jahan (Imam) Sq; mains from IR250,000; ⌚11.30am-10pm; 🖉) Esfahan's most atmospheric restaurant is located in the shadow of the Masjed-e Shah and features an internal courtyard with fountain, tiled walls and painted vaulted ceilings with mirror inlay – truly gorgeous. Dishes such as *khoresh-e beh* (stewed lamb and quince) and *khoresh-e alu* (stewed chicken and plum) are consistently delicious. There's a cover charge for tea, worth paying just to enjoy the delightful interior.

Haj Mahmood Beryani IRANIAN $
(www.beryaniazam.com; Bazar Engelab Blind Alley; beryani IR140,000; ⌚9am-3pm Sat-Thu) Famous for its *beryani* (which is served with a glass of *dugh;* churned sour milk or yoghurt mixed with water), Azam has several branches. This one inside the bazaar is a recommended lunch option – the queuing, the shunting into seats, the quick turn-around and the chomping on whole onions is all part of this fun experience.

★Abbasi Teahouse & Traditional Restaurant IRANIAN $$
(www.abbasihotel.ir; Abbasi Hotel, Shahid Medani St; noodle soup IR200,000; ⌚4-10.30pm; 📶) Set into a flank of the Abbasi Hotel's elegant main courtyard, this delightful little restaurant (not to be confused with the hotel's main restaurant) attract legions of locals in the early evening. The signature dish is *ash-e reshte* (noodle soup with beans and vegetables; IR200,000) and big bowls of this wholesome soup fly out of the kitchen in record numbers when it's cold.

★Shahrzad IRANIAN $$
(☎031-1220 4490; www.shahrzad-restaurant.com; Abbas Abad St; mains IR500,000; ⌚11.30am-10.30pm) Opulent Qajar-style wall paintings, stained-glass windows and battalions of black-suited waiters contribute to the Shahrzad's reputation as the best restaurant in Esfahan. House specialities include lamb cutlets, and *chelo fesenjan* (pomegranate and walnut stew). At the end of the meal complimentary pieces of *gaz* flavoured with almond and rose water complete the meal. Booking isn't encouraged so queues are common.

Malek Soltan Jarchi Bashi IRANIAN **$$**
(☎031-3220 7453; www.jarchibashi.com; Bagh-e Ghalandarha Alley, Hakim St; mains IR450,000; ⊙noon-3.30pm & 7.30-10.30pm) This sumptuous renovation of a 400-year-old bathhouse is a highly romantic venue for dinner, especially on Wednesday and Saturday nights (or on Thursday and Friday at noon) when live music adds to the atmosphere. The vaulted interior has been beautifully restored with fountains and splendid murals. The food is not the best but it's worth having something just to enjoy the ambience.

Chehel Sotun Restaurant IRANIAN **$$**
(www.abbasihotel.ir; Abbasi Hotel, Shahid Medani St; mains IR450,000; ⊙7-10.30pm) It's probably fair to say that the food in this beautiful restaurant is not the best, but if this isn't the prime concern, then it's worth a night out here to enjoy the company of Esfahanis celebrating a special occasion in surroundings fit for a shah. The sweeping staircase, mirror work and elaborate murals are a visual feast.

Drinking & Nightlife

Roozegar CAFE
(☎031-3223 4357; Espadana Inn, off Naqsh-e Jahan (Imam) Sq; ⊙10am-10.45pm; 🛜) After a few laps of the square, this little cafe is a lovely spot to pause and relax. Soothing music, rich honey cake, good coffee and herbal teas served with *nabat* (crystallised sugar) help restore energy levels. The cafe is in a small courtyard north of the Masjed-e Sheikh Lotfollah.

Azadegan Teahouse TEAHOUSE
(Chaykhaneh-ye Azadegan; off Naqsh-e Jahan (Imam) Sq; ⊙7am-midnight) In a lane off the northeastern corner of Naqsh-e Jahan (Imam) Sq, this popular teahouse sports an enormous collection of bric-a-brac hanging from its walls and ceiling. Enter down the passageway lined with scooters, lamps and old radios.

Shopping

Esfahan has a wide selection of handicrafts, including carpets, hand-painted miniatures on camel bone, metalwork and enamelware.

Hossein Fallahi ARTS & CRAFTS
(Miniature Art Gallery and Workshop; ☎031-3220 4613; www.miniatureart.org; Posht Matbak St, off Naqsh-e Jahan (Imam) Sq; miniature painted box from US$25; ⊙9am-9pm) In this studio it's possible to watch the master at work, peering through a magnifying glass as he applies tiny brushstrokes of paint, applied with a cat's hair and pigeon feather, to a miniature painting or a box made of bone.

Paradise Handicrafts CARPETS
(☎031-3220 4860; paradisecarpets@yahoo.com; 19 Afarinesh Bazaar, Naqsh-e Jahan (Imam) Sq; ⊙9am-1pm & 3-7pm Sat-Thu) This friendly father-and-son team specialise in nomadic carpets from all over Iran. High-quality pieces are available and postage can be arranged.

Orientation

Most sites are within easy walking distance of the main street, Chahar Bagh Abbasi, which has lots of accommodation options.

Information

MEDICAL SERVICES

Al-Zahra Hospital (☎031-3620 2020; Soffeh St) Best hospital in Esfahan. English-speaking doctors.

MONEY

Sepah St off Naqsh-e Jahan (Imam) Sq has several exchange agencies.

Jahan-e Arz Money Changer (Sepah St; ⊙8.30am-3pm Sat-Thu) Offers good rates.

TOURIST INFORMATION

Tourist Office (☎031-3221 6831; Naqsh-e Jahan (Imam) Sq; ⊙7.30am-2pm Sat-Thu) Under the Ali Qapu Palace; the English-speaking staff hand out maps and brochures about the city and the surrounding area.

TRAVEL AGENCIES

Donyaye Parvaz Tour & Travel Agency (☎031-3667 3101; donyayeparvaz@aol.com; 8 Chahar Bagh-e Bala St; ⊙8.30am-5pm Sun-Thu) Located at the southern end of the Si-o-Seh Pol, this professional outfit can arrange tours and visas, book accommodation, and organise train, air and ferry tickets. Staff member Mr Morshedi speaks excellent English and is extremely helpful.

OFF THE BEATEN TRACK

DESERT VILLAGES

Rather than barrelling down the Esfahan–Yazd highway in a direct bus, take some time to detour East to the Dasht-e Kavir desert, stopping at **Toudeshk**, **Na'in** and farther-flung **Mesr** and **Garmeh**. All have appealing sleeping options and activities include 4WD, camel or hiking excursion to explore the remarkable desert landscape. Trips out this way are highly recommended and easily organised through a licensed driver guide (p166).

Iran Travel & Tourism (☎031-3222 3010; irantravel1964@yahoo.com; Shahid Medani St; ⏰8.30am-7pm Sat-Thu) Opposite Abbasi Hotel; can book plane, train and even ferry tickets.

VISA EXTENSIONS

The **Department of Aliens Affairs** (Rudaki St; ⏰8am-2pm Sat-Thu) is in a large, drab-looking government building. Passports must be shown at the gate and paperwork picked up from the office in the courtyard. Same-day service (three to four hours) is possible if the application is lodged early. Women applicants must wear *hijab* in the required photographs. Showing proof of a prebooked onward plane/bus ticket helps.

Getting There & Away

AIR

Esfahan international airport (http://enisfahan.airport.ir) is located about 25km northeast of town. Destinations include Mashhad (US$84, daily), Shiraz (US$50, 2 weekly) and Tehran (US$80, daily).

BUS

Esfahan has a few bus terminals.

Kave bus terminal (Kave Blvd) in the north is the busiest and most commonly used by travellers. It services Tehran, Kashan and Yazd. A *dar bast* taxi to Kave from the centre of town should cost around IR160,000.

Jey bus terminal (Jey St) Offers hourly departures to Yazd between 6am and 1am (VIP IR260,000, six hours). To get here, take a shuttle taxi from Takhti Junction (IR20,000).

Buses from Esfahan

DESTINATION	FARE (IR)	DURATION (HR)
Kashan	115,000	4
Mashhad	780,000	16
Shiraz	360,000	6
Tabriz	650,000	12
Tehran	330,000	6
Tehran Airport	350,000	5
Yazd	260,000	5

TRAIN

The train station *(istgah-e ghatah)* is on the southern edge of the city. It can be reached by bus from a stop outside Kowsar International Hotel, although the wait and the journey can take over an hour. A taxi costs IR300,000. Train tickets must be booked (most easily through a travel agent) well in advance, particularly on weekends or in holiday periods. Destinations include Kashan (IR220,000, 4½ hours), Mashhad (IR100,000, 18 hours) and Tehran (IR370,000, 7½ hours).

Getting Around

TO/FROM THE AIRPORT

There is no airport bus service. A *dar bast* taxi costs around US$9.

BUS & MINIBUS

Local buses and minibuses leave the bus terminal near Chehel Sotun Palace every few minutes. Books of tickets can be bought at booths along the routes.

METRO

Esfahan's new **metro** (www.esfahanmetro.org) is still being constructed.

TAXI

Depending on the distance – not to mention negotiating skills – a fare in a private taxi around inner Esfahan costs anything from IR120,000 to IR320,000.

The long Chahar Bagh Abbasi St is the city's main thoroughfare, and every couple of seconds a shuttle taxi goes *mostaghim* (straight ahead) for about IR500 per kilometre.

Yazd يزد

☎035 / POP 1,110,000 / ELEV 1229M

With its winding lanes, forest of *badgirs*, mud-brick houses and delightful places to stay, Yazd is a 'don't miss' destination. On a flat plain ringed by mountains, the city is wedged between the northern Dasht-e Kavir and southern Dasht-e Lut and is every inch a city of the desert. It may not have the big-ticket sights of Esfahan or Shiraz, but, with its atmospheric alleyways and centuries of history, it exceeds both in its capacity to enchant. Yazd warrants a lazy approach – rambling around the maze of historic lanes (referred to locally as Yazd's 'historical texture'), popping into random teahouses or pausing to work out calligraphic puzzles in the city's exquisite tilework.

Yazd has a long and important history as a trading post. When Marco Polo passed this way in the 13th century he described Yazd as 'a very fine and splendid city and a centre of commerce'. It was spared destruction by Genghis Khan and Tamerlane, and flourished in the 14th and 15th centuries, with silk, textile and carpet production the main home-grown industries. Like most of Iran, Yazd fell into decline when the Safavids were defeated and remained little more than a provincial outpost until the railway line from Tehran was extended here by the last shah. Today, it is a thriving city of over a million inhabitants.

Sights

★Masjed-e Jameh
MOSQUE

(مسجد جامع, Jameh Mosque; Masjed-e Jameh St; IR80,000; ⏱8am-8pm, museum 8-11am) FREE Soaring above the old city, this magnificent building is graced with a tiled entrance portal (one of the tallest in Iran), flanked by two 48m-high minarets and adorned with inscriptions from the 15th century. The exquisite mosaics on the dome and mihrab, and the tiles above the main western entrance to the courtyard are masterpieces of calligraphy.

★Amir Chakhmaq Mosque Complex
NOTABLE BUILDING

(مجموعه امیر چخماق; Amir Chakhmaq Sq) The stunning three-storey facade of this Hosseinieh is one of the largest such structures in Iran. The rows of perfectly proportioned sunken alcoves are at their best and most photogenic in late afternoon, when the copper-coloured sunlight is captured within each alcove and the towering exterior appears to glow against the darkening sky.

★Old City
AREA

(بافت قدیم) With its numerous *badgirs* rising above a labyrinth of adobe roofs, the historic old city of Yazd is one of the oldest towns on earth. Listed as a Unesco World Heritage site, it encompasses thousands of ancient dwellings, screened from the narrow *kuches* (lanes) by imposing mud walls. For the visitor, the old city offers a treasure trove of hidden courtyards and teahouses, shops selling crafts and houses converted into atmospheric hotels. Altogether, it is one of Iran's don't miss sights.

Saheb A Zaman Zurkhaneh
CULTURAL CENTRE

(زور خانه صاحب الزمان; off Amir Chakhmaq Sq; IR200,000; ⏱reservoir 6am-9pm, workouts 7-8pm Sat-Thu) The cavernous *ab anbar* (water reservoir), built around 1580, resembles a 29m-high standing egg from the inside. Crowned with five burly *badgirs*, this impressive piece of architecture stored water for much of the city until modern irrigation made it redundant. The building has found a new purpose as a *zurkhaneh* (house of strength) in which *javan mard* (gentlemen) exercise using heavy wooden clubs to build muscle.

Bagh-e Dolat Abad
PAVILION, GARDENS

(باغ دولت آباد; ☎035-3627 0781; Shahid Raja'i St; IR150,000; ⏱7am-11pm) Once a residence of Persian regent Karim Khan Zand, this small pavilion set amid Unesco-listed gardens was built around 1750. The interior of the pavilion is superb, with intricate latticework and

THE CLASSIC YAZD DAY TRIP

There are many interesting places within a day trip of Yazd. These are most easily visited on a tour. Full-day loops around local desert villages cost US$50 by taxi or US$85 for a driver-guide. Half-day trips to nearer destinations, such as Zein-o-din cost US$30 by taxi and US$65 with a driver-guide. It's best to stick to licensed guides.

Kharanaq

The virtually deserted and crumbling mudbrick village of Kharanaq (Kharanagh) is in a valley about 70km north of Yazd and a very picturesque spot for a wander.

Chak Chak

This isolated cliff-face **fire temple** is Iran's most important Zoroastrian pilgrimage site. Legend has it that after the Arab invasion in AD 637, the Sassanian princess Nikbanuh fled here. Short of water, she threw her staff at the cliff and water began dripping out – *chak, chak* means 'drip, drip'. The site protects the source of the water and offers dramatic views across the desert.

Meybod

Meybod is an ancient mud-brick town with several intriguing buildings. In the centre, crumbling **Narin castle** (Rashiddadin Ave; IR150,000; ⏱8am-sunset) dates from Sassanian times but has Achaemenid foundations and evidence of much earlier settlement beneath. A cluster of sights in the west of town include a beautifully restored **caravanserai**, with craft shops, a restaurant, and a *zeilo* (prayer rug) **museum** (IR80,000 incl coffee; ⏱9.30am-sunset). Alongside is a 300-year-old **post house** (Chapar-khaneh; US$1.50; ⏱9am-3pm Sat-Thu), ask at the caravanserai if it's closed. It's in front of an *ab anbar* (reservoir) and opposite a conical-roofed Safavid-era **icehouse** (same ticket as the *zeilo* museum).

As you leave town towards Yazd, stop at the impressive **pigeon house**, with 4000 niches.

Yazd

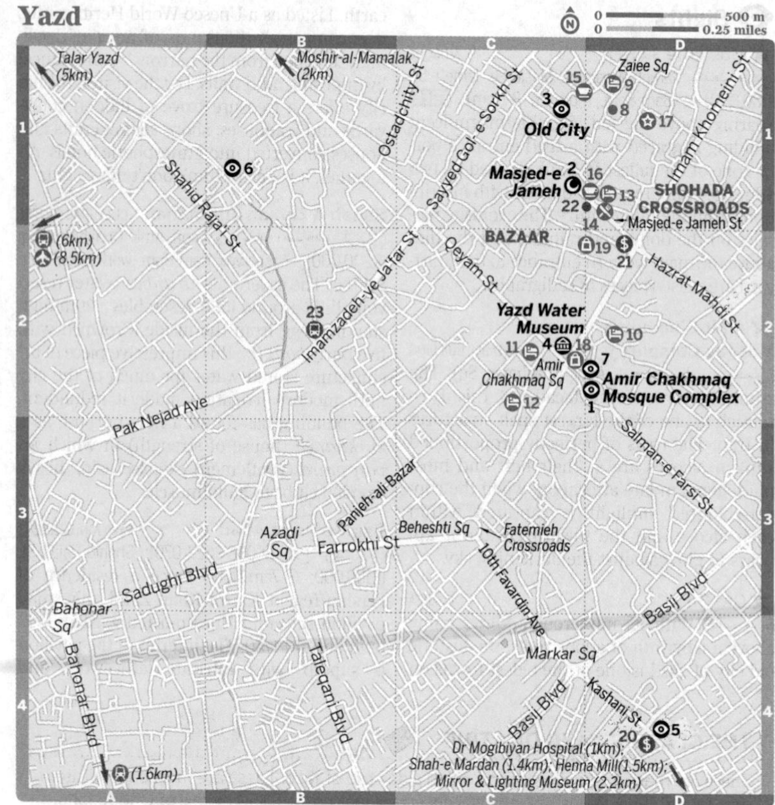

exquisite stained-glass windows. The pavilion also boasts Iran's loftiest *badgir;* standing over 33m tall, it was rebuilt in the 1960s.

Henna Mill MILL

(Mazari-ha Alley) FREE The lanes off Kashani St, near the quirky **Mirror & Lighting Museum** (Kashani St; IR80,000; ⏲8am-8pm), are home to a number of henna mills. With their huge grinding stones, rotated against a flat plate on a brick plinth, these mills have been producing henna for well over a hundred years. A few are still in operation and make for an interesting quick visit en route to lunch in **Shah-e Mardan** (☎035-3824 4039; cnr Mazari-ha & Kashani St; 3-person tray IR510,000; ⏲11am-4pm lunch & 7-11pm dinner), one of the renovated mills now serving as a restaurant.

Tours

Yazd is a base for tours, with the most popular being a half-day in the desert (including camel-riding) or a trip to Kharanaq, Chak Chak and Meybod. You can get a driver-guide to do the latter circuit for under US$30 but better licensed guides usually charge more.

Mojtaba Heidari TOURS

(☎0935 066 2366; www.mojirantrip.com) With detailed knowledge about Yazd and the desert, and a willingness to share a wealth of cultural insights, this driver-guide is fluent in English and endearing, if a tad eccentric. Experienced in giving help with obtaining visa codes.

Mohsen Hajisaeid OUTDOORS

(☎035-3622 7828, 0913 351 4460; www.iranpersiatour.com) Mohsen has the well-deserved reputation as being one of the best licensed guides in Iran. Based here in Yazd, he's also an executive of the Yazd Tourism Associations Council. Check the website for a full list of tours.

Mazieh Mandegari HIKING

(☎0913 453 3833; maziehmandegari@yahoo.com; same-day or 24hr mountain ascent per person

Yazd

Top Sights
1 Amir Chakhmaq Mosque Complex D2
2 Masjed-e Jameh C1
3 Old City C1
4 Yazd Water Museum C2

Sights
5 Ateshkadeh D4
6 Bagh-e Dolat Abad B1
7 Saheb A Zaman Zurkhaneh D2

Activities, Courses & Tours
8 Yazd Tourist Information Office D1

Sleeping
9 Fahadan Museum Hotel D1
10 Hotel Vali D2
11 Malek-o Tojjar C2
12 Narenjestan Traditional House C2
13 Silk Road Hotel D1

Eating
Malek-o Tojjar .... (see 11)
14 Silk Road Hotel Restaurant D1

Drinking & Nightlife
15 Art House C1
16 Fooka Cafe D1

Entertainment
17 Traditional Persian Night D1

Shopping
18 Haj Khalifeh Ali Rahbar C2
19 Khan Bazaar D2

Information
20 Hadad Exchange D4
21 Khaki Exchange D2
Persian Odyssey .... (see 22)
22 Starsland Tour & Travel D1
Tourist Office .... (see 1)

Transport
23 Local Buses to Main Bus Terminal B2

US$100, up to 6 people) This licensed, trained and highly experienced mountain guide operating out of Yazd offers hikes up Shirkouh at any time of year, although she recommends spring and autumn as the best time to see wildflowers and for the climate.

Sleeping

★ Nartitee Ecolodge HOMESTAY $
(Pomegranate Flower Ecolodge; ☎0919 405 7118, 035-3262 2853; www.nartitee.ir; Khayam Alley, off Rahatabad St, Taft; per person US$15, incl tea & fresh fruit from garden, dinner IR200,000; P❄📶) For a rewarding off-the-beaten track experience, spending a night in this licensed homestay is highly recommended. Located close to Yazd in the neighbouring village of Taft, the ecolodge is housed in a 100-year-old adobe building, painstakingly restored by the grandchildren of the original Zoroastrian owners.

★ Narenjestan Traditional House HOMESTAY $
(☎035-3627 3231, 0913 455 6598; www.narenjestanhouse.com; Shahid Sadoughi Alley, off Imam Khomeini St; r from US$35) This licensed homestay, in the heart of the old city, is a real find. The couple who run it speak excellent English (the husband gained his PhD in New Zealand) and have committed their time and energies both to restoring the 200-year-old family home and to perfecting the art of hospitality.

Fahadan Museum Hotel HOTEL $$
(☎035-3630 0600; www.mehrchainhotels.com; Fahadan St; s/d/tr IR2,120,000/3,160,000/4,000,000; ❄📶) Arranged around delicately painted courtyards, this beautiful little establishment is more museum than hotel and some of the rooms are exquisite. With a flamboyant, moustachioed manager, a location in the heart of the old city, a popular teahouse in the main courtyard and a rooftop with spectacular views, this is one hotel that's well worth booking in advance.

Hotel Vali HOTEL $$
(☎035-3622 8050; www.valihotel.com; off Imam Khomeini St; s/d/tr US$58/70/94; P❄📶) This restored caravanserai attracts large crowds of travellers from around the country, congregating over *chay* from the samovar in the canvas-covered courtyard. The gem of this antique establishment is the upholstered basement room with a pool fed by the *qanat* (underground aqueduct).

Silk Road Hotel HOSTEL, HOTEL $$
(☎035-3625 2730, 091 3151 6361; www.silkroadhotel.net; 5 Tal-e Khakestary Alley, off Masjed-e Jameh St; dm/s/d/tr US$10/35/60/70; ❄@📶) Two minutes' walk from the Masjed-e Jameh, the Silk Road's courtyard setting, delicious Indian-style food and sociable atmosphere attracts a steady stream of backpackers. The standard rooms aren't the the major draw here: it's the ambience that counts. Beware overbooking.

★Malek-o Tojjar HOTEL $$$
(☎035-3622 4060; www.mehrchainhotels.com; Panjeh-ali Bazar, Qeyam St; d/tr/VIP IR3,530,000/4,470,000/8,400,000; P❄📶) Hidden along a narrow, lamp-lit passage from the Panjeh-ali Bazar lies Yazd's original traditional hotel. The small sign above a modest door gives no hint of the treasure trove of exquisite details that are a feature of this Qajar-era house. For those on honeymoon or celebrating a special occasion, the VIP rooms are something very special with superbly painted ceilings, extravagant mirror work and bathrooms with Jacuzzi.

Eating

Traditional hotels have courtyard teahouse-restaurants: atmospheric places for a meal or drink, though the quality in most is mediocre. Camel meat is available in stews and at certain kabab stalls.

In the passage under the Amir Chakhmaq building kababis specialise in *jigar* (liver) and other meats (30¢ to US$1 per skewer).

Silk Road Hotel Restaurant INDIAN $
(☎035-3625 2730; www.silkroadhotel.ir; 5 Tal-e Khakestary Alley, off Masjed-e Jameh St; mains from IR150,000; ⏲7am-10.30pm) While the Iranian food here is very good, the delicious subcontinental curries are the most popular dishes among travellers, particularly those who've run out of patience with kababs. The sociable courtyard atmosphere makes for a pleasant evening. A wide choice of teas and fresh juices makes this a good place to pause while on a walking tour.

★Talar Yazd IRANIAN $$
(☎035-3522 6661; www.talareyazd.ir; Ghandehaeri Alley, off Jomhuri-e Eslami Blvd; mains IR250,000; ⏲noon-4.30pm & 7-11pm) Elegant but uncomplicated, the Talar, with its prim white tablecloths and waiters wheeling trolleys, has a 1950s appeal. Its short menu of classic Iranian dishes, including slow-roast lamb, is delicious and the kababs are perfect. It's an 8km ride from central Yazd (IR150,000 in a cab) but worth it to spend time in the company of Yazdis out for lunch at the weekend.

Malek-o Tojjar IRANIAN $$
(☎035-3622 4060; www.mehrchainhotels.com; Panjeh-ali Bazar, off Qeyam St; buffets from IR450,000; ⏲breakfast 7.30-9.30am, lunch noon-3pm, dinner 7-10pm) The highly decorated main hall of this classic Iranian restaurant makes for a romantic setting for a special evening. The menu is complemented with several regional variations, including *kufteh Yazdi* (Yazdi meatballs).

YAZD'S ZOROASTRIAN CONNECTION

Originally settled 5000 years ago, Yazd has an interesting mix of people, 10% of whom follow the ancient religion of Zoroastrianism. An elegant **ateshkadeh** (آتشکده, Sacred Eternal Flame; Kashani St; IR80,000; ⏲8-11.45am & 4-6.45pm, to 7.45pm in summer) (fire temple) near the city centre shelters an eternal flame and visitors are welcome and it's possible to visit the now-abandoned **Dakhmeh-ye Zartoshtiyun** (برج خاموشی, Towers of Silence; IR80,000; ⏲7am-2pm winter, 8am-noon summer) on the outskirts of Yazd where the Zoroastrians once buried their dead.

Drinking & Nightlife

★Art House TEAHOUSE
(House of Mehdi Malek Zadeh; next to Chehel Mehrab Mosque, Fahadan district; ⏲8am-11pm) This tiny, friendly rooftop teahouse is the perfect place to enjoy soup, or an uncomplicated tea and cake (IR160,000) with one of the best views in town. There's a craft shop and workshop downstairs.

Fooka Cafe CAFE
(☎035-3620 8520; Masjed Jameh St; ⏲8am-midnight) As a refreshingly modern alternative to the traditional teahouses of old Yazd, this stylish cafe, with its installation of hanging coffee cups, is a popular meeting place for Yazd's younger in-crowd. A full menu of traditional favourites (mains from IR150,000) is available and there's rooftop seating.

Entertainment

Traditional Persian Night LIVE MUSIC
(☎0935 935 7123; www.tpersiannight.com; Kohan Traditional Hotel, Alley 40, off Imam Khomeini St, Fahadan district; child/adult IR550,000/690,000; ⏲7-10pm, seasonal) The Kohan Traditional Hotel offers an evening of classical entertainments over a Persian dinner in the fine setting of its beautiful courtyard garden. The price includes live *setar* music, story-telling and a three-course meal, including Yazdi cake with bitter orange blossom tea.

Shopping

Haj Khalifeh Ali Rahbar CONFECTIONER
(www.hajkhalifehalirahbar.com; cnr Amir Chakhmaq Sq & Imam Khomeini St; ⏲9am-1pm & 5-9pm Sat-Thu) The best of Yazd famous sweets can be

found in this centenarian-old store. Customers survey the samples, write down what they want on the form provided, take it to the counter for boxing, pay at the cashier and then collect the sweets on the way out.

Khan Bazaar MARKET

(entrance on Imam Khomeini St; 9am-1pm & 3.30-8pm Sat-Thu) The alleyways of this covered bazaar extend back to the 9th century and make for a diverting hour or so's meander. Many stores sell various grades of cloth that have been handwoven in Yazd for centuries.

THE BADGIRS OF YAZD

Any summer visitor will understand immediately why the city's roofscape is a forest of *badgirs* (windtowers, pronounced 'bad-*gears*'). These ancient systems of natural air-conditioning are designed to catch even the lightest breeze and direct it to the rooms or water reservoir below. To appreciate the effect, just stand beneath one.

Information

DANGERS & ANNOYANCES

Problems for backpackers include offering cheap but unlicensed (and therefore illegal) homestay accommodation. It might sound like a saving or an adventure but it's not worth the risk.

Insist on seeing a guide's license. To be bona fide, this must include a photograph, hologram and expiry date.

Women should avoid walking around alone at Yazd at night as there are occasional reports of harassment.

MEDICAL SERVICES

Dr Mogibiyan Hospital (035-5624 0061; Kashani St) For emergency treatment.

MONEY

Hadad Exchange (035-3624 7220; Kashani St; 9.30am-2pm & 4-7pm Sat-Wed, 9.30am-2pm Thu) On the 2nd floor of a building opposite the *ateshkadeh*.

Khaki Exchange (Imam Khomeini St) Good rates.

TOURIST INFORMATION

Tourist Office (Amir Chakhmaq Sq; 5-8pm Sat-Thu high season only; wi-fi) Located in the Amir Chakhmaq Mosque Complex, this office supplies maps and advice, makes hotel bookings, books desert tours and offers free wi-fi.

Yazd Tourist Information Office (035-621 6542; Ziaee Sq; 8.30am-7pm, to 8pm summer) Stocks a few maps and brochures, but is mainly dedicated to selling tours. It also rents bikes for IR60,000 per hour.

TRAVEL AGENCIES

Persian Odyssey (Shirdal Airya Travel & Tours; 0912 427 9943, 035-3627 1620; www.persianodyssey.com; 6th Alley, Masjed-e Jameh St) is an award-winning enterprise run by a dynamic team of young entrepreneurs with many years of experience in licensed-tour guiding.

Starsland Tour & Travel (035-1827 0091; starsland91@yahoo.com; Masjed-e Jameh St; 9am-2.30pm & 3.30-6pm) is also very helpful for arranging tours and onward travel on trains, planes or buses.

VISA EXTENSIONS

A visa can be extended in Yazd in under an hour. The **Tourist Police Office** (110; Kashani St, near Abuzar Sq; 8am-2pm Sat-Wed, to noon Thu), close to Abuzar Sq, processes same-day applications.

Getting There & Away

AIR

Located to the west of Yazd city centre, **Shahid Sadooghi International Airport** (Yazd Airport; 035-3721 4444; www.yazd.airport.ir; Azadegan St) offers a couple of useful services. Iran Air and ATA fly to Tehran (from US$62, 70 minutes, twice daily) and Mashad (from US$75, 80 minutes, four times weekly).

BUS

Most buses leave from the **main bus terminal** (Shahrak-e Sanati) about 10km west of the old city of Yazd (IR150,000, 20 minutes by *dar bast* taxi). It is accessible by shuttle taxi from Beheshti and Azadi Sqs.

Buses from Yazd

DESTINATION	FARE (IR - VIP)	DURATION (HR)
Esfahan	260,000	5
Kashan	500,000	5
Mashhad	600,000	12
Shiraz	360,000	6
Tabriz	800,000	14
Tehran	490,000	7

TRAIN

In the south of the city, the **train station** (Rah Ahan) offers limited services. Train tickets are more easily purchased at travel agencies.

Destinations include Mashhad (IR900,000, 14 hours) and Tehran via Kashan (IR310,000, eight hours).

DON'T MISS

QANATS

For at least 2000 years Iranians have been digging *qanats* (underground aqueducts) for irrigation and drinking water. Some of these impressive engineering feats are dozens of kilometres long. While modern irrigation projects now take priority, *qanats* are still important and the brave men who built them are honoured in the excellent **Yazd Water Museum** (Amir Chakhmaq Sq; IR150,000; ⏲8am-2.30pm & 3.30-7pm). Housed in a mansion with a *qanat* flowing underneath, the displays (mostly in English) give a fascinating glimpse of the challenges of life lived at the edge of a desert.

Getting Around

Dar bast taxis start at about IR100,000 for short trips, and cost IR150,000 to IR200,000 from the airport or main bus terminal to the city centre. Taxis are more expensive at night.

Local buses (IR30,000) travel between the main bus terminal and the **bus stand** near the corner of Imamzadeh-ye Ja'far and Shahid Raja'i Sts near the old city.

Shiraz شیراز

☎071 / POP 1,460,665 / ELEV 1506M

Celebrated as the heartland of Persian culture for over 2000 years, Shiraz has become synonymous with education, nightingales, poetry and wine. It was one of the most important cities in the medieval Islamic world and was the Iranian capital during the Zand dynasty (AD 1747–79), when many of its most beautiful buildings were built or restored.

History

The encouragement of enlightened rulers and the presence of artists and scholars helped make Shiraz one of the greatest cities in the Islamic world throughout the 13th and 14th centuries. Centuries of decline followed until Karim Khan of the short-lived Zand dynasty made it his capital in 1750.

Sights

A city of poets, Shiraz is home to the garden shrines of **Hafez** (آرامگاه حافظ, Tomb of Hafez; Golestan Blvd; IR200,000; ⏲7.30am-10pm, to 10.30pm summer) and **Sa'di** (آرامگاه سعدی, Tomb of Sa'di; Bustan Blvd; IR200,000; ⏲7.30am-10pm, to 10.30pm summer), both major pilgrimage sites for Iranians. It's also home to exquisite mosques and whispered echoes of ancient sophistication that reward those who linger beyond the customary excursion to nearby Persepolis.

★Bagh-e Naranjestan PALACE

(Citrus Garden; Lotf Ali Khan Blvd; IR200,000; ⏲8am-7pm) Named after the bitter oranges that line the central courtyard, this is Shiraz's smallest but most lovely garden. Enclosing the delightful **Naranjestan-e Ghavam Pavilion** (Lotf Ali Khan Blvd; IR200,000; ⏲8am-7pm), it was laid out as part of a complex owned by one of Shiraz's wealthiest Qajar-era families. The pavilion's mirrored entrance hall opens onto rooms covered in a myriad of intricate tiles, inlaid wooden panels and stained-glass windows. Particularly noteworthy are the ceilings of the upstairs rooms, painted with European-style motifs, including Alpine churches and busty German fräuleins.

★Masjed-e Nasir Al Molk MOSQUE

(مسجد نصیرالملک, Nasir Al Molk Mosque, Pink Mosque; off Lotf Ali Khan Blvd; IR150,000; ⏲7.30-11.30am & 2.30-5pm) One of the most elegant and most photographed pieces of architecture in southern Iran, the Pink Mosque was built at the end of the 19th century and its coloured tiling (an unusually deep shade of blue) is exquisite. There are some particularly fine *muqarnas* in the small outer portal and in the northern *iwan,* but it is the stained glass, carved pillars and polychrome faience of the winter prayer hall that dazzle the eye when the sun streams in.

★Bagh-e Nazar GARDENS

(باغ نظر, Eye-catching Garden; Karim Khan-e Zand Blvd; ⏲8.30am-1.30pm & 2.30-5.30pm) This formal garden encompasses an octagonal pavilion, which is now home to the **Pars Museum** (موزه پارس; IR150,000; ⏲8.30am-1.30pm & 2.30-5.30pm). Karim Khan once received foreign dignitaries in the pavilion, which, with its stunning stalactite ceiling and delightful murals of lovers courting, scholars reading and horsemen hunting, is a highlight in its own right. Exhibits include Karim Khan Zand's sword and some interesting old ceramics.

Aramgah-e Shah-e Cheragh SHRINE

(آرامگاه شاهچراغ, Mausoleum of Sayyed Mir Mohammad; Ahmadi Sq; ⏲variable, often 24hr) FREE Sayyed Mir Ahmad, one of Imam Reza's 17 brothers, was hunted down and killed by the caliphate on this site in AD 835 and his remains are housed in a dazzling shrine of mirrored tiles. A mausoleum was first erected over the tomb during the 12th century, but the courtyard and tile work represent relatively modern embellishments from the late-Qajar period and the Islamic Republic. The blue-tiled dome and dazzling gold-tipped minarets form a magnificent context for the Shiite rituals at this revered centre of pilgrimage.

Bazar-e Vakil BAZAAR
(بازار وکیل; off Karim Khan-e Zand Blvd; ⌚8am-9pm Sat-Thu) The city's ancient trading district is home to several bazaars dating from different periods. The finest and most famous of these is the Bazar-e Vakil, a cruciform structure commissioned by Karim Khan as part of his plan to make Shiraz into a great trading centre. The bazaar encompasses the **Shamshirgarha Bazaar**, dedicated to tribal handicrafts, and the **Seray-e Moshir**, a tastefully restored two-storey caravanserai, set around an attractive tree-filled courtyard with a pool and fountains. **Masjed-e Vakil**, next to the tribal arts arcade, is notable for its rose-pink tiles and 48 diagonally fluted columns.

Hammam-e Vakil HISTORIC BUILDING
(حمام وکیل, Regent's Bath; off Taleqani St; IR150,000; ⌚7.30am-8pm Sat-Thu) The vaulted central chamber of this Zand-era bathhouse features some fine plasterwork and candy-twist columns. A series of costumed mannequins illustrate how Shirazis would have relaxed by the fountain after taking a bath in the handsome heat room, which has a vaulted ceiling, pillars and a small (empty) pool.

Arg-e Karim Khan FORTRESS
(ارگ کریمخان, Citadel of Karim Khan; Shohada Sq; IR200,000; ⌚7.30am-9pm summer, 8am-8pm winter) Dominating the city centre, this burly fortress was built in the early Zand period and formed part of the royal court that Karim Khan hoped would rival Esfahan. The high walls feature ornamental brickwork and are punctuated by four attractive 14m-high circular towers. The southeastern tower has a noticeable lean, having subsided into the underground cistern that served as the Arg's bathhouse.

Tours

Tours can be arranged through almost every hotel in town.

Shahram Rafie OUTDOORS
(☎0939 625 0511; www.steptoiran.com) An expert on Persepolis and the Shiraz region, but also greatly knowledgeable about the whole of Iran, Shahram is a refreshingly calm licensed driver-guide whose manner as much as his knowledge recommends him.

Iran Travel Service TOURS
(☎0917 300 3249; www.irantravelservice.com) Run by Mojtaba Rahmanian, who has excellent English and is a mine of information on the country.

Sleeping

★ **Forough Hotel** BOUTIQUE HOTEL $
(☎071-3222 5877; foroughhotel@gmail.com; Namazi Junction, Dastghieb St; d/tr US$45/65; ❄📶) This newly restored old house offers homely rooms that come with pristine duvets and freshly laundered towels. The hotel offers half-price entrance to the delightful little **Museum of Iranian Fine Arts** (Namazi Junction, Dastgheib St; IR200,000; ⌚8.30am-noon & 3.30-8pm) next door.

★ **Niayesh Boutique Hotel** BOUTIQUE HOTEL $
(☎071-3223 3622; www.niayeshhotels.com; 10 Shahzadeh Jamaili Lane; s/d/tr/q US$35/50/68/85; P❄📶) One of only a handful of traditional hotels in Shiraz, this delightful, sociable hotel in the heart of the old quarter is a firm backpacker favourite. The most characterful rooms are arranged around the central courtyard of the original house.

Parhami Traditional House HOTEL $
(☎071-3223 2015; www.parhamihouse.com; off Lotf Ali Khan Zand Blvd; s/d US$30/35; 📶) This attractive hotel, run by an enterprising family who has renovated the surrounding lanes over the past five years, is located in a traditional house wrapped around a citrus-filled courtyard with a blue pool. Homely rooms are decorated with rugs, and the home cooking attracts local youngsters into the courtyard restaurant.

★ **Shiraz Hotel** HOTEL $$
(☎071-3227 4820; www.shiraz-hotel.com; Quran Sq; r from US$95) This is currently Shiraz's most desired residence, attracting international visitors to its conference facilities and well-heeled Iranian travellers in town for business. The rooms are luxurious and spacious, with panoramic views of the city, and a number of eating options, including a revolving restaurant.

Shiraz

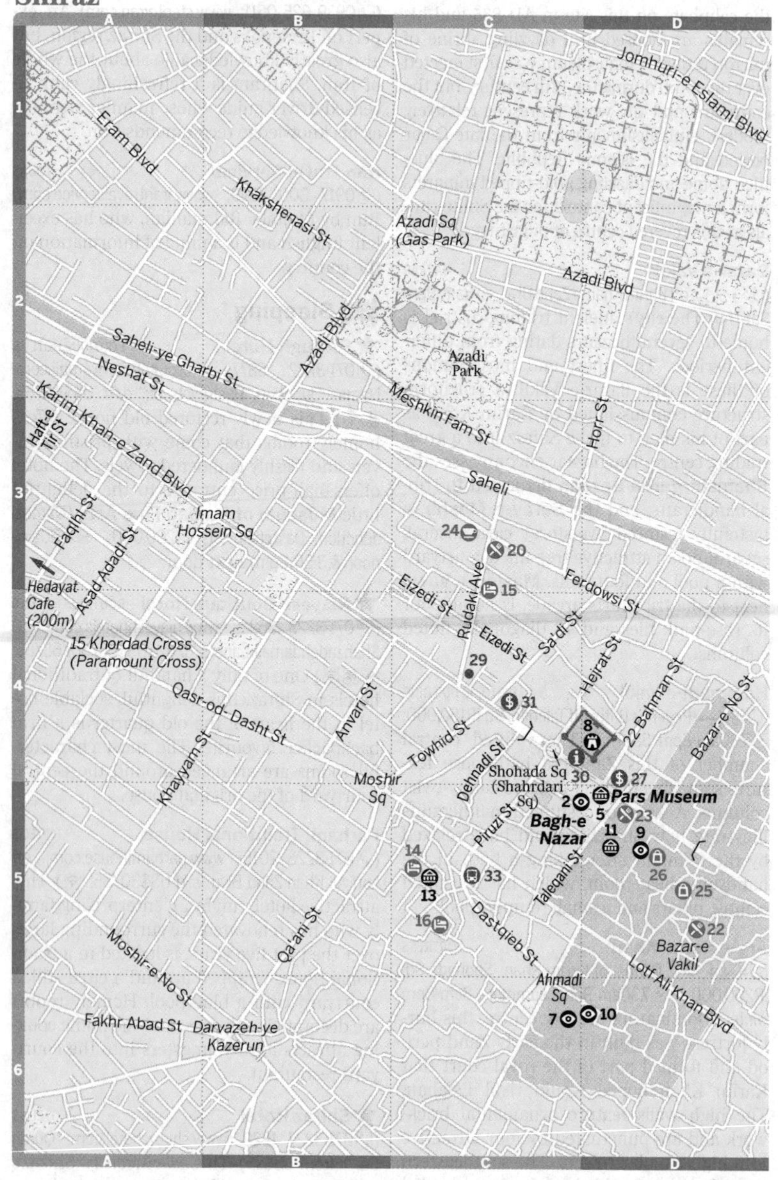

★**Karim Khan Hotel** HOTEL $$
(071-3223 5001; www.karimkhanhotel.com; Rudaki Ave; d US$63; P ❄ @) This centrally located hotel with its stained-glass windows casting lozenges of light across the foyer in a modern take on an ancient theme is a characterful choice in a city with few outstanding hotels. The rooms don't quite live up to the promise of the lobby and are made dark by the same stained-glass motifs – but this is a minor criticism.

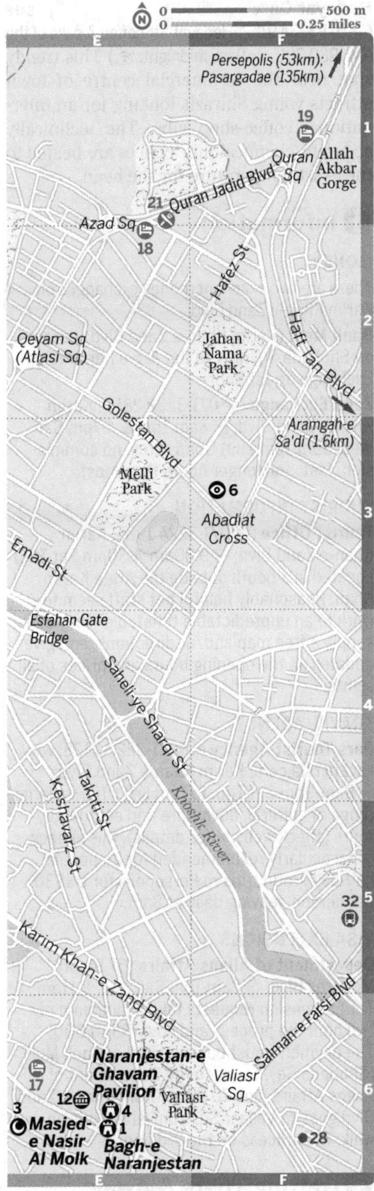

Shiraz

Top Sights
1 Bagh-e Naranjestan E6
2 Bagh-e Nazar C5
3 Masjed-e Nasir Al Molk E6
4 Naranjestan-e Ghavam Pavilion E6
5 Pars Museum D5

Sights
6 Aramgah-e Hafez F3
7 Aramgah-e Shah-e Cheragh C6
8 Arg-e Karim Khan D4
9 Bazar-e Vakil D5
10 Bogh'e-ye Sayyed Mir Mohammed D6
11 Hammam-e Vakil D5
12 Khan-e Zinat ol-Molk E6
13 Museum of Iranian Fine Arts C5

Sleeping
14 Forough Hotel C5
15 Karim Khan Hotel C3
16 Niayesh Boutique Hotel C5
17 Parhami Traditional House E6
18 Royal Shiraz Hotel E2
19 Shiraz Hotel F1

Eating
20 Ghavam C3
21 Haft Khan E1
22 Seray-e Mehr Teahouse D5
23 Sharzeh Traditional Restaurant D5

Drinking & Nightlife
24 Ferdowsi Cafe C3

Shopping
25 Seray-e Moshir D5
26 Shamshirgarha Bazaar D5

Information
27 Bank Melli D4
28 Department of Aliens Affairs F6
29 Pars Tourist Agency C4
30 Tourist Office C4
31 Zand Exchange C4

Transport
32 Karandish Bus Terminal F5
33 Local Bus Terminal C5

Royal Shiraz Hotel HOTEL $$
(071-3227 4356; www.royalshirazhotel.com; Quran Jadid Blvd; d/ste/extra bed IR2,870,000/7,325,000/760,000; P ❄ @ ≋) With a popular restaurant on the 6th floor, a sports complex including a pool, sauna and Jacuzzi, this new and stylish hotel is giving the larger upper-end options a run for their money. Located by the Quran Gateway, there are views over the city and fashionable eating options nearby.

Eating

Local staples include ice-cream-and-noodle concoction *faludeh* and Shirazi salad, a refreshing melange of onion, tomato and cucumber. But the famous Shiraz (Syrah) grape is no longer made into the wine that inspired Hafez to poetry.

★Ghavam IRANIAN $
(☎071-3235 9271; Rudaki Ave; dizi IR210,000; ⏰6.30am-1.30pm & 4.30-11pm; ❄☑) This tiny restaurant, more shop than diner, is an absolute favourite with locals, foreign expats and the odd tour group whose guide is in the know. Would-be diners queue up on the street to find a place at the tightly packed tables, drawn to the delicious home-cooked fare.

★Seray-e Mehr Teahouse TEAHOUSE $
(Seray-e Mehr, just off Rouhollah Bazaar, Bazar-e Vakil; meals from IR250,000, tea IR40,000; ⏰9.30am-9.30pm) This serendipitous little jewel in the middle of the Bazar-e Vakil is hidden behind a small door next to the Seray-e Moshir caravanserai. Decorated with painted panels and antiques on the wall, this split-level teahouse has a small menu of tasty favourites (think *dizi, kubideh, zereshk polo*) and a delightfully relaxed atmosphere in which to sit, eat and sip tea.

Sharzeh Traditional Restaurant IRANIAN $$
(☎071-3224 1963; Vakil St, off Karim Khan-e Zand Blvd; meals US$5-13; ⏰noon-3pm & 8-11pm) Near Masjed-e Vakil, this popular restaurant is in the basement of an arcade with galley-style seating around the upper of the two floors. It's best for lunch, when *bazaris* (shopkeepers) flock here to eat hearty local dishes.

★Haft Khan IRANIAN $$$
(☎071-3227 0000; www.haftkhanco.com; cnr 17th Alley & Quran Jadid Blvd; buffet IR750,000, à la carte mains from IR250,000; ⏰10am-midnight; P❄📶☑) Wildly popular with fashionable Shirazis, this enormous restaurant complex near Quran Gateway offers four types of dining experience: there's a generous buffet on the ground floor, a fast-food court on the 2nd floor, an à la carte restaurant on the 3rd floor serving Iranian barbeque and a teahouse on the roof.

Drinking & Nightlife

Ferdowsi Cafe CAFE
(Ferdosi St; ⏰9am-11pm; 📶) Attracting a loyal local crowd of liberally minded young Shirazis, overseen by a genial boss, this cafe does a range of brilliant flavoured teas – the sour one is a particular assault on the tastebuds.

Hedayat Cafe CAFE
(☎071-3234 9152; Hedayat St; coffee & cake of the day IR80,000; ⏰9am-midnight; 📶) This trendy spot near the commercial centre of town attracts young Shirazis looking for an international coffee-shop vibe. The technically accurate 'chemical mix' coffees are heated to the exact temperature for the bean.

Information

MONEY

There are two excellent money exchanges on Karim Khan-e Zand Blvd:

Bank Melli (Karim Khan-e Zand Blvd) Located on Shohada Sq, next to the Arg-e Karim Khan. Exchange on 1st floor.

Zand Exchange (☎071-3222 2854; Karim Khan-e Zand Blvd; ⏰8am-1pm & 4-7pm Sat-Wed, 8am-1pm Thu) Good rates, no commission, fast, and longer hours than most.

TOURIST INFORMATION

Tourist Office (☎071-3224 1985; Karim Khan-e Zand Blvd; ⏰9.30am-4.30pm Sat-Thu) Located in a booth outside the Arg-e Karim Khan. Reasonably helpful but staff seem to work to an unpredictable timetable. They can supply a free map and/or directions, and give updates on the opening hours and prices of all sights.

TRAVEL AGENCY

Pars Tourist Agency (☎071-3222 2428; www.key2persia.com; Karim Khan-e Zand Blvd; ⏰9am-9pm Sat-Thu, to 1pm Fri) Offers a large range of cultural, adventure and ecofriendly tours (check website for details), this agency is particularly recommended for its popular half-day group trips to Persepolis for US$30 per person, leaving daily at 8am.

VISA EXTENSIONS

Department of Aliens Affairs (57 St, off Modares Blvd; ⏰8am-1pm Sat-Wed, 8-11am Thu) Extension requests take a minimum of two hours to process and cost IR340,000. The payment must be deposited at Bank Melli (Shohada Sq). To reach the Department of Aliens Affairs, bus 70 from Karim Khan-e Zand Blvd goes to Valiasr Sq, from where it is an easy walk; the office is on the 3rd floor.

Getting There & Away

AIR

It's easy to start or finish a trip to Iran in Shiraz because several airlines operate direct flights from **Shiraz International Airport** (☎flight info 071-3711 8890; www.shiraz.airport.ir) to Gulf cities and İstanbul. Destinations include Esfahan (from US$35, two weekly), Mashhad (from US$70, two weekly) and Tehran (from US$82, daily).

BUS & TAXI

Most long-distance buses and savaris operate from **Karandish terminal** (Terminal-e Bozorg; Salman-e Farsi Blvd).

Buses from Shiraz

DESTINATION	FARE (IR; VIP)	DURATION (HR)
Esfahan	300,000	8
Kashan	450,000	10
Mashhad	790,000	20
Tabriz	790,000	20
Tehran	570,000	13
Yazd	300,000	6½

Getting Around

Most people get around town by shuttle taxis, which ply the streets for around IR20,000 per trip. A typical short-hop *dar bast* taxi in the centre of town costs around IR100,000. A *dar bast* taxi between the airport and the city centre costs around IR250,000.

Short-hop journeys around the city originate from the local bus terminal and trips cost around IR10,000.

Persepolis پرسپولیس

071 / ELEV 1634M

One of the great wonders of the ancient world, Persepolis embodies not just a grand architectural scheme but also a grand idea. It was conceived by Darius the Great who, in 520 BC, inherited the responsibility for ruling the world's first known empire founded by his predecessor, Cyrus the Great. Embracing tenets such as cultural tolerance and fair treatment of all subjects, Darius sought to reflect these concepts in the design of the magnificent palace complex at Persepolis, inviting architects from the furthest corner of the Persian Empire to contribute to its construction. The result is an eclectic set of structures, including monumental staircases, exquisite reliefs and imposing gateways, that testified to the expanse of Darius' domain.

History

Work here began with Darius I (the Great), who took the throne in 520 BC, and it was added to by subsequent kings. It was a ceremonial capital at the heart of an enormous empire, a showcase designed to awe visitors with its scale and beauty. During the annual No Ruz (New Year) celebration, subjects came from across the empire to pay homage and tribute to the ruler. Persepolis was burned to the ground during Alexander the Great's visit in 330 BC.

Sights

Persepolis sits on top of a great plinth of stone blocks and today, as in ancient times, visitors seeking entry to the city must approach this elevated complex of wonders from a tree-lined avenue across the plain, before ascending to the entrance via the monumental **Grand Staircase**. The stairs were carved from massive blocks of stone, but each step was shallow so that Persians in long elegant robes could ascend the 111 steps gracefully. A small **museum** on site houses some interesting finds.

★Apadana Staircase RUINS

The stairs, which are guarded by stone soldiers, are decorated by an exceptionally finely crafted frieze in three panels. Each panel is divided into several tiers depicting the reception of various visitors to Persepolis and these can be read, by those with the expertise, almost like a history text book. As such, this is one sight that really repays the engagement of a qualified guide.

★Xerxes' Gateway GATE

The bronze trumpets that once heralded the arrival of important foreign delegations (a fragment of which is on display in the museum) may now be silent, but it is still possible to capture the sense of awe on approaching the colossal main gateway. Built during the reign of Xerxes I, who called this his Gate of All Nations, the pillared entrance is guarded by bearded and hoofed mythical figures in the style of Assyrian gate-guards.

★Apadana Palace PALACE

Constructed on a stone terrace by Xerxes I, the Apadana Palace lies largely in ruins. It's thought that this is where foreign delegations would have been received by the king and the splendour accompanying their audience is captured in the bas-reliefs on the northern wall.

Private Palaces PALACE

The palaces in the southwestern corner of the site are believed to have been constructed during the reigns of Darius and Xerxes. The **Tachara** is easily the most striking,

Persepolis

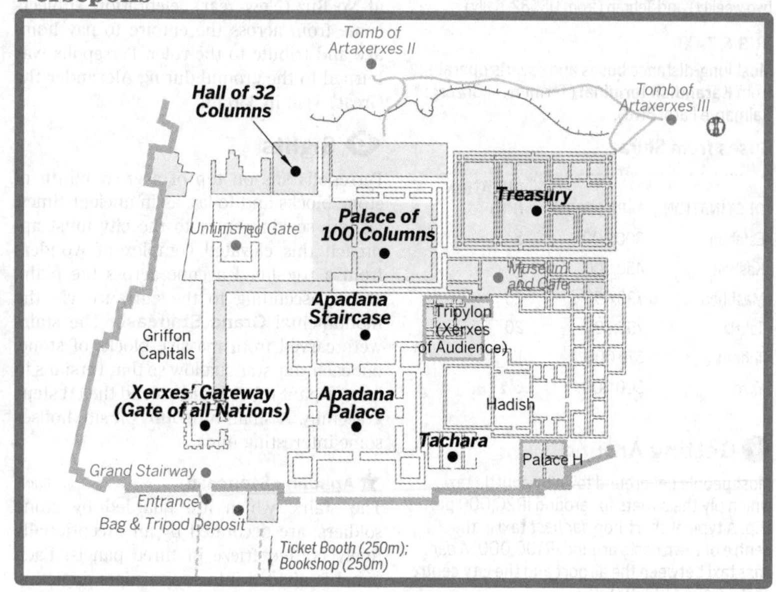

with many of its monolithic doorjambs still standing and covered in bas-reliefs and cuneiform inscriptions. The stairs on the southern side bear highly skilled reliefs and are some of the most photogenic. The palace opens onto a royal courtyard flanked by two palaces.

Tomb of Artaxerxes II TOMB

On the hill above the Treasury are two rock-hewn tombs. The larger and more elaborate of the two belongs to Artaxerxes II, and clambering up to this remarkable structure allows something of an aerial perspective on Persepolis and a better appreciation of its scale.

Palace of 100 Columns PALACE

With an extravagant hall measuring almost 70 sq metres and supported by 100 stone columns, this palace formed one of two principal reception areas in Persepolis. Built during the reigns of Xerxes and Artaxerxes I, some believe it was used to receive the military elite upon whom the empire's security rested. Today, enough of the broken columns remain to give an idea of the palace's former grandeur, and fine reliefs show a king, soldiers and representatives of 28 subject nations.

Tours

Just about every hotel in Shiraz organises tours to Persepolis, and prices are usually based on the rates set by the local cultural heritage and tourism office. Accredited guides generally have foreign-language skills and must carry a badge with a hologram, photograph and expiry date, and many drive their own vehicle. Their expertise obviously entitles them to charge more than a non-accredited driver – US$60 for up to three people for a half-day tour of Persepolis, Naqsh-e Rostam and Naqsh-e Rajab (US$85 for a whole-day tour including Pasargadae).

Pars Tourist Agency (p174) in Shiraz operates a daily half-day group bus tour with guide for US$30 per person, including entry fees (US$55 for day-trip including Pasargadae). Some travellers opt for a driver who speaks English (but doesn't guide) to ferry them around for a half-day (IR800,000 plus IR160,000 for each extra hour).

Sleeping

Hotel Persepolis HOTEL $$

(☎071-4334 1550; www.persepolis-apadana-hotel.com; s/d US$43/74, d with view of Persepolis US$96; P ❄) Guests at this gracious hotel, with its attractive porch and fine garden, can enjoy the perfect shaded view of the ruins of Persepolis while sipping tea from white china. Rooms are comfortable and the service charming. There's also a rather grand restaurant with a menu of Persian favourites, such as a daily stew with rice (IR250,000).

Getting There & Away

While tours, especially with licensed driver-guides, offer the most rewarding way of visiting Persepolis, it is possible to visit the ruins by other means. A return taxi costs IR400,000 from Shiraz, including an hour's waiting time. Minibuses from Karandish bus terminal in Shiraz to Marvdasht cost IR40,000, from where a *dar bast* taxi to Persepolis should cost IR160,000, although local taxi drivers tend to charge foreigners a premium.

Taxis wait outside the entrance gate to Persepolis for the return trip to Shiraz and are usually willing to add in quick stops at Naqsh-e Rostam and Naqsh-e Rajab for IR800,000.

There's no public transport linking Persepolis with Pasargadae, 84km to the northeast.

Naqsh-e Rostam & Naqsh-e Rajab

نقش رستم و نقش رجب

In the cliffs neighbouring Persepolis are two ancient sites featuring rock-hewn tombs that are well worth a visit. Naqsh-e Rajab is the closest to Persepolis but Naqsh-e Rostam is the more spectacular of the two sites.

Most tours to Persepolis also stop at Naqsh-e Rostam and Naqsh-e Rajab. It's feasible to walk the 6km from Persepolis to Naqsh-e Rostam, stopping off at Naqsh-e Rajab en route in winter but this is not an option in the heat of summer. Alternatively, a round trip in a *dar bast* taxi from Persepolis costs IR500,000 including waiting time.

Sights

★Naqsh-e Rostam TOMB

(Marv Dasht–Sarooie Rd; IR200,000; ⏲8am-6pm winter, 7.30am-8pm summer) The spectacular rock tombs at Naqsh-e Rostam are a must-see. Hewn out of a cliff high above the ground, the four tombs are believed to be those of Darius II, Artaxerxes I, Darius I and Xerxes I (from left to right facing the cliff), although historians are still debating this. The seven Sassanian stone reliefs cut into the cliff depict vivid scenes of imperial conquests and royal ceremonies; signboards below each relief give a detailed description in English.

Naqsh-e Rajab RUINS

(off Marv Dasht–Sarooie Rd; IR80,000; ⏲8am-6pm winter, 7.30am-8pm summer) On the old Shiraz–Esfahan road, these rock carvings could easily escape notice if it weren't for the sign and the entry kiosk. Four fine Sasanian bas-reliefs are hidden here from the road by the folds of a rocky hill and depict various scenes from the reigns of Ardashir I and Shapur the Great.

Getting There & Away

Taxis waiting outside the entrance gate to Persepolis for the return trip to Shiraz can be persuaded to make a detour at Naqsh-e Rostam and Naqsh-e Rajab with a brief stop at each for IR800,000. These two sites are also usually included in a guided tour to Persepolis from Shiraz.

Pasargadae پاسارگاد

071 / POP 400 / ELEV 1847M

The village of Pasargadae, lying south of the Abarkuh Desert, stands on a lonely, windswept plain surrounded by arid mountains. The sole reason to journey out to this remote town is to visit the ancient monuments from which it takes its name. Marked by an austere beauty, these ruins of empire will enthral historians and those with a detective interest in piecing together the clues of an ancient civilization. It has to be said, there are not that many clues to go on, but enough to suggest that the ancients were sophisticated in their tastes and grand in their design.

Begun under Cyrus the Great in about 546 BC, Pasargadae developed into a city of some significance until it was superseded by Darius I's magnificent palace at Persepolis. The key sights in this isolated plain are the Tomb of Cyrus, Darius' Garden and Cyrus' Private Palace. The whole site can be visited in a couple of hours – an hour less with private transport.

Sights

★Tomb of Cyrus TOMB

Proud and alone on the Morghab Plain, the Tomb of Cyrus is the first of the monuments encountered on entering the site of Pasargadae. The tomb consists of a modest rectangular burial chamber perched on six tiered plinths. Its unique architecture is a totem of conquest, combining elements of all the major civilisations captured by Cyrus.

Cyrus' Private Palace RUINS
'I am Cyrus, the Achaemenid King' reads the cuneiform inscription on a pillar of Cyrus' palace complex. The minimal ruins of what must have been a grand set of structures lie about 1km north of the king's tomb. Archaeologists note the unusual plan of the palace with its central hall of 30 columns (the stumps of which remain), and its two great opposing verandahs, but it takes a bit of imagination to reassemble the fallen masonry.

Prison of Solomon RUINS
Around 500m north of Cyrus' Private Palace are the remains of the Prison of Solomon (Zendan-e Soleiman), variously thought to be a fire temple, tomb, sundial or store. On the hill beyond is the **Tall-e Takht** – a monumental 6000-sq-metre citadel used from Cyrus' time until the late Sassanian period. Local historians believe the references to Solomon date from the Arab conquest, when the inhabitants of Pasargadae renamed the sites with Islamic names to prevent their destruction.

ℹ Getting There & Away

The easiest way to reach Pasargadae by public transport is to board a bus between Shiraz and Yazd or Esfahan (or vice versa) along Hwy 65 and alight at the Pasargadae junction. From here taxis cover the 5.5km along Pasargad Rd to the ruins (IR100,000). More conveniently, it is easy to find a taxi from Shiraz for the 84km round trip (around IR2,400,000, with a one-hour wait).

NORTHEASTERN IRAN
شمال شرقی ایران

Mashhad مشهد

☎051 / POP 2,965,000 / ELEV 975M

Mashhad is Iran's holiest and second-biggest city. Its *raison d'être* and main sight is the beautiful, massive shrine complex commemorating the AD 817 martyrdom of Shiite Islam's eighth Imam, Reza. Tens of millions converge here yearly to pay their respects; witnessing the emotion is profoundly moving. During major pilgrim periods, accommodation and transport books out.

Sights

★**Haram-e Razavi** ISLAMIC SITE
(حرم امام رضا; www.imamrezashrine.com; 24hr) FREE Imam Reza's Holy Shrine is enveloped in a vast series of sacred precincts collectively known as the Haram-e Razavi, or Haram for short. This magical city-within-a-city sprouts dazzling clusters of domes and minarets in blue and pure gold behind courtyards and magnificent arched arcades. It's one of the marvels of the Islamic world, and it's worth savouring its moods and glories more than once by visiting at different times of day.

Holy Shrine ISLAMIC SHRINE
(Haram Complex) Amid tearful prayer and meditation, the climax to any Mashhad pilgrimage is touching and kissing the *zarih* (gold-latticed cage), which covers Imam Reza's tomb in the Haram's central shrine beneath the iconic golden dome. Non-Muslims are generally excluded from visiting this inner sanctum but can see a *zarih* on display in the Haram's Central Museum.

Imam Khomeini Ravagh ISLAMIC SITE
(Haram Complex; 24hr) All a-dazzle with intricate, mirror-faceted tiling, this former courtyard is now enclosed and entirely covered by a sparkling ceiling held in place by large, well-spaced columns that spread up and out like conical trees. Sunset prayers are often led from here, with both sexes worshipping together in the large, carpeted space.

Carpet Museum MUSEUM
(موزه فرش; Kausar Courtyard, Haram Complex; IR5000; 8am-12.30pm Sat-Wed, to 11.30am Thu, to noon Fri) Arguably the Haram's best museum. Rugs displayed here range from beautiful classics through to garish coral gardens and a Tabriz-made carpet-portrait of WWI bogeyman Kaiser Wilhelm II. Tying the staggering 30 million knots for *Seven Beloved Cities* took 14 years.

Central Museum MUSEUM
(موزه مرکزی; Kausar Courtyard, Haram Complex; IR10,000; 8am-5.45pm Sat-Thu, to noon Fri) This eclectic museum kicks off with chunks of now-superseded shrine decor interspersed with contemporary sporting medals presented by pious athletes, while the basement **stamp collection** includes a 1983 commemorative featuring the 'Takeover of the US Spy Den'. The 1st-floor **Visual Arts Gallery** offers you the opportunity to shower money (or hats) down onto the top of the Holy Shrine's fourth *zarih* tomb encasement (replaced in 2001).

Tours

Faramarz Aminian OUTDOORS
(☎0915 508 5420; aminian.faramarz@gmail.com) Offers imaginative, tailor-made itineraries, including saffron field tours in October and visits to nomad areas around Kalat in spring.

Central Mashhad

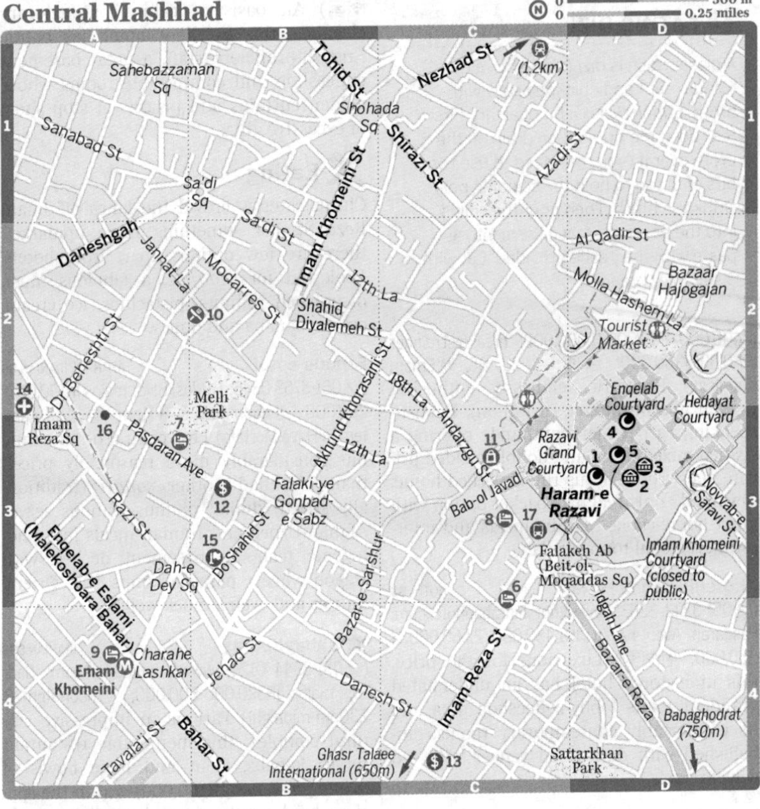

Central Mashhad

Top Sights
1 Haram-e Razavi D3

Sights
2 Carpet Museum D3
3 Central Museum D3
4 Holy Shrine D3
5 Imam Khomeini Ravagh D3

Sleeping
6 Javad Hotel C3
7 Khorshid Taban Hotel A3
8 Kosar Ghods Hotel C3
9 Vali's Non-Smoking Homestay A4

Eating
10 Hezardestan Traditional Teahouse B2

Shopping
11 Carpet Bazaar C3

Information
12 Baghoi Exchange B3
13 Ghasr International Hotel C4
14 Imam Reza Hospital A2
15 Turkmen Consulate B3

Transport
16 Adibian Travel & Tours A3
17 Andarzgu Bus Stop C3
HGH724 .... (see 9)

Sleeping

Hundreds of apartment-hotels cater to pilgrim groups. In peak season, prices soar. Standards and cleanliness vary considerably.

★ **Vali's Non-Smoking Homestay** HOSTEL **$**
(☎051-3851 6980, 0939 250 1447; www.valishomestay.com; 277, Malekoshoara Bahar 38th Alley; dm/s/d without bathroom

EATING DIZI

A classic dish is *dizi* (abgusht), a delicious meat and chickpea stew with broth. Eating *dizi* is a bit of an art. First, tear up some bread then drain off the broth over it (you may need to use two bits of bread to hold the scalding pot). Drink the broth. Then pour the solids into the bowl and mash them into a paste with the pestle provided. Eat with a spoon or bread.

IR400,000/800,000/1,000,000, breakfast/dinner IR80,000/180,000; ; 83, 86, Emam Khomeini) Eccentric, endlessly enthusiastic Vali is a hospitable (if full-on), English-speaking carpet merchant/guide offering a six-bed mixed dorm and double-bedded private guest room in his rug-bedecked home. Mashhad's only real backpacker option with great home-cooked family meals and interesting regional tours available.

Khorshid Taban Hotel HOTEL $$
(051-3222 2263; www.khorshidtabanhotel.com; Pasdaran Ave; s/d/tr IR1,480,000/2,560,000/3,150,000;) Luxurious for the price, this nine-storey hotel has an understated grandeur to its lobby/coffeeshop area and its comfortably contemporary rooms, embellished with dark-wood veneer with red velvet panels.

Kosar Ghods Hotel HOTEL $$
(www.kosaronline.com; Andarzgu St, btwn 2nd & 4th Alley; s/d IR994,000/1,520,000;) With an unbeatable Haram-front location staring straight at the main entrance gates, the Kosar Ghods' compact rooms are fairly modest but bright and clean, with gleaming tiled floors. It's between 2nd and 4th alleys, signed in Farsi and Arabic (but not in English).

★**Ghasr Talaee International** HOTEL $$$
(051-38038; www.ghasrtalaee.com; Imam Reza St; s IR2,790,000, d IR3,990,000-4,990,000;) A gigantic chandelier, tinkling piano music and suavely personable, English-speaking staff welcome guests into this lush five-star hotel with 650 rooms spread over 20 storeys.

★**Javad Hotel** HOTEL $$$
(051-3222 4135; www.javadhotel.com; Imam Reza St; full season s/d IR2,200,000/3,800,000, off-season IR1,500,000/2,800,000;) An oasis of calm, contemporary elegance, this excellent hotel has polite, English-proficient staff, a great basement coffeeshop and comfortable rooms whose golden curtains add pizazz yet stop short of excessive glitz.

Eating

Cheap eateries crowd the lanes off Imam Reza St. For something more upmarket, there are few options apart from hotels. Look out for *maajun*, a fabulous mush of crushed walnuts, pistachios, ice cream, cream, banana and honey.

Fanous-e Abi AFGHANI, IRANIAN $$
(051-3768 0345; Ferdosi Blvd; mains IR100,000-290,000; noon-4pm & 8-11pm; 12 to Aparteman Haye Mortafa) Less central or authentic but considerably more reasonably priced than Mashhad's other *sonati* (traditionally styled) dining options, Fanous serves Afghan-Uzbek and Iranian meals in a photogenic teahouse basement decked with wagon wheels, paraffin lamps, 'Old Orient' murals and even a mock well.

★**Babaghodrat** IRANIAN $$$
(051-3344 0124; www.babaghodrat.com; Sadr 16; mains IR320,000-600,000; noon-4pm & 7.30pm-midnight) Part of an impressive cultural complex, this memorable restaurant serves kababs, trout and huge bowls of *mirza ghasemi* (IR160,000) within the spacious brick vaults of a Qajar-era caravanserai. It's around 10 minutes' walk from the southeast end of the Reza covered bazaar.

★**Hezardestan Traditional Teahouse** IRANIAN $$$
(051-3222 2943; Jannat Lane; mains IR287,500-540,500; 11am-4pm & 6-11pm) Hezardestan is one of Iran's most beautiful teahouse-restaurants, with a museum-like basement full of of carpets, samovars, antique metalwork and countless knick-knacks around a small fountain. The menu is limited to *ghormeh*, chicken kabab, *dizi* or mashed *halim bademjan* (lamb and mashed aubergine).

Shopping

Mashhad is great for buying carpets (browse the **Carpet Bazaar** (Andarzgu 13th Alley; approx 9am-1pm & 4pm-sunset)) in distinctive Khorasan styles. Other purchases include turquoise, saffron and shrine souvenirs of debatable taste.

Information

MEDICAL SERVICES

Imam Reza Hospital (☎051-3854 3031; www.mums.ac.ir; Ibn-e Sina St) Good, accessible hospital with 24-hour pharmacy.

MONEY

Baghoi Exchange (☎051-3853 3438; Imam Khomeini St; ⏰9am-2pm & 5-7pm Sat-Wed, 9am-1pm Thu)

Ghasr International Hotel (Imam Reza St, cnr 16th Alley; ⏰24hr) for after-hours exchange.

VISAS FOR ONWARD TRAVEL

Turkmen Consulate (☎051-3854 7066; Do Shahid St, off Dah-e Dey Sq; ⏰8.30-noon Mon-Thu & Sat) Allow at least 10 days to get a five-day transit visa (US$55 to $85, depending on nationality).

TRAVEL AGENTS

Very professional **Adibian Travel & Tours** (☎051-5513 2539; www.adibian.com; Pasdaran Ave, cnr 4th Alley; ⏰8am-7pm Sat-Wed, to 6pm Thu, 9am-noon Fri) is an English-speaking agency that sells air and train tickets. **HGH724** (☎051-3806 9000; www.hgh724.com; Malekoshoara Bahar St; ⏰8.30am-7pm Sat-Thu; Ⓜ Imam Khomeini) is also reliable for air tickets.

Getting There & Away

During peak seasons long-distance transport can be booked up months ahead.

AIR

To Tehran there are over two dozen daily flights (IR2,000,000 to IR2,800,000) on at least seven airlines. There are at least three flights daily to Esfahan, Shiraz, Tabriz and Yazd, none costing over IR3,000,000.

Iran Aseman (www.iaa.ir) has flights to Dushanbe, Tajikistan (from IR6,100,000, Thursday) and other international connections are available.

BUS

The huge **Imam Reza Bus Terminal** (end of Imam Reza St; 🚌84) handles most long-distance services. Pre-purchase tickets for most routes. Destinations include Esfahan (IR780,000, VIP; 22 hours), Tehran (IR685,000, VIP; 12 hours) and Yazd (IR645,000, VIP; 16 hours).

TRAINS

Destinations include the following:

Esfahan (IR720,000, 18 hours)
Tabriz (IR440,000, 24 hours)
Tehran (IR1,130,000, 12 hours)
Yazd (IR900,000, 14 hours)

Getting Around

TO/FROM THE AIRPORT

The airport, 5km east of Imam Reza Bus Terminal, has three terminals. The metro station is at Terminal 1 but trains are infrequent. Bus 77 leaves on the hour (6am to 8pm) from stops just west of Terminal 1 and outside Terminal 2. It returns from the Enghelab City Terminal on the half-hour.

Most travellers use taxis, which should cost around IR120,000 to the central area.

BUS

Buses cost IR5000 per hop, or IR3500 if you pay using an electronic, pre-paid MAN-card (IR50,000 deposit). Most buses stop running after 9pm. Useful services include bus 83, which goes from the main bus terminal to the train station via central Mashhad.

METRO

Tickets for two/six rides on the 24-station metro line 1 cost IR20,000/40,000 from shops in the station.

UNDERSTAND IRAN

Iran Today

At a Crossroads

Modern Iran seems to be forever sitting at a crossroads between Islam and the West, between reformists and conservatives, between rogue state and responsible international citizen. Whichever of these Irans is in ascendance, the country remains one of the Middle East's most important regional powers. And just as relations between Iran and 'the Great Satan' (USA) appeared to be thawing, along came Donald Trump.

Liberal–Conservative Divide

For most of the last 100 years, power in Iran has swung like a pendulum between two very different views of the world. On one side, the liberals and Reformists, those who enjoyed the social freedoms of the Shah's Iran and rejoiced as President Khatami led a mini-revolution in the way the Islamic Revolution saw itself.

Although it is always dangerous to generalise, it is the young and the urban who most often define this stream of Iranian society. Pitted against them all too often are the conservatives led by the clerical establishment, the guardians of the Islamic Revolution, and with a loyal rural heartland. They are the Ayatollah Khomeini's footsoldiers, and those who swept (former president) Mahmood Ahmadinejad to power in 2005 and kept him there.

Regional Meddling

Few countries hold as much power in the Middle East right now as Iran. Having taken up the mantle of defender of Shiites and their interests across the region, and having spent decades channelling funds into the coffers of friendly governments and movements, Iran now has a powerful voice in what happens in some of the world's most important conflicts.

Iranian-backed Hezbollah is widely credited with propping up the Syrian government, fighting alongside government troops to turn back the march of Islamic State and other groups who would overthrow the Assad regime. In Lebanon and Iraq, both countries with Shiite majorities like Iran, Iran has advisors on the ground and provides financial support to ensure that its view of politics prevails. In this role, Iran provides a counterpoint to Saudi Arabia and the Gulf States as regional powers.

Iran & the USA

Iran's relationship with the West, particularly the United States, has long defined the image the country has of itself and which it projects onto the world stage. Relations between Iran and the West began to thaw under President Khatami. After many years of tough negotiations, sanctions and brinkmanship finally culminated in a mutual victory whereby Iran's nuclear program would come under international supervision in return for the lifting of sanctions. Iran was, it seemed, finally about to come in from the cold. And then, along came Donald Trump who has made the nuclear deal one of the foreign policy platforms of his campaign. The rapprochement between Iran and the West is currently holding but who knows for how long.

TOMANS

Visitors quickly discover the idiosyncratic local practice of talking about prices in 'tomans' rather than rials. One toman is worth 10 rials.

Worse, many people will knock off the thousands, so 'five' becomes shorthand for 5000 tomans, ie 50,000 rials.

However confusing this sounds, once you get a feel for what things cost, you'll get the hang of it quickly.

In the interim, get the price written down, and double-check ask whether it's in rials or tomans.

History

Elam & the Aryans

A prominent early civilisation was Elam, a kingdom influenced by Sumer and regularly at war with them. The Elamites' capital, Susa (Shush), is Iran's most important archaeological site.

In the late 2nd millennium BC, Indo-European Aryan tribes began arriving from the north. Persians settled in central Iran, bringing the teachings of Zoroaster and the worship of Ahuramazda, traditions that would coalesce into what we now know as Zoroastrianism.

Achaemenids

The Persians and northwesterly Medes were unified under Cyrus, who ascended the throne in 559 BC and within 20 years created the greatest empire the world had known.

Darius I expanded the empire and created the magnificent ceremonial complex at Persepolis to serve as imperial showcase. The defeat of his son Xerxes at Salamis in Greece in 480 BC began a slow decline culminating in Alexander the Great's conquest 150 years later.

Parthians & Sassanians

After Alexander's death, Persia was controlled by the Seleucids, but the Parthians, expert horseriders and archers, took over in the 3rd century and ruled for five centuries, punctuated by regular skirmishes with the Romans.

The Sassanians (Sassanids), went one better. In AD 260 King Shapur defeated the Romans at Edessa and actually captured Emperor Valerian.

Arab Conquest, Seljuks & Mongols

The Arabs defeated the Sassanians twice in 637, effectively ending the dynasty. The Persians adopted Islam but Iranian culture and administration enormously influenced the Arabs as they spread across the Middle East.

As caliphate power waned in the 9th century, local tribes established their own dynasties, eventually ousted by the Seljuks, a Turkic people who captured Esfahan in 1051, making it the capital. Their rule heralded a new era in Persian art, architecture, literature and science but their political power soon fragmented.

In the early 13th century, they came to a bloody end when rampaging Mongols under Genghis Khan and later his grandson, swept across the Iranian plateau, leaving devastation in their wake. Despite the destruction, they eventually became great arts patrons and endowed many fine monuments.

However, in a story repeated throughout Iranian history, the tough conquerors found that the seductive Persian culture with its poetry, wine and romance soon rendered them ripe for conquest by the next hardcase who showed up on their borders.

That was Tamerlane, who came from Central Asia and conquered Persia, becoming famous for both his penchant for the arts and his bloodthirstiness.

Safavid Iran & the 18th century

Synonymous with the glory of Iran, the Safavids ruled from the early 16th-century. They turned Persia Shiite and ushered in a great national revival, especially under Shah Abbas I (r 1587–1629) who made Esfahan a wondrous city.

Things fell apart again in the 18th century, but two notable figures were Nader Shah, a military genius whose wars finally bankrupted the country, and Karim Khan Zand, a more dove-ish figure responsible for a golden age in Shiraz.

Foreign Powers

Constant meddling in Iranian affairs by Britain and Russia characterised the 19th century and Qajar dynasty. The pattern continued through the 20th century, with the pro-democracy Constitutional movement put down partly by Russia, then British-backed Reza Shah staging a coup and founding the Pahlavi dynasty.

Meanwhile, oil was drilled by the Anglo-Persian company (now BP) but outdated original agreements didn't fairly compensate Iran. When reforming prime minister Mohammad Mossadegh tried for a better deal in the 1950s, the British refused, so he nationalised the industry. The CIA, paranoid about the spread of socialism, helped orchestrate a coup and Mossadegh was toppled in 1953.

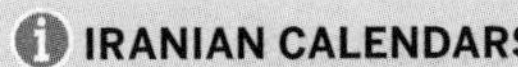

IRANIAN CALENDARS

The Persian solar calendar is in official and everyday use; the Muslim lunar calendar is used for Islamic religious matters; and the Western (Gregorian) calendar is used in dealing with foreigners. For conversions, refer to www.iranchamber.com/calendar/converter/iranian_calendar_converter.php

The Islamic Revolution

Under Pahlavi rule, resistance had smouldered. Secular, communist and Islamic groups had a common desire to remove the shah, whose reforms were too slow for some and too un-Islamic for others. Exiled Ayatollah Khomeini was an inspirational figure, but much of the organising was done by unionists, communists and ordinary middle-class citizens. On 16 January 1979, Shah Mohammad Reza Pahlavi and his third wife, Farah Diba fled. Khomeini took the reins and moved fast, eliminating opposition and establishing a theocracy under the principle of *velayat-e faqih* (rule of Islamic jurists).

A brutal war with Western-backed Saddam Hussein's Iraq followed, and the sacrifice, often religiously inspired, of the Iranians became legendary: these *shuhada* (martyrs) are revered nationwide.

Khomeini died in 1989 and the supreme leadership passed to Ali Khamenei. Under him, presidents have ranged from smooth operator Akbar Hashemi Rafsanjani (1989–97) to reformist cleric Mohammad Khatami (1997–2005) and populist, hardline Mahmood Ahmadinejad (2005–2013). The election of Hassan Rouhani, seen as a moderate and a reformer, in 2013 sparked hope for systemic change.

A GUIDE TO KABABS

In any restaurant, most main-dish options will be kabab. These are served either with bread or with buttery rice *(chelo kabab)*. Kababs are yummy, healthy and cooked shish-style over charcoal. Fish kababs are often available, and very tasty. Other common incarnations include the following:

Barg Pieces of lamb or beef

Bakhtiari *Barg* and *juje*

Juje Marinated chicken pieces

Kubideh Minced mutton, breadcrumbs and onion

Sheesh/Shishlik Grilled meat pieces with bone, often lamb chops

Soltani *Kubideh* and *barg*

Food & Drink

Iran is home to a diverse cuisine with great regional variations. Restaurant menus are over-dominated by kababs and fast food, so you'll sometimes have to make a bit of an effort to find other specialities.

Dishes to look out for include *zereshk polo ba morgh* (chicken on rice tangy with barberries), *ghorme sabzi* (meat, beans and vegetables, served with rice) and *khoresht* (thick stew) including *fesenjan* (a pomegranate and walnut stew, normally with chicken).

Teahouses are venues for tea and *qalyan* waterpipes but also characterful spots for eating.

Soups – usually barley-based, often with barberries – and salads are the traditional accompaniments to a meal. Upmarket restaurants may have a salad bar.

Iran produces a head-spinning array of freshly made *shirini* (sweets): every town has its local specialties.

In the absence of alcohol, fruit-flavoured soft drinks are popular. 'Lemon beer' is a sweet, malt-based tipple with a shandy-ish flavour.

Arts

Architecture

Iranian architecture has influenced building throughout much of the Islamic world. Marvelling at mosques such as the small but perfect Masjed-e Sheikh Lotfollah in Esfahan will be among the highlights of your trip.

The defining aspects of Persian architecture are its monumental simplicity and lavish use of ornamentation and colour. Standard elements include: a courtyard and arcades, lofty entrance porticoes and four *iwan* (barrel-vaulted halls opening onto the courtyard).

These basic features are often so densely covered with decoration that observers are led to imagine the architecture is far more complex than it actually is. The decorations are normally geometric, floral or calligraphic.

Carpets

The best-known Iranian cultural export, the Persian carpet, is far more than just a floor covering to an Iranian. A Persian carpet is a display of wealth, an investment, an integral aspect of religious and cultural festivals, and part of everyday life.

Carpets come in almost as many different designs as there are ethnic groups and major urban centres. Some are inspired by religion; other common motifs include amulets to avert the evil eye and other, pre-Islamic motifs, such as stylised trees of life. They may also be inspired by whatever surrounds the weaver, such as animals and flowers, particularly the lotus, rose and chrysanthemum. Gardens are commonly depicted.

In general, designs are classified as either 'tribal' or 'city' carpets. Tribal designs vary greatly depending on their origin, but are typically less ornate. City carpets are the classic Persian rugs, usually highly ornate floral designs around one or more medallions.

Millions of Iranians work in the industry but maintaining the brand is increasingly difficult with cheaper 'Persian carpets' being produced in India and Pakistan, and fewer young Iranians interested in learning to weave.

Poetry

Iranians venerate their great poets, who are seen as guardians of Persian culture and have mausolea that are popular pilgrimage sites. For more on Iranian poets, see p547.

Cinema

Iranian filmmakers are hugely popular in the Western art-house scene, though you're unlikely to see much of their work while in

Iran, where locally made action films and dubbed Bollywood flicks dominate. Worth looking for: *A Separation* by Asghar Farhadi, *10* by Abbas Kiarostami, *Time For Love, Kandahar* or *Gabbeh* by Mohsen Makhmalbaf; *Blackboards* or *The Apple* by his daughter Samira Makhmalbaf; *Children of Heaven* or *The Willow Tree* by Majid Majidi; *The White Balloon* by Jafar Panahi; or *The Lizard* (Marmulak) by Kamal Tabrizi.

Held in April, the **Fajr International Film Festival** (www.fajriff.com/en/) is Iran's premier film festival and features Iranian and international films and red-carpet events in more than 20 cinemas across Tehran.

SURVIVAL GUIDE

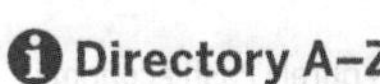

Directory A–Z

ACCOMMODATION

Hotels Upmarket hotels are few but on the increase. Midrange has the greatest choice with converted courtyard hotels (*hotel sonnati*) the country's most atmospheric option.

Mosaferkhanehs Basic lodging houses or very basic hotels with dorm beds, shared bathrooms, a predominantly local male clientele and very simple facilities.

Camping There are very few official camping areas and camping is rarely appropriate.

ACTIVITIES

With its mountainous terrain and position on a bird migration route, Iran is a great place for climbing, skiing and birdwatching. The following agencies can help with specialist tours:

Iran Mountain Zone (www.mountainzone.ir)

Sepid Mountaineering Company (0917-313 2926, 0711-235 5939; www.iransightseeing.com)

Iran Ski Federation (021-2256 9595; www.skifed.ir)

Birding Pal (http://birdingpal.org/Iran)

DANGERS & ANNOYANCES

In general, Iran is one of the world's safest countries for travellers.

Crossing the road is a different story: Iranian traffic is a gloriously (but perilously) anarchic free-for-all. Watch how the locals cross, and then go: boldly but cautiously.

Police won't usually give you any hassle unless you're breaking the law. Don't take photographs of bridges, borders, airports, and sensitive areas.

EMBASSIES & CONSULATES

For Iranian embassies see the **Iranian Ministry of Foreign Affairs** (www.mfa.ir) site. Addresses here are in Tehran; consulates are listed under Tabriz and Mashhad.

Afghan Embassy (Map p142; 021-8873 7050; www.afghanembassy.ir; cnr 4th & Pakistan Sts, off Beheshti Ave; 8am-2pm Sat-Wed; M Shahid Beheshti) Issue of tourist visas (for most nationalities around US$100) is unpredictable.

Australian Embassy (Map p142; 021-8386 3666; www.iran.embassy.gov.au; 2 23rd St, off Khaled Eslamboli St; 7.30am-noon & 12.30-3.30pm Sun-Wed, to 2.45pm Thu; M Mosalla)

Azerbaijani Embassy (Map p146; 021-2256 3146; www.tehran.mfa.gov.az; 16 Rastovan St; 9am-12.30pm Sat-Wed; M Shariati) It costs €60 for a 30-day tourist visa for most; ready in a day – you can pick it up between 5pm to 6pm.

Dutch Embassy (Map p146; 021-2366 0000; http://iran.nlembassy.org; 60 West Arghavan St; 7.30am-4pm Sun-Wed, to 1.30pm Thu; M Nobonyad)

French Embassy (Map p142; 021-6409 4000; www.ambafrance-ir.org; 64 Nofl Loshato St; 8.30am-noon Mon-Thu; M Teatr-e Shahr)

German Embassy (Map p142; 021-3999 0000; www.teheran.diplo.de; 324 Ferdowsi St; 7am-3.30pm Sun-Thu; M Sa'di)

Italian Embassy (Map p142; 021-6672 6955; www.ambteheran.esteri.it; 68 Nofl Loshato St; 9am-1pm Sun-Thu; M Teatr-e Shahr)

New Zealand Embassy (Map p146; 021-2612 2175; www.mfat.govt.nz/en/countries-and-regions/middle-east/iran/new-zealand-embassy; cnr 2nd Park Alley, Sosan St, North Golestan Complex, Aghdasiyeh St; 8.30am-12.30pm & 1-3pm Sun-Thu)

Pakistani Embassy (Map p142; 021-6694 1388; www.mofa.gov.pk/iran; 1 Etemadzadeh Ave; 8.30am-1.30pm Sat-Wed; M Meydan-e Enghelab Eslami) Only visas for Iranians.

SLEEPING PRICE RANGES

The following price ranges refer to a double room including tax and breakfast unless stated. Prices in Tehran and Central Iran range from $50 to over $200.

$ less than US$40

$$ US$40 to US$150

$$$ more than US$150

Turkish Embassy (Map p142; ☎021-3595 1100; http://tehran.emb.mfa.gov.tr; 337 Ferdowsi St; ⏲9am-5pm Sun-Thu; Ⓜ Sa'di)

Turkmenistan Embassy (Map p146; ☎021-2220 6306; http://iran.tmembassy.gov.tm; 5 Barati St, off Vatanpour St; ⏲9.30-11am Sun-Thu; Ⓜ Tajrish, then taxi)

UK Embassy (Map p142; ☎021-6405 2000; www.gov.uk; 198 Ferdowsi St; ⏲7.30am-2pm Sun-Thu; Ⓜ Sa'di) Still closed at time of research but rumoured to be opening soon.

US Interests Section of Swiss Embassy (Map p146; ☎021-2200 6002; www.eda.admin.ch/tehran; 2 Yasaman St, off Sharifi Manesh Ave; ⏲8am-noon Sun-Thu; Ⓜ Sadr)

ETIQUETTE

Ta'arof is a system of formalised politeness ubiquitous in Iran. For example, an offer of food will be turned down several times, giving the person making the offer the chance to save face if in reality they don't have the ability to provide a meal. A good rule is to refuse any offer three times but, if they continue to insist, do accept. However, if a taxi driver or shopkeeper refuses payment, do remember that this is just *ta'arof* and insist on paying. Generally, Iranians realise that foreigners may not understand *ta'arof*, so you're unlikely to offend.

GAY & LESBIAN TRAVELLERS

Homosexuality is punishable in some cases by death.

Barbaric laws aside, there is no reason why gay and lesbian travellers shouldn't visit Iran. It makes sense not to advertise that you're part of a same-sex couple; discretion is the better part of valour.

HEALTH

- Iran has a good system of medical care, and it's usually easy to find an English-speaking doctor.
- Tap water is safe to drink.
- Pay for medical and health care then claim it back on insurance. Costs are very low.

> **EATING PRICE RANGES**
>
> The following price ranges refer to a main course in most of Iran.
>
> **$** less than US$5 (IR200,000)
>
> **$$** US$5–US$10 (IR200,000–IR375,000)
>
> **$$$** more than US$10 (IR375,000)
>
> In Tehran and central Iran, prices are almost double.

INSURANCE

- Travel insurance is compulsory.
- Shop around: some insurers consider the region a 'danger zone' and exclude it or charge large premiums.

INTERNET ACCESS

- Wi-fi is widespread, though speeds are slow.
- Internet cafes are known as *coffeenets*.
- Access to thousands of websites is blocked, from news sites to Twitter and Facebook (but not Skype). To get around this, most Iranians use a VPN client: set one up before leaving home.

LEGAL MATTERS

- All drug and alcohol use is illegal.
- Having unmarried sex with an Iranian can be very harshly dealt with.
- Deliberate refusal to wear correct hejab (woman's headscarf) is a crime.

MONEY

- Iran for the visitor is a purely cash economy. Bring enough cash in US dollars or euros for the duration of your trip. You cannot use credit or debit cards, travellers cheques or ATMs in Iran to withdraw money.
- Getting your hands on money once you're inside Iran is expensive and a nightmare.
- Currency is the Iranian rial and inflation high.
- It's easy to change euros, US dollars and some other currencies in Tehran and other big cities.
- Changing money on the street is common but illegal.
- The coins you'll see are IR250, IR500, IR1000, IR2000 and IR5000.The main notes are IR500, IR1000, IR2000, IR5000, IR10,000, IR20,000, IR50,000, IR100,000 and IR500,000.

Bargaining

As a general rule the prices of groceries, food, sights, transport (except private taxis) and most things with a price tag attached are fixed. But virtually all prices in the bazaar are negotiable, particularly for souvenir-type products and always for carpets. In touristed areas, bargaining is essential.

Tipping

Tipping is not a big deal. In most restaurants a service charge is added to the bill anyway.

OPENING HOURS

Opening and closing times can be erratic, but you can rely on most businesses closing Thursday afternoons and Friday (the Iranian weekend). Businesses and sights typically open longer hours in the summer months.

BUYING A CARPET

Iranians have had more than 2500 years to perfect the art of carpet making – and just as long to master the art of carpet selling. If you don't know your warp from your weft, it might be worth reading up before visiting Iran, or taking an Iranian friend when you go shopping (bearing in mind that professional 'friends' who make a living from commission are a fact of life).

If you know what you're doing you might pick up a bargain, but unless you're an expert, don't buy a carpet or rug as an investment – buy it because you like it. Before buying, lie the carpet flat to check for bumps or other imperfections. Small bumps will usually flatten out with wear but big ones are probably there to stay. To check if a carpet is handmade, turn it over; on most handmade pieces the pattern will be distinct on the underside (the more distinct, the better the quality).

TELEPHONE

- To dial out call 00; dialling in, drop the initial 0.
- Your home SIM won't work in Iran. A pay-as-you-go SIM card is easily bought.
- Irancell has a one-month tourist SIM card sold at a booth upstairs in Tehran's Imam Khomeini International Airport for IR500,000. The SIM gives IR200,000 worth of calls and texts plus 5GB of data.
- Credit can be topped up at vendors displaying yellow and blue MTN signs for an extra 10% on the value of the card.

TOILETS

- Almost all public toilets are squats: use the hose or carry toilet paper.
- Hotels usually have a choice of squat or throne and have toilet paper. Put used paper in the bin.

TOURS

Tours of Iran are a good way to make the most of a large, complex country. Recommended agencies include **Lupine Travel** (www.lupinetravel.co.uk), **Persian Voyages** (www.persianvoyages.com; UK) and **Distant Horizons** (www.distant-horizons.com; USA).

VISAS

- A visa is required by nearly all nationalities.
- Some nationalities can supposedly get a visa on arrival by air but this is not always reliable; to be on the safe side, apply for a visa two months in advance of travel.
- Reputable Iranian travel agencies can assist with the formalities on line.
- The standard tourist visa is 30 days, extendable for another 30 days while in Iran. Shiraz is reported to be the best place to do this.
- Costs vary by nationality.
- Israelis are refused entry and so is anyone with an Israeli stamp in their passport or a stamp from a border with Israel.
- Citizens of the USA (plus Canada and the UK at the time of research) must contract a ministry-approved driver/guide and submit a pre-planned itinerary when applying for a visa.

WOMEN TRAVELLERS

- Women travelling alone regularly report groping on public transport: sit in the back of taxis and use women-only carriages on the metro.
- On intercity buses, sit next to another woman or your male companion. On city buses, you must sit in the women's area at the back.
- Tampons are difficult to find.
- Greet men by placing your hand over your heart rather than shaking hands.

Modest Clothing

- All women visitors must wear figure-disguising clothing and cover their hair.
- Loose-fitting clothes should cover the neck, arms and backside (mid-thigh length). Jeans are ok but not skirts.
- At shrines, chadors (cover-all cloth) are usually compulsory but can be borrowed on-site.

Getting There & Away

ENTERING THE COUNTRY

Assuming you have a visa, border crossing is easy. Women need to be modestly dressed on arrival.

Imam Khomeini International Airport, Tehran Fixed-price taxi into town: IR750,000, depending on vehicle type; rip-offs are unusual if you use the official taxi queue. Bus to Metro station: IR75,000, plus IR7000 for Metro ticket to city centre

Shiraz International Airport Taxi into town: US$5

Turkish border at Bazargan Taxi to Maku: US$10. Onward bus to Tabriz: US$2

AIR

Most international flights arrive in Tehran, but there are also international flights to Tabriz, Shiraz, Esfahan and Mashhad.

BORDER CROSSINGS

It's possible to travel by land between Iran and seven neighbouring countries. Crossing from Turkey is easy and from Armenia, Azerbaijan and Turkmenistan is do-able with varying degrees of hassle. The borders to Afghanistan and Pakistan are straightforward, but check security before you head to these – both were off-limits at the time of writing. Foreigners cannot cross into Iraq proper, though the border to Iraqi Kurdistan is open intermittently.

Afghanistan

The border at Dogharon, 20km east of Taybad, is open but we strongly warn against crossing this border.

Armenia

There is one crossing point at Norduz. Armenian visas are issued at the border, though sometimes the bus leaves before you have your visa! Apart from that, it's pretty smooth.

Azerbaijan

Three recognised crossings: first, between Astara (Azerbaijan) and Astara (Iran), and second, between Culfa (Azerbaijan) and Jolfa (Iran), the latter leading to the exclave of Nakhchivan, from where you must fly to get to Baku. The third option, good if you want to go to Jolfa from Baku, is at Bilesuva, the border used by Baku–Nakhchivan buses. Visas not issued at border.

Iraq

Western government advisories contain strong warnings against travel in the areas in which any of Iraq's border crossings with Iran are located.

Pakistan

The only recognised crossing for foreigners is between Mirjaveh (Iran) and Taftan (Pakistan). Crossing this border is considered highly dangerous for Western travellers.

Turkey

The main road crossing to/from Turkey is at Gürbulak (Turkey) and Bazargan (Iran) where there are hotels, moneychanging facilities and regular transport on either side of the border.

Turkmenistan

There are three border posts open to foreigners: inconvenient and little-used Incheh Borun/Gyzyl-Etrek, Bajgiran linking Mashhad and the Turkmen capital Ashgabat, and Sarakhs and Saraghs for those heading east; the area around the latter should be visited with caution. You must change transport at all three crossings. **Stantours** (www.stantours.com) can help with the organisation and paperwork needed to cross these borders.

All airlines are based in Tehran except for Taban Air, which is in Mashhad. International flights are available on **Kish Air** (Code Y9; www.kishairline.com), **Mahan Air** (Code W5; www.mahan.aero), **Taban Airlines** (Code TBM; www.taban.aero), **Caspian Airlines** (Code RV; www.caspian.aero) and **Iran Air** (p148).

LAND

Bus

Buses run from Tabriz and Tehran to Ankara, İstanbul (about 36 to 42 hours and costing around US$60) and other Turkish cities. There are also services to Baku (Azerbaijan) and Yerevan (Armenia).

Train

The train from İstanbul to Tehran via Ankara and Tabriz is called the Trans-Asia Express. It runs weekly in either direction and, at the time of writing, trains on the 2968km journey departed İstanbul on Tuesday, and left Tehran on Wednesday; it takes 70 hours and costs about €50 each way. Seating is in comfortable 1st-class couchettes with four berths. Check www.raja.ir or the Turkish railways website at www.tcdd.gov.tr for the latest info.

SEA

The main shipping agency for trips across the Persian Gulf is **Valfajr-8** (www.valfajr.ir) but as services are infrequent, oft-delayed and more expensive than flying, few people travel by sea.

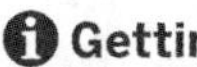

Getting Around

Transport is frequent, fairly modern and cheap. Travel agents will book planes, trains and, sometimes, buses, saving the trip to a transport terminal.

AIR

Domestic air fares in Iran are low and flights on most routes are frequent and reliable. Check out www.parvazyab.com or more usefully use the services of an in-country travel agent.

BUS

- Buses are cheap, comfortable and frequent. There are two general types of bus: normal *(mahmooly)* and VIP, which has reclining seats and more space, costing around 50% more.
- Some buses have toilets.
- Most services provide a meal or snack.
- At bus terminals, timetables are rarely in English but staff help foreigners board the right bus.
- Tickets, best bought in advance, are in Farsi, so learn the numerals.

CAR & MOTORCYCLE

You can hire cars in Iran, hire a driver-guide or, less popular these days, bring your own vehicle. City driving is hair-raising but roads are generally in good condition.

HITCHING

Hitching is never completely safe in any country and we do not recommend it. In Iran, hitching is a novel concept and women should not attempt it. Occasionally drivers will offer foreigners a free ride in return for practising their English or out of simple hospitality. You should offer to pay something, although it will usually be turned down.

LOCAL TRANSPORT

- Towns and cities have local buses, shuttle taxis, private taxis and, increasingly, a metro (only useful at present in Tehran).
- Bus numbers and destinations are usually only marked in Farsi. Tickets usually have to be bought at booths before boarding. Women and small kids board and sit at the back.
- Minibuses service local suburban routes and are often crammed: no room for segregation. Pay in cash when you get on.

Taxis

Shared shuttle taxis travel between major *meydans* (squares) and along main roads. Shout your destination at the driver through the window and they'll stop if going that way. Prices are low (from a few cents to a couple of dollars).

NA DAR BASTE!

If you hail an empty taxi the driver will hope you are hiring it privately, which is known as 'dar baste', literally 'closed door'. If you want to share – cheaper for you, less money for the driver – say *'na dar baste'*, and they'll let you know if they're interested.

Any taxi can be chartered, as can many private cars. Tell the driver where you want to go, and ask *'chand toman?'* Bargain to get 20% off the quoted price.

Agency taxis, or 'telephone' taxis, are ordered by phone – from the hotel if requested. Tehran and Yazd have women-only taxi companies.

Private Taxi

Almost every car in the country is available for private hire. Needless to say, prices are open to negotiation. One way to avoid getting ripped off is to ask the driver of a savari for the price per person of a certain trip then multiply it by four.

Savari

Savaris are shared taxis that run between towns up to a few hours apart. They're quicker but less comfortable than buses. A total of four passengers is normal: you wait for the savari to fill then depart. Passengers can agree to pay for empty seats between them.

Savaris usually leave from the relevant bus terminal. If in doubt, charter a private taxi and tell the driver *'savari'* and your destination.

TRAIN

- Iran's rail network is excellent, with largely modern trains.
- For routes and prices in English, check the non-official www.iranrail.net.
- The majority of trains have two classes. Some have bus-style seating, some compartments.
- From Tehran, there is at least one daily service to Mashhad, Esfahan and Tabriz. Trains usually depart on time. For stops en route, arrival times are often in the middle of the night.
- On overnight trains (usually to/from Tehran), the 1st-class carriages have sleeper couchettes *(ghazal)* with four or six bunks. There's a single-sex sleeper. Food is available on board.
- It's recommended you book ahead (not currently possible online). This is often easier to do with a travel agent than at the station itself.

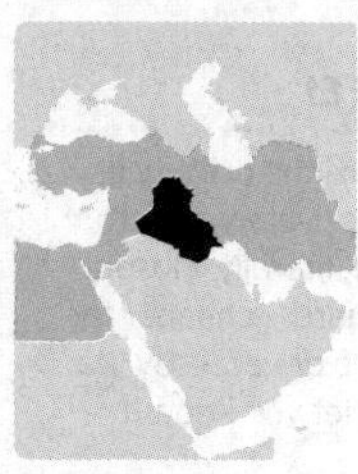

Iraq

Includes ➡

Iraq Explained............191
History.........................192
People & Society 197
Further Information... 198

Fast Facts

Area 438,317 sq km

Currency Iraqi dinar (ID)

Languages spoken Arabic, Kurdish

Population 38.15 million

Time Arabia Time Zone (GMT/UTC plus three hours)

Understand

Torn between its glorious past and its recent bloody history, Iraq is a country in turmoil. Just as the place was beginning to recover from the 2003 US-led invasion and its aftermath, jihadist group Isis took control of large swathes of the country's north in 2014. The tide may have turned back in favour of the Iraqi government with the recapture of Mosul and other cities in 2017, but most of Iraq remains extremely dangerous.

The country's attractions include breathtaking mountains, vibrant cities and numerous archaeological sites, not to mention a warm and hospitable population. But Western governments continue to advise against all but essential travel to parts of Iraqi Kurdistan and the south of the country, and against all travel to most of the north and west of Iraq. Follow their advice and postpone your visit until peace returns.

Resources

Iraqi Ministry of Foreign Affairs (www.mofa.gov.iq) Includes government-approved news and listings of Iraqi embassies abroad.

Kurdistan Regional Government (www.krg.org) Website of the Kurdish government with a brief history and news from a Kurdish perspective.

Kurdistan – The Other Iraq (www.theotheriraq.com) Focusing on all things Kurdish.

UNAMI (www.uniraq.org) UN Assistance Mission for Iraq with news on humanitarian issues.

BBC News (www.bbc.com/news/world/middle_east) Comprehensive news on the region.

International Crisis Group (www.crisisgroup.org/middle-east-north-africa/gulf-and-arabian-peninsula/iraq) In-depth reports on the country's pressure points and recent history.

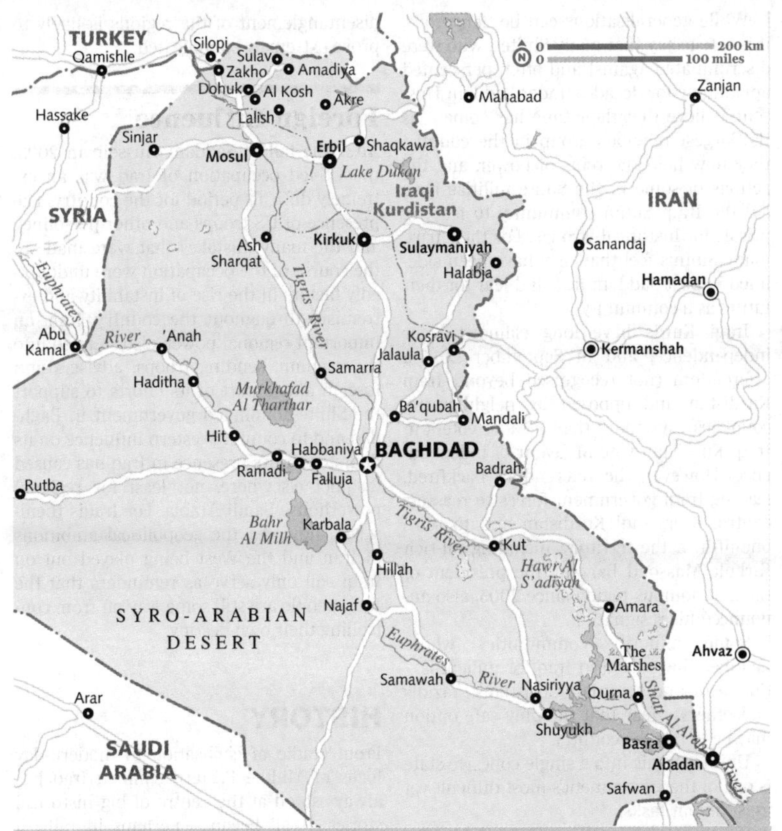

IRAQ EXPLAINED

Not for the first time in recent decades, Iraqis are emerging from a major conflict. In each of the last four decades, beginning with the 1980s, Iraq has been devastated by a massive war fought on its territory, leaving a conflict-weary population wondering if peace will ever come. Questions of reconstruction – of devastated cities and infrastructure, of the very idea of Iraq – lie at the centre of what comes next for Iraq and its long-suffering people.

Isis

When Isis seized Mosul and a swath of cities across northern and western Iraq in 2014, they seemed like an unstoppable force. The Iraqi Army surrendered in places almost without a fight, and only the rearguard action by the Peshmerga forces of Iraqi Kurdistan stopped Isis from reaching Baghdad and the predominantly Kurdish cities of the northeast. While the self-declared caliphate played on the fears of Sunni Muslims who worried about what would happen at the hands of a Shiite-dominated government, their brutality and targeting of minority Christian, Yazidi and Kurdish populations was anathema to many in a country that had always been predominantly Muslim but also strongly secular in outlook. The bloody conflict to wrest control of cities like Tikrit, Ramadi and especially Mosul back from Isis took a terrible toll. But if nothing else, it reinforced for many Iraqis that intolerance and extremism should have no future role in governing Iraq.

A Divided Country

It would be highly misleading to suggest that the unity of Iraqis in fighting Isis indicates a newfound national unity.

While generalisations can be dangerous, it is safe to say that many Shiites, who were discriminated against and often persecuted appallingly for decades under Saddam Hussein, believe that their time has come – as the largest religious group in the country, they now hold the reins of power, and the actions of some in the Shiite militias have led the Iraqi Sunni community to fear reprisals for historical wrongs. For their part, many Sunnis feel that they have been sidelined in post-Saddam Iraq and fear for their future as a community.

Iraqi Kurds have long clamoured for independence, and in September 2017 a referendum (not recognised beyond Iraqi Kurdistan and opposed by neighbouring countries) saw more than 90% of voters in Iraqi Kurdistan vote in favour of independence. However, the referendum backfired, leading Iraqi government forces to reassert control over Iraqi Kurdistan and to seize one-fifth of the territory, including oil-rich Kirkuk. Massoud Barzani, the president of the autonomous region since 2005, also announced his resignation.

Some minority communities whose members have lived in Iraq for millennia – Chaldean and Assyrian Christians, Yazidis and others – fear that the only safe option may be to flee the country.

Uniting Iraqis into a single cohesive state is one of the government's most difficult yet most urgent tasks.

The Break-Up of Iraq?

Analysts have long said that Iraq – created by foreign powers in the wake of WWII – is in fact three countries.

Kurdish independence is a perennial hot topic in Iraqi Kurdistan, and recent events have only reinforced the Kurdish conviction that they alone can be relied upon to defend their people. At the height of Isis' advance, 'disputed areas' like oil-rich Kirkuk were largely abandoned by an inefficient Iraqi Army and swiftly filled by Kurdish soldiers. Kirkuk has now been seized from the Kurds by Iraqi government forces.

The 2017 referendum on Kurdish independence was rejected by Iraq's central government, Iraq's neighbours and all major powers, but 92% of voters in Iraqi Kurdistan voted in favour of independence. However, with so many oil-rich lands close to the borders between Kurdish and Arab Iraq, any disentanglement of the regions is likely to prove extremely complicated.

Foreign Influence

After the fall of Saddam Hussein in 2003, the US-led occupation of Iraq was an extremely difficult period for the country. The presence of US troops and other personnel, and the many mistakes that were made in the course of the occupation were undoubtedly factors in the rise of instability and extremism throughout the country. Iran, an important regional power, also stepped into the vacuum, sending troops, advisers and foreign aid as part of its efforts to support the Shiite-dominated government in Baghdad and to counter Western influence on its doorstep. Iran's presence in Iraq has caused disquiet elsewhere, not least for regional powerhouse Saudi Arabia. For Iraqis themselves, however, the geopolitical ambitions of Iran and the West being played out on Iraqi soil only serve as reminders that the Iraqi people are still some way off from controlling their own destiny.

HISTORY

From cradle of civilisation to modern-day locus of Middle Eastern conflict, Iraq has always stood at the centre of big historical stories. It all began – perhaps literally, if claims that the Garden of Eden lay between the Tigris and Euphrates Rivers are true – in Mesopotamia, and then Islam arose in neighbouring Arabia. Then, as now, Iraq took centre stage in the issues that divide the faith, with foreign powers seeking to control the country down through the ages.

Ancient Mesopotamia

Iraq's story begins with the Sumerians, who flourished in the rich agricultural lands surrounding the Tigris and Euphrates Rivers from around 4000 BC. In 1750 BC, Hammurabi seized power and went on to dominate the annals of the Babylonian empire. He developed the Code of Hammurabi, the first written code of law in recorded history. Despite constant attacks from the Hittites and other neighbouring powers, Babylon would dominate the region until the 12th century BC, after which it went into a slow decline.

IRAQ'S FUTURE

Much of Iraq's future remains extremely uncertain. The US-led invasion in 2003, the takeover of large swaths of the north and west of the country by Isis in 2014, and battles to drive Isis from Mosul and elsewhere in 2017 have each added a layer of devastation and insecurity to an already war-weary land.

Although the Iraqi government has gradually reasserted its control over many territories formerly held by Isis, the situation remained volatile at the time of writing. Isis still controls large areas of northern Iraq and eastern Syria, from where it is capable of launching terrorist attacks, military combat operations and suicide bombings. These threats are in addition to the ongoing dangers posed by improvised explosive devices (IEDs) and landmines left behind from the conflict, and the sectarian violence that the conflict has potentially fostered. Elsewhere, landmines still litter the Iran–Iraq border, making it a dangerous place.

As a result of these issues, Arab Iraq, particularly in the country's north, is completely off-limits to independent travellers.

Iraq's semi-autonomous Kurdistan region has, at various points in the last few years, been designated as reasonably safe for visitors, although this relative stability has become more fragile since the Kurdish bid for independence in September 2017. Western governments warn against all but essential travel to the region. The Iraqi government suspended international flights to and from Erbil and Sulaymaniyah airports after the referendum and has said it's preparing to take control of Kurdistan border crossings. Quite apart from the danger you could face if you ignore this advice and travel to the area, be aware that your travel insurance policy may not be valid.

By the 7th century BC, the rival Assyrian civilisation had reached its high point under Ashurbanipal, whose capital at Nineveh was one of the great cities of the world, with cuneiform libraries, luxurious royal courts and magnificent bas-reliefs. His expensive military campaigns against Babylonia and other neighbours, however, drained the kingdom of its wealth and manpower. In 612 BC, Nineveh and the Assyrian Empire fell to Babylonian King Nabopolassar.

The Neo-Babylonian Empire returned Babylon to its former glory. Nabopolassar's son, Nebuchadnezzar II, built the famous Hanging Gardens of Babylon and conquered Jerusalem. In 539 BC, Babylon finally fell to the Persian Empire of Cyrus the Great. The Persians were in turn defeated by Alexander the Great, who died in Babylon in 323 BC. For the next 1000 years, Mesopotamia was ruled by a string of empires, among them the Seleucid, Parthian and Sassanid.

Islamic Iraq

In AD 637 the Arab armies of Islam swept north from the Arabian Peninsula and occupied Iraq. Their most important centres became Al Kufa, Baghdad and Mosul.

In 749, the first Abbasid caliph was proclaimed at Al Kufa, and the Abbasids would go on to make Iraq their own. The founding of Baghdad by Al Mansur saw the city become, by some accounts, the greatest city in the world. In 1258 Hulagu – grandson of the feared Mongol ruler Genghis Khan – laid waste to Baghdad and killed the last Abbasid caliph. Political power in the Muslim world shifted elsewhere.

By 1638, Iraq had come under Ottoman rule. After a period of relative autonomy for the region, the Ottomans centralised their rule in the 19th century, and Iraqi dislike of foreign occupation crystallised even as the Ottomans undertook a massive program of modernisation. The Ottomans held on until 1920, when the arrival of the British saw Iraq submit to yet another occupying force, which was first welcomed but then resented by the Iraqis.

Independent Iraq

Iraq gained its independence from the British in 1932, in a decision-making process that left the Kurdish population with very little hope for their own independent state. By then the Kurdish independence movement had gained momentum and included a successful military branch, the Peshmerga (literal meaning: 'those who face death'). The Peshmerga were a key component in the Kurdish struggle for independence and eventually became the official armed force of the Kurdistan Regional Government.

The period that followed was distinguished by a succession of coups and counter-coups and by the discovery of massive reserves of oil. During WWII, the British again occupied Iraq over fears that the pro-German government would cut oil supplies to Allied forces. On 14 July 1958, Iraq's pro-British monarchy was overthrown in a military coup, and Iraq became a republic. In 1968 a bloodless coup brought the Ba'ath Party to power.

In 1961 the first Iraqi-Kurdish war began, lasting until 1970. During this period Mustafa Barzani – the father of the current president of Iraqi Kurdistan, Massoud Barzani – led the struggle to create an independent Kurdish state in Iraq.

The war ended in stalemate and the signing of the Iraqi-Kurdish Autonomy Agreement, under which a Kurdish autonomous region comprising three governorates was created. In 1974 a second Iraqi-Kurdish war broke out, resulting in Baghdad retaking control of Kurdistan.

While the Kurds faced numerous struggles, the 1970s marked a glorious decade for the rest of Iraq. The oil boom of the 1970s brought wealth and prosperity. Oil profits were heavily invested in education, health care and infrastructure.

Iraq's heyday ended on 16 July 1979, when an ambitious Ba'ath official named Saddam Hussein Abd Al Majid Al Tikriti worked his way into power. Saddam's first action as president was to secure his authority by executing political and religious opponents.

Iran–Iraq War

Meanwhile, next door, the Islamic Revolution was busy toppling Iran's pro-Western government. Saddam – a secular Sunni Muslim – became increasingly concerned about the threat of a Shiite revolution in his own country. After several months of sabre rattling, Iraq invaded Iran on 22 September 1980 with the full support of the US, the Soviet Union, and several Arab and European states.

At first Iraq had the upper hand, but it soon found itself at an impasse. The eight years of war were characterised by Iranian human-wave infantry attacks and Iraq's use of chemical weapons against Iranian troops and civilians. The Iran–Iraq war ended in stalemate on 20 August 1988. Each side suffered at least 200,000 deaths and incurred US$100 billion in war debts.

Even throughout the war with Iran, Saddam continued his systematic murder of Kurds. In 1983, more than 8000 boys and men of the Barzani tribe were killed, in an attempt to get rid of all the men of military serving age.

In March 1988, Saddam's cousin and the chief of Iraq's intelligence services, Ali Hassan Al Majid, ordered a chemical attack on the city of Halabja. About 5000 civilians died as a result of the five-hour bombing, and many more still bear physical and psychological scars. Some experts say that Saddam attacked Halabja because both Kurdish and Iranian soldiers had sought shelter in the city.

In the closing months of the war, Saddam launched Al Anfal ('the spoils of war'), a genocidal campaign against the Kurds and a small number of other minorities that lasted from February to September 1988. Dissident male Kurds were imprisoned in concentration camps and later killed in mass executions. The women were segregated and often died as a result of the prisons' inhumane conditions.

The exact number of dead has never been fully ascertained, but Iraqi prosecutors put the figure at 182,000 (other sources give a significantly higher figure). In addition, around 4500 Kurdish villages were destroyed.

Gulf War & Sanctions

The wounds of the Iran–Iraq war had barely healed when Saddam turned his attention to Kuwait. In July 1990 Saddam accused the Kuwaitis (with some justification) of waging 'economic warfare' against Iraq by attempting to artificially hold down the price of oil, and of stealing oil by slant-drilling into the Iraqi side of the border. On 2 August 1990, Iraq invaded Kuwait, whose small armed forces were quickly overrun. Six days later, Iraq annexed Kuwait as its 19th province. It was a costly miscalculation.

Led by US president George HW Bush, an international coalition of nearly one million troops from 34 countries amassed on Iraq's borders. On 17 January 1991, Operation Desert Storm began with a massive five-week bombing campaign, followed by a ground offensive that drove Iraqi forces from Kuwait. Widely varied figures estimate that between 20,000 and 100,000 Iraqis were killed. As part of the ceasefire agreement, the UN ordered Iraq to destroy all chemical, nuclear and biological weapons and long-range missiles.

Shortly before the war ended, Iraqi Shiites and Kurds took up arms against Saddam, encouraged by the impending victory and promises of coalition support. But help never arrived. Saddam's forces quickly crushed the rebellion, leaving thousands more dead.

In Kurdistan a series of uprisings organised by the Kurdistan Democratic Party and the Patriotic Union of Kurdistan swept through the north, taking control of every town and city except for Mosul and Kirkuk. This was followed by fierce retaliation by Saddam and the exodus of Kurdish civilians to Iran and Turkey. Each year on 5 March, Kurdistan commemorates the uprisings.

Other opponents of Saddam were imprisoned or tortured or simply vanished. Coalition forces later established no-fly zones in southern and northern Iraq to protect the Shiites and Kurds. For the latter, this was the beginning of the end of their oppression.

In the meantime, the UN had imposed a stringent sanctions regime on Iraq that was first enforced in August 1990. The original stated purpose of the sanctions was to compel Iraq to withdraw from Kuwait, pay reparations and disclose any weapons of mass destruction. The removal of Saddam, although never officially a goal, was believed by many to be a non-express aim of the sanctions. Whether this is true or not, the sanctions did little to undermine Saddam's regime, but they did bring untold misery to the people of Iraq in the form of malnutrition, poverty, inadequate medical care and lack of clean water. The hardest-hit group was children. Estimates of the number of children who died because of the effects of the sanctions and the collateral effects of war vary hugely, but Unicef estimated the figure to be around 500,000. When Madeleine Albright (at the time US ambassador to the UN) was questioned in 1996 about whether the death of so many children was too high a price for the removal of Saddam Hussein, she replied, 'I think this is a very hard choice, but the price – we think the price is worth it'.

IRAQ IN PEACETIME

Many tragedies have befallen Iraq, but one of the least reported is the disruption to the country's vibrant social and cultural life.

The predominantly Shiite south has traditionally been Iraq's most conservative corner; it's a deeply religious land with one eye turned west towards the Arab world and the other looking east towards its coreligionists across the border in Iran. The sacred cities of Najaf and Karbala still attract Shiite pilgrims from around the world, and the region is awash with legend, from the Garden of Eden to the port city of Basra, from where Sinbad the Sailor is said to have set out on his epic journeys.

Central and western Iraq are the country's Sunni Arab heartland. More than anywhere else, it was the Sunni towns that prospered under Saddam Hussein. While this often came at the expense of other Iraqi regions and communities, these regions were, for much of the 20th century, some of the most liberal in Arab Iraq. The touchstones of Arab life in the Middle East, too, have always thrived here, from the big celebrations that once brought large extended families and even entire neighbourhoods together to the coffee shops and bazaars that functioned as the meeting places of public life.

Connecting Sunni and Shiite Iraq is a string of stirring historical sites, many of which flourished in ancient times in the fertile lands between the Tigris and Euphrates Rivers. The ancient Sumerian city of Ur, 15km south of Nasiriyya, is one of the most impressive archaeological sites in Iraq, dating back to at least 4000 BC. Little remains of ancient Babylon except for several mounds and the famous Lion of Babylon, a basalt statue carved more than 2500 years ago.

It all comes together, as it always has, in Baghdad, one of the great meeting places and cultural powerhouses of the Middle East. Baghdad may be battered and suspicious, but it remains true to its roots as a city of storytellers and of streets lined with booksellers; it's a polyglot place ruled by cosmopolitan and conservative influences in equal measure.

LONELY PLANET & THE IRAQ WAR

In a 2007 BBC documentary, former US ambassador Barbara Bodine said that an outdated copy of Lonely Planet's *Middle East* guide was used during the planning stages of the Iraq invasion and postwar reconstruction. 'It's a great guidebook, but it shouldn't be the basis of an occupation', she told the BBC.

2003 Iraq War

In a speech to the UN General Assembly on 12 September 2002, US president George W Bush set the stage for war by declaring – among other claims – that Iraq was manufacturing weapons of mass destruction (WMDs) and harbouring Al Qaeda terrorists. Saddam disputed the claims but reluctantly agreed to allow weapons inspectors back into the country. UN inspectors concluded that Iraq had failed to account for all its weapons but insisted that there was no evidence WMDs had existed. Meanwhile, a 'coalition of the willing' led by American and British troops was massing in Kuwait. On 20 March 2003 – without UN authority – the coalition launched its second war on Iraq. Allied forces easily overran Iraqi forces, with relatively few casualties. Baghdad fell on 9 April 2003, but Saddam escaped. On 1 May 2003, Bush declared victory under a banner that read 'Mission Accomplished'. But the war was just beginning.

While the initial optimism quickly vanished in Arab Iraq, the Kurds largely welcomed the allied forces as liberators and even co-operated with them in the overrunning of northern cities like Mosul and Kirkuk. An American-Kurdish joint operation also pushed members of extremist group Ansar Al Islam into Iran.

Throughout the rest of the country, it soon became clear that planning for postwar Iraq had been woefully inadequate. The country descended into chaos and anarchy. The Iraqi Army was disbanded in a process known as 'debathification', by which former Ba'ath Party members were excluded from the new Iraqi government, leaving millions of unemployed men on the street. The country was spiralling into a guerrilla war with a growing insurgency.

In December 2003, a dishevelled and bearded Saddam was found cowering in a spider hole near his hometown of Tikrit. Saddam was executed in December 2006 for crimes against humanity. This was the ultimate green light for the Kurds to start rebuilding their homeland.

In 2004 things went from bad to worse for Arab Iraq. The insurgency exploded, led by such groups as Al Qaeda. That same year, photographs emerged of American soldiers abusing Iraqi prisoners at Abu Ghraib prison, creating an international backlash against the occupation. Two major battles in the Sunni city of Fallujah did little to stem the bloodshed. On 22 February 2006, the holy Shiite shrine in Samarra was bombed, kicking off a wave of sectarian violence that pitched Iraqi Sunnis and Shiites against one another and left thousands dead. Kurds were reluctant to take military action in a sectarian war they did not see as their own.

The tide finally started to turn in 2007 when the US launched a troop surge that saw an extra 20,000 troops being sent to Iraq. Subsequently, the levels of violence began to fall, and foreign troops began to leave. Britain ended its combat operations in 2009 and the US in 2010, with the last US troops leaving at the end of 2011.

By the time of the final US withdrawal, the death toll from the war and subsequent insurgency in Iraq had reached an estimated 105,000 to 115,000 Iraqi civilians (based on figures provided by Iraq Body Count – other sources give a different figure), 10,125 Iraqi soldiers and police, 4800 coalition soldiers (mostly from the US) and 150 journalists. Tens of thousands more have been injured or maimed. The UN High Commissioner on Refugees estimates that at least 3.4 million Iraqis either have fled the country or were internally displaced as a result of the war.

In a seemingly parallel universe, the Kurds had quietly but quickly established the foundations to build a state and by the time the US troops left, theirs was already considered a safe and modern region amid chaos.

Growing Pains

In 2006, when Iraqis elected their first permanent democratic government, led by Nouri Al Maliki, hope for stability was high. By the time the last US troops left Iraq at the end of 2011, violence had fallen dramatically, but problems between Maliki's party and Iraq's Sunni and Kurdish population were brewing under the surface.

The cracks in the government were already showing in 2012 when the fragile Shiite-majority coalition came close to collapse. At the end of that year, Sunni-led protests swept through Anbar Province – Iraqi Sunnis felt they were being marginalised and targeted by Maliki's government. Protests continued until violence escalated in January 2014 and the Iraqi government lost the city of Fallujah to Isis.

During that same month, Baghdad failed to transfer the Kurdish share of Iraq's federal budget to Erbil, angering the Kurdistan Regional Government. The lack of money gave the Kurds the perfect excuse to begin exporting their crude oil independently, putting further strain on Erbil–Baghdad relations. In August 2014, Maliki stepped down and was replaced by Haider Al Abadi, appointed by the new president, Kurdish Fuad Masum.

In June 2014 a greater threat materialised in the form of Isis, presenting Baghdad and Erbil with a common enemy. An amalgamation of disillusioned civilians, former members of Saddam Hussein's Ba'ath Party and foreigners, Isis began operating in Iraq under an extreme version of Sharia law, displacing more than a million people and killing thousands. The group encouraged the Iraqi and Kurdish military to take up arms and foreign powers to intervene with air strikes.

PEOPLE & SOCIETY

Iraq's political and security situations may have been in a state of flux for more than two decades, but the country's social touchstones – family, religion, ethnicity – remain largely unchanged. In fact, while the relationship between various groups has become extremely problematic, the bonds uniting members *within* these groups have perhaps become stronger than ever. Whether Iraq as a country can one day rival these groups as a source of unified identity remains to be seen.

Modern Iraqi Society

Iraq is one of the most culturally and socially diverse countries in the Middle East. About 75% to 80% of the population is Arab, 15% to 20% Kurdish and the rest made up of Turkomans, Assyrians, Persians, Chaldeans, Palestinians, Yazidis and nomadic Bedouin. Islam is the official religion of Iraq. Muslims make up 97% of the population – about 60% to 65% of them Shiite and 35% to 40% Sunni. There are also small but historically significant communities of Christians who belong to various sects, including Chaldeans, Assyrians, Syrian and Roman Catholics. Other religious minorities are the Shabaks, Yazidis, Sabeans, Mandeans (followers of John the Baptist) and a handful of Jews (a number of whom have ancestors who converted to Islam and no longer consider themselves Jewish).

Arabic and Kurdish are the official languages of Iraq. Arabic is spoken by 80% of the population. The Kurds speak a language that is widely known as Kurdish, but in reality Kurds speak one of two Indo-European languages: Kurmanji and Sorani. In Iraqi Kurdistan, English education is now compulsory, so many young people understand at least a bit of English. Many young Kurds don't speak Arabic, while the older generations were forced to learn it at school as children.

Kurdish tradition has recently become intertwined with modernity, brought about by a wave of returning diaspora Kurds – young men and women who were forced to flee Kurdistan during the 1970s and '80s and were largely raised in the West. While the majority consider themselves Kurdish, they are strongly influenced by their Western upbringing, offering traditional Kurdistan a window into a different culture and at times clashing with Kurdish conservatism. While the big cities have embraced a form of Western pop culture, it only takes a quick drive to the outskirts to see that rural Kurdistan remains untouched by Western luxuries, and a sense of 'Kurdishness' prevails.

Daily Life in Iraq

Arab and Kurdish Iraqi life revolves around the family and extended family, a bond that took on added significance during years of war, sanctions and international isolation. Honour and reputation are matters of great importance. It's a paternalistic, patriarchal and conservative society, especially in rural areas, although this is less the case in Kurdish cities like Sulaymaniyah.

Iraq is primarily a tribal society. Allegiance to one's ethnic group often takes precedence over any party, provincial or national loyalties, and ethnic interests play a key role in the shaping of government and public policy.

The role of women is complex. Legally, men and women have the same rights. Women are commonplace in government, politics, media, private business and universities. Nevertheless, women are still expected to take on the traditional roles of wife and mother. Arranged marriages are common, usually between first cousins – although this is less so in Kurdistan. So-called honour killings are not uncommon, although in one well-publicised case – the murder of 15-year-old Dunya at the hands of her 45-year-old polygamous husband in 2014 – the fact that a large number of civilians and politicians spoke out publicly against honour killings may suggest that things are changing.

The rise of Isis and the sectarian violence that swept through Arab Iraq in recent decades forced many women back into the home and to adopt a more conservative style of dress. In the cities of Kurdistan, things are more relaxed and women play a bigger part in daily street life.

Many an Iraqi's favourite pastime is picnicking. The Kurds in particular have turned the humble picnic into an art form, and every Friday throughout the warmer months Kurds descend en masse on the nearest park or beauty spot for a family picnic.

FURTHER INFORMATION

Books on Modern Iraq

➡ *Iraq: The Cost of War* (Jeremy Greenstock; 2017) Fascinating portrait of the country's travails by a former UK ambassador to the UN.

➡ *The Rise of Islamic State: ISIS and the New Sunni Revolution* (Patrick Cockburn; 2015) Isis in Iraq, from one of the region's finest analysts.

➡ *The Modern History of Iraq* (Phebe Marr and Ibrahim Al Marashi; 2017) Updated with a 4th edition in 2017.

➡ *The Unravelling: High Hopes and Missed Opportunities in Iraq* (Emma Sky; 2015) Firsthand account of the complications of modern Iraq.

Books on Iraqi History

➡ *Iraq: A History* (John Robertson; 2016) Readable overview of Iraq's long and storied history.

➡ *Republic of Fear: The Inside Story of Saddam's Iraq* (Kanan Makiya and Samir Al Khalil; 1990) Searing account of Saddam Hussein's Iraq.

➡ *Road Through Kurdistan: Travels in Northern Iraq* (AM Hamilton and David McDowall; 2004) An engaging account of road-building in 1928.

➡ *The Marsh Arabs* (Wilfred Thesiger; 1964) Classic study of traditional life in southern Iraq in the pre-Saddam era.

➡ *Baghdad Sketches: Journeys Through Iraq* (Freya Stark; 1932) Brilliant account of a journey through colonial Iraq.

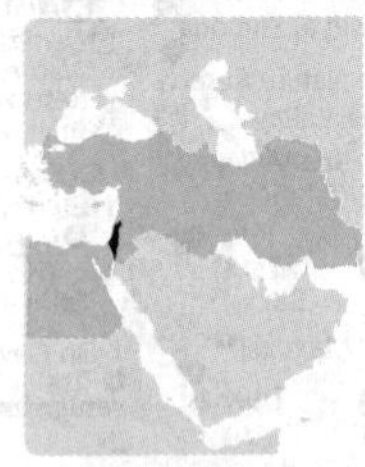

Israel & the Palestinian Territories

Includes ➡

Jerusalem 201
Tel Aviv-Jaffa (Yafo)..... 221
Haifa 231
Akko 236
Sea of Galilee 242
Dead Sea 249
Eilat 252
West Bank 256
Ramallah 256
Bethlehem 261
Understand Israel & the Palestinian Territories 267
Survival Guide 275

Best for Nature

- ➡ Ein Gedi Nature Reserve (p249)
- ➡ Makhtesh Ramon (p252)
- ➡ Hula Nature Reserve (p246)
- ➡ Red Sea snorkelling (p253)

Best for Culture

- ➡ Israel Museum (p215)
- ➡ Tel Aviv's theatres and live music venues (p218)
- ➡ Tsfat's art galleries (p244)
- ➡ Ramallah (p256)

Why Go?

At the intersection of Asia, Europe and Africa, Israel and the Palestinian Territories have been a meeting place of cultures, empires and religions since the dawn of history. Cradle of Judaism and Christianity, and sacred to Muslims and Baha'is, the Holy Land offers visitors the opportunity both to immerse themselves in the richness and variety of their own religious traditions and to discover the beliefs, rituals and architecture of other faiths. Distances are short, so you can relax on a Mediterranean beach one day, spend the next rafting down the Jordan River or floating in the mineral-rich waters of the Dead Sea, and the day after that scuba diving in the Red Sea. Hikers can follow spring-fed tributaries of the Jordan, discover verdant oases tucked away in the arid bluffs above the Dead Sea, and explore the multicoloured sandstone formations of Makhtesh Ramon. And ancient sites such as Jericho and the Roman cities of Caesarea and Beit She'an will leave history buffs in awe.

When to Go

Jerusalem

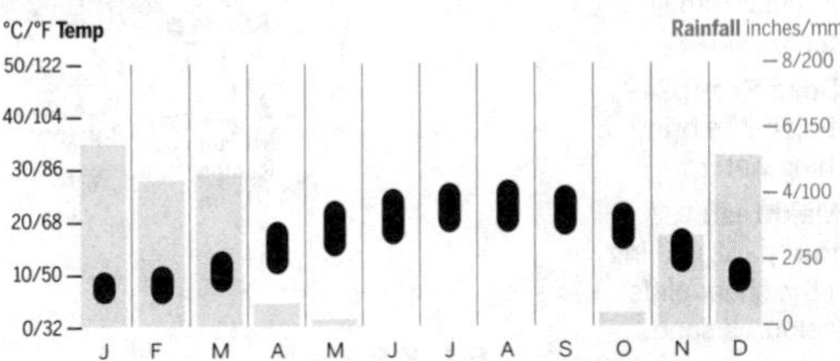

Feb–Apr Hillsides and valleys are carpeted with wildflowers; the ideal season for hiking.

Jul–Aug Warm and dry in Jerusalem, humid in Tel Aviv and infernal around Jericho, Eilat and the Dead Sea.

Sep–Oct Jewish holidays generate a spike in domestic tourism – and room prices.

Israel & the Palestinian Territories Highlights

1. **Church of the Holy Sepulchre** (p203) Visiting the place believed to be the site of Jesus's crucifixion. Also, admiring the magnificent **Dome of the Rock** (p208), and placing a note between the ancient stones of the **Western Wall** (p206).
2. **Masada** (p251) Ascending the Snake Path before dawn and watching the sun rise.
3. **Tel Aviv-Jaffa** (Yafo; p221) Taking a dip in the warm Mediterranean.
4. **Church of the Nativity** (p261) Exploring the nooks and crannies of this church in Bethlehem.
5. **Tsfat** (Safed; p244) Wandering the narrow alleyways of this town, a centre of Kabbalah (Jewish mysticism) since the 16th century.
6. **Haifa** (p231) Admiring the breathtaking sea views from the spectacular Baha'i Gardens.
7. **Dead Sea** (p249) Floating in the briny, soothing waters.
8. **Makhtesh Ramon** (p252) Hiking amid the sheer cliffs and coloured sands.

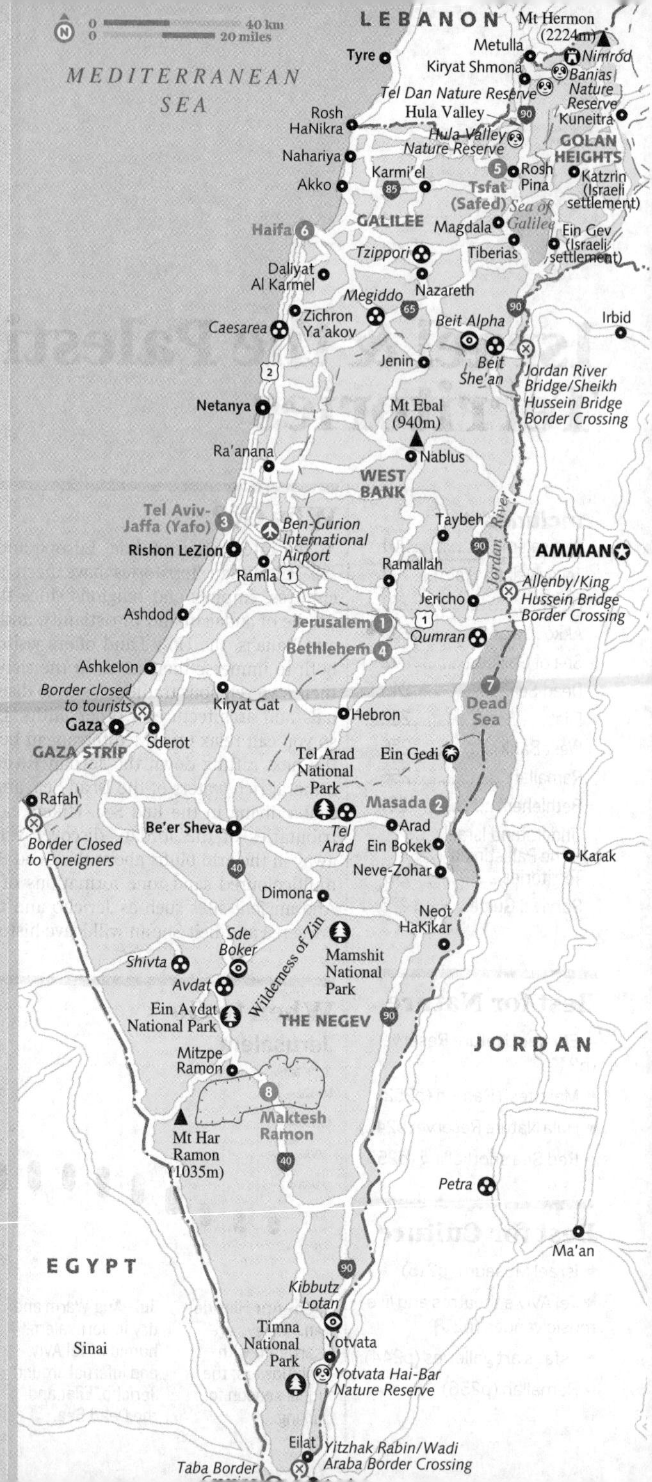

JERUSALEM ירושלים القدس

02 / POP 865,721

Holy to Jews, Christians and Muslims, Jerusalem is one of the world's foremost pilgrimage destinations – you can walk in the footsteps of prophets, pray in buildings built by order of kings and caliphs, and overnight in hospices where Crusaders and cardinals have slumbered. Even for the nonreligious, it's hard not to be moved by the emotions and history that come alive in the narrow alleyways of the Old City.

History

According to the American historian Eric H Cline (in his 2004 book *Jerusalem Besieged*), Jerusalem has been destroyed at least twice, placed under siege 23 times, attacked another 52 times and captured and recaptured 44 times.

The first settlement on the site of Jerusalem was a small Jebusite village south of Mt Moriah (the Temple Mount), where the Bible says Abraham almost sacrificed his son Isaac. In 997 BC King David captured the city and made it his capital. His son, King Solomon, built the First Temple, which was destroyed in 586 BC by Babylonian king Nebuchadnezzar, who exiled the Jews to Babylonia. In 538 BC they were allowed to return and almost immediately began construction of the Second Temple, consecrated in 516 BC.

Power in Jerusalem shifted between Jewish rulers, such as the Maccabees, and various regional empires, until the Romans took control in 63 BC, installing Herod the Great as king of Judea. He launched a massive building campaign, significantly expanding the Second Temple. The city was then ruled by a series of procurators; it was the fifth of these, Pontius Pilate, who ordered the crucifixion of Jesus.

Growing Jewish discontent with Roman rule exploded in AD 66 with the Great Jewish Revolt (the First Jewish-Roman War), which ended with the sacking of Jerusalem and the destruction of the Second Temple in AD 70. After the Bar Kochba Rebellion (AD 132–35), the Jews were banished from Jerusalem. Emperor Hadrian rebuilt the city as Aelia Capitolina, whose street grid forms the basis of today's Old City.

During the Byzantine era (4th to early 7th century AD), Christianity became the official state religion, forcing the conversion of many local Jews and Samaritans. Many Christian shrines were built; work on the Church of the Holy Sepulchre, for instance, commenced in AD 326.

NEED TO KNOW

Capitals Jerusalem, Ramallah

Country Codes 972 (I), 972 or 970 (PT)

Languages Hebrew and Arabic (I), Arabic (PT)

Populations Israel 8.8 million, West Bank 2.8 million, Gaza 1.8 million

Currency Israeli new shekel (NIS or ILS)

Mobile phones Generally excellent 900/1800 MHz coverage

Money ATMs widely available in Israel, less so in the Palestinian Territories

Visas Israeli on-arrival visas available for most nationalities

Exchange Rates

Australia	A$1	2.71NIS
Egypt	E£10	2NIS
Euro zone	€1	4.29NIS
Jordan	JD1	4.93NIS
UK	UK£1	4.85NIS
USA	US$1	3.50NIS

For current exchange rates see www.xe.com.

Resources

Israel Nature & Parks Authority (www.parks.org.il)

This Week in Palestine (www.thisweekinpalestine.com)

Israel Ministry of Tourism (www.goisrael.com)

In AD 638 Byzantine Jerusalem fell to the armies of Islam and came under the sway of Arab civilisation. The Dome of the Rock, instantly recognisable thanks to its gleaming gold dome, was completed in AD 691 on the site of the long-destroyed Jewish Temple and, according to Quranic tradition, Muhammad's ascent to heaven. But despite its significance to Islam, Jerusalem's political and economic fortunes fell into decline, in part because of the city's distance from the imperial capitals of Damascus and Cairo.

In the 11th century, Palestine fell to the Seljuk Turks, who stopped Christian pilgrims from visiting Jerusalem. The response of Western European Christians was a series of Crusades – and Crusader kingdoms – that lasted from 1095 to 1270. The Crusaders took Jerusalem in 1099, but lost it in 1187 to Saladin (Salah ad-Din), Kurdish founder of the Muslim Ayyubid dynasty.

In 1250 the city came under the influence of the Mamluks, successors to the Ayyubids, who ruled from Egypt and turned the city into a centre of Islamic learning. In 1517 the Ottoman Turks absorbed Jerusalem into their expanding empire, where it would remain, something of a backwater, for the next 400 years.

In the 19th century the first road linking Jerusalem with Jaffa was built, greatly increasing the number of Jewish and Christian pilgrims. By about 1850, Jews constituted the majority of the city's 25,000 residents. The first neighbourhood built outside the walls of the Old City was Yemin Moshe, established in 1860. Access to the city became quick and easy with the completion of the Jaffa–Jerusalem rail line in 1892.

The British captured Jerusalem from the Ottomans in December 1917 and later made it the capital of the British Mandate of Palestine. Tensions between Jews and Arabs flared in the 1920s and 1930s. After the British left Palestine in 1948, fighting between the new State of Israel and Jordan's Arab Legion resulted in the city's partition. West Jerusalem became the capital of Israel; East Jerusalem, including the entire Old City, was annexed by Jordan.

The barbed wire and fortifications dividing the city came down after Israel captured the eastern part of the city during the 1967 Six Day War. Shortly afterwards, Israel annexed East Jerusalem, declaring the entire city to be its 'eternal capital'. The Palestinians claim East Jerusalem as the capital of a future independent state of Palestine. Israel's separation barrier – in many places around Jerusalem an 8m-high concrete wall – cuts the mostly Arab East Jerusalem off from the West Bank.

Sights

Jerusalem is divided into three main areas: the walled Old City, with its four quarters; the predominantly Arab neighbourhoods of East Jerusalem; and mostly Jewish West Jerusalem.

Christian Quarter

The narrow streets of the Old City's 18.2-hectare Christian Quarter are lined with religious institutions, hospices, hostels, artisans' workshops and souvenir shops belonging to 20 different Christian denominations.

The Church of the Holy Sepulchre incorporates the final five Stations of the Cross (the other nine are along the Via Dolorosa, in the Muslim Quarter). The destruction of the church in 1009 by the mad Fatimid caliph Al Hakim helped spark the Crusades. The present-day church is more or less a Crusader structure of Byzantine origin; what is believed to be the tomb of Jesus, inside the Aedicule (burial shrine), was opened and restored in 2016.

To keep the peace between the Church of the Holy Sepulchre's notoriously fractious Christian denominations, a Muslim family, the Nusseibehs, keeps the keys, unlocking the doors each morning and securing

ISRAEL & THE PALESTINIAN TERRITORIES IN...

Ten Days

Spend three days exploring the wonders of **Jerusalem**, then take the slow train to **Tel Aviv** and spend a couple of days in cafes, at museums, cycling, and on the beach. Rent a car, if you can, and head north, spending two days at the **Sea of Galilee** and hiking at **Tel Dan** or **Banias**. Finally, drive west to **Haifa** to visit the gorgeous **Baha'i Gardens**, then down the coast to the ancient ruins of **Caesarea**. From Tel Aviv, fly home or head by bus to **Eilat** and, via the Yitzhak Rabin/Wadi Araba border crossing, to **Petra**, Jordan.

Two Weeks

Follow the 10-day itinerary but make additions. From **Jerusalem** take a day trip below sea level to **Qumran**, where the Essenes hid the Dead Sea Scrolls, and **Masada**, where Jewish Zealots defied the Roman legions, then swim in the **Dead Sea**. Take another day trip from Jerusalem, southward to friendly, engaging **Bethlehem** and the troubled city of **Hebron**. In the Lower Galilee, visit **Nazareth**, Jesus's boyhood stomping ground, and dine there. In the Upper Galilee, explore spiritual **Tsfat (Safed)**, centre of Kabbalah (Jewish mysticism).

them again at night. Visitors should dress modestly – the guards are very strict and refuse entry to those with bare legs, shoulders or backs.

★Church of the Holy Sepulchre CHURCH
(Map p212; ☎02-626-7000; Christian Quarter; ⊙5am-9pm Easter-Sep, to 8pm Sun, 4am-7pm Oct-Easter) Four magnificent arches, their lintels richly decorated with Crusader crosses, herald the entrance to one of Christianity's most sacred sites. The church is believed by many Christians to be built over the biblical Calvary, or Golgotha, where Jesus was nailed to the cross, died and rose from the dead. For the past 16 centuries pilgrims have travelled far to worship here; expect crowds rather than quiet contemplation, unless you arrive early. The easiest access is via Christian Quarter Rd.

Ethiopian Monastery RELIGIOUS SITE
(Deir Es Sultan; Map p212; Christian Quarter; ⊙daylight hours) Sequestered on the rooftop of the Church of the Holy Sepulchre (p203), this monastery houses a few monks from the Church of Ethiopia who live among the ruins of a medieval cloister erected by the Crusaders. The cupola in the middle of the roof section admits light to St Helena's crypt below. A door in the southeastern corner leads through a chapel and downstairs to the courtyard of the Holy Sepulchre itself.

Muslim Quarter

Running from the Old City's Damascus Gate south and southeast towards the Temple Mount, this is the liveliest area of the Old City; it's also the most claustrophobic, confusing and crowded. You'll inevitably get lost in the tangle of teeming humanity and be enchanted by the tempting aromas wafting out of the spice merchants, coffeehouses, bakeries and tiny restaurants. Wander the area's Mamluk and medieval alleyways and you'll be transported back to another time.

The main entrance to the Muslim Quarter is Damascus Gate, which dates in its present form from the time of Süleyman the Magnificent, although there had been a gate here long before the arrival of the Turks: this was the city's main gate as early as the time of Agrippa, who ruled in the 1st century BC.

Via Dolorosa RELIGIOUS SITE
(Way of the Sorrows; Map p212; Muslim Quarter) The road leading from **Lions' Gate** (St Stephen's Gate; Map p204; Muslim Quarter) into the heart of the Old City is known as Via Dolorosa or the Stations of the Cross. It's the route that many Christians believe was taken by the condemned Jesus as he carried his cross to Calvary. Plaques mark each of the nine 'stations' (some are easy to miss); the final five are inside the Church of the Holy Sepulchre.

St Anne's Church CHURCH
(Map p204; Sha-ar HaArayot Rd, Muslim Quarter; adult/student & child 10/8NIS; ⊙8am-noon & 2-6pm Apr-Sep, to 5pm Mon-Sat Oct-Mar) The finest example of Crusader architecture in Jerusalem, St Anne's was completed in 1138 on a site thought to have been the home of Joachim and Anne, the parents of the Virgin Mary. One of the sunken pools accessed from the rear of the church compound is traditionally thought to be the biblical **Pool of Bethesda** where Jesus is said to have healed a sick man (John 5:1-18).

Souq Al Qattanin MARKET
(Cotton Market; Map p212; Muslim Quarter; ⊙daylight hours) Food and clothing vendors are framed by soaring vaults in this mid-14th-century shopping arcade. The part closest to Al Wad St dates from the Crusader period; the Mamluks extended it in the middle of the 14th century. A cotton bazaar once stood here, though these days lamps, souvenirs, snacks and bric-a-brac are on sale, creating an atmospheric diversion for visitors to the Muslim Quarter.

Armenian Quarter & Mt Zion

Armenia became the first nation to officially embrace Christianity when their king converted in AD 303. After the Armenians' kingdom disappeared at the end of the 4th century, they adopted Jerusalem as their spiritual capital and have had an uninterrupted presence here ever since. The city's Armenian population, now numbered at about 1500, grew significantly in the early 1900s, when immigrants arrived – both to work on retiling the Dome of the Rock and to escape Ottoman Turkish persecution.

Mt Zion is situated outside Zion Gate from the Old City's Armenian Quarter.

St James' Cathedral CHURCH
(Couvent Armenien St-Jacques; Map p212; ☎religious-service info 02-628-2331; https://armenian-patriarchate.com; Armenian Orthodox Patriarchate Rd, Armenian Quarter; ⊙morning prayers 6.30am, vespers 3pm, Mass 8am Sat & 8.30am Sun) Accessible only for services, the interior of this 12th-century cathedral is infused with incense smoke. Blue-and-white tiles and glittering icons adorn its walls, and richly patterned

Inner Jerusalem

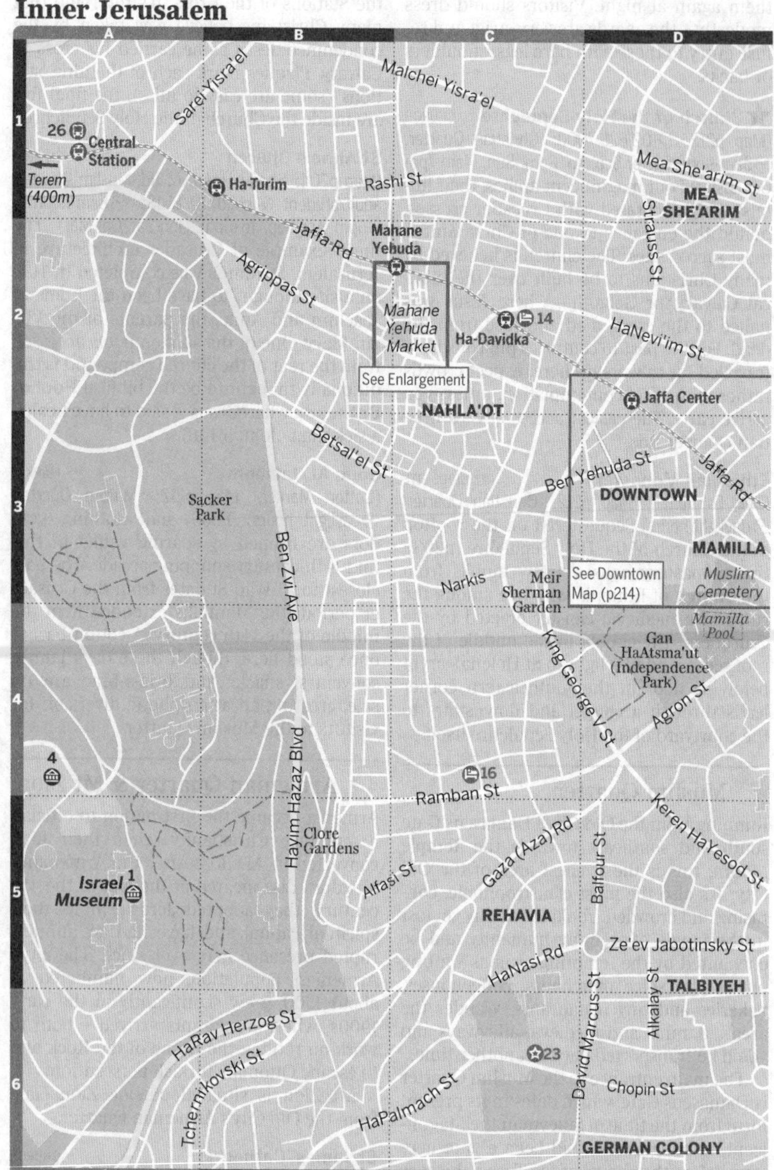

carpets are strewn across the floor. At other times, you can enter the courtyard to see the exterior, which is decorated with *khatchkars* (Armenian stone crosses surrounded by intricate tracery) and tiled murals depicting the Last Judgement and the Apostles.

Room of the Last Supper CHRISTIAN SITE
(Cenacle, Coenaculum; Map p204; Mt Zion; ⏲8am-6pm) **FREE** Medieval beliefs about the location of the Last Supper have embedded the Coenaculum (Latin for dining hall) in Christian tradition. Most historians agree that this hall

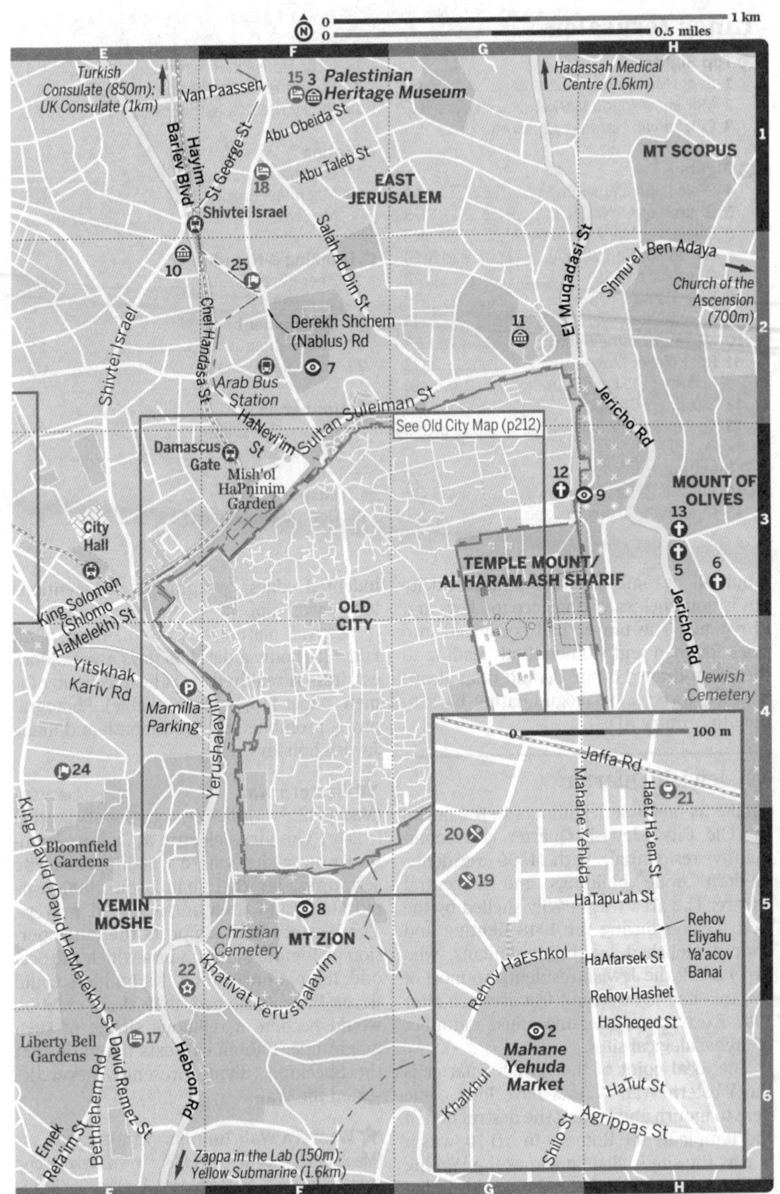

is unlikely to be built on the spot where Jesus ate his final meal. Nonetheless, this elegantly rib-vaulted chamber (formerly part of the 4th-century Holy Zion church) usually teems with pilgrims. Retained in the 14th-century Crusader structure that replaced the original church, it was converted to a mosque during the Ottoman period.

King David's Tomb RELIGIOUS SITE

(Map p204; Mt Zion; 8am-5pm Sun-Thu, to 1pm Fri) **FREE** Erected by Crusaders two millennia after King David's death, this

Inner Jerusalem

Top Sights
1 Israel Museum....A5
2 Mahane Yehuda Market....G6
3 Palestinian Heritage Museum....F1

Sights
4 Bible Lands Museum....A4
5 Church of All Nations....H3
6 Church of Mary Magdalene....H3
Garden of Gethsemane....(see 5)
7 Garden Tomb....F2
8 King David's Tomb....F5
9 Lions' Gate....H3
10 Museum on the Seam....E2
11 Rockefeller Museum....G2
Room of the Last Supper....(see 8)
12 St Anne's Church....G3
13 Tomb of the Virgin Mary....H3

Sleeping
14 Abraham Hostel....C2
15 American Colony Hotel....F1
16 Little House in Rehavia....C4
17 St Andrew's Scottish Guesthouse....E6
18 St George's Guesthouse....F1

Eating
19 Ishtabach....G5
20 Machneyuda....G5
Modern....(see 1)

Drinking & Nightlife
21 Beer Bazaar....H4

Entertainment
22 Cinematheque....E5
23 Jerusalem Theatre....C6

Information
24 French Consulate....E4
25 US Consulate....F2

Transport
26 Central Bus Station....A1

ground-floor tomb is of dubious authenticity but is nonetheless a holy place for Jews and Christians. The prayer hall is divided into sides for men and women, both leading to the velvet-draped tomb. Behind is an alcove believed to be a synagogue dating back to the 5th century AD.

Jewish Quarter

Unlike its bustling neighbours to the north, the Old City's Jewish Quarter is predominantly residential, with 4500 residents, modern stone buildings and a central square. The area was heavily shelled by the Arab Legion during the 1948 fighting and later demolished by the Jordanians, who expelled all the Jewish residents, so most of the area had to be rebuilt from scratch after 1967. Excavations have unearthed a number of archaeological sites.

The focal point of the Jewish Quarter is the Western Wall – Jews have long come here to mourn and lament the destruction of the Temple by the Romans in AD 70, which is why the site is also known as the Wailing Wall, a name that Jews tend to avoid. Today, the area immediately in front of the wall serves as a great open-air synagogue, with a southern section for women and a larger northern section for men (plans for a mixed area have met fierce opposition from the ultra-Orthodox). Stuffed between the huge Herodian-era stones (identifiable by their indented edges) are prayers and petitions left by worshippers.

The wall plaza is open to members of all faiths 24 hours a day, 365 days a year. Modest dress is required, as is head covering for men (paper kippot are available). Photography is prohibited on the Sabbath and many Jewish holidays.

★Western Wall JEWISH SITE
(Map p212; www.thekotel.org; Jewish Quarter; 24hr) The air is electric at Judaism's holiest prayer site, where worshippers recite scriptures, lay their hands on 2000-year-old stone and utter impassioned prayers. The Western Wall supports the outer portion of Temple Mount, upon which the Second Temple once stood. Its builders could never have fathomed that their creation would become a religious shrine of such magnitude. Rabbinical texts maintain that the Shechina (divine presence) never deserted the Wall.

★Western Wall Tunnels ARCHAEOLOGICAL SITE
(Map p212; 02-627-1333; www.thekotel.org; Jewish Quarter; adult/student & child 35/19NIS; by tour only 8.30am-5pm) Guided tours of the Western Wall tunnels offer an entirely different perspective on Herod's epic construction: visitors are led along a 488m passage following the northern extension of the Wall. The excavated tunnel burrows down to the original street level, allowing visitors to tread the same ground as the

ancients. Guides give fascinating insights into how these mighty walls were erected – Herod's stone masons chiselled blocks up to 14m long and weighing almost 600 tons apiece.

You can only visit the tunnels on 75-minute guided tours (Hebrew and English multiple times a day; French, Spanish and Russian less regularly in summer only); try to book at least a week ahead.

Jerusalem Archaeological Park & Davidson Centre HISTORIC SITE
(Map p212; ☎02-627-7550; www.archpark.org.il; Jewish Quarter; adult/student & child 30/16NIS, guided tour 160NIS, audio guide 5NIS; ⏲8am-5pm Sun-Thu, to 2pm Fri) Pore over the remains of streets, columns, gates, walls, plazas and *mikve'ot* (Jewish ritual baths) at this archaeological site near **Dung Gate** (Map p212; Old City). An audio guide is a helpful accompaniment at the open-air portion of the site; meanwhile, video presentations (in Hebrew and English) at the visitor centre give an overview of the main excavations in the 1970s and reconstruct the site as it looked 2000 years ago.

Cardo Maximus HISTORIC SITE
(Map p212; Jewish Quarter) Cutting a broad north–south swath, the sunken Cardo Maximus, with its art boutiques, is the reconstructed main street of Roman and Byzantine Jerusalem. At one time it would have run the whole breadth of the city, up to what's now Damascus Gate, but in its present form it starts just south of David St (the tourist souq), serving as the main entry into the Jewish Quarter from the Muslim and Christian areas.

DON'T MISS

THE OLD CITY & ITS GATES

The magical, mysterious Old City consists of the Temple Mount (Al Haram Ash Sharif) and four quarters: Muslim, Christian, Jewish and Armenian, each with a distinct atmosphere. The sturdy walls (built 1553–42) are the legacy of Ottoman Sultan Süleyman the Magnificent.

Commanding a prominent elevated location overlooking the Old City, the **Citadel** (Tower of David; Map p212; ☎info 02-626-5333, tour reservations 02-626-5347; www.tod.org.il; Omar Ibn Al Khattab Sq, Old City; adult/student/child 40/30/18NIS; ⏲9am-4pm Sat-Thu, to 5pm Jul & Aug, 9am-2pm Fri) started life as the palace of Herod the Great. Also used as a palace by the Romans and Crusaders, the structure was extensively remodelled by the Mamluks and Ottomans and is now home to the impressive **Museum of the History of Jerusalem**, which tells the story of the city in a series of chronologically arranged exhibits starting in the second millenium BC and finishing in 1948.

Jaffa Gate (Map p212; Old City), the main entrance to the Old City from West Jerusalem, leads directly to the Christian and Armenian Quarters; it is so named because the old road to Jaffa started here. Moving clockwise, the **New Gate** (1887), built by Sultan Abdul Hamid, also gives access to the Christian Quarter. Down the hill, Damascus Gate, the most attractive and crowded (and politically volatile) of all the city gates, links the Muslim Quarter with the bustling centre of East Jerusalem.

It was near **Herod's Gate** in 1099 that the Crusaders first breached Jerusalem's walls. **Lions' Gate** (p203), facing the Mount of Olives, is also called St Stephen's Gate, after the first Christian martyr, who was stoned to death nearby. It was from here that Israeli paratroops took the Old City in the 1967 Six Day War. **Dung Gate** links the Western Wall (the Jewish Quarter) with the **City of David** excavations, a bit down the slope to the south. **Zion Gate**, affording access to the Armenian and Jewish Quarters, is still pocked with reminders of the fierce fighting that took place here in 1948.

Truth be told, the idea of the 1km **walk** (Map p212; Old City; adult/child 18/8NIS; ⏲both sections 9am-4pm Sat-Thu Oct-Mar, to 5pm Apr-Sep, southern ramparts 9am-2pm Fri year-round) atop the ramparts is better than the reality. Views aren't all that impressive (they're better from the Citadel), and there's no shade, which makes it a real slog in high summer. Tickets are purchased from the 'Jerusalem Tourist Information Center' near Jaffa Gate. Because the ramparts around the Temple Mount are off limits, there are two stretches: from Jaffa Gate south to Dung Gate, and from Jaffa Gate north to St Stephen's (Lions) Gate.

TEMPLE MOUNT

There are few patches of ground as holy – or as disputed – as the **Temple Mount** (Map p212; Old City; ⏲8.30-11.30am & 1.30-2.30pm Sun-Thu Apr-Sep, 7.30-10am & 12.30-1.30pm Sun-Thu Oct-Mar) FREE, known to Muslims as **Al Haram Ash Sharif** (the Noble Sanctuary) and Jews as **Har HaBayit** (the Temple Mount). This is Judaism's holiest site and Islam's third-holiest site, after Mecca and Medina.

The huge, open stone plaza, dotted with cypress trees, was built over the biblical Mt Moriah, the location, according to Jewish tradition, of the Foundation Stone of the world itself. It was here, says the Talmud, that Adam, Cain, Abel and Noah performed ritual sacrifices, and where Abraham offered his son Isaac to God in a supreme test of faith (Genesis 22:1-19). It was also the site of Solomon's First Temple, where the Ark of the Covenant was housed, and the Second Temple, destroyed by the Romans in AD 70. The Romans subsequently erected a temple to Zeus on the site, which later served as a Christian church.

The centrepiece of the Temple Mount today is the mosaic-adorned **Dome of the Rock** (Qubbet Al Sakhra; Map p212; Old City), completed in AD 691. Topped by a gold dome, it shelters the slab of stone from which Muslim tradition says Mohammed ascended to heaven on the Mi'raj (Night Journey). **Al Aqsa Mosque** is believed to be a partial conversion of a 6th-century Byzantine church.

The Temple Mount has nine gates and though anyone can leave the compound by most of them, non-Muslims are allowed to enter only at the Bab Al Maghariba/Sha'ar HaMugrabim (Gate of the Moors), reached from the Western Wall plaza. Line up early for security checks (hours for non-Muslim visitors are limited) and bear in mind that the Mount closes on Muslim holidays. Modest dress is required. Non-Muslims can walk around the plaza, but are not allowed to enter the Dome of the Rock or Al Aqsa Mosque.

City of David ARCHAEOLOGICAL SITE
(Map p212; ☎info 02-626-8700, tour reservations 077-996-6726; www.cityofdavid.org.il; Kidron Valley; adult/child 29/15NIS, movie 13NIS, biblical city tour adult/child 60/45NIS; ⏲8am-5pm Sun-Thu, to 2pm Fri Oct-Mar, to 7pm Sun-Thu, to 4pm Fri Apr-Sep; 🚌1, 2, 38) As teeming with controversy as it is with ancient history, the City of David is one of Jerusalem's most active archaeological sites. The oldest part of Jerusalem, it was a settlement during the Canaanite period; David is said to have captured the city and to have brought the Ark of the Covenant here 3000 years ago. Excavations began in the 1850s and are ongoing, as are arguments over the development and expansion of the site (in Silwan, East Jerusalem). Allow at least three hours.

From Dung Gate, head east (downhill) and take the road to the right; the entrance is then on the left. Many visitors find it useful to join a guided tour.

If you intend to walk through **Hezekiah's Tunnel** (8th century BC) – and we suggest that you do – you can change into a swimming costume in the bathrooms and leave your gear in a locker (10NIS); alternatively, wear shorts. You will also need suitable footwear (flip-flops or waterproof shoes).

Mount of Olives

For Christians, this hillside is where Jesus took on the sins of the world, was arrested and later ascended to heaven. A half-dozen churches commemorate events in Jesus's life.

According to the Old Testament's Book of Zechariah, this is where God will redeem the dead on the Day of Judgement, which is why the Mount of Olives has served as a Jewish cemetery since the time of the First Temple.

The panorama of the Old City from the summit is spectacular – visit early in the morning for the clearest views.

Church of the Ascension CHURCH
(www.evangelisch-in-jerusalem.org; cnr Anbar St & Martin Buber St, Mount of Olives; 5NIS; ⏲8am-1pm Mon-Sat; 🚌275) In 1898 the Ottomans granted Germany 8 hectares of land on the Mount of Olives. This was set aside for a church and hospice, and the complex was named after Augusta Victoria, wife of Kaiser Wilhelm II. Completed in 1910, the church is decorated with mosaics and frescos, and has a 60m-high bell tower that can be climbed by visitors (there are 203 steps).

Church of All Nations CHURCH

(Basilica of Gethsemane; Map p204; Mount of Olives; ⌚8am-5.50pm Apr-Sep, to 4.50pm Oct-Mar) Built above the remains of two previous churches, a Franciscan basilica crowns the site where Jesus is believed to have prayed through the night before he was betrayed (Matthew 26:36). Inside the church, also referred to as the Sanctuary of the Agony of Jesus, light is muted by stained-glass windows and the vaulted ceiling is spangled with stars to evoke the mood of Jesus's nocturnal prayers in the Garden of Gethsemane.

Garden of Gethsemane GARDENS

(Map p204; Mount of Olives; ⌚8.30am-noon & 2.30-5pm Mon-Wed, Fri & Sat, to 4pm Sun & Thu) FREE After a night of feverish prayer, Jesus is believed to have been arrested in this garden (Mark 14:26, 32-50), now attached to the Church of All Nations (p209). It has some of the world's oldest olive trees (in Hebrew *gat shmanim* means 'oil press'), though testing has failed to prove conclusively that these were the same trees beneath which Jesus prayed and his disciples slept. A railing protects the remaining trees from visitors (scotching pilgrims' attempts to snap off branches).

Church of Mary Magdalene CHURCH

(Map p204; Mount of Olives; ⌚10am-noon Tue & Thu) A glint of St Petersburg on the Mount of Olives, this shapely church was constructed in the style of a 17th-century Russian Orthodox church. Built in 1888 by Alexander III in memory of his mother, the church is now a convent and guards the relics of two Russian saints. Its seven golden onion-shaped domes form one of Jerusalem's most attractive and surprising landmarks.

Tomb of the Virgin Mary CHRISTIAN SITE

(Map p204; Mount of Olives; ⌚5am-noon & 2.30-5pm Apr-Sep, from 6am Oct-Mar) FREE Centuries of candle smoke have blackened the walls of this subterranean shrine, one of Christianity's holiest sites. According to tradition, this is the resting place of Mary, mother of Jesus. Though strung with countless lanterns and crowded with icons, the space is faintly lit. A central shrine is cloaked in velvet and pilgrims can duck inside.

East Jerusalem

Modern, workaday and predominantly Arab, East Jerusalem is filled with plenty of hustle and bustle, especially along north–south Nablus Rd and roughly parallel Salah ad-Din St. The pre-1967 border between Israel and Jordan ran along Cheyl HaHandasa Rd, now followed by the Jerusalem light-rail line.

★**Palestinian Heritage Museum** MUSEUM

(Dar Al Tifel Al Arabi Foundation; Map p204; ☎02-627-2531; www.dta-museum.org; American Colony, Al Jarrah St, East Jerusalem; adult/child 20/10NIS; ⌚8am-4pm Mon-Thu & Sat) Within the American Colony (p216) complex in a 19th-century building, this museum provides a useful primer on ancient and modern Palestinian culture. Displays on embroidery, basket weaving and agrarian implements offer a glimpse into age-old village traditions. The museum also details the displacement of the Palestinian people, including lists of formerly Arab villages, and memorialises events such as 1948's Deir Yassin massacre.

Rockefeller Museum MUSEUM

(Map p204; ☎02-670-8074; 27 Sultan Suleiman St, East Jerusalem; ⌚10am-3pm Sun, Mon, Wed & Thu, to 2pm Sat; 🚊Damascus Gate) FREE Though overlooked by many visitors to the city, this archaeological museum is well worth a visit. The atmosphere is as enjoyable as the contents; make for the **Cloisters**, where Roman-era antiquities are arranged around a gushing water feature. Other highlights include 9th-century mosaics, Roman ossuary vessels and Byzantine-era blocks featuring early Christian inscriptions.

Garden Tomb GARDENS

(Map p204; ☎02-539-8100; www.gardentomb.org; East Jerusalem; ⌚8.30am-5.15pm Mon-Sat; 🚊Damascus Gate) FREE A tranquil patch of green in the middle of East Jerusalem's mayhem, this site is considered by its trustees to be both the garden and sepulchre of Joseph of Arimathea, and the place where Jesus was crucified, buried and resurrected. While enjoying little support for their claims, the trustees have provided a walled and attractively landscaped space that is more conducive to contemplation than the better-known site said to be that of the crucifixion, the Church of the Holy Sepulchre.

Museum on the Seam GALLERY

(Map p204; ☎02-628-1278; www.mots.org.il; 4 Chel Handasa St; adult/student 30/25NIS; ⌚10am-5pm Mon, Wed & Thu, to 2pm Fri, 2-8pm Tue; 🚊Shivtei Israel) Located on the 'seam' (border) between East and West Jerusalem, this gallery presents rotating contemporary art exhibitions, often exploring themes of identity, multiplicity and faith. Expect anything from neon multimedia installations

Temple Mount/ Al Haram Ash Sharif

A TOUR OF TEMPLE MOUNT/ AL HARAM ASH SHARIF

Temple Mount/Al Haram Ash Sharif encompasses multiple sites that span an area the size of one or two city blocks. A visit requires a little planning and may need to be accomplished over a couple of days.

Ascend the rickety wooden ramp at the Western Wall plaza to reach Temple Mount/Al Haram Ash Sharif at the Bab Al Maghariba (Gate of the Moors). Passing through the gate, continue ahead to view the understated facade of the ❶ **Al Aqsa Mosque** and the sumptuous detail of the ❷ **Dome of the Rock**. Take a slow turn around the Dome to admire its surrounding structures, including the curious ❸ **Dome of the Chain** and the elegant ❹ **Sabil of Qaitbay**. Don't miss the stunning view of the Mount of Olives seen through the stone arches known as the ❺ **Scales of Souls**.

Exit Temple Mount/Al Haram Ash Sharif at the ❻ **Bab Al Qattanin (Gate of Cotton Merchants)** and return to the Western Wall plaza, where you can spend some time at the ❼ **Western Wall** and visit the ❽ **Jerusalem Archaeological Park & Davidson Centre**.

TOP TIPS

➡ Opening hours for Temple Mount/ Al Haram Ash Sharif are limited for non-Muslims and lines can be long during the busy summer season, so queue early (gates open at 7.30am).

➡ An interesting way to reach the Jerusalem Archaeological Park is to take the underground tunnel that starts 600m away in the City of David (tickets for the park are sold at the City of David).

Scales of Souls

Muslims believe that scales will be hung from the column-supported arches to weigh the souls of the dead.

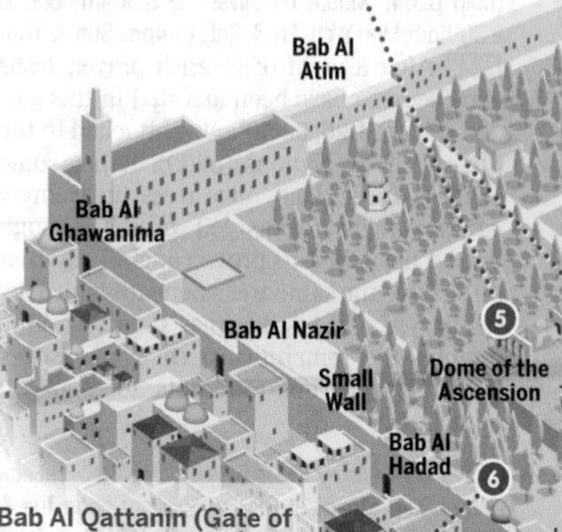

Bab Al Qattanin (Gate of Cotton Merchants)

This is the most imposing of the sanctuary's gates. Make a point of departing through here into the Mamluk-era arcaded Souq Al Qattanin (Cotton Market).

Sabil of Qaitbay

This three-tiered, 13m-high structure was built by Egyptians in 1482 as a charitable act to please Allah and features the only carved-stone dome outside Cairo.

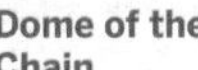

Dome of the Chain

Some believe this structure was built as a model for the Dome of the Rock. Legend has it that Solomon hung a chain from the dome and those who swore falsely while holding it were struck by lightning.

Dome of the Rock

The crown jewel of Jerusalem's architectural heritage, the Dome famously contains the enormous foundation stone that Jews believe is the centre of the earth and Muslims say is the spot where Mohammed made his ascent.

Al Aqsa Mosque

One of the world's oldest mosques, Al Aqsa (the Furthest Mosque) is 75m long and has a capacity for more than 5000 worshippers. The Crusaders renamed it Solomon's Temple and used it as a royal palace and a stable for their horses.

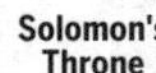

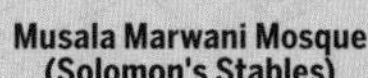

Western Wall

Today it's the holiest prayer site on earth for Jews and an important cultural nexus on Shabbat, when Jews from around the city come to sing, dance and pray by the Wall.

Jerusalem Archaeological Park & Davidson Centre

This is the place to see Robinson's Arch, the steps that led up to Temple Mount and ancient *mikve'ot* (Jewish ritual baths) where pilgrims washed prior to entering the holy temple.

AL KAS FOUNTAIN

Al Kas Fountain, located between Al Aqsa Mosque and the Dome of the Rock, is used for ritual washing before prayers.

Old City

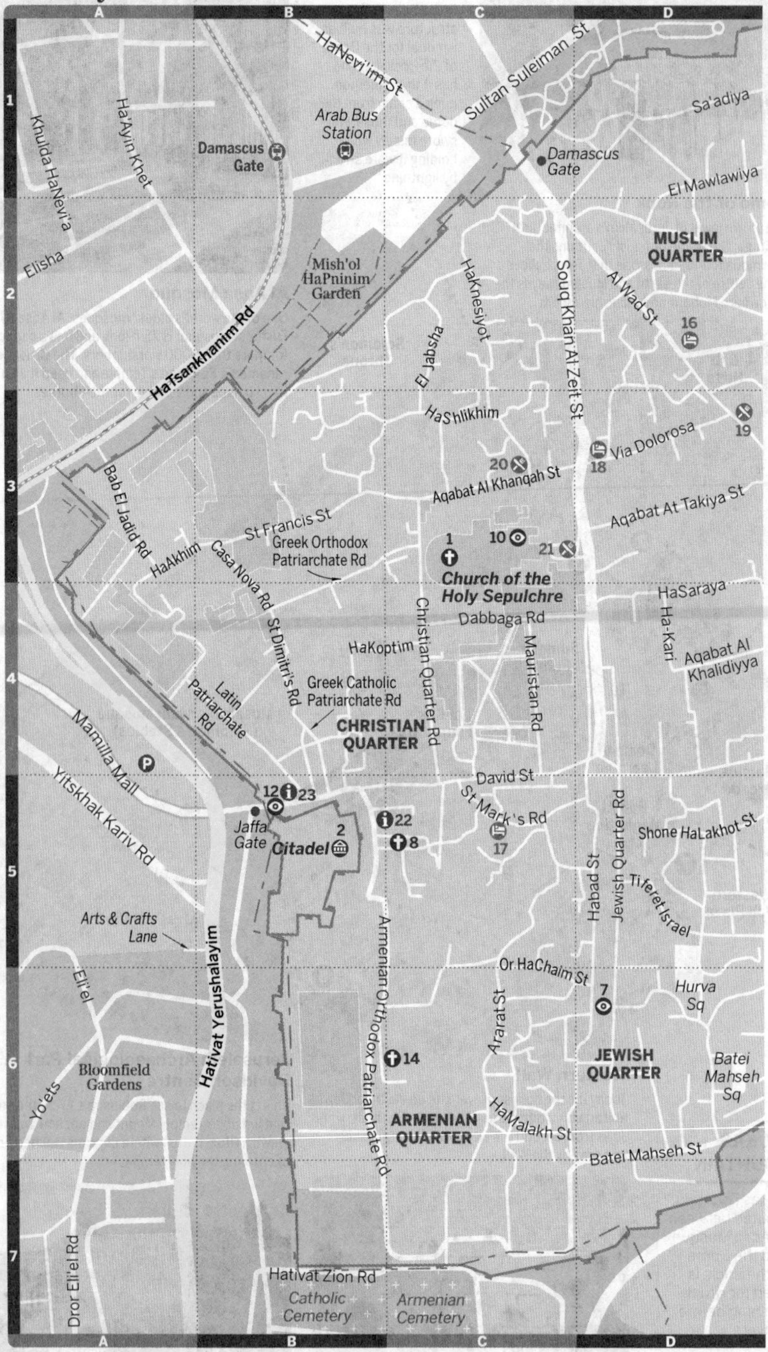

A
B
C
D
1
2
3
4
5
6
7
HaNevi'im St
Sultan Suleiman St
Sa'adiya
Khulda HaNevi'a
Ha'Ayin Khet
Arab Bus Station
Damascus Gate
Damascus Gate
El Mawlawiya
MUSLIM QUARTER
Elisha
Mish'ol HaPninim Garden
HaKnesiyot
Souq Khan Al Zeit St
Al Wad St
16
HaTsankhanim Rd
El Jabsha
HaShlikhim
19
Via Dolorosa
20
18
Aqabat Al Khanqah St
Bab El Jadid Rd
Aqabat At Takiya St
St Francis St
Greek Orthodox Patriarchate Rd
1
10
21
HaAkhim
Casa Nova Rd
Church of the Holy Sepulchre
HaSaraya
Dabbaga Rd
Christian Quarter Rd
St Dimitri's Rd
HaKoptim
Mauristan Rd
Ha-Kari
Aqabat Al Khalidiyya
Latin Patriarchate Rd
Greek Catholic Patriarchate Rd
Mamilla Mall
CHRISTIAN QUARTER
David St
Yitskhak Kariv Rd
12
23
22
St Mark's Rd
Jewish Quarter Rd
Shone HaLakhot St
Jaffa Gate
Citadel
2
8
17
Habad St
Tiferet Israel
Arts & Crafts Lane
Hativat Yerushalayim
Armenian Orthodox Patriarchate Rd
Or HaChaim St
Eli'el
Ararat St
7
Hurva Sq
14
JEWISH QUARTER
Batei Mahseh Sq
Bloomfield Gardens
Yo'ets
ARMENIAN QUARTER
HaMalakh St
Batei Mahseh St
Dror Eli'el Rd
Hativat Zion Rd
Catholic Cemetery
Armenian Cemetery

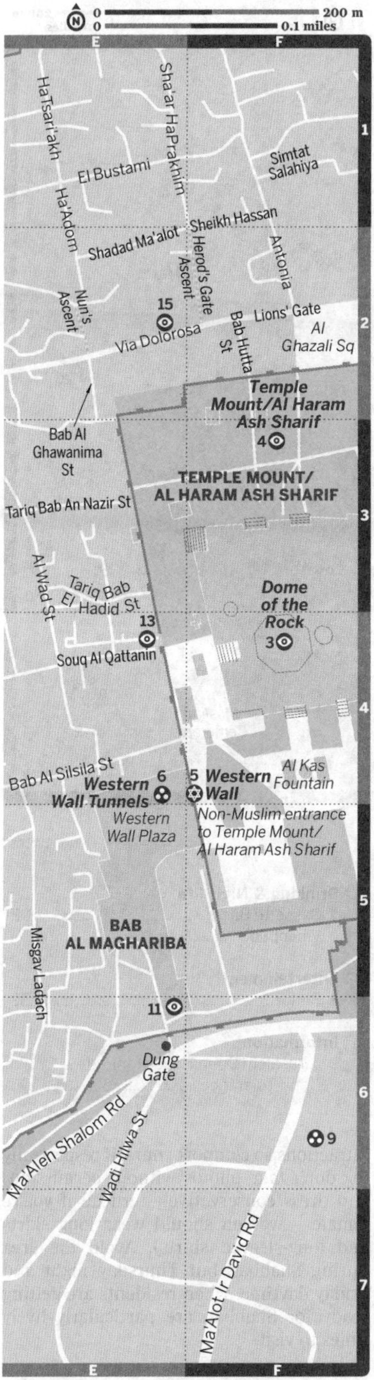

Old City

Top Sights

1 Church of the Holy Sepulchre C3
2 Citadel B5
3 Dome of the Rock F4
4 Temple Mount/Al Haram Ash Sharif F3
5 Western Wall F4
6 Western Wall Tunnels E4

Sights

7 Cardo Maximus D6
8 Christ Church C5
9 City of David F6
10 Ethiopian Monastery C3
11 Jerusalem Archaeological Park & Davidson Centre E6
12 Ramparts Walk B5
13 Souq Al Qattanin E4
14 St James' Cathedral C6
15 Via Dolorosa E2

Sleeping

16 Austrian Hospice D2
Christ Church Guesthouse .... (see 8)
17 Citadel Youth Hostel C5
18 Hashimi Hotel D3

Eating

19 Abu Shukri D3
Christ Church Cafe .... (see 8)
20 Lina Restaurant C3
21 Zalatimo C3

Drinking & Nightlife

Viennese Café .... (see 16)

Information

22 Christian Information Centre C5
23 Jaffa Gate Tourist Office B5

to searing recreations of biblical scenes; whatever is on display is sure to be thought provoking. The building itself served as a forward military position for the Israeli army from 1948 to 1967 and still bears the scars of war.

City Centre

Jerusalem's city centre is northwest of the Old City. Its central axis is Jaffa Rd, which links **Jaffa Gate** (and the western tip of the Old City) with Mahane Yehuda Market (and, further west, the Central Bus Station). Midway between the Jaffa Gate and the market, about 1km from each, is **Zion Square**, a handy landmark and meeting point. Pedestrianised Ben Yehuda

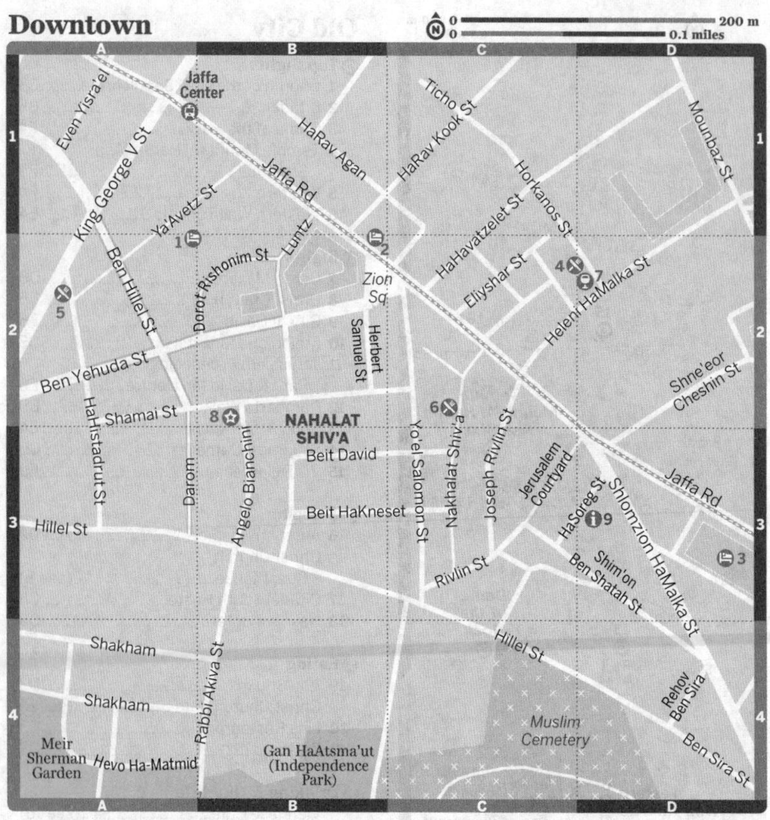

Downtown

Sleeping
1 Arthur Hotel A2
2 Jerusalem Hostel & Guest House B2
3 Post Hostel D3

Eating
4 Darna C2
5 Pinati A2
6 T'mol Shilshom C2

Drinking & Nightlife
7 Cassette Bar D2
Videopub .... (see 7)

Entertainment
8 Bimot B2

Information
9 Jerusalem Open House for Pride and Tolerance D3

St connects Zion Sq – and adjacent, crafts-shop-lined **Yoel Solomon St** – with **King George V St**, creating a triangle.

The ultra-Orthodox neighbourhood of **Mea She'arim** is centred on **Shabbat Square** (Kikar HaShabbat), which – like the area's main drag, Mea She'arim St – is 600m north along Strauss St from the intersection of Jaffa St and King George V St. It's one of the world's most reluctant tourist attractions so comport yourself respectfully (eg don't take photos without permission) and dress conservatively (crucial if you're female – women should wear long skirts and long-sleeved shirts). Avoid the area during Shabbat, but Thursday night and Friday daytime, when residents are getting ready for Shabbat, are particularly lively times to visit.

★Mahane Yehuda Market MARKET
(Map p204; www.machne.co.il; Jaffa Rd, Downtown; ⏲8am-7pm Sun-Thu, 9am-3pm Fri; 🚊Mahane Yehuda) All of Jerusalem meets in Mahane Yehuda, from first-time visitors to residents loading their trolleys with fruit and veg. Market tables are laden with wheels of halvah (sesame-paste nougat), olives larger than thumbs, glistening poppy-seed pastries and almost everything that can be made or grown locally. At night it reinvents itself as a restaurant and bar hub where local foodies and tourists hang out.

Mount of Remembrance

The Mount of Remembrance (Har HaZikaron) is 5km west of the city centre. The JLR's Mt Herzl stop is a 10-minute walk away.

★Yad Vashem MEMORIAL, MUSEUM
(☎info 02-644-3749, tour reservations 02-644-3802; www.yadvashem.org; Hazikaron St, Har Hazikaron; ⏲9am-5pm Sun-Wed, to 8pm Thu, to 2pm Fri; 🚊Mt Herzl) FREE Israel's official memorial to the six million Jews who died at the hands of the Nazis is powerful, poignant and sobering. In the **Holocaust History Museum**, galleries trace the genocide chronologically and thematically using artefacts, films, personal testimonies (on video), photographs and art installations. Photos of those who perished cover the ceiling of the **Hall of Names**, and books filled with their names are arranged all around. A hole in the floor symbolises the lost unknown: victims whose names will never be recorded because they, their entire families, all their friends and everyone else who had known them was killed, leaving no one to bear witness or say the Kaddish (the Jewish mourning prayer). Minimum age 10. Allow at least three hours.

Giv'at Ram

Home to the Knesset, Israel's Supreme Court and the Hebrew University's Faculty of Science, Giv'at Ram is about 2.5km southwest of the city centre.

★Israel Museum MUSEUM
(Map p204; ☎02-670-8811; www.imj.org.il; 11 Ruppin Blvd, Museum Row; adult/student/child 5-17yr 54/39/27NIS; ⏲10am-5pm Sat-Mon, Wed & Thu, 4-9pm Tue, 10am-2pm Fri; 🚌7, 9, 14, 32) More than 5000 years of cultural treasures are assembled around the vast Israel Museum's indoor and outdoor galleries. Highlights are the titanic statues of the **Archaeological Wing**, while the **Fine Arts Wing** showcases 20th-century Israeli art from carpet weaving to sculpture. Newcomers to Jewish culture will appreciate the **Rhythm of Life Room**'s lavish displays on birth, marriage and death ceremonies. The prize exhibit is the **Dead Sea Scrolls**: housed in a distinctive shrine, these are among the world's oldest biblical manuscripts.

Bible Lands Museum MUSEUM
(Map p204; ☎02-561-1066; www.blmj.org; 21 Stefan Wise St, Museum Row; adult/student & child 44/22NIS; ⏲9.30am-5.30pm Sun-Tue & Thu, to 9.30pm Wed, 10am-2pm Fri & Sat; 🚌7, 9, 14, 35, 66) Exploring the people and civilisations who populate the Bible, this museum displays a wealth of artefacts showing how their different cultures were interrelated. The organisation of the exhibits can be a little confusing, so we recommend taking the free guided tour, which starts Sunday to Friday at 10.30am (English) and 11am (Hebrew), Wednesday at 5.30pm (English) and 6pm (Hebrew), and Saturday at 11.30am (Hebrew).

Tours

Green Olive Tours (☎03-721-9540; www.greenolivetours.com), a well-regarded company with Israeli and Palestinian owners, offers a daily walking tour of the Old City (three hours, 165NIS), a twice-weekly walking and light-rail day tour of West Jerusalem including Yad Vashem (260NIS), and a fascinating weekly walking tour of the East–West divide (three hours, 140NIS). It also runs a number of tours into the West Bank, including a Banksy tour of Bethlehem and a visit to Hebron.

Jerusalem-based **Abraham Tours** (www.abrahamtours.com) offers day tours (from 150NIS) around Jerusalem and to the West Bank, the Dead Sea, Masada, Caesarea and the Galilee, as well as trips to Petra and Wadi Rum in Jordan.

Sleeping

Most budget accommodation is located in the Old City or the city centre. Decent midrange options are thin on the ground, but there are plenty of top-end choices, including atmospheric Christian hospices in the Old City and boutique hotels downtown.

If you want atmosphere, by all means stay in the Old City – but note that the area is inconvenient if you have a car and/or lots of luggage. If you are after proximity to restaurants, bars, cafes and public transport, you are much better off staying in the city centre or the German Colony.

Old City

Citadel Youth Hostel HOSTEL $

(Map p212; ☎02-628-5253; www.citadelyouthhostel.com; 20 St Mark's Rd, Armenian Quarter; mattress on roof 50NIS, dm 63NIS, d 207NIS, s/d with shared bathroom 123/177NIS; @ 📶) Seconds away from the markets, steeped in history, yet somewhat shabby, the Citadel is a perfect example of a hostel with unrealised potential. Parts of the building date back 700 years and while the stone-walled rooms have atmosphere, the beds are worn and the bathrooms poorly maintained.

★**Austrian Hospice** GUESTHOUSE $$

(Map p212; ☎02-626-5800; www.austrianhospice.com; 37 Via Dolorosa, Muslim Quarter; dm/s/d/tr €32/97/140/198; @ 📶) Stepping into this gated complex feels like discovering a treasure. This castle-like guesthouse first opened in 1863 and its gardens, archways and stone walls ooze history. Private rooms are simply furnished but large, with good beds. Single-sex dorms are in the basement, where there are also squeaky-clean shared bathrooms.

Hashimi Hotel HOTEL $$

(Map p212; ☎02-628-4410; www.hashimihotel.com; 73 Souq Khan Al Zeit St, Muslim Quarter; s/d/tr from US$80/110/280; @ 📶) An oasis in the Old City, this hotel in a 400-year-old building has light-flooded, floral-patterned rooms (ask for a corner room with a view). There are a few rules (no alcohol anywhere, and no unmarried couples in the same room), but they'll be nothing as you sip mint tea on the rooftop overlooking extraordinary views of the Dome of the Rock (p208).

Christ Church Guesthouse GUESTHOUSE $$$

(Map p212; ☎02-627-7727; www.cmj-israel.org; Omar Ibn Al Khattab Sq, Old City; s/tw/ste/q 430/645/710/985NIS; P @ 📶) This wonderfully maintained guesthouse gets high marks for its period atmosphere, multilingual staff, prime location and garden setting. The simply furnished rooms have stone floors, domed ceilings and comfortable beds, and there are lounges where guests can relax over free tea and coffee.

East Jerusalem

★**American Colony Hotel** HISTORIC HOTEL $$$

(Map p204; ☎02-627-9777; www.americancolony.com; 1 Louis Vincent St, East Jerusalem; s from US$320, d US$320-550, ste US$675-875; P @ 📶 🏊) East Jerusalem's VIP choice is this luxurious complex based around a mid-19th-century building. The American Colony Hotel retains much of its historic charm – think mother-of-pearl inlaid furniture and intricate tile work – though rooms sprinkle just the right amount of modernity into the mix. Standard rooms have a classic style (hardwood beds, flowing drapes), while some suites have chandelier windows and four-posters.

St George's Guesthouse GUESTHOUSE $$$

(Map p204; ☎02-628-3302; www.stgeorgesguesthouse.org; 20 Derekh Shchem (Nablus) Rd, East Jerusalem; s/d standard US$110/150, deluxe US$150/180; P @ 📶; 🚊Shivtei Israel) Within a century-old Anglican church, this tranquil guesthouse has been welcoming pilgrims since 1923 (the buildings previously housed the choir school and clergy). Twin guest rooms, with crisp linens, satellite TV and kettle, are set around a courtyard garden; the deluxe versions, with stone walls, extra space and modernised bathrooms, are worth the extra charge.

City Centre & Around

★**Abraham Hostel** HOSTEL $

(Map p204; ☎02-650-2200; https://abrahamhostels.com; 67 HaNevi'im St, Davidka Sq, Downtown; dm 85-115NIS, s 270-330NIS, d 300-420NIS, f 490-620NIS; @ 📶; 🚊Ha-Davidka) Lively Abraham Hostel has earned its popularity. Its friendly crew easily covers traveller essentials – 24-hour reception, laundry (12NIS), shared kitchen – and ups the ante with a sweet bar and lounge, nightly events and culturally enriching tours. Choose from male, female or mixed dorms, or basic but clean en suite rooms. Mingle with the international crowd and sigh at the rooftop views: you've arrived.

★**Post Hostel** HOSTEL $

(Map p214; ☎02-581-3222; http://theposthostel.com; 23 Jaffa Rd, Downtown; dm US$24-32, d US$105-125, tr US$145; 📶; 🚊City Hall) On the 3rd floor of an old post office is this airy and well-run hostel. Bold red and navy decor and postal-themed murals pay homage to the building's past, and the digs are simple but spotless, ranging from private rooms to dorms (single sex and mixed). The bar, roof terrace and chill-out area with pool table promote a relaxing, convivial vibe.

Jerusalem Hostel & Guest House HOSTEL $

(Map p214; ☎02-623-6102; www.jerusalem-hostel.com; 44 Jaffa Rd, Zion Sq, Downtown; dm 80-90NIS, d 240-330NIS; @ 📶; 🚊Jaffa Center) An old-school backpacker ambience infuses the well-maintained Jerusalem Hostel. Rooms might be plain, but the common areas are given a lift with antiques, old photos, Judaica and (in the entrance vestibule) huge columns. There's a choice of en suite rooms and single-sex and mixed dorms, as well as a communal kitchen and a roof terrace with couches to chill on.

★Arthur Hotel BOUTIQUE HOTEL $$$
(Map p214; ☎02-623-9999; www.atlas.co.il/arthur-jerusalem; 13 Dorot Rishonim St, Downtown; d from US$184; P@; Jaffa Center) Rooms at the nostalgic Arthur Hotel employ fur-lined cushions, embroidered headboards and antique furnishings to conjure the 1920s. Jewel-toned rooms vary in style, but bathrooms are glossy and well maintained; try to get a balcony room in the rear of the building.

German Colony & Rechavia

St Andrew's Scottish Guesthouse GUESTHOUSE $$
(Map p204; ☎02-673-2401; www.scotsguesthouse.com; 1 David Remez St, Yemin Moshe; s/d/ste US$135/170/380; P@) St Andrew's feels like a bit of Scotland transported to the Middle East. Set on a hill overlooking the Old City, with leafy gardens and an imposing stone facade, it has something of a school-dormitory feel, but rooms are sizeable, with high ceilings and surgically clean bathrooms, and Scottish flavour has been infused throughout (including generous use of tartan).

Little House in Rehavia HOTEL $$
(Map p204; ☎02-563-3344; www.jerusalem-hotel.co.il; 20 Ibn Ezra St, Rehavia; s/d/q/f US$139/153/190/243;) A midrange gem in a pretty residential neighbourhood, Little House's 1929 stone building has plenty of character, and the staff is just as charming. Twenty-eight simple but clean rooms have well-kept, beige-tiled bathrooms. The hotel is a little bare but great value, especially with the roof terrace and Israeli breakfast buffet, best eaten in the cat-patrolled garden.

Eating

A significant percentage of Jerusalem's restaurants are kosher and thus closed on Shabbat and Jewish holidays; when almost everything in the city's Jewish neighbourhoods shuts down, one option is to head to East Jerusalem.

For a self-catering extravaganza, visit the Mahane Yehuda Market, where stalls sell the city's finest produce – and innovative eateries offer grungy-chic gourmet.

Old City

Most Old City restaurants stick to hummus, kebabs, shwarma and other Middle Eastern fare. The only exceptions are around Jaffa Gate, where there are a few Mediterranean-style places, and at Hurva Sq in the Jewish Quarter, where there are American-style fast-food joints. Finding a meal after dark can be challenging as the Old City shuts down when the crowds go home.

Many places in the Muslim Quarter close during Ramadan.

★Abu Shukri MIDDLE EASTERN $
(Map p212; ☎02-627-1538; 63 Al Wad St, Muslim Quarter; hummus 20NIS; 9am-4pm;) Abu Shukri is so popular that it's spawned imitators around Jerusalem. The standard platter includes a bowl of rich, smooth hummus – topped with chickpeas, tahina (sesame-seed paste), *fuul* (stewed fava beans) or pine nuts – crunchy veg and a basket of pita bread. Be sure to add a side order of falafel (10NIS). Cash only.

Lina Restaurant MIDDLE EASTERN $
(Map p212; ☎02-627-7230; Aqabat Al Khanqah St, Muslim Quarter; hummus 20NIS; 9am-5pm) The main rival to legendary Abu Shukri is this excellent Middle Eastern place, whose hummus – usually glistening with olive oil – is among Jerusalem's best. There are two dining rooms on opposite sides of the street, though this unassuming spot is easy to miss.

City Centre

The City Centre is jam-packed with restaurants, cafes, pizzerias, and hummus, felafel and shwarma joints.

★Pinati MIDDLE EASTERN $$
(Map p214; ☎02-625-4540; http://pinati.co.il; 13 King George V St, Downtown; mains 25-60NIS; 8am-7pm Sun-Thu, to 3pm Fri; ; Jaffa Center) Locals swear by the hummus, served with pita and piquant garlic-chilli paste, but Pinati's well-seasoned mains are worth sampling, too: slow-stewed moussaka, schnitzels, bean soups and shakshuka (egg and tomato bake). Casual dining and comforting kosher food is a winning formula, so you may have to battle crowds at lunchtime.

Ishtabach KURDISH $$
(Map p204; ☎02-623-2997; cnr Shikma St & Beit Ya'akov St, Downtown; mains 40-65NIS; noon-1am; Mahane Yehuda) Nestled on the outskirts of the Mahane Yehuda Market,

Ishtabach is famous for delicious (and filling) *shamburak,* Kurdish pastry stuffed with various meats or vegetables and served with unique sauces (like garlic jam) for added flavour. Come hungry for the *siske* filling – beef that's been slow cooked for more than 15 hours.

T'mol Shilshom CAFE **$$**

(Map p214; ☎02-623-2758; www.tmol-shilshom.co.il; 5 Yo'el Salomon St, Downtown; mains 40-55NIS; ⌚8.30am-11pm Sun-Thu, to 2pm Fri; 📶; 🚊Jaffa Center) Whether you settle into the book-lined interior or the shaded courtyard, T'mol Shilshom is one of Jerusalem's most relaxing brunch spots. This friendly kosher joint is best known for its shakshuka: classic, spicy or cheese-laden versions of the Middle Eastern egg-and-tomato bake are on offer, always with a mountain of fresh bread, salad and olive tapenade.

★**Machneyuda** INTERNATIONAL **$$$**

(Map p204; ☎02-533-3442; www.machneyuda.co.il; 10 Beit Ya'akov St, Downtown; mains 86-175NIS, tasting menu 295NIS; ⌚12.30-4pm & 6.30-11pm Sun-Thu, to 3pm Fri; 🚊Mahane Yehuda) Is it New York comfort food, Italian fine dining or haute cuisine? This superb restaurant near Mahane Yehuda Market (p215) has won local acclaim for its playful menu, which offers Catalan-style calamari, black linguine with crab and good ol' fashioned steak and potatoes. Book well in advance, and pray there's semolina cake.

Darna MOROCCAN **$$$**

(Map p214; ☎02-624-5406; www.darna.co.il; 3 Horkanos St, Downtown; mains 75-155NIS, set menus 175-240NIS; ⌚noon-3pm & 6.30pm-midnight Sun-Thu, after Shabbat-10pm Sat; 🚊Jaffa Center) Aromatic and delicious dishes from Morocco – including plenty of tagine and couscous choices – are served in atmospheric surrounds at this long-standing kosher favourite. Be sure to try the *pastilla fassia* (filo pastry stuffed with poussin and almonds) and consider the *mechoui* (slow-cooked lamb shoulder).

> **USEFUL JERUSALEM WEBSITES**
>
> **www.gojerusalem.com** Handy tourist website that includes events information.
>
> **www.itraveljerusalem.com** Extremely useful website operated by the municipality; includes itineraries.
>
> **www.jerusalem.com** Overview of the city, its attractions and events; includes virtual tours of important sites.

Drinking & Nightlife

Jerusalem's city centre is well endowed with bars. The best are in the Mahane Yehuda Market area and, in the vicinity of Zion Sq, on Rivlin, Ben Shatah, Helene HaMalka and Dorot Rishonim Sts. East Jerusalem bars tend to be inside hotels, while the Old City is almost as dry as the Negev.

Beer Bazaar CRAFT BEER

(Map p204; ☎02-671-2559; www.facebook.com/Beer.Bazaar.Jerusalem; 3 Haetz Ha'em St, Mahane Yehuda Market, Downtown; ⌚11am-late Sun-Thu, to 5pm Fri, from 8pm Sat; 🚊Mahane Yehuda) Glug your way through more than 100 craft beers (including dozens of Israeli brews) at this enormously friendly bar in Mahane Yehuda Market (p215). The popular Jerusalem location of a Tel Aviv microbrew chain, Beer Bazaar rotates both the beers on tap and the entertainment, which ranges from 'beer yoga' to live music.

Cassette Bar BAR

(HaCasetta; Map p214; 1 Horkanos St, Downtown; ⌚8pm-5am Sat-Thu, 2pm-6am Fri; 🚊Jaffa Center) Accessed from the street (look for the metal door covered with old cassette tapes) or through the rear of the Record Bar next door, this pint-sized bar is a long-standing hipster haunt. The crowd drinks well into the night, serenaded by alternative tracks.

Upstairs is **Videopub** (Map p214; https://sites.google.com/site/videopubjerusalem; 1st fl, 1 Horkanus St, Downtown; ⌚8pm-4am Mon-Thu, Sat & Sun, from 10pm Fri; 🚊Jaffa Center), a popular gay bar.

Entertainment

Tickets for concerts, theatre and other events can be booked through **Bimot** (Map p214; ☎02-623-7000; https://tickets.bimot.co.il; 8 Shamai St, Downtown; ⌚9am-7pm Sun-Thu, to 1pm Fri; 🚊Jaffa Center).

Cinematheque CINEMA

(Map p204; ☎02-565-4333; www.jer-cin.org.il; 11 Hebron Rd, near Old City; tickets 39NIS) The Jerusalem Cinematheque, with its quality foreign films and miniature festivals on themes from gay cinema to China on the silver screen, is a hang-out for true movie connoisseurs. It's a favoured haunt of secular, left-leaning Jerusalemites and the home of the respected **Jerusalem Film Festival** (www.jff.org.il; ⌚mid-Jul).

Yellow Submarine LIVE MUSIC
(☎02-679-4040; www.yellowsubmarine.org.il; 13 HaRechavim St, Talpiot) Does Middle Eastern dance music or Balkan pop sound like your jam? How about soft jazz or Jewish spiritual song, or stand-up comedy (in English)? An impressively diverse program of musical and spoken-word talent takes the stage at Yellow Submarine; browse the website for upcoming events.

Zappa in the Lab LIVE MUSIC
(☎box office 03-762-6666; www.zappa-club.co.il; 28 Hebron Rd, Abu Tor; ⌚box office 9am-9pm) Crafted out of a disused railway warehouse, this venue has an industrial feel and an attractive bar backlit against weathered stone. Zappa stages jazz, folk, rock and pop concerts, with a smattering of tribute bands and comedy. Events are almost nightly; check the website for details (it's worth booking).

Jerusalem Theatre PERFORMING ARTS
(Jerusalem Centre for the Performing Arts; Map p204; ☎02-560-5755; www.jerusalem-theatre.co.il; 20 David Marcus St, Talbiyeh; ⌚box office 9.30am-7.30pm Sun-Thu, to 1pm Fri) This complex includes a concert hall, a cinema, theatres and a cafe. This is the place to catch a performance by the Jerusalem Symphony Orchestra, as well as comedy, music, children's theatre and dance performances.

Information

The best deals for changing money are at the private, commission-free exchange offices in the New City (around Zion Sq), East Jerusalem (Salah ad-Din St) and in the Old City (Jaffa Gate). Note that except in East Jerusalem many close early on Friday and remain closed all day Saturday.

ATMs are plentiful around Zion Sq in the city centre.

Christian Information Centre (Map p212; ☎02-627-2692; www.cicts.org; Omar Ibn Al Khattab Sq, Old City; ⌚9am-5.30pm Mon-Fri, 8.30am-12.30pm Sat) This office opposite the entrance to the Citadel is operated by the Franciscans and provides information on the city's Christian sites.

Hadassah Medical Centre Mount Scopus (☎emergency room 02-584-4333, info 02-584-4222; www.hadassah.org.il; 🚌19) The Mt Scopus campus of this nonprofit hospital has a 24-hour emergency department and a specialist paediatric emergency department that is also open 24 hours.

Jaffa Gate Tourist Office (Map p212; ☎02-627-1422; www.itraveljerusalem.com; Jaffa Gate; ⌚8.30am-5pm Sat-Thu, to 1.30pm Fri) Main tourist office for Jerusalem. It supplies free maps, organises guides and provides information and advice.

Jerusalem Open House for Pride and Tolerance (Map p214; ☎02-625-3191; www.joh.org.il; 1st fl, 2 HaSoreg St; 🚊City Hall) For more information on the local LGBT community, contact the Jerusalem Open House to learn about upcoming events, some of which are English-speaker friendly.

Terem (☎1-599-520-520; www.terem.com; 80 Yirmiyahu St, Romema; ⌚24hr; 🚊Central Station) Efficient multilingual walk-in medical clinic that handles everything from minor ailments to emergencies. It's a five-minute walk from the Central Bus Station.

DANGERS & ANNOYANCES

Demonstrations and marches by both Jews and Arabs are pretty common in Jerusalem and while they are usually peaceful, it's a good idea to remain vigilant in case things get rowdy (Damascus Gate and Temple Mount are regular flashpoints). The Mount of Olives has not always been the friendliest area to walk in and some female travellers strolling there alone have been hassled. If possible, visit the area in pairs. Ultra-Orthodox Jewish groups sometimes stone buses, burn garbage bins and confront the police at Shabbat Sq in Mea She'arim, which even on quiet days can turn hostile when tourists (especially immodestly dressed ones) saunter in.

Getting There & Away

BUS

Buses to major cities and towns across Israel leave from the **Central Bus Station** (Map p204; www.bus.co.il; Jaffa Rd; 🚊Central Station). Book your ticket to Eilat in advance, as these services are often full.

If you are headed into northern areas of the West Bank such as Ramallah (bus 18, 7NIS), use the **Arab bus station** (East Jerusalem Central Bus Station; Map p204; Derekh Shchem (Nablus) Rd, East Jerusalem) on Derekh Shchem (Nablus) Rd, the street straight in front of Damascus Gate. The buses that leave from here are green and white.

For Bethlehem, take bus 21 (8NIS) from the **Arab bus station** (Map p212; Sultan Suleiman St, East Jerusalem) west of the Damascus Gate next to the tram stop. The buses that leave from here are blue and white. For Hebron, take bus 21, alight at Bab Al Zqaq and then take a Hebron bus (5NIS).

Check the latest information with the **East Jerusalem Transport Association** (☎ 02-627-2881). The general rule is that blue-and-white buses go to southern West Bank destinations and green-and-white buses go to northern West Bank destinations.

SHERUT (SHARED TAXI)

Sheruts (*servees* in Arabic; shared taxis) depart more frequently than buses and often cost only a few shekels more; on Shabbat they're the only public transport to destinations in Israel. Sheruts for Tel Aviv (from 24NIS per person on weekdays, 30NIS on weekends and after midnight) depart from the corner of HaRav Kook St and Jaffa Rd, near Zion Sq; in Tel Aviv, they stop just outside the Central Bus Station.

TRAIN

Jerusalem's **train station** (Jerusalem Malcha; ☎ 02-577-4000; www.rail.co.il; Yitzhak Moda'i St, Malcha; ⏲ ticket booth 6-10am & 3.15-7.45pm Sun-Thu, 8.45am-2pm Fri) is located in the southwest of the city, near the Jerusalem Mall; to get there, take bus 18 from King George St or bus 6 from the Central Bus Station. Hourly trains reach Tel Aviv's Savidor Merkaz, HaHagana and HaShalom stations (20NIS, 1½ hours). To get to the coast and Haifa you have to transfer in Tel Aviv.

Starting in April 2018 it will take just 28 minutes to travel between Jerusalem and Tel Aviv thanks to a US$2 billion high-speed rail line that will also serve Ben Gurion Airport.

ℹ Getting Around

TO/FROM THE AIRPORT

Ben Gurion Airport is 52km northwest of Jerusalem. **Nesher Service Taxis** (☎ 02-625-7227, 072-264-6059; www.neshertours.co.il) operates 24-hour sheruts that take you from Ben Gurion to the Jerusalem address of your choice. They depart when full from the rank in front of the international arrivals hall and charge 64NIS per passenger. To get to Ben Gurion from Jerusalem, call Nesher a day in advance to schedule pickup. There is also now a bus (485) that goes every hour between Ben Gurion and Jerusalem's Central Bus Station for 16NIS.

A private taxi costs 268NIS on weekdays, and 320NIS at night (9pm to 5.30am) and on Shabbat and Jewish holidays.

BUS

Jerusalem is laced with a good network of city bus routes (5.90NIS per ride), with some of them feeder lines for the light-rail system. To access information about routes, schedules and to download handy public transport maps, see www.jet.gov.il.

To get to parts of East Jerusalem such as the Mount of Olives (bus 75, 5NIS), use the Arab bus station located on Sultan Suleiman St in East Jerusalem, near Herod's Gate. The buses that leave from here are blue and white.

LIGHT RAIL

Jerusalem Light Rail (www.citypass.co.il) consists of a single line that runs from Mt Herzl in the west of the city to Heyl HaAvir in Pisgat Ze'ev, in the city's far northeast. There are 23 stops along a 13.9km route, including the Central Bus Station, Mahane Yehuda Market and Damascus Gate. The service runs every 10 minutes or so from 5.30am to midnight daily except on Shabbat: on Friday services stop 90 minutes before Shabbat begins, and Saturday services start one hour after Shabbat concludes. Tickets (5.90NIS) can be purchased from the machines on tram stops and must be validated on board the tram. Multiple journeys can be loaded onto a Rav-Kav card (p283).

TAXI

Plan on spending between 25NIS and 50NIS for trips anywhere within the central part of town. Insist that the driver uses the meter; between 5.30am and 9pm (except Shabbat), the meter should start on 12.30NIS. Call **Hapalmach Taxi** (☎ 02-679-3333) or find taxi services by neighbourhood (and sample fares) on JerusalemTaxis (http://jerusalemtaxies.com).

BUSES FROM JERUSALEM

DESTINATION	BUS NUMBER	PRICE (NIS)	DURATION (HR)	FREQUENCY
Be'er Sheva	446, 470	27	1¾	2 hourly
Eilat	444	70	5	4 daily
Haifa	940, 947	37.50	2½–3	every 15min
Masada	444, 486	37.50	2½	almost hourly
Tel Aviv (Arlozorov Bus Station)	480	16	1	every 15min
Tel Aviv (Central Bus Station)	405	16	1	every 15min
Tiberias	961, 962	37.50	2½	almost hourly

Drivers at Jaffa Gate and those who wait next to the Tomb of the Virgin Mary on the Mount of Olives are notorious for refusing to use the meter and then overcharging.

MEDITERRANEAN COAST

Stretching for 273km from Gaza to the Lebanese border, Israel's Mediterranean coastline has some fine beaches, first-rate archaeological sites, and many of the country's wealthiest and most innovative towns and cities.

Tel Aviv-Jaffa (Yafo)

تل ابيب-يافا תל אביב–יפו

03 / POP 432,892

When the State of Israel hits the headlines, the state of Tel Aviv sits back with a cappuccino. Nicknamed 'the Bubble', Tel Aviv (or TLV) is a city of outdoor cafes, boutiques, bistros, leafy boulevards and long sandy beaches - and a favourite with Europeans looking for some year-round sun. All over the city, classic Bauhaus buildings are getting a well-needed facelift, while nearby skyscrapers rise towards the heavens. Yet the real Tel Aviv is best sought out in humble hummus joints, wine bars hidden down alleyways, fresh fruit-shake stalls, quiet pocket parks and chaotic marketplaces.

Sights

City Centre

Rabin Square SQUARE

(Map p222) Used for Independence Day celebrations, political rallies and peace vigils, this huge public space was renamed after the assassination of Prime Minister Yitzhak Rabin in 1995; a **memorial** marks the site where he was shot. The square also has an 'ecological pond' filled with lotus flowers and koi, two fountains and some cool cafes around the perimeter. On the northern edge towers City Hall, which looks like a 1960s communist-style block - though not on nights when the facade is turned into an enormous Tetris game.

★**Tel Aviv Museum of Art** GALLERY

(Map p222; 03-607-7020; www.tamuseum.com; 27 Shaul HaMelech Blvd; adult/student/child under 15yr 50/40NIS/free; 10am-6pm Mon-Wed & Sat, to 9pm Tue & Thu, to 2pm Fri; P; 7, 9, 18, 38, 42, 70, 82) The modern 'envelope' building by American architect Preston Scott Cohen is one of many reasons to visit this impressive museum. There's a huge amount to see here (including art activities for kids), but the highlight is modern and contemporary Israeli art. The impressionist and post-impressionist collection includes works by Renoir, Gauguin, Degas, Pissarro, Monet, Picasso, Cézanne, Van Gogh, Vuillard, Matisse, Soutine and Chagall.

Independence Hall HISTORIC SITE

(Beit Haatzmaut; Map p222; 03-510-6426; http://eng.ihi.org.il; 16 Rothschild Blvd; adult/student/child 24/18/16NIS; 9am-5pm Sun-Thu, to 2pm Fri) This building, still in need of some restoration work, was originally the home of Meir Dizengoff, one of the city's founding fathers and its first mayor. It was here, on 14 May 1948, that David Ben-Gurion declared the establishment of the state of Israel. Entry includes a short introductory film and a tour of the room where Israel's Declaration of Independence was signed.

Haganah Museum MUSEUM

(Map p222; 03-560-8624; http://eng.shimur.org/hagana; 23 Rothschild Blvd; adult/student & child 15/10NIS; 8am-4pm Sun-Thu) Splendidly located on Rothschild Blvd, this museum chronicles the formation and activities of the Haganah, the paramilitary organisation that was the forerunner of today's Israel Defence Forces (IDF). A civilian guerrilla force protecting kibbutzim (Israeli farms and cooperatives) from attack in the 1920s and '30s, the Haganah went on to assist in the illegal entry of more than 100,000 Jews into Palestine after the British Government's 1939 white paper restricting immigration. After WWII, Haganah fighters carried out anti-British operations.

★**Carmel Market** MARKET

(Shuk HaCarmel; Map p222; 8am-late afternoon Sun-Thu, to mid-afternoon Fri) Tel Aviv's busiest street market is, in many ways, the heart of the city. It's a crowded and noisy place where vendors hawk everything from cut-price beachwear to knock-off designer accessories, and where locals come to buy olives, pickles, nuts, fruit, vegetables, cheese and freshly baked bread.

Neve Tzedek

Founded in 1887, Jaffa's first Jewish suburb - its old houses are now some of the most expensive real estate in town - is well worth a wander. The district's cute boutiques, cafes, wine bars and restaurants

Central Tel Aviv

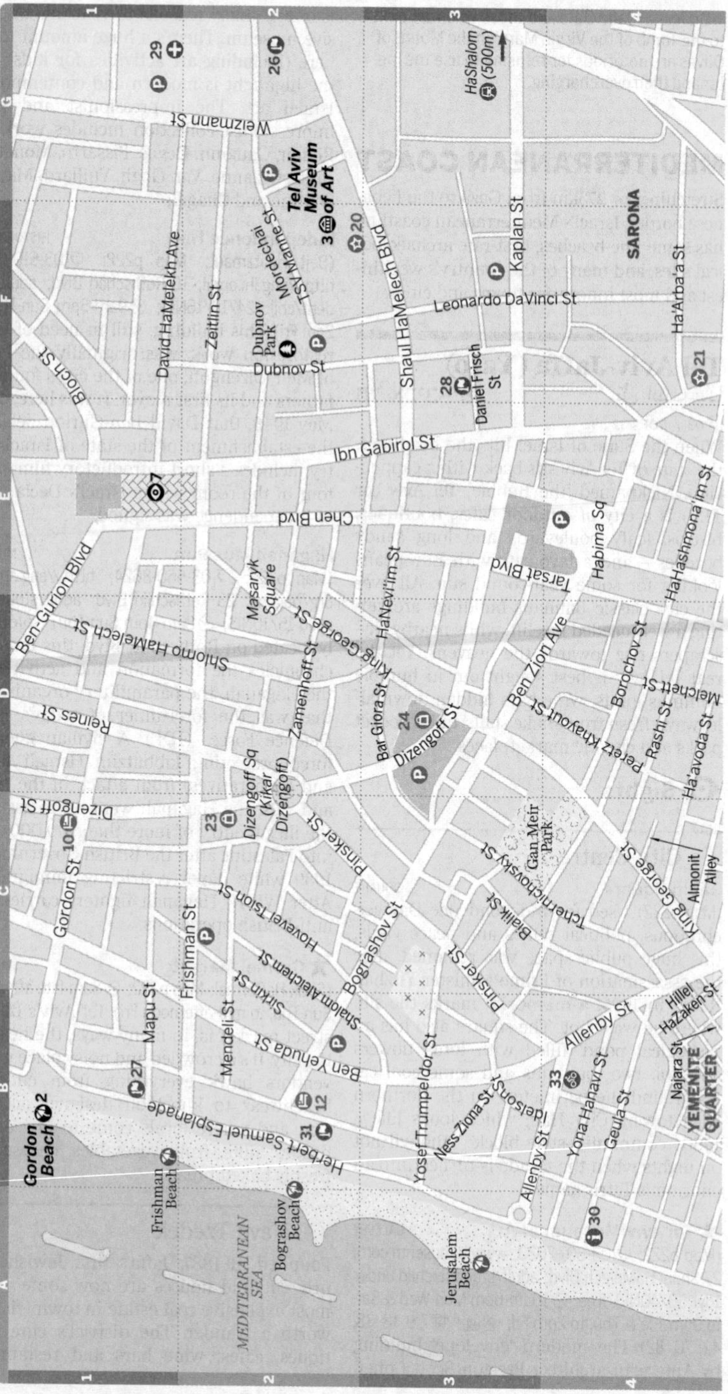

0 400 m
0 0.2 miles

A B C D E F G
1 2 3 4

Gordon Beach 2
Gordon St
10
Dizengoff St
Reines St
Ben-Gurion Blvd
Bloch St
27
Mapu St
Shlomo HaMelech St
7
David HaMelekh Ave
29
Weizmann St
Frishman Beach
Frishman St
Zeitlin St
23
Mendeli St
MEDITERRANEAN SEA
Herbert Samuel Esplanade
Sirkin St
Hovevei Tsion St
Dizengoff Sq (Kikar Dizengoff)
Masaryk Square
Dubnov Park
Dubnov St
Mordechai TSV Manne St
26
Bograshov Beach
31
12
Ben Yehuda St
Shalom Aleichem St
Pinsker St
Zamenhoff St
King George St
Chen Blvd
Tel Aviv Museum of Art 3
20
Bograshov St
Bar Giora St
HaNevi'im St
Ibn Gabirol St
Shaul HaMelech Blvd
24
Yosef Trumpeldor St
Dizengoff St
Ness Ziona St
Jerusalem Beach
28
Daniel Frisch St
Leonardo DaVinci St
HaShalom (500m)
Pinsker St
Idelson St
Bialik St
Tchernichovsky St
Gan Meir Park
Ben Zion Ave
Tarsat Blvd
Kaplan St
Allenby St
33
Yona Hanavi St
Allenby St
Peretz Khayout St
Habima Sq
30
Geula St
Borochov St
SARONA
King George St
Rashi St
Melchett St
Najara St
Hillel HaZaken St
YEMENITE QUARTER
Almonit Alley
Ha'avoda St
HaHashmona'im St
Ha'Arba'a St
21

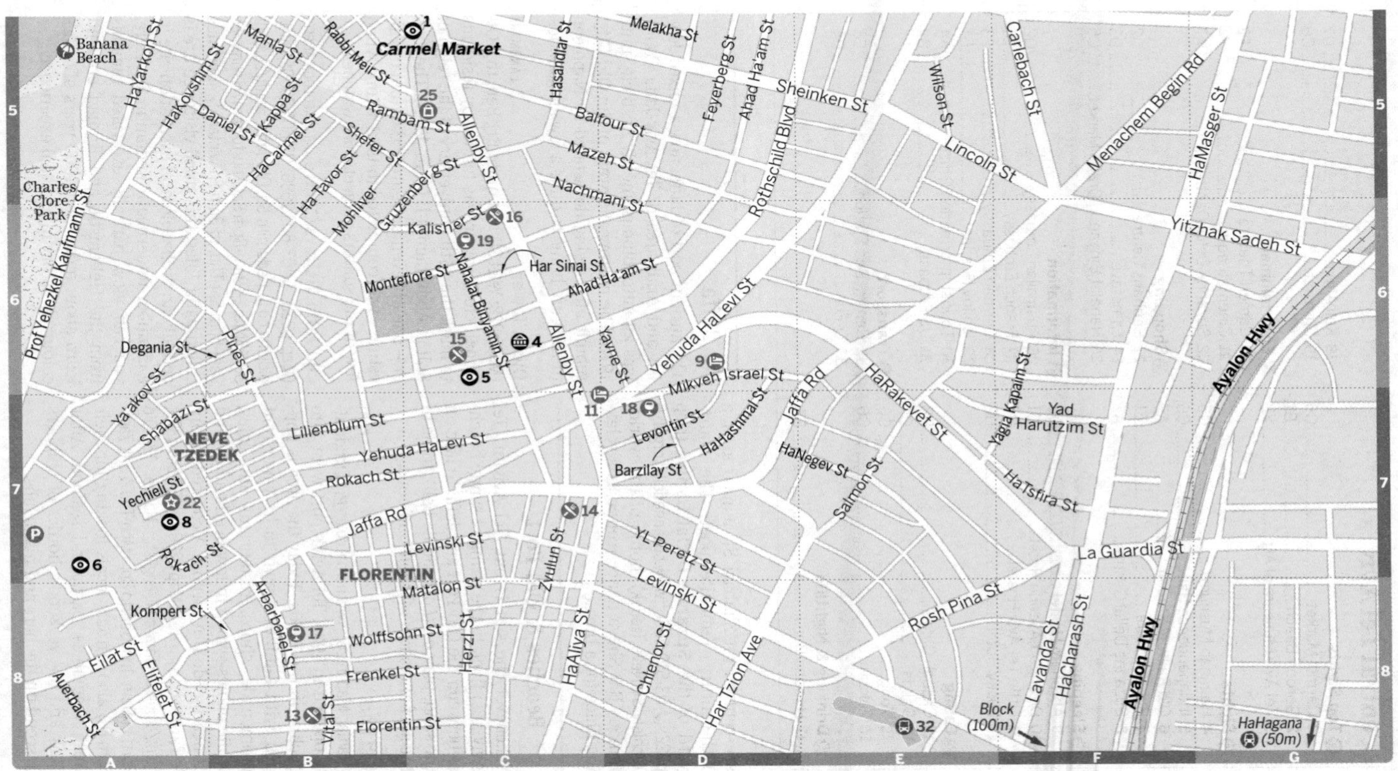

Banana Beach
HaYarkon St
HaKovshim St
Manla St
Rabbi Meir St
Carmel Market
Melakha St
Hasandlar St
Feyerberg St
Ahad Ha'am St
Sheinken St
Wilson St
Carlebach St
Menachem Begin Rd
HaMasger St
Daniel St
Kappa St
HaCarmel St
Rambam St
Shefer St
Ha Tavor St
Mohliver
Gruzenberg St
Allenby St
Balfour St
Mazeh St
Nachmani St
Rothschild Blvd
Lincoln St
Yitzhak Sadeh St
Charles Clore Park
Prof Yehezkel Kaufmann St
Kalisher St
Har Sinai St
Ahad Ha'am St
Montefiore St
Nahalat Binyamin St
Yavne St
Yehuda HaLevi St
Mikveh Israel St
Jaffa Rd
HaRakevet St
Yagia Kapaim St
Yad Harutzim St
Ayalon Hwy
Degania St
Pines St
Ya'akov St
Shabazi St
NEVE TZEDEK
Lilienblum St
Yehuda HaLevi St
Rokach St
Levontin St
HaHashmal St
Barzilay St
HaNegev St
Salmon St
HaTsfira St
Yechieli St
Jaffa Rd
Levinski St
Zvulun St
YL Peretz St
La Guardia St
Rokach St
FLORENTIN
Matalon St
Levinski St
Rosh Pina St
Kompert St
Arbarbanel St
Wolffsohn St
Herzl St
HaAliya St
Chlenov St
Har Tzion Ave
Lavanda St
HaCharash St
Eilat St
Elifelet St
Auerbach St
Frenkel St
Vital St
Florentin St
Block (100m)
HaHagana (50m)

Central Tel Aviv

Top Sights
1 Carmel Market....C5
2 Gordon Beach....B1
3 Tel Aviv Museum of Art....F2

Sights
4 Haganah Museum....C6
5 Independence Hall....C6
6 Old Railway Station....A7
7 Rabin Square....E1
8 Suzanne Dellal Centre....A7

Sleeping
9 Abraham Hostel....D6
10 Dizengoff Avenue Hotel....C1
11 Little Tel-Aviv Hostel....C7
12 Lusky Hotel....B2

Eating
13 Casbah Cafe....B8
14 Dalida....C7
15 Vong....C6
16 Zakaim....C6

Drinking & Nightlife
17 Hoodna Bar....B8
18 Kuli Alma....D7
19 Shpagat....C6

Entertainment
20 Cameri Theatre....F2
21 Cinematheque....F4
22 Suzanne Dellal Centre....A7

Shopping
23 Bauhaus Centre....C2
24 Lametayel....D3
25 Nahalat Binyamin Crafts Market....C5

Information
26 Australian Embassy....G2
27 French Embassy....B1
28 German Embassy....F3
29 Ichilov Hospital....G1
30 Tourist Information Office....A4
31 US Embassy....B2

Transport
32 Central Bus Station....E8
33 O-Fun....B4

are centred on Shabazi St, named after a 17th-century Yemenite poet. The courtyard of the **Suzanne Dellal Centre** (Map p222; ☎03-510-5656; www.suzannedellal.org.il; 5 Yechiely St, Neve Tzedek), home of the world-famous Bat Sheva dance troupe, is a relaxing place for a break.

Beaches & Old Port

Whenever the sun is out, Tel Avivim (Tel Avivians) flock to the string of sandy beaches between the Old Port and Jaffa to laze on the sand, play *matkot* (paddle ball), frolic in the surf and show off their buff bods.

Old Port PORT

(Namal; Map p226; www.namal.co.il; P) Originally opened in 1936, Tel Aviv's port went into decline in the 1960s. Today the area is popular with families drawn to its waterfront promenade, shops, restaurants and cafes, while planes swoop in low overhead to land at nearby Sde Dov airport. A covered organic **farmers market** (Map p226; ☎077-541-1393; http://shukhanamal.co.il/english; Hangar 12, Old Port; ⏲9am-4pm Sun, to 8pm Mon-Thu & Sat, 7am-5pm Fri) also attracts locals looking for their fresh vegetables, pasta and seafood. After dark and on weekends, hordes of clubbers descend on the bars and nightclubs.

Jaffa

The ancient port of Jaffa, now a mixed Jewish and Arab area of Tel Aviv-Jaffa (Yafo), was an autonomous, mostly Arab city until 1948. The narrow alleyways of the **Old City**, rebuilt after being devastated by Napoleon in 1799, are home to quite a few art galleries.

Clock Tower LANDMARK

(Map p228; Yefet St) Not quite Big Ben, this Ottoman clock tower was funded by residents to mark the 25th anniversary of the reign of Sultan Abdulhamid II (1876–1909). The tower – one of seven built around Ottoman Palestine – was completed in 1903, a time when few of the sultan's subjects had watches.

Old Jaffa Visitors Centre ARCHAEOLOGICAL SITE

(Map p228; ☎03-603-7686, 03-603-7000; www.oldjaffa.co.il; Kedumim Sq, Old Jaffa; adult/student 30/15NIS; ⏲9am-8pm Sat-Thu, to 5pm Fri summer, 9am-5pm Sat-Thu, to 3pm Fri winter) Sometimes called 'Jaffa Tales', this small visitor centre is actually an archaeological excavation site in a chamber underneath Kedumim Sq. Here, you can view partially excavated remains from the Hellenistic and Roman era and learn about more than 4000 years of Jaffa's colourful history in a virtual experience.

★**Jaffa Flea Market** MARKET
(Shuk HaPishpeshim; Map p228; ⏲stalls 10am-3pm Sun-Fri, to late Thu; 🚌Dan 10, 18, 25, 41) In recent years, lots of energy has gone into giving Jaffa's Old City a tourism-triggered makeover, and the results are undeniably attractive. However, the real draw in this part of the city is considerably more dishevelled. Spread over a grid of streets south of the clock tower, Jaffa's much-loved *pishpeshuk* or *shuk ha-pishpeshim* (flea market) is full of boutiques, laid-back cafes, pop-up bars and colourful street stalls selling vintage clothes, objects and furniture.

Old Railway Station HISTORIC SITE
(HaTachana; Map p222; www.hatachana.co.il; Neve Tzedek; ⏲10am-10pm Sat-Thu, to 5pm Fri; P; 🚌18, 10, 100) Once the terminus of the Jerusalem–Jaffa train line, this station near the southern end of the beachfront promenade operated between 1892 and 1948 and was subsequently used by the IDF as a storage facility before being converted into a retail and entertainment complex. Now the old station houses are home to shops, cafes, bars and a branch of the popular ice-cream chain Vaniglia; it's known locally as HaTachana (The Station).

Maine Friendship House MUSEUM
(☎03-681-9225; www.jaffacolony.com; 10 Auerbach St; ⏲noon-3pm Fri, 2-4pm Sat) The first neighbourhood outside Jaffa's city walls, the American Colony was established by a group of American Christians in the 1860s. The story of their star-crossed (some would say hare-brained) settlement scheme is told at the engaging Maine Friendship House museum. The colony area, run-down but charming, is centred on the corner of Auerbach and Be'er Hoffman Sts, 1km northeast of Jaffa's old city.

Ramat Aviv

Ramat Aviv is the area north of the Yarkon River and **Park HaYarkon**, which stretches east from the Old Port (Namal) area.

Beit Hatfutsot MUSEUM
(Museum of the Jewish People; ☎03-745-7808; www.bh.org.il; Gate 2, Tel Aviv University, 2 Klausner St, Ramat Aviv; adult/child under 5yr 45NIS/free; ⏲10am-7pm Sun-Wed, to 10.30pm Thu, 9am-2pm Fri, to 3pm Sat; P; 🚌Dan 7, 13, 25, 45) Beit Hatfutsot recounts the epic story of Jewish exile and the Jewish diaspora using objects, photographs, audiovisual presentations and databases. New permanent exhibitions include Heroes, an interactive exhibit on Jewish greats like Einstein (for children) and Hallelujah!, displaying intricate models of synagogues past and present (including one from China). Opened in 1978 and once known as the Diaspora Museum, it is located on the leafy campus of Tel Aviv University.

Eretz Israel Museum MUSEUM
(Land of Israel Museum; Map p226; ☎03-641-5244; www.eretzmuseum.org.il; 2 Chaim Levanon St, Ramat Aviv; adult/student 52/32NIS, child under 18yr free, incl planetarium adult/child 84/35NIS; ⏲10am-4pm Sun-Wed, to 8pm Thu, to 2pm Fri, to 3pm Sat, planetarium shows 11.30am & 1.30pm Sun-Thu, 11am & noon Sat; P; 🚌Dan 7, 13, 24, 25, 45, 127) Incorporating the archaeological excavations of a 12th-century BC port, this museum sports a huge and varied range of exhibits. Highlights include pavilions with glass and coin displays, a reconstructed

TEL AVIV'S BAUHAUS HERITAGE

Tel Aviv has more sleek, clean-lined Bauhaus (International Style) buildings than any other city in the world, which is why it was declared a Unesco World Heritage Site in 2003. The ideas and ideals of Bauhaus were brought from Germany to Palestine in the 1930s by Jewish architects fleeing Nazi persecution.

Tel Aviv's Bauhaus heritage is easy to spot, even through the modifications and dilapidation of the past 70 years. Look for structures with horizontal lines, curved corners (eg of balconies), 'thermometer stairwells' (stairwells with a row of vertical windows to provide light), and a complete absence of ornamentation.

The **Bauhaus Center** (Map p222; ☎03-522-0249; www.bauhaus-center.com; 99 Dizengoff St; ⏲10am-7.30pm Sun-Thu, to 2.30pm Fri; 📶) sells a variety of architecture-related books and city plans, including a 1:6000 preservation map and guide to Tel Aviv-Jaffa. It has two Bauhaus walking tour offerings (each 80NIS per person): one self-guided with a rented audio headset, the other a two-hour guided walking tour of the same streets at 10am Friday. A free English-language Bauhaus tour run by the Tel Aviv Tourist Office departs from 46 Rothschild Blvd (corner Shadal St) every Saturday at 11am.

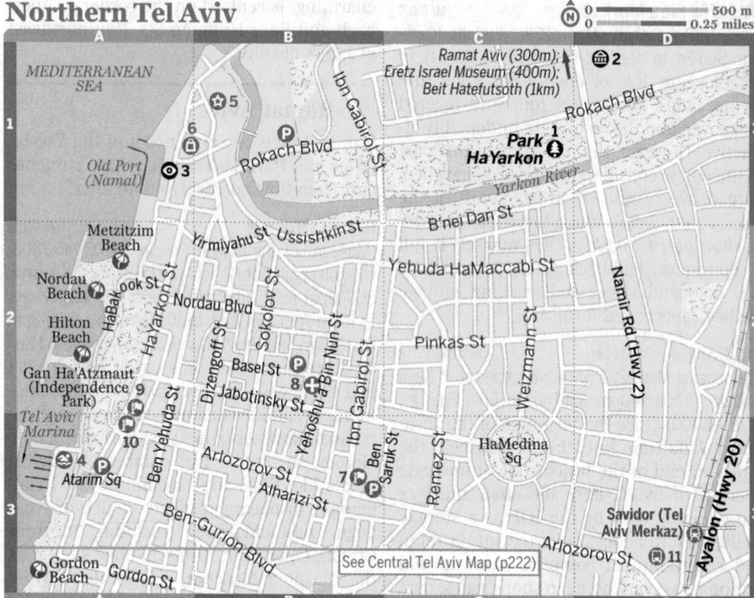

Northern Tel Aviv

Top Sights
1 Park HaYarkon C1

Sights
2 Eretz Israel Museum D1
3 Old Port A1

Activities, Courses & Tours
4 Gordon Swimming Pool A3

Entertainment
5 Shablul Jazz Club B1

Shopping
6 Old Port Farmers' Market A1

Information
7 Egyptian Embassy B3
8 Tel Aviv Doctor B2
9 Turkish Embassy A2
10 UK Embassy A3

Transport
11 Arlozorov Bus Terminal D3

flour mill and olive-oil plant, an ethnography and folklore collection, and a garden built around a gorgeous Byzantine bird mosaic.

Yitzhak Rabin Centre MUSEUM
(☎03-745-3358; www.rabincenter.org.il; 14 Chaim Levanon St; self-guided tour adult/student & child 50/25NIS, guided tour 60/35NIS; ⏰9am-5pm Sun, Mon & Wed, to 7pm Tue & Thu, to 2pm Fri; P; Dan 7, 29, 85) Established in 1997 to promote democratic values, narrow socio-economic gaps and address social divisiveness, this centre is also home to the **Israeli Museum**, which includes 150 films and 1500 photographs telling the story of modern Israel's struggle for peace with its neighbours. Visitors can take a self-guided tour using a multi-language audio device or book in advance to join a guided tour in Hebrew or English.

Activities

★ Park HaYarkon PARK
(Ganei Yehoshua; Map p226; www.park.co.il; Rokach Blvd; P) Park HaYarkon is Tel Aviv's answer to Central Park or Hyde Park. Joggers, cyclists, skaters, footballers and frisbee-throwers should head for this 3.5-sq-km stretch of grassy parkland, Tel Aviv's largest green space, along the Yarkon River. The **Sportek Centre** here has a climbing wall, basketball courts, a skate park and trampolines. Starting from Tel Aviv's Old Port, the

park opens out into wide fields and a large lake as you get closer to Ramat Gan.

★**Gordon Beach** BEACH

(Map p222; P) South from Hilton Beach, this is Tel Aviv's main beach. Well equipped with sun loungers, ice-cream shops, an outdoor gym and beach restaurants, it's popular with Tel Avivians, tourists and *matkot* (paddle ball) players. On Saturdays, you'll likely see group folk dancing on the boardwalk. The **Gordon Swimming Pool** (Map p226; 03-762-3300; www.gordon-pool.co.il; Tel Aviv Marina; adult/student & child Sun-Fri 69/59NIS, Sat 79/70NIS; 6am-9pm Mon-Thu, to 7pm Fri, 7am-6pm Sat, 1.30-9pm Sun;) is at the nearby marina.

Sleeping

Many of Tel Aviv's accommodation options are in the city centre, so you can spend the day on the beach and pop back for a shower before heading out on foot for the night.

In all price categories, book ahead during July, August and the Jewish holidays of Sukkot, Rosh Hashanah, Hanukkah and Passover, when overseas tourists (especially from France) flock to the city.

★**Abraham Hostel** HOSTEL $

(Map p222; 03-624-9200; https://abraham-hostels.com; 21 Levontin St; dm/s/d/ste from 95/460/470/520NIS;) This mammoth hostel is one of the best places to meet other travellers, and it has some of the cleanest and best-kept hostel rooms you'll find. It also offers excellent suites for couples or families with bathroom, kitchenette and TV. Friendly, multicultural and multilingual staff (we met Palestinian and Swiss receptionists); also operates tours in Tel Aviv and around Israel. The huge dining hall doubles as a venue for (often loud) live bands and comedy.

Little Tel-Aviv Hostel HOSTEL $

(Map p222; 03-559-5050; www.littletlvhostel.com; 51 Yehuda HaLevi St; dm/d 130/450NIS;) A hostel that sets high standards, Little Tel-Aviv is not so little once inside. Housed in a renovated building in the heart of the action, it offers mixed dorms or female dorms, plus very clean private rooms. Guests can enjoy hanging out in the hostel's cute garden, common kitchen and bar. The age limit for dorms is under 35.

Dizengoff Avenue Hotel BOUTIQUE HOTEL $$$

(Map p222; 03-694-3000; www.d-avenue.co.il; 133 Dizengoff St; s/d 550/732NIS;) This pretty, urban hotel is bang in the middle of Dizengoff, one of the main shopping streets, but you'd be forgiven for missing it. A simple doorway with a side entrance leads to this simple boutique hotel that's slightly cheaper than its counterparts. Nice touches include free ice popsicles at reception and a happy hour with Israeli wine for guests.

Lusky Hotel HOTEL $$$

(Map p222; 03-516-3030; www.luskyhtl.co.il; 84 HaYarkon St; s/d/ste US$165/180/300; P) This family-run choice offers well-appointed rooms featuring large windows letting in lots of light. Most of these have kitchenettes, and a number have balconies with sea views – the pick of the bunch is undoubtedly the one-bedroom penthouse, which has a huge balcony overlooking the beach. Drivers will appreciate the free underground parking.

Eating

Tel Aviv is all about the food. Because of its location smack bang in the middle of the Middle East, it mixes Mediterranean, Balkan, Arab and Asian influences, and it's also one of the most vegan-friendly cities on earth. There really is something for all tastes, from great seafood to Greek-inspired restaurants, and more recently a boom in East Asian–style eateries.

Coinciding with the boutique makeover that the city is undergoing, there is a rising crop of 'chef restaurants' (ie eateries run by celebrity chefs). From Sunday to Friday, many restaurants offer good-value 'business lunch' deals. Fast-food joints selling local favourites such as falafel and shwarma are never more than a few steps away, with a particularly good selection along Ben Yehuda, Allenby and Ibn Gabirol Sts.

Casbah Cafe CAFE $

(Map p222; 03-518-2144; 3 Florentin St; mains from 34NIS; 8am-2am Mon-Sat, to midnight Sun;) One of the most popular cheap eateries in the hip neighbourhood of Florentin, Casbah is run by the same people behind the equally cool Hoodna Bar (p229), just around the corner. It has a lazy, laid-back feel and has many dishes for vegetarians, such as the Balkan shakshuka, cauliflower curry or the vegan burger with sweet-potato fries.

Vong VIETNAMESE $$

(Map p222; 03-633-7171; www.vong.co.il; 15 Rothschild Blvd; mains 57-65NIS, banhs from 42NIS; noon-midnight;) If you're looking for huge bowls of Vietnamese food, then Vong is for you. Located on Rothschild Blvd, opposite Independence Hall, it's now an institution. Dishes include bok choy (Chinese

Jaffa (Yafo)

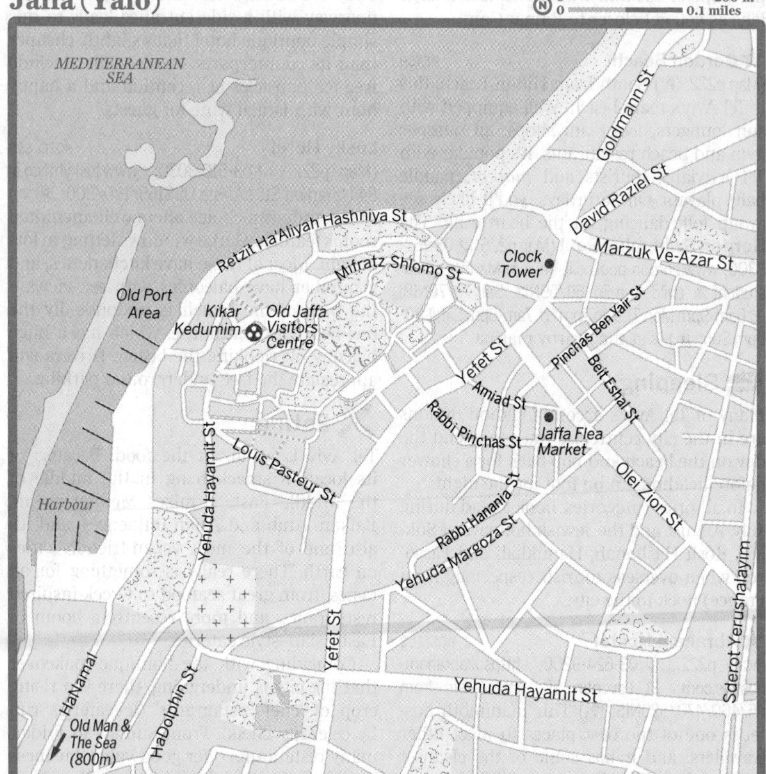

cabbage), spicy dien-dien noodles and bahns, soft rolls with beef, fish, curry or tofu fillings. Check out the cocktails with names like Forrest Jump and Lady Ga.

Zakaim VEGAN $$
(Map p222; ☎03-613-5060; 20 Simtat Beit Hashoeva; mains 49-62NIS; ⏲6pm-late Sun-Thu, noon-late Fri & Sat; ✍) Despite its 100% vegan menu, chef Harel Zakaim's restaurant – hidden down an alleyway off 98 Allenby St – is a taste-fest for non-vegans. Dishes range from Persian rice (cooked with crispy potatoes on top) to red peppers stuffed with vegetables and lentils, to vegan pizzas, to chips served in a brown paper bag. There are even cocktails and chocolate truffles.

★**Dalida** FUSION $$$
(Map p222; ☎03-536-9627; http://en.dalidatlv.co.il; 7 Zvulun St; mains 84-142NIS, sharing platters 159NIS; ⏲5pm-2am Sun-Thu, from noon Fri & Sat; 📶✍) One of Florentin's finest, Dalida is named after and inspired by the former Miss Egypt and iconic '60s singer who, like the food here, blended Arab, Italian and French styles. High-class but homely, Dalida offers a half-price menu from 5pm to 7pm Sunday to Thursday. Try the Arabic cabbage with seared calamari or lamb, pistachios and halloumi kebab.

🍷 Drinking & Nightlife

The city has a fantastic bar scene – there are drinking dens to suit every taste and budget. Some are hipster hotspots, others are neighbourhood joints so chilled they're almost comatose. When it comes to clubbing, dance bars and bars hosting live gigs dominate the scene. Dress codes are relaxed.

★**Kuli Alma** BAR
(Map p222; ☎03-656-5155; http://kulialma.com; 10 Mikveh Israel St; ⏲10pm-5am; 📶) Mystical and just downright cool, Kuli Alma is a TLV nightlife institution with an emphasis on art and

music. Behind the unimposing entrance, locals and not-so locals mingle in the patio dotted with plants, graffiti and an outdoor gallery. There's a vegetarian menu, and it hosts an eclectic mix of DJ and live music nights.

★Block CLUB
(www.block-club.com; 157 Shalma/Salame Rd, Neve Sha'anan; early arrivals 50-70NIS, late arrivals 70-90NIS; ⏲11pm-late Thu-Sat) In the Central Bus Station building, Block is known as Tel Aviv's best club for good reason, hosting big-name international DJs playing anything from funk, hip-hop and Afrobeat to drum 'n' bass, house and trance. There's an impressive sound system and a smokers' lounge.

Hoodna Bar BAR
(Map p222; 13 Arbarbanel St, Florentin; ⏲6pm-late Sun-Thu, from 1pm Fri & Sat; 📶) Hoodna (truce in Arabic) is a carpenter's workshop zone by day but transforms itself at night, when tables and sofas are dragged into the street to create a chilled-out drinking space. Inside there are almost daily live or DJ sets. In the last week of February, it hosts the Southern Wind indie rock festival.

Shpagat GAY & LESBIAN
(Map p222; ☎03-560-1785; 43 Nahalat Binyamin St; ⏲7pm-late Sat-Thu, noon-5pm Fri) A hip gay bar on Nahalat Binyamin St, Shpagat attracts big crowds most nights. In the early evening, it's a peaceful spot to grab a drink, but later on the DJs take over and the volume goes up a notch or 10.

☆ Entertainment

★Barby LIVE MUSIC
(☎03-518-8123; www.barby.co.il; 52 Kibbutz Galuyot St) This Tel Aviv institution at the southernmost point of the city is a favourite venue for reggae, electronica, funk and alternative bands. Occasionally hosts big name acts and the vibe is always positive with a capital 'P'. Check the website for line-ups.

★Cinematheque CINEMA
(Map p222; ☎03-606-0800; www.cinema.co.il/english; 1 Ha'Arba'a St; from 30NIS; ⏲10am-midnight Sun-Fri, from 11am Sat) Features classic, retro, foreign, avant garde and experimental films. It often holds film festivals, such as **DocAviv** (www.docaviv.co.il/org-en; ⏲May).

Suzanne Dellal Centre DANCE
(Map p222; ☎03-510-5656; www.suzanneddellal.org.il; 5 Yechieli St) Home to the world-famous Bat Sheva dance company, it stages performances of modern dance, music and ballet.

Cameri Theatre THEATRE
(Map p222; ☎03-606-0960; www.cameri.co.il; 30 Leonardo da Vinci St) Hosts first-rate theatre performances in Hebrew, on some nights with simultaneous English translation or English-language subtitles.

Shablul Jazz Club JAZZ
(Map p226; ☎03-546-1891; www.shabluljazz.com; Hangar 13, Old Port) Cool jazz, blues, salsa and world music take centre stage at this intimate venue on the Old Port. Shablul hosts nightly live music. Check the Facebook page (www.facebook.com/shabluljazz) for an events calendar.

🔒 Shopping

The most interesting boutiques are found in the Jaffa Flea Market, Shabazi St in Neve Tzedek, and Sheinkin St in the city centre. At the **Nahalat Binyamin Crafts Market** (Map p222; www.nachlat-binyamin.com; ⏲10am-5pm Tue, to 6pm or 7pm summer, 10am to 4.30pm

ESSENTIAL FOOD & DRINK

Amba Iraqi-style mango chutney

Bourekas Flaky Balkan pastries filled with Bulgarian cheese, spinach or mushrooms

Challah Braided bread traditionally eaten by Jews on the Sabbath

Cholent A heavy meat and potato stew simmered overnight and served for Sabbath lunch

Labneh (labaneh) Thick, creamy yoghurt cheese, often smothered in olive oil and sprinkled with zaatar

Sabich A pita filled, in the Iraqi-Jewish tradition, with fried eggplant, boiled potato, hard-boiled egg, tahina, amba and freshly chopped vegies

S'chug Yemenite hot chilli paste

Shakshuka A spicy Moroccan egg and tomato stew, usually eaten for breakfast

Zaatar A spice blend that includes hyssop, sumac and sesame seeds

Fri) – a great place to walk around and soak up Tel Aviv's exuberant atmosphere – artists sell ceramics, jewellery, glasswork and Judaica they have made.

Lametayel (Map p222; 077-333-4501; www.lametayel.co.il; top fl, 50 Dizengoff St, Dizengoff Center; 10am-9pm Sun-Thu, to 2.30pm Fri), Israel's largest camping and travel equipment shop, carries a full range of Lonely Planet guides and is a prime source of information for Israeli backpackers heading overseas.

Orientation

Tel Aviv is centred on five north–south streets that parallel the middle part of the city's 6km of seafront. Nearest the sand is Herbert Samuel Esplanade, while hotel-lined HaYarkon St – which heads north to the Yarkon River – lies a block inland. East of HaYarkon St is Ben Yehuda St, followed by once-chic Dizengoff St – the area between Dizengoff Sq and Dizengoff Centre serves as the focal point of the city centre. Restaurant-lined Ibn Gabirol St forms the eastern boundary of the city centre.

The Neve Tzedek and Florentin districts mark the southernmost reaches of the city centre – south of there is Jaffa – while Park HaYarkon and, on the coast, the Old Port (Namal) mark the northernmost.

Information

The best currency exchange deals are at the private bureaux that don't charge commission, for example on Dizengoff, Allenby and Ben Yehuda Sts. Most post offices change cash and travellers cheques, commission-free.

Ichilov Hospital (Tel Aviv Sourasky Medical Centre; Map p222; 03-697-4444; www.tasmc.org.il; 6 Weizmann St; emergency 24hr) Near the city centre, Ichilov is the city's big central hospital, with 24-hour emergency room and a travellers' clinic (the Malram Clinic) for immunisations.

Tel Aviv Doctor (Map p226; 054-941-4243, toll-free 1-800-201-999; www.telaviv-doctor.com; 46 Basel St, near Basel Sq) A well-equipped medical clinic with multilingual doctors and staff. Has direct billing for some major insurance companies and also offers home and hotel visits.

Tourist Information Office (Map p222; 03-516-6188; www.visit-tel-aviv.com; 46 Herbert Samuel Esplanade; 9.30am-5.30pm Sun-Thu, to 1pm Fri Nov-Mar, to 6.30pm Sun-Thu, to 2pm Apr-Oct) Tel Aviv's main tourist-information office has super-helpful staff and can provide maps, brochures and plenty of advice.

Getting There & Away

During Shabbat and on Jewish holidays, taxis and sheruts (share taxis) offer the only public transport.

BUS

Most intercity buses depart from the 6th floor of Tel Aviv's enormous, confusing and filthy Central Bus Station (Map p222), where there's also an information desk. Suburban and city buses use the 4th and 7th floors. Tickets can be bought from the driver or from ticket booths.

Egged buses (www.egged.co.il) leave for Jerusalem (405; 16NIS, one hour, every 20 minutes); Haifa (921; 27NIS, 1½ hours, every 25 minutes); Tiberias (836; 37.50NIS, 2½ hours, every 30 minutes); Nazereth (826; 34NIS, 2¾ hours, every 45 minutes); and Eilat (393, 394 and 790; 70NIS, 5½ hours, hourly). You'll need to book tickets to Eilat in advance (call *2800 or go to www.egged.co.il), as these services are usually full. Metropoline buses travel to/from Be'er Sheva (353, 369 and 370; 15NIS, 1½ hours, every 30 minutes).

Tel Aviv's second bus station, the open-air Arlozorov Bus Terminal (Map p226), adjoins the Tel Aviv Savidor Merkaz train station. If staying in the centre or the north of the city, Egged bus 480 (16NIS, one hour, every 10 minutes) is the most convenient service to Jerusalem.

CAR

Most car-rental companies have offices on HaYarkon St.

SHERUT

Seven days a week, sheruts (shared taxis, in most cases yellow minibuses) depart from Tsemach David St outside the Central Bus Station and head to Jerusalem (26NIS, on Shabbat 36NIS) and Haifa (30NIS, on Shabbat 45NIS).

TRAIN

Tel Aviv has four train stations: Savidor Merkaz, HaHagana, HaShalom and University. Destinations include Haifa (27.50NIS, one hour, two or three hourly except Shabbat) and Akko (35.50NIS, 1½ hours).

Getting Around

TO/FROM THE AIRPORT

Ben-Gurion Airport is 18km southeast of central Tel Aviv.

The fastest way to get to/ from the airport is by train (14NIS, twice an hour, 24 hours a day except on Shabbat, ie Friday afternoon to Saturday night, and Jewish holidays). Airport trains serve all four Tel Aviv stations except between midnight and 5am, when they stop only at Savidor Merkaz station (and run just once an hour).

Check the Israel Railway website (www.rail.co.il/en) for details.

Prices for taxis are controlled, and either meters or pre-set official prices are used; there's an orderly taxi rank just outside the international terminal building. Depending on traffic, the ride into central Tel Aviv takes about 20 minutes and should cost 160NIS (day rate) and 200NIS (9pm to 5.30am and Shabbat). There's usually an extra charge of 5NIS per suitcase.

BICYCLE

Getting around the compact centre is easiest by bicycle – two wheels are a great way to avoid traffic snarls, packed buses and unscrupulous taxi drivers. The city has 120km of dedicated bike paths that run along the beachfront and thoroughfares such as Rothschild Blvd, Chen Blvd, Ben-Gurion Blvd and Ibn Gabirol St. For rentals, try **O-Fun** (Map p222; 03-522-0488; http://ofun.co.il; 32 Allenby St; 10am-7pm Sun-Thu, to 2pm Fri).

BUS

Tel Aviv city buses are operated by the Dan cooperative (www.dan.co.il) from 5.30am to midnight, except Shabbat. A ticket for a single ride costs 5.90NIS and a one-day pass *(hofshi yomi)* allowing unlimited bus travel around Tel Aviv and its suburbs costs 13.50NIS (plus 5NIS for a Rav-Kav travel card).

TAXI

Plan on 40NIS to 50NIS for most trips within the central city. The most popular taxi app in town is Gett Taxi (https://gett.com).

Caesarea קיסריה قيسارية

04 / POP 4800

Caesarea (Qeysarya; pronounced kay-*sar*-ee-ya in Hebrew), gorgeously situated on the shores of the sparkling, turquoise Mediterranean, was one of the great ports of antiquity, rivalling storied harbours such as Alexandria and Carthage. Today, **Caesarea National Park** (www.parks.org.il; adult/child 39/24NIS, harbour only 14NIS; 8am-5pm Sat-Thu, to 4pm Fri Apr-Oct, 8am-4pm Sat-Thu, to 3pm Fri Nov-Mar, last entry 1hr before closing) is one of the Levant's most impressive Roman sites (rivalled, in Israel, only by Beit She'an). Roman highlights include a 4000-seat **theatre** and an **amphitheatre** once used for chariot races and bloody gladiatorial contests.

Cafes and restaurants add to the scene – you can dine al fresco by the sea until late at night.

Caesarea National Park is 40km south of Haifa and 57km north of Tel Aviv.

Haifa חיפה حيفا

04 / POP 278,900

Haifa is one of the world's most beautiful port cities. The views from the top of majestic Mt Carmel (546m) are breathtaking, especially from the Baha'i Gardens, but almost everywhere you look in the city there are interesting, if not always beautiful, urban landscapes, many from the late Ottoman and Mandate (Bauhaus) periods.

Sights

The bustling streets of **Hadar**, the city's mid-20th-century commercial centre, are lined with eateries and inexpensive shops.

★Baha'i Gardens GARDENS

(04-831-3131; www.ganbahai.org.il; 45 Yefe Nof St, Panorama Tour; lower gardens 9am-5pm, closed Baha'i holidays & Yom Kippur; P) FREE The best way to see these truly breathtaking gardens – a Unesco World Heritage Site – is to take a free, 45-minute **Upper Terrace Tour** from the top of the gardens. Except on Wednesday, an English-language tour starts at noon, with additional tours in Hebrew, Arabic or Russian on most days at 11am, 11.30am and 1.30pm (see the website for the monthly schedule). It's first come, first served, so get there a half-hour ahead. Both men and women must wear clothing that covers their shoulders (a shawl is OK) and knees.

To get to the start of the Panorama Tour from Carmel Centre, walk 1km north along Yefe Nof St, which affords the city's finest bay views. The tour finishes at the lower gardens down on HaTziyonut Blvd – to get back up to Carmel Centre, there is usually a sherut (10NIS) waiting; count on paying about 30NIS for a taxi.

In the lower gardens, the gold-domed **Shrine of the Báb** is the tomb of the Báb, the spiritual predecessor to the Baha'i faith's main prophet Baha'ullah; his remains were brought here from Persia in 1909. The interior can be visited daily from 9am to noon.

Tikotin Museum of Japanese Art MUSEUM

(04-838-3554; www.tmja.org.il; 89 HaNassi Ave; adult/child 35/23NIS; 10am-7pm Sat-Thu, to 1pm Fri) Founded by Felix Tikotin in 1957, this museum – unique in the Middle East – puts on superb exhibits of Japanese art.

★Hecht Museum MUSEUM

(04-825-7773; http://mushecht.haifa.ac.il; 199 Abba Hushi Blvd, Haifa University; 10am-4pm Sun, Mon, Wed & Thu, to 7pm Tue, to 1pm Fri, to 2pm Sat; P) FREE The pièce de résistance

Haifa

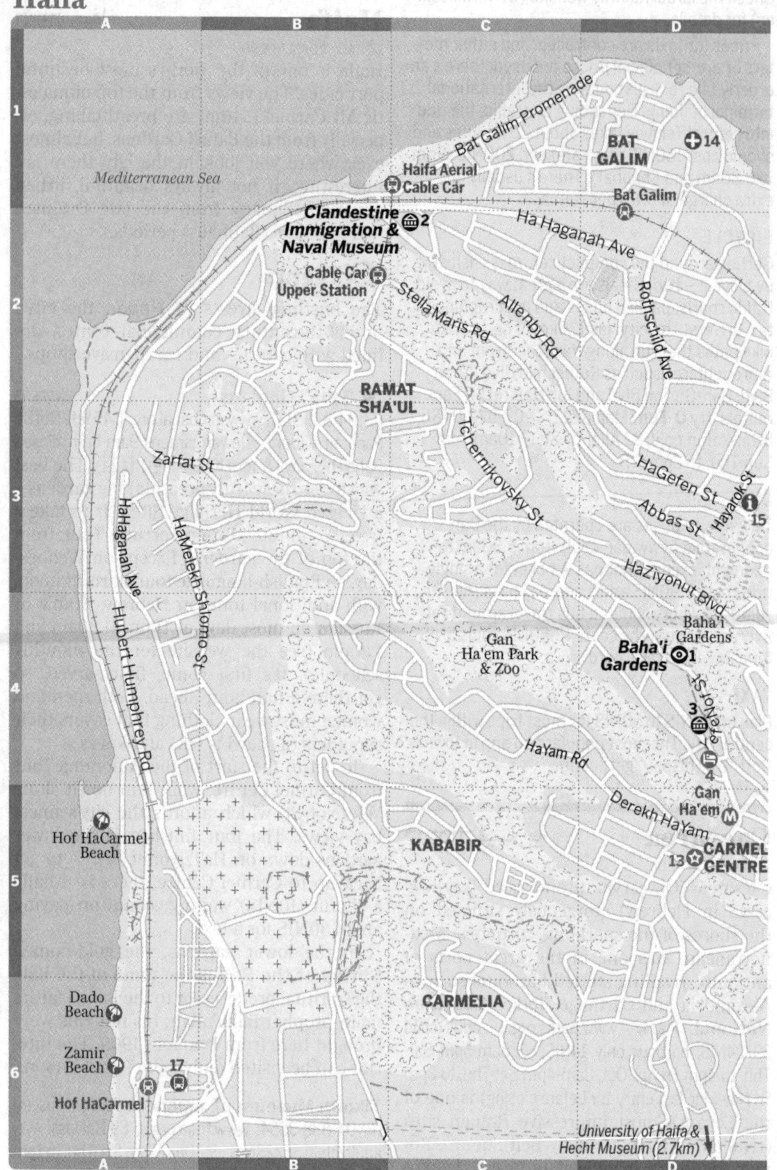

at this superb museum of archaeology and art is the **Ma'agan Mikhael Shipwreck**, a 2400-year-old merchant vessel unearthed in 1985. The art wing assembles mostly impressionist and post-impressionist works (part of founder Dr Reuben Hecht's own collection), including works by luminaries like Van Gogh and Modigliani.

★Clandestine Immigration & Naval Museum MUSEUM
(☎04-853-6249; http://eng.shimur.org/clandestine-immigration; 204 Allenby Rd; adult/child

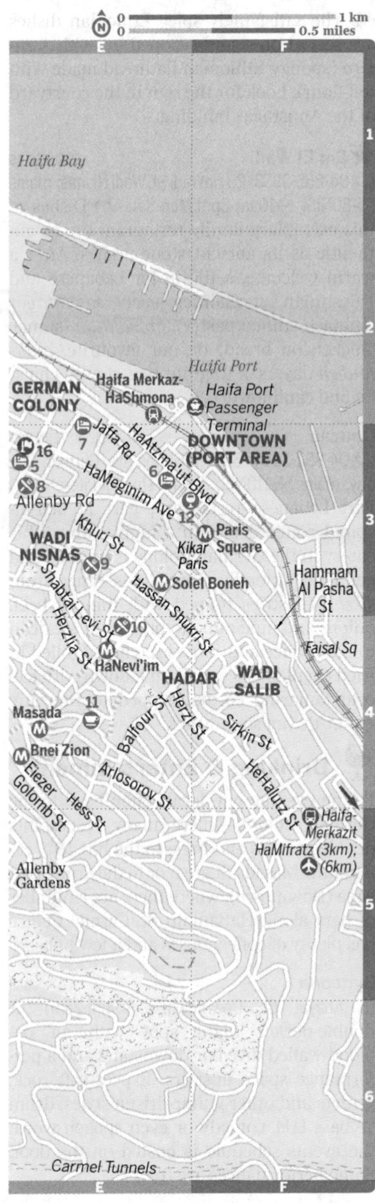

15/10NIS; ⌚10am-4pm Sun-Thu; Ⓟ) Using a series of powerful video testimonials, this fascinating museum showcases the Zionist Movement's determined efforts to infiltrate Jewish refugees from Europe into British-blockaded Palestine from 1934 to 1948. The centrepiece is a WWII landing craft rechristened the *Af-Al-Pi-Chen* ('nevertheless' in Hebrew) that carried 434 refugees to Palestine in 1947; intercepted by the British, they were sent to internment camps on Cyprus. The museum is run by the Ministry of Defense, so you'll need your passport to get in.

Haifa

Top Sights

1	Baha'i Gardens	D4
2	Clandestine Immigration & Naval Museum	C2

Sights

3	Tikotin Museum of Japanese Art	D4

Sleeping

4	Beth Shalom Hotel	D4
5	Colony Hotel Haifa	E3
6	Port Inn	E3
7	Saint Charles Guesthouse	E3

Eating

8	Douzan	E3
9	Ein El Wadi	E3
10	HaMis'ada Shel Ima	E4

Drinking & Nightlife

11	Cafe Masada	E4
12	Syncopa	E3

Entertainment

13	Haifa Cinematheque	D5

Information

14	Rambam Medical Centre	D1
15	Tourist Office	D3
16	US Consulate	E3

Transport

17	Haifa-Hof HaCarmel Bus Station	A6

Sleeping

★Port Inn GUESTHOUSE $

(☎04-852-4401; www.portinn.co.il; 34 Jaffa Rd, Port Area; dm/s/d/tr/q 100/290/340/450/550NIS, d/tr with shared bathroom 260/300NIS; @📶) Budget travellers rightly flock to this charming guesthouse. A library and lounge are decked out with Turkish carpets, zany artwork and creeper plants, there's a garden out back offering journal-writing space on tiled tables, and the rooms are plain but perfectly clean. Mixed dorm rooms have five or nine beds; single-sex dorms have nine.

Saint Charles Guesthouse GUESTHOUSE $
(04-855-3705; https://saintcharlesguesthouse.wordpress.com; 105 Jaffa Rd, Port Area; s/d/f 180/300/390NIS;) Slow-moving nuns, swishing their robes, are your hosts at the sedate, boarding-school-like Saint Charles. Operated by the Latin Patriarchate Rosary Sisters, the guesthouse offers high-ceilinged (if bare) rooms within an 1880 building. Antique tiles and an inner garden add to the contemplative feel, while the shared kitchen and port location round out a good-value package. Curfew is generally 10pm. Cash only.

Colony Hotel Haifa BOUTIQUE HOTEL $$
(04-851-3344; www.colonyhaifa.com; 28 Ben-Gurion Ave, German Colony; d US$90-245; @) This tastefully updated Templer building is the ideal spot to soak up the German Colony's history and atmosphere. Its 40 rooms have large windows, high ceilings, all-marble bathrooms and antique-themed furniture such as four-poster beds. Throw in a roof terrace, an excellent Mediterranean breakfast buffet and a Swedish massage (from 160NIS) and Colony Hotel is a winning package.

Beth Shalom Hotel HOTEL $$
(04-837-7481; www.beth-shalom.co.il; 110 HaNassi Ave, Carmel Centre; s/d/tr US$85/110/140; P) Run by a Swiss family, this great-value guesthouse feels a bit institutional, but it's a well-oiled machine. Pine-accented, white-walled rooms are compact but spotlessly clean, with adequate bathrooms and perks like safes and hairdryers. Family-friendly amenities include a small play area with ball pit, table tennis, a library and a lounge area with complimentary hot drinks.

Eating

More than a dozen excellent restaurants, some owned by Arab celebrity chefs, line elegant Ben-Gurion Ave in the German Colony. Almost all are open seven days a week. Carmel Centre has a nice mix of upscale restaurants, sleek cafes and takeaway joints. In Hadar, there are felafel, shwarma and other cheap eats along the northwestern part of Herzl St.

HaMis'ada Shel Ima ETHIOPIAN $
(Mother's Restaurant; 20 HaNevi'im St, cnr Shabtai Levi, Hadar; mains 35-40NIS; noon-10pm Sun-Fri, sundown-10pm or 11pm Sat;) Stepping into this unpretentious eatery is like a quick trip to Addis Ababa, raucous soundtrack included. The satisfyingly spicy Ethiopian dishes are served on – and scooped up with – *injera* (spongy Ethiopian flatbread made with teff flour). Look for the sign in the courtyard of the Amisragas building.

★**Ein El Wadi** LEBANESE $$
(04-855-3353; 26 HaWadi St, Wadi Nisnas; mains 55-80NIS; 10am-8pm Mon-Sat;) Dishes at this exemplary family restaurant are as authentic as its ancient stone arches. After a warm welcome, settle in for Lebanese and Palestinian specialities such as *fatayer* (spinach-stuffed pastry), *musakhan* (sumac chicken on bread) or, our favourite, *makloubeh* (layers of fragrant rice, stewed chicken and cauliflower).

Douzan MIDDLE EASTERN $$$
(04-852-5444; 35 Ben-Gurion Ave, German Colony; mains 55-110NIS; 9am-11pm or later;) Part Lebanese restaurant, part French-inspired coffee den with a hippie ethos, this eatery in the German Colony is original and genuinely friendly. Specialities range from *sfeeha* (pastries topped with minced beef, onions and pine nuts) to prawns in Mexican tomato sauce and *rolettini* (cheese rolled in fried eggplant slices). Wash it down with ice-cold tamarind cordial, sipped to Douzan's guitar-driven soundtrack.

Drinking & Entertainment

For an evening out, locals often head to the German Colony, where many restaurants double as cafes and bars; to the hip, lefty cafes of the Masada St area; or to the grimy Port Area (Downtown), where there are a number of bars along HaBankim St. Carmel Centre has plenty of coffeehouses and a few pubs.

Syncopa BAR
(5 Khayat St, Downtown; 9pm-2am) A double-decker night spot with an ox-blood-walled dive bar downstairs and a performance space upstairs. Expect soft rock, grunge and other guitar-driven styles, drum 'n' bass DJs, comedy or even spoken word; the events schedule is posted on the door. Some performances are free.

Cafe Masada CAFE
(16 Masada St, Hadar; 8am-2am, from 9am Sat;) Save the world over a coffee at this spirited hang-out, prowled by as many cats as art-lovers and activists. Eavesdrop the lively debate over shakshuka and sandwiches, or mingle with locals over a beer – it's an

open-minded joint with a crowd that enjoys a good chinwag.

Haifa Cinematheque CINEMA
(☎04-833-8888; www.haifacin.co.il; 142 HaNassi Ave, Carmel Centre; ticket 35NIS) Screens avant-garde, off-beat and art films in two halls. It's key venue for Haifa's **film festival** (www.haifaff.co.il; per screening 45NIS; ⏰mid-Oct).

Orientation

As you ascend the slopes of Mt Carmel, the views get better and the neighbourhoods get wealthier.

The gritty Downtown (Ir Tachtit) and adjacent Port Area (Ezor HaNamal), built during the late Ottoman period and the British Mandate, are on the flats adjacent to Haifa Port. Landmarks include the Haifa Merkaz-HaShmona train station, which affords easy access to Ben-Gurion airport, Tel Aviv and Akko; and Paris Sq (Kikar Pariz), the lower terminus of the Carmelit funicular railway (a steep, six-station metro). About 1km west of there, directly below the Baha'i Gardens, is Ben-Gurion Ave, the elegant main thoroughfare of the German Colony. The mostly-Arab neighbourhood of Wadi Nisnas is in a little valley midway between Paris Sq and the German Colony.

About 1km south (up the slope) from Paris Sq is Herzl St, the heart of Hadar HaCarmel, universally known as Hadar. The HaNev'im stop on the Carmelit is 350m northwest of the corner of Herzl and Balfour Sts (the heart of Hadar) and 350m southeast of Wadi Nisnas' main drag, HaWadi St.

Around the Carmelit's upper terminus, Gan HaEm, is Carmel Centre (Merkaz HaCarmel), the commercial and dining heart of the affluent neighbourhoods that are strung out along the ridge of Mt Carmel.

Free street maps are available at most hotels and the Haifa tourist office.

Information

Rambam Medical Centre (Rambam Health Care Campus; ☎1-700-505-150, emergency room 04-777-3300; www.rambam.org.il; 8 HaAliya HaShniya St, Bat Galim; ⏰24hr) Northern Israel's largest hospital and one of the country's best equipped. Take a Bat Galim–bound bus (43 from Hof HaCarmel bus station, 16 or 136 from Lev HaMifratz, and 24 or 36 from the university) to get there.

Tourist Office (Haifa Tourist Board; ☎04-853-5606; www.visit-haifa.org; 48 Ben-Gurion Ave, German Colony; ⏰8.30am-6pm Sun-Thu, to 1pm Fri) Situated near the top of Ben-Gurion Ave. Free maps offered.

Getting There & Away

BOAT

Ferries connect **Haifa port** (www.haifaport.co.il; Kdoshei Bagdad St) with Old Akko's marina twice daily on weekdays and three times on a Saturday; the journey takes 45 minutes, depending on sea conditions. Buy tickets up to an hour before departure time.

BUS

Haifa has two central bus stations.

Haifa-Hof HaCarmel, used by buses heading south along the coast (ie towards Tel Aviv), is on the Mediterranean (western) side of Mt Carmel. It's 8km around the base of Mt Carmel from the German Colony. Destinations include Jerusalem (Egged bus 940, 37.50NIS, two hours, every 30 to 90 minutes except Friday evening to sundown Saturday). The fastest way to get to Tel Aviv is by train.

Haifa-Merkazit HaMifratz, on the Haifa Bay side of Mt Carmel, is used by most buses to destinations north and east of Haifa. It is 8km southeast of the German Colony, a few hundred metres – through the giant Lev HaMifratz shopping mall – from the Lev HaMifratz train station. Train is the fastest way to Akko and Nahariya.

Destinations include the following:

Akko (Nateev Express buses 271 and 361, 16NIS, 35 to 45 minutes, every 10 minutes) Bus 271 continues north to the Baha'i Gardens.

Jerusalem (Egged bus 960, 37.50NIS, two hours, one or two times an hour except Friday afternoon to sundown Saturday)

Nazareth (buses 331 and 332, shared between Nazareth Tourism & Transport and GB Tours; 19NIS to 26NIS, one hour, twice hourly Sunday to Friday, hourly all day Saturday)

Tiberias (Egged buses 430 and 434, 21.50NIS, 1¼ hours, three times per hour except Friday afternoon to sundown Saturday)

Tsfat (Nateev Express bus 361, 1¾ hours, twice an hour) via Akko (45 minutes).

TRAIN

Haifa has four train stations: **Haifa-Hof HaCarmel** (near the Haifa-Hof HaCarmel bus station); **Haifa Merkaz-HaShmona** (Haifa Center-HaShmona; in the Downtown/Port area); **Haifa-Bat Galim** (near Ramban hospital); and **Lev HaMifratz** (near the Haifa-Merkazit HaMifratz bus station). Travel by train within Haifa, between any of the following stations (departing every 10 to 20 minutes), costs 7.50NIS.

Services leave from all four stations to Ben Gurion airport (35.50NIS, 1¼ to 1¾ hours, twice hourly), Akko (13.50NIS, 30 minutes, four times an hour) and Tel Aviv (27.50NIS to 32.50NIS, one to 1¼ hours, two or three times an hour).

Getting Around

The Carmelit metro (closed since a 2017 fire) is great for getting up and down the mountain, but for travel along Mt Carmel's flanks you'll need buses (run by Egged, Nateev Express and Omni Express). Much faster is Metronit, a three-line bus service inaugurated in 2013 that's as fast as light rail thanks to its dedicated lanes and synchronised traffic lights. Unlike standard buses, you must buy tickets (5.90NIS, valid for 90 minutes) before boarding; ticket machines are at each stop.

Metronit line 1 links the two central bus stations, Haifa-Merkazit HaMifratz and Haifa-Hof HaCarmel, via the Port Area and the German Colony at least twice an hour (every five minutes at peak times) 24 hours a day, seven days a week (yes, including Shabbat!). Line 2 links Bat Galim (Rambam hospital) with Haifa-Merkazit HaMifratz, also via the German Colony and the Port Area.

Akko עכו عكا

04 / POP 47,675

Marco Polo passed through Akko (Acre; Akka in Arabic) around 750 years ago and much of the place hasn't changed a lot since then. Today, Old Akko seduces visitors with towering ramparts, deep moats, green domes, slender minarets, church towers, secret passageways and subterranean vaults. It was awarded Unesco World Heritage status in 2001. Akko can easily be visited on a day trip from Haifa.

Sights

Step into the towering, stone-vaulted **Knights' Halls** (Hospitaller Fortress; adult/child 25/22NIS; 8.30am-5pm Sat-Thu, to 4pm Fri), built 800 years ago by the Hospitallers (a monastic military order), and it's not hard to envision the medieval knights who once lived and dined here. A few blocks away, the extraordinary **Templars' Tunnel** (adult/child 15/12NIS; 9.30am-6.30pm Sat-Thu, to 5.30pm Fri, closes 1hr earlier in winter), 350m long, was built by the Knights Templar (another military order) to connect their main fortress, just north of the black-and- white-striped **lighthouse** at Old Akko's southwestern tip, with **Khan Al Umdan**, next to the **marina**.

City Walls HISTORIC SITE

Fortified, wrecked and refortified by Muslims, Crusaders and Mamluks, Old Akko is encircled by a sea wall to the west, south and southeast, and by ramparts (that you can walk on). A dry moat was dug to the north and northeast, mainly between 1750 and 1840.

Souq Al Abiad MARKET

(White Market; Salah Ad Din St; 8am-late afternoon) This old city market brims with stalls. Sugar cane is squeezed into juice, sacks of saffron seem full to bursting, *kunafeh* is sliced, and sellers holler about the peerless craftsmanship of sandals, lanterns and scarves.

Sleeping

Akko Gate Hostel HOSTEL $

(04-991-0410; www.akkogate.com; 13/14 Salah Ad Din St; dm/d/tr/q US$20/78/110/125;) Run by the friendly Walid, this long-running hostel has an enviable old-city location near the market and falafel joints on Salah Ad Din St. Wrought-iron bed frames and tiled floors characterise the well-worn rooms within this Ottoman-era building, each with mini-fridges and TVs.

HI Knights Hostel HOSTEL $$

(02-594-5711, reservations 1-599-510-511; www.iyha.org.il; 2 Weizmann St; dm 135-155NIS, d 380-500NIS;) Looking more like part of the old city walls than a modern hostel, this 76-room IYHA hostel runs like clockwork. The clean dorm and private rooms feel institutional, but the building has unique features, including an ancient aqueduct running through it and ruins in the courtyard. Book well ahead as it's popular with groups.

Eating

Old Akko has some excellent dining options, particularly if you're in the mood for fish or seafood. For cheap eats, there are quite a few places selling hummus, felafel and/or shwarma along Salah ad-Din St.

Hummus Said MIDDLE EASTERN $

(04-991-3945; hummus 17NIS; 6am-2.30pm Sun-Fri;) Cheap and immensely satisfying, Said's velvety hummus is the best in Akko and comes served with plenty of pickles, salads and pita, plus a bonus garnish of fava beans or garlic. Expect queues.

★**Uri Buri** SEAFOOD $$$

(04-955-2212; HaHaganah St; mains 82-134NIS, half portions 51-78NIS; noon-midnight;) Dining at Uri Buri is enough of a reason to place Akko on your travel itinerary. Lovers of seafood will quickly understand why chef Uri is

Akko

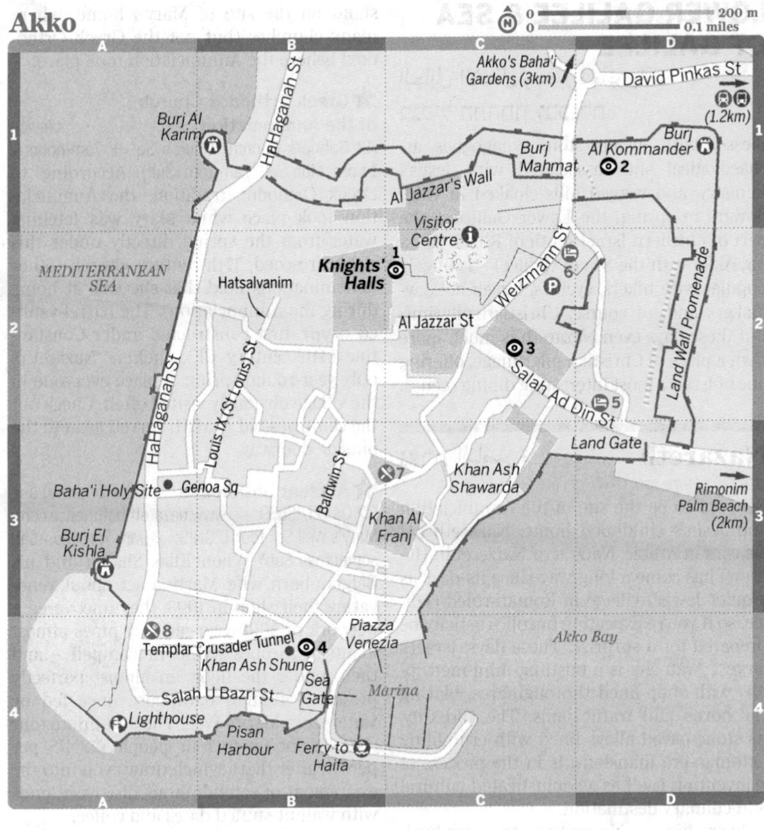

Akko

Top Sights
1 Knights' Halls C2

Sights
2 City Walls D1
3 Souq Al Abiad C2
4 Templars' Tunnel B4

Sleeping
5 Akko Gate Hostel D2
6 HI Knights Hostel C2

Eating
7 Hummus Said C3
8 Uri Buri A4

so legendary. Start with wafer-thin salmon sashimi freshened by wasabi sorbet, followed by huge prawns and artichoke swirled into buttery, black-rice noodles, or sea bass simmered in coconut milk and apple.

Information

Visitor Centre (04-995-6706; www.akko.org.il; 8.30am-6.30pm summer, to 4.30pm winter, closes 2hr earlier Fri;) Get a free map, see a scale model of the city and watch an eight-minute introductory film (available in nine languages). Tickets are sold at a kiosk out the front; pick up a free audio guide at a second kiosk, just after the entrance to the Knights' Halls (ID deposit required).

Getting There & Away

Akko's train and bus stations are about 1.5km northeast of the Old City.

Train is the fastest and most scenic way to travel to/from Haifa Merkaz-HaShmona (13.50NIS, 30 minutes, three times per hour), Tel Aviv (35.50NIS, 1¾ hours, twice hourly) and Ben Gurion airport (44NIS, two hours, twice hourly).

LOWER GALILEE & SEA OF GALILEE

الجليل الاسفل وبحيرة طبريا
בגליל התחתון ובכנרת

Blessed with ancient stone synagogues, archaeological sites associated with Jesus's ministry, and rugged hills cloaked in wildflowers in spring, the Lower Galilee – the part of northern Israel south of Rte 85 (linking Akko with the Sea of Galilee) – is hugely popular with hikers, cyclists, Israeli holidaymakers and, of course, Christian pilgrims. But these days even Nazareth is much more than a place of Christian pilgrimage, offering one of Israel's most interesting dining scenes.

Nazareth נצרת الناصرة

☎04 / POP 75,700

Believed to be the site of the Annunciation and Jesus's childhood home, Nazareth (Al Naasira in Arabic, Natzrat or Natzeret in Hebrew) has come a long way since its days as a quiet Jewish village in Roman-ruled Galilee, so if you're expecting bucolic rusticity be prepared for a surprise. These days, Israel's largest Arab city is a bustling mini-metropolis with shop-lined thoroughfares, blaring car horns and traffic jams. The Old City, its stone-paved alleys lined with crumbling Ottoman-era mansions, is in the process of reinventing itself as a sophisticated cultural and culinary destination.

Everything in Nazareth is open for business on Shabbat (Friday night and Saturday). On Sunday, on the other hand, while attractions and pastry shops are open, other shops and most restaurants are not.

Sights

The peaceful rooftop gardens of the **Centre International Marie de Nazareth** (☎04-646-1266; www.cimdn.org; 15 Al Bishara St; recommended donation 50NIS; ⏲9.30am-noon & 2.30-6pm Mon-Sat, last entry 5pm), landscaped with plants mentioned in the Bible, afford 360-degree panoramas of the city.

★**Basilica of the Annunciation** CHURCH
(☎04-565-0001; www.nazareth-en.custodia.org; Al-Bishara St; ⏲Upper Basilica 8am-6pm, Grotto of the Annunciation 5.45am-6pm, silent prayer 6-9pm) Dominating the Old City's skyline is the lantern-topped cupola of this Franciscan-run Roman Catholic basilica, an audacious modernist structure. Constructed from 1960 to 1969, it's believed by many Christians to stand on the site of Mary's home, where many churches (but not the Greek Orthodox) believe the Annunciation took place.

★**Greek Orthodox Church of the Annunciation** CHURCH
(St Gabriel's Church; Church Sq; ⏲7am-noon & 1-6pm Mon-Sat, 7am-1pm Sun) According to Greek Orthodox tradition, the Annunciation took place while Mary was fetching water from the spring directly under this richly frescoed, 17th-century church (other denominations hold that she was at home during the Annunciation). The barrel-vaulted **crypt**, first constructed under Constantine (4th century CE), shelters Nazareth's only year-round spring, a place everyone in the village obviously visited often. Check out the centuries-old **graffiti** carved around the outside doorway.

★**Ancient Bathhouse** ARCHAEOLOGICAL SITE
(☎04-657-8539; www.nazarethbathhouse.com; Mary's Well Sq; tour 120NIS; ⏲9am-7pm Mon-Sat, sometimes Sun) When Elias Shama and his Belgian-born wife Martina set about renovating their shop in 1993, they uncovered a network of 2000-year-old clay pipes almost identical to ones found in Pompeii – and then, under the floor, an almost perfectly preserved Roman bathhouse once fed by water from Mary's Well. The 30-minute tour (120NIS for up to four people, 28NIS per person after that), which draws you into the excitement of serendipitous discovery, ends with walnut-stuffed dates and coffee.

Sleeping

Vitrage Guesthouse B&B $
(☎052 525-8561, 04-657-5163; www.vitrage-guesthouse.com; No 4 6083 St; s/d/tr with shared bathroom 210/234/270NIS, small rooms 150/198/250NIS; 📶) More a homestay than a B&B, this simply furnished nine-room guesthouse is run by Bishara, a retired *vitrage* ('stained glass' in French) artisan, who grew up here (and was baptised in the garden pool), and his wife. He's happy to show visitors how stained glass is made and often invites guests to dine with the family. Excellent value.

★**Fauzi Azar Inn** GUESTHOUSE $$
(☎04-602-0469; www.abrahamhostels.com; dm 85-100NIS, d 335-385NIS, all excl breakfast; @📶) Hidden away in a gorgeous, two-century-old stone house in the Old City, this place has oodles of charm – and so do the staff. The 14 rooms are simple but tasteful, though they're no match for the lounge's arched windows,

Lower Galilee & Sea of Galilee

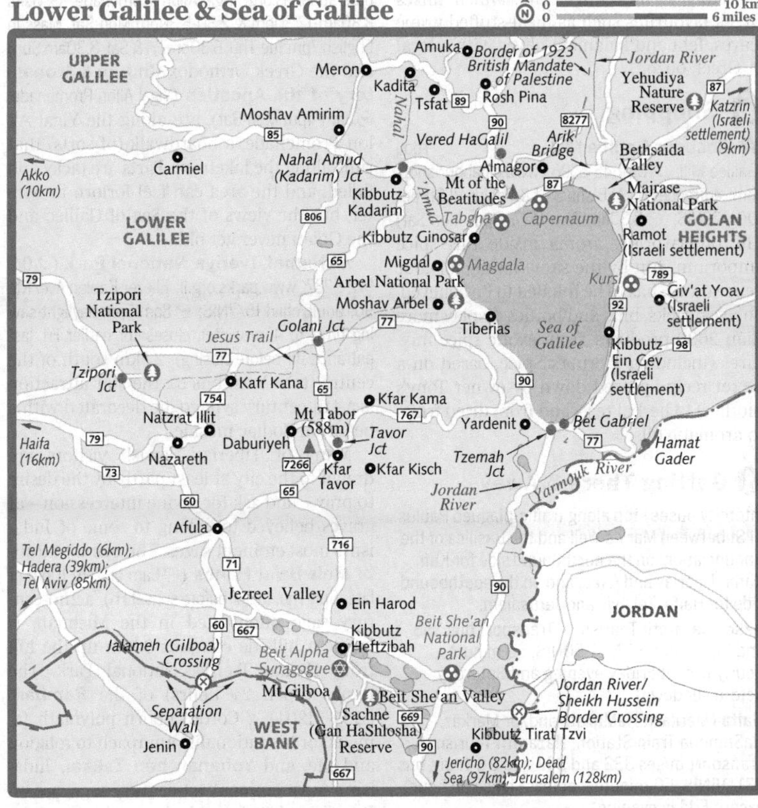

marble floors and 5m-high frescoed ceiling. A great place to meet other travellers – or to volunteer (see website).

★Al Mutran Guest House GUESTHOUSE $$
(☎04-645-7947; www.al-mutran.com; Bishop's Sq; d US$110-140, q US$200; 📶) Adjacent to the residence of Nazareth's Greek Orthodox *mutran* ('bishop' in Arabic), this family-run gem, with 11 rooms, occupies a gorgeous, 200-year-old mansion with 4.5m-high ceilings, Ottoman arches and antique floor tiles. Breakfast is served in the stylish lobby, decorated with embroidered pillows and Bedouin textiles.

Eating

Foodies around Israel and beyond know that Nazareth's delicious dining scene is worth braving the traffic for. The buzzword is 'fusion', with European-inspired dishes blended with local seasonings and then served with a generous helping of Arab hospitality.

★Abu Ashraf MIDDLE EASTERN $
(Diwan Al Saraya; ☎04-657-8697; 6134 St; mains 20NIS; ⊙8am-8pm Mon-Sat; 🖉) This old-time coffeehouse is famous all over town for its *katayef* (sweet pancakes folded over goat's cheese or cinnamon walnuts and then doused with geranium syrup), coffee (a special mix of five kinds of bean plus cardamom) and collection of antiques. Also serves excellent vegetable salads, *freekeh* (roasted green wheat), *labneh* (thick yoghurt) and *kibbeh* (meat-filled cracked-wheat croquettes). Ebullient owner Abu Ashraf loves to share stories about Nazareth.

Avra GREEK $$
(☎04-659-1547; Mary's Well Sq; mains 32-86NIS; ⊙8.30am-midnight or later Mon-Sat) 'Avra' means 'good atmosphere' in Greek, and that's exactly what this cafe-restaurant has, along with delicious Greek and Palestinian dishes and a soundtrack of traditional and modern Greek instrumental music. The

speciality is the Ouzo Plate, which mixes Greek favourites such as meat-stuffed grape leaves, feta and kalamata olives with a local or Greek ouzo.

Shopping

★Elbabour Galilee Mill FOOD
(Galilee Mill; 04-645-5596; www.elbabour-shop.com; entrances on Al Bishara St & Paulus VI St; per 100g 25NIS; 8.30am-7pm or 7.30pm Mon-Sat) The otherworldly aroma inside this spice emporium, run by the same family for four generations, has to be inhaled to be believed. Shelves, sacks, bins and bottles display more than 2600 products, from exotic spice mixtures (including Pierina's Spice, based on a secret recipe passed down by owner Tony's mother) to herbal teas, and from dried fruits to aromatic oils.

Getting There & Away

Intercity buses stop along traffic-plagued Paulus VI St between Mary's Well and the Basilica of the Annunciation: on the northbound side for Kafr Kana, Tiberias and Akko, and on the southbound side for Haifa, Tel Aviv and Jerusalem.

Akko (Nazareth Tourism & Transport bus 353 and Egged bus 343, 21.50NIS, 50 minutes, hourly except Friday evening and Saturday before sundown)

Haifa (Merkazit HaMifratz and/or Merkaz HaShmona Train Station, Nazareth Tourism & Transport buses 332 and 342 and GB Tours bus 331, 16NIS, 50 minutes, at least twice an hour except Friday evening)

Tiberias (Nazareth Tourism & Transport bus 431, 16NIS, one hour, hourly except Friday evening and Saturday before sundown) Some buses stop on Nazareth's ring road, Rte 75, instead of on Paulus VI St.

Buses to Amman, Jordan, are run by Nazarene Tours (p282).

Tiberias טבריה طبريا

04 / POP 42,600

Tiberias is one of the four holy cities of Judaism, the burial place of venerated Jewish sages, and a very popular base for Christians visiting holy sites around the Sea of Galilee. It's also one of the most aesthetically challenged resort towns in Israel, its sunbaked lakeside strip marred by eyesores from the 1970s.

Sights

Most of Tiberias' sights, including Catholic **St Peter's Church** (04-672-0516; www.saintpeterstiberias.org; Yigal Allon Promenade; visits 8.30am-12.30pm & 2.30-5.30pm Mon-Sat, Mass in English 7pm Tue-Thu, 6.30pm Fri & Sat, 8.30am Sun) and the Greek Orthodox **Church & Monastery of the Apostles** (Yigal Allon Promenade; 8am-4pm Mon-Sat), are along the Yigal Allon Promenade, a boardwalk (of sorts) that runs along the lakefront. Parts are tacky and faded, and the area can feel forlorn in winter, but the views of the Sea of Galilee and the Golan never get old.

At **Hamat Tveriya National Park** (04-672-5287; www.parks.org.il; Eliezer Kaplan Ave/Rte 90; adult/child 15/7NIS; 8am-5pm daylight-saving time, to 4pm winter, closes 1hr earlier Fri, last entrance 1hr before closing), 2.5km south of the centre (take local bus 5), the star attraction is a 4th-century synagogue decorated with a beautiful Zodiac mosaic.

Many of Tiberias' Jewish visitors are drawn to the city at least partly by the desire to pray – and ask for divine intercession – at graves believed to belong to some of Judaism's most eminent sages. The **tomb of Rabbi Meir Ba'al Hanes** (6am or 7am-10pm or later Sun-Thu, to 2hr before sunset Fri), a 2nd-century sage often cited in the Mishnah, is inside a hillside complex 300m up the hill from Hamat Tveriya National Park. The tombs (open 24 hours) of the **Rambam** (1135– 1204), a Cordova-born polymath famous for his rationalist approach to religion and life, and **Yohanan ben Zakkai**, Judaism's most eminent 1st-century sage, are on Ben Zakkai St four blocks northeast of the central bus station.

Sleeping & Eating

Tiberias has some of the Galilee's cheapest beds. The Yigal Allon Promenade has a number of places to grab a bite or sip a beer, as does the perpendicular Midrahov (pedestrian mall) and a nearby section of HaBanim St. **Supersol Express** (HaBanim St; 7.30am-8pm Sun-Thu, to 4.30pm Fri summer, to 2pm Fri winter) has picnic supplies.

★Tiberias Hostel HOSTEL $
(Rabin Sq; dm 75-100NIS, s 180-250NIS, d 230-350NIS; @) Yet another excellent ILH hostel, this place has a real backpacker vibe, a rooftop chill-out area with fairy lights, a full kitchen for guests and friendly staff who are happy to provide tips on local sights and activities. Breakfast costs just 15NIS; the non-meat Friday dinner is also a bargain (15NIS to 35NIS).

Tiberias

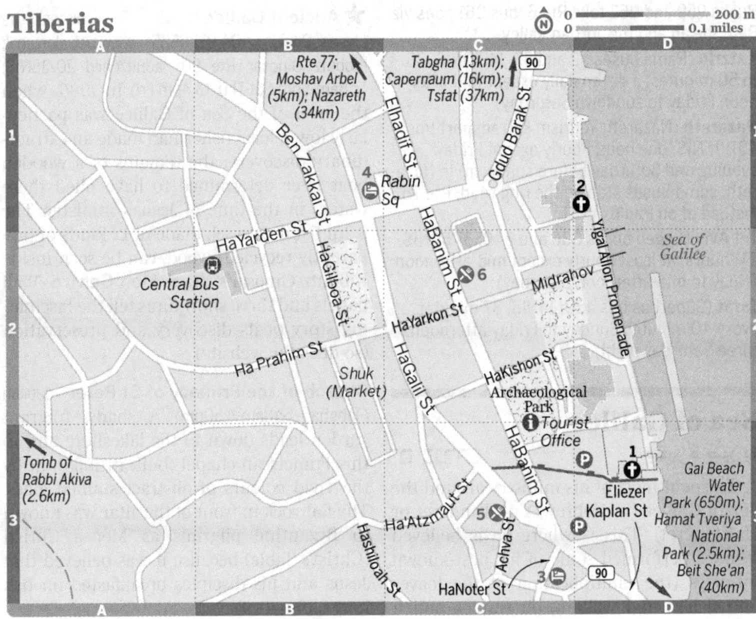

Aviv Holiday Flats — HOTEL $$

(☎04-671-2272; http://aviv-hotel.xwx.co.il; 2 HaNoter St; s/d/tr/q excl breakfast 300/400/500/600NIS; 📶) The 30 handsome, modern studio apartments have at least 30 sq metres of space, balconies, kitchenettes, comfy sheets and new mattresses for 2017. One of the best deals in town. A copious buffet breakfast costs 50NIS.

Guy — ISRAELI $$

(☎04-672-3036; HaGalil St, cnr Achva St; mains 38-75NIS; ⊙noon-9pm or 10pm Sun-Thu, to 2.30pm Fri winter, to 4pm Fri summer; 🖉) An unpretentious, old-time Mizrahi (Oriental-Jewish) restaurant featuring home-style grilled meats, soups (winter only) and a delicious array of stuffed vegetables, as well as Ashkenazi-style chopped liver, Iraqi-style *kibbeh* (spiced meat balls in tangy soup) and Lebanese-style *kibbeh* (a fried cracked-wheat dumpling stuffed with chopped meat). Cash only.

Information

Tourist office (☎04-672-5666; HaBanim St; ⊙8am-4pm Sun-Thu, to noon Fri) Has loads of free brochures on the Sea of Galilee, including Christian sites, and worthwhile hiking and cycling maps.

Tiberias

Sights

1 Church & Monastery of the Apostles ... D3
2 St Peter's Church ... D1

Sleeping

3 Aviv Holiday Flats ... C3
4 Tiberias Hostel ... B1

Eating

5 Guy ... C3
6 Supersol Express ... C2

Getting There & Away

Most intercity buses stop at the 1970-style **central bus station** (www.bus.co.il; HaYarden St); some short-haul lines also stop along HaGalil St. Destinations:

Beit She'an (Superbus bus 28; 14NIS, 35 minutes, every 45 minutes Sunday to Thursday, hourly until mid-afternoon Friday and after sundown Saturday)

Haifa-Merkazit HaMifratz (Egged buses 430 and 434; 21.50NIS, 1¼ hours, twice an hour except Friday afternoon to sundown Saturday)

Jerusalem (Egged buses 959, 961 and 962; 37.50NIS, 2¾ hours, every one or two hours except Friday evening to sundown Saturday)

Buses 959 and 962 take Rte 6, bus 961 goes via Beit She'an and the Jordan Valley.

Katzrin (Rama buses 52 and 57; 14.50NIS, 35 to 50 minutes, a dozen daily except mid-afternoon Friday to sundown Saturday)

Nazareth (Nazareth Tourism & Transport bus 431; 16NIS, one hour, hourly except Friday evening and Saturday before sundown) In Nazareth, some buses stop on the ring road, Rte 75, instead of on Paulus VI St.

Tel Aviv (Egged buses 836 and 840; 37.50NIS, 2¾ hours, at least hourly except mid-afternoon Friday to mid-afternoon Saturday)

Tsfat (Superbus bus 450; 14NIS, 37 minutes, every 40 minutes Sunday to Friday afternoon, three Saturday night)

Sea of Galilee

بحيرة طبريا　　ים כנרת

Jesus spent most of his ministry around the Sea of Galilee (in Hebrew, Yam Kinneret or HaKinneret). This is where he is believed to have performed some of his best-known miracles (the multiplication of the loaves and fishes, and walking on water), and it was overlooking the Kinneret that he delivered the Sermon on the Mount.

The shores of the Sea of Galilee, by far Israel's largest freshwater lake, are lined with great places to relax: beaches, camping grounds, cycling trails and walking tracks.

Sights

Heading north from Tiberias and then around the Sea of Galiliee, it's about 6km to Magdala, 8km to the Ancient Galilee Boat, 13km to Tabgha, 16km to Capernaum and 33km to Kursi. The Mount of the Beatitudes is 3km by car up the hill (Rte 90) from Tabgha – or, on foot, you can take a 1km trail.

Magdala ARCHAEOLOGICAL SITE

(☎04-620-9900; www.magdala.org; Migdal Junction, Rte 90; adult/child 15/10NIS; ⊗8am-6pm) When the Legionnaires of Christ, a Catholic congregation based in Mexico, began building a spiritual retreat in 2009, they were astonished to discover a synagogue from the 1st century AD, dated to the time of Jesus by a local coin minted in AD 29. The excavations – work continues every summer – are now an open-air museum. It's situated on the site of the ancient town of Magdala (Migdal in Hebrew), home of Mary Magdalene.

★**Ancient Galilee Boat** HISTORIC SITE

(Jesus Boat; ☎04-911-9585; www.bet-alon.co.il; Kibbutz Ginosar, Rte 90; adult/child 20/15NIS; ⊗8am-5pm Sat-Thu, to 4pm Fri) In 1986, when the level of the Sea of Galilee was particularly low, a local fisherman made an extraordinary discovery: the remains of a wooden boat later determined to have plied these waters in the time of Jesus's ministry. The 8.2m fishing vessel, made of 12 kinds of (apparently recycled) wood, can be seen inside Kibbutz Ginosar's **Yigal Alon Centre**. Wall panels and three short films tell the fascinating story of its discovery and preservation (so does the website).

Church of the Primacy of St Peter CHURCH

(Tabgha; ⊗8am-4.50pm) A shady, fragrant garden leads down to the lakeshore and to this Franciscan chapel (built in 1933), lit by the vivid colours of abstract stained glass. The flat rock in front of the altar was known to Byzantine pilgrims as Mensa Christi (Christ's Table) because it was believed that Jesus and his disciples breakfasted on fish here (John 21:9).

★**Mount of the Beatitudes** CHURCH

(Har HaOsher; ☎04-671-1223; Rte 90; per car 10NIS; ⊗gate & church 8-11.45am & 2-4.45pm) Since at least the 4th century, this landscaped hillside is believed to be where Jesus delivered his Sermon on the Mount (Matthew 5–7), whose opening lines – the eight Beatitudes – begin with the phrase 'Blessed are...'. The sermon also includes the Lord's Prayer and oft-quoted phrases such as 'salt of the earth', 'light of the world' and 'judge not, lest ye be judged'. The tranquil gardens have breathtaking views of the Sea of Galilee.

Capernaum ARCHAEOLOGICAL SITE

(Kfar Nachum, Kfar Nahum; 5NIS; ⊗8am-5pm, last entry 4.30pm) The New Testament says that the prosperous lakeside village of Capernaum (estimated population 1500), on the imperial highway from Tiberias to Damascus, was Jesus's base during the most influential period of his Galilean ministry (Matthew 4:13, Mark 2:1, John 6:59). It is mentioned by name 16 times: this is where Jesus is believed to have preached at the synagogue (Mark 1:21), healed the sick and recruited his first disciples: fishers Peter, Andrew, James and John and Matthew the tax collector.

Kursi National Park ARCHAEOLOGICAL SITE
(☎04-673-1983; www.parks.org.il; cnr Rte 92 & Rte 789; adult/child 14/7NIS; ⊙8am-4pm Oct-Mar, to 5pm Apr-Sep, closes 1hr earlier Fri, last entry 30min before closing) Mentioned in the Talmud as a place of idol worship, this Gentile fishing village – discovered by chance in the early 1970s – is where Jesus is believed to have cast a contingent of demon spirits out of two men and into a herd of swine (Mark 5:1–13, Luke 8:26–39). The beautifully conserved ruins feature an impressive 5th-century Byzantine monastery.

Sleeping

Camping is possible on almost all Sea of Galilee beaches.

★**Genghis Khan in the Golan** HOSTEL $$
(☎052 371-5687; www.gkhan.co.il; Giv'at Yoav; dm/6-person tent 100/750NIS, linen & towel per stay 20NIS) Hosts Sara and Bentzi Zafrir offer the warmest of welcomes and a fantastic independent-travel vibe here. Inspired by the yurts *(gers)* used by the nomads of Mongolia, they designed and handmade five colour-coded yurts with space for up to 10 on comfortable foam mattresses. Situated 13km southeast of Kursi (Kursy) Junction (the intersection of Rte 92 and Rte 789).

★**Pilgerhaus Tabgha** GUESTHOUSE $$$
(☎04-670-0100; www.dvhl.de; s/d Sat-Wed 500/680NIS, Thu & Fri 600/880NIS; @☜) Opened in 1889, this 72-room German Catholic guesthouse – geared to Christian pilgrims but open to all – is a tranquil place with glorious gardens, right on the shores of the Sea of Galilee. Renovated in 2016, it's ideal for meditation and reflection amid exemplary Germanic cleanliness and order. Wheelchair accessible. Reserve well in advance, especially in the spring and autumn. It's about 500m from Capernaum Junction.

Getting There & Around

Rte 90 runs along the entire western edge of the Sea of Galilee, Rte 92 follows the eastern shore and Rte 87 connects the two, running along the lake's northwestern shore.

The entire shoreline is served by two Rama buses that link Tiberias with the Golan town of Katzrin. Bus 52 goes via the Sea of Galilee's western and northwestern shores, including Tabgha and Capernaum, while slower bus 57 follows the lake's southwestern and eastern shores, passing by Ein Gev and Kursi National Park.

Beit She'an בית שאן بيسان

☎04 / POP 17,300

Founded sometime in the 5th millennium BC, Beit She'an – today a struggling modern town – has the most extensive Roman-era ruins in Israel.

Sights

Beit She'an National Park (☎04-658-7189; www.parks.org.il; Rte 90; adult/child 28/14NIS; ⊙8am-4pm Oct-Mar, to 5pm Apr-Sep, closes 1hr earlier Fri, last entry 30min before closing) is the best place in the country to get a sense of what it might have been like to live, work and shop in the Roman Empire. Colonnaded streets, a 7000-seat theatre, two bathhouses and piles of columns crumpled by the AD 749 earthquake evoke the aesthetics, grandeur, self-confidence and decadence of Roman provincial life in the centuries after Jesus.

The extraordinarily well-preserved mosaics (including a 12-panel zodiac circle) at the **Beit Alpha Synagogue** (☎04-653-2004; www.parks.org.il; Kibbutz Heftzibah; adult/child 22/9NIS; ⊙8am-4pm or 5pm, closes 1hr earlier Fri, last entry 1hr before closing), 8km west of town, are among the most dazzling ever found in Israel. Served by Kavim bus 412 (at least hourly).

Sleeping

HI – Beit She'an Guest House HOSTEL $$
(☎02-594-5644; www.iyha.org.il; 129 Menahem Begin Ave/Rte 90; s/d 400/530NIS, additional adult/child 160/125NIS; @☜≋) Within easy walking distance of Beit She'an's antiquities, this hostel has 80 rooms (18 of them added in 2017), attractive public areas, a great rooftop patio and a pool (open April to Sukkot). Rooms are practical and clean and have five beds; individual dorm beds are not available. Situated a bit south of the intercity bus stops. Wheelchair accessible.

Getting There & Away

Beit She'an does not have a proper bus station. Rather, buses stop along Menahem Begin Ave (Rte 90) about 100m north of the Beit She'an Guest House (youth hostel).

Jerusalem (Egged buses 943, 961 and 966, 37.50NIS, 2¼ hours, every 30 to 90 minutes Sunday to Friday afternoon and Saturday night)

Tiberias (Superbus bus 28, 14NIS, 35 minutes, every 45 minutes Sunday to Thursday, hourly until mid-afternoon Friday and after sundown Saturday)

To get to Nazareth, change buses in Afula.

The legendary Rakevet HaEmek (Jezreel Valley rail line) reopened in 2016, linking Beit She'an's train station, situated 2.5km northwest of the national park, with Haifa-Merkaz HaShmona (20NIS, 45 minutes, hourly).

Travellers headed to Jordan can make use of the Jordan River/Sheikh Hussein border crossing, 8km east of town.

UPPER GALILEE & GOLAN HEIGHTS

الجليل الاعلى وهضبة الجولان

הגליל העליון רמת הגולן

The rolling, green hills of the Upper Galilee (the area north of Rte 85) and, to the east, the wild plateaux and peaks of the occupied Golan Heights offer an incredible variety of activities to challenge the body and the soul – and nourish the stomach and the mind. Domestic tourists flock to the area; some are looking for luxurious *tzimmerim* (B&Bs), boutique wineries and gourmet country restaurants, while others come in search of superb hiking, cycling and horse riding, white-water rafting and even skiing. Yet other visitors are attracted by the dazzling carpets of spring wildflowers, some of the world's best birdwatching and the spiritual charms of Tsfat, long a hugely important centre of Kabbalah (Jewish mysticism). The entire region, its summits refreshingly cool in summer, is just a short drive from the Christian sites and cooling beaches of the Sea of Galilee.

Tsfat (Safed) צפת صفد

04 / POP 33,350 / ELEV 900M

The mountaintop city of Tsfat is an ethereal place to get lost for a day or two. A centre of Kabbalah (Jewish mysticism) since the 16th century, it's home to an otherworldly mixture of Hasidic Jews, artists and devout-but-mellow former hippies, more than a few of them American immigrants who turned to mysticism in a 1960s-inspired search for spirituality and transcendental meaning.

On Shabbat (Friday night and Saturday until sundown), commerce completely shuts down. While this may be inconvenient if you're looking for a bite to eat, the lack of traffic creates a meditative, spiritual Sabbath atmosphere through which joyful Hasidic tunes waft from hidden synagogues and unseen dining rooms.

Sights

Synagogue Quarter

Tsfat's long-time Jewish neighbourhood spills down the hillside from **HaMaginim Sq** (Kikar HaMaginim; Defenders' Sq), which dates from 1777. All of Tsfat's historic Kabbalist synagogues are a quick (if often confusing) walk from here. The main alley in the Synagogue Quarter, called **Alkabetz St** and **Beit Yosef St** (Yosef Caro St), is lined with joyously colourful **art galleries**. The **tombs of famous Kabbalists** are in the cemetery down the slope from the Synagogue Quarter.

Synagogue hours tend to be irregular, especially in winter, and unannounced closings (eg for Monday and Thursday morning bar mitzvahs) are common. Visitors should wear modest clothing (no shorts or bare shoulders); kippas/yarmulkes are provided for men (or you can wear any hat). Caretakers appreciate a small donation (5NIS). Synagogues are closed to tourists on Shabbat and Jewish holidays.

★Ashkenazi Ari Synagogue SYNAGOGUE

(Najara St; approx 9.30am-7pm Sun-Thu, to 1pm Fri, closed during prayers) Founded in the 16th century by Sephardic Jews from Greece, this venerable synagogue looks much as it did 150 years ago. It stands on the site where, according to tradition, the great Kabbalist Yitzhak Luria (Isaac Luria; 1534–72; often known as the Ari) used to greet the Sabbath. In the 18th century it came to serve Tsfat's Ashkenazi Hasidic community, hence the synagogue's name (the Jerusalem-born Ari himself had a Sephardic mother and an Ashkenazi father).

★Caro Synagogue SYNAGOGUE

(04-692-3284, Eyal 050 855-0462; Beit Yosef St; donation 5NIS; 9am-5pm or 6pm Sun-Thu, closes 1hr earlier in winter, 9am-noon Fri) Decorated with Middle Eastern arches, hanging lamps and bookshelves heavy with holy texts, this synagogue – like the street it's on – is named in honour of Toledo-born Rabbi Yosef Caro (1488–1575), author of the Shulchan Aruch (the most authoritative codification of Jewish law). It was founded as a house of study in the 1500s but was rebuilt after the earthquakes of 1759 and 1837 – and again in 1903.

Artists' Quarter

The neighbourhood south of the Ma'alot Olei HaGardom stairway used to be Tsfat's Arab quarter, as you can see from the min-

Upper Galilee & the Golan Heights

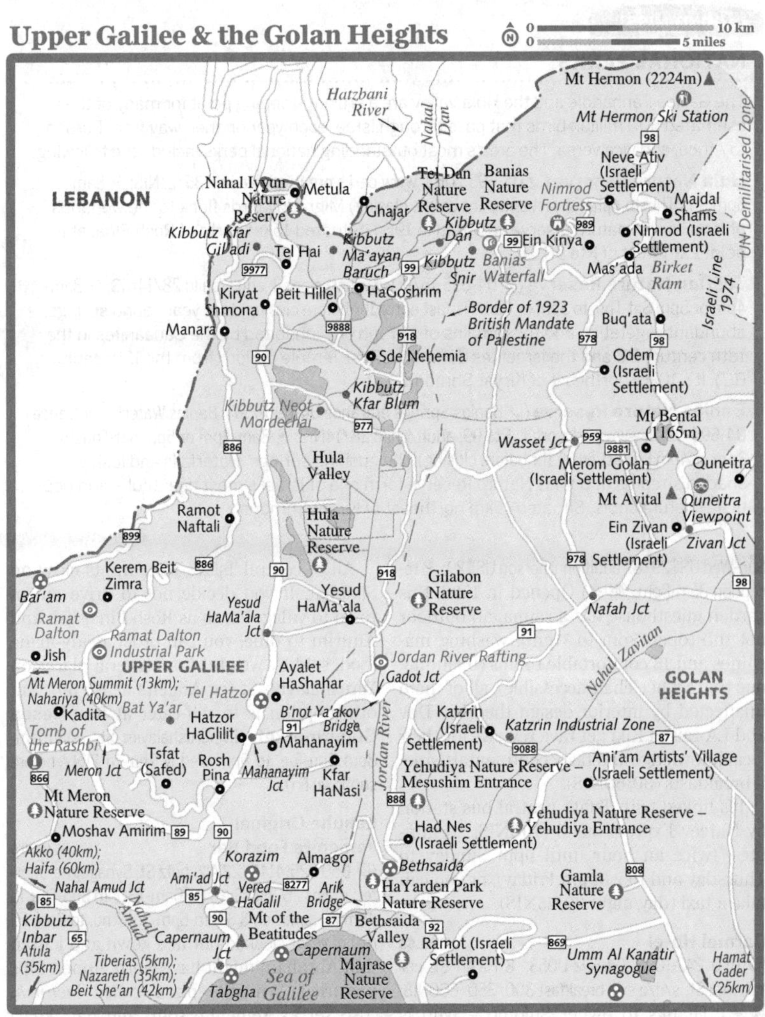

arets, but after the 1948 war the area was developed as an Israeli artists' colony. Most of the galleries and studios around the quarter are open to visitors, with many artists are happy to talk about their work and even happier to make a sale.

Courses

Tzfat Kabbalah Center RELIGIOUS

(International Center for Tzfat Kabbalah; ☎04-682-1771; www.tzfat-kabbalah.org; 1st fl, Fig Tree Courtyard, 28 Alkabetz St, Synagogue Quarter; ⏲9am-6pm Sun-Thu, to 1pm Fri) Adherents of all religions, or none at all, are welcome to drop by for an introduction to Jewish mysticism and on-the-spot meditation. Hour-long personalised workshops with Eyal Riess, who lectures around the world on the Tsfat Kabbalah tradition, cost 150NIS to 250NIS. Screens films on the subject in Hebrew, English, Spanish and Russian and sells Kabbalah amulets and jewellery.

Sleeping

★ **Safed Inn** GUESTHOUSE $$

(Ruckenstein B&B; ☎04-697-1007; www.safedinn.com; cnr HaGdud HaShlishi St & Merom Kna'an St, Mt Canaan; dm/d excl breakfast US$29/100,

DON'T MISS

NATIONAL PARKS

The Galilee Panhandle and the Hula Valley are a crucial stopping point for many of the estimated 500 million birds that pass through Israel each year on their way from Europe to Africa, and vice versa. The area's most outstanding national parks include the following:

Hula Nature Reserve (☎04-693-7069; www.parks.org.il; adult/child 35/21NIS; ⏲8am-5pm Sun-Thu, to 4pm Fri, last entry 1hr before closing) Migrating birds flock to the wetlands of Israel's first nature reserve, founded in 1964. Situated 15km north of Rosh Pina, at a point 2km west of Rte 90.

Tel Dan Nature Reserve (☎04-695-1579; www.parks.org.il; adult/child 28/14NIS; ⏲8am-4pm or 5pm Sat-Thu, to 3pm or 4pm Fri, last entry 1hr before closing) Has year-round springs, abundant vegetation and the remains of a grand city inhabited by the Canaanites in the 18th century BC and the Israelites during the First Temple period (from the 12th century BC). It's 10km northeast of Kiryat Shmona.

Banias Nature Reserve (☎Banias Springs entrance 04-690-2577, Banias Waterfall entrance 04-695-0272; www.parks.org.il; Rte 99; adult/child 28/14NIS; ⏲8am-4pm or 5pm Sat-Thu, to 3pm or 4pm Fri, last entry 1hr before closing) The gushing springs, waterfalls and lushly shaded streams of Banias Nature Reserve form one of Israel's most beautiful – and popular – nature spots. Situated 15km northeast of Kiryat Shmona.

Sun-Wed US$29/87, additional person US$29; ⏲reception 8am-8pm; @📶) Opened in 1936, this garden guesthouse has a sauna, an outdoor hot tub (open 8pm to 11pm), washing machines and 18 comfortable rooms (including one that's wheelchair accessible), all of them unaffected by interior design theories. Dov and LA-raised Riki get rave reviews for their local knowledge and tasty continental/Israeli breakfasts (30/60NIS).

It's linked with Tsfat's central bus station by Nateev Express bus 3 (4.10NIS, 20 minutes, twice an hour until 9pm Sunday to Thursday and to 2.30pm Friday), or you can take a taxi (day/night 20/25NIS).

Carmel Hotel HOTEL **$$**
(☎050 242-1092, 04-692-0053; 8 Ha'Ari St, cnr Ya'avetz St; s/d/q excl breakfast 300/350/600NIS; @📶) Thanks to owner Shlomo – who is likely to insist that you try his limoncello – staying here is like having the run of a big, old family house. Some of the 12 simply furnished rooms are romantic and some aren't, but they're all clean and practical and some have fantastic views.

Eating

All along Yerushalayim St, more than a dozen small eateries sell falafel, *sabich* (a pita stuffed with deep-fried eggplant and egg), shawarma, pizza and baked goods. There are several more places to eat at around HaMaginim Sq, on the edge of the Synagogue Quarter.

All of central Tsfat's restaurants close on Shabbat. If you decide not to drive out of town to villages such as Rosh Pina, Jish and Amirim to dine, you can order ready-made food, sold by weight, from several places on Yerushalayim St (eg Araleh's at No 59). Another option is to self-cater at **Rav-Hesed Supermarket** (13 Yerushalayim St; ⏲7.15am-8pm Sun-Tue, to 9pm Wed & Thu, to 2½hr before sundown Fri).

Lahuhe Original Yemenite Food Bar YEMENI **$**
(☎050 225-4148; 22 Alkabetz St, Synagogue Quarter; mains 25-35NIS; ⏲8.30am-7.30pm Sun-Thu, to 4pm Fri summer, 8.30am-6pm Sun-Thu, to 2pm Fri rest of year) Decked out in a gown and kaftan that Abraham might have worn, Ronen flips pan-fried 'Yemenite pizza' called *lachuch*. Also serves Yemenite soup and qat (khat) juice, which is illegal in many Western countries but not in Israel.

★**Elements Cafe** VEGETARIAN **$$**
(☎054 653-0668; www.elementscafe.co.il; 5 HaMaginim Sq, 3m down an alley; mains 25-55NIS; ⏲11am-6pm or later Sun-Thu year-round, 11.30am-2.30pm Fri summer; 📶🖉) 🍃 Serving wholesome food that nourishes both body and soul, this cafe offers a menu that's 100% vegan and gluten-free, a healthful, positive vibe and reasonable prices. Specialities include soup, pizza, homemade sauerkraut, stir-fried rice or quinoa (45NIS), and desserts such as coconut-chai ice cream and

smoothies made with almond milk, dates, chia seeds and carob.

★**HaAri 8** ISRAELI **$$$**
(☎04-692-0033; www.haari8.rest.co.il; 8 Ha'Ari St; mains 68-134NIS; ⊙noon-10pm Sun-Thu;) When the mayor has VIP guests, this is where he brings them. Specialities include grilled meats, steak and Moroccan pastry 'cigars', and fish. Vegetarian options include fresh salads, soups, pasta, quiche and grilled portobello mushrooms. Has a playroom for kids.

Orientation

Central Tsfat's main thoroughfare, lined with shops and eateries, is north–south Yerushalayim St (Jerusalem St). West of there, a broad staircase called Ma'alot Olei HaGardom divides the Synagogue Quarter (to the north) from the Artists' Quarter (to the south).

Information

For information on Tsfat's history, attractions, accommodation and study options – and some colourful local personalities – check out www.safed.co.il.

The English-speaking staff at the **Tourist Information Center** (☎04-692-4427; www.livnot.org; 17 Alkabetz St, Synagogue Quarter; ⊙8.30am-5pm Sun-Thu, 9am-1pm or 2pm Fri) are happy to provide information on visiting Tsfat and on local volunteering opportunities for both non-Jews and Jews.

Getting There & Away

The **central bus station** (www.bus.co.il; HaAtzma'ut St), situated about 700m east of the Synagogue Quarter, has numerous services.

Haifa-Merkazit HaMifratz (Nateev Express bus 361; 22.40NIS, 1½ hours, twice an hour) Goes via Akko (one hour).

Jerusalem (Nateev Express bus 982; 37.50NIS, 3¼ hours, six to nine daily Sunday to Friday afternoon and on Saturday night)

Tiberias (Superbus bus 450; 14NIS, 37 minutes, every 40 minutes Sunday to Friday afternoon, three Saturday night)

The fastest way to get to Tel Aviv is to take Nateev Express bus 361 to Akko and then hop on a train.

Golan Heights

رمת הגולן هضبة الجولان

Offering commanding views of the Sea of Galilee and the Hula Valley, the volcanic Golan plateau is dry and tan in summer, and lush, green and carpeted with wildflowers in spring. Its fields of basalt boulders – and, on its western edge, deep canyons – are mixed with cattle ranches, orchards, vineyards and middle-class communities, both Israeli and Druze.

Israel's control of the Golan Heights has been a source of tension between Israel and Syria since 1967, when the area was captured from Syria. In the bitterly fought 1973 Yom Kippur War, Syrian forces briefly overtook much of the Golan before being pushed back. The disengagement 'buffer' zone between the two regions is staffed by the blue-helmeted soldiers of the UN Disengagement Observer Force. In 1981, Israel unilaterally annexed the area – a move that has not been recognised internationally or by the UN – and has developed settlements across it. Despite the ongoing political

RAFTING THE JORDAN

First-time visitors are often surprised at the Jordan's creek-sized proportions, but first-time rafters are often bowled over – sometimes into the soup – by how powerful its flow can be. Several excellent outfits offer rafting and kayaking down the Jordan (from 97NIS) – competition is as fierce as the current, which means standards of service and safety are high. Discounts of 20% or more are often available on the internet if you book at least 24 hours ahead, and from locally distributed coupon books.

Kfar Blum Kayaks (☎04-690-2616; www.kayaks.co.il; Beit Hillel; ⊙trips begin 10am-3pm, open approx Passover-Sukkot) A refreshing **4km descent** (1¼ hours; minimum age five) in an inflatable two-person kayak or a raft (for two to six) costs 97NIS, while a more challenging **8km route** (2½ hours; minimum age 10) costs 129NIS.

Ma'ayan-Hagoshrim Kayaks (☎077 271-7500; www.kayak.co.il; Kibbutz Ma'ayan Baruch; ⊙trips begin 9am or 10am-3pm or 4pm Apr-Oct) The 1½-hour **Family Route** (5km; minimum age five) costs 97NIS per person; the wilder, two-hour **Challenge Route** (6km; minimum age 10) is 117NIS. Has a campground (125NIS per person, including tent and mattress).

dispute, the Druze and Israeli communities exist in harmony here, and travellers shouldn't expect to experience any tension on the ground.

Katzrin קצרין كتسرين

☎04 / POPULATION 6900

By far the Golan's largest Israeli settlement, Katzrin (Qazrin) makes an excellent base for exploring the central and southern Golan and stocking up on picnic supplies.

Sights

★Golan Archaeological Museum MUSEUM
(☎04-696-1350; Merkaz Eitan; adult/child 19/16NIS, incl Ancient Katzrin Park 28/20NIS; ⏲9am-4pm Sun-Thu, to 2pm Fri) A real gem of a museum. Highlights include extraordinary basalt lintels and Aramaic inscriptions from 32 Byzantine-era Golan synagogues; coins minted during the Great Jewish Revolt (AD 66–70); a model of Rujum Al Hiri, a mysterious Stone Age maze 156m across, built some 4500 years ago; and a film (available in nine languages) that brings to life the Roman siege of Gamla.

Ancient Katzrin Park ARCHAEOLOGICAL SITE
(Ancient Qazrin; ☎04-696-2412; adult/child 26/18NIS, incl Golan Archaeological Museum adult/child 28/20NIS; ⏲9am-4pm Sun-Thu, to 2pm Fri, 10am-4pm Sat, closes 1hr later in Aug) To get a sense of life during the Talmudic period (3rd to 6th centuries AD) when the Golan had dozens of Jewish villages, drop by this partly reconstructed Byzantine-era village. Situated 1.6km east of the Merkaz Eitan commercial centre.

DON'T MISS

NIMROD FORTRESS

Built by Muslims in the 13th century to protect the road from Tyre to Damascus, **Nimrod Fortress** (☎04-694-9277; www.parks.org.il; Rte 989; adult/child 22/9NIS; ⏲8am-4pm or 5pm Sat-Thu, closes 1hr earlier Fri, last entry 1hr before closing) rises fairy-tale-like on a long, narrow ridge (altitude 815m) on the southwestern slopes of Mt Hermon. The work that went into building such a massive fortification – 420m long and up to 150m wide – on the top of a remote mountain ridge boggles the mind. If you're going to visit just one Crusader-era fortress during your trip, this should be it.

Sleeping

Golan Garden Hostel HOSTEL $
(☎053 430-3677; www.golangarden.com; 12 Hukuk St; dm/d with shared bathroom 100/300NIS; @📶) This mellow 18-bed place – run by super-friendly Alon and Daniel – has a chill-out lounge with bean-bag chairs, a full kitchen for self-caterers, dorm rooms with four or six beds, a hammock on the back patio, and guitars and drums for guests to play.

Information

Run by the regional council, the town's **information centre** (☎04-696-2885; www.tourgolan.org.il; Hutzot HaGolan Mall, Katzrin Industrial Zone; ⏲9am-4pm Sun-Thu) has brochures and free maps in Hebrew, English and Russian, and can supply details on accommodation, hiking and winery visits. Situated in the shopping centre 2km east of the town centre, behind the round fountain.

Get a free consultation with experienced SPNI guides about Golan hiking options at **SPNI Hiking Information** (Merkaz Hadracha; ☎04-770-9460; www.teva.org.il; SPNI Golan Field School, 2 Zavitan St; ⏲8.30am-5pm Sun-Thu). You can also phone with questions. Sells 1:50,000-scale hiking maps (90NIS).

Getting There & Away

Katzrin is the Golan's only real bus hub. **Rama buses** (☎04-373-2099; www.golanbus.co.il) head to virtually every part of the plateau as well as to Tiberias, Rosh Pina and Kiryat Shmona.

Long-haul Egged services include the following:

Haifa – Lev HaMifratz (bus 503; 37.50NIS, 2½ hours, four daily Sunday to Thursday, two on Friday)

Jerusalem (bus 966; 42.50NIS, four hours, one to three daily)

Tel Aviv – Central Bus Station (bus 843; 42.50NIS, 3½ hours, four or five daily Sunday to Thursday, one on Friday, one on Saturday)

Majdal Shams מג'דל שמס مجدل شمس

☎04 / POPULATION 10,640

The largest of Golan's four Druze towns, Majdal Shams is the commercial and cultural focal point of the area's Druze community. Druze flags (with five horizontal stripes) flutter in the wind, and you often see men with elaborate moustaches sporting traditional Druze attire, including a black *shirwal* (baggy trousers) and a white fez. That said, the town is considerably less conservative than many Druze villages in the area: young people dress like their secular Israeli counterparts, and alcohol is available in several pubs.

In the centre of town, in the middle of a traffic circle, stands a heroic **equestrian statue** of Sultan Pasha Al Atrash, Druze hero of the 1925 uprising against French colonial rule in Syria. Towering **Mt Hermon**, snow-capped in winter, is 9km up the hill from Majdal Shams along Rte 98.

Sleeping

Narjis Hotel HOTEL $$
(Malon Butik Narkis; ☎04-698-2961; www.narjishotel.com; Rte 98; d in summer/winter 500/680NIS; ⏲reception 9am-6pm; 📶) This stylish hotel, owned by a Majdal Shams family, has 18 huge, romantic rooms with modern decor, jacuzzis, balconies and fridges. Reserve ahead. Situated 200m towards Mt Hermon from Hermon Junction, the roundabout at the intersection of Rte 989 and Rte 98.

Getting There & Away

Majdal Shams is 50km north of Katzrin and 30km east of Kiryat Shmona. It is served by Rama bus 58 from Kiryat Shmona.

DEAD SEA ים המלח البحر الميت

The lowest place on the face of earth, the Dead Sea (431m below sea level) brings together breathtaking natural beauty and compelling ancient history.

Getting There & Around

It's possible, though a bit fiddly, to explore the Dead Sea by public bus. To avoid hanging around wilting under the sun, plan your itinerary in advance.

Egged buses (www.egged.co.il) link sites along Rte 90 (including Ein Gedi Nature Reserve, Masada and Ein Bokek) with the following destinations:

Eilat Egged bus 444 (42.50NIS, 2¾ hours to Ein Bokek, eight per day Sunday to Thursday, three on Friday, three Saturday afternoon and evening)

Jerusalem Egged buses 444 and 486 (34NIS, one hour to Ein Gedi, about hourly 6.30am to 4.45pm Sunday to Thursday, until 2pm Friday, at least one Saturday night)

Tel Aviv Egged bus 421 (48.40NIS, 2½ hours to Ein Bokek, three daily Sunday to Thursday, one on Friday). In Tel Aviv departs from the Arlozorov Bus Terminal; goes via Hwy 6.

Abraham Hostels (https://abrahamtours.com) offers one-day excursions to the Dead Sea for 150NIS to 280NIS from Jerusalem and Tel Aviv.

QUMRAN

World-famous for having hidden the Dead Sea Scrolls (documents written from 200 BC to AD 68 that include the oldest known manuscripts of the Hebrew Bible), **Qumran** (☎02-994-2235; www.parks.org.il; Rte 90 near Kalya; adult/child 29/15NIS; ⏲8am-4pm or 5pm Sat-Thu, to 3pm or 4pm Fri, last entry 1hr before closing) was the site of a small Essene settlement destroyed by the Romans two years before they laid waste to Jerusalem. Situated in the West Bank 35km east of Jerusalem, 20km south of Jericho and 35km north of Ein Gedi. All Jerusalem–Dead Sea buses pass by here.

Ein Gedi عين جدي עין גדי

Nestled in two dramatic canyons that plunge from the arid moonscape of the Judean Desert to the shores of the Dead Sea, Ein Gedi Nature Reserve is one of Israel's most magical desert oases. Its freshwater pools (wear your bathing suit), cool streams, Eden-like waterfalls and luxuriant vegetation, fed by four year-round springs, are a haven for wildlife such as the majestic Nubian ibex (*ya'el* in Hebrew) and the boulder-dwelling hyrax (dassie or rock rabbit; *shafan sela* in Hebrew).

Sights & Activities

Ein Gedi Nature Reserve (☎08-658-4285; www.parks.org.il; ⏲8am-4pm or 5pm) consists of two roughly parallel canyons, **Wadi David** (the more popular of two) and **Wadi Arugot**, each of which has its own entrance complex and ticket office. The key to a successful hike in the reserve is the excellent **colour-coded map-brochure** given out when you buy your tickets. Food is not allowed in the reserve.

Situated about midway between the Wadi David and Wadi Arugot ticket offices, a 5th-century AD **synagogue** sports a superb mosaic floor.

Ein Gedi Beach is closed due to sinkholes.

Activities

Ein Gedi Spa SPA
(☎08-620 1030; www.eingediseaofspa.co.il; Rte 90; adult without/with lunch 95/155NIS, child 5-12yr 56/110NIS; ⏲9am-5pm Sat-Thu, 8am-4.30pm Fri) Situated 3km south of Kibbutz Ein Gedi,

Dead Sea

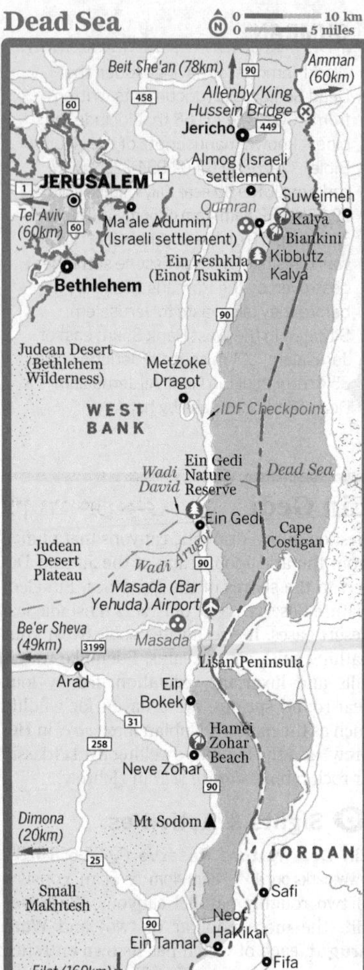

this spa – owned by the kibbutz – is a popular place to catch a float and coat yourself with invigorating natural black mud. The shoreline has receded 1.3km since the spa opened in 1984, so beach-goers take a little train (every 20 minutes) to the water's edge. Wheelchair accessible.

Sleeping & Eating

Don't show up without reservations. There are few dining options in the Ein Gedi area so arrive with picnic supplies and consider having dinner at your hostel.

Ein Gedi Youth Hostel HOSTEL $
(Beit Sarah; 02-594-5600; www.iyha.org.il; near Ein Gedi Nature Reserve; dm/s/d 132/321/410NIS, additional adult/child 120/94NIS;) The sensational setting and simple but contemporary rooms, with three to five beds, make this 87-room hostel madly popular. Dinner is often available for 62NIS (71NIS on Friday). Offers discounts of 15% to 20% on various area attractions. Situated 200m up the slope from the Rte 90 turn-off to Ein Gedi Nature Reserve. Reserve well ahead.

Khan Ein Gedi HUT $
(Ein Gedi Camp Lodge; Avi 052 606-3666, Ben 052 933-1019; www.facebook.com/eingedicamplodge; Kibbutz Ein Gedi; dm in a hut 120NIS; year-round;) Situated just outside the gate to Kibbutz Ein Gedi, this mellow, hillside operation has eight basic huts, each with five mattresses on the floor. Bathroom and kitchen facilities are shared. There's wi-fi in the chill-out area, whose wooden bar, open 24/7, sells pizzas.

Kolbo Grocery SUPERMARKET $
(Kibbutz Ein Gedi; 7.30am-8pm Sun-Thu, to 2pm Fri, 11am-2pm Sat) The only proper food shop in the area. Situated next to Kibbutz Ein Gedi's dining hall.

Masada מצדה مسعدة

No place in Israel is as evocative of life in 1st-century Roman Judea as Masada, an isolated desert mesa where the last Jewish resistance to Roman rule was crushed in AD 73 after a dramatic, bloody siege. Today, visitors to the complex, declared a Unesco World Heritage Site in 2001, can see palaces built by King Herod, structures used by the Jewish Zealots and, far below, the remains of the 10th Legion's siege bases. For a supremely romantic experience, climb to the top at dawn to watch the sunrise

After the Romans conquered Jerusalem in AD 70, almost a thousand Jews – men, women and children – made a desperate last stand atop Masada, a desert mesa edged by sheer cliffs. From AD 72 the mesa was surrounded by a ring of military encampments belonging to Rome's feared 10th Legion. As a Roman battering ram was about to breach the walls of their fastness, Masada's defenders chose suicide over enslavement, so when Roman soldiers swarmed onto the top of the flat-topped mountain they were met with... silence.

Sights & Activities

The easy way to get to the top of **Masada** (Metzada; ☎08-658-4207, 08-658-4208; www.parks.org.il; adult/child 28/14NIS; ⏲8am-4pm or 5pm Sat-Thu, to 3pm or 4pm Fri, last entry 1hr before closing) is to take the cable car, which whisks you from the Visitors Centre to the top in Swiss comfort in just three minutes.

But if you're up for it, hiking up the **Snake Path** will give you a much better appreciation of Masada's geography – and a good workout. This famously serpentine footpath winds its way up the mountain's eastern flank, starting from near the Visitors Centre. Walking up takes 45 to 60 minutes; count on spending 30 minutes to come back down. If you'd like to watch sunrise from the summit (highly recommended!), get to the trailhead an hour before the sun comes up, ie sometime between 4.30am (in June) and 5.30am (in December). Before 8am, access is from the security barrier near the youth hostel.

You can also ascend Masada from the western side, via the Roman-built **Siege Ramp Trail**, which is accessible only from Arad (via Rte 31 and then Rte 3199).

The **Masada Museum** (Visitors Centre; incl audio guide atop Masada 20NIS; ⏲8.30am-4pm or 5pm Sat-Thu, to 3pm or 4pm Fri, last entry 30min before closing), inside the Visitors Centre, offers a vivid introduction to Masada's archaeology and history – highly recommended!

Sleeping & Eating

The only place to stay right at Masada is the **Masada Guest House** (☎02-594-5623; www.iyha.org.il; dm/s/d 170/400/530NIS; @ 📶 ❄), an 89-bed hostel situated a few hundred metres below the Visitors Centre.

Inside the Visitors Centre complex, falafel, shawarma, sandwiches, salads, cafeteria meals and cold beer are available at the **food court** (eastern entrance, Masada National Park; mains from 25NIS; ⏲8am-4pm or 4.30pm; ✎).

Getting There & Away

Masada's Visitors Centre, on the eastern side of the mountain, is 21km south of the Ein Gedi Nature Reserve; the access road from Rte 90 is 3km long. All intercity buses serving the Dead Sea stop a few hundred metres from the Visitors Centre. Bus times are posted at Visitors Centre ticket windows.

Ein Bokek عين بوقيق עין בוקק

☎08

Sandwiched between the turquoise waters of the southern Dead Sea and a dramatic tan bluff, Ein Bokek's strip of luxury hotels is the region's main tourist zone. Ein Bokek (also spelled En Boqeq) has the Dead Sea's nicest **beach** (⏲24hr) FREE – perfect for a soothing dip (changing rooms available) in the briny, healing waters.

Sleeping

Unless you camp on the beach (free), there's no budget (or even midrange) accommodation in Ein Bokek's two hotel zones. But if you're up for a splurge there are loads of options – the area's dozen hotels offer crisply air-conditioned facilities, gorgeous swimming pools, state-of-the-art spas and buffet bonanzas. Good options include the 203-room **Hod HaMidbar** (☎08-668-8222; www.hodhotel.co.il; d incl half-board 1000-1800NIS; @ 📶 ❄).

THE NEGEV النقب הנגב

The Negev is the only part of Israel that feels vast and boundless. Stretching from the Red Sea north for 250km, the region's rocky, treeless hills and dry gullies have been attracting travellers, traders and nomads since the time of Abraham. These days, sun-seekers, scuba divers, birdwatchers and hikers flock to the resort city of Eilat, where the sun shines 360 days a year. Perched on the rim of Israel's multi-hued 'grand canyon', hip Mitzpe Ramon is a magnet for creative minds, quirky entrepreneurs and serenity seekers.

Mitzpe Ramon

متسبيه ريمون מצפה רמון

☎08 / POP 5000 / ELEVATION 900M

The Hebrew word *mitzpe* means 'lookout' and Mitzpe Ramon, spectacularly sited on the northern edge of Makhtesh Ramon – Israel's 'grand canyon' – well and truly lives up to its name. Views are of the take-your-breath-away variety and help draw artists and visionary people looking for a less pressured and more creative lifestyle. The wide, open spaces that surround Mitzpe, far from crowds and city lights (the stargazing here is superb), are equally suited to those seeking solitude and visitors looking for an activity-triggered adrenaline rush.

EN AVDAT NATIONAL PARK

En Avdat National Park (☎08-655-5684; www.parks.org.il; adult/child 28/14NIS; ⏲8am-4pm winter, to 5pm summer, closes 1hr earlier Fri) comes as a huge surprise in the otherwise bone-dry Negev Desert: a year-round, freshwater spring that miraculously flows over a waterfall and through a narrow, winding ravine with steep sides of soft white chalk. Caves along the trail were inhabited by monks during the Byzantine period.

The two most popular trails begin at the Lower Parking Lot, a 3km drive from the northern entrance. The Short Route (start at least 1½ hours before the park closes) is a 1.6km circuit that takes you to En Avdat pool and the waterfall and back. The one-way Long Route (start at least 2½ hours before the park closes) goes to the park's southern entrance; because one section involves ladders that you can climb but not descend, this route cannot be done in the other direction.

The park has two entrances. The northern one, Zinim (Tzinim) Cliff, is just outside Midreshet Ben-Gurion's big yellow gate, while the southern one – which offers panoramas but no trails down into the wadi – is on Rte 40, 4km north of the Nabataean ruins of Avdat National Park.

Park staff can provide you with a map and details on hiking options.

Sights

Makhtesh Ramon Nature Reserve (www.parks.org.il; ⏲24hr) FREE is a spectacular 300m deep, 9km wide and 40km long. Perched on the crater's rim, the **Makhtesh Ramon Visitors Center** (☎08-658-8691; adult/child 28/14NIS; ⏲8am-4pm or 5pm, closes 1hr earlier Fri, last entry 1hr before closing) has extremely helpful staff and exhibits on the area's geology.

Mitzpe Ramon's most dynamic neighbourhood, the **Spice Route Quarter**, is a cluster of hangars and warehouses built decades ago as an industrial zone. These days, this is the best place in town to feel Mitzpe's tremendous creative energy – check out the artisanal factories, artists' studios, tiny boutique hotels, yoga studios, cafes and pubs, as well as a weaving museum, a superb bakery and even a nationally prominent jazz club.

Sleeping

Green Backpackers HOSTEL $
(☎08-653-2319; www.thegreenbackpackers.com; 2/2 Nahal Sirpad St; dm 88-100NIS, d 385NIS, d with shared bathroom 285NIS; @📶) Run with enthusiasm by keen hikers Lee and Yoash, this home-style hostel on the edge of town, with 24 beds, is the local backpacker hub. There's a tiny lounge with DVD library, a book exchange, communal kitchen and laundry facilities (25NIS per load). Tea and coffee are free, and a basic breakfast costs 10NIS.

Silent Arrow LODGE $
(Hetz BaSheket; ☎052 661-1561; http://silentarrow.com; Mitzpe HaKochavim St; dm/s/d/q with shared bathroom & excl breakfast 90/170/270/470NIS) Seeking the tranquillity and simplicity of the desert? This encampment may fit the bill. A 20-minute (1.5km) walk from town, it offers basic accommodation, a spotless bathroom block, a chill-out courtyard, a fully equipped communal kitchen and a herb garden. Choose a mattress in a 30-bed communal tent or a private dome tent. All electricity is solar.

Getting There & Away

Metropoline buses 60, 64 and 65 travel between Mitzpe and Be'er Sheva (15NIS, 1¾ hours, at least hourly) from 5am to 9.30pm. None of these services operate on Shabbat.

To get to Eilat (39.50NIS, 2¼ hours, four to six daily Sunday to Thursday, one Friday), take Egged bus 392, which starts its run in Be'er Sheva. In Mitzpe, it stops along Rte 40.

Eilat אילת ايلات

☎08 / POP 49,700

Hugely popular with Israeli families looking for a beach break and Europeans taking refuge from bone-chilling winters back home, the Red Sea resort of Eilat is brash, ugly and almost inevitably crowded. The turquoise waters of the Red Sea offer snorkelling, diving and water-sports opportunities galore, while nearby mountains and canyons offer superb desert hiking. The average daily high is 21°C in January and 40°C in July.

Sights & Activities

The Red Sea's coral reefs offer some of the world's most thrilling **scuba diving**. All you need to do is pop your head underwater to see all sorts of extraordinary fish and coral (the area is thought to have 1200 species of fish and 250 of coral), making Eilat a great place for kids as well as for adult beginners looking to do a PADI scuba course.

Eilat has more than a dozen dive centres offering courses and equipment rental, almost all of them along South Beach. Most are open daily from 8am or 8.30am to 5pm or 5.30pm. Prices vary but average around 230NIS for an introductory dive and 550NIS for a half-day PADI Discover Scuba Diving session, including equipment hire. To dive or snorkel independently, count on paying around 40NIS to rent a snorkel, mask and fins (a wetsuit costs an additional 40NIS to 60NIS), and 155NIS for a full scuba set; a tank refill is 25NIS.

Hundreds of millions of migrating birds pass through Eilat twice a year as they fly between Europe and Africa. The best place to spot them is the International **Birding & Research Center in Eilat** (IBRCE; Eilat Birding Center; Map p253; ☎050 767-1290; www.eilatbirds.com; ⏱park 24hr, office 8am-4pm Sun-Thu) FREE, 6km northeast of town.

★Coral Beach Nature Reserve DIVE SITE
(Map p253; ☎08-632-6422; www.parks.org.il; adult/child 35/21NIS; ⏱9am-5pm or 6pm, closes 1hr earlier Fri, last entrance 1hr before closing; 🚌15) The crystal-clear waters of this 1km-long reserve are the best place on the Israeli Red Sea coast for snorkelling. Snorkelling kit can be rented for 23NIS (100NIS deposit). For picnic supplies, head to the supermarket across the street.

Underwater Observatory Marine Park AQUARIUM
(Map p253; ☎08-636-4200; www.coralworld.co.il; Coral Beach; adult/child 109/89NIS; ⏱ticket sales 8.30am-4pm, site open to 6pm summer, to sundown rest of year; 🚌15) The standout feature of this aquarium complex, which is hugely popular with families, is the **observatory**, which takes you 12m below the surface of the Red Sea into the living reef for a scuba diver's view of the fish and corals. Other highlights include **Shark World**, a 7m-deep tank that's home to sharks and stingrays, and the excellent **Rare Fish Aquarium**. Tickets are valid for three days, but to come back you need to get a photo re-entry ticket (free).

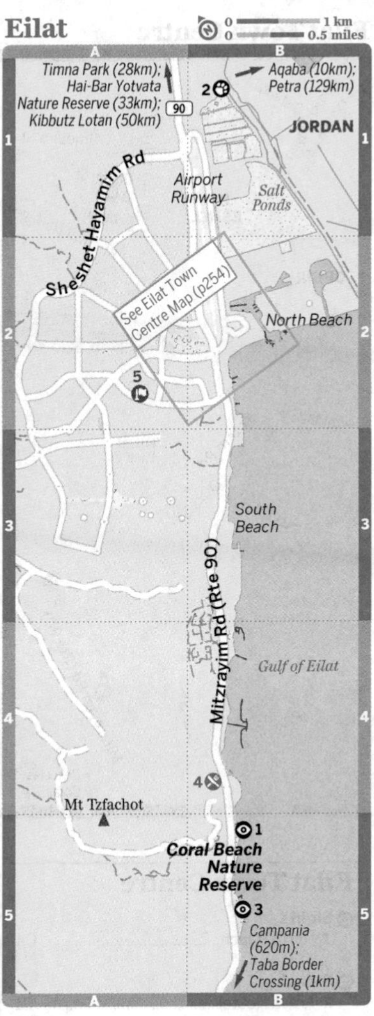

Eilat

Top Sights
1 Coral Beach Nature Reserve B5

Sights
2 International Birding & Research Center in Eilat B1
3 Underwater Observatory Marine Park B5

Eating
4 Fish Market B4

Information
5 Egyptian Consulate A2

Eilat Town Centre

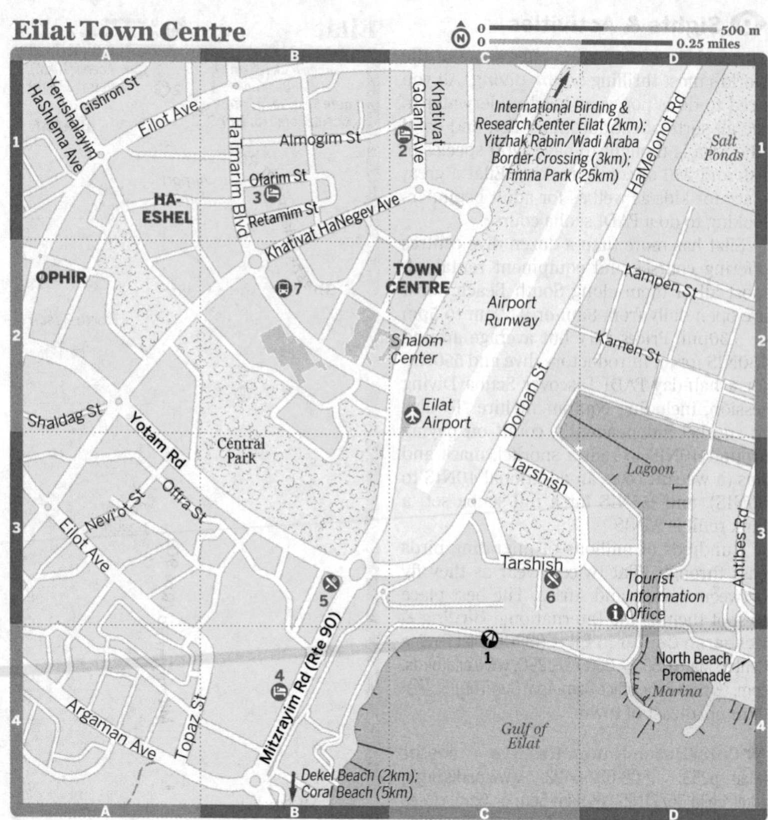

Eilat Town Centre

Sights

1 North Beach C4

Sleeping

2 Arava Hostel C1
3 Blue Hotel B1
4 Eilat Youth Hostel & Guest House B4

Eating

5 New Tourist Center B3
6 Pastory C3

Transport

7 Central Bus Station B2

North Beach BEACH

(Map p254; 24hr) Pebbly North Beach and its promenade are often very crowded – for some people, that's one of the main draws. This is by far the most popular place in Eilat to see and be seen. The promenade's restaurants, cafes and bars are another enticement and ensure that the area is full of action until the wee hours. Public showers, bathrooms and a few changing booths can be found at the edge of the beach.

Sleeping

Eilat has about 50 hotels with 15,000 hotel rooms. Some of the most comfortable are along North Beach Promenade; prices tend to drop as you move inland. Inexpensive but decent places can be found on the side streets around the central bus station, 1.5km northwest of North Beach. Prices rise by about 25% at weekends and 50% (or more) during Israeli school holidays and in July and August.

Arava Hostel HOSTEL $

(Map p254; 08-637-4687; www.aravahostel.com; 106 Almogim St; dm/s/d 80/200/240NIS; @) The only place in Eilat with an authentic backpacker vibe, the ILH-affiliated, 100-bed Arava won't win any awards for its spartan rooms and dark, cramped dorms, or for its location. There are compensations, though: a date-palm-shaded front garden that's perfect for sunset beers, a communal kitchen, laundry facilities (20NIS per load) and free parking.

Blue Hotel HOTEL $$
(Map p254; ☎08-632-6601; www.bluehotel.co.il; 123 Ofarim St; s 216-342NIS, d 240-380NIS; @📶) Run by a friendly Israeli-Irish couple, this place has 34 well-priced rooms – reached via open-air hallways – that are nothing to write home about but do have useful amenities (fridge, cable TV and kettle). There are bicycles for hire and guests receive discounts on diving packages with the Reef Diving Group.

Eilat Youth Hostel & Guest House HOSTEL $$
(Map p254; ☎02-594-5605; www.iyha.org.il; 18 Mitzrayim Rd/Rte 90; dm 126-155NIS, s 300-376NIS, d 380-500NIS; @📶) This recently renovated 107-room hostel is an extremely attractive option, thanks to its location and its modern, clean and comfortable rooms and dorms. Often hosts school groups. There are plans to add a pool.

Eating

Visitor-oriented restaurants, cafes and pubs can be found on the North Beach Promenade and on the streets around the lagoons. The **New Tourist Center** (Map p254; cnr Rte 90 & Yotam Rd; mains 35-110NIS) is home to a number of reasonably priced eateries. For self-caterers, a number of little supermarkets can be found a block inland from North Beach and at various points along South Beach (Mitzrayim Rd/Rte 90).

★ **Pastory** ITALIAN $$
(Map p254; ☎08-634-5111; http://pastory.co.il; 7 Tarshish St; mains 48-158NIS; ⏲1-11pm) This family-friendly place behind the Leonardo Plaza Hotel serves antipasti platters packed with flavourful morsels, al dente pasta with rustic sauces, piping-hot pizza with quality toppings and an irresistible array of homemade desserts and gelato.

★ **Fish Market** SEAFOOD $$$
(Shuk HaDagim; Map p253; ☎08-637-9830; http://shokdagim.rest.co.il; Almog Beach, Rte 90; mains incl salads 79-119NIS; ⏲12.30-11pm; 📶) Fresh fish from the Red Sea, the Mediterranean and Egypt's Nile Delta and beef from the Golan are the stars at this Greek-inflected fish restaurant – some say it's Eilat's best. Every meal begins with a selection of Mediterranean salads.

Drinking & Nightlife

The drinking scene in Eilat is largely confined to raucous pubs on and around North Beach and in the New Tourist Center. The club scene is healthy, but venues have short lifespans and hot spots change every season – staff at your hotel should be able to give you the low-down.

Information

The extremely helpful **tourist information office** (Map p254; ☎08-630-9111; www.goisrael.com; Bridge House, North Beach Promenade; ⏲8.30am-5pm Sun-Thu, 8am-1pm Fri; 📶) answers questions, supplies free maps and brochures, and gives away secondhand books in English, French, German and other languages. You can use your smartphone to photograph (legally) walking guides to eight area hikes. Has free wi-fi and sockets to charge smartphones and tablets. Free city-run wi-fi is available all over town (download the free Eilat Plus app).

Getting There & Away

The Yitzhak Rabin/Wadi Araba border crossing between Israel and Jordan is about 5km northeast of Eilat, while the Taba border crossing with Egypt is about 9km southwest.

AIR

Ramon International Airport (www.iaa.gov.il), in the Arava Valley 18km north of Eilat, will replace Eilat's city centre **airport** (Map p254; ☎08-637-1515; www.iaa.gov.il) and **Ovda Airport** (☎08-367-5387; www.iaa.gov.il), long used by charter carriers from Europe. It will also serve as Israel's second full-service international airport.

Both Arkia (www.arkia.com) and Israir (www.israirairlines.com) link Eilat with Ben Gurion Airport (35 minutes) and Tel Aviv's Sde Dov several times a day. Arkia also goes to Haifa. Prices vary depending on demand, ranging from as low as 86NIS to 420NIS one way to/from Tel Aviv.

Low-cost airlines such as Finnair, Ryanair, Scandinavian, Transavia and Wizz offer nonstop services to Eilat from a wide variety of European cities. Many services are seasonal (winter and spring).

BUS

Eilat's **central bus station** (Map p254; www.bus.co.il; HaTemarim Blvd), about 1.5km northwest of North Beach, has excellent bus connections to the rest of Israel.

Dead Sea (Egged bus 444; 42.50NIS, 2¾ hours to Ein Bokek, eight per day Sunday to Thursday, three on Friday, three Saturday afternoon and evening)

Jerusalem (Egged buses 444 and 445; 70NIS, 4¼ to five hours, 10 on Sunday, four daily Monday to Wednesday, seven on Thursday, three on Friday, three Saturday afternoon and evening) Bus 445 is an express service.

Mitzpe Ramon (Egged bus 392; 39.50NIS, 2¼ hours, four to six daily Sunday to Thursday, one Friday)

Tel Aviv (Egged buses 390, 393, 394 and 790; 70NIS, five to 5¾ hours, every hour or two) From Sunday to Thursday, there are departures from 4am or 5am to 7pm or 8pm, with a red-eye at 1am. On Friday, the last bus leaves around 3pm; service resumes on Saturday at 11am. To reserve a seat (highly recommended), go to www.egged.co.il (click 'Book Tickets Online') or call *2800; reservations can be made up to 14 days ahead.

Getting Around

Egged bus 15 leaves from the central bus station and travels via the North Beach hotels and the South Beach beaches to the Taba border crossing with Egypt (4.20NIS, 36 minutes) every hour from about 8am to 9pm Sunday to Thursday, 8am to 3pm or 4pm Friday and 9am to 7pm Saturday. Travelling north from Taba, the bus changes its number to 16. A taxi from the city centre all the way to the border crossing costs 50NIS to 60NIS.

WEST BANK

الضفة الغربية הגדה המערבית

You hear the word 'welcome' a lot in the West Bank. Whether it is shouted by a vendor in a bustling souq, said with a smile over a plate of falafel or roared over Arabic music blasting from a taxi, Palestinians always want to make tourists feel appreciated.

Given its association with political strife and violence, this can come as a surprise to first-time visitors. But while the West Bank is a political tinderbox, it is something else too: an addictive tapestry of bustling souqs and chaotic streets, of rolling hills and chalky desertscapes, of thick, black coffee served in porcelain cups and of cities so steeped in history that it is humbling.

Ramallah

רמאללה رام الله

☎02 / POP 65,000

In a region where the lives of cities can often be measured in terms of millennia, Ramallah – little more than a hamlet until the late 19th century – is a veritable new kid on the block. But the de facto capital of the Palestinian Territories has made up for lost time: today it is a vibrant, bustling and cosmopolitan city that is the West Bank's political and economic heart.

Sights

★**Yasser Arafat Museum** MUSEUM

(Muqata'a; Al Itha'a St; 5NIS; ⏲10am-6pm Tue-Sun) Next to the ornate tomb of the late Palestinian leader Yasser Arafat is a new museum that bears his name. Divided into two parts, the first half traces Arafat's life alongside that of his Fatah movement and other Palestinian factions.

Those less interested in Palestinian politics may prefer the second section, where Arafat spent his final years under Israeli siege from 2001 to 2004. The restored facility includes his bedroom, where khaki uniforms still hang in the wardrobe.

Dar Zahran Heritage Building GALLERY

(www.darzahran.org; ⏲11am-7pm Mon-Sat) FREE One of Ramallah's oldest buildings, Dar Zahran was restored and converted into a gallery-cum-museum in 1990, and plans are now under way for a coffee shop on the upper floor. Built 250 years ago when Ramallah was little more than a hamlet, the building has photographs from as far back as 1850 and exhibitions of contemporary Palestinian art.

Sleeping

★**Area D Hostel** HOSTEL $

(☎056 934-9042; http://ramallahhostel.com; Vegetable Market St; dm/d/apt 70/200/250NIS; P @ ☏) Area D is one of only a handful of international standard hostels in the West Bank and by far the best for visitors to Ramallah. Its spotless dorms and double rooms are basic, but the shared lounge is a great place to relax, meet other travellers and plan excursions.

The hostel is located above Ramallah's service taxi garage, opposite the bus station for Jerusalem. Area D is a reliable place to organise tours to other cities, including Hebron, and staff have a wealth of information about travel inside the West Bank and beyond.

Hostel in Ramallah HOSTEL $

(☎02-296-3555; www.hostelinramallah.com; Al Nuzha St; dm/s/d 50/105/130NIS; ☏) This quirky hostel a five-minute walk from Yasser Arafat Sq is spread over three floors of

WORTH A TRIP

TAYBEH

Taybeh, on a remote hillside 15km outside of Ramallah, was just another West Bank village until local lad Nadim Khoury returned from university in the US and decided to start brewing beer. Now Taybeh beer has become an empire, sold throughout the West Bank (and increasingly even over the Green Line in Israel) as well as in Germany, Sweden and the US.

Taybeh's annual **Octoberfest** attracts thousands of locals, expatriates and tourists and with its new winery and hotel, the Khoury family are hoping to encourage visitors to spend a little longer in the village, believed to be the place Jesus and his disciples stayed in the hours before his death.

To get there, take a shared taxi from the service taxi garage below Area D Hostel in Ramallah.

Taybeh Brewing Company (☎02-289-8868; www.taybehbeer.net; ⊙8am-4pm) offers free tours daily, often given by master-brewer Madees Khoury herself. Visitors can observe the beer-making – and occasionally bottling – process and learn about how this tiny Christian village ended up exporting beer across the West Bank, Israel and the wider world.

an apartment building, with a half-dozen dorms and a range of single and double rooms. Staffed by a rotating cast of international volunteers, it has one of the best roof terraces in the city.

Millennium Ramallah HOTEL $$$
(☎02-298-5888; Emil Habibi St; s/d US$185/200; P 🛜 ≋) Formerly the Mövenpick (and still referred to as such by taxi drivers), the Millennium is probably Ramallah's smartest hotel and the go-to place for business travellers. It has huge rooms, excellent staff and great facilities, including a gym and pool (summer only).

Eating

★La Vie Cafe INTERNATIONAL $$
(☎02-296-4115; Castel St; mains 35-70NIS; ⊙10am-midnight Sat-Thu, 4pm-midnight Fri) Tucked away on a quiet street just 10 minutes' walk from Al Manara, this place has a diverse menu of pasta, pizza and sandwiches, with much of its produce grown in owners Saleh and Morgan's roof garden. On weekends, La Vie is a popular nightspot, serving a range of beers, wines and cocktails.

Pronto Resto-Café ITALIAN $$
(Al Muntazah; mains 45-75NIS; ⊙7am-11pm) It's no longer the only place to get pizza in Ramallah, but it is easy to see how Pronto has survived since 1997 in a city where many restaurants barely last a year. From the fish (from Jaffa) to the wine (from Bethlehem), Bassem Khoury and family prioritise local ingredients and Pronto remains the only place for real Italian food in Ramallah.

Drinking & Nightlife

★Snowbar BAR
(☎02-296-5571; www.al-snowbar.com; ⊙noon-late May-Oct) For two decades, Snowbar has been the place to see and be seen in Ramallah. Although it has an often deserved reputation as a late-night party spot, on weeknights Snowbar has a chilled-out vibe with a mostly local crowd lounging over cocktails, beers and shisha. It's a 20NIS ride from downtown Ramallah; all the taxi drivers know it.

★Berlin Pub COCKTAIL BAR
(⊙5pm-late; 🛜) Berlin is the latest hip spot on Ramallah's ever-changing nightlife scene. The barman trained in Germany before opening this tiny cocktail bar and pub and prides himself on the lack of a menu, preferring punters to just tell him what they like.

Radio BAR
(⊙noon-late; 🛜) Ramallah veterans who remember the infamous Beit Aneeseh can rest assured that Radio, located in the same building, is filling the gap that the late-night bar left when it was shut down in 2014. Radio has a similar grungy vibe, with live music, shisha and cheap beers either inside or in the garden.

Entertainment

Al Kamandjati ARTS CENTRE
(☎02-297-3101; www.alkamandjati.com; Old City) This small conservatory, which features an ancient arch with an edgy, modern copper entryway, offers intimate concerts and recitals.

Khalil Sakakini Centre CULTURAL CENTRE
(☎02-298-7374; www.sakakini.org; Al Muntazah) Hosts art exhibitions by the locally and internationally renowned, along with a whole host of other cultural pursuits. Check the website for upcoming events.

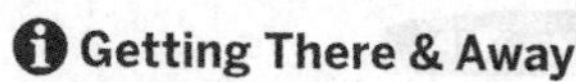

Getting There & Away

From the old Arab bus station in East Jerusalem, take bus 218 or 219 to Ramallah (30 minutes).

As a rule of thumb, the smaller the bus, the faster the journey. Buses to/from Ramallah operate from 6am to 9.30pm or 10pm in summer

CHECKPOINTS

Checkpoints (in Hebrew, *machsomim*) control the flow of travellers between the West Bank and Israel. There are also some checkpoints inside the West Bank, although these tend to be less stable, shifting locations, shutting down altogether or popping up in new locations.

Most checkpoints are run by the Israel Defence Forces (IDF), although some have been outsourced to private contractors. The latter tend to be more troublesome and more likely to question foreigners and search their bags.

Operating hours of checkpoints vary, but most of the major ways in and out of the West Bank are now open 24 hours; these include Checkpoint 300 in Bethlehem and Qalandia, near Ramallah. Jalameh, north of Jenin, is only open 8am to 7pm.

In general, travellers are not checked when going into the West Bank – only when travelling from the West Bank back into Israel.

Foreign-passport holders are allowed to travel through IDF checkpoints into areas under the control of the Palestinian Authority, but by military order, Israeli citizens are forbidden from doing so.

There is no cost involved with crossing a checkpoint, and foreign-passport holders do not need any special documentation. Just show your passport and visa and put your bags through an X-ray machine. The procedure is generally fast, but with waiting time you can expect to be at a checkpoint for 15 to 20 minutes (or longer if lines have formed).

Try to avoid passing through a checkpoint in the early morning (7am to 9am) or on Muslim or Jewish holidays because of long lines.

Foreigners can take a vehicle into and out of the West Bank (if you've got a rental car, make sure your insurance policy covers travel to the Palestinian Territories – most don't), but there can sometimes be delays upon your return to Israel because the soldiers may inspect the vehicle for explosives.

The following are some of the main checkpoints into and out of the West Bank:

Qalandia Between Jerusalem and Ramallah. Use this checkpoint for Ramallah, Nablus and Jenin. Qalandia is one of the busiest checkpoints, and it sports some grim metal corrals and locking turnstiles of the sort you'd expect to see at a maximum-security prison. Be aware that Qalandia is occasionally the scene of violence between Israeli soldiers and stone-throwing Palestinian youths, particularly on Fridays or when political tension is high.

Checkpoint 300 Located south of Jerusalem at the entrance to Rachel's Tomb. One road leads to the checkpoint for cars and one for pedestrians. This is an indoor checkpoint, and the conditions are better than at Qalandia. It is open 24/7.

Bethlehem (highway) You will go through this checkpoint if you take bus 231 from Bethlehem. It resembles a toll gate, and security is very light. Tourists may remain on the bus during the passport check (Palestinian passengers are asked to line up outside the bus). It's open 24/7.

Jalameh Located 10km south of Afula, this checkpoint is one of the best in terms of ease and accessibility. However, long lines have been reported, and it is only open between 8am and 7pm.

Abu Dis This checkpoint connects East Jerusalem to Abu Dis, from where travellers can connect to Jericho. It is a pedestrian-only checkpoint and is usually closed at night.

For more details on the conditions at individual checkpoints, visit the website of the left-wing Israeli group Machsom Watch (www.machsomwatch.org).

or until 7pm in winter, after which you can take a service taxi from Ramallah to Qalandia and then a taxi to Jerusalem, or vice versa.

You will not need to get off the bus on the way into the West Bank, but on the way out, all passengers disembark and go through airport-style security. Have your passport and Israeli visa ready to show the soldiers behind the bullet-proof glass. Also hold onto your ticket to show to the driver once you're on the other side of the checkpoint.

The bus station in Ramallah is a five-minute walk from Al Manara Sq and a two-minute walk from the service garage, where shared taxis leave to destinations throughout the West Bank.

Getting Around

Everything within the Ramallah area is 10 minutes or less by private taxi and should cost 15NIS to 20NIS, but agree on the price with the driver before setting off.

A cheaper way of getting around during the day is by service taxi. You can hail them on any street and ask for your destination. Most will drop you off at Al Manara for 3NIS.

Jericho & Around יריחו اريحا

02 / POP 20,300

Whether you are walking around ancient ruins or observing epic monasteries carved into the Judean mountains, it is impossible not to feel a sense of history in Jericho, which is proudly dubbed the 'world's oldest continuously inhabited city' by the local authorities.

It is no idle boast: archaeological evidence traces settlement here back more than 10,000 years, and the ashes of the empires that have fought and conquered Jericho over the millennia can be seen throughout the city.

Sights

The **Tree of Zacchaeus**, on Ein Al Sultan St, is said to be the very same sycamore that Zacchaeus, a wealthy publican, climbed 2000 years ago for a better view of the preaching Jesus (Luke 19:1-10).

Tel Al Sultan RUINS

(Ancient Jericho; adult/student/child 10/7/5NIS; 8am-5pm) It is impossible not feel a sense of history strolling around the mounds and ruins at Tel Al Sultan, where remains of dwellings and fortifications dating back some 10,000 years have been unearthed. You will see what look like sand dunes and stairways (the oldest known stairways in the world); underneath, the layers of civilisation beneath go back even further into the mists of time.

Mount of Temptation & Monastery of the Qurantul RELIGIOUS SITE

(8am-4pm Mon-Fri, to 2pm Sat & Sun) FREE One of Jericho's – indeed, the entire West Bank's – most impressive sights is the Monastery of Qurantul, built on the spot where the Bible says Jesus resisted Satan after his 40-day fast in the desert.

It is an incredible feat of engineering, cut into the cliff face with dramatic views over the Dead Sea to Jordan.

Opening times for the monastery are sporadic, but as with all tourist attractions in the Palestinian Territories, it is best to go early – or at least a couple of hours before sunset. Note that the caretaker may lock the door if he is showing big groups around, so it is worth hanging around a few minutes if you find it closed.

Cable cars (www.jericho-cablecar.com; 60NIS; 8am-7pm Mon-Thu, to 10pm Fri) stop just before the monastery, and even the short climb up the stairs to the front gate can be a struggle in the midday heat. The juice sellers and a couple of restaurants provide a good spot to catch your breath.

★**Hisham's Palace** RUINS

(Khirbet Al Mafjar; 10NIS; 8am-6pm) A short drive north of Tel Al Sultan, this is a spot not to be missed. The sprawling winter hunting retreat of Caliph Hisham Ibn Abd al Malik must have been magnificent on its creation in the 8th century, with its baths, mosaic floors and pillars – so much so that archaeologists have labelled it the 'Versailles of the Middle East'. It was not fated to last, however – it was destroyed by an earthquake soon after its creation.

St George's Monastery MONASTERY

(9am-1pm) FREE The spectacular St George's Monastery is a must-see in **Wadi Qelt**, built into the cliff face in the 5th century. The paintings inside the main chapel are worth the walk, and parts of the original mosaic floors are visible below perspex screens. Up another flight of stairs there is a beautiful cave chapel.

From the car park, it is a gruelling 10-minute hike to the monastery – expect to be hassled by donkey-taxi vendors the entire way.

ISRAELI SETTLEMENTS

Israeli colonies set up in the Palestinian Territories are most often referred to as 'settlements'. There are approximately 350,000 Israeli settlers in the West Bank, living in more than 100 settlements, with hundreds of thousands more living in parts of Jerusalem captured by Israel in 1967.

Settlements range in size from a collection of caravans on a remote hilltop to large urban areas, such as Ma'ale Adumim near Jerusalem, home to tens of thousands of Israelis and now effectively a suburb of Jerusalem. There are a variety of reasons cited by settlers for why they live on the West Bank: most commonly, cheaper housing prices than in Israel and, among the religious, the fulfilment of biblical prophecy and an extension of the will of God.

Under almost all interpretations of international law, which forbids the transfer of civilians to land under military occupation, Israeli settlements in the West Bank and in East Jerusalem are illegal. The Israeli right disputes this interpretation of international law. Key complaints against Israeli settlements are that they often occupy private Palestinian land (as opposed to state-owned land), divert precious water resources from surrounding Palestinian cities, towns and villages and, most significantly, fragment the territory of the West Bank, making the establishment of a coherent, contiguous and viable Palestinian state impossible.

The US and European Union have declared the settlements an obstacle to peace, but Israeli Prime Minister Benjamin Netanyahu's right-wing coalition government has continued to construct housing in Israeli settlements in the West Bank and in East Jerusalem.

To find out more, visit the websites of Palestinian NGO Al Haq (http://alhaq.mits.ps) or left-wing Israeli organisation B'Tselem (www.btselem.org). For a settler perspective, the Israeli settlement of Gush Etzion, near Bethlehem, has a visitor centre and museum (www.gush-etzion.org.il).

Sleeping & Eating

★Sami Youth Hostel GUESTHOUSE $

(☎02-232-4220; eyad_alalem@live.com; r 120-150NIS;) One of the West Bank's best budget stays, Sami Youth Hostel is nestled deep in the refugee camp on the outskirts of Jericho, with a dozen clean and quiet rooms in an enigmatically furnished two-storey building. By far the best thing about Sami Youth Hostel is Sami himself, who speaks fluent English and treats his guests more like family members than customers.

Oasis Hotel HOTEL $$$

(☎02-231-1200; www.oasis-jericho.ps; s 450-550NIS, d 550-650NIS; @) Formerly the Intercontinental (the logo of which is still visible on the side of the building), the Oasis Hotel is expensive, but its clean modern rooms, helpful staff and choice of two swimming pools make it a popular high-end choice. Its location, just off the Jerusalem–Jericho road, make it a great hub for exploring not only Jericho but also the Dead Sea and beyond.

★Abu Omar MIDDLE EASTERN $

(Ein Al Sultan St; mains 20-50NIS; ⊙6am-midnight) Next to the main square, this local favourite serves the best roast chicken in the West Bank, period. It is double the price for a sit-down meal versus taking away, but grabbing a table is well worth it.

Al Essawe MIDDLE EASTERN $

(Main Sq; mains 15-45NIS; ⊙6am-11pm) On a corner overlooking Jericho's main square, Al Essawe's lovely 2nd-floor terrace is an excellent place to watch the world go by. The owner speaks English, and the restaurant serves the usual Arabic fare: kebabs, falafel and mezze. Don't miss the fresh lemonade.

Information

Tourist Information Centre (☎02-231-2607; Main Sq; ⊙8am-5pm;) An essential first stop for independent travellers. The staff at this excellent booth in the city's main square speak perfect English and are a wealth of information on what to see and how to get there. It can arrange tours, recommend hotels and help travellers plan their day, or longer stay, in Jericho.

Getting There & Away

Service taxis from Jerusalem to Jericho go from the Abu Dis checkpoint (12NIS), but are awkward to catch and travellers often opt to go via Ramallah (18NIS) or Bethlehem (21NIS).

Alternatively, you can hire a cab driver in Bethlehem or Ramallah for a day trip to Jericho and its surroundings. Most drivers will ask for at least 200NIS to 250NIS a day. If you hire a taxi in Jerusalem, it can be double that.

Jericho is not a very walkable city away from downtown: it is dusty and humid and many of its sights are on opposite sides of the city. Service taxis (about 3NIS) serve many of the sights, but it is quicker and easier to negotiate a rate with a local driver (20NIS to 30NIS an hour is fair).

Even if you only visit Jericho for the day, do not forget your passport as Israeli checkpoints on the road out of the city are common.

Bethlehem בית לחם بيت لحم

☎02 / POP 47,000

Bethlehem may no longer be the 'little town' of Christmas carols, but you don't have to go far in what is now a pulsating city to see the stories of Mary and Joseph, stars, mangers and a saviour hardwired into every paving stone, street and church.

Like Jerusalem, every Christian denomination – Lutheran, Syriac, Catholic, Orthodox – is present here and the city positively hums with activity, its winding streets congested with traffic and its main square filled with snap-happy pilgrims scrambling to keep up with their guides.

But there is plenty to see and do for even for the nonreligious. There's a lively Old City and bazaar and numerous sites around town, including the epic Mar Saba Monastery. Many tourists also come for the street art – particularly several stencils by British street artist Banksy – that have turned the Israeli Separation Wall that now divides Bethlehem from Jerusalem into a vast canvas.

Sights

Old City

The narrow limestone streets and exotic shopfronts of Manger Sq and the Old City are a scene from another age, particularly Pope Paul VI St, Star St and the narrow alleys connecting the two. Visit on a Sunday to experience some church services. Most in attendance will be Palestinians and resident monks and nuns, but visitors are welcome to attend or stop in for a few moments of contemplation.

Church of the Nativity CHURCH

(6.30am-7.30pm spring-autumn, to 6pm winter) FREE For the millions of pilgrims who descend on the Holy Land every year, the Church of the Nativity is the main reason for visiting Bethlehem. The church, believed to be built on the spot where Jesus was born, was originally commissioned in AD 326 by Emperor Constantine and has seen innumerable transformations since. A restoration project is under way to preserve the building.

To really get the most out of a visit, negotiate a price from one of the handful of tour guides you'll find milling about outside.

You'll have to duck to get through the tiny Ottoman-era door into the church, aptly named the **Door of Humility**. At the front of the nave, descend the stairs to enter the **Grotto of the Nativity**. Atmospherically lantern-lit and redolent with mystery, a **14-pointed silver star** marks the spot where Jesus is said to have been born.

St Catherine's Church CHURCH

(Manger Sq; 6.30am-7.30pm spring-autumn, to 6pm winter) FREE Midnight Mass at this pink-toned church, next door to the Church of the Nativity, is broadcast across the world on Christmas Eve, but there's nothing like being there in person for an atmospheric – if rather lengthy – Christmas experience.

Bethlehem Museum MUSEUM

(☎02-274-2589; www.arabwomenunion.org; Star St; 10NIS; 8am-1pm & 2-5pm Mon-Sat) The museum, housed in a typical 19th-century Palestinian home, is made up of three rooms recreated as a traditional Bethlehem family abode, with many exhibits dating back more than 200 years. Your entrance fee gets you a rather cursory tour by one of the staff, as well access to the gift shop, where you can buy embroidery produced by the Bethlehem Arab Women's Union.

Outskirts of Town

Shepherds' Field PARK

(9am-3pm Mon-Sat) FREE If you've always wondered where exactly 'shepherds watched their flocks by night', drop into Shepherds' Field, a parklike area just outside Beit Sahour. As well as the strollable grounds, you'll find a Byzantine cave housing a chapel and the 1953 Italian-designed Church of the Angels.

Around Bethlehem, Ramallah & Jericho

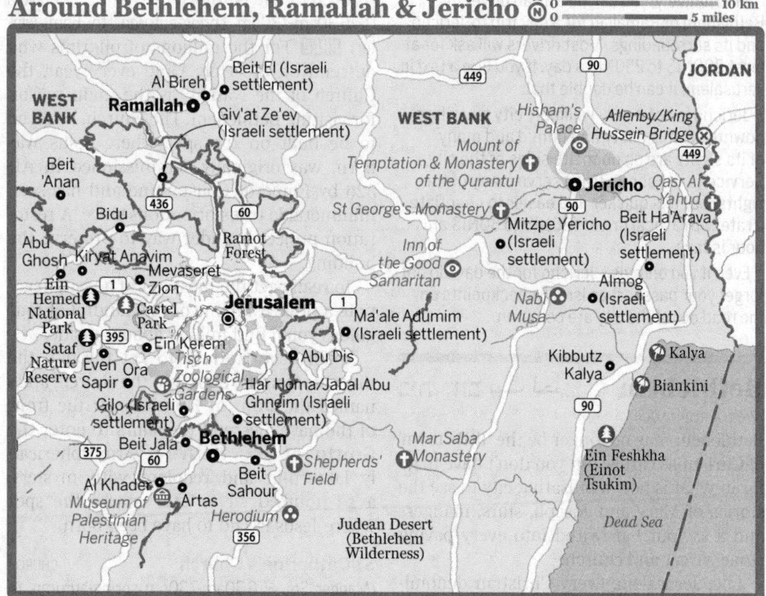

Museum of Palestinian Heritage MUSEUM
(8am-4pm Sat-Thu) FREE This impressive museum in the new complex of buildings opposite Soloman's Pools is the personal collection of one man, Ishaq Al Hroub, who gathered this remarkable selection of traditional Palestinian exhibits over five decades in his basement in Dura, near Hebron.

Around Bethlehem

★**Mar Saba Monastery** MONASTERY
(8am-5pm Sat-Tue & Thu) A must-see on any journey through the Holy Land is Mar Saba Monastery, a bleak and beautiful 20km drive east of Bethlehem (beyond Beit Sahour).

Women must view the phenomenal cliff-clinging copper-domed hermitage, founded in AD 439, from the opposite slope, but men are permitted inside, where tours are available with one of the 15 monks in residence.

Herodium PALACE
(Herodion; adult/child 29/15NIS; 8am-5pm Apr-Sep, 8am-4pm Oct-Mar) King Herod's spectacular fortress-palace, Herodium, built between 23 and 15 BC, was known through the centuries to Arab inhabitants as the Mountain of Paradise. It rises from the Judean Desert like a flat-topped caricature of a volcano (the top is actually an extension of the natural hill, hollowed out to hold Herod's palace), 9km south of Beit Sahour.

Sleeping

Since most hotels in Bethlehem cater to a pilgrim crowd, expect to pay 30% to 50% more at Christmas or Easter time, and book your room well in advance.

Ibdaa Cultural Centre Guesthouse GUESTHOUSE $
(02-277-6444; www.ibdaa48.org; Dheisheh Refugee Camp; dm/d 50/100NIS; @) A great little hostel in the cultural centre of the same name, Ibdaa is located in the narrow streets of Dheisheh refugee camp, a 20-minute drive out of town towards Hebron. Facilities are basic, but as a window into Palestinian life away from the tourist hordes, it is unparalleled.

★**Hosh Al Syrian Guesthouse** BOUTIQUE HOTEL $$
(02-274-7529; www.hoshalsyrian.com; d $70-140;) Every now and then a hotel comes along and raises the game, and Fadi Kattan's beautiful Hosh Al Syrian Guesthouse has done just that. Tucked away in the Syrian quarter, a two-minute walk from Manger Sq, some rooms have terraces overlooking the roofs of the Old City.

Manger Square Hotel HOTEL $$
(www.mangersquarehotel.com; Manger St; s/d/tr US$90/130/150;) This four-star hotel over the road from Manger Sq was built in 2012 and is excellent value considering the location. Some rooms have views over the valley behind Bethlehem, others over the Old City. Staff are polite and helpful and in summer there is a rooftop pool.

Eating

For fast food, stroll along Manger St or head up to the small souq just off Pope Paul VI St. Here you'll find fist-size falafel, sizzling shawarma and lots of tempting produce for picnics or self-catering.

Afteem MIDDLE EASTERN $
(Manger Sq; mains 6-35NIS) A Bethlehem institution for decades, top-notch hummus and *masabacha* (warm hummus with whole chickpeas) are just two of the dishes on the menu at this popular eatery close to Manger Sq.

Peace Center Restaurant SANDWICHES, ITALIAN $
(Manger Sq; mains 20-45NIS; 9am-11pm Mon-Sat) This Manger Sq eatery is the place to go for traditional Palestinian food downtown, with a range of dishes including *makloubeh* ('upside down' chicken, under rice cooked with nuts and spices) and *mansaf* (chicken or lamb over rice with a thick, meaty broth) on its varied and reasonable menu.

★**Hosh Al Jasmine** MIDDLE EASTERN $$
(Beit Jala: mains 30-55NIS) This local restaurant on a hillside in Beit Jala serves homely Palestinian food, beer and wine on the grounds of an organic farm, with hens clucking, birds singing and fantastic views over the hills of the southern West Bank. Lunch and dinner are served on rickety wooden tables perched on the very edge of the valley, while couches and tree-house-like raised platforms are a great place to relax and enjoy a shisha. The best time to come is at sunset.

Drinking & Nightlife

★**Rewined** BAR
(7pm-late Thu-Sun) This uber-trendy haunt a 15-minute walk downhill from the Old City serves a variety of local beer and wine, as well as cocktails and shisha, to a mostly local crowd relaxing on couches on a terrace overlooking Manger St.

Information

The information desk at the **Peace Center** (02-276-6677; 8am-3pm Mon-Thu & Sat;) gives away city maps and provides helpful hints on accommodation and transport. It often holds art and photography exhibitions.

Getting There & Away

Bus 231 from Jerusalem to Bethlehem (30 minutes) departs every 15 minutes between 6am and 9pm (until 6.30pm in winter) from the Damascus Gate bus station, via Beit Jala.

Alternatively, take bus 234 from Jerusalem to the main Bethlehem checkpoint (Checkpoint 300) and get a taxi into Bethlehem (20NIS).

The best way to get from Bethlehem to the sites that surround it is by taxi, and drivers will clamour to offer visits to multiple sites for a fixed price (something around 50NIS an hour is standard, but you'll need to haggle). It is actually pretty good value, especially if you are in a small group, and many drivers speak good English and

DON'T MISS

WALLED-OFF HOTEL

For 10 years British street artist Banksy has been stencilling his work on and around the wall that separates Bethlehem from Jerusalem. Now he's opened the **Walled Off Hotel** (02-277-1322; www.walledoffhotel.com; 182 Caritas St; dm US$30, d US$215-265, ste US$965; P) opposite the wall that promises 'the worst view in the world'. The view may be unconventional, but the hotel itself is slick and stylish – and surreal (one suite has a tiki bar).

Home to a museum, a piano bar and an art gallery, Walled Off also boasts some of the most high-end dorms in the Middle East, if not the world, with fresh towels, mini-fridges and in-room music.

The hotel was built in secret and was only due to stay open for a year, but in September 2017 began taking bookings for the winter season, suggesting that it may remain. The hotel offers useful and informative tours to nearby Aida refugee camp as well as to other nearby cities, such as Jericho and Hebron.

can answer your questions. Drivers generally congregate outside Checkpoint 300, Manger Sq or the 231 bus stop to Jerusalem.

Nablus שכם نابلس

☎09 / POP 126,000

Set between Mt Gerizim and Mt Ebal, Nablus (Shechem in Hebrew) has historically been an exporter of olive oil, cotton and carob, but is best known these days for its soap factories, olive-wood carving and *kunafeh*, a syrupy wheat and cheese pastry famous throughout the Middle East.

Nablus today is a bustling, exciting and vibrant metropolis, with a stunningly beautiful Old City that rivals Jerusalem's – not least because of the lack of tour groups clogging its narrow alleyways.

Sights & Activities

The focal point for visitors to Nablus is **Al Qasaba** (Casbah or Old City), where you'll find an Ottoman-era rabbit warren of shops, stalls and pastry stands, spice sacks and vegetable mounds. Amid the clamour are dozens of contemplative mosques, including the **Al Kebir Mosque** (7am-10pm, closed during prayers). For more information on things to do and see, go to www.nablusguide.com.

Jacob's Well CHURCH
(donations appreciated; 8am-noon & 2-4pm) Near the entrance to Balata, the largest refugee camp in the West Bank, is the spot where Christians believe a Samaritan woman offered Jesus a drink of water, before he revealed to her that he was the Messiah (John 4:13–14). A Byzantine church destroyed in the Samaritan revolt of AD 529 was replaced by a Crusader church, which itself fell into ruins in the Middle Ages. The current church, St Photina the Samaritan, was built in the 1860s by the Greek Orthodox Patriarchate.

★**Hammam Al Shifa** BATHHOUSE
(35NIS; men 8am-10pm, women 8am-5pm Sun & Tue only) Hand over your valuables before changing into a towel (or swimming costume, if you have one). The hammam has a hot room (a heated platform for lying on), a sauna and steam room. Massages are not for the faint-hearted. This hammam can be hard to find, but locals will point the way.

Sleeping

★**Khan Al Wakalah** HOTEL $$
(s/d 180/250NIS, d without air-con 100NIS) Set in a beautifully restored Mamluk-Ottoman-era currency exchange in the Old City, Khan Al Wakalah has been a pit stop for travellers between Damascus and Jerusalem (as well as religious pilgrims on their way to Mecca and Medina) for centuries. Its 24 rooms are set around a shaded courtyard with big comfy beds and stunning interiors of wood and traditional Nablus stone.

ISRAEL'S SEPARATION WALL

From 1967 until the Second Intifada (2000–05), most Palestinians were still able to cross into Israel from the West Bank with relative ease, many commuting on a daily basis.

But in the mid-1990s and even more so during the Second Intifada, scores of suicide bombers crossed into Israel from the West Bank, killing hundreds of Israeli civilians. Israel responded with military incursions into areas controlled by the Palestinian Authority, and both security experts and the Israeli public called on the government to build a security barrier.

From the point of view of the Israeli left, a barrier would only further the Oslo Accords process (which had as its goal the establishment of two separate states), along the lines of 'good fences make good neighbours'. But there was opposition, from Jewish settlers not wanting to find themselves on the West Bank side of the wall, and from West Bank Palestinians, whose villages and fields were bisected by the wall, and whose access to Jerusalem the borders made difficult or impossible.

Except in Jerusalem, most of the barrier (about 5% of which is a concrete anti-sniper wall up to 8m high) matches the Green Line (the 1949 armistice between Israel and Jordan) – but only roughly. Quite a few sections loop and scoop around Israeli settlements, separating Palestinians from their communities, businesses, schools and crops. Palestinians call the separation wall the 'Apartheid Wall' and see it as part of a concerted campaign to grab land wherever possible. Israel – where the barrier is seen as a security success – says that the route of the wall can always be modified, for example, if there is a final status accord on borders.

Al Yasmeen Hotel HOTEL $$
(☎09-233-3555; www.alyasmeen.com; s/d/tr US$60/75/90; @☎) Al Yasmeen's location in the heart of the Old City makes it a perennially popular choice with both local and international tourists visiting Nablus. Staff are polite and helpful, and although many of the rooms are in dire need of refurbishment (ask to see a few), they are clean, quiet and affordable.

Eating

The Nablus speciality is sweets, including Arabic pastries, halva, Turkish delight and especially *kunafeh* (vermicelli-like pastry over a cheese base soaked in syrup).

★Al Aqsa ARABIC $
(Old City; kunafeh 6NIS; ⏲1-7.30pm Sat-Thu) This tiny eatery next door to the Al Kebir Mosque in the Casbah is unanimously considered to produce the finest *kunafeh* in the Palestinian Territories. Every day the warm, elastic cheese and syrup-soaked wheat shreds (it works, trust us) is divvied up from huge circular trays and dispensed to a throng of hungry customers. Do as the locals do and eat standing in the street outside.

Al Aqqad ARABIC $
(Hitten St; mains 10-30NIS; ⏲8am-late Sat-Thu) This is a classic sawdust-on-the-floor Nablusi eatery just a short walk from the main gate into the Old City. Staff speak little English but will happily serve you a delicious shawarma pita packed with chicken or lamb, pickles and fiery chilli.

Information

Good Samaritan Center (⏲9am-4pm Sun-Fri) An excellent place for information about the Samaritans and Mt Gerizim.

Getting There & Away

There is no direct bus service to Nablus from Jerusalem. The best way to reach the city is from Ramallah, where buses leave from the central bus station throughout the day. A taxi from Qalandia checkpoint will cost around 100NIS. There is a shared taxi stand to the north of Martyrs Sq, where you can take service taxis to Ramallah and Jenin.

Jenin ג'נין جنين

☎04 / POP 40,000

Jenin possesses a raffish, ramshackle sort of charm but has struggled to recover from the violence of the Second Intifada and today still feels like a city down on its luck. The Jenin Cinema reopened in 2010 with German funding but struggled to make ends meet and was recently demolished, bringing an end to a project that had once heralded the city's rebirth. But whether you are getting lost in the alleys of its packed **souq** for an hour, checking out the world-famous Freedom Theatre or spending a night or two staying with olive-oil farmers in nearby villages, Jenin feels very much off the traditional tourist trail.

> DON'T MISS
>
> **MT GERIZIM**
>
> One of the world's last communities of Samaritans (an ancient religion closely related to Judaism) lives on Mt Gerizim, one of the hills that overlooks Nablus. Learn more about them at the excellent **Samaritan Museum** (☎02-237-0249; 15NIS; ⏲9am-3pm Sun-Fri) before walking the ruins of the **Platform** (adult/child 22/10NIS; ⏲8am-4pm Sat-Thu, to 3pm Fri) – the site of the ruined Samaritan Temple – built on land which the faithful believe was the first created by God. From the centre of Nablus, Mt Gerizim can be reached by taxi in around 10 minutes; it's a 50NIS to 70NIS journey including wait time.

Sights

Masjid Jenin Al Kabir MOSQUE
With its unmissable green roof, Masjid Jenin Al Kabir (Jenin Great Mosque), was built in 1566 on the orders of Fatima Khatun, then wife of the Governor of Damascus. Even given the West Bank's huge roster of impressive mosques, Jenin's is worth a visit both for its Ottoman architecture and as a centrepiece to the **Old City**.

★Freedom Theatre THEATRE
(☎04-250-3345; www.thefreedomtheatre.org; ⏲9am-5pm) FREE Set in Jenin's refugee camp, the Freedom Theatre has persevered in the face of unimaginable odds, including the assassination of its founder, Juliano Mar Khamis, by masked gunmen in 2011. Palestinian filmmakers, actors and directors who worked in the theatre since it was established have also had to put up with significant Israeli restrictions on movement. Despite this, the theatre holds regular performances and visitors are always warmly received. Drop them an email to let them know you are coming.

WORTH A TRIP

HEBRON & THE TOMB OF THE PATRIARCHS

For Jews, Christians and Muslims alike, Hebron (Al Khalil in Arabic) is believed to be the burial place of Abraham, biblical patriarch of all three 'Abrahamic' religions. Sadly, shared faith has done little to improve local relations between the major monotheistic religions, and Hebron has long been a focus of religious violence. In 1929 Arab nationalists attacked the city's Jews – all of them non-Zionist ultra-Orthodox – and killed 67 of them, causing the rest of the community to flee; and in 1994 a Brooklyn-born Israeli settler killed 29 men and boys inside the Ibrahimi Mosque. Jewish settlements within the city centre have also created considerable tension.

The focal point of the city is the **Ibrahimi Mosque/Tomb of the Patriarchs** (8am-4pm Sun-Thu, except during prayers), or Cave of Machpelah, the collective tomb of Abraham, Isaac and Jacob, along with their wives Sarah, Rebecca and Leah (Rachel is believed to be buried near Bethlehem). Be aware of the strict security and separate prayer spaces for Jews and Muslims. When entering the mosque, you will be asked to remove your shoes, and women will be handed a head covering. When entering the synagogue, men will be offered kippas and women a scarf to cover their shoulders.

Canaan Fair Trade FACTORY
(04-243-1991; www.canaanfairtrade.com; 8am-5pm Sun-Thu) Located 2km beyond Buqi'in, this olive-oil factory practises fair-trade policy with its farmers. A tour of the factory includes a tasting, and if you want to get to know the olive farmers, they can set you up with a homestay.

Greek Orthodox Church of St George CHURCH
(8am-6pm, closed 1-3pm Sun) FREE On the periphery of Burqi'in, the Greek Orthodox Church of St George is built on the site where Jesus is said to have healed 10 lepers. Believed to be one of the world's oldest surviving churches (dating from the 4th or 5th century AD), it is built around the cave where the lepers were living when Jesus passed through the village.

Service taxis (3NIS) go here from a station about 300m west of the Masjid Jenin, close to Cinema Guesthouse.

Sleeping & Eating

★**Cinema Guesthouse** GUESTHOUSE $
(059 931-7968; www.cinemajenin.org; 1 Azzaytoon St; dm/s/d 75/125/250NIS;) A quiet spot in the heart of chaotic Jenin, this is a great place to meet other travellers (or NGO workers, journalists, activists and the like) and unwind for a day or two. It has three spacious dorm rooms, a couple of tiny private rooms and a nice kitchen for cooking communal meals. Breakfast is an extra 10NIS. The English-speaking manager is a fount of information on the area. It's opposite the central bus station.

Aawtar INTERNATIONAL, MIDDLE EASTERN $
(Cinema Circle; mains 20-60NIS; 8am-midnight) Head up to Aawtar's spacious roof garden for a choice of Arabic and Western dishes under the stars. Even on cool evenings, the terrace is packed with groups drinking, eating and chatting over shisha. Downstairs, the restaurant has bay windows overlooking the street and serves Arab staples as well as pizza, burgers and enormous salads.

Getting There & Away

There are frequent buses between Nablus and Jenin (15NIS) and between Jenin and the northern checkpoint of Jalameh (4NIS to 5NIS) for travellers heading to Afula, Haifa or Nazareth.

Note that unlike other West Bank checkpoints, which operate 24 hours, Jalameh is open only from 8am to 7pm.

GAZA STRIP

قطاع غزة רצועת עזה

Gaza has been off the to-do list for travellers for some time – and for good reason. Israel has blockaded the tiny strip from land, air and sea since just after Islamist party Hamas took control in 2006, keeping Gaza's 1.8 million residents in and, with the exception of a handful of journalists, politicians and aid workers, the world out. Even if it were possible to visit Gaza, it would not be recommended: Hamas has fought three wars with Israel between 2006 and 2014 and the strip remains unstable and dangerous.

At 45km long and 10km wide, Gaza is one of the most densely populated places in the world – but it remains desperately poor, with hundreds of thousands of people living either in ramshackle refugee camps or heavily bombed towns and cities. It doesn't need to be: literacy levels are upwards of 97% and its seas hold untapped natural gas reserves worth up to US$7 billion. Its historic sites go back three millennia and it is home to one of the most beautiful coastlines in the Mediterranean.

Over the last few years billions have been pledged internationally to rebuild the strip, but it is difficult to see how any serious change can take place while the Israeli and Egyptian blockade continues and the Palestinian militants who control Gaza remain committed to establishing a Palestine 'from the river to the sea' (the Jordan to the Mediterranean) – leaving little room for their Israeli neighbours.

UNDERSTAND ISRAEL & THE PALESTINIAN TERRITORIES

Israel & the Palestinian Territories Today

Optimism about peace was widespread among both Israelis and Palestinians in the heyday of the Oslo peace process, back in the mid-1990s. But years of suicide bombings, rocket attacks from Hamas-controlled Gaza and Islamist calls for Israel's destruction have made many Israelis pessimistic about the chances for real peace and wary of new, potentially risky initiatives. A variety of factors have had a similar impact on the assessment of many Palestinians: continuing settlement construction, incidents of Israeli army brutality, daily humiliation at checkpoints and the right-wing, populist drift of Israeli politics.

Israeli Prime Minister Binyamin Netanyahu has publicly declared his support for a two-state solution to the Israeli-Palestinian conflict, but since his latest right-wing coalition government came to power in 2015, it has aggressively expanded Jewish settlements and offered only vague answers to Palestinian questions about eventual borders. The 2016 election of Donald Trump, who promised to move the US embassy in Israel to Jerusalem, has emboldened both Netanyahu and the furthest-right parties in his coalition.

The leadership of the Palestinian Authority (PA) is also hamstrung. Although PA President Mahmoud Abbas and his prime minister, Rami Hamdallah, have a long record of support for a two-state solution, they too have seemed reluctant to make any bold moves. Instead, Abbas has been putting efforts into having the State of Palestine recognised by international bodies such as the UN and demanding that the international community set a date for an end to Israel's occupation.

History

Ancient Times

Israel and the Palestinian Territories have been inhabited by human beings for some two million years. Between 10,000 and 8000 BC – a little later than in nearby Mesopotamia – people in places such as Jericho switched from hunting to the production of grain and the domestication of animals.

Around 1800 BC, Abraham is believed to have led his nomadic tribe from Mesopotamia (Iraq) to a land the Bible calls Canaan. His descendants were forced to relocate to Egypt because of drought and crop failure, but according to the Bible Moses led them out of slavery and back to the Land of Israel in about 1250 BC. Conflicts with the Canaanites and Philistines pushed the Israelites to abandon their loose tribal system and unify under King Saul (1050–1010 BC) and his successors, King David and King Solomon, builder of the First Temple in Jerusalem.

After Solomon's reign (965–928 BC), the Jews entered a period of division and periodic subjugation. Two rival entities came into being: the Kingdom of Israel, in what is now the northern West Bank and the Galilee; and the southern Kingdom of Judah, with its capital at Jerusalem. After Sargon II of Assyria (r 722–705 BC) destroyed the Kingdom of Israel in 720 BC, the 10 northern tribes disappeared from the historical record.

The Babylonians captured Jerusalem in 586 BC, destroying the First Temple and exiling the people of Judah to Babylonia (now Iraq). Fifty years later Cyrus II, king of Persia, defeated Babylon and allowed the Jews to return to the Land of Israel. They immediately set about constructing the Second Temple, consecrated in 516 BC.

Greeks & Maccabees, Romans & Christians

Greek rule over the Land of Israel began in the late 4th century BC. When the Seleucid king Antiochus IV Epiphanes (r 175–164 BC) banned Temple sacrifices, Shabbat and circumcision, the Jews, led by Judah Maccabee, revolted. Using guerrilla tactics, they captured Jerusalem and rededicated the temple – an event celebrated by the Jewish holiday of Hanukkah.

The Maccabees also established the Hasmonean dynasty, but infighting made it easy for Rome to take over in 63 BC. At times the Romans ruled the Roman province of Judea (also spelled Judaea or Iudaea) directly through a procurator – the most famous of whom was Pontius Pilate – but they preferred a strong client ruler like Herod the Great (r 37–4 BC), whose major construction projects included expanding the Second Temple.

The 1st century AD was a time of tremendous upheaval in the Roman province of Judea, not least between approximately AD 26 and 29, when it is believed that Jesus of Nazareth carried out his ministry. The tension exploded in AD 66, when the Jews launched the Great Jewish Revolt against the Romans, also known as the First Jewish-Roman War. Four years later, Titus, the future emperor, crushed the rebels and laid waste to the Second Temple (Rome's Arch of Titus celebrates the victory). The mountaintop Jewish stronghold of Masada fell in AD 73, putting an end to even nominal Jewish sovereignty for almost 1900 years.

In the years following Jesus's crucifixion, which some experts believe took place in AD 33, Jews who believed him to be the Messiah and those who didn't often worshipped side by side. But around the time the Gospels were written (late 1st century AD), theological and political disagreements emerged and the two communities diverged.

With the Temple destroyed and the elaborate animal sacrifices prescribed in the Torah suspended, Jewish religious life was thrown into a state of limbo. In an effort to adapt to the new circumstances, Jewish sages set about reorienting Judaism towards prayer and synagogue worship.

After another failed Jewish revolt, the Bar Kochba Rebellion (AD 132–35), the triumphant Romans – in an attempt to erase Jews' connection to the country – renamed Jerusalem 'Aelia Capitolina' and the province of Judea 'Syria Palaestina'.

Muslims & Crusaders

Islam and the Arabs arrived in Palestine around AD 638 – just six years after the death of the Prophet Mohammed – when Caliph Omar (Umar), the second of the Prophet Mohammed's successors, accepted the surrender of Jerusalem. Jews were again permitted to settle in Jerusalem and Christian shrines, including those established by Helena (Constantine the Great's mother), were preserved.

Omar's successors built Al Aqsa Mosque and the Dome of the Rock on the Temple Mount (known to Muslims as Al Haram Ash Sharif), believed to be the site of Mohammed's Night Journey (Mi'raj) to behold the celestial glories of heaven.

Christian pilgrimage to the holy sites in Jerusalem was blocked in 1071 by the Seljuk Turks. In response, in 1095 Pope Urban II issued a call for a crusade to restore the site of Jesus's Passion to Christianity. By the time the Crusades began, the Seljuks had been displaced by the Fatimid dynasty, which was quite happy to allow the old pilgrimage routes to reopen. But it was too late. In 1099 the Crusaders overwhelmed Jerusalem's defences and massacred its Muslims and Jews.

In 1187 the celebrated Kurdish-Muslim general Saladin (Salah ad-Din) defeated a Crusader army at the Horns of Hattin in Galilee (near Arbel) and took Jerusalem. The final Crusaders left the Middle East with the fall of Akko (Acre) in 1291.

Ottomans, Zionists & British

The Ottoman Turks captured Palestine in 1516, and two decades later Sultan Süleyman the Magnificent (r 1520–66) built the present massive walls around Jerusalem's Old City. For most of the 400 years of Ottoman rule, Palestine was a backwater run by pashas more concerned with tax collection than good governance.

While a small numbers of Jews had remained in Palestine continuously since Roman times, and pious Jews had been immigrating whenever political conditions permitted, organised Zionist immigration to agricultural settlements didn't begin until 1882, sparked by pogroms in Russia. For slightly different reasons, Jews from Yemen began arriving the same year. But until the 1920s, the vast majority of Palestine's Jews belonged to the old-line Orthodox community, most of it uninterested in Zionism (the movement to establish a Jewish state in Palestine), and lived in Judaism's four holy cities: Hebron, Tsfat (Safed), Tiberias and Jerusalem (which became Jewish-majority in about 1850).

In November 1917 the British government issued the Balfour Declaration, which stated that 'His Majesty's Government view with favour the establishment in Palestine of a National Home for the Jewish People'. The next month, British forces under General Edmund Allenby captured Jerusalem.

After the end of WWI Jews resumed immigration to Palestine, this time to territory controlled by a British mandate – approved by the League of Nations – that was friendly, modernising and competent. Among the Jewish immigrants were young, idealistic socialists, many of whom established kibbutzim (communal settlements) on marginal land purchased from absentee Arab landlords, sometimes displacing Arab peasant farmers. In the 1930s they were joined by refugees from Nazi Germany.

The Arab Revolt (1936–39), aimed both at the Zionists and British forces, was suppressed by the Mandatory government with considerable violence. However, it convinced the British – who, in case of war with Germany, would surely need Arab oil and political goodwill – to severely limit Jewish immigration to Palestine. Just as the Jews of Europe were becoming increasingly desperate to flee Hitler, the doors of Palestine slammed shut.

Independence & Catastrophe

By 1947 the British government, exhausted by WWII and tired of both Arab and Jewish violence in Palestine, turned the 'Palestine problem' over to the two-year-old UN. In a moment of rare agreement between the US and the Soviet Union, in 1947 the UN General Assembly voted in favour of partitioning Palestine into two independent states – one Jewish, the other Arab – with Jerusalem under a 'special international regime'. Palestinian Jews accepted the plan in principle, but Palestinian Arabs and nearby Arab countries rejected it. Arab bands immediately began attacking Jewish targets, beginning the 1948 Arab–Israeli War.

As soon as the British left, at midnight on 14 May 1948, two things happened: the Jews proclaimed the establishment of an independent Jewish state; and the armies of Egypt, Syria, Jordan, Lebanon and Iraq invaded Palestine. But to the Arab states' – and the world's – surprise the 650,000 Palestinian Jews were not defeated but rather took control of 77% of Mandatory Palestine (the Partition Plan had offered them 56%), though without Jerusalem's Old City. Jordan occupied (and annexed) the West Bank and East Jerusalem; Egypt took control of the Gaza Strip.

As a result of the 1948 Arab–Israeli War, Israel achieved independence. The establishment of a sovereign Jewish state guaranteed that Jews fleeing persecution would always have a country that would take them in.

But for the Palestinian Arabs, the war is remembered as Al Naqba, the Catastrophe. Approximately 700,000 of the Arabs living in what was to become Israel fled or were expelled by the end of the year. While many fled their homes to escape fighting, others were forced out of their towns and villages by Israeli military units.

After Israel became independent, impoverished Jewish refugees began flooding in, including Holocaust survivors and refugees from Arab countries whose ancient Jewish communities had been targets of anti-Jewish violence. Within three years, Israel's Jewish population had more than doubled.

War, Terrorism & Three Peace Treaties

In the spring of 1967, Arab capitals – especially Cairo – were seething with calls to liberate all of historic Palestine from what they saw as an illegitimate occupation by Israel. Egyptian President Gamal Abdel Nasser ordered UN peacekeeping forces to withdraw from Sinai and closed the Straits of Tiran to Israeli shipping.

On 6 June Israel launched a pre-emptive attack on Egypt, virtually wiping out its air force and, in less than a week, captured Sinai and Gaza from Egypt, the West Bank and East Jerusalem from Jordan, and the Golan from Syria. The conflict came to be known as the Six Day War (see www.sixdaywar.co.uk for the Israeli perspective).

In 1973 Egypt and Syria launched a surprise, two-front attack on Yom Kippur, the holiest day of the Jewish calendar. Unprepared because of intelligence failures, Israel was initially pushed back. Although in tactical and strategic terms Israel eventually achieved victory on the battlefield, it came away from the war feeling defeated, in part because the early Egyptian and Syrian advances, coming just six years after the stunning victory of 1967, were so bloody and traumatic.

Egyptian President Anwar Sadat stunned the world in 1977 by travelling to Jerusalem. He offered to make peace with Israel in return for an Israeli withdrawal from Sinai and promises (never fulfilled) of progress towards a Palestinian state. The Camp David Accords, the first peace treaty between Israel and an Arab state, were signed in 1978.

A popular uprising against Israeli rule broke out in the West Bank and Gaza in 1987. Known as the Intifada (Arabic for 'shaking off'), this spontaneous eruption of strikes, stones and Molotov cocktails gave Palestinians a renewed sense of hope and purpose.

In 1988 Yasser Arafat, then president of the PA, publicly renounced terrorism. Five years later, Israel and the Palestine Liberation Organization (PLO) signed the Oslo Accords, under which Israel handed over control of territory to the Palestinians in stages, beginning with the major towns of the West Bank and Gaza. The toughest issues – the future of Jerusalem and Palestinian refugees' 'Right of Return' – were to be negotiated at the end of a five-year interim period. The Oslo formula was, essentially, 'land for peace' based on the two-state solution proposed by the UN in 1947.

In 1994 Israel and Jordan sign a peace treaty, delimiting their long border and guaranteeing Jordan a share of Jordan River water.

Renewed Violence & Stalemate

But the Oslo Accords didn't bring real peace to Israelis and Palestinians. Rather, the treaty drove those on both sides who opposed compromise to pursue their goals through violence. In November 1995 a right-wing, Orthodox Jewish Israeli assassinated Prime Minister Yitzhak Rabin at a peace rally in Tel Aviv; and Hamas and Islamic Jihad launched suicide bombings against Israeli civilians.

The Al Aqsa (Second) Intifada (2000–05) brought an unprecedented wave of Palestinian suicide bombings against Israeli civilian targets, including buses, supermarkets, cafes and discos. Prime Minister Ariel Sharon, a tough-talking former general, sent tanks to occupy West Bank towns previously ceded to the PA and made frequent, bloody incursions into Gaza. Depressed and sick, Arafat's command of events and – according to some aides – reality weakened until his death in November 2004.

Over the course of the Second Intifada, over 1000 Israelis, 70% of them civilians, were killed by Palestinians and some 4700 Palestinians, more than 2000 of them civilians, were killed by Israelis, according to the Israeli human-rights group B'Tselem (www.btselem.org).

In 2005 Sharon – completely contradicting his reputation as an incorrigible hardliner – evacuated all 8600 Israeli settlers from the Gaza Strip and four settlements in the northern West Bank. Like many other hawkish Israeli leaders before and after, he had come to the conclusion that Israel's continued occupation of the territories captured in 1967 was against Israeli interests and, in the long run, geopolitically and demographically untenable.

Palestinian legislative elections were held in 2006 and Hamas – an Islamist political and militant group classified as a terrorist organisation by the United States, Canada, the UK and the European Union – won. The following year Hamas gunmen ran their Fatah counterparts out of the Gaza Strip after bloody fighting, leaving the West Bank and Gaza under rival administrations. A reconciliation agreement was signed in 2017 but has since stalled.

Israel and the Shiite Lebanese militia Hezbollah, backed by Iran, fought a brief war in the summer of 2006. Thousands of rockets rained down on Israeli cities, towns and villages, bringing life in northern Israel to a terrified halt. The scale of Israel's bombing attacks on Lebanese towns was widely condemned, but in early 2018 a tenuous ceasefire was still holding despite Israeli air attacks against Iranian weapons deliveries to Hezbollah transiting through Syria.

In response to years of rocket fire from Gaza, very late in 2008 Israel launched a major offensive, dubbed Operation Cast Lead, aimed at halting the attacks. Israel and Hamas again clashed in late 2012 and, even more violently, in the summer of 2014. During the 50-day Hamas-Israel war, missiles and mortars were fired into Israel, many of which were intercepted by the pioneering Iron Dome antimissile defence system. Israeli air and ground attacks on Gaza killed more than 2100 Palestinians (69% of them civilians, according to a UN estimate) and left some 60,000 Palestinians homeless. The war ended with few real gains for either side.

In 2017 Israel began constructing a high-tech barrier around the Gaza Strip to prevent the infiltration tunnels from crossing into Israeli territory.

People

Israel

As the only Jewish state, Israel and its society are unique in the Middle East – and the world. Three-quarters of Israelis are Jewish, but Israeli society is surprisingly diverse, encompassing communities of Muslim and Christian Arabs, Bedouins, Druze, Circassians, asylum seekers from Africa (especially Eritrea and Sudan) and foreign workers (eg eldercare helpers from the Philippines and agricultural workers from Thailand).

The ancestors of about half of Israeli Jews immigrated from Europe (especially Russia, Romania, Poland, Germany and Hungary) and the Americas, with the other half coming from Africa (eg Morocco and Ethiopia) and Asia (especially Iraq, Iran, Yemen and India). Despite their diversity of background, Israeli Jews are bound together by a collective memory of exile and persecution, especially the Holocaust (1939–45), in which six million of the world's 18 million Jews perished.

The Israeli army, to which Jewish, Druze and Circassian men and most Jewish women are drafted at the age of 18 (men for three years, women for two), serves as a unifying force, although army-based bonds and social networks leave out groups that do not serve, including most Arab Israelis and most ultra-Orthodox Jews. The country is always in a state of security vigilance, in recent times as a result of rocket attacks and attempted infiltrations from Gaza, Hezbollah's huge Iranian-supplied arsenal in Lebanon, instability in Sinai and Syria, and Iran's nuclear program.

In the economic sphere, Israel has forged strong links with Europe, the USA and South, Southeast and East Asia. It has the world's 25th-highest per-capita GDP, fuelled by a keen sense of entrepreneurism and world-class capacity in fields such as computers, chemistry and medical research.

Palestinian Territories

The perspectives and dreams of the residents of the Palestinian Territories have been forged by a century of loss, deprivation and violence. While Islam plays a major role in Palestinians' world view (only 2% of West Bankers and 0.3% of Gazans are Christians), the defining characteristic of Palestinian society is the desire for an independent homeland. For many Palestinians, years of unemployment, poverty and shortages have led to a collective sense of desperation and powerlessness, though some continue to work on building the institutions, infrastructure and economic structures of a future Palestinian state.

Government & Politics

Israel

Israel is a parliamentary democracy headed by a prime minister. Government decisions are made by the cabinet, presided over by the prime minister; its members (ministers) have executive responsibility for government ministries. The 120-member Knesset is elected by national proportional representation every four years (although elections are almost always called early). Israel also has a president – since 2014 the post has been held by Reuven Rivlin – whose role is largely ceremonial; he or she is elected by the Knesset for a term of seven years.

Since 2009 Israel's prime minister has been Binyamin Netanyahu, head of the right-wing Likud Party. The coalition he formed after the 2015 elections is the most ideologically right-wing in Israeli history.

Palestinian Territories

The Palestinian Authority (Palestinian National Authority; PA or PNA) is an interim administrative body set up in 1994 under the Oslo Accords to rule parts of the West Bank and Gaza for five years, until the establishment of a Palestinian state. Final-status negotiations have dragged on – and so has the PA, now 20 years past its envisioned replacement by a fully independent State of Palestine.

As part of the Oslo peace process, the PA assumed control of civil and security affairs in the major cities of the West Bank; covering about 3% of the land area of the West Bank, they are known collectively as Area A. A further 25% of the West Bank (including most villages), known as Area B, is under PA civil control, with Israel maintaining responsibility for security affairs. The rest of the West Bank (some 72% of the land area) is designated as Area C, under full Israeli civil and security control.

The PA is headed by an executive president, directly elected – at least in theory – once every four years. Yasser Arafat held the post from 1994 until his death in 2004. In January 2005 Mahmoud Abbas (also known as Abu Mazen) was elected and has served as PA president ever since, despite the absence of subsequent elections.

The Palestinian Legislative Council (PLC), also known as the Palestinian parliament, has 132 members elected from 16 districts in the West Bank and Gaza. The last elections, won by Hamas, took place in 2006. A Fatah-Hamas reconciliation agreement was signed in 2017 but implementation has stalled.

The United Nations General Assembly upgraded the status of the Palestinians to that of a nonmember observer state in 2012.

Religion

Judaism

One of the oldest religions still practised, Judaism is based on a covenantal relationship between the Jewish people and God. The most succinct summary of Jewish theology and Judaism's strict monotheism is to be found in the Shema prayer, which reads, 'Hear O Israel, the Lord is your God, the Lord is One'.

Judaism is based on the Torah (the first five books of the Hebrew Bible, ie the Old Testament) and the Oral Law, as interpreted by rabbis and sages in works such as the Mishna (edited in the 2nd and 3rd centuries AD) and the Talmud (edited from the 4th to 6th centuries AD).

Orthodox Judaism (the most conservative of the religion's streams) holds that the Oral Law, in its entirety, was given at Mt Sinai. The Reform, Conservative and Reconstructionist Movements believe that Judaism has always been dynamic and proactive, changing and developing over the generations as it faced new circumstances and ideas. All three accord equal status to women, while Orthodoxy does not.

Islam

Islam was founded by the Prophet Mohammed (AD 570–632), who lived in what is now Saudi Arabia. It is based on belief in the absolute oneness of God (Allah) and in the revelations of his final prophet, Mohammed. The Arabic word *islam* means 'absolute submission' to God and his word. Islam's sacred scripture is the Quran (Koran), which was revealed to Mohammed and is believed to be God's infallible word.

Islam and Judaism share common roots, and Muslims consider Adam, Noah, Abraham, Isaac, Jacob, Joseph and Moses to be prophets. As a result, Jews and Muslims share a number of holy sites, including the Temple Mount/Al Haram Ash Sharif in Jerusalem and the Ibrahimi Mosque/Tomb of the Patriarchs in Hebron. Because of their close scriptural links, Muslims consider both Jews and Christians to be an *Ahl Al Kitab,* a 'people of the Book'. Judaism has always seen Islam as a fellow monotheistic faith (because of the Trinity, Jewish sages weren't always so sure about Christianity).

Christianity

Christianity is based on the life and teachings of Jesus of Nazareth, a Jew who lived in Judea and Galilee during the 1st century AD; on his crucifixion by the Romans; and on his resurrection three days later, as related in the New Testament. Christianity started out as a movement within Judaism, and Jesus's closest disciples, known as the Apostles, were all Jews. But after his death, the insistence of Jesus's followers that he was the Messiah caused Christianity to become increasingly distinct from Judaism.

The ownership of holy sites in Israel and the Palestinian Territories has long been a subject of contention among the country's various Christian denominations, which include Armenians, Assyrians, Copts and Ethiopians. At a number of sites in Jerusalem and Bethlehem, relations are still governed by a 'status quo' agreement drawn up in Ottoman times.

The Holy Land's largest denomination, the Greek Orthodox Church – almost all of whose local members are Arabic-speaking

Palestinians – has jurisdiction over more than half of Jerusalem's Church of the Holy Sepulchre, and a large portion of Bethlehem's Church of the Nativity.

Other Belief Systems

The Druze religion is an 11th-century offshoot of Islam. Many Druze live in northern Israel (including Mt Carmel) as well as in Lebanon and Syria.

Haifa is the world centre of the Baha'i faith, founded in Persia in the mid-1800s.

Arts

Literature

Israelis are enormously proud of the revival of the Hebrew language and the creation of modern Hebrew literature, seeing them as the crowning cultural achievements of the Zionist movement. Some highly regarded names to keep an eye out for (their major works are available in English translation) include Yehuda Amichai (1924–2000), Aharon Appelfeld (1932–2018), AB Yehoshua (b 1936), Amos Oz (b 1939) and David Grossman (b 1954).

The most widespread form of literary expression among Palestinians has long been poetry, the leading voice of which remains Mahmoud Darwish (1941–2008; www.mahmouddarwish.com). Emile Habibi (1922–96) and Tawfiq Zayad (1929–94) – both of whom represented the Israeli Community Party in the Knesset – wrote highly regarded works of fiction. Habibi's *The Secret Life of Saeed the Pesoptimist* (1974) is a brilliant, tragicomic tale dealing with the difficulties facing Palestinian Arabs who became Israeli citizens after 1948. The stunning debut work of Ghassan Kanafani (1936–72), *Men in the Sun* (1963), delves into the lives, hopes and shattered dreams of its Palestinian characters.

Music

Israeli music mixes modes, scales and vocal styles from both East and West.

In the realms of classic Israeli pop and rock, names to listen for include Shlomo Artzi, Arik Einstein, Matti Caspi, Shalom Hanoch, Yehudit Ravitz, Assaf Amdursky and, more recently, Aviv Geffen. Idan Raichel introduced Ethiopian melodies to a mainstream audience.

Mizrahi (Oriental or Eastern) music, with its Middle Eastern and Mediterranean scales and rhythms, has its roots in the melodies of North Africa (especially Umm Kulthum-era Egypt and mid-century Morocco), Iraq and Yemen.

Over the past decade, mainstream performers such as Etti Ankri, Ehud Banai, David D'Or, Kobi Oz, Berry Sakharof and Gilad Segev have turned towards traditional – mainly Sephardic and Mizrahi – liturgical poetry and melodies, producing works with massive mainstream popularity.

Born in the *shtetls* (Jewish villages) of Eastern Europe, klezmer (Jewish soul) can take you swiftly from ecstasy to the depths of despair. Israel also has a strong Western classical tradition thanks to Jewish refugees from Nazism and post-Soviet immigrants from Russia. The Israel Philharmonic Orchestra (www.ipo.co.il) – whose first concert, in 1936, was conducted by Arturo Toscanini – is world renowned.

Visitors to the West Bank and Arab areas of Israel may come across traditional Palestinian folk music featuring the sounds of the *oud* (a stringed instrument shaped like half a pear), the *daf* (tambourine) and the *ney* (flute). Palestinian rap, such as the works of Lod-based DAM (www.damrap.com), frequently deals with the themes of occupation, the difficulties of daily life, and resistance.

Theatre & Dance

Many contemporary Israeli plays tackle the hot political and social issues of the day – in recent years, the West Bank occupation, suicide, homosexuality within Orthodox Judaism and the Holocaust have all been explored onstage. Tel Aviv, Jerusalem and Haifa have a profusion of companies, venues and festivals both large and small; some offer English supertitle translations.

Long an important expression of Palestinian national aspirations, Palestinian theatre has been censored by the British, suppressed and harassed by the Israelis, battered by conflict and closures and, most recently, targeted by Islamists. Nevertheless, Palestinian actors and directors carry on. Juliano Mer Khamis (1958–2011), the Palestinian-Israeli founder of Jenin's Freedom Theatre (www.thefreedomtheatre.org), was murdered by masked gunmen in Jenin, but the theatre continues to function in the city's refugee camp to this day.

Cinema

In recent years, Israeli films – many of which take a highly critical look at Israeli society and policies – have been garnering prizes at major film festivals, including Cannes, Berlin, Toronto and Sundance. For a database of made-in-Israel movies, see the website of the Manhattan-based Israel Film Center (www.israelfilmcenter.org). There are film festivals and thriving cinematheques in Jerusalem (www.jer-cin.org.il), Tel Aviv (www.cinema.co.il) and Haifa (www.haifacin.co.il).

Most feature-length Palestinian movies are international co-productions. In 2014 *Omar,* a political thriller about trust and betrayal directed by Hany Abu-Assad, garnered Palestine's second Oscar nomination.

Sadly both of the West Bank's movie venues – the Al Kasaba Theater & Cinematheque in Ramallah and the internationally supported Cinema Jenin – had closed as of 2017.

Food & Drink

Israelis and Palestinians disagree about many things, but what they find tasty isn't one of them. Favourites among both peoples include hummus (chickpea paste), felafel (fried chickpea balls served with salad and hummus in a pita pocket), shwarma (chicken, turkey or lamb grilled on a giant spit and stuffed into a pita) and pita bread, both with and without the pocket.

Few countries offer a better selection of vegetarian options than Israel and the Palestinian Territories. Almost all restaurants serve giant – and often creative – salads, and even in meat-heavy Arab and Levantine restaurants, the mezze-style appetisers and salads can serve as a tasty, inexpensive meatless meal. Tel Aviv, Haifa, Jerusalem and Nazareth are known for their excellent restaurants serving both Levantine classics and dishes from around the world.

In both Israel and the Palestinian Territories, tipping 10% or 15% of the bill is as much of an established practice as it is in the English-speaking world.

Daily Life

Israeli society was founded on socialist principles, exemplified by the kibbutz (communal village). These days, though, the vast majority of Israelis have shifted to a decidedly bourgeois and individualistic outlook that embraces aspirations whose fulfilment depends on middle-class paycheques. Hiking, cycling, windsurfing, backpacking, camping and other outdoor activities are hugely popular.

Gaza is largely controlled by Islamic fundamentalists, but much of the West Bank retains a moderate outlook, and Ramallah in particular exhibits the trappings of modern, Western living, including shiny cars, health clubs and late-night bars.

Israeli women enjoy a freedom, opportunity and status on a par with their European counterparts and have historically played significant roles in the economy, politics and even the military. (Israel was one of the first countries to elect a female prime minister: Golda Meir, in 1969.) Though Palestinian women have traditionally assumed the role of home-based caregiver, recent years have seen more women encouraged to enter higher education and to work outside the home. However, as in Ottoman times, marriage and divorce in both Israel and the Palestinian Territories remain in the hands of very conservative religious establishments that tend to favour male prerogatives over women's rights. As there is no civil marriage in Israel, couples of mixed religious background and same-sex couples wishing to wed must do so outside of Israel (eg in Cyprus).

The annual per-capita GDP in the Palestinian Territories is just US$4300, compared with Israel's US$36,200.

Language

Israel's two official languages are Hebrew and Arabic; the official language of the Palestinian Authority is Arabic. On the streets of Israel you'll also hear a lot of Russian, French, English and Amharic spoken by immigrants. Some ultra-Orthodox Jews and older Ashkenazim continue to speak Yiddish (the Germanic language of the Jews of Eastern Europe), and a small number of Sephardic Jews still use Ladino (Judeo-Espanyol), a blend of Hebrew and Spanish traditionally written – like Yiddish – using the Hebrew alphabet. Most Israelis and many Palestinians speak at least some English.

Israeli road signs generally appear in Hebrew, Arabic and English, but often with baffling transliterations. Caesarea, for example, may be rendered Qesariyya, Kesarya, Qasarya and so on; and Tsfat may appear as Zefat, Zfat or Safed. The V sound is often rendered, as in German, using a W.

Environment

Israel and the Palestinian Territories, which cover an area of 28,000 sq km, are bordered to the east by the 6000km-long Great Rift Valley (also known as the Syrian-African Rift), to which the Sea of Galilee, the Dead Sea and the Red Sea all belong. Between this mountain-fringed valley and the Mediterranean Sea lie the Judean Hills (up to 1000m high), which include Jerusalem and Hebron, and the fertile coastal plain, where the bulk of Israel's population and agriculture is concentrated. The arid, lightly populated Negev, the country's southern wedge, consists of plains, mountains, wadis and makhteshes (erosion craters).

Situated at the meeting point of two continents (Asia and Africa) and very near a third (Europe), Israel and the Palestinian Territories are home to a mix of habitats and ecologies found nowhere else on earth. Asian mammals such as the Indian porcupine live alongside African tropical mammals like the rock hyrax (dassie) and creatures more often found in European climes such as the stone marten. National parks and nature reserves encompass around 25% of Israel's total area.

Some 500 million birds from an incredible 283 species migrate through Israel and the Palestinian Territories each year – check out www.birds.org.il, www.natureisrael.org/birding, www.eilat-birds.org and www.wildlife-pal.org to find out more.

Environmental Issues

Israel is one of only two countries in the world to have entered the 21st century with more trees than it had at the beginning of the 20th (the other is the United States). But while afforestation programs re-created forest habitats, and innovative desert agriculture (using technologies such as drip irrigation, which was invented here) 'made the desert bloom', demands on the land from urbanisation have resulted in the same problems found in many parts of the world: air and water pollution, overuse of natural resources and poor waste management. Things are even worse on the coast of Gaza, where the problem of surface pollution is accompanied by seawater seepage into the aquifers.

Because of pumping from the Jordan River, its tributaries and the Sea of Galilee, the amount of water flowing into the Dead Sea each year is one billion cu metres (over 90%) less than it would be naturally. As a result of evaporation, the water level is dropping by about 1.2m per year, causing the seashore to recede and creating dangerous sinkholes. In 2013 an agreement was signed by Israel, the Palestinian Authority and Jordan to build a 110km-long canal from Aqaba; as of 2018 implementation was slowly moving ahead. Environmentalists are concerned about the impact on the Dead Sea of introducing seawater carrying living organisms and a different mix of minerals.

SURVIVAL GUIDE

Directory A–Z

ACCOMMODATION

B&B (Tzimmer)

The most popular form of accommodation in the Galilee and Golan is the tzimmer (or zimmer), which we translate as B&B, though not all serve breakfast. For a double room, count on paying 400NIS or 500NIS at the very least. To find a tzimmer, check out www.zimmeril.com.

Camping

Camping is forbidden inside Israeli nature reserves, but various public and private bodies run inexpensive camping sites (www.campingil.org.il) at about 100 places around the country, including 22 operated by the Israel Nature & Parks Authority (www.parks.org.il) next to nature reserves. Some are equipped with shade roofs (so you don't need a tent), lighting, toilets,

SLEEPING PRICE RANGES

Israel: the following prices are for double rooms with breakfast on weekends and in high season. Prices are slightly higher in Tel Aviv compared with the rest of the country.

$ less than 350NIS

$$ 350NIS to 600NIS

$$$ more than 600NIS

Palestinian Territories: the following price ranges are for double rooms with breakfast on weekends in high season.

$ less than 200NIS

$$ 200NIS to 400NIS

$$$ more than 400NIS

showers and barbecue pits. In Hebrew, ask for a *chenyon laila* or an *orchan laila*.

Camping is particularly popular on the shores of the Sea of Galilee. Some organised beaches – offering toilet facilities, a decent shower block and security – charge per-person admission fees, but others are free if you arrive on foot (visitors with wheels pay a per-car fee).

In the Palestinian Territories, camping should be avoided because of general security concerns.

Hostels

Almost three dozen independent hostels and guesthouses belong to Israel Hostels (www. hostels-israel. com), whose members offer dorm beds for 100NIS, good-value doubles and unmatched opportunities to meet other travellers.

Israel's 19 official Hostelling International (HI) hostels and guesthouses – significantly upgraded since the days of no-frills dorms and timer-activated hall showers – offer spotless, institutional rooms that are ideal for families, and also serve copious breakfasts. For details, check out the website of the Israel Youth Hostels Association, www. iyha.org.il.

The Society for the Protection of Nature in Israel (www.natureisrael.org) runs nine field schools *(beit sefer sadeh)* in areas of high ecological value. Offering basic but serviceable accommodation, they're popular with school groups and families. Book well ahead, especially during school vacation periods.

Hotels

Both Israel and the Palestinian Territories offer accommodation options for every budget and style of travel. In Israel, expect prices – though not always standards – on a par with Western Europe. In recent years an increasing number of small, stylish boutique hotels have opened. The West Bank is quite a bit cheaper, with many of the best options clustered in Ramallah and Bethlehem. Israeli hotels are famous for their generous buffet breakfasts. Although most hotel restaurants serve only kosher food, they remain open on Shabbat and Jewish holidays.

Seasonal Rates

Accommodation prices in Israel vary enormously with the day of the week and the season. Weekday rates generally run from Saturday or Sunday night through Wednesday or Thursday night. Weekend rates apply on Friday and sometimes Thursday (many Israelis don't work on Friday) and/or Saturday night. High-season pricing is in force during July and August and on Jewish holidays such as Rosh HaShanah, Shavu'ot and the week-long Passover and Sukkot festivals. At these times, book well in advance.

In the West Bank, room prices remain fairly constant year-round, the exception being Bethlehem, where rates rise around Christmas and Easter. Book well ahead if you are planning on travel at these times.

ACTIVITIES

Cycling

Mountain biking has become hugely popular in Israel in recent years, especially among hitech yuppies with SUVs (a stereotype, but not an untrue one). Shvil Net (www.shvilnet.co.il) publishes Hebrew-language cycling guides that include detailed topographical maps.

Hiking

With its unbelievably diverse terrain – ranging from the alpine slopes of Mt Hermon to the parched makhteshes (erosion craters) of the Negev – and almost 10,000km of marked trails, Israel offers some truly superb hiking. Don't forget to bring a hat and plenty of water, and plan your day so you can make it back before dark. Tiuli (www.tiuli.com) has details in English on hiking options around the country.

At national parks and nature reserves run by the Israel Nature and Parks Authority (www. parks.org.il), walking maps with English text are usually handed out when you pay your admission fee. In other areas, the best maps to have – in part because they indicate the location of minefields and live-fire zones used for Israel Defense Forces training – are the 1:50,000-scale topographical maps (in Hebrew) produced by the Society for the Protection of Nature in Israel (SPNI), sold at bookshops and some nature reserves.

In the West Bank, it's generally not a good idea to wander around the countryside unaccompanied. Consult local organisations for up-to-date information on areas considered safe; Jericho and environs are usually a good bet.

Water Sports

The Red Sea has some of the world's most spectacular and species-rich coral reefs. Good-value dive packages and scuba courses are available in Eilat.

EATING PRICE RANGES

Israel: the following price ranges refer to a main course. Prices are higher in Tel Aviv compared with the rest of the country.

$ less than 35NIS

$$ 35NIS to 70NIS

$$$ more than 70NIS

Palestinian Territories: the following price ranges refer to a main course.

$ less than 35NIS

$$ 35NIS to 55NIS

$$$ more than 55NIS

SECURITY SITUATION

There is no getting around the fact that, although rare in recent years, terrorist attacks and/or rocket fire are a possibility in Israel and the Palestinian Territories. When travelling here, you should regularly check the media for news about possible safety and security risks.

Israel has some of the most stringent security policies in the world. When entering all sorts of public venues, your bags are likely to be searched and in some cases X-rayed. Abandoned shopping bags, backpacks and parcels are picked up by bomb-squad robots and may be blown up.

Road passage between many Palestinian West Bank towns and Israel is regulated by Israeli army roadblocks, where you'll need to show a passport and may have to answer questions about your reason for travel. The situation in the West Bank can change quickly, so monitor the news. Some good rules of thumb:

- Always carry your passport.
- Travel during daylight hours.
- Use caution when approaching roadblocks and checkpoints. Remember: soldiers may have no idea that you're just a curious tourist.
- Don't wander into refugee camps on your own – go with a local guide.
- Avoid political demonstrations, which often get out of hand and can turn into violent confrontations.

Israel's Mediterranean beaches, including those in Tel Aviv, are generally excellent, offering ample opportunities to swim, windsurf and sail. For freshwater swimming head to the Sea of Galilee. The supersaline Dead Sea offers that quintessential 'floating' experience.

CHILDREN

Travel with children in Israel and the Palestinian Territories is generally a breeze: the food's varied and tasty, the distances are short, there are child-friendly activities at every turn, and the locals absolutely love children.

Beaches are usually clean, well equipped with cafes and even playgrounds, and great for a paddle, a sandcastle or a swim. Most Israeli shopping malls have play areas. As wheelchair access to nature reserves has improved in recent years, so has the ease of getting around with a pram (stroller).

In the vast majority of hotels, guesthouses and B&Bs, babies and toddlers can sleep in their parents' room for free; older children (often from age three) are welcome for an extra charge. In hostels and SPNI field schools, rooms generally have at least four beds, making them ideal for families.

In the West Bank, getting through Israeli checkpoints can involve hassles and delays.

CUSTOMS REGULATIONS

Israel allows travellers aged 18 and over, including those heading to the West Bank, to import duty-free up to 1L of spirits and 2L of wine, 250ml of perfume, 250g of tobacco products (200 cigarettes) and gifts worth no more than US$200. Bringing drugs, drug paraphernalia, mace (self-defence tear gas), laser jammers (to confuse police-operated laser speed guns), fresh meat and pornography is prohibited.

DANGERS & ANNOYANCES

Israel is generally a very safe place to travel and violent crime against tourists is extremely rare. However, the country has some unique challenges visitors should be aware of.

- Be careful when visiting border regions, particularly those close to Syria and Lebanon or between Israel and the West Bank.
- Keep your eye on the news and don't be afraid to ask at your hotel or hostel for advice.
- Avoid demonstrations, particularly in Jerusalem, which can quickly descend into violence.
- If you are asked about the political situation, be aware that feelings run high and discussions can quickly get heated.
- Use hotel safes where available. Don't leave valuables unattended, particularly on the beach.

In the West Bank, hostility towards visitors is almost unheard of. However, visitors should exercise caution as the area is under military occupation and clashes between the Israeli military and Palestinian youths (eg at checkpoints) are common, particularly on Fridays and after major events such as Palestinian funerals. Steer clear of demonstrations.

EMBASSIES & CONSULATES

While Israel may claim Jerusalem as its capital, unresolved political issues have led most diplomatic missions to set up shop in or near Tel Aviv. A few countries maintain consulates in Jerusalem, Haifa and Eilat.

Australian Embassy (Map p222; ☎03-693-5000; www.israel.embassy.gov.au; 28th fl, Discount Bank Tower, 23 Yehuda HaLevi St; ⊙8am-12.30pm & 1-4pm Mon-Thu, to 1pm Fri)

Canadian Embassy (☎03-636-3300; www.canadainternational.gc.ca/israel; 3 Nirim St; ⊙8am-4pm Mon-Thu, to 1.30pm Fri)

Egyptian Embassy (Map p226; ☎03-546-4151; www.egyptembassy.net; 54 Basel St; ⊙9-11am Sun-Tue) There's also a consulate in Eilat (Map p253; ☎08-637-6882; www.egyptembassy.net; 68 Efroni St; ⊙9.30-noon Sun-Thu).

French Embassy (Map p222; ☎03-520-8500; www.ambafrance-il.org; 112 Herbert Samuel Esplanade; ⊙8am-12.30pm Mon-Fri) There's also a consulate (Map p204; ☎02-629-8500; www.consulfrance-jerusalem.org; 5 Paul Émile Botta St) in Jerusalem.

German Embassy (Map p222; ☎03-693-1313; www.tel-aviv.diplo.de; 19th fl, 3 Daniel Frisch St; ⊙8-11.30am Mon, Tue, Thu & Fri)

Irish Embassy (☎03-696-4166; www.embassyofireland.co.il; 2 Jabotinski St, Ramat Gan; ⊙10am-12.30pm Mon-Thu)

Jordanian Embassy (☎03-751-7722; 10th fl, 14 Abba Hillel St, Ramat Gan; ⊙9.30am-3pm Sun-Thu)

Netherlands Embassy (☎03-754-0777; www.netherlandsworldwide.nl/countries/israel; 13th fl, 14 Abba Hillel St, Ramat Gan; ⊙9am-4pm Mon-Thu, to 1pm Fri)

Turkish Embassy (Map p226; ☎03-524-1101; 202 HaYarkon St; ⊙9am-noon Mon-Fri) There's also a consulate (☎02-591-0555; http://jerusalem.cg.mfa.gov.tr; 87 Derekh Shchem (Nablus) Rd, Sheikh Jarrah; ⊙8am-5pm Mon-Fri) in Jerusalem.

UK Embassy (Map p226; ☎03-725-1222; www.ukinisrael.fco.gov.uk; 192 HaYarkon St; ⊙8am-4pm Mon-Thu, to 1.30pm Fri) There's also a consulate (☎02-541-4100; www.ukinjerusalem.fco.gov.uk; 15 Nashashibi St, Sheikh Jarrah; ⊙8am-4pm Mon-Thu, to 2pm Fri) in Jerusalem.

US Embassy (Map p222; ☎03-519-7475; https://il.usembassy.gov; 71 HaYarkon St; ⊙8am-noon Mon-Fri by appointment only) There are also consulates in Haifa (☎04-853-1470; https://il.usembassy.gov; 26 Ben-Gurion Ave, German Colony) and Jerusalem (America House; Map p204; ☎02-622-7230; https://jru.usconsulate.gov; 18 Derekh Shchem (Nablus) Rd, East Jerusalem). President Trump has announced that the embassy will soon move to Jerusalem.

GAY & LESBIAN TRAVELLERS

Israel has a very lively gay scene. Tel Aviv has lots of rainbow-coloured flags, a huge Gay Pride Parade and plenty of hang-outs. Haifa and Jerusalem have smaller gay communities. The resort town of Eilat is gay friendly, although the scene is mostly Israeli tourists. Most local organisations offering support, information, contacts and events are based in Tel Aviv and Jerusalem.

Orthodox Judaism, Islam and almost all of the Holy Land's Christian churches adamantly oppose homosexuality, so it's appropriate to be circumspect in religious neighbourhoods. There are no laws in Israel against homosexuality. Israel does not have gay marriage but recognises gay and lesbian marriages performed abroad.

Outside of Ramallah, the West Bank is conservative, and homosexuality and gay culture are very much taboo. Even in Ramallah and Bethlehem, there is no LGBT nightlife scene as such, and just as elsewhere in the Arab world, open displays of affection would certainly be frowned upon – and could be quite dangerous.

INTERNET ACCESS

Wi-fi hot spots can be found all over Israel and in quite a few places in the Palestinian Territories. In Israel, wi-fi is also available on many intercity buses and trains, and Tel Aviv offers free wi-fi in public spaces all over the city.

MONEY

ATMs

ATMs are widespread, and Visa, MasterCard and, increasingly, American Express and Diners cards are accepted almost everywhere. Most – but not all – ATMs do Visa and MasterCard cash advances.

Note: ATMs are not available at border crossings with Jordan and Egypt.

Bargaining

Most of your bargaining experiences will happen at souqs, flea markets or in taxis, which despite being required by law to use a meter, rarely miss the chance to fleece tourists for a few shekels. As with bargaining across the world, it pays to keep your cool and – particularly with souvenirs – remember that as the buyer you ultimately have the advantage.

Moneychangers

The best exchange deals are available at Israeli post office branches able to handle foreign currency and from independent exchange bureaux, neither of which charge commissions.

OPENING HOURS

In Israel, shops, banks and offices are generally open from Sunday to Thursday and on Friday until sometime between 12.30pm and 3pm. Many restaurants, pubs and places of entertainment (cinemas and performance venues) remain open on Shabbat (Friday evening to Saturday night) and most Jewish holidays.

In predominantly Muslim areas (eg East Jerusalem, Akko's Old City and the West Bank) businesses may be closed on Friday (but remain open on Saturday).

Christian-owned businesses (eg in Nazareth, Haifa's Wadi Nisnas, Bethlehem and the Armenian and Christian Quarters of Jerusalem's Old City) are often closed on Sunday.

PUBLIC & RELIGIOUS HOLIDAYS

In addition to the main Islamic holidays, the following are observed in Israel and the Palestinian Territories (dates below include the holiday eves):

New Year's Day Official holiday in the Palestinian Territories but not in Israel (1 January).

Christmas (Orthodox) Celebrated by Eastern Orthodox churches on 6–7 January and by Armenians in the Holy Land on 18–19 January.

Passover (Pesach) Weeklong celebration of the liberation of the Israelites from slavery in Egypt (19–26 April 2019, 8–15 April 2020, 27 March to 3 April 2021).

Easter Sunday (Western) For Catholics and Protestants, 21 April 2019, 12 April 2020 and 4 April 2021.

Easter Sunday (Orthodox) For Eastern Orthodox and Armenians (28 April 2019, 19 April 2020, 2 May 2021).

Holocaust Memorial Day (Yom HaSho'ah) Places of entertainment closed. At 10am sirens sound and Israelis stand silently at attention (1–2 May 2019, 20–21 April 2020, 8–9 April 2021).

Memorial Day (Yom HaZikaron) Commemorates soldiers who fell defending Israel. Places of entertainment closed. At 8pm and 11am sirens sound and Israelis stand silently at attention (7–8 May 2019, 27–28 April 2020, 14–15 April 2021).

Israel Independence Day (Yom Ha'Atzma'ut) Celebrated on 8–9 May 2019, 28–29 April 2020 and 15–16 April 2021.

International Labour Day Public holiday in both Israel and the Palestinian Territories (1 May).

Nakba Day Palestinian commemoration of the *nakba* (catastrophe) of 1948 (15 May).

Shavuot (Pentecost) Jews celebrate the giving of the Torah at Mt Sinai (8–9 June 2019, 28–29 May 2020, 16–17 May 2021).

Tish'a B'Av (Ninth of Av) Jews commemorate the destruction of the Temples in Jerusalem. Restaurants and places of entertainment closed (10–11 August 2019, 29–30 August 2020, 17–18 July 2021).

Rosh HaShanah (Jewish New Year) Celebrated 29 September to 1 October 2019, 18–20 September 2020 and 6–8 September 2021.

Yom Kippur (Jewish Day of Atonement) Solemn day of reflection and fasting. Israel's airports and land borders close, all transport ceases (8–9 October 2019, 27–28 September 2020, 16–17 September 2021).

Sukkot (Feast of the Tabernacles) Weeklong holiday that recollects the Israelites' 40 years of wandering in the desert (13–20 October 2019, 2–9 October 2020, 20–27 September 2021).

Hanukkah (Festival of Lights) Jews celebrate the rededication of the Temple after the Maccabean revolt; no closures (2–10 December 2018, 22–30 December 2019, 10–18 December 2020, 28 November to December 6 2021).

Christmas (Western) Public holiday in the West Bank, but not in Israel or Gaza. Celebrated by Catholics and Protestants on 24–25 December.

SAFE TRAVEL

Some parts of Israel and the Palestinian Territories – particularly along the Jordanian border and around the periphery of the Golan Heights – are sown with antipersonnel mines. Known mined areas are fenced with barbed wire sporting dangling red (or rust) triangles and/or yellow and red 'Danger Mines!' signs. Flash floods sometimes wash away old mines, depositing them outside of marked minefields. Wherever you are, never, ever touch anything that looks like it might be an old artillery shell, grenade or mine!

TELEPHONE

International Calling

Israel's country code is 972, while the Palestinian Territories use both 972 and 970.

In Israel, several competing companies, each with their own three-digit international access code, offer international dialling. International direct-dial rates can be as high as 3.80NIS a minute, but if you sign up in advance, fees can be remarkably cheap (as little as 0.05NIS a minute). Companies include 012 Smile (www.012.net), Netvision (http://netvision. cellcom.co.il), Golan Telecom (www.golantelecom.co.il) and Hot Mobile (www.hotmobile.co.il).

Mobile Phones

Israel's various mobile phone operators, including Orange (www. orange.co.il), Pelefone (www. pelephone.co.il), Cellcom (www.cellcom.co.il), Hot Mobile (www.hotmobile.co.il) and Golan Telecom (www. golantelecom.co.il), offer pay-as-you-go SIM cards as well as cheap monthly plans with a variety of data options. A number of online companies sell Israeli SIMs internationally.

ISRAELI BORDER CONTROL

Israel's rigorous entrance procedures are a source of annoyance for some and a breeze for others. Don't be surprised if you are asked questions about your reasons for travelling, trips you've recently made, your occupation, your acquaintances in Israel and the Palestinian Territories, and possibly your religious or family background.

If you are meeting friends or family, you might want to have their full name, address and phone number handy (a letter confirming you're staying with them is ideal). If you have hotel reservations, a printout may help – or be completely superfluous.

If border officials suspect that you're coming to take part in pro-Palestinian political activities or if you have an Arab or Muslim name, they may ask some probing questions; on occasion they have even searched laptops. Sometimes they take an interest in passport stamps from places like Lebanon or Iran, but often they don't. The one sure way to get grilled is to sound evasive or to contradict yourself – the security screeners are trained to try to trip you up. Whatever happens, remain calm and polite.

Israeli airport security is the strictest in the business. It unabashedly uses profiling, but not necessarily in the way you think. In 1986, a pregnant Irish woman, Anne Mary Murphy, almost boarded an El Al 747 in London with Semtex explosive hidden in her luggage – it had been placed there without her knowledge by her Jordanian boyfriend, Nezar Hindawi, who is still in prison in the UK. Ever since then, Israeli security officials – at Ben Gurion Airport and at airports abroad – have been on the lookout for anyone who might unwittingly serve as a suicide bomber, with young, unmarried Western women near the top of the profiling list.

In the Palestinian Territories, SIM cards can be easily bought from either Jawwal and Wataniya – the two Palestinian networks – and used in unlocked phones.

TRAVELLERS WITH DISABILITIES

In Israel, access to public amenities for people with disabilities, including those in wheelchairs, is approaching the levels of Western Europe and North America. Almost all hotels and HI hostels are required to have one or more rooms outfitted for wheelchair users, and many tourist attractions, including museums, archaeological sites and beaches, are wheelchair accessible to a significant degree. Quite a few nature reserves offer trails designed for wheelchairs (see www.parks.org.il and www.kkl.org.il), with new ones are being added each year. Restaurants are a mixed bag because few have fully wheelchair-accessible bathrooms. Kerb ramps for wheelchairs are widespread. For details on accessibility, check out the website of Access Israel, www.aisrael.org

The Palestinian Territories are less well equipped than Israel, and getting around is made more difficult by Israel Defense Forces checkpoints, which often have to be crossed on foot and sometimes require moving over and around barriers.

VISAS

In general, Western visitors to Israel and the Palestinian Territories are issued free, on-arrival tourist (B/2) visas by Israel. For specifics on who qualifies, visit www.mfa.gov.il (click on 'Consular Services' and then 'Visas').

On-arrival visas are usually valid for 90 days. But some travellers, such as those entering by land from Egypt or Jordan, may be given just 30 days or even two weeks – it's up to the discretion of the border-control official. If there is any indication that you are coming to participate in pro-Palestinian protests, plan to engage in missionary activity or are seeking illegal employment, you may find yourself on the next flight home.

Israel no longer stamps tourists' passports (though it retains the right to do so). Instead, visitors are given a small loose-leaf entry card to serve as proof of lawful entry. It's easy to lose, but keep it somewhere safe as it's your only proof that you're in the country legally (eg to pass through a roadblock to/from the West Bank). For info on potential issues with Israeli passport stamps, see p39.

We've heard reports of Israeli authorities at Allenby/King Hussein Bridge and Ben Gurion Airport issuing 'Palestinian Authority Only' entry permits to travellers with family or personal connections in the West Bank, making it difficult or impossible to get past the IDF roadblocks that regulate traffic from the West Bank into Israel, including Jerusalem.

Extension

To extend a tourist (B/2) visa, you have a couple of options:

➡ Do a 'visa run' to Jordan, Egypt or overseas. This might get you an additional three months – or just one. Ask other travellers for the latest low-down.

➡ Apply to extend your visa (90NIS). Extensions are granted by the Population & Immigration Authority (www.piba.gov.il), part of the Ministry of the Interior, whose offices include bureaux in Jerusalem, Tel Aviv and Eilat.

VOLUNTEERING

Israel abounds with volunteer opportunities. These are often on archaeological digs, at ILH hostels or environmental organisations. Check the websites of the National Council for Volunteering in Israel (www.ivolunteer. org.il) or Israel Hostels (www.hostels-israel.com/volunteer-in-a-hostel).

If you're between 18 and 35, it's also possible to volunteer on a kibbutz. Volunteers interested in a taste of the lifestyle at these communal agricultural communities can expect to spend two to six months helping with manual labour, which could include anything from gardening to washing dishes to milking cows. Food and accommodation are provided and sometimes there's a small weekly allowance. For more information, visit www.kibbutz.org.il/eng.

In the Palestinian Territories, volunteer opportunities often involve helping the many NGOs working to improve everyday life for Palestinians, such as Medical Aid for Palestinians (www.map-uk.org). Doing due diligence is essential as some outfits are more reputable than others.

Getting There & Away

AIR

Israel's main gateway is **Ben Gurion International Airport** (TLV; www.iaa.gov.il), 50km northwest of Jerusalem and 18km southeast of central Tel Aviv. It handles about 20 million passengers a year.

Ramon International Airport (www.iaa.gov.il), in the Arava Valley 18km north of Eilat, is scheduled to open sometime in 2018 as Israel's second international airport. It replaces Eilat's city-centre airport (no more turboprops swooping in low over North Beach!) and will handle the low-cost flights that previously used Ovda (Uvda) airbase.

Israeli airport security is very tight so international travellers should check in at least three hours before their flight – when flying both to and from Israel.

The only Middle Eastern cities with direct air links to Tel Aviv are Amman, served by Royal Jordanian (www.rj.com); Cairo, served by Air Sinai (a low-profile but astonishingly expensive subsidiary of Egyptair); and Istanbul, served by Turkish Airlines (www.turkishairlines.com). There is no airport in the Palestinian Territories so the only way to get to the West Bank by air is to fly via either Israel or Jordan.

LAND

Egypt

Taba crossing, on the Red Sea 10km south of Eilat, is the only border post between Israel and Egypt that's open to tourists. Check travel advisories before taking this route as the security situation in Sinai is changeable.

You can get a 14-day Sinai-only entry permit at the border, allowing travel to Red Sea resorts stretching from Taba to Sharm El Sheikh, plus St Katherine's. It's no longer possible to travel overland to Cairo via Sinai because of the security situation. Egyptian visas valid for the whole country are available at the consulate in Eilat or the embassy in Tel Aviv.

Getting There & Away Egged buses 15 and 16 link Eilat's central bus station with Taba (4.20NIS, 36 minutes, daily except Friday evening). A taxi from the city centre costs 50NIS to 60NIS.

Jordan

While the two land crossings between Israel and Jordan are quick and efficient, the Allenby/King Hussein Bridge crossing between the Israeli-controlled West Bank and Jordan is not always as smooth.

Jordan River/Sheikh Hussein Crossing

Generally far less busy than Allenby/King Hussein Bridge, this crossing is in the Jordan Valley 8km east of Beit She'an, 30km south of the Sea of Galilee, 135km northeast of Tel Aviv and 90km northeast of Amman. Jordan issues on-arrival visas for many nationalities. The crossing is open from 7am to 8.30pm Sunday to Thursday and 8.30am to 6.30pm Friday and Saturday.

The Israeli side lacks an ATM, but you can get a cash advance at the currency exchange window, open whenever the terminal is.

For travellers heading to Jordan, getting through Israeli border formalities usually takes no more than half an hour. You then have to take a bus to cross to the Jordanian side of the river (walking across is forbidden).

Getting There & Away Taxis that wait at the border can take you to Beit She'an (40NIS, but you'll need to haggle hard) and destinations around Israel, including Tiberias, Jerusalem and Tel Aviv.

BORDER CLOSINGS

Yom Kippur All Israeli land borders and airports closed.

Eid Al Hijra/Muslim New Year Land crossings with Jordan closed.

Eid Al Adha Taba crossing with Egypt and Palestinian wing of the Allenby/King Hussein Bridge closed.

Ramadan All crossings may close early

On the Jordanian side, regular service taxis travel to/from Irbid's West bus station.

Nazarene Tours (☎04-601-0458; 3 Marj Ibn Amer St; 80NIS; ⏲departures 8.30am Tue, Thu & Sat) links Nazareth with Amman via the Jordan River/Sheikh Hussein crossing on Sunday, Tuesday, Thursday and Saturday. Departures are at 8.30am from the company's Nazareth office, near the Bank of Jerusalem and the Nazareth Hotel (not to be confused with the office of Nazarene Transport & Tourism in the city centre), and at 2pm from Amman's Royal Hotel (University St). Reserve by phone at least two days ahead.

Yitzhak Rabin/Wadi Araba Crossing

Located just 3km northeast of Eilat, this crossing is handy for trips to Aqaba, Petra and Wadi Rum. It is open from 6.30am to 8pm Sunday to Thursday and from 8am on Friday and Saturday. Note: Jordanian visas are no longer issued on arrival here so you'll need to get one in advance.

Getting There & Away A taxi ride to the border to/from Eilat costs 50NIS. If you're coming by bus from the north (eg Jerusalem, Tel Aviv or the Dead Sea), it may be possible to get off on Rte 90 at the turn-off to the border or at Kibbutz Eilot, but from there it's 2km on foot through the desert (along Rte 109).

Once you're in Jordan, you can take a cab to Aqaba. If you're heading to Petra, you can catch a minibus for the 120km ride in Aqaba; vehicles depart when full between 6am and 7am and 11am and noon. Alternatively, bargain for a taxi all the way from the border to Petra.

Allenby/King Hussein Bridge

Linking the Israeli-controlled West Bank with Jordan, this busy crossing is 46km east of Jerusalem, 8km east of Jericho and 60km west of Amman. It is the only crossing that people with Palestinian Authority travel documents, including West Bank Palestinians, can use to travel to and from Jordan and the outside world, so traffic can be heavy, especially on Sunday, around holidays and on weekdays from 11am to 3pm.

Try to get to the border as early in the day as possible – times when tourists can cross may be limited and delays are common. Israeli citizens (including dual citizens) are not allowed to use this crossing.

Jordan does not issue on-arrival visas at the Allenby/King Hussein crossing – you'll have to arrange a visa in advance at a Jordanian embassy, such as the one in Ramat Gan, near Tel Aviv. However, if your visit to the Palestinian Territories and/or Israel started in Jordan, you won't need a new visa to cross back into Jordan through Allenby/King Hussein Bridge, provided you do so within the period of validity of your Jordanian visa – just show your stamped exit slip.

The bus across the frontier costs JD7, plus JD1.50 per piece of luggage. Jordan has doubled the cost of Jordanian visas from JD30 to JD60.

Bring plenty of cash (Jordanian dinars are the most useful) and make sure you have small change. There are no ATMs, but both sides have exchange bureaux.

This crossing can be frustratingly delay-prone, especially if you're travelling into the West Bank and/or Israel. Chaotic queues, intrusive security, luggage X-rays (expect to be separated from your bags) and impatient officials are the norm; expect questions from Israeli security personnel if your passport has stamps from places like Lebanon or you're headed to less touristed parts of the West Bank. There are separate processing areas for Palestinians and tourists.

The border is (officially) open from 8am to midnight Sunday to Thursday and 8am until 3pm on Friday and Saturday, but arrive after 6pm and you risk not being able to cross.

Getting There & Away Shared taxis run by Abdo (☎02-628-3281) and Al Nijmeh (☎02-627-7466), most frequent before 11am, link the blue-and-white bus station opposite Jerusalem's Damascus Gate with the border (40NIS, 30 minutes); the charge per suitcase is 5NIS. Private taxis can cost as much as 300NIS, with hotel pick-up as an option.

Egged buses 948, 961 and 966 from West Jerusalem's Central Bus Station to Beit She'an (and points north) stop on Rte 90 at the turn-off to Allenby Bridge (12.50NIS, about hourly, 40 minutes). Walking the last few kilometres to the crossing is forbidden, so you'll have to take a taxi (50NIS).

To get to/from Amman's Abdali or South bus stations, you can take a servees (shared taxi) or minibus (JD8, 45 minutes); a taxi costs about JD22. JETT (www.jett.com.jo) runs a daily bus to the border from Abdali (JD8.50, one hour, departure at 7am).

Getting Around

AIR

Daily flights to Eilat from Ben Gurion Airport's domestic terminal are handled by Arkia (www.arkia.com) and Israir (www.israirairlines.com). Arkia also flies to Haifa. Deals are often available online, with one-way tickets sometimes going for as little as 86NIS to or from Ben Gurion – the price of a bus ticket!

BICYCLE

Cycling is a great way to get around Israel. The distances between cities, villages, nature reserves and archaeological sites are relatively short; many highways have wide shoulders (though drivers can politely be described as erratic, and cycling is forbidden on some major intercity routes); and there is a growing number of off-road bike trails and scenic byways. Biking is also a great way to meet people and experience the country at ground level. Best of all, it's free and environmentally friendly.

The main drawback to cycling, other than the risk of being run over, is the heat. Always set off as early in the day as possible and carry plenty of water. Choose your route carefully: while the coastal plain is flat enough, the Upper Galilee, the Golan and the Dead Sea region have lots of steep hills, and the Negev Desert and the Jordan Valley can be mercilessly hot.

Bicycles can be taken on intercity buses for no charge and are allowed on all trains – including those serving Ben Gurion Airport – except during rush hour (6am to 9am and 3pm to 7pm) Sunday to Thursday and on Saturday evening (there's no rush hour on Friday and the eves of Jewish holidays so all trains are bike-friendly then). Folding bikes can travel with you inside buses and can be taken on all trains.

Palestinian roads are not designed for cycling, and it is relatively rare to see bicycles in the West Bank. But a growing number of tour groups cater to cyclists, including Bike Palestine (www.bikepalestine.com).

BUS

Almost every town, village and kibbutz has bus service at least a few times a day – except, that is, from mid-afternoon on Friday until Saturday in the late afternoon or evening, when the vast majority of intercity lines don't run at all (exceptions include services to Eilat and Majdal Shams).

Tickets are sold at bus station ticket windows and by bus drivers; exact change is not needed. Return tickets, available on a few lines (eg to Eilat), cost 15% less than two one-way tickets.

Most discounts are available only if you have a rechargeable Rav-Kav smartcard, which comes in two versions: personalised *(ishi)*, which has your picture on it and requires filling out an application; and anonymous *(anonimi)*, which is sold at stations (5NIS) and by drivers (10NIS) and is transferable but qualifies you for only limited discounts. The good news is that both get you 20% off all fares; the bad news is that at present, you need a separate Rav-Kav account for each bus company (a single card can hold up to eight accounts).

Israel no longer has a bus duopoly (the Egged and Dan cooperatives used to divide the country between them). Rather, there are now about 20 companies, including Egged and Dan, that compete for routes in Ministry of Transport tenders. The Public Transportation Info Center (www.bus.co.il), a snap to use once you figure it out, provides details in English on all bus companies' routes, times and prices. Smartphone apps for Android and iPhones can be downloaded from the website.

> **DRIVING ON SHABBAT**
>
> According to most interpretations of Halacha (Jewish law), driving a motor vehicle violates the sanctity of Shabbat (the Sabbath), in part by contravening prohibitions against lighting fire and travelling more than 2000 cubits. As a result, certain streets, neighbourhoods and villages populated almost exclusively by Orthodox and ultra-Orthodox Jews are closed to traffic from sundown on Friday until an hour after sundown on Saturday, as well as on many Jewish holidays. If you come upon a street blocked by a barrier, don't drive around it or you may find yourself facing angry locals or even having stones thrown at you.
>
> By tradition (though not law), no one in Jewish areas – except for emergency services – drives a motor vehicle on Yom Kippur.

Bus companies you're likely to run across:

Afikim (www.afikim-t.co.il)
Dan (www.dan.co.il)
Egged (www.egged.co.il)
Kavim (www.kavim-t.co.il)
Metropoline (www.metropoline.com)
Nateev Express (www.nateevexpress.com)
Nazareth Tourism & Transport (www.ntt-buses.com)
Rama (www.golanbus.co.il)

The only bus tickets that need to be (or can be) ordered in advance are Egged tickets to/from Eilat, which can be reserved up to 14 days ahead via www.egged.co.il, by smartphone app or by phone (dial 2800 or 03-694-8888). Note: the system may only accept Israeli credit cards; PayPal may also be an option.

CAR & MOTORCYCLE

To drive a vehicle, all you need is your regular driving licence; an international driving licence is not required. Israel's automobile association is known as Memsi (www.memsi.co.il).

Car Hire

Having your own wheels lets you travel at your own pace, stay in out-of-the-way B&Bs, get lost along back roads and cover a lot of ground in a short amount of time. It doesn't make much sense to have a car in Jerusalem or Tel Aviv – parking can be a huge hassle – but it's a great idea in hilly Haifa and in the Galilee, Golan and Negev, where many towns and villages are served by just a handful of buses a day. Gasoline/petrol costs about US$2 per litre (US$7.60 per US gallon).

Car hire with insurance and unlimited kilometres costs as little as 140NIS per day, US$200 per week or US$600 per month (the incredibly cheap prices advertised online don't include insurance). Most major international rental companies have offices in Israel. If you get parking or traffic tickets, the rental company may forward them to you, tacking on a handling fee of 60NIS. Some companies require that renters be at least 25 years old.

Note: most rental agencies forbid you to take their cars into parts of the West Bank defined in the Oslo Accords as Areas A and B; exceptions include Green Peace (www.greenpeace.co.il), Dallah (www.dallahrentacar.com) and Goodluck (www.goodluckcars.com). It's no problem, though, driving a car rented in Israel on Rte 1 from Jerusalem to the Dead Sea or Rte 90 from the Dead Sea to the Sea of Galilee.

Road Rules

Seat belts are required at all times. Unless you have a hands-free set, using a mobile phone while driving is illegal and subject to a fine of 1000NIS. From November to March, car headlights must be turned on whenever you're driving on an intercity road.

Israeli road signs are marked in English, Hebrew and (usually) Arabic; be prepared for some quirky transliterations. The best road maps are produced by Mapa (www.mapa.co.il/maps) and are available at all bookshops.

Police cars always have their blue (sometimes red and blue) lights flashing, so seeing police lights in your rear-view mirror doesn't mean you're in trouble (if you are, they'll make that clear with a megaphone).

LOCAL TRANSPORT

Bicycle

Bike paths have been going up in cities all over Israel, but the most developed network is in Tel Aviv, which has a municipal bike-rental program, aimed at commuters (bikes are free for the first 30 minutes), called Tel-O-Fun (www.tel-o-fun.co.il).

Taxi

Taking a 'special' (speshel; ie nonshared) taxi can be very convenient but, at times, a bit of a hassle because some unscrupulous drivers overcharge tourists. The best way to avoid getting ripped off is to sound like a confident old hand as you give the street address, including a cross street. It's almost always to your advantage to use the meter (by law the driver has to put it on if you ask); make sure it is reset to the flag-fall price after you get in.

In Israel, flag fall is 12.30NIS (10.50NIS in Eilat). Tariff 2 (25% more expensive than Tariff 1) applies between 9pm and 5.30am and on Shabbat and Jewish holidays. Wait time costs 94NIS per hour.

Many Israelis now use the mobile phone app GetTaxi (www.gettaxi.co.il), available in Android and iPhone versions, to order and pay for taxis in all parts of Israel (except Eilat). Uber launched in Israel in 2014.

Taxi drivers do not expect tips, but in the absence of a rip-off attempt, it's fine to leave a shekel or two in change.

SHERUT

Sheruts (sheh-*roots*), known in the Palestinian Territories as a *servees* (sehr-*vees*), are a useful way to get around. These vehicles, often 13-seat minivans, operate on a fixed route for a fixed price. They're like a bus except that they don't have pre-set stops. If you don't know the fare, ask your fellow passengers.

Sheruts (Hebrew plural: *moniyot sherut* – the word *sherutim* means 'bathrooms'!) are generally quicker than buses. They begin their runs from a recognised taxi rank and leave only when they're full, so you may have to hang around for a while, though rarely more than 20 minutes. You can get out anywhere you like but will probably have to pay the full fare to the final destination. Many sheruts operate 24/7 and are the only means of public transport in Israel on Shabbat and Jewish holidays, eg between Tel Aviv and Jerusalem. Prices are the same or slightly lower than buses except on Shabbat, when they rise slightly.

TRAIN

Israel Railways (www.rail.co.il) runs a comfortable and convenient network of passenger rail services; details on departure times are also available from the Public Transportation Info Center (www.bus.co.il). Trains do not run from mid-afternoon Friday until after sundown on Saturday, or on some Jewish holidays. Return tickets are 10% cheaper than two one-way tickets; children aged five to 10 get a 20% discount. Unlike buses, Israel's rail system is wheelchair accessible.

Israel Railway's oldest line, inaugurated in 1892 and famously scenic, links three Tel Aviv stations with southern Jerusalem (23.50NIS, 1½ hours). The system's heavily used main line runs along the coast at least twice an hour, affording fine views of the Mediterranean as it links Tel Aviv with Haifa (32NIS, one hour). Tel Aviv also enjoys convenient services to Ben Gurion Airport (16NIS, 18 minutes, at least hourly 24 hours a day except Shabbat), as does Haifa.

In late 2018 a US$2 billion high-speed rail line between Jerusalem and Tel Aviv is scheduled to open, shortening the travel time between the cities to just 28 minutes. The line will also serve Ben Gurion Airport.

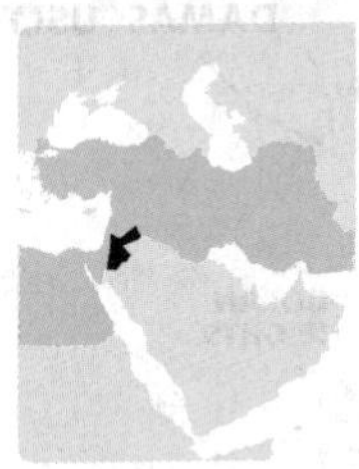

Jordan

Includes ➡

Amman 288
Jerash 301
Dead Sea & the West.................307
Mujib Biosphere Reserve 310
Madaba 313
Dana Biosphere Reserve 318
Petra & Wadi Musa.....320
Wadi Rum..................333
Aqaba 337
Understand Jordan....343
Survival Guide...........347

Why Go?

Ahlan wa sahlan! – 'Welcome!' From the Bedouin of Wadi Rum to the taxi drivers of Amman, you'll be on the receiving end of this open-armed welcome every day. It's this, and a sense of stability amid a problematic neighbourhood, that makes travel in Jordan such a delight.

With heavyweight neighbours pulling big historical punches, Jordan easily holds its own. Amman, Jerash and Umm Qais were cities of the Roman Decapolis, while biblical sites include Bethany-Beyond-the-Jordan, where Jesus was baptised, and Mt Nebo, where Moses reputedly surveyed the Promised Land. Grandest of all is the impressive Nabataean capital of Petra, carved from vertical cliffs.

But Jordan is not just about antiquities – it also offers the great outdoors. Whether diving in Aqaba, trekking in the camel-prints of Lawrence of Arabia or hiking through stunning canyons, Jordan's eco-savvy nature reserves offer the best of adventures in the Middle East.

Best for Nature

- Ajloun Forest Reserve (p305)
- Dana Biosphere Reserve (p318)
- Shaumari Wildlife Reserve (p311)
- Wadi Rum Protected Area (p333)

Best for History

- Petra (p320)
- Jerash (p301)
- Umm Qais (Gadara; p306)
- Madaba (p313)

When to Go

Amman

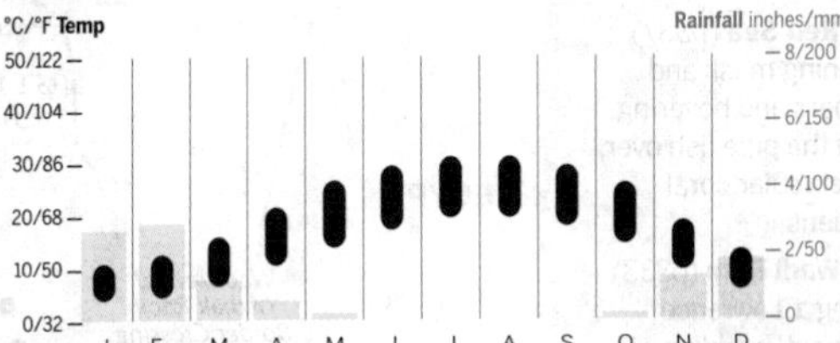

Mar–May The weather is perfect, with warm days, cool nights and spectacular wildflowers.

Sep–Nov A good time to go hiking, with fewer visitors and relief after intense summer heat.

Dec–Feb The Red and Dead Seas offer balmy dips, while upland Jordan shivers with winter chills.

Jordan Highlights

1. **Amman** (p288) Encountering modern Jordan in the cafes and malls of this vibrant capital.
2. **Jerash** (p301) Wandering among the impressive Roman ruins, and enjoying community engagement in nearby Ajloun.
3. **Jordan Trail** (p305) Hiking sections of this trail in Mujib or Dana Biosphere Reserves.
4. **Dead Sea** (p308) Descending below zero for a bob in this sea, the lowest point on earth.
5. **Madaba** (p313) Piecing together early Christian history in the mosaics here.
6. **Karak Castle** (p317) and **Shobak Castle** (p320) Listening to the thunder of ghostly hooves at Jordan's most impressive Crusader forts.
7. **Petra's Siq** (p321) Treading the path of history, with the sheer-sided chasm leading to an ancient world.
8. **Red Sea** (p337) Donning mask and flippers and hovering with the pipe fish over spectacular coral gardens.
9. **Wadi Rum** (p333) Living a 'Lawrence moment' by riding through the desert on a camel.
10. **The Badia** (p311) Exploring this region with its desert castles and Shaumari Wildlife Reserve.

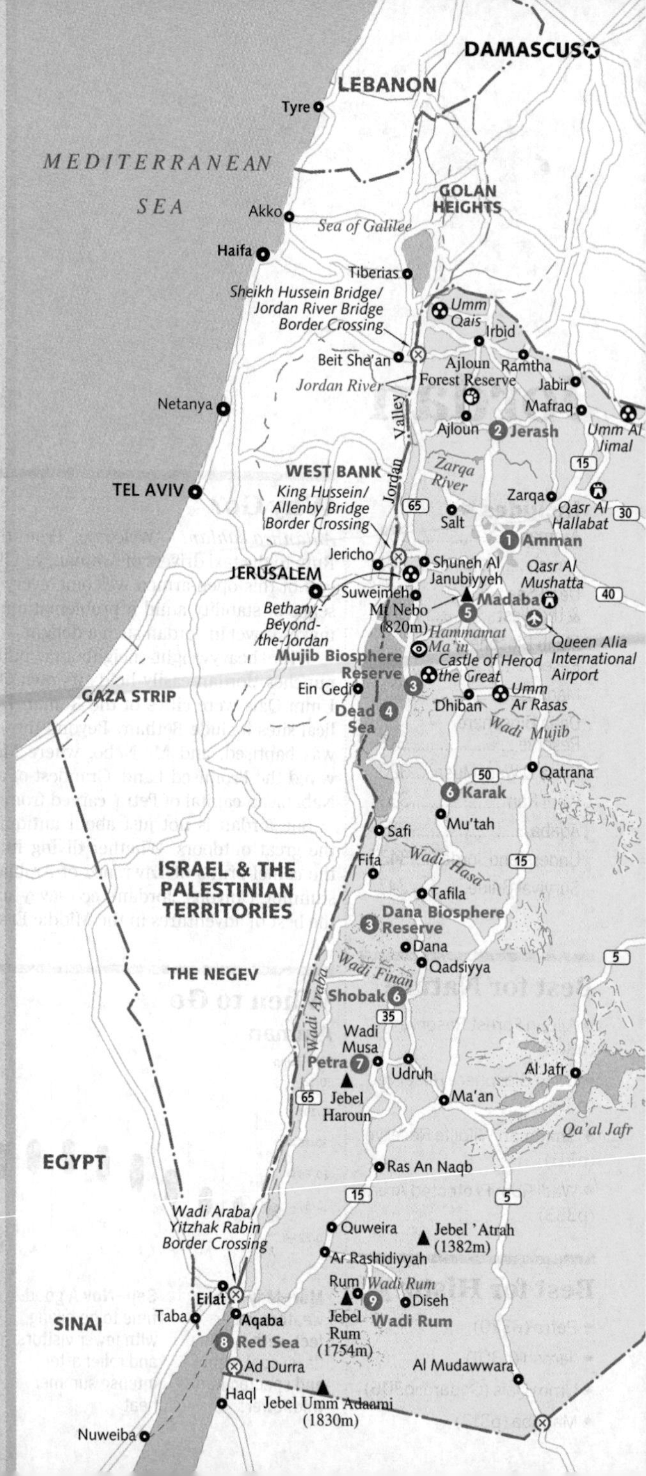

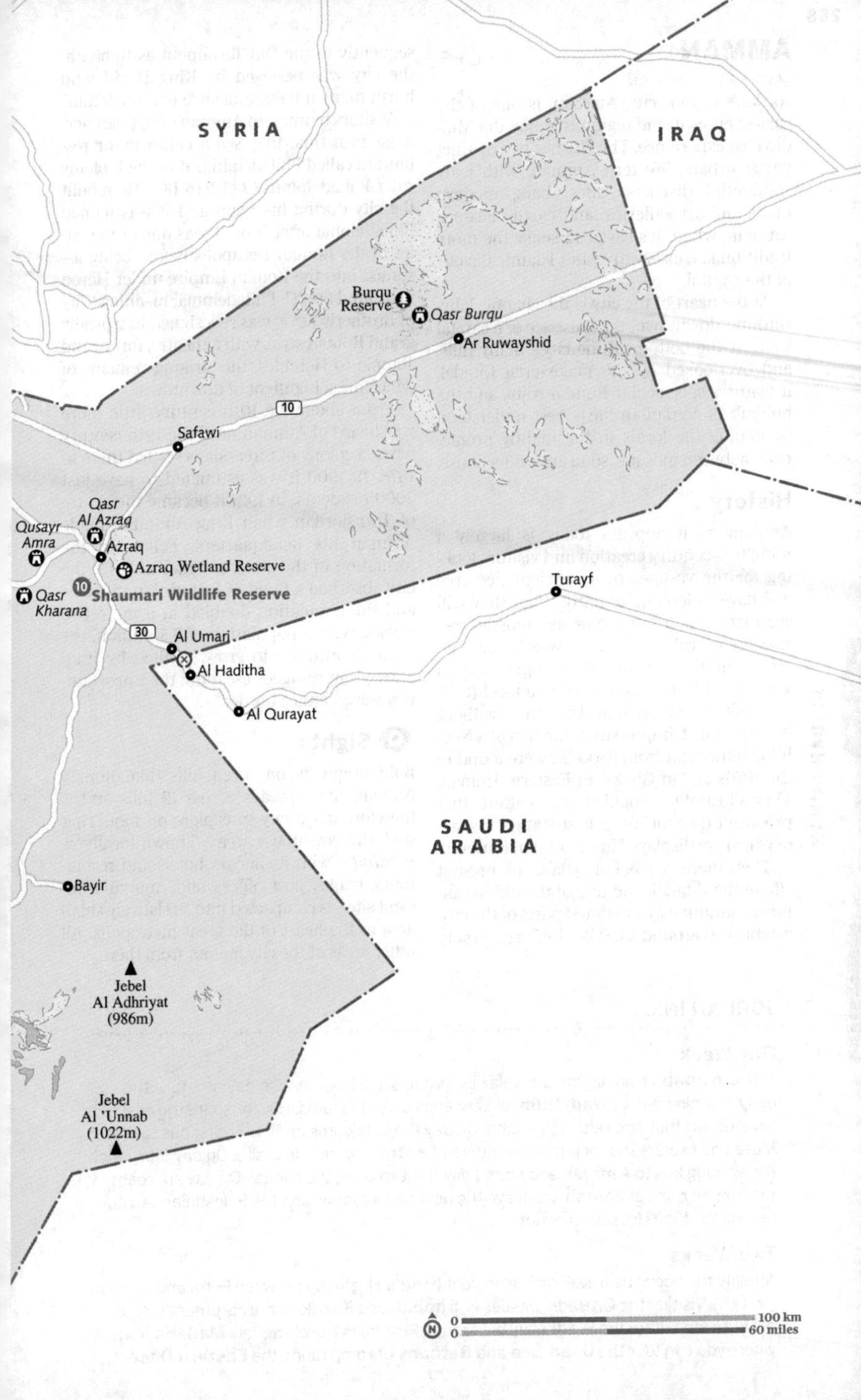

SYRIA
IRAQ
Burqu Reserve
Qasr Burqu
Ar Ruwayshid
10
Safawi
Qasr Al Azraq
Qusayr Amra
Azraq
Azraq Wetland Reserve
10
Shaumari Wildlife Reserve
Qasr Kharana
30
Al Umari
Al Haditha
Al Qurayat
Turayf
SAUDI ARABIA
Bayir
Jebel Al Adhriyat (986m)
Jebel Al 'Unnab (1022m)
0 100 km
0 60 miles

AMMAN عمان

06 / POP 3.5 MILLION

Jordan's capital city, Amman, is one of the easiest cities in the region to enjoy the Middle East experience. The city has two distinct parts: urbane Western Amman, with leafy residential districts, cafes, bars, modern malls and art galleries; and earthy Eastern Amman, where it's easier to sense the more traditional, conservative and Islamic flavour of the capital.

At the heart of the city is the chaotic, labyrinthine 'downtown', the must-see of a capital visit. At the bottom of the city's many hills, and overlooked by the magisterial Citadel, it features spectacular Roman ruins and the hubbub of Jordanian life – best understood by joining the locals in the nightly promenade between mosque, souq and coffeehouse.

History

Amman as it appears today is largely a mid-20th-century creation and visitors looking for the vestiges of its ancient pedigree will have to look quite hard. What they will see instead is a homogeneous, mostly low-rise, cream-coloured city of weathered concrete buildings, some sparklingly clad in white marble, others in need of a facelift.

That's not to say that Amman is without history. In fact, impressive remnants of a Neolithic settlement from 8500 BC were found in the 1970s at Ain Ghazal in Eastern Amman. They illustrate a sophisticated culture that produced the world's earliest statues – some of which are displayed in the Jordan Museum.

Then there is Jebel al-Qala'a, the present site of the Citadel, and one of the oldest and most continuously inhabited parts of the city, established around 1800 BC. Referred to subsequently in the Old Testament as Rabbath, the city was besieged by King David who burnt many inhabitants alive in a brick kiln.

Visitors bump into Amman's Egyptian heritage each time they see a company or restaurant called Philadelphia, after the Ptolemy ruler Philadelphius (283–246 BC). He rebuilt the city during his reign and it was named Philadelphia after him. It was one of the cities of the Roman Decapolis before being assumed into the Roman Empire under Herod in around 30 BC. Philadelphia, meaning 'City of Brotherly Love', was redesigned in typically grand Roman style, with a theatre, forum and Temple to Hercules, the striking remains of which are a highlight of downtown.

From about the 10th century little more was heard of Amman until the 19th century when a colony of Circassians settled there in 1878. In 1900 it was estimated to have just 2000 residents. In 1921 it became the centre of Transjordan when King Abdullah made Amman his headquarters. Following the formation of the state of Israel in 1948, the city absorbed a flood of Palestinian refugees and the population doubled in a mere two weeks. With a population of 3.5 million, the capital continues to grow, swelled by Iraqi and Syrian refugees escaping the uncertainties across either border.

Sights

Built originally on seven hills (like Rome), Amman now spreads across 19 hills and is therefore not a city to explore on foot. That said, the downtown area – known locally as *il-balad* – with its budget hotels and restaurants, banks, post offices and Amman's ancient sites, is compacted into a relatively small area in the heart of the great metropolis. All other areas of the city fan out from there.

JORDAN IN...

One Week

Arrive in **Aqaba** from Egypt, and relax in Jordan's holiday town. On day two, take the early-morning bus to **Wadi Rum**, of Lawrence of Arabia fame. Hike or share the cost of a 4WD desert tour and return to Aqaba. On day three, take the early-morning bus to Wadi Musa and explore the rock-hewn wonders of **Petra**, a world-class site. On day four, catch the evening bus to **Amman** and spend day five exploring the capital. On day six, roam the Roman ruins of **Jerash** and leave the next day for Israel and the Palestinian Territories via the King Hussein crossing.

Two Weeks

Amplify the above by travelling the ancient **King's Highway** between Petra and Amman (by taxi), visiting the Crusader castles of **Shobak** and **Karak**, the escarpment village of **Dana**, and dramatic **Wadi Mujib** en route. Rest up in travel-friendly **Madaba** from where you can tour the **Dead Sea** and **Bethany**,or romp round the **Eastern Desert**.

Downtown

★Citadel RUINS

(Map p292; ☎06 463 8795; Jebel Al Qala'a; JD2, free with Jordan Pass; ⏰8am-7pm Sat-Thu Apr-Sep, to 4pm Sat-Thu Oct-Mar, 10am-4pm Fri year-round) The area known as the Citadel sits on the highest hill in Amman, Jebel Al Qala'a (about 850m above sea level), and is the site of ancient Rabbath-Ammon. Occupied since the Bronze Age, it's surrounded by a 1700m-long wall, which was rebuilt many times during the Bronze and Iron Ages, as well as during the Roman, Byzantine and Umayyad periods. There's plenty to see, but the Citadel's most striking sights are the Temple of Hercules and the Ummayad Palace.

★Darat Al Funun GALLERY

(House of Arts; Map p292; ☎06 464 3251; www.daratalfunun.org; 13 Nadim Al Mallah St, Lweibdeh; ⏰10am-7pm Sat-Thu, closed Aug) FREE On the hillside to the north of the downtown area, this cultural haven is dedicated to contemporary art. The main building features an excellent art gallery with works by Jordanian and other Arab artists, an art library, and workshops for Jordanian and visiting sculptors and painters. A schedule of upcoming exhibitions and events is available on the website.

★Roman Theatre THEATRE

(Map p292; JD2, incl Museum of Popular Traditions, free with Jordan Pass; ⏰8am-4pm Sat-Thu, 9am-4pm Fri Oct-Mar, 8am-7pm Apr-Sep) This magnificently restored theatre is the most obvious and impressive remnant of Roman Philadelphia, and is the highlight of Amman for most foreign visitors. The theatre itself is cut into the northern side of a hill, and has a seating capacity of 6000. The best time for photographs is the morning, although the views from the top tiers just before sunset are also superb.

Duke's Diwan MUSEUM

(Map p292; Al Malek Faisal St; ⏰8am-dusk) FREE This historic townhouse, built in 1924, has served as a post office (Amman's first), the Ministry of Finance and a hotel. Today, it has been restored with period furnishings by a prominent Jordanian businessman, who is also the duke of the village of Mukhaybeh. The collection of old photos of Amman provide an interesting glimpse of a bygone age.

Museum of Popular Traditions MUSEUM

(Map p292; ☎06 465 1670; Roman Theatre complex; admission incl in Roman Theatre ticket, free with Jordan Pass; ⏰8am-4pm Sat-Thu, 9am-4pm Fri Oct-Mar, 8am-7pm Apr-Sep) This small museum, immediately to the left as you enter the Roman Theatre, has well-presented displays of traditional costumes, jewellery and face masks, along with mannequins dressed in the traditional costumes of Jordan's different ethnic groups. A separate gallery displays mosaics from Jerash and Madaba.

NEED TO KNOW

Capital Amman

Country code ☎962

Language Arabic (English widely spoken)

Official name Hashemite Kingdom of Jordan

Population 10 million

Currency Jordanian dinar (JD)

Mobile phones SIM cards widely available

Money ATMs widespread; credit cards (except Amex) widely accepted

Visas Available on arrival

Exchange Rates

Australia	A$1	JD0.56
Egypt	E£1	JD0.04
Euro zone	€1	JD0.88
Israel & the Palestinian Territories	1NIS	JD0.2
UK	£1	JD1
USA	US$1	JD0.71

For current exchange rates see www.xe.com.

Resources

Bible Places (www.bibleplaces.com) Biblical sites.

Jordan Tourism Board (www.visitjordan.com)

Royal Society for the Conservation of Nature (www.rscn.org.jo) Nature reserves.

Jebel Amman & Around

★Royal Automobile Museum MUSEUM

(☎06 541 1392; www.royalautomuseum.jo; King Hussein Park; JD3, with audio guide JD5; ⏰10am-7pm Wed-Mon, from 11am Fri) You really don't have to be a car enthusiast to enjoy this museum,

Amman

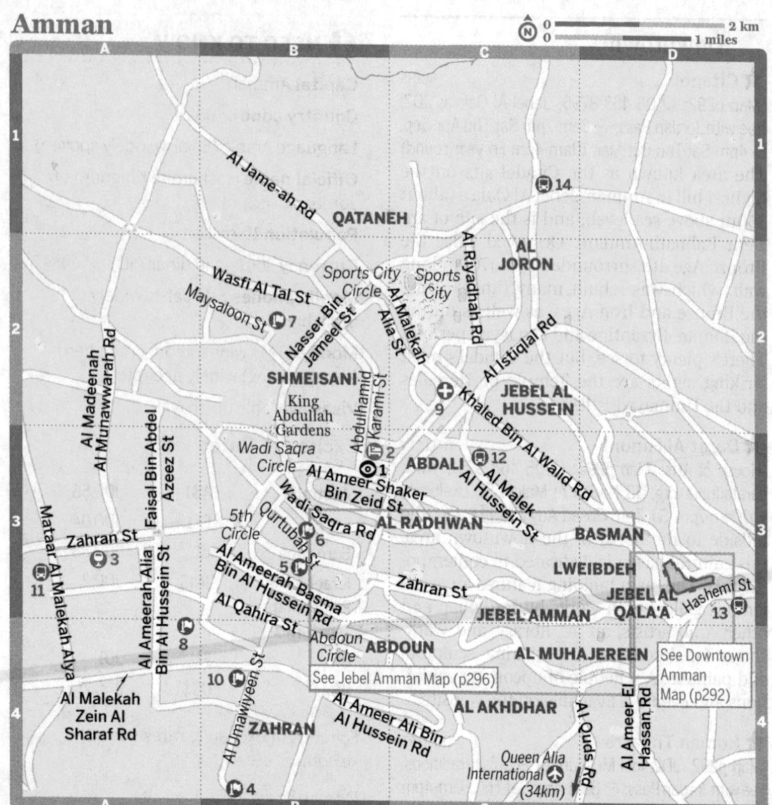

which displays more than 70 classic cars and motorbikes from the personal collection of King Hussein. It's something of a gem, and a great way to recount the story of modern Jordan. Vehicles range from pre-1950s glories to modern sports cars, taking in chrome-clad American cruisers to regal Rolls Royces along the way, with accounts of presidential visits, Hollywood stars and defunct Middle Eastern monarchies enlivening the narrative.

★ Jordan National Gallery of Fine Arts GALLERY

(Map p296; ☎06 463 0128; www.nationalgallery.org; Hosni Fareez St, Jebel Lweibdeh; JD5; ⏱9am-5pm Wed-Mon) This small but impressive gallery is a wonderful place to gain an appreciation of contemporary Jordanian painting, sculpture and pottery. The attractive space highlights contemporary art from around the Middle East and the wider Muslim world. Temporary exhibitions here are of high quality and serve as a valuable introduction (or refresher) to the world of Islamic art. The gallery is signposted from Suleiman Al Nabulsi St, opposite the King Abdullah Mosque.

Rainbow Street STREET

(Abu Bakr As Siddiq St; Map p292) This street in Jebel Amman is a destination in itself. Ammanis come here every evening to promenade and to visit the many great cafes and restaurants – to see and be seen. There are plenty of shops if you come in the daytime (the area is good for souvenirs), but either way it's best explored by foot as the narrow one-way street easily clogs with traffic any time of day or night.

★ Qasr Al Abad RUINS

(Palace of the Slave; ⏱daylight hours) FREE The small but impressive Qasr Al Abad, west of Amman, is one of the very few examples of pre-Roman construction in Jordan. Mystery surrounds the palace, and even its precise age isn't known, though most scholars believe that Hyrcanus of the powerful Jewish Tobiad

Amman

Sights
1 Haya Cultural Centre........................B3

Activities, Courses & Tours
Experience Jordan.......................(see 3)

Sleeping
2 Kempinski Amman..............................B3

Drinking & Nightlife
3 Rovers Return....................................A3

Information
4 Australian Embassy............................B4
5 Canadian Embassy.............................B3
6 Egyptian Embassy..............................B3
7 Israeli Consulate.................................B2
8 Netherlands Embassy........................A4
9 Palestine Hospital...............................C2
10 US Embassy...B4

Transport
11 JETT (7th Circle)................................A3
12 JETT (Abdali).......................................C3
13 Raghadan Bus Station........................D3
14 Tabarbour Bus Station........................C1

family built it sometime between 187 and 175 BC as a villa or fortified palace. Although never completed, much of the palace has been reconstructed, and remains an impressive site.

Activities

Al Pasha Turkish Bath HAMMAM
(Map p292; ☎06 463 3002; www.pashaturkishbath.com; Al Mahmoud Taha St; JD25; ⌚9am-2am, last booking midnight) A popular hammam (Turkish bath) where you'll be steam cleaned, scrubbed and pummelled until you're pink and glowing. It can be an intense experience, especially if you're not familiar with having a stranger take a scourer to almost every inch of your body, but it's incredibly rejuvenating – you'll come out feeling cleaner than you have in years.

Sleeping

Downtown Amman has many budget hotels. Places listed below all promise hot water and some even deliver. Midrange hotels are mostly in the Jebel Amman area, while top-end hotels are located in Jebel Amman and Shmeisani.

Downtown

★**Jordan Tower Hotel** HOTEL $
(Map p292; ☎06 461 4161; www.jordantoweramman.com; 50 Hashemi St; s/d/tr JD25/35/45, dm/s/d/tr with shared bathroom JD12/18/25/35; @☎) This warm and friendly hotel has a winning location: you couldn't be closer to the key sights without offering beds in the Forum. Rooms are bright and snug with flat-screen TVs; there's also a big, bright and homely reception-cum-lounge area and rooftop restaurant.

Sydney Hotel HOTEL $
(Map p296; ☎06 464 1122; www.sydneyhotelamman.com; 9 Sha'aban Rd; dm without breakfast JD7, s/d JD26/37; ☎) Halfway between Jebel Amman and downtown, this hotel has big rooms that have been recently renovated. There's a huge communal area surrounding reception. Breakfast isn't included for the dorm rate, but the hotel remains a great-value option.

Cliff Hotel HOTEL $
(Map p292; ☎06 462 4273; Al Malek Faisal St; s/d/tr/q with shared bathroom JD7/12/14/21; ☎) This long-standing shoestring option has basic, dark rooms and a bit of a grungy entrance, but there's a big bright lounge area that acts as a sociable meeting place. The shared bathrooms have hot water. A popular choice among younger shoestringers. It offers day trips to the Dead Sea, Petra and other sites. Breakfast costs JD2.

Caravan Hotel HOTEL $
(Map p296; ☎06 566 1195; www.caravanhotel.net; Al Ma'moun St; s/d/tr/q JD22/28/33/38; ☎) Situated on a quiet street near King Abdullah Mosque, this hotel has long been a favoured choice, but these days possibly more for its

DON'T MISS

JORDAN MUSEUM

The **Jordan Museum** (Map p296; www.jordanmuseum.jo/en; btwn Omar Matar & Ali Bin Abi Taleb Sts; JD5; ⌚10am-2pm Sat-Mon, Wed & Thu), located next to the City Hall, is one of the best in the Middle East. Housed in a grand modern building, a series of beautifully presented and informative displays tell Jordan's epic history from the earliest civilisations known to humankind to the present era. Highlights include the oldest-known human statues (the strikingly modern 9500-year-old plaster mannequins of Ain Ghazal), Jordan's share of the Dead Sea Scrolls, and a host of remains from Petra and surrounds.

Downtown Amman

A B C D
1 2 3 4 5 6 7

LWEIBDEH
JEBEL AL QALA'A
Nimer Bin Adwan St
Al Malek Ali Bin Al Hussein St
Al Malek Al Hussein St
Yaqout Al Hamawi St
Sa'id Khair St
Nadim Al Mallah St
Citadel 1
29
17
8
Darat Al Funun 2
Omar Al Khayyam St
15
Cinema Al Hussein St
Yaqout Al Hamawi St
Sa'id Khair St
Shabsough St
Al Amir Mohammed St
Service Taxi 4
16
14
10
19
11
4
Al Malek Faisal St
Service Taxi 7
Service Taxi 2
28
Basman St
Service Taxi 6
Hashemi St
9
Othman Bin Affan St
Ibn Al Atheer St
Service Taxi 3
Service Taxi 38
Service Taxi 1
24
Fruit & Vegetable Souq
Italian St
Moh'd Al Shabeebi St
Fawzi Al Malouf St
12
25
26
27
22
Hardware Souq
18
Rainbow St (Abu Bakr As Siddiq St)
Al Qabartay St
Petra St
6
Quraysh St
Al Mahmoud Taha St
21
23
Khirfan St (Al Malek Faysal Al Awal St)
7
Service Taxi 35
Service Taxi 27
Omar Bin Al Khattab St (Mango St)
Fruit & Vegetable Souq
Al Malek Talal St
Italian St
Quraysh St
Service Taxi 25 & 26
Hashemi St

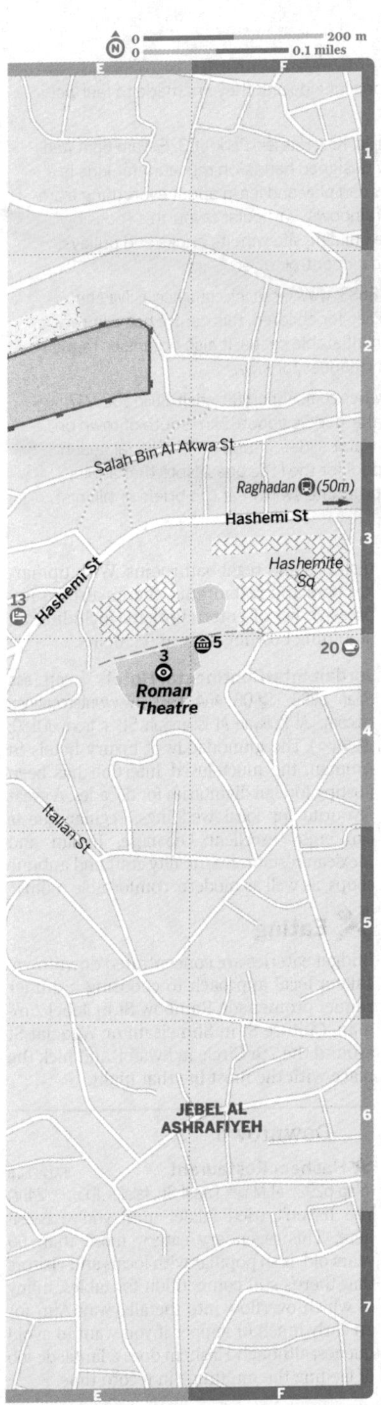

Downtown Amman

Top Sights
1 Citadel ... D2
2 Darat Al Funun ... B3
3 Roman Theatre ... E4

Sights
4 Duke's Diwan ... C4
5 Museum of Popular Traditions ... F4
6 Rainbow Street ... A5

Activities, Courses & Tours
7 Al Pasha Turkish Bath ... A6
8 Beit Sitti ... A2
9 Wild Jordan ... B4

Sleeping
10 Art Hotel ... B3
11 Cliff Hotel ... B4
12 Jabal Amman Hotel ... B5
13 Jordan Tower Hotel ... E3

Eating
14 Afrah Restaurant & Coffeeshop ... B3
15 Habibah ... B3
16 Hashem Restaurant ... B3
17 Najla's Kitchen ... A2
18 Sufra ... A5
Wild Jordan Center ... (see 9)
19 Zajal ... B4

Drinking & Nightlife
20 Al Hail Restaurant & Café ... F4
21 Books@café ... B6
Montage ... (see 23)
22 Shaher's Penthouse Cafeteria ... C5

Entertainment
23 Royal Film Commission ... B6

Shopping
24 Al Afghani ... C5
25 Balian ... B5
26 Jordan River Foundation ... A5
27 Souk Jara ... B5
Wild Jordan Center ... (see 9)

Information
28 Al Madeenah Police Station ... C4
29 Citadel Ticket Office ... D2

reliable service than its dated fixtures. The big clean rooms have a bright aspect.

Art Hotel HOTEL $$

(Map p292; ☎06 463 8900; www.arthoteljordan.com; 30 Al Malek Faisal St; s/d/tr JD40/50/70; 📶) This stylish new hotel occupies a good spot downtown. Rooms are well finished in crisp white with good fittings, and each is decorated idiosyncratically with fun street-art murals.

AMMAN FOR CHILDREN

Amman has an increasing number of attractions for kids and they are made to feel welcome, even in a restaurant late at night.

Children's Museum (06 541 1479; www.cmj.jo; King Hussein Park; JD3; 9am-6pm Wed-Thu & Sat-Mon, 10am-7pm Fri;) This brilliantly designed hands-on museum for kids is a complete joy. In its many zones, young visitors can play and learn about everything from the working of the human body to lasers and rainbows. Particular favourites (possibly because they also involve dressing up) are the building site with its bricks and pulleys, and the mocked-up Royal Jordanian plane and air control tower.

Haya Cultural Centre (Map p290; 06 568 8633; www.facebook.com/hccjo; Ilya Abu Madhi St; 9am-6pm Sat-Thu) Designed especially for children, this centre has a library, a playground, an interactive ecomuseum and an inflatable castle. It also organises regular activities and theatre, puppet and music performances for kids.

Amman Waves (06 412 1704; www.ammanwaves.com; Airport Rd; adult/child JD23/17; 10am-7pm) This enormous Western-style water park is about 15km south of town on the highway to the airport. There are multiple water slides, a tube ride, artificial beach with wave machine and a children's paddling pool for the little ones. Note that adults should respect local sensibilities and wear appropriate swimwear (no briefs or bikinis).

Jebel Amman

★La Locanda BOUTIQUE HOTEL $$
(Map p296; 06 460 2020; www.locandahotel.com; 52 Al Ba'ouniyah St, Lweibdeh; r JD75-95;) This lovely themed boutique hotel – with each of the stylish rooms decorated to match an Arabic music icon – boasts fine fabrics and slick modern bathrooms. There's a relaxed atmosphere and good food and drink at the hotel's Maestro bar (p297).

Hisham Hotel HOTEL $$
(Map p296; 06 464 4028; www.hishamhotel.com.jo; Mithqal Al Fayez St; s/d from JD50/70;) This hotel in the leafy embassy district is an excellent choice if you're looking for a hotel removed from the hustle and bustle of the city while still within easy reach of downtown. The rooms are modern, the decor is attractive and there's a convivial bar next door.

Jabal Amman Hotel HOTEL $$
(Map p292; 06 463 7733; www.jabalammanhotel.com; Rainbow St, Bldg 2; s/d from JD58/88;) Compact, subtle and modern, this conveniently located hotel provides a retreat from city life, with a series of studio apartments in varying sizes. Each comes with a small kitchenette allowing guests to prepare their own food, though breakfast is included in the daily rate.

★Kempinski Amman HOTEL $$$
(Map p290; 06 520 0200; www.kempinski.com; Abdul Hamid Shouman St, Shmeisani; r from JD190;) Amman's most chic and sophisticated hotel has immaculate rooms, designer furnishings and regal bathrooms. With upmarket bars and restaurants, there's also an impressive list of entertainment, including an adjoining bowling alley and cinema.

Jordan InterContinental Hotel HOTEL $$$
(Map p296; 06 464 1361; www.intercontinental.com; Al Kulliyah Al Islamiyah St; r from JD180;) The granddaddy of luxury hotels in Amman, the much-loved InterCon has been hosting foreign dignitaries for decades. A great favourite for local weddings, regular guests can enjoy excellent Lebanese, Indian and Mexican restaurants, quality craft and antique shops, as well as modern, comfortable rooms.

Eating

Budget eateries are concentrated downtown. Take a local approach to choosing a dinner venue: promenade Rainbow St in Jebel Amman, Culture St in Shmeisani or Waqalat St around the 7th Circle in Swafei, and pick the place with the most life that night.

Downtown

★Hashem Restaurant FALAFEL $
(Map p292; Al Malek Faisal St; falafel JD3; 24hr) You haven't tried falafel until you've eaten here. This legendary eatery, more than 50 years old, is so popular with locals and visitors that there's stiff competition for tables, many of which overflow into the alleyway. Aim for an early lunch or supper if you want to avoid queues, although Hashem does a fantastic job of feeding the multitude in record time.

Habibah DESSERTS $
(Map p292; Al Malek Al Hussein St; pastries from 500 fils; ⏲8am-10pm) This legendary shop is a good bet for Middle Eastern sweets and pastries. Sweet tooths of all ages line up for honey-infused, pistachio-topped variations on the region's most famous desserts.

Zajal JORDANIAN $$
(Map p292; Al Amir Mohammed St; mains JD4-8; ⏲9am-2am) This low-key cafe-restaurant attracts a young crowd with its open areas and terrace plus good cheap food. The *manakeesh* (bread with *zaatar*, a blend of spices) is particularly good value.

Afrah Restaurant & Coffeeshop JORDANIAN $$
(Map p292; ☎06 461 0046; Al Malek Faisal St; mains JD5-10; ⏲9am-1am) This popular restaurant in the heart of downtown is as much about the ambience as the traditional Jordanian food. Live Arab pop entertainment is offered most nights from around 9pm.

Jebel Amman

★**Al Quds** FALAFEL $
(Map p296; Rainbow St; falafel 500 fils) One of the best falafel spots in Amman, Al Quds has been serving up tasty sandwiches for more than 50 years. Watch out for lunchtime queues when the office workers descend.

★**Reem Cafeteria** MIDDLE EASTERN $
(Map p296; 2nd Circle; shawarma JD1; ⏲11am-late) There are hundreds of shoebox-sized shawarma kiosks in Amman, but few that have the customers queuing down the street at 3am. Look for the red-and-white awning (with milling crowds) on 2nd Circle.

★**Jasmine House** MEDITERRANEAN $$
(Map p296; ☎06 461 1879; Al Baouniyah St, Lweibdeh; mains around JD7; ⏲4.30-11.30pm Mon-Sat) The scent of the jasmine blooms on the terrace make dining a fragrant experience here. The restaurant, in a 1950s villa, takes inspiration from the Italian homes of the period. Ingredients are fresh and the homemade pasta is superb.

★**Zuwwadeh Restaurant** JORDANIAN $$
(☎06 472 1528; Fuheis; mains JD5-16; ⏲noon-12.30am Fri-Wed, to 1am Thu) Highly popular with Fuheis locals and discerning expats from Amman, the ambience at Zuwwadeh is lively and warm. The food is delicious, especially the *fatteh* (fried bread) with hummus, meat or chicken and pine nuts.

★**Sufra** JORDANIAN $$$
(Map p292; ☎06 461 1468; www.facebook.com/SufraRestaurant; 28 Rainbow St, Jebel Amman; starters from JD3.350, mains from JD10; ⏲noon-11pm Sun-Thu, from 10am Fri & Sat) Housed in a lovely old villa with a terrace garden, this really is the place to eat traditional Jordanian cuisine The signature *mansaf* (lamb with rice and nuts, with a yoghurt sauce) is a delight.

★**Rosa Damascena** SYRIAN $$$
(Map p296; ☎06 461 0010; 2nd Circle; mezze JD2-3, mains JD7-10) Rosa Damascena offers a variety of hot and cold mezze – make particular space on your plate for dips of *mohammara be jouz* (ground walnuts with pomegranate and chilli), along with tasty mains like *jidi bel zeit* (stewed lamb with cracked wheat) and *musakhan* (baked chicken on bread with sumac).

LOCAL KNOWLEDGE

COOKING WITH GRANDMA

If you want to learn the secrets of Jordanian cooking, head for **Beit Sitti** (Map p292; ☎07 7755 7744; www.beitsitti.com; 16 Mohammad Ali Al Sadi St; lessons JD35) – 'Grandmother's House'. This villa is on the edge of Lweibdeh, where chef-sisters Maria, Dina and Tania Haddad have opened the kitchen of their old family home to share their love of good eating.

Over two hours you'll tackle a handful of classic and lesser-known recipes and then sit down to a mouth-watering four-course feast prepared by your own hands. Lessons are available for breakfast, lunch and dinner and you're welcome to take a bottle of wine to enjoy with your meal. Recently, Beit Sitti has started to work with local refugee women to introduce Syrian, Iraqi and Palestinian dishes to their menu to showcase the many regional influences on Jordan's food, as well as arranging occasional visits to organic farms just outside the city for a real farm-to-table experience.

If cooking isn't your thing, pop into **Najla's Kitchen** (Map p292; ☎07 9515 5566; 16 Mohammed Ali Al Saedi St; set meals JD15; ⏲12.30-6pm), the spin-off restaurant next door, and let the Haddad family rustle up a main course for you.

Jebel Amman

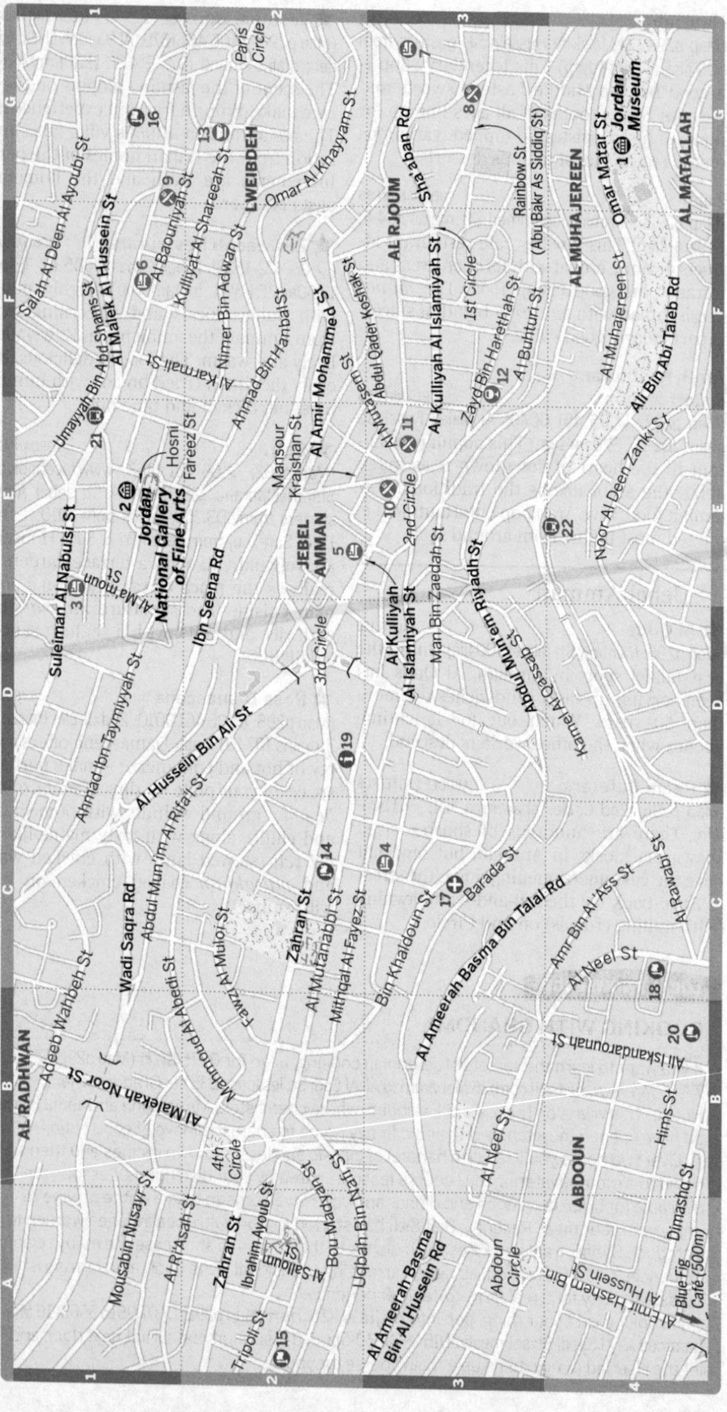

0 500 m
0 0.25 miles
N
A
B
C
D
E
F
G
1
2
3
4
AL RADHWAN
Adeeb Wahbeh St
Al Malekah Noor St
Mousabin Nusayr St
Wadi Saqra Rd
Al Ri'Asah St
Abdul Mun'im Al Rifa'i St
Mahmoud Al Abedi St
Zahran St
4th Circle
Tripoli St
Ibrahim Ayoub St
Al Salloum St
15
Fawzi Al Muloi St
Zahran St
Al Mutanabbi St
14
Bou Madyan St
Uqbah Bin Nafi St
Mithqal Al Fayez St
19
4
Al Ameerah Basma Bin Al Hussein Rd
Bin Khaldoun St
Al Ameerah Basma Bin Talal Rd
17
Barada St
Abdoun Circle
Al Neel St
ABDOUN
Al Emir Hashem Bin Al Hussein St
Ali Iskandarounah St
Amr Bin Al 'Ass St
Al Neel St
18
Hims St
20
Dimashq St
Blue Fig Café (500m)
Al Rawabi St
Ahmad Ibn Taymiyyah St
Al Hussein Bin Ali St
Suleiman Al Nabulsi St
3
Al Ma'moun St
2
Jordan National Gallery of Fine Arts
Hosni Fareez St
Ibn Seena Rd
3rd Circle
JEBEL AMMAN
5
Al Kulliyah Al Islamiyah St
Man Bin Zaedah St
Abdul Mun'em Riyadh St
Kamel Al Qassab St
22
Mansour Kraishan St
Al Amir Mohammed St
10
2nd Circle
11
Al Mutasem St
Abdul Qader Koshak St
Umayyah Bin Abd Shams St
21
Al Malek Al Hussein St
Salah Al Deen Al Ayoubi St
6
Al Karmali St
Al Baouniyah St
9
16
Kulliyat Al Shareeah St
13
Nimer Bin Adwan St
Ahmad Bin Hanbal St
LWEIBDEH
Paris Circle
Omar Al Khayyam St
AL RJOUM
Sha'aban Rd
7
Al Kulliyah Al Islamiyah St
1st Circle
8
Zayd Bin Harethah St
12
Al Buhturi St
Rainbow St (Abu Bakr As Siddiq St)
AL MUHAJEREEN
Noor Al Deen Zanki St
Al Muhajereen St
Omar Matar St
1
Jordan Museum
Ali Bin Abi Taleb Rd
AL MATALLAH

Jebel Amman

Top Sights
1 Jordan Museum G4
2 Jordan National Gallery of Fine Arts E1

Sleeping
3 Caravan Hotel E1
4 Hisham Hotel C3
5 Jordan InterContinental Hotel E2
6 La Locanda F1
7 Sydney Hotel G3

Eating
8 Al Quds G3
9 Jasmine House G1
10 Reem Cafeteria E3
11 Rosa Damascena E3

Drinking & Nightlife
12 District F3
Maestro Music Bar .... (see 6)
13 Rumi G2

Information
14 French Embassy C2
15 German Embassy A2
16 Irish Consulate G1
17 Khalidi Hospital C3
18 Lebanese Embassy C4
19 Ministry of Tourism D2
Tourist Police .... (see 19)
20 UK Embassy B4

Transport
21 Abdali Bus Station E1
22 Muhajireen Bus Station E4

Drinking & Nightlife

Some of the cafes in downtown are perfect hangouts for blog writing, tweeting a friend, meeting locals and playing backgammon. A dozen or more cafes can be found around Hashemite Sq – a great place for people-watching in summer. Alternatively, there are lots of popular cafes around Abdoun Circle and you could easily make a night of it by walking along Rainbow St and popping in to the cafes and bars that are dotted along it.

Downtown

Shaher's Penthouse Cafeteria CAFE
(Map p292; Al Malek Talal St, Downtown; 9.30am-11pm) This cosy cafe has a traditionally decorated indoor dining area as well as an outdoor terrace overlooking the street below. There's frequently someone playing the oud (lute) or violin to provide a cultured counterpoint to the street noise below.

Al Hail Restaurant & Café CAFE
(Map p292; Hashemite Sq, Downtown; 9am-midnight) A glass of mint tea here comes with perhaps the best view of the Citadel on offer downtown.

Jebel Amman

★**Rumi** CAFE
(Map p296; www.facebook.com/rumicafejo; 14 Kulliyat Al Shareeah St, Lweibdeh; 7am-midnight Sun-Thu, from 9am Fri & Sat;) Tea is the thing here: choose from blends from Bahrain (flavoured with rosewater), Iraq (cardamom), Morocco (mint) and more besides.

★**Maestro Music Bar** BAR
(Map p296; www.facebook.com/maestrobaramman; 52 Al Baouniyah St, Lweibdeh; 9am-midnight) The big draw here is the live music, with bands playing every Friday night, open mic jam sessions on Mondays and jazz through the sound system on other nights. Maestro also hosts sessions for the **Amman Jazz Festival** (www.ammanjazzfestival.com; Apr).

Carakale Brewery BREWERY
(07 9728 5192; www.carakale.com; Fuheis; 6-10pm Thu, from 2pm Fri & Sat) Jordan doesn't sound like the place where you can drink at a local microbrewery, but you can at Fuheis just outside Amman, where Carakale has opened a bar to taste its ales on-site.

District BAR
(Map p296; 07 7001 7517; www.facebook.com/DistrictAmman; Zayd Bin Harethah St, Jebel Amman; 5pm-1am) Catch the sunset over the old city while sipping a happy-hour cocktail (50% off from 5pm to 8pm) on District's rooftop terrace. The casual chic vibe, industrial-modern design, year-round outdoor seating, creative cocktails and well-dressed crowd make this one of Amman's most popular night spots.

Rovers Return PUB
(Map p290; 06 581 4844; Ali Nasouh Al Taher St, Sweifieh; 1pm-late) This popular, cosy English pub in Sweifieh has wood panelling and a lively atmosphere. The comfort food includes authentic fish and chips, and roast beef with gravy. The *Coronation Street* theme is carried off well; we half-expected to be served a pint of Newton & Ridley.

WORTH A TRIP

WILD JORDAN

The best way to organise trips to (and reserve accommodation in) any of the reserves run by Jordan's Royal Society for the Conservation of Nature (RSCN) is to pay a visit to their flagship centre, **Wild Jordan** (Map p292; ☎06 461 6523; www.wildjordan.com; Othman Bin Affan St, Downtown). While you're pondering which reserves to visit, have a smoothie in their stylish, health-focused **Wild Jordan Cafe** (☎06 463 3542; mains JD7-12; ⏲9am-11pm;) or mooch through the **craft shop** (☎06 463 3718; www.wildjordancenter.com; ⏲10am-10pm) where all profits are either returned to the craftspeople or contribute to nature-reserve projects. Before you leave, pick up a downtown walking trail brochure for some backstreet revelations.

Books@café CAFE
(Map p292; ☎06 465 0457; Omar Bin Al Khattab St; ⏲10am-midnight;) You may need to keep your sunglasses on when you enter this place – the retro walls in psychedelic colours are a fun throwback to the '70s. This is typical modern Jordanian coffeehouse chic. Alcohol is served, and on Thursday nights it is one of Amman's rare openly gay-friendly haunts.

☆ Entertainment

Royal Film Commission CINEMA
(Map p292; ☎06 464 2266; www.film.jo; 5 Omar Bin Al Khattab St) The home of the Jordanian film industry, the commission holds screenings and festivals featuring the best of local and international cinema. The outdoor amphitheatre is a great place to see a film, while the stylish on-site **Montage** (⏲9am-11pm;) cafe is worth a visit at any time of day.

Shopping

Amman is a good place to shop for souvenirs in Jordan, with everything from tourist kitsch to high-quality handicraft boutiques, many of which are run to benefit local communities. Prices are fixed. Rainbow St is good for a browse.

Jordan River Foundation ARTS & CRAFTS
(Map p292; ☎06 593 3211; www.jordanriver.jo; Bani Hamida House, Fawzi Al Malouf St, Jebel Amman; ⏲8.30am-7pm Sat-Thu, 10am-5pm Fri) Supporting top-notch worthy causes by selling equally top-notch crafted items, this shop is an Amman institution. The showroom supports handloomed rugs from Bani Hamida and exquisite Palestinian-style embroidery. Cushions, camel bags, embroidery, baskets and Dead Sea products make it an excellent place to buy stylish decor.

Balian CERAMICS
(Map p292; www.armenianceramics.com; 8 Rainbow St; ⏲9am-6pm Sat-Thu) The Balian family came to Amman from Jerusalem in the early 1920s, and have been selling their traditional hand-painted tiles ever since. While you might not be able to decorate an entire bathroom, their individual tiles make lovely souvenirs.

Al Afghani GIFTS & SOUVENIRS
(Map p292; Talal St; ⏲10am-10pm Sat-Thu, from 2pm Fri) If we call this souvenir shop long-established, we mean it: the original family business goes back to 1870s Palestine. It's jammed to the rafters with shopping delights big and small.

Souk Jara MARKET
(Map p292; www.facebook.com/soukjara; Rainbow St; ⏲10am-10pm Fri) A weekly open-air flea market selling a variety of handicrafts (though recently there's been a big influx of plastic tat). It's good fun to browse, and there are some great food and drink stalls and occasional live music to add to the atmosphere.

ℹ Information

EMERGENCY

Ambulance, fire & police ☎911

INTERNET ACCESS

Wi-fi is widely available in Amman, often even in the most unassuming of coffeeshops.

MEDICAL SERVICES

Amman has some of the best medical facilities available in the region. The English-language *Jordan Times* lists hospitals and doctors on night duty. It also publishes a list of pharmacies open after hours. Most pharmacists speak good English.

Khalidi Hospital (Map p296; ☎06 464 4281; http://khmc.jo; Bin Khaldoun St) One of the best hospitals in the country, with 24-hour facilities.

Palestine Hospital (Map p290; ☎06 560 7071; www.palestinehospital.org.jo; Al Malekah Alia St, Shmeisani) Recommended hospital with emergency ward.

MONEY

Changing money in Amman is quick and easy, especially since there are dozens of banks downtown and in Jebel Amman, the two areas in which most visitors are likely to find themselves.

➡ Banks with ATMs are plentiful, and most accept international cards. You'll usually be charged around JD2 per ATM transaction. Arab Bank, Cairo Amman Bank, Jordan Gulf Bank and Bank Al Etihad are all reliable.

➡ Many moneychangers are located along Al Malek Faisal St in downtown.

TOURIST INFORMATION

A useful free map to pick up is *99 Things To Do In Amman*, produced by the Jordan Tourist Board. The *Curating the Best Culinary & Cultural Spaces of Amman* map by Plurality (www.facebook.com/pluralityME) is another useful guide.

Ministry of Tourism (Map p296; ☎ ext 254 06 460 3360; ground fl, Al Mutanabbi St, Jebel Amman; ⏲ 8am-9pm) is the most useful place for information. It's also the centre for the **tourist police** (☎ 06 460 3360, ext 254; ⏲ 8am-9pm). The staff are friendly and speak good English.

Wild Jordan Center (p298) provides information and bookings for activities and accommodation in any of Jordan's nature reserves, including Dana and Wadi Mujib.

Getting There & Away

AIR

The only domestic air route is between Amman and Aqaba.

BUS, MINIBUS & SERVICE TAXI

Amman has quite a few different bus stations, and the one you want depends on your destination. Most towns and cities are actually served by minibuses rather than bus, which are white with the route written on the side in Arabic. Service taxis between towns are also available at most stations. Either way, they usually don't follow fixed schedules unless noted, and depart when the driver deems them full enough. All departures are more frequent in the morning, and most dry up completely after sunset.

Alternatively, JETT runs services to several cities from its own stations, as well as tourist services to Petra and the Dead Sea (a link to Wadi Rum is expected to open in 2018).

Private Bus

Private coach company **JETT** (Map p290; ☎ 06 566 4146; www.jett.com.jo; Al Malek Al Hussein St, Shmeisani) has two bus stations: in Abdali and at **7th Circle** (Map p290; ☎ 06 585 4679). Abdali is slightly busier, with least six daily services each to Aqaba (four hours, JD7) and Irbid (two hours, JD2), as well as a daily 6.30am departure to Wadi Musa (for Petra, four hours, JD10). You'll need your passport to book a ticket.

For international travellers, Abdali also has a daily 7am departure for the King Hussein Bridge (one hour, JD10). The bus takes you to Israeli immigration, but must be booked no later than a day in advance. Services to Cairo are also offered (around 20 hours, JD35). Schedules vary so check in advance and ensure your visas are in order before booking.

There are a similar number of Aqaba and Irbid departures from 7th Circle, along with a daily VIP Aqaba service that includes more comfortable seating, drinks and snacks (JD17) and a daily 9am tourist service to the Dead Sea resort area (one hour, JD7), which returns at 5pm.

Public Bus

The two main public bus stations are Tabarbour (North Bus Station) and Wihdat (South Bus Station), serving the northern and southern parts of Jordan respectively.

Fairly regular minibuses and service taxis depart from **Tabarbour Bus Station** (North Bus Station; Map p290) for Ajloun (JD1, every 30 minutes, two hours), Jerash (JD1, hourly, 1¼ hours) and Irbid (JD1, two hours). Change at Irbid for Umm Qais. You can also get connections to Deir Alla (for Pella, one hour), Fuheis (45 minutes), Irbid (two hours), Ramtha (two hours), Salt (45 minutes) and Zarqa (for Azraq, 30 minutes); all these services cost under JD1. Heading south, Tabarbour also has frequent minibuses to Madaba (800 fils, 45 minutes).

From **Wihdat Bus Station** (South Bus Station) there are minibuses to Aqaba (JD5.500, five hours) leaving every two hours or so until 9pm. For Petra, minibuses and service taxis (JD5, four hours) depart for Wadi Musa when full from the far corner of the lot between about 7am and 4pm (but travel early in the day where possible). There are regular buses to Karak (JD1.800, two hours) until 5pm, Shobak (JD4, 2½ hours) and Ma'an (JD3, three hours). For Dana, take a bus to Tafila (JD2.750, 2½ hours) and change, but note that most accommodation in Dana offers cheap direct transfers from Amman.

For the Dead Sea, minibuses leave from **Muhajireen Bus Station** (Map p296; Al Ameerah Basma Bin Talal St), near 3rd Circle. There are no direct services: the route involves a minibus to Shuneh Al Janubiyyeh (South Shuna, JD1, 45 minutes) and then a wait for another minibus to Suweimeh. At Suweimeh, you'll have to hire a taxi, which is an unreliable option – it's easier to take the JETT bus. There are also services to Madaba (800 fils, 45 minutes) between 6am and 5pm.

Raghadan Bus Station (Map p290) downtown has minibuses and service taxis to Salt, Fuheis and Madaba.

CAR

There are many car-rental agencies to choose from around King Abdullah Gardens and all the major hotels have car-rental offices.

Getting Around

TO/FROM THE AIRPORT

Queen Alia International Airport (☎ 06 401 0250; www.qaiairport.com) is less than an hour's journey south of Amman. The Airport Express Bus (JD3) runs to Amman every 30

JORDAN IN A HURRY? TAKE A TOUR!

Do you usually shy away from tours? Well Jordan is one place to make an exception, especially if you're short of time or on a tight budget. Tours run by budget hotels in Amman and Madaba have filled the public transport gaps to destinations like the Eastern Desert, the Dead Sea and the King's Highway. The 'tours' are often just transport, so don't expect much from the guide-cum-driver. They do, however, offer a chance to meet fellow travellers and share costs.

The Cliff (p291) and Jordan Tower (p291) hotels in Amman offer popular day trips to the Eastern Desert castles; another top excursion is to Jerash, Ajloun and Umm Qais. Good-value tours along the King's Highway leave Amman in the morning and travel to Petra (9½ hours) via Madaba, Wadi Mujib, Karak, Shobak and Dana. The Black Iris Hotel (p314) and the Mariam Hotel (p314) in Madaba can arrange similar itineraries. Transport is generally in a four-seater taxi or minibus and prices vary depending on the number of fellow passengers, stops, time and distance.

There are a few tour companies with a good reputation for comprehensive (but more expensive) tours around Jordan; try Petra Moon (p327) in Wadi Musa to get an idea of what's on offer or **Engaging Cultures** (800 731 0655; https://engagingcultures.com), which focuses on community-based tourism. For activities, **Experience Jordan** (Map p290; 07 7041 7711; www.experiencejordan.com; 44 Ali Nasouh Al Taher St, Sweifieh) is recommended for hiking tours while **Bike Rush** (07 9945 4586; www.facebook.com/bikerush; Al Jafn St, 8th Circle; noon-9pm Sat-Thu) organises cycling tours.

minutes (from 6.30am to 5pm); the night bus runs hourly (5pm to midnight). Taxis cost JD20 to downtown Amman (around 45 minutes). Car hire is available in the arrivals hall.

PRIVATE TAXI

Private taxis are painted yellow. They are abundant, can be flagged anywhere, have cheap fares and most drivers automatically use the meter. A taxi from downtown to Shmeisani, for example, costs JD2.500, and it's JD3 to Tabarbour.

Careem (www.careem.com/amman), a Middle East–wide ride-hailing company, operates in Amman, and you can book lifts from your phone app. Uber (www.uber.com) also operates in Amman.

SERVICE TAXI

These white cabs are shared taxis that stick to specific routes and are not permitted to leave the city limits. Fares cost around 400 fils per seat, and you usually pay the full amount regardless of where you get off. After 8pm, the price for all service taxis goes up by 25%. There can be long queues at rush hour (8am to 9am and 5pm to 6pm). The cars queue up and usually start at the bottom of a hill – you get into the last car and unusually the whole line rolls back a car space and so on.

Service taxi 1 (Map p292) From Basman St for 4th Circle.

Service taxi 2 (Map p292) From Basman St for 1st and 2nd Circles.

Service taxi 3 (Map p292) From Basman St for 3rd and 4th Circles.

Service taxi 4 (Map p292) From the side street near the central post office for Jebel Lweibdeh.

Service taxi 6 (Map p292) From Cinema al Hussein St for the Ministry of the Interior Circle, past Abdali station and JETT international and domestic offices.

Service taxi 7 (Map p292) From Cinema Al Hussein St, up Al Malek Al Hussein St, past Abdali station and King Abdullah Mosque, and along Suleiman Al Nabulsi St for Shmeisani.

Service taxis 25 & 26 (Map p292) From Italian St, downtown, to the top of Jebel Al Ashrafiyeh and near Abu Darwish Mosque.

Service taxi 27 (Map p292) From Italian St to Middle East Circle for Wahadat station.

Service taxi 35 (Map p292) From opposite the Amman Palace Hotel, passing close to the Muhajireen Police Station.

Service taxi 38 (Map p292) From Basman ST to Makkah Al Mukarramah Rd.

JERASH & THE NORTH

You might expect that the far north of Jordan, with its exceptional Roman ruins, biblical associations, lively cities and complex terrain, would feature as a standard part of any visitor's trip to the country. This, however, is not the case and the region receives relatively few visitors compared with Petra and the South. In recent years the area has grown a reputation for sustainable tourism with small-scale enterprises offering a genuine chance for visitors to engage in local activities for the benefit of local communities.

To make the most of the homestays, interactive craft activities and local hikes, it is worth spending a few days in this ancient region of pine forests and olive groves. The availability of public transport and friendly accommodation facilitate this, and if the springtime flowers happen to be blooming, it will prove to be a hard region to leave.

Jerash جرش

02 / POP 50,750 / ELEV 618M

The beautifully preserved **Roman ruins** (JD8, with Jordan Pass free; 8am-4.30pm Oct-Apr, to 7pm May-Sep) of Jerash, 51km north of Amman, are deservedly one of Jordan's major attractions. Archaeological digs have been ongoing for 85 years, but it is estimated that 90% of the city is still unexcavated. In its heyday the ancient city, known in Roman times as Gerasa, had a population of around 15,000.

Allow at least three hours to do Jerash justice. The best times to visit are before 10am or after 4pm, but this is tricky if you are relying on public transport.

In July and August, there's the **Jerash Festival** (www.facebook.com/Festival.Jarash), which features local and overseas artists, music and drama performances in the ancient city, and displays of traditional handicrafts.

History

Although inhabited from Neolithic times, and settled as a town during the reign of Alexander the Great, Jerash was largely a Roman creation and the well-preserved remains of all the classic Roman structures are easily distinguishable among the ruins.

In the wake of Roman general Pompey's conquest of the region in 64 BC, Gerasa became part of the Roman province of Syria and, soon after, a city of the Decapolis. The city reached its peak at the beginning of the 3rd century AD, when it was bestowed with the rank of Colony, after which time it went into a slow decline as trade routes shifted.

By the middle of the 5th century, Christianity was the region's major religion and many churches were constructed in the area at this time. With the Sassanian invasion from Persia in 614, the Muslim conquest in 636 and a devastating earthquake in 747, Jerash's heyday passed and its population shrank to about a quarter of its former size.

Sights

The entrance to the site is south of the ancient city, close to **Hadrian's Arch**. Also known as the Triumphal Arch, it was built in AD 129 to honour the visit of Emperor Hadrian. Behind the arch is the **hippodrome**, which once hosted chariot races watched by up to 15,000 spectators.

The **South Gate**, originally one of four along the city wall and built in AD 130, leads into the city proper. The Oval Plaza (forum) is one of the most distinctive sites of Jerash, unusual because of its shape and huge size (90m long and 80m at its widest point). Fifty-six Ionic columns surround the paved limestone plaza, linking the cardo maximus with the **Temple of Zeus**.

The elegant remains of the Temple of Zeus, built around AD 162, can be reached from the **forum** – a worthwhile climb if just for the view. Next door, the **South Theatre** was built in the 1st century AD with a capacity of 5000 spectators. From the upper stalls, the acoustics are still wonderful as demonstrated by the occasional roving minstrel or drummer.

To the northeast of the forum lies the **cardo maximus**, the city's main thoroughfare, also known as the colonnaded street. Stretching for 800m to the **North Gate**, the street is still paved with the original stones, rutted by the thousands of chariots that once jostled along its length.

The colonnaded street is punctuated by the **nymphaeum**, the main fountain of the city, before giving rise to a superb **propylaeum** or monumental gateway, and a staircase. The **Temple of Artemis**, towering over Jerash at the top of the stairs, was dedicated to the goddess of hunting and fertility. Built between AD 150 and 170, the temple remains are flanked by 11 or the original 12 elaborately carved Corinthian columns; built of sandstone, they appear to glow in the late afternoon sun. Alas, the rest of the temple was dismantled to provide masonry for new churches under Theodorius in AD 386.

Further to the north is the **North Theatre**, built originally in AD 165 and now restored to former glory. It's worth ending the visit in the small **museum** (02 631 2267; 8.30am-6pm Oct-Apr, to 5pm May-Sep) FREE, which contains a collection of artefacts from the site; they help indicate something of the wealth and grandeur associated with the city in its heyday.

Sleeping & Eating

Although Jerash can be visited as a day trip from Amman, an overnight stop (it's best to book accommodation in advance) is more rewarding and may be necessary if you're trying to visit by public transport. The

Jerash

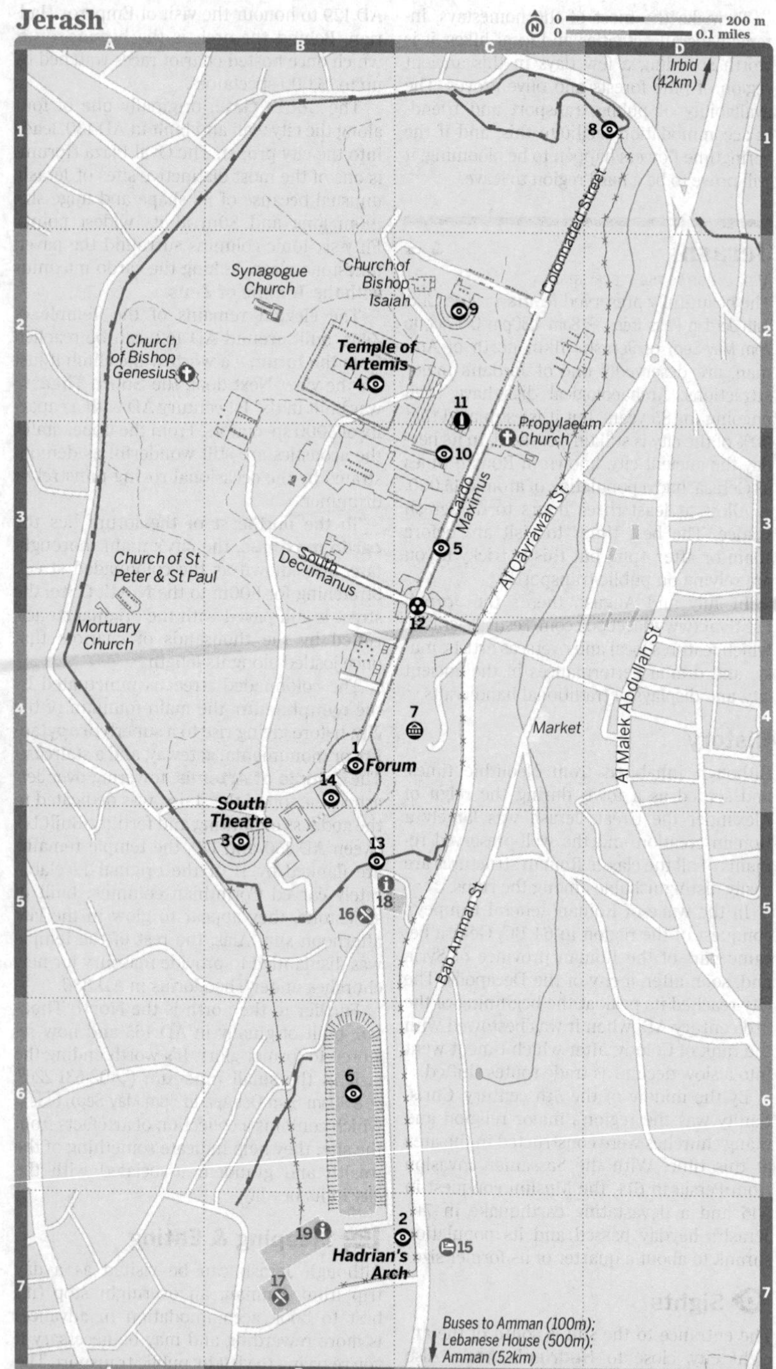

N
0 200 m
0 0.1 miles
A
B
C
D
1
2
3
4
5
6
7
Irbid (42km)
8
Colonnaded Street
Church of Bishop Isaiah
Synagogue Church
9
Church of Bishop Genesius
Temple of Artemis
4
11
Propylaeum Church
10
Cardo Maximus
Al Qayrawan St
5
Church of St Peter & St Paul
South Decumanus
12
Mortuary Church
7
Market
Al Malek Abdullah St
1
Forum
14
South Theatre
3
13
18
16
Bab Amman St
6
19
2
15
Hadrian's Arch
17
Buses to Amman (100m); Lebanese House (500m); Amman (52km)

Jerash

Top Sights

1 Forum B4
2 Hadrian's Arch C7
3 South Theatre B5
4 Temple of Artemis B2

Sights

5 Cardo Maximus C3
6 Hippodrome B6
7 Museum C4
8 North Gate D1
9 North Theatre C2
10 Nymphaeum C3
11 Propylaeum C2
12 Roman Ruins of Jerash C3
13 South Gate B5
14 Temple of Zeus B4

Sleeping

15 Hadrian Gate Hotel C7

Eating

16 Jerash Rest House B5
17 Jordan House Restaurant B7

Information

18 Ticket Checkpoint B5
19 Ticket Office B7

modern town of Jerash, which encompasses the ruins of the Eastern Baths, comes to life after sunset and is a pleasant place to explore in the early evening.

Olive Branch Resort HOTEL $$
(☎02 634 0555; www.olivebranch.com.jo; s/d/tr from JD37/52/63, campsites per own/hired tent JD10/12;) Around 7km from Jerash on the road to Ajloun, this hilltop hotel is situated amid olive groves and pine trees. Refurbished rooms are neat and spacious, some with balconies, others in a separate annexe below the gardens. Country fare is served in the airy restaurant.

Hadrian Gate Hotel HOTEL $$
(☎07 7779 3907; s/d/tr/penthouses from JD25/40/50/70;) The only hotel in Jerash boasts a spectacular location overlooking Hadrian's Arch. Breakfast is served on the rooftop terraces, boasting a panoramic view of the Temple of Artemis to the west and Jerash's market gardens to the east. A range of private rooms with shared bathrooms are humble but spotless; the host's hospitality makes up for the simple amenities.

Jordan House Restaurant BUFFET $$
(buffet JD7; ⌚8am-9pm;) Serving a comprehensive buffet between 11am and 5pm, this friendly establishment at the entrance to the Jerash ruins is a good place for a Turkish coffee before starting out, and a fresh lemon and mint drink over lunch on your return.

★**Lebanese House** LEBANESE $$$
(☎02 635 1301; www.facebook.com/LebaneseUmKhalil; meals JD10-18; ⌚11am-1am;) Nicknamed 'Umm Khalil', this rambling restaurant, a 10-minute walk from Jerash's centre, has been a national treasure since it opened in 1977. On offer are plenty of sizzling and cold mezze and freshly baked bread, as well as superior salads and mouth-watering grills. If you can't decide what to sample, try the set menu for a selection of the best dishes.

Information

Near the South Gate, the visitor centre has informative descriptions and reconstructions of many buildings in Jerash, as well as a good relief map of the ancient city. The site's **ticket office** (☎02 635 1272) is in a modern souq with souvenir and antique shops, a post office and a semi-traditional coffeehouse. Keep your ticket, as you'll have to show it at the South Gate.

Knowledgeable guides (JD20) at the ticket checkpoint can help navigate the huge complex. Walking at a leisurely pace and allowing time for resting on a fallen column, you can visit the main ruins in three to four hours.

The site is exposed with little shade, so a hat and water is essential for most of the year. Toilets are available at the site entrance (inside the souvenir souq), at **Jerash Rest House** (☎02 635 1437; buffet JD8; ⌚noon-8pm) and at the visitor centre.

Getting There & Away

Jerash is approximately 50km north of Amman, and the roads are well signposted from the capital, especially from 8th Circle. If you're driving, note that this route can get extremely congested during the morning and afternoon rush hours.

From the North Bus Station (Tabarbour) in Amman, public buses and minibuses (800 fils, 1¼ hours) leave regularly for Jerash, though they can take an hour to fill up. Leave early for a quick getaway, especially if you're planning a day trip.

Jerash's bus and service-taxi station is a 15-minute walk southwest of the ruins, at the second set of traffic lights, behind the big white building. You can pick up a minibus to the station from outside the visitor centre for a few fils. From here there are also plenty of minibuses travelling regularly to Irbid (JD1, 45 minutes) and Ajloun (500 fils, 30 minutes) until around 4pm.

ESSENTIAL JORDANIAN FOOD & DRINK

Fuul medames Fava-bean dish drizzled with fresh-pressed olive oil; served with unleavened Arabic bread, sour cream, local salty white cheese and a sprinkling of *zaatar* (thyme and other herbs).

Maqlubbeh Pyramid of steaming rice garnished with cardamom and sultanas; topped with slivers of onion, meat, cauliflower and fresh herbs.

Mensaf Bedouin dish of lamb, rice and pine nuts, combined with yoghurt and the liquid fat from the cooked meat.

Kunafa Dessert of shredded dough and cream cheese, smothered in syrup.

Marrameeya Sage-based herbal tea, especially delicious at Dana.

You can cook your own Jordanian speciality at Petra Kitchen (p326) in Wadi Musa.

You can normally flag down the bus to Amman from the main junction in front of the site to save the trek to the bus station.

Transport drops off significantly after 5pm. Service taxis sometimes leave up to 8pm (later during the Jerash Festival) from the bus station, but this is not guaranteed. With a bit of determined bargaining, a private taxi between Amman and Jerash should cost around JD20 each way. From Jerash, a taxi to Irbid costs around JD15.

Ajloun عجلون

☎02 / ELEV 744M / POP 10,000

Ajloun (Ajlun) is a popular and easy day trip from Amman, and can be combined with a trip to Jerash if you leave early. Better still, stay in nearby Ajloun Forest Reserve.

Sights

★Ajloun Castle CASTLE

(Qala'at Ar Rabad; JD3, with Jordan Pass free) This castle was built atop Mt 'Auf (1250m) between 1184 and 1188 by one of Saladin's generals, 'Izz ad Din Usama bin Munqidh (who was also Saladin's nephew). The castle commands views of the Jordan Valley and three wadis leading into it, making it an important strategic link in the defensive chain against the Crusaders and a counterpoint to the Crusader Belvoir Fort on the Sea of Galilee in present-day Israel and the Palestinian Territories.

With its hilltop position, Qala'at Ar Rabad was one in a chain of beacons and pigeon posts that enabled messages to be transmitted from Damascus to Cairo in a single day. The rearing of pigeons is still a popular pastime in the area. There is a useful explanation in English just inside the main gate, and a small museum containing pots, snatches of mosaics and some medieval hand grenades.

The castle is a tough 3km uphill walk from the town centre, but minibuses very occasionally go to the top (about 100 fils). Alternatively, take a taxi from Ajloun (JD1 to JD2 each way). The visitor centre and ticket office is about 500m downhill from the castle entrance; there's a small scale model of the castle on display here and, perhaps more usefully, clean toilets.

Sleeping & Eating

There are a few places for a snack and a drink inside Ajloun Castle. For something more substantial, both **Abu Alezz Restaurant** (Abdallah bin Hussein St; meals JD2-4; ⏲10am-9pm) and **Barhoum** (Abdallah bin Hussein St; meals JD2-6; ⏲10am-9pm) near the main roundabout in Ajloun offer standard Jordanian fare. Or head into the surrounding hills for a picnic.

Ajloun Hotel HOTEL $

(☎02 642 0524; s/d JD27/35; 📶❄) This is a handy option for an early-morning visit to the castle, as it's just 1km down the road. There's a comfortable lounge area in the foyer, and decent basic rooms. Choose a top-floor room for grand views of the countryside.

Mountain Castle Hotel HOTEL $

(☎07 9565 6726, 02 642 0202; s/d from JD28/38; 📶) This busy little hotel boasts a gorgeous garden terrace of flowering jasmine, grapevines and roses – enjoying your meals here will be a highlight of your stay. The decor is a tad tired and the furnishings on the minimal side, but there are expansive views from many of the rooms.

Getting There & Away

Ajloun is around 75km northwest of Amman and 30km northwest of Jerash. The castle can be seen from most places in the area – if you're driving or walking, take the signposted road (Al Qala'a St) heading west at the main roundabout in the centre of Ajloun. The narrow streets of the town centre can be horribly congested at times.

From the centre of town, minibuses travel regularly to Jerash (800 fils, 30 minutes, along a scenic road) and Irbid (JD1, 45 minutes).

From Amman (JD1, two hours), minibuses leave half-hourly from the North Bus Station.

Ajloun Forest Reserve
محمية عجلون الطبيعية

Located in the Ajloun Highlands, this small (13 sq km) but vitally important **nature reserve** (02 647 5673; www.wildjordan.com; per day JD2.500) was established by the RSCN in 1988 to protect forests of oak, carob, pistachio and strawberry trees (look for the peeling, bright orange bark and no, they don't produce strawberries!). The reserve also provides sanctuary for the endangered roe deer. To reach the reserve, charter a taxi for the 9km from Ajloun (around JD5 to JD7 one way).

Sights & Activities

House of Calligraphy WORKSHOP
(Orjan; by appointment via Wild Jordan) Reinforcing Islamic heritage, the women in this workshop aim to educate visitors about Arab culture, and there's even an opportunity to try your hand at calligraphy as you use a reed to write your name in Arabic.

Biscuit House WORKSHOP
(Orjan; by appointment via Wild Jordan) Delicious Jordanian delicacies are prepared for sale in RSCN Nature Shops in this cottage-industry kitchen. The on-site cafe sells locally produced herbal teas, olive-oil crisps, and molasses and tahini sandwich cookies.

Soap House WORKSHOP
(Orjan; by appointment via Wild Jordan) Local women demonstrate the art of making all kinds of health-promoting soaps using natural local ingredients and comprising 90% pure olive oil. Pomegranate is one of a dozen exotic fragrances.

★ **Al Ayoun Society** HIKING
(07 9682 9111, 07 7973 4776; www.facebook.com/alayounsociety; Orjan) This excellent local-tourism cooperative based in Orjan village can arrange guides for the Al Ayoun Trail as well as homestays in Orjan and Rasoun. Taking one of the society guides on a trail is one of the best ways to discover the Jordanian countryside and village life.

Sleeping & Eating

The Ajloun Forest Reserve operates **tented bungalows** (02 647 5673; s/d/tr with shared bathroom from JD82/93/105, deluxe cabins JD105/116/128). The ablution block contains composting toilets and solar-heated showers. There are also cabins available, equipped with private bathroom and terrace. Bring mosquito repellent in the summer. You can walk to the recommended **Al Ayoun Homestays** (07 9682 9111, 07 7973 4776; www.facebook.com/alayounsociety; homestays around JD20-40) within the reserve or dine in the tented **rooftop restaurant** (02 647 5673; buffet JD14).

Information

At the entrance to the reserve is a modest **visitor centre** (www.wildjordan.com; dawn-dusk) with a helpful reception where you'll find information and maps on the reserve and its flora and fauna. There's also a Nature Shop selling locally produced handicrafts.

You should book accommodation and meals in advance with the RSCN through its Wild Jordan Center (p298) in Amman. If you're planning to take a guided hike, you must book 48 hours ahead. Guided hikes require a minimum of four people and start at JD9 per person, depending on the choice of trail.

Getting There & Away

You can reach the reserve by hiring a taxi from Ajloun (around JD6, 9km); ask the visitor centre to book one for your departure. If you're driving, the reserve is well signposted from Ajloun,

THE JORDAN TRAIL

More than 650km from top to toe, the newly established 36-day Jordan Trail (www.jordantrail.org) covers the entire length of Jordan and threads through some of the country's most iconic landscapes, including Ajloun, Petra and Wadi Rum. The trail is segmented into eight legs averaging around 80km each.

Those who have already completed this route recommend taking 42 days to cover the distance, allowing for one or two rest days along the way. The Jordan Trail Association, established to preserve the trail and help ensure its accessibility, maintains a useful website that describes each leg of the trail and recommends tour operators who can facilitate travel along all or parts of its length. These include Experience Jordan (p300). The Dana to Petra stage is particularly rewarding and has been described by *National Geographic* as one of the best 15 hikes in the world.

Irbid إربد

02 / ELEV 582M / POP 502,700

Jordan's second-largest city is a university town, and one of its more lively and progressive. Irbid is also a good base for exploring the historic sites of Umm Qais. The town comes alive at night, especially in the energetic area around the university, where the streets are lined with restaurants and internet cafes.

Sights

Dar As Saraya Museum MUSEUM
(02 724 5613; Al Baladia St; JD2, with Jordan Pass free; 8am-6pm) Located in an old villa of basaltic rock just behind the town hall, this museum is an interesting diversion. Built in 1886 by the Ottomans, the building is typical of the caravanserai established along the Syrian pilgrimage route. It was used as a prison until 1994 and now houses a delightful collection of local artefacts illustrating Irbid's long history.

Museum of Archaeology & Anthropology MUSEUM
(02 721 1111; 10am-1.45pm & 3-4.30pm Sun-Thu) FREE One of the highlights of this museum is a reconstruction of a traditional Arab pharmacy and smithy. The Numismatic Hall has some fascinating displays on the history of money over 2600 years. All displays are labelled in English.

Sleeping & Eating

It has to be said that the standard of hotels in Irbid is not great. The redeeming feature is the warmth of the welcome.

Omayah Hotel HOTEL $
(02 724 5955; omayahhotel@yahoo.com; King Hussein St; s/d JD24/32) Decent value for money, this budget hotel boasts satellite TV and fridges, as well as large picture windows overlooking the heart of the city. The friendly proprietor is kind and helpful, and solo women will feel comfortable here. Rooms towards the back of the property and away from the main road are a bit quieter.

Al Joude Hotel HOTEL $$
(02 727 5515; s/d/tr from JD35/40/55; @) Near the campus of Yarmouk University, off University St. Rooms are spacious but tired. The hotel has a popular cafe and restaurant.

Clock Tower Restaurant JORDANIAN $
(Al Jaish St; meals JD3-5; 8.30am-11.30pm) The name of this popular local is written in Arabic, but as it's right next to the clock tower and has a huge spit of shawarma roasting in the window, it's hard to miss. There's a family seating area upstairs for a bit of peace and quiet, and the Jordanian staple dishes are cheap, cheerful and delicious.

Al Joude Garden Restaurant JORDANIAN $$
(mixed-grill meals JD5-10) Students, visiting parents and local families crowd into the courtyard outside Al Joude Hotel to sip fresh fruit juices and smoke a strawberry shisha. The waiters are kept in a constant state of rush in this venue as they are summoned for hot embers and top-ups of Turkish coffee – expect long waits for food orders. It's off University St. The Western-style **News Cafe** (pizza JD2.500; 10am-midnight) in the same complex is a popular meeting place and serves good coffee and pizza.

Getting There & Away

Approximately 85km north of Amman, Irbid is home to three main minibus/taxi stations.

From the **North Bus Station** (Tabarbour), there are minibuses to Umm Qais (45 minutes, JD1). From the large **South Bus Station** (new Amman bus station; Wahadat), air-conditioned Hijazi buses (JD2, 90 minutes) leave every 15 to 20 minutes between 6am and 7pm for Amman's north bus station. Minibuses also leave the South Bus Station for Ajloun (45 minutes) and Jerash (45 minutes); fares are around 800 fils.

From the **West Bus Station** (Mujamma Al Gharb Al Jadid), about 1.5km west of the centre, minibuses go to Sheikh Hussein Bridge (for Israel and the Palestinian Territories; 45 minutes) and Shuneh Ash Shamaliyyeh (North Shuna; one hour); fares are between 800 fils and JD1.200.

Getting Around

Getting between Irbid's bus stations is easy, with service taxis (200 fils) and minibuses (100 fils) shuttling between them and the city centre. Service taxis and minibuses to the South Bus Station can be picked up on Radna Al Hindawi St; for service taxis to the North Bus Station, head to Prince Nayef St. For the West Bus Station, take a bus from Palestine St, just west of the roundabout.

Umm Qais (Gadara) أم قيس

02 / ELEV 310M / POP 6100

Tucked in the far northwest corner of Jordan, and about 25km from Irbid, are the ruins of Umm Qais, site of both the ancient Roman city of Gadara and an Ottoman-era village. The hilltop site offers spectacular views over the Golan Heights in Syria, the Sea of Galilee (Lake Tiberias) to the north, and the Jordan Valley to the south.

Sights

★ West Theatre RUINS

Entering Umm Qais from the south, the first structure of interest is the well-restored and brooding West Theatre. Constructed from black basalt, it once seated about 3000 people. This is a place to sing or declaim a soliloquy – the acoustics are fantastic.

Decumanus Maximus ROMAN SITE

Still paved to this day, the main road through the site once linked Gadara with other nearby ancient cities such as Abila and Pella. In its heyday, the road extended as far as the Mediterranean coast.

Museum MUSEUM

(☎02 750 0072; ⌚8am-6pm Sat-Thu, to 4pm Fri) FREE This modest museum is set around a tranquil courtyard of fig trees. The main mosaic on display (dating from the 4th century and found in one of the tombs) illustrates the names of early Christian notables. Another highlight is the headless white-marble statue of the Hellenic goddess Tyche, which was found sitting in the front row of the West Theatre.

Sleeping & Eating

Umm Qais Hotel HOTEL $

(☎02 750 0080; s/d from JD15/20) With modest rooms above a bakery (guess where the bread for breakfast comes from?), and located a stone's throw from the ruins, this is a friendly, family-run hotel. Home-cooked Jordanian meals are available on request from the landlady. Half-day trips into the countryside can be organised from here.

★ Beit Al Baraka B&B $$

(☎07 9661 5738; www.barakadestinations.com; tw with shared bathroom JD70) This friendly, charming B&B offers simple rooms sharing two bathrooms (with some nice toiletries). The roof terrace has great views over the hills, but the particular treat is the breakfast spread, piled high with jams, cheeses, olives and other locally sourced foods.

★ Umm Qais Resthouse JORDANIAN $$

(☎02 750 0555; mezze JD1.500-3, mains around JD7; ⌚10am-7pm Oct-May, to 10pm Jun-Sep; ✎) Without doubt one of the best parts of visiting the Gadara site is pausing to take refreshment at the Umm Qais Resthouse, perched atop a small hill in the heart of the ruins. With stunning views over the Sea of Galilee, the Golan Heights and the peaks of Lebanon, it's the perfect venue for lunch or an early dinner.

Galsoum's Kitchen JORDANIAN $$$

(☎07 9661 5738; www.barakadestinations.com; meals JD15) Book ahead to enjoy a traditional north Jordanian meal using locally sourced produce, served up in cook Galsoum's home in Umm Qais. Menus depend on the season. Directions to get here are given after you book.

Information

There are minimal signs in Gadara, so it's worth collecting the brochure about Umm Qais from the ticket office. *Umm Qais: Gadara of the Decapolis* (JD3), published by Al Kutba, is ideal for anyone who wants further information. Guides (JD10) are available at the ticket office.

Baraka Destinations (☎07 9661 5738; www.barakadestinations.com) has an office near the ruins offering information about the various community-tourism projects in the area.

Note that there are no ATMs in Umm Qais.

Getting There & Away

Umm Qais village, and the ruins 200m to the west, are about 25km northwest of Irbid and about 110km north of Amman. Minibuses leave Irbid's North Bus Station (800 fils, 45 minutes) on a regular basis. There's no direct transport from Amman. Umm Qais is a 25-minute drive from the Sheikh Hussein Bridge border crossing with Israel and the Palestinian Territories.

DEAD SEA & THE WEST

There are several excellent reasons to visit the Dead Sea region, not least for a float in the sea itself. Bethany-Beyond-the-Jordan is an important archaeological site that pinpoints a major event in the life of Jesus to a remarkably specific location on the banks of the Jordan River. For something completely different, beautiful Mujib Biosphere Reserve offers some of Jordan's wettest and wildest adventure opportunities.

Public transport is unreliable on the Dead Sea Hwy; consider renting a car or taxi for the day. Most budget travellers visit the Dead Sea as part of an organised day trip from a hotel in Amman or Madaba.

Bethany-Beyond-the-Jordan (Al Maghtas) المغطس

This important site is claimed by Christians to be the place where Jesus was baptised by John the Baptist, where the first five apostles met, and where, at Tell Ellias, the prophet Elijah ascended to heaven in a chariot. It wasn't until the 1994 peace treaty with Israel that the remains of churches, caves and baptism pools were unearthed. Pope John Paul II authenticated the site in March 2000.

Entry to Al Maghtas (Baptism Site) includes a mandatory guided tour, partly by shuttle bus, partly on foot. Tours often return via the House of Mary the Egyptian and a two-room hermit cave.

Sights

Site of Jesus's Baptism RUINS

The main archaeological site comprises the remains of three churches, one on top of the other. Steps lead down to the original water level and a building nearby marks the likely site of Jesus's baptism. Byzantine churches were built to mark the site during the 5th and 6th centuries, and rebuilt on the same site after they were destroyed by flooding. All that remains today are traces of original mosaic.

Jordan River RIVER

A walking trail passes a golden-roofed Greek Orthodox church and leads to a shaded wooden platform by the river, which here is little more than a creek lined with reeds. You can be baptised in the Jordan if accompanied by a priest; there's also a font accessible to all that is filled with water from the river (but note that, despite its holy status, the river itself is quite polluted, so the water shouldn't be drunk).

Tell Elias RUINS

Tell Elias is where Elijah is said to have ascended to heaven, although there is little to see here. The rebuilt arch marks the 5th- to 6th-century pilgrim chapel, where Pope John Paul II authenticated the site in 2000. The nearby 3rd-century rectangular prayer hall is one of the earliest Christian places of worship ever discovered, dating from a period when Christianity was still illegal.

Getting There & Away

The site is near Shuneh Al Janubiyyeh, at the southern end of the Jordan Valley. Coming from Amman, follow signs to the Baptism Site along the main road to the Dead Sea. Tours from budget hotels in Amman and Madaba often include this site in a trip that also takes in the Dead Sea and Mt Nebo (from around JD60 for a taxi carrying four people).

There is no public transport to the Baptism Site; the closest you can get is 5km away at the Al Maghtas junction, on a Suweimah-bound minibus from Amman.

Dead Sea البحر الميت

ELEV -425M

The Dead Sea is at the lowest point on earth and has such high salinity (due to evaporation) that nothing but the most microscopic of life forms can survive in it. Indeed, the only things you're likely to see in the Dead Sea are a few over-buoyant tourists. A dip in the sea is one of those must-do experiences, but be warned: you'll discover cuts you didn't know you had, so don't shave before bathing! Sadly, the Dead Sea is under threat from shrinking water levels.

Sights & Activities

The most luxurious way to swim on the Jordanian side of the Dead Sea is at one of the upmarket resorts that offer day access to their private beaches and swimming pools. Access to their spas costs extra. The resorts and public areas are very busy on Fridays – useful for finding a ride back to Amman if

DEAD SEA FAST FACTS

- The Dead Sea is part of the Great Rift Valley; it is the lowest spot on earth at 425m below sea level and more than 390m deep.
- It is not actually a sea, but a lake filled with incoming water with no outlet.
- It is the second-saltiest body of water on earth (after Lake Aral in Djibouti) with a salt content of 31%.
- Egyptians used Dead Sea mud (bitumen) in their mummification process; the last lump of floating bitumen surfaced in 1936.
- The majority of Dead Sea minerals (including calcium and magnesium) occur naturally in our bodies and have health-giving properties.
- The Dead Sea is three million years old, but has shrunk by 30% in recent years (half a metre per year) due to evaporation and the demands of the potash industry, one of Jordan's most valuable commodities.

DON'T MISS

BRAVING LUXURY IN A DEAD SEA SPA

Even if you're a die-hard, old-school traveller who feels that sleeping on a bed with a soft mattress is a sign of weakness, there's a certain gratification in succumbing to the spa experience. You'll be in good company: Herod the Great and Cleopatra, neither noted as wimpish types, both dipped a toe in spa waters. So ditch the hiking boots for a day, step into a fluffy bathrobe and brave the clinically white entrance hall of a Dead Sea pleasure dome.

The spa experience (from around JD30) usually begins with a mint tea and a spa bag to stow your worldly goods – this isn't going to be a chlorinated swim in the municipal pool back home. You'll then be shown to the mirrored changing rooms, with Dead Sea soaps and shampoos and more towels than you'll have body to towel down. This marks the point of no return: the silent-padding assistants waft you from here along marble corridors to the opulent bathhouses.

All the spas offer a range of cradling Dead Sea waters with different levels of salinity. There's usually a foot spa and a float in a Damascene-tiled Jacuzzi. Outside pools assault visitors with a variety of bullying jet sprays. Best of all are the little pots that bubble when you sit in them and ought to be X-rated.

Luxury of this kind is an extreme sport and by the time you reach the spa's private infinity pool, you'll be so seduced by the ambience you won't have the energy to try the saunas, steam rooms or tropical sprays, let alone the gym. Lie instead under an oleander by the pool, sip a chilled carrot juice and wonder why you resisted the spa experience for so long.

For the best Dead Sea spa experience, try the **Resense Spa** (☎05 356 8888; www.kempinski.com; Kempinski Ishtar Hotel, Dead Sea Resort Zone; day spa JD68; ⏰10am-10pm) or the **Zara Spa** (☎05 349 1310; www.movenpick.com; Mövenpick Resort & Spa, Dead Sea Resort Zone; guests/nonguests JD20/50; ⏰8.30am-8.30pm) – both offer a full range of treatments.

you missed the last bus. Take lots of water, as the humidity and heat is intense (over 40°C in summer) and there's little shade.

Amman Beach BEACH

(☎05 356 0800; Dead Sea Hwy; adult/child JD25/15, restaurant buffet JD14; ⏰9am-8pm, restaurant 11am-5pm) This public beach and pools complex, 2km south of the main resort strip, gives affordable access to the Dead Sea. The grounds are attractively landscaped and the beach is clean, with sun umbrellas and freshwater showers. Locals generally swim fully clothed.

Oh Beach BEACH

(☎05 349 2000; www.ohresort.net; Dead Sea Hwy; adult/child JD15/10, with lunch JD40/25; ⏰9am-6pm) This private beach, stepped down the hillside in a series of landscaped terraces and infinity pools, is a great way to enjoy the Dead Sea in comfort without paying for a night in one of the neighbouring hotels. There are several restaurants and bars, a weekend buffet and a range of spa treatments.

Dead Sea Panoramic Complex Lookout VIEWPOINT

(JD2; ⏰8am-10pm) Walk among cacti to this lookout, high above the Dead Sea, and then watch raptors wheel in the wadis below, and you will have to pinch yourself to think that you are standing at sea level. This complex houses an interesting geology **museum** and an excellent restaurant with lovely views, especially on a crisp day in winter when the Judaea Mountains across the water seem as if they are just an arm's stretch away.

Al Wadi Resort WATER PARK

(☎05 349 3333; www.alwadideadsea.com; Dead Sea Resort Zone; adult/child JD25/18; ⏰9am-6pm Sat-Thu, to 7pm Fri) This huge water park has a giant pool with a wave machine and epic slides, in pleasantly landscaped surroundings. There are two restaurants, one poolside offering light food, and a larger buffet restaurant. Children are measured on entry: those under 95cm are admitted free.

Sleeping

About 5km south of Suweimeh is a strip of opulent pleasure palaces that offer the latest in spa luxury. There are no budget or midrange options and the resorts featured here are two of several five-star options.

★**Mövenpick Resort & Spa** RESORT **$$$**

(☎05 356 1111; www.moevenpick-hotels.com; Dead Sea Resort Zone; d JD180; Ⓟ📶) This green haven boasts a river that ambles through the village-style complex of rustic two-storey apartments. Wooden screens and balconies allow guests to enjoy sea or garden views in private, while secluded seating areas around a superb infinity pool add to the ambience. The Zara Spa is particularly well-regarded.

Kempinski Hotel Ishtar RESORT **$$$**
(05 356 8888; www.kempinski.com; Dead Sea Resort Zone; s/d JD200/220; P) This grand resort isn't shy in its bid to be the best. Floor-to-ceiling windows stretch the length of the Dead Sea vista, a Sumerian-style lobby overlooks a spectacular, circular infinity pool, and a series of water features tumble down to the Dead Sea. A palace among hotels, the hotel's Resense Spa is a destination in its own right.

Holiday Inn Resort Dead Sea RESORT **$$$**
(05 349 5555; www.ihg.com; Dead Sea Resort Zone; s/d JD120/145; P) This excellent resort with a series of epic pools stretching down to the beach will appeal to families, as its access to the Dead Sea is quicker and easier than the steep descent at other resorts. It charges nonguests JD25 on weekdays and JD45 at weekends and holidays for access to its beach and pools.

Getting There & Away

JETT buses offer a daily service to the resort strip south of Suweimeh from Amman (JD8 return) at 9am, returning at 5pm. The bus leaves from the JETT office near 7th Circle. Check with the JETT office (p299) in Amman for the latest timetable.

Minibuses from Muhajireen bus station only run as far as Suweimeh. A return taxi from Amman to Amman Beach costs about JD50 including three hours' waiting time (minimum required to make the trip worthwhile) or JD20 for a one-way journey.

Some budget hotels in Amman and most hotels in Madaba organise day trips via Mt Nebo, the Dead Sea Panoramic Complex and Hammamat Ma'in.

Mujib Biosphere Reserve محمية الموجب

The 215-sq-km **Mujib Biosphere Reserve** (06 461 6523; Dead Sea Hwy) was established by the RSCN for the captive breeding of the Nubian ibex, but it also forms the heart of an ambitious ecotourism project. It's a great place for hiking and canyoning, with water year-round. There's no public transport to the reserve so you'll need to rent a car or take a taxi from Amman, Madaba or Karak.

Sights & Activities

A trip to this reserve begins at the **visitor centre** (07 9720 3888; 8am-8pm), which lies along the Dead Sea Hwy, next to the suspension bridge about 20km south of the Dead Sea resorts. Bring a swimming costume, a towel and a watertight bag for valuables as some of the trails are wet. Guides are compulsory for all but the Siq trail and should be booked in advance through the Wild Jordan Centre (p298) in Amman. There are some information boards about the reserve, but few facilities. Children under 18 years are not allowed on the trails.

Sleeping

★ **Mujib Chalets** CHALET **$$**
(07 9720 3888; www.wildjordan.com; s/d/tr JD52/64/75;) Wild Jordan operates 15 stylish and modern en-suite chalets overlooking the Dead Sea. You need to book accommodation and meals in advance, either by calling the chalet manager directly or when booking your hike through the RSCN. The chalets have double or twin beds, a fridge and a shaded patio overlooking the Dead Sea, in a plot that is still under development.

AZRAQ & THE EAST

The landscape east of Amman quickly turns into a featureless stone desert, known as the *badia*, cut by twin highways running to Iraq and Saudi Arabia. It has its own haunting, if barren, beauty, partly because it seems so limitless: indeed this is what 80% of Jordan looks like, while supporting only 5% of its population. If you stray into this territory, you'll be surprised to find you're not the first to do so. A whole assortment of ruined hunting lodges, bathhouses and pleasure palaces, known collectively as 'desert castles', have lured people into the wilderness for centuries. Most of these isolated outposts were built or adapted by the Damascus-based Umayyad rulers in the late 7th and early 8th centuries.

Accommodation and public transport are almost non-existent out here, so most travellers visit the region on a tour from budget hotels in Amman. Alternatively, hire a car and make a thorough job of it by staying overnight in Azraq. Avoid straying too close to the Syrian or Iraqi borders, and don't pick up hitchhikers.

Hallabat قصر الحلابات

With a fair proportion of masonry still standing, some beautifully restored archways and a desolate perch on the edge of the Eastern Desert, **Qasr Al Hallabat Fort** (daylight hours) FREE is a good introduction to the history of the region. Hallabat once boasted elaborate baths, intricate frescoes and mosaics, a mosque and several reservoirs, and served as a focus for a thriving farming community. Restoration of a substantial part of the site under Spanish direction has restored an inkling of the castle's former stature.

Part of the neighbouring fort complex in Hallabat, **Hammam As Sarah** (daylight hours) FREE has been extensively restored, revealing the underfloor piping system that was used to heat the bathing rooms. The hammam is located along the main road to Hallabat village, about 3km east of Qasr Al Hallabat and 5km from the main road. The minibus to Hallabat village drives past Hammam As Sarah and can drop you off on request. The site is unlocked – just push open the gate.

Azraq الأزرق

The oasis town of Azraq (meaning 'blue' in Arabic) lies 80km east of Amman. For centuries an important meeting of trade routes, the town is still a junction of truck roads heading northeast to Iraq and southeast to Saudi Arabia. South Azraq was founded early last century by Chechens fleeing Russian persecution, while North Azraq is home to a minority of Druze, who fled French Syria in the 1920s.

Sights

★Shaumari Wildlife Reserve WILDLIFE RESERVE
(Mahmiyyat Ash Shaumari; www.rscn.org.jo; JD4; 8am-4pm) Established in 1975 by the RSCN, this 22-sq-km reserve, 7km from Azraq, was created with the aim of reintroducing wildlife that has disappeared from the region, most notably the highly endangered Arabian oryx, Persian onagers (wild asses), Dorcas gazelles and houbara bustards. The reserve has recently undergone a radical overhaul. For the best experience, visit the enclosures for a close-up view of the desert animals before joining a jeep safari (JD20, three hours, minimum of four people) around the reserve.

★Azraq Wetland Reserve NATURE RESERVE
(05 383 5017; JD2.500; 9am-6pm Mar-Aug, to 4pm Sep-Feb) For several millennia, the Qa'al Azraq (Azraq Basin) comprised a huge area of mudflats, pools and marshlands, which led to the establishment of Azraq as one of the most important oasis towns in the Levant. Since the mass pumping of water to thirsty Amman, however, the wetlands have almost disappeared. Thankfully, the RSCN has worked to preserve the remainder, and they remain a fascinating place to visit. The **Marsh Trail** (1.5km, 30 minutes) follows natural paths made by water buffalo and includes a bird hide.

★Qasr Al Azraq CASTLE
(JD1, ticket also valid for Qusayr Amra & Qasr Kharana, free with Jordan Pass; daylight hours) On the edge of dusty Azraq, this imposing fort dates back to the Roman emperor Diocletian (AD 300), but owes its current form to the beginning of the 13th century. During WWI Sherif Hussein (father of King Hussein) and TE Lawrence made it their desert headquarters in the winter of 1917–18, during the Arab Revolt against the Ottomans.

Lawrence, who famously wrote in the Seven Pillars of Wisdom of the 'Roman legionaries who languished here', stayed in the room directly above the southern entrance, while his loyal followers braved the elements in other areas of the fort. They were holed up here for several months in crowded conditions with little shelter from the intense cold – gaping holes in the roof were patched up with nothing but palm branches and clay.

Sleeping & Eating

★Azraq Lodge HOTEL $$
(05 383 5017; s/d/tr from JD70/82/93; P) This former British 1940s military hospital in south Azraq has been atmospherically renovated by the Royal Society for the Conservation of Nature (RSCN) as a base from which to explore the Eastern Desert. The RSCN has succeeded in preserving the

TOURING THE DESERT CASTLES

Jumping on an organised tour of the desert castles from Amman makes a lot of sense if you're short of time or on a tight budget. Tours can be arranged at the Palace, Farah and Cliff hotels in Amman, which charge about JD15 to JD20 per person for a full-day trip. You're unlikely to get a better deal by negotiating directly with the driver of a service taxi or private taxi in Amman, and regular taxi drivers are rarely keen on leaving the city. Tours, which can also be arranged from the Black Iris Hotel (p314) and Mariam Hotel (p314) in Madaba, usually encompass the big three – Al-Azraq, Amra and Kharana.

historic building while adding a modern extension, so thankfully there's no need to rough it on bare stretchers.

Azraq Palace Restaurant JORDANIAN $$
(☎07 9503 0356; buffet JD10; ⊙11am-4pm & 6-11pm) This busy restaurant attracts tour groups on desert-castle excursions. The standard Jordanian fare of rice, grills, salads and dips is tasty and filling and the management is helpful.

Getting There & Away

Minibuses run up and down the road along northern and southern Azraq in search of passengers before joining the highway to Zarqa (JD1.500, 1½ hours). If you are driving, you have the choice here of joining Hwy 5, which leads south after at least three or four hours of utter desolation to southern Jordan. The drive to Amman along either Hwy 30 or Hwy 40 takes around two hours. Fill up with petrol when you see a station, as pumps are few and far between.

Around Azraq

The sights around Azraq are hard to access by public transport and the most feasible way to visit them is either with your own car or on a taxi tour from Amman or Madaba.

Sights

★Qusayr Amra CASTLE
(JD1, ticket also valid for Qasr Al Azraq & Qasr Kharana, free with Jordan Pass; ⊙8am-6pm May-Sep, to 4pm Oct-Apr) One of the best-preserved desert buildings of the Umayyads, the Unesco World Heritage Site of Qusayr Amra is the highlight of a trip into the Eastern Desert. Part of a much greater complex that served as a caravanserai, bathhouse and hunting lodge, the *qusayr* (little castle) is renowned for its rather risqué 8th-century frescoes of wine, women and wild times.

DESERT CASTLES

There are dozens of ruins belonging to the Umayyad dynasty scattered across the gravel plains of the Eastern Desert, so how do you choose which ones to visit?

Below is a list of the main castles and a guide to their accessibility. The castles fall into two convenient sets. The most famous ones lie on the so-called 'desert castle loop'. These are accessible on a day trip from Amman via Azraq, by tour or by car. Individual castles can be reached with more difficulty by a combination of minibus and taxi.

The other set lies on the so-called 'Eastern Desert Highway', or Hwy 10, which leads from the town of Mafraq to the Iraqi border. These are much more time-consuming to visit.

Each of the two sets takes a long, full day to cover. You can combine the two sets by staying the night in Azraq and using Hwy 5 to cut between the two.

Desert Castle Loop

CASTLE NAME	PUBLIC TRANSPORT	4WD	BY TOUR	WORTHWHILE?
Qasr al-Hallabat	Yes	No	Sometimes	✓✓
Qasr al-Azraq	Yes	No	Yes	✓✓✓
Qasr 'Uweinid	No	Yes	No	✓
Qusayr Amra	Taxi from Azraq	No	Yes	✓✓✓
Qasr Kharana	Taxi from Azraq	No	Yes	✓✓✓
Qasr Al-Mushatta	Taxi from Amman	No	No	✓✓

Eastern Desert Highway

CASTLE NAME	PUBLIC TRANSPORT	4WD	BY TOUR	WORTHWHILE?
Umm al-Jimal	Yes	No	Sometimes	✓✓
Qasr Deir al-Kahf	No	No	No	✓
Qasr Aseikhin	No	No	No	✓
Qasr Burqu	No	Yes	No	✓✓

★**Qasr Kharana** CASTLE

(JD1, ticket also valid for Qusayr Amra & Qasr Al Azraq, free with Jordan Pass; 8am-6pm May-Sep, to 4pm Oct-Apr) Located in the middle of a vast, treeless plain, this imposing thick-walled structure was the most likely inspiration for the 'desert castle' moniker and is arguably the most photogenic of all the desert castles.

★**Umm Al Jimal Ruins** RUINS

(daylight hours) FREE The unpretentious urban architecture of Umm Al Jimal, near the Jordanian-Syrian border, encompasses more than 150 buildings standing one to three storeys above ground, including 128 houses and 15 churches. Together, these buildings provide a fascinating insight into rural life during the Roman, Byzantine and early Islamic periods.

MADABA & THE KING'S HIGHWAY مادبا والطريق الملوكي

Of Jordan's three north–south highways (only one of which is a dual carriageway), the King's Highway is by far the most interesting and picturesque, with a host of attractions lying on the road or nearby. The highway connects the mosaic town of Madaba to the pink city of Petra via Crusader castles, Roman forts, biblical sites, a windswept Nabataean temple and some epic landscapes – including the majestic Wadi Mujib and a gem of a nature reserve at Dana.

Unfortunately, public transport along the King's Highway is patchy and stops altogether at Wadi Mujib, between Dhiban and Ariha, meaning that the only feasible travel along its length is by car or taxi. Helpfully, the Palace Hotel in Amman and budget hotels in Madaba organise daily transport for like-minded travellers.

Madaba مادبا

The amiable market town of Madaba is best known for a collection of Byzantine-era mosaics. The most famous of these is the mosaic map on the floor of St George's Church, but there are many others carpeting different parts of the town, many of which are even more complete and vibrant in colour. Look for the chicken – there's one in most mosaics, and trying to spot it may save 'mosaic-fatigue' syndrome.

One-third of Madaba's population is Christian (the other two-thirds are Muslim), making it one of the largest Christian communities in Jordan. The town's long tradition of religious tolerance is joyfully – and loudly – expressed on Friday. This is one day when you shouldn't expect a lie-in. The imam summons the faithful to pray before dawn, the carillon bells bid the Orthodox Christians to rise at first light, and finally Mammon gets a look in with the honks and groans of traffic when the shops open.

Unlike most other towns along the highway, Madaba has a good choice of hotels and restaurants. Less than an hour by public transport from Amman, it makes an alternative base for exploring King's Highway and Dead Sea highlights. By taxi, you can even travel directly from Queen Alia International Airport in around 20 minutes.

Sights

A combination ticket (JD2) covers admission to the Archaeological Park, the Church of the Apostles and Madaba Museum.

★**St George's Church & Mosaic Map** CHURCH

(Talal St; adult/child under 12yr JD1/free; 9.30am-5pm Fri year-round, 8am-5pm Sat-Thu Nov-Mar, to 6pm Sat-Thu Apr-Oct) This rather modest 19th-century Greek Orthodox church houses a treasure of early Christianity. Imagine the excitement in 1884 when Christian builders came across the remnants of a Byzantine church on their construction site. Among the rubble, having survived wilful destruction, fire and neglect, the flooring they discovered wasn't just another mosaic but one with extraordinary significance: to this day, it represents the oldest map of Palestine in existence and provides many historical insights into the region.

★**Church of the Beheading of John the Baptist** MUSEUM

(Latin Church; 05 324 4065; Talal St; adult/child under 12yr JD1/free; 9am-5pm Oct-Apr, to 7pm May-Sep) This operational early-20th-century Roman Catholic church has been transformed into an intriguing destination for visitors and pilgrims by the restoration of the ancient sites upon which it sits. The gem of the complex is the **Acropolis Museum**, housed in the vaulted underbelly of the church. Here a well dating to the Moabite era, 3000 years ago, is still operational.

OFF THE BEATEN TRACK

CANYONING IN JORDAN

The central part of Jordan is riven with wadis and canyons, some of which only come alive during a flash flood and others which are home to permanent watercourses that push their way through the rocky landscape to the Dead Sea. Along the way the presence of water creates beautiful semi-tropical oases of palms, oleander and ferns. Often hidden from the road, these secret gardens are among the treasures of Jordan.

While thankfully the most spectacular canyons (such as those of the lower Wadi Mujib) are protected and made safely accessible by the RSCN, there is nothing to stop a visitor exploring other canyons off the beaten track.

To go it alone, the essential companion for canyoning is the widely available hikers' bible, *Jordan: Walks, Treks, Caves, Climbs & Canyons*, by Di Taylor and Tony Howard (4th edition 2007). For escorted trips (recommended given the unpredictability of flash flooding), contact the RSCN at Wadi Mujib or Dana, Feynan Ecolodge (p319) or the Black Iris Hotel and **Queen Ayola Hotel** (☎05 324 4087; Talal St) in Madaba.

Church of the Apostles CHURCH
(King's Hwy; adult/child under 12yr JD3/free, with Jordan Pass free; ⏲9am-4pm Oct-Apr, 8am-5pm May-Sep) This insignificant-looking church contains a remarkable mosaic dedicated to the Twelve Apostles. The embroidery-like mosaic was created in AD 568 and is one of the few instances where the name of the craftsman (Salomios) is included. The central portion shows Thalassa, a female personification of the sea, surrounded by fish and slippery marine creatures. Native animals, birds, flowers, fruit and cherubic faces decorate the corners.

Madaba Archaeological Park I & Virgin Mary Church ARCHAEOLOGICAL SITE
(☎05 324 6681; Abu Bakr As Seddiq St; adult/child under 12yr JD3/free, with Jordan Pass free; ⏲8am-4pm Oct-Apr, to 5pm May-Sep) Some careful restoration and excavation in the early 1990s led to the creation of this open-air museum, which houses a collection of ruins and fine mosaics from the Madaba area. The Church of the Virgin Mary is also included in the site; built in the 6th century and unearthed beneath the floor of a private house in 1887, the church boasts a central mosaic, thought to date from 767, that is a masterpiece of geometric design.

Sleeping

★**Black Iris Hotel** GUESTHOUSE $
(☎05 324 1959; www.blackirishotel.com; s/d/tr JD25/35/48; 📶) For a home-away-from-home feeling, it's hard to beat this tidy hotel near Al Mouhafada Circle. The rooms are cosy and there's a spacious communal sitting area. The breakfast spreads are notably excellent (try the date molasses with tahina). The kindly and knowledgeable travel assistance makes the Black Iris ever popular with readers; women travelling alone will feel comfortable here.

Moab Land Hotel GUESTHOUSE $
(☎05 325 1318; www.moablandhotel.com; Talal St; s/d/tr JD26/32/40) With grand views of St George's Church (p313) and beyond, this family-run hotel couldn't be more central. The prize draw, apart from the welcome, is the glorious rooftop terrace where breakfast is served in summer. Reception is on the upper floor.

★**Mariam Hotel** HOTEL $$
(☎05 325 1529; www.mariamhotel.com; Aisha Umm Al Mumeneen St; s/d/tr/q JD26/38/46/55; @📶🏊) The well-regarded Mariam offers good facilities, including a bar, a poolside restaurant and a cheerful communal area. There's also a restaurant-bar on the 5th floor offering views across town. Reservations are recommended. The hotel arranges transport and tours for guests.

Mosaic City Hotel HOTEL $$
(☎05 325 1313; www.mosaiccityhotel.com; Yarmouk St; s/d JD42/52; 📶) This well-kept, central, family-run hotel has bright and spacious rooms. Some have balconies overlooking lively Yarmouk St, but windows are double glazed, keeping street noise to a minimum. The reception staff is ever amiable and facilities include bar and mini gym. A family room with double-size bathroom sleeps four (JD87).

Madaba 1880 Hotel HOTEL $$
(☎05 325 3250; www.madaba1880.com; Talal St; s/d/tr JD48/72/85; 📶) Reopened in 2016

after a complete refurbishment and under new management, this central hotel punches well above its price range, with modern, comfortable rooms and a plush lobby. The San George bar is a good place for an evening drink, whether you're a guest or not.

Eating

For freshly baked Arabic bread, head for the ovens opposite the Church of the Apostles. There are several grocery stores in town.

★Al Mandi JORDANIAN $
(05 325 3256; Al Quds St; meals JD3; 11am-9pm) Al Mandi knows the adage: do one thing and do it well. Come for an enormous plate of *mandi* – delicious barbecued chicken with portions of different types of rice, topped with nuts and dried fruit and served with broth and a salad.

Abu Yousef JORDANIAN $
(Ash Shuhada St; mains JD1-2; 8am-1pm;) Little more than a hole in the wall, Abu Yousef's establishment is part of the fabric of the town, serving fresh hummus and falafel daily to those in the know. Found opposite the parking lot of Haret Jdoudna restaurant, this modest place has supported owner Abu Yousef (now very elderly) and his family for more than 30 years.

Ayola Coffeeshop & Bar CAFE $
(05 325 1843; Talal St; snacks around JD2.500; 8am-11pm;) If you want a toasted sandwich (the steak and cheese option is unexpectedly good), Turkish coffee, a beer or a glass of arak with the locals, or simply a comfortable perch on which to while away some time with fellow travellers, then this is the place to come.

Adonis Restaurant & Cafe JORDANIAN $$
(05 325 1771; Ishac Al Shuweihat St; mixed grill JD7; 11am-2am) Housed in a beautifully restored typical Madaba residence and run by one of the town's returning sons, this excellent restaurant has quickly become the place to be at weekends. Serving typical Jordanian fare in a space that expands almost magically into unseen corners, Adonis has the added charm of live music on Thursday and Friday nights.

★Haret Jdoudna JORDANIAN $$$
(05 324 8650; Talal St; mains JD8-15; noon-midnight;) Popular with locals and with discerning diners from Amman, and set in a restored Ottoman house, this restaurant is always worth a visit. Sit indoors by a roaring fire in winter or in the leafy courtyard in summer and sample traditional Jordanian dishes such as *mutaffi bethanjan* (fried eggplant with sesame). Book ahead for Thursday or Friday nights.

Shopping

Haret Jdoudna Complex ARTS & CRAFTS
(05 324 8650; Talal St; 10.30am-11pm) Selling an extensive range of crafts, including mosaics, ceramics, textiles and clothing, this shop, attached to the restaurant of the same name, stocks particularly exquisite embroidery. Many of the items are sponsored by the Arab Cultural Society. Indeed, most items come from local nonprofit organisations, including the Jordan River Foundation.

Lawrence Arts & Crafts GIFTS & SOUVENIRS
(07 9550 4121; Prince Hassan St) Visit this private workshop for an insight into the painstaking process of laying out mosaics. You can purchase your own copy of the Madaba map or a more modest Tree of Life (from JD8, depending on size).

OFF THE BEATEN TRACK

BRONZE AGE BURIAL CHAMBERS

Near to Madaba, **Wadi Jadid** (24hr) is locally renowned for its remarkable collection of around 40 early Bronze Age burial chambers and stone memorials. Known as dolmens ('dolmen' means stone table), they date between 5000 and 3000 BC and consist of two upright stones capped by a bridging stone. How the huge bridging stones were winched into position remains unknown: it's little wonder that social anthropologists regard them as proof of early social cohesion.

From the road, it takes about 30 minutes to walk to the nearest dolmen and an hour to reach more distant groups. The site is near the village of Al Fiha, 10km southwest of Madaba, but you need to be in the know to find it. The best way to visit is by checking on directions with the Mariam Hotel in Madaba, downloading a map from the hotel website or joining a tour (JD12, plus JD3 for each hour spent at the site).

Information

The **Visitors Centre** (05 325 3563; Abu Bakr As Seddiq St; 8am-6pm Oct-Apr, to 7pm May-Sep) has a 10-minute video on Madaba's highlights, a brochure called *Madaba and Mount Nebo*, toilets and a handy car park.

There are plenty of banks with ATMs in town, clustered around Sameh Al Farah St.

Getting There & Away

The bus station is about 15 minutes' walk east of the town centre on the King's Highway.

A taxi costs JD90 to JD120 per car (maximum of four passengers) to Petra along the King's Highway with stops en route. Some hotels arrange taxi share with other tourists. **Ammar Damseh** (07 9727 1688, 07 7640 3515; lanatours2017@gmail.com) is a recommended independent English-speaking operator who can arrange taxi tours locally and as far afield as Petra and Jerash.

Note there is no public transport between Madaba and Karak along the King's Highway.

Getting Around

Madaba is small enough to explore on foot, though the walk from the bus station to the centre of town is quite a hike with bags. Taxis (around JD1) are plentiful. If you're driving, note that it's not possible to park outside some of the cheaper hotels, as they're on busy, narrow streets.

Mt Nebo جبل نيبو

Mt Nebo, on the edge of the East Bank plateau and 9km from Madaba, is where Moses is said to have seen the Promised Land. He then died (allegedly aged 120!) and was buried in the area, although the exact location of the burial site is the subject of conjecture.

Sights

★ Memorial Viewpoint VIEWPOINT

(JD2, with Moses Memorial Church free; 8am-4pm Oct-Apr, to 6pm May-Sep) Moses' view of the Promised Land towards ancient Gilead, Judah, Jericho and the Negev is marked by an Italian-designed bronze memorial next to the Moses Memorial Church. The ironwork, symbolising the suffering and death of Jesus on the cross and the serpent that 'Moses lifted up' in the desert, stands in the middle of an invariably windy viewing platform. Markers indicate notable points in the often-hazy distance, including the Golan Heights, Jerusalem (just 46km away) and the Dead Sea.

Moses Memorial Church CHURCH

(Mt Nebo; JD2; 8am-4pm Oct-Apr, to 6pm May-Sep) On top of Mt Nebo, this modest church, or more accurately basilica, was built around 4th-century foundations in 597 and has just undergone major reconstruction. It houses some of the best mosaics in Jordan, dating from around 530. The masterpiece is a hunting and herding scene interspersed with an assortment of African fauna, including a zebu (humped ox), lions, tigers, bears, boars, zebras, an ostrich on a leash and a camel-shaped giraffe.

Eating

★ Nebo Restaurant & Terrace BUFFET $$

(05 324 2442; buffet JD10; 11.30am-6pm Sat-Thu, to late Fri) The spectacular view and warm welcome from the owners make this restaurant worth a trip to Mt Nebo in its own right. The panoramic windows and the roof terrace make the very best of the vista, and the restaurant has its own ovens for baking fresh Arabic bread.

Asa Moses Restaurant BUFFET $$

(Siyagha Restaurant; 05 325 0226; buffet JD10; noon-4.30pm;) This trestle-tabled restaurant opposite the Ayoun Musa junction produces a daily lunch buffet of traditional Jordanian dishes, including *maqlubbeh* (an 'upside down' dish of rice, meat and vegetables) if ordered an hour ahead. The stone pillars and reed ceiling add to the been-here-forever ambience. Try a local Mt Nebo wine and sink into the *majlis* cushions for a nap.

Getting There & Away

From Madaba, shared taxis to Mt Nebo cost around JD1; a private taxi from Madaba costs JD5 (JD8 return, with one hour waiting time). It's common for Madaba drivers to offer trips to Mt Nebo, in conjunction with the baptism site at Bethany, for around JD20.

Machaerus (Mukawir) قلية مكاور

Just beyond the village of Mukawir is the spectacular 700m-high hilltop perch of Machaerus, the castle of Herod the Great. The ruins themselves are only of moderate interest, but the setting is breathtaking and commands great views out over the surrounding hills and the Dead Sea.

DON'T MISS

WADI MUJIB وادي الموجب

Stretching across Jordan from the Desert Hwy to the Dead Sea is the vast Wadi Mujib, proudly known as the 'Grand Canyon of Jordan'. This spectacular valley is about 1km deep and over 4km from one edge to the other. The canyon forms the upper portion of the Mujib Biosphere Reserve, which is normally accessed from the Dead Sea Hwy.

Even if you are not intending to make the crossing, it's worth travelling to the canyon rim. Just after **Dhiban**, the road descends after 3km to a spectacular **lookout**. Some enterprising traders have set up a tea stall here, and fossils and minerals from the canyon walls are for sale. This is the easiest point on the road to stop to absorb the view, take a photograph and turn around if you're heading back to Madaba.

Dhiban is where almost all transport south of Madaba stops. The only reliable way to cross the mighty Mujib from Dhiban to Ariha (about 30km) is to charter a taxi from Madaba to Karak. Hitching is not advisable in the current climate.

Sights

Castle of Herod the Great CASTLE
(Machaerus; JD1.500, with Jordan Pass free; 8am-6pm) Machaerus is known locally as Qala'at Al Meshneq (Castle of the Gallows), a fitting name given that it is renowned as the place where John the Baptist was beheaded by Herod Antipas, the successor of Herod the Great. The castle is about 2km past Mukawir village and easy to spot. If you don't feel in the mood for a climb, it's worth coming this way just to see the hilltop fortress framed by sea and sky.

Shopping

★Bani Hamida Weaving Centre & Gallery ARTS & CRAFTS
(www.jordanriver.jo; 8am-3pm Sun-Thu, 10am-6pm Fri, to 4pm winter) This women's cooperative in Mukawir village (by the side of the road leading to the castle) is run by the Bani Hamida Centre and is a good place to buy colourful kilims and cushions. Designs reflect both contemporary tastes and traditional Bedouin patterns. The fixed prices fairly reflect the labour invested in the weaving.

Getting There & Away

Frequent minibuses (600 fils, one hour) leave from outside Madaba bus station for Mukawir village, via Libb (the last is at around 5pm). From there, it's a 2km downhill stroll to the foot of the castle.

Karak الكرك

03

Lying roughly halfway along the King's Highway, the typical central Jordanian town of Karak may well have escaped attention but for the evocative ancient Crusader castle that looms over its dusty streets. Most people spend an hour visiting the battlements and leave, but there is accommodation in Karak and the bustling market town atmosphere has its own attraction.

Always something of a politically charged town, Karak was the scene of a terrorist attack in 2016. As a result, Karak has seen a notably increased police presence around the castle.

Sights

Karak Castle CASTLE
(03 235 1216; JD2, with Jordan Pass free; 8am-4pm Oct-Mar, to 7pm Apr-Sep) The evocative ancient Crusader castle of Karak became a place of legend during the 12th-century battles between the Crusaders and the Muslim armies of Saladin (Salah ad-Din). Although among the most famous, the castle at Karak was just one in a long line built by the Crusaders, stretching from Aqaba in the south to Turkey in the north. The ticket office – and guides, charging around JD10 for a tour – can be found near the entrance at the southern end of Al Qala'a St through **Ottoman's Gate**.

At one point in its chequered history, the castle belonged to a particularly unsavoury knight of the cross, Renaud de Chatillon. De Chatillon arrived from France in 1148 to take part in the Crusades. Hated by Saladin for his treachery, he was renowned for his sadistic delight in torturing prisoners and throwing them off the walls into the valley 450m below; he even went to the trouble of having a wooden box fastened over their heads so they wouldn't lose consciousness before hitting the ground.

Inside the castle, down the hill from the entrance, is the excellent **Islamic Museum**. In a semi-subterranean room with a vaulted ceiling, this evocatively lit collection houses some of the finds from the castle and excavations in the surrounding area.

Sleeping

Qairwan Hotel BOUTIQUE HOTEL $
(Cairwan Hotel; 03 239 6022; King's Hwy; s JD27, with shared bathroom JD10, d/tr JD30/40, 5-bed Jacuzzi ste with kitchen JD45;) This homely, family-run establishment has plenty of personality. Each of the nine rooms is unique, with quirky decoration. Unexpectedly, stairs lead to a cavernous disco. The hotel is 500m from the bus station, just outside Karak town. Breakfast costs an extra JD4, and dinner is available on request.

Towers Castle Hotel HOTEL $
(03 235 4293; Al Qala'a St; s/d/tr JD20/30/35) Near the castle, this friendly hotel is a good option. The reception area is unassuming, but the floral rooms are clean, and many open onto balconies with views across Wadi Karak. Staff can help with onward travel.

Eating

Most restaurants are near the castle on Al-Mujamma St or near the statue of Saladin. Shwarma stands are clustered around Al-Jami St.

King's Restaurant JORDANIAN $
(03 235 4293; Al Mujamma St; mezze 500 fils, mains from JD4; 8am-10pm) This boulevard restaurant with tables on the pavement attracts travellers at all times of the day and night. It offers grills, pizzas and sandwiches, and local, home-cooked Jordanian dishes like *maqlubbeh* (an 'upside down' dish of rice, meat and vegetables).

King's Castle Restaurant JORDANIAN $$
(03 239 6070; mains JD5, buffet JD10; noon-4pm) At busier tourist times, groups come here for the daily lunch buffet. With pleasant outdoor seating, castle views and a host of salads to choose from, it's easy to understand why. At quieter times, there's no buffet, so order off the menu. The eastern building is worth a visit for its impressive relief display of the castle.

Getting There & Away

From the bus station – outside the town, at the bottom of the hill by the junction of the King's Highway – several daily buses go direct to Amman's south bus station (JD2, around two hours) via the Desert Hwy. Minibuses also run about every hour along the King's Highway from Karak to Tafila (JD1.500, one hour), the best place for connections to Qadsiyya (for Dana Biosphere Reserve) and Shobak. To Wadi Musa (for Petra), take a minibus to Ma'an (JD2.500, two hours), which leaves around 1pm daily, and change there.

Buses to Aqaba (JD5, three hours) travel in the mornings via the Dead Sea Hwy about four times a day.

From Karak, taxi fares are around JD50 to Amman or Madaba, JD45 to Dana and JD65 to Petra. There's a taxi stand near the vegetable market.

Tafila الطفيله

Tafila is a busy transport junction and you may have to change transport here. Minibuses run frequently from Karak (JD1.500, one hour) across the dramatic gorge of **Wadi Hasa**. There are also direct minibuses to/from the South bus station in Amman (JD2.800, 2½ hours) via the Desert Hwy; Aqaba (JD2.500, 2½ hours) via the Dead Sea Hwy; Ma'an (JD1.500, one hour) via the Desert Hwy; and Qadsiyya (for Dana Biosphere Reserve; JD1.300, 30 minutes) down the King's Highway.

Dana Biosphere Reserve محمية ضانا الطبيعية

The RSCN-run **Dana Biosphere Reserve** (adult/student per day JD8/4, with RSCN lodging or hikes free) is one of Jordan's hidden gems and is its most impressive ecotourism project. The gateway to the reserve is the charming 15th-century stone village of **Dana**, which clings to a precipice overlooking the valley and commands exceptional views. It's a great place to spend a few days hiking and relaxing. Most of the reserve is accessible only on foot.

The reserve is the largest in Jordan and includes a variety of terrain – from sandstone cliffs over 1500m high near Dana to a low point of 50m below sea level in Wadi Araba. Sheltered within the red-rock escarpments are protected valleys that are home to a surprisingly diverse ecosystem. About 600 species of plants (ranging from citrus trees and juniper, to desert acacias and date palms), 180 species of birds and over 45 species of mammals (of which 25 are endangered) – including ibexes, mountain gazelles, sand cats, red foxes and wolves –

thrive in the reserve. Dana is also home to almost 100 archaeological sites, including the 6000-year-old copper mines of **Khirbet Feynan**.

A fascinating little **museum** illustrates the various wildlife at 1500m on the King's Highway, at 1100m at Dana Village and 50m below sea level in Wadi Araba.

There are hiking and mountain bike trails of different lengths and difficulty available, some guided, some self-guided. For full details of activities within the reserve, check the Wild Jordan website (www.wildjordan.com/eco-tourism-section/ecotourism) and be ready to make reservations for longer guided trails in the spring and autumn.

Sleeping & Eating

Dana Hotel HOTEL $
(☎07 9559 7307, 02 227 0537; www.suleimanjarad.webs.com; half board per person in villas JD25, s/d JD12/20) A warm welcome is assured at this hotel, run by the Sons of Dana, a local tourism cooperative. Deservedly popular, and the oldest established hotel in Dana, it has very simple rooms in its original building, but it has also expanded across the square into an attractively built house with villas and a terrace overlooking the valley.

Al Nawatef Camp CAMPGROUND $
(☎02 227 0413, 07 9639 2079; www.alnawatefcamp.com; half board in tented chalets with shared shower block JD15) Perched at the edge of an escarpment, this wonderful camp is run by a hospitable local who knows the area 'because', he says, 'it runs in my blood'. The goat-hair chalets with beds, linen and blankets boast balconies with exceptional views. The camp is signposted 2km off the King's Highway, 5km south of the Dana turning in Qadsiyya.

Rummana Campground CAMPGROUND $$
(☎06 461 6523; www.wildjordan.com; s/d/tr/q tent JD53/64/76/87, deluxe tent JD70/82/93/105; ⏲15 Mar-31 Oct) Prices at this camp may seem steep, but waking up to the sound of Dana's wildlife, it's easy to see why reservations are necessary. Views from the campsite down the valley are incredible, and with great hiking trails just beyond the tents, you've got easy access to the reserve. Tents have comfy beds and a shared bathroom block.

★**Dana Guest House** LODGE $$$
(☎02 227 0497; www.rscn.org.jo; incl park entrance fee s/d/tr/q JD87/99/110/122, with shared bathroom JD64/76/87/90) With panoramic views across the reserve, a roaring fire in winter and enthusiastic park rangers, this ecolodge is run by the Royal Society for the Conservation of Nature (RSCN). All but two of the minimalist, stone-walled rooms have a balcony. Heating and hot water are provided by solar panels. Delicious fare is served in the restaurant.

★**Feynan Ecolodge** LODGE $$$
(☎06 464 5580; www.ecohotels.me/feynan; Wadi Feynan; full board incl park entrance fee from s/d/tr JD101/127/170; ⏲Sep-Jun) Owned by the RSCN, this unique ecolodge – frequently rated one of the world's best – is accessible on foot from Dana (a day's hike) or by 4WD from the Dead Sea Hwy. Powered by solar energy (including the hot water), and with its mud-rendered architecture lit entirely by locally made candles, Feynan has a magical caravanserai ambience.

Feynan Way Restaurant JORDANIAN $
(dinner JD3-10; ⏲7am-midnight) Occupying a tree-shaded terrace, this simple restaurant provides an opportunity for breakfast or lunch after the long hike from the campground, or a welcome chance to 'go out' from your hotel in the evening.

Shopping

Nature Shop ARTS & CRAFTS
(Dana Guest House; ⏲9am-5.30pm) With a wide range of quality crafts inspired by nature, plus workshops and a food-drying centre for making organic food, this shop is well worth a visit. Villagers are given the opportunity to make quality local crafts (organic herbs, fruit rolls, jams, olive-oil soaps, candles and silver jewellery) that are sold by the RSCN throughout Jordan.

Information

The **visitor centre** (☎03 227 0497; www.rscn.org.jo; ⏲8am-3pm) at Dana is the first port of call for a visit to the reserve, unless you're staying at Rummana Campground (though it can call ahead to arrange your transfer). The ticket office closes at 3pm, so if you're planning a sunset hike, make sure you arrive before then. Stop here for further information about the reserve and its hiking trails and to arrange a guide.

Reservations for guides are advisable in spring and autumn, as there's a daily maximum of people permitted on certain trails.

Admission fees are included in the price of RSCN accommodation.

Getting There & Away

The easiest way to get to Dana by public transport is from Tafila. Minibuses run every hour or so between Tafila and Qadsiyya (JD1, 30 minutes). The turn-off to Dana village is 1km north of Qadsiyya; from here it's a steep 2.8km downhill walk to the village (there's no bus).

There are three early-morning buses to Amman (JD3, three hours); the first leaves Qadsiyya at 4.30am, the next at 5am and the third at around 6am.

The non-RSCN Dana guesthouses all offer transfers to/from Dana village (usually free) and can arrange pickups. Minibus transfers from Amman's south bus station cost JD5 if you book with your guesthouse in advance. A taxi to Dana from Karak costs around JD40 one way. A taxi from Dana to Petra costs JD36, or JD12 per person in a shared taxi from your hotel.

Shobak الشوبك

The landscape around the small town of Shobak shifts from the fertility of the uplands to the semi-aridity that marks the upper reaches of mighty Wadi Araba. Hidden within the dazzlingly white, sheep-meandered hills is Shobak Castle, the Crusader gem at the end of the King's Hwy. With some interesting cultural activities and beautiful hiking routes, it's worth overnighting to explore what the region has to offer.

Sights

★Shobak Castle CASTLE

(Mont Real, Montreal; JD1, with Jordan Pass free; daylight hours) Perched in a wild, remote landscape, Shobak Castle wins over even the most castle-weary visitor, despite being less complete than its sister fortification at Karak (p317). It's especially imposing when seen from a distance, as it sits on a dramatic hill (formerly called Mons Realis, or the Royal Mountain), imposing its might on the surrounding countryside. Local guides, who really know their stuff, are available at the gate for around JD10. There are toilets and some limited information at the visitor centre at the bottom of the castle mound.

Sleeping

Jaya Tourist Camp CAMPGROUND $

(07 9595 8958; www.jayatouristcamp.yolasite.com; half/full board per person JD20/25) With a variety of basic tents in a tranquil spot on high ground opposite Shobak Castle, this friendly campground set in a garden of hollyhocks has a clean shower block and Bedouin goat-hair tents for relaxing. Hiking, including to Dana, can be arranged in advance. The campground is poorly signed but is downhill from the larger Montreal Hotel.

Montréal Hotel HOTEL $$

(07 7695 1714; www.jhrc.jo; r/ste JD50/90;) This hotel, with a spectacular view of the castle, has some lovely features including a stylish lounge around a central gas fire. The rooms are simple but comfortable. The hotel takes a sustainable approach and has solar panels for hot-water heating and electricity. Dinner (JD9) is available.

Getting There & Away

Early-morning minibuses link Shobak village with Amman's south bus station (JD5, 2½ hours), Aqaba and Karak. Some minibuses travelling between Wadi Musa and Ma'an also pass through Shobak. For the 3km from Shobak village to the castle, you can charter a taxi (around JD6 return including waiting time) or walk.

If you're driving, there are well-signposted roads from both the King's Highway and the Desert Hwy to the castle and further signs from Shobak village.

PETRA & THE SOUTH

Travel along the King's Highway and you'll notice that somewhere after Dana the character of the countryside changes. As the fertile hilltop pastures of the north give way to the more arid landscapes of the south, you suddenly find you're in epic country – the country that formed the backdrop for *Lawrence of Arabia* and *Indiana Jones and the Last Crusade.*

To make the most of this exciting part of Jordan, with its unmissable world wonders at Petra and Wadi Rum, you need to spend a day or two more than the map might suggest. Find some time to hike and stay with the Bedouin, and the experience is sure to become a highlight of your entire Middle Eastern trip.

Before catching the ferry to Egypt or crossing into Israel and the Palestinian Territories, spare an evening for Aqaba, a popular place for a night out with travellers.

Petra & Wadi Musa

بترا &وادي موسى

The ancient Nabataean city of Petra, with its elaborate architecture chiselled out of the pink-hued cliffs, is not just the leading highlight of a country blessed with more than its fair share of top sites: it's a wonder of the world. It lay hidden for centuries, known only to the Bedouin who made it their home, until the great Swiss explorer, Jean Louis Burckhardt, happened upon it in 1812.

Built partly in honour of the dead, the Petra necropolis retains much of its sense of hidden mystery thanks to its inaccessible location in the heart of a windblown landscape. Reached via the Siq, a narrow rift in the land whose cliffs cast long shadows across the once-sacred way, the path suddenly slithers into sunlight in front of the Treasury – a spectacle that cannot fail to impress. Add to this the cheerfulness of the local Bedouin, and it's easy to see what makes Petra a must to visit.

History

The Nabataeans, who arrived in the region around the 6th century BC, are the nomadic tribe from western Arabia who built most of the monuments in the Ancient City that are visible today. They were organised traders and over the next 500 years they used their wealth to build the city of Petra. In its heyday, under King Aretas IV (r 8 BC–AD 40), the city was home to around 30,000 people, including scribes and expert hydraulic engineers who built dams, cisterns and water channels to protect the site and its magnificent buildings.

By AD 106, as trade routes shifted from Petra to Palmyra and new sea trade routes via the Red Sea to Rome bypassed Petra altogether, the Romans assumed control of the weakened Nabataean empire. Far from abandoning the city of Petra, however, the invaders recast the ancient city with familiar Roman features, including a colonnaded street and baths.

Earthquakes in 363 and 551 ruined much of the city and Petra became a forgotten outpost, a 'lost city' known only to local Bedouin who preferred to keep its whereabouts secret. Part of the continuing allure of the 'rose red city' is that despite many years of scrutiny by archaeologists since Burckhardt's visit in 1812, Petra still has many secrets yet to be discovered.

Sights

From the entrance (near the Visitor's Centre in Wadi Musa), a walk of at least two hours (return) is required to visit any of the main sights within Petra, so comfortable footwear is a must. Hats and sunscreen are also useful. Hotels will provide their guests with a packed lunch or there is the **Basin Restaurant** (Map p324; lunch buffet JD16, fresh orange juice JD4; noon-4pm;) for something more substantial. Plenty of stalls dotted around the site sell tea, coffee, soft drinks and snacks. A variety of four-legged transport is available for hire if you get tired on the walk back – it's a long slog uphill all the way!

PETRA TICKETS

- The ticket office is in the Petra visitor centre in Lower Wadi Musa.
- Entry fees are JD50/55/60 for one-/two-/three-day passes (payable only in Jordanian currency). Multiday tickets are nontransferable. For more information, see p331.
- Children under 12 are admitted free.
- If you are visiting Petra as a day trip from Israel the entry fee is JD90.
- Those with a Jordan Pass (p347) can enter Petra for free.

★ Siq CANYON

(Map p324) The 1.2km Siq, or canyon, with its narrow, vertical walls, is undeniably one of the highlights of Petra. The walk through this magical corridor, as it snakes its way towards the hidden city, is one full of anticipation for the wonders ahead – a point not wasted on the Nabataeans who made the passage into a sacred way, punctuated with sites of spiritual significance.

★ Treasury TOMB

(Al Khazneh; Map p324) Known locally as the Treasury, this tomb is where most visitors fall in love with Petra. The Hellenistic facade is an astonishing piece of craftsmanship. Although carved out of iron-laden sandstone to serve as a tomb for the Nabataean King Aretas III (c 100 BC–AD 200), the Treasury derives its name from the story that an Egyptian pharaoh hid his treasure here (in the facade urn) while pursuing the Israelites.

Street of Facades RUINS

(Map p324) From the Treasury, the passage broadens into what is commonly referred to as the Outer Siq. Riddling the walls of the Outer Siq are over 40 tombs and houses built by the Nabataeans in a 'crow step' style reminiscent of Assyrian architecture. Colloquially known as the Street of Facades, they are easily accessible, unlike many tombs in Petra.

Petra

A WALKING TOUR

Splendid though it is, the Treasury is not the full stop of a visit to Petra that many people may imagine. In some ways, it's just the semicolon – a place to pause after the exertions of the Siq, before exploring the other remarkable sights and wonders just around the corner.

Even if you're on a tight schedule or worried the bus won't wait, try to find another two hours in your itinerary to complete this walking tour. Our illustration shows the key highlights of the route, as you wind through Wadi Musa from the ❶ **Siq**, pause at the ❷ **Treasury** and pass the tombs of the broader ❸ **Outer Siq**. With energy and a stout pair of shoes, climb to the ❹ **High Place of Sacrifice** for a magnificent eagle's-eye view of Petra. Return to the ❺ **Street of Facades** and the ❻ **Theatre**. Climb the steps opposite to the ❼ **Urn Tomb** and neighbouring ❽ **Silk Tomb**: these Royal Tombs are particularly magnificent in the golden light of sunset.

Is the thought of all that walking putting you off? Don't let it! There are donkeys to help you with the steep ascents and Bedouin stalls for a reviving herb tea. If you run out of steam, camels are on standby for a ride back to the Treasury.

TOP TIPS

- From around 7am in summer and 8am in winter, watch the early morning sun slide down the Treasury facade.
- Stand opposite the Royal Tombs at sunset (around 4pm in winter and 5pm in summer) to learn how Petra earned its nickname, Pink City.
- Petra's oleanders flower in May.

MARK READ/LONELY PLANET ©

Treasury

As you watch the sun cut across the facade, notice how it lights up the ladders on either side of Petra's most iconic building. These stone indents were most probably used for scaffolding.

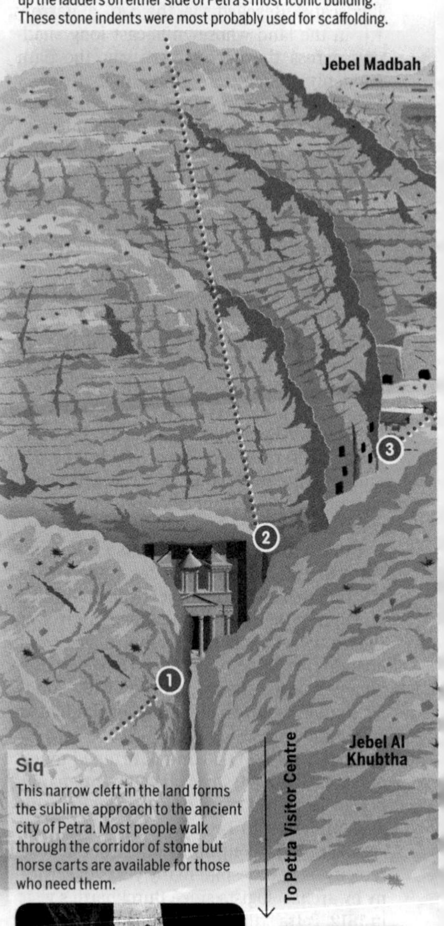

Siq

This narrow cleft in the land forms the sublime approach to the ancient city of Petra. Most people walk through the corridor of stone but horse carts are available for those who need them.

MARK READ/LONELY PLANET ©

ANOTHER WAY DOWN

A superb walk leads from the High Place of Sacrifice, past the Garden Tomb to Petra City Centre.

High Place of Sacrifice

Imagine the ancients treading the stone steps and it'll take your mind off the steep ascent. The hilltop platform was used for incense-burning and libation-pouring in honour of forgotten gods.

CHRISTOPHE CAPPELLI/SHUTTERSTOCK ©

CLAUDIOVIDRI/SHUTTERSTOCK ©

Outer Siq

Take time to inspect the tombs just past the Treasury. Some appear to have a basement but, in fact, they show how the floor of the wadi has risen over the centuries.

Street of Facades

Cast an eye at the upper storeys of some of these tombs and you'll see a small aperture. Burying the dead in attics was meant to deter robbers – the plan didn't work.

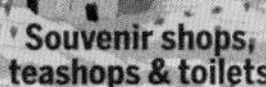

HEAD FOR HEIGHTS

For a regal view of Petra, head for the heights above the Royal Tombs, via the staircase.

Urn Tomb

Earning its name from the urn-shaped finial crowning the pediment, this grand edifice with supporting arched vaults was perhaps built for the man represented by the toga-wearing bust in the central aperture.

Silk Tomb

Perhaps Nabataean builders were attracted to Wadi Musa because of the colourful beauty of the raw materials. Nowhere is this more apparent than in the weather-eroded, striated sandstone of the Silk Tomb.

Theatre

Most stone amphitheatres are freestanding, but this one is carved almost entirely from the solid rock. Above the back row are the remains of earlier tombs, their facades sacrificed in the name of entertainment.

WAJ/SHUTTERSTOCK ©

NAEBLYS/SHUTTERSTOCK ©

ALBERT H. TEICH/SHUTTERSTOCK ©

Petra

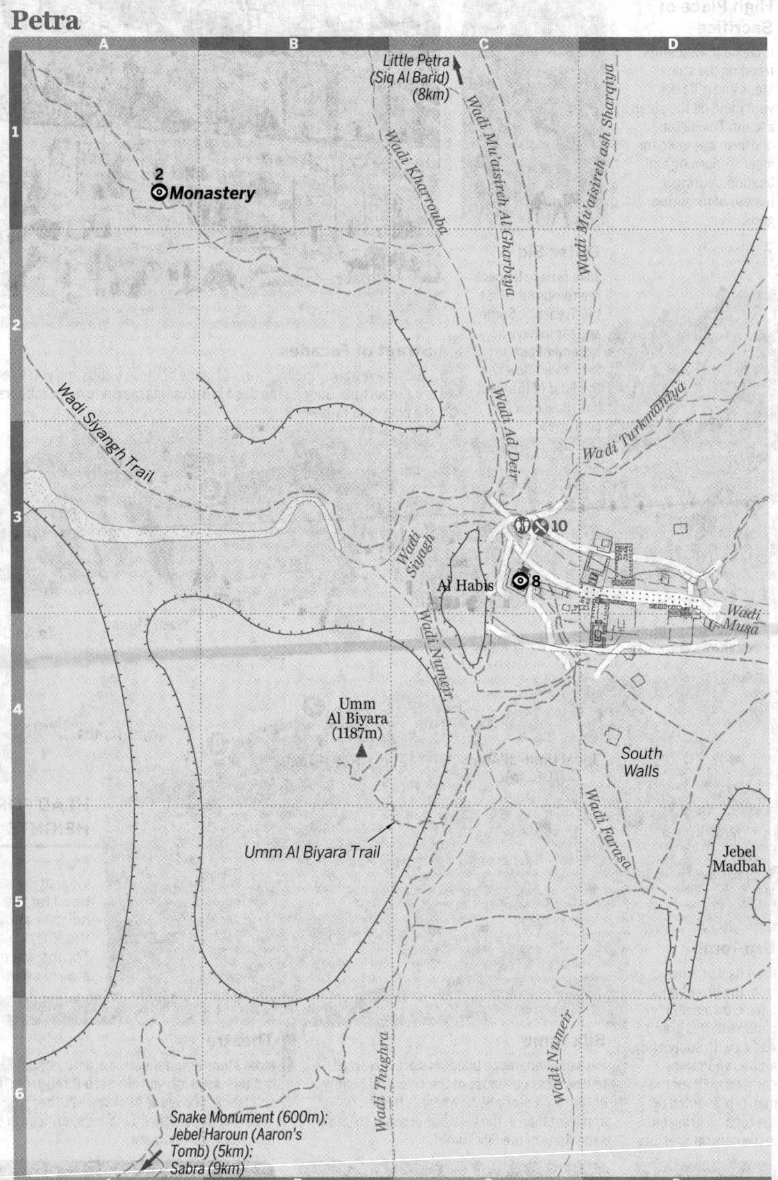

★ **High Place of Sacrifice** VIEWPOINT
(Al Madbah; Map p324) The most accessible of Petra's 'High Places', this well-preserved site was built atop Jebel Madbah with drains to channel the blood of sacrificial animals. A flight of steps signposted just before the Theatre leads to the site: turn right at the **obelisks** to reach the sacrificial platform. You can ascend by donkey (about JD10 one way), but you'll sacrifice both the sense of achievement on reaching the summit and the good humour of your poor old transport.

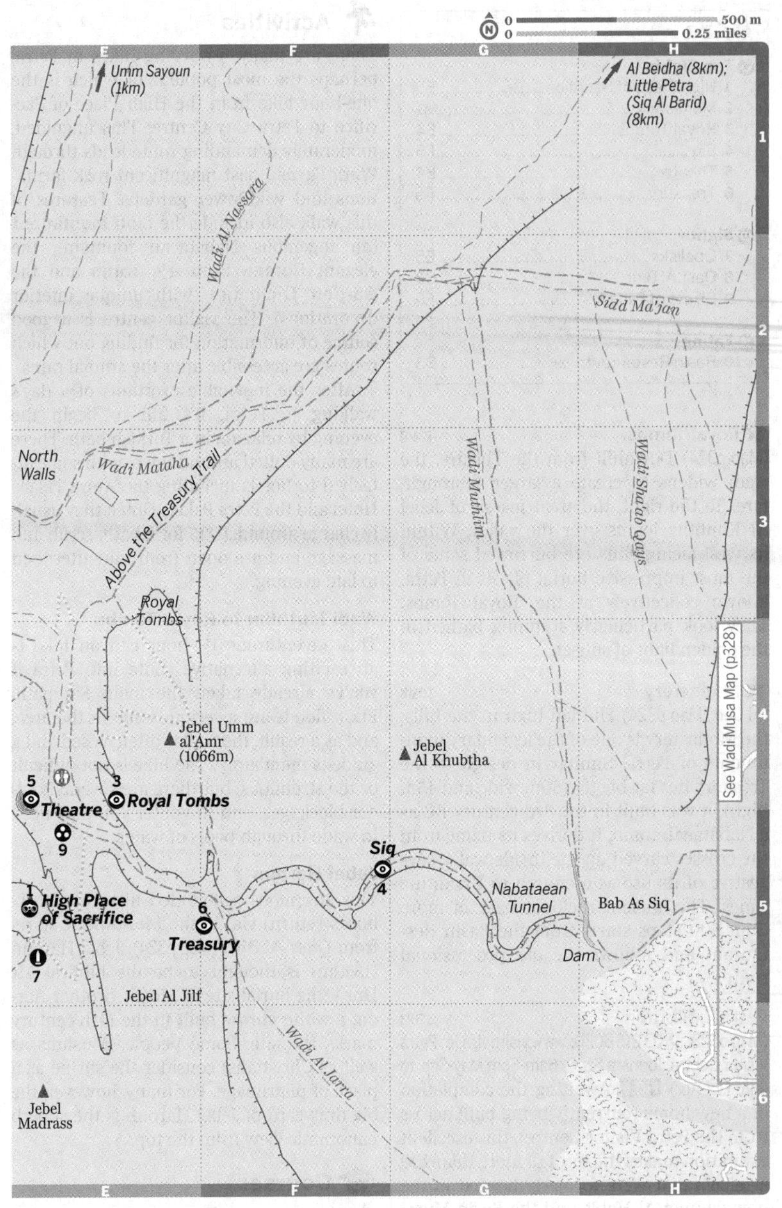

★Theatre THEATRE

(Map p324) Originally built by the Nabataeans (not the Romans) more than 2000 years ago, the Theatre was chiselled out of rock, slicing through many caves and tombs in the process. It was enlarged by the Romans to hold about 8500 (around 30% of the population of Petra) soon after they arrived in AD 106. Badly damaged by an earthquake in AD 363, the Theatre was partially dismantled to build other structures but it remains a Petra highlight.

Petra

Top Sights

1	High Place of Sacrifice	E5
2	Monastery	A1
3	Royal Tombs	E4
4	Siq	F5
5	Theatre	E4
6	Treasury	F5

Sights

7	Obelisks	E5
8	Qasr Al Bint	C3
9	Street of Facades	E5

Eating

10	Basin Restaurant	C3

★Royal Tombs TOMB

(Map p324) Downhill from the Theatre, the wadi widens to create a larger thoroughfare. To the right, the great massif of Jebel Al Khubtha looms over the valley. Within its west-facing cliffs are burrowed some of the most impressive burial places in Petra, known collectively as the 'Royal Tombs'. They look particularly stunning bathed in the golden light of sunset.

★Monastery TOMB

(Al Deir; Map p324) Hidden high in the hills, the Monastery is one of the legendary monuments of Petra. Similar in design to the Treasury but far bigger (50m wide and 45m high), it was built in the 3rd century BC as a Nabataean tomb. It derives its name from the crosses carved on the inside walls, suggestive of its use as a church in Byzantine times. The ancient rock-cut path of more than 800 steps starts from the Basin Restaurant and follows the old processional route.

Petra Exhibition MUSEUM

(Map p328; ☎03 215 6020; www.visitpetra.jo; Petra Visitor Centre, Tourism St; ⏲6am-6pm May-Sep, to 4pm Oct-Apr) FREE Awaiting the completion of a new home (currently being built across from the Petra Visitor Centre), this excellent exhibition makes the most of more than 200 artefacts that were formerly housed in the now-defunct Al Habis and the Basin Museums in the Ancient City. The exhibition is divided into different display areas, including Petra through the ages, art and architecture, religion, politics and society, and trade, and helps to give a tangible context to the site itself.

Activities

There are many rewarding hikes in Petra, perhaps the most popular of which is the one-hour hike from the High Place of Sacrifice to Petra City Centre. This unguided, moderately demanding route leads through **Wadi Farasa** past magnificent rock formations and wildflower gardens. Features of this walk also include the **Lion Monument** (an ingenious Nabataean fountain), the elegant **Roman Soldier's Tomb** and the **Garden Triclinium** (with unique interior decorations). The visitor centre is a good source of information for finding out which routes are accessible after the annual rains.

After the inevitable exertions of a day's walking in Petra, it's fun to begin the evening by relaxing in a Turkish bath. There are many dotted around town, with some attached to hotels including the Amra Palace Hotel and the Petra Palace Hotel; they usually charge around JD25 for a bath, scrub and massage and are open from mid-afternoon to late evening.

Wadi Muthlim to Royal Tombs

This adventurous 1½-hour canyon hike is an exciting alternative route into Petra if you've already taken the main Siq path. Flash floods are a serious issue in the area, and as a result, the trail is often closed and a guide is mandatory. The hike is not difficult or too strenuous, but there are several boulder blockages, and in winter you may need to wade through pools of water.

Jebel Haroun

This strenuous self-guided hike (about six hours return) via **Snake Monument** starts from **Qasr Al Bint** (Map p324). Jebel Haroun (1350m) is thought to be the biblical Mt Hor – the burial site of Moses' brother Aaron; a white **shrine** built in the 14th century marks the site. Some people (Muslims as well as Christians) consider the shrine as a place of pilgrimage. For many, however, the big drawcard of Jebel Haroun is the superb panoramic view from the top.

Courses

★Petra Kitchen COOKING

(Map p328; ☎03 215 5900; www.petrakitchen.com; Tourism St; cookery course per person JD35; ⏲6-9pm) For those wanting to know how to prepare wonderful hummus or bake the perfect baklava, Petra Kitchen offers a practical course, delivered in a single evening. Located 100m up the main road from the Mövenpick Hotel, it offers nightly cookery courses for those wanting to learn from locals how to cook Jordanian mezze, soup and main dishes in a relaxed family-style atmosphere.

Tours

Mohammed Al Hasanat TOURS
(07 7738 0884; explorerone69@yahoo.com) A licensed national guide since 1979, he organises camping tours over several days, including camel and horse safaris.

Petra Moon Tourism Services TOURS
(Map p328; 07 9617 0666; www.petramoon.com; Tourism St; all-day horse rides to Jebel Haroun US$100, min 3 people) The most professional agency in Wadi Musa for arranging trips inside Petra and around Jordan (including Wadi Rum and Aqaba).

Sleeping

You can't overnight in Petra itself, but there are plenty of hotels in neighbouring Wadi Musa – the town that acts as the gateway to the ancient city. The town comprises a string of hotels, restaurants and shops stretching about 5km from Ain Musa, the head of the valley, down to the entrance to Petra. The village centre is at Shaheed roundabout, with shops, restaurants and budget hotels, while midrange hotels are strung out along the main road for the remaining 2km towards the visitor centre and the entrance to Petra.

Lower Wadi Musa

The following hotels are located at the bottom end of town, within walking distance to the entrance to Petra.

★ **Petra Guest House Hotel** HOTEL $$
(Map p328; 03 215 6266; www.guesthouse-petra.com; off Tourism St; r from JD75; P 📶) Guests can't get closer to the entrance to Petra without sleeping in a tomb, and indeed the hotel's bar – the famous Cave Bar (p330) – is located in one. Accommodation ranges from spacious, motel-like chalets to sunny

TREATMENT OF ANIMALS IN THE ANCIENT CITY OF PETRA

If there's one area of complaint that understandably upsets visitors more than others in the Ancient City, it's the mistreatment of animals. Indeed, many visitors are now quick to admonish any incidents of animal mishandling, particularly from the younger boys, some of whom mete out the kind of treatment to animals that a harsh environment often delivers to them. This, of course, is no excuse, and the local community, together with the Petra administration, have come together over recent years to try to improve the welfare of the animals who form an essential part of the Bedouin family livelihood and whose presence helps to greatly enhance the pleasure of the site for visitors. These efforts are beginning to bear fruit, and animals appear generally in better condition, are better nourished and are on the whole better treated than in former times. While most owners take responsibility for their animals very seriously, incidents of ill treatment still occur. Some visitors have suggested a ban on animal use, but this is more likely to encourage neglect of the family assets as Bedouin incomes are extremely limited and don't stretch to supporting a redundant 'family member'. And in all likelihood, this would lead to the dispiriting prospect of a Petra without the people and animals who have been minding this valley for centuries, replaced by technological alternatives, such as golf buggies and electric carts.

While some Bedouin animal handlers resent tourists interfering in the way they treat their animals, most are now sensitive to the fact that their actions are under scrutiny. A word of encouragement to the animal handler about an alternative way of cajoling their charges into action is appreciated more than a diatribe against animal cruelty. All ill treatment should be reported to the tourist police at the Petra Visitor Centre, preferably with photographic or video evidence. This approach is already having a positive impact, and the attitudes of handlers towards the various animals at work in Petra are slowly changing.

If you do decide that you'd like to ride a horse, ensure that you find a provider who offers animals that are capable of carrying their mount. You should also pay the appropriate fare (as given at the Petra Visitor Centre) for the services you commission. It is largely as a result of cut-price fares that handlers feel pressured to return more quickly to base (thereby putting their animals at risk) to recoup the loss with an additional fare.

Wadi Musa

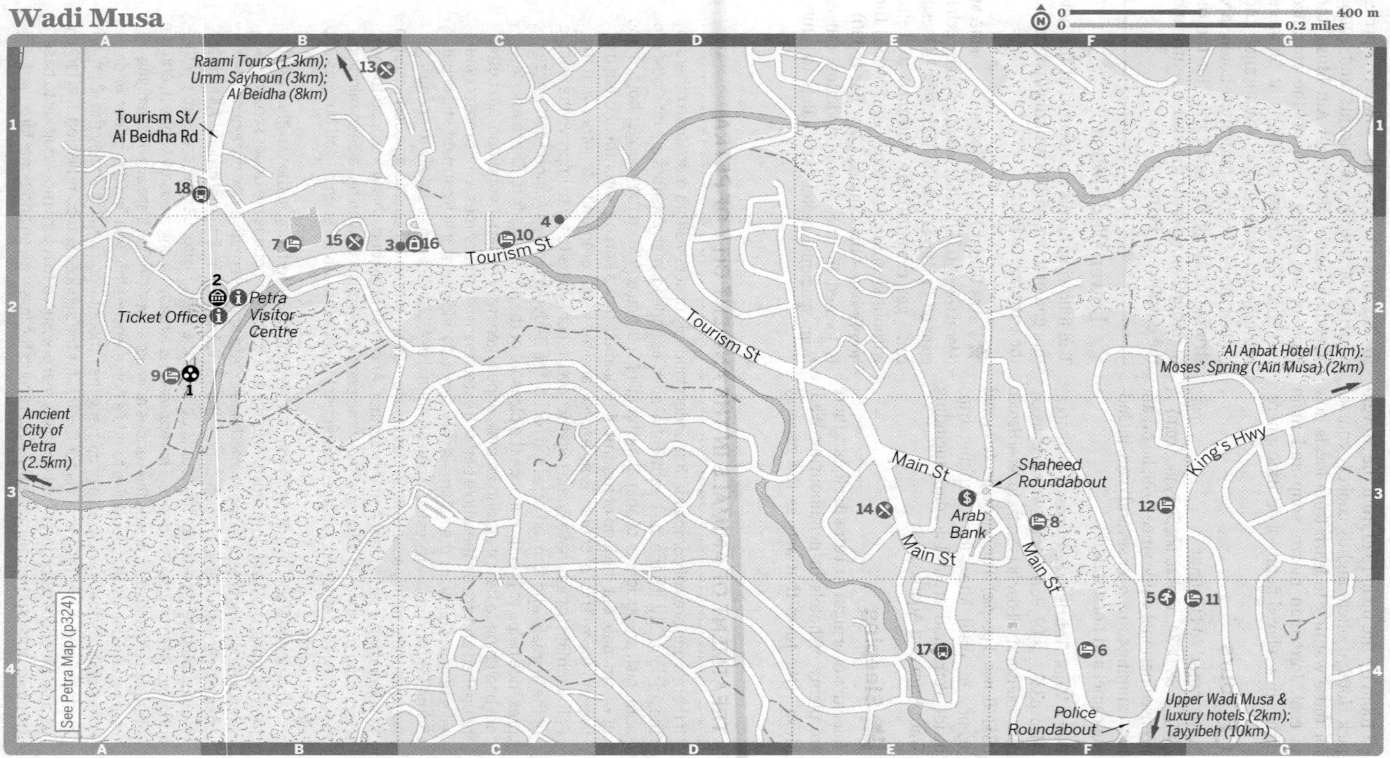

0 400 m
0 0.2 miles

Raami Tours (1.3km); Umm Sayhoun (3km); Al Beidha (8km)
Tourism St/ Al Beidha Rd
Tourism St
Main St
Ticket Office
Petra Visitor Centre
Ancient City of Petra (2.5km)
See Petra Map (p324)
Shaheed Roundabout
Arab Bank
Police Roundabout
King's Hwy
Al Anbat Hotel I (1km); Moses' Spring ('Ain Musa) (2km)
Upper Wadi Musa & luxury hotels (2km); Tayyibeh (10km)
1 2 3 4 5 6 7 8 9 10 11 12 13 14 15 16 17 18
A B C D E F G

Wadi Musa

Sights
1 Entrance to Ancient City of Petra A2
2 Petra Exhibition B2

Activities, Courses & Tours
Petra by Night .... (see 2)
3 Petra Kitchen C2
4 Petra Moon Tourism Services C2
5 Sella Turkish Bath F4

Sleeping
6 Cleopetra Hotel F4
7 Mövenpick Hotel B2
8 Peace Way Hotel F3
9 Petra Guest House Hotel A2
10 Petra Palace Hotel C2
11 Petra Sella Hotel G4
12 Rocky Mountain Hotel F3

Eating
13 Al Qantarah B1
14 Bin Bukhara Restaurant E3
15 Oriental Restaurant B2

Drinking & Nightlife
Cave Bar .... (see 9)
English Bar .... (see 10)

Shopping
16 Made in Jordan C2

Transport
17 Bus Station E4
18 JETT Bus Stop A1

(if cramped) rooms in the main building. The staff are unfailingly delightful and the breakfast buffet is superior to most. Offers excellent value for money.

Petra Palace Hotel HOTEL $$
(Map p328; ☎03 215 6723; www.petrapalace.com.jo; Tourism St; s/d/tr/q JD41/55/76/96; @☎) Located 500m from the entrance to Petra, this well-established hotel, with its palm-tree entrance, big bright foyer and helpful management, offers rooms around a swimming pool. Corridors and grounds are looking tired, but the sociable English Bar and a good restaurant compensate. A mixed Turkish bath (JD20 per person) is open from 8am to 10pm.

★**Mövenpick Hotel** HOTEL $$$
(Map p328; ☎03 215 7111; www.moevenpick.com; Tourism St; r from JD500; P@) This beautifully crafted Arabian-style hotel, 100m from the entrance to Petra, is worth a visit simply to admire the inlaid furniture, marble fountains, wooden screens and brass salvers. As the hotel is in the bottom of the valley there are no views, but the large and super-luxurious rooms all have huge windows regardless. The buffet breakfast and dinner are exceptional.

Wadi Musa Town Centre

The following hotels are near the bus station. Free transport to and from the entrance to Petra is usually offered once a day.

★**Cleopetra Hotel** HOTEL $
(Map p328; ☎03 215 7090; www.cleopetrahotel.com; Main St; s/d/tr JD18/25/32; @) One of the friendliest and most efficiently run budget hotels in town, Cleopetra has bright, fresh rooms. There's a communal sitting area in the lobby where wi-fi is available for JD2. The hotel can arrange overnight 4WD trips to Wadi Rum (JD50 per person for a minimum of three) and the ever-helpful Mosleh can organise other transport.

★**Peace Way Hotel** BOUTIQUE HOTEL $
(Map p328; ☎03 215 6963; peaceway_petra@yahoo.com; Main St; s/d/tr JD16/22/35;) This hotel has undergone the most remarkable transformation from budget to boutique. The makeover includes blue-lit ceilings, carved wooden doors and a chocolate brown theme to the corridors and rooms, contrasted with cream-coloured marble. Even more remarkable is that the hotel has kept its budget prices, making this central option very good value. Unusually, it's pet-friendly too.

Upper Wadi Musa

★**Rocky Mountain Hotel** HOTEL $
(Map p328; ☎03 215 5100, 07 9694 1865; www.rockymountainhotel.com; King's Hwy; s/d/tr/q JD26/39/50/60; @) This backpacker-friendly hotel has caught just the right vibe to make it Petra's most successful travellers' lodge. There's a cosy communal area with free tea and coffee and the *majlis*-style roof terrace makes the most of the impressive sweeping views. A free shuttle service to the Petra entrance leaves at 7.30am and 8.30am, returning at 4pm and 5pm.

Petra Sella Hotel HOTEL $$
(Map p328; ☎03 215 7170; www.sellahotel.com; King's Hwy; s/d/tr JD45/65/85; @) This newly renovated hotel has luxurious rooms,

decked in stylish stone tiles with split ceilings and marble sinks in the bathrooms – almost boutique for Wadi Musa. There are good views from front rooms, but rooms at the back are bigger. The hotel runs the spotless **Sella Turkish Bath** (Map p328; ☎03 215 7170; www.sellahotel.com; King's Hwy; ⏰5.30-10pm) opposite.

Eating

All of the following places are in Wadi Musa.

Bin Bukhara Restaurant KEBAB $
(Map p328; off Main St; mains JD4; ⏰11am-midnight) Selling rotisserie-style barbecued chicken and kebabs, this popular restaurant on the one-way loop round the centre of Wadi Musa (diagonally opposite Petra Butchery BBQ) is just the place to satisfy an appetite after the long slog up from Petra.

★**Oriental Restaurant** JORDANIAN $$
(Map p328; ☎03 215 7087; Tourism St; mains JD6; ⏰11am-9.30pm) This main-street favourite offers tasty grills and Jordanian fare, such as *mensaf* (a lamb and rice dish). The outdoor terrace, bedecked with Doric columns, makes a sociable hangout after the long hike back from Petra. The neigbouring Red Cave and Sandstone restaurants offer similar fare and an equal welcome.

★**Al Qantarah** JORDANIAN $$$
(Map p328; ☎03 215 5535; www.al-qantarah.com; Lower Wadi Musa; lunch/dinner JD10/12; ⏰lunch 11.30am-4.30pm, dinner 7-10pm; P 🌿) Wadi Musa's best restaurant specialises in Jordanian food and serves up to 500 people in one lunch sitting. There is no menu – lunch and dinner are buffet style with 15 kinds of salads and mezze, eight meat and soup dishes and eight kinds of dessert. There's a cooking station and live music every day in the delightful, traditional dining rooms.

Drinking & Nightlife

★**Cave Bar** BAR
(Map p328; ☎03 215 6266; www.guesthouse-petra.com; Petra Guesthouse, near Petra Visitor Centre; ⏰3-11pm) It's almost a crime to visit Petra and miss the oldest bar in the world. Occupying a 2000-year-old Nabataean rock tomb, this atmospheric Petra hotspot has been known to stay open until 4am on busy summer nights. Sitting among the spirits, alcoholic or otherwise, gives a flavour of Petra that's in animated contrast to the bar's ancient origins.

English Bar BAR
(Map p328; ☎03 215 6723; Petra Palace Hotel, Tourism St; ⏰2-11pm) The Petra Palace Hotel runs this sociable bar, decorated with assorted local memorabilia. It is one of the few dedicated bars in town, and it makes for a particularly cosy spot in winter when the alternative rooftop bars are closed.

Shopping

Made in Jordan ARTS & CRAFTS
(Map p328; ☎03 215 5900; Tourism St; ⏰8.30am-11pm) This shop sells quality crafts from local enterprises. Products include olive oil, soap, paper, ceramics, table runners, nature products from Wild Jordan in Amman, jewellery from Wadi Musa, embroidery from Safi, camel-hair shawls, and bags from Aqaba as well as Jordan River Foundation goods. The fixed prices reflect the quality and uniqueness of each piece; credit cards are accepted.

FINDING YOUR OWN PACE IN PETRA

Instead of trying to 'see it all' (the quickest way to get monument fatigue), make Petra your own by sparing time to amble among unnamed tombs or sip tea at a Bedouin stall.

Half day (five hours) Stroll through the Siq, savouring the moment of revelation at the Treasury. Climb the steps to the High Place of Sacrifice and take the path through Wadi Farasa, passing a paintbox of rock formations.

One day (eight hours) Complete the half-day itinerary, but pack a picnic. Visit the Royal Tombs, walk along to Qasr al-Bint and hike the wadi that leads to Jebel Haroun as far as Snake Monument – an ideal perch for a snack and a snooze. Save some energy for the climb to the Monastery, a fitting finale for any Petra visit.

Two days Spend a second day scrambling through exciting Wadi Muthlim and restore your energies over a barbecue at the Basin Restaurant. Sit near the Theatre to watch the Royal Tombs at sunset – the best spectacle in Petra. Reward your efforts with a Turkish bath and a drink in the Cave Bar – the oldest pub in the world.

DON'T MISS

PETRA BY NIGHT

Like a grumbling camel caravan of snorting, coughing, laughing and farting miscreants, 200 people and one jubilantly crying baby make their way down the Siq 'in silence'. Asked to walk in single file behind the leader, breakaway contingents surge ahead to make sure they enjoy the experience 'on their own'. And eventually, sitting in 'reverential awe' outside the Treasury, the collected company shows its appreciation of Arabic classical music by lighting cigarettes from the paper bag lanterns, chatting energetically, flashing cameras and audibly farting some more.

Welcome to public entertainment in the Middle East! If you really want the Siq to yourself, come in the winter, go at 2pm or take a virtual tour on the internet.

But despite the promotional literature to the contrary, silence and solitude is not what the **Petra by Night Tour** (Map p328; Petra Visitor Centre, Tourism St; adult/child under 10yr JD17/free; ⏲8.30-10.30pm Mon, Wed & Thu) is all about. What this exceptional and highly memorable tour does give you is the fantastic opportunity to experience one of the most sublime spectacles on earth in the fever of other people's excitement. Huddles of whispering devotees stare up at the candlelit god blocks, elderly participants are helped over polished lozenges of paving stones and the sound of a flute wafts along the neck-hairs of fellow celebrants – this is surely much closer to the original experience of the ancient city of Petra than walking through the icy stone corridor alone.

Information

DANGERS & ANNOYANCES

From September to March, dangerous flash floods can catch hikers unaware. Checking the forecast is essential.

Some solo women travellers have reported being hoodwinked into relationships with local Bedouin men. The best advice is to treat with scepticism offers of hospitality from attractive men, declarations of undying love and promises of platonic nights under the stars.

MONEY

There are several ATMs dotted around town, including at the **Arab Bank** (Map p328; Main St) in central Wadi Musa and at the Mövenpick Hotel near the Petra Visitor Centre. Many hotels will change money, albeit at a poor rate. The banks are open from about 8am to 2pm Sunday to Thursday and (sometimes) 9am to 11am on Friday.

TOURIST INFORMATION

The ticket office is in the **Petra Visitor Centre** (Map p328; ☎03 215 6044; www.visitpetra.jo; Tourism St; ⏲6am-4pm May-Sep, to 6pm in summer), just before the entrance to Petra at Wadi Musa. Although tickets are not sold after 4pm, you can remain in Petra until sunset (7pm in summer, 5pm in winter).

Entry fees are JD50/55/60 for one-/two-/three-day passes (payable in Jordanian currency or by credit card). If visiting Petra as a day trip, including from Israel and the Palestinian Territories, the entry fee is JD90. Children aged under 12 and visitors with disabilities are admitted free. The Jordan Pass (p347), which represents great value for money, gives free entry to Petra.

The ticket includes the price of a horse ride along the Bab Al Siq (the pathway between the Visitor Centre and the opening of the Siq) and a guided tour for a minimum of five people. The tour is not mandatory but is recommended; it runs on the hour between 7am and 3pm and lasts for two hours, helping to highlight the key points of interest along the main trail to Qasr Al Bint (near the Basin Restaurant).

Tickets are non-transferable between visitors, and you have to show your passport when buying a ticket. Multiday tickets must be used on consecutive days, and they don't include the cost of the Petra by Night experience.

Getting There & Away

Public transport to and from Wadi Musa is less frequent than may be expected, given that it's the top tourist attraction in Jordan. The best place to find information about minibuses and other transport is to ask at any of the hotels or one of the restaurants around the Shaheed roundabout.

BUS

A daily JETT bus connects Amman with Petra, largely designed for those wanting to visit on a day trip. The service leaves at 6.30am from the JETT office, near Abdali bus station (JD10 each way, four hours) and drops off passengers at the **JETT bus stop** (Map p328; ☎06 566 4141; www.jett.com.jo; Tourism St), just up the Al Beidha Rd, a two-minute walk from the Petra Visitor Centre in Wadi Musa. The return bus leaves at 5pm in summer, 4pm in winter.

WALKING TIMES TO KEY SIGHTS IN PETRA

The following table indicates one-way walking times at a leisurely pace. At a faster pace without stopping, you can hike from Petra Visitor Centre to the Treasury in 20 minutes and the museum in 40 minutes along the main thoroughfare. Don't forget to double the time for the uphill return journey.

DIRECT ROUTE	TIME (MIN)	DIFFICULTY
Visitor Centre to Siq entrance	15	Easy
Siq entrance to Treasury	20	Easy
Treasury to Royal Tombs	20	Easy
Treasury to Obelisk at High Place of Sacrifice	45	Moderate
Obelisk to Museum (via main thoroughfare)	45	Easy
Treasury to Museum	30	Easy
Museum to Monastery	40	Moderate

MINIBUS

Minibuses leave from the **bus station** (Map p328) in central Wadi Musa. Most minibuses won't leave unless they're at least half full, so a wait is almost inevitable. If there are insufficient passengers, they may not leave at all. It's possible the driver may suggest payment for the empty seats. This is not a scam: it's just an attempt by the driver to cover the cost of the journey. As such, passengers should establish the fare before departing. There are far fewer services on Fridays. Passengers may well be charged extra for luggage (around JD3), especially if it takes up a seat that could be used for a paying customer.

The following services run when full from Wadi Musa bus station:

Amman (JD5 to JD6, four hours) Regular minibuses travel daily between Amman's South bus station (Wahadat) and Wadi Musa via the Desert Hwy. These buses leave Amman and Wadi Musa when full every hour or so between around 6am and noon. From Amman there are services until around 4pm; from Wadi Musa there may be an additional journey or two depending on demand. Schedules change frequently but hotels in Wadi Musa can give up-to-date advice.

Aqaba (JD5, 2½ hours) These leave at about 6am, 8.30am and possibly at 3pm – timings can be checked through a hotel the day before.

Karak (JD7, two hours) A minibus sometimes leaves at around 7am and sometimes at noon, but demand is low so it doesn't leave every day and there is no service on Fridays. Alternatively, travel is possible via Ma'an.

Ma'an (JD0.5, 45 minutes) Minibuses leave fairly frequently throughout the day (more often in the morning), stopping briefly at the university, about 10km from Ma'an. From Ma'an there are connections to Amman, Aqaba and the Wadi Rum junction.

Wadi Rum (JD7, two hours) There is a daily minibus around 6am. It's necessary to reserve a seat the day before – hotels normally contact the driver on guests' behalf. If the service isn't operating, an alternative is to take the minibus to Aqaba, get off at the Ar Rashidiyyah junction and catch another minibus (hitching is not recommended, though possible) the remainder of the journey to Rum. Cleopetra Hotel, among other hotels, organises competent overnight tours to Wadi Rum as an alternative to the patchy public transport.

TAXI

Private (yellow) taxis are easy to find in Wadi Musa. One-way taxi fares cost JD45 to Wadi Rum (one hour) or JD80 return with a one-hour wait. A few 4WD taxis are available for much the same cost, but they are not of much benefit as Wadi Rum visitors still have to join a 4WD tour from the Wadi Rum Visitor Centre to explore the protected area.

The one-way fare to Aqaba (1½ hours) is JD45; to Shobak (40 minutes) it is JD30 or JD60 return including a one-hour wait; and to Karak (1½ hours) it's JD75 or JD150 return including a one-hour wait. To travel to Madaba or Amman via the scenic King's Highway, with stops at Shobak, Dana and Karak, the fare is JD120 to JD150. Nonstop to the airport, Madaba and Amman along the dull and badly surfaced Desert Hwy, the fares are JD70, JD75 and JD100 respectively.

Getting Around

There are usually plenty of yellow taxis with green plates travelling up and down the main road of Wadi Musa towards the entrance for Petra, especially in the early morning and late afternoon. They congregate outside Petra Visitor Centre. It's best to stick with these taxis as other cars offering taxi services are unlicensed and often uninsured. Taxis are unmetered, but the fares are kept pretty much standard. Between lower and central Wadi Musa it costs JD4;

between lower and upper Wadi Musa (Moses' Spring) it costs JD7.

Within Petra, the only way to reach most sites is by walking (strong, comfortable footwear is essential!) or by taking a camel, donkey or mule to more distant and uphill sites.

Wadi Rum وادي رم

Western visitors have been fascinated by the magnificent landscape of Wadi Rum ever since TE Lawrence wrote so evocatively about its sculpted rocks, dunes and Bedouin encampments in *Seven Pillars of Wisdom* in the early 20th century. David Lean's *Lawrence of Arabia,* which was party filmed here, not only contributed to the myth of the man who took part in the Arab Revolt, but also gave epic status to Wadi Rum itself.

Wadi Rum is everything you'd expect of a quintessential desert: extreme in summer heat and winter cold; violent and moody as the sun slices through chiselled siqs at dawn or melts the division between rock and sand at dusk; exacting on the Bedouin who live in it; and vengeful on those who ignore its dangers. For most visitors, on half- or full-day trips from Aqaba or Petra, Wadi Rum offers one of the easiest and safest glimpses of the desert afforded in the region. For the lucky few who can afford a day or two in their itinerary to sleep over at one of the desert camps, it can be an unforgettable way of stripping the soul to basics.

Sights

Named in honour of Lawrence's book, the **Seven Pillars of Wisdom** is a large rock formation with seven fluted turrets, which is easy to spot from the visitor centre. Further along Wadi Rum, the enormous, dramatic **Jebel Rum** (1754m) towers above Rum Village. Of the sites closest to Rum Village (distances from the Rest House in brackets), there's a 1st-century BC **Nabataean temple** (400m) and good views from **Lawrence's Spring** (3km), named after Lawrence because he wrote so evocatively of it in *Seven Pillars of Wisdom.*

Visitor Centre Museum MUSEUM

(8am-6pm) FREE While you are buying your ticket to enter Wadi Rum, spare half an hour to visit the informative museum (next to the restaurant), which helps to give a human context to the desert. The displays also explain environmental issues through information panels in English and natural history exhibits. Ask to see the 10-minute film on some of the highlights of Wadi Rum, shown in the purpose-built cinema.

Activities

There are several rewarding hikes in the area, though bear in mind that many of them require walking through soft sand – a tiring activity at the best of times and dangerously exhausting in the summer.

HIGHLIGHTS OF WADI RUM

The main highlights of Wadi Rum are shown below (distances from the visitor centre in brackets):

Barrah Siq (14km) A long, picturesque canyon accessible on foot or by camel.

Burdah Rock Bridge (19km) This impressive 80m-high bridge can be viewed from the desert floor or, better still, you can scramble up to it with a guide (one hour).

Jebel Khazali (7km) Narrow siq with rock inscriptions.

Lawrence's House/Al-Qsair (9km) Legend has it that Lawrence stayed here during the Desert Revolt. The remote location and supreme views of the red sands are the main attractions.

Sand Dunes/Red Sands (6km) Superb red sand dunes on the slopes of Jebel Umm Ulaydiyya that seem to catch alight at sunset.

Sunset and Sunrise Points (11km) The places to be at dawn and dusk if you want to see the desert at its most colourful.

Umm Fruth Rock Bridge (13km) Smaller and more visited than Burdah, this bridge is tucked into an intimate corner of the desert.

Wadak Rock Bridge (9km) Easy to climb, this little rock bridge offers magnificent views across the valley.

KATALEEWAN INTARACHOTE/SHUTTERSTOCK ©

1. Petra's Siq (p321)
Wander the path of history, with the sheer-sided chasm leading to an ancient world.

2. Shobak (p320)
Marvel at the ruins of this Crusader castle at the end of the King's Hwy.

3. Treasury, Petra (p321)
Carved out of iron-laden sandstone, the Hellenistic facade is an astonishing piece of craftsmanship.

4. Wadi Rum (p333)
Have a *Lawrence of Arabia* moment among the fire-coloured dunes of this unforgettable desert.

JOHN WALKER/SHUTTERSTOCK ©

3

A **camel ride** offers one of the best ways to understand the rhythms of the desert. A two-hour trip costs JD10. Full-day camel hire costs JD60 per day – see the rates posted at the visitor centre. Be aware that after one hour of camel riding, most people choose to get off and walk!

For ideas on more adventurous trips, see www.bedouinroads.com.

★ **Rum Horses** HORSE RIDING
(☎07 9580 2108; rumhorses@yahoo.co.uk; from per hr JD25) The highly recommended and long-established Rum Horses is the best horse-trekking agency in the region. The owner, Atallah Swillheen, trained and qualified in horse management and endurance racing in Europe, and currently stables 11 horses. Riders must be experienced – beginners aren't catered for. As well as short rides, fully supported multiday treks can also be arranged, from around JD130 per day.

Royal Aero Sports Club of Jordan BALLOONING
(☎03 205 8052; www.rascj.com) For a magnificent eagle-eye view of Wadi Rum, take to the air by balloon (JD140 per person for a minimum of two people). Trips take a minimum of two hours and are dependent on the weather. Bait Ali Lodge acts as the local facilitator for this company, and the easiest way to book is through the lodge.

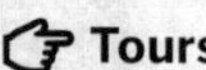

Tours

★ **Rum Stars** OUTDOORS
(☎07 9512 7025; www.rumstars.com) Camel rides, 4WD trips, hiking and scrambling, led by the erudite Ahmed Ogla Al Zalabey, who was born in a tent near the Rum Stars campsite.

★ **Shabab Sahra** ADVENTURE
(☎07 7697 6356, 07 7724 7899; www.shababsahra.com; climbing JD50-70, overnight camping JD20) Wadi Rum's only climbing outfit with internationally trained and accredited guides from the Rum area. Prices vary according to the number of climbers. Shabab Sahra has created a handful of bolted climbing routes near Rum village, and offers overnight camping to access more remote climbing and scrambling areas.

Rahayeb Desert Camp Activities OUTDOORS
(☎07 9690 9030; www.rahayebdc.com; per person from JD50) Brush up on your desert skills by being a 'Bedouin for a Day'. This camp arranges a day with a local family, sampling bread and coffee and learning how to milk sheep, goats and camels. It's harder than it looks and, unless you're a dairy farmer, is likely to elicit guffaws of laughter from your expert hosts.

Bedouin Lifestyle OUTDOORS
(☎07 7913 1803; www.bedouinlifestyle.com) Run by Atalla Ablawi, offering tented camps, hiking and camel and jeep tours.

Sleeping

There are no hotels in Wadi Rum, but camping in the reserve ranges from a goat-hair blanket under the stars at an isolated Bedouin camp to a mattress under partitioned canvas or beds in a comfortable cabin. To stay within the reserve, make contact with any of the companies listed under Tours.

In addition, accommodation is available outside the reserve at Bait Ali and in neighbouring Diseh. This village is signposted off the Wadi Rum approach road, 16km from the Desert Hwy. Diseh camps include the secluded **Rahayeb Camp** (☎07 9690 9030; www.rahayebdc.com; Diseh; half board per person JD35, deluxe tents JD60); the sociable but basic **Zawaideh Desert Camp** (☎07 9584 0664; zawaideh_camp@yahoo.com; Diseh; half board per person JD20) popular with young Jordanians, close to the road and accessible by car; **Captain's Camp** (☎07 9551 0432, 03 201 6905; captains@jo.com.jo; Diseh; half board s/d JD45/85), a well-run midrange camp with hot showers, snug seating areas and good buffets; and a couple of luxury options such as **Wadi Rum Night Luxury Camp** (☎03 215 7070; www.wadirumnight.com; tent with half board JD120-160). Hitch a ride near the police checkpoint to the village (8km – be prepared for a wait), or request someone from the camp come to meet you.

At all the camps, mattress, blankets and food are provided, but not always linen.

★ **Bait Ali Lodge** CAMPGROUND $$
(☎07 9925 7222, 07 9554 8133; www.baitali.com; tent per person from s/d JD35/70, cabin from s/d JD53/84, deluxe chalet s/d JD100/137;) If you want to stay in the desert but are not wild about roughing it, Bait Ali is a recommended compromise. Tucked behind a hill, with a fine view of the wilderness, this ecofriendly camp is clearly signposted just off the road, 15km from the Desert Hwy and 9km before the Wadi Rum visitor centre. The lodge offers advice on a range of activities in the area.

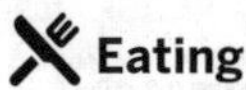

Eating

Rest House BUFFET $$
(breakfast JD5, lunch JD12, dinner buffet JD12; 8am-6pm) Dining here is open-air and buffet-style, though if tourist numbers are low (at hotter times of the year, for example), selections are restricted to what's in stock for the à la carte menu. Late afternoon with food and a cold drink while watching the sun's rays light up Jebel Umm Al Ishrin is the perfect way to finish the day.

Rum Gate Restaurant BUFFET $$
(03 201 5995; Wadi Rum visitor centre; snacks JD5, buffet lunch JD12; 8am-5pm;) The buffet at this restaurant at the visitor centre is popular. Outside lunchtime, the restaurant is a meeting place for guides, weary hikers and independent travellers who congregate over a tea and a chicken sandwich.

Entertainment

Film Bus CINEMA
(www.film.jo; JD7) Jordan's Royal Film Commission has been piloting cinema under the stars in Wadi Rum, showing films connected to the area. If you ever wanted to see *Lawrence of Arabia* in situ (or *The Martian* – also filmed in Wadi Rum), this is for you.

Information

If you are camping (including at the Rest House), bring along a torch (flashlight), a book to read and a padlock (many tents are lockable).

The Bedouin are a conservative people, so dress appropriately. Long shorts and sleeveless T-shirts for men and women are just about acceptable around the Rest House, but baggy trousers/skirts and modest shirts/blouses will save you sunburn and earn you respect from the Bedouin, especially in the desert.

The **visitor centre** (03 209 0600; www.wadirum.jo; 7am-7pm) is situated at the entry to the protected area, about 30km east of the Desert Hwy and 7km north of Rum village. This is where you buy your entry ticket, book a 4WD or camel excursion, organise accommodation at a camp and book a guide. There are no ATMs or credit card payment facilities in Wadi Rum, nor is there a petrol station. There is a restaurant, craft shops, an excellent museum, clean toilets and parking area. You can also ask to see a 10-minute film on some of the highlights of Wadi Rum, shown in the purpose-built cinema.

Getting There & Away

There's at least one minibus a day to Aqaba (JD3, one hour) at around 7am. A second sometimes runs a little later in the morning, but check with your camp operator first. To Wadi Musa (JD7, 1½ hours), there is a fairly reliable daily minibus at 8.30am. Check current departure times at the visitor centre, Rest House or camp operator when you arrive in Wadi Rum.

For Ma'an, Karak or Amman, the minibuses to either Aqaba or Wadi Musa can drop you off at the Ar Rashidiyya crossroads with the Desert Hwy (JD2, 20 minutes), where it is easy to hail onward transport.

A JETT bus link from Amman was rumoured to be starting in 2018. It's expected to cost JD10 to JD12. Check JETT's website for the latest (www.jett.com.jo).

Occasionally taxis hang around the visitor centre (and very occasionally the Rest House) waiting for a fare back to wherever they came from – normally Aqaba, Wadi Musa or Ma'an. It costs JD20 to Aqaba, and JD35 to Wadi Musa (Petra). A taxi jeep from Rum village to the Ar Rashidiyya crossroads with the Desert Hwy costs around JD10. Some camps organise onward transport at competitive rates for their guests.

Aqaba العقبة

03

The most important city in southern Jordan, Aqaba is located at the far eastern end of the Gulf of Aqaba and therefore enjoys a narrow access to the spectacular waters of the **Red Sea**. Ringed by high desert mountains and enjoying a pleasant climate for most of the year, Aqaba has become Jordan's main holiday destination, but despite this it has retained the relaxed small-town atmosphere of a seaside town.

Many visitors are drawn to the diving and snorkelling clubs just south of the town, and of course the big destinations of Wadi Rum and Petra lie a couple of hours' drive to the northeast. It's also an amiable place to break a journey to/from Egypt or Israel and the Palestinian Territories.

Sights

Aqaba is more about sea than sights, but there are a couple of sights of interest, including the limited ruins of **Ayla** (Corniche; 24hr) FREE, the ancient **port of Aqaba** (next to the Mövenpick Resort) and **Aqaba Fort** (off King Hussein St), which is currently closed for long-term renovation. Built between 1510 and 1517, the fort was used as a khan (travellers' inn) for pilgrims on their way to Mecca. The Ottomans occupied the castle until WWI when, in 1917, it was all but destroyed by shelling from the

Aqaba

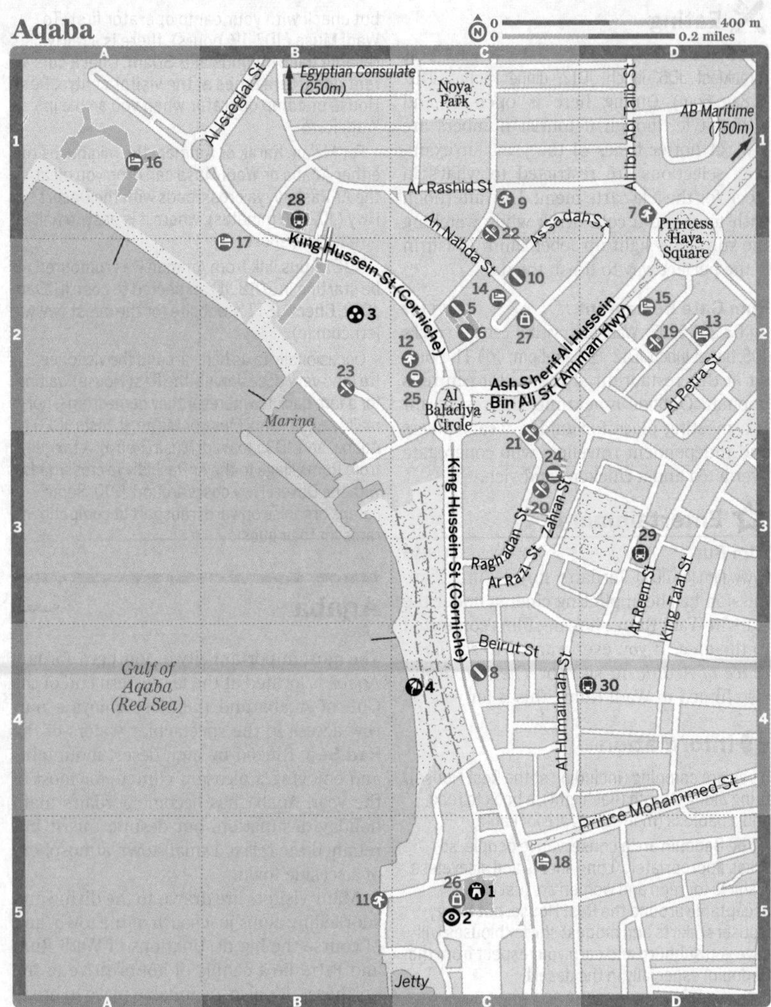

British Royal Navy. It houses some interesting artefacts, including an old Roman milestone.

Packed at the weekend and on public holidays, the **public beach** FREE is a stretch of rather minimal sand beneath palm trees, which nonetheless offers a fun and sociable way to engage with Jordanians at play. During *Eid*, the family parties extend well into the night.

Aqaba Bird Observatory BIRD SANCTUARY
(☎03 205 8825; www.facebook.com/aqababirds; Wadi Araba Border Rd; JD7; ⏲8am-3pm Sun-Thu) Run by the RSCN, this bird sanctuary with its population of white-eyed gulls is an artificially created wetland that's become host to a variety of species that use the area as a stopping-off point on the great bird migrations between Africa, Europe and Asia. There's a 1.5km walking trail around the cluster of lakes, and in winter especially the place is thick with ducks and waders.

Arab Revolt Flagpole LANDMARK
Standing a massive 137m high and with a flag measuring 20m by 40m, this is Aqaba's most easily spotted landmark by some degree. Look closer however and you'll see the flag isn't Jordanian as you might expect.

Aqaba

Sights
1 Aqaba Fort C5
2 Arab Revolt Flagpole C5
3 Ayla B2
4 Public Beach C4

Activities, Courses & Tours
5 Aqaba Adventure Divers Office C2
6 Aqaba International Dive Centre Office C2
7 Aquamarina Sea Breeze D1
8 Arab Divers C4
9 Bab Al Hara C1
10 Dive Aqaba Office C2
11 Glass-Bottom Boat Dock B5
Red Sea Dive Centre Office .... (see 5)
12 Sindbad C2

Sleeping
13 Amir Palace Hotel D2
14 Captain's Hotel C2
15 Dweik 3 Hotel D2
16 InterContinental Hotel A1
17 Kempinski Hotel B2
18 Yafko Hotel C5

Eating
19 Al Mohandes D2
20 Al Tarboosh Restaurant C3
21 Ali Baba Restaurant C3
Captain's Restaurant .... (see 14)
22 Floka Restaurant C1
23 Romero at Royal Yacht Club B2

Drinking & Nightlife
24 Al Fardos Coffee Shop C3
25 Rovers Return C2

Shopping
26 Noor Al Hussein Foundation C5
27 Souk by the Sea C2

Transport
28 JETT Bus Office B1
29 Main Bus & Minibus Station D3
30 Minibus & Service Taxi Station to Karak D4

Instead, it's the banner of the Great Arab Revolt, whose centenary was celebrated in 2017. The capture of Aqaba was a key moment in the revolt against Ottoman rule in the Middle East.

Activities

Many people head to Aqaba for the opportunity it affords to experience the Red Sea. Most hotels in town can organise boat trips and water sports but for diving and snorkelling, visitors generally head to the dive centres that lie along the narrow strip between Aqaba and the Saudi border. These all offer accommodation or are easily accessed as a day trip from Aqaba by shuttle bus or taxi. The luxurious Tala Bay complex, at the Aqaba end of the southern coast, offers a more glamorous range of hotel rooms and water sports but perhaps lacks the traveller vibe of the dive camps.

Diving & Snorkelling

According to the Jordan Royal Ecological Society (www.jreds.org), the Gulf of Aqaba has over 110 species of hard coral, 120 species of soft coral and about 1000 species of fish, with some great sites for diving and snorkelling.

Aqaba's dive agencies are very professional. A typical two-dive trip from a boat (some sites have shore access) with tanks and weights costs around JD80, with an additional JD25 for full equipment rental. Night dives and PADI courses (from JD280) are available. Flippers, mask and snorkel can be hired for JD5 per day or all-inclusive snorkelling boat trips cost around JD45 per person.

Red Sea Dive Centre Office DIVING
(☎03 202 2323; www.aqabascubadiving.com; King Hussein St) One of the most established dive centres in Aqaba.

Dive Aqaba Office DIVING
(☎03 210 8883; www.diveaqaba.com; An Nahda St) A highly professional training centre known for its high-quality teaching staff.

Darna Divers Village DIVING
(☎07 9671 2831; www.aqabadivers.com) Scuba operator based at the south beach near Tala Bay.

Aqaba Adventure Divers Office DIVING
(☎07 9584 3724; www.aqaba-diving.com; King Hussein St) Well-regarded scuba outfit.

Arab Divers DIVING
(☎03 203 1808; www.aqabadive.com; King Hussein St) Recommended scuba operator.

Aqaba International Dive Center Office DIVING
(☎07 9694 9082; www.aqabadivingcenter.com) Popular, well-equipped scuba operator.

Water Sports & Hammans

The cafe-lined public beaches of Aqaba are aimed at sunset strollers rather than swimmers. The Tala Bay complex, south of Aqaba, features a huge sandy bay in attractively landscaped gardens, surrounded by upmarket hotels and lends itself better to water sports.

★Berenice Beach Club WATER SPORTS
(www.berenice.com.jo; JD15; ⊙9am-sunset) The only dedicated, private beach club on the south coast, Berenice has pools, a jetty giving access to a coral reef, a dive centre, water sports, boat trips, restaurants and spotless changing rooms. It attracts record crowds on Fridays. It offers a 50% discount for guests of many Aqaba hotels and operates a regular free shuttle bus service (check the website for the current schedule).

Tala Bay Beach Club WATER SPORTS
(☎03 943 0949; www.aqababoat.com; JD10) With three pools, a pool bar, restaurants, waterskiing, jet-skiing, parasailing, windsurfing, kite boarding, kayaking, sailing, diving and snorkelling, this beach club, within the Tala Bay complex, caters to all levels of energy. Day entry to the beach includes transport on the shuttle bus from Aqaba.

Bab Al Hara HAMMAM
(☎07 9966 3800; Ar Rashid St; JD25; ⊙9am-10pm) This spotlessly clean, friendly establishment offers steam bath, jacuzzi, foot and body massage and sauna, and there's a separate pool for women and families. A one-hour oil massage costs an additional JD25.

Boat Trips

Aquamarina Sea Breeze CRUISE
(☎07 9950 0731; www.aquamarina-aqaba.com; Shwaikini Bldg, Princess Haya Sq; 1hr sunset cruise per person JD15) With four or five boats operational in Aqaba, this company is leading the way in boat trips. It offers trips to Pharaoh Island (adult/child under 12 years JD45/20), three-hour glass-bottom boat rides between 3pm and 6pm and popular one-hour sunset trips at 6pm. Prices include soft drinks.

Sindbad CRUISE
(☎07 7543 4150; www.sindbad.jo; Aqaba Gateway) Operates a number of popular cruises around the Gulf of Aqaba either from the marina or from Berenice Beach Club. Popular trips include a four-hour snorkelling cruise (adult/child under 12 years JD25/12) and a sunset cruise from 6pm to 9.30pm including a BBQ dinner on the beach (adult/child JD25/12).

Neptune Submarine Vision BOATING
(☎07 7722 3375, 07 7943 0969; www.facebook.com/pg/NeptuneBoat) A glass-bottom boat with a difference, the *Neptune* has a glass hull that is fully submersed allowing for a 360-degree view in what the company describes as a dry-dive experience. The self-styled 'underwater observatory' leaves daily from the Tala Bay marina, on the south coast.

Glass-Bottom Boat Dock BOATING
(30min/1hr JD25/40; ⊙6am-sunset) Boats, which operate between 6am and sunset, congregate along the jetty in front of Aqaba Fort. The rate charged is per boat, which holds about 10 people. Prices reflect demand so be prepared to bargain when it's busy. During any of the trips, you can swim, snorkel or fish (bring your own equipment).

Sleeping

Unless otherwise stated, budget places listed here offer (nonsatellite) TV, air-conditioning and a private bathroom with hot water (not always reliable); they don't include breakfast. Midrange places have a fridge, satellite TV, telephone and hot water, and prices include breakfast.

Yafko Hotel HOTEL $
(☎03 204 2222; www.yafko.com; cnr Corniche & Prince Mohammed St; s/d without breakfast JD27/38;) Set back from the Corniche you can sit in bed at this slick hotel and enjoy the sea views. Some rooms are an odd shape, but the furnishings and stone trim make this an attractive choice. It is conveniently located near the fort and transport hubs plus plenty of cafes (breakfast isn't offered here).

★Captain's Hotel BOUTIQUE HOTEL $$
(☎03 206 0710; www.captains.jo; An Nahda St; s/d/tr JD55/65/85;) Aqaba's version of a boutique hotel, the Captain's began life as a fish restaurant – still flourishing on the ground floor – and slowly evolved into this stylish accommodation. With copper-tiled flooring and compact rooms with Arabian-style furniture, sauna and jacuzzi, this is an upmarket choice for a midrange price.

Dweik 3 Hotel HOTEL $$
(☎03 203 5919; atalla_dweik@yahoo.com; Amman Hwy; s/d/tr JD50/60/70;) An excellent midrange hotel with a great location close to all the action. Rooms are generously sized and

well kept, and those at the front have pleasant balconies. Not to be confused with the nearby Dweik 1 or Dweik 2 Hotels.

Amir Palace Hotel HOTEL $$
(☎03 206 3113; www.amirpalacehotel.com; Al Petra St; r JD25-45; 📶) Unpretentious but reliable hotel just off the main thoroughfare in Aqaba, with helpful staff and comfortable spotless rooms. Rooms facing the side street are slightly cooler, as they avoid the full day-long blast of the sun.

★Kempinski Hotel RESORT $$$
(☎03 209 0888; www.kempinski.com; King Hussein St; r from JD245; P @ ≋) Lavish, multilayered swimming pools, six restaurants and bars (including the renowned Fish Inn and Black Pearl) and a spa make this super-luxury hotel worth top dollar. The beachfront setup is tremendous, and the service is flawless.

★InterContinental Hotel RESORT $$$
(☎03 209 2222; www.intercontinental.com; King Hussein St; r from JD134; P @ ≋) An imposing full stop at the end of the bay, the InterCon boasts less of an infinity pool than an infinity sea: on a calm day, the Gulf of Aqaba stretches in one seamless ripple all the way to Egypt. With exceptional landscape gardening, pools and a lazy river, the InterCon has stolen the top spot in Aqaba's luxury accommodation.

Eating

Aqaba's speciality is fish, particularly *sayadieh:* it's the catch of the day, delicately spiced, served with rice in an onion and tomato (or tahina) sauce.

★Al Mohandes JORDANIAN $
(At Tabari St; mains JD1; ⊙7am-1am) This canteen restaurant is as unpretentious as it comes, but it's always busy whatever the time of day. Bowls of hummus, falafel and *fuul* (fava bean paste) are quickly served with mint tea. Women are directed to the family salon upstairs.

Al Tarboosh Restaurant BAKERY $
(☎03 201 8518; Raghadan St; pastries from 200 fils; ⊙7.30am-midnight) A handy pastry shop that offers a great range of meat, cheese and vegetable *sambusas* (samosas). Order a bag for taking away or sit and eat them straight from the oven at the tables outside.

★Ali Baba Restaurant JORDANIAN $$
(☎03 201 3901; Raghadan St; mains JD9; ⊙8am-midnight; 🍷) No longer quite the star draw with locals that it once was, this evergreen restaurant still pulls in a tourist crowd. The outdoor seating area is a good vantage point for people-watching, though you'll need to sit inside if you want to have alcohol with your meal. The food is traditional Jordanian, with a seafood slant.

★Captain's Restaurant SEAFOOD $$$
(☎03 201 6905; An Nahda St; mains JD8-18; ⊙noon-11pm) Serving consistently good quality seafood, including *sayadieh* and a delicious seafood curry, this is a perennially popular choice for locals with something to celebrate.

★Romero at Royal Yacht Club ITALIAN $$$
(☎03 202 2404; www.romero-jordan.com; Royal Yacht Club; mains JD7-16; ⊙noon-11pm; 🍷) With views of the marina, this elegant, wood-panelled restaurant is the place to savour a romantic sunset and mingle with Aqaba's nouveau riche. The mostly Italian menu includes Mediterranean flavours, homemade vegetarian pasta, seafood salads – and an unexpected line in sushi. Reservations are recommended.

Floka Restaurant SEAFOOD $$$
(☎03 203 0860; An Nahda St; mains JD8-15; ⊙12.30-11.30pm) A friendly, unpretentious establishment, where you choose from the catch of the day (which normally includes sea bream, silver snapper, grouper and goatfish) and select how you would like it cooked. Service can be a little slow, but there's indoor and outdoor seating.

Drinking & Nightlife

Rovers Return PUB
(☎03 203 2030; Aqaba Gateway complex; ⊙12.30pm-12.30am) This 'English' pub attracts a young crowd, plus those curious to see how the iconic pub of soap opera *Coronation Street* has ended up by the Red Sea (check the wall of fame and then order Betty's Hotpot to find out). There's a traditional English pub menu and Guinness on tap. The interior can get smoky, but there's an outdoor terrace.

Al Fardos Coffee Shop COFFEE
(off Zahran St; ⊙10am-midnight) Just off Zahran St, this is a traditional coffeehouse where local men sip *qahwa* (coffee), play backgammon and smoke shisha. It has a pleasant outdoor setting, and foreign women are welcome.

Shopping

Noor Al Hussein Foundation ARTS & CRAFTS
(☎ 03 560 7460; www.nooralhusseinfoundation.org; Aqaba Fort) The Noor Al Hussein Foundation is a national vocational training organisation, with one of its arms making handicrafts with local cooperatives. The fruits of their labours are on sale here – the needlework products are particularly fine.

Souk by the Sea MARKET
(Fri evenings Oct-May) A fun tourist market with local handicrafts, carpets and the like.

Information

There are dozens of banks and ATMs around the city. Many are located along the southern side of Amman Highway, near Baladiya Circle.

Numerous moneychangers are congregated around the corner of Zahran and Ar Razi Sts. They keep longer hours than the banks.

Foreign women may feel less conspicuous wearing loose shirts and baggy shorts over a swimsuit, or, better still, using the facilities of one of the beachside hotels in town or along the southern coast. Bikinis are acceptable in either of the latter locations.

Getting There & Away

AIR

Aqaba has Jordan's only commercial **airport** (☎ 03 203 4010; www.aac2.info) outside Amman. Royal Jordanian (www.rj.com) flies twice daily between the two cities. One-way tickets cost around JD49.

Aqaba's King Hussein International Airport is 10km north of town, close to the border with Israel and the Palestinian Territories. There's no bus to the airport, so take service taxi 8 (around JD2, 15 minutes) from the main bus and minibus station, or take a taxi for around JD10.

BOAT

AB Maritime (☎ 03 209 2000; www.abmaritime.com.jo; Amman Hwy) runs two services to Egypt: a fast catamaran to Taba and a slower ferry to Nuweiba. Western governments warn against travel to some parts of the Sinai; check the latest advisories before travelling.

Minibuses (JD1) leave from near the entrance to Aqaba Fort on King Hussein St and go by the southern beaches, camps, dive sites and Royal Diving Centre, passing the ferry terminal for boats to Egypt. A taxi from central Aqaba to the ferry terminal costs JD8.

BUS

There are buses to Amman and Irbid from Aqaba. It's worth paying for the comfort, speed and air-conditioning of a JETT private bus. Ordinary public buses travel between the main bus and minibus station in Aqaba and Amman's south (Wahadat) station (JD6, four hours) about every hour between 7am and 5pm.

From the **JETT Bus Office** (☎ 03 201 5222; King Hussein St) next to the Mövenpick hotel, coaches run six times daily to Amman (JD8, four hours) between 7am and 5pm. Different departures go to different bus stations in Amman – Abdali, Tarbaboor or the JETT station on 7th Circle – so check before booking. There's also a twice-daily VIP service to 7th Circle (JD17, four hours), which includes complimentary snacks and more comfortable seating. Book a day in advance (take your passport). JETT also have three coaches a day to Irbid (JD10, five hours).

MINIBUS

To Wadi Musa (for Petra), two minibuses (JD5, 2½ hours) leave when full, departing between 6am and 7am and between 11am and noon; the exact departure times depend on the number of passengers, and you may have a long wait as very few locals use this service. Drivers often offer passengers the option, however, to leave with a minimum of four to five people providing each passenger pays extra.

There's one daily minibus to Wadi Rum (JD2, one hour) at around 1.30pm.

Minibuses to Amman's south station (JD6, five hours) leave when full, approximately every three hours throughout the day.

All of the above minibuses leave from the **main bus and minibus station** (Ar Reem St). Minibuses to Karak and Tafila (JD3.500, three hours), via Safi and the Dead Sea Hwy, are the exception, leaving from the small station next to the mosque on Al Humaimah St.

TAXI

From the main bus and minibus station, service taxis head to Amman (JD10, five hours), but far less regularly than buses and minibuses. To Karak (JD6, three hours), they leave from the small station on Al Humaimah St. Service taxis start lining up at either station at 6am, and many have left by 8am, so get there early. Chartering a taxi costs around JD45 one way to Petra and JD25 to Wadi Rum.

Chartering a taxi to the south coast beaches costs JD10. Between Aqaba and the Israel and the Palestinian Territories border is also JD10.

Getting Around

Hundreds of green air-conditioned taxis cruise the streets beeping at tourists. They are unmetered, but most rides around town cost from JD1 to JD2. A one-way ride to Tala Bay/Berenice is a set fare of JD10.

UNDERSTAND JORDAN

Jordan Today

In common with other parts of the Middle East, Jordan traditionally favours strong, centralised government under an autocratic leader – what might be called 'benign dictatorship'. This does not preclude voicing an opinion, however, and in November 1989 the first full parliamentary elections since 1967 were held, and women were allowed the vote. Four years later most political parties were legalised and able to participate in parliamentary and municipal elections. Despite these concessions, democracy in Jordan is still something of an alien concept – as illustrated by the brief and largely unremarkable demonstrations at the start of the decade that contrasted with the more urgent 'Arab Spring' uprisings in neighbouring countries. Perceived as promoting the interests of the individual over those of the community, many in Jordan see democracy as running, to some extent, against the grain of tribal traditions where respect for elders is paramount.

A lack of uniform appetite for democracy does not equate, however, with a lack of enthusiasm for modernity, and King Abdullah is widely regarded as a modernising monarch in touch with the sensibilities of a globalised world, supportive of social and economic reform and committed to stamping out corruption. He has proved adept at handling foreign affairs – imperative, considering the neighbourhood Jordan shares.

Occupying the calm eye of the storm in the Middle East, the country has a long tradition of absorbing the displaced peoples of its troubled neighbours. Currently coping with the fourth influx of refugees in 50 years, Jordan is now home to 620,000 registered and an estimated 780,000 unregistered Syrian refugees. War-weary subjects, with little chance of repatriation in the foreseeable future, many Syrians are confined to camps such as Za'atari that is equivalent in size to Jordan's largest cities. With each new flood of asylum seekers, Jordan's resources and the patience of its citizens are stretched to breaking point.

Despite the mixed origins of its people, the current political and economic difficulties, the insecurity of life in a volatile region and the threat from extremists hovering over the border, Jordanians remain united in their pride for their country.

History

In Jordan history is not something that happened 'before'. It's a living, breathing part of everyday life, witnessed not just in the pragmatic treatment of ancient artefacts but also in the way people live. Jordanians value their heritage and are in no hurry to eschew ways of life that have proved successful for centuries. Each period of history thus features in the experiences of a visitor, not only through a pile of fallen columns, but in the taking of tea with old custodians of the desert or the bargaining for a kilim with designs inherited from the Byzantine era.

Early Settlements

Just step foot in Jordan and you begin your encounter with history. Visit the dolmens near Madaba, for example, and you'll be entering the cradle of civilisation; dating from 4000 BC, the dolmens embody the sophistication of the world's first villages.

The copper and bronze ages helped bring wealth to the region (1200 BC). You can find forgings from Jordan's ancient copper mines in the Dana Biosphere Reserve. Trading in these metals had a cohesive impact – travel the King's Highway and not only will you walk on the path of royalty, but you'll also see how this route helped unify city-states into a recognisable Jordan between 1200 BC and 333 BC.

Great Empires

The Greeks, Nabataeans and Romans dominated Jordan's most illustrious historical period (333 BC to AD 333), leaving the magnificent legacies of Petra and Jerash. Located at the centre of the land bridge between Africa and Asia, the cities surrounding the King's Highway profited from the caravan routes that crossed the deserts from Arabia to the Euphrates, bringing shipments of African gold and South Arabian frankincense via the Red Sea ports in present-day Aqaba and Eilat.

By the 4th century BC, the growing wealth of Arab lands attracted the attention of Alexander the Great. The precocious 21-year-old stormed through the region in 334 BC, winning territories from Turkey to Palestine and bringing access to the great intellectual treasures of the classical era.

Trade was the key to Jordan's golden era (8 BC to AD 40), thanks to the growing importance of a nomadic Arab tribe from the south, known as the Nabataeans. The Nabataeans produced only copper and bitumen (for waterproofing boat hulls), but they knew how to trade in the commodities of neighbouring nations. They never possessed an 'empire' in the common military and administrative sense of the word; instead, from about 200 BC, they established a 'zone of influence' that stretched from Syria to Rome – one that inevitably attracted the conquering tendencies of the Roman Empire.

You only have to visit Jerash for five minutes, trip over a fallen column and notice the legions of other columns beside, to gain an immediate understanding of the importance of the Romans in Jordan. This magnificent set of ruins indicates the amount of wealth the Romans invested in this outpost of their empire. It's perhaps a fitting legacy of their rule that the Jordanian currency, the dinar, derives its name from the Latin *denarius* (ancient Roman silver coin).

Spirit of the Age

Under the influence of Rome, Christianity replaced the local gods of the Nabataeans, and several hundred years later Islam took its place. The arrival of Islamic dynasties is evident from the 7th century onwards, literally strewn over the deserts of eastern Jordan in the form of the intriguing Umayyad structures that dot the stark landscape. The conflict between Islam and Christianity, evident at Jordan's crusader castles in Ajloun, Karak and Shobak, is a defining feature of the next thousand years.

British imperialism dominates Jordan's history prior to the Arab Revolt of 1914; ride a camel through Wadi Rum and cries of 'To Aqaba!' hang in the wind. And so does the name of Lawrence, the British officer whose desert adventures have captured the imagination of visitors to such an extent that whole mountains are named after him. The Arab Revolt may not have immediately achieved its goal during peace negotiations, but it did lead directly to the birth of the modern state of Jordan. A series of treaties after 1928 led to full independence in 1946, when Abdullah was proclaimed king.

Modern State of Jordan

Jordan's modern history is about independence, modernisation (under the much loved King Hussein and his son and heir, the current King Abdullah). It's also marked by cohabitation with difficult neighbours. Much of the conflict stems from the creation of a Jewish national homeland in Palestine, where Arab Muslims accounted for about 90% of the population. Their resentment informed the dialogue of Arab-Israeli relations for the rest of the 20th century. Today, after the settlement of successive waves of refugees, the majority of the population of Jordan is made up of Palestinians.

On 26 October 1994, Jordan and Israel and the Palestinian Territories signed a momentous peace treaty, and for the past two decades Jordan has been preoccupied with its neighbours to the east rather the west – a shift in focus necessitated firstly by the Gulf War and subsequently by the US-led invasion of Iraq, which led to a further influx of refugees, this time from Iraq. Ironically, the refugees brought their relative prosperity with them – a windfall that has stimulated the economy throughout the past decade and helped turn Amman, in particular, into a cosmopolitan, modern city.

BOOKS ON JORDAN

Lonely Planet publishes a detailed *Jordan* guide. Other key reading includes the following:

- *Seven Pillars of Wisdom* (TE Lawrence; 1935) Describes Lawrence's epic adventures in Jordan and the part he played in the Arab Revolt (he wrote some of it in Amman).
- *Petra: Lost City of the Ancient World* (Christian Augé and Jean-Marie Dentzer; 2000) An excellent, portable background introduction to Petra.
- *Married to a Bedouin* (Marguerite van Geldermalsen; 2006) An idea of life with the Bedouin at Petra.
- *Walking in Jordan* (2001) and *Walks & Scrambles in Rum* (Tony Howard and Di Taylor; 1993) Describe dozens of hikes in Jordan, from wadi walks to climbing routes.

People & Society

Bedouin Roots

A strong tradition of hospitality and a lively sense of humour make it easy to connect with Jordanians. These are traits that belong to the Bedouin tradition. In fact, over 98% of Jordanians are Arab, descended from the original desert dwellers of Arabia. Living a traditional life of livestock rearing, the few remaining nomadic Bedouin are concentrated mainly in the Badia – the great desert plains of eastern Jordan. The majority of Jordan's indigenous population, however, now enjoy the benefits of settlement and education. While many are wistful about the stories of their grandparents, they are not nostalgic about the hardships they faced.

The most easily identifiable aspect of the Bedouin inheritance is an ingrained tribal respect for local elders, or sheikhs. This characteristic is extended to the ultimate leaders of the country. Claiming unbroken descent from Prophet Mohammed, Jordan's Hashemite royal family is a nationally beloved and regionally respected institution associated with benign and diplomatic governance and a history of charitable works. Despite protests against the government in the 2011 Arab Spring, there was no popular demand for a republic.

Importance of Family

Family ties are all-important to both modern and traditional Jordanians, and paying respect to parents is where the sense of obeisance to elders is engendered. Socialising generally entails some kind of get-together with the extended family, with lines drawn loosely between the genders. This is reflected in terms of physical divisions within the house, where separate seating areas are reserved for men and women.

In Jordan, a woman's 'honour' is still valued in traditional society, and sex before marriage or adultery is often dealt with harshly by other members of the woman's family. Traditional concepts of *ird* (honour) run deep but sit uneasily with the freedoms many affluent Jordanian women have come to expect, largely thanks to universal access to one of the region's best education systems. A minimum of six women MPs is guaranteed by royal decree and while only 14% of the labour force was made up of women in 1991, today (according to UN data) this has risen to over one quarter.

Urbanisation

There is an increasing polarisation in Jordanian society between town and country. In Amman, modern Western-leaning middle- and upper-class youths enjoy the fruits of a good education, shop in malls, drink lattes in Starbucks and obsess over the latest fashions. In rural areas, meanwhile, unemployment is high and many populations struggle with making ends meet. For this reason, economic migration is common in Jordan, and many working-class families have at least one male who is temporarily working away from home – whether in Amman, the Gulf States, or further afield.

Religion

Over 92% of the population are Sunni Muslims. A further 6% are Christians living mainly in Amman, Salt, Madaba and Karak. There are tiny Shiite and Druze groups.

Most Christians belong to the Greek Orthodox Church, but there are also some Greek Catholics, a small Roman Catholic community, and Syrian, Coptic and Armenian Orthodox communities.

Arts & Crafts

Walk the streets of Madaba, with bright coloured kilims flapping in the wind, hike to the soap-making villages of Ajloun, or watch elderly Bedouin women threading beads at Petra, and it will become immediately apparent that the country has a strong handicraft tradition. The authorities have been quick to support this aspect of Jordan's heritage and now craft cooperatives are widespread, resulting in benefits for local communities and ensuring that Jordan's rich legacy endures for future generations. Taking an interest in Jordanian crafts, then, is not a remote aesthetic exercise – it represents sustainable tourism at its best.

Kilims

Jordan has a long-established rug-making industry dating back to the country's pre-Islamic, Christian communities. *Mafrash* (rugs) are usually of the flat, woven kind, compared with carpets that have a pile. To this day, especially in Madaba and Mukawir, it's possible to watch kilims based on early Byzantine designs being made.

Embroidery

This is an important skill among Jordanian women and most learn the craft at a young age. Teenagers traditionally embroider the clothes they will need as married women. Embroidery provides an occasion for women to socialise, often with a pot of tea spiced up with a pinch of local gossip.

Mosaic

With a noble and distinguished lineage in Jordan, mosaics are made from tiny squares of naturally coloured rock called tesserae – the more tesserae per centimetre, the finer and more valuable the mosaic. Portable pieces are available.

Food & Drink

Though little known outside the country, Jordan has a distinctive culinary tradition, largely thanks to the Bedouin influence.

The Bedouin speciality is *mensaf* – delicious spit-roasted lamb, basted with spices until it takes on a yellow appearance. It's served on a platter of rice and pine nuts, flavoured with the cooking fat, and often centrally garnished with the head of the lamb. Honoured guests are served the eyes (which have a slightly almond flavour); less honoured guests are offered the tongue (a rich-flavoured, succulent meat). The dish is served with a sauce of yoghurt, combined with the cooking fat.

In Wadi Rum you might be lucky enough to be offered a Bedouin barbecue from the *zarb,* a pit oven buried in the desert sand.

JORDAN BIKE TRAIL

The biking equivalent of hiking's Jordan Trail (p305), the epic Jordan Bike Trail (www.jordanbiketrail.com) navigates a path from Umm Qais to the Red Sea. The website has detailed information on the route, including GPS waypoints and elevation charts for each stage, and is highly challenging, even for experienced riders. Described as not very technical, this canyon-crossing trail does, however, include lots of stiff climbs.

Another Jordanian favourite is *maqlubbeh* (sometimes called 'upside down') – steamed rice pressed into a pudding basin, topped with meat, eggplant, tomato and pine nuts.

Dessert here, as in many parts of the Middle East, may be *kunafa* or *muhalabiyya* (a milk custard containing pistachio nuts).

If you fancy learning how to make your own Jordanian cuisine, try an evening course at Petra Kitchen (p326).

The universal drink of choice is sweet black tea (coffee comes a close second); most social exchanges, including haggling over a kilim, are punctuated with copious glasses that are usually too hot to handle. Other options include *yansoon* (aniseed herbal tea) and *zaatar* (thyme-flavoured tea).

Bottled mineral water is widely available, as are the usual soft drinks, Amstel beer and locally produced wines.

Environment

The Land

Jordan can be divided into three major geographic regions: the Jordan Valley, the East Bank plateau and the desert. The fertile valley of the Jordan River is the dominant physical feature of the country's western region, running from the Syrian border in the north, along the border with Israel and the Palestinian Territories and into the Dead Sea. Part of the larger African Rift Valley, the Jordan Valley continues under the name Wadi Araba and extends to the Gulf of Aqaba, where Jordan claims a sneeze-sized stretch of the Red Sea. The majority of the population lives in a hilly 70km-wide strip running the length of the country, known as the East Bank plateau. The remaining 80% of the country is desert, stretching into Syria, Iraq and Saudi Arabia.

Wildlife

Spring is the best time to see some of Jordan's 2000 flowers and plants, including the black iris, Jordan's redolent national flower.

Two of Jordan's most impressive wild animals are the Arabian oryx and Nubian ibex, resident at the Shaumari Wildlife Reserve and Mujib Biosphere Reserve respectively. Jordan is an important corridor for migratory birds en route to Africa and southern Arabia.

Nature Reserves

The Royal Society for the Conservation of Nature (RSCN; www.rscn.org.jo) operates six reserves in Jordan, of which Mujib and Dana Biosphere Reserves are, scenically at least, the undoubted highlights. Shaumari Wildlife Reserve in Azraq reopened to the public in 2017 after an impressive make-over and offers jeep safaris in the desert terrain. The Azraq Wetland Reserve, located nearby, is a good place for birdwatching, while the Ajloun Forest Reserve in Northern Jordan protects a beautiful area of woodland, perfect for hiking.

Environmental Issues

The RSCN has pioneered models for sustainable development and tourism by working closely with local communities and making them stakeholders in conserving local reserves. The society has also been responsible for reintroducing several endemic animals in Jordan, including the endangered oryx.

Despite these welcome initiatives, there are still major problems, including a chronic lack of water, the pressure of tourism on fragile sites such as at Petra and in Wadi Rum, and increasing desertification through overgrazing.

Solutions to these problems are constantly under review and there are ambitious plans to build a pipeline, known as the 'Peace Conduit', connecting the Red and Dead Seas to provide desalinated water and to raise the diminishing level of the Dead Sea.

SURVIVAL GUIDE

Directory A–Z

ACCOMMODATION

Jordan has accommodation to suit most budgets in the main cities but limited choice elsewhere. It's generally not necessary to book ahead except in the two peak seasons (September to October, and March to mid-May). Holiday weekends are peak times in Aqaba and at the Dead Sea resorts.

RSCN Eco-lodges Some of the best accommodation in Jordan is offered at sustainable lodges in the country's nature reserves.

Hotels Most hotels in Jordan are family-run enterprises with a long tradition of hospitality towards travellers.

SLEEPING PRICE RANGES

Prices in reviews are for double rooms in high season (September to October, and from March to early May) and include private bathroom and breakfast unless otherwise indicated.

$ less than JD40

$$ JD40 to JD90

$$$ more than JD90

Resorts Five-star luxury can be found at resorts in Amman, Aqaba, Wadi Musa and the Dead Sea.

ACTIVITIES

With the opening of the Jordan Trail (p305) and Jordan Bike Trail, Jordan has become a hotspot for outdoor activities. There is camel riding and ballooning in Wadi Rum, organised through Bait Ali Lodge (p336), water sports and birdwatching easily arranged through hotels and dive centres in Aqaba, and 4WD driving along the Eastern Badia Trail to Burqu through the RSCN.

Hiking is particularly well organised in Jordan at Petra and in the RSCN reserves, including Dana Biosphere Reserve, Wadi Rum Protected Area and Mujib Biosphere Reserve. Mujib offers some great canyoning and rappelling while Wadi Rum is the Middle East's premier climbing destination.

CHILDREN

Children are universally adored in Jordan, so you'll find that taking the kids adds a welcome dimension to your trip. Children are instant ice breakers and will guarantee contact with local people, especially as foreign families are still something of a novelty.

JORDAN PASS

The Jordan Pass (www.jordanpass.jo) is a highly recommended discount scheme offered by the Ministry of Tourism and Antiquities. It is easily obtained and readily recognised throughout Jordan. If passes are purchased online before arrival, the cost of a tourist visa for three or more nights' stay in Jordan is waived, in addition to giving free entry to Petra, Jerash and more than 40 other attractions.

There are three categories of pass that differ only in the number of days of entry covered at Petra – Jordan Wanderer (JD70; one day at Petra), Jordan Explorer (JD75; two days at Petra) and Jordan Expert (JD80; three days at Petra).

EATING PRICE RANGES

Prices in reviews represent the cost of a standard main-course dish, unless stated otherwise.

$ less than JD5

$$ JD5 to JD10

$$$ more than JD10

CUSTOMS REGULATIONS

- 1L of alcoholic spirits or two bottles of wine
- 200 cigarettes or 25 cigars or 200g of tobacco
- A 'reasonable amount of perfume for personal use'
- Gifts up to the value of JD50 or the equivalent of US$150
- Prohibitions include drugs, weapons, and pornographic films and magazines
- Exporting anything more than 100 years old is illegal, so don't buy any souvenir (including 'ancient' coins or oil lamps) that is deemed to be 'antique'. If you're unsure about an item's provenance, contact the Customs Department (www.customs.gov.jo).

EMBASSIES & CONSULATES

Most embassies and consulates are in Amman. In general, offices are open 9am to 11am Sunday to Thursday for visa applications and 1pm to 3pm for collecting visas.

Australian Embassy (Map p290; ☎06 580 7000; www.jordan.embassy.gov.au; 41 Kayed Al Armoti St, Abdoun)

Canadian Embassy (Map p290; ☎06 590 1500; www.canadainternational.gc.ca/jordan-jordanie; Zahran St)

Egyptian Embassy (Map p290; ☎06 560 5175; 22 Qortubah St, Jebel Amman; ⏲9am-noon Sun-Thu); there's also a consulate (☎03 201 6171; cnr Al Isteglal & Al Akhatal Sts; ⏲8am-3pm Sun-Thu) in Aqaba.

French Embassy (Map p296; ☎06 460 4630; www.ambafrance-jo.org; Al Mutanabbi St, Jebel Amman)

German Embassy (Map p296; ☎06 590 1170; www.amman.diplo.de; 31 Bin Ghazi St, Jebel Amman) Between 4th and 5th Circles.

Irish Consulate (Map p296; ☎06 553 3616; ireland_consulate@gmk.com.jo; Al Malek Al Hussein St, Jebel Amman)

Israeli Consulate (Map p290; ☎06 550 3500; http://embassies.gov.il/amman-en; Maysaloon St, Rabiyah)

Lebanese Embassy (Map p296; ☎06 592 9111; 17 Muhammad Ali Badir St) Near the UK embassy.

Netherlands Embassy (Map p290; ☎06 590 2200; www.nederlandwereldwijd.nl/landen/jordanie; 3 Abu Bakr Siraj Ad Din St) Near the 4th Circle.

UK Embassy (Map p296; ☎06 590 9200; www.gov.uk/government/world/organisations/british-embassy-amman; Dimashq St, Abdoun)

US Embassy (Map p290; ☎06 590 6000; https://jo.usembassy.gov; 20 Al Umawiyeen St, Abdoun)

FOOD

Eating in Jordan is primarily a social experience, whether conducted over a chat in Amman's cafes or sitting in cross-legged silence in a Bedouin tent. Anyone venturing beyond the bus-station kebab stands will quickly find that Jordanian food is not a tedious affair of falafel sandwiches but deliciously varied and culturally nuanced. Jordan is also beginning to be noted for its home-grown wines. The range of mezze, or side dishes, available with every meal ensures that vegetarians are well catered for.

GAY & LESBIAN TRAVELLERS

Homosexuality is illegal in most Islamic countries in the Middle East, but in Jordan gay sex is legal, and the age of consent is 16. Public displays of affection by heterosexuals are frowned upon, and the same rules apply to gays and lesbians, although same-sex hand-holding is a common sign of friendship in Jordan.

The legality of homosexuality shouldn't be confused with full societal acceptance, and discrimination and harassment is common. There is a subdued underground gay scene in Amman – if you're keen to explore it, keep your enquiries discreet.

Check www.gayguide.net/middle_east and the gay and lesbian thread of Lonely Planet's Thorn Tree bulletin board (www.lonelyplanet.com/thorntree) for more information.

INTERNET ACCESS

Wi-fi is standard (and mostly offered free) in hotels of most budgets, as well as many cafes and restaurants.

MONEY

The currency in Jordan is the dinar (JD) – known as the *jay-dee* among hip young locals – and is made up of 1000 fils. A piastre refers to 10 fils. Often when a price is quoted, the ending will be omitted, so if you're told that something is 25, it's a matter of working out whether it's 25 fils, 25 piastre or 25 dinars! Although it sounds confusing, most Jordanians wouldn't dream of ripping off a foreigner, with the possible exception of taxi drivers.

ATMs

It is possible to travel in Jordan almost entirely on plastic. ATMs giving cash advances abound in all but the smaller towns. There are no local charges on credit-card cash advances.

Visa is the most widely accepted card at ATMs, followed by MasterCard. Other cards, such as Cirrus and Plus, are also accepted by many ATMs (eg Jordan National Bank and HSBC).

Credit Cards

Credit cards are widely accepted in midrange and top-end hotels and restaurants, and a few top-end shops. A commission (up to 5%) is often added.

Moneychangers

It's easy to change money in Jordan. Most major currencies are accepted in cash. US dollars, UK pounds and euros are easier to change than Australian or New Zealand dollars. Travellers cheques are all but obsolete in Jordan.

There are no restrictions on bringing dinars into Jordan. It's possible to change dinars back into some foreign currencies in Jordan.

Lebanese, Egyptian and Israeli currency can all be changed in Amman. Egyptian and Israeli currency are also easily changed in Aqaba. Banks and moneychangers charge about the same for exchanging cash, but large hotels charge more. There are small branches of major banks at the borders and airports.

Tipping

Tips of 10% are generally expected in better restaurants. A service charge of 10% is automatically added at most midrange and top-end restaurants.

OPENING HOURS

Opening times vary widely across the country. Many sights, government departments and banks close earlier in winter and during Ramadan. The following opening hours are therefore a rough guide only. The official weekend in Jordan is Friday and Saturday, so expect curtailed hours on these days.

Banks 8am–3pm Sunday to Thursday
Bars and clubs 9pm–1am daily
Cafes 9am–midnight daily
Restaurants noon–midnight daily
Shops 9am–8pm Saturday to Thursday; some close 2pm–4pm
Souqs 9am–8pm daily

PHOTOGRAPHY

Digital accessories and memory cards are widely available.

Ask before taking taking shots of people, particularly women and the elderly, as some Jordanians object to being photographed. Avoid photographing border zones and any military installations or checkpoints.

POST

For postal information, Jordan Post (www.jordanpost.com.jo) has an informative website.

Reliable courier companies include FedEx (www.fedex.com/jo), which has an office in Amman, and DHL (www.dhl.com), which has offices in Amman and Aqaba.

PRACTICALITIES

Media

Radio Popular radio stations include Radio Jordan (96.3 FM), BBC World Service (1323 AM) and Popular hits (99.6 FM).

Newspapers The key English-language newspaper is the *Jordan Times* (www.jordantimes.com).

TV Jordan's Channel 2 (French and English) and satellite channels (BBC, CNN, MTV and Al Jazeera) are available in most midrange and top-end hotels.

Discount Cards

It makes sense for most travellers to buy a Jordan Pass (www.jordanpass.jo) online before entering the country: this waives the cost of a visa in addition to giving free access to many sites in Jordan, including Petra.

Smoking

There are laws banning smoking in public places, but these are not always enforced, except in top-end hotels and restaurants in Amman, the Dead Sea and Aqaba.

Weights & Measures

Jordan uses the metric system.

PUBLIC HOLIDAYS

In addition to the main Islamic holidays, Jordan observes the following:

New Year's Day 1 January
Good Friday March/April
Labour Day 1 May
Independence Day 25 May
Army Day and Anniversary of the Great Arab Revolt 10 June
Christmas Day 25 December

SAFE TRAVEL

Jordan is very safe to visit and, despite local dissatisfaction with issues such as Iraqi immigration, the Syrian refugee crisis, unemployment and high inflation, you are unlikely to feel any hint of the turmoil of neighbouring countries.

TELEPHONE

Mobile Phones

There is expansive coverage in Jordan for mobile phone networks. Local SIM cards can be used for international calls and can be topped up with readily available prepaid cards; 4G is increasingly available.

Two main service providers are Zain (www.zain.com) and Orange (www.orange.jo), both of which offer a full range of plans and prepaid SIM cards (ID required to purchase).

Phone Codes

962	Jordan country code
00	International access code

Area codes precede six- or seven-digit landline, mobile and info numbers.

02	Northern Jordan
03	Southern Jordan
05	Jordan Valley, central and eastern districts
06	Amman district
07	Prefix for eight-digit mobile phone numbers
0800	Prefix for toll-free numbers
1212	Local directory assistance (Amman)
131	Local directory assistance (elsewhere)
132 or 133	International directory assistance

TIME

Jordan is two hours ahead of GMT/UTC in winter and three hours ahead between 1 April and 1 October.

TOILETS

Most hotels and restaurants, except those in the budget category, now have Western-style toilets. Squat toilets come with either a hose or water bucket provided for cleaning and flushing. Toilet paper should be thrown in the bin provided, as the sewerage system is not designed for paper. Public toilets are generally best avoided except at Petra.

TOURIST INFORMATION

Jordan runs a good network of visitor centres inside the country, and the Jordan Tourism Board (www.visitjordan.com) has a comprehensive website.

TRAVELLERS WITH DISABILITIES

Jordan is not well set up for travellers with disabilities, but there is some good news:

- Wheelchair access is now mandatory in all new public buildings.
- Entry to some attractions, including Petra, is free for those with disabilities.
- Horse-drawn carriages are provided at Petra to help with access to the Siq and Treasury.
- A useful website (www.accessiblejordan.com) provides advice for travellers.

VISAS

Visas, required by all visitors, are available on arrival (JD40 for most nationalities) at the international airports and most of Jordan's land borders. The Jordan Pass (www.jordanpass.jo) is recognised at all land borders.

If you arrive in Jordan's southern city of Aqaba by air on an international flight or by sea from Nuweiba in Egypt, you are entitled to a free visa as part of the free-trade agreement with the Aqaba Special Economic Zone Area (ASEZA).

Exceptions

Currently visas for Jordan are issued at Sheikh Hussein Bridge from Israel, but not at King Hussein Bridge or Wadi Araba. Check the latest status of Jordan's border crossings on the Jordan Tourism Board website (http://international.visitjordan.com/GeneralInformation/GettingAround/Bordercrossings.aspx).

Extensions

In Amman and Aqaba visas can easily be extended, for a charge of JD40, for stays of up to three months. The maximum stay allowed on an extended tourist visa is six months. Failure to register results in a fine of JD1.500 for every day you have overstayed. This is payable when you extend, or on departure from Jordan at a counter just before immigration at Queen Alia International Airport in Amman.

In Amman, you can start the process of lodging your visa extension paperwork at **Al Madeenah Police Station** (Map p292; 06 465 7788; 1st fl, Al Malek Faisal St, Downtown), opposite the Arab Bank.

WOMEN TRAVELLERS

Women are on the whole unlikely to feel uncomfortable travelling alone in Jordan. To avoid harassment, it's best to dress conservatively, wear shorts and a loose T-shirt over swimwear on public beaches (it's not necessary to cover your head) and be cautious of unsolicited declarations of love. Many restaurants usher female customers into their family areas and women don't sit next to the driver in taxis.

WORK

There's not much in the way of casual work in Jordan as all such jobs are in hot demand from refugees. Skilled employment is best sought in advance of arrival.

Getting There & Away

Jordan can be entered from Egypt by boat or from Israel and the Palestinian Territories by bus or taxi; you can bring your own car or motorcycle (but not hire car). Leaving Jordan by land requires a little more planning and onward travel in the region can be problematic after visiting Israel and the Palestinian Territories. Check the latest situation in northern Sinai in Egypt, and around Jerusalem in Israel and the Palestinian Territories before venturing across the border.

AIR

Queen Alia International Airport (☎06 401 0250; www.qaiairport.com), about 35km south of Amman, is the country's main gateway. Car-rental agencies are located in the arrivals building.

The only other international airport is at Aqaba, where some international carriers stop en route to Amman. Flights to Sharm El Sheikh in Egypt are handled from here.

The national airline, Royal Jordanian (www.rj.com), is well established with a good safety record. It has direct flights to most major cities in Europe and all Middle Eastern capitals, and runs short flights from Amman to Aqaba (twice daily). Royal Wings (www.royalwings.com.jo), a subsidiary of Royal Jordanian, has smaller planes and runs expensive charter flights.

A number of airlines fly to Jordan:

Air Arabia (www.airarabia.com)
Air France (www.airfrance.com)
British Airways (www.ba.com)
Emirates (www.emirates.com)
Fly Dubai (www.flydubai.com)
Gulf Air (www.gulfair.com)
Iraqi Airways (www.ia.com.iq)
KLM (www.klm.com)
Kuwait Airways (www.kuwaitairways.com)
Lufthansa Airlines (www.lufthansa.com)
Qatar Airways (www.qatarairways.com)
Saudi Arabian Airlines (www.saudia.com)
Turkish Airlines (www.turkishairlines.com)

> **BEWARE THE TRICKS OF THE TRADE**
>
> **Taken for a ride** The taxi fare quoted on the meter is in fils, not in dinars, and visitors often misunderstand this when paying. Perhaps understandably, it is rare for a taxi driver to point out this mistake.
>
> **Crafty business** Shop owners often claim something is genuinely locally crafted as part of a profit-share scheme, when in fact it is imported from abroad.
>
> **Money for old rope** So-called 'antiques' are often merely last year's stock that has gathered an authentic-looking layer of dust. Similarly, 'ancient' oil lamps and coins are seldom what they are purported to be.

LAND

It's easy to reach Jordan by land from Israel and the Palestinian Territories. Foreign residents of Saudi Arabia (and transit passengers who can show they have no other way of reaching Jordan) are also able to cross Saudi Arabia and enter Jordan by land.

Saudi Arabia

Getting a visa, even a transit visa, to Saudi Arabia is very difficult. If you are eligible for a visa, the main land route for public transport is at Al Umari, south of Azraq. The other two crossing points are Ad Durra, south of Aqaba, and further east at Al Mudawwara. Several companies run services to and from Jeddah and Riyadh from Amman's Abdali bus station.

The air-conditioned JETT bus travels to Jeddah, Riyadh and Dammam.

Israel & the Palestinian Territories

There are currently no direct services between Amman and Jerusalem or Tel Aviv. Of the three border crossings, Sheikh Hussein Bridge, King Hussein Bridge and Wadi Araba, King Hussein Bridge is the most commonly used and easiest to reach from Amman, but may require extra time and patience as there are often delays.

The borders are closed for Yom Kippur and the Islamic New Year.

Sheikh Hussein Bridge (Jordan River)

Regular service taxis travel between the West bus station at Irbid and the border (JD15, 45 minutes). Private taxis cost JD50 from Irbid. You can ask Jordanian immigration not to stamp your passport here.

Buses cross the bridge (around JD2) run roughly every 30 minutes.

DEPARTURE TAX

Jordan's departure tax for travellers is JD8 by land and sea, and JD15 by air. If you are leaving by air, the departure tax is generally included in the ticket price.

Taxis go to the Beit She'an bus station (10 minutes) for onward connections. To get to Tel Aviv, it's quickest to get from Beit She'an to Afula and change there.

Travelling in the other direction, take a bus to Tiberias and change at Beit She'an (6km from the border). From there, take another bus to the Israeli border (arrive early because there are few buses).

Israeli exit tax is 100NIS at this border. The transfer bus across the bridge to the Jordanian side costs around 10NIS.

The border is open 8am to 10pm Sunday to Thursday and 9am to 8pm Friday and Saturday.

King Hussein Bridge (Allenby Bridge)

Take a service taxi from Amman's **Abdali bus station** (Map p296; Al Malek Al Hussein St, Jebel Amman) to King Hussein Bridge (JD10, 45 minutes) or there's a single daily JETT bus (JD10, one hour, 7am). A private taxi to the bridge costs around JD25. Public transport stops at the immigration terminal for locals; make sure you're dropped at the second terminal, for foreigners.

The two border posts are 5km apart. Buses (JD7 plus JD1.5 per piece of luggage, 10 minutes to one hour – depending on waiting time) shuttle between the two borders (expect long delays). It's not possible to walk or take a private vehicle across this border.

Jordanian immigration officials won't stamp your passport here – you're given an exit form instead. If you're coming back to Jordan, you can return at this crossing within two weeks without needing a new visa. There's an exit fee of JD8.

Be prepared for slow progress (around two hours) at the border. If you're in a rush, a VIP service at the terminal is available for around JD80.

To get to Jerusalem from the border, take a sherut (Israeli shared taxi; around 42NIS plus 5NIS for luggage, 30 minutes) to Jerusalem's Damascus Gate.

Travelling in the other direction, there's an Israeli exit tax of 174NIS. If you intend to return to Israel, keep the Jordanian entrance form safe – you will have to present it on exiting the border.

The border is open 8am to 8pm Sunday to Thursday and 8am to 1pm Friday and Saturday.

Wadi Araba (Yitzhak Rabin)

Taxis run between Aqaba and the border (JD10, 15 minutes). There's an exit fee of JD8. You can walk the short distance across the border in a matter of minutes.

Buses run to central Eilat, 2km away (five minutes). Taxis cost around 50NIS.

Travelling in the other direction, buses from Jerusalem to Eilat will stop at the turn-off for the border (five minutes), a short walk away.

Israeli exit tax is 100NIS at this border. Currently you can't obtain a visa for Jordan at this border.

The border is open 6.30am to 8pm Sunday to Thursday and 8am to 8pm Friday and Saturday.

Other Destinations

To travel between other destinations in the Middle East and Jordan, travellers need time, patience and, most importantly, the necessary visas. Most trips involve long, hot journeys with frustrating delays so most people end up flying. It remains inadvisable to travel to Syria or Iraq at the present time.

JETT has a coach service to Cairo (JD35), twice per week departing from the international bus office in Amman. Check with the JETT office ahead of your departure as schedules and prices change frequently.

SEA

Visiting Egypt is a popular side trip from Aqaba or feasible as part of an onward journey. Most nationalities can obtain Egyptian tourist visas on the boat or on arrival at Nuweiba (the Egyptian consulate in Aqaba also issues visas). Note that full visas are not issued in Taba, only the two-week Sinai Visitor Pass.

There are two main boat services to Egypt, which leave from the passenger terminal just south of Aqaba. Departure times are often subject to change so check with Arab Bridge Maritime (www.abmaritime.com.jo), which operates the services, before travelling.

The fast boat to Taba (US$60, one hour) leaves daily at 10pm. Fares for children aged between six and 12 are US$38 (under six US$32). The return ferry leaves Taba at 1.30pm.

There is also a slower regular service (US$45, three hours) departing twice daily at 11am and 2pm. Fares are reduced for children aged under eight (US$23). It's notorious for being delayed. Services from Nuweiba leave at noon and 1pm.

Departure tax (JD8) is not included in the ticket prices. You need to show your passport to buy tickets. Note that fares from Nuweiba must be paid for in US dollars, but there are currency exchange facilities at the terminals at Aqaba and Nuweiba. Passports are collected on the boat in both directions and handed back on arrival at immigration.

ℹ Getting Around

Public transport is designed primarily for the locals and as it is notoriously difficult to reach many of the sights of interest (especially the

Dead Sea, desert castles and King's Highway) consider hiring a car or using tours organised by hotels in Amman and Madaba.

AIR

There is only one domestic air route, between Amman and Aqaba.

Royal Jordanian (www.rj.com) Flights twice daily (one way around JD52, one hour).

Royal Wings (www.royalwings.com.jo) A subsidiary of Royal Jordanian, offering expensive charter flights.

BICYCLE

Cycling can be fun or sheer folly depending on the time of year. From March to May and September to November are the best times to get on your bike – you won't have to battle with the stifling summer heat or the bitter winter winds. Spare parts aren't always common in Jordan. Bike hire is available from Bike Rush (p300) in Amman.

BUS & MINIBUS

The national bus company JETT (p299) operates air-conditioned, nonstop services between Amman and Aqaba, King Hussein Bridge border crossing (7am daily) and Petra (6.30am daily).

Public minibuses are the most common form of public transport. They normally only leave when full and tickets are bought on the bus.

CAR

Hiring a car is a good way to visit Jordan as public transport caters almost solely to local needs. Driving in Jordan is relatively easy (with the exception of chaotic Amman), and there are some spectacular routes. International Driving Permits (IDP) are not necessary for hiring a car. Road conditions are reasonable but petrol stations are scarce along the King's Highway and Dead Sea Hwy.

Hire

There are many car-hire agencies in Amman (around King Abdullah Gardens in Shmeisani), a few in Aqaba and one or two at Queen Alia International Airport and the King Hussein border with Israel and the Palestinian Territories. Drivers must be over 21 and some companies stipulate an upper age limit of 65 years.

Daily rates are around JD50 with a deposit of up to JD400 payable upon pick-up (usually by credit card) and refunded upon return of the car. It's not possible to drive a hire car from Jordan into neighbouring countries.

Insurance

If you're driving into Jordan in a private vehicle, compulsory third-party insurance must be purchased at the border from about JD40 (valid for one month). You also pay a nominal customs fee of JD5 for 'foreign car registration' (obtainable at the borders with Jordan and the ferry terminal in Nuweiba, Egypt).

Road Rules

Vehicles drive on the right-hand side of the road in Jordan. The general speed limit inside built-up areas is 50km/h or 70km/h on multilane highways in Amman, and 90km/h to 110km/h on the national highways.

Wearing a seatbelt is compulsory. Traffic police are positioned at intervals along the highways and you should keep your passport, licence and rental paperwork handy for the many checkpoints.

HITCHING

Hitching is never entirely safe, and we don't recommend it. Travellers who hitch should understand that they are taking a small but potentially serious risk. Hitching is sometimes used as a means of transport in Jordan in areas where public transport is limited or nonexistent, such as parts of the King's Highway and to the desert castles east of Amman.

LOCAL TRANSPORT

Local city buses are generally packed, routes are confusing and the chances of being pickpocketed are higher. Take a service taxi instead.

Private taxis are good value in the cities. Note that metered fares are displayed in fils not dinars, and if you proffer the fare in dinars by mistake, the driver is unlikely to correct you.

White service taxis are a little more expensive than minibuses and don't cover as many routes, but they are generally faster and take less time to fill up (there are generally only four seats).

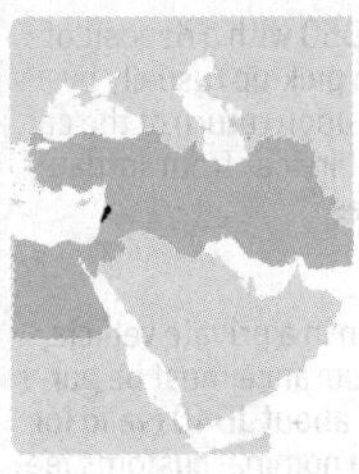

Lebanon

Includes ➡

Beirut 356
Byblos (Jbail) 373
Batroun 375
Tripoli (Trablous) 377
The Qadisha Valley 380
Sidon (Saida) 382
Tyre (Sour) 385
Chouf Mountains 387
Baalbek 390
Understand Lebanon 392
Survival Guide 401

Best Places to Eat

- Liza (p367)
- Baron (p367)
- Mayrig (p367)
- Onno (p365)
- Feniqia (p375)

Best Places to Stay

- Saifi Urban Gardens (p362)
- Hotel Albergo (p364)
- The Grand Meshmosh Hotel (p362)
- L'Auberge de la Mer (p376)
- Smallville Hotel (p363)

Why Go?

This diminutive Mediterranean nation is a fascinating nexus point of the Middle East and the West; of Christianity and Islam; of tradition and modernity. It's a place where culture, family and religion are all-important, but where sectarian violence can too often erupt – claiming lives and scarring both the landscape and the national psyche.

Home to a glorious national cuisine, a string of sexy beach resorts and the Middle East's most glamorous, hedonistic city (Beirut), this is also a country where the fiery orators and fierce foot soldiers of Hezbollah are based, and where huge populations of Palestinian and Syrian refugees currently shelter. Damaged by decades of civil war and the invasions and interventions of neighbouring nations, Lebanon is nonetheless blessed with magnificent mountain vistas, majestic ancient ruins and an indomitable, hospitable people. Lebanon rewards the traveller with food for thought and a feast for the senses and the stomach.

When to Go

Beirut

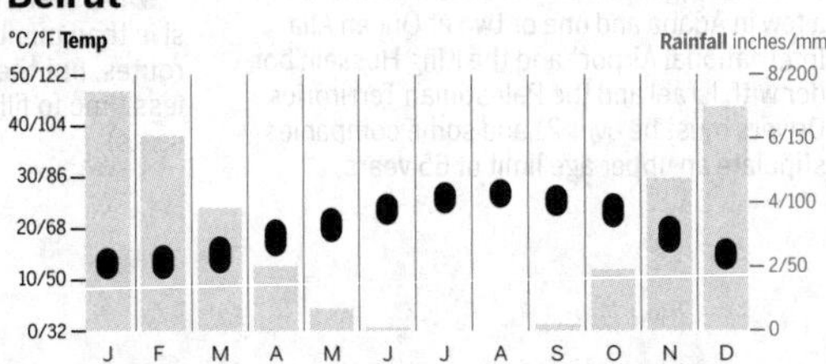

Dec–Apr Skiing – and après-ski parties – in the mountains.

May–Sep The perfect time to go hiking along wild trails and through cedar forests.

Jun–Aug Beirut's famous beach lounges and nightclubs beckon.

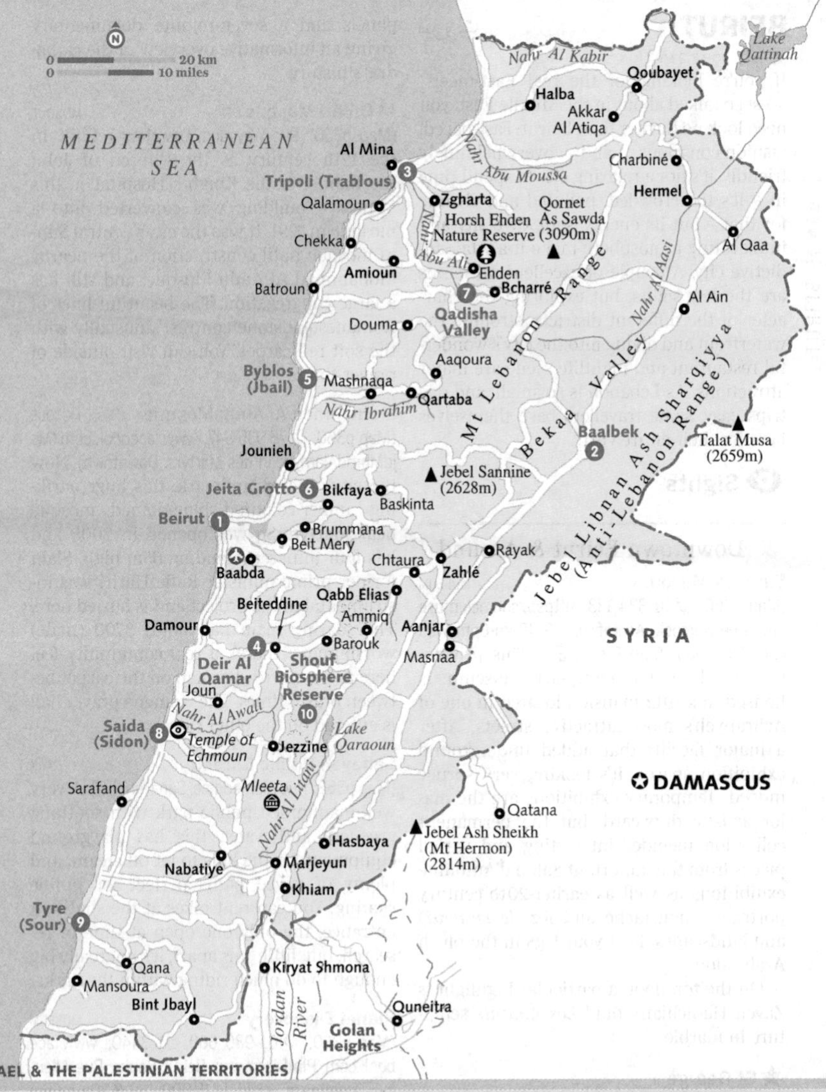

Lebanon Highlights

1. **Beirut** (p356) Partying at beach lounges and rooftop bars.
2. **Baalbek** (p391) Gazing at one of the best-preserved of all Roman temples.
3. **Tripoli** (p377) Soaking up the atmosphere of the traditional souq area.
4. **Deir Al Qamar** (p389) Taking in the atmosphere of one of Lebanon's most beautiful villages.
5. **Byblos** (p373) Wandering through ruins and celebrating a Mediterranean sunset.
6. **Jeita Grotto** (p373) Marvelling at the glittering stalactites and stalagmites.
7. **Qadisha Valley** (p380) Hiking past rock-cut monasteries and gushing waterfalls.
8. **Saida** (p383) Exploring the historic centre of this traditional seaside town.
9. **Tyre** (p385) Walking in the footsteps of the Romans and bathing in crystal-clear waters.
10. **Shouf Biosphere Reserve** (p388) Breathing in crisp, cedar-scented air.

BEIRUT بيروت

☎01 / POP 2.2 MILLION

If you're looking for the real East-meets-West so talked about in the Middle East, you need look no further than Beirut. Fast-paced, fashion-conscious and overwhelmingly friendly, it's not a relaxing city to spend time in – it's too crowded, polluted and chaotic for that – but its energy, soul, diversity and intoxicating atmosphere make it a vital, addictive city. A couple of excellent museums are the key sights, but exploring the character of the different districts, strolling the waterfront and diving into the city's wonderful restaurant and nightlife scene are major attractions. As Lebanon is so small, and day trips easy, some travellers base themselves here for their entire visit.

Sights

Downtown Beirut & Around

Sursock Museum MUSEUM

(Map p360; ☎01 334 133; https://sursock.museum; Rue Sursock, Achrafiyeh; ⊙10am-6pm Wed & Fri-Mon, noon-9pm Thu) FREE This privately owned contemporary-art museum is housed in a 1912 mansion located in one of Achrafiyeh's most attractive streets. After a major facelift that added underground exhibition spaces, it's looking very spruce indeed. Temporary exhibitions are the major artistic drawcard, but the permanent collection includes interesting and varied pieces from the important Salon d'Automne exhibitions as well as earlier-20th-century portraits (moustache and fez *de rigueur*) and landscapes. Rest your legs in the plush Arab salon.

On the top floor, a particular highlight is Zaven Hadichian's fluid *Les Amants* sculpture in marble.

★St George Crypt Museum ARCHAEOLOGICAL SITE

(Map p360; Pl d'Étoile, Downtown; adult/child 5000/1000LL; ⊙10am-6pm Tue-Sun) When a bomb fell on the **Orthodox cathedral** in 1975, the only silver lining was that it revealed these ruins beneath. Though the area is small, an excellent and atmospheric archaeological display outlines elements from different parts of the city's history: Seleucid to medieval, with the highlights being Byzantine mosaic floors and a number of spooky tombs. There are good information panels and a seven-minute documentary giving an informative overview of the cathedral's history.

Al Omari Mosque MOSQUE

(Map p360; Rue Weygand, Downtown) Built in the 12th century as the Church of John the Baptist of the Knights Hospitaller, this attractive building was converted into a mosque in 1291. It was the city's central Sunni mosque until construction of the nearby Mohammad Al Amin Mosque, and still has a large congregation. The beautiful lines of Romanesque stone contrast unusually with the soft red carpet. You can visit outside of prayer time.

Mohammed Al Amin Mosque MOSQUE

(Map p360; ☎76 935 847; www.facebook.com/MsjdMhmdAlamyn; Pl des Martyrs, Downtown) Now the city's major landmark, this huge, striking amber-coloured blue-domed mosque near Martyrs Sq was opened in 2008 and has four minarets standing 65m high. Slain former prime minister Rafic Hariri was instrumental in the project and is buried here. The soaring main hall holds 3700 (male) worshippers; there's a real community feel here as people read or nap on the carpet between prayer times. The women's prayer hall is entered on the other side.

Sanayeh Public Garden PARK

(Map p362; Rue Alameddine, Sanayeh; 👪) A very well-maintained public park with soothing greenery and water, this has playground equipment for the kids to let off steam, and plenty of paved paths perfect for in-line skating. You can rent bikes at the southern entrance, the only one open at time of research, but, little 'uns apart, it's not really big enough to do much riding within the park.

Planet Discovery MUSEUM

(Map p360; ☎01 980 660, ext 3440; www.facebook.com/PlntDiscovery; Beirut Souks, Rue Allenby, Downtown; child LL15,000; ⊙8.30am-6pm Mon-Fri, 10.30am-7pm Sat & Sun; 👪) This activity centre and interactive science museum in the Souks shopping arcades is aimed at young children and offers a science museum that's very hands on and engaging. There's a separate art workshop where kids can mould clay or paint ceramics (from 7500LL); they are supervised, so parents sometimes park their kids here to browse some shops. Puppet shows are held at 4pm and 5pm most Fridays to Sundays, and there are other regular events.

Cardo Maximus RUINS

(Map p360; Rue Emir Bechir, Downtown) The 'cardo maximus' was the principal north–south street of a Roman city, and you can see the evocative remains of Beirut's cardo maximus between the city's major religious buildings, showing that this area has been the city centre for a long time. There's little interpretation available, but you can make out the course of the road and the foundations of what were probably shops alongside.

Maronite Cathedral of St George CATHEDRAL

(Map p360; Rue Emir Bechir, Downtown) The neo classical facade of this late 19th-century cathedral, next to the Mohammed Al Amin mosque, was inspired by the Basilica di Santa Maria Maggiore in Rome. It's the seat of the city's Maronite archdiocese. The interior is done out in marble, with volute-topped columns, a gilt coffered ceiling and an ornate baldachin over the altar.

Hamra & Western Beirut

Dar El Nimer CULTURAL CENTRE

(Map p362; 01 367 013; www.darelnimer.org/en; Rue d'Amerique, Hamra; 11am-7pm Mon-Sat) FREE Housed in a gorgeous 1930s villa, Dar El Nimer features rotating art exhibits and an impressive permanent collection including decorative arts, glass, coins and manuscripts spanning 10 centuries from Palestine and the Levant. Check the website for upcoming music or literature events, usually free and almost always worth attending.

Pigeon Rocks NATURAL FEATURE

(Roches de Raouché; Map p358; Ave du Général de Gaulle, Raouché) These limestone outcrops just offshore are prime selfie territory and a Beirut landmark. They are impressive; one has an archway eroded through it. A couple of cafes here do awful food but are decent spots to sit and admire the view with a shisha or beer.

American University of Beirut UNIVERSITY

(AUB; Map p362; www.aub.edu.lb; Rue Bliss, Hamra; visitor office 10am-4pm Mon-Fri) One of the Middle East's most prestigious and expensive universities, the AUB was founded in 1866 by American Protestant missionary Daniel Bliss. Spread over 28 tree-filled hectares, it is a true oasis in this fume-filled city. The on-site **archaeological museum** (01 340 549; www.aub.edu.lb/museum_archeo/Pages/index.aspx; 9am-4pm Mon-Fri, closed university holidays) FREE was founded in 1868, and has a fine collection of Lebanese and Middle Eastern artefacts dating back to the early Stone Age. Inside the university gate, a visitor office can arrange a free tour of the campus.

NEED TO KNOW

Capital Beirut

Country code 961

Languages Arabic, English, French

Official name Republic of Lebanon

Population 6.4 million (unofficial estimate including refugees)

Currency Lebanese lira/pound (LL); US dollar (US$)

Mobile phones Coverage extends throughout most of the country.

Visas Free one-month, single-entry tourist visas are available at Rafic Hariri International Airport for citizens of many countries.

Exchange Rates

Australia	A$1	LL1201
Canada	C$1	LL1230
Euro zone	€1	LL1754
Israel & the Palestinian Territories	1NIS	LL424
Japan	¥100	LL1354
New Zealand	NS$1	LL1112
UK	UK£1	LL1957
USA	US$1	LL1508

For current exchange rates, see www.xe.com.

Southern Beirut

★**National Museum of Beirut** MUSEUM

(Mathaf; Map p358; 01 426 703; www.beirutnationalmuseum.com; cnr Rue de Damas & Ave Abdallah Yafi, Badaro; adult/child LL5000/1000; 9am-5pm Tue-Sun) Located on the former Green Line, this is Beirut's major cultural institution. Its impressive, magnificently displayed collection of archaeological artefacts offers a great overview of Lebanon's history and the civilisations that impacted this cultural crossroads. Highlights include

Greater Beirut

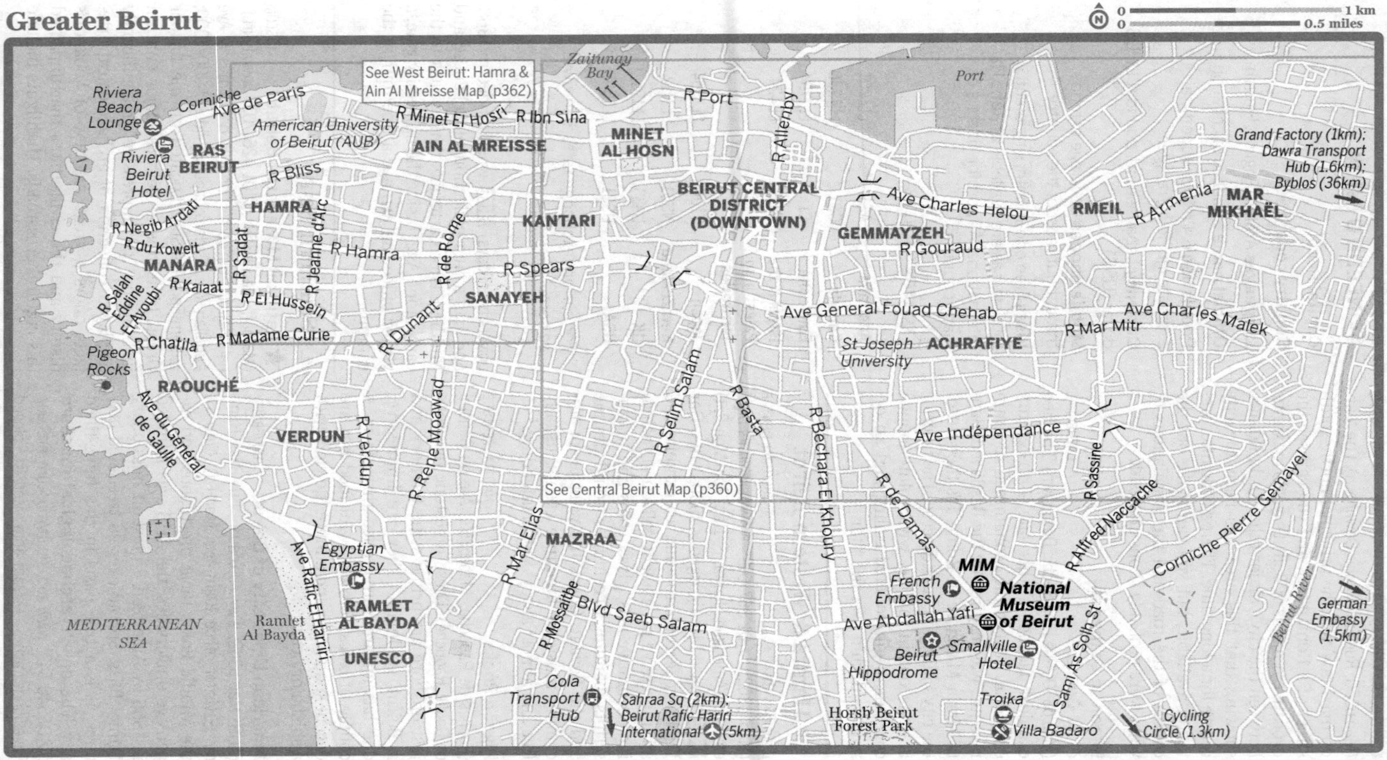

0 — 1 km
0 — 0.5 miles

See West Beirut: Hamra & Ain Al Mreisse Map (p362)
See Central Beirut Map (p360)

Zaitunay Bay
Port
Riviera Beach Lounge
Corniche
Ave de Paris
American University of Beirut (AUB)
R Minet El Hosri
R Ibn Sina
MINET AL HOSN
R Port
R Allenby
Grand Factory (1km); Dawra Transport Hub (1.6km); Byblos (36km)
Riviera Beirut Hotel
RAS BEIRUT
AIN AL MREISSE
R Bliss
BEIRUT CENTRAL DISTRICT (DOWNTOWN)
Ave Charles Helou
MAR MIKHAËL
RMEIL
R Armenia
HAMRA
R Negib Ardati
R du Koweit
MANARA
R Sadat
R Jeanne d'Arc
R Hamra
R de Rome
KANTARI
GEMMAYZEH
R Gouraud
R Spears
R Kaiaat
R El Hussein
SANAYEH
R Salah Eddine El Ayoubi
Ave General Fouad Chehab
Ave Charles Malek
R Mar Mitr
R Dunant
R Chatila
R Madame Curie
St Joseph University
ACHRAFIYE
Pigeon Rocks
RAOUCHÉ
Ave du Général de Gaulle
VERDUN
R Verdun
R Rene Moawad
R Selim Salam
R Basta
R Bechara El Khoury
Ave Indépendance
R Sassine
R de Damas
R Alfred Naccache
Corniche Pierre Gemayel
Beirut River
MAZRAA
R Mar Elias
Egyptian Embassy
Ave Rafic El Harriri
MIM
French Embassy
National Museum of Beirut
German Embassy (1.5km)
MEDITERRANEAN SEA
Ramlet Al Bayda
RAMLET AL BAYDA
R Mossaitbe
Blvd Saeb Salam
Ave Abdallah Yafi
Sami As Solh St
Beirut Hippodrome
Smallville Hotel
UNESCO
Cola Transport Hub
Sahraa Sq (2km); Beirut Rafic Hariri International (5km)
Horsh Beirut Forest Park
Troika
Villa Badaro
Cycling Circle (1.3km)

the famous, much-photographed Phoenician gilded bronze figurines found buried near the Obelisk Temple at Byblos; a series of human-faced Phoenician sarcophagi and a frescoed Roman tomb, these latter in the outstanding basement, reopened in 2016.

At the start of your visit, leave your passport at the front desk and borrow one of the museum's complimentary iPads so that you can scan labels on significant pieces in the collection to receive a commentary about each (bring your own headphones if possible). You may also wish to view the 12-minute documentary that is screened in the audiovisual room off the foyer, which plays every hour on the hour between 9am and 4pm. This details how curators saved the museum's collection during the civil war and subsequently restored it to its former glory.

It's worth starting your visit on the upper floor (take the right-hand stairs to go chronologically forwards) as this gives you an overview of the sweep of Lebanese history and lets you sort out your Seleucids from your Phoenicians. The collection of Bronze Age artefacts here is of extraordinary quality: as well as the Byblos figurines, admire the obsidian-and-gold coffer and Egyptian gold pectorals found in the same royal necropolis, and the exquisite ivory make-up boxes from Saida. Other highlights include an extraordinary Attic drinking vessel in the shape of a pig's head; a marble head of Bacchus from the Roman period; and a magnificent collection of Phoenician glass.

On the ground floor, some excellent Byzantine mosaics are notable, as well as two wonderful carved sarcophagi from Tyre dating from the 2nd century AD: one depicts drunken cupids and the other the legend of Achilles. Also here are the much-loved Phoenician statues of baby boys; these were commissioned by aristocrats from Saida as ex-votos to Echmoun, the Phoenican god of healing, to thank him for saving their children.

The atmospheric and beautifully presented basement (easily missed; look behind the stairs) is a standout, holding the eerie series of human-faced sarcophagi from Saida as well as an intriguing reconstruction of a 2nd-century AD collective tomb from Tyre, with wall paintings depicting mythological scenes. Much earlier Chalcolithic pot burials are also interesting, while three evocatively mummified bodies and perfectly preserved clothing tell a poignant 13th-century story. Perhaps fleeing from the Crusader wars, they died in a Qadisha Valley cave still clutching the title deeds to their land, foreshadowing a story repeated in refugee camps across Lebanon today.

★MIM MUSEUM

(Map p358; ☎01 421 672; www.mim.museum; Rue de Damas, Ras Al Nabaa; adult/teen/child LL6000/2000/free; ⏲10am-1pm & 2-6pm Tue-Sun) Under the St Joseph university, this atmospheric and beautifully designed museum presents an extraordinary collection of exquisitely selected and presented minerals. The otherworldly colours and forms produced in the earth's hidden recesses are astonishing. No less so is a room of fabulous fish fossils from Mémoire du Temps (p375) in Byblos, as well as a rare, perfectly preserved pterosaur. Interactive and innovative displays add to the experience. It's very close to the National Museum, accessed via the university's main glass doorway.

Activities

Cycling Circle CYCLING

(The Bike Kitchen; ☎03 126 675; www.cycling-circle.com; Rue 45, Fourn El Chabak; ⏲3.30-8pm Mon-Fri) A pioneer in promoting cycling culture in Lebanon, this friendly set-up organises cycling tours in Beirut and around the country, and is an excellent source of cycling advice. They also rent out bikes from their shop.

Riviera Beach Lounge SWIMMING

(Map p358; ☎01 373 210; www.rivierahotel.com.lb; Ave de Paris, Ras Beirut; adult/child weekdays LL33,000/20,000, weekends LL43,000/25,000; ⏲9am-6pm May-Oct; 👪) The pool/beach parties at Riviera resemble those held in Las Vegas or Ibiza, with international DJs and free-flowing alcohol. Families tend to congregate at 'Little Riviera', a kids pool and cafe serving kid-friendly food. You can hire jet skis, go diving or try out parasailing. You can also hire pool beds or private bungalows.

Saint George Yacht Club and Marina SWIMMING

(Map p360; ☎01 356 065; www.stgeorges-yacht-club.com; Zaitunay Bay, Downtown; adult weekday/weekend US$23/27, child US$20/23; ⏲9am-6pm; 👪) Though the famous hotel that this was part of is still in legal dispute over a planned forced acquisition, this is one of the most family-friendly of the beach clubs. There's no party scene here, so it's a good choice if you're interested in relaxation rather than raunch. It's right on the marina boardwalk.

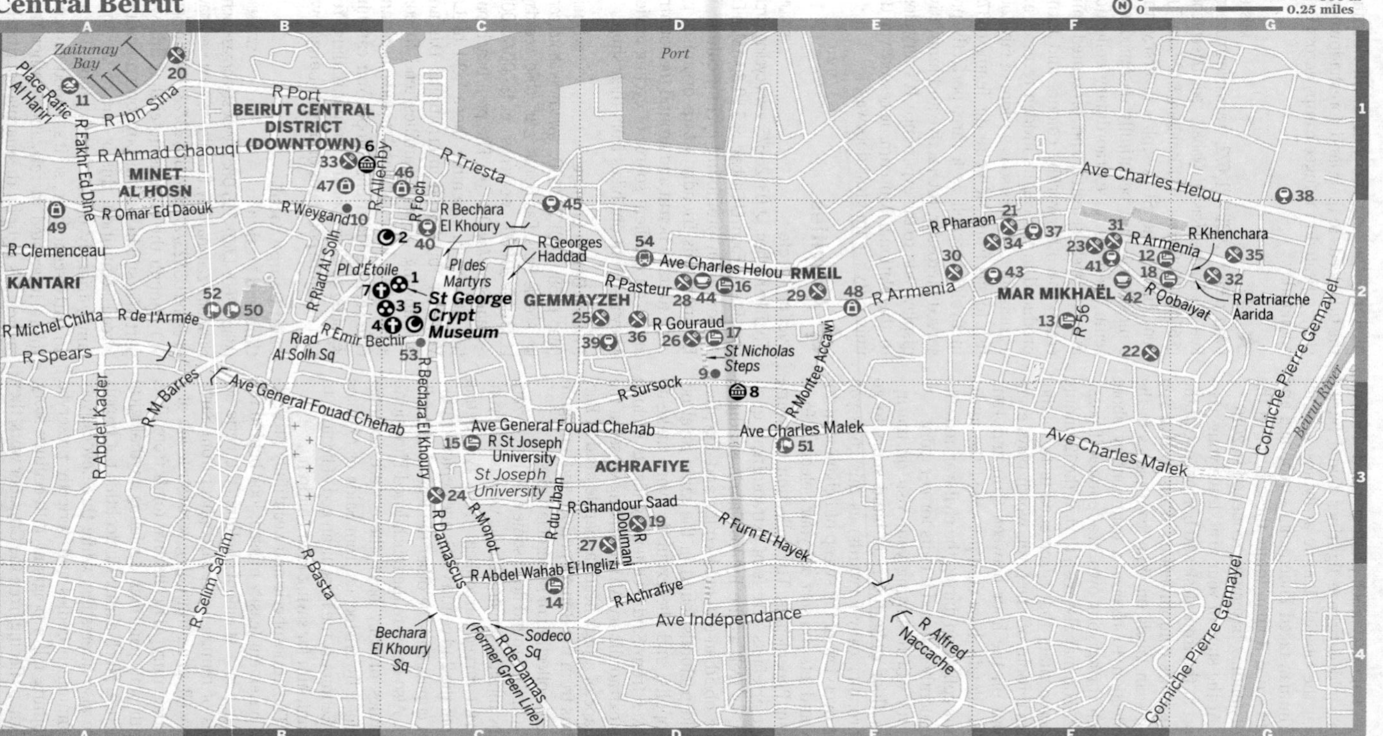
Central Beirut
500 m
0.25 miles
Port
Zaitunay Bay
Place Rafic Al Hariri
Beirut River
BEIRUT CENTRAL DISTRICT (DOWNTOWN)
MINET AL HOSN
KANTARI
GEMMAYZEH
RMEIL
MAR MIKHAËL
ACHRAFIYE
St George Crypt Museum
R Port
R Ibn Sina
R Fakhr Ed Dine
R Ahmad Chaouqi
R Omar Ed Daouk
R Clemenceau
R Michel Chiha
R de l'Armée
R Spears
R Abdel Kader
R M Barres
R Selim Salam
R Basta
R Weygand
R Allenby
R Foch
R Riad Al Solh
Pl d'Étoile
R Emir Bechir
Riad Al Solh Sq
R Bechara El Khoury
Pl des Martyrs
R Triesta
R Georges Haddad
Ave Charles Helou
R Pasteur
R Gouraud
St Nicholas Steps
R Sursock
R Montee Accawi
R Armenia
R Pharaon
R Khenchara
R Qobaiyat
R Patriarche Aarida
R 56
Corniche Pierre Gemayel
Ave General Fouad Chehab
Ave Charles Malek
R St Joseph University
St Joseph University
R Damascus
R Monot
R du Liban
R Ghandour Saad
R Doumani
R Furn El Hayek
R Abdel Wahab El Inglizi
R Achrafiye
Ave Indépendance
R Alfred Naccache
Bechara El Khoury Sq
Sodeco Sq
R de Damas (Former Green Line)

Central Beirut

Top Sights
1 St George Crypt Museum ... C2

Sights
2 Al Omari Mosque ... C2
3 Cardo Maximus ... C2
4 Maronite Cathedral of St George ... C2
5 Mohammed Al Amin Mosque ... C2
6 Planet Discovery ... B1
7 St George Greek Orthodox Cathedral ... B2
8 Sursock Museum ... D3

Activities, Courses & Tours
9 Alternative Beirut ... D2
10 Free Walking Tour Beirut ... B2
11 St George Yacht Club ... A1

Sleeping
12 Baffa House ... F2
13 Hostel Beirut ... F2
14 Hotel Albergo ... C4
15 O Monot ... C3
Plan Bey ... (see 23)
16 Saifi Urban Gardens ... D2
17 The Grand Meshmosh Hotel ... D2
18 Villa Clara ... F2

Eating
19 Bab Sharki Le Jardin ... D3
20 Babel Bay ... A1
21 Baron ... F2
Café Em Nazih ... (see 16)
22 El Brimo ... F2
23 Enab ... F2
24 Falafel Sayhoun ... C3
25 Kahwet Leila ... D2
26 Le Chef ... D2
27 Liza ... D3
28 Loris ... D2
29 Mayrig ... E2
30 Oslo ... E2
31 Samakati ... F2
32 Seza ... G2
33 Souk El Tayeb ... B1
34 Tavolina ... F2
35 Tawlet ... G2
36 Urbanista ... D2

Drinking & Nightlife
37 Anise ... F2
38 B 018 ... G1
39 Dragonfly ... D2
40 Iris ... C2
41 Junkyard ... F2
42 Kalei Coffee Company ... F2
43 L'Osteria ... F2
44 Madame Om ... D2
45 Posh ... C2
Torino Express ... (see 39)

Shopping
46 Aïshti ... C1
47 Beirut Souks ... B1
48 L'Artisan du Liban ... E2
49 Orient 499 ... A2

Information
50 Australian Embassy ... B2
51 Netherlands Embassy ... E3
52 UK Embassy ... B2

Transport
53 Advanced Car Rental ... C2
54 Charles Helou Bus Station ... D2

Courses

American Language Center LANGUAGE
(Map p362; ☎01 741 262; www.alcbeirut.com; 9th fl, 108 Rue Sourati, Hamra; ⏲9am-9pm Mon-Fri) Offers three levels of colloquial Arabic courses (beginner, intermediate and advanced) and are happy to cater to short-term visitors.

Tours

★Living Lebanon TOURS
(☎03 222 781; www.living-lebanon.com) This excellent setup runs a great range of tours of Lebanon, with private customisable trips and Saturday group excursions departing from Beirut and investigating a particular area or theme. Prices are very fair: think around US$50 for group tours. They also run walking tours of Beirut, hiking trips and winery visits. Their website has excellent information on the whole country.

They are also willing and helpful contacts for booking rural accommodation and advice on the current security situation for independent travel. Book tours via their Facebook page (www.facebook.com/LivingLovingLebanon).

Alternative Beirut WALKING
(Map p360; www.alternative-beirut.com; walking tour US$16.50; ⏲noon Sat) Every Saturday, this four-hour walking tour leaves from the top of the St Nicholas steps in Gemmayzeh and takes in non-touristy Beirut, getting under the skin of the city. There's no need to book; just turn up.

Free Walking Tour Beirut WALKING
(Map p360; http://freewalkingtourbeirut.com) Runs 2½-hour walking tours of Beirut, meeting at the main entrance of Beirut Souks on Rue Weygand. You pay what you think they

West Beirut: Hamra & Ain Al Mreisse

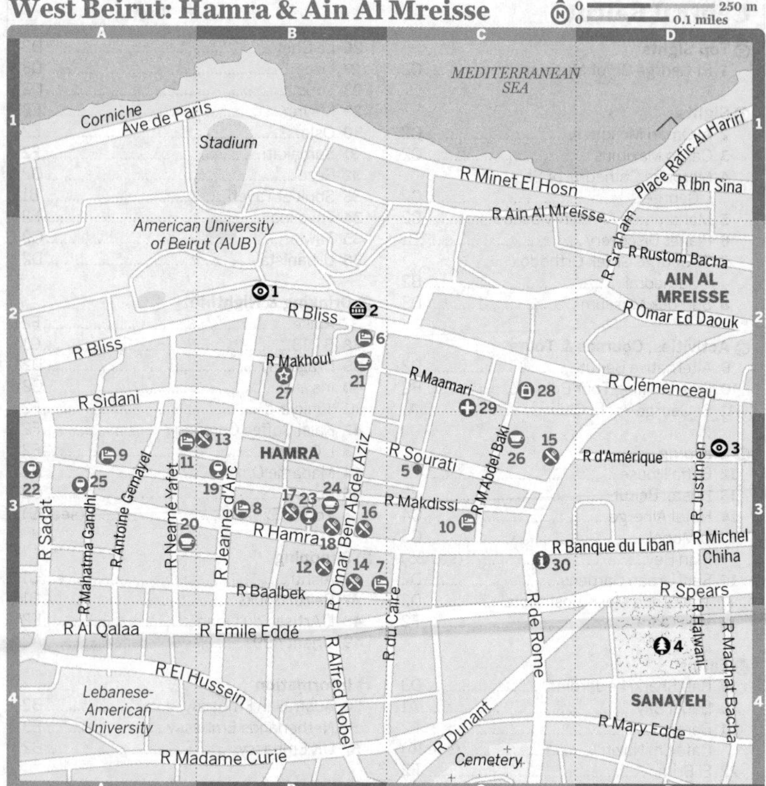

are worth. In the pipeline are thematic tours such as one based on the Civil War. See the website for days and times.

Festivals & Events

Beirut International Film Festival FILM
(☎01 448 141; www.beirutfilmfestival.org; ⊙Oct) Held in October, this festival showcases films from Lebanon and the Middle East.

Beirut Holidays PERFORMING ARTS
(www.facebook.com/beirutholidays; ⊙Jul-early Aug) A loosely associated series of concerts, comedy and other performances that keep Beirut jumping through summer.

Beirut International Marathon SPORTS
(☎05 959 262; www.beirutmarathon.org; ⊙Nov) Held each autumn, usually in November, and popular with international athletes. It starts and finishes downtown.

Sleeping

★**Saifi Urban Gardens** HOSTEL $
(Map p360; ☎01 562 509; www.saifigardens.com; Rue Pasteur, Gemmayzeh; dm/s/d US$18/50/54; 📶) This hopping joint in the shadow of the Charles Helou motorway has a range of rooms and single-sex dorms, a communal lounge, a garden nargileh cafe that is a popular hangout for local arty types, and a rooftop pub. Dorms are comfortable, with en-suite bathrooms; new furniture was going in as we last visited, too.

★**The Grand Meshmosh Hotel** HOSTEL $
(Map p360; ☎01 563 465; www.thegrandmeshmosh.com; St Nicholas Stairs, Rue Gouraud, Gemmayzeh; dm US$24-28, d with shared bathroom US$62-68, d US$100-109; 📶) Nestled on the flank of one of Beirut's iconic stairways, this place enjoys a privileged position in the heart of the Gemmayzeh district, with great bars and eateries just steps away. Rooms

West Beirut: Hamra & Ain Al Mreisse

Sights
1 American University of Beirut B2
2 AUB Museum B2
3 Dar El Nimer D3
4 Sanayeh Public Garden D4

Activities, Courses & Tours
5 American Language Center C3

Sleeping
6 1866 Court & Suites B2
7 35 Rooms B3
8 Casa d'Or B3
9 Gems Aparthotel A3
10 Hamra Urban Gardens C3
11 Mayflower Hotel A3

Eating
12 Abu Naim B3
13 Bagatelle B3
14 Beit Halab B3
15 Dar C3
16 Mezyan B3
17 Onno B3
18 T Marbouta B3

Drinking & Nightlife
19 Bedivere B3
20 Café Younes A3
21 Café Younes B2
22 Captain's Cabin A3
23 Dany's B3
24 de Prague B3
25 Ferdinand A3
26 Salon Beyrouth C3

Entertainment
27 Blue Note Cafe B2

Shopping
28 Librairie Internationale C2

Information
29 American University of Beirut Hospital C2
30 Tourist Information Office C3
Tourist Police .... (see 30)

and dorms are luminous and attractive, with blonde wood and comfortable beds. The ensuite rooms are up several flights of stairs but worth the climb. Management is warmly welcoming.

Among the perks of the place are a selection of Lebanese beers, a well-decorated outdoor patio and tasty homemade meals. The hotel hosts gigs and art exhibitions that attract a local crowd; good for mingling.

Hamra Urban Gardens HOTEL, HOSTEL $
(Map p362; 01 742 390; www.hamragardens.com; Rue Abdel Baki, Hamra; dm US$22, r US$70-80;) Offering excellent value and facilities, this recently opened hostel-hotel in Hamra has smart modern rooms with commodious beds, a proper gym, on-site cafe and a great rooftop bar/pool area. Unsurprisingly, it's pretty popular, so you'd better book ahead.

Hostel Beirut HOSTEL $
(Map p360; 01 568 966; http://hostelbeirut.com; 11 Rue 56, Mar Mikhaël; dm US$21-25;) On the hill above Mar Mikhaël in a typical residential neighbourhood, this friendly hostel is an NGO that uses all profits to help refugees go to university. It's a simple, likeable place with a sociable common area and balcony; dorms have plenty of space and most are air-conditioned. It's a little tricky to find, so note the directions on the website.

★ **Gems Aparthotel** HOTEL $$
(Map p362; 01 746 067; www.gemshotel.com.lb; Rue Makdissi, Hamra; r US$85-125;) Great for Hamra bar-hopping: it's opposite a whole string of them, and this modern hotel offers an excellent standard for the fair prices charged. Rooms are spacious and well appointed, with a cooktop, fridge and microwave; bathrooms feature spacious, powerful showers. Decor is elegant and restrained and noise isolation works well. Downstairs is an appealing lounge and stylish bar-restaurant.

★ **Smallville Hotel** HOTEL $$
(Map p358; 01 619 999; http://thesmallville.com; Rue de Damas, Badaro; r/ste without breakfast US$130/170; P@) Sophie the superhero is your host at this strikingly original hotel with an exuberantly contemporary design, all reds, whites and quirks. There's plenty of fun in the decor, red bow-tied staff and outrageously colourful street-side bar, but rooms offer serious comfort and style. We actually prefer the spacious standard rooms to the two-room suites; both offer fine views from floor-to-ceiling windows with balconies. Breakfast is an extra US$22 per person.

The rooftop pool and bar is a highlight but often books out for noisy parties at weekends.

Baffa House B&B $$
(Map p360; ☎81 668 221; www.baffahouse.com; Rue Patriarche Aarida, Mar Mikhaël; r US$120;) Helpful multilingual host Samir has done a great job of maintaining the essence of this characterful old house that's very handy for the boutiques and restaurants hereabouts. The airy, high-ceilinged common areas are tastefully decorated with a nod to local and family history, while four simply furnished, comfortable rooms make very pleasant bases for exploring this intriguing area.

35 Rooms HOTEL $$
(Map p362; ☎01 345 676; www.35rooms.com; Rue Baalbek, Hamra; s/d/ste from US$100/150/220; P) This small hotel in the centre of Hamra provides its guests with location, a friendly welcome, generally clean and well-equipped rooms, and excellent value for money. The executive rooms and suites have kitchenettes with fridge, kettle and microwave; the basic ones have fridge only.

Riviera Beirut Hotel HOTEL $$
(Map p358; ☎01 373 210; www.rivierahotel.com.lb; Ave de Paris, Ras Beirut; r from US$150; P @) This four-star hotel is one of the best Beirut summer options, as it has the most impressive beach club in the city. It also has a history of offering excellent discounts via bookings sites. Rooms are large and comfortable; some have balconies with sea views. It doesn't cost much extra to upgrade to these: well worth it.

Casa d'Or HOTEL $$
(Map p362; ☎01 347 850; www.casadorhotel.com; Rue Jeanne d'Arc, Hamra; s US$70-100, d US$90-130; P @) Recently renovated rooms in this well-located hotel in the heart of Hamra are on the bland side but offer plenty of space, low beds and desks. Some have a hot plate. Management is helpful; prices are reasonable and slightly negotiable.

Plan Bey B&B $$
(Map p360; ☎01 444 110; www.plan-bey.com; Rue Armenia, Mar Mikhaël; r US$140-150;) Actually part of an exhibition space run by this Mar Mikhaël gallery, this designer double room and its exquisite associated bathroom makes for an unusual place to stay. At time of research, they planned to create further rooms in the area.

Mayflower Hotel HOTEL $$
(Map p362; ☎01 340 680; www.mayflowerbeirut.com; Rue Neamé Yafet, Hamra; s/d US$99/121; P @) A Beirut institution, the Mayflower's rooms are looking worn, but they're clean, comfortable enough and well priced. There's shabby charm to the dated decor: the newest things on show are faded DVDs (remember them?) for sale in a display cabinet. Extras include a small rooftop pool and the venerable **Duke of Wellington bar**.

★**Hotel Albergo** HOTEL $$$
(Map p360; ☎01 339 797; www.albergobeirut.com; 137 Rue Abdel Wahab El Inglizi, Achrafiyeh; ste US$262-440; P @) As classy as they come, the Albergo is undoubtedly Beirut's best hotel and is a wonderful choice for those who can afford the hefty price tag. Guests enjoy decor rich in art and antiques, a rooftop pool, the city's best Italian restaurant and highly professional service. Breakfast costs an extra US$25 to -30.

★**1866 Court & Suites** HOTEL $$$
(Map p362; ☎01 371 866; www.1866beirut.com; Rue Bliss, Hamra; standard r US$145-180, deluxe r US$225-260; P) It's not often a hardened hotel reviewer catches their breath on entering a room, but that's what we did here with the sheer scope of the glorious wrap-around sea view from the floor-to-ceiling windows of this tower hotel. City vistas are pretty special too, but if the upgrade is small, go for the Med. Rooms are effortlessly stylish and service most helpful.

There's a complex of cafe-restaurants here, so there's dining on the doorstep.

O Monot BOUTIQUE HOTEL $$$
(Map p360; ☎01 338 777; www.omonot.com; Rue Monot, Achrafiyeh; r from US$248; P) On first glance, the location of this boutique hotel doesn't look auspicious. But if you ignore the fact that a busy motorway is next door, the fact that Achrafiyeh, Gemmayzeh and Downtown are on the doorstep makes it extremely convenient. Rooms are very handsome, quiet and romantically lit; service is slick. The rooftop pool is a major draw.

Superior rooms have an enhanced bathroom with tub and a better outlook. Approach the hotel directly when reserving for decent pay-upfront discounts.

Villa Clara BOUTIQUE HOTEL $$$
(Map p360; ☎70 995 739; http://villaclara.fr; Rue Khenchara, Mar Mikhaël; s/d US$182/204;) Its French restaurant is well known, but the seven rooms in this boutique option remain a bit of a secret. On the 1st floor, they are chic and comfortable, albeit light on amenities. The location just off the Mar Mikhaël bar strip is excellent and the building, an elegant old villa, is a lovely place to spend a few days.

Eating

★Café Em Nazih LEBANESE, CAFE $

(Map p360; ☎76 711 466; http://saifigardens.com; Rue Pasteur, Gemmayzeh; dishes LL4000-12,000; ⏲8am-4am; 📶) Tucked away in true urban style under a hostel and in the shade of an overpass, this excellent semi-open space brings together locals and foreigners, students and artists. It's a venue for cheap beer, weekend gigs or a sociable waterpipe as well as the food (order and pick up at the counter inside), which is decent and very fairly priced.

Turn off Pasteur at the Coral petrol station, then turn right down the stairs, or descend via the Saifi Gardens hostel entrance.

Falafel Sayhoun LEBANESE $

(Map p360; ☎01 633 188; http://falafelsahyoun.com; Rue Damascus, Achrafiyeh; falafel LL3000; ⏲9.30am-11.30pm) The best falafel in town can be sourced at Falafel Sayhoun, which has been serving its sensational falafel rolls since 1933. It's just a hole in the wall really, but a mighty impressive operation: just watch them at work.

Beit Halab SYRIAN $

(Map p362; ☎71 885 088; Rue Baalbek, Hamra; mains LL10,000-15,000; ⏲8am-midnight) Cheap and cheerful, Beit Halab is considered by Syrians to be among the best Syrian food in Beirut. Nibble traditional Levantine mezze to start and then get stuck into one of the rotating special dishes, which are hard to find outside the kitchen of a Syrian grandmother. Grab a seat on the mezzanine, where you can overlook passersby on the busy street below.

T Marbouta LEBANESE, CAFE $

(Map p362; ☎01 350 274; www.facebook.com/tmarbouta; Rue Hamra, Hamra; mains LL14,000-20,000; ⏲10am-midnight Sun-Thu, to 1am Fri & Sat; 📶) Tucked away in the corner of a shopping plaza, this socially focused cafe and restaurant is quite a surprise to discover, with its buzzy garden atrium. Good-quality food is served in generous portions at a decent price; the meat platters come with pita, chips and hummus and are a substantial feed by themselves. Service is very scatty.

Le Chef LEBANESE $

(Map p360; ☎01 446 769; Rue Gouraud, Gemmayzeh; mains LL6000-10,000; ⏲8am-midnight Mon-Sat) Don't miss lunch at this beloved Beiruti institution where waiters dish up vast platefuls of 'workers' food' to all and sundry. There's little atmosphere, but the food is good value.

MARKET EATING

Few things embody the Lebanese culture like its food does. To sample homemade food, visit the weekly open-air **Souk El Tayeb** (Map p360; www.soukeltayeb.com; Beirut Souks, Downtown; ⏲9am-2pm Sat), known as 'the good market', where small-scale farmers sell products prepared according to traditional recipes. You can buy *labneh* cheese or eat a *saj* (flatbread cooked on a metal dome) sandwich on the go.

This outdoor Saturday market in the Beirut Souks is particularly recommended, but there are also other locations and days: noon to 6pm Wednesday at the Gefinor Centre, Clemenceau, and 11am to 6pm Thursdays at the Village Dbayeh.

Oslo ICE CREAM $

(Map p360; ☎01 569 313; www.osloicecream.com; Rue Armenia, Mar Mikhaël; ice cream LL6000; ⏲11am-8pm) Oslo is a charming shop founded by a Lebanese confectioner who made it big in LA and returned to Beirut to shake up the ice-cream scene. The shop scoops Western-style creamy ice cream with a Lebanese twist (rose lokum, pomegranate, mulberry), as well as delightful cookies and madeleines.

★Loris LEBANESE $$

(Map p360; ☎01 567 568; www.loris.restaurant; Rue Pasteur, Gemmayzeh; mains LL15,000-25,000; ⏲11am-1.30am; 📶🍷) It's an upbeat, social scene at this enjoyable cafe-bar-restaurant hybrid. The elegant garden and glitzy interior of this sizeable villa make it look like a high-end spot, but prices are surprisingly reasonable. Great mixed grills, a top house *muttabal* (aubergine dip) and a variety of other stews, Lebanese pizzas and other creatively enhanced traditional offerings make this a fine spot.

★Onno LEBANESE, ARMENIAN $$

(Map p362; ☎01 740 948; Rue Ibrahim Abdul Aal, Hamra; mains LL18,000-34,000; ⏲noon-midnight Sun-Thu, to 1am Fri & Sat) Exceptionally welcoming service and a convivial atmosphere make this one of Hamra's best dining choices for traditional food. A range of tasty hummus dips and salads are accompanied by lamb's brains, ram testicles and fried sparrows for the adventurous. The range of Armenian mains, including meats in sour-cherry sauce, is delicious. Let yourself be guided by the staff.

★Tawlet LEBANESE **$$**

(Map p360; ☎01 448 129; www.tawlet.com; 12 Rue Armenia, Mar Mikhaël; buffet incl arrack US$33, daily special Mon-Fri US$15; ⊙1-4pm Mon-Fri, from noon Sat; ✎) There are loads of great restaurants in Beirut, but there's only one that commands the respect of every farmer, chef and foodie in the country – and that's Tawlet. Showcasing farm-fresh (often organic) produce and providing a venue where traditional recipes can be tested and sampled, this chic eatery offers a daily lunch buffet (detailed online) cooked by a visiting chef.

To find it, head east along Rue Armenia. Tawlet is the end of the alley behind the Anthurium flower shop, on the northern side of the road. They also run **cooking classes** and all manner of other foodie things; check the website.

Mezyan MIDDLE EASTERN **$$**

(Map p362; ☎071 293 015; www.facebook.com/mezyanpub; Rasamany Bldg, Rue Hamra, Hamra; mains from LL15,000; ⊙11am-2am) Mezyan is a Hamra institution. This restaurant-bar has occupied a few locations over the years, serving small plates of Lebanese, Syrian and Armenian mezze to a lefty crowd. Friday nights at the latest incarnation, down an alley next to a bureau de change on Hamra St, are famous for their revelry. Book a table and come ready to shake your hips to Arabic pop tunes.

Dar CAFE **$$**

(Map p362; ☎01 373 348; http://darbistroandbooks.com; Alley 83, off Rue de Rome, Hamra; mains LL15,000-30,000; ⊙8am-midnight) Dar, or 'home' in Arabic, is cosily tucked away at the end of an alley in bustling Hamra. The peaceful restaurant and bookstore space spill out of a mid-century Lebanese house (increasingly rare for the area) into a colourful garden. Drop by for a sandwich or salad under jasmine and frangipani; stay through the evening for a reading and Lebanese wine.

Seza ARMENIAN, LEBANESE **$$**

(Map p360; ☎01 570 711; Rue Patriarche Aarida, Mar Mikhaël; mains LL23,000-35,000; ⊙noon-5pm & 7pm-midnight) On a quiet Mar Mikhaël corner, this sweet family-run spot offers cuisine true to this traditional Armenian area. There's a cute little plant-shaded terrace out front, and a attractive vintage chic interior. The food is authentic, unpretentious and very tasty. The coriander-marinated fish is excellent, while the sheep-foot soup will appeal to nose-to-tailers.

Samakati SEAFOOD **$$**

(Map p360; ☎01 561 560; Rue Armenia, Mar Mikhaël; fish per kilo LL50,000-90,000; ⊙noon-midnight) This sweet little fish restaurant on the Armenia strip has appropriately nautical blue-and-white check tables. There's a range of seafood mezze: delicious whole grilled calamari and tasty crab, avocado and mango salad. Pick your fish from the display: they aren't quite straight off the boats but tastily chargrilled with thyme. Prices are per kilo.They also do a great chargrilled-fish pita roll.

Villa Badaro INTERNATIONAL **$$**

(Map p358; ☎01 385 155; www.facebook.com/villabadaro; Rue de l'Hôpital Militaire, Badaro; mains LL18,000-39,000; ⊙10am-1am; 📶) In the heart of the Badaro eating and drinking area, this appeals for its tables in the handsome covered streetside garden of a villa. The menu is relatively short, with Japanese and American influences showing in a range of creative salads, tuna dishes, burgers and steaks. It's all pretty tasty and well presented.

Bagatelle MEDITERRANEAN **$$**

(Map p362; ☎01 342 842; www.bagatellebeirut.com; Rue Jabre Doumit, Hamra; mains LL18,000-40,000; ⊙11am-midnight; 📶) Set in a very charming historic house pleasantly screened by greenery from this quiet street, this is a likeably discreet spot that does a pleasing line in salads, pizzas and fuller meals, inspired by France, Greece and Italy and accompanied by decent wines.

Bab Sharki Le Jardin MIDDLE EASTERN **$$**

(Map p360; ☎01 218 450; Rue Trabaud, Achrafiyeh; mains LL18,000-30,000; ⊙noon-midnight) In the ultra-elegant part of Achrafiyeh, Bab Sharki offers a wide selection of Levantine dishes, including Iraqi, Armenian and Aleppian cuisine. Its relaxing garden is a fine urban retreat, while inside there's live traditional instrumental music. A must-try is the Armenian *mante* – small pastries filled with meat or spinach that the waiter will mix with yoghurt and spicy sauce at your request.

Kahwet Leila LEBANESE **$$**

(Map p360; ☎01 561 888; www.kahwetleila.com; Rue Gouraud, Gemmayzeh; mezze LL7000-13,500, platters LL14,500-26,000; ⊙10am-1am; 📶✎) Old Beirut lives on through clever recreations such as this chic coffeehouse, which is designed to evoke the city's 'Paris of the East' past. The menu features mezze and a choice of platters (burgers, shawarma, brochettes, falafel), but many head here for coffee and a nargileh, making good use of the cafe's backgammon sets and packs of cards.

Urbanista CAFE $$

(Map p360; ☎01 567 811; www.weare-urbanista.com; Rue Gouraud, Gemmayzeh; light meals LL13,000-20,000, mains LL24,000-42,000; ⏰8am-midnight; 📶) As international as it name would suggest, this industrial-chic cafe is as popular with expats as it is with locals. It has individual and communal tables, a courtyard, comfy armchairs and a laid-back vibe. The widely influenced menu is strong on comfort food and salads.

El Brimo LEBANESE $$

(Map p360; ☎70 444 199; off Orthodox Hospital St, Geitawi; mezze LL7000-15,000; ⏰10.30am-4.30am; 📶) Supremely out of place in the sleepy Geitawi neighborhood, El Brimo's Vegas-style facade hides an elegantly restored manor house with a garden. The mezze are excellent, the staff friendly, and the shisha comes in wild flavors like guava and melon. Come for after-dinner drinks at the weekend for some of the best people-watching in the city.

Abu Naim LEBANESE $$

(Map p362; ☎01 750 480; www.facebook.com/abunaimhamra; Rue Abdel Aziz, Hamra; dishes LL7000-22,000; ⏰noon-midnight) Despite Hamra's buzzing scene, it's not that easy to find a straight-up Lebanese restaurant without a hipster slant or burger menu. This fits the bill: run by an extremely friendly family, it doles out reliable, tasty, no-frills home cooking just off the strip.

Enab LEBANESE $$

(Map p360; ☎01 444 441; www.facebook.com/enabbeirut; Rue Armenia, Mar Mikhaël; mezze LL7000-17,000, grills LL17,000-28,000; ⏰10am-1am; 📶) Head up the wooden staircase to access this huge and ultra-popular restaurant and then choose between a garden table or one in the attractively decorated front salons. The menu features all of the usual Levantine favourites, with a few wildcards – try the eggplant *fatteh* (pita with yoghurt and other toppings) and you won't be disappointed.

★Baron LEBANESE $$$

(Map p360; ☎01 565 199; www.baronbeirut.com; Rue Pharaon, Mar Mikhaël; mains LL19,000-65,000; ⏰noon-3pm & 7.30-11.30pm, to 4pm lunchtime Sat & Sun, to midnight Fri & Sat, shorter hours winter; 📶✍) 🍃 Located in the Mar Mikhaël design district, this locavore restaurant is very much at the forefront of Beirut culinary trends. Innovative, modern creations using traditional Lebanese ingredients are the signature, with well-selected ingredients and influences from other Mediterranean countries rounding out a great seasonal menu. Decent wines, an elegantly bohemian air and excellent service seal the deal. Vegetarian choices are brilliant here.

★Mayrig ARMENIAN, LEBANESE $$$

(Map p360; ☎01 572 121; www.mayrigbeirut.com; 282 Rue Pasteur, Gemmayzeh; mezze LL6000-17,000, mains LL24,000-33,000; ⏰noon-11.30pm; 📶) Beirutis of Armenian descent tend to head to this elegant restaurant in Gemmayzeh if they want to celebrate a special occasion, and once you've eaten here you'll understand why. The food here is among the best in the city and provides a nice change from the usual Levantine menu. The sour-cherry kebab is particularly delicious.

Also on offer are pastry dishes, *kibbeh* (meat-filled cracked-wheat croquettes), *soujouk* (Armenian sausage) and *mante* (dumplings). Booking is recommended.

★Liza LEBANESE $$$

(Map p360; ☎01 208 108; www.lizabeirut.com; 1st fl, Metropolitan Club, Rue Doumani, Achrafiyeh; mezze LL10,000-25,000, mains LL25,000-49,000; ⏰12.30-3.30pm & 8-11.30pm Mon-Sat, noon-4pm & 8-11.30pm Sun; 📶) Epitomising Beiruti chic, Liza serves expertly prepared nouvelle Lebanese food in surroundings that have graced the pages of many international design magazines. Prices are remarkably reasonable considering the quality – especially at lunch when the daily plat du jour and a salad costs LL28,500 – and there's an expertly curated wine list by both the glass and bottle. Simply splendid.

Babel Bay LEBANESE $$$

(Map p360; ☎01 370 846; Zaitunay Bay, Downtown; mains LL35,000-70,000; ⏰noon-11.30pm) On the boardwalk around the marina, a seat on the raised platform terrace here is a prime Beirut spot on a sunny day. Unlike some of the other places in this strip, the food is classy and worthwhile, with fresh fish a highlight, along with a broad wine selection. Portions are generous if not cheap.

Tavolina ITALIAN $$$

(Map p360; ☎01 442 244; www.facebook.com/tavolinarestaurant; Rue Kamille Yousef Chamoun, Mar Mikhaël; pizzas & pastas LL15,000-30,000, mains

LL30,000-50,000; ⏲12.30-11.30pm) Every suburb needs an Italian trattoria, and it would certainly be nice if all were as impressive as this one. Serving up plump bruschetta, handmade pasta, piping hot pizzas and well-executed classics such as *cotoletta alla Milanese* (crumbed veal cutlet), this place deserves its spot on the list of Beirut's best Italian eateries. The only downside is the car-park-and-tower-block outlook.

Drinking & Nightlife

Cafes

Café Younes CAFE
(Map p362; ☎01 742 654; www.cafeyounes.com; Rue Abdel Aziz, Hamra; ⏲7.15am-11pm Mon-Sat, from 10am Sun; 📶) The aroma of freshly ground coffee beans has been enticing patrons into this friendly cafe near the American University of Beirut since 1935, rewarding them with the best coffee in Beirut (espresso, filter, decaf and traditional Middle Eastern styles). There's another branch in nearby **Rue Neamé Yafet** (Map p362; ☎01 750 975; Rue Neamé Yafet, Hamra; ⏲8am-11pm Mon-Sat, from 10am Sun; 📶).

Kalei Coffee Company CAFE
(Map p360; ☎03 780 342; www.kaleicoffee.com; off Rue Qobaiyat, Mar Mikhaël; ⏲9am-11pm; 📶) Very popular with Beiruti hipsters and expat workers, this arty place is a little tucked-away haven: it's very pleasant to sit outside and slowly realise you can't hear any car horns. It's not cheap, but the coffee is carefully selected and delicious; there's also a range of brunchy fare like smashed avocado, granola and salads, as well as beers and wines.

To find it, turn off Rue Armenia past the Union petrol station, follow the street around the corner and then turn right.

de Prague CAFE
(Map p362; ☎01 744 864; www.facebook.com/deprague; Rue Makdissi, Hamra; ⏲9am-2am Mon-Sat, from 10am Sun; 📶) Popular with AUB students, intellectuals and artists, this spacious bohemian cafe has comfy chairs and low-set tables, and feels like a large lounge room. Bring your laptop or you'll look out of place.

Salon Beyrouth CAFE
(Map p362; ☎79 185 790; Rue Mohamed Abdel Baki, Hamra; ⏲9.30am-1am Sun-Thu, to 2am Fri & Sat; 📶) This gorgeously renovated house doubles down on the speakeasy vibe with art deco furnishings and decor, a black-and-white tiled floor and throwback cocktails like the Rob Roy and Vieux Carré. On weekends, the restaurant morphs into a venue with sexy lighting to facilitate dancing to local bands and DJs.

Troika CAFE
(Map p358; ☎01 384 517; www.facebook.com/troikabadaro; Military Hospital St, Badaro; ⏲4pm-1am Mon-Thu, to 2am Fri & Sat, to midnight Sun) Troika is where the art kids smoke and dance and carry on in Badaro. Weekend DJ nights are some of Beirut's most interesting, and it's pretty entertaining to watch people who may have had one too many try to dance around people drinking at tables (if you sit, do so away from the DJ booth). The nights are in strange juxtaposition to the cocktails, which can be unimaginative.

Bars & Pubs

★**Ferdinand** PUB
(Map p362; ☎01 355 955; www.facebook.com/ferdinandthepub; Rue Mahatma Gandhi, Hamra; ⏲5pm-1am; 📶) Self-assured and welcoming, this is a convivial evening spot with a softer musical footprint than most. They do a fine cocktail, the smoked burgers are dripping with taste and served with showbiz flair, while the whisky shelves groan under the weight of an excellent selection. Charismatic Walid is an ideal host and good for local advice.

Junkyard BAR, CLUB
(Map p360; ☎03 945 961; www.facebook.com/junkyardbeirut; Rue Qobaiyat, Mar Mikhaël; ⏲6pm-2am) A stack of well-worn shipping containers converted into a fashionable bar/party venue hybrid, Junkyard has a great rooftop terrace showcasing recycled materials: check out the bucket lamps. Downstairs features a huge glass atrium and has live music at weekends that segues into DJ sets. Excellent cocktails make for a popular scene: it's best to reserve on Friday and Saturday nights.

Access is via the street with the green United petrol station on the corner.

Iris ROOFTOP BAR
(Map p360; ☎03 090 936; www.irisbeirut.com; An Nahar Bg, off Rue Weygand, Downtown; ⏲6pm-3am, from 5pm Oct-Apr) Beirut has some great rooftops and this is one of the best, a cracking place to be at sunset sipping a (pricey) cocktail and admiring the excellent view. The romance gradually morphs into party mode as the evening continues, the place fills up and the music pumps so loud you can hear it blocks away.

Dragonfly BAR

(Map p360; ☎01 561 112; Rue Gouraud, Gemmayzeh; ⏲6pm-1am) Attracting a 30s-something arty crowd, this long-standing bar has a Parisian-style decor and cocktail waiters smartly decked out in ties and lab coats. And there's certainly plenty of chemistry going on in their delicious cocktails. When we last visited, they were infusing gin with Earl Grey tea to create a sensational sour.

Anise BAR

(Map p360; ☎70 977 926; www.facebook.com/anisecorridorbar; Rue Alexander Fleming, Mar Mikhaël; ⏲6pm-late; 📶) This is the place to come if you are interested in getting to know arrack, the aniseed-flavoured Lebanese spirit. An unobtrusive clutch of cleanskin bottles behind the bar holds a range of smooth and flavoursome craft-distilled offerings from around the country; the bar staff will guide you. They also do cocktails, with herby sensations like sage margarita recommendable. It's happy hour until 9pm.

Bedivere PUB

(Map p362; ☎01 748 909; www.bediverelb.com; Rue Jeanne d'Arc, Hamra; ⏲9am-1am Mon-Sat, from 5pm Sun; 📶) With a lightly worn medieval theme and mellow soundtrack, this inviting hideaway has cute outdoor tables and an interior dominated by sociable bar-counter seating. With interesting cocktails and the tasty 961 Lebanese craft beer on tap, it's a fine place to while away a hot afternoon or meet locals in the evening. You get a discount if you lock your phone away. They've also got a full menu of dishes from breakfast eggs to pasta, steaks and burgers.

L'Osteria WINE BAR

(Map p360; ☎01 566 175; www.facebook.com/losteria.beirut; Rue Armenia, Mar Mikhaël; ⏲5pm-2am) There's a Little Italy vibe to Mar Mikhaël and this place slots right in, with its Chianti and prosciutto in an atmospheric faux-vaulted stone chamber, though the Chat Noir painted on the wall is a little off-message. It's a nice scene that gets lively as the evening goes on, with 30-somethings dancing in the restricted space to upbeat Eurotrash sounds from the DJ.

Dany's BAR

(Map p362; www.danyslb.com; off Rue Makdissi, Hamra; ⏲10am-2.30am; 📶) This little bar, moved a few blocks over in 2017 from its original location, has a laid-back and inclusive vibe and packs out the indoor/outdoor alley space. In yeasty harmony, it shares workspace with a bakery restaurant, a happy combination for a decent evening out. Happy hour runs all day until 8pm but isn't that cheap.

Torino Express BAR

(Map p360; ☎01 443 797; Rue Gouraud, Gemmayzeh; ⏲10am-2am; 📶) One of Beirut's longest-serving hipster hangouts, this neighbourhood place functions as a cafe during the day but hits its stride at night when the DJ spins a wildly eclectic collections of tracks and the barmen work their magic.

Captain's Cabin BAR

(Map p362; ☎01 740 516; Rue Adonis, Hamra; ⏲6pm-3am) Countless bars have come and gone in Beirut, but Captain's Cabin, in the Hamra district, has weathered decades of war. Founded in 1964, it still maintains its original decor – with a vintage pool table, darts and tottering wooden chairs. The prices are among the fairest in town and the owner is an infinite source of knowledge on the city's history.

Madame Om CAFE, PUB

(Map p360; ☎01 572 050; www.facebook.com/MadameOm; Rue Pasteur, Gemmayzeh; ⏲11am-late Mon-Sat) Named after the Egyptian diva Om (Umm) Kulthum, this cosy gay-friendly cafe-pub hybrid is a popular choice in the afternoon and early evening on weekdays, when drinks are discounted by 30%. Check its Facebook page for event info. You'll find it in the blue building down the side of the Coral petrol station – follow the signs for the restaurant Goya.

Nightclubs

Posh CLUB

(Map p360; www.facebook.com/poshnights; Rue Jamerek, Saifi; ⏲11pm-5am Thu, Sat & Sun) In Saifi near Downtown, this club is party central for a mixed crowd: it's a mainstay of the Beirut LGBT scene. A state-of-the-art lighting-and-sound system is used to great advantage, with patrons strutting their stuff to a pulsing background of house, R'n'B, rave, techno and electro-Arabic. Entrance is US$13 for women and US$20 to US$27 for men. On Saturdays the action moves east to a rooftop near the water in Bourj Hammoud.

Grand Factory CLUB

(☎Fri 70 885 882, Sat 71 694 469; www.facebook.com/thegrandfactorybeirut; Rue Al Rehban, Karantina; entry US$20-30; ⏲10pm-4am Fri & Sat)

Beirut's fame as a party city is in part due to Grand Factory, located on the panoramic roof of a former industrial site. The venue hosts live concerts and international DJ sets. While it privileges electronic beats, its line-up is varied enough to please all tastes. Friday night parties are renowned as the best. Catch a cab as it's not easy to find.

Entry gets pricier as the night gets later and includes two drinks before midnight and one thereafter.

B 018 CLUB

(Map p360; ☎01 580 018; www.facebook.com/b018beirut; Lot 317, La Quarantine, Mar Mikhaël; US$20; ⏲10pm-7am Thu-Sat) Easily the most famous club in town, this gay-friendly underground place a couple of kilometres east of Downtown is known for its mock-horror interior and sliding roof, which always opens at some point during the night. Drinks are horrendously expensive, and the staff have plenty of attitude. Thursday is '80s night, and hard house dominates at the weekend.

To get here, ask a cab driver to take you to the Forum de Beyrouth and follow the clubbers from there.

☆ Entertainment

Blue Note Cafe JAZZ

(Map p362; ☎01 743 857; www.bluenotecafe.com; Rue Makhoul, Hamra; ⏲noon-late Mon-Sat; 📶) This is one of the very best places to hear jazz and blues in Lebanon. Local – and sometimes international – acts perform each Wednesday, Thursday, Friday and Saturday. Check the website for the programme.

Beirut Hippodrome HORSE RACING

(Map p358; ☎01 632 515; Abdallah El Yafi, Barbir; ⏲24hr Sun) Beirut's 'new' Hippodrome (dating from the 19th century instead of the Roman era) has an extremely chequered past. In the 1960s, it was one of the busiest racetracks in the world; in 1982, it was occupied by the Israeli army during the Lebanese civil war. (The occupation is memorably depicted in the film *Waltz With Bashir*.) These days, the horses run on Sundays, and it's quite the jolly to watch them among Beirut's salt-of-the-earth types (mostly old men).

Shopping

★Orient 499 HOMEWARES

(Map p360; ☎01 369 499; www.orient499.com; 499 Rue Omar Ed Daouk, Downtown; ⏲10.30am-6pm Mon-Sat) Entranced by Middle Eastern design, Frank Luca and Aida Kawas decided to establish this atelier and boutique, where they design and make some objects (including Aida Kawas' wonderful clothing) and also sell products and artefacts sourced from other countries in the region. Expensive but exquisite homewares, handmade soaps, ceramics, metalwork, toys and furniture are on offer.

Aïshti DEPARTMENT STORE

(Map p360; ☎01 991 111; www.aishti.com; Al Moutran St, Downtown; ⏲10am-10pm; 📶) Lebanon's premier luxury department store, Aïshti is a draw for fashionistas across the Middle East. Come to browse international designers as well as local darlings like Zuhair Murad, Elie Saab and Reem Acra. For those without a black AmEx, Aïzone offers (slightly) more affordable garments and accessories.

Librairie Internationale BOOKS

(Map p362; ☎01 743 285; Centre Gefinor, Rue Clemenceau, Hamra; ⏲8am-7pm Mon-Sat) This venerable bookstore near the American Hospital holds a wide range of English-language titles among quality French and Arabic books.

L'Artisan du Liban ARTS & CRAFTS

(Map p360; ☎01 564 907; www.lartisanduliban.com; Centre Saint Antoine, Rue Gouraud, Gemmayzeh; ⏲9.30am-7pm Mon-Fri, 9.30am-5pm Sat) Head down the marble passageway between Pasteur and Gouraud to find this shop, which sells ceramics, silverware, traditional clothing, soap, embroidery, textiles and toys, all made by Lebanese artisans.

Beirut Souks MALL

(Map p360; ☎01 989 041; www.beirutsouks.com.lb; Rue Saad Zaghloul, Downtown; ⏲10am-10pm; 📶) The historic Beirut markets were destroyed during the Civil War; their place has now been taken by this swish complex that includes shops, eateries and a cinema. Architecturally it's all rather impressive and interesting to wander its different levels and appreciate its creative use of indoor and outdoor space, but the phalanx of monolithic, upmarket global brands is depressingly familiar.

ⓘ Information

DANGERS & ANNOYANCES

Most foreign embassies advise their citizens not to travel to the southern suburbs of Beirut because of the possibility of rocket attacks and car bombs. The southern suburbs are defined as the area south of the Camille Chamoun Sports Stadium to the airport and east of the main airport road, and include Chiyah, Ghobeire,

DON'T MISS

ACTIVE LEBANON

With a mountainous interior and long coast, Lebanon offers plenty of scope for activity.

Hiking opportunities are good, with the Qadisha Valley area particularly appealing. For a longer challenge, the **Lebanon Mountain Trail** runs along the spine of the country. Various operators including **Liban Trek** (01 329 975; www.libantrek.com), **Living Lebanon** (p361), **33 North** (03 454 996; www.33-north.com) and **Lebanese Adventure** (03 081 620; www.lebanese-adventure.com) can arrange hiking trips and other outdoor activities.

In winter, skiing is popular and the resorts have the advantage of being within easy range of the coast. **Ski Lebanon** (70 103 222; www.skileb.com) has all the information you need on winter sports.

Cycling is still a nascent pursuit in Lebanon but is growing fast. Cycling Circle (p359) is an excellent point of contact and information.

Along the coast, several operators offer diving and snorkelling, including **Stingray Diving** (70 001 552; www.facebook.com/stingrayleb; Bel Azur Hotel, Rue Sea Side) in Jounieh.

Haret Hreik, Bir El Abed, Borj El Barajne, Mraije, Roueiss, Lailake, Hay El Sellom and Tahouitit El Ghadir. Also off limits were the suburbs west of the airport highway to the coast, and south from Adnon El Hakim Rd to Abbas El Mousawi Rd.

The biggest annoyance in Beirut is the traffic. Rules both on and off the road are nonexistent, and pedestrians should take particular care when crossing the road. The pack-a-day air pollution is also noticeable.

For complaints or problems (including robbery), contact the **tourist police** (Map p362; 1735; Rue de Rome, Hamra; English hotline 8am-1pm Mon-Fri) at this office adjacent to the tourist information office.

MEDICAL SERVICES

American University of Beirut Hospital (Map p362; 01 350 000; www.aubmc.org; Rue Sourati, Hamra; 24hr) Considered one of the best hospitals in the Middle East, with English and French spoken.

TOURIST INFORMATION

Beirut's friendly, very helpful multilingual**Tourist Information Office** (Map p362; 01 343 073; www.mot.gov.lb; cnr Rue Banque du Liban & Rue de Rome, Hamra; 9am-4pm Mon-Thu, to 1pm Fri & Sat, closes 1hr earlier Mon-Fri Nov-Mar) has good information on the whole country and is a useful oracle for decoding the complex transport system.

Look out for the excellent *Best of Beirut* booklets, with a good range of listings and handy fold-out maps of each suburb.

Getting There & Away

AIR

Beirut–Rafic Hariri International Airport (01 628 000; www.beirutairport.gov.lb) is about 9km south of Beirut's city centre.

There is no public transport to the airport; the closest spot to catch a minibus or servees (shared taxi) is at the roundabout beyond the checkpoint, about a 1km walk.

Taxis are available outside the arrivals area, but you'll need to negotiate your fare with the driver. The trip to Hamra, Downtown, Achrafiyeh or Gemmayzeh should cost no more than US$25 (LL40,000). It can be cheaper to prebook online with taxi companies such as White Taxi (p372) or Lebanon Taxi (p372); you can also use Allotaxi (http://allotaxi.com.lb) or Uber (www.uber.com). Showing a quote from one of these companies to the taxi drivers at the airport is also a useful way of negotiating a reasonable fare.

BUS, MINIBUS & SERVICE TAXI

Buses, minibuses and service taxis to destinations north of Beirut leave from Gemmayzeh's **Charles Helou bus station** (Map p360; Rue Trieste, Gemmayzeh) and the **Dawra transport hub** (Coastal Hwy, Dawra), 7km east of town. To destinations south, east and southeast (and some northern destinations), they mostly leave from the **Cola transport hub** (Map p358; Rue Salim Salam, Malaab), about 2km south of the centre. Express transports to Tyre leave from the **Kuwait Embassy roundabout** (Rue Hafez al Assad, Bir Hassan), further south again (but still considered safe to access).

Charles Helou is the only formal station. At the other transport hubs, ask any driver for your bus (if someone doesn't find you first).

Getting Around

BICYCLE

Biking Beirut can sound like a recipe for disaster, but growing community pressure means the city is slowly (glacially) becoming more cycle-friendly. An urban collective is producing graffiti propaganda promoting cycling culture and Cycling Circle (p359) is an active group that organises bike tours in and outside Beirut and offers hire in its Beirut shop.

A bike-share scheme was just starting up in Beirut at time of research, but only had one stand, yet to be inaugurated. Check www.next-bike.net or www.bikeforall-lb.com for news.

BUS & MINIBUS

Beirut is well serviced by its network of slow, crowded but good-value buses and minibuses. They operate on a 'hail-and-ride' system: just wave at the driver and, in theory at least, the bus will stop. There are no timetables, but buses generally run from around 5.30am to 7pm daily at intervals of 15 minutes or so.

Pick up a copy of *Best of Beirut*, which has a very useful simple bus-route map. Check out, too, www.busmap.me, a project to develop a detailed map of the city's public transport system.

The LCC bus routes most useful to travellers are listed below. A short trip will almost always cost LL1000, a longer ride LL1500.

No 2 Hamra-Antelias Rue Sadat (Hamra), Rue Emile Eddé, Radio Lebanon, Sassine Sq, Dawra transport hub, Antelias

No 4 AUB Medical Centre–Lebanese University AUB Medical Centre, Hamra, Bechara El Khoury Sq (Downtown), Mazraa, Lebanese University

No 6 Cola-Byblos Antelias, Jounieh, Byblos (Jbail)

No 7 National Museum–Bharssaf National Museum, Beit Mery, Brummana, Baabdat, Bharssaf

No 24 Hamra–National Museum Hamra, Cola, National Museum (Mathaf)

CAR & MOTORCYCLE

If you have nerves of steel and a penchant for *Grand Theft Auto*, you may well enjoy driving in and around Beirut. Expect awful traffic and no quarter given or asked.

The best local car-rental company is **Advanced Car Rental** (Map p360; ☎01 999 884; www.advancedcarrent.com; Azarieh bldg, Rue Emir Bachir, Downtown), which offers great discounts on its published rates. Other international companies are present at the airport (p371) and Downtown.

Be aware that online navigation aids often don't take account of road closures in the centre.

TAXI

Taxis can either be hired privately ('taxi') or shared ('service', pronounced *servees*); just tell the driver the suburb you are going to and they will accept or not. Drivers don't use meters, so you'll need to agree to a fare in advance or pay something reasonable at the end. Within Beirut, private taxis charge anywhere from LL5000 to LL20,000, depending on your destination. Service taxis charge from LL2000 to LL4000. You'll often find that your driver will drive you private for a while and then lapse and start picking up passengers, so gauge what you think is a fair fare.

Reliable bookable taxi services include **White Taxi** (☎01 513 593; www.whitetaxi.me) and **Lebanon Taxi** (☎01 353 153; www.lebanontaxi.com), while international operators like Allotaxi (http://allotaxi.com.lb) and Uber (www.uber.com) are also active.

CENTRAL LEBANON

The central area of Lebanon soars from the coastal towns of the Mediterranean into the mountainous interior of the first of the country's parallel ranges, Mt Lebanon. There's a world of difference between the baking-hot beaches of the busy summer resorts and the crisp cedar-scented air over two vertical kilometres higher, yet they are so close that, as you gaze out from a hilltop over the littoral, you almost feel that you could lob a pine cone into the sea.

Of the coastal towns in this region, Byblos is by far the most captivating, with a carefree charm, good sleeping and eating choices, and a complex of interesting ruins at its heart.

Jeita Grotto مغارة جعيتا

One of the Middle East's greatest natural wonders, the stunning **Jeita Grotto** (☎09 220 841; www.jeitagrotto.com; adult/child under 15yr LL18,150/10,175, discounted if lower caves closed; ⏲9am-5pm Tue-Sun, closed late Jan-early Feb) cave system extends around 6km into the mountains 18km, northeast of Beirut. The simply extraordinary upper cavern, accessed via a cable car from the ticket office, has strategically positioned coloured lights that showcase the stalactites and stalagmites in all their crystalline glory. The flooded lower caves, reached via a tacky toy train, are explored by rowing boat and are closed when the flood levels rise too high.

Discovered in 1836 and opened as a tourist attraction in 1969, the caves were used as an ammunition store during the civil war, despite the flooding from the Nahr El Kalb (or Dog River) for which they form the source.

Bear in mind that there's no photography allowed: you can stow your camera in lockers at the mouth of the caverns. The ticket price includes the toy train and cable-car rides, grotto entrance and a 20-minute video presentation about the caves (screened at different times of the day in English, French and Arabic). Allow 90 minutes for your visit. There's also a tourist office here.

To get to the grotto, take a minibus (LL1500) or LCC bus 6 (LL1500) from Dawra and ask the driver to drop you at the Jeita turn-off on the Beirut–Jounieh Hwy. From here, negotiate a return price with a waiting taxi for the 5km journey (around US$15 to US$20, according to demand), and make sure to figure in waiting time. Alternatively, a return taxi trip from Beirut should cost around US$60 including waiting time.

Byblos (Jbail) جبيل

☎09 / POP 35,000

A pretty fishing port with an ancient harbour, medieval town centre, Crusader-era castle and atmospheric archaeological site, Byblos (Jbail in Arabic) is a wonderful choice for those wanting a night or two out of Beirut, but it's also an easy and enjoyable day trip. The seaside, good accommodation and eating options, and a lively party scene in the old souq make it a likeably hedonistic place that packs out in summer.

Sights

Byblos Archaeological Site HISTORIC SITE

(☎09 540 001; adult/child LL8000/2000; ⌚8am-6.30pm) A well-restored **Crusader castle** dominates Byblos' atmospheric archaeological site, which incorporates Neolithic, Chalcolithic, Greek and Roman ruins – stirring evidence of what is one of the world's oldest continuously inhabited towns. There are panoramic views over the ruins and harbour from the castle's rooftop and crenellated towers – be sure to climb the stone staircases to the top of the keep to appreciate these. Then stroll the picturesque ruins; most buildings are fairly fragmentary but the site is full of wildflowers and sea views.

The castle sits just inside the entrance and is a logical first stop. After exploring it, backtrack to the site entrance and turn left to explore the ruins, which include the remains of **city ramparts** dating from the 3rd and 2nd millennium BC; several temples; and a Roman theatre overlooking the sea. In the Roman period (64 BC–395 AD), the streets here were lined with colonnades and sculptures adorned most public places. Interestingly, the layout wasn't according to the usual Roman grid, instead being adapted to the existing monuments on the site.

The L-shaped **Temple of Resheph** dates from the 3rd millennium BC and is thought to have been burned down during the Amorite invasions. It was replaced by the **Obelisk Temple**, which now lies alongside; the 1500 gold-covered votive offerings in the shape of human figures discovered here in the 20th century are displayed at Beirut's National Museum (p357).

The site's oldest temple, the **Temple of Baalat Gebal** (the Mistress of Byblos), dates back to the early 3rd millennium BC and was dedicated to the goddess of the city. Destroyed by the Amorites, it was reconstructed several times and dedicated to Aphrodite during the Roman period. Many temple findings, including alabaster vase fragments inscribed with the names of Old Kingdom pharaohs, are today housed in the National Museum. The six standing columns approaching the temple are the vestiges of a Roman colonnaded street dating from c 300 AD.

West of the Temple of Baalat Gebal is the **Roman theatre**, a reconstruction that's one-third the size of the original. This is situated near the cliff edge and has great views across the sea. Behind this are nine **royal tombs**, cut in vertical shafts deep into the rock in the 2nd millennium BC. Some of the sarcophagi found here are now housed in the National Museum, including that of King Hiram, whose sarcophagus has one of the earliest Phoenician alphabet inscriptions in the world. His grave shaft also is inscribed, this time with the eerie phrase, 'Warning here. Thy death is below.'

Other remains include the **King's Spring** (Ayn El Malik), a source of water for the city for millennia (and where, according to legend, Isis sat weeping on her search for Osiris); and, around an elegant 19th-century house, intriguing **remnants** of Neolithic (5th millennium BC) and Chalcolithic (4th millennium BC) enclosures, houses and huts. Here, too, is a monumental Bronze Age structure on a platform that might have been a royal palace of sorts.

Church of St John the Baptist CHURCH

(Eglise St Jean Marc) Construction of this heart-warmingly beautiful Romanesque church in the medieval streets above the harbour commenced in 1115 and the structure was extended and improved over subsequent centuries. It's thus an interesting mixture of Arab and Western European designs, with remains of Byzantine mosaics from an earlier structure scattered about the area. The unusual open-air baptistry sits against the

Byblos (Jbail)

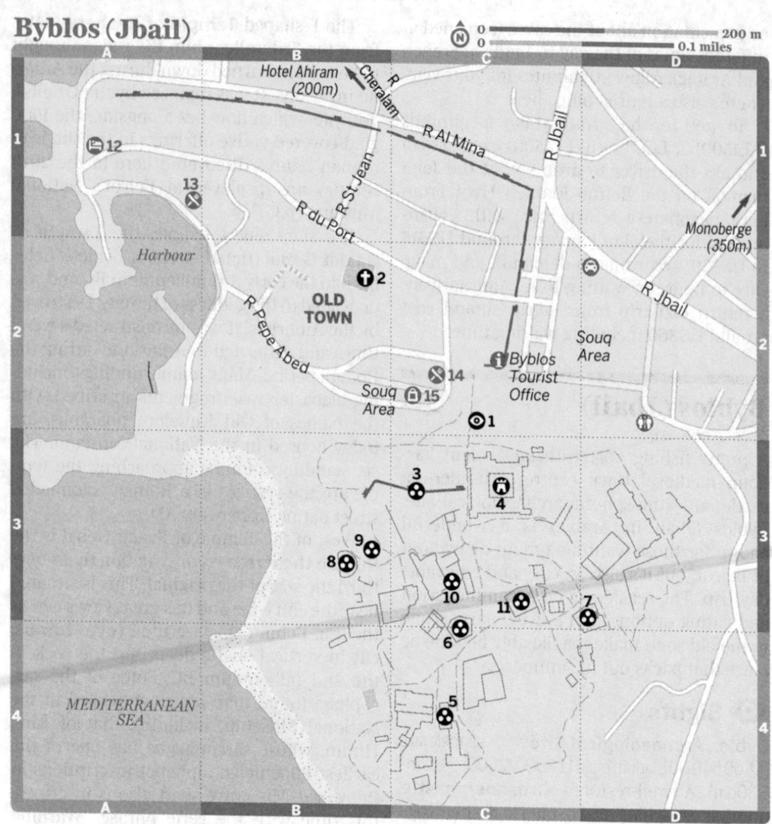

Byblos (Jbail)

Sights

1 Byblos Archaeological Site............ C2
2 Church of St John the Baptist............ B2
3 City Ramparts............ C3
4 Crusader Castle............ C3
5 Early Settlements............ C4
6 King's Spring............ C4
7 Obelisk Temple............ D3
8 Roman Theatre............ B3
9 Royal Tombs............ B3
10 Temple of Baalat Gebal............ C3
11 Temple of Resheph............ C3

Sleeping

12 Byblos Sur Mer............ A1

Eating

13 Bab El Mina............ A1
14 Feniqia............ C2

Shopping

15 Mémoire du Temps............ C2

north wall, its arches and four supporting pillars topped by a dome. It's not usually open except around 5pm mass.

Festivals & Events

Byblos International Festival MUSIC
(www.byblosfestival.org; Jul-early Aug) Byblos hosts local and international performers at its popular annual summer festival. There are usually five or six concerts through the duration, typically featuring quite a mix of styles. Performances take place on a spectacular stage built over the water. Check the website for events listings and ticketing details.

Sleeping

★ **Monoberge** HOTEL $$
(09 550 999; www.monoberge.com; Rue Principale; s/d US$110/127; P) Modern and friendly, this is an excellent choice a short stroll from the historic part of Byblos. The standard rooms are huge, with brushed

concrete floors, in-room router, comfortable king beds and good facilities. Staff are helpful and it offers excellent value. The only downside is the proximity of the busy highway, but the rooms aren't noisy.

Hotel Ahiram HOTEL $$
(☎09 540 440; www.ahiramhotel.com; Rue Cheralam; s/d/tr US$110/132/154; P 📶) A popular three-star choice, this unassuming place has friendly staff, direct access to a small, pebbly beach, and a variety of room types (request one with a balcony and sea view). Ask about substantial off-season discounts.

Byblos Sur Mer HOTEL $$$
(☎09 548 000; www.byblossurmer.com; Rue du Port; s/d US$264/286, ste s/d from US$363/385; P @ 📶 🏊) Hugely popular with young couples enjoying romantic breaks away from Beirut, this classy hotel overlooking the harbour has spacious renovated rooms (many with balconies), a seafront pool and a sunny breakfast room where a lavish buffet is served. Public spaces include a waterside seafood restaurant, a summer-only shisha lounge and a ground-floor restaurant with a glass-panelled floor floating above excavated ancient ruins.

Eating

★Feniqia LEBANESE $$
(☎09 540 444; Old Souq; mains LL25,000-33,000; ⊙9am-3am) There's a golden rule in the Med: restaurants outside archaeological sites are awful. But Feniqia is a glorious exception. A beautifully decorated rustic semi-open pavilion, it serves quality Lebanese dishes presented with real flair. The dark tahini with toast-your-own-pita is a sensational free appetiser, while meat platters come arrayed on serious hardware. The charismatic owner always revs up a fun atmosphere.

It packs out most nights, but there's counter seating as well, so they'll find you a spot soon enough.

Bab El Mina SEAFOOD $$
(☎09 540 475; www.babelmina.com; Rue Pepe Abed; mains LL17,000-37,000; ⊙noon-midnight) Substantially better than the rest of the restaurants overlooking the port, this has a lovely location and is a prime sundowner spot. It serves decent seafood: calamari, octopus, prawns and fish in various manifestations, including fish *kibbeh* (cracked wheat croquettes) and ceviche.

Shopping

★Mémoire du Temps GIFTS & SOUVENIRS
(☎09 540 555; www.memoryoftime.com; Byblos souq; ⊙9am-6pm, to 8pm Jun-Aug) This family were pioneers in extracting the fish fossils that have garnered worldwide attention; dropping in here for a gaze is a Byblos must-do. They are simply extraordinary; 100-million-year-old rays, sharks, swordfish and even an octopus are perfectly preserved. Fossils start at US$5; all come with a certificate of authentication and can be legally taken out of the country.

It's the second fossil shop on the left as you enter the souq that's opposite the tourist office.

Information

Byblos Tourist Office (☎09 540 325; www.mot.gov.lb; ⊙8.30am-5pm Mon-Sat) This helpful tourist office is located across from the entrance to the archaeological site.

Getting There & Away

Northbound buses from Beirut's Charles Helou bus station stop on the highway at the entrance. LCC bus 6 (LL1500, 50 minutes) and private minibuses (LL1500, 50 minutes) travel from the Cola and Dawra transport hubs in Beirut and stop on Rue Jbail. The taxi stand is across the road from the Banque Libanaise pour le Commerce in Rue Jbail. Private taxis charge LL35,000 to Dawra (30 minutes) and LL15,000 to Batroun (15 minutes); note that unreliable traffic makes this a minimum travel time.

NORTH LEBANON

Northern Lebanon includes the city's second city, Tripoli, with an intriguingly traditional Sunni old town and an enchanting waterside district, Al Mina. South of here, the casual seaside town of Batroun is ideal for a relaxed break. Inland, the marvellous Qadisha Valley offers wintertime skiing and great hiking between venerable monasteries clinging to the rocky cliffs.

Batroun البترون

☎06 / POP 15,000

It may lack sprawling medieval souqs and handsome ancient ruins, but this small town has a semi-somnolent and highly atmospheric old neighbourhood near the water that rewards leisurely exploration.

LEMONADE

The town of Batroun is surrounded by citrus groves, and lemonade is a local speciality. The best places to sample this are **Limonade Tony Daou** (⏲8am-10pm) and **Hilmi's** (☎70 173 036; ⏲8am-9pm), where the lemonade is made by rubbing lemons against each other rather than being pressed. The juice is then mixed with sugar and orange-blossom water and served in a long glass. The former is on the main road in town; the latter by the side of the highway 7km south.

Founded by the Phoenician king Ithobaal I, Batroun was a busy port in ancient times but was levelled by an earthquake and mudslides in AD 551. Many historians believe that the town's large natural harbour was formed at this time.

The majority of the town's residents are Christian, and there are many historic churches to visit in the old town's narrow cobbled streets. There's a notable Down Under connection; lots of Batroun emigrants settled there, and there are plenty of Aussie accents to be heard on the streets here as the next generation explore their roots.

Sights

Sea Wall RUINS
Between the old town and the sea, sections of what is labelled the Phoenician sea wall still stand. It actually dates from the 2nd and 3rd centuries AD and was built to enable quarrying of the seaside's sandstone.

St George's Church CHURCH
The most interesting of the town's places of worship, this Byzantine-style Greek Orthodox church was built in the 19th century and features an elegant decorated doorway, dome, vaulted stone ceiling and icon screen.

Our Lady of the Sea CHURCH
(Sadiyat Al Bahr) Overlooking the remains of the sea wall, this simple Greek Orthodox church is built right on the water's edge and has a charming terrace with an arched belvedere framing sea views. The small church has a vaulted ceiling, stone walls and a marble iconostasis in front of the altar.

St Stephen's Church CHURCH
Batroun's main Maronite church is set on a square right next to the harbour. The stone building with its arched entrance, decorated facade and square crenellated towers is quietly imposing and usually packed with worshippers on a Sunday.

Festivals & Events

Batroun International Festival MUSIC, FOOD
(www.batrounfestival.org; ⏲early Aug-early Sep) Running through the later part of summer, this features some big-name concerts, a film festival and a food-and-wine knees-up.

Sleeping

★ **L'Auberge de la Mer** BOUTIQUE HOTEL $$$
(☎06740824; www.laubergedelamer.com; r US$242-330; P 📶) Tucked between the churches of St Stephen and St George and commanding sea views from its upper floors, this upmarket but casual hotel is a delightful option for a romantic break. The individually decorated rooms are elegant; some have sea-facing balconies. There's a magnificent vaulted foyer lounge, a breakfast room overlooking the harbour and a rooftop jacuzzi.

Eating

Simple eateries cluster around the souq and the main road through town. A fish restaurant of hit-and-miss service and quality is the main waterside option in the old centre.

Drinking & Nightlife

Colonel MICROBREWERY
(☎06 743 543; www.colonelbeer.com; Rue Bayadir; ⏲4pm-midnight Mon-Thu, to 1am Fri, 10am-1am Sat & Sun; 📶) This excellent craft brewery offers not just very tasty brews on tap, but a mighty attractive indoor space and outdoor deck and garden for drinking them. Flights are available so you can quickly identify your favourite, and there's a range of soak-it-up food on offer. Ring ahead for a free tour.

Information

Batroun Tourist Office (☎06 741 522; www.mot.gov.lb; Old Souq; ⏲8am-4pm Mon-Sat Jun-Sep, to 2pm Mon-Thu & Sat, to 8-11am Fri Oct-May)

Getting There & Away

Tripoli-bound buses from Beirut's Charles Helou station will drop passengers on the main highway at the Batroun exit; the fare should cost between LL2500 and LL6000 (one hour). From here, it's a relatively short walk to the harbour. Private taxis charge LL15,000 for the trip to Byblos (15 minutes) and LL50,000 to the Dawra transport hub in Beirut (50 minutes). Note that unreliable traffic makes these travel times minimums.

Tripoli (Trablous) طرابلس

☎06 / POP 315,000

Captivating Tripoli (Trablous in Arabic), Lebanon's second-largest city, is famous for its medieval Mamluk architecture, including a bustling and labyrinthine souq that is the best in the country and full of atmosphere. The city is also blessed with handsome examples of Crusader- and Ottoman-era architecture.

The largely Sunni population is known for its piety, so bar-hopping in the Old City isn't on offer; fortunately, the city's justly famous sweets provide compensation. It's a different story in Al Mina, where Phoenician Tripoli originally stood. Now a port district 3km from the centre, this is a charming neighbourhood whose substantial Christian population means there is a lively and up-and-coming bar scene.

Tripoli has had an unsettled recent history, and clashes between factions were formerly regular. The risk of extremist violence is still present and some embassies counsel their citizens not to enter the city. Be absolutely sure to check the security situation in detail before visiting here.

History

Tripoli was a thriving trading post as early as the 8th century BC thanks to the constant comings and goings of traders from Tyre, Saida and Arwad (the latter in present-day Syria). Each community settled in its own area, a fact reflected in the city's name, which derives from the Greek word *tripolis*, meaning 'three cities'.

Conquered in turn by the Seleucids, Romans, Umayyads, Byzantines and Fatimids, the city was invaded by the Crusaders in AD 1102, who held on to it for 180 years and built its imposing – and still-standing – hilltop fortress, the Citadel of Raymond de Saint-Gilles. In 1289, the Mamluk Sultan Qalaun took control of the city and embarked upon an ambitious building program; many of the mosques, souqs, madrasas (schools for study of the Quran) and khans that remain in the Old City today date from either the Crusader period or subsequent Sultan Qalaun era. The Turkish Ottomans took over the city in 1516 and ruled in relative peace until 1920, when it became part of the French mandate of Greater Lebanon.

With a large influx of Palestinian refugees from 1948 onwards, the city became the site of ferocious fighting during the civil war. Huge UN-administered refugee camps still hug Tripoli's outskirts, including the Nahr El Bared camp, now infamous for its protracted Palestinian/Lebanese army deadlock in 2007, during which nearly 400 Palestinians and Lebanese soldiers died. Until recently, factional clashes in Tripoli's suburbs were also a problem.

Sights

Tripoli comprises two main areas: the city proper, which includes modern Tripoli and the Old City; and Al Mina, the rather enchanting port suburb, 3km west along the seafront. The geographical centre of town is Saahat At Tall, a large square by the clock tower.

The old city sprawls east of Saahat At Tall, while the modern centre is west of the square, along Rue Fouad Chehab.

Tripoli's major sight is its Crusader fortress, but visitors should be sure not to miss the compact and wonderfully atmospheric Old City to the citadel's northwest. Dating from the Mamluk era (14th and 15th centuries), this is a sizeable maze of narrow alleys, colourful souqs, hammams, khans, mosques and madrasas. It's a lively and fascinating place where craftspeople, including tailors, jewellers, soap makers and coppersmiths, continue to work as they have done for centuries. The **Souq Al Sayyaghin** (the gold souq), **Souq Al Attarin** (for perfumes and spices), the medieval **Souq Al Haraj** and **Souq An Nahhassin** (Rue Malik Faisal), the brass souq, are highlights.

Women should dress modestly in the Old City, and check with the custodian before entering mosques.

Khan Al Khayyatin HISTORIC BUILDING
(Khan of the Tailors; Bab Al Hadid; ⌚24hr) One of the most beautiful buildings in the old city, this semi-open vaulted-roofed khan was formerly a Crusader hospital and is today a beautifully restored 14th-century tailors' souq lined with small workshops. These specialise in women's clothing ranging from niqabs to leopard-print leggings.

Citadel of Raymond de Saint-Gilles CASTLE
(Rue Emir Fakreddine; 8am-sunset) FREE Towering above Tripoli and the river, this Crusader fortress was originally built during the period from 1103 to 1104. Burned down in 1297, it was partly rebuilt the following century by a Mamluk emir and is still used by the Lebanese military. Today, it's an impressive structure whose most impressive element is the imposing entrance with its moat and three gateways (one Ottoman, one Mamluk, one Crusader). Inside, there are decent information panels as well as a small museum.

The existence of this castle eventually led to the city of Tripoli being centred here, rather than down by the water at Al Mina. Look out for the *mashhad* (octagonal mausoleum) that was the centre of a Fatimid cemetery. The views from the ramparts are excellent.

At time of research the castle was being partly used as a barracks so entrance was free, but admission fees may return.

Hammam Al Jadid HISTORIC BUILDING
(Rue Vieille de Beirut; 8am-sunset) While certainly not new – Hammam Al Jadid was built around 1740 – it was in use until the 1970s and is very well preserved. It was donated as a gift to the city by Asad Pasha Al Azem, governor of Damascus, and no expense was spared in its construction. Draped over the ornate portal is a representation of a 14-link chain carved from a single block of stone.

A huge, glass-pierced dome dominates the main chamber and brings a dim light to the pool and fountain below. The floor and fountain are laid with slabs of marble in contrasting colours. Several smaller chambers, also with glass-pierced domes, lead off the main room.

Madrasa Al Qartawiyya ARCHITECTURE
(Souq Al Attarin) Attached to the east side of the Great Mosque is Madrasa Al Qartawiyya, which was built by a Mamluk governor of the same name in the early 1300s, over the baptistery of the old cathedral. Famed for its fine workmanship, the madrasa has an elegant facade of black-and-white stone facings, topped by a honeycomb-patterned half-dome above the portal. The back wall is also made with black-and-white stone and has some beautiful Arabic inscriptions.

Inside, the prayer hall is topped by Tripoli's only oval dome and has a finely decorated south-facing wall and *minbar* (pulpit).

Taynal Mosque MOSQUE
(Rue Cheikh Ramez al Malak) Standing on its own to the south of the souqs on the outskirts of the Old City, but well worth the walk, is this restored green-domed mosque by the central Muslim cemetery. Dating from 1336, it represents probably the most outstanding example of Islamic religious architecture in Tripoli. The prayer hall is a marvellous space with an ornate inlaid pulpit, elegant lamps and stone vaulting. Note the re-used columns and capitals from Byzantine-era buildings.

Khan Al Misriyyin HISTORIC BUILDING
(Khan of the Egyptians; Souq Al Bazerken; 24hr) Believed to date from the 14th century when it was used by Egyptian merchants, this dilapidated khan is home to several friendly soapmakers, including, upstairs, one of the city's most famous businesses, **Sharkass**, which has been making olive-oil soap since 1803, and downstairs, **Tripoli Soap**, comparative youngsters dating from 1937. The city's soap is famous, and the family operations here will happily talk you through the process. The atrium is decorated with faded Lonely Planet quotes.

Hammam Ezzedine NOTABLE BUILDING
(Souq Al Bazerken; 8am-sunset) FREE Used from the 13th-century right up until 1975, this historic hammam is an extensive complex that is undergoing an elegant restoration. There's a typically indirect entrance to the *mashlah* (main cold room set around a fountain) and good information and intriguing plasterwork through the whole building. Note the relief of the Lamb of God on the entrance door: the block was reused from a former Crusader pilgrim hospice.

Great Mosque MOSQUE
(Rue Emir Khaled Chéhab) Built on the site of a 12th-century Crusader cathedral and incorporating some of its features, this mosque has a magnificent entrance and an unusual minaret that was converted from the cathedral bell tower. Inside, a harmonious stone courtyard gives on to a surprisingly compact prayer hall covered by a cupola.

Khan As Saboun HISTORIC BUILDING
(Khan of Soapmakers; Souq Al Sayyaghin; 24hr) In the centre of the souq, the Khan As Saboun was built in the 16th century and first used as an army barracks; since then, it has for generations functioned as a point of sale for Tripoli's famous soaps. Crumbling arch-

es, trees and a down-at-heel water feature in the middle gives it the feel of a gently declining oasis.

Al Muallaq Mosque MOSQUE
(Hanging Mosque; Rue Vieille de Beirut) You have to glance up to see this small and unusual 14th-century mosque with its delicate octagonal minaret. The prayer hall unusually stretches across the street, with bustling shoppers passing underneath. It's a picturesque space with stone vaulting and columns.

Madrasa Al Nouriyat ARCHITECTURE
(Souq Al Sayyaghin) On a little square in the vicinity of the Great Mosque, this religious school has distinctive black-and-white stonework and a beautiful inlaid *mihrab* (vaulted niche in a mosque wall showing the direction of Mecca). It's still in use today.

★Al Mina AREA
An enticing blend of tradition and modernity, the web of narrow streets of Tripoli's port quarter makes for wonderful strolling. The Phoenician city stood here; these days quiet neighbourhood lanes hold both venerable coffeehouses and a string of modern boutiques and bars. The population is principally a blend of Orthodox and Sunni faiths. Along the waterfront, the corniche road is a venue for promenading or getting a boat trip out to nearby islands.

Activities

Offshore from Al Mina is a string of tiny islets that the city is very proud of. From the corniche, boat trips head out to sail around them; you can also charter a water taxi. If you prefer to stay on land, you can hire bikes on the corniche, too.

Courses

★Levantine Institute LANGUAGE
(☎71 586 508; www.levantineinstitute.com; Rue Patriarch Dowaihi Zahrieh; ⏲8am-9pm Mon-Fri) This is a great opportunity to learn Arabic (either classical or vernacular Lebanese) as well as help out by teaching disadvantaged Syrian refugee children, who struggle with the trilingual school system here as they lack previous exposure to English and French.

Sleeping

The characterful waterside district of Al Mina, 3km from the centre, is the best place to base yourself, with a couple of excellent choices. There are no decent accommodation options in the Old City.

★Beit El Nessim B&B **$$**
(☎06 200 893; www.beitelnessim.com; off Rue Labban, Al Mina; r US$100, with shared bathroom US$75; 📶❄) Utterly charming, this rambling, historic dwelling has been repurposed for guests without sacrificing any of its traditional feel. Artfully combined with a few Indian touches, it makes for a most relaxing retreat in the heart of this intriguing area and very close to the bar and restaurant scene. All rooms are different but quirky, comfortable, furnished with antiques and strikingly attractive.

★Via Mina BOUTIQUE HOTEL **$$$**
(☎06 222 227; www.viamina.com; Rue Farah Antoun, Al Mina; r US$160-195; P❄📶) Tucked away in the depths of the port quarter, this enchanting spot is a brilliant renovation of a noble 19th-century mansion. Rooms are simply elegant, with sumptuous dark-wood floorboards and white materials lending a colonial feel. There's a great garden patio to relax in, a host of other facilities and thoughtful touches, and extremely helpful staff.

Eating

Tripoli's eating options include an excellent and authentic street-food scene in the Old City, where vendors sell sweet corn, falafel, pastries and other delights. Rue Riad Al Solh has a plethora of budget fast-food joints. If you want to drink alcohol with your meal, head to the restaurants in Al Mina.

The local speciality is *haliwat al jibn*, a super-sweet confection made from curd cheese and served with syrup.

A string of restaurants along the corniche and bar-eateries on Rue Labban are the main eating strips in the Al Mina port district.

Silver Shore SEAFOOD **$$**
(☎06 212 223; www.facebook.com/chatekalfoddi; Corniche, Al Mina; mains LL20,000-35,000; ⏲11am-9pm) Tripoli's best seafood is found here in an elegant dining room with views over the water. The very courteous and professional staff will guide you through what's available, which includes an excellent array of fishy mezze and select-your-own catch of the day. They specialise in whole fish bathed in a tangy tahini sauce. Delicious.

Drinking & Nightlife

The Old City is a sober place with appealingly straight-up cafes for smoking shisha. Rue Labban in the Al Mina district is the hub of Tripoli bars, with a handful of inviting places run by the local Christian community.

Wood BAR
(☎78 845 247; www.facebook.com/woodresto; Rue Labban, Al Mina; ⏰5pm-2am or 3am; 📶) Compact but lively, this is one of a series of appealing bars tucked away on this street in the port quarter. A sociable, hipstery crowd of 20- and 30-somethings and a welcoming boss make for good times. Food offerings were set to be revamped when we passed by, so see what's on offer.

Getting There & Away

Several companies run bus services from Beirut to Tripoli. All leave from Charles Helou bus station (p371) in Beirut; there's no need to book ahead.

Connex (www.connex.com.lb) has 20 buses daily in either direction (LL5000, 90 minutes via Jounieh and Byblos, every 30 minutes from around 7am to 8.30pm). Other companies are slightly cheaper but significantly slower.

Ahdab also runs minibuses from Tripoli to Beirut (LL3000, around two hours, every 15 minutes from 6am to 8pm). All bus and minibus services depart from Rue Fouad Chehab and Rue Tall in Tripoli. Service taxis leave about every half-hour to Beirut (LL6000, 1½ hours) from near the service-taxi booth, just in front of the clock tower.

Daily minibuses to Bcharré (LL4000, 80 minutes, three to four services between 9am and 5pm) leave from outside the Marco Polo travel agency, which is about 25m from the **tourist office** (Abdel Hamid Karami Sq). For the Cedars, organise a taxi at Bcharré (around LL20,000).

A service taxi from Tripoli to Bcharré costs LL6000 (from 6am to 5pm) and to the Cedars it's LL10,000; both leave from Al Koura Sq.

The Qadisha Valley

وادي قاديشا

The trip up to the mountain village of Bcharré takes you through some of the most beautiful scenery in Lebanon. The road winds along mountainous slopes, continuously gaining in altitude and offering spectacular views of the Qadisha Valley, a Unesco World Heritage–listed site that is home to isolated rock-cut monasteries, wildflowers and plenty of wildlife. Red-roofed villages perch atop hills or cling precariously to the mountainsides; the Qadisha River, with its source just below the Cedars ski resort, runs along the valley bottom; and Lebanon's highest peak, Qornet As Sawda (3090m), soars overhead. With plentiful opportunities for hiking quiet valley trails or scaling isolated mountain landscapes, this is the perfect antidote to the urban mayhem of Beirut.

Bcharré

بشري

☎06 / POP 22,000 / ELEV 1500M

Bcharré is the only settlement of any size in the Qadisha Valley and is particularly famous as the birthplace of the artist and poet Khalil Gibran. Outside the ski season (when the Cedars resort, further up the mountain road, should be your winter-sports base), it's an excellent base for those hiking in the Qadisha Valley and is a pleasant, relaxed spot.

Sights

Gibran Museum MUSEUM
(☎06 671 137; www.gibrankhalilgibran.org; admission LL8000, audio guide LL3000; ⏰10am-6pm Mar-Nov Tue-Sun, to 5pm Nov-Mar) According to his wishes, the body of poet and artist Khalil Gibran (1883–1931), author of the much-loved *The Prophet* (1923), was interred in the chapel of this 19th-century monastery built into the rocky slopes of a hill on the eastern outskirts of the town. Now a museum, the monastery building houses a large collection of Gibran's paintings: dreamlike, symbolist nudes in the main. If you haven't read *The Prophet,* consider prioritising other attractions, as much of the art's context will be lost.

It's a pleasant, relaxing spot though. Look out for Elvis' signature on a copy of Gibran's masterwork. Stairs behind the museum lead to the site of some **Phoenician tombs**.

Qadisha Grotto CAVE
(☎03 568 251; adult/child LL5000/2000; ⏰9.30am-sunset, closed mid-Dec–mid-May) Extending around 500m into the mountain, this small grotto contains some impressive limestone formations. Though not as spectacular as Jeita Grotto near Beirut, its evocative setting makes it worth a visit. The grotto is a 7km walk or drive from Bcharré off the road to the Cedars; follow the signs to L'Aiglon Hotel and then take the concrete footpath opposite (also accessible from the hairpin bend before the hotel). It's then a 1.5km walk to the grotto. A simple restaurant (☎03 771 363) operates here in summer. If you're relying on this, it's best to phone ahead.

HIKING THE QADISHA VALLEY MONASTERIES

The soaring rocky hillsides and secluded floor of the Qadisha Valley are home to historic Maronite monasteries, grottoes, hermitages and chapels that are atmospheric stops when hiking through the area. The main route into the valley is via a winding road accessed from just south of Bcharré. Near where this road hits the valley floor is one of the most important monasteries, **Deir Mar Elisha** (St Élisée, St Eliseus; 9am-sunset) FREE, which can be accessed by car and now functions as a simple museum. Hewn out of the rock face, its centrepiece is a vaulted 19th-century church that houses an 8th-century icon of St Elisha.

From here, it's a 5km (1½ to two-hour) walk to the serene, still-working convent of **Deir Qannoubin**, probably the oldest religious community in the valley (some sources date the building to as early as the 4th century). The permanent residence of the Maronite Patriarchs between 1440 and 1790, its church features a fresco of the Coronation of the Virgin being witnessed by a group of Patriarchs. Just beyond Qannoubin is the **Chapel of Mar Marina**, a female saint who, disguised as a man, lived as a monk at Qannoubin for many years before being accused of paternity of an illegitimate child. Other versions have her saving an abandoned child by breast-feeding it herself. Mothers unable to produce breast milk sometimes make the pilgrimage here to plead for the saint's intervention.

Those who don't have the time and energy to walk between Deir Mar Elisha and Deir Qannoubin should be able to organise a ride in the all-terrain jeeps that are parked outside the restaurant next to the stream on the valley floor. The drivers usually charge around LL5000 per person and drop you a 10-minute stroll short of the monastery.

Beyond here, the path continues another 4.5km to 13th-century **Saydet Hawqa** (Our Lady of Hawqa), below the village of Hawqa. It's a picturesque, rustic place built into a cave. From Hawqa, it's a 6.5km walk back along the road to Bcharré; you might find a share taxi to pick you up.

Other monasteries that can be visited include the working monastery of **Deir Mar Antonios Qozhaya** between the villages of Hawqa and Ehden in the northern section of the valley. It's a sizeable spot, accessible by road, that was the Maronite see in the 12th century and has been in use ever since. Another, simpler spot is the **Deir Mar Semaan** (St Simon's Hermitage) hermitage cut into the rock face on the southern side of the valley, accessed via a path just over a kilometre past the road down to the valley floor.

For a list of trekking guides working in the Qadisha Valley, see the 'Hike the LMT' section of the Lebanon Mountain Trail website (www.lebanontrail.org).

Sleeping & Eating

Tiger House HOSTEL $

(03 378 138; tigerhousepension@hotmail.com; Rue Cèdre; dm US$15, d with shared/en suite bathroom US$40/45; wi-fi) Friendly and cosy, this is a genial family-run option offering little privacy but a warm welcome. Bunks and beds could have better mattresses, and there's no heating, cooling or communal kitchen, but it's a likeable spot. Home-style evening meals are available.

Hotel Chbat HOTEL $$

(03 292 494; www.hotelchbat.net; Rue Khalil Gibran; s/d/tr US$85/115/145; P wi-fi pool) Genial owner Wadih Chbat loves helping his guests to take skiing lessons, trek through the valley and visit the local monasteries. Rooms at his old-fashioned chalet-style hotel are clean but in need of refurbishment; ask for valley views. Twins are quite a bit more spacious than doubles. There's also a welcoming lounge with pot-belly stove and a terrace restaurant. Wi-fi is in the lobby only.

Masa INTERNATIONAL $

(06 672 729; Rue Khalil Gibran; light meals LL5000-20,000; noon-midnight; wi-fi) This modern cafe-bar on the main road (opposite the more noticeable RTC restaurant) makes a pleasant venue for tasty grilled meats served with fresh-cut chips, poutine, pizzas or a beer on the small deck with valley views. It's friendly and family-run.

La Montagnard INTERNATIONAL $$

(06 672 222; www.hotelchbat.net; Main St; meals LL6000-28,000; 9am-midnight; wi-fi) Situated on the street directly below Hotel Chbat, this

bar and restaurant succeeds in channelling a rustic mountain theme, with wooden furniture and a fireplace being the decorative focus. The menu is dominated by snacks and comfort food (subs, pastas, burgers, pizzas).

Getting There & Away

Bcharré's **minibus office** (06 671 108) is located next to the St Saba Church. Minibuses (two to three hours) travel from the Dawra transport hub in Beirut 10 to 12 times daily between 7.30am and 7.30pm, and from Bcharré to Dawra between 4.30am and 4.30pm. Tickets cost between LL7000 and LL10,000, depending on individual drivers. At Dawra, you'll need to go to the Abou Artine gas station near the Armenian statue to buy a ticket.

The Cedars الأرز

One of Lebanon's most attractive ski resorts, the Cedars is also its oldest and most European in feel. The village takes its name from one of the country's few remaining groves of cedar trees, which stands on the right-hand side of the road as you head up towards the ski lifts. A few of these slow-growing trees are thought to be approaching 1500 years old and fall under the protection of the Patriarch of Lebanon, who holds a festival here each August.

Activities

Cedars Paragliding School PARAGLIDING
(03 544 449; www.cedarsparagliding.com) Lebanon's impressive verticality makes it a great paragliding destination, and this set-up has long experience. Depending on seasonal offers, tandem flights cost around US$125 and packages including accommodation and meals are available. A full course is US$1500.

Sleeping & Eating

Le Cedrus HOTEL $$$
(06 678 777; www.cedrushotel.com; r US$220-250, ste US$350-500; P@) If you plan to stay at the Cedars, this ivy-clad Alpine-style hotel is the most comfortable option. On the main street, well-run and with the popular Le Pichet bar-restaurant on the ground floor, it offers 22 large, attractive and well-maintained rooms with mountain views. Prices are substantially cheaper on weekdays and even cheaper outside the ski season.

Le Pichet INTERNATIONAL $$
(06 678 777; www.cedrushotel.com; mezze LL7000-13,000, mains LL15,000-40,000; 9am-11pm;) The restaurant at Le Cedrus Hotel is the best at the Cedars, offering everything from fondue for two to burgers, pastas and Levantine mezze and grills. The bar tends to stay open later on weekends.

Getting There & Away

The Cedars is 5km southeast of Bcharré. A taxi between Bcharré and the Cedars costs around LL20,000 (10 minutes): during the ski season it is sometimes possible to take a service taxi (LL8000, 10 minutes). Both leave from in front of St Saba Church.

SOUTH LEBANON

The southern Lebanese have had plenty to endure through recent decades, with war, occupation, militias and air strikes composing a depressing recent history. Peace is always a fingers-crossed concept here. Nevertheless, while you shouldn't venture close to the Israeli border, this is a really enticing slice of Lebanon that shouldn't be missed.

South of Beirut on the coast, the historic towns of Saida and Tyre offer plenty for the visitor, including good clean beaches. The former appeals for its character-packed souq and traditional Sunni ambience, while Tyre's Roman ruins, boutique hotels and whiff of hedonism give it a distinctive feel.

Inland, the mighty Chouf mountains rise steeply, harbouring pretty villages and the famed palace at Beiteddine. Higher yet are the cedar reserves where you can admire the nation's iconic and impressive tree. On the foothills on the other side are some of the nation's famous wineries.

Sidon (Saida) صيدا

07 / POP 90,000

Set amid thick citrus and banana groves, the port town of Saida, also called Sidon, was once a rich and flourishing Phoenician city, with tight trade links to ancient Egypt and a globally renowned glass-making industry. Later the capital of the Persian satrapy, these days it's best known for its fresh fruit and its sweets (the local speciality is a crumbly cookie called *senioura*).

Traces of Saida's rich history can still be found all over town, with many ancient remnants in the Old City. The history is very much part of everyday life, and while this means that options for accommodation and eating out are fairly limited, it also offers a

SECURITY IN SOUTH LEBANON

With a tragic history marred by frequent Israeli incursions and local sectarian fighting, South Lebanon has been subjected to more violence and disruption than any other region since the early days of the civil war. Unfortunately, this continues to the present day.

Rocket attacks from southern Lebanon into Israel have been regular over the years, and Israel often responds/pre-empts with artillery fire or other attacks. These events can happen without warning. Tension in Saida between Sunnis and Shiites has triggered violent confrontations; at time of research most foreign embassies were advising their citizens to avoid parts of Saida and all areas south of the Litani River, with the exception of the city of Tyre. Before heading this way, check with your embassy as to the current security situation.

While travelling in the far south, don't venture too far off the main roads between Saida and Tyre. The land itself is still littered with unexploded mines and cluster bombs, so it's definitely not the place to set off on any kind of impromptu hike. Civilian casualties from unexploded ordnance (UXO) are tragically regular.

stronger sense of DIY exploration than some of Lebanon's busier destinations.

The local Sunni population is conservative, so dress and behave accordingly.

Sights

★Saida Souq — SOUQ

Along with Tripoli's, Saida's old city is Lebanon's most characterful and authentic souq area. It's a delight to wander the narrow lanes, ducking into tunnels and discovering venerable buildings along the way. Pick up a map of it at the Soap Museum, or just get lost in it for a while. Look out for traditional sweets being made along the way.

Khan Al Franj — HISTORIC BUILDING

(8am-10pm) FREE A highlight of the souq area is the Khan Al Franj (Inn of the Foreigners), the most beautiful and best preserved of all the limestone khans built by Fakhreddine (Fakhr Ad Din Al Maan II) in the 17th century. Wonderfully restored courtesy of the Hariri Foundation (www.hariri-foundation.org), it consists of vaulted arcades surrounding a large rectangular courtyard with a central fountain, and now houses Saida's tourist office and the ateliers of some craftspeople.

Great Omari Mosque — MOSQUE

(Port Rd) Facing the northern tip of the harbour, the Omari (Great) Mosque is said to be one of the finest examples of Islamic religious architecture of the 13th century and was converted from a fortified Knights Hospitaller structure; it's a muscular buttressed edifice from outside. The interior has been beautifully restored after war damage and features fine stonework and arching. It's open to non-Muslims outside prayer times.

Bab As Saray Mosque — MOSQUE

Just behind the Khan Al Franj, on a picturesque square, the Bab As Saray Mosque is the oldest in Saida, dating from 1201, and is filled with beautiful stonework, including hefty black columns. You can visit outside of prayer times; ask the attendant first.

Musée du Savon — MUSEUM

(Soap Museum; 07 733 353; www.fondationaudi.org; Rue al Moutran; adult/teen/child LL5000/2500/free; 8.30am-5pm) Located in a beautifully restored stone-vaulted soap factory dating from the 17th century, this is a museum of what has traditionally been an important Saida export. Well laid out, with trilingual explanations (Arabic, English, French) on the art of 'saponification', the museum also has a stylish cafe and a boutique with some lovely illustrated history and cookery books. The audiovisual is worthwhile, giving a helpful visual illustration of how the process works. Pick up a helpful map of the souq here.

Palace Debbané — MUSEUM

(07 720 110; www.museumsaida.org; Rue Al Moutran; 9am-6pm Sat-Thu) FREE Entered from the souq via a tall staircase marked with a sign, this former Ottoman aristocrat's building built in 1721 has intricate Mamluk decoration, including tile work and cedar wood ceilings, and interesting historical exhibits. It was closed for renovations at last visit but was due to reopen in 2018.

OFF THE BEATEN TRACK

MLEETA

An intriguing mix of memorial, museum and theme park, the **Mleeta Resistance Tourist Landmark** (☎07 210 211; www.mleeta.com; LL4000; ⏲9am-sunset), on Mt A'mel near Nabatieh, celebrates and commemorates Hezbollah's fight against the 1982–2000 Israeli occupation of Lebanon and the month-long 2006 Israel-Hezbollah War. This bleak but strategically important mountaintop, covered in oak trees and rocky caves, was one of the spots where Hezbollah resistance fighters were garrisoned during the occupation.

The principal exhibits include a rousing 12-minute film about the occupation and resistance, an introductory exhibition and 'The Abyss', a bizarre pit structure filled with armoured vehicles and weapons abandoned by the Israelis. Landmine and cluster bomb remnants serve as a reminder of the brutality inflicted on Lebanese civilians. From here, you can follow paths that the fighters took through the forest, enter the tunnel system where they sheltered, and admire the views from their lookout points. Well-maintained rose gardens commemorate the dead.

There's nothing balanced about the historical narrative being recounted here; elements of the very real Lebanese tragedy and cynical global realpolitik that exacerbated it are juxtaposed with dogmatic fantasy. The insight that it offers into the Hezbollah point of view is fascinating; there's nothing else in Lebanon quite like it. Guides (free) speak many languages.

Mleeta is an 82km (approximately 90-minute) drive southeast of Beirut, via Saida. Tyre is another 50km (one hour) south. You'll need a car to get here, as there is no public transport. Allow two hours for your visit.

Sea Castle CASTLE

(Qalat Al Bahr; adult/child under 10 LL4000/free; ⏲9am-sunset) Erected in 1228 by the Crusaders, this picturesque castle sits on a small island that was formerly the site of a temple dedicated to Melkart, the Phoenician version of Hercules, and is connected to the mainland by a fortified stone causeway. Largely destroyed by the Mamluks to prevent the Crusaders returning to the region, it was renovated by Fakhreddine in the 17th century. On calm days, you can see numerous broken rose-granite columns lying on the surrounding sea floor.

Temple of Echmoun RUINS

(Bustan Al Sheikh; ⏲8am-dusk) FREE About 3km northeast of Saida, this is Lebanon's only Phoenician site boasting more than mere foundations. Begun in the 7th century BC, the temple complex was devoted to Echmoun, god of the city of Saida; the highlight is undoubtedly the throne of Astarte, flanked by two winged sphinxes. Later constructions are visible around it, including a Roman-era villa (right at the end of the site) and Byzantine church, both with interesting mosaics in the process of restoration.

There are no signboards, so interpretation can be tricky; the temple is the large construction on your right just after the metal staircase; other elements are from later structures. From central Saida, you can take a taxi (LL10,000) to the ruins. By minibus (LL1000), get off the highway just beyond Centrepoint shopping centre, parallel with the big stadium. You'll see a car on a pole; head down this road and the site is just over a kilometre along this orchard-lined road. Although admission is free, it is polite to tip the volunteer caretaker LL5000.

Eating

Tawlet Saida LEBANESE $$

(☎07 733 899; www.soukeltayeb.com/tawlet-saida; Rue du Port; mains US$10-25, weekend buffet US$30; ⏲noon-4pm Tue-Fri, 1-5pm Sat & Sun) Perched high over the old town with views over the fishing harbour, this outpost of Beirut's foodie maestros focuses on local traditions, so seafood is a highlight. It's a fabulous space that will entice you to linger. Look for the green sign; entrance is via a tunnel underneath the building. Weekend lunch buffets should be prebooked if possible.

Getting There & Away

Minibuses (LL3000, 30 to 45 minutes) and service taxis (LL5000) from Beirut to Saida sometimes leave from the Cola transport hub, but are more likely to travel to/from Sahraa Sq, between Cola and the airport. There are also minibuses (LL2000, 50 minutes) and service taxis (LL5000) between Saida and Tyre.

Tyre (Sour) صور

07 / POP 143,000

The storied city of Tyre, once famous across the known world for its purple dye made from murex sea snails (Tyrian purple), has a wonderful seaside location and extensive Roman ruins. It's a popular holiday destination for Beirutis, with excellent accommodation choices and what are Lebanon's best, cleanest beaches; you might even swim with turtles.

Tyre (called Ksour or Sour in Arabic), a predominantly Shiite town, is the power base of Hezbollah's Secretary-General Hassan Nasrallah and also home to the United Nations peacekeeping mission (UNIFIL). The town's foundations date back to approximately 2750 BC, after which it was ruled by the Egyptians and then the famous King Hiram, under whom it prospered. Later colonised variously by the Assyrians, Neo-Babylonians, Greeks, Seleucids, Romans, Byzantines, Arabs, Crusaders, Mamluks and Ottomans, the settlement began to languish from the 13th century onwards and, despite many attempts, never quite recovered its former glory.

Sights

The old part of Tyre lies on the peninsula jutting out into the sea. The modern town is on the left-hand side as you arrive from Beirut. Behind the port is the Christian quarter, with its tiny alleys and old houses with shaded courtyards, several of them hotels.

In 1984 Tyre was declared a Unesco World Heritage site, and its archaeological remains are divided into three parts: **Al Mina** (Areas 1 and 2) on the south side of the city, **Al Bass** (Area 3) on the original mainland section, and a **medieval site** in the centre of town.

★Al Bass Archaeological Site — ARCHAEOLOGICAL SITE

(07 740 530; Route 51; adult/child LL6000/1000; 8am-7pm or sunset) This sprawling site lies 2km east of the centre, entered off the highway. Just past the entrance is a vast **funerary complex**, with hundreds of ornate sarcophagi and tombs, several still filled with bones. Next to it, a well-preserved **Roman road** stretches through an impressive 20m-high **monumental archway**, probably dating from Hadrian's 2nd-century-AD reign. Beyond it is a large and well preserved Roman **hippodrome** built in the 2nd century AD; this once held more than 20,000 spectators.

The site's museum is under gradual restoration, but don't expect it to open any time soon.

Al Mina Archaeological Site — ARCHAEOLOGICAL SITE

(07 740 115; Rue Abou Deeb; adult/child LL6000/1000; 8am-7pm or sunset) Dating from the 3rd millennium BC, these atmospheric ruins cover a large area leading down to an ancient **submerged harbour**. Highlights include a street paved with geometrical Roman and Byzantine **mosaics**, on each side of which are rows of large columns. Look out also for the unusually large public **Roman bathhouse** from the 2nd or 3rd century AD and a 4th-century **rectangular arena** that would have held up to 2000 spectators, perhaps to watch some sort of ancient water sport.

A five-minute walk north of the main Al Mina site brings you to the ruins of a 12th-century **Crusader cathedral** (Rue Joudi), along with a network of Roman and Byzantine roads. Ask at the main ruins, as it's not always open.

Sleeping

There are a couple of lovely places to stay tucked away by the water in the Christian quarter, between the beach and the fishing port.

Asamina Boutique Hotel — HOTEL $$

(07 344 499; www.asaminatyr.com; Rue Saydet Al Behar; s/d US$110/130, ste from US$220;) Modern and comfortable, this hotel in the pedestrian part of the old city has rooms with flowery bedspreads contrasting with the rough-cut stone walls. Bathrooms feature elegant tilework and the best rooms look out over the water; it's about a minute's stroll to a swimmable beach. It's run by a kind family who put on an excellent breakfast.

Hotel Al Fanar — HOTEL $$

(07 741 111; www.alfanarresort.com; Rue Saydet Al Behar; s/d/q US$80/120/160;) With its toes almost in the water, this hotel's location next to Tyre's small white *fanar* (lighthouse) is its principal draw. Family run, it's in need of renovation but is clean and offers some rooms with excellent sea views, including a couple with porthole windows. There's a gorgeous shared waterside balcony, as well as a great bar/restaurant terrace right over the sea.

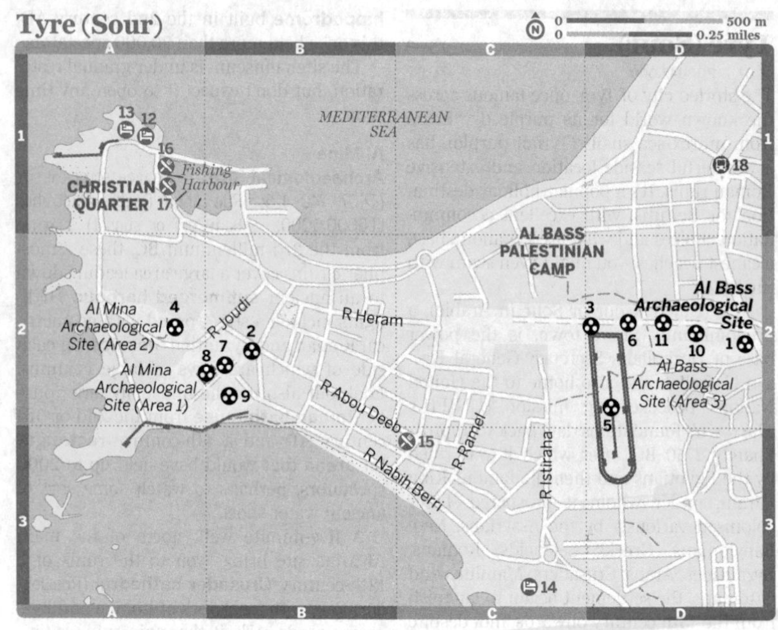

Tyre (Sour)

Top Sights

1 Al Bass Archaeological Site D2

Sights

2 Al Mina Archaeological Site B2
3 Aqueducts D2
4 Crusader Cathedral A2
5 Hippodrome D2
6 Monumental Archway D2
7 Mosaic Street B2
8 Rectangular Arena B2
9 Roman Bathhouse B2
10 Roman Necropolis D2
11 Roman Road D2

Sleeping

Asamina Boutique Hotel .... (see 13)
12 Dar Alma A1
13 Hotel Al Fanar A1
14 Rest House C3

Eating

15 Abou Deeb C3
16 Le Phénicien A1
Restaurant Al Fanar .... (see 13)
17 Tony's A1

Transport

18 Minibuses to Saida & Beirut D1

★ **Dar Alma** BOUTIQUE HOTEL $$$

(07 740 082; www.daralmatyre.com; Rue Saydet Al Behar; r standard/superior US$154/220;) Beautiful tiles and comfortable mattresses give both style and substance to the excellent rooms at this enchanting hotel overlooking the water in the heart of the old town. The outlook is lovely, whether from the superior rooms or the restaurant, which serves delicious breakfasts and romantic lunches and dinners with a small-producer ethos. Book ahead, as it's very popular.

You can't quite reach here by car, but it's a short walk from either side of the pedestrian area.

Rest House HOTEL $$$

(07 742 000; www.resthouse-tyr.com.lb; Rue Istiraha; r US$176-253, ste US$220-330;) A true resort, this huge place near the Al Bass Archaeological Site has its own expansive stretch of sandy beach plus a huge pool, gym, restaurant, summer-only beach cafe and landscaped gardens. The tiled rooms come with patios or balconies and large

beds but feel in need of renovation and more amenities for this price. Significant low-season discounts apply.

Eating

Tony's SEAFOOD $
(70 108 641; Fishing Harbour; salads LL6000, fish LL10,000-25,000; 9am-midnight) At first glance, this simple, informal place opposite the port doesn't appear to offer much to the diner. But after sampling Tony's ultra-fresh fish and shrimp, you're sure to become an instant devotee.

Dine on whatever is freshest, accompanied by *fattoush* salad, a bowl of hummus and ice-cold beer, and you'll leave happy and replete.

Abou Deeb LEBANESE $
(07 740 808; Rue Abou Deeb; meals LL3,000-25,000; 8am-2am Mon-Sat, to midnight Sun) On a busy intersection in the centre, you can't miss the huge signage of this place. It's a friendly spot, doing a range of great falafel and shawarma rolls, as well as larger kebab meals and fresh fruit juices.

Restaurant Al Fanar LEBANESE $$
(07 741 111; www.alfanarresort.com; Rue Saydet Al Behar; pub mains LL10,000-35,000, sushi per piece LL1500-6000; pub 10am-late, restaurant 4-11.30pm Tue-Thu, from 2pm Fri & Sat;) Hotel Al Fanar has a pub with a marvellous seaside terrace, a prime spot for a late-afternoon drink. They do a range of classic Lebanese dishes and also turn out OK sushi.

Le Phénicien SEAFOOD $$$
(07 740 564; Old Port; mezze LL5500-20,000, fish priced by kg; 11am-11pm) Also known locally as 'Hadeed', this place is famous for its fresh fish, which is served fried or grilled. A pleasant outdoor terrace overlooks the fishing harbour – book ahead to score a seat here in summer or on weekends through the year. Service is extremely unmotivated, but that's life.

Getting There & Away

Minibuses (LL5000, one to 1½ hours) travel between Tyre and Sahraa Sq or the Cola transport hub (p371) in Beirut, stopping en route in Saida (LL2000, 50 minutes).

Direct minivans leave from the Kuwait Embassy roundabout (p371). Service taxis charge LL10,000 to Beirut and LL5000 to Saida.

CHOUF MOUNTAINS

جبال الشوف

The southernmost part of the Mt Lebanon Range, this mountainous region southeast of Beirut is wild and isolated in some parts, and covered with small villages and terraced agricultural plots in others. It's an easily reached and pleasant place for a day or two of exploration. Deir Al Qamar is one of the country's most enchanting villages, while nearby Beiteddine Palace, a sumptuous restored 19th-century palace, is a major draw. High up in the range, Lebanon's famous and protected cedars overlook the nation from their lofty vantage point.

Sights

Beiteddine Palace NOTABLE BUILDING
(05 500 077; www.beiteddine.org; Beit Ed Dine; adult/child LL10,000/3000; 9am-5.15pm Tue-Sun Apr-Oct, to 3pm Nov-May) Sitting majestically on a hill surrounded by terraced gardens and orchards, Beiteddine Palace is one of the highlights of the Chouf Mountains. This restored 19th-century gem features sumptuous interiors, views over the surrounding hills and an important archaeological collection. Although conceived by Italian architects, the palace incorporates many traditional forms of Arab design and is a model of elegance. In summer, it's the venue of a well-known arts **festival** (01 999 666; www.beiteddine.org; late Jun-early Aug). The village is around 50km southeast of Beirut.

Beiteddine Palace was built over a period of 30 years in the early 19th century by Emir Bashir Chehab II, Ottoman-appointed governor of the region. Its name means 'House of Faith', acknowledging the older Druze hermitage that originally occupied the site. During the French mandate the palace was used for local administration, and after 1930 it was declared a historic monument. In 1943 Lebanon's first president after independence declared it his summer residence. The palace was extensively damaged during the Israeli invasion; it's estimated that up to 90% of the original contents were lost during this time. When fighting ended in 1984, the site was claimed by the Druze militia, and Walid Jumblatt, the Druze leader, ordered its restoration. In 1999 the Druze returned it to the government.

The main gate opens onto a 60m-wide **outer courtyard** (Dar Al Baraniyyeh) that's walled on three sides only; the fourth side has views over the surrounding valleys and hills. The archaeological collection off this space was closed for restoration at last visit.

A double staircase on the outer courtyard's western side leads into a smaller **central courtyard** (Dar Al Wousta) with a fountain. Beyond this courtyard (accessed from its northern side) is the third – and last – **inner courtyard** (Dar Al Harim). This was the centre of the family quarters, and incorporates a beautiful **hammam** and huge kitchens.

Underneath the Dar Al Wousta (accessed via a doorway near the staircase) are the former stables, now home to an outstanding collection of 5th- and 6th-century **Byzantine mosaics**. Found at Jiyyeh, 30km south of Beirut, they were brought by Walid Jumblatt to Beiteddine in 1982. Whatever you do, don't miss them: they're truly stunning. During the arts festival, this area serves as the backstage area and is likely off limits.

The only food options in Beiteddine are a few snack bars. You'll need to eat at the nearby Mir Amin Palace or bring a picnic with you to eat in the palace garden beside the beautiful open-air mosaics.

Minibuses ('Chouf Buses') from Beirut's Cola transport hub can drop passengers at Douwwar, which is within walking distance of Beiteddine (LL3000, 45 minutes, every 30 minutes between 7.30am and 4pm). Taxis waiting there can take you to Deir Al Qamar, wait while you explore there and then bring you back to the palace (US$40). Alternatively, it's a picturesque but hilly one-hour walk between Deir Al Qamar and the palace.

A taxi will charge around US$125 to take you from Beirut to to Deir Al Qamar and Beiteddine, wait while you explore both, and then return you to Beirut.

★**Shouf Biosphere Reserve** NATURE RESERVE
(☎05 350 150; www.shoufcedar.org; LL7000; ⏲10am-6pm Jun-Sep, to 3.30pm Oct-May) The largest of Lebanon's three natural protectorates, comprising an incredible 5% of the total land area, this is the largest natural cedar reserve in the country and has more than 250km of hiking trails. It's wonderful to see these beautiful trees in their natural environment, and the cool mountain climate makes a welcome change from the sweltering coast. There are several entrances, all with short-distance hiking trails to observe the cedars and access to longer trails.

At the entrances (Ain Zhalta, Barouk, Maasser, Niha, Mrusti and Aammiq) you will find ranger huts with restrooms – you should be able to negotiate to hire a hiking guide at each of these or obtain information about hiking trails. Those wanting to overnight nearby should check the website for details of the reserve's guesthouses.

The most interesting of the nodes is **Maasser**, where you can stroll for an hour or so among the trees, see a particularly venerable one and rest under the famous Lamartine cedar, whose spreading boughs cover a little nest in the rock. Both here and at Barouk, the trees are some 6km above the village.

Within the park are ancient rock-cut fortress remains as well as six of the country's last remaining cedar forests, some with trees thought to be around 2000 years old. More than 200 species of birds and mammals (including wolves, gazelles, porcupines and wild boar) inhabit or regularly pass through the area. The reserve incorporates the Ammiq Wetland, a remnant of the extensive marshes and lakes that once covered parts of the Bekaa Valley. The last significant wetland in Lebanon, it's an important staging and wintering area for migratory water birds en route between Europe and Africa.

Sleeping & Eating

Mir Amin Palace HOTEL $$$
(☎05 501 315; www.miraminpalace.com; Beit Ed Dine; r from US$270; P @ 🛜 🏊) Wealthy Beirutis in search of fresh air dominate the guest list at this elegant place. Built in the 19th century as an emir's residence, it opened as a hotel in the 1970s and has been well maintained – though not noticeably refurbished – since then. All of the rooms are large, but the executive doubles and Imperial Suite are the pick of the bunch.

Getting There & Away

Minibuses leave from Beirut's Cola transport hub heading for various Chouf destinations, such as Kfarhim (LL3000, 50 minutes) and Douwwar (LL3000, 45 minutes, every 30 minutes). There are no direct minibuses to popular destinations like Deir Al Qamar and Beiteddine Palace, but it's easy to reach them from nearby stops.

Deir Al Qamar دير القمر

☎05 / POP 2000 / ELEV 800M

One of Lebanon's loveliest villages, the pretty Chouf settlement of Deir Al Qamar ('Convent of the Moon') was the seat of Lebanon's emirs during the 17th and 18th centuries, and retains a number of handsome buildings from this time. It's a popular weekend escape for Beirutis. Beiteddine Palace (p387) is a few kilometres further down the road.

Sights

★Main Square SQUARE
(Pl Dany Chamoun) The main square is a showcase of fine Arab architecture, including the **Mosque of Emir Fakhreddine Maan**, built in 1493, and, behind it, a **cobbler's souq** housing touristy shops. Above and behind the souq is a beautiful silk khan built in 1595 that now houses a cultural centre. Nearby are the buildings that once housed a **Jesuit school** and a **synagogue**, as well as the **Palace of the poet Nicolas El Turq**, which has a cafe on its ground floor.

Qaisariye NOTABLE BUILDING
(Souq de la Soie) This harmonious khan just above the square was built in the late 16th century and chiefly served as a souq for silk and jewel traders. These days a French cultural centre is installed here.

Serail of Youssef Chehab HISTORIC BUILDING
(Palais de Justice; Pl Dany Chamoun; 9am-5pm Mon-Fri) On the main street opposite the main square is this beautiful 18th-century palace, which now serves as the town hall (look for the two carved lions above the doorway, which represent justice). The entrance leads to an attractive courtyard, off which there is an apartment with wooden panelling, domed ceiling and a window offering views over the valley.

Behind this building it's worth exploring steep and narrow cobbled streets, honey-hued stone houses and two churches: the 17th-century **Our Lady of the Rosary** and the 18th-century **Church of St Elie**.

Sleeping & Eating

Beit Al Qamar BOUTIQUE HOTEL $$
(05 511 722; www.beitalqamar.com; r US$145-170; P) Combine rural relaxation with the grassroots food ethos of the Tawlet mini-empire, and you have a seriously enticing place to stay. It's a traditional Chouf house in the hills northeast of town. The garden grows some of the produce which features in the outdoor kitchen's work, while the colourful, lovably kitschy furniture and simple but enticing pastel-shaded rooms are tops.

The weekend lunch buffet is wildly popular, so your country haven becomes a little less peaceful for a few hours.

Deir Al Oumara B&B $$
(05 511 557; www.deiraloumara.com; r US$110-140; P) A stunning two-level arched loggia gives onto a lovely courtyard whose open side reveals a peaceful panorama of tree-clad hillside. The dozen rooms don't have quite the same wow factor, but are recently modernised and mostly very spacious (one is split-level). Breakfast and other meals with that view are a delight and the manager is keen to help.

Al Midane CAFE $
(05 511 651; Pl Dany Chamoun; mains LL10,000-25,000; 10am-10pm or later, closed Mon Dec-Mar;) Popular with locals and tourists alike, this cafe on the square has an attractive outdoor terrace and is a great spot to linger over a light meal or coffee. The menu covers pasta, pizza, pita rolls and salads. The friendly owner is proud of his town and knowledgeable about its history – he'll happily supply sightseeing tips.

Getting There & Away

To get here from Beirut, get a minibus from the Cola intersection (p371) to Kfarhim (LL3000, 50 minutes) and then take a service or taxi the last 4km from there. Think US$40 for a taxi direct from Beirut, and US$120 for a day trip including Beiteddine Palace and waiting time.

BEKAA VALLEY وادي البقاع

Heavily cultivated over millennia (the valley was one of Rome's breadbaskets), the fertile, pastoral Bekaa Valley is actually a high plateau between the Mt Lebanon and Jebel Libnan Ash Sharqiyya (Anti-Lebanon) ranges. It's idyllically beautiful in parts and is home to the marvellous ruins of Baalbek. Caution is required here though: the valley is Hezbollah heartland and also produces a significant illegal marijuana crop. Its proximity to Syria means that the security situation can change rapidly: be sure to have up-to-date information before visiting.

Though less agriculturally productive than in centuries past because of a combination of deforestation and poor crop planning, the Bekaa's plentiful vineyards have gained an international reputation for their wines. Several wineries are visitable.

SECURITY IN THE BEKAA VALLEY

The Bekaa Valley is Hezbollah's heartland, but its proximity to Syria has meant that some factional violence has erupted in the past. At time of research, this was restricted to the far-northern end of the valley. Some Western governments were advising against travel to Baalbek, and travel beyond Baalbek was strongly discouraged because of Isis presence in the valley's far north. There's also a history of kidnappings in the valley: before travelling, it is essential to check the security situation with the Ministry of Tourism (p371) in Beirut.

Even when safe to travel, this is a sensitive area. Hezbollah command centres and an active drug trade are both present in the valley, so be very careful of where you take photos: best stick to snapping Roman temples.

Though you'll see Hezbollah's yellow flag fluttering around Baalbek, you'll find the locals (a mixture of Christians and Shiites) a welcoming lot.

Sights

Chateau Ksara WINERY

(☎08 813 495; www.chateauksara.com; Ksara; ⏰9am-6pm Apr-Oct, to 5pm Mar, Nov & Dec, to 4pm Mon-Sat Jan & Feb) A winery that you don't have to prebook, Ksara is a reliable producer that offers tours and tastings. The tour includes a visit to an atmospheric Roman-era cave complex where some of the wines are cellared. There's also a restaurant here.

Chateau Kefraya WINERY

(☎08 645 333; www.chateaukefraya.com; Kafraiya; tourist train ride LL10,000; ⏰10am-6pm, restaurant noon-9pm) One of only a couple of wineries in Lebanon that you can currently visit without pre-booking, this produces quality wines of all three colours. You might pass up the tour, which includes a tourist train ride through the vines to Roman-era tombs, and concentrate on lunch in the restaurant and a tasting session in the shop.

Activities

Rafting Squad RAFTING, KAYAKING

(☎03 080 790; www.raftingsquad.com) White-water rafting and kayaking on the Orontes River is organised by this company, which can also do guided hikes in the area and offers camping and bungalow accommodation.

Eating

★Tawlet Ammiq LEBANESE $$

(☎03 004 481; www.soukeltayeb.com; Ammiq Old Village, West Bekaa; set lunch US$44; ⏰1-4pm Sat & Sun Apr-Nov; P) Ask any Lebanese foodie to nominate their top choice for a weekend culinary adventure, and they are likely to say Tawlet Ammiq, the Bekaa Valley branch of Souk El Tayeb, a Beirut-based outfit that runs a **farmers market** highlighting rural produce, as well as a hugely popular **restaurant** where a constantly changing cast of cooks from across the country showcase their regional culinary traditions.

Set in the fertile Western Bekaa Valley bordering the Ammiq Wetlands – part of the Shouf Biosphere Reserve – Tawlet Ammiq gives local producers the opportunity to showcase their traditions, crops and techniques. It also acts as a test kitchen where local cooks are rediscovering and refining traditional recipes and customs.

Weekend lunches here are leisurely affairs, with diners choosing from a buffet piled high with delicacies. Those in the know arrive mid-morning to sample fresh *manakeesh* (baked flatbread with toppings like cheese and minced meat) cooked on a *saj* (metal dome over coals) in the garden and then often zip off to enjoy a wine-tasting at nearby Chateau Kefraya before returning for lunch. Seating is outside in warm weather, and around a pot-belly stove inside when the weather is cool.

The restaurant building is a model of sustainable design, and has sweeping views of the valley. You'll need a car to get here, as there is no public transport. It's 28km southwest of Chtaura.

Baalbek بعلبك

☎08 / POP 35,000 / ELEV 1160M

Known as the Heliopolis or 'Sun City' of the ancient world, Baalbek's ruins comprise the most impressive ancient site in Lebanon and are arguably the best preserved in the Middle East. The temples here, which were built on an extravagant scale, have enjoyed a stellar reputation throughout the centuries, yet still manage to maintain the appealing air of an undiscovered wonder because of their semi-rural setting. The town itself, which is

86km northeast of Beirut, is the administrative headquarters for both the Bekaa Valley and the Hezbollah party.

At time of research, Western governments were advising against travel to Baalbek: it is important to check the security situation before visiting.

Sights

★Baalbek Ruins — ARCHAEOLOGICAL SITE

(☎08 376 812; adult/child LL15,000/5000; ⏲8am-5.30pm) Dominating the centre of modern Baalbek, this wonderful Roman temple complex is one of the Middle East's major archaeological highlights. The monumental Temple of Jupiter impresses by its sheer scale, while the adjacent Temple of Bacchus is astoundingly well preserved, with exquisite carved decoration. A **museum in a tunnel** under the complex has good information. The much smaller Temple of Venus is opposite the main entrance. In summer the ruins are the atmospheric venue for the Baalbeck International Festival.

Other excavations near the main complex include remnants of a Roman theatre and other structures.

★Temple of Bacchus — RUINS

Baalbek's Temple of Bacchus is often described as the most beautifully decorated temple in the Roman world, and it's certainly one of the best preserved. The portico has eight columns along the facade and 15 along the sides, supporting a rich entablature and an exterior ceiling of curved stone that is decorated with vivid scenes: Mars, a winged Victory, Diana drawing an arrow, Tyche with a cornucopia, Vulcan with his hammer, Bacchus, and Ceres holding a sheaf of corn.

The temple was begun during the reign of Nero in the mid-1st century AD; its attribution to the god of wine – appropriate enough in the Bekaa – is uncertain but based on reliefs showing vines and other Bacchic themes. Examine the carvings around the doorways closely for their exquisite detail; a fallen section of the ceiling also allows you to examine this up close. For a tip, loitering guides can be good at pointing out elements that are otherwise easily missed, but take their fanciful interpretations of what is being depicted with a grain of salt. There's a small two-level **museum in the medieval tower** at the corner of the temple area, with Arab-era finds upstairs and sarcophagi downstairs, with good descriptions of Roman burial practices.

Temple of Jupiter — RUINS

This temple was built on a monumental scale and is one of the largest Roman temples known. Dedicated to Jupiter Heliopolitanus, it was built from the 1st century BC onwards on an immense substructure more than 90m long. Though largely ruinous, it impresses by its sheer size.

At the entrance, a staircase leads to a *propylaea* (entrance) that gives on to an unusual hexagonal courtyard, a 2nd-century-AD addition. Beyond here is the massive central courtyard, with two high altars flanked by ritual columns in grey and pink granite. Another enormous staircase led from here to the temple itself, consisting of a *cella* in which the statue of the god was housed and a surrounding portico of 10 columns along the facade and 19 columns along the side. These columns are the largest known from antiquity – 22.9m high with a girth of 2.2m. Today only six of these remain standing with the architrave still in position.

It was probably built over an earlier Phoenician temple and, as was common in antiquity, the 'Sun City' Jupiter preserved some solar and cosmic attributes of Ba'al, the deity he was superseding.

Temple of Venus — RUINS

Opposite the entrance to the main ruins is the exquisite Temple of Venus, which preserves a section of a circular building with fluted columns. During the early Christian era, this was turned into a basilica and dedicated to St Barbara (who joined the saintly ranks when her pagan father tried to kill her for converting to Christianity – he got his comeuppance when a bolt of lightning reduced him to a smouldering heap). Next to it is a fragmentary **Temple of the Muses**.

This temple area wasn't open to the public at time of last visit, but is easily admired from the pavement around it.

Festivals & Events

Baalbeck International Festival — PERFORMING ARTS

(www.baalbeck.org.lb; ⏲early Jul–mid-Aug) This famous festival brings jazz, rock, ballet and opera to a stage in front of the splendid Temple of Bacchus over a series of summer nights. It attracts some big international names and extra transport is laid on from Beirut for the event.

Sleeping

Hotel Palmyra HISTORIC HOTEL $

(☎03 371 127; s/d US$50/75; 📶) This grand old hotel, opened in 1874, is a nostalgic and beautiful reminder of Baalbek's glory days of tourism: Kaiser Wilhelm, Einstein and de Gaulle all slept here. Faded, dusty and creaky, it's a very long way from those days now but is still charming. Despite no resources, the staff (some have been here for decades) still just about keep things going.

Some of the rooms have been slightly modernised and offer OK comfort, with high ceilings, fans and, from some, views of the ruins. Wi-fi and hot water both work, perhaps surprisingly. Impressively, through wars and hard times, the hotel has never closed in nearly a century and a half of existence. The courteous staff will show you reminders of other famous guests.

Eating & Drinking

A handful of reliable but unmemorable eateries can be found opposite the ruins and on the main road leading through the souq.

Baalbek is pretty much a dry town, though there are takeaway alcohol shops. There are plenty of cafes along the central streets that get lively in the evenings.

Getting There & Away

The only public transport options from Beirut to Baalbek are minibuses and service taxis. From the Cola transport hub (p371), a minibus to Baalbek costs LL8000 (1½ hours); a service taxi costs LL15,000. The bus stop in Baalbek is by the Palmyra Hotel, and the service taxi stand is in the souq area.

In summer, you can negotiate a private taxi to take you across the barren, beautiful mountains to the Cedars or Bcharré (1½ hours) for around US$80 to US$100.

UNDERSTAND LEBANON

Lebanon Today

Pity the poor Lebanese, who, after having lived through a bloody and protracted civil war and equally bloody and protracted invasions by Israel, have then had to cope with the awful violence in neighbouring Syria. With 1.5 million Syrian refugees joining the already significant number of Palestinian refugees in Lebanon, the country's infrastructure and economy have been put under severe pressure. Damage to the social fabric is also evident: the number of people needing support has drained Lebanese patience and pockets, leading to growing resentment. Hezbollah's involvement in the Syrian war, fighting on the government side, has also polarised the country: many Lebanese are understandably antagonistic to the Assad regime after so many years of Syrian occupation.

The country's political system has been in disarray and was briefly pushed into the international news cycle by the odd incident in late 2017 when Prime Minister Saad Hariri unexpectedly resigned after travelling to Saudi Arabia. Weeks later, when he finally returned to Beirut, Hariri agreed to stay on, at least for now. With other international interests pulling the political strings in Lebanon, the machinery of the government is regularly paralysed, and constant wrangling in the highly factionalised national parliament has left it basically dysfunctional. At time of research, there had been no elections in eight years, but things seem to be looking up slightly, with a decent chance of elections in 2018.

History

Early Empires

The area of modern-day Lebanon lays claim to having one of the oldest civilisations in the world; its shores have likely been permanently settled since around 10,000 BC. The archaeological remains at Byblos, in particular, show several millennia of constructions.

By around 2500 BC, the coast was colonised into city-states by a Semitic group who came to be known as the Phoenicians. For more than 1500 years, they would watch the ebb and flow of great civilisations before the tide ebbed for them, too.

The emerging city-states were very much independent entities. They were first brought together under the rule of the Akkadians, who marched out of Mesopotamia (modern-day Iraq) in search of conquest and natural resources. Under the rule of Sargon of Akkad (r 2334–2279 BC) the eastern Mediterranean area flourished, particularly ports such as Byblos. This grew wealthy on trade with the Egyptians, who needed plentiful supplies of timber (from Mt Lebanon), a resource lacking in their own country.

By about 1550 BC Egypt had removed itself from under the occupation of Asiatic Hyksos invaders, who had fought to control the country for more than a century. To completely banish the threat, the pharaohs pursued their former tormentors north, leading to a period of expansion of the Egyptian empire.

In 1480 BC, a revolt organised by more than 300 local rulers was easily crushed as Egypt was firmly established in what is now the Palestinian Territories and southern Syria. In the north, however, the various principalities coalesced to form the Mitanni empire. They held off all Egyptian attempts at control, helped in part by their invention of the horse-drawn chariot.

The Mitanni empire was subsumed by the encroachments of the Hittites (1365 BC) from a region corresponding with today's central Turkey. By 1330 BC all of Lebanon was firmly under Hittite control. The region became a battleground for the Egyptian and Hittite superpowers. They clashed at the bloody Battle of Kadesh on the Nahr Al Aasi (Orontes River) in Syria around 1300 BC, the battle seeing the Egyptians retreat south. Finally, the two opposing forces signed a treaty of friendship in 1284 BC. It left the Egyptians with the south and the Hittites with what corresponds to modern-day Syria and Lebanon.

Still living in tandem with the Egyptians and Hittites were the Phoenicians, who occupied several towns along the Mediterranean coast and successfully traded with Egypt to the south, Mesopotamia to the east and Anatolia to the north. Having no military ambitions, they were not seen as a threat to the great powers of the region. Despite their innovations and skills as artisans and traders, the Phoenicians never became unified politically, and instead remained independent city-states along the Lebanese coast. Gebal (Byblos, later Jbail) and Tyre (also known as Sour) were the most important of these cities, followed by Sidon (Saida) and Berytus (Beirut).

Greeks & Romans

Alexander the Great defeated the forces of King Darius III at Issus (333 BC) in what is now southeast Turkey, opening the way for his armies to storm through Syria and Palestine on his way to Egypt. On his death, his nascent empire was divided among his bickering generals. Ptolemy I gained Egypt and southern Syria, while Seleucus I Nicator established a kingdom in Babylonia that spread to include the north Syrian centres of Antioch, Apamea, Lattakia and Cyrrhus.

The Seleucids disputed the Ptolemiac dynasty's claim to Lebanon and the Palestine and finally succeeding in ousting them in 198 BC, under the leadership of Antiochus III. A further aggressive campaign of expansion by the Seleucids brought them up against the new power of Rome. In the resulting clash, the Seleucids were defeated and in 188 BC Antiochus was forced to cede all his territories in Asia Minor. However, it wasn't until 64 BC that the Roman legate Pompey finally abolished the Seleucid kingdom, making it a province of Rome with its capital at Antioch.

After emperor Constantine converted to Christianity in AD 313, the new religion, now legitimised, soon dominated the empire. This rosy state of affairs was abruptly shattered in the 7th century when the Persians once again descended from the north, taking Damascus and Jerusalem in 614 and eventually Egypt in 616, although Byzantine fortunes were revived when the emperor Heraclius invaded Persia and forced the Persians into a peace agreement. In the south, however, the borders of the empire were being attacked by Arab raiders. This was no new thing, but these Arabs were different. They were ambitious followers of the teachings of a prophet named Mohammed, and they called themselves Muslims.

The Advent of Islam

With the Byzantine empire severely weakened by the Persian invasion, the Muslims met with little resistance and in some cases were welcomed. In 636, the Muslim armies led by Khaled ibn Al Walid won a famous victory at Yarmouk, near the modern border between Jordan and Syria. The Byzantine forces could do little but fall back towards Anatolia. Jerusalem fell in 638 and soon all of Lebanon and Syria was in Muslim hands.

Because of its position on the pilgrims' route to Mecca, Syria became the hub of the new Muslim empire that, by the early 8th century, stretched from Spain across northern Africa and the Middle East to Persia (modern Iran) and India. Muawiyah, the governor of Damascus, had himself declared the fifth caliph (successor to Mohammed) in 658 and then went on to found a dynasty, the Umayyads, which would last for nearly 100 years.

Umayyad rule was overthrown in 750, when the Abbasids seized power. This new and solemn religious dynasty moved the capital of the Arab world to Baghdad, relegating Syria to backwater status. By 980 Lebanon had fallen under the rule of the Fatimid dynasty, whose capital was Cairo.

The Crusades

A plea from Pope Urban II in November 1095 for the recapture of the Church of the Holy Sepulchre in Jerusalem resulted in a Crusade of hundreds of thousands of people on the road to the Holy Land. All along their route, cities such as Antioch, Aleppo, Apamea, Damascus, Tripoli, Beirut and Jerusalem, weakened by their own rivalries and divisions, were exposed to the invaders' untempered violence.

The atrocities inflicted on the population of Maarat Al Numan in December 1098 were perhaps the nadir of Crusading behaviour, but the same excesses of savagery also marked the taking of Jerusalem on 15 July 1099, when only a handful of Jewish and Muslim inhabitants escaped alive.

Following the capture of the Holy City, the Crusaders built or took over a string of castles. Nureddin (Nur ad Din), the son of a Turkish tribal ruler, was able to unite all of Syria not held by the Franks and defeat the Crusaders in Egypt. His campaign was continued by Saladin (Salah ad Din), who recaptured Palestine and most of the inland Crusader strongholds. Saladin's compromise with the Assassins led to the Crusaders remaining on the coast.

Prosperity returned with the rule of Saladin's dynasty, known as the Ayyubids, who parcelled up the empire on his death. They were succeeded by the Mamluks, the freed slave class of Turkish origin that had taken power in Cairo in 1250, just in time to repel the onslaught from the invading Mongol tribes from Central Asia in 1260. Led by the fourth of their sultans, Beybars – a great warrior hero of Islam – the Mamluks finally managed to rid the Levant of the Crusaders by capturing their last strongholds, taking Acre in 1291 and the fortified island of Ruad (Arwad) in 1302.

The Ottoman Turks

By 1516 the Ottoman Turks occupied the Levant and would remain there for the next four centuries. Up until the early 19th century, the region prospered under Turkish rule. By the 19th century, though, groups of Arab intellectuals in Syria and Palestine, many influenced by years of study in Europe, had set an Arab reawakening in train. The harsh policies of the Young Turk movement of 1908 further encouraged both opposition to Turkish rule and the growth of Arab nationalism.

World War I & the French Mandate

During WWI, the region was the scene of fierce fighting between the Turks, who had German backing, and the British based in Suez. The enigmatic British colonel TE Lawrence, better known as Lawrence of Arabia, and other British officers involved with the Arab Revolt encouraged Arab forces to take control of Damascus, and urged Emir Faisal, the leader of the revolt, to set up a government in 1918.

When Arab nationalists proclaimed Faisal king of Greater Syria (an area that included Palestine and Lebanon) and his Hashemite brother, Abdullah, king of Iraq in March 1920, the French moved swiftly to force Faisal into exile. Later the French were formally awarded the mandate over Syria and Lebanon by the League of Nations.

Under pressure from the Lebanese Christian Maronites, the French employed what amounted to a divide-and-rule policy. They split their mandate into Lebanon (including Tyre, Beirut and Tripoli); a Syrian Republic, whose Muslim majority resented their presence; and the two districts, Lattakia and Jebel Druze.

The French attempt to create a Lebanese nation fell foul of growing Arab nationalist sentiment, which held that Arabs should live in a greater Arab homeland, rather than arbitrarily drawn nation states. For the Maronites, who looked towards Europe, Arab nationalism was a threat. Hostility to the French led to uprisings in 1925 and 1926.

Scant attention was paid to the opposition, and in 1926 the French and their Maronite allies drew up and passed a new constitution for Lebanon, sowing the seeds of the country's troubled future. The document formalised a largely symbolic power-sharing formula, but Maronites still managed to secure a virtual monopoly on positions of power. Sunni Muslims boycotted the constitution, which was suspended in 1932. In 1936, the Franco-Lebanese treaty was signed, promising eventual independence for Lebanon; the following year a new constitution was drawn up but not ratified by the French.

World War II & Independence

When France fell to the Germans in 1940, Syria and Lebanon came under the control of the puppet Vichy government until July 1941, when British and Free French forces took over. The Free French promised independence – and delivered it five years later

– but only after violent clashes (and French bombing) in Syria in 1945 had compelled Britain to intervene.

In Lebanon, the various religious and political factions came together in 1943 to draw up the Lebanese National Covenant, an unwritten agreement dividing power along sectarian lines on the basis of the 1932 census. The president was to be Maronite, the prime minister a Sunni, and the speaker of the house a Shiite. Parliamentary seats were divvied up between Christians and Muslims in the ratio of six to five. The Maronites were also given control of the army, with a Druze chief of staff. Dividing the country along sectarian lines from the very start was to be a major source of strife for years to come.

In November 1943, the fledgling Lebanese government of President Bishara Al Khouri went a step further and passed legislation removing all references to French Authority in the constitution. The French retaliated by arresting the president and members of his cabinet, and suspending the constitution. Britain, the US and the Arab states supported the Lebanese cause for independence, and in 1944 the French began the transfer of all public services to Lebanese control, followed by the withdrawal of French troops. Independence was declared in 1946.

Early Years of Independence

The early years of independence for the fledgling government weren't easy. First came economic strife and next, on 14 May 1948, the declaration of Israeli independence in former Palestine. Immediately, Lebanese soldiers joined pan-Arab armies and Palestinian fighters in the struggle against Israel. During 1948 and 1949, while war raged, Palestinian refugees flooded north into Lebanon; Amnesty International claims that the tiny nation absorbed more Palestinians than any other country, more than 100,000 by the end of 1949 alone. Though initially welcomed into Lebanon, the Maronite majority soon became uneasy about the refugees, mostly Sunni Muslims, who threatened to tilt their precarious balance of power. In 1949 Lebanon accepted an armistice with Israel, but although 1948's UN Resolution 194 stated that refugees should be allowed to return home if they wanted to, in most cases this didn't eventuate. The Palestinian refugees, largely against their own and locals' will, were in Lebanon to stay.

By the 1950s the National Assembly was once again struggling against economic crisis. In 1952 staunchly pro-Western president Camille Chamoun quickly garnered Muslim enemies by refusing all notions of pan-Arabism (the creation of a united Arab entity in the Middle East), and in 1958, when his term was about to end, the unpopular president tried to extend his presidency to a second term. Lebanon's first civil war soon erupted, with pro-Western Maronites pitted against largely Muslim, pan-Arabist opponents. Chamoun panicked, turning to the US for help, and on 15 July 1958, 15,000 US troops landed in Beirut.

The presence of US troops quelled trouble, and Chamoun was finally persuaded to resign, to be replaced by a new president,

PALESTINIAN REFUGEES

Most Palestinians who fled to Lebanon in 1948 during the Arab–Israeli War were relegated to refugee camps administered by the UN Relief and Works Agency (UNRWA), and 12 of the original 16 camps still house most of Lebanon's Palestinian population today. The area of land allocated for these camps has not increased since their establishment, despite significant population growth, leading to situations whereby families of up to 10 members are forced to live in a single room.

According to UNRWA, there are now about 450,000 registered Palestinian refugees in Lebanon. Amnesty International estimates that there are another 3000 to 5000 second-generation unregistered refugees living illegally and without rights. Other UN agencies place the total number of registered and unregistered refugees at 655,000.

Palestinian refugees in Lebanon suffer from a lack of opportunities, being prohibited from joining many professions, largely barred from owning or improving property and having only limited access to public health care, education and welfare programs. Most are still provided for by the UNRWA, which runs the camps' schools, hospitals, women's centres and vocational training programs.

For more information, see www.unrwa.org.

HEZBOLLAH

Often described as a 'State within a State', Hezbollah (aka the Party of God or Party of Allah) is a Lebanese Shiite Islamist political party and militant group with an armed wing known as the Jihad Council. It wields enormous influence in the country – particularly in the south – and currently holds 12 seats in the national parliament, including two cabinet positions. It also has its own radio station, TV network and countrywide network of social services.

After the 1982 Israeli invasion of Lebanon, Iranian revolutionary guards began to preach to Lebanon's disaffected Shiites, who proved receptive to their message of overthrowing Western imperialism and the anti–Muslim Phalange. Hezbollah was formed at this time. Alongside suicide bombings, its ruthless armed wing also resorted to taking hostages, including CIA bureau chief William Buckley, who was kidnapped, tortured and killed in 1984–85. Other victims included Associated Press bureau chief Terry Anderson, kidnapped in 1985 and held until 1991; and UK envoy Terry Waite, kidnapped in 1987 and held until 1991.

Many in Lebanon and the Arab world credit Hezbollah with ending the Israeli occupation of Lebanon in 2000, an achievement celebrated at the Resistance Tourist Landmark in Mleeta (p384) near Nabitiyeh in the country's south. Their solid resistance to the Israeli invasion in 2006 also won them credit across the country, though it was their anti-Israel activity that arguably provoked that invasion in the first place.

Hezbollah's current leader and public face is Hassan Nasrallah (b 1960), whose base is in the village of Bazourieh, near Tyre. Nasrallah has studied Islamic theology in Lebanon, Iraq and Iran, and is known for his charismatic and evocative brand of rhetoric.

Admired for its welfare and education projects, and feared for its military capability and history of violence, Hezbollah is branded a terrorist organisation by a number of Western governments and is known for its rocket attacks on Israel, kidnap missions against that country's soldiers and attacks on Israeli citizens abroad. Hezbollah is heavily backed by the fellow Shiite Iranian government and has been intimately involved in the Syrian Civil War, fighting alongside government forces.

Fouad Chehab. With Chehab's talent for smoothing ruffled feathers, Lebanon soon prospered. Civil war, believed the optimistic Lebanese, was a thing of the past.

Swinging Sixties?

By the mid-1960s, Beirut, the newly crowned 'Paris of the East', was booming, but Palestinian refugees and the Shiites of the south remained in poverty. As Beirut basked in newfound riches, the less fortunate grew bitter and restive, and the good times were already numbered.

The outbreak of the 1967 Arab–Israeli Six Day War brought yet more Palestinian refugees into Lebanon. Refugee camps soon became centres of guerrilla resistance, and the government watched impotently as Palestinian attacks on Israel from Lebanese soil rapidly increased.

In May 1968, Israeli forces retaliated across the border. Meanwhile, with sectarian tensions growing, the Lebanese army clashed violently with Palestinian guerrillas. Palestinian forces proved too strong an opponent for the army, and in November 1969 Lebanon signed the Cairo Agreement with the Palestinian Liberation Organisation (PLO), agreeing to large-scale autonomy of its refugee camps and refugees' freedom 'to participate in the Palestinian revolution'.

Maronite opposition to the agreement was immediate. Many Muslims, on the other hand, felt an innate sympathy for their fellow Palestinians. In response, a group of Christians known as Phalangists began to arm and train young men, and by March 1970 fighting between Phalangists and Palestinians had erupted on Beirut's streets as southern Lebanon suffered under Israeli reprisals against relentless guerrilla attacks. Rapidly, the country factionalised and took up arms.

Civil War

It's widely agreed that Lebanon's civil war began on 13 April 1975 when Phalangist gunmen attacked a Beirut bus, killing 27 Palestinian passengers. Soon, there was outright chaos. In December, Phalangists stopped

Beirut traffic and killed Muslim travellers. Muslims retaliated, prompting 'Black Saturday' during which around 300 people died.

The slaughter rapidly reached horrific proportions. In January 1976, Phalangists led a massacre of some 1000 Palestinians in Karantina, a Beirut slum. Two days later, Palestinians attacked the southern coastal town of Damour and killed more than 500 Christians. In August, Phalangists set their sights on the Tel Al Zaatar refugee camp in northeast Beirut, killing between 2000 and 3000 Palestinian civilians.

Soon Beirut was divided along the infamous Green Line, which split the city in two, with Christian enclaves to the east and Muslims to the west. Though allegiances and alliances along its border would shift many times in the coming strife, the Green Line would remain in place for 15 years.

Syria & Israel Intervene

In 1976 the civil war gave Syria a reason to send tens of thousands of troops into Lebanon. Though initially sympathetic to the Palestinians and the pan-Arab cause, it wasn't long before Syria switched allegiance to the Maronite side, occupying all but the far south and angering other Arab countries. Nevertheless, in October 1976 the Arab League brokered a deal with Syria, allowing it to keep 40,000 troops in Lebanon as part of a peacekeeping 'Arab Deterrent Force'. Syria was left in primary control of Lebanon, and the first of the civil war's 150 short-lived ceasefires was declared.

At the same time, Palestinian attacks on Israel continued, prompting Israel to launch 'Operation Litani' in 1978, swiftly occupying most of southern Lebanon. Immediately, the UN demanded Israel's withdrawal and formed the UN Interim Force in Lebanon (UNIFIL) to 'restore international peace'. Though Israel withdrew to a 19km 'security zone', it simultaneously installed a puppet South Lebanon Army (SLA) and proclaimed an 1800-sq-km region south of Nahr Al Litani (the Litani River) 'Free Lebanon'. For the coming years, this area was mired in war.

In 1982 Israeli 'Operation Peace for Galilee' troops marched into Lebanon headed for Beirut, supported tacitly by Maronite and Phalangist leaders. By 15 June, Israeli forces had surrounded and besieged West Beirut, bombarding 16,000 PLO fighters entrenched there. Heavy fighting ensued, and in just two months the city was in ruins – 20,000 people, from both sides of the Green Line, were dead. The infamous Sabra and Shatila massacres, perpetrated by Phalangist forces in refugee camps under Israeli control, were particularly horrific. On 21 August the PLO left Beirut, guaranteed safe passage by multinational forces. By now, however, battle was also raging in the Chouf Mountains, the historic preserve of Druze and Christians, until then free from the ravages of war. The Lebanese army joined the Phalangists and Israelis against the Druze, who themselves were aided by the Shiite militia Amal, until the US intervened and another ceasefire was brokered.

By this time the US was becoming increasingly entrenched in the war, appearing to favour Israel and Lebanon's beleaguered government. In 1983 came the reprisals. In April, an Islamic Jihad–organised suicide attack on the US embassy in Beirut left 63 dead. In October, suicide bombers hit the US and French military headquarters in Beirut, killing more than 300. In 1984 abductions and the torture of foreigners – whose involvement in Lebanese affairs the abductors deeply resented – began. The following year, international forces hastily left Lebanon.

Battle of the Camps

In early 1985 the last Israeli troops finally withdrew to their self-proclaimed 'security zone', leaving their interests in the hands of the SLA and Christian militias, who immediately clashed with Druze and Shiite opponents around Saida. In West Beirut fighting continued between Shiite, Sunni and Druze militias, all battling for the upper hand.

In the midst of the chaos, PLO forces began to return to Lebanon. Concerned, however, that this would lead to a renewed Israeli invasion of the south, the Shiite Amal fought to remove them. Heavy fighting battered the Palestinian refugee camps during 1986, causing many more thousands of casualties.

To add to the confusion, in 1987 the National Assembly government finally fell apart and split in two, with a Muslim government to the west of Beirut and a Christian administration to the east. Fighting along the Green Line continued to rage as Christian leaders attempted to drive Syria from Lebanon, angering Syria still more by accepting arms from Iraq, Syria's gravest enemy. It wasn't until 1989 that a road to peace finally seemed viable, with the drafting of the Taif Accord.

SYRIAN REFUGEES

The civil war in neighbouring Syria has had a huge impact on Lebanon. In 2017, the seventh year of the conflict, the UN Refugee Agency (UNHCR) estimated that there were more than five million Syrian refugees in the region, nearly 1.5 million of whom were in Lebanon. This was an enormous burden to shoulder for a country with a native population of only four million, and though the UNHCR and other international aid organisations were in the country to assist, the task of housing, feeding, educating and providing health care for the refugees was placing a huge burden on Lebanon's weak economy and inadequate infrastructure.

At the time of writing, there are no official Syrian refugee camps in Lebanon – the Lebanese wouldn't countenance the possibility of hosting more Palestinian-style permanent refugee settlements – so many of the Syrian refugees are living in appalling conditions without proper housing, heating, running water or electricity. None are able to work legally (even illegal jobs are scarce) and only a small percentage of Syrian children attend school. For more information, see www.unhcr.org.

Peace & Reconstruction

The 1989 Taif Accord established a comprehensive ceasefire and a parliament equally divided between Christians and Muslims. The country saw peace for the first time in 15 years, and the civil war officially ended on 13 October 1990.

Syria's continued presence in Lebanon beyond the civil war was justified with reference to Lebanon's weak national army and the government's inability to carry out Taif Accord reforms, including dismantling militias, alone.

From 1993 onwards, the Lebanese army and life were slowly rebuilt and Rafic Hariri, a Lebanese-born multimillionaire and entrepreneur, became prime minister.

Meanwhile, the south remained impoverished and was the base for Israeli-Hezbollah skirmishes. Israeli offensives in 1993, 1996 and 1999, in response to Hezbollah and Palestinian attacks, devastatated rebuilt structures and killed many civilians.

Sustained Israeli losses led to calls within that country for military withdrawal, and its army finally withdrew from southern Lebanon on 24 May 2000.

In Lebanon, discontent rumbled on. Maronite groups opposed Syria's refusal to withdraw from Lebanon, while Shiites and Hezbollah continued to support its presence. On 2 September 2004, the UN issued Security Council Resolution 1559, which called 'upon all remaining foreign forces to withdraw from Lebanon'. Syria still did not comply, and on 20 October 2004, Prime Minister Hariri tendered his resignation, announcing that he would not be a candidate to head the next government.

Killing of Rafic Hariri

On 14 February 2005, a massive Beirut car bomb killed the former prime minister, Rafic Hariri, and 21 others. Many Lebanese placed the blame firmly on Syria and attended demonstrations calling for Syrian withdrawal from Lebanon. Syria finally bowed to pressure, withdrawing its 14,000 remaining troops from Lebanon on 27 April 2005 after almost 30 years of occupation. For the first time in more than two decades, Lebanon was completely free from military forces other than its own.

The 2005 parliamentary elections, the first after Syria's withdrawal, saw a majority win for the March 14 Alliance led by Saad Hariri, with Fouad Siniora elected Lebanon's new prime minister. The elections also saw Hezbollah become a legitimate governmental force, winning 14 seats in parliament, while in the south its fighters continued to launch attacks on Israeli troops and towns.

In 2006 Israel again invaded southern Lebanon, aiming to reduce Hezbollah capacity. A ceasefire was brokered a month later after a military stalemate that inflicted significant civilian casualties.

Food & Drink

The equivalent of Italian antipasto or Spanish tapas, Lebanese mezze are the most famous elements of the Lebanese menu and are the perfect way to start a meal...or, with enough little dishes, to form a meal in themselves. The following form the nucleus of the Lebanese mezze menu and are almost always served with pita bread.

Hummus Chickpea-and-tahini (sesame-seed paste) dip

Kibbeh Croquettes of finely ground meat and minced onion encased in burghul (cracked wheat) and either fried or cooked in broth; a popular vegetarian version features spiced pumpkin

Kibbeh labaniyye Kibbeh balls cooked in a warm yoghurt sauce

Kibbeh nayyeh Raw spiced minced lamb topped with herbs and olive oil

Labneh Thick yoghurt seasoned with olive oil and garlic

Moujaddara Lentils cooked with rice and onions

Muttabal Eggplant-and-tahini dip

Sambusas Fried cheese or meat pastries, similar to samosas

Shanklish Strong-tasting aged cow- or sheep-milk cheese, often rolled into balls and covered in dried *zaatar* or thyme

Warak arish Stuffed vine leaves (also known as *wara anaib*)

Three popular salads are often ordered alongside mezze:

Fattoush Toasted pita bread, cos lettuce, cucumbers, tomatoes and sumac

Roca and wild-thyme salad

Tabouleh Parsley, tomato, spring onion, burghul salad and mint

Main courses tend to be meat or fish dominated, and include the following:

Kofta Mincemeat with parsley and spices grilled on a skewer

Sayadieh Fish and rice topped with onion sauce

Shish tawooq Chicken marinated in olive oil, lemon, parsley and sumac and then grilled on skewers

There are also tasty fast-food options on offer:

Falafel Deep-fried balls of spiced chickpeas and/or fava beans served on a platter or wrapped in pita bread

Lahme baajin Spiced ground meat and tomato pizza

Manakeesh Thyme-and-olive-oil pizza

Shawarma Thin slices of marinated meat garnished with fresh vegetables, pickles and tahini, wrapped in pita bread

Drinking

Arabic/Turkish coffee is particularly popular in Lebanon, while delicious freshly squeezed juices are on offer almost everywhere throughout the summer. Alcohol, too, is widely available; Beirut is awash with craft beer and cocktails, but the most popular alcoholic old-timer is the potent aniseed-flavoured arrack, mixed liberally with water and ice.

Nightlife is excellent in Beirut and along the coast, especially in summer, when rooftop bars and beach clubs are pumping.

The standard local beer is Almaza, which lives up to its name ('diamond' in Arabic) when served ice-cold. There's a burgeoning craft-beer scene and local wines are impressive – the best-known producers are Chateau Ksara (p390) and Chateau Kefraya (p390) at the southern end of the Bekaa Valley, and Chateau Musar in Ghazir, north of Beirut. The best of the boutique wineries are DomaineWardy in Zahlé, Massaya near Chtaura and **IXSIR** (restaurant 71 773 770, tours 71 631 613; www.ixsir.com.lb; Basbina; 10am-5pm Tue-Sun) near Batroun.

Religion

Lebanon hosts 18 'official' religious sects, which are Muslim (Shiite, Alawite, Ismaili and Sunni), Christian (Maronite, Greek Orthodox, Greek Catholic, Armenian Catholic, Gregorian, Syrian Orthodox, Jacobite, Nestorian, Chaldean, Copt, Evangelical and Roman Catholic), Druze and Jewish. There are also small populations of Baha'is, Mormons, Buddhists and Hindus.

Muslims are today estimated to comprise around 54% of the population, though before the civil war unofficial statistics put the Muslim to Christian ratio closer to 50:50. The shift is attributed to the mass emigration of Christians during and since the civil war, and to higher birth rates among Muslims. Christians comprise 40.5% of the overall population and Druze 5.6%.

Traditionally, Muslim Shiites have largely inhabited the south of the country, the Bekaa Valley and southern suburbs of Beirut. Sunnis, meanwhile, have been concentrated in Beirut, Tripoli and Saida; the Druze in the Chouf Mountains; and Maronite Christians (the largest Christian group) in the Mt Lebanon region. Though recent years have seen geographical population shifts, particularly in Beirut, this still largely holds true today.

Environment

Though Lebanon is one of the smallest countries in the world, its terrain is surprisingly diverse. Four main geographical areas run almost parallel to each other from north to south. They are (from west to east): the coastal plain, the Mt Lebanon Range, the Bekaa Valley and the Jebel Libnan Ash Sharqiyya (Anti-Lebanon) range.

The Mt Lebanon Range includes Lebanon's highest summit, Qornet As Sawda (3090m). Jebel Libnan Ash Sharqiyya marks the border between Lebanon and Syria. Its highest summit is Jebel Ash Sheikh (Mt Hermon), at 2814m.

Literature

Though it was the publishing powerhouse of the Middle East for much of the 20th century, Beirut suffered during the civil war and much of its recent literary output has been shaped by this long drawn-out and horrific event. Even today, a great deal of Lebanon's literary output remains concerned with themes drawn from these 15 years of hardship.

Of the writers who remained in Lebanon during the civil war, Emily Nasrallah (b 1931) is a leading figure who is best known for her award-winning debut novel *The Birds of September*. Those who work overseas include Canada-based Rawi Hage (b 1964), whose Beirut-set debut novel *De Niro's Game* garnered strong international reviews; London-based Tony Hanania (b 1964), whose novel *Unreal City* is set in Beirut; and French-based Amin Maalouf (b 1949), two of whose novels are set in Lebanon: *Balthasar's Odyssey* in Jbail (Byblos), and *The Rock of Tanios* in a rural village. The latter was awarded the prestigious Prix Goncourt in 1993.

Of other authors widely available in translation, Lebanon's two major figures are Elias Khoury (b 1948) and London-based feminist author Hanan al-Shaykh (b 1945). Al-Shayk's *Story of Zahra* is a harrowing account of the civil war, while her *Beirut Blues* is a series of long letters that contrast Beirut's cosmopolitan past with the book's war-torn present. Elias Khoury has published 10 novels, many available in translation: his 1998 novel *Gate of the Sun* has achieved particular international acclaim.

Up-and-coming Lebanese novelists include Rabee Jaber (b 1972), author of *The Druze of Belgrade,* which was awarded the International Prize for Arabic Fiction in 2012.

Poet Khalil Gibran (1883-1931) remains the celestial light in Lebanon's poetry scene. Interestingly, today poetry is once again flourishing in the largely Shiite south, partly due to a movement known as Shu'ara Al Janub (Poets from the South), for whom poetry has become a means of expressing the frustrations and despair of life in that most war-ravaged of regions.

Music

With the 2014 death of the hugely popular singer and actress Sabah, Lebanon is left with two reigning divas: living legend Fay-

THE CEDARS OF LEBANON

The most famous of the world's several species of cedar tree are the cedars of Lebanon, mentioned in the Old Testament, and once covering great swaths of the Mt Lebanon Range.

Jerusalem's original Temple of Solomon was made from this sort of cedar wood, and the ancient Phoenicians, attracted by its fragrance and durability, also used it in their buildings. Unfortunately, a long history of deforestation has meant that today just a few pockets of cedars remain in Lebanon – despite the tree appearing proudly on the nation's flag.

Cedrus libani is a beautiful evergreen of the conifer family with a very distinctive flat-branched shape. In Lebanon it grows mostly from 1200m to 1900m of elevation. Up in the mountains here there are some exceptionally ancient examples.

Of these remnants of a once-abundant arboreal past, the best places to view the remaining cedars of Lebanon are either at the Chouf Cedar Reserve, or at the small grove at the Cedars ski resort in the north of the country.

rouz (b 1934) and Najwa Karam (b 1966), known as the 'Sun of Lebanese song'.

Fayrouz has enjoyed star status since her first recordings in Damascus in the 1950s, and later became an icon for Lebanon during the civil war (which she sat out in Paris). Now in her 80s, her most recent album is 2017's *Bebalee*.

Najwa Karam rose to stardom during the 1990s. With 19 albums under her belt, including the 2001 blockbuster *Nedmaneh,* she remains a driving force on the Lebanese music scene. Her most recent release is 2017's *Menni Elak*.

Mainstream pop artists include Nancy Ajram and Haifa Wehbe, both producing catchy tunes and raunchy videos. More interesting are alt-rock band Mashrou' Leila, which specialises in satirical lyrics and themes; and oud (lute) player Marcel Khalife, who marries classical Arabic music with contemporary sounds.

In the bars and clubs of Beirut's Hamra and Mar Mikhaël districts, contemporary fusions of oriental trip-hop, lounge, drum and bass and traditional Arabic music are popular, alongside Western retro, mainstream and indie tracks.

SURVIVAL GUIDE

Directory A–Z

ACCOMMODATION

Beirut has a wide range of hotel accommodation as well as some backpacker hostels. Decent hotels are a bit thin on the ground in some parts of the country; coastal resorts like Jounieh and Byblos offer the most choice.

High season is June to September – except for the Cedars ski area, where it's December to March. Low-season discounts are sometimes available, so it's always worth checking.

Hostels & Homestays

Hostelling International has eight affiliated hostels in Lebanon. Most are in small, rural villages, offering a taste of real local life, and offer dorm beds for between US$15 and US$25 per person per night.

For upscale homestays across the country, L'Hote Libanais (www.hotelibanais.com) can organise a single stay or an entire itinerary for reasonable prices. Check www.diyafa.org for a list of rural Lebanese guesthouses that can be booked online.

SLEEPING PRICE RANGES

Prices are for rooms in high season and include bathrooms, breakfast and taxes unless otherwise indicated.

$ less than LL112,500 (US$75)

$$ LL112,500 to LL262,500 (US$75 to US$175)

$$$ more than LL262,500 (US$175)

BARGAINING

Bargaining isn't as much a part of life in Lebanon as in other parts of the Middle East, but in traditional shopping districts, it's still standard practice.

DANGERS & ANNOYANCES

Many countries, including the UK, Australia and the USA, have been counselling their citizens to reconsider their need to travel to all or certain parts of Lebanon. Most specifically, foreign offices advised against travel to the southern suburbs of Beirut, Saida, areas south of the Litani River (with the exception of Tyre), the upper Bekaa Valley, all areas bordering Syria and northern Lebanon north of a line from Tripoli to Sir Ed Dinniyeh and Arsal. Some also advised against travel to Baalbek and Tripoli.

- Before travelling to Lebanon, register your travel with your country's foreign affairs department so that you can be sent security updates. When in the country, monitor the *Daily Star* or *L'Orient–Le Jour* for up-to-the-minute news and regularly check the websites of foreign embassies for security updates. Be aware that the political and security situation in Syria can impact Lebanon and compromise its stability, and that Israeli missiles are sometimes fired into southern Lebanon. Also be aware that there are currently no safe land exits from the country and that airport access is sometimes blocked at time of strife, making it impossible to leave the country.
- Bekaa Valley is Hezbollah's heartland, but Isis (Islamic State) were still present in the far north. There's also a history of foreigners being kidnapped for ransom here.
- At time of research, Tripoli was still regarded as unsafe by some foreign governments, with the risk of being caught up in factional violence and terrorist attacks a real one.
- While central Beirut was seen as safe to visit by most governments, the risk of a terrorist attack on the city remained high.
- Throughout the country, be very aware when taking photographs, as there are numerous guard posts, military installations and sensitive areas.

Government Travel Advice

The following government websites offer travel advisories and information:

Australian Department of Foreign Affairs & Trade (www.smarttraveller.gov.au)

British Foreign Office (www.gov.uk/foreign-travel-advice)

Canadian Department of Foreign Affairs (https://travel.gc.ca/travelling/advisories)

France Diplomatie (www.diplomatie.gouv.fr/fr/conseils-aux-voyageurs)

German Auswärtiges Amt (www.auswaertiges-amt.de)

US State Department (http://travel.state.gov)

EMBASSIES & CONSULATES

All embassies are in or near Beirut. Nationals of New Zealand and Ireland should contact their embassies in Cairo for assistance.

Australian Embassy (Map p360; ☎01 960 600; www.lebanon.embassy.gov.au; Serail Hill, Downtown; ⏱8.30am-4pm Mon-Thu, to 1.30pm Fri)

Canadian Embassy (☎04 726 700; www.canadainternational.gc.ca/lebanon-liban; 1st fl, Coolrite Bldg, Autostrade, 43 Jal Ad Dib Hwy)

Egyptian Embassy (Map p358; ☎01 825 566; www.mfa.gov.eg; Rue Dr Muhammed El Bethri 5, Be'er Hassan; ⏱9am-4pm Mon-Fri)

French Embassy (Map p358; ☎01 420 000; www.lb.ambafrance.org; Rue de Damas, Ras Al Nabaa; ⏱8.15am-1pm & 2-5pm Mon-Fri)

German Embassy (☎01 504 600; www.beirut.diplo.de; Regent Park Tower, Rue Barbar Abou Jawdeh, Dekwaneh; ⏱8.30am-4pm Mon-Fri)

Italian Embassy (☎05 954 955; www.ambbeirut.esteri.it; Rue du Palais Presidentiel, Baabda; ⏱9am-1pm Mon-Fri)

Jordanian Embassy (☎05 922 500; www.mfa.gov.jo; Rue Elias Helou, Baabda; ⏱8.30am-2.30pm Sun-Thu)

Netherlands Embassy (Map p360; ☎01 211 150; http://lebanon.nlembassy.org; Netherlands Tower, Ave Charles Malek, Achrafiyeh; ⏱8.30am-4.30pm Mon-Fri)

UK Embassy (Map p360; ☎01 960 800; www.gov.uk/government/world/organisations/british-embassy-beirut; Rue de l'Armée, Downtown; ⏱8am-4pm Mon-Thu, to 2pm Fri)

EATING PRICE RANGES

Prices represent the cost of a standard main-course dish.

$ less than LL15,000 (US$10)

$$ LL15,000 to LL30,000 (US$10 to US$20)

$$$ more than LL30,000 (US$20)

US Embassy (☎04 543 600; http://lebanon.usembassy.gov; Main St, Awkar, Antelias; ⏱8am-4.30pm Mon-Fri)

EMERGENCY & IMPORTANT NUMBERS

Lebanon's country code	☎961
International access code	☎00
Ambulance & emergencies	☎140
Fire	☎175
Police	☎112
General security information	☎1717

INTERNET ACCESS

Wi-fi is widely available, offered for free in nearly every accommodation choice and commonly in restaurants, cafes and bars.

Mobile phone coverage is good across the country, so buying a local SIM card and data package is the easiest way to get online.

LGBTIQ TRAVEL

Despite some encouraging recent judicial decisions, homosexuality is still illegal in Lebanon. Nevertheless, there's a thriving – if clandestine – gay scene in Beirut. Gay-friendly cafes, bars and clubs include B 018 (p370), Posh (p369) and Madame Om (p369).

There have been spells of police harassment of gay men in Beirut, with the arrests of patrons in some hammams and cinemas. There were also reports of invasive body searches being perpetrated on men in police custody. Before attending known gay venues, check the current situation with Helem (www.helem.net), a protection organisation for LGBTIQ people.

MONEY

ATMs

ATMs are reliable and available, and dispense cash in both Lebanese lira and US dollars. ATM fees vary very widely for withdrawing money with foreign cards, so try a few. At last research, SGBL and Banque Libano-Française worked best.

Cash

Lebanon's currency is the Lebanese lira (LL), also known as the Lebanese pound (LBP). Banknotes are of the following denominations: 1000, 5000, 10,000, 20,000, 50,000 and 100,000 lira; there are also 25, 50, 100, 250 and 500 lira coins.

US dollars are a second currency here and higher-end establishments rarely quote prices in anything else. You'll often get change in a mixture of the two currencies.

Tipping

Tipping is widespread in Lebanon. For hotel porters and parking valets, somewhere around LL4000, depending on the level of service, will be appreciated. For waiters usually tip around 10% to 15%, but check your bill before doing so: some places automatically add a 15% service charge.

OPENING HOURS

Banks 8.30am to 2pm Monday to Friday, to noon Saturday

Post offices & government offices 8am to 5pm Monday to Friday, to 1.30pm Saturday

Restaurants Nonstandard; roughly 11am to 1am

Shops 10am to 7pm Monday to Friday, to mid-afternoon Saturday

PUBLIC HOLIDAYS

New Year's Day 1 January

Orthodox Christmas Day 6 January

Feast of Saint Maroun 9 February – feast of the patron saint of the Maronites

Easter March/April – Good Friday to Easter Monday

Labour Day 1 May

Martyrs' Day 6 May

Assumption 15 August

All Saints' Day 1 November

Independence Day 22 November

Christmas Day 25 December

Muslim holidays are also observed.

SMOKING

Though a law restricting smoking indoors exists, it isn't widely enforced.

The Lebanese are enthusiastic smokers, recently ranking third worldwide in consumption per capita. Smoking shisha pipes is a very common social activity in cafes.

TAXES & REFUNDS

An 11% value-added tax (VAT) applies to most purchases in Lebanon and is nearly always included in the quoted price. You can claim back VAT on purchases in shops of over US$100 either through the shop itself or at the airport on departure.

TELEPHONE

Mobile Phones

Mobile-phone coverage extends throughout most of the country (bar a few remote, mountainous areas). Check with your mobile provider before leaving home whether you'll have roaming service in Lebanon.

SIM Cards

Local Touch and Alfa SIM cards are widely available from phone stores, cost around US$35 (including some credit and data), are activated immediately and can be easily recharged.

Phone Codes

The country code for Lebanon is ☎961, followed by the local area code (minus the zero), then the subscriber number. The area code when dialling a mobile phone is ☎03 or 70. The international access code (to call abroad from Lebanon) is ☎00.

TOURIST INFORMATION

The Lebanese Ministry of Tourism (www.destinationlebanon.gov.lb) runs several helpful tourist offices across the country. Brochures and maps on various towns and regions are available for download from their website.

VISAS

Free one-month, single-entry tourist visas renewable for three months are available at Rafic Hariri International Airport for citizens of many countries, including Australia, Canada, China, France, Germany, Ireland, Italy, Japan, the Netherlands, New Zealand, Spain, the UK and the USA. A paid visa-on-arrival system was in place for some other countries. For the most up-to-date information, visit the website of Lebanon's General Security Office (www.general-security.gov.lb/en).

Lebanon denies entry to all travellers with evidence of a visit to Israel in their passport. If asked at a border crossing or at the airport if you've ever been to Israel, bear in mind that saying 'yes' (if you have) will mean you won't be allowed into the country.

To extend your one-month visa to a three-month visa, go to the General Directorate of General Security in Beirut a few days before your first month ends; you'll find the office across the road from the National Museum – head to the 2nd floor. Take your passport, two passport photos, and two photocopies of your passport ID page and the page where your entry visa was stamped.

Once your application is processed, you will be given a receipt and told to return in seven days to collect your passport with its extended visa.

WOMEN TRAVELLERS

Lebanon is a relatively easy destination for solo female travellers. Western-style clothes are common in Beirut, and revealing beach wear is acceptable in the beach clubs that line the sands from Saida up to Byblos. However, modest clothing is recommended for areas outside Beirut and the beach.

In mosques or religious sites, women should cover their shoulders and heads, and avoid wearing shorts or short skirts. In taxis, it's best to sit in the back seat.

Getting There & Away

AIR

With the land border with Israel closed and the Syrian border off limits, most travellers to Lebanon arrive and depart by air.

Beirut–Rafic Hariri International Airport (p371) is Lebanon's only airport and main entry point into the country. The national carrier, Middle East Airlines (www.mea.com.lb), has an extensive network including flights to and from Europe and to the Arab world. Many other Middle Eastern airlines fly into Beirut, as well as some European ones.

LAND

The only land crossings from Lebanon are into Syria, which has been off limits for several years. The Israel–Lebanon land border has not been open for many years.

SEA

There has previously been a ferry service from Turkey to Tripoli in Lebanon, but it was suspended at time of research.

Getting Around

AIR

There are no air services operating within Lebanon, but the country is so small that you don't really need them (you can drive from one end to the other in half a day).

BUS

Minibuses travel between Beirut and all of Lebanon's major towns; the only route that has large, Pullman-style buses is Beirut–Tripoli. The best of the buses on that route are operated by Connexion (www.connexion-transport.com) and will drop passengers off at any point along the Beirut–Tripoli highway on request.

Buses usually have a route number and the destination displayed in the front window, but this is usually in Arabic only. Government-run buses have red number plates, and there are a number of independently owned microbuses that cover the same routes; note that the embassies of foreign countries recommend using the government-run buses only. You pay for your ticket on board, either at the start or end of the journey.

Some towns, including Beirut, have privately owned buses that operate a hail-and-ride system. Fares are generally LL1000 for intracity destinations and LL1500 for intercity destinations.

CAR & MOTORCYCLE

You need to be a competent driver with very steady nerves to contemplate driving in Lebanon, since rules are cheerfully flouted. A three-lane road, for example, can frequently become seven lanes and intersections are a survival-of-the-fittest experience. Hairpin bends and potholed roads are frequent in the mountains, and few roads are gritted after a snowfall.

Beirut's traffic is often heavy, and road signs (where there are any at all) can be cryptic or misleading. In addition to being generally cautious, remember to stop at military checkpoints and have your passport and car-hire papers ready for inspection.

That said, car-hire prices are very competitive compared to the cost of hiring a driver, and grabbing a vehicle can make the most of limited time. Make sure you've got phone data: navigation with online maps makes things much easier.

TAXI

Most routes around Lebanese towns and cities are covered by service, or shared, taxis, which are usually elderly Mercedes with red licence plates and a taxi sign on the roof. You can hail them at any point on their route and also get out wherever you wish by saying '*anzil huun*' (drop me off here). Be sure to ask '*servees?*' before getting in (if it's an empty car), to ensure the driver doesn't try to charge you a private taxi fare. Going rates are generally LL1500 to LL4000 for trips within a town, and LL3000 to LL10,000 for trips to outlying areas.

If you want to engage a private taxi, make sure the driver understands exactly where you want to go and negotiate the fare clearly before you get in.

Reputable Beirut-based taxi companies that have English-speaking drivers and well-maintained cars include White Taxi (p372) and Lebanon Taxi (p372). Both charge around US$100 for a half-day hire and US$150 for a full-day hire.

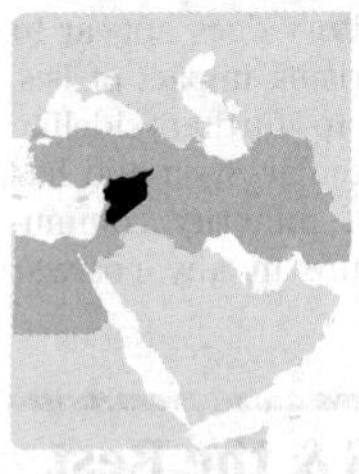

Syria

Includes ➡

Syria Explained..........406
History.........................407
People & Society 410
Further Information....412

Fast Facts

Area 185,180 sq km

Currency Syrian pound (£)

Language Spoken Arabic

Population 17.19 million

Time Eastern European Time (UTC/GMT plus two hours)

Understand

At the time of writing, Syria was one of the most dangerous places on the planet. To put it simply, you can't go. And if you can, you shouldn't. The uprising against the Assad regime that began in early 2011 long ago became a civil war. Syrians themselves have paid the heaviest price: as many as 475,000 people have died in the conflict and millions have been forced into exile. Westerners, including journalists and aid workers, have also been targeted, very publicly, both for kidnapping and for execution. In addition to the human cost, entire cities have been laid waste and untold damage has been done to some of the Middle East's most important historical and archaeological sites. Put simply, Syria is a war zone, and peace seems as far away as at any time since war began in 2011.

Resources

International Crisis Group (www.crisisgroup.org) Respected international NGO known for its objective, detailed coverage of conflicts worldwide.

Syrian Observatory for Human Rights (www.syriahr.com/en) Tireless collating of deaths and battles from inside Syria.

Syria News Wire (www.newsfromsyria.com) A blog on the Syrian conflict coming out of Damascus and London.

Unesco (www.unesco.org) Go to the 'Safeguarding Syrian Cultural Heritage' section for the most comprehensive coverage of the threat to Syria's cultural heritage.

BBC News (www.bbc.com/news/world/middle_east) Comprehensive, up-to-the-minute news on the region.

Al Jazeera (www.aljazeera.com/topics/regions/middleeast.html) Reporting from an Arab perspective.

SYRIA EXPLAINED

Syria is in ruins. Divided up into devastated fiefdoms ruled by warring armies, the country has become a battleground for the major players vying for influence in the Middle East, among them Russia and the US, Isis and Hezbollah, Iran and the Gulf States. While at one level a proxy war for those who would use Syria to further their own interests, Syria's civil war has been nothing short of a catastrophe for its people.

Assad & the Alawites

One of the few things that all sides opposing the Syrian government can agree on is that President Bashar Al Assad must go. If only it were that simple. In his community, and among some secular-minded Syrians, Assad is a hero, seen as the last bulwark against Islamic extremism in the country. As an Alawite, he is seen as the protector of his community, a people who represent around 11% of Syria's population and whose homeland is in the country's west. The Assad family, and therefore the Alawites, have held power in Syria since the 1970s, and the Alawites fear that Assad's removal would put the entire community at risk of revenge and sectarian violence. For those opposed to the Assad regime, however, he remains the greatest obstacle to peace, a leader with blood on his hands and whose authoritarian rule and bloody response to calls for democracy mean that he can never be part of postwar Syria. Until a way can be found around this impasse over Assad's future role, peace will remain a distant dream.

Isis

Of all the players in Syria's tragic civil war, it is Isis and its extremist ideology that have come to symbolise the brutality of the conflict. Since 2014, the provincial Syrian city of Raqqa has been the capital of the self-declared caliphate and a base from which Isis has extended its control of vast swaths of Syria – at the peak of its powers, it controlled nearly half of the country's territory, and an estimated 10 million civilians lived under its rule in Syria and Iraq. Campaigns to drive Isis from its strongholds continue at the time of writing, and the group was estimated in 2017 to have lost around 60% of the territory it formerly controlled. While the group's territory does appear to be shrinking, the polarising impact of Isis' presence has helped to further sideline those who call for a secular Syria and has deepened the fears of minority communities about their future in any postwar outcomes.

Russia, the US & the Rest

It is difficult for any of the foreign powers operating in Syria to complain about international meddling in the Syrian conflict – they're all at it. The US has long been a player by backing the largely secular Free Syrian Army, while Russia has, since 2015, provided critical military backing for the Syrian government and has possibly saved it in the process. Iran and Hezbollah, too, have seen opportunities to increase their regional influence by siding with the Syrian government, even as the oil-rich Arab Gulf States have sought to combat Iranian meddling by lavishing funds across all manner of rebel groups, including, according to some reports, Al Qaeda–backed Al Nusra Front. Wary of growing Kurdish influence in northern Syria, Turkey, too, has become a major player, maintaining a delicate balancing act by opposing both Isis and those best placed to remove it. The result is a complex entangling of geopolitical rivalries that has only served to escalate the conflict and make worse the lives of ordinary Syrians.

Paths to Peace

Peace in Syria can at times seem like an impossible dream, such is the level of division – between those who support Assad and those who want him tried for war crimes, between those fighting for an Islamic Syria and those who believe in a secular future – in the country. Add to this the apocalyptic levels of human misery and the physical devastation of cities and infrastructure, and Syria's future looks bleak indeed. For a peaceful Syria to emerge from the morass, a united international community is a necessity. Despite the best efforts of UN-appointed mediators, such unity is a long way off, and the numerous UN-backed peace conferences that have been held have, not surprisingly, come to nothing. Another prerequisite for peace would seem to be some unity of vision among Syrians

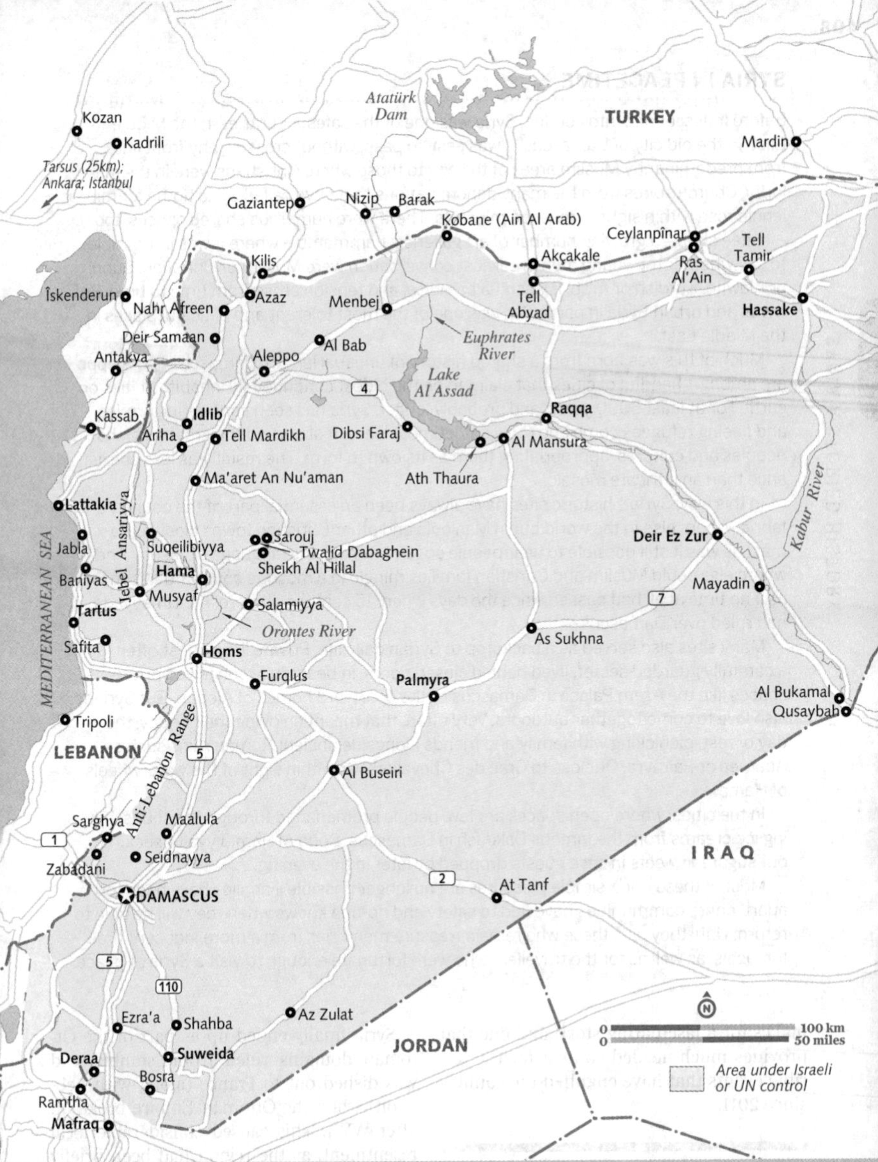

themselves as to what postwar Syria will look like. That, too, appears unlikely without major concessions by all sides. The only consolation for Syrians is that, as difficult as such prospects may be to realise, the dangers of not doing so are even more difficult to contemplate. Such tenuous shreds of positive thinking are as close as Syria comes to hope in the present climate.

HISTORY

Syria may be passing through the most difficult of times, but this is a country that has seen it all before. Through the centuries, Syria has stood at the crossroads of empires and civilisations, and its territory has been the scene for invading armies and era-defining wars. Damascus and Aleppo are among the oldest cities on earth. It all

SYRIA IN PEACETIME

Before it descended into conflict, Syria was one of the safest countries in the Middle East. In the old city of Damascus, it was easy to pass, without crossing any front line, from predominantly Muslim areas of the city to those where Christians were in the majority. Church spires from the many denominations that have called Syria home for millennia rose within sight of mosque minarets. There were numerous shared spaces, too – coffee shops, a growing number of art galleries, hammams – where it was impossible to say whether the young men in earnest conversation were Muslim or Christian, Sunni or Alawite, Kurdish or Arab. It wasn't a paradise, and tension arose from time to time. But Syria, and urban Syria in particular, was one of the most tolerant and peaceful places in the Middle East.

Much of this was born from a shared history of unusual length. Damascus and Aleppo are among a handful of cities that claim to be the oldest continuously inhabited cities on earth. For at least 5000 years, and probably longer, Syria has seen conquering armies and fleeing refugees come and (only sometimes) leave. It absorbed the great religions, peoples and cultures, appropriating them as its own to form. The result was less coexistence than an intricate mosaic.

In this way, Syria's historic sites have always been an essential part of the country's fabric. Where else in the world but in Maaloula and other Christian towns close to Damascus was it still possible to hear people speak Aramaic, the language of Jesus? And where else could Muslim and Christian families mingle in a mosque courtyard at sunset as if no time at all had passed since the days when, 15 centuries before, the Umayyads had ruled over Damascus?

Many sites also served as a backdrop to Syrian daily life. Private life is most often a carefully guarded secret, lived behind closed doors, in beautifully conceived private spaces like the Azem Palace in Damascus or the courtyard homes of Aleppo. But Syrians also love to come together outdoors. Very often, that meant enjoying their Friday, the day of rest, picnicking with family and friends alongside ancient Roman ruins such as Apamea or Palmyra. Or close to Crac des Chevaliers. Or within sight of the waterwheels of Hama.

In the cities, where open spaces are few, people promenaded through the souqs, buying ice creams from the famous Bakdash in Damascus' Souq Al Hamidiyya or seeking out sugared sweets in case guests dropped by later in the evening.

Most of these once-simple pleasures are no longer possible. Families have been torn apart, entire communities have fled to safety and no-one knows when they will be able to return. Until they can, these who remain treasure memories from a more innocent time – for locals, as well as for the travellers who were fortunate enough to visit a Syria at peace.

makes for a fascinating story, and one that provides much-needed context for the terrible events that have engulfed the country since 2011.

A Storied History

Historically, Syria included the territories that now make up modern Jordan, Israel and the Palestinian Territories, Lebanon and Syria itself. Because of its strategic position, its coastal towns were important Phoenician trading posts. Later, the area became a pivotal part of the Egyptian, Persian and Roman Empires, and of many others in the empire-building business.

Syria finally ended up as part of the Ottoman domains ruled from Istanbul and was dished out to France (along with Lebanon) when the Ottoman Empire broke up after WWI. This caused considerable local resentment, as the region had been briefly independent from the end of WWI until the French took over in 1920.

France never had much luck with its Syria-Lebanon mandate. Local opposition to its policy of carving up the country into mini-states (Grand Liban, Lebanon, Aleppo and Damascus) and minority enclaves (for the Druze and Alawites) led to revolts against French rule. Elections were held in 1928 and 1932, but moves to establish a constitution were stymied by the occupying power, which compounded its unpopularity in 1939 when it ceded the northern cities of Antioch (Antakya) and Alexandretta (Iskenderun) to encourage Turkey's neutrality in WWII.

A nationalist government was formed under Shoukri Al Quwatli in August 1943, but the French continued to be in denial about the waning of their influence in the region, bombing Damascus after locals had demonstrated in support of a final handover of administrative and military services to the new government. The situation was only resolved after the British intervened and oversaw the final departure of all French troops and administrators at the end of the war.

Post WWII

By 1954, after several military coups, the nationalist Ba'ath Party ('Ba'ath' means 'renaissance') took power virtually unopposed. A brief flirtation with the pan-Arabist idea of a United Arab Republic (with Egypt) in 1958 proved unpopular, and coups in 1960, 1961 and 1963 saw the leadership change hands yet again. By 1966 the Ba'ath Party was back in power, but it was severely weakened by losses in two conflicts: the Six Day War with Israel in 1967 and the Black September hostilities in Jordan in 1970. At this point, defence minister Hafez Al Assad seized power.

Assad maintained control longer than any other post-independence Syrian government, with a mixture of ruthless suppression and guile. The most widely condemned example of the former came on 2 February 1982, when Assad ordered the shelling of the old city in Hama in response to a growing campaign by the Muslim Brotherhood. He followed this with a warning that anyone left in the city would be declared a rebel. In the fighting that followed, between 10,000 and 25,000 people were killed out of a total population of 350,000, and mosques, churches and archaeological sites were damaged and destroyed.

In 1998, Assad was elected to a fifth seven-year term with a predictable 99.9% of the vote. It took failing health to finally remove him from power; his death was announced on 10 June 2000.

Disappointment

Following the death of Assad senior, his son Bashar acceded to the presidency, continuing the minority Alawites' hold on power. A new government was formed in December 2001 with a mandate to push forward with political, economic and administrative reforms. For a while, a wave of change swept Syria, the so-called 'Damascus Spring' buzzing with a proliferation of private newspapers, internet bloggers, and public debate not seen in the country in decades. Foreign goods flooded into Syria, private banks were allowed to open, and mobile phones made a belated but wildly popular appearance.

But 'not so fast' was the message that came from the old guard that had surrounded Bashar's father – anything perceived as opposing the government was quickly shut down. Reforming the country's unwieldy bureaucracy, of which membership depends more on political patronage and nepotism than merit, also proved a bridge too far, as did any hope of curbing the state's far-reaching powers under the emergency laws brought in in 1963, after the coup that brought the Ba'ath Party to power.

As a result, while many of the economic reforms were left untouched, political reforms stalled. There was more freedom and less fear than during the rule of Assad senior, but Syrians suffered low wages and rising prices. The country appeared to be going through a boom – certainly a tourism boom – as a result of an improving international standing (even the US reopened its embassy in Damascus), and there was an influx of investment and hope, in some places. But life for the majority of Syrians continued to be difficult, with around a quarter of young people out of work. This tense situation was finally ignited by the 'Arab Spring' uprisings that swept across the region from late 2010.

Uprising & War

Small-scale public protests that began in Deraa in March 2011 may not have escalated had security forces not killed four unarmed protestors and then killed one of the mourners at the funeral. President Assad's brother, Maher Assad, then led an armoured division to suppress any further dissent. The death of dozens of unarmed people in the assault led to protests around the country. By mid-May, the UN reported that at least 1000 people had been killed by security forces and by *shabiha* – pro-Assad armed gangs. *Shabiha* have also been involved in torture, which Amnesty International says is now widespread, with many of the cases coming from Deraa.

President Assad did make some concessions, ending the emergency laws and promising electoral reform, but armed resistance to the regime grew along with the security forces' use of heavy weapons, including tanks and the air force. Defecting soldiers from the Syrian Army formed the basis for the creation of the Free Syrian Army. In October 2011, the Syrian National Council (www.syriancouncil.org) – an organisation of dissidents and defected politicians made up predominantly of Sunni Muslims, including the Islamist Muslim Brotherhood – announced its mission to replace the Assad government. Based outside Syria and promising to uphold democratic rights and abide by the rule of law, it soon won support from Western governments, while Russia continued to support Assad.

The result has been years of conflict, with the Syrian government pitched against Islamist, secular and ethnic militias, all supported by their foreign backers.

PEOPLE & SOCIETY

Daily Life

In the current climate of civil war, daily life in Syria is primarily a battle for survival, with families torn apart and every day a fraught and perilous struggle for the basic necessities of existence. Before everything fell apart, family ties were extremely close, families were large, and extended families often lived together. Rural–urban migration over recent years meant that about half of the country's population lived in the cities.

Before the outbreak of conflict in 2011, and before the collapse of the country's social networks and education system, Syrians faced a number of challenges common to the region. On one level, prewar Syrians were well educated, with an overall literacy rate of around 80% (86% for men, 74% for women). School attendance was compulsory for children aged between six and 12, and there were four national public universities with combined enrolments of almost 200,000. At the same time, unemployment was far higher than the official rate of 10% suggested. Compounding the problem, wages were low – average government salaries were just US$300 per month and university graduates such as doctors rarely earned more than US$700. The consequence was that the country faced a serious 'brain drain', with many graduates heading overseas to find better-paying work. The obligatory 30 months' military service by all 18-year-old men also played its part.

Arts

Syria has contributed some of the Arab world's best-loved cultural figures, but cultural life fell into decline during the reign of Hafez Al Assad, thanks largely to government repression and a critical lack of government funding. Now writers, musicians and cinematographers are starting to make waves again.

Literature

Most Syrian writers to have made their name beyond Syria's borders have done so from exile. The most famous contemporary example is Rafik Schami (b 1946), who left Syria in 1971. His *A Hand Full of Stars* (1990) is an outstanding work for teenagers, but *The Dark Side of Love* (2004) is his best-known (and most widely available) work.

Zakariya Tamir (b 1931), Syria's master of the children's story, deals with everyday city life marked by the frustration and despair born of social oppression. Having been virtually forced to leave Syria in 1980, he was awarded the Syrian Order of Merit in 2002. His *Tigers on the Tenth Day and Other Stories* (1978) is wonderful.

But not everyone was forced to leave. The Damascene Nizar Qabbani (1923–98) became one of the Arab world's most beloved poets, credited with transforming formal Arabic poetry with the use of everyday language. He was adored in the 1950s for his love poems, and later for his expressions of the Arabs' collective feelings of humiliation and outrage after the wars with Israel.

Of the noted writers who remained in Syria, the most celebrated and outspoken was Ulfat Idilbi (1912–2007), who wrote about the late Ottoman Empire and French Mandate and the drive for liberation and independence. *Sabriya: Damascus Bitter Sweet* (1995) is critical of the mistreatment of women by their families, much of its anger stemming from Idilbi's own experience

PRESERVING SYRIA'S HISTORICAL SITES

The loss of human life during the Syrian conflict has been well documented. Less is known about the damage caused to Syria's historic sites. As Unesco's Director-General, Irina Bokova, warned in 2014, 'We are reaching the point of no return where Syria's cultural heritage is concerned. The destruction of heritage represents a cultural haemorrhage in addition to the tragic humanitarian crisis and suffering experienced by the people of Syria.'

The Desecration of Cultural Sites

All of Syria's six Unesco World Heritage–listed sites – Aleppo's Old City, the Old City of Damascus, Palmyra, Bosra, the Crac des Chevaliers and a series of historic villages in northern Syria – were added by Unesco to its list of World Heritage Sites in Danger in 2013. All six have been extensively damaged during the conflict.

In Aleppo, the Great Umayyad Mosque has been reduced to rubble, and 121 historic buildings and 1500 shops have been destroyed in the covered souq. The citadel, surrounding buildings and many gates to the Old City have also been badly damaged, while the Yalbogha Hammam is, at the time of writing, occupied by military groups.

The Crac des Chevaliers, Syria's iconic Crusader-era castle, has been repeatedly hit in the fighting. Although its superstructure remains largely intact, the interior has been badly damaged. Looting and damage has also occurred in the ancient cities of Palmyra, Bosra and Apamea.

The core of the Old City in Damascus has thus far largely escaped serious damage. Some mosaics on the facade of the Umayyad Mosque have been damaged by mortar rounds, although the mosaics have since been repaired by the government's General Directorate of Archaeology and Museums. The national museum remains undamaged and, remarkably, open for visitors.

The 2015 occupation of Palmyra by Isis, and its return in late 2016 into early 2017, saw widespread looting and the deliberate destruction of important monuments in the ancient city, including the iconic tetrapylon, Roman theatre, Temple of Baalshamin and Arch of Triumph.

Beyond World Heritage Sites, Isis has repeatedly targeted Islamic shrines revered by locals, denouncing them as un-Islamic. It has also targeted Christian churches. The Armenian Genocide Martyrs' Memorial Church in Deir Al Zour, for example, was deliberately destroyed in 2014, along with its priceless library devoted to the events in Turkey at the end of WWI that are recognised by several reputable international bodies as a genocide against the Armenian people.

What's Being Done

In 2014, UN Security Council Resolution 2139 called on all parties to 'immediately end all violence which has led to human suffering in Syria, save Syria's rich societal mosaic and cultural heritage, and take appropriate steps to ensure the protection of Syria's World Heritage Sites'.

Although it's unable to physically prevent or monitor attacks on most threatened sites within Syria, Unesco has put in place measures to stop illegal trafficking in looted antiquities, working closely with Interpol and customs authorities in neighbouring countries and around the world.

In a section on its website, Unesco (www.unesco.org/new/en/safeguarding-syrian-cultural-heritage) also publishes comprehensive reports and photographic evidence of attacks on historic sites in a bid 'to monitor the situation of cultural heritage in Syria and help international cooperation to protect the country's heritage'.

For its part, the Syrian government has launched a national campaign called 'Save Syria's History' and says that many of its workers have been killed trying to protect the country's ancient sites. The government's critics argue that indiscriminate bombing by the government itself has caused widespread damage to historic and cultural sites.

of being married off at 16 to a man twice her age. *Grandfather's Tale* (1997) is also worth tracking down.

Since the war began in 2011, writing has very much taken a back stage, although two excellent works worth seeking out are *The Home That Was Our Country: A Memoir of Syria* (Alia Malek; 2016) and *No Knives in the Kitchens of This City* (Khaled Khalifa; 2016).

Music

Syria's most famous musical star, Farid Al Atrache (1915–74), spent most of his career in Cairo and remains Syria's most beloved musical export across the region. Sometimes called the 'Arab Sinatra', he was a highly accomplished oud player and composer who succeeded in updating Arabic music by blending it with Western scales and rhythms and the orchestration of the tango and waltz. His melodic improvisations on the oud (he's still known as 'King of the Oud') and his *mawal* (a vocal improvisation) were the highlights of his live performances, and recordings of these are treasured. By the time of his death, he was considered – and still is by many – to be the premier male Arabic music performer.

After a quiet period on the Syrian music scene, there were signs of a revival before the conflict, thanks to the local success of albums by Kulna Sawa *(All Together)*, Itar Shameh, Anas and Friends, Gene and InsaniT, and by the charismatic Lena Chamamian *(Shamat)*. A sold-out Woodstock-type concert that toured the country in 2007 featured many of these bands. One of the biggest voices to have emerged from Syria in recent years is that of singer Omar Souleyman. Coming from deep up-country, near the Turkish border, his fast-paced renditions of local folk songs have morphed, thanks to a collaboration with Icelandic singer Björk, into a global sound.

Cinema

Cairo has long been regarded as the home of Arab cinema, a status now being challenged by the Gulf States. Syrian film-makers have long resented this, none more so than the country's leading director, Nabil Maleh. Maleh's *The Extras* (1993) captured the stifling repression of the Assad regime in its tale of an unmarried couple looking for a space to have an affair. In April 2011, Maleh and many other Syrian film-makers issued a call for solidarity by film-makers everywhere in protest at the fact that 'peaceful Syrian citizens are being killed today for their demands of basic rights and liberties'.

FURTHER INFORMATION

➡ *Syria: Descent into the Abyss* (Patrick Cockburn, Robert Fisk and Kim Sengupta; 2015) Reportage by respected journalists of long standing.

➡ *Syria Speaks: Art and Culture from the Frontline* (edited by Malu Halasa, Zaher Omareen and Nawara Mahfoud; 2014) Work by more than 50 artists and writers from wartime Syria.

➡ *My House in Damascus: An Inside View of the Syrian Revolution* (Diana Darke; 2014) Rare insider account of the war's context and daily life.

➡ *Syrian Dust* (Francesca Borri; 2015) Unflinching and courageous reportage from Aleppo at war.

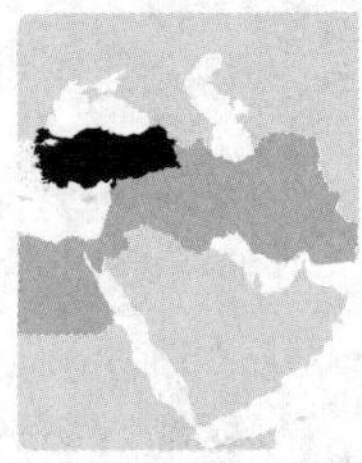

Turkey

Includes ➡

Istanbul 416
Aegean Coast 436
Gallipoli Peninsula 441
Selçuk 446
Ephesus 449
Bodrum Town 453
Mediterranean Coast 458
Antalya 463
Cappadocia 475
Understand Turkey 486
Survival Guide 488

Best Places to Eat

- ➡ Antiochia (p429)
- ➡ Topdeck Cave Restaurant (p477)
- ➡ Ney (p457)
- ➡ Kalamaki Restaurant (p461)
- ➡ Vanilla (p466)

Best Places to Stay

- ➡ Sota Cappadocia (p479)
- ➡ Hideaway Hotel (p462)
- ➡ Hotel Empress Zoe (p428)
- ➡ Akay Pension (p460)
- ➡ Angora House Hotel (p471)

Why Go?

Turkey is where Asia and Europe meet and meld together. The 'bridge between continents' tag may be a cliché, but this nation's juxtaposition of modern sophistication and ancient tradition is a surprising and heady brew that turns many travellers' first perceptions on their head. Steeped in age-old culture but imbued with a contemporary go-getting pulse, Turkey defies being pinned down and is the perfect introduction to the Middle East.

Every empire builder worth their salt has left their mark here. Stare in wonder at İstanbul's deluge of Byzantine and Ottoman finery or explore the rambling ruins of Ephesus – actually just trip over a rock in Turkey and it's probably going to be rubble from some long-gone empire's era of glory. Afterwards, hike the lunarscape of Cappadocia or sunbake on a beach backed by lush Mediterranean coastline and you'll discover a countryside just as mesmerising as its monuments.

When to Go

Istanbul

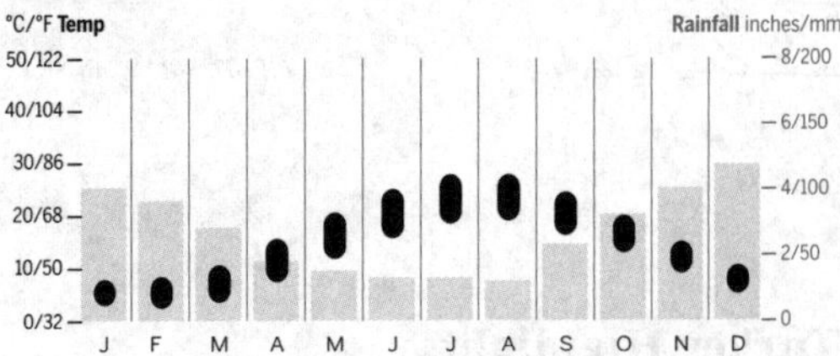

Apr–May Spring is perfect for tackling Turkey's long-distance Lycian Way.

Jul–Sep Sun-sloth time. The Mediterranean coast sizzles and the sand beckons.

Oct Prices drop but Turkish weather forgets it's off season. Blue sky days without the crowds.

Turkey Highlights

1 **İstanbul** (p416) Craning your neck to gaze at Byzantine frescoes and Ottoman artistry.

2 **Ephesus** (p449) Channelling your inner Roman amid the ruins.

3 **Cappadocia** (p475) Hiking amid this geological wonderland of 'fairy chimney' rock crags.

4 **Pamukkale** (p452) Scaling the blinding-white calcium hillside to dip your toes in thermal pools.

5 **Konya** (p473) Watching the dervishes whirl in the gardens of the Mevlana Museum.

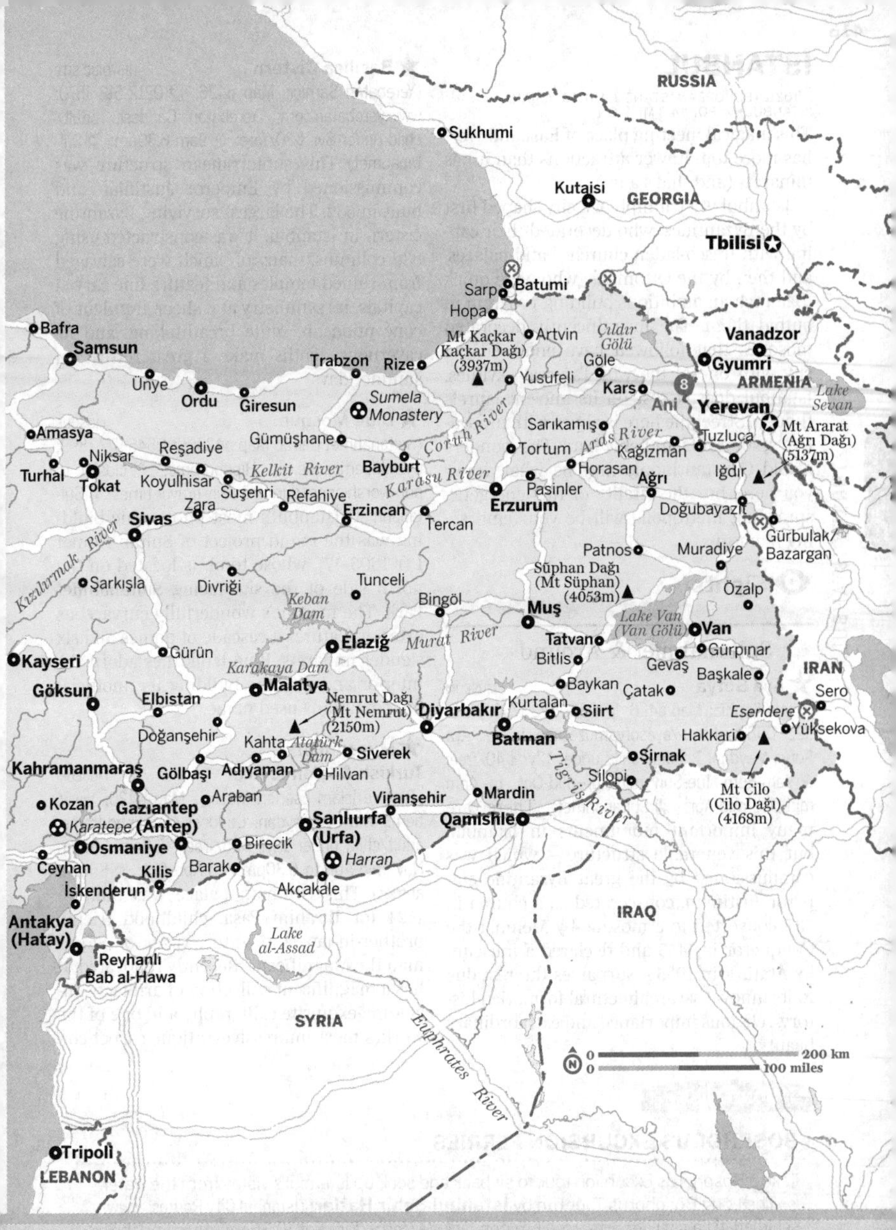

6 **Antalya** (p463) Strolling Kaleiçi's alleys then heading out of town to ramble city ruins.

7 **Gallipoli Peninsula** (p441) Remembering the fallen at the WWI battlefields.

8 **Ani** (p485) Exploring the crumbling churches of this ancient Armenian capital.

9 **Kaş** (p461) Discovering Turkey's lush Mediterranean scenery on a hike, boat or kayak trip.

10 **Safranbolu** (p472) Soaking up the old-world atmosphere in Turkey's best preserved Ottoman town.

İSTANBUL

0212 (EUROPEAN İSTANBUL), 0216 (ASIAN İSTANBUL) / POP 14.8 MILLION

This magical meeting place of East and West has more top-drawer attractions than it has minarets (and that's a lot).

İstanbul is a triumph of a city shaped first by the Byzantines, who decorated their capital with fresco-laden churches and palaces, and then by the Ottomans, who were quick to launch an ambitious building program to outbid them. The magnificently decorated mosques that followed have endowed the city with one of the world's great skylines. İstanbul doesn't rest on its ancient laurels though. Street life here is abuzz with innovative restaurants and chic bars. The wonders of old Constantinople may be what draws you here, but the vitality of this energetic, sprawling metropolis will be your embracing memory.

Sights

Sultanahmet & Around

★Aya Sofya MUSEUM

(Hagia Sophia; Map p426; 0212-522 1750, 0212-522 0989; http://ayasofyamuzesi.gov.tr/en; Aya Sofya Meydanı 1; adult/child under 12yr ₺40/free; 9am-6pm Tue-Sun mid-Apr–mid-Oct, to 4pm mid-Oct–mid-Apr; Sultanahmet) There are many important monuments in İstanbul, but this venerable structure – which was commissioned by the great Byzantine emperor Justinian, consecrated as a church in 537, converted to a mosque by Mehmet the Conqueror in 1453 and declared a museum by Atatürk in 1935 – surpasses the rest due to its innovative architectural form, rich history, religious importance and extraordinary beauty.

★Basilica Cistern HISTORIC SITE

(Yerebatan Sarnıçı; Map p426; 0212-512 1570; www.yerebatan.com; Yerebatan Caddesi; adult/child under 8yr ₺20/free; 9am-6.30pm; Sultanahmet) This subterranean structure was commissioned by Emperor Justinian and built in 532. The largest surviving Byzantine cistern in İstanbul, it was constructed using 336 columns, many of which were salvaged from ruined temples and feature fine carved capitals. Its symmetry and sheer grandeur of conception are quite breathtaking, and its cavernous depths make a great retreat on summer days.

★Blue Mosque MOSQUE

(Sultanahmet Camii; Map p426; 0545 577 1899; www.bluemosque.co; Hippodrome; closed to non-worshippers during 6 daily prayer times; Sultanahmet) İstanbul's most photogenic building was the grand project of Sultan Ahmet I (r 1603–17), whose tomb is located on the north side of the site facing Sultanahmet Park. The mosque's wonderfully curvaceous exterior features a cascade of domes and six slender minarets. Blue İznik tiles adorn the interior and give the building its unofficial but commonly used name.

★Museum of Turkish & Islamic Arts MUSEUM

(Türk ve Islam Eserleri Müzesi; Map p426; www.tiem.gov.tr; Atmeydanı Caddesi 46, Hippodrome; adult/child under 12yr ₺25/free; 9am-4.30pm Nov–mid-Apr, to 6.30pm mid-Apr–Oct; Sultanahmet) This Ottoman palace was built in 1524 for İbrahim Paşa, childhood friend, brother-in-law and grand vizier of Süleyman the Magnificent. Recently renovated, it has a magnificent collection of artefacts, including exquisite calligraphy and one of the world's most impressive antique carpet col-

DON'T MISS

BOSPHORUS EXCURSION FERRIES

Take a Bosphorus Excursion tour to sit back and soak up İstanbul's vistas from the water.

The Long Bosphorus Tour run by **İstanbul Şehir Hatları** (İstanbul City Routes; www.sehirhatlari.com.tr) departs from Eminönü *iskele* (ferry dock) at 10.35am, travelling the entire length of the strait up to Anadolu Kavağı in a 95-minute trip and returning at 3pm (return adult/child/under six years ₺25/12.50/free). The same company also run a Short Bosphorus Tour. It's not possible to get on and off the ferry at stops along the way using the same ticket.

The hop-on/hop-off Palace Tour ferry run by **Dentur Avrasya** (444 6336; www.denturavrasya.com) departs from Kabataş *iskele* at 12.45pm, 1.45pm, 2.45pm and 3.45pm, stopping at Emirgan and Küçüksu Kasrı on its way to to Beylerbeyi Palace. You can hop on and hop off at all the stops. One-way tickets cost ₺15.

lections. Some large-scale carpets have been moved from the upper rooms to the **Carpet Museum** (Halı Müzesi; Map p426; ☎0212-518 1330; www.halimuzesi.com; cnr Babıhümayun Caddesi & Soğukçeşme Sokak; ₺10; ⏰9am-6pm Tue-Sun mid-Apr–mid-Oct, to 4pm mid-Oct–mid-Apr; 🚊Sultanahmet or Gülhane), but the collection remains a knockout with its palace carpets, prayer rugs and glittering artefacts such as a 17th-century Ottoman incense burner.

★**Topkapı Palace** PALACE
(Topkapı Sarayı; Map p426; ☎0212-512 0480; www.topkapisarayi.gov.tr; Babıhümayun Caddesi; palace adult/child under 12yr ₺40/free, Harem adult/child under 6yr ₺25/free; ⏰9am-6.45pm Wed-Mon mid-Apr–Oct, to 4.45pm Nov–mid-Apr, last entry 45min before closing; 🚊Sultanahmet) Topkapı is the subject of more colourful stories than most of the world's museums put together. Libidinous sultans, ambitious courtiers, beautiful concubines and scheming eunuchs lived and worked here between the 15th and 19th centuries when it was the court of the Ottoman empire. A visit to the palace's opulent pavilions, jewel-filled Treasury and sprawling Harem gives a fascinating glimpse into their lives.

★**İstanbul Archaeology Museums** MUSEUM
(İstanbul Arkeoloji Müzeleri; Map p426; ☎0212-520 7740; Osman Hamdi Bey Yokuşu Sokak, Gülhane; adult/child under 12yr ₺20/free; ⏰9am-7pm Tue-Sun mid-Apr–Sep, 9am-4pm Tue-Sun Oct–mid-Apr; 🚊Gülhane) This superb museum showcases archaeological and artistic treasures from the Topkapı collections. Housed in three buildings, its exhibits include ancient artefacts, classical statuary and an exhibition tracing İstanbul's history. There are many highlights, but the sarcophagi from the Royal Necropolis of Sidon are particularly striking. Note that the ticket office closes one hour before the museum's official closing time.

NEED TO KNOW

Capital Ankara

Country code 09

Language Turkish

Official name Türkiye Cümhuriyeti (Republic of Turkey)

Population 79 million

Currency Turkish lira (₺)

Mobile phones Foreign phones can use a local SIM card for 120 days

Money ATMs widespread; credit cards accepted

Visas 90-day tourist e-visas should be purchased before travel (www.evisa.gov.tr)

Exchange Rates

Australia	A$1	₺2.98
Euro zone	€1	₺4.68
Iran	IRR10,000	₺1.01
Iraq	ID100	₺0.31
UK	£1	₺5.28
USA	US$1	₺3.76

For current exchange rates see www.xe.com.

Resources

Lonely Planet (www.lonelyplanet.com/turkey) Destination information, hotel bookings, traveller forum and more.

Turkish Cultural Foundation (www.turkishculture.org) Culture and heritage; useful for archaeological sites.

Go Turkey (www.goturkeytourism.com) Official tourism portal.

Hürriyet Daily News (www.hurriyetdailynews.com) The best English-language daily news site.

Bazaar District

★**Grand Bazaar** MARKET
(Kapalı Çarşı, Covered Market; Map p430; www.kapalicarsi.org.tr; ⏰8.30am-7pm Mon-Sat, last entry 6pm; 🚊Beyazıt Kapalıçarşı) The colourful and chaotic Grand Bazaar is the heart of İstanbul's Old City and has been so for centuries. Starting as a small vaulted *bedesten* (warehouse) built by order of Mehmet the Conqueror in 1461, it grew to cover a vast area as lanes between the *bedesten*, neighbouring shops and *hans* (caravanserais) were roofed and the market assumed the sprawling, labyrinthine form that it retains today.

★**Süleymaniye Mosque** MOSQUE
(Map p430; Professor Sıddık Sami Onar Caddesi; ⏰dawn-dusk; Ⓜ Vezneciler) The Süleymaniye crowns one of İstanbul's seven hills and

Aya Sofya

A TIMELINE

537 Emperor Justinian, depicted in one of the church's famous **❶mosaics**, presides over the consecration of Byzantium's new basilica, Hagia Sophia (Church of the Holy Wisdom).

557 The huge **❷dome**, damaged during an earthquake, collapses and is rebuilt.

843 The second Byzantine Iconoclastic period ends and figurative **❸mosaics** begin to be added to the interior. These include a depiction of the Empress Zoe and her third husband, Emperor Constantine IX Monomachos.

1204 Soldiers of the Fourth Crusade led by the Doge of Venice, Enrico Dandolo, conquer and ransack Constantinople. Dandolo's **❹tomb** is eventually erected in the church whose desecration he presided over.

1453 The city falls to the Ottomans; Mehmet II orders that Hagia Sophia be converted to a mosque and renamed Aya Sofya.

1577 Sultan Selim II is buried in a specially designed tomb, which sits alongside the **❺tombs** of four other Ottoman Sultans in Aya Sofya's grounds.

1847–49 Sultan Abdül Mecit I orders that the building be restored and redecorated; the huge **❻Ottoman Medallions** in the nave are added.

1935 The mosque is converted into a museum by order of Mustafa Kemal Atatürk, president of the new Turkish Republic.

2009 The face of one of the four **❼seraphs** is uncovered during major restoration works in the nave.

2012 Restoration of the exterior walls and western upper gallery commences.

TOP TIP

Bring binoculars if you want to properly view the mosaic portraits in the apse and under the dome.

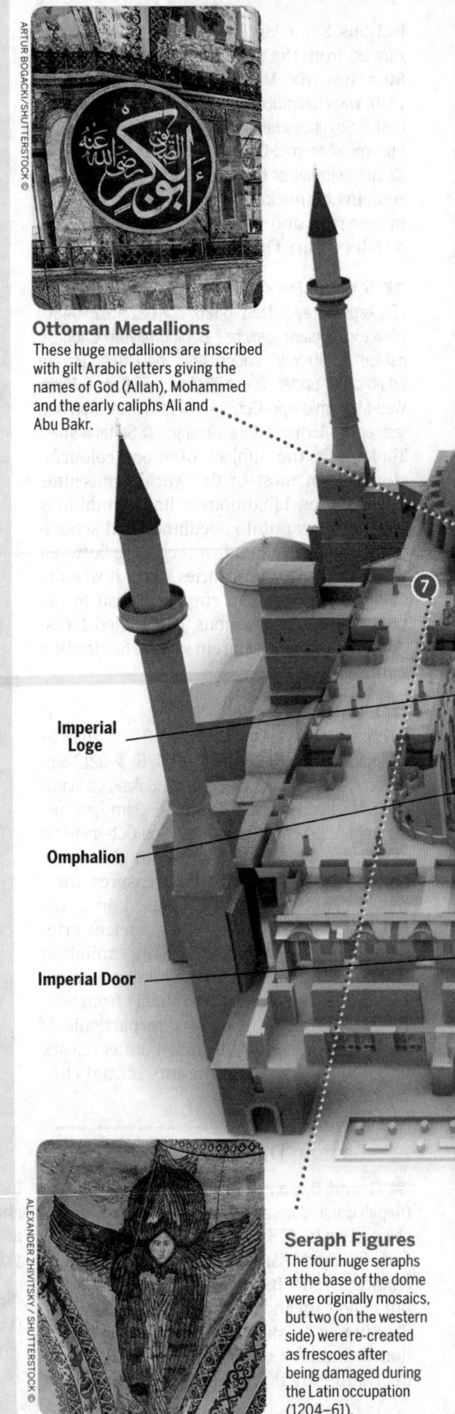

Ottoman Medallions
These huge medallions are inscribed with gilt Arabic letters giving the names of God (Allah), Mohammed and the early caliphs Ali and Abu Bakr.

Seraph Figures
The four huge seraphs at the base of the dome were originally mosaics, but two (on the western side) were re-created as frescoes after being damaged during the Latin occupation (1204–61).

MARK READ/LONELY PLANET ©

Dome
Soaring 56m from ground level, the dome was originally covered in gold mosaics but was decorated with calligraphy during the 1847–49 restoration works overseen by Swiss-born architects Gaspard and Giuseppe Fossati.

Christ Enthroned with Empress Zoe and Constantine IX Monomachos
This mosaic portrait in the upper gallery depicts Zoe, one of only three Byzantine women to rule as empress in their own right.

BYELIKOVA OKSANA/SHUTTERSTOCK ©

Ottoman Tombs
The tombs of five Ottoman sultans and their families are located in Aya Sofya's southern corner and can be accessed via Babıhümayun Caddesi. One of these occupies the church's original Baptistry.

Grave of Enrico Dandolo
The Venetian doge died in 1205, only one year after he and his Crusaders had stormed the city. A 19th-century marker in the upper gallery indicates the probable location of his grave.

Constantine the Great, the Virgin Mary and Emperor Justinian
This 11th-century mosaic shows Constantine (right) offering the Virgin Mary the city of Constantinople. Justinian (left) is offering her Hagia Sophia.

STIG ALENAS / SHUTTERSTOCK ©

İstanbul

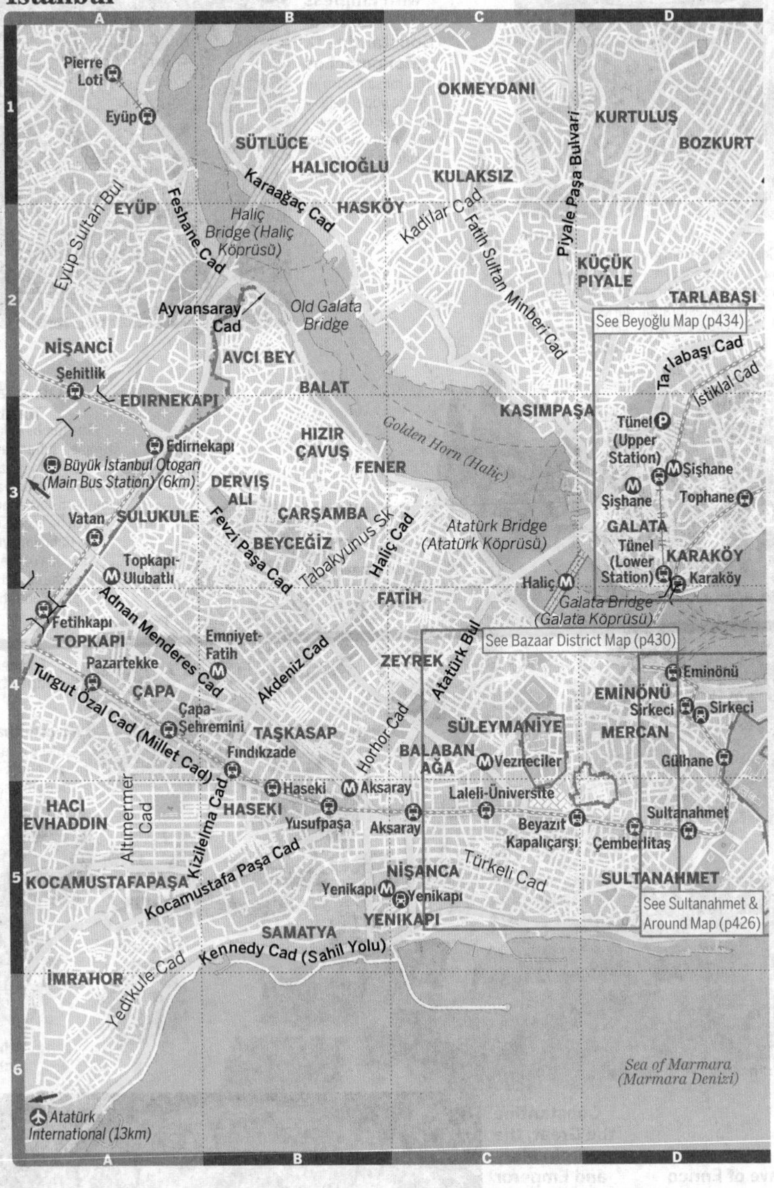

dominates the Golden Horn, providing a landmark for the entire city. Though it's not the largest of the Ottoman mosques, it is certainly one of the grandest and most beautiful. It's also unusual in that many of its original *külliye* (mosque complex) buildings have been retained and sympathetically adapted for reuse.

★ Spice Bazaar MARKET

(Mısır Çarşısı, Egyptian Market; Map p430; ☎0212-513 6597; www.misircarsisi.org; ⏲8am-7.30pm

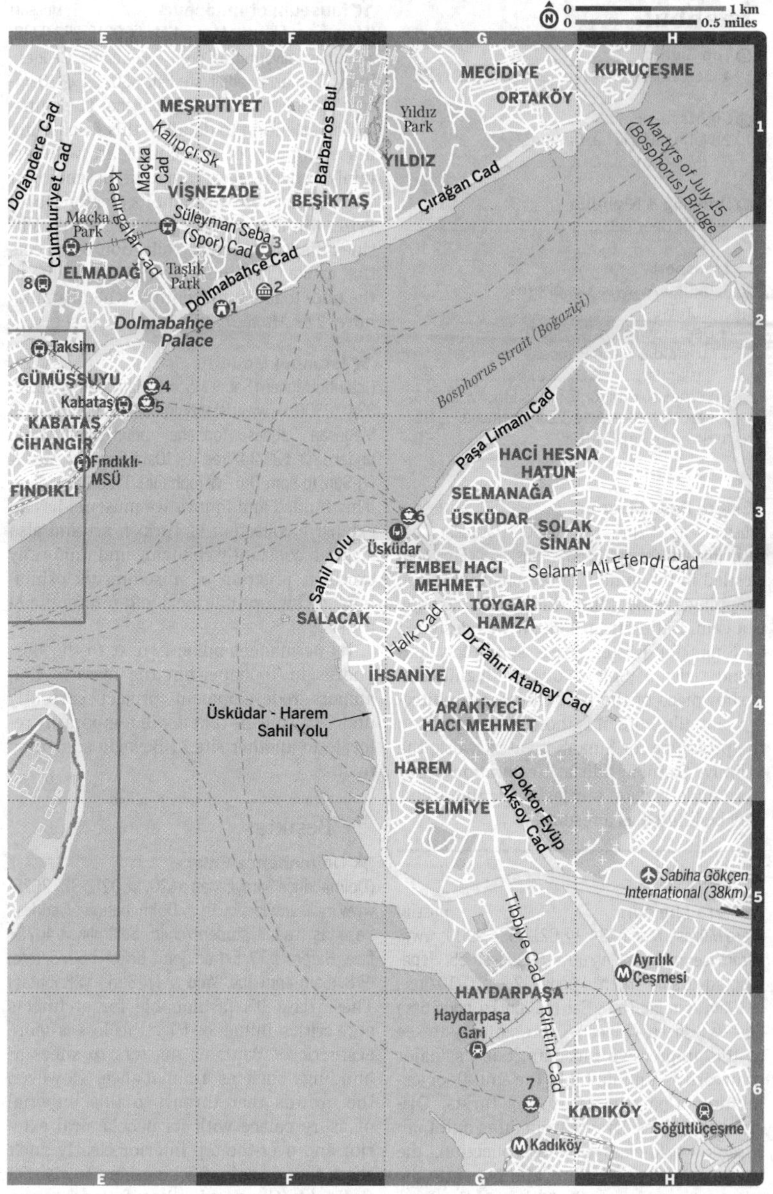

Mon-Fri, 8am-8pm Sat, 9.30am-7pm Sun; Eminönü) Vividly coloured spices are displayed alongside jewel-like *lokum* (Turkish delight) at this Ottoman-era marketplace, providing eye candy for the thousands of tourists and locals who make their way here every day. Stalls also sell caviar, dried herbs, honey, nuts and dried fruits. The number of stalls selling tourist trinkets increases annually, yet this remains a great place to stock up on edible souvenirs, share a few jokes with vendors and marvel at the well-preserved building.

İstanbul

Top Sights
1 Dolmabahçe Palace.....F2

Sights
2 National Palaces Painting Museum.....F2

Drinking & Nightlife
3 Craft Beer Lab.....F2

Transport
4 Dentur Avraysa Bosphorus Cruises.....E2
5 Dentur Avraysa Ferries to Üsküdar & the Princes' Islands.....E2
6 Ferries to Eminönü & Beşiktaş.....G3
7 Ferries to Karaköy & Eminönü.....G6
8 Havataş Airport Bus.....E2

Rüstem Paşa Mosque MOSQUE
(Rüstem Paşa Camii; Map p430; Hasırcılar Caddesi, Rüstem Paşa; dawn-dusk; Eminönü) Nestled in the middle of the busy Tahtakale shopping district, this diminutive mosque is a gem. Dating from 1560, it was designed by Sinan for Rüstem Paşa, son-in-law and grand vizier of Süleyman the Magnificent. A showpiece of the best Ottoman architecture and tile work, it is thought to have been the prototype for Sinan's greatest work, the Selimiye Camii in Edirne. Restoration works were underway on our last visit, and access may be limited as a result.

Beyoğlu

★**Pera Museum** MUSEUM
(Pera Müzesi; Map p434; 0212-334 9900; www.peramuseum.org; Meşrutiyet Caddesi 65, Tepebaşı; adult/student/child under 12yr ₺20/10/free; 10am-7pm Tue-Thu & Sat, to 10pm Fri, noon-6pm Sun; Şişhane, Tünel) There's plenty to see at this impressive museum, but its major drawcard is undoubtedly the 2nd-floor exhibition of paintings featuring Turkish Orientalist themes. Drawn from Suna and İnan Kıraç's world-class private collection, the works provide fascinating glimpses into the Ottoman world from the 17th to 20th centuries and include the most beloved painting in the Turkish canon – Osman Hamdı Bey's *The Tortoise Trainer* (1906). Other floors host high-profile temporary exhibitions (past exhibitions have showcased Warhol, de Chirico, Picasso and Botero).

★**Museum of Innocence** MUSEUM
(Masumiyet Müzesi; Map p434; 0212-252 9738; www.masumiyetmuzesi.org; Çukurcuma Caddesi, Dalgıç Çıkmazı 2; adult/student ₺30/15; 10am-6pm Tue-Sun, to 9pm Thu; Tophane) The painstaking attention to detail in this fascinating museum/piece of conceptual art will certainly provide every amateur psychologist with a theory or two about its creator, Nobel Prize–winning novelist Orhan Pamuk. Vitrines display a quirky collection of objects that evoke the minutiae of İstanbullu life in the mid- to late 20th century, when Pamuk's novel *The Museum of Innocence* is set.

★**İstanbul Modern** GALLERY
(İstanbul Modern Sanat Müzesi; Map p434; 0212-334 7300; www.istanbulmodern.org; Meclis-i Mebusan Caddesi, Tophane; adult/student/child under 12yr ₺25/14/free; 10am-6pm Tue, Wed & Fri-Sun, to 8pm Thu; Tophane) This large, lavishly funded and innovative museum has an extensive collection of Turkish art and also stages a constantly changing and uniformly excellent program of mixed-media exhibitions by high-profile local and international artists.

Its permanent home is next to the Bosphorus in Tophane, but the massive Galataport redevelopment project currently underway means that it will temporarily relocate to another site in Beyoğlu sometime in 2018.

Beşiktaş

★**Dolmabahçe Palace** PALACE
(Dolmabahçe Sarayı; Map p420; 0212-327 2626; www.millisaraylar.gov.tr; Dolmabahçe Caddesi, Beşiktaş; adult/student/child Selâmlık ₺40/5/free, Harem ₺30/5/free, joint ticket ₺60/5/free; 8.45am-4pm Tue, Wed & Fri-Sun; Kabataş) These days it's fashionable for architects and critics influenced by the less-is-more aesthetic of Bauhaus masters to sneer at buildings such as Dolmabahçe. However, the crowds that throng to this imperial pleasure palace with its neoclassical exterior and over-the-top interior clearly don't share that disdain, flocking here to visit its **Selâmlık** (Ceremonial Suites), **Harem** and **Veliaht Dairesi** (Apartments of the Crown Prince). The latter houses the **National Palaces Painting Museum** (Milli Saraylar Resim Müzesi; Map p420; 0212-236 9000; adult/student/child ₺15/5/free; 9am-4pm Tue, Wed &

DON'T MISS

PLEASURES OF THE BATH

After a long day's sightseeing, few things could be better than relaxing in a hamam. Here are our top soapy-scrub experiences guaranteed to leave your skin rosy pink and silky soft.

Kılıç Ali Paşa Hamamı (Map p434; ☎0212-393 8010; http://kilicalipasahamami.com; Hamam Sokak 1, off Kemeraltı Caddesi, Tophane; traditional hamam ritual ₺190; ⊙women 8am-4pm, men 4.30pm-midnight; Tophane) It took seven years to develop a conservation plan for this 1580 Mimar Sinan–designed building and complete the meticulous restoration. Fortunately, the result was well worth waiting for. The hamam's interior is simply stunning and the place is run with total professionalism, ensuring a clean and enjoyable Turkish bath experience. Services include a traditional hamam ritual (₺190) and massage (from ₺150).

Ayasofya Hürrem Sultan Hamamı (Map p426; ☎0212-517 3535; www.ayasofyahamami.com; Aya Sofya Meydanı 2; bath treatments €70-140, massages €40-75; ⊙8am-10pm; Sultanahmet) This meticulously restored twin hamam dating to 1556 offers the most luxurious traditional bath experience in the Old City. Designed by Mimar Sinan, it was built just across the road from Aya Sofya by order of Süleyman the Magnificent and named in honour of his wife Hürrem Sultan, commonly known as Roxelana.

Fri-Sun; Akaretler, Kabataş), which can be visited on a Selâmlık or Harem ticket.

Tours

★İstanbul Walks WALKING
(Map p426; ☎0554 335 6622, 0212-516 6300; www.istanbulwalks.com; 1st fl, Şifa Hamamı Sokak 1; tours €35-140; Sultanahmet) Specialising in cultural tourism, this company is run by history buffs and offers a large range of guided walking tours conducted by knowledgeable English-speaking guides. Tours concentrate on İstanbul's various neighbourhoods, but there are also tours of major monuments, a Turkish coffee trail, and a Bosphorus and Golden Horn cruise by private boat. Significant discounts for children aged under seven.

Courses

Cooking Alaturka COOKING
(Map p426; ☎0212-458 5919; www.cookingalaturka.com; Akbıyık Caddesi 72a, Cankurtaran; classes per person incl meal €65; ⊙10.30am & 4.30pm by reservation Mon-Sat; Sultanahmet) Established in 2002, this culinary school has changed hands recently but is still cooking up a storm under its Turkish-Italian ownership. Suitable for both novices and experienced cooks, its convivial two-hour classes give a great introduction to Turkish cuisine, from classic meze to Ottoman dishes such as *imam bayıldı* (aubergine dish). The results are then enjoyed over a two-hour meal.

Sleeping

Sultanahmet & Around

★Marmara Guesthouse PENSION $
(Map p426; ☎0212-638 3638; www.marmaraguesthouse.com; Terbıyık Sokak 15, Cankurtaran; s €25-45, d €30-50, f €50-70; Sultanahmet) Few of Sultanahmet's family-run pensions can compete with the Marmara's cleanliness, comfort and thoughtful details. Owner Elif and team go out of their way to welcome guests, offering advice aplenty and serving a delicious breakfast on the vine-covered, sea-facing roof terrace. Rooms have comfortable beds, good bathrooms (small in some cases) and double-glazed windows.

Cheers Hostel HOSTEL $
(Map p426; ☎0212-526 0200; www.cheershostel.com; Zeynep Sultan Camii Sokak 21, Sultanahmet; dm €15-22, s €40, d €60-70, tr €75; P@; Gülhane) The five- to 10-bed dorms at Sultanahmet's best hostel are worlds away from the barrack-like quarters at many of its competitors. Bright and airy, they feature air-conditioning, lockers and comfortable beds. Bathrooms (one shower per eight beds) are clean. The excellent central position is a major draw, as is the cosy rooftop bar with its open fire and great view.

Metropolis Hostel HOSTEL $
(Map p426; ☎0212-518 1822; www.metropolishostel.com; Terbıyık Sokak 24, Cankurtaran; dm €10-16, s €28, d €36, tw with shared bathroom €29;

Topkapı Palace

DAILY LIFE IN THE IMPERIAL COURT

A visit to this opulent palace compound, with its courtyards, harem and pavilions, offers a fascinating glimpse into the lives of the Ottoman sultans. During its heyday, royal wives and children, concubines, eunuchs and servants were among the 4000 people living within Topkapı's walls.

The sultans and their families rarely left the palace grounds, relying on courtiers and diplomats to bring them news of the outside world. Most visitors would go straight to the magnificent ❶**Imperial Council Chamber**, where the sultan's grand vizier and Dîvân (Council) regularly met to discuss affairs of state and receive foreign dignitaries. Many of these visitors brought lavish gifts and tributes to embellish the ❷**Imperial Treasury**.

After receiving any guests and meeting with the Dîvân, the grand vizier would make his way through the ornate ❸**Gate of Felicity** into the Third Court, the palace's residential quarter. Here, he would brief the sultan on the deliberations and decisions of the Dîvân in the colonnaded ❹**Audience Chamber**.

Meanwhile, day-to-day domestic chores and intrigues would be underway in the ❺**Harem** and servants would be preparing feasts in the massive ❻**Palace Kitchens**. Amid all this activity, the ❼**Marble Terrace** was a tranquil retreat where the sultan would come to relax, look out over the city and perhaps regret his sequestered lifestyle.

DON'T MISS

There are spectacular views from the terrace above the Konyalı Restaurant and also from the Marble Terrace in the Fourth Court.

ZZVET/SHUTTERSTOCK ©

Harem
The sultan, his mother and the crown prince had sumptuously decorated private apartments in the Harem. The most beautiful of these are the Twin Kiosks (pictured), which were used by the crown prince.

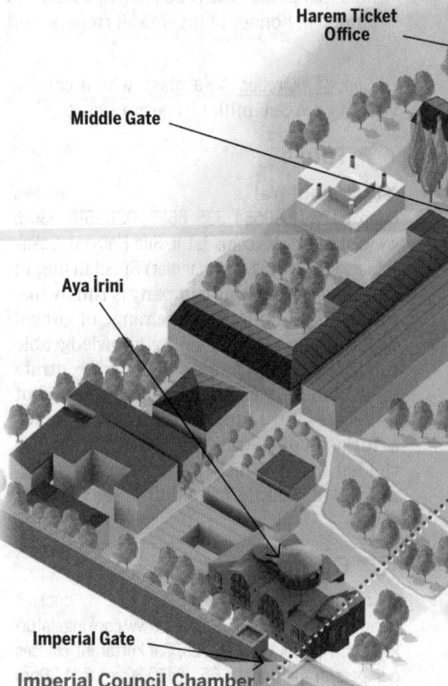

Imperial Council Chamber
This is where the Dîvân (Council) made laws, citizens presented petitions and foreign dignitaries were presented to the court. The sultan sometimes eavesdropped on proceedings through the window with the golden grille.

BRIAN MAUDSLEY/SHUTTERSTOCK ©

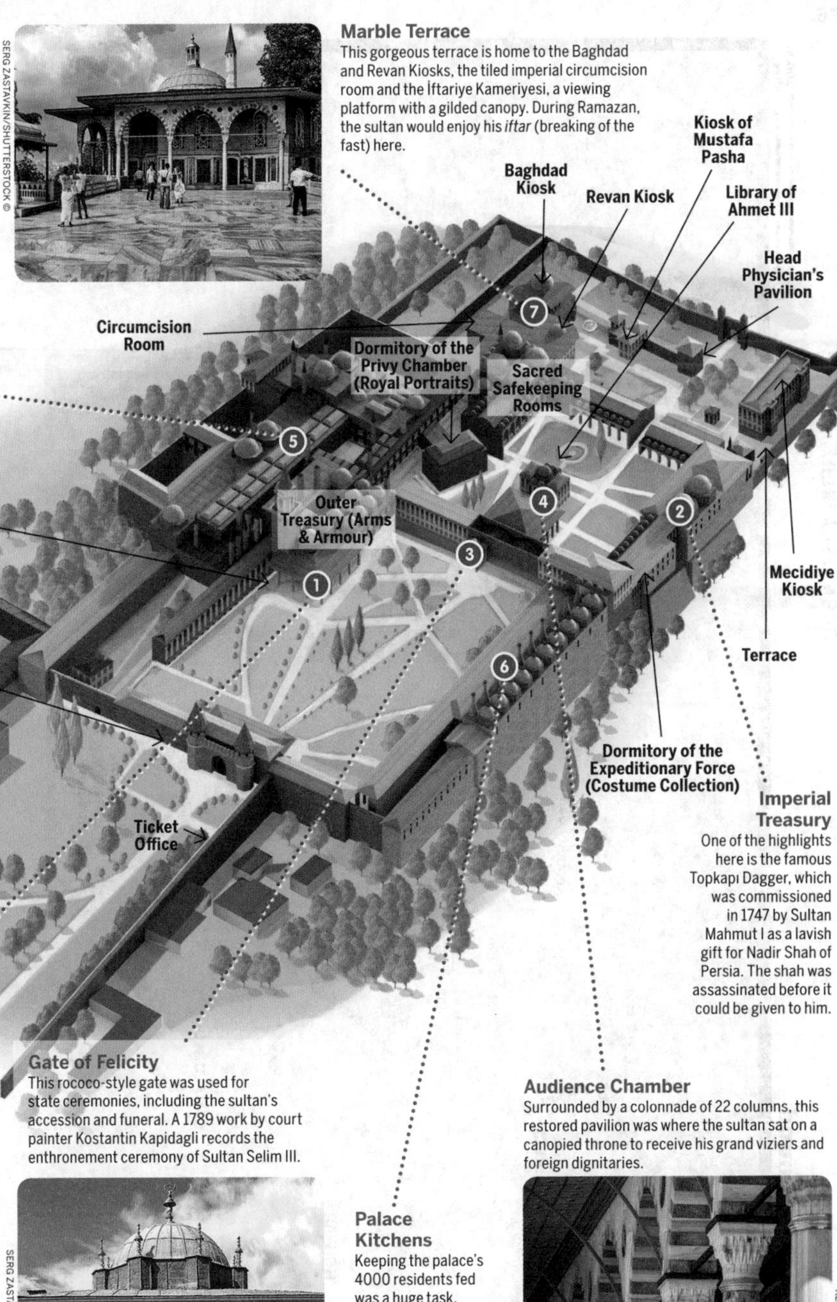

SERG ZASTAVKIN/SHUTTERSTOCK ©

Marble Terrace

This gorgeous terrace is home to the Baghdad and Revan Kiosks, the tiled imperial circumcision room and the İftariye Kameriyesi, a viewing platform with a gilded canopy. During Ramazan, the sultan would enjoy his *iftar* (breaking of the fast) here.

Imperial Treasury

One of the highlights here is the famous Topkapı Dagger, which was commissioned in 1747 by Sultan Mahmut I as a lavish gift for Nadir Shah of Persia. The shah was assassinated before it could be given to him.

Gate of Felicity

This rococo-style gate was used for state ceremonies, including the sultan's accession and funeral. A 1789 work by court painter Kostantin Kapidagli records the enthronement ceremony of Sultan Selim III.

Audience Chamber

Surrounded by a colonnade of 22 columns, this restored pavilion was where the sultan sat on a canopied throne to receive his grand viziers and foreign dignitaries.

SERG ZASTAVKIN/SHUTTERSTOCK ©

Palace Kitchens

Keeping the palace's 4000 residents fed was a huge task. Topkapı's kitchens occupied 10 domed buildings with 20 huge chimneys, and were workplace and home for 800 members of staff.

KLUBLU/SHUTTERSTOCK ©

Sultanahmet & Around

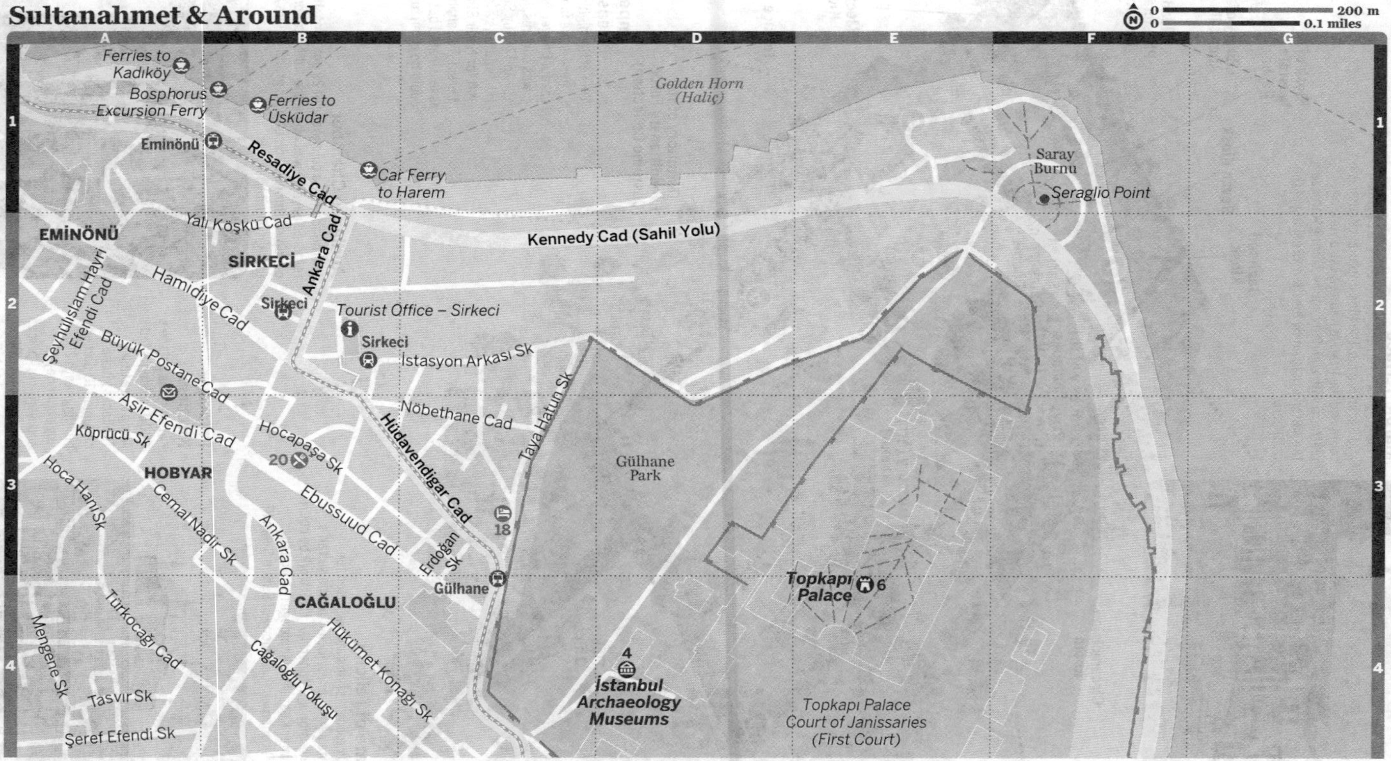

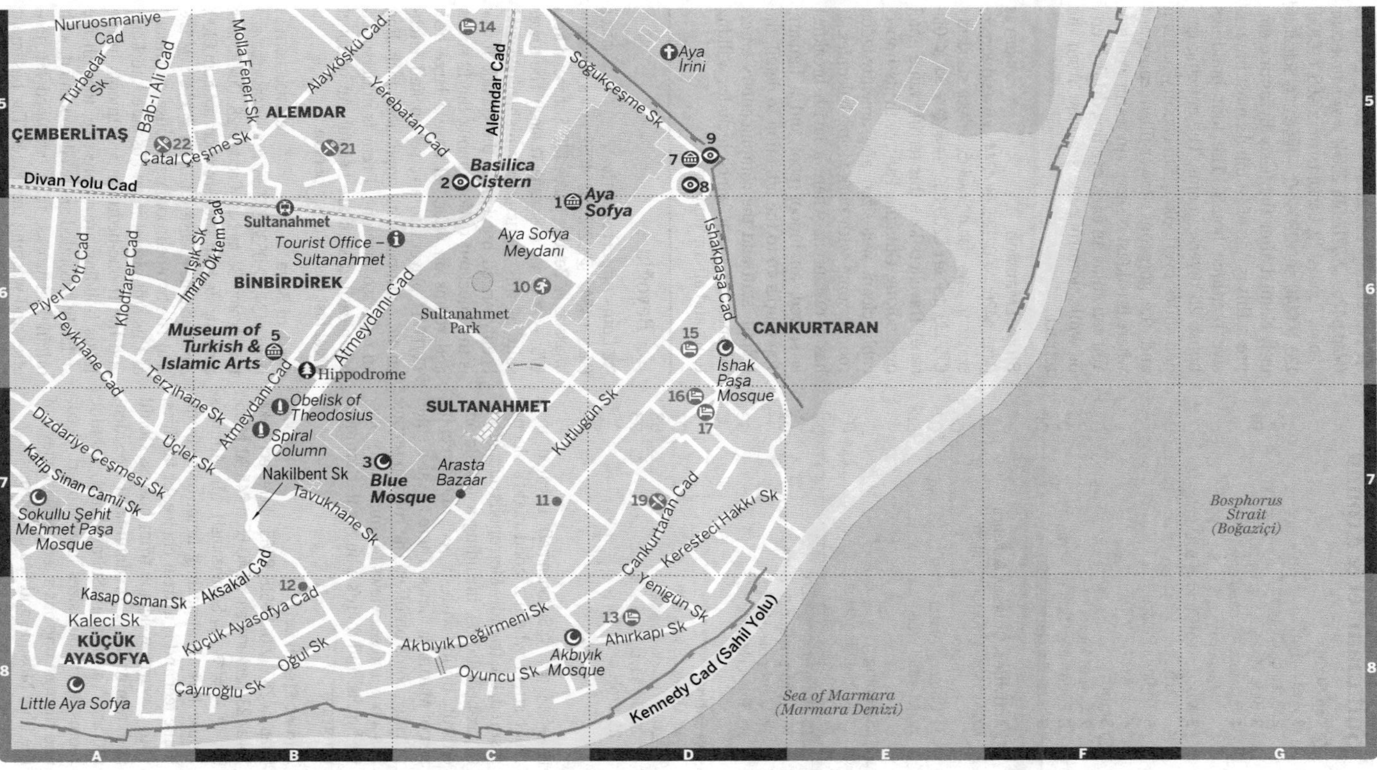
Nuruosmaniye Cad
Türbedar Sk
Bab-ı Ali Cad
Molla Feneri Sk
Alayköşkü Cad
Yerebatan Cad
Alemdar Cad
14
Aya İrini
Soğukçeşme Sk
ALEMDAR
ÇEMBERLİTAŞ
22
Çatal Çeşme Sk
21
9
7
Basilica
2 Cistern
Divan Yolu Cad
8
1 Aya Sofya
Sultanahmet
Tourist Office – Sultanahmet
Aya Sofya Meydanı
Piyer Loti Cad
Klodfarer Cad
Işık Sk
İmran Öktem Cad
BİNBİRDİREK
10
Atmeydanı Cad
İshakpaşa Cad
Sultanahmet Park
CANKURTARAN
Peykhane Cad
Museum of Turkish & Islamic Arts
5
Hippodrome
15
İshak Paşa Mosque
Terzihane Sk
Atmeydanı Cad
Obelisk of Theodosius
SULTANAHMET
Kutlugün Sk
16
17
Dizdariye Çeşmesi Sk
Spiral Column
Üçler Sk
3 Blue Mosque
Arasta Bazaar
Katip Sinan Camii Sk
Nakilbent Sk
Tavukhane Sk
11
19
Cankurtaran Cad
Kerestecì Hakkı Sk
Sokullu Şehit Mehmet Paşa Mosque
Bosphorus Strait (Boğaziçi)
Aksakal Cad
12
Kasap Osman Sk
Küçük Ayasofya Cad
Yenigün Sk
Kaleci Sk
Akbıyık Değirmeni Sk
13
Ahırkapı Sk
KÜÇÜK AYASOFYA
Oğul Sk
Akbıyık Mosque
Oyuncu Sk
Çayıroğlu Sk
Little Aya Sofya
Kennedy Cad (Sahil Yolu)
Sea of Marmara (Marmara Denizi)
A
B
C
D
E
F
G
5
6
7
8

Sultanahmet & Around

Top Sights
1 Aya Sofya C6
2 Basilica Cistern C5
3 Blue Mosque B7
4 İstanbul Archaeology Museums D4
5 Museum of Turkish & Islamic Arts B6
6 Topkapı Palace E4

Sights
7 Carpet Museum D5
8 Fountain of Sultan Ahmet III D5
9 Imperial Gate D5

Activities, Courses & Tours
10 Ayasofya Hürrem Sultan Hamamı C6
11 Cooking Alaturka C7
12 İstanbul Walks B8

Sleeping
13 Ahmet Efendi Evi D8
14 Cheers Hostel C5
15 Hotel Empress Zoe D6
16 Marmara Guesthouse D7
17 Metropolis Hostel D7
18 Sirkeci Mansion C3

Eating
19 Balıkçı Sabahattin D7
20 Birecikli B3
21 Deraliye B5
22 Erol Lokantası A5

P ⊖ ❄ @ 🛜; 🚊Sultanahmet) Located in a quiet street where a good night's sleep is assured, the friendly Metropolis offers four- to six-bed dorms, including a female-only en suite option with six beds and sweeping Sea of Marmara views. There are also small private rooms on offer. The rooftop terrace has a bar and sea views to equal many pricier hotels, and there's a busy entertainment program.

Ahmet Efendi Evi PENSION **$**
(Map p426; ☎0212-518 8465; Keresteci Hakkı Sokak 23, Cankurtaran; s €40-65, d €45-80, f €65-95; P ⊖ ❄ 🛜; 🚊Sultanahmet) Mr Ahmet's House has an appealing home-away-from-home feel and is a great choice for families, with a warm welcome from hostess Gönül and family. In a predominantly residential area (a rarity in Sultanahmet), its nine rooms of various sizes have modern decor and fittings; one has a terrace with views of the Blue Mosque and Sea of Marmara.

★**Hotel Empress Zoe** BOUTIQUE HOTEL **$$**
(Map p426; ☎0212-518 2504; www.emzoe.com; Akbıyık Caddesi 10, Cankurtaran; s €65, d €100-120, tr €140, ste €180-250; ⊖ ❄ 🛜; 🚊Sultanahmet) Named after the feisty Byzantine empress, this is one of İstanbul's most impressive boutique hotels. The four buildings house 26 diverse rooms. The enticing garden suites overlook a 15th-century hamam and the gorgeous flower-filled courtyard where breakfast is served in warm weather. You can enjoy an early evening drink there, or while admiring the sea view from the terrace.

Sirkeci Mansion HOTEL **$$**
(Map p426; ☎0212-528 4344; www.sirkecimansion.com; Taya Hatun Sokak 5, Sirkeci; standard r €79-139, deluxe r €209-259; ⊖ ❄ @ 🛜 ≋; 🚊Gülhane) Travellers love this terrific-value hotel overlooking Gülhane Park, with its impeccably clean, well-sized and amenity-laden rooms, some with park-facing balconies. It has a restaurant where a lavish breakfast is served, an indoor pool and a hamam. Top marks go to the attention to detail, the helpful staff and the complimentary entertainment program, which includes walking tours and afternoon teas.

Beyoğlu

★**Louis Appartements** HOTEL **$**
(Map p434; ☎0212-293 4052; www.louis.com.tr/galata; İlk Belediye Caddesi 10, Şişhane; d from €75; ⊖ ❄ @ 🛜; Ⓜ Şişhane, 🚊Tünel) The tower suite at this meticulously maintained and keenly priced hotel near the Galata Tower is the knockout option among the 12 suites and rooms on offer. All have a large bed, TV/DVD player, ironing set-up and kitchenette equipped with appliances, including an espresso machine. Decor is understated but pleasing; staff are helpful. An optional breakfast costs €6 per person.

Casa di Bava BOUTIQUE HOTEL **$$**
(Map p434; ☎0538 377 3877; www.casadibavaistanbul.com; Bostanbaşı Caddesi 28, Çukurcuma; economy ste from €90, 1-bedroom apt from €100, 2-bedroom penthouse €320; ⊖ ❄ 🛜 🐾; Ⓜ Taksim) The two-bedroom penthouse apartment at this suite hotel is an absolute knockout, and the 11 one-bedroom apartments in the 1880s building are impressive, too. All are stylishly decorated and well appointed, with original artworks, fully equipped kitchenettes and washing machines. The basement

suites are smaller and less expensive; all have daily maid service. Breakfast is available on request.

Witt Istanbul Hotel BOUTIQUE HOTEL **$$**
(Map p434; ☎0212-293 1500; www.wittistanbul.com; Defterdar Yokuşu 26, Cihangir; d ste €86-165, terrace ste €180-325; ❄@🛜; Ⓜ Taksim, 🚊 Tophane) Showcasing nearly as many designer features as an issue of *Architectural Digest,* this stylish apartment hotel in Cihangir offers spacious suites with seating area, CD/DVD player, espresso machine, king-size bed and swish bathroom. Most have kitchenettes and a few have panoramic terraces (there's also a communal rooftop terrace). It's a short but steep climb from the Tophane tram stop.

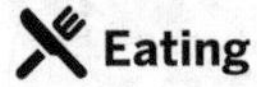

Eating

Sultanahmet & Around

★ **Birecikli** ANATOLIAN **$**
(Map p426; ☎0212-513 77 63; www.birecikli.com/sirkeci; Hocapaşa Camii Sokak 2B, Sirkeci; pides ₺16-18, kebaps ₺12-33; ⏲9am-10.30pm) Those keen on robust flavours and the liberal application of chilli in their food will be instantly enamoured of the dishes served at this bustling eatery in Hocapaşa. Choose from an array of liver options, meat kebaps, pides and *lahmacun* (Arabic-style pizza), and be sure to start with a delicious *sarımsaklı Antep lahmacin* (thin, crispy Antep-style pizza). No alcohol.

Erol Lokantası TURKISH **$**
(Map p426; ☎0212-511 0322; Çatal Çeşme Sokak 3, Cağaloğlu; soups ₺4.50-5.50, portions ₺9-22; ⏲11am-6pm Mon-Sat; ✍; 🚊 Sultanahmet) One of Sultanahmet's last *lokantas* (eateries serving ready-made food), Erol wouldn't win any awards for its interior design but might for its warm welcome and food. The dishes in the bain-marie are made fresh daily using seasonal ingredients by the Erol family members, who have collectively put in several decades in the kitchen.

★ **Balıkçı Sabahattin** SEAFOOD **$$$**
(Map p426; ☎0212-458 1824; www.balikcisabahattin.com; Şeyit Hasan Koyu Sokak 1, Cankurtaran; mezes ₺10-40, fish ₺40-60; ⏲11am-10pm; 🛜; 🚊 Sultanahmet) Balıkçı Sabahattin is an enduring favourite with discerning Turks from near and far, who enjoy the limited menu of meze and seafood, including fish from red mullet to sole. This is Sultanahmet's most prestigious restaurant and its best food, although the service can be harried. You'll dine under a leafy canopy in the garden (one section smoking, the other nonsmoking).

Deraliye TURKISH **$$$**
(Map p426; ☎0212-520 7778; www.deraliyerestaurant.com; Ticarethane Sokak 10; mezes ₺15-55, mains ₺28-69; ⏲noon-4pm & 6-11pm; ❄🛜; 🚊 Sultanahmet) Offering a taste of the sumptuous dishes once served in the great Ottoman palaces, Deraliye offers diners the chance to order delights such as the goose kebap served to Süleyman the Magnificent or Mehmet II's favourite lamb stew. Those with less adventurous palates can opt for modern standards such as kebaps. There are whirling dervish and Ottoman music performances on weekends.

Bazaar District & Around

Hamdi Restaurant KEBAP **$$**
(Map p430; ☎0212-444 6463; www.hamdirestorant.com.tr; Kalçın Sokak 11, Eminönü; mezes ₺12-28, kebaps ₺29-50; ⏲noon-midnight; 🅿❄👪; 🚊 Eminönü) One of the city's best-loved restaurants, this place near the Spice Bazaar is owned by Hamdi Arpacı, who started out as a street-food vendor in the 1960s. His tasty Urfa-style kebaps were so popular that he soon graduated from his modest stand to this building, which has views of the Old City, Golden Horn and Galata from its top-floor terrace.

Beyoğlu

Karaköy Güllüoğlu SWEETS, BÖREK **$**
(Map p434; ☎0212-293 0910; www.karakoygulluoglu.com; Katlı Otopark, Kemankeş Caddesi, Karaköy; portion baklava ₺11-19, portion börek ₺9-9.50; ⏲7am-11pm Sun-Thu, 8am-11.30pm Fri & Sat; 👪; 🚊 Karaköy) This much-loved *baklavacı* (baklava shop) opened in 1949 and was the first İstanbul branch of a business established in Gaziantep in the 1820s. There are other Güllüoğlu offshoots around town, but this remains the best. Pay for a *porsiyon* (portion) of whatever takes your fancy at the register, then order at the counters.

★ **Antiochia** ANATOLIAN **$$**
(Map p434; ☎0212-244 0820; www.antiochiaconcept.com; General Yazgan Sokak 3, Tünel; mezes & salads ₺16-22, pides ₺24, kebaps ₺30-65; ⏲noon-11pm Mon-Fri, 3pm-midnight Sat; ❄🛜👪; 🚊 Tünel) Dishes from the southeastern city of Antakya (Hatay) are the speciality here.

Bazaar District

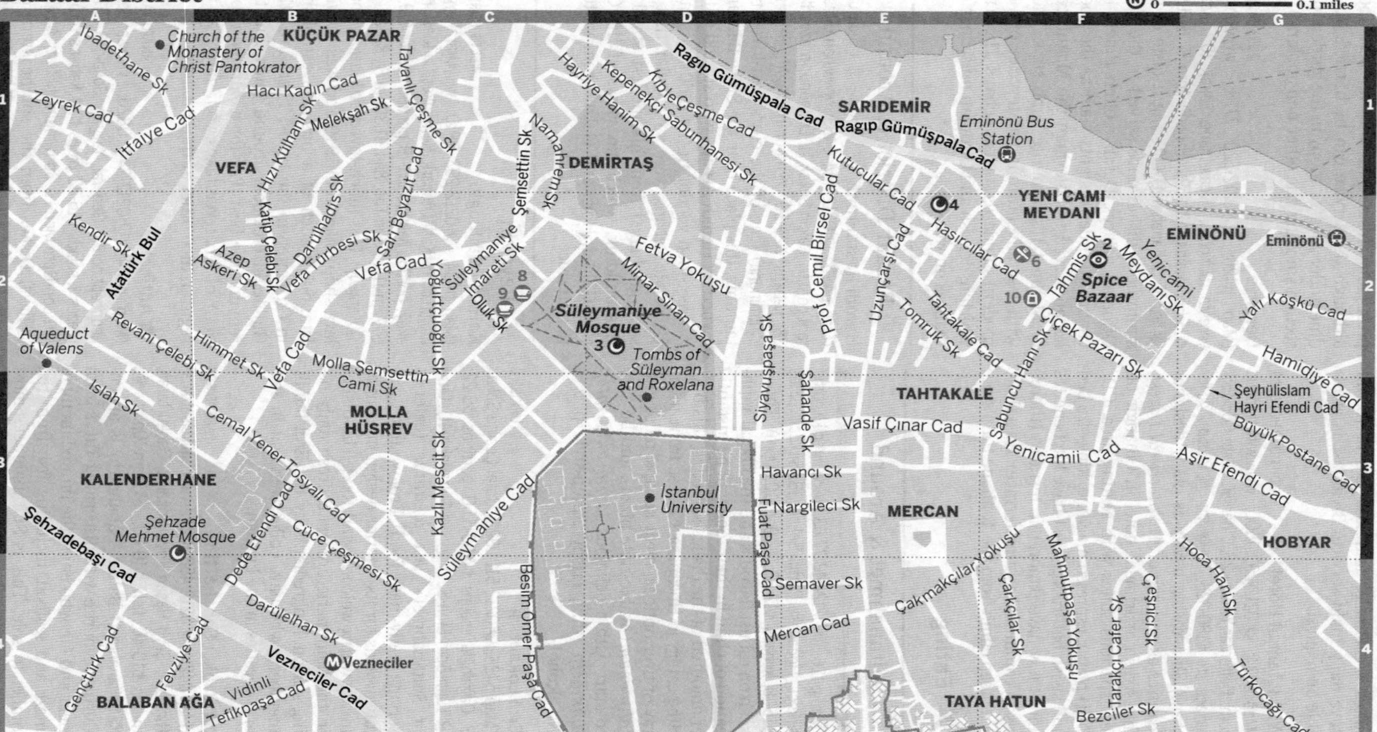

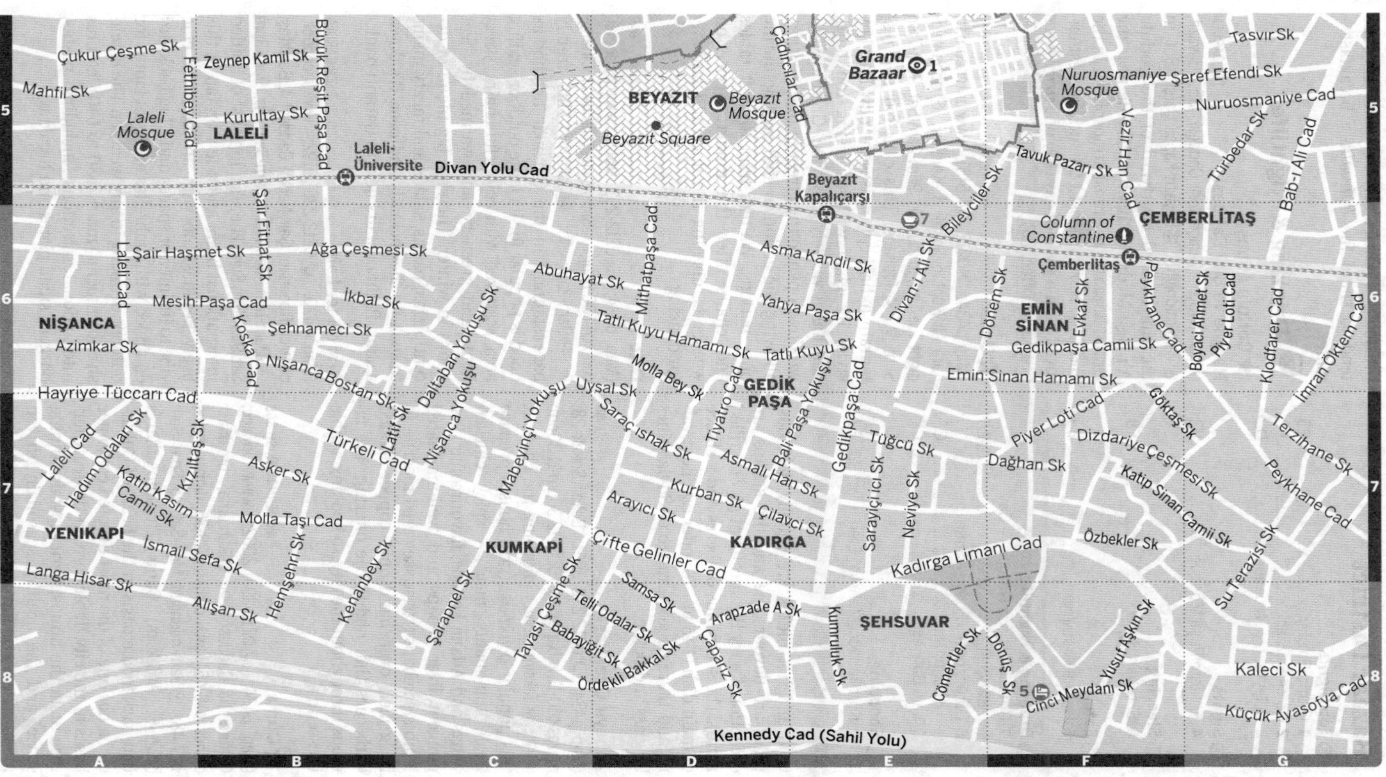

5
6
7
8
A
B
C
D
E
F
G
Çukur Çeşme Sk
Zeynep Kamil Sk
Fethibey Cad
Büyük Reşit Paşa Cad
Mahfil Sk
Laleli Mosque
Kurultay Sk
LALELİ
Laleli-Üniversite
Divan Yolu Cad
BEYAZIT
Beyazit Mosque
Beyazit Square
Çadırcılar Cad
Grand Bazaar
1
Nuruosmaniye Mosque
Nuruosmaniye Şeref Efendi Sk
Tasvır Sk
Nuruosmaniye Cad
Türbedar Sk
Bab-ı Ali Cad
Vezir Han Cad
Tavuk Pazarı Sk
Bileyciler Sk
Beyazit Kapalıçarşı
7
Column of Constantine
ÇEMBERLİTAŞ
Çemberlitaş
Laleli Cad
Şair Haşmet Sk
Şair Fitnat Sk
Ağa Çeşmesi Sk
Mithatpaşa Cad
Abuhayat Sk
Asma Kandil Sk
Divan-ı Ali Sk
Dönem Sk
Evkaf Sk
Peykhane Cad
Boyacı Ahmet Sk
Piyer Loti Cad
Klodfarer Cad
İmran Öktem Cad
NİŞANCA
Mesih Paşa Cad
İkbal Sk
Koska Cad
Şehnameci Sk
Azimkar Sk
Daltaban Yokuşu Sk
Yahya Paşa Sk
EMİN SİNAN
Gedikpaşa Camii Sk
Tatlı Kuyu Hamamı Sk
Tatlı Kuyu Sk
Nişanca Bostan Sk
Molla Bey Sk
GEDİK PAŞA
Tiyatro Cad
Bali Paşa Yokuşu
Gedikpaşa Cad
Emin Sinan Hamamı Sk
Hayriye Tüccarı Cad
Nişanca Yokuşu
Mabeyinci Yokuşu
Uysal Sk
Saraç İshak Sk
Piyer Loti Cad
Göktaş Sk
Terzihane Sk
Laleli Cad
Hadım Odaları Sk
Kızıltaş Sk
Türkeli Cad
Latif Sk
Tüğcü Sk
Dizdariye Çeşmesi Sk
Dağhan Sk
Katip Kasım Camii Sk
Asker Sk
Asmalı Han Sk
Kurban Sk
Sarayiçi Ici Sk
Neviye Sk
Katip Sinan Camii Sk
Peykhane Cad
Arayıcı Sk
Çilavcı Sk
YENİKAPI
Molla Taşı Cad
KUMKAPI
KADIRGA
Özbekler Sk
İsmail Sefa Sk
Çifte Gelinler Cad
Kadırga Limanı Cad
Su Terazisi Sk
Langa Hisar Sk
Hemşehri Sk
Kenanbey Sk
Şarapnel Sk
Tavaşi Çeşme Sk
Samsa Sk
Telli Odalar Sk
Arapzade A Sk
Kumruluk Sk
ŞEHSUVAR
Yusuf Aşkın Sk
Alişan Sk
Babayiğit Sk
Ördekli Bakkal Sk
Çapariz Sk
Cömertler Sk
Dönüş Sk
5
Cinci Meydanı Sk
Kaleci Sk
Küçük Ayasofya Cad
Kennedy Cad (Sahil Yolu)

Bazaar District

Top Sights

1 Grand Bazaar E5
2 Spice Bazaar F2
3 Süleymaniye Mosque D2

Sights

4 Rüstem Paşa Mosque E2

Sleeping

5 Saruhan Hotel F8

Eating

6 Hamdi Restaurant F2

Drinking & Nightlife

7 Çorlulu Alipaşa Nargile ve Çay Bahçesi E6
8 Darüzziyafe (Former Soup Kitchen) C2
9 Lale Bahçesi C2

Shopping

10 Kurukahveci Mehmet Efendi F2

Cold and hot mezes are equally delicious, pides are flavoursome and the kebaps are exceptional – try the succulent *şiş et* (grilled lamb). The set menus of mezes and a choice of main dish (₺45 to ₺78) offer excellent value and there's a good range of Suvla wines by glass and bottle.

Zübeyir Ocakbaşı KEBAP $$

(Map p434; 0212-293 3951; Bekar Sokak 28; mezes ₺10-11, kebaps ₺30-70; 12.30pm-11.30pm; Taksim) Every morning the chefs at this popular *ocakbaşı* (grill house) prepare fresh, top-quality meat – spicy chicken wings and Adana kebaps, flavoursome ribs, pungent liver kebaps and well-marinated lamb *şiş* kebaps (roast skewered meat) – to be grilled over handsome copper-hooded barbecues that night. The offerings are famous throughout the city, so booking a table is essential.

★Cuma MODERN TURKISH $$$

(Map p434; 0212-293 2062; www.cuma.cc; Çukurcuma Caddesi 53a, Çukurcuma; breakfast dishes ₺18-45, lunch dishes ₺28-35, dinner mains ₺27-48; 9am-midnight Mon-Sat, to 8pm Sun; Taksim) Banu Tiryakioğulları's laid-back foodie oasis in the heart of Çukurcuma has one of the most devoted customer bases in the city. Tables are on the leafy terrace or in the atmospheric upstairs dining space, and the healthy, seasonally driven menu is heavy on flavour and light on fuss – breakfast is particularly delicious (regulars tend to share the *kahvaltı* – breakfast – plate).

Drinking & Nightlife

★Çorlulu Alipaşa Nargile ve Çay Bahçesi TEA GARDEN

(Map p430; Yeniçeriler Caddesi 35, Beyazıt; 7am-midnight; Beyazıt-Kapalı Çarşı) Set in the vine-covered courtyard of the Çorlulu Ali Paşa Medrese, this nargile cafe near the Grand Bazaar is the most atmospheric in the Old City. Nargiles cost ₺25 and are best enjoyed with a glass of çay (₺2) or *Türk kahve* (Turkish coffee, ₺5).

★Unter BAR

(Map p434; 0212-244 5151; www.unter.com.tr; Kara Ali Kaptan Sokak 4, Karaköy; noon-midnight Tue-Thu, to 2am Fri, 9am-2am Sat, 9am-7pm Sun; Tophane) This cafe, bar and restaurant hybrid epitomises the new Karaköy style: it's glam without trying too hard, and has a vaguely arty vibe. Ground-floor windows open to the street in fine weather, allowing the action to spill outside during busy periods. Waiters tend to shift tables and chairs after the dinner service on weekends, opening the floor and laneway for dancing.

Otto BAR

(Map p434; 0212-293 9617; www.facebook.com/OTTOCihangir; Sıraselviler Caddesi, Cihangir; 9am-2am; Taksim) This trendy bar-restaurant in the Cihangir neighbourhood is popular for its large outdoor seating area, scattered with colourful chairs, street lights and greenery, and warmed by heat lamps in winter. There's a big menu of decent pizzas, pastas, salads and meaty mains to soak up the cocktails and beer. It's down a short flight of stairs next to Garanti bank.

Craft Beer Lab BEER GARDEN

(Map p420; 0212-236 9192; www.facebook.com/craftbeerlab; Şair Nedim Caddesi 4, Beşiktaş; 10am-1am Mon-Thu, 10am-3am Fri, 9am-3pm Sat, 9am-1am Sun) There's a long list of bottled international beers and a few on tap at this lively Beşiktaş pub with an industrial-chic vibe to its interior spaces and a big backyard equipped with umbrellas and heat lamps for outdoor drinking in any weather. The extensive food menu (mains ₺30 to ₺40) features international selections, including pastas, burgers, small plates and breakfast.

Information

DANGERS & ANNOYANCES

Theft is not generally a big problem but travellers should take normal precautions. Areas in which to be particularly careful are the Grand Bazaar (pickpocket central) and near the historic city walls (don't walk here alone or after dark).

In 2016 a wave of terrorist attacks in İstanbul, some in areas and facilities frequented by tourists, led many governments to issue travel advisories for the city. These have since been lifted.

MEDICAL SERVICES

Memorial Sişli Hospital (☎0212-314 6666, 0212-444 7888; www.memorial.com.tr/en; Piyalepaşa Bulvarı, Sişli; Ⓜ Şişli) Emergency department, eye centre and pediatric clinic.

TOURIST INFORMATION

The main tourist office is in **Sultanahmet** (Map p426; ☎0212-518 1802; Hippodrome, Sultanahmet; ⏲9.30am-6pm mid-Apr–Sep, 9am-5.30pm Oct–mid-Apr; 🚊Sultanahmet).

Getting There & Away

AIR

The city's main airport, **Atatürk International Airport** (IST, Atatürk Havalımanı; ☎444 9828; www.ataturkairport.com), is located in Yeşilköy, 23km west of Sultanahmet.

The city's second international airport, **Sabiha Gökçen International Airport** (SAW, Sabiha Gökçen Havalımanı; ☎0216-588 8888; www.sgairport.com), is at Pendik/Kurtköy on the Asian side of the city.

Due to both airports operating at capacity, a new airport is under construction, 50km north of the centre. Phase one opening is planned for October 2018, after which some scheduled flights will move from Atatürk Airport.

BUS

The **Büyük İstanbul Otogarı** (Big İstanbul Bus Station; ☎0212-658 0505; www.otogaristanbul.com) is the city's main bus station. it's located at Esenler about 10km west of Sultanahmet.

The metro between Aksaray and Atatürk Airport stops here (Otogar stop). From the Otogar take the metro to Zeytinburnu and then connect with a tram to Sultanahmet or Kabataş/Taksim.

TRAIN

The nightly *İstanbul–Sofia Expressi* departs Halkali station at 10.40pm daily; ticket prices start at ₺120. A transfer bus to Halkali departs from Sirkeci Station (where you can buy the train tickets) at 9.30pm.

A fast-train service operates between Ankara and Pendik, 20km southeast of Kadıköy on the Asian side of the city. This takes approximately four hours and ticket prices start at ₺70. Unfortunately, Pendik is difficult to access.

Getting Around

Rechargeable **İstanbulkarts** (travelcards) offer discounts on fares on all public transport. Purchase and recharge at street kiosks and machines near transport stops. *Jetons* (single-journey ticket tokens) can also be purchased at ticket machines. You must have an İstanbulkart to use a bus.

TO/FROM THE AIRPORT

Atatürk International Airport

There's an efficient metro service between the airport and Yenikapı, from where you can connect to the M2 metro. This stops at Şişhane and Taksim in Beyoğlu en route. To get to Sultanahmet, alight from the metro at Zeytinburnu, from where it's easy to connect with the tram to Sultanahmet.

The **Havataş airport bus** (Map p420; ☎444 2656; http://havatas.com) departs from in front of the arrivals hall to Taksim Meydanı. Buses leave every 30 minutes; tickets cost ₺12.

In a taxi it's around ₺50 to Sultanahmet; ₺60 to Beyoğlu.

Many hotels can book (slow) door-to-door airport shuttles.These cost around ₺25.

Sabiha Gökçen International Airport

Havataş airport buses (p433) travel from the airport to Taksim Meydanı between 3.30am and 1am. Tickets cost ₺15 to Taksim (1½ hours).

Shuttle-bus services from hotels to the airport cost up to ₺80 and are infrequent – check details with your hotel.

BOAT

Major ferry docks are at the mouth of the Golden Horn (Eminönü and Karaköy) and at Beşiktaş. The Kabataş *iskele* (ferry dock) has been closed for redevelopment since 2016 with a tentative reopening date of late 2018.

BUS

Major bus stands are underneath Taksim Meydanı and at Beşiktaş, Kabataş, Eminönü, Kadıköy and Üsküdar.

METRO

The M1A connects Yenikapı with the airport; the M2 connects Yenikapı with Hacıosman via Taksim; and the Marmaray connects Kazlıçeşme, west of the Old City, with Sirkeci before crossing under the Bosphorus to Üsküdar and Ayrılık Çeşmesi.

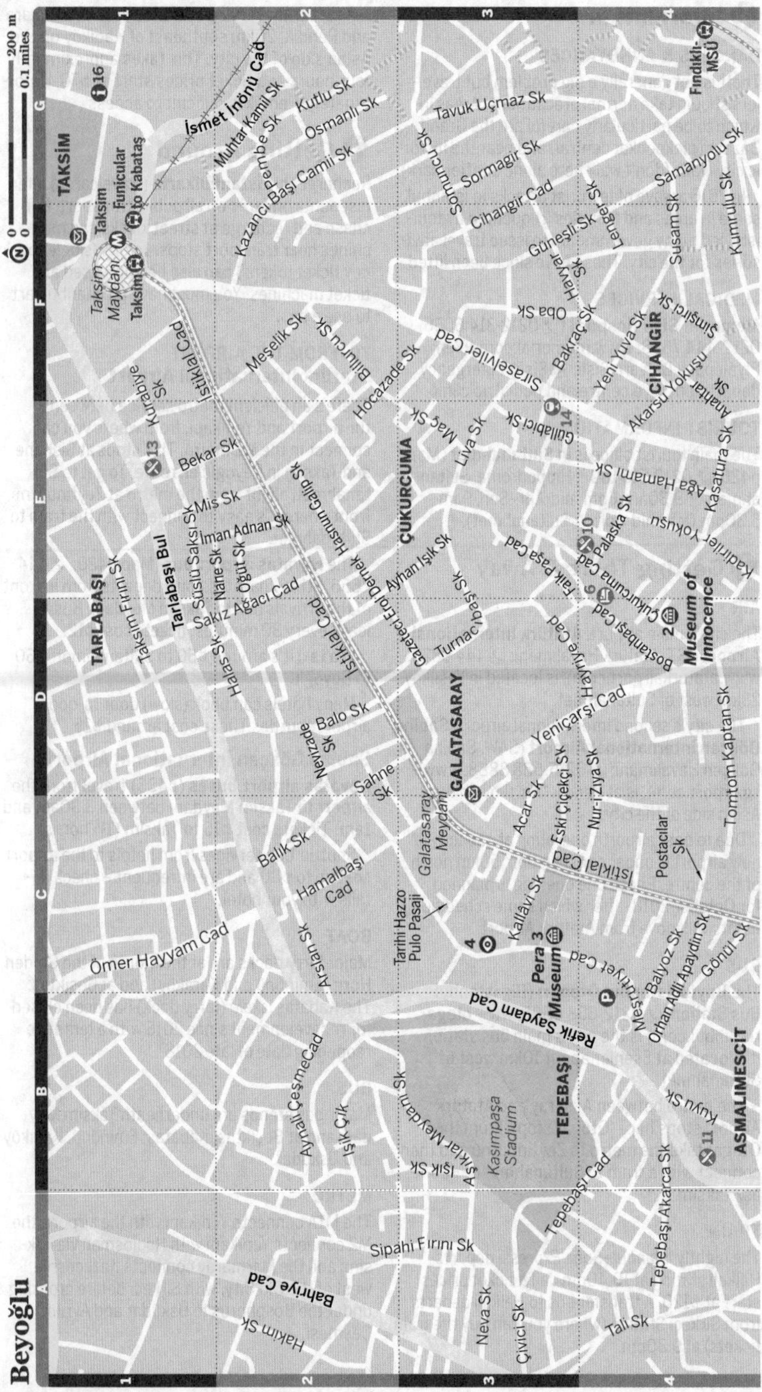

Beyoğlu

0 200 m
0 0.1 miles
TAKSİM
Taksim Maydanı
Taksim
Funicular to Kabataş
16
TARLABAŞI
Taksim Fırını Sk
13
Kurabiye Sk
Tarlabaşı Bul
Süslü Saksı Sk
İstiklal Cad
İsmet İnönü Cad
Halas Sk
Sakız Ağacı Cad
Nane Sk
İman Adnan Sk
Mis Sk
Bekar Sk
Öğüt Sk
Muhtar Kamil Sk
Kazancı Başı Camii Sk
Pembe Sk
Kutlu Sk
Osmanlı Sk
Hakim Sk
Bahriye Cad
Ömer Hayyam Cad
Aynali ÇeşmeCad
Arslan Sk
Hamalbaşı Cad
Balık Sk
Nevizade Sk
Balo Sk
Hasnun Galip Sk
Meşelik Sk
Billurcu Sk
Işik Çik
Sahne Sk
Gazeteci Erol Dermek
Ayhan Işık Sk
Hocazade Sk
ÇUKURCUMA
Sipahi Fırını Sk
Işık Sk
Aşıklar Meydanı Sk
Tarihi Hazzo Pulo Pasaji
Galatasaray Meydanı
GALATASARAY
Turnacıbaşı Sk
Maç Sk
Liva Sk
Somuncu Sk
Tavuk Uçmaz Sk
Neva Sk
Kasımpaşa Stadium
4
Çivici Sk
Refik Saydam Cad
Kallâvi Sk
Acar Sk
Yeniçarşı Cad
Faik Paşa Cad
Gullabici Sk
Sıraselviler Cad
Oba Sk
Cihangir Cad
Sormagir Sk
Pera Museum 3
TEPEBAŞI
Tepebaşı Cad
Eski Çiçekçi Sk
Hayriye Cad
14
Bakraç Sk
Havyar Sk
Güneşli Sk
Lenger Sk
Nur-i Ziya Sk
Meşrutiyet Cad
6
Çukurcuma Cad
10
Palaska Sk
Ağa Hamamı Sk
Yeni Yuva Sk
Tali Sk
Bostanbaşı Cad
Tepebaşı Akarca Sk
Balyoz Sk
Postacılar Sk
2
CİHANGİR
Akarsu Yokuşu
Susam Sk
Samanyolu Sk
Orhan Adli Apaydin Sk
Museum of Innocence
Kadiriler Yokuşu
Şimşirci Sk
Fındıklı-MSÜ
11
Kuyu Sk
Gönül Sk
Tomtom Kaptan Sk
Kasatura Sk
Anahtar Sk
Kumrulu Sk
ASMALIMESCİT

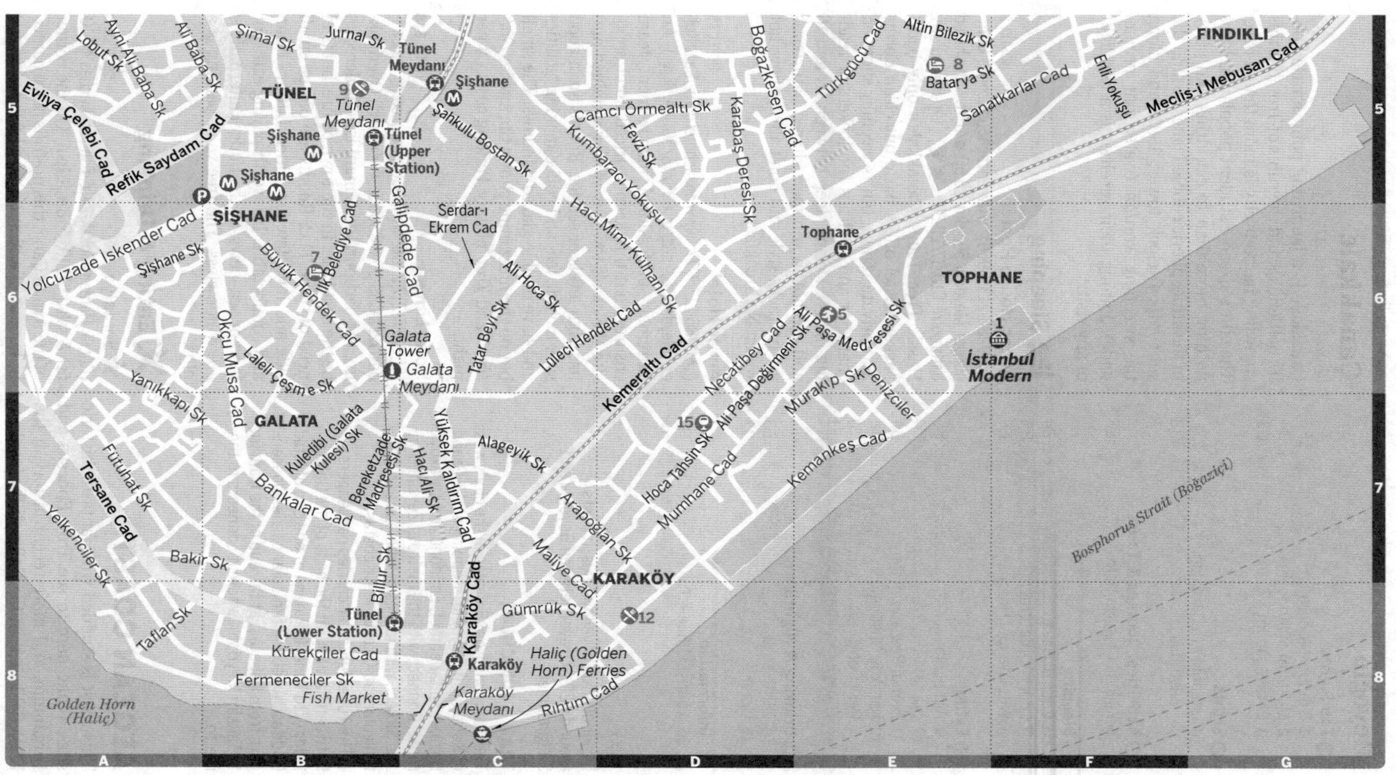
FINDIKLI
Meclis-i Mebusan Cad
Enli Yokuşu
Altin Bilezik Sk
8
Batarya Sk
Sanatkarlar Cad
Türkgücü Cad
Boğazkesen Cad
Karabaş Deresi Sk
Camcı Örmealtı Sk
Fevzi Sk
Kumbaracı Yokuşu
Hacı Mimi Külhanı Sk
Tophane
TOPHANE
1
İstanbul Modern
Ali Paşa Medresesi Sk
5
Necatibey Cad
Ali Paşa Değirmeni Sk
Murakıp Sk
Denizciler
15
Hoca Tahsin Sk
Mumhane Cad
Kemankeş Cad
Bosphorus Strait (Boğaziçi)
Kemeraltı Cad
Lüleci Hendek Cad
Ali Hoca Sk
Tatar Beyi Sk
Serdar-ı Ekrem Cad
Şimal Sk
Jurnal Sk
Tünel Meydanı
Şişhane
TÜNEL
9
Tünel Meydanı
Tünel (Upper Station)
Şahkulu Bostan Sk
Ayni Ali Baba Sk
Lobut Sk
Ali Baba Sk
Evliya Çelebi Cad
Refik Saydam Cad
Şişhane
ŞİŞHANE
Yolcuzade İskender Cad
Şişhane Sk
7
İlk Belediye Cad
Büyük Hendek Cad
Galipdede Cad
Okçu Musa Cad
Laleli Çeşme Sk
Galata Tower
Galata Meydanı
Yanıkkapı Sk
GALATA
Kuledibi (Galata Kulesi) Sk
Bereketzade Medresesi Sk
Hacı Ali Sk
Yüksek Kaldırım Cad
Alageyik Sk
Bankalar Cad
Fütuhat Sk
Tersane Cad
Yelkenciler Sk
Bakir Sk
Billur Sk
Arapoğlan Sk
Maliye Cad
KARAKÖY
Gümrük Sk
12
Karaköy Cad
Taflan Sk
Tünel (Lower Station)
Kürekçiler Cad
Fermeneciler Sk
Fish Market
Karaköy
Haliç (Golden Horn) Ferries
Karaköy Meydanı
Rıhtım Cad
Golden Horn (Haliç)
TURKEY İSTANBUL

Beyoğlu

Top Sights
1 İstanbul Modern F6
2 Museum of Innocence D4
3 Pera Museum C3

Sights
4 İstanbul Arastırmaları Enstitüsü C3

Activities, Courses & Tours
5 Kılıç Ali Paşa Hamamı E6

Sleeping
6 Casa di Bava E4
7 Louis Appartements B6
8 Witt Istanbul Hotel E5

Eating
9 Antiochia B5
10 Cuma E4
11 Hamdi Restaurant Pera B4
12 Karaköy Güllüoğlu D8
Pera Café ......(see 3)
13 Zübeyir Ocakbaşı E1

Drinking & Nightlife
14 Otto E3
15 Unter D7

Information
16 Tourist Office – Taksim G1

TAXI

İstanbul is full of yellow taxis. It costs around ₺20 to travel between Beyoğlu and Sultanahmet.

TRAM & FUNICULAR

The tram runs from Bağcılar, in the city's west, to Kabataş, in Beyoğlu, stopping at the Grand Bazaar, Sultanahmet, Eminönü and Karaköy en route. Connect with the metro at Zeytinburnu and Sirkeci, with ferries at Eminönü and with funiculars at Karaköy and Kabataş.

The Tünel funicular carries passengers between Karaköy, at the base of the Galata Bridge, to Tünel Meydanı, at one end of İstiklal Caddesi. A second funicular carries passengers from Kabataş, at the end of the tramline, to Taksim Meydanı, where it connects to the metro.

AEGEAN COAST

This coast is studded with fantastic historic sites. Come here to see Troy, Ephesus and Pergamum, and more recent history at the battlefield sites on the Gallipoli Peninsula.

Çanakkale

0286 / POP 165,517

Çanakkale is a launching point for Gallipoli's battlefields and the ruins of Troy, but this sprawling harbour city is more than a base. The citie's sizeable student population loves nothing more than to eat, drink and party in the atmospheric cobbled lanes around the *saat kulesi* (clock tower; 1897) and along the sweeping *kordon* (waterfront promenade). Joining their revelries is a highlight of any visit.

Sleeping

Anzac House Hostel HOSTEL $
(0286-213 5969; www.anzachouse.com; Cumhuriyet Meydanı 59; dm €6.50, s/d/tr with shared bathroom €10/17/22.50;) Operated by Hassle Free Tours, Çanakkale's only backpacker hostel offers basic but clean dorms and private rooms, but is woefully short on character and facilities (no lockers or reading lights). Dorms sleep between six and 16 and are hot in summer; shared bathrooms are barracks-style and don't always have hot water. No breakfast.

Anzac Hotel HOTEL $$
(0286-217 7777; www.anzachotel.com; Saat Kulesi Meydanı 8; s/d/tr €35/45/50; P) An extremely professional management team ensures that this keenly priced hotel opposite the clock tower is well maintained and has high levels of service. Rooms are a good size, include tea- and coffee-making facilities and have double-glazed windows. The small bar on the mezzanine shows the movies *Gallipoli* and *Troy* nightly. Parking costs €3 per night.

Hotel Limani HOTEL $$$
(0286-217 2908; www.hotellimani.com; Yalı Caddesi 12; s €35-55, d €35-75; P@) Overlooking the harbour, the Limani is considered to be the best hotel in the town centre, but is in need of some TLC. Rooms are on the small side and have few amenities, but are clean and comfortable. It's worth paying extra for land or sea views, as the budget alternatives are windowless. The free valet parking is a plus.

Eating & Drinking

★**Sardalya** SEAFOOD $
(Küçük Hamam Sokak 24b; fish sandwiches ₺7-10, fish & salad ₺11-19; 8am-11pm) On the corner of the Aynalı Çarşı, this no-frills place named in honour of a plentiful local fish (*sardalya*

Aegean Coast

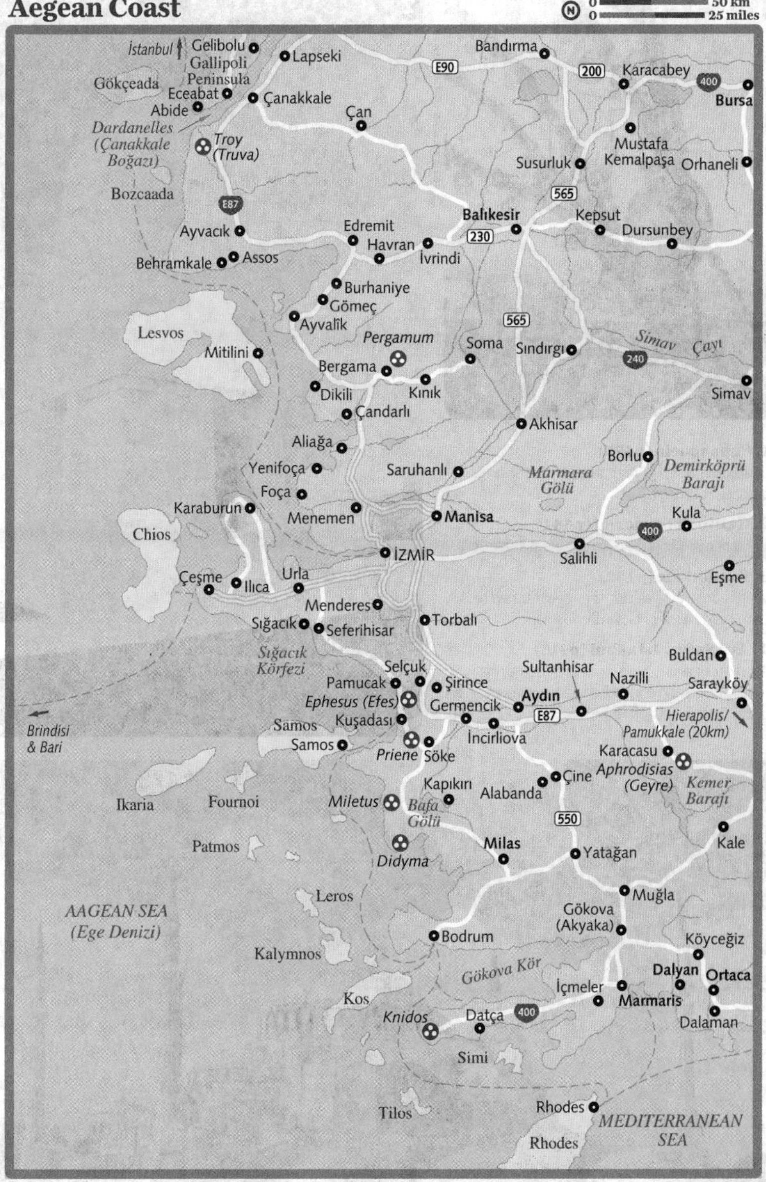

means sardine) serves everything from superfresh *balık ekmek* (fish sandwiches) to tasty plates of *midye tava* (fried mussels) or deep-fried fish. Sit at the counter on the street and chat with the locals between tasty mouthfuls, or order to go.

Yalova SEAFOOD **$$**

(☎0286-217 1045; www.yalovarestaurant.com; Gümrük Sokak 7; mezes ₺5-35, mains ₺25-65; ⏲12.30pm-1am) Locals have been coming here for slap-up meals since 1940. A two-storey place on the *kordon*, it serves seafood that often comes straight off the fishing

A LITTLE WORLD/SHUTTERSTOCK ©

GVICTORIA/SHUTTERSTOCK ©

1. Cappadocia (p475)
Be seduced by this geological wonderland of 'fairy chimney' rock crags.

2. Gallipoli memorial (p441)
Pay your respects to the fallen soldiers at Anzac Cove.

3. Pamukkale (p452)
Venture down the gleaming white calcite travertines (terraces) to dip your toes in thermal pools.

4. Aya Sofya, İstanbul (p416)
Appreciate the innovative architectural form, rich history, religious importance and extraordinary beauty of this venerable structure.

S-F/SHUTTERSTOCK ©

3

MURATART/SHUTTERSTOCK ©

boats moored out the front. Head upstairs to choose from the meze and fish displays, and be sure to quaff some locally produced Suvla wine with your meal.

★**Yalı Hanı** TEA GARDEN, BAR
(Fetvane Sokak 26; ⌚8am-10pm, closed winter) Hidden in the wisteria-covered courtyard of a late-19th-century caravanserai is this atmospheric hybrid *çay bahçesi* (tea garden) and bar that doubles as a performance and film-festival venue. It's a favourite haunt of boho types, who linger over glasses of wine and earnest conversation after checking out the art exhibitions that are often held in the upstairs space.

Information

ATMs are located right by the docks.

Tourist office (☎0284-217 1187; İskele Meydanı 67; ⌚8.30am-5.30pm Mon-Fri, 9.30am-12.30 & 1.30-4pm Sat & Sun) This office can supply city maps, information about Gallipoli battlefields and dolmuş timetables.

Getting There & Away

BOAT

Most ferries depart from the main **ferry** dock. To Eceabat (₺3/35 per person/car, 25 minutes) ferries depart hourly between 7am and midnight.

BUS

The city's **otogar** (bus station) is around 7km east of the centre, but many buses pick up and drop off at the ferry dock.

Services include Ankara (₺90, 10 hours, 10 daily), Bursa (₺45 4½ hours, two daily), Edirne (₺45, 4½ hours, at least two daily), İstanbul (₺65, six hours, regular services) and İzmir (₺55 to ₺60, 5¾ hours, at least two daily).

Troy

While not the most dramatic of Turkey's ancient sites, **Troy** (☎0286-283 0536; adult/child under 12yr ₺25/free; ⌚8.30am-7pm Apr-Oct, 8am-5pm Nov-Mar) is testament to the importance of myth to the human experience. Some imagination is needed to reconstruct the city's former splendour; fortunately, an informative audio guide (₺10) helps to evoke the ancient city for those who are visiting without a tour guide.

As you approach the ruins, take the stone steps up on the right. These bring you out on top of what was the **outer wall of Troy VIII/IX**, from where you can gaze on the fortifications of the **east wall gate** and **tower of Troy VI**.

Go back down the steps and follow the boardwalk to the right, between thick stone walls and up a knoll, from where you can look at some original (as well as some reconstructed) red-brick **walls of Troy II/III**. The curved protective roof above them is the same shape and height as the Hisarlık mound before excavations began in 1874.

Continue following the path, past the northeast bastion of the heavily fortified city of Troy VI, the site of a Graeco-Roman Troy IX **Temple of Athena** and further walls of Troy II/III. You can make out the stone foundations of a **megaron** (building with porch) from the same era.

Next, beyond traces of the wall of Early/Middle Troy (Troy I **south gate**) are more remains of megarons of Troy II, which were inhabited by a literal 'upper class' while the poor huddled on the plains.

The path then sweeps past Schliemann's original **trial trench**, which cut straight through all the layers of the city. Signs point out the nine city strata in the trench's 15m-high sides.

Just round the corner is a stretch of wall from what is believed to have been the two-storey-high Troy VI **Palace Complex**, followed by traces from Troy VIII/IX of a sanctuary to unknown deities. Later, a new sanctuary was built on the same site, apparently honouring the deities of Samothrace. Eventually, the path passes in front of the **Roman Odeon**, where concerts were held and, to the right, the **Bouleuterion** (Council Chamber), bringing you back to where you started.

Getting There & Away

Dolmuşes (minibuses) to Troy (₺7, 35 minutes, hourly) leave on the half-hour between 9.30am and 5pm from a station at the northern end of the bridge over the Sarı River in Çanakkale and drop passengers at the archaeological site's car park.

Eceabat

☎0286 / POP 8947

Eceabat (ancient Maydos) is an unremarkable waterfront town on the southern shore of the Dardanelles. It is notable only for its proximity to the main Gallipoli battlefields. Ferries dock by the main square (Cumhuriyet Meydanı), which is ringed by hotels, restaurants and bus-company offices.

Sleeping & Eating

Hotel Crowded House HOTEL $$

(☎0286-810 0041; www.hotelcrowdedhouse.com; Hüseyin Avni Sokak 4; s/d/tr €19/43/39; ❄📶) Conveniently located near the ferry port, Crowded House offers basic rooms with comfortable beds and clean bathrooms plus a simple breakfast.

★**Kilye Suvla Lokanta** MODERN TURKISH $$

(☎0286-814 1000; www.suvla.com.tr; Suvla Winery, Çınarlıdere Mevkil 11; mains ₺19-35; ⏲lokanta noon-3pm, tasting room & concept store 8.30am-5.30pm; ✍) Suvla's 60 hectares of certified organic vineyards are located near Kabatepe on the opposite side of the peninsula, but its winery, complete with an ultra-stylish garden restaurant, tasting room and produce shop, is on Eceabat's outskirts. Worth a dedicated visit, its menu features simple modern twists on Turkish classics such as *köfte* (meatballs), plus fresh salads, pastas and Turkish-style pizzas.

Getting There & Away

Buses to İstanbul stop in front of the ferry port.

Gestaş (☎444 0752; www.gdu.com.tr) ferries cross the Dardanelles between Eceabat and Çanakkale (per person/car ₺3/35, 25 minutes) hourly between 7am and midnight.

Gallipoli Peninsula

☎0286

Today, the Gallipoli (Gelibolu) Peninsula battlefields are covered in pine forests and fringed by idyllic beaches and coves. However, the bloody battles fought here in 1915 are still alive in Turkish and foreign memories and hold important places in the Turkish, Australian and New Zealand national narratives. Australians and New Zealanders view the peninsula, now protected as the **Gallipoli Campaign Historic Site**, as a place of pilgrimage and visit in their tens of thousands each year; they are outnumbered by Turks who, drawn by the legend of the courageous 57th regiment and its commander, Mustafa Kemal (the future Atatürk), also travel here in ever-increasing numbers to pay their respects.

Tours

★**Crowded House Tours** TOURS

(☎0286-814 1565; www.crowdedhousegallipoli.com; Zubeyde Hanim Meydani 28, Eceabat) Based at spacious new premises right on the Eceabat waterfront, this is the most professional of the tour companies operating on the Gallipoli Peninsula and is heartily recommended, especially if you can join a tour led by the affable and extremely knowledgable

TOURING THE GALLIPOLI BATTLEFIELDS

Start your tour at the extremely impressive **Çanakkale Epic Promotion Centre** (Çanakkale Destanı Tanıtım Merkezi; ☎0286-810 0050; http://canakkaledestani.milliparklar.gov.tr; Kabatepe; simulation experience & museum adult/child ₺13/free, museum only adult/child ₺3/free; ⏲9am-4pm), 1km east of the village of Kabatepe. Heading north from Kabatepe, on the coast road brings you to **Anzac Cove** where the ill-fated Allied landing began on 25 April 1915. Another 300m along is the **Arıburnu Sahil Anıtı** (Arıburnu Coastal Memorial), a moving Turkish monument with Atatürk's famous words of peace and reconciliation, spoken in 1934. Just beyond the memorial is **Arıburnu Cemetery** and, 750m further north, **Canterbury Cemetery**. Between them is the Anzac **Commemorative Site** (Anzac Tören Alanı) at North Beach, where dawn services are held on Anzac Day.

Returning to the Çanakkale Epic Promotion Centre, follow the signs to **Lone Pine** (Kanlısırt), just under 3km uphill. En route, you pass the **Mehmetçiğe Derin Saygı Anıtı**, dedicated to 'Mehmetçik' (Little Mehmet, the Turkish 'tommy' or 'digger') who carried a Kiwi soldier to safety. Lone Pine, 400m uphill, is a moving Anzac cemetery stood on the grounds of the 6 August 1916 battle where over 4000 men died. From here, it's another 3km up the one-way road to the New Zealand Memorial Cemetery at **Chunuk Bair** (Conkbayırı Yeni Zelanda Mezarlığı ve Anıtı).

About 1km uphill from Lone Pine, across the road from the Little Mehmet statue, is the **57 Alay Cemetery** (57 Alay Şehitliği) for the Ottoman 57th Regiment, which was led by Mustafa Kemal and was almost completely wiped out on 25 April while halting the Anzac attempt to advance to the high ground of Chunuk Bair.

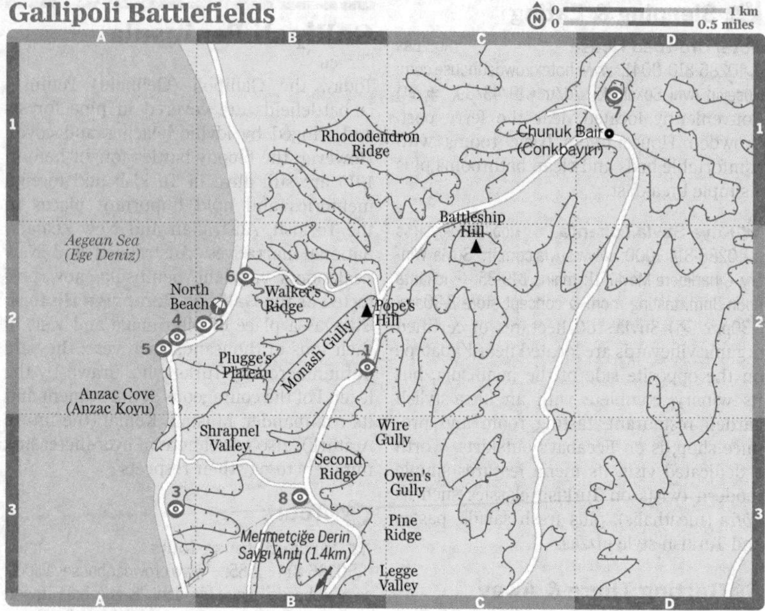

Gallipoli Battlefields

Sights

1 57 Alay Cemetery ... B2
2 Anzac Commemorative Site ... B2
3 Anzac Cove (Anzac Koyu) ... A3
4 Arıburnu Cemetery ... A2
5 Arıburnu Sahil Anıtı ... A2
6 Canterbury Cemetery ... B2
7 Chunuk Bair New Zealand Cemetery & Memorial ... D1
8 Lone Pine Cemetery ... B3

Bülent 'Bill' Yılmaz Korkmaz. Its core offering is a half-day tour of the main Anzac battlefields and cemeteries (€25).

Bursa

0224 / POP 1,907,305

Modern, industrial Bursa is built around the mosques, mausoleums and other sites from its incarnation as first Ottoman capital. For some fresh air after pounding the markets, the soaring peaks of Mt Uludağ are nearby, with Çekirge's thermal hamams en route.

Sights

It's worth taking a cable-car ride – the world's longest – up to the views and cool, clear air of nearby **Uludağ National Park** (www.bursa.com.tr; per car ₺15). Hiking to the summit of Uludağ takes three hours. The cable car can be reached by bus, taxi or dolmuş from Bursa.

★ **Muradiye Complex** HISTORIC SITE

(off Kaplıca Caddesi) FREE Set in a shady park, this Ottoman-era complex incorporates a handsome *medrese* (seminary; 1426) and the equally handsome **Sultan Murat II (Muradiye) Camii** (also 1426), but its most interesting elements are the 13 imperial *türbes* (tombs) in the cemetery. A number of these are exquisitely decorated with tiles, painted calligraphy and inlaid woodcarving. Don't miss the 14th-century tomb of Cem Sultan (the third son of Mehmet the Conqueror) and 16th-century tombs of Şehzades Mahmud and Ahmed, the sons of Beyazıt II.

★ **Yeşil Camii** MOSQUE

(Green Mosque; Yeşil Caddesi) Built for Mehmet I, the Yeşil (Green) Camii was completed in 1422 and represents a departure from the previous, Persian-influenced Seljuk architecture that dominated Bursa. Exemplifying Ottoman stylings, it contains a harmonious facade and beautiful carved marble work around the central doorway. The mosque was named for the interior wall's greenish-blue tiles.

Sleeping & Eating

Hotel Çeşmeli HOTEL $$
(☎0224-224 1511; Gümüşçeken Caddesi 6; s/d/tr €22/35/48; ❄📶) Run by women, the Çeşmeli is located near the market and is a friendly but sometimes noisy option. Although the rooms are dated and have uncomfortable beds, they are spotlessly clean.

★**Kitap Evi** BOUTIQUE HOTEL $$$
(☎0224-225 4160; www.kitapevi.com.tr; Burç Üstü 21; s/d from €55/70, s/d ste from €70/95; ❄@) Tucked inside the citadel battlements far above Bursa's minarets and domes, this Ottoman mansion and one-time book bazaar offers 13 individually styled rooms and larger suites (one suite boasts a marble-lined hamam). There's also a gorgeous rear courtyard with fountain where drinks and meals are served (open 8am to midnight). We applaud the free pick-up/drop-off from the BUDO/İDO seaports or otogar.

Lalezar Türk Mutfağı TURKISH $
(☎0224-221 8424; Ünlü Caddesi 14; soups ₺7-10, portions ₺10-25; ⏲7am-9pm, closed Sun summer) The impeccably clean and comfortable surrounds and ultra-friendly staff raise this long-standing favourite above most of Bursa's cheap eateries. There's an ever-changing array of soups, pilavs and vegetable and meat dishes on offer in the gleaming bain-marie as you enter. Don't leave without trying some of Bursa's best *fırın sütlac* (rice pudding). No alcohol.

★**Kebapçı İskender** KEBAP $$
(Ünlü Caddesi 7; İskender portions ₺35; ⏲11am-9pm) This refuge for serious carnivores is famous nationwide – it is one of two eateries in Bursa claiming to be where the legendary İskender kebap was created in 1867. The wood-panelled interior with tiled pillars and stained-glass windows is a pleasant environment in which to taste the renowned dish. There's no menu; simply order *bir* (one) or *bir buçuk* (1½) portions.

Getting There & Away

BOAT

The best way to travel between Bursa and İstanbul is by seabus. From Bursa's city centre, take bus F3 (₺10) to the **BUDO** (Bursa Deniz Otobüsleri, Bursa Sea Buses; ☎0850 850 9916; https://budo.burulas.com.tr/) seaport at Mudanya, 30km northwest of the city centre, from where eight ferries per day travel to/from İstanbul Eminönü (adult/child ₺29/24, two hours).

DON'T MISS

BURSA'S DERVISH LODGE SEMA

Every evening inside Bursa's 200-year-old *tekke* (dervish lodge), known as the **Karabaş-i Veli Kültür Merkezi** (Mevlâna Cultural Centre; ☎0224-222 0385; www.osmangazi.bel.tr; Çardak Sokak 32; ⏲winter 8pm, summer 9.30pm) FREE, you can watch the *şeyh* (master dervish) lead his students through a *sema* (whirling dervish ceremony). Saturday night is a major event, with various dervish groups participating. Get here early to absorb the wonderful community atmosphere in the *tekke's çay bahçesi* (tea garden) before the ceremony.

BUS

Bursa's **otogar** (☎0850-850 9916; Yeni Yalova Yolu 8km, Alaşarköy Mahallesi) is 10km north of the centre. From the otogar to the city centre, take bus 38 (₺4.40, one hour). Heading to the otogar, wait at the **stop** on Atatürk Caddesi opposite the *eski belediye* (old town hall).

Destinations include the following:

Ankara (₺50, 6½ hours)
Çanakkale (₺40, five hours)
Denizli (₺80, nine hours)
İstanbul (₺40, three hours)
İzmir (₺40, 5½ hours)

Bergama (Pergamum)

☎0232 / POP 102,090

The laid-back market town of Bergama is the modern successor to the once-powerful ancient city of Pergamum. Unlike Ephesus, which heaves with tourists year-round, Pergamum is for the most part a site of quiet classical splendour.

Sights

★**Bergama Acropolis** ARCHAEOLOGICAL SITE
(Bergama Akropol; Akropol Caddesi 2; ₺25; ⏲8am-4.30pm Oct-Mar, to 6.30pm Apr-Sep) One of Turkey's most impressive archaeological sites, Bergama's acropolis is dramatically sited on a hill to the northeast of the town centre. There's plenty to see in this ancient settlement, with ruins large and small scattered over the upper and lower cities. Chief among these are the Temple of Trajan; the vertigo-inducing 10,000-seat Hellenistic theatre, the Altar of Zeus (sadly denuded of its magnificent frieze, which now resides in Berlin) and the whimsical mosaic floors in Building Z.

Asklepion RUINS
(Prof Dr Frieldhelm Korte Caddesi 1; ₺20; ⌚8am-4.30pm Oct-Mar, to 6.30pm Apr-Sep) The Asklepion may not be as dramatic as the Acropolis, but in some ways it is even more extraordinary. One of the most important healing centres of the Roman world, it had baths, temples, a theatre, a library, treatment centres and latrines in its heyday. Remnants of many of these structures have been preserved on site, and what we see now is quite similar to how the centre would have appeared in the time of Emperor Hadrian.

Bergama Archaeology Museum MUSEUM
(Bergama Müze Müdürloğu; ☎0232-483 5117; Cumhuriyet Caddesi 6; ₺5; ⌚8am-4.30pm Nov-Mar, to 6.30pm Apr-Oct) Boasting a small but impressive collection of artefacts, Bergama's museum is well worth a visit. On exhibit are reliefs from the Acropolis, including a wonderful Roman-era relief from the Demeter Terrace, and a Hellenistic frieze and architrave from the Athena Terrace. Also impressive are the many statues from the Asklepion and a mosaic floor featuring Medusa's head that was originally in the Lower Agora. The ethnography gallery focuses on the crafts, costumes and customs of the Ottoman period.

Sleeping & Eating

Odyssey Guesthouse PENSION $
(☎0232-631 3501; www.odysseyguesthouse.com; Abacıhan Sokak 13; dm/s/d/tr €6/16/22/29, s/d without bathroom €10/17; ⌚closed Jan–mid-Feb; ❄📶) Superb views of all three archaeological sites from the upstairs terrace lounge is one of many enticements at this friendly pension. There are nine simple rooms spread over two buildings, a book exchange and a communal kitchen. Breakfast costs ₺15.

★**Aristonicus Boutique Hotel** BOUTIQUE HOTEL $$
(☎0232-632 4141; Taksim Caddesi 37; s/d/tw/tr & q €30/55/55/65; P❄📶) Offering extraordinarily good value, this relatively new operation has converted two old stone houses into an attractive hotel offering six immaculate rooms with satellite TV, kettle and minibar. The singles are tiny and some of the doubles have slightly cramped bathrooms, but the comfort levels are generally more than acceptable. Breakfast is in a shady courtyard.

★**Arzu** PIDE, KEBAP $
(☎0232-612 8700; İstiklal Meydanı 35; soups ₺6-9, pides ₺10-14, İskender kebap ₺14; ⌚6am-midnight) Located on a busy corner, this ultrafriendly *pidecı* (pide place) is probably the most popular eatery in town. The pides (Turkish-style pizzas) are excellent and there are also soups and kebaps on offer.

Bergama Sofrası TURKISH $
(☎0232-631 5131; Bankalar Caddesi 44; soup ₺7, portions ₺10-12; ⌚9am-9pm) One of a number of *lokantas* (eateries serving ready-made food) that can be found on the town's main drag, this friendly place next to the hamam has indoor and outdoor seating, and an open kitchen. The spicy *köfte* (meatball) is the speciality. The usual *lokanta* rule applies – eat here at lunch when the food is still fresh.

Information

Tourist Office (☎0232-631 2851; bergamaturizm@kultur.gov.tr; Cumhuriyet Caddesi 11; ⌚8.30am-noon & 1.30-5.30pm Mon-Fri) This helpful office is just north of the museum.

Getting There & Away

BUS

Bergama's **otogar** (Tepeköy) lies 7km from the centre. From the otogar, half-hourly dolmuşes head to the Soma Garaj in town (₺2.50).

Bus services from the otogar include Ankara (₺80 to ₺85, 8½ hours, 480km, nightly); Çanakkale (₺30 to ₺35, 220km, 4½ hours); and İzmir (₺13, two hours, 110km, every 30 minutes).

Getting Around

A *teleferik* (cable car; Bergama Akropolis Teleferik; ☎0232-631 0805; Akropol Caddesi; one-way/return ₺10/15; ⌚8am-5pm Apr-Sep, to 7pm Oct-Mar) links the Acropolis with the lower car park on Akropol Caddesi.

İzmir

☎0232 / POP 2.79 MILLION

Turkey's third-largest city is proudly liberal and deeply cultured. Garlanded around the azure-blue Bay of İzmir, it has been an important Aegean port since ancient times, when it was the Greek city of Smyrna.

Foreign visitors are few. The reason for this is a mystery to us, as the city is home to one of Turkey's most fascinating bazaars, an impressive museum of history and art, and a local lifestyle as laid-back as it is welcoming.

Sights

★**Kemeraltı Market** MARKET
(Kemeraltı Çarşısı; ⌚8am-7pm Mon-Sat; M Çankaya, Konak) A labyrinthine bazaar stretching from Konak Sq through to the ancient Agora, Kemeraltı dates back to the 17th century and is

home to shops, eateries, artisans' workshops, mosques, coffeehouses, tea gardens and synagogues. Spending a day exploring its crowded and colourful streets, historic places of worship, hidden courtyards and grand caravanseries reveals the real İzmir. Highlights include the cafes between the Hisar Mosque and the Kızlarağası Han, which serve the city's famous *fincanda pişen Türk kahvesi* (Turkish coffee boiled in the cup).

★İzmir Museum of History & Art MUSEUM

(İzmir Tarih ve Sanat Müzesi; 0232-445 6818; near Montrö Meydanı entrance, Kültürpark; ₺5; 8am-6.30pm Apr-Oct, 8.30am-5pm Nov-Mar; 12, 253, Basmane) This museum is overlooked by many visitors to the city, who do themselves a great disservice in the process. Spread over three pavilions, it is one of the richest repositories of ancient artefacts in the country and its Sculpture pavilion – crammed with masterpieces from ancient Smyrna, Teos, Miletos and Pergamon – is simply sensational. The Precious Objects and Ceramics pavilions contain jewellery, coins and pots, all displayed in a somewhat dated fashion but with informative labelling in English.

Agora RUINS

(Agora Caddesi; ₺10; 8am-6pm mid-Apr–Sep, to 4.30pm Oct–mid-Apr; Çankaya) Dating from the end of the 4th century BC, Smyrna's ancient agora was ruined in an earthquake in AD 178 but soon rebuilt by order of the Roman emperor Marcus Aurelius. The reconstructed Corinthian colonnade and Faustina Gate are eye-catching, but the vaulted chambers and cisterns in the basements of the two stoas (basilicas) are even more interesting, giving visitors a good idea of how this rectangular-shaped, multilevel marketplace would have looked in its heyday. Archaeological investigations are still underway.

Sleeping

InHouse Hostel HOSTEL $

(0232-404 0014; www.inhousehostel.com; 1460 Sokak 75, Alsancak; dm €8-9.50, s/d with shared bathroom €27/29; 12, 253, Alsancak) Opened in 2015, this hostel offers 56 beds in private rooms and in cramped dorms sleeping between three and 10. Dorms have under-bed lockers, hard bunk beds and clean but limited shared bathrooms. There's 24-hour reception, a kitchen for common use, a small foyer lounge and an entertainment program predominantly consisting of nightly pub crawls. The Alsancak location is excellent.

Hotel Baylan Basmane HOTEL $

(0232-483 0152; www.hotelbaylan.com; 1299 Sokak 8, Basmane; standard s/d/tr €21/30/37, deluxe s/d/tr €24/34/42; Basmane) A sound three-star choice, the Baylan has a loyal business clientele so you'll need to book in advance to snaffle a room. One of the cleanest and most professionally run hotels in the city, it has free on-site parking and a variety of room types, including deluxe rooms with private terraces, cramped twins and some singles with light-well windows only.

★Swissôtel Büyük Efes HOTEL $$

(0232-414 0000; www.swissotel.com/hotels/izmir; Gazi Osmanpaşa Bulvarı 1; standard/executive r from €100/132; Çankaya) Guests here have been known not to leave the premises at all during their city stay. Frankly, we're not at all surprised. Rooms are comfortable and well appointed, but it's the hotel's gorgeous garden and impressive facilities that are the real attraction. These include indoor and outdoor swimming pools, tennis court, spa, gym and rooftop bar with panoramic bay views.

Eating

★Ayşa TURKISH $

(0232-489 8485; Abacıoğlu Han, Anafartalar Caddesi 228, Kemeraltı Market; meze plates ₺9-10, portions from ₺10; 8am-6pm Mon-Sat; Konak, Çankaya) Serving Bosnian food that is remarkably similar to Turkish home cooking, this stylish *lokanta* (eatery with readymade food) offers both indoor and outdoor seating. Choose from the DIY meze display and be sure to snaffle a piece of *börek* (filled pastry) if it's on offer. Main dishes include both meat and vegetable choices.

Veli Usta Balık Pişiricisi SEAFOOD $$$

(0232-464 2705; www.balikpisiricisiveliusta.com; Atatürk Caddesi 212a, Alsancak; mezes ₺6-32, mains from ₺33; noon-11pm; 12, 253) In İzmir, three ingredients make for the perfect meal: *balık* (fish), *roca* (rocket) and rakı (aniseed brandy). This friendly terrace restaurant on the *kordon* is a great spot to sample all three, and is hugely popular with locals. Be sure to order the rolled sole, grouper or dory (described as *şiş* on the menu), which is the signature dish.

Getting There & Away

AIR

Many domestic and European flights arrive at İzmir's **Adnan Menderes Airport** (444 9828; www.adnanmenderesairport.com;), 15km south of the city centre.

BUSES FROM İZMIR'S OTOGAR

DESTINATION	FARE (₺)	DURATION (HR)	FREQUENCY
Ankara	65	8	hourly
Antalya	65	7	hourly
Bergama	13	2	half-hourly
Bodrum	35	3	hourly
Bursa	40	5	hourly
Çanakkale	60	6	hourly
Denizli	35	3	half-hourly
İstanbul	80-85	8	hourly
Konya	60	10½	6 daily
Kuşadası	19	1¼	hourly
Marmaris	48	4	hourly
Selçuk	12	1	frequent

BUS

İzmir's **otogar** (www.izotas.com.tr; Kemalpaşa Caddesi) lies 6.5km east of the city centre. Tickets can also be purchased from the bus companies' offices in the city centre; most of these are located in Dokuz Eylül Meydanı in Basmane and offer free *servises* (shuttle buses) to the otogar.

TRAIN

Six daily trains go to Selçuk from **Basmane station** (₺6.50, 1½ hours) between 7.45am and 6.25pm.

Getting Around

İzmir's Kent Kart (rechargeable transport card; ₺6) covers all public transport. They can be purchased and recharged at stations, piers and shops with the Kent Kart sign.

TO/FROM THE AIRPORT

Havaş (www.havas.net; 1-way ₺11) buses (one hour) travel between the domestic terminal and Gazi Osmanpaşa Bulvarı outside the Swissôtel Büyük Efes hourly. The city's commuter rail system İzban runs between the airport and Alsancak in the city centre.

METRO

İzmir Metro (www.izmirmetro.com.tr; fare ₺2.60; 6am-0.20am) is clean, quick and cheap. There are currently 17 stations running from Fahrettin Altay to Evka-3 via Konak, Çankaya, Basmane and Ege Universitesi (Aegean University).

TRAIN

The city's commuter rail system is called **İzban** (www.izban.com.tr). The northern line runs from Aliağa, near Bergama, to **Alsancak** (Alsancak Garı; 0232-464 7795); the southern line runs from Alsancak to Cumaovası, south of the city, where passengers can connect with services to Tepeköy near Selçuk.

Selçuk

0232 / POP 35,960

This farming village, speckled with ruins topped with storks' nests, is a likeable, down-to-earth place. Although best known as the gateway to Ephesus, there's plenty in town to explore, including Roman/Byzantine aqueduct arches, a lone pillar remaining from one of the Seven Wonders of the Ancient World, and the hilltop Byzantine ruins of the Basilica of St John and Ayasuluk Fortress. It's a relaxing place to cool your heels.

Sights

Ephesus Museum MUSEUM
(0232-892 6010; Uğur Mumcu Sevgi Yolu Caddesi; ₺10; 8am-6.30pm Apr-Oct, to 4.30pm Nov-Mar) An essential stop on every Ephesus itinerary, this small museum contains artefacts from the ancient city, including scales, jewellery and cosmetic boxes as well as coins, funerary goods and ancient statuary. Highlights include the famous phallic terracotta effigy of Bes in **room 2**, the huge statue of a resting warrior in **room 4** and the two extraordinary multibreasted marble statues of Artemis in **room 7**. The timelines on the walls are extremely useful for placing objects into their historical context.

Basilica of St John CHURCH
(Aziz Yahya Kilisesi; St Jean Caddesi; incl Ayasuluk Fortress ₺10; 8am-6pm Apr-Oct, to 4pm Nov-Mar) Despite a century of restoration, the once-great basilica built by Byzantine Emperor Justinian (r 527–565) remains a skeleton of its former self. Nonetheless, it is an atmospheric site with excellent hilltop

views, and the best place in the area for a sunset photo. The information panels and scale model highlight the building's original grandeur, as do the marble steps and monumental gate.

Ayasuluk Fortress FORTRESS

(Ayasuluk Kalesi; St Jean Caddesi; incl Basilica of St John ₺10; ⏲8am-6pm Apr-Oct, to 4pm Nov-Mar) Selçuk's crowning achievement is accessed on the same ticket as the Basilica of St John (p446), once the citadel's principal structure. Earlier and extensive excavations here, concluded in 1998 after a quarter century, proved that there were castles on Ayasuluk Hill going back beyond the original Ephesian settlement to the Neolithic age. The fortress' partially restored remains, about 350m north of the church, date from Byzantine, Seljuk and Ottoman times and are well worth a visit.

Temple of Artemis RUINS

(Temple of Artemision, Artemis Tapınağı; off Dr Sabri Yayla Bulvarı; ⏲8am-7pm Apr-Oct, 8.30am-6pm Nov-Mar) FREE In an empty field to the west of the centre, this lone reconstructed pillar is all that remains of the massive Temple of Artemis (or Artemision), one of the Seven Wonders of the Ancient World. At its zenith, the temple counted 127 columns; today, the only way to get any sense of its grandeur is to visit Didyma's better-preserved Temple of Apollo (which had a 'mere' 122 columns).

Sleeping

★Homeros Pension PENSION $

(☎0535 310 7859, 0232-892 3995; www.homerospension.com; 1048 Sokak 3; s/d €15/28, with shared bathroom €10/17; ❄📶) This long-time family-run favourite offers 10 rooms in two buildings. The decor features colourful hanging textiles and handcrafted furniture made by owner Derviş, a carpenter, antiques collector and ultra-welcoming host. Enjoy some of the best views in town on the roof terraces (one at each house). The six rooms in the newer (main) building are the nicest.

★Boomerang Guesthouse GUESTHOUSE $$

(☎0232-892 4879, 0534 055 4761; www.boomerangguesthouse.com; 1047 Sokak 10; dm/s/d/f €8/30/40/70, s/d with shared bathroom €20/30; ❄@📶) People keep coming back to this welcoming Turkish/Australian-Chinese operation to spend chilled-out evenings among the trees in the stone courtyard with its popular bar-restaurant. The best of the 10 rooms have balconies (ie Nos 13 and 14); all have kettles and fridges. The windowless basement dorm has 12 single beds, shares two bathrooms and has fans rather than air-con.

Hotel Bella BOUTIQUE HOTEL $$

(☎0232-892 3944; www.hotelbella.com; St Jean Caddesi 7; s €35-49, d €39-53, tr €60, f €67; ❄📶) This boutique hotel on a sloping street opposite the start of the aqueduct has 11 well-designed rooms with Ottoman flourishes in the decor. Some of these are small. Antiques and artefacts decorate the rooftop lounge and restaurant. Top marks are awarded for the free transfers to Ephesus.

★Ayasoluk Hotel BOUTIQUE HOTEL $$$

(☎0541 565 3545, 0232-892 3334; www.ayasolukhotel.com; 1051 Sokak 12; r €60-140; ❄📶🏊) Selçuk has more than its fair share of good small hotels, but this one stands out for the elegance of its decor, extent of its facilities (swimming pool, bar, restaurant) and friendliness of its staff. Rooms have extremely comfortable beds, modern bathrooms and satellite TVs, and the pool terrace commands sweeping views.

Eating

Ramazan Usta Gaziantep Kebap KEBAB $

(☎0232-892 8383; Siegburg Caddesi 11; kebaps ₺15-20; ⏲5-11pm Sun, Mon & Thu, 6pm-midnight Tue & Sat, 5pm-midnight Wed) A pocket-sized outpost of Turkey's southeast located in a pedestrianised street near the aqueduct, Master Ramazan's *kebapçı* (kebap eatery) serves the best meat dishes in town for some of the cheapest prices. It even serves beer. No wonder it's popular with locals and tourists alike.

Seçkin & Firuze TURKISH $

(☎0232-892 1184; Cengiz Topel Caddesi 20; mezes ₺14-20, mains ₺15-35; ⏲8am-11pm) This lovely family-run eatery on Selçuk's 'restaurant row' serves grills and seafood dishes that taste just like *ana* (mum) makes because that's just who's preparing them in the kitchen. Excellent mezes too.

Boomerang Garden Restaurant CHINESE $

(☎0232-892 4879, 0534 055 4761; 1047 Sokak 10; mezes ₺6, mains ₺15-30; ⏲8am-midnight; 🌿) If you really can't last another day without a fix of rice and noodles and sweet-and-sour whatever, head for this delightful courtyard restaurant (and bar) that boasts its own Chinese cook. But don't limit yourself, if you want Turkish – from kebaps to cheese *köfte* – or even vegetarian fare, Candy (Çağıran) can oblige. Always a warm welcome.

Selçuk

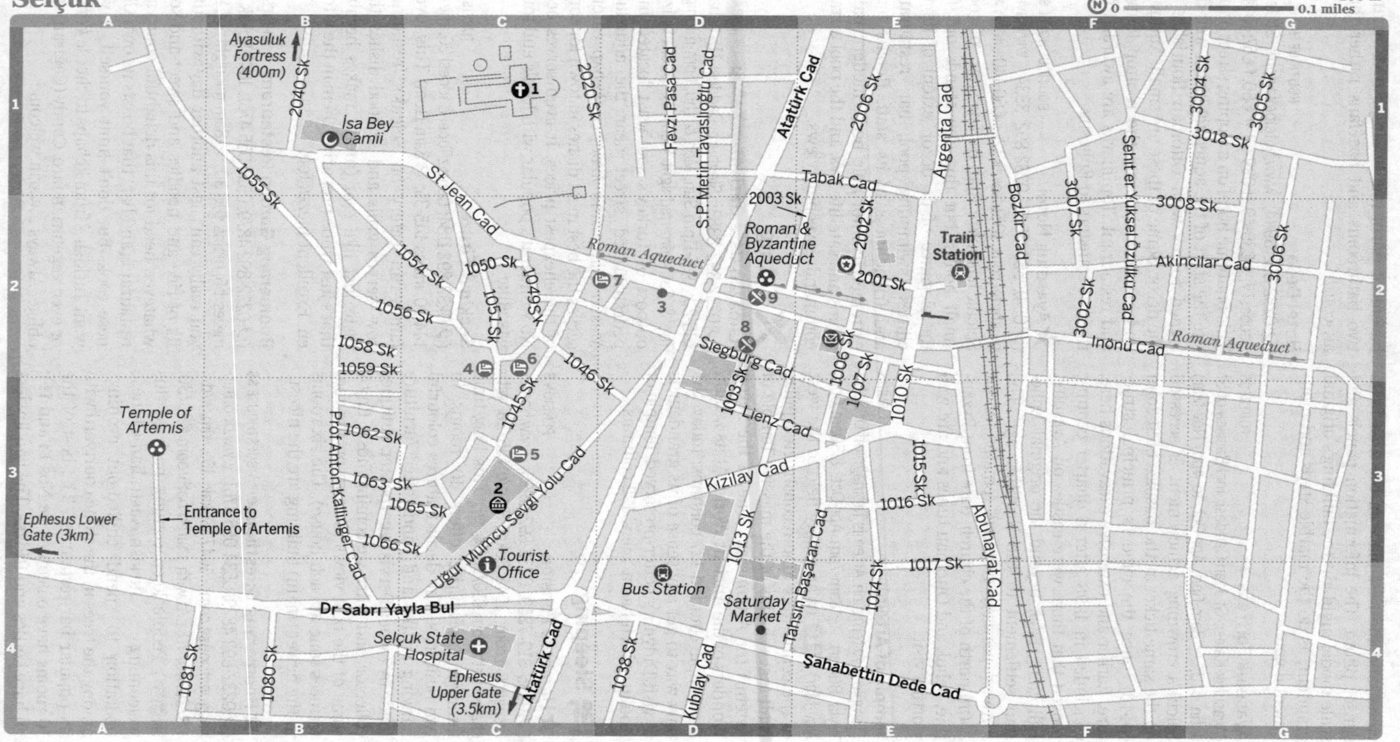

Selçuk
0 200 m
0 0.1 miles
Ayasuluk Fortress (400m)
2040 Sk
İsa Bey Camii
1055 Sk
St Jean Cad
1054 Sk
1050 Sk
1049Sk
1051 Sk
1056 Sk
1058 Sk
1059 Sk
1046 Sk
1045 Sk
2020 Sk
Roman Aqueduct
Fevzi Paşa Cad
S.P. Metin Tavaslioğlu Cad
Atatürk Cad
2006 Sk
Tabak Cad
2003 Sk
Roman & Byzantine Aqueduct
2002 Sk
2001 Sk
Argenta Cad
Train Station
Bozkir Cad
3007 Sk
Sehit er Yuksel Özülkü Cad
3008 Sk
3004 Sk
3018 Sk
3005 Sk
3006 Sk
Akincilar Cad
3002 Sk
İnönü Cad
Roman Aqueduct
Siegburg Cad
1003 Sk
1006 Sk
1007 Sk
1010 Sk
Lienz Cad
Temple of Artemis
1062 Sk
Prof Anton Kallinger Cad
1063 Sk
1065 Sk
1066 Sk
Uğur Mumcu Sevgi Yolu Cad
Entrance to Temple of Artemis
Ephesus Lower Gate (3km)
Tourist Office
Kizilay Cad
1015 Sk
1016 Sk
1013 Sk
Tahsin Başaran Cad
Abuhayat Cad
1017 Sk
1014 Sk
Bus Station
Saturday Market
Dr Sabrı Yayla Bul
Selçuk State Hospital
Ephesus Upper Gate (3.5km)
Atatürk Cad
1038 Sk
Kubilay Cad
Şahabettin Dede Cad
1081 Sk
1080 Sk

Selçuk

Sights
1 Basilica of St John C1
2 Ephesus Museum C3

Activities, Courses & Tours
Enchanting Tours .... (see 7)
3 No Frills Ephesus Tours D2

Sleeping
4 Ayasoluk Hotel C2
5 Boomerang Guesthouse C3
6 Homeros Pension C2
7 Hotel Bella D2

Eating
Boomerang Garden Restaurant .... (see 5)
8 Ramazan Usta Gaziantep Kebap D2
9 Seçkin & Firuze D2

Getting There & Away

BUS & DOLMUŞ

Dolmuşes (minibuses) depart from the **otogar** (Atatürk Caddesi) to İzmir (₺12, one hour, every 40 minutes from 6.30am to 8.30pm); and Kuşadası (₺6, 25 minutes) via Pamucak (₺3.50, 10 minutes), every 30 minutes from 6.30am to midnight.

Intercity bus services head to Ankara (₺85, eight hours, four services daily); Bursa (₺68, six hours, nine daily); Göreme (₺72, 10½ hours, one service daily); Denizli for Pamukkale (₺35, three hours, at least two departures daily); Fethiye (₺50, 5½ hours, one daily); and İstanbul (₺90 to ₺100, nine hours, two daily). There are also three direct services daily to Pamukkale (₺30, three hours). Otherwise, change in Denizli.

Train

There are six express trains per day to/from İzmir's Basmane Garı (₺6.50, 1½ hours) between 7.45am and 6.25pm, via the airport. These travel on to Denizli.

Ephesus

The Greco-Roman world truly comes alive at **Ephesus** (Efes; www.ephesus.us; main site adult/child ₺40/free, Terraced Houses ₺20, parking ₺7.50; 8am-6.30pm Apr-Oct, to 4.30pm Nov-Mar). After more than a century and a half of excavation, the city's recovered and renovated structures have made Ephesus Europe's most complete classical metropolis – and that's with 80% of the city yet to be unearthed!

As capital of Roman Asia Minor, Ephesus was a vibrant city of over 250,000 inhabitants, the fourth largest in the empire after Rome, Alexandria and Antioch. Adding in traders, sailors and pilgrims to the Temple of Artemis, these numbers were even higher, meaning that in Ephesus one could encounter the full diversity of the Mediterranean world and its peoples. So important and wealthy was Ephesus that its Temple of Artemis, on the western edge of present-day Selçuk, was the biggest on earth, and one of the Seven Wonders of the Ancient World.

Sights

★Terraced Houses — RUINS

(₺20) The roofed complex here contains seven well-preserved Roman homes built on three terraces, which are well worth the extra visiting fee. As you ascend the stairs through the enclosure, detailed signs explain each structure's evolving use during different periods. Even if you aren't a history buff, the colourful mosaics, painted frescoes and marbles provide breathtaking insight into the lost world of Ephesus and its aristocracy.

Curetes Way — RUINS

Named for the demigods who helped Lena give birth to Artemis and Apollo, the Curetes Way was Ephesus' main thoroughfare, 210m long and lined with statuary, religious and civic buildings, and rows of shops selling incense, silk and other goods, workshops and even restaurants. Walking this street is the best way to understand Ephesian daily life.

Library of Celsus — RUINS

This magnificent library dating from the early 2nd century AD, the best-known monument in Ephesus, has been extensively restored. Originally built as part of a complex, the library looks bigger than it actually is: the convex facade base heightens the central elements, while the middle columns and capitals are larger than those at the ends. Facade niches hold replica statues of the Four Virtues. From left to right, they are: Sophia (Wisdom), Arete (Goodness), Ennoia (Thought) and Episteme (Knowledge).

Temple of Hadrian — RUINS

One of Ephesus' star attractions and second only to the Library of Celsus, this ornate, Corinthian-style temple honours Trajan's successor and originally had a wooden roof when completed in AD 138. Note its main arch; supported by a central keystone, this

Ephesus

architectural marvel remains perfectly balanced, with no need for mortar. The temple's designers also covered it with intricate decorative details and patterns: Tyche, goddess of chance, adorns the first arch, while Medusa wards off evil spirits on the second.

Great Theatre RUINS

Originally built under Hellenistic King Lysimachus, the Great Theatre was reconstructed by the Romans between AD 41 and 117 and it is thought St Paul preached here. However, they incorporated original design elements,

Ephesus

Top Sights

1 Terraced Houses........ B5

Sights

2 Asclepion........ B6
3 Baths of Scholasticia........ B5
4 Baths of Varius........ C5
5 Brothel........ B4
6 Church of St Mary........ A2
7 Columns of the Evangelists........ A3
8 Curetes Way........ B5
9 Ephesus........ B4
10 Gate of Hadrian........ B4
11 Great Theatre........ B4
12 Gymnasium of Vedius........ C1
13 Harbour Baths........ A3
14 Harbour Street........ A3
15 Hercules Gate........ B5
16 Hydreion........ B5
17 Latrines........ B5
18 Library of Celsus........ B4
19 Lower Agora........ B4
20 Lower Gate........ B3
21 Marble Street........ B4
22 Memmius Monument........ B5
23 Necropolis........ C6
24 Odeon........ C5
25 Pollio Fountain........ B5
26 Prytaneum........ C5
27 Sanctuary of the Mother Goddess Cybele........ D2
28 Stadium........ C2
29 Temple of Domitian........ B5
30 Temple of Hadrian........ B5
Temple of Hestia........ (see 26)
31 Temple of Isis........ C5
32 Temple of Serapis........ A4
33 Tomb of St Luke........ C6
34 Trajan Fountain........ B5
35 Upper Agora........ C5
36 Upper Gate (Magnesian Gate)........ C6

including the ingenious shape of the *cavea* (seating area), part of which was under cover. Seating rows are pitched slightly steeper as they ascend, meaning that upper-row spectators still enjoyed good views and acoustics – useful, considering that the theatre could hold an estimated 25,000 people.

Tours

Selçuk-based operators such as **Enchanting Tours** (☎0535 245 3548, 0232-892 6654; www.enchantingtoursturkey.com; St John Caddesi 3/B, Hotel Bella) and **No Frills Ephesus Tours** (☎0545 892 8828, 0232-892 8828; www.nofrillsephesustours.com; St Jean Caddesi 3/A; half-/full-day tour from €40/55; ⊙9am Apr-Oct) offer recommended tours.

Getting There & Away

Selçuk is roughly a 3.5km walk from both entrances. Dolmuşes (minibuses) serve the Lower Gate (₺2.50) every half-hour in summer, hourly in winter. A taxi from Selçuk to either gate costs about ₺20.

Kuşadası

☎0256 / POP 107,000

Kuşadası is a popular package-tour destination and, as the coastal gateway to Ephesus, Turkey's busiest cruise port. Lacking the sights and ambience of Bodrum, though it does have a little Byzantine **castle** (Güvercin Adası; ⊙8am-11pm May-Aug, 9am-9pm Sep-Apr) FREE, Kuşadası remains a runner-up on the Aegean party scene. But if you prefer to mix your Ephesus visit with nightlife and sea views rather than the rural ambience of Selçuk, then Kuşadası offers some good hotels and restaurants.

Sleeping & Eating

★**Liman Hotel** HOTEL $$
(☎0256-614 7770; www.limanhotel.com; cnr Kıbrıs & Güvercinada Caddesis; s/d/tr €35/45/55;) Run by seasoned traveller Hasan 'Mr Happy' Değirmenci, the Harbour Hotel is a welcoming haven for travellers. The 14 rooms (accessed by lift!) are simple but comfortable, and all have satellite TV, kettle and balcony (six are sea-facing). The real pleasure of staying here is the general vibe of holiday camaraderie, especially on the rooftop terrace.

★**Villa Konak** BOUTIQUE HOTEL $$$
(☎0256-614 6318; www.villakonakhotel.com; Yıldırım Caddesi 55; standard r €60, deluxe r €60-75, f €120; ⊙closed late Oct-early Apr;) In a quiet old quarter far above the harbour, Villa Konak is cobbled together from seven houses of varying ages (one a 160-year-old stone house), all decorated with Ottoman knick-knacks and offering amenities including satellite TV. There are 17 rooms, a gorgeous garden with pool and comfy deckchairs, a cafe/bar and a library. No child guests under six.

★**Hasan Kolcuoğlu Kebap** KEBAB $$
(☎0256-614 9979; Güvercinada Caddesi 37, Efe Boutique Hotel; kebaps ₺27-34; ⊙8.30am-11pm) This upscale kebap house below the Efe Boutique Hotel has seating on a sprawling terrace with dress-circle views of the castle. The speciality is spicy Adana kebap, which groups love to order by the metre (₺49). Breakfast (₺26) is

good value, as is the ₺65 fixed menu offering mezes, kebap and dessert. All main courses come with three free mezes.

★ Kazım Usta SEAFOOD $$$
(☎0256-614 1226; Liman Caddesi 4; mezes ₺12-35, mains ₺28-50; ⊙11am-midnight) Still going strong after well over 60 years, Kazım Usta offers a warm welcome and is Kuşadası's top (and priciest) fish restaurant, serving dishes ranging from swordfish kebap to farmed bream and meat options. Order fish by the kilo (1kg is ₺80 to ₺130) and book well ahead to bag a waterfront table in summer. It closes earlier in winter.

ℹ Getting There & Away

BOAT

Meander Travel (☎0256-612 8888; www.meandertravel.com; Mahmut Esat Bozkurt Caddesi 14/B; ⊙7am-11pm Apr-Oct, 9am-6pm Mon-Sat Nov-Mar) operates a daily **ferry** to the Greek island of Samos (single/same-day return/open return €35/40/55) from April to October. Boats depart Kuşadası at 9am and Samos at 5pm or 6pm.

BUS & DOLMUŞ

Kuşadası's **otogar** (Garaj Caddesi) is at the southern end of Süleyman Demirel Bul. Free *Servises* (shuttle buses) run to/from the bus companies' offices on İsmet İnönü Bulvarı.

To Bodrum (₺30, 2½ hours) there are three departures daily in summer; otherwise take a dolmuş (minibus) to Söke, from where they run half-hourly. To İzmir (₺19, one hour) buses run every 30 minutes in summer, hourly in winter.

> **WORTH A TRIP**
>
> **PRIENE, MILETUS & DIDYMA**
>
> Selçuk and Kuşadası are good bases for visits to the superb ancient cities of **Priene** (₺5; ⊙8.30am-7pm Apr-Oct, to 5pm Nov-Mar), **Miletus** (Milet; ₺10, parking ₺4, audio guide ₺10; ⊙8.30am-7pm Apr-Oct, to 5pm Nov-Mar) and **Didyma** (₺10, audio guide ₺10; ⊙8.30am-7pm mid-May–mid-Sep, to 5pm mid-Sep–mid-May), all to the south. If you're pushed for time, a 'PMD' tour from Selçuk or Kuşadası costs between €45 and €60.
>
> Perched high on the craggy slopes of Mt Mykale, Priene has a beautiful windswept setting; Miletus boasts a spectacular theatre and Didyma hosts the stupendous Temple of Apollo.

Dolmuşes to Selçuk (₺6, 20 minutes), via Pamucak and the turn-off for Ephesus Lower gate, and to Söke (₺6, 30 minutes) both leave from the roundabout at the southern end of Candan Tarhan Bulvarı every 20 to 30 minutes.

Pamukkale

☎0258 / POP 337,444

Walking down Pamukkale's gleaming white calcite travertines (terraces), overrunning with warm, mineral-rich waters, remains one of Turkey's singular experiences. Just above the travertines lies Hierapolis, once a Roman and Byzantine spa city, which has considerable ruins and a museum. While the photogenic travertines get busloads of day-trippers, staying overnight allows you to visit the site at sunset and dodge some of the crowds.

◉ Sights

★ Travertines NATURE RESERVE
(₺35 incl Hierapolis; ⊙8am-6.45pm, extended hours Jun–mid-Sep, reduced hours Nov-Mar) The World Heritage–listed saucer-shaped travertines (or terraces) of Pamukkale wind sideways down the powder-white mountain above the village, providing a stunning contrast to the clear blue sky and green plains below. To protect the unique calcite surface that overruns with warm, mineral-rich waters, guards oblige you to go barefoot (or in socks or shower shoes), so if you're planning to walk down to the village via the travertines, be prepared to carry your shoes with you.

★ Hierapolis RUINS
(adult/child ₺35/free incl travertines; ⊙8am-6.45pm, extended hours Jun–mid-Sep, reduced hours Nov-Mar) Hierapolis' location atop Pamukkale's tourist-magnet travertines is quite spectacular, and the ruins of this ancient spa city are beautifully maintained. Founded as a curative centre around 190 BC by Eumenes II of Pergamum, it prospered under both the Romans and Byzantines, when large Jewish and Orthodox Christian communities comprised most of the population. Recurrent earthquakes brought disaster, and Hierapolis was finally abandoned after an AD 1334 tremor. When visiting, don't miss the Roman Theatre, the Agora and the on-site **museum** (adult/child ₺5/free; ⊙8.30am-6.45pm Apr-Oct, 8am-4.45pm Nov-Mar).

Sleeping

Beyaz Kale Pension PENSION $

(☎0258-272 2064; www.beyazkalepension.com; Oguzkaan Caddesi 4; s/d/tr/f €19/27/34/38;) On a quiet street just outside the village centre, this excellent, friendly pension has 10 spotless rooms on two floors, some more modern than others. It serves some of the best local pension fare (veg/meat menus ₺25/30) in the rooftop restaurant. The family room sleeps six.

Melrose Viewpoint HOTEL $$

(Melrose Suites; ☎0544 498 9114; www.melroseviewpoint.com; Çay Sokak 7; s/d/tr/f from €22/26/36/46;) A tall building with a jaunty blue-and-white colour scheme, this hotel has 26 attractively decorated rooms, some of which have wonderful views of the travertines. Room amenities include satellite TV and kettle, and facilities include a large swimming pool and on-site restaurant (menu ₺25). When we last visited, construction of a basement spa was planned.

Getting There & Away

Inter-city buses arrive at and depart from Denizli. **Dolmuşes** (minibuses; ₺3.50, 40 minutes) run frequently between Pamukkale and Denizli's **otogar** (İzmir Bulvarı) between 6.30am and 11pm.

Destinations from Denizli's otogar include the following:

Ankara (₺60, seven hours, every two hours)
Antalya (₺40, four hours, every two hours)
Bodrum (₺35, five hours, six daily)
Bursa (₺75, 10 hours, every two hours)
İstanbul (₺95, 12 hours, frequent)
Izmir (₺30, four hours, hourly)
Konya (₺55, six hours, every two hours)
Marmaris (₺36, four hours, five daily)
Nevşehir (for Cappadocia; ₺65, nine hours, four daily)
Selçuk (₺30, three hours, two daily)

Bodrum Town

☎0252 / POP 37,815

Although more than a million tourists flock to its beaches, restaurants and clubs each summer, the town of Bodrum (ancient Halicarnassus) never seems to lose its cool. More than any other Turkish seaside getaway, it has an enigmatic elegance that pervades it, from the town's crowning castle and glittering marina to its flower-filled cafes and white-plastered backstreets. Even in the most hectic days of high summer, you can still find little corners of serenity in the town.

OFF THE BEATEN TRACK

AFRODISIAS

Added to Unesco's World Heritage List in 2017, **Afrodisias** (₺15; 8am-6.30pm Apr-Oct, to 4.30pm Nov-Mar) in the Anatolian hinterland trumps many of Turkey's ancient sites for its sheer scale and magical surrounds (Roman poplars, green fields and warbling birds). It also has an extremely impressive on-site museum housing sculptures and friezes excavated on site. Highlights include the marble reliefs in the museum's Sevgi Gönül Salonu, the Temple of Aphrodite, the bouleuterion, the white marble theatre and the stunning 270m-long stadium with its 30,000 overgrown seats.

The site is an easy detour for those driving between Pamukkale and the Aegean coast.

Sights

★**Bodrum Castle** CASTLE

(Bodrum Kalesi; ☎0252-316 2516; www.bodrum-museum.com; İskele Meydanı) There are splendid views from the battlements of Bodrum's magnificent castle, built by the Knights Hospitaller in the early 15th century and dedicated to St Peter. In recent years it has housed the **Museum of Underwater Archaeology** (Sualtı Arkeoloji Müzesi), arguably the most important museum of its type in the world. At the time of research, the castle and museum were closed for a €25 million restoration and weren't predicted to re-open until summer 2019.

Mausoleum RUINS

(Mausoleion; Turgutreis Caddesi; ₺10; 8am-7pm Apr-Oct, to 5pm Nov-Mar) One of the Seven Wonders of the Ancient World, the Mausoleum was the greatest achievement of Carian King Mausolus (r 376–353 BC), who moved his capital from Mylasa (today's Milas) to Halicarnassus. The only ancient elements to survive are the pre-Mausolean stairways and tomb chambers; the narrow entry to Mausolus' tomb chamber and a huge granite stone that blocked it; the Mausolean drainage system; precinct wall bits; and some large fluted marble column drums.

Sleeping

Eskici Hostel HOSTEL $

(☎0252-316 8072, 0535 573 3203; info@eskicihostel.com; Papatya Sokak 24; dm €10-13, d & tw €40, tr €50;) Head to the Eskici ('Junk') if you're

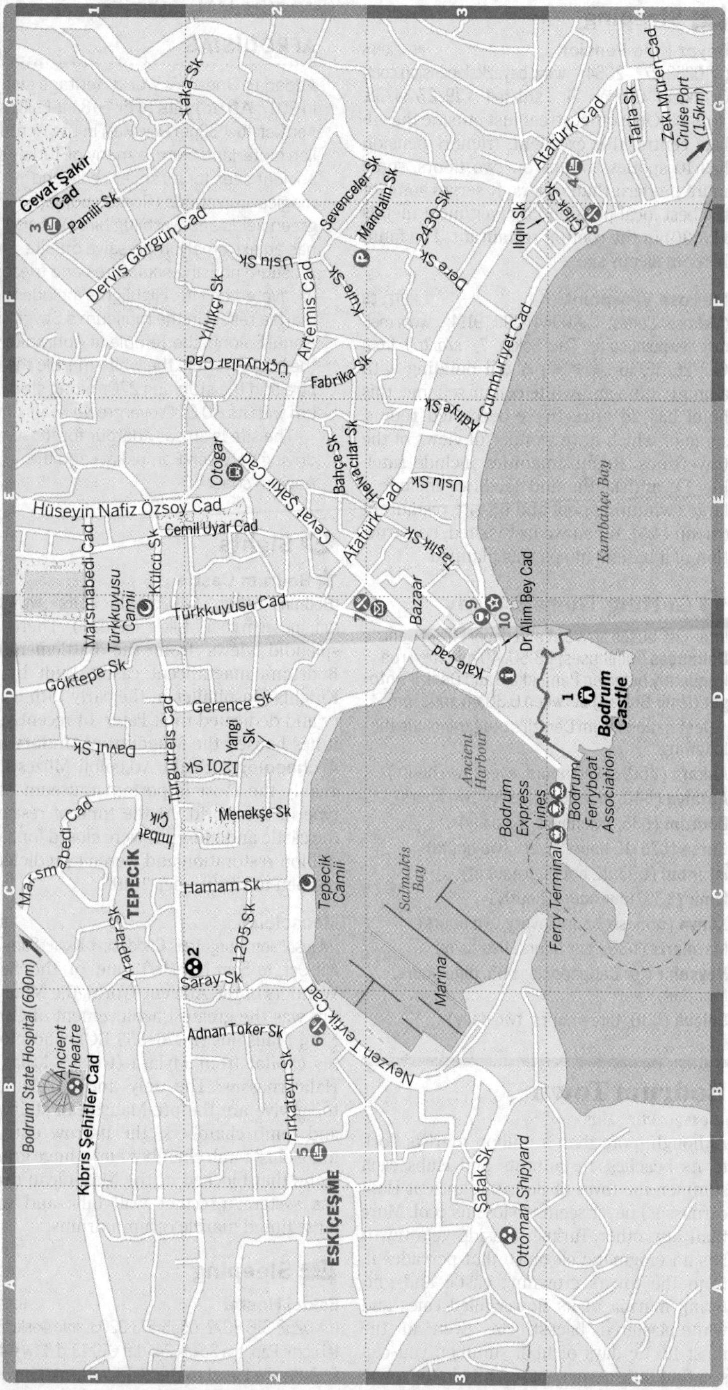

Bodrum

0 400 m
0 0.2 miles
N
A
B
C
D
E
F
G
1
2
3
4
Bodrum State Hospital (600m)
Ancient Theatre
Kıbrıs Şehitler Cad
Marsmabedi Cad
Araplar Sk
TEPECİK
İmbat Çık
Davut Sk
Göktepe Sk
Marsmabedi Cad
Türkkuyusu Camii
Külcü Sk
Hüseyin Nafiz Özsoy Cad
Cemil Uyar Cad
Turgutreis Cad
2
Saray Sk
Adnan Toker Sk
1205 Sk
Hamam Sk
Menekşe Sk
1201 Sk
Yangi Sk
Gerence Sk
Türkkuyusu Cad
Otogar
Cevat Şakir Cad
Üçkuyular Cad
Yıllıkçı Sk
Uslu Sk
Artemis Cad
Derviş Görgün Cad
Yaka Sk
3
Cevat Şakir Cad
Pamili Sk
Fırkateyn Sk
5
6
ESKİÇEŞME
Neyzen Tevfik Cad
Tepecik Camii
Salmakis Bay
Marina
7
Bahçe Sk
Helvacılar Sk
Atatürk Cad
Fabrika Sk
Kule Sk
Sevenceler Sk
Mandalin Sk
Bazaar
Taşlık Sk
Uslu Sk
Adliye Sk
Dere Sk
2430 Sk
Şafak Sk
Ottoman Shipyard
Ancient Harbour
Kale Cad
9
10
Dr Alim Bey Cad
Cumhuriyet Cad
Bodrum Express Lines
Ferry Terminal
Bodrum Ferryboat Association
1
Bodrum Castle
Kumbahçe Bay
Ilgın Sk
Çilek Sk
Atatürk Cad
4
8
Tarla Sk
Zeki Müren Cad
Cruise Port (1.5km)

Bodrum

Top Sights
1 Bodrum Castle........D4

Sights
2 Mausoleum........C2

Sleeping
3 El Vino Hotel........F1
4 Eskici Hostel........G4
5 Ha lâ Bodrum........B2

Eating
6 Gemibaşı........B2
7 Nazik Ana........D2
8 Ox........F4

Drinking & Nightlife
9 Dada Salon........D3

Entertainment
10 Club Catamaran........D3

keen to party while in Bodrum. And we mean party big time. Opened in 2017, it has a small pool in the downstairs garden, a fab rooftop bar with castle and sea views, and an array of private rooms and mixed dorms (most with air-con and bathroom). Sadly, when we visited it could have done with a good clean.

★Ha lâ Bodrum BOUTIQUE HOTEL $$

(☎0532 368 1411; www.halabodrum.com; Davalcu Ali Sokak 17; r €60-120; ❄📶) This may well be the most eccentric and charming hotel in Turkey. A 550-year-old stone house filled with authentic Ottoman furnishings and objets d'art, it offers five rooms with beds made with antique cotton and silk linen. The 2-hectare garden filled with lemon trees and bougainvillea is an enchanting spot in which to while away summer evenings over cocktails and dinner.

El Vino Hotel BOUTIQUE HOTEL $$

(☎0252-313 8770; www.elvinobodrum.com; Pamili Sokak; r/ste from €145/185; ❄📶🏊) This beautiful 'urban resort' with 31 rooms is contained in several stone buildings spread over an enormous garden in the backstreets of Bodrum that you'd never know was there. Try for a room with views of both the pool/garden and the sea (eg room 303). The rooftop restaurant is one of the best hotel ones in Bodrum. Great off-season rates.

Eating

Nazik Ana TURKISH $

(☎0252-313 1891; www.nazikanarestaurant.com; Eski Hükümet Sokak 5; mezes ₺9-12, portion ₺10-22.50, pides ₺15-25; ⏰8am-11pm; ❄) This simple, back-alley place with folksy, rustic decor offers hot and cold prepared dishes, viewable *lokanta*-style at the front counter, allowing you to sample different Turkish traditional dishes at shared tables. You can also order pides (Turkish-style pizzas) and *köfte* (meatballs). It gets busy with workers at lunchtime, offering one of Bodrum's most authentic and friendly eating experiences.

Gemibaşı SEAFOOD $$

(☎0252-316 1220; www.gemibasi.com/restaurant; Neyzen Tevfik Caddesi 132; mezes ₺13-25, mains ₺35-45; ⏰7pm-midnight) The 'Ship's Captain' is often described as the quintessential Bodrum eatery, popular with locals and with people who have holidayed here for decades. Located opposite the marina, it's an old-fashioned *meyhane* (tavern) serving fresh mezes and fish to a rakı-addled clientele. Book ahead to score a table on the streetside terrace.

Ox BURGERS $$$

(☎0532 356 7652; Cumhuriyet Caddesi 155; burgers ₺39-79; ⏰noon-midnight) Craving a break from kebaps and grilled fish? This upmarket and highly fashionable burger bar overlooking Bodrum's castle and beach may be exactly what you're looking for. Grab a streetside table and order one of its speciality burgers – toppings include everything from cheddar cheese to foie gras and truffle. There's a good range of beer and wine to choose from.

Drinking & Nightlife

★Dada Salon COCKTAIL BAR

(☎0252-316 0038; www.dadasalon.com.tr; Dr Alim Bey Sokak 44; ⏰9pm-5am) Occupying an old sponge warehouse, this bohemian speakeasy is owned by Okan Bayulgen, a well-known TV, film and theatre actor. An intimate venue for cabaret, theatre and live-music acts, it occupies three floors and has two bars, one on the ground floor and another on the roof terrace. Gay friendly.

Club Catamaran CLUB

(☎0542 451 5425, 0542 451 5424; www.clubcatamaran.com; Dr Alim Bey Caddesi 10; entrance ₺50-60 incl one drink; ⏰11.30pm-5am Jun-Sep) Europe's biggest floating disco, this party boat sails at 1am, keeping the licentiousness offshore for a good three hours. Its transparent dance floor can pack in 2000 clubbers plus attendant DJs. A free shuttle operates every 10 minutes to the eastern bay.

BUSES FROM BODRUM OTOGAR

DESTINATION	FARE (₺)	DURATION (HR)	FREQUENCY (PER DAY)
Ankara	100	12	1
Antalya	65	8	1
Denizli	35	5	3
İstanbul	120	12	6
İzmir	35	3½	hourly
Konya	80	12	3 daily
Kuşadası	30	3	1 evening
Muğla	17	2	hourly
Söke	20	2½	hourly

Information

ATMs line Cevat Şakir Caddesi and waterfront streets on both bays.

Tourist Office (0252-316 1091; Kale Meydanı 48; 8am-noon & 1-5pm Mon-Fri)

Getting There & Away

AIR

Milas-Bodrum Airport (BJV; 444 9828; www.milas-bodrumairport.com), 39km northeast from Bodrum, has flights to İstanbul and Ankara.

Havaş (www.havas.net/en) and **Muttaş** (0542 683 4800; www.muttas.com.tr) shuttle between the airport and the otogar (bus station; ₺15, 40 minutes) in Bodrum Town almost every 30 minutes.

BOAT

Bodrum's **ferry terminal** is a good departure point to the Greek Islands, with daily sailings to Kos between May and September, and a couple of services weekly to Rhodes and Symi between June and September. Ferry operators include **Bodrum Express Lines** (0252-316 1087; www.bodrumexpresslines.com; Kale Caddesi 18; 8am-11pm May-Sep, to 8pm Oct-Apr) and **Bodrum Ferryboat Association** (Bodrum Feribot İşletmeciliği; 0252-316 0882; www.bodrumferryboat.com; Kale Caddesi 22; 8am-7pm May-Sep, to 6pm Oct-Apr).

BUS

Bodrum otogar is on Cevat Şakır Caddesi.

Marmaris

0252 / POP 33,761

A popular resort town that swells to over a quarter-million people during summer, Marmaris is loud, brash and in your face, all over town all of the time. That said, if it's a last night out, a *gület* (Turkish yacht) cruise along the coast or a ferry to Greece that you're after, then this tourist haven is pretty much the full Monty. It's not all beers on Bar St though. The pretty harbour with teensy old quarter is crowned with a castle.

Sights & Activities

Marmaris Bay day trips (₺35 to ₺40 including lunch, soft drinks and pickup) offer coastal views and inviting swimming stops. Boats offering these trips (usually from 10.30am to 4.30pm May to October) are practically bumping into one another on the docks. Before signing up, confirm all details (exact boat, itinerary, lunch etc). 'All-inclusive' (including beer) costs ₺50 to ₺60. Be aware that the vast majority of these trips include loud pumping music and various live 'entertainments' put on by the crew. If this isn't your cup of tea, it's best to give them a wide berth.

Marmaris Castle & Museum CASTLE
(Marmaris Kalesi ve Müzesi; 30 Sokak; ₺8; 8am-6.30pm Apr-Oct, to 5pm Nov-Mar) Marmaris' hilltop castle (1522) was Süleyman the Magnificent's rallying point for 200,000 troops, used to recapture Rhodes from the Knights Hospitaller. The castle hosts small **Marmaris Museum**, which exhibits amphorae, tombstones, figurines, oil lamps and other finds from surrounding archaeological sites, including from Knidos and Datça. Saunter along the castle's walls and ramparts and gaze down on the bustling marina.

Sleeping

Maltepe Pansiyon PENSION $
(0252-412 1629; www.maltepepansiyon.com; 66 Sokak 9; s/d/tr/q ₺50/100/150/200;) The shady garden where guests can drink *elma çay* (apple tea) under a grape arbour is just

one of the attractions of this 22-room pension, a backpacker favourite for decades. Rooms are small but spotless, and the friendly manager Mehmet (Memo) goes out of his way to help. A self-catering kitchen is available, as are cheaper rooms with shared bathroom.

Marina Apart Otel APARTMENT, HOTEL $$
(☎0252-412 2030; www.marinaapartotel.com; Mustafa Kemal Paşa Sokak 24; d/q €35/40; ❄@📶🏊) The 10 hotel rooms and 40 self-catering apartments for up to four people are bare but quite good value, each with the full complement of cooking implements, cutlery, sofa and balcony. There's a cafe-bar in reception and a neighbouring bakery for provisions. Rates include breakfast, and hotel services such as Dalaman Airport transfers (€50) are available.

Otel Dost HOTEL $$
(☎0252-412 1343; www.oteldost.com; General Mustafa Muğlalı Caddesi 74; s/d/tr/apt €30/45/60/100; ❄📶🏊) Turkish-British couple İbrahim and Natalie offer 18 well-equipped modern rooms and a vine-covered terrace for breakfast. Across the road is a pool and snack bar, and the self-catering penthouse apartment has two bedrooms with views of the surrounding hills. Help with tours, transfers, rental cars and ferry tickets. Suite 206 is the choicest.

Eating

Köfteci Ramiz KÖFTE $
(☎0532 441 3651; www.kofteciramiz.com; General Mustafa Muğlalı Caddesi 5/A; mains ₺14.90-29.90; ⌚9am-midnight) At lunchtime, local suits queue for this long-established *köfte* chain's salad bar (₺7.50), not to mention the award-winning *köfte*, kebaps and other grills. Meal deals abound. Founded by two brothers from Macedonia, it's been here since 1928.

★**Ney** TURKISH $$
(☎0252-412 0217; 26 Sokak 24; mezes ₺11, mains ₺20-30; ⌚noon-midnight) Tucked away up some steps from the western end of the marina is this tiny but delightful restaurant in a 250-year-old Greek stone house with Bugül at the stove. Decorated with seashells and wind chimes, it offers delicious home cooking such as *tavuklu mantı* (Turkish ravioli with chicken), *et güveç* (meat casserole) and wonderful mezes.

Fellini ITALIAN $$
(☎0252-413 0826; Barbaros Caddesi 71; mains ₺25-45; ⌚8am-1am) With cheery yellow chairs and faux flower arrangements, this popular waterfront restaurant now in its 25th year serves great thin-crust pizzas, pasta, seafood, steaks and kebaps.

Drinking

Marmaris by night offers more neon than Vegas, and almost as many drunks certain they're just one shot away from the big score. Away from the infamous debauchery of Bar St, there are quieter spots for drinks and harbour views, including the more tranquil waterfront bar-restaurants lining Barbaros Caddesi and the marina.

Information

Tourist Office (☎0252-412 1035; İskele Meydanı 2; ⌚8am-noon & 1-5pm Mon-Fri mid-Sep–May, daily Jun–mid-Sep) The exceptionally helpful staff here dispense solid information and give out free maps.

Getting There & Away

AIR

The closest airport is Dalaman (p491), 95km southeast.

Havaş (www.havas.net/en) runs a regular shuttle bus between Dalaman Airport and Marmaris otogar (₺17.50, 1½ hours).

BOAT

From late April to October, daily catamarans serve Rhodes (one-way or same-day return/open return €39/70, one hour) from the pier 1km southeast of Marmaris, departing at 9.15am and 5pm.

Travel agencies, including **Yeşil Marmaris** (☎0533 430 7179, 0252-412 1033; www.rhodesferry.com; Barbaros Caddesi 13; ⌚9am-11.30pm) in town and **Marmaris Ferry** (☎0252-413 0230; www.marmarisferry.com; Mustafa Munir Elgin Bulvarı, Marmaris Cruise Port; ⌚8am-7pm) sell tickets.

BUS

Marmaris' small **otogar** (Mustafa Münir Elgin Bulvarı) is 3km north of the centre. There are six services daily to Antalya (₺60, 6¼ hours); and İstanbul (₺120, 13 hours); and hourly buses to İzmir (₺45, 4¼ hours). For Bodrum, catch a dolmuş (minibus) to Muğla (₺15, one hour) and then the bus to Bodrum (₺20, two hours). There are hourly Marmaris Koop buses via Dalaman to Fethiye (₺24, 3¼ hours).

Getting Around

Frequent dolmuşes (₺2.50) run between the otogar and the centre of town and the bay.

MEDITERRANEAN COAST

Also known as the 'Turquoise Coast', Turkey's Mediterranean region is blessed with sand-lined coves, backed by craggy mountain slopes, and home to more ancient ruins than you can shake a stick at. Whether you're here to explore the atmospheric Lycian ruins that litter the hillsides, get some sandcastle action in Patara or head out on a sailing trip, you really can't go wrong.

Fethiye

☎0252 / POP 91,244

Fethiye's natural harbour is perhaps the region's finest, tucked into the southern reaches of a broad bay scattered with pretty islands. This prosperous western Mediterranean hub is a major launching pad for *gület* (Turkish yacht) cruises. It also makes a good base for visiting Ölüdeniz, one of Turkey's seaside hot-spots, and many interesting sites in the surrounding countryside, including the ghost town of Kayaköy (also called Karmylassos or Levissi) just over the hill.

Sights

In Town

Fethiye Museum MUSEUM

(☎0252-614 1150; www.lycianturkey.com/fethiye-museum.htm; 505 Sokak; ₺5; ⊙9am-7pm mid-Apr–mid-Oct, 8am-5pm mid-Oct–mid-Apr) Focusing on Lycian finds from Telmessos as well as the ancient settlements of Tlos and Kaunos, this small museum exhibits pottery, jewellery, small statuary and votive stones (including the important Grave Stelae and the Stelae of Promise). Its most prized significant possession, however, is the so-called **Trilingual Stele** from Letoön, dating from 338 BC, which was used partly to decipher the Lycian language with the help of ancient Greek and Aramaic.

Tomb of Amyntas TOMB

(117 Sokak; ₺5; ⊙9am-7pm) Fethiye's most recognisable sight is the mammoth Tomb of Amyntas, an Ionic temple facade carved into a sheer rock face in 350 BC, in honour of 'Amyntas son of Hermapias'. Located south of the centre, it is best visited at sunset. Other, smaller rock tombs lie about 500m to the east.

Around Fethiye

★Kayaköy (Levissi) Abandoned Village RUINS

(₺5; ⊙9am-7pm Apr-Oct, 8am-5pm Nov-Mar) The tumbledown ruins of Levissi are highly atmospheric. The roofless, dilapidated stone houses sit on the slopes like sentinels over the modern village below.

Not much is intact except the two churches. The 17th-century **Kataponagia Church**, with an ossuary containing the mouldering remains of the long-dead in its churchyard, is on the lower part of the slope, while the **Taxiarkis Church** is near the top of the hill. Both retain some of their painted decoration and black-and-white pebble mosaic floors.

Ölüdeniz Beach & Lagoon BEACH

(Ölüdeniz Caddesi; lagoon adult/child ₺7/3.50, bicycle/car parking ₺7/25; ⊙9am-7pm) The beach is why most people visit Ölüdeniz. While the decent strip of shore edging the village is free, the famed lagoon beach is a protected national park (Ölüdeniz Tabiat Parkı) that you pay to enter. Both the public beach and lagoon get heavily crowded in summer, but, with the mountains soaring above you, it's still a lovely place to while away a few hours. There are showers, toilets and cafes, and sunshades, loungers and paddle boats can be rented.

Activities & Tours

Many visitors not joining the longer blue voyages opt for the **12-Island Tour** (per person incl lunch ₺50-60; ⊙10.30am-6.30pm mid-Apr–Oct), a day-long boat trip around Fethiye Körfezi (Fethiye Bay). The boats usually stop at five or six islands and cruise by the rest, but either way it's a great way to experience the coastline. Hotels and travel agencies sell tickets or you can deal directly with the boat companies along the waterfront parade at the marina.

Tandem paragliding is big business in Ölüdeniz. The descent from 1960m Baba Dağ (Mt Baba) can take up to 40 minutes, with amazing views over the Blue Lagoon, Butterfly Valley and, on a clear day, as far as Rhodes. Operators include **Easy Riders** (☎0252-617 0148; Ölüdeniz Caddesi; ⊙9am-9pm) and **Gravity Tandem Paragliding** (☎0252-617 0379; www.flygravity.com; Denizpark Caddesi; ⊙9am-10pm), who typically charge around ₺200.

DON'T MISS

BLUE VOYAGES

For many travellers a four-day cruise on a *gület* (Turkish yacht) – known as a 'blue voyage' *(mavi yolculuk)* – is the highlight of their trip. Usually advertised as travelling between Fethiye and Olympos, the boats actually stop (or start) at Kale and the trip to/from Olympos (1¼ hours) is by bus. From Fethiye, boats call in at Ölüdeniz and Butterfly Valley and stop at Kaş, Kalkan and/or Kekova, with the final night at Gökkaya Bay. Food is usually included in the price, but you sometimes have to pay for water and soft drinks and always for alcohol. All boats are equipped with showers, toilets and smallish double cabins. In practice, most people sleep on mattresses on deck. In summer prices typically range between €200 and €300. While it makes sense to shop around, note that cheaper companies may skimp on food. Make sure the crew speak English, and don't be swayed by gimmicks such as free water sports. Most of all, steer clear of street touts selling voyages and avoid buying your ticket in İstanbul. We recommend the following owner-operated outfits for running a tight ship:

Alaturka (☎0252-612 5423; www.alaturkacruises.com; Fevzi Çakmak Caddesi 29/B; 3-night cruise per person from €220)

Before Lunch Cruises (☎0535 636 0076; www.beforelunch.com; Kordon Gezi Yolu; 3-night cruise per person €250-350)

Ocean Yachting (p459)

Ocean Yachting Travel Agency OUTDOORS
(☎0252-612 4807; www.gofethiye.com; Fevzi Çakmak Caddesi; 3-night cruise €175-220; ⏰8am-8pm) As well as blue cruises, Ocean Yachting sells a bundle of local tours and activities, including paragliding (€110), day-long rafting trips (from €45), jeep safaris to Saklıkent and Tlos (€45), Dalyan tours (€50) and the 12-island boat trip (€45). It also has a swag of seven-night cruise choices and is a good option for chartering an entire *gület*.

Sleeping & Eating

★Duygu Pension PENSION $
(☎0535 796 6701, 0252-614 3563; www.duygupension.com; 16 Sokak 54; s/d/tr €17/24/34; P⊖❄@令≋) Cute as a button, this warm and welcoming family-run pension near the Karagözler 2 marina has 10 homely rooms brightened by colourful wall stencils and frilly touches, while the rooftop terrace has blinding sea views. Birol is your man and a great source of information.

Minu Hotel HOTEL $$
(☎0252-612 2050; www.minuhotel.com; 40 Sokak 4; s/d €30/45; ❄令) All white-on-white minimalism in the rooms and friendly, highly efficient service, the Minu is a fantastic central Fethiye find. Breakfast is a feast and the beds are among the comfiest in town.

Be aware though, it's slap-bang amid the main eating and nightlife area (the music dies down at midnight) so early-to-bedders may want to give it a miss.

★Fish Market SEAFOOD $$
(Balık Pazarı, Balık Halı; Hal ve Pazar Yeri, btwn Hukumet & Belediye Caddesis; ⏰11am-10pm) This circle of fishmongers ringed by restaurants is Fethiye's most atmospheric eating experience: buy fresh fish (per kilo ₺10 to ₺35) and calamari (₺45), take it to a restaurant to have them cook it, and watch the fishmongers competing for attention with the waiter-touts, flower sellers and roaming *fasıl* (gypsy music) buskers.

Meğri Lokantasi TURKISH $$
(☎0252-614 4047; www.megrirestaurant.com; Çarşı Caddesi 26; dishes ₺12-60; ⏰11am-10pm; 🌶) Looking for us at lunchtime in Fethiye? We're usually here. You can pick a meaty grill off the (more expensive) menu, but do as the locals do: head inside and mix and match a plate (large mixed plate, ₺20) from their glass counter display of hearty, home-style vegetable and meat dishes. It's pretty much all delicious.

Getting There & Away

BOAT

Ferries sail to Rhodes in Greece (one-way/same-day return/open return €50/60/75, 1½ hours) from Fethiye pier, opposite the tourist office. They operate daily June through to September with fewer services during the rest

DON'T MISS

WALKING THE LYCIAN WAY

Acclaimed as one of the world's top-10 long-distance walks, the **Lycian Way** follows signposted paths around the Teke Peninsula to Antalya. The 500km route leads through pine and cedar forests beneath mountains rising almost 3000m, past villages, stunning coastal views and an embarrassment of ruins at Lycian cities. For those who don't have plenty of time to trek the entire trail, it can easily be walked in individual sections.

Get information on hiking all, or some of the sections, of the trail at www.cultureroutesinturkey.com.

of the year. Tickets are available near the pier from **Ocean Yachting Travel Agency** (p459) and **Yeşil Dalyan** (☎0252-612 8686; www.yesildalyantravel.com; Fevzi Çakmak Caddesi; ⏱8am-7pm).

BUS

Fethiye's **otogar** (Fethiye Bus Station; İnönü Bulvarı) is 2.5km east of the town centre.

Buses taking the coastal route to Antalya (₺45, six hours) leave around every hour in high season. Buses taking the quicker inland road direct to Antalya (₺30, 3½ hours) leave at 7.30am, 9.30am, 11.30am, 1.30pm, 3.30pm and 6.30pm. Heading north to Marmaris (₺24, two hours) dolmuşes (minibuses) leave every hour between 7.45am and 10.45pm.

Getting Around

Dolmuşes heading for destinations in the local region stop at a **dolmuş stand** (Akdeniz Caddesi) in the town centre, near the new mosque. Destinations include Kayaköy (₺5.50), Ölüdeniz (₺5.50), Faralya and Kabak (₺6.50) and Saklıkent (₺11).

Patara

☎0242 / POP 950

Patara claims Turkey's longest uninterrupted beach as well as a swag of atmospheric Lycian ruins. Just inland, 1.5km from the beach and ruins, is the laid-back village of **Gelemiş**. This is the perfect spot to mix ruin rambling with some dedicated sun worship. Once a stop on the hippie trail (visitors now mostly arrive on the Lycian Way; p460), Gelemiş remains refreshingly unspoiled and traditional village life goes on.

Sights

Ancient Patara ARCHAEOLOGICAL SITE

(₺15 incl Patara Beach; ⏱9am-7pm mid-Apr–Oct, 8am-5pm Nov–mid-Apr) Patara's grand monuments lie scattered along the road to the beach. The main section of ruins is dominated by the dilapidated 5000-seat **theatre**. Next door is the **bouleuterion**, ancient Patara's 'parliament', where it is believed members of the Lycian League met. It has been thoroughly restored, following a two-year, ₺8.5-million reconstruction. The **colonnaded street**, with re-erected columns, runs north from here. This would have been Patara's grandest boulevard, lined by shops and with the agora at its southern end.

Patara Beach BEACH

(₺15 incl Patara ruins) Backed by large sand dunes, this splendid, 18km-long sandy beach is one of Turkey's best. Due to its length, you can find a quiet spot even in the height of summer. Sunshades (small ₺7.50, large ₺10) and loungers (₺7.50) can be rented and there's a cafe for when you get peckish. Depending on the season, parts of the beach are off limits as it is an important nesting ground for sea turtles. It closes at dusk and camping is prohibited.

Sleeping

★ **Akay Pension** PENSION $$

(☎0532 410 2195, 0242-843 5055; www.pataraakaypension.com; Gelemiş; s/d/tr/apt €25/36/45/65; P ⊖ ❄ 📶 ≋) Run by keen-to-please Kazım and his wife Ayşe, the Akay has a comfy Ottoman-style lounge to hang out in and meet other travellers, and 11 well-maintained, sweetly decorated rooms with new bathrooms, and balconies overlooking citrus groves. There's a pair of two-bedroom apartments for families, too. Ayşe's cooking is legendary; sample at least one set meal (from ₺26) while here.

Flower Pension PENSION $$

(☎0242-843 5164, 0530 511 0206; www.patarafl owerpension.com; Gelemiş; s/d/tr/apt €24/33/40/75; P ⊖ ❄ @ 📶 ≋) Run by knowledgeable manager Bekir, the Flower has 15 bright and airy rooms with balconies overlooking the garden, including two self-catering studios and two apartments with well-equipped kitchens and two bedrooms. Bekir's mum Ayşe presides over the kitchen, producing Turkish food at its best (dinner ₺25 to ₺30), with biweekly barbecues in summer.

Getting There & Away

Gelemiş has roughly hourly dolmuşes (minibuses) in summer to Kalkan (₺7, 20 minutes) and Kaş (₺9, 45 minutes).

Kalkan

0242 / POP 3396

Kalkan is a well-to-do harbourside town built largely on hills that look down on an almost-perfect bay. It's as justly popular for its excellent restaurants and its compact old town. Just be aware that Kalkan is pricier and more dominated by British holiday-home residents and tourists than most other coastal spots. Gorgeous **Kaputaş Beach**, which often makes the covers of travel guides and magazines, is 7km from town towards Kaş.

Sleeping

Caretta Hotel HOTEL $$

(0505 269 0753, 0242-844 3435; www.carettahotelkalkan.com; İskele Sokak 6; s/d €30/45;) This boutique-hotel-cum-pension is a perennial favourite for its swimming platforms, homestyle cooking, warm welcome and away-from-it-all appeal. The 14 bright, sunny rooms have excellent terraces and modern Ottoman decorative touches. A private beach, boat trips and sea taxi from Kalkan harbour are offered.

Gül Pansiyon PENSION $$

(0242-844 3099; www.kalkangulpansiyon.com; 7 Nolu Sokak 10; s/d/apt €30/35/45;) The 'Rose' has a rooftop with million-dollar views, small but tidy rooms with balconies, and three apartments with kitchenettes and washing machines. Try to bag one of the rooms on the 3rd floor for the views and the light. There are discounts outside of peak summer, when it's a popular pit stop for hikers.

White House Pension PENSION $$

(0532 443 0012, 0242-844 3738; www.kalkanwhitehouse.co.uk; 5 Nolu Sokak 19; s/d €35/55-60;) On a quiet corner at the top of the old-town hill, this attentively run pension has 10 compact, breezy rooms – four with balconies – in a spotless family home. The real winner here, though, is the view from the terrace and friendly owners Halıl and Marion.

Eating & Drinking

Cafe Del Mar CAFE $

(0242-844 1068; www.cafedelmarkalkan.com; Hasan Altan Caddesi 61a; mains ₺17-35, cakes & desserts ₺12-15; 11am-10pm;) Inviting blue saloon-style doors lead to this little cafe brimming with antiques and curios, hanging lanterns and curvy metalwork furniture. Come here for a light lunch a sneaky mid-afternoon coffee and cake pick-me-up, or early evening cocktails (₺29). Up top is a grill restaurant with sea views.

★ **Kalamaki Restaurant** MODERN TURKISH $$$

(0242-844 1555; Hasan Altan Caddesi 47a; mains ₺35.90-69.90; 11am-10pm;) A modern venue with a very stylish minimalist pub on the terrace and restaurant upstairs, serving superb Turkish dishes with a European twist. Try the scrumptious lamb with prunes and almonds or the vegetarian *şiş* kebap (roasted on a skewer). Host Tayfur takes it all in his stride – even when celebs like Gordon Ramsay come a-calling.

Botanik Garden Bar BAR

(0535 470 9099; Süleyman Yilmaz Caddesi; 4pm-late;) By far the most kicked-back venue for a beer or cocktail in Kalkan is at a table under the canopy of this garden's mature, leafy trees. Be aware though, with both hammocks and a tree house to sloth in, many find it so relaxing that one late-afternoon drink easily turns into spending the rest of the evening here.

Getting There & Away

Buses to Fethiye (₺16, 1½ hours) leave from the **otogar** (Şehitler Caddesi) every one to 1½ hours.

Kalkan is on the Kaş–Kınık local dolmuş (minibus) route with regular dolmuşes heading west to Patara (₺7, 25 minutes) and east to Kaş (₺7, 35 minutes).

Kaş

0242 / POP 7801

It may not sport the region's finest beaches but its mellow atmosphere and menu of adventure activities have made Kaş an ideal base for forays into the surrounding area. For divers this is Turkey's hub for underwater exploits, while a plethora of boat trips, kayaking tours and hikes are also easily arranged from here.

The 6km-long Çukurbağ Peninsula extends west of the pretty old quarter. At the start of it, you'll find a well-preserved ancient theatre, all that's left of ancient Antiphellos. Just offshore, dominating the harbour view, is the geopolitical oddity of the Greek island of Meis (Kastellorizo), which can be visited on a day trip.

Activities & Tours

The nearby Kekova area with its underwater ruins, lush coastal scenery and pretty villages of Üçağız and Kaleköy is ideal for hiking and other activities.

Dragoman OUTDOORS
(0242-836 3614; www.dragoman-turkey.com; Uzun Çarşı Sokak 15; 1-dive/6-dive pack €26/148, sea-kayaking tours €29-55; 9am-9pm) This dynamic outdoor activities centre has built a reputation for its diving with professional and knowledgeable dive instructors. Its outdoor activities include sea kayaking day and multiday tours exploring the coast around Kekova and further afield, excellent hiking and mountain biking trips, and stand-up paddleboarding (SUP). For something more relaxing, there's also full-day boat trips tootling around the Kekova area (€45).

Sleeping

Anı Pension PENSION $
(0242-836 1791, 0533 326 4201; www.motelani.com; Süleyman Çavuş Caddesi 12; dm/s/d €10/18/24;) With a seven-bed dorm and kitchen for guest use, the Anı leads the way for budget digs in Kaş, having recently been renovated by hosts Ömer and brother Ahmet. The decent-sized rooms all have balconies and the roof terrace is a hub where you can kick back, cool off with a beer and swap travel stories with fellow guests.

★ **Hideaway Hotel** HOTEL $$
(0242-836 1887; www.hotelhideaway.com; Anfitiyatro Sokak 7; s/d/ste €49/55-75/89;) Run by the unstoppable Ahmet, a fount of local information, this lovely hotel has large, airy rooms (some with sea views) with a fresh white-on-white minimalist feel and gleaming modern bathrooms. There's a pool for cooling off and a chilled-out roof terrace that's the venue for morning yoga and sundowners at the bar with Meis views.

Olea Nova Boutique Hotel BOUTIQUE HOTEL $$$
(0242-836 2660; www.oleanova.com.tr; Demokrasi Caddesi 43; r/f/ste from €120/220/310;) Set amid olive groves and villas, 6km from Kaş's centre, with panoramic views across the water to the Greek island of Meis, this swish boutique hotel is just the ticket for those seeking a peaceful break. The 20 rooms and suites are all pristine white minimalism, while the kidney-shaped pool, adjoining bar-restaurant and private beach are slothing central.

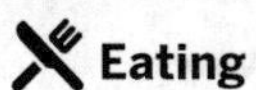

Eating

Havana Balık Evi SEAFOOD $
(0242-836 4111; Öztürk Sokak 7; mains ₺12-27; 9am-midnight;) Head to the 'Atmospheric Fish House' for cheap and cheerful *balık ekmek* (₺12), the simple fish sandwich that is a staple in coastal Turkey. Keeping up with the fishy theme, there are also hearty bowls of *balık guveç* (fish casserole) and *hamsı tava* (pan-fried Turkish anchovies).

Bi Lokma ANATOLIAN $$
(0242-836 3942; www.bilokma.com.tr; Hükümet Caddesi 2; mains ₺22-40; 9am-midnight;) Also known as 'Mama's Kitchen', this place has green tables in a terraced garden high above the harbour. The 'mama' in question is Sabo, whose daughters have taken the culinary baton, turning out traditional Turkish soul food, including excellent meze, and their famous house *mantı* (Turkish ravioli) and *börek* (filled pastry).

★ **Retro Bistro** INTERNATIONAL $$$
(0242-836 4282; İbrahim Serin Caddesi; mains ₺25-69; 11am-10pm;) Retro devotes considerable energy and creativity to its homemade pasta, pizza bases, bread and *sous vide* (water bath) cooking, serving inventive creations such as 48-hour braised *osso buco* (veal shanks) with teriyaki gravy, great burgers, a delicately spiced curry and a Black Sea pizza, with a squid-ink-infused black Napolitana base.

Getting There & Away

BOAT

The **Meis Express ferry** (0242-836 1725; www.meisexpress.com; adult €25, child under 12yr €20, under 7yr free) sails throughout the year at 10am and returns at 4pm (3pm in winter). The voyage takes 20 minutes. Take your passport to the **ticket office** (0242-836 1725; www.meisexpress.com; Cumhuriyet Meydanı; 8.30am-7pm) the day before to book.

BUS

From Kaş otogar, Batı Antalya dolmuşes (minibuses) head every 30 minutes to Antalya (₺30, 3½ hours). The same company has departures to Fethiye (₺20, 2½ hours) every one to 1½ hours between 7am and 6.15pm.

In summer, local Öz Kaş dolmuşes to Kalkan (₺7, 35 minutes) leave every 20 to 45 minutes from the otogar between 8am and 9.30pm; this same service continues on to Patara (₺9, 45 minutes).

Olympos & Çıralı

0242

About 65km northeast of Demre, past Finike and Kumluca, a road leads southeast from the main highway (veer to the right then follow the signs for 11km) to ancient Olympos with its tumble of beachside **ruins** (0242-238 5688; Olympos; incl Olympos Beach ₺20, parking ₺4; 9am-7pm Apr-Oct, 8am-5pm Nov-Mar) and backpacker camp community. On the other side of the mountain, and over the narrow Ulupınar Stream, is Çıralı, a holiday hamlet that's home to that most enigmatic of classical icons: the eternal flame of the **Chimaera** (₺6; 24hr).

Sleeping

Olympos

★Şaban Pension BUNGALOW $

(0242-892 1265; www.sabanpansion.com; Yazırköyü, Olympos; incl half-board dm €9, bungalows s/d/tr €24/33/43, tree houses without bathroom s/d €19/24;) Our personal favourite, this is the place to lounge in a hammock in the orchard or on a wooden platform by the stream enjoying sociable owner Meral's home cooking. Şaban isn't a party spot; it's a tranquil getaway where relaxed conversations strike up around the bonfire at night. Accommodation is in charming cabins and tree houses.

Kadır's Tree Houses BUNGALOW $

(0532 347 7242, 0242-892 1250; www.kadirstreehouses.com; Yazırköyü; incl half-board dm €10-12, s/d/tr with air-con €27/35/53;) The place that put Olympos on the map looks like a Wild West boom town that just kept a-growin' and not the Japanese POW camp that some others resemble. Accommodation includes four-bed dorms with private bathroom, five-bed tree house dorms without, and private bungalows. Its bars are the valley's liveliest and the **Olympos Adventure Center** (0532 686 1799; www.olymposadventurecenter.com; climbing trips 3hr/full-day from €40/70) is here.

Çıralı

★Orange Motel PENSION $$

(0242-825 7328; www.orangemotel.net; Yanartaş Yolu, Çıralı; s/d/tr €50/60/75, bungalows €70-90;) In the middle of an orange grove, the Orange feels like a farm despite its central location. Come here in spring and you'll never forget the overwhelming scent and buzz of bees. The garden is hung with hammocks, rooms are veritable wooden suites and there's a house travel agency. Breakfast features homemade orange and lemon marmalades and orange-blossom honey.

Hotel Canada HOTEL $$

(0242-825 7233, 0538 647 9522; www.canadahotel.net; s/d from €30/40, 4-person bungalows from €75;) This is a beautiful place, offering the quintessential Çıralı experience: warmth, friendliness and homemade honey. The main house rooms are comfortable and the garden is filled with hammocks, citrus trees and 11 bungalows. Canadian Carrie and foodie husband Şaban also offer excellent set meals. It's 750m from the beach; grab a free bike and pedal on down.

Information

Çıralı has an ATM; Olympos does not.

Getting There & Away

Buses taking the coastal road between Fethiye and Antalya drop off and pick up at the Olympos and Çıralı junctions. Just make sure you specify which one you want as they are 500m apart. From there, dolmuşes (minibuses) leave for both destinations, though transport to Çıralı is considerably less regular than to Olympos.

If you book in advance, many hotels will pick you up from the highway.

Antalya

0242 / POP 1,068,099

Once seen simply as the gateway to the Turkish Riviera, Antalya today is very much a destination in its own right. At its core is the preserved old-city district of Kaleiçi (literally 'within the castle'), which offers atmospheric accommodation in the finely restored Ottoman houses on its winding lanes. The old city wraps around a Roman-era harbour with clifftop views of hazy-blue mountain silhouettes that are worth raising a toast to. Just outside of the central city are two beaches and one of Turkey's finest museums.

Sights

★Kaleiçi HISTORIC SITE

Antalya's historic district is a sight in itself and you could happily spend an hour or so strolling the narrow lanes here while admiring the mix of finely restored and creakily dilapidated Ottoman-era architecture.

Antalya

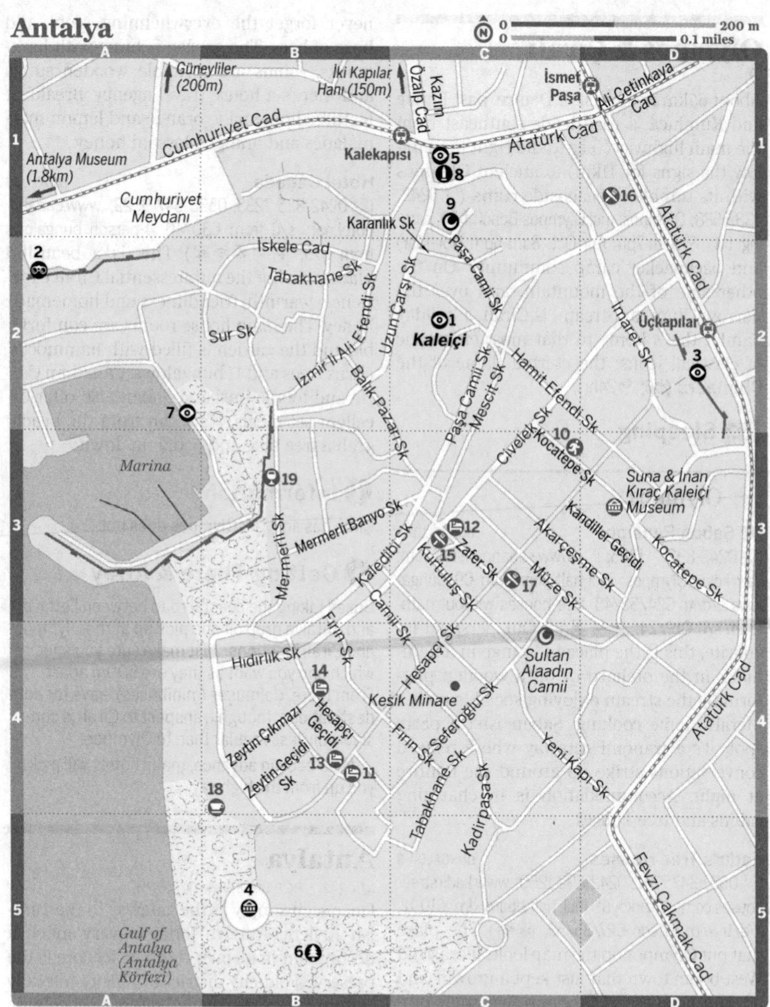

The district begins at the main square, **Kale Kapısı** (Fortress Gate), which is marked by the old stone **Saat Kulesi** (Clock Tower) and statue of Attalus II, the city's founder. To the north is the **İki Kapılar Hanı** (Old Bazaar; ⏲10.30am-10pm), a sprawling covered bazaar dating to the late 15th century. Walk south along Uzun Çarşi Sokak, the street that starts opposite the clock tower. Immediately on the left is the 18th-century **Tekeli Mehmet Paşa Camii** (Paşa Camii Sokak), a mosque built by the Beylerbey (Governor of Governors), Tekeli Mehmet Paşa, and repaired extensively in 1886 and 1926. Note the beautiful Arabic calligraphy in the coloured tiles above the windows and along the base of the dome.

Wander further into this protected zone, where many of the gracious old **Ottoman houses** have been restored and converted into pensions, boutique hotels and shops. To the east, at the top of Hesapçi Sokak, is the monumental **Hadrian's Gate** (Hadriyanüs Kapısı; Atatürk Caddesi), also known as Üçkapılar or the 'Three Gates', erected for the Roman emperor's visit to Antalya in AD 130.

The **Roman Harbour** (İskele Caddesi) at the base of the slope was Antalya's lifeline from the 2nd century BC until late in the 20th cen-

Antalya

Top Sights
1 Kaleiçi C2

Sights
2 Elevator A2
3 Hadrian's Gate D2
4 Hıdırlık Kalesi B5
5 Kale Kapısı C1
6 Karaalioğlu Parkı B5
7 Roman Harbour A2
8 Saat Kulesi C1
9 Tekeli Mehmet Paşa Camii C1

Activities, Courses & Tours
10 Sefa Hamamı C3

Sleeping
11 Lazer Pension B4
12 Mediterra Art Hotel C3
13 Sabah Pansiyon B4
14 White Garden Pansion B4

Eating
15 ÇaY-Tea's C3
16 Dönerciler Çarşısı D1
17 Vanilla C3
Yemenli .... (see 13)

Drinking & Nightlife
18 Castle Café B4
19 Kale Bar B3

tury, when a new port was constructed about 12km to the west, at the far end of Konyaaltı Plajı. The harbour was restored during the 1980s and is now a marina for yachts and excursion boats. An **elevator** (Asansör) descends the cliff to the harbour from the western end of Cumhuriyet Meydanı.

At the southwestern edge of Kaleiçi, on the corner of **Karaalioğlu Parkı** (Atatürk Caddesi), a large, attractive, flower-filled park with panoramic sea views, rises **Hıdırlık Kalesi**, a 14m-high tower dating to the 1st or 2nd century AD. It was built as a mausoleum and later, due to its excellent position above the bay, played an important role in the city's defences as a watchtower and lighthouse.

★Antalya Museum MUSEUM
(0242-238 5688; www.antalyamuzesi.gov.tr/en; Konyaaltı Caddesi; ₺20; 8am-7pm Apr-Oct, to 5pm Nov-Mar) Do not miss this comprehensive museum with exhibitions covering everything from the Stone and Bronze Ages to Byzantium. The Hall of Regional Excavations exhibits finds from ancient cities in Lycia (such as Patara and Xanthos) and Phrygia, while the Hall of Gods displays beautiful and evocative statues of 15 Olympian gods, many in excellent condition. Most of the statues were found at Perge, including the sublime *Three Graces* and the towering *Dancing Woman* dominating the first room.

Activities

Excursion boats tie up in Kaleiçi's Roman Harbour. One-, two- and six-hour trips are offered (€10/15/30 at the top end; your accommodation can likely get you a better deal).

Sefa Hamamı HAMAM
(0532 526 9407, 0242-241 2321; www.sefahamam.com; Kocatepe Sokak 32; soak & steam ₺65, soak, soap, scrub & steam ₺100; 11am-8pm Mon-Sat) This atmospheric hamam retains much of its 13th-century Seljuk architecture. Men and women bathe separately, though mixed bathing is also available.

Sleeping

Lazer Pension PENSION $
(0242-242 7194; www.lazerpansiyon.com; Hesapçı Sokak 61; s/d/tr €15/23/32;) Recommended by Antalya regulars, this excellent no-frills option has spacious rooms with modern bathrooms, an upstairs terrace and a courtyard decorated with pot plants. Much care has been taken to ensure the rooms are shipshape, giving this old-town pension the edge on its competitors.

Sabah Pansiyon PENSION $
(0242-247 5345, 0555 365 8376; www.sabahpansiyon.com; Hesapçı Sokak 60; s/d/tr €15/20/30, 2-bedroom self-catering apt €75-100;) The Sabah has long been the first port of call for travellers watching their kuruş, thanks to the Sabah brothers who run the show and organise transport and tours aplenty. Rooms vary in size but all are sweet, simple and superclean. The courtyard is prime territory for meeting other travellers and their onsite restaurant Yemenli (p466) turns out decent Turkish classics.

★White Garden Pansion PENSION $$
(0242-241 9115; www.whitegardenpansion.com; Hesapçı Geçidi 9; s/d €30/40, self-catering apt €95-140;) A positively delightful place to stay, combining quirky Ottoman character, modern rooms with an old-world

veneer, and excellent service from Metin and team. The building itself is a fine restoration and the courtyard is particularly charming with its large pool. The breakfast also gets top marks.

Mediterra Art Hotel BOUTIQUE HOTEL $$
(0242-244 8624; www.mediterraarthotel.com; Zafer Sokak 5; r from €35;) This upscale masterpiece of wood and stone once housed a Greek tavern, with 19th-century frescoes and graffiti to prove it. It offers sanctuary by the courtyard pool, summer and winter restaurants and 33 small, though modestly luxurious, rooms in four buildings. Lovely touches include headboards carved with stars, and wall paintings of Ottoman characters on the landing.

Eating

ÇaY-Tea's CAFE $
(0542 732 7000; http://cay-teas.com; Hıdırlık Sokak 3; mains ₺20; 9am-midnight Apr–Oct, shorter hours Nov-Mar;) Çay and coffee is served with ribbon-wrapped shortbread and a posy of fake flowers at this eclectic Dutch-Turkish cafe, where vintage furniture spills into the street and a wine cellar houses an inviting country-kitchen-style space. The menu is great light-lunch territory with sandwiches, omelettes, crepes, vegan specialities and homemade cakes, including a lavender cheesecake.

Dönerciler Çarşısı KEBAP $
(Market of Döner Makers; Inönü Caddesi; mains ₺12-30; 11am-11pm) Its street sign says 'Inönü Caddesi' and the canopy of umbrellas has given it the nickname 'Şemsiye Sokak' (Umbrella St). Locals, however, refer to this pedestrianised lane and the gloomy arcade to the east as the Dönerciler Çarşısı. The entire street is devoted to kebap shops churning out grilled-meat dishes.

Yemenli TURKISH $
(0242-247 5345; Hesapçı Sokak 60; mains ₺16.50-38; noon-11pm;) Tried-and-true Turkish favourites are served up by the team behind Sabah Pansiyon, with tables spilling out onto the street. Service is friendly and on the ball, and a large Efes beer is only ₺10.

★ **Vanilla** INTERNATIONAL $$$
(0242-247 6013; www.vanillaantalya.com; Hesapçı Sokak 33; mains ₺32-77; 11.30am-midnight;) This outstanding, ultramodern restaurant, led by British chef Wayne, has a streamlined, unfussy atmosphere with its banquettes, glass surfaces and pleasant outside area dotted with cane-backed chairs. The menu is a beacon for vegetarians and anyone needing a kebap-break, with Mediterranean-inspired dishes such as panko-crusted goat's-cheese salad and avocado risotto sitting alongside a Thai-style curry, pizzas and steak.

WORTH A TRIP

ASPENDOS & PERGE

Antalya is an excellent base for excursions to the ancient sites of Perge and Aspendos. Since Antalya's 2017 AntRay line extension, a trip to Perge is now as simple as hopping on the tram. Both sites can also easily be visited from the town of Side.

Aspendos (Aspendos Yolu, Belkıs; ₺25, parking ₺5; 9am-7pm mid-Apr–mid-Oct, 8am-5pm mid-Oct–mid-Apr) People come in droves to this ancient site near the modern-day village of Belkıs for one reason: to view the awesome **theatre**, considered the best-preserved Roman theatre of the ancient world. It was built during Aspendos' golden age in the reign of Emperor Marcus Aurelius (AD 161–80), and was used as a caravanserai by the Seljuks during the 13th century. The history of the city, though, goes all the way back to the Hittite Empire (800 BC).

Perge (Atatürk Caddesi, Aksu; ₺25; 9am-7pm mid-Apr–mid-Oct, 8am-5pm mid-Oct–mid-Apr; Aksu) Some 17km east of Antalya and 2km north of Aksu on highway D400, Perge was one of the most important towns of ancient Pamphylia. Inside the site, walk through the massive **Roman Gate** with its four arches. To the left is the southern **nymphaeum** and well-preserved **baths**, and to the right, the large square-shaped **agora**. Beyond the **Hellenistic Gate**, with its two huge towers, is the fine **colonnaded street**, where an impressive collection of columns still stands.

BUSES FROM ANTALYA OTOGAR

DESTINATION	FARE (₺)	DURATION (HR)	FREQUENCY (DAILY)
Alanya	25	3	every 20min
Ankara	75	8	frequent
Çanakkale	110	12	2 morning, 2 afternoon & 2 evening
Denizli (Pamukkale)	40	4	hourly
Fethiye (coastal)	45	6	hourly
Fethiye (inland)	30	3½	several
Göreme/Ürgüp	60-70	9	2 morning & 3 evening
İstanbul	100	11½	6 morning & hourly in evening
İzmir	70	8	hourly
Kaş	30	3½	every 30min
Konya	50	5	4 morning, 5 afternoon & 6 evening
Olympos/Çıralı	14	1½	every 30min
Side/Manavgat	14	1½	every 20min in season

Drinking & Nightlife

★Castle Café CAFE, BAR

(☎0242-248 6594; Hıdırlık Sokak 48/1; ⏲8am-11pm) This lively hang-out along the cliff edge is a local favourite, attracting a crowd of young Turks with its affordable drinks (300mL beer ₺11). Service can be slow, but the terrace's jaw-dropping views of the beaches and mountains west of town more than compensate, as does the well-priced menu (mains ₺14 to ₺24) featuring fish and chips and burgers.

Kale Bar BAR

(☎0242-248 6591; Mermerli Sokak 2; ⏲11am-midnight) This patio bar attached to the CH Hotels Türkevi may well command the most spectacular harbour and sea view in all of Antalya. Cocktails are accordingly priced north of ₺20.

Getting There & Away

AIR

Antalya's **international airport** (Antalya Havalımanı; ☎0242-444 7423; www.aytport.com; Serik Caddesi) is 10km east of the city centre. There are direct connections to several Turkish cities, including direct flights to Cappadocia.

BUS

Antalya's **otogar** (Antalya Bus Station; Adnan Selekler Caddesi) is 4km north of the city centre.

Getting Around

To ride any public transport, you must buy an **Antalyakart** (rechargeable transport card; ₺5). Purchase from kiosks near tram stops.

TO/FROM THE AIRPORT

On the AntRay tram, it's 12 stops from the airport (Havalimanı) stop to İsmet Paşa stop, the closest stop to Kaleiçi. A taxi will cost ₺40 to ₺50.

TRAM

Antalya's AntRay tram line runs from the northern areas of the city via the otogar (bus station) into the centre and then heads east via the airport and Aksu (for Perge).

Antalya's original 6km-long single-track *antik* or *nostalji tramvay* (tram) stops at Kale Kapısı at 12 and 42 minutes past the hour, heading to Antalya Museum (Müze stop).

Side

☎0242 / POP 12,128

Down at Side harbour, the re-created colonnade of the Temple of Athena marches towards the blue sea, while at the top of Side old town, the 2nd-century theatre lords it up over the surrounding countryside. Between these two ancient relics, the lanes of this once-docile fishing village are a shameless souvenir-peddling tourist trap, but the liberal scattering of glorious Roman and Hellenistic ruins still make it a worthwhile stopover.

Sights

★Temples of Apollo & Athena RUINS

(Side Harbour) FREE This compact site is one of the most romantic on the Mediterranean coast. Apollo and Athena were Side's deities, although Apollo eventually became more important. The Temple of Athena dates from the 2nd century BC, and a half-dozen columns have been placed upright in their original spots with a frieze of Medusa heads.

Theatre RUINS

(Çağla Caddesi; ₺20; ⊙8am-7pm late Apr-late Oct, to 5pm late Oct-late Apr) Built in the 2nd century AD, Side's spectacular theatre could seat up to 20,000 spectators and rivals the nearby theatre of Aspendos for sheer drama. Look at the wall of the *skene* (stage building) for reliefs of figures and faces, including those of Comedy and Tragedy.

Sleeping & Eating

★Beach House Hotel HOTEL $$

(☎0242-753 1607; www.beachhouse-hotel.com; Barbaros Caddesi; s/d/f €23/46/56;) Once the celebrated Pamphylia Hotel, which was a magnet for celebrities in the 1960s, the Beach House's prime seafront location and welcoming Turkish-Australian owners lure a loyal band of regulars. Most rooms face the sea and all have balconies. We love the roof terrace (with teensy pool), the library full of beach-reads and the garden that's complete with Byzantine ruins.

★Ocakbaşı TURKISH $$$

(☎0242-753 1810; Zambak Sokak 46; mains ₺32-56; ⊙11am-10pm;) With excellent service and a huge menu of tasty Turkish grills, mezes, seafood, stews and vegetarian dishes, Ocakbaşı has been a popular dinner spot since 1986. The restaurant atmospherically overlooks a spotlit 2nd-century Roman bath. In summer it can get noisy and crowded, so dine early (before 7.30pm) if you don't fancy being squeezed between tables of large tour groups.

Getting There & Away

Side's otogar (Side Bus Station; Side Caddesi) is just east of the old town; an easy walk into the centre. Frequent dolmuşes (minibuses) connect Side otogar with the Manavgat otogar (₺3), 4km to the northeast, from where buses go to Antalya (₺14, 1½ hours), Alanya (₺15, 1½ hours) and Konya (₺40, 4½ hours).

Alanya

☎0242 / POP 109,656

A former seaside bastion for a succession of Mediterranean powers, Alanya has boomed in recent decades. At night, the downtown area's bar strip resembles 'Vegas by the Sea' but climbing up the hillside is an impressive fortress complex sprinkled with traditional red-tile-roofed houses. Alanya is a tale of two cities if ever we saw it.

Sights & Activities

★Alanya Castle FORTRESS

(Alanya Kalesı; Kaleyolu Caddesi) FREE Surmounting Alanya's rocky peninsula is its awesome Seljuk-era castle, wrapped in 6.5km of walls and tentatively awaiting Unesco World Heritage listing. Climb to it through the steep streets of the Tophane district to get a sense of its scale, and wonderful views across the city and Cilician mountains. Right at the top is the **İç Kale** (Inner Fortress; ₺15; ⊙8am-7pm Apr-Oct, to 5pm Nov-Mar), within which are plentiful (though poorly preserved) ruins, including a half-dozen cisterns and the shell of an 11th-century Byzantine church.

Red Tower HISTORIC BUILDING

(Kızılkule; İskele Caddesi; ₺5, combined ticket with Tersane & guard house ₺10; ⊙9am-7pm) This five-storey octagonal defence tower, measuring nearly 30m in diameter, more than 30m in height and with a central cistern within for water storage, looms over the harbour at the lower end of İskele Caddesi. Constructed in 1226 by Seljuk Sultan Alaeddin Keykubad I (who also built Alanya Castle), it was the first structure erected after the Armenian-controlled town surrendered to the sultan, and is now symbolic of the city. It's worth visiting, not least for the interesting museum within.

Excursion Boats BOATING

(per person incl lunch ₺70) Every day at around 10.30am, boats leave from near Rıhtım Caddesi for a six-hour voyage around the promontory, visiting several caves, as well as **Cleopatra's Beach** (Kleopatra Plajı). If you're after a relaxing day at sea, be aware that some boats, made up to look like pirate ships, are essentially floating parties – complete with foam-filled dance floors.

Sleeping

Temiz Otel HOTEL $$

(☎0242-513 1016; www.temizotel.com.tr; İskele Caddesi 12; s/d €19/28;) If you want to be smack in the centre of the city action, the Temiz has 32 decently sized, if bland, rooms. Those at the front have balconies, but light sleepers should ask for a room at the back as the thumping noise from the bars goes on into the wee hours.

★Centauera BOUTIQUE HOTEL $$$
(☎0242-519 0016; www.centauera.com; Andızlı Camii Sokak 4, Tophane; r €70-80; P❄📶) A 10-minute (750m) stroll from the harbour, the blissful Centauera is a world away from central Alanya, with views across the elegant sweep of bay and only birdsong to disturb your mornings. This restored Ottoman house is packed full of old-world elegance and ably run by friendly owner Koray. With just five rooms, it's an intimate choice.

Eating & Drinking

★İskele Sofrası TURKISH $$
(Tophane Caddesi 2b; mezes ₺9, mains ₺20-50; ⏲9.30am-1am; 📝) Three generations of the friendly Öz family run this restaurant, uphill from the harbour. There are never fewer than 10 mezes on at once – perhaps *girit ezmesi,* an unforgettable mash of feta, walnuts and olive oil. All the usual grills and loads of seafood headline the menu, but special lamb hotpots can be cooked, with a day's notice.

Lokanta Su MEDITERRANEAN $$$
(☎0242-512 1500; Damlataş Caddesi 16; mains ₺43-52; ⏲10am-11pm; ❄👪) One of the most prominent and clearly upmarket places on touristy Damlataş Caddesi, this is a lovely courtyard restaurant, with one of the best wine lists in town. The food's good and it has a kids menu, and even a kids cocktail list.

Tudors Pub BAR
(☎0546-532 1160; www.tudorsantalya.com; İskele Caddesi 80; ⏲2pm-3am) Live music and decent beer are the draws at this slick, multistorey venue by the harbour. There's not too much about it that's reminiscent of a certain 16th-century royal house from Wales, but it can provide a regal night of fun.

Getting There & Away

The otogar is on the coastal highway, 3km west of the centre. Buses leave hourly to Antalya (₺25, 2½ hours) and eight times daily to Adana (₺60, nine hours).

CENTRAL ANATOLIA

Ankara

☎0312 / POP 4.7 MILLION

Turkey's capital may not have showy Ottoman palaces or regal facades, but Ankara thrums to a vivacious, youthful beat unmarred by the tug of history. Drawing comparisons with İstanbul is pointless – the flat, modest surroundings are hardly the stuff of national poetry – but the beautifully conceived Museum of Anatolian Civilisations and the Anıt Kabir, a colossal tribute to Atatürk, modern Turkey's founder, provide more than enough of a reason to visit.

Sights

★Museum of Anatolian Civilisations MUSEUM
(Anadolu Medeniyetleri Müzesi; ☎0312-324 3160; www.anadolumedeniyetlerimuzesi.gov.tr; Gözcü Sokak 2; ₺20; ⏲8.30am-7pm; MUlus) The superb Museum of Anatolian Civilisations is the perfect introduction to the complex weave of Turkey's ancient past, with beautifully curated exhibits housing artefacts cherry-picked from just about every significant archaeological site in Anatolia.

The central hall houses reliefs and statuary, while the surrounding halls take you on a journey of staggering history from Palaeolithic, Neolithic, Chalcolithic, Bronze Age, Assyrian, Hittite, Phrygian, Urartian and Lydian periods. Downstairs is a collection of Roman artefacts unearthed at excavations in and around Ankara.

★Anıt Kabir MONUMENT
(Atatürk Mausoleum & Museum; www.anitkabir.org; Gençlik Caddesi; audioguide ₺10; ⏲9am-5pm; MAnadolu) FREE The monumental mausoleum of Mustafa Kemal Atatürk (1881–1938), the founder of modern Turkey, sits high above the city with its abundance of marble and air of veneration. The tomb itself actually makes up only a small part of this complex, which consists of **museums** and a **ceremonial courtyard**. For many Turks a visit is virtually a pilgrimage, and it's not unusual to see people visibly moved. Allow at least two hours in order to visit the whole site.

Citadel AREA
(Ankara Kalesi; Gözcü Sokak; MUlus) The imposing *hisar* (citadel) is the most interesting part of Ankara to poke about in. This well-preserved quarter of thick walls and intriguing winding streets took its present shape in the 9th century AD, when the Byzantine emperor Michael II constructed the outer ramparts. The inner walls date from the 7th century.

Ankara

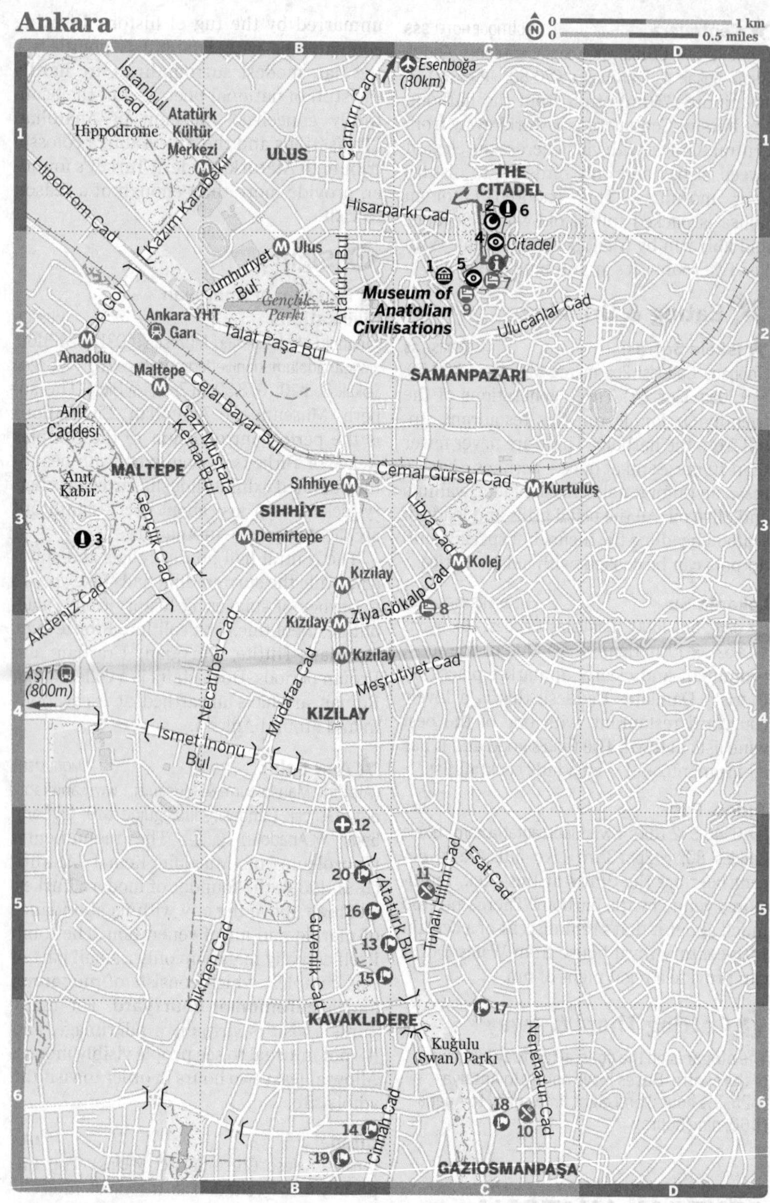

Sleeping

★ **Deeps Hostel** HOSTEL $

(☎0312-213 6338; www.deepshostelankara.com; Ataç 2 Sokak 46; dm/s/d without breakfast €12/17/25; ; MKızılay) At Ankara's best budget choice, friendly owner Şeyda has created a colourful, light-filled hostel with spacious dorms and small private rooms with squeaky-clean, modern shared bathrooms. It's all topped off by masses of advice and information, a fully equipped kitchen and a cute communal area downstairs where you can swap your Turkish travel tales.

Ankara

Top Sights
1 Museum of Anatolian Civilisations C2

Sights
2 Alaettin Camii C1
3 Anıt Kabir A3
4 Citadel C2
5 Parmak Kapısı C2
6 Şark Kulesi C1

Sleeping
7 Angora House Hotel C2
8 Deeps Hostel C3
9 Divan Çukurhan C2

Eating
10 Balıkçıköy C6
11 Mangal C5
Mezzaluna .... (see 18)

Information
12 Bayındır Hospital B5
13 Bulgarian Embassy B5
14 Canadian Embassy B6
15 French Embassy B5
16 German Embassy B5
17 Iranian Embassy C6
18 Iraqi Embassy C6
19 Russian Embassy B6
20 US Embassy B5

★ Angora House Hotel HISTORIC HOTEL $$
(☎0312-309 8380; www.angorahouse.com.tr; Kale Kapısı Sokak 16; s/d/tr €30/55/75; ; Ⓜ Ulus) Be utterly charmed by this restored Ottoman house, which oozes subtle elegance at every turn. The six spacious rooms are infused with old-world atmosphere, featuring dark wood accents and colourful Turkish carpets, while the walled courtyard garden is the perfect retreat from the citadel streets. Delightfully helpful staff and a feast of a breakfast add to the appeal.

Divan Çukurhan HISTORIC HOTEL $$$
(☎0312-306 6400; www.divan.com.tr; Depo Sokak 3, Ankara Kalesi; r from €70, ste from €130; ; Ⓜ Ulus) This fabulous upmarket hotel offers guests a chance to soak up the historic ambience of staying in the 16th-century Çukurhan caravanserai. Set around a dramatic glass-ceilinged interior courtyard, each individually themed room blends ornate decadence with sassy contemporary style. Ankara's best bet for those who want to be dazzled by oodles of sumptuous luxury and sleek service.

Eating

Mangal TURKISH $
(☎0312-466 2460; www.mangalkebap.com; Bestekar Sokak 78; mains ₺15-25; ⏲9am-10pm) For over 20 years this neighbourhood star has been churning out perfectly prepared pide and every kind of kebap or grilled meat you can think of, as well as many you can't. It's fairly smart, which makes the decent prices an unexpected surprise.

Balıkçıköy SEAFOOD $$
(☎0312-466 0450; Kırlangıç Sokak 3; mains ₺20-45; ⏲noon-midnight) Ankara's favourite seafood restaurant. Take the waiter's recommendations for the cold meze, then take your pick of the fried and grilled fish – the fried whitebait is a favourite – all perfectly cooked and quick to the table. Book ahead to avoid disappointment.

Mezzaluna ITALIAN $$$
(☎0312-467 5818; Turan Emeksiz Sokak 1; mains ₺30-64; ⏲noon-11pm;) There comes a time when you need a kabap break. Luckily, the capital's classiest Italian restaurant can help you out with that. The menu covers pasta (all homemade), seafood and steaks, but trust us, you're here for the pizza. Mezzaluna's thin-crust, wood-fired pizzas are superb. We like their house special with eggplant, mushrooms, Parmesan and proper Parma ham. Delicious.

Information

Bayındır Hospital (☎0312-428 0808; www.bayindirhastanesi.com.tr; Atatürk Bulvarı 201, Çankaya; ⏲24hr) An up-to-date private hospital.

Tourist Office (☎0312-310 3044; Kale Kapısı Sokak; ⏲10am-5pm; Ⓜ Ulus) Inside the Citadel. Gives out a free map of town.

Getting There & Away

AIR

Esenboğa Airport (p491) is 33km north of Ankara. Turkish domestic carriers have direct flights to many centres including İstanbul, İzmir and Trabzon.

Belko Air airport buses (☎444 9312; www.belkoair.com; arrivals floor, AŞTI otogar; ₺15) link the airport with the AŞTİ otogar (45 minutes) and Kızılay (one hour) every 30 minutes between 5am and midnight.

BUS

Every Turkish city or town of any size has direct buses to Ankara. The gigantic otogar (bus station), called the **AŞTİ** (Ankara Şehirlerarası

Terminali İşletmesi; Mevlâna Bulvarı), is at the western end of the Ankaray metro line, 4.5km west of Kızılay. Buses to/from İstanbul (₺65 to ₺70, six hours), Antalya (₺75, nine hours), İzmir (₺75, eight hours) and other major destinations leave numerous times daily.

TRAIN

Ankara's flash new **train station** (Ankara YHT Garı; www.tcdd.gov.tr; Celal Bayar Bulvarı), inaugurated in September 2016, has high-speed train services to Eskişehir (₺30, 1½ hours, 13 trains daily); İstanbul Pendik (a suburb 25km east of central İstanbul; ₺70, four hours, eight trains daily); and Konya (₺30, two hours, 10 trains daily).

In 2017, engineering work on the train lines used for long-distance services heading east, which normally begin and end in Ankara, meant that those services were beginning from Irmak station in Kırıkkale district (60km east of Ankara). Check for up-to-date information on these long distance services at Ankara train station's information desk.

Getting Around

Single-journey tickets for bus and metro journeys cost ₺4. An **Ankara Kart** (rechargeable transport card; ₺1), available at kiosks and metro stations, gives you discounted fares.

METRO

Ankara's underground train network is the easiest way to get between Ulus and Kızılay and the otogar. There are two lines: the Ankaray line running between AŞTİ otogar in the west through Maltepe and Kızılay to Dikimevi in the east; and the Metro line running from Kızılay northwest via Sıhhiye and Ulus to Batıkent. The two lines interconnect at Kızılay.

Safranbolu

0370 / POP 44,000

Safranbolu's old town, known as Çarşı, is a vision of red-tiled roofs and meandering alleys chock-a-block full of candy stores and cobblers. Steeped in a heady scent of yesteryear, spending the night here is all about soaking up the enchanting Ottoman scene within the muddle of timber-framed mansions now converted into quirky boutique hotels. A day at the old hamam or browsing the market shops and revelling in cobblestoned quaintness is about as strenuous as it gets.

Sights & Activities

★Çarşı ARCHITECTURE

The real joy of Safranbolu is simply wandering the cobblestone alleys. Everywhere you look in Çarşı is a feast for the eyes. Virtually every house in the neighbourhood is an original, and what little modern development there is has been held in check. Many of the finest historic houses have been restored and, as time goes on, more and more are being saved from deterioration and turned into hotels, shops or museums.

Cinci Hamam HAMAM

(0370-712 2103; Kazdağlıoğulu Meydanı; soak & scrub ₺35; men 6am-11pm, women 9am-10pm) One of the most renowned bathhouses in all of Turkey, with separate baths for men and women. If you're going to get scrubbed down to rosy-pink skin just once on your Turkey travels, this is the place to do it.

Sleeping & Eating

Efe Guesthouse PENSION $

(0370-725 2688; www.efeguesthouse.com; Kayadibi Sokak 8; dm/s/d €9/17/25;) This place dishes up all of Safranbolu's Ottoman charm at a smidgen of the cost of other hotels. There's a basic dorm for those really saving their lira and the snug private rooms are packed full of local character.

★Kahveciler Konağı BOUTIQUE HOTEL $$

(0370-725 5453; Mescit Sokak 7; s/d €25/45;) The eight large rooms here have whitewashed walls, glorious wood-panel ceilings and lovely views of red-tiled roofs. Amiable host Erşan has transformed his grandfather's house into a comfortable home away from home topped off by a genuine welcoming vibe. As a bonus for those less agile, the bathrooms are big by Safranbolu standards and require no climbing into cupboards.

★Atış Cafe ANATOLIAN $

(Celal Bayer Caddesi; mains ₺10-15; 10am-10pm;) Safranbolu has cute cafes dishing up regional cuisine aplenty but Atış is our favourite for its genuinely friendly management and solid home-style cooking. Dig into local dishes of *peruhi* (pasta parcels drenched in a butter sauce) and *Rum mantı* (Turkish ravioli served in a soy-sauce broth) on the itsy-bitsy terrace or inside in the delightfully cosy floral-styled salon.

Taşev MODERN TURKISH $$

(0370-725 5300; www.tasevsanatvesarapevi.com; Hıdırlık Yokuşu Sokak 14; mains ₺17-40; 10am-11pm Tue-Sun;) This is Safranbolu's bona fide contemporary dining option and it delivers with thick steaks and creamy pasta dishes. The Turkish cheese platter is a must for cheese lovers. Service is warm and they'll helpfully explain menu items and help you choose from the extensive wine list.

Information

Tourist Office (☎0370-712 3863; www.safranboluturizmdanismaburosu.gov.tr; Kazdağlıoğulu Meydanı; ⏲9am-5.30pm) Informed, multilingual staff can provide tips and advice, and will even help with booking bus tickets.

Getting There & Away

Most buses stop in Karabük first and then finish at **Kıranköy otogar** (Adnan Menderes Bulvarı, Kıranköy), called 'Safranbolu otogar' but in Kıranköy or upper Safranbolu. From the otogar most bus companies provide a free *servis* (shuttle bus) that deposits you in central Kıranköy, near the **dolmuş (minibus) stand**. From there, regular dolmuşes trundle down the hill to Çarşı.

There are regular bus departures to Ankara (₺22 to ₺26, three hours) and İstanbul (₺60, seven hours).

Konya

☎0332 / POP 1.2 MILLION

An economic powerhouse that is religiously inspired and a busy university city that's as conservative as they come: Konya treads a delicate path between its historical significance as the home town of the whirling dervish orders and a bastion of Seljuk culture, and its modern importance as an economic boom town. The city derives considerable charm from this juxtaposition of old and new, with ancient mosques and the maze-like market district rubbing up against contemporary Konya around Alaaddin Tepesi.

Sights

★Mevlâna Museum MUSEUM

(☎0332-351 1215; Asanlı Kışla Caddesi; audioguide ₺10; ⏲9am-6.30pm, to 5pm Nov-Apr; 🚊Mevlâna) FREE For Muslims and non-Muslims alike, the main reason to come to Konya is to visit the Mevlâna Museum, the former lodge of the whirling dervishes and home to the tomb of Celaleddin Rumi (later known as Mevlâna), who we have to thank for giving the world the whirling dervishes. This is one of the biggest pilgrimage centres in Turkey, and the building's fluted dome of turquoise tiles is one of Turkey's most distinctive sights.

★Tile Museum MUSEUM

(Karatay Medresesi Çini Müzesi; ☎0332-351 1914; Ankara Caddesi, just off Alaaddin Meydanı; ₺5; ⏲9am-7pm, to 5pm Nov-Apr) Gorgeously restored, the interior central dome and walls of this former Seljuk theological school (1251) showcase some finely preserved blue-and-white Seljuk tilework. There is also an outstanding collection of ceramics on display including exhibits of the octagonal Seljuk tiles unearthed during excavations at Kubad Abad Palace on Lake Beyşehir. Emir Celaleddin Karatay, a Seljuk general, vizier and statesman who built the medrese (seminary), is buried in one of the corner rooms.

Sleeping

Ulusan Otel HOTEL $

(☎0332-351 5004, 0532 488 2333; ulusanhotel@hotmail.com; Çarşi PTT Arkasi 4; s/d €10/20; 🚭📶) This is the pick of the Konya cheapies. The rooms may be totally basic, but they're bright and spotlessly clean. Shared bathrooms are immaculately kept (some rooms have private bathrooms) and the communal area is full of homey knick-knacks.

DON'T MISS

WATCHING THE DERVISHES WHIRL

The Mevlevi worship ceremony, or *sema*, is a ritual dance representing union with the divine; it's what gives the dervishes their famous whirl, and appears on Unesco's third Proclamation of Masterpieces of the Oral and Intangible Heritage of Humanity. Watching a *sema* can be an evocative, romantic, unforgettable experience. There are many dervish orders worldwide that perform similar rituals, but the original Turkish version is the smoothest and purest, more of an elegant, trancelike dance than the raw energy seen elsewhere.

Year-round the dervishes perform on Saturday at the **Mevlâna Culture Centre** (www.emav.org; Aslanlı Kışla Caddesi; ⏲7pm Sat; 🚊Mevlâna Kültür Merkezi) FREE. Also, during summer (from early June to late September) there is a wonderfully intimate Thursday night **performance** (entry through east gate; ⏲8.45pm Thu Jun-Sep) FREE outdoors in the garden of the Mevlâna Museum.

Konya

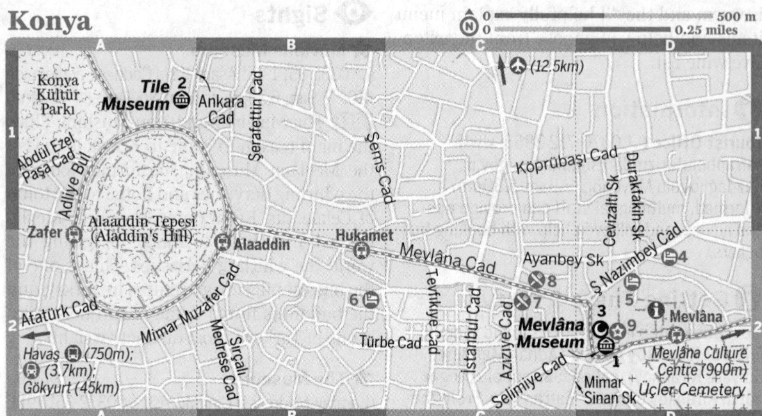

Konya

Top Sights

1 Mevlâna Museum D2
2 Tile Museum A1

Sights

3 Selimiye Camii D2

Sleeping

4 Derviş Otel D2
5 Hich Hotel D2
6 Ulusan Otel B2

Eating

7 Bolu Lokantası C2
8 Konya Mutfağı C2

Entertainment

9 Mevlâna Museum Whirling Dervish Performance D2

★ Derviş Otel BOUTIQUE HOTEL **$$**

(☎0332-350 0842; www.dervishotel.com; Güngör Sokak 7; r €50-60, f €100;) This airy, light-filled, 200-year-old house has been converted into a rather wonderful boutique hotel. All of the seven spacious rooms have lovely soft colour schemes with local carpets covering the wooden floors, comfortable beds and modern bathrooms to boot. With enthusiastic management providing truly personal service, this is a top-notch alternative to Konya's more anonymous hotels.

★ Hich Hotel BOUTIQUE HOTEL **$$$**

(☎0332-353 4424; www.hichhotel.com; Celal Sokak 6; r €80-150;) This design hotel mixes contemporary furnishings and luxurious touches such as espresso coffee machines in the rooms with the elegant original structure of the two 150-year-old buildings it occupies. There are gorgeous floor tiles and stained-glass window features in abundance. Outside is a sunny garden terrace cafe and you can spin your way to the Mevlâna Museum in but a moment.

Eating & Drinking

★ Bolu Lokantası ANATOLIAN **$**

(☎0332-352 4533; Aziziye Caddesi 27/B; etli ekmek & ayran ₺13; ⏲10am-10pm) Konya's king of *etli ekmek* (the local version of pide); Bolu is tiny, basic and always crammed. There's no menu; just order *etli ekmek,* with a jug of *ayran* (yoghurt drink) to wash it down, squeeze over the lemon, sprinkle liberally with spice, then roll up the slices and eat with charred peppers. It's the best lunch in town.

Konya Mutfağı ANATOLIAN **$**

(☎0332-350 4141; Mevlâna Caddesi 71; mains ₺15-27; ⏲11.30am-11pm) Run by the *belediye* (town council), this restaurant offers up the regional tastes of Konya. It's a great place to sample *patlıcan közleme kebabı* (roasted eggplant, peppers and tomatoes topped with grilled lamb) and *tirit* (a traditional wedding dish of bread, lamb and peppers topped with yoghurt and browned butter). Then cleanse your palate with a tamarind sherbet.

Information

Tourist Office (☎0332-353 4020; off Aslanı Kışla Caddesi; ⏲9am-5pm Mon-Sat) This helpful tourist office has free city maps and brochures and has information on the whirling dervish shows.

Getting There & Away

AIR

Konya Airport (Konya Havalimanı; www.konya.dhmi.gov.tr; off Ankara Caddesi) is about 13km northeast of the city centre. There are several flights daily to İstanbul.

Havaş (☎0332-239 0105; www.havas.net; Ferit Paşa Caddesi; ₺11) runs an airport shuttle-bus service between the airport and central Konya.

BUS

Konya's **otogar** (Dr Halil Ürün Caddesi; Otogar) is about 7km north of Alaaddin Tepesi. Regular buses serve all major destinations, including Ankara (₺35, four hours); Antalya (₺50, five hours); İstanbul (₺85, 11½ hours); and Nevşehir and Göreme (₺35 to ₺40). There are bus company ticket offices on Mevlâna Caddesi.

To get to the city centre from the otogar take the tram signed for Alaaddin from the east side of the station.

TRAIN

The **train station** (Alay Caddesi) is about 3km southwest of the centre. There are 10 high-speed train links between Konya and Ankara daily (₺30, two hours); and three to İstanbul's Pendik station (₺85, 4¼ hours) via Eskişehir (₺35, 1¾ hours).

Getting Around

In order to use Konya's public transport you need to have a **Konya ElKart** (rechargeable transport card; ₺1), which can be bought from the signed metal booths adjoining any of the larger tram and bus stops.

The main line runs from Selçuk Üniversite, via the otogar into the centre of town, terminating at Alaaddin. The second line starts at Zafer (on the western side of Alaaddin Tepisi), stops at Alaaddin, and then runs east along Mevlâna Caddesi, past the Mevlâna Museum and Mevlâna Culture Centre.

CAPPADOCIA

Cappadocia is a geological oddity of honeycombed hills and towering boulders of otherworldly beauty. People have long utilised the region's soft stone, seeking shelter underground and leaving the countryside scattered with fascinating cavern architecture. The fresco-adorned rock-cut churches of Göreme Open-Air Museum and the subterranean refuges of Derinkuyu and Kaymaklı are the most famous sights, while simply bedding down in one of Cappadocia's cave hotels is an experience in 21st-century cave living.

Getting There & Away

Two airports serve central Cappadocia: **Kayseri Airport** (Kayseri Erkilet Havalimanı; ☎0352-337 5494; www.kayseri.dhmi.gov.tr; Kayseri Caddesi) and **Nevşehir Airport** (Nevşehir Kapadokya Havalimanı; ☎0384-421 4451; www.kapadokya.dhmi.gov.tr; Nevşehir Kapadokya Havaalanı Yolu, Gülşehir). Both have several flights daily to/from İstanbul.

Most buses from İstanbul and other western Turkey destinations travel to Cappadocia overnight. At Nevşehir, it's common for the bus to terminate there and passengers to transfer to a bus-company *servis* (shuttle bus) for the final 20-minute journey to Uçhisar, Göreme, Avanos, Ortahisar or Ürgüp.

Getting Around

TO/FROM THE AIRPORT

Airport shuttle-bus services operate between both Cappadocia airports and the various villages. They must be pre-booked. Most hotels will do this for you.

There are a few companies to choose from but **Helios Transfer** (☎0384 271 2257; www.heliostransfer.com; Adnan Menderes Caddesi 25/A, Göreme; per passenger to/from Nevşehir Airport €8, to/from Kayseri Airport ₺10; 9am-6pm) and **Cappadocia Express** (☎0384-271 3070; www.cappadociatransport.com; Iceridere Sokak 3, Göreme; per passenger to/from Nevşehir Airport ₺20, to/from Kayseri Airport ₺25; 9am-6pm) are the most recommended.

DON'T MISS

CAPPADOCIA FROM ABOVE

If you've never taken a flight in a hot-air balloon, Cappadocia is one of the best places in the world to try it. Flight conditions are especially favourable here, with balloons operating most mornings throughout the year. Seeing this area's remarkable landscape from above is a truly magical experience and many travellers judge it to be the highlight of their trip.

Be aware that, despite the aura of luxury that surrounds the hot-air ballooning industry, this is an adventure activity and is not without its risks. There have been several fatal ballooning accidents here over the past decade. It's your responsibility to check the credentials of your chosen operator carefully. The following agencies have good credentials.

Butterfly Balloons (☎0384-271 3010; www.butterflyballoons.com; Uzundere Caddesi 29; 1hr flight €140; ⏲9.30am-6pm)

Royal Balloon (☎0384-271 3300; www.royalballoon.com; Dutlu Sokak 9; 1hr flight €175; ⏲9.30am-5.30pm)

DOLMUŞ TRANSPORT BETWEEN VILLAGES

Dolmuşes (minibuses; ₺3 to ₺4 depending on where you get on and off) travel between Ürgüp and Avanos via Ortahisar, the Göreme Open-Air Museum, Göreme, Çavuşin, Paşabağı and Zelve. The services leave Ürgüp otogar hourly between 8am and 7pm. Starting from Avanos, the dolmuşes operate hourly between 8am and 8pm. You can hop on and off anywhere along the route.

Göreme

☎0384 / POP 2200

Surrounded by epic sweeps of golden, moonscape valley, this remarkable honey-coloured village hollowed out of the hills has long since grown beyond its farming-hamlet roots. Nearby, the Göreme Open-Air Museum is an all-in-one testament to Byzantine life, while if you wander out of town you'll find storybook landscapes and little-visited rock-cut churches at every turn. With its easy-going allure and stunning setting, it's no wonder Göreme continues to send travellers giddy.

Sights

★Göreme Open-Air Museum HISTORIC SITE
(Göreme Açık Hava Müzesi; ☎0384-271 2167; Müze Caddesi; ₺30; ⏲8.30am-7pm Apr-Nov, to 5pm Dec-Mar) One of Turkey's Unesco World Heritage sites, the Göreme Open-Air Museum is an essential stop on any Cappadocian itinerary and deserves a two-hour visit. First an important Byzantine monastic settlement that housed some 20 monks, then a pilgrimage site from the 17th century, this splendid cluster of monastic Byzantine artistry with its rock-cut churches, chapels and monasteries is 1km uphill from Göreme's centre. Note that the museum's highlight – the **Karanlık Kilise** (Dark Church) – has an additional ₺10 entrance fee.

★Güllüdere (Rose) Valley AREA
FREE The trails that loop around Güllüdere Vadısı (Rose Valley) are easily accessible to all levels of walkers and provide some of the finest fairy chimney–strewn vistas in Cappadocia. As well as this, though, they hide fabulous, little-visited rock-cut churches boasting vibrant fresco fragments and intricate carvings hewn into the stone. If you only have time to hike through one valley in Cappadocia, this is the one to choose.

Tours

Heritage Travel TOURS
(☎0384-271 2687; www.turkishheritagetravel.com; Uzundere Caddesi; day tours per person cash/credit card €45/55; ⏲8.30am-5.30pm) This highly recommended local agency offers day-tour itineraries that differ from most operators in Cappadocia, including an 'Undiscovered Cappadocia' trip that visits Soğanlı, Mustafapaşa and Derinkuyu Underground City. It also offers private day trips for those with particular interests, including jeep safaris, tours to Hacıbektaş and a fresco trip exploring Cappadocia's Byzantine heritage.

Yama Tours TOURS
(☎0384-271 2508; www.yamatours.com; Müze Caddesi 2; group tours north/south €29/34; ⏲9.30am-6pm) This popular backpacker-friendly travel agency runs daily Cappadocia North (Göreme Open-Air Museum, Paşabağı and Avanos) and South (Ihlara Valley and Derinkuyu Underground City) tours. They can also organise a bag full of other Cappadocia adventures and activities for you, including private trips to Hacibektaş and Soğanlı that take in plenty of sights along the way, and three-day trips to Mt Nemrut.

Sleeping

Dorm Cave HOSTEL **$**

(0384-271 2770; www.travellerscave.com; Hafız Abdullah Efendi Sokak 4; dm/d €7/25, ste from €45;) This hostel offers three spacious cave-dorms that share small bathrooms across the courtyard and three petite private rooms upstairs. Next door, they've branched out with new comfortable suite-style rooms, but if you're in that price range you're better off heading further up the hill for terrace views.

★**Kelebek Hotel** BOUTIQUE HOTEL **$$**

(0384-271 2531; www.kelebekhotel.com; Yavuz Sokak 31; s €44-56, d €55-70, fairy chimney s €56-84, d €70-105, s/d without bathroom €44/55, s/d ste from €68/85;) Local guru Ali Yavuz leads a charming team at one of Göreme's original boutique hotels, which has seen a travel industry virtually spring from beneath its stunning terraces. Exuding Anatolian inspiration at every turn, the rooms are spread over a labyrinth of stairs and balconies interconnecting two gorgeous stone houses, each with a fairy chimney protruding skyward.

Kismet Cave House GUESTHOUSE **$$**

(0384-271 2416; www.kismetcavehouse.com; Kağnı Yolu 9; d €65-110, f €130;) Kismet's fate is assured. Guests consistently rave about the intimate experience here, created by welcoming, well-travelled host Faruk. Rooms (some in actual fairy chimneys) are full of local antiques, carved wood features, colourful rugs and quirky artwork, while communal areas are home to cosy cushion-scattered nooks. This honest-to-impending-greatness Anatolian cave house is delightfully homey in every way.

Eating

Fırın Express PIDE **$**

(0384-271 2266; Camı Sokak; pide ₺7-13; 10am-10pm;) Simply the best pide in town is found in this local haunt. The cavernous wood oven fires up meat and vegetarian options and anything doused with egg. We suggest the *patlıcanı* (aubergine) pide or *ıspınaklı kaşarlı* (spinach and cheese) pide and adding an *ayran* (yoghurt drink) to wash it down with, for a bargain feed.

★**Topdeck Cave Restaurant** ANATOLIAN **$$**

(0384-271 2474; Hafız Abdullah Efendi Sokak 15; mains ₺28-45; 6-11pm) If it feels as though you're dining in a family home, it's because you are. Talented chef Mustafa (aka Topdeck) and his gracious clan have transformed an atmospheric cave room in their house into a cosy restaurant where the kids pitch in with the serving and diners dig into hearty helpings of Anatolian favourites with a spicy twist.

Pumpkin Cafe ANATOLIAN **$$$**

(0542 808 5050; İçeridere Sokak 7; set menu incl soft drinks, tea & coffee ₺60, vegetarian ₺50; 6-11pm;) With its dinky balcony decorated with whimsically carved-out pumpkins, this cute cafe is one of the cosiest dining picks in Göreme. The daily-changing four-course set menu (with a choice of main) is a fresh feast of home-style dishes, all presented with delightful flourishes and topped off by some of the friendliest service in town.

Getting There & Away

There are daily long-distance buses to all over Turkey from Göreme's **otogar** (Belediye Caddesi). For most services heading west, you're ferried to Nevşehir's otogar by a free *servis* (shuttle bus) first.

BUSES FROM GÖREME'S OTOGAR

DESTINATION	FARE (₺)	DURATION (HR)	FREQUENCY (DAILY)
Ankara	45	4½	5 morning, 3 afternoon & 1 evening
Antalya	70	9	3 morning & 4 evening
Bodrum	90	13	3 evening
Çanakkale	100	16	1 evening
Denizli (for Pamukkale)	60-70	11	7 evening
Fethiye	80	14	2 evening
İstanbul	80	11-12	2 morning, 1 afternoon & 4 evening
İzmir	70	11½	3 evening
Kayseri	15	1	6 morning, 1 afternoon & 3 evening
Konya	35	3	2 morning, 3 afternoon & 6 evening
Selçuk	70	11	1 evening

Getting Around

As well as the Ürgüp–Avanos dolmuş (p476), Göreme has a regular bus service to Nevşehir (₺3) via Uçhisar (₺2) every 30 minutes between 7.30am and 10pm.

Around Göreme

From Göreme, an easy 3km walk through **Pigeon (Güvercinlik) Valley** (or take the Göreme–Nevşehir dolmuş) brings you to **Uçhisar Castle** (Uçhisar Kalesi; ₺6.50; ⌚8am-7pm) with awesome views of the lunarscape below. Hike through **Rose (Güllüdere)** and **Red (Kızılçukur) Valleys** to Çavasın village to visit the **Church of St John the Baptist** FREE, high up in the cliff overlooking the old village ruins.

Between Göreme and Avanos (hop on the Ürgüp–Avanos dolmuş) is the valley of **Paşabağı**, with some of Cappadocia's most famous fairy chimney formations. Further along the road is an old monastic settlement that is now **Zelve Open-Air Museum** (Zelve Açık Hava Müzesi; ₺10; ⌚8am-7pm).

Southwest of Göreme is a series of ancient underground cities first carved out by the Hittites and once occupied by Byzantine Christians taking refuge from Persian and Arab armies. The largest of these is **Derinkuyu** (Derinkuyu; ₺25; ⌚8am-7pm), which, unbelievably, once sheltered 10,000 people and their livestock. Another at **Kaymaklı** (Kaymaklı; ₺25; ⌚8am-7pm) is located 10km to the north. There is little in the way of information at either site, so it's worthwhile hiring a guide.

Continuing southwest you reach **Ihlara Valley** (Ihlara Vadısı; incl Selime Monastery, Güzelyurt's Monastery Valley & Aksaray Museum ₺20; ⌚8am-6.30pm), a beautiful canyon full of rock-cut churches dating back to Byzantine times. A hiking trail threads the length of the gorge following the course of the river, Melendiz Suyu, which flows for 13km from Selime village and its rock-hewn **monastery** (Selime village; ₺20 incl Ihlara Valley, Güzelyurt's Monastery Valley & Aksaray Museum; ⌚8am-6pm) to Ihlara village.

Derinkuyu and Kaymaklı are easily reached by public transport. Take any dolmuş to Nevşehir's central dolmuş stand and catch the Derinkuyu Koop dolmuş ((₺5, 45 minutes, every 30 minutes between 9am and 6.30pm), which runs past both sites. Due to having to make bus changes in both Nevşehir and Aksaray, Ihlara Valley can't be done on a day trip by public transport.Taking a tour, or hiring a car, are the best options.

Avanos

☎0384 / POP 13,533

The Kızılırmak (Red River) is the slow-paced pulse of this provincial town and the unusual source of its livelihood; the distinctive red clay that, mixed with a white, mountain mud variety, is spun to produce the region's famed pottery. Up from the river an old quarter of gently decaying Greek-Ottoman houses snakes up the hillside, while riverside is the place to ponder the sunset as you sip your umpteenth çay.

Sleeping & Eating

★Kirkit Hotel BOUTIQUE HOTEL **$$**
(☎0384-511 3148; www.kirkithotel.com; Genç Ağa Sokak; s/d/tr/f €25/40/45/50; 📶) This Avanos institution, right in the centre of town, is a rambling stone house with rooms full of kilims (pileless woven rugs), old B&W photographs, intricately carved cupboards and *suzanis* (Uzbek bedspreads), all set around a courtyard brimming with plants and quirky antiques. Looked after by incredibly knowledgeable and helpful management, Kirkit is the perfect base for trips around Cappadocia.

★Hanım Eli ANATOLIAN **$**
(Atatürk Caddesi; mains ₺8-16; ⌚11am-9pm) This modest diner serves wholesome local dishes packed full of fresh, local flavour. This is home-style cooking executed brilliantly and without any pretentious flourish. The *manti* (Turkish ravioli) we had here was the best in Cappadocia. Wily diners looking for Anatolian soul food without the price tag of Göreme and Ürgüp's restaurants would do well to lunch here.

Getting There & Around

You can book long-distance buses at Avanos' small **otogar** (Kapadokya Caddesi), a 10-minute walk from the centre. The bus companies all provide a *servis* (shuttle bus) to Nevşehir.

As well as the dolmuş (minibus) to Ürgüp, Avanos has dolmuşes to Nevşehir (₺4) every 20 minutes between 7am and 7pm.

Ürgüp

☎0384 / POP 20,700

Ürgüp is the rural retreat for those who don't fancy being too rural, with its bustling, modern downtown area a direct foil to the old village back lanes still clinging to the hillside rim. There's not a lot to do in town itself. Instead, Ürgüp has cleverly positioned itself as the connoisseur's base for exploring the geographical heart of Cappadocia, with boutique-hotel frippery at your fingertips.

Sleeping

Hotel Elvan PENSION $

(0384-341 4191; www.hotelelvan.com; Barbaros Hayrettin Sokak 11; s/d/f €20/30/36, deluxe €22/32/38;) Bah – who needs boutique style when you have pensions like the Elvan, where Hasan and family dish out oodles of homespun hospitality. Set around an internal courtyard brimming with colourful pot plants, the 22 neat rooms feature daisy bedspreads and sparkling-clean bathrooms. On the ground floor, stone-arch deluxe rooms come with snazzy onyx-travertine bathrooms and TVs.

Canyon Cave Hotel BOUTIQUE HOTEL $$

(0384-341 4113; www.canyoncavehotel.com; Sair Mahfi Baba 3 Sokak 9; s/d €50-55/55-60, ste €70-100;) Host Murat İşnel creates a fun and sociable atmosphere at his nine-room hilltop pad with its rooftop bar overlooking the entire sweep of Ürgüp and the majestic peak of Erciyes Dağı (Mt Erciyes) beyond. Rooms (both half- and full cave) are generously sized and simply furnished, and breakfast is a slap-up feast featuring cafetière coffee and banana bread.

★ **Sota Cappadocia** BOUTIQUE HOTEL $$$

(0384-341 5885; www.sotacappadocia.com; Burhan Kale Sokak 12; r/ste from €130/180;) Ürgüp's hippest hotel. Nil Tuncer, with help from acclaimed interior decorator Oytun Berktan, has stamped the eight rooms with a minimalist design as much at home in New York as within the swirling natural coloured caves. Dramatic black accenting, repurposed *gözleme*-pans as statement wall art, hanging lamps salvaged from a Russian tanker – Sota's swaggering style shakes up the Cappadocia scene.

Eating

Zeytin Cafe TURKISH $

(0384-341 7399; Atatürk Bulvarı; dishes ₺7-18; 10am-10pm;) Our top lunchtime spot in Ürgüp is this thoroughly welcoming, modern *lokanta* (eatery serving ready-made food) dishing up wholesome homemade stews, *mantı* (Turkish ravioli) and Turkish staples. Head inside to the counter and choose from the daily-changing selection.

Yeni Lokanta TURKISH $$

(0384-341 6880; Postane Sokak 3; mains ₺14-45; 10.30am-10pm) This new-wave *lokanta* is a roaring success. Yeni Lokanta drags the traditional working-man's canteen into the 21st century with smart-attired waiters, a contemporary dining room and some impressive dish presentation. The *izgara köfte* (grilled meatballs) here are lush.

★ **Ziggy Cafe** MODERN TURKISH $$$

(0384-341 7107; www.ziggycafe.com; Tevfik Fikret Caddesi 24; meze set menus ₺60-65, mains ₺20-45; 11.30am-11pm;) This tribute to the adored pet dog of charismatic host Selim is a luscious success. The two-tiered terrace fills day and night with a hip clientele enjoying strong cocktails while feasting on the finest meze menu in Cappadocia, created by chef Ali Ozkan. Ziggy's has nailed the essence of casual-yet-classy Cappadocian dining.

Getting There & Around

Ürgüp's **otogar** (Güllüce Caddesi) is in the middle of town and offers similar bus services as Göreme. From the otogar, dolmuşes (minibuses) travel to Nevşehir every 15 minutes from 7am to 8pm (₺4, 25 minutes), along with the dolmuş to Avanos (p476).

Kayseri

0352 / POP 1.3 MILLION

Mixing Seljuk tombs, mosques and modern developments, Kayseri is both Turkey's most Islamic city after Konya and an economic powerhouse. Most travellers whizz through town on their way from the airport to Cappadocia's villages, but the city centre is full of surprises. An afternoon pottering within the narrow bazaar streets and poking about the Seljuk and Ottoman monuments – all loomed over by mighty Erciyes Dağı (Mt Erciyes) – is an interesting contrast to exploring the more famous fairy-chimney vistas to the city's west.

Sights

★ **Museum of Seljuk Civilisation** MUSEUM

(Selçuklu Uygarlığı Müzesi; Mimar Sinan Parkı; ₺2; 9am-5pm Tue-Sun) This excellent museum is set in the restored Çifte Medrese, a 13th-century twin hospital and seminary built at the bequest of Seljuk sultan Keyhüsrev I and his sister Gevher Nesibe Sultan. It's thought to be one of the world's first medical training schools.The strikingly serene architecture is offset by beautiful exhibits of Seljuk artistry, culture and history, complemented by up-to-the-minute multimedia displays. Our one grumble is that not enough of the information panels have English translations.

Kayseri Castle CASTLE
(Kayseri Kalesi; Cumhuriyet Meydanı) The monumental black-basalt walls of Kayseri castle were first constructed under Roman emperor Gordian III and rebuilt by the Byzantine emperor Justinian 300 years later. The imposing edifice you see today though is mostly the work of 13th-century Seljuk sultan Alaattin Keykubat.

The castle is undergoing a mammoth restoration project, now in its final phase. Once finished (estimated for 2018) the interior will become the new home of Kayseri's Archaeological Museum, as well as providing space for an art centre.

Sleeping & Eating

★İmamoğlu Paşa Hotel HOTEL $$
(☎0352-336 9090; www.imamoglupasaotel.com.tr; Kocasinan Bulvarı 24; s/d €25/35; ❄📶) Kayseri's standout midranger is a pleasant shock. Contemporary rooms come complete with wide-screen satellite TVs, rain showers, kettles, probably the most comfortable beds in town, and minibars (yes, there's beer). You want a room on the 5th floor or higher for views of Erciyes Dağı (Mt Erciyes). It's on the road opposite the train station, next door to the police station.

★Alamet-i Farika ANATOLIAN $
(☎0532-232 1080; Deliklitaş Caddesi 8; mains ₺10-24; ⏲10am-10pm) The interior is all European-style elegance, but the food is top-notch Anatolian. Tuck into the *mantı* (Turkish ravioli), devour the meaty speciality *çentik kebap* (grilled meat served atop potatoes with a yoghurt and tomato sauce) and save room for the naughtily sweet desserts. Finish up with Turkish coffee, served in dainty teacups with a shot glass of lemonade on the side.

Dalyan Balıkçılık SEAFOOD $
(☎0352-222 9928; Sivas Caddesi 12/B; fish sandwich ₺8-9, mains ₺17.50-25; ⏲10am-10pm) Walk through the fishmongers by the door to this rather brilliant fish restaurant on the terrace out back. As well as cheap and filling *balık ekmek* (fish sandwiches), which make for a tasty lunch, the seafood mains are great value and come loaded down with salads. Service is spot on.

Getting There & Away

AIR

Kayseri Airport (p475) is 9km north of the centre. A taxi from the central city to the airport costs around ₺35.

BUS

Kayseri's **otogar** (☎0352-336 4373; Osman Kavuncu Bulvarı) is 9km west of the centre. Nearly all bus companies provide a free *servis* (shuttle bus) into the central city. To Göreme, most buses run by Metro will drop you in the village on their way to Nevşehir.

Destinations include the following:

Ankara (₺50; five hours; hourly)
Erzurum (₺65 to ₺72; nine hours; six evening)
Göreme (₺15; one hour; two morning, one afternoon, six evening)
Nevşehir (₺15; 1½ hours; regular – hourly to every 1½ hours)
Trabzon (₺90; 11½ hours; one morning, one afternoon and five evening)

BLACK SEA COAST & NORTHEASTERN ANATOLIA

Trabzon

☎0462 / POP 766,782

Founded by Greek traders from Miletus in the 8th century BC, Trabzon has been handballed down the years between Cimmerians, Medes, Hellenes, Byzantines and a succession of other peoples. Once an important stop on the Silk Road, it remains the Black Sea's busiest port. Somewhat louche, it's the most sophisticated city in the region, too caught up in its own whirl of activity to worry about what's happening in far-off İstanbul or Ankara.

Most travellers come here to see Sumela Monastery, 46km to the south, but Trabzon's medieval church (now mosque) and bazaar district are worthy of a stopover themselves.

Sights

Sumela Monastery MONASTERY
(Sümela Manastırı; Meryemana; ☎0462-326 0748; www.sumela.com; Altındere Vadisi, Maçka; ₺25; ⏲9am-7pm Apr-Oct, 8am-4pm Nov-Mar) The Greek Orthodox Monastery of the Virgin Mary, better known as Sumela Monastery, is one of the Black Sea's highlights. It has been

shut for restoration though since 2015. Check the latest information in Trabzon; on our last visit locals were doubtful work would finish by the original 2018 reopening date.

While shut, you can still get views of the monastery, clinging improbably to a sheer cliff, high above evergreen forests, by driving the road up to the car park.

★Aya Sofya Mosque & Museum MOSQUE, MUSEUM
(Aya Sofya Müzesi ve Camii; ☎0462-223 3043; Ayasofya Caddesi; ⏲9am-7pm Jun-Aug, to 6pm Apr, May, Sep & Oct, 8am-5pm Nov-Mar) FREE Originally called Hagia Sophia (Church of Divine Wisdom), Aya Sofya sits 4km west of Trabzon's centre on a terrace close to the sea. Built between 1238 and 1263, it was influenced by Georgian and Seljuk design, although the wall paintings and mosaic floors follow the prevailing Constantinople style of the time. It was converted to a mosque after Ottoman conquest in 1461, and later used as an ammunition-storage depot and hospital by the Russians, before restoration in the 1960s.

Bedesten MARKET
(Covered Bazaar; Çarşı) On the site of a marketplace built by the Genoese, Trabzon's current covered bazaar was put up by the Ottomans, perhaps in the 16th century. With a single dome (unusual among Turkish bazaars) and a pleasing internal symmetry of arches, it's a lovely place to sip çay and contemplate your purchases.

Sleeping & Eating

Adelante HOSTEL $
(☎0462-544 4344; www.trabzonhostel.com; Saray Atik Cami Sokak 5; dm/d €15/40; 📶) Within the old city, this very decent hostel provides squeaky-clean dorm accommodation with shared bathrooms, and is enthusiastically run by English-speaking Elif. *Kuymak, kaygana* and other local specialities feature in the breakfast. There's also a couple of private double rooms, but it's the good-value dorm beds that make this place shine.

Hotel Nur HOTEL $$
(☎0462-323 0445; Cami Sokak 15; s/d €40/58; ❄📶) A long-standing travellers' favourite, with Black Sea views from the rooftop breakfast room and very helpful staff, the Nur has clean, modern and comfortably outfitted rooms all with satellite TV, kettle and fridge. Be aware though, solo travellers usually get stuck with a pint-sized room and the nearby mosque doesn't skimp on the dawn call to prayer.

> OFF THE BEATEN TRACK
>
> **DRIVING THE BLACK SEA COAST**
>
> To see the best of the Black Sea, travel the glorious, vertigo-inducing curves on the coastal road from **Amasra**, with its Roman and Byzantine ruins, to the fortified town of **Sinop**. Carry on east – passing through the busy port of Samsun – to **Ünye** with an old town of preserved Ottoman houses that is ripe for wandering. Finish up in **Ordu** for breathtaking Black Sea vistas from the cable car that trundles up the hill behind town.

★Kalender TURKISH $
(☎0462-323 1011; Zeytinlik Caddesi 16b; dishes ₺8-16; ⏲8.30am-9pm Mon-Sat; ❄) This welcoming cafe-restaurant, just south of Trabzon's museum, has a cosmopolitan vibe and a daily changing menu of wholesome and hearty Turkish dishes including *menemen* (scrambled eggs with peppers and tomatoes) and *kuymak*. Choose a mixed plate of four dishes to get stuck into local flavours.

Cemilusta TURKISH $$
(☎0462-321 6161; www.cemilusta.com.tr; Atatürk Alanı 6; mains ₺7-35; ⏲9am-10pm; 🖉) The front terrace here, overlooking the *meydan* (square), is nearly always jam-packed with both locals and Turkish tourists happily munching on tasty Black Sea specialities of *lahana sarma* (stuffed cabbage rolls) and *kuymak* or digging into grilled fish, lamb chops or *köfte* (meatballs).

Information

Tourist Office (☎0462-326 4760; Atatürk Alanı; ⏲8am-5.30pm Jun-Sep, to 5pm Mon-Fri Oct-May) Staff are helpful and some speak a little English. They give out a decent free map.

Getting There & Away

AIR

Trabzon Airport (Trabzon Havalimanı; www.trabzon.dhmi.gov.tr; off Atatürk Bulvarı) is 5.5km east of the city centre. There are several flights daily from İstanbul and Ankara, and regular services to Adana, Antalya and İzmir.

A taxi costs around ₺25 between the airport and the central city at Atatürk Alanı.

BUS

Trabzon's otogar is 3km east of the port. Bus companies, such as **Metro** (www.metroturizm.com.tr; Limonlu Sokak; ⊙9am-6pm Mon-Sat) and **Ali Osman Ulusoy** (www.aliosmanulusoy.com.tr; Limonlu Sokak; ⊙9am-6pm Mon-Sat), have central booking offices scattered around Atatürk Alanı. Destinations include the following:

Ankara (₺70 to ₺75, 12½ hours, eight morning, 13 afternoon and eight evening)

Erzurum (₺35, five hours, four morning, one afternoon and six evening)

Hopa (₺25, 2½ hours, hourly 8am to 7pm)

İstanbul (₺120, 17½ hours, one morning, regular after 1pm)

Kayseri (₺80 to ₺90, 11 hours, seven afternoon and four evening)

Rize (₺12, 1½ hours, hourly 8am to7pm)

Samsun (₺35 to ₺40, 5½ hours, regular; frequent after 1pm)

Tbilisi, Georgia (via Batumi; ₺60, 9½ hours, one evening)

Getting Around

Dolmuşes (minibuses; ₺2) to the otogar, Aya Sofya and many other destinations leave from under the flyover on Limonlu Sokak, just off the southeastern corner of Atatürk Alanı.

Erzurum

☎0442 / POP 418,000

Lovers of architecture and history will be in paradise in Erzurum, where fantastic Seljuk, Saltuk, Mongol and Ottoman mosques and *medreses* (seminaries) line the main drag. The surrounding mountains and steppe form a heavenly backdrop to the jumble of billboards and minarets.

Erzurum is not a city resting on its considerable historically significant laurels; the vibrant life coursing along its shopping-centre-lined streets has earned it a reputation as a modern metropolis and an eastern Turkish hub.

Sights

★Yakutiye Medresesi MUSEUM

(Turkish-Islamic Arts & Ethnography Museum; Cumhuriyet Caddesi; ₺5; ⊙8am-7pm Apr-Oct, to 5pm Nov-Mar) Dominating Erzurum's central park, this handsome Mongol *medrese* dates from 1310. The Mongols borrowed the basics of Seljuk architecture and developed their own variations, as seen on the facade and sides of the main portal that feature geometric, plant and animal motifs. The southern minaret sports superb mosaic tile work that wouldn't look out of place in Central Asia. Inside, are nicely curated exhibits on traditional regional crafts, costumes and local life.

★Çifte Minareli Medrese ISLAMIC SITE

(Twin Minaret Seminary; Cumhuriyet Caddesi; ⊙9am-5pm) The Seljuk-style Çifte Minareli Medrese, dating from the second half of the 13th century, is for most people Erzurum's most splendid building. The twin, fluted brick minarets, decorated with eye-catching small blue tiles, rise above a beautifully carved main portal. The portal, which has interestingly different motifs on each side, leads into a long, dignified, porticoed courtyard. The grand 12-sided, domed hall at the far end of the courtyard may have served as the tomb of the *medrese's* founder.

Ulu Cami MOSQUE

(Grand Mosque; Cumhuriyet Caddesi) This restrained but elegant mosque was built in 1179 by Erzurum's Saltuk Turkish emir. Seven aisles run north–south and six run east–west, resulting in a forest of columns and pointed arches. In the central north-south aisle, a stalactite dome opens to the heavens above the third bay. The bay before the *mihrab* (niche indicating the direction of Mecca), at the central aisle's southern end, sports two 'elephant-eye' windows and a traditional *kırlangıç* (swallow) dome of overlapping wooden-beams.

Sleeping & Eating

Hekimoğlu Otel HOTEL $

(☎0442-234 3049; hekimogluotelomer@hotmail.com; Kazım Karabekir Caddesi 66; s/d €15/25; 📶) With a jovial, welcoming team at reception, the Hekimoğlu is a good-value option in Erzurum's main hotel area. Rooms are simple and on the small side, but are clean and the pink bedspreads add a touch of colour. There's a busy *lokanta* (eatery serving ready-made food) downstairs, so that's everything sorted after a long Anatolian bus ride.

★Otel Zade HOTEL $$

(☎0442-233 1616; www.otelzade.com.tr; İsmet Paşa Caddesi 27; s/d €40/60 deluxe €50/75; ❄📶) The best thing that's happened in the Erzurum accommodation scene for years. Spacious, supercomfortable rooms have slick, contemporary furniture and come kitted out

Erzurum

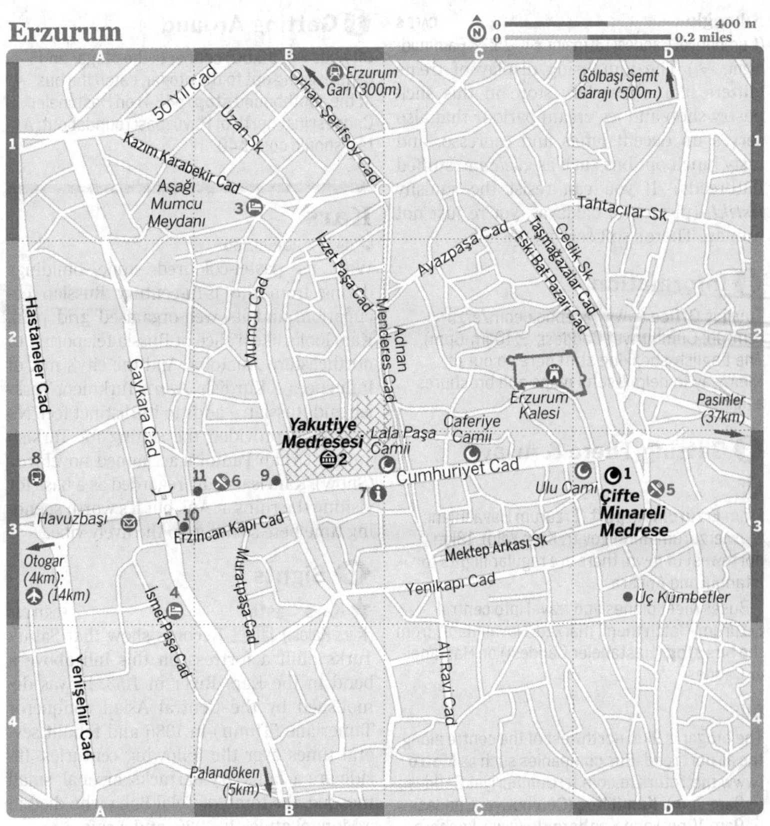

Erzurum

Top Sights
1 Çifte Minareli Medrese ... D3
2 Yakutiye Medresesi ... B3

Sleeping
3 Hekimoğlu Otel ... B1
4 Otel Zade ... A3

Eating
5 Emirşeyh Nedim ... D3
6 Kılıçoğlu ... B3

Information
7 Tourist Office ... B3

Transport
8 Buses to Airport & Otogar ... A3
9 Kamil Koç Office ... B3
10 Kanberoğlu Office ... A3
11 Metro ... B3

with kettles, minibars, big built-into-the-wall satellite TVs and complimentary fruit. Even the soap in the bathroom is nice. Upgrade to a deluxe room to stretch out on the sofa after a long day on the Anatolian road.

★ **Emirşeyh Nedim** KEBAP $
(www.emirseyh.com.tr; Yenikapı Caddesi 172; mains ₺12-32; ⌚9am-11pm) Erzurum's choice meat-eating experience is a lovely two-storey building with carved stone pillars and painted recessed ceilings. With very good food and friendly service, it's popular with everyone from families to couples and groups of friends.

You won't go wrong with the Emirşeyh *köfte* (meatballs), any of the kebaps or a *karışık ızgara* (mixed grill), all prepared at open ranges.

Kılıçoğlu CAFE $

(Cumhuriyet Caddesi 13; mains ₺10-15; ⏲6am-midnight; 📶) The tantalising display of treats glitters like a jewellery store in this slick pastry shop and ice-cream parlour that also serves up decent lattes and espresso, and tasty lunch options such as *gözleme* (stuffed flatbreads). If you can resist the squishy *fıstıklı* (pistachio) baklavas, you're just not human. There's soft seating upstairs.

Information

Tourist Office (www.facebook.com/erzurumtdb; Cumhuriyet Caddesi; ⏲10am-6pm) The English-speaking staff here go out of their way to help. Useful maps and brochures available.

Getting There & Away

AIR

From **Erzurum Airport** (Erzurum Havalimanı; www.erzurum.dhmi.gov.tr; Kars Yolu), 13km northwest of town, there are regular flights to İstanbul and Ankara.

Buses meet planes and travel into central Erzurum. Catch them, marked 'Havalimanı', from the **bus stop** (Hastaneler Caddesi) on Hastaneler Caddesi.

BUS

The otogar is 9km northwest of the centre along the airport road. Bus companies such as **Metro** (www.metroturizm.com.tr; Cumhuriyet Caddesi; ⏲9am-7pm), **Kamil Koç** (Cumhuriyet Caddesi; ⏲9am-10pm) and **Kanberoğlu** (www.kanberoglu.com.tr; Çaykara Caddesi) have central ticket offices and provide a free *servis* (shuttle bus) to the otogar. Destinations include the following:

Ankara (₺80 to ₺95; two morning, four afternoon and regular in evening)

Doğubayazıt (₺25; three early morning)

İstanbul (₺110 to ₺130; regular in afternoon and nine evening)

Kayseri (₺60; three morning, five afternoon and four evening)

Trabzon (₺35; three morning, six afternoon and nine evening)

Van (₺60; three morning, four afternoon and three evening)

TRAIN

The daily **Doğu Ekspresi** train (www.tcdd.gov.tr) departs at 2.46pm to Kars (₺16.50, 4½ hours), and at 12.21pm to Ankara (₺41, 20 hours), via Sivas (₺23, 10 hours) and Kayseri (₺29, 13½ hours). Engineering work on the rail line at Ankara in 2017 meant that the train was terminating at Irmak (60km east of Ankara).

Getting Around

City bus K4 (₺2.50) connects the otogar and centre: going out to the otogar, catch the bus at the southbound **stop** (p484) on Hastaneler Caddesi just north of Havuzbaşı roundabout. A taxi should cost ₺40.

Kars

☎0474 / POP 79,300

With its pastel-coloured stone buildings dating from the 19th-century Russian occupation, and its well-organised grid plan, Kars looks like a slice of Russia teleported to northeastern Anatolia. And the city's mix of influences – Kurdish, Azeri, Turkmen, Turkish and Russian – adds to its distinct feel. No wonder it provided the setting for Turkish author Orhan Pamuk's acclaimed novel *Kar* (Snow). Kars is usually regarded as a base for visiting the ruins at Ani, but it's worth spending time here soaking up the lively vibe.

Sights

★**Kars Castle** FORTRESS

(Kars Kalesi) FREE Records show that Saltuk Turks built a fortress on this hill above a bend in the Kars River in 1153. It was demolished by the Central Asian conqueror Tamerlane (Timur) in 1386 and rebuilt several times over the following centuries. Inside are a Janissary barracks, arsenal, small mosque, the tomb of Celal Baba who died in a Mongol attack in 1239, and a cafe.

Sleeping & Eating

Hotel Temel HOTEL $

(☎0474-223 1376; Yenipazar Caddesi 9; s/d €15/22; 📶) The rooms at 'Hotel Base' may be frayed around the edges and needing a bit of maintenance, but they're neatly kept and come with a cheerful blue-and-yellow colour scheme. Staff are a friendly bunch.

Hotel Katerina Sarayı HOTEL $$

(☎0474-223 0636; www.katerinasarayi.com; Celalbaba Caddesi 52; s/d/tr €30/45/55; P 📶) This old Russian military hospital, dating from 1879, has a tranquil riverside setting right beneath the castle yet is only 10 minutes' walk from the centre. Be aware though that it's set up with Turkish tourists in mind, which means amusingly over-the-top fake gilt bedheads and furniture in the smallish rooms and no coffee (just tea) at breakfast.

WORTH A TRIP

ANI

The ruins of **Ani** (₺8; ⏲8am-7pm Apr-Oct, to 5pm Nov-Mar; Ⓟ), 45km east of Kars, are an absolute must-see. Your first view is stunning: wrecks of great stone buildings adrift on a sea of undulating grass, landmarks in a ghost city that was once the stately Armenian capital and home to nearly 100,000 people, rivalling Constantinople in power and glory. The poignant ruins, the windswept plateau overlooking the Turkish–Armenian border, and the total lack of crowds make for an eerie and unforgettable ambience.

The best transport option for Ani is a round-trip (car or minibus) from Kars organised by the knowledgeable, English-speaking driver-guide **Celil Ersözoğlu** (☎0532 226 3966; celilani@hotmail.com; return transport to Ani 1-2 people ₺150, ₺50 per person for 3 or more). The trip includes about three hours' waiting time and a rundown on Ani's history en route. He also offers optional guiding services: ₺200 for either the main plateau site or the 'underground city'; ₺350 for both (five to six hours).

★**Ocakbaşı Restoran** TURKISH $
(☎0474-212 0056; www.kaygisizocakbasi.com; Atatürk Caddesi; mains ₺13-22; ⏲8am-11pm; 📶🍃) This classy 40-year-old favourite with a large upstairs dining room serves tasty and unusual regional and Turkish dishes, such as its speciality *alinazik* (aubergine purée with yoghurt and ground *köfte;* you can ask for *et siz* for a vegetarian version) and some good pide with unusual ingredient combinations (including vegetarian options).

Çeşni Ev Yemekleri ANATOLIAN $
(Atatürk Caddesi; mains ₺8-10; ⏲10am-10pm) This friendly cafe, right in the centre of town, is a good place to head when you're grilled out. The small menu of village-cooking favourites dishes up excellent *mantı* (Turkish ravioli) and a decent *karnıyarık* (stuffed aubergines), as well as regional specialities of *kete* (Anatolian butter bread) and *hangel* (pasta in a yoghurt sauce).

Getting There & Away

Kars Airport (Kars Harakani Havalimanı; www.dhmi.gov.tr; İsmail Aytemiz Bulvarı), 6km south of the town centre, has daily flights to İstanbul and Ankara.

Kars' **otogar** (Bus Station; Main Kars–Ardahan Rd) for long-distance services is 4km northeast of the centre. Free *servises* (shuttle buses) ferry passengers to/from the bus companies' city-centre offices.

Destinations include Erzurum (₺20 to 25, three hours, six buses between 11am and 4pm), Trabzon (₺80, seven hours, Kanberoğlu bus at 12.30pm) and Ankara (₺90, 17 hours, Doğu Kars bus at 5pm). **Metro** (www.metroturizm.com.tr; Faikbey Caddesi) has a daily service to İstanbul (₺130, 22 hours) at 11am.

Dolmuşes (minibuses) to local towns leave from the **Eski Otogar** (Halitpaşa Caddesi). If you're heading to Doğubayazıt, take a dolmuş to Iğdır (₺25, 2½ hours, 7am, 8am, 8.30am, 10am, 12.30pm, 2pm and 5pm) and change there.

Doğubayazıt

☎0472 / POP 77,000

Doğubayazıt's setting is superb. To the north, the talismanic Mt Ararat (Ağrı Dağı; 5137m), Turkey's highest mountain, lords it over the landscape. To the south, the beautiful İshak Paşa Palace surveys town from a rocky perch beneath jagged peaks. The town itself doesn't have too much charm, but it's the obvious base for climbing Mt Ararat (when open to climbers) and the main kicking-off point for the overland trail through Iran (the border is 35km away).

Sights & Activities

The twin peaks of Mt Ararat have figured in legends since time began, most notably as the supposed resting place of Noah's ark. The western peak, Büyük Ağrı (Great Ararat), is 5137m high, while Küçük Ağrı (Little Ararat) rises to 3925m. Climbing Great Ararat is a fantastic and challenging experience. Sadly for climbers, in 2016 Ararat was declared a military restricted zone and climbers were banned from the mountain. It is hoped that the ban will be lifted for the 2018 climbing season, though this didn't seem likely on our last research trip. Check locally for up-to-date information.

When open again, all climbers must have a permit (US$70) and must go with a licensed guide. Typically, agencies charge about €400 per person to lead a four-person group on a four- to five-day trek from Doğubayazıt. Most reputable agencies recommend five-day treks to allow acclimatisation before tackling the summit.

★İshak Paşa Palace PALACE
(İshak Paşa Sarayı; İshak Paşa Sarayı Yolu; ₺5; 9am-6pm Apr-Oct, 8am-4pm Nov-Mar; P) The splendid İshak Paşa Palace stands on a small plateau beneath stark cliffs 6km southeast of town. Combining Ottoman, Seljuk, Georgian, Persian and Armenian design, the palace was begun in 1685 and completed in 1784 by an Ottoman general, İshak Paşa. Dolmuşes (minibuses; ₺2.50) rattle to the palace until about 5pm from a stop behind the *belediye* (city hall), leaving when about half-full. Taxis charge ₺25 one way, or ₺30 return with a one-hour wait.

Sleeping & Eating

★Tehran Boutique Hotel BOUTIQUE HOTEL **$$**
(0472-312 0195; www.tehranboutiquehotel.com; Büyük Ağrı Caddesi 72; s/d €31-44/44-56, deluxe €51;) Supercomfortable and spacious rooms, some with Ararat views and balconies, have their own tea- and coffee-making equipment, minibars stocked with beer and soft drinks, and gleaming, up-to-date bathrooms with spacious rain-shower compartments. A good breakfast spread is served on the top floor (which has the best views), and there's a bar and inviting seating in the lobby.

Hotel Doğus HOTEL **$$**
(0472-312 6161; http://dogushotel.net; Belediye Caddesi 100; s/d/tr €18/34/42;) The Doğus provides bright, spotless rooms with wood-surfaced furnishings and tiled bathrooms, and a good breakfast.

Yoresel Yemekleri ANATOLIAN **$**
(Dr İsmail Beşikçi Caddesi; mains ₺7-11; 7am-8pm Mon-Sat;) There's no sign so look for the menu blackboard on the pavement outside then head up the stairs to this clean, family-run place that serves up a variety of Kurdish and Anatolian dishes with different daily specials. There's hearty soups and vegetarian dishes, as well as the regional speciality *abdigör köfte*.

Getting There & Away

BUS & DOLMUŞ

The otogar (bus station) is 3km west of the centre. Tickets for most destinations can be bought at the **Ağrı Doğuş office** (Belediye Caddesi; 9am-7pm) in the central city. Buses to Erzurum (₺35, four hours) mostly leave between 10am and 3pm.

Dolmuşes (minibuses) to **Iğdır** (Abdurrezzak Aladaş Sokak), where you can change for Kars, and **Van** (Abdurrezzak Aladaş Sokak) leave from separate stops in central Doğubayazıt.

TO/FROM IRAN

Dolmuşes (Ağrı Caddesi) leave from Ağrı Caddesi in the centre to the border at Gürbulak (₺8, 30 minutes) from 6am to about 5pm. On the Iranian side, pay ₺1 for a shared taxi to Bazargan (3km), where you can change money and find onward transport. The border is open 24 hours.

UNDERSTAND TURKEY

Turkey Today

After nearly two decades of strong economic growth, Turks have seen their standard of living rise significantly, but long-standing issues remain – including the Kurdish conflict and tensions between Islamic and secular lifestyles and belief systems. The failed coup in 2016 increased these tensions and led to draconian reprisals against any elements of the society considered to be anti-government. This has in turn led to organisations including Amnesty International, Human Rights Watch and Reporters Without Borders (RSF) raising concerns about diminishing civil, political and human rights in the country, including press freedom.

History

Few countries can claim to have played such a significant role in the history of human civilisation as Turkey, and the country's location on the major trade routes between Europe and Asia identified it as a strategic target for empire builders across the ages.

Early Anatolian Civilisations

The Hittites, the greatest early civilisation in Anatolia, were a force to be reckoned with from 2000 to 1200 BC, ruling their empire from their capital, Hattuşa (east of present-day Ankara). After the collapse of the Hittite empire, Anatolia splintered into small states and it wasn't until the Graeco-Roman period that parts of the country were reunited. Christianity later spread through the region, preached by the apostle Paul, who crossed Anatolia on the new Roman roads.

Rome, then Byzantium

In AD 330 the Roman emperor, Constantine, founded a new imperial city at Byzantium (İstanbul). Renamed Constantinople, it became the capital of the Eastern Roman Empire and was the centre of the Byzantine Empire for 1000 years. During the European Dark Ages, the Byzantine Empire kept alive the flame of Roman culture, although it was intermittently threatened from the east (Persians, Arabs, Turks) and west (European powers such as the Goths and Lombards).

Seljuks & Ottomans

The Byzantine Empire began to decline from 1071, when the Seljuk Turks defeated its forces at Manzikert, north of Lake Van. The Seljuks overran most of Anatolia, establishing a provincial capital at Konya. The Byzantines endeavoured to protect Constantinople and reclaim Anatolia, but during the Fourth Crusade (1202–04), which was supposedly instigated to save Eastern Christendom from the Muslims, an unruly Crusader force sacked Constantinople.

The Seljuks, meanwhile, were defeated by the Mongols at Köse Dağ in 1243. The region fractured into a mosaic of Turkish *beyliks* (principalities) and Mongol fiefdoms, but by 1300 a single Turkish bey, Osman, had established the Ottoman dynasty.

Having captured Constantinople in 1453, the Ottoman Empire reached its zenith a century later under Süleyman the Magnificent. It expanded deep into Europe, Asia and North Africa, but when its march westward stalled at Vienna in 1683, the rot set in. By the 19th century, European powers had begun to covet the Ottomans' domains.

Nationalism swept Europe after the French Revolution, and Greece, Romania, Montenegro, Serbia and Bosnia all won independence from the Ottomans. The First Balkan War removed Bulgaria and Macedonia from the Ottoman map, while Bulgarian, Greek and Serbian troops advanced on İstanbul. The empire was now known as the 'sick man of Europe'.

Republic

WWI stripped the Turks of Syria, Palestine, Mesopotamia (Iraq) and Arabia, and the victorious Europeans intended to share most of Anatolia among themselves, leaving the Turks virtually nothing.

Enter Mustafa Kemal Atatürk, the father of modern Turkey. Atatürk made his name by repelling the British and Anzac forces in their attempt to capture Gallipoli. Rallying the tattered Turkish army, he outmanoeuvred the Allied forces in the War of Independence and, in 1923, pushed the invading Greeks into the sea at Smyrna (İzmir).

After renegotiation of the WWI treaties, a new Turkish Republic, reduced to Anatolia and part of Thrace, was born. Atatürk embarked on a modernisation program, introducing a secular democracy, the Roman script, European dress and equal rights for women. The capital shifted from İstanbul to Ankara. Many of the sweeping changes did not come easily and their reverberations can still be felt today. In population exchanges with Greece, around 1.5 million Greeks left Turkey and nearly half a million Turks moved in.

Since Atatürk's death in 1938, Turkey has experienced three military coups and, during the 1980s and '90s, the government and the PKK waged a vicious conflict in the southeast over the PKK's aims to create a Kurdish state.

After a wobbly decade of weak coalition governments in the 1990s, Recep Tayyip Erdoğan's AKP won government in 2002, heralding an era of societal reforms and economic recovery.

People

Turkey has a population of almost 80 million, the great majority of whom are Muslim and Turkish. Kurds form the largest minority (numbering approximately 15 million), but there is an assortment of other groups – both Muslim and non-Muslim. Since the 1950s there has been a steady movement of people into urban areas, so today 70% of the population lives in cities. Whether urban or rural, Muslim or Christian, Turkish, Kurdish or otherwise, the peoples of Turkey tend to be family-focused, hospitable, gregarious and welcoming.

PRACTICALITIES

Electricity 230V, using the European two round-pin plug.

Security Checkpoints are common on main roads; always have your passport on hand.

Smoking Illegal in hotels, restaurants and public buildings though outside of İstanbul and major tourist areas this isn't strictly enforced.

Water Tap water is safe but due to heavy chlorination many people prefer to use bottled water.

Weights and measures Turkey uses the metric system.

Religion

Roughly 80% of the population is Sunni Muslim, however, many Turks take a relaxed approach to religious duties and practices. Islam's holy days and festivals are observed, but for many Turks Islamic holidays are the only times they'll visit a mosque. An additional 19.8% of the population are Alevi Muslims, living mainly in the east of the country.

Of the remaining 0.2%, the two most significant Christian minorities are the Armenians (formerly from Anatolia) and the Greeks (formerly spread throughout the country), though both groups now live mainly in İstanbul. A small Jewish community of around 25,000 also lives mostly in İstanbul, while a declining community of Nestorian and Assyrian Orthodox Christians is based in the southeast of the country.

Food

Kebaps and *köfte* (meatballs) in all their variations may be the mainstay of restaurant meals, but Turkish food is more complex than just grilled meat (as succulent as that grilled meat may be).

The king of cheap eats is a döner kebap (spit-roasted lamb slices) sandwich – called a *dürüm* – but pide (Turkish pizza) with both vegetarian and meat toppings, and *lahmacun* (Arabic-style pizza), which has a paper-thin base spread with a meat-and-tomato topping, come a close second.

Meze is where Turkish cuisine really comes into its own, and for vegetarians is an excellent way to ensure a varied diet. *Acılı ezme* (spicy tomato-and-onion paste), *fasulye pilaki* (white beans cooked with tomato paste and garlic), and *yaprak sarma* (vine leaves stuffed with rice, herbs and pine nuts) are just a few of the myriad meze dishes on offer.

Main dishes are usually meat-based. *Saç kavurma* (stir-fried cubed meat dishes) and *güveç* (meat and vegetable stews cooked in a terracotta pot) are just as common as kebap. Those with a sweet-tooth are in luck as Turkey outdoes itself on syrupy treats. Baklava and *lokum* (Turkish delight) are well worth chucking away your calorie-counter for.

SURVIVAL GUIDE

Directory A–Z

ACCOMMODATION

Turkey has accommodation options to suit all budgets, with concentrations of good, value-for-money hotels, pensions and hostels in places most visited by independent travellers (eg İstanbul and Cappadocia).

ESSENTIAL TURKISH FOOD & DRINK

- **Ayran** Refreshing salty yoghurt drink.
- **Baklava** Syrupy pistachio pastries, sent to tempt the weak.
- **Gözleme** Flatbread typically stuffed with cheese, spinach or potato.
- **İman Bayıldı** Slow-cooked aubergines stuffed with tomato, onion and garlic.
- **İskender kebap** Döner meat served on yoghurt-doused pide bread and drowned in a tomato and butter sauce.
- **Mantı** Teensy pasta parcels of cheese or meat smothered in tomato sauce and yoghurt.
- **Rakı** Aniseed-flavoured clear spirit that turns white when mixed with water.

Rooms are discounted by 20% to 50% during the low season (October to April; November to late March in İstanbul), but not during Christmas and Easter periods and major Islamic holidays.

Accommodation options in more Westernised spots such as İstanbul, İzmir and the coastal resorts often quote tariffs in euros; establishments in less touristy locations generally quote in lira.

DISCOUNT CARDS

The Ministry of Culture and Tourism offers various discount cards covering museums and sights. Visit www.muze.gov.tr/en/museum-card for more information.Two of the most useful:

Museum Pass: İstanbul The five-day card (₺85) offers a possible ₺165 saving on entry to the city's major sights, including Aya Sofya, and allows holders to skip admission queues.

Museum Pass: Cappadocia The three-day card (₺45) covers the major sights including Göreme Open-Air Museum, offering a possible ₺98 saving.

EMBASSIES & CONSULATES

Embassies are in Ankara.

Australian Embassy (☎ for initial appointment 0312-459 9500; www.turkey.embassy.gov.au; 7th fl, MNG Bldg, Uğur Mumcu Caddesi 88, Gaziosmanpaşa; ⊙8.30am-4.45pm Mon-Fri)

Azerbaijani Embassy (☎0312-491 1681; http://ankara.mfa.gov.az; Diplomatik Site, Bakü Sokak 1, Oran; ⊙9am-noon & 4-5pm Mon-Fri)

Bulgarian Embassy (☎0312-467 2071; www.mfa.bg/embassies/turkey; Atatürk Bulvarı 124, Kavaklıdere; ⊙9am-noon Mon-Fri)

Canadian Embassy (☎0312-409 2700; http://turkey.gc.ca; Cinnah Caddesi 58, Çankaya; ⊙8am-noon & 12.30-4.45pm Mon-Thu, 8am-12.30pm Fri)

Dutch Embassy (☎0312-409 1800; www.hollandavesen.nl; Hollanda Caddesi 5, off Turan Güneş Bulvarı; ⊙8.30am-4pm Mon-Fri)

French Embassy (☎0312-455 4545; www.ambafrance-tr.org; Paris Caddesi 70, Kavaklıdere; ⊙9am-4pm Mon-Fri)

Georgian Embassy (☎0312-491 8030; www.turkey.mfa.gov.ge; Diplomatik Site, Kılıç Ali Sokak 12, Oran; ⊙9am-noon Mon-Fri)

German Embassy (☎0312-455 5100; www.ankara.diplo.de; Atatürk Bulvarı 114, Kavaklıdere; ⊙9am-4pm Mon-Thu, 9am-2pm Fri)

Greek Embassy (☎0312-448 0647; www.mfa.gr/ankara; Zia Ür Rahman Caddesi 9-11, Gaziosmanpaşa; ⊙9am-2pm Mon-Fri)

Iranian Embassy (☎0312-468 2821; http://iranembassy-tr.ir; Tahran Caddesi 10, Kavaklıdere; ⊙8.30am-noon Mon-Fri)

ℹ SLEEPING PRICE RANGES

Ranges are based on the cost of a double room in high season.

İstanbul, İzmir & Bodrum Peninsula

$ less than €80

$$ €80–180

$$$ more than €180

Rest of Turkey

$ less than €25

$$ €26–60

$$$ more than €60

Iraqi Embassy (☎0312-468 7421; www.mofamission.gov.iq; Turan Emeksiz Sokak 11, Gaziosmanpaşa; ⊙9am-noon Mon-Fri)

Irish Embassy (☎ for initial appointment 0312-459 1000; www.embassyofireland.org.tr; 1st fl, MNG Bldg, Uğur Mumcu Caddesi 88, Gaziosmanpaşa; ⊙9am-1pm & 2-5pm Mon-Fri)

New Zealand Embassy (☎0312-446 3333; www.nzembassy.com/turkey; Kizkulesi Sokak 11, Gaziosmanpaşa; ⊙8.30am-5pm Mon-Fri)

Russian Embassy (☎0312-439 2122; www.turkey.mid.ru; Karyağdı Sokak 5, Çankaya; ⊙9.30am-noon Mon, Wed & Fri)

UK Embassy (☎0312-455 3344; www.gov.uk/world/turkey; Şehit Ersan Caddesi 46a, Çankaya; ⊙8.45am-5pm Mon-Fri)

US Embassy (☎ for initial appointment 0312-455 5555; https://tr.usembassy.gov; Atatürk Bulvarı 110, Kavaklıdere; ⊙9am-4pm Mon-Fri)

GAY & LESBIAN TRAVELLERS

Homosexuality is not a criminal offence in Turkey, but prejudice remains strong and there are sporadic reports of violence towards gay people – the message is discretion.

İstanbul has a flourishing gay scene, as does Ankara. For more on the challenges facing LGBT people in Turkey, visit www.outrightinternational.org/region/turkey.

BHN Mavi Tours (www.turkey-gay-travel.com) Gay-friendly İstanbul travel agent, with useful links on its website.

Kaos GL (www.kaosgl.com) Based in Ankara, the LGBT rights organisation publishes a gay-and-lesbian magazine and its website has news and information in English.

MONEY

Turkey's currency is the Türk lirası (Turkish lira; ₺). The lira comes in notes of five, 10, 20, 50, 100 and 200, and coins of five, 10, 25 and 50 kuruş and one lira.

EATING PRICE RANGES

Price ranges reflect the cost of a standard main-course dish.

$ less than ₺25

$$ ₺25–40

$$$ more than ₺40

ATMs

ATMs dispense Turkish lira, and occasionally euros and US dollars. Machines generally offer instructions in foreign languages including English.

It's possible to get around Turkey using only ATMs if you draw out money in the towns to tide you through the villages that don't have them.

Credit Cards

Visa and MasterCard are widely accepted by hotels, shops and restaurants, although often not by pensions and local restaurants outside the main tourist areas.

Moneychangers

The Turkish lira is weak against Western currencies, and you will probably get a better exchange rate in Turkey than elsewhere. US dollars and euros are the easiest currencies to change.

Tipping

- **Hotel porter** €2 per bag (mid-range hotel), €5 per bag (top-end hotel).
- **Restaurants** A few coins in budget eateries; 10% of the bill in midrange and top-end establishments.
- **Taxis** Round up metered fares to the nearest lira.

OPENING HOURS

The following are standard opening hours.

Bars 4pm-late

Government departments, offices and banks 8.30am-noon and 1.30-5pm Monday to Friday

Nightclubs 11pm-late

Restaurants 11am-10pm

Shops 9am-6pm Monday to Friday (longer in tourist areas and big cities – including weekend opening)

Tourist information 9am-12.30pm and 1.30-5pm Monday to Friday

PUBLIC HOLIDAYS

New Year's Day (Yılbaşı) 1 January

National Sovereignty & Children's Day (Ulusal Egemenlik ve Çocuk Günü) 23 April

Labor & Solidarity Day (May Day) 1 May

Commemoration of Atatürk, Youth & Sports Day (Gençlik ve Spor Günü) 19 May

Şeker Bayramı (Sweets Holiday) See Eid Al Fitr (p568)

Democracy and National Solidarity Day 15 July

Victory Day (Zafer Bayramı) 30 August

Kurban Bayramı (Festival of the Sacrifice) See Eid Al Adha (p568)

Republic Day (Cumhuriyet Bayramı) 29 October

SAFE TRAVEL

Although Turkey is by no means a dangerous country to visit, it's always wise to be a little cautious.

Despite the terrorist attacks in 2016, the likelihood of being caught in such incidents remains small. Coastal resorts have not been targeted to date, and, although attacks have hit İstanbul and Ankara, the usual targets are government and military installations or convoys.

Currently most government travel advisories warn against all travel within 10km of the Syrian border and issue cautionary advise on travelling within southeastern Anatolia.

Marches and demonstrations are a regular occurrence in Turkish cities, especially İstanbul. These are best avoided as they can lead to clashes with the police.

Be aware of cultural differences, for example the lese-majesty rule about not insulting the Turkish Republic.

TELEPHONE

Turkey's country code	90
International access code from Turkey	00
Ambulance	112
Fire	110
Police	155

Mobile Phones

If your mobile (cell) phone is unlocked, you can purchase a prepaid SIM card (SIM *kart*). Local SIMs will work in a foreign mobile for 120 days. After that period, the networks detect and bar the phone. For longer stays, you need to register your phone within a month of arrival.

There are three major networks: Turkcell (www.turkcell.com.tr), Vodafone (www.vodafone.com.tr) and Türk Telekom (www.turktelekom.com.tr). SIM cards and *kontör* (credit) are widely available – at kiosks and shops as well as mobile phone outlets. You will need your passport to purchase a SIM.

SIM cards cost around ₺85 (including ₺30 in local call credit). An internet data pack with the SIM will cost around ₺25/30/40/60 for 1/2/4/8 GB.

TIME

Turkey is on Eastern European Summer Time all year round (GMT/UTC plus three hours).

VISAS

For stays of up to 90 days nationals of countries including Denmark, Finland, France, Germany, Greece, Israel, Italy, Japan, New Zealand, Sweden and Switzerland don't need a visa to visit Turkey. Most other Western nationalities should purchase an e-visa in advance from www.evisa.gov.tr.

 Getting There & Away

Land borders with Bulgaria and Greece funnel visitors through to Asia via İstanbul, while ferry services link the Mediterranean's coastal cities and resorts with nearby Greek islands. In the east, Hopa is the gateway to Georgia and the rest of the Caucasus, Doğubayazıt is the last major centre before the Gürbulak crossing into Iran, and Silopi has taxi services to Iraqi Kurdistan. There are frequent, and well-priced, flights to Lebanon and Egypt (and not so well-priced ones to Jordan) from İstanbul.

AIR

The main international airports:

Atatürk International Airport (p433) İstanbul's main airport.

Sabiha Gökçen International Airport (p433) On İstanbul's Asian side; popular with low-cost European airlines.

Antalya International Airport (p467) Receives flights from across Europe.

Adnan Menderes Airport (p445) Many European services use İzmir's airport.

Milas-Bodrum Airport (BJV; ☎444 9828; www.milas-bodrumairport.com) Mainly charter flights and budget airlines.

Dalaman International Airport (☎0252-792 5555; www.dalaman.dhmi.gov.tr) Seasonal flights from many European cities.

Esenboğa Airport (☎0312-590 4000; www.esenbogaairport.com; Özal Bulvarı, Balıkhisar) Good international connections although İstanbul's airports offer more choice.

LAND

Due to the current conflict, attempting to cross into Syria cannot be recommended – and is downright dangerous.

Iran

Gürbulak–Bazargan This busy post, 35km southeast of Doğubayazıt (Turkey), is open 24 hours. There are regular dolmuşes from Doğubayazıt.

Esendere–Sero Southeast of Van, this road crossing was not recommended for security reasons at the time of research.

Iraq

Between Silopi (Turkey) and Zahko (Kurdish Iraq), there's no town or village at the **Habur–Ibrahim al-Khalil crossing**.

A taxi from Silopi to Zakho costs between US$50 and US$70. Border formalities can take longer than an hour. Your driver will manoeuvre through a maze of checkpoints and handle the paperwork. Coming into Turkey, watch out for taxi drivers slipping contraband into your bag.

There are five direct buses daily, run by Can Diyarbakır Turizm, from Diyarbakır, and three from Batman, to Dohuk (₺70, six hours) or Erbil (₺80, nine hours) in Kurdish Iraq.

Note that currently most Western governments issue warnings against all travel to Diyarbakır and cautionary advisories against travelling in southeastern Anatolia and crossing the Iraqi border. This situation is unlikely to change in the near future.

 Getting Around

AIR

Domestic flights are a good option in such a large country, and competition between the airlines keeps tickets affordable. Turkey's domestic airlines:

Anadolu Jet (☎444 2538; www.anadolujet.com/tr)

Atlasglobal (☎0850-222 0000; www.atlasglb.com/en)

Onur Air (☎0850-210 6687; www.onurair.com.tr)

Pegasus Airlines (☎0888-228 1212; www.flypgs.com/en)

 BORDER CROSSINGS

Turkey shares borders with Armenia, Azerbaijan, Bulgaria, Georgia, Greece, Iran, Iraq and Syria. The land border with Armenia remains closed.

Turkey's relationships with most of its neighbours tend to be tense, which can affect when and where you can cross. Check for the most up-to-date information; sources of information include Lonely Planet's Thorn Tree forum (www.lonelyplanet.com/thorntree), your embassy in Turkey and the Turkish embassy in your country.

Border procedures can often be long and frustrating with baggage checks on both sides of the border regardless of the country.

Sun Express (☎444 0797; www.sunexpress.com)

Turkish Airlines (☎1800-874 8875; www.turkishairlines.com)

BUS

Turkey's intercity bus system is as good as any you'll find, with modern, comfortable coaches crossing the country at all hours and for very reasonable prices. On the journey, you'll be treated to hot drinks and snacks.

A town's otogar (bus station) is often on the outskirts, but bigger bus companies often have free *servises* (shuttle buses) to ferry you into the centre and back again. Major bus companies with extensive route networks include **Kamil Koç** (☎444 0562; www.kamilkoc.com.tr), **Metro Turizm** (☎0850-222 3455; www.metroturizm.com.tr) and **Ulusoy** (☎0850-811 1888; www.ulusoy.com.tr).

DOLMUŞ

These privately owned minibuses run between small towns and villages (as well as providing transport within cities and towns). Most dolmuşes depart on set schedules, but in a few places they wait until every seat is taken. On dolmuş routes between towns, you can flag one down anywhere along the route. To let the driver know that you want to hop out, say *'inecek var'* (someone wants to get out).

CAR

Driving Licence

An international driving permit (IDP) may be useful if your licence is from a country likely to seem obscure to a Turkish police officer.

Fuel

Turkey has the world's second-highest petrol prices. Petrol/diesel cost about ₺5.30 per litre.

Hire

You need to be at least 21 years old, with a year's driving experience, to hire a car in Turkey. Most car-hire companies require a credit card. Most hire cars have standard (manual) transmission; you'll pay more for automatic. The majority of the big-name companies charge hefty one-way fees. Stick to the major companies, as the local agencies often do not have insurance.

Insurance

You must have international insurance, covering third-party damage, if you are bringing your own car into the country (further information is available at www.turing.org.tr/international-traffic-insurance-greencard/). Buying it at the border is a straightforward process (one month car/motorcycle €65.62/52.50).

Road Rules & Safety

Maximum speed limits, unless otherwise posted, are 50km/h in towns, 90km/h on highways and 120km/h on *otoyols* (freeways).

Road accidents claim about 10,000 lives each year. To survive on Turkey's roads:

- Drive cautiously and defensively.
- Do not expect your fellow motorists to obey road signs or use indicators.
- Avoid driving at night, when you won't be able to see potholes, animals, or even vehicles driving without lights, with lights missing, or stopped in the middle of the road. Drivers sometimes flash their lights to announce their approach.

TRAIN

The **Turkish State Railways** (TCDD; www.tcdd.gov.tr) network covers the country fairly well, with the notable exception of the coastlines.

The following are useful routes for travellers:

High-speed routes:

İstanbul Pendik–Eskişehir–Ankara

İstanbul Pendik–Eskişehir–Konya

Ankara–Konya

Other routes:

İzmir–Selçuk–Aydın–Denizli

İstanbul Pendik–Eskişehir–Denizli

Eskişehir–İzmir

İzmir–Afyon–Konya

Kayseri–Sivas–Erzurum–Kars

Understand the Middle East

THE MIDDLE EAST TODAY **494**

The Middle East is in turmoil, caught between peace and conflict like never before. We tell you how and why.

HISTORY **496**

Join us on a journey at this crossroads of cultures, from ancient civilisations to the Arab Spring.

RELIGION **526**

We explore the three great monotheistic faiths – Judaism, Christianity and Islam – which were all born in the Middle East.

ARCHITECTURE **531**

Pyramids, mosques and everything in between – we give you the lowdown on the region's human-made structures.

MIDDLE EASTERN CUISINE **536**

Our comprehensive guide takes you on a delicious journey through the kitchens of the Middle East.

THE ARTS **543**

We delve into the Middle East's rich artistic heritage, from cinema to books and music.

LANDSCAPE & ENVIRONMENT **552**

We cover the signature Middle Eastern landforms and the region's most pressing environmental issues.

The Middle East Today

For a region with a reputation for being so volatile, remarkably little changes when it comes to the bigger picture. War continues in Syria and in parts of Iraq, Israel and the Palestinians seem as far away from a peaceful resolution as ever, while Iran continues to be everyone's favourite bogeyman. Turkey has experienced more turmoil than it has become used to, but remains essentially stable, as does Jordan, while Egypt and Lebanon are at peace, if only just.

Best on Film

Lawrence of Arabia (1962) Evokes the complicated, early-20th-century Middle East.

Once Upon a Time in Anatolia (2011) Acclaimed evocation of the Turkish soul and steppe.

A Separation (2011) Oscar-winning film that portrays the angst of modern Iran.

Omar (2014) Oscar-nominated film about the fatal entwining of Palestinians and Israelis.

Queen of the Desert (2015) Hollywood portrait of Gertrude Bell touches on issues of gender, landscape and the colonial Middle East.

Best in Print

The Innocents Abroad (Mark Twain; 1869) Still many people's favourite travel book about the region, 150 years later.

The Thousand and One Nights Resonates with all the allure and magic of the Middle East.

No Knives in the Kitchens of This City (Khaled Khalifa; 2016) Aleppo at war provides a backdrop to a family facing its own disintegration.

Arab Spring Then and Now: From Hope to Despair (Robert Fisk & Patrick Cockburn; 2017) The state of the Middle East by two of its most respected journalists.

Iran Rising

Iran always seems to be in the news these days, whether looming large over President Trump's election campaign and subsequent foreign policy rhetoric, or using its influence in Syria, Iraq, Bahrain and Saudi Arabia to back up its claims to being a regional political player; the impasse between Qatar and its Gulf neighbours in 2017 owed much to Iran's perceived meddling in regional affairs. At one level, Iran's hand was forced by Isis's deliberate targeting of Shiite communities as apostates, prompting the Islamic Republic to position itself as the protector of and advocate for Shiites across the region. At the same time, it is a role that Iran appears more than happy to play, building on its close historical ties with Hezbollah in Lebanon and the Assad government in Syria. So complicated were things in Iraq for a time that US troops were essentially fighting on the same side as Iranian advisors in the 2017 battle for Mosul. Whether such realpolitik survives once the common enemy has been defeated remains to be seen.

The Bad News

Sadly, there is bad news in abundance in the Middle East. Syria is nothing short of a catastrophe with no end in sight, while Iraq always seems to be at war with itself; the utter devastation wrought upon Mosul and the wholesale persecution of religious minorities in the country – Iraqi Christians, the Yazidis – have been epic in scale, threatening communities with ancient roots in the soil of the country. Elsewhere, the democratic spark seems to have gone out in Egypt as a price for stability, while Israelis and Palestinians continue to stare out across the barbed wire and increasingly high walls with the same level of mutual incomprehension that they have had for more than 60 years – peace conferences no longer even happen. Lebanon, too, remains fragile, its border regions off-limits, its resources and infrastructure strained by the presence of more than one million refugees from the conflict in Syria.

The Good News

The Middle East may be a tough neighbourhood, but it's not all doom and gloom – although sadly, good news stories rarely make the headlines. One of those delightfully boring headlines could read: 'Another Peaceful Day in Jordan'. Despite extraordinary challenges – around 600,000 refugees, wars on its northern and eastern borders, and a population sometimes impatient for change – Jordan goes quietly about its business, at peace and moderately prosperous. For all its critics, Israel is a dynamic, multicultural country whose urban spaces, Tel Aviv in particular, are transforming into some of the most happening places in the Mediterranean. Turkey, too, seems well equipped to deal with the robust domestic and international challenges to its stability. And while they may have their problems, Lebanon and Egypt remain at relative peace, despite constant and sometimes seemingly existential threats.

Turkey in Turmoil

Few leaders in the Middle East have quite the same power to influence events as Turkey's president, Recep Tayyip Erdoğan. Close to the summit of Turkish politics since 2003, he has struck a difficult balance between Islamic principles and Turkey's secular democratic system. However, his largely unassailable popularity has taken a battering in recent times. Large-scale protests in 2013 and a failed coup attempt in July 2016 have prompted media crackdowns and, in the aftermath of the 2016 coup attempt, widespread arrests and targeting of political opponents. Added to these domestic difficulties are the spillover consequences of the war in neighbouring Syria, with around 800,000 refugees having fled to Turkey, placing extraordinary strain on the country's resources. The state's troubled relationship with its Kurdish population has been further complicated by the prominent role (often backed by the US and its allies) played by Kurdish militias in Syria and Iraq. That Turkey remains stable and democratic is admirable considering the pressures. But for the first time in a while, the strain is showing.

AREA: **4,183,436 SQ KM**

POPULATION: **340.13 MILLION**

LANGUAGES SPOKEN: **ARABIC, FARSI, HEBREW AND TURKISH; ENGLISH AND FRENCH WIDELY SPOKEN**

if Middle East were 100 people

48 would be Arab
22 would be Persian
19 would be Turkish
8 would be Kurds
2 would be Jewish
1 would be other

belief systems

(% of population)

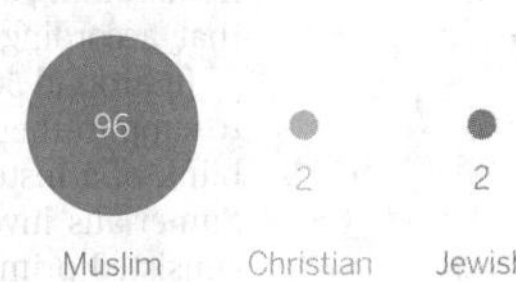

population per sq km

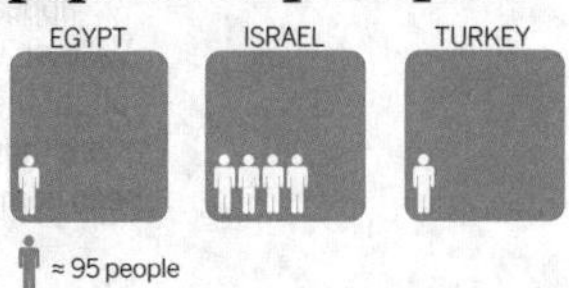

History

The Middle East *is* history, home to a roll call of some of the most important landmarks ever built. Mesopotamia (now Iraq) was the undisputed cradle of civilisation. Damascus (Syria), Aleppo (Syria), Byblos (Lebanon), Jericho (Israel and the Palestinian Territories) and Erbil (Iraq) all stake compelling claims to be the oldest continuously inhabited cities on earth. And it was here in the Middle East that the three great monotheistic religions – Judaism, Christianity and Islam – were born.

Ancient Middle East

Cradle of Civilisation

The Great Pyramid of Khufu (built in 2570 BC) remained the tallest human-built structure in the world until the building of the Eiffel Tower in 1889.

The first human beings to walk the earth did just that: they walked. In their endless search for sustenance and shelter, they roamed the earth, hunting, foraging plants for food and erecting makeshift shelters as they went. The world's first nomads, they carried what they needed; most likely they lived in perfect harmony with nature and left next to nothing behind for future generations to write their story.

The first signs of agriculture, arguably the first major signpost along the march of human history, grew from the soils surrounding Jericho in what is now the Palestinian Territories, around 8500 BC. Forced by a drying climate and the need to cluster around known water sources, these early Middle Easterners added wild cereals to their diet and learned to farm them. In the centuries that followed, these and other farming communities spread east into Mesopotamia (a name later given by the Greeks, meaning 'Between Two Rivers'), where the fertile soils of the Tigris and Euphrates floodplains were ideally suited to the new endeavour. For some historians, this was a homecoming of sorts for humankind: these two rivers are among the four that, according to the Bible, flowed into the Garden of Eden.

In around 5000 BC, the Sumerians became the first to build cities and to support them with year-round agriculture and river-borne trade. In the blink of a historical eye, although almost 2000 years later in reality, the Sumerians invented the first known form of writing: cuneiform, which consisted primarily of pictographs and would later evolve into alphabets on which some modern writing systems are based. With agriculture and writing mastered, the world's first civilisation had been born.

TIMELINE

250,000 BC

The earliest traces of human presence appear in the Nile Valley. Little is known about them, but they are thought to have been nomadic hunter-gatherers.

5000 BC

Al Ubaid culture, the forerunner to the great civilisations that would earn Mesopotamia (now Iraq) the sobriquet of the cradle of civilisation, rises between the Tigris and Euphrates rivers.

4000 BC

The Sumerian civilisation takes hold in Mesopotamia. They would rule the region until the 24th century BC and invent cuneiform, the world's first writing.

Elsewhere across the region, in around 3100 BC, the kingdoms of Upper and Lower Egypt were unified under Menes, ushering in 3000 years of Pharaonic rule in the Nile Valley.

Birth of Empire

The moment in history when civilisations evolved into empires is unclear, but by the 3rd century BC, the kings of what we now know as the Middle East had heard the fragmented news brought by traders of fabulous riches just beyond the horizon.

The Sumerians, who were no doubt rather pleased with themselves for having tamed agriculture and invented writing, never saw the Akkadians coming. One of many city-states that fell within the Sumerian realm, Akkad, on the banks of the Euphrates southwest of modern Baghdad, had grown in power, and, in the late 24th and early 23rd centuries BC, Sargon of Akkad conquered Mesopotamia and then extended his rule over much of the Levant. The era of empire, which would convulse the region almost until the present day, had begun.

Although the Akkadian Empire would last no more than a century, Sargon's idea caught on. The at-once sophisticated and war-like Assyrians, whose empire would, from their capital at Nineveh (Iraq), later encompass the entire Middle East, were the most enduring power. Along with their perennial Mesopotamian rivals, the Babylonians, the Assyrians would dominate the human history of the region for almost 1000 years.

The 7th century BC saw the conquest of Egypt by Assyria and, far to the east, the rise of the Medes. In 550 BC the Medes were conquered by Cyrus the Great, widely regarded as the first Persian shah (king). In the 7th century BC the king of one of the Persian tribes, Achaemenes, created a unified state in southern Iran, giving his name to what would become the First Persian Empire, the Achaemenids. His 21-year-old great-grandson Cyrus II ascended the throne in 559 BC, and within 20 years it would be the greatest empire the world had known up until that time.

Having rapidly built a mighty military force, Cyrus the Great (as he came to be known) ended the Median Empire in 550 BC. Within 11 years, Cyrus had campaigned his way across much of what is now Turkey, east into modern Pakistan, and finally defeated the Babylonians. It was in the aftermath of this victory in 539 BC that Cyrus established a reputation as a benevolent conqueror. Over the next 60 years Cyrus and his successors, Cambyses (r 525–522 BC) and Darius I (r 521–486 BC), battled with the Greeks for control over Babylon, Egypt, Asia Minor and parts of Greece.

Egypt won independence from the Persians in 401 BC, only to be reconquered 60 years later. The second Persian occupation of Egypt was brief: little more than a decade after they arrived, the Persians were again driven out of Egypt, this time by the Greeks. Europe had arrived on the scene and held sway in some form for almost 1000 years until the birth of Islam.

The Cyrus Cylinder, which is housed at the British Museum with a replica at the UN, is a clay tablet with cuneiform inscriptions, and is widely considered to be the world's first charter of human rights.

The Epic of Gilgamesh, written in 2700 BC and one of the first works of world literature, tells the story of a Sumerian king from the ancient city of Uruk (which gave Iraq its name).

3100 BC
Menes unites the kingdoms of Upper and Lower Egypt. Thus begins one of the great civilisations of antiquity, the ancient Egypt of the pharaohs, who would rule for almost 3000 years.

2400 BC
Sargon of Akkad, ruler of the city-state of Akkad in Sumerian Mesopotamia, conquers the region, taking much of what we now know as the Levant.

1800 BC
According to the Book of Genesis, Abraham, the great patriarch of the Jewish faith and prophet in both Christianity and Islam, is born in Ur of the Chaldees in Mesopotamia.

1750 BC
The Babylonian kingdoms are first united under Hammurabi, creating the capital, the Hanging Gardens of Babylon. They would rule the Tigris–Euphrates region for more than 500 years.

PHOENICIANS

The ancient Phoenician Empire (1500–300 BC), which thrived along the Lebanese coast, may have been the world's first rulers of the sea. Their empire was the Mediterranean Sea and its ports, and their lasting legacy was to spread the early gains of Middle Eastern civilisation to the rest of the world.

An offshoot of the Canaanites in the Levant, the Phoenicians first established themselves in the (now Lebanese) ports of Tyre and Saida. Quick to realise that there was money to be made across the waters, they cast off in their galleys, launching in the process the first era of true globalisation. From the unlikely success of selling purple dye and sea snails to the Greeks, they expanded their repertoire to include copper from Cyprus, silver from Iberia and even tin from Great Britain.

As their reach expanded, so too did the Phoenicians' need for safe ports around the Mediterranean rim. Thus it was that Carthage, one of the greatest cities of the ancient world, was founded in what is now Tunisia in 814 BC. Long politically dependent on the mother culture in Tyre, Carthage eventually emerged as an independent, commercial empire. By 517 BC the powerful city-state was the leading city of North Africa, and by the 4th century BC Carthage controlled the North African coast from Libya to the Atlantic.

But the nascent Roman Empire didn't take kindly to these Lebanese upstarts effectively controlling the waters of the Mediterranean Sea, and challenged them both militarily and with economic blockades. With Tyre and Saida themselves severely weakened and unable to send help, Carthage took on Rome and lost, badly. The Punic Wars (Phoenician civilisation in North Africa was called 'Punic') between Carthage and Rome (264–241 BC, 218–201 BC and 149–146 BC) reduced Carthage, the last outpost of Phoenician power, to a small, vulnerable African state. It was razed by the Romans in 146 BC, the site symbolically sprinkled with salt and damned forever.

Greeks

The definition of which territories constitute 'the Middle East' has always been a fluid concept. Some cultural geographers claim that the Middle East includes all countries of the Arab world as far west as Morocco. But most historians agree that the Middle East's eastern boundaries were determined by the Greeks in the 4th century BC.

In 336 BC Philip II of Macedon, a warlord who had conquered much of mainland Greece, was murdered. His son Alexander assumed the throne and began a series of conquests that would eventually encompass most of Asia Minor, the Middle East, Persia and northern India. Under Alexander, the Greeks were the first to impose any kind of order on the Middle East as a whole. In 331 BC, just five years after taking control, Alexander the Great's armies swept into what is now Libya. Greek rule extended as far east as what is now the Libyan city of Benghazi, beyond which the Romans

1600–609 BC

The Assyrian Empire rules from its capital at Nineveh (present-day Iraq) over a territory that reaches as far as Egypt. Its heyday is around 900 BC.

1500 BC

The Phoenicians set out to conquer the waters of the Mediterranean from their base in Tyre and Saida (modern-day Lebanon). They rule the seas for 1200 years.

15th century BC

Hieroglyphic tablets make reference to a city called 'Dimashqa', conquered by the Egyptians. It's the first written record of a city that may date back to 3000 BC.

663 BC

After a series of military and diplomatic confrontations, Ashurbanipal, King of the Assyrians, attacks Egypt, sacks Thebes and loots the Temple of Amun.

would hold sway. Ever since, the unofficial but widely agreed place where the Middle East begins and ends has been held to be Cyrenaica in Libya.

Upon Alexander's death in 323 BC, his empire was promptly carved up among his generals. This resulted in the founding of three new ruling dynasties: the Antigonids in Greece and Asia Minor; the Ptolemaic dynasty in Egypt; and the Seleucids. The Seleucids controlled the swath of land running from modern Israel and Lebanon through Mesopotamia to Persia.

But, this being the Middle East, peace remained elusive. Having finished off a host of lesser competitors, the heirs to Alexander's empire then proceeded to fight each other. It took an army arriving from the west to again reunite the lands of the east – this time in the shape of the legions of Rome.

Under Ptolemaic patronage and with access to a library of 700,000 written works, scholars in Alexandria calculated the earth's circumference, discovered it circles the sun and wrote the definitive edition of Homer's work.

Pax Romana

Even for a region accustomed to living under occupation, the news of massed, disciplined ranks of Roman legions marching down across the plains of central Anatolia must have struck fear into the hearts of people across the Middle East. But this was a region in disarray and the Romans chose their historical moment perfectly.

Rome's legionaries conquered most of Asia Minor (most of Turkey) in 188 BC. Syria and Palestine soon fell, if not without a fight then without too much difficulty. When Cleopatra of Egypt, the last of the Ptolemaic dynasty, was defeated in 31 BC, the Romans controlled the entire Mediterranean world. Only the Sassanids in Persia held Rome at bay.

Foreign occupiers they may have been, but the Romans brought much-needed stability and even a degree of prosperity to the region. Roman goods flooded into Middle Eastern markets, improving living standards in a region that had long ago lost its title as the centre of the world's sophistication. New methods of agriculture increased productivity across the region and the largely peaceful Roman territories allowed the export of local products to the great markets of Rome. Olive trees, with their origins in Turkey and the Levant, were, like the oilfields of today, a lucrative product, with insatiable demand in Rome driving previously unimaginable growth for local Middle Eastern economies.

What the Mesopotamians began with their city-states, the Romans perfected in the extravagant cities that they built to glorify the empire but which also provided new levels of comfort for local inhabitants. Their construction or development of earlier Phoenician and Greek settlements at Ephesus, Palmyra, Baalbek and Jerash announced that the Romans intended to stay.

Five out of the Seven Wonders of the Ancient World were within the boundaries of the modern Middle East: the Temple of Artemis (Turkey), the Mausoleum of Halicarnassus (Turkey), the Hanging Gardens of Babylon (Iraq), Pharos of Alexandria (Egypt) and the Pyramids of Giza (Egypt).

Jewish Revolt

So was the Roman Middle East a utopia? Well, not exactly. As just about any foreign power has failed to learn right up to the 21st century, Middle Easterners don't take kindly to promises of wealth in exchange for

586 BC

Babylonia's King Nebuchadnezzar marches on Jerusalem, destroys the Jewish temple and carries the Jewish elite and many of their subjects into Mesopotamian exile.

550 BC

Cyrus the Great forms one of the ancient world's most enlightened empires in Persia, known for its tolerance and the freedoms granted to its subjects.

536 BC

Cyrus the Great overruns Babylon, frees the Jewish exiles and helps them to return home to Jerusalem, complete with funds to rebuild the temple.

525 BC

The Persian king Cambyses conquers Egypt, rules as pharaoh and then disappears with his army in the Saharan sands as he marches on Siwa.

ALEXANDER THE GREAT

One of the greatest figures to ever stride the Middle Eastern stage, Alexander (356–323 BC) was born into greatness. His father was King Philip II of Macedon, who many people believed was a descendant of the god Hercules, and his mother was Princess Olympias of Epirus, who counted the legendary Achilles among her ancestors. For his part, the precocious young Alexander sometimes claimed that Zeus was his real father.

Alexander was the ultimate alpha male, as well versed in poetry as in the ways of war. At the age of 12, the young Alexander tamed Bucephalus, a horse that the most accomplished horsemen of Macedonia dared not ride. By 13, he had Aristotle as his personal tutor. His interests were diverse: he could play the lyre, learned Homer's *Iliad* by heart and admired the Persian ruler Cyrus the Great for the respect he granted to the cultures he conquered.

He rode out of Macedonia in 334 BC to embark on a decade-long campaign of conquest and exploration. His first great victory was against the Persians at Issus in what is now southeast Turkey. He swept south, conquering Phoenician seaports and thence into Egypt where he founded the Mediterranean city that still bears his name. In 331 BC the armies of Alexander the Great made a triumphant entrance into Cyrenaica. After the Oracle of Ammon in Siwa promised Alexander that he would indeed conquer the world, he returned north, heading for Babylon. Crossing the Tigris and the Euphrates, he defeated another Persian army before driving his troops up into Central Asia and northern India. Eventually fatigue and disease brought the drive to a halt and the Greeks turned around and headed back home. En route, Alexander succumbed to illness (some say he was poisoned) and died at the tender age of 33 in Babylon. The whereabouts of his body and tomb remain unknown.

In 333 BC, Persian Emperor Darius III, facing defeat by Alexander, abandoned his wife, children and mother on the battlefield. His mother was so disgusted she disowned him and adopted Alexander as her son.

sovereignty. The Jews living in Palestine in particular found themselves stripped of political power and operating in an ever-diminishing space of religious and economic freedom. By the middle of the 1st century AD, Jews across the Roman Empire had had enough. Primary among their grievances were punitive taxes, the Roman decision to appoint Jewish high priests and the not-inconsiderable blasphemy of Emperor Caligula's decision in AD 39 to declare himself a deity. Anti-Roman sentiment had been bubbling away for three decades, in part because of one rebellious orator – Jesus of Nazareth – and due also to a Jewish sect called the Zealots, whose creed stated that all means were justified to liberate the Jews.

Led by the Zealots, the Jews of Jerusalem destroyed a small Roman garrison in the Holy City in AD 66. Infighting within the revolt and the burning of food stockpiles to force wavering Jews to participate had disastrous consequences. Jerusalem was razed to the ground and up to 100,000 Jews were killed in retaliation; some Jewish historians claim that the number of dead over the four years of the revolt reached a million.

The failed uprising and the brutal Roman response (which came to be known as the First Jewish-Roman War) would have consequences that

334 BC

A youthful Alexander the Great of Macedonia marches out of Greece and doesn't stop until a vast empire stretching from Libya to India is within his grasp.

323 BC

Alexander the Great dies aged just 33. His empire is carved up among his generals: the Antigonids (Greece and Asia Minor); the Ptolemaic dynasty (Egypt); and the Seleucids (everywhere else).

3rd century BC

The Nabataeans build their rock-hewn fortress of Petra and hold out against the Romans until AD 106, through entrepreneurial guile, military might and carefully negotiated treaties.

188 BC

The massed ranks of the Roman legionnaires conquer Asia Minor (Turkey) and then continue south sweeping all before them. The Romans would rule the Middle East in some form for more than six centuries.

have rippled down through the centuries. Jerusalem was rebuilt as a Roman city and the Jews were sent into exile (which, for many Jews, ended only with the creation of the State of Israel in 1948). Few people in the Middle East dared to challenge the Romans after that.

Byzantines

In AD 331 the newly converted Emperor Constantine declared Christianity the official religion of the 'Holy Roman Empire', with its capital not jaded, cynical Rome but the newly renamed city of Constantinople (formerly Byzantium, later to become İstanbul). Constantinople reached its apogee during the reign of Justinian (AD 527–65), when the Byzantine Empire consolidated its hold on the eastern Mediterranean.

But the Byzantine (or Eastern Roman) Empire, as it became known, would soon learn a harsh lesson that the Ottomans (ruling from the same city) would later fail to heed. Spread too thinly by controlling vast reaches of the earth and riven with divisions at home, they were vulnerable to the single most enduring historic power in Middle Eastern history, stirring in the deserts of Arabia: Islam.

The Court of the Caliphs (Hugh Kennedy; 2004) is the best account of Abbasid Baghdad in its prime, blending careful scholarship and Arab sources with a lively and compelling style.

Islamic Middle East

Arrival & Spread of Islam

No one in sophisticated Constantinople, an opulent city accustomed to the trappings of world power, could have imagined that the greatest threat to their rule would come from a small oasis community in the desert wastes of Arabia. The Byzantines, it is true, were besieged in their coastal forts of the southern Mediterranean, their power extending scarcely at all into the hinterland. And the Sassanid empire to the east was constantly chipping away at poorly defended Byzantine holdings. But there was little to suggest to the heirs of the Roman domain that these were anything more than minor skirmishes on the outer reaches of their empire.

In the 7th century AD, southern Arabia lay beyond the reach of both the Byzantines and the Sassanids. The cost and difficulty of occupying the Arabian Peninsula simply wasn't worth the effort, home as it was only to troublesome nomads and isolated oases. Thus it was that when, far from the great centres of power, in the nondescript town of Mecca (now in Saudi Arabia), a merchant named Mohammed (b AD 570) began preaching against the pagan religion of his fellow Meccans, no one in Constantinople paid the slightest attention.

Mohammed died in 632, but within a few short decades the entire Middle East would be under the control of his followers. Under Mohammed's successors, known as caliphs (from the Arabic word for 'follower'), the new religion spread rapidly, reaching all of Arabia by 634. By 646 Syria, Palestine and Egypt were all in Muslim hands, while most of Iraq,

64 BC

Pompey the Great abolishes the Seleucid kingdom, annexes Syria and transforms it into a province of the Roman Empire. Rome sets its sights on Egypt.

31 BC

The Romans defeat Cleopatra, bringing to an end the era of the pharaohs and drawing Egypt under their control. Unable to bear the ignominy, Cleopatra commits suicide.

AD 0

Jesus of Nazareth, founder of the Christian faith, is born in Bethlehem (in the present-day Palestinian Territories), which was, at the time, fully incorporated into the Roman Empire.

AD 33

Jesus is crucified by the Romans in Jerusalem. According to Christian tradition, he rises from the dead three days later and then ascends to heaven. His followers spread out across the world.

BAGHDAD THE BEAUTIFUL

When Haroun Ar Rashid came to power in AD 786, Baghdad, on the western bank of the Tigris, had only been in existence for 24 years. By the time he died, it had become one of the world's pre-eminent cities. Haroun Ar Rashid tried to rename the city Medinat As Salaam (City of Peace). Although the name never caught on, everything else that Haroun Ar Rashid and his immediate successors did was an unqualified success. Baghdad was remade into a city of expansive pleasure gardens, vast libraries and distinguished seats of learning, where the arts, medicine, literature and sciences all flourished. It was soon the richest city in the world. The crossroads of important trade routes to the east and west, it rapidly supplanted Damascus as the seat of power in the Islamic world, which stretched from Spain to India. Al Maamun, Haroun's son and successor, founded the Beit Al Hikmah (House of Wisdom), a Baghdad-based academy dedicated to translating Greek and Roman works of science and philosophy into Arabic. It was only through these translations that most of the classical literature we know today was saved for posterity.

Iran and Afghanistan were wrested from the Sassanids by 656. By 682 Islam had reached the shores of the Atlantic in Morocco.

Umayyads

Having won the battle for supremacy over the Muslim world, Mu'awiyah, the Muslim military governor of Syria and a distant relative of Mohammed, who became the fifth caliph, moved the capital from Medina to Damascus and established the first great Muslim dynasty – the Umayyads. Thanks to the unrelenting success of his armies, Mu'awiyah and his successors found themselves ruling an empire that held sway over almost a third of the world's population. The decision to make Damascus the capital meant that, for the first time in the Middle East's turbulent history, the region was ruled from its Levantine heartland. The Umayyads gave the Islamic world some of its greatest architectural treasures, including the Dome of the Rock in Jerusalem and the Umayyad Mosque in Damascus – lavish monuments to the new faith, if a far cry from Islam's simple desert origins.

History, however, has not been kind to the Umayyads. Perhaps seduced by Damascus' charms, they are remembered as a decadent lot, known for the high living, corruption, nepotism and tyranny that eventually proved to be their undoing. News of Umayyad excesses never sat well with the foot soldiers of Islam and even confirmed their long-held suspicions about their adherence to Islamic tenets.

Abbasids

In 750 the Umayyads were toppled in a revolt fuelled, predictably, by accusations of impiety. Their successors, and the strong arm behind the revolt, were the Abbasids. The Abbasid caliphate created a new capital in Bagh-

AD 39

The Roman emperor Caligula, not content with ruling much of the world, declares himself a deity, adding to the resentment already felt by Jews and Christians living across the Roman Empire.

AD 66–70

The Jews in Jerusalem and elsewhere revolt against oppressive Roman rule. The uprising is brutally put down, the Jewish temple destroyed and, within four years, more than 100,000 Jews are killed.

224

The Sassanids commence almost four decades of rule in Persia. For most of their rule, Zoroastrianism is the dominant faith.

267–71

Queen Zenobia seizes power in Palmyra, defeats the Roman legion sent to dethrone her, briefly occupies Syria, Palestine and Egypt, and declares herself independent of Rome. Rome is not amused.

dad, and the early centuries of its rule constituted what's often regarded as the golden age of Islamic culture in the Middle East. The most famous of the Abbasid caliphs was Haroun Ar Rashid (r 786–809) of *The Thousand and One Nights* fame. Warrior-king Haroun Ar Rashid led one of the most successful early Muslim invasions of Byzantium, almost reaching Constantinople. But his name will forever be associated with Baghdad, which he transformed into a world centre of learning and sophistication.

After Haroun Ar Rashid's death, the cycle that had already scarred Islam's early years – a strong, enlightened ruler giving way upon his death to anarchy and squandering many of the hard-won territorial and cultural gains of his reign – was repeated.

Seljuks

By the middle of the 10th century, the Abbasid caliphs were the prisoners of their Turkish guards, who spawned a dynasty of their own, known as the Seljuks (1038–1194). The Seljuks extended their reach throughout Persia, Central Asia, Afghanistan and Anatolia, where the Seljuk Sultanate of Rum made its capital at Konya. The resulting pressure on the Byzantine Empire was intense enough to cause the emperor and the Greek Orthodox Church to swallow their pride and appeal to the rival Roman Catholic Church for help. What happened next would plant the seeds for a clash of civilisations, whose bitterness would reverberate throughout the region long after the swords of Islam and Christianity had been sheathed.

Genghis Khan & the Mongol Invasion

In the early 13th century, the Seljuk Empire came to a final and bloody end when the rampaging Mongols swept across the Persian plateau on their horses, leaving a trail of cold-blooded devastation and thousands of dismembered heads in their wake.

Under the leadership first of Genghis Khan, and then his grandsons, including Hulagu, the Mongol rulers managed to seize all of Persia, as well as an empire stretching from Beijing (China) to İstanbul (Turkey). Eventually they established a capital at Tabriz. The Mongols destroyed many of the Persian cities they conquered, obliterating much of Persia's documented history. But they also became great arts patrons, leaving many fine monuments. The empire fragmented when Abu Said died without a successor, and soon succumbed to invading forces from the east led by Tamerlane (Lame Timur).

The Crusades Through Arab Eyes (Amin Maalouf; 1983) is brilliantly written and captures perfectly why the mere mention of the Crusades still arouses the anger of many Arabs today.

The Crusades & Their Aftermath

Preparing for War

With the Muslim armies gathering at the gates of Europe, and already occupying large swaths of Iberia, Pope Urban II in 1095, in response to the eastern empire's alarm, called for a Western Christian military

331
Emperor Constantine declares Christianity the official religion of the Roman Empire and moves his capital to Constantinople (previously known as Byzantium). This event marks the birth of the Byzantine Empire.

527–65
Emperor Justinian reigns over the Byzantine Empire whose realm extends through the Mediterranean, including coastal North Africa and most of the Middle East.

570
The Prophet Mohammed is born in Mecca (present-day Saudi Arabia). Despite his humble origins, he will become the 25th and most revered prophet of the world's second-largest religion.

622
When his message from Allah, imparted to Mohammed by the Archangel Gabriel, is rejected by powerful Meccans, the Prophet flees to Medina. In the Islamic calendar, this flight is known as the Hejira and marks Year Zero.

expedition – a 'Crusade' – to liberate the holy places of Jerusalem. Rome's motives were not entirely benevolent: Urban was eager to assert Rome's primacy in the east over Constantinople. The monarchs and clerics of Europe attempted to portray the Crusades as a 'just war'. In the late 11th century, such a battle cry attracted zealous support.

Bitterly fought on the battlefield, the Crusades remain one of the region's most divisive historical moments. For the Muslims, the Christian call to arms was a vicious attack on Islam itself, and the tactics used by the Crusaders confirmed the Muslim suspicion that Christianity's primary concern was imperial conquest. So deep does the sense of grievance run in the region that US President George W Bush's invasion of Iraq in 2003 was widely portrayed as the next Christian crusade. In the Christian world view, the Crusades were a necessary defensive strategy, lest Islam sweep across Europe and place Christianity's very existence under threat.

Christian Invasion

Whatever the rights and wrongs, the crusading rabble enjoyed considerable success. After linking up with the Byzantine army in 1097, the Crusaders successfully besieged Antioch (modern Antakya, in Turkey) and then marched south along the coast before turning inland, towards Jerusalem, leaving devastation in their wake. A thousand Muslim troops held Jerusalem for six weeks against 15,000 Crusaders before the city fell on 15 July 1099. The victorious Crusaders then massacred the local population – Muslims, Jews and Christians alike – sacked the non-Christian religious sites and turned the Dome of the Rock into a church.

Saladin in his Time (PH Newby; 1983) reads like a novel, except that it's all true, with surprising plot twists, epic events and picaresque characters brought to life.

Curiously, even after the gratuitous violence of the Crusades, Christians and Muslims assimilated in the Holy Land. European visitors to Palestine recorded with dismay that the original Crusaders who remained in the Holy Land had abandoned their European ways. They had become Arabised, taking on Eastern habits and dress – perhaps it was not an unwise move to abandon chain mail and jerkins for flowing robes in the Levantine heat. Even with their semi-transformation into locals, the Crusaders were never equipped to govern the massive, newly resentful Middle East. A series of Crusader 'statelets' arose through the region during this period.

Muslim Backlash

These statelets aside, the Middle East remained predominantly Muslim, and within 50 years the tide had begun to turn against the Crusaders. The Muslim leader responsible for removing the Crusaders from Jerusalem (in 1187) was Salah Ad Din Al Ayyoub, better known in the West as Saladin.

Saladin and his successors (a fleeting dynasty known as the Ayyubids) battled the Crusaders for 60 years until they were unceremoniously removed by their own army, a strange soldier-slave caste, the Mamluks, who

632

After returning to Mecca at the head of Islam's first army in 630, the Prophet Mohammed dies in Mecca. Despite squabbles over succession, his followers carry the new religion across the world.

642

Islam's battle for succession reaches its critical moment with the death of Hussein, the son of Ali. Ever since this date, the Muslim world has been divided into strains – Sunni and Shiite.

646

Barely a decade after the death of Mohammed, Syria, Palestine and Egypt have all been conquered by the followers of Islam. Modern Israel aside, they have been predominantly Muslim ever since.

656

Islam takes hold in Iraq, Persia and Afghanistan, defeating the ruling Sassanids and building on the expansion of Islam, which had been born just a few decades before.

SALADIN – THE KURDISH HERO OF ARAB HISTORY

Saladin – or Salah Ad Din (Restorer of the Faith) Al Ayyoub – was born to Kurdish parents in 1138 in what is modern-day Tikrit in Iraq. He joined other members of his family in the service of Nureddin (Nur Ad Din) of the ruling Zangi dynasty. By the time Nureddin died in 1174, Saladin had risen to the rank of general and had already taken possession of Egypt. He quickly took control of Syria and, over the next 10 years, extended his authority into parts of Mesopotamia. In 1187 Saladin crushed the Crusaders at the Battle of Hittin and captured Jerusalem, precipitating the Third Crusade and pitting himself against Richard I (the Lionheart) of England. After countless clashes, the two rival warriors signed a peace treaty in 1192, giving the coastal territories to the Crusaders and the interior to the Muslims. Saladin died three months later in Damascus, where he is buried.

ran what would today be called a military dictatorship. The only way to join their army was to be press-ganged into it – non-Muslim boys were captured or bought outside the empire, converted to Islam and raised in the service of a single military commander. They were expected to give this commander total loyalty, in exchange for which their fortunes would rise (or fall) with his. Sultans were chosen from among the most senior Mamluk commanders, but it was a system that engendered vicious, bloody rivalries, and rare was the sultan who died of natural causes.

The Mamluks were to rule Egypt, Syria, Palestine and western Arabia for nearly 300 years (1250–1517), and it was they who finally succeeded in ejecting the Crusaders from the Near East, prising them out of their last stronghold of Acre (modern-day Akko in Israel) in 1291.

Defending Constantinople, Emperor Constantine XI placed a chain across the Golden Horn to prevent Ottoman ships entering. Mehmet II ordered his ships over land – rolled over oiled logs – to breach the blockade and demoralise the Byzantine defenders.

The Ottoman Middle East

Rise of the Ottomans

Turkey, saved for now from an Islamic fate by the Crusaders, had remained largely above the fray. But the Byzantine rulers in Constantinople felt anything but secure. The armies of Islam may have been occupied fighting the Crusaders (and each other) in the so-called Holy Lands, but the Byzantines looked towards the south nervously, keeping their armies in a state of high readiness. Little did they know that their undoing would come from within.

In 1258, just eight years after the Mamluks seized power in Cairo and began their bloody dynasty, a boy named Osman (Othman) was born to the chief of a Turkish tribe in western Anatolia. He converted to Islam in his youth and later began a military career by hiring out his tribe's army as mercenaries in the civil wars, then besetting what was left of the Byzantine Empire. Payment came in the form of land.

660

Mu'awiyah moves the capital of the Muslim world from Arabia to Damascus, shifting Islam's balance of power. The Umayyad caliphate rules over an empire that encompasses almost the entire Middle East.

711

The armies of Islam cross from North Africa into Europe and the Iberian Peninsula is soon under their control. Al Andalus, in southern Iberia, becomes a beacon for tolerance and the arts.

750

The first Arab dynasty, the Umayyad caliphate in Damascus, falls amid accusations of impiety, and power shifts to Baghdad, the base for the Abbasids.

786–809

Haroun Ar Rashid rules the Abbasid world from his capital of Baghdad. This was the Abbasid heyday and provides the setting for tales in *The Thousand and One Nights*.

Rather than taking on the Byzantines directly, Osman's successors (the Ottomans) deliberately picked off the bits and pieces of the empire that Constantinople could no longer control. By the end of the 14th century, the Ottomans had conquered Bulgaria, Serbia, Bosnia, Hungary and most of present-day Turkey. They had also moved their capital across the Dardanelles to Adrianople, today the Turkish city of Edirne. In 1453 came their greatest victory, when Sultan Mehmet II took Constantinople, the hitherto unachievable object of innumerable Muslim wars almost since the 7th century.

Lords of the Horizons: A History of the Ottoman Empire (Jason Goodwin; 1998) is anecdotal and picaresque but still manages to illuminate the grand themes of Ottoman history.

Sixty-four years later, on a battlefield near Aleppo, an army under the gloriously named sultan Selim the Grim routed the Mamluks and assumed sovereignty over the Hejaz. At a stroke, the whole of the eastern Mediterranean, including Egypt and much of Arabia, was absorbed into the Ottoman Empire. By capturing Mecca and Medina, Selim the Grim claimed for the Ottomans the coveted title of the guardians of Islam's holiest places. For the first time in centuries, the Middle East was ruled in its entirety by a single Islamic entity.

Golden Age

The Ottoman Empire reached its peak, both politically and culturally, under Süleyman the Magnificent (r 1520–66), who led the Ottoman armies west to the gates of Vienna, east into Persia, and south through the holy cities of Mecca and Medina and into Yemen. His control also extended throughout North Africa. A remarkable figure, Süleyman was noted as much for codifying Ottoman law (he is known in Turkish as

OTTOMAN CONQUEST OF EUROPE

Just as the forces of Christian Europe were on the verge of expelling Al Andalus, the Islamic civilisation that ruled southern Spain from Christian soil, the Ottoman Turks, gathering in the east, opened a new front.

Horse-borne, and firing arrows from the saddle, the Ottoman Turks emerged from the Anatolian steppe in the 14th century, eager to gain a foothold on European soil. It was the boldest of moves, considering that the Abbasid advance on Constantinople had prompted the fierce European backlash of the Crusades. But the Ottomans were better equipped to take on war-weary Europe and advanced so swiftly – so seemingly miraculously – into Eastern Europe that Martin Luther openly wondered whether they should be opposed at all. The Ottoman Empire, at its greatest extent, reached from western Libya to the steppes of Hungary.

The end of Ottoman expansion is variously pinpointed as the failed Vienna campaign in 1683 or the treaty of Karlowitz (in which the Ottomans lost the Peloponnese, Transylvania and Hungary) in 1699 when the Ottomans sued for peace for the first time.

969 The Shiite general Jawhar lays the foundations for a new palace city, Al Qahira (Cairo). Two years later, a new university and mosque complex, Al Azhar, is founded.

1038–1194 The Seljuks, the former Turkish guards of the Abbasids, seize power, effectively ruling the Abbasid Empire. In addition to Turkey, they take Afghanistan, Persia and much of Central Asia.

1097 In response to a cry for help from the besieged Byzantines in Constantinople, the Christian Crusaders sweep down across the Middle East, trying to end Muslim rule in the Holy Land.

1099 After a withering siege, the Crusaders enter Jerusalem, massacre thousands regardless of their religion and claim the city for Christianity. The Dome of the Rock is turned into a church.

Süleyman Kanunı – law bringer) as for his military prowess. Süleyman's legal code was a visionary amalgam of secular and Islamic law, and his patronage of the arts saw the Ottomans reach their cultural zenith.

Another hallmark of Ottoman rule, especially in its early centuries, was its tolerance. In general, Christian and Jewish communities were accorded the respect the Quran outlines for them as 'People of the Book' and were given special status. The Ottoman state was a truly multicultural and multilingual one, and Christians and Muslims rose to positions of great power within the Ottoman hierarchy. In a move unthinkable for a Muslim ruler today, Sultan Beyazıt II even invited the Jews expelled from Iberia by the Spanish Inquisition to İstanbul in 1492.

But as so often happened in Middle Eastern history upon the death of a charismatic leader, things began to unravel soon after Süleyman died fighting on the Danube. The Ottomans may have held nominal power throughout their empire for centuries to come, but the growing decadence of the Ottoman court and unrest elsewhere in the countries that fell within the Ottoman sphere of influence ensured that, after Süleyman, the empire went into a long, slow period of decline.

Under Attack

Only five years after Süleyman's death, Spain and Venice destroyed virtually the entire Ottoman navy at the Battle of Lepanto (in the Aegean Sea), thereby costing the Ottomans control over the western Mediterranean. North Africa soon fell under the sway of local dynasties. Conflict with the Safavids – Persia's rulers from the early 16th century to the early 18th century – was almost constant.

To make matters worse, within a century of Süleyman's death, the concept of enlightened Ottoman sultans had all but evaporated. Assassinations, mutinies and fratricide were increasingly the norm among Constantinople's royals, and the opulent lifestyle was taking its toll. Süleyman was the last sultan to lead his army into the field, and those who came after him were generally coddled and sequestered in the fineries of the palace, having minimal experience of everyday life and little inclination to administer or expand the empire. The Ottomans remained moribund, inward looking and generally unaware of the advances that were happening in Europe – the Ottoman clergy did not allow the use of the printing press until the 18th century, a century and a half after it had been introduced into Europe.

Just as it had under the similarly out-of-touch Umayyads in the 8th century, the perceived impiety of the sultans and their representatives gave power to local uprisings. The Ottoman Empire lumbered along until the 20th century, but the empire was in a sorry state and its control over its territories grew more tenuous with each passing year.

Süleyman the Magnificent was responsible for achievements as diverse as building the gates of Jerusalem and introducing to Europe, via Constantinople, the joys of coffee.

1171

The Kurdish-born general Salah Ad Din Al Ayyoub (Saladin) seizes power from the Fatimid Shiite caliph in Egypt, restores Sunni rule and establishes the Ayyubid dynasty.

1187

Saladin retakes Jerusalem from the Crusaders and forever after becomes a hero to Muslims around the world. Fighting elsewhere between Saladin's forces and the Crusaders continues.

1192

Saladin signs a peace treaty with his long-time enemy, Richard the Lionheart. The Crusaders get the coast, the Muslims get the interior and Saladin dies three months later.

1250

The Mamluks, a military empire forged from the ranks of the Muslim armies, seize power for themselves and begin a 300-year rule over Egypt, Syria and Palestine.

European Incursions

Europe had begun to wake from its medieval slumber and the monarchs of France and Great Britain, in particular, were eager to bolster their growing prosperity by expanding their zones of economic influence. More than that, the prestige that would accompany colonial possessions in lands that had held an important place in the European imagination was undeniable. The reflected glory of 'owning' the Holy Lands or becoming the rulers over what was once the cradle of civilisation was too much for these emerging world powers to resist, and fitted perfectly within their blueprint for world domination. They may have talked of a 'civilising mission'. They may even have believed it. But it was prestige and greed that ultimately drove them as they cast their eye towards the Middle East.

In 1798 Napoleon invaded Egypt. It was not by accident that he chose the Middle East's most populous country as his first conquest in the region. By conquering the one-time land of the pharaohs, this ruler with visions of grandeur and an eye on his place in history announced to the world that France was the world power of the day. The French occupation of Egypt lasted only three years, but left a lasting mark – even today, Egypt's legal system is based on a French model.

The British, of course, had other ideas. Under the cover of protecting their own Indian interests, they forced the French out of Egypt in 1801.

Decline

At the Battle of the Pyramids, Napoleon's forces took just 45 minutes to rout the Mamluk army, killing 1000 for the loss of just 29 of their own men.

Four years later, Mohammed Ali, an Albanian soldier in the Ottoman army, emerged as the country's strongman and he set about modernising the country. As time passed it became increasingly obvious that Constantinople was becoming ever more dependent on Egypt for military backing rather than the reverse. Mohammed Ali's ambitions grew. In the 1830s he invaded and conquered Syria, and by 1839 he had effective control of most of the Ottoman Empire.

While it might have appeared to have been in Europe's interests to consign the Ottoman Empire to history, they were already stretched by their other colonial conquests and holdings (the British in India, the French in Africa) and had no interest, at least not yet, in administering the entire region. As a consequence, the Europeans prevailed upon Mohammed Ali to withdraw to Egypt. In return, the Ottoman sultan gave long-overdue acknowledgement of Mohammed Ali's status as ruler of a virtually independent Egypt, and bestowed the right of hereditary rule on his heirs (who continued to rule Egypt until 1952). In some quarters the Ottoman move was viewed as a wise strategy in keeping with their loose administration of their empire. In truth, they had little choice.

The emboldened Europeans were always at the ready to expand their influence in the region. In 1860 the French sent troops to Lebanon after a massacre of Christians by the local Druze. Before withdrawing,

1258

Baghdad is sacked by the Mongol hordes sweeping down out of Central Asia, destroying the city and officially ending the Abbasid Cailphate. Osman (founder of the Ottomans) is born.

1291

With energy drained from the Crusader cause, the Mamluks drive the last Crusaders from their coastal fortress of Acre (now Akko in Israel) and from the Middle East.

1453

After encircling the city during his Eastern European conquests, Sultan Mehmet II of the Ottoman Empire captures Constantinople, which had never before been in Muslim hands.

1492

Muslim Al Andalus falls to the Christian armies of the Spanish Reconquista, ending seven centuries of enlightened but increasingly divided rule. Jewish people begin arriving across the Middle East.

the French forced the Ottomans to set up a new administrative system for the area guaranteeing the appointment of Christian governors, over whom the French came to have great influence.

While all of this was happening, another import from the West – nationalism – was making its presence felt. The people of the Middle East watched with growing optimism as Greece and the Ottomans' Balkan possessions wriggled free, marking the death knell of Ottoman omniscience and prompting Middle Easterners to dream of their own independence. In this they were encouraged by the European powers, who may have paid lip service to the goals of independence, but were actually laying detailed plans for occupation. Mistaking (or, more likely, deliberately misinterpreting or ignoring) the nationalist movement as a cry for help, the European powers quickly set about filling the vacuum of power left by the Ottomans.

A Peace to End All Peace: Creating the Modern Middle East, 1914–1922 (David Fromkin; 1989) is an intriguing account of how the map of the modern Middle East was drawn arbitrarily by European colonial governments.

The Ottoman regime, once feared and respected, was now universally known as the 'sick man of Europe'. European diplomats and politicians condescendingly pondered the 'Eastern question', which in practice meant deciding how to dismember the empire and cherry-pick its choicest parts. In 1869 Mohammed Ali's grandson Ismail opened the Suez Canal. But within a few years, his government was so deeply in debt that in 1882, the British, who already played a large role in Egyptian affairs, occupied the country. It was a sign of things to come.

Colonial Middle East

Broken Promises

With the exception of Napoleon's stunning march into Egypt, Britain and France had slowly come to occupy the Middle East less by conquest than by stealth. European advisers, backed by armed reinforcements when necessary, were increasingly charting the region's future and it would not be long before their efforts were rewarded.

With the outbreak of WWI in 1914, the Ottoman Empire made its last serious (and ultimately fatal) error by throwing its lot in with Germany. Sultan Mohammed V declared a jihad (holy war), calling on Muslims everywhere to rise up against Britain, France and Russia (who were encroaching on Eastern Anatolia). When the British heard the Ottoman call to jihad, they performed a masterstroke – they negotiated an alliance with Hussein bin Ali, the grand sherif (Islamic custodian and descendant of the Prophet Mohammed) of Mecca, who agreed to lead an Arab revolt against the Turks in return for a British promise to make him 'King of the Arabs' once the conflict was over. This alliance worked well in defeating the Ottomans.

There was just one problem. With the Ottomans out of the way, the British never had any serious intention of keeping their promise. Even as they were negotiating with Sherif Hussein, the British were talking with the French on how to carve up the Ottoman Empire. These talks yielded the 1916 Sykes-Picot Agreement – the secret Anglo-French accord that

1520-66

Süleyman the Magnificent rules over the golden age of the Ottoman Empire, expanding the boundaries of the empire down into Arabia (including the holy cities of Mecca and Medina), Persia and North Africa.

1571

Five years after the death of Süleyman the Magnificent, Spain and Venice defeat the Ottomans at the Battle of Lepanto in the Aegean. Ottoman power has peaked and will never be as strong again.

1683

The Ottoman armies march on Vienna, but their defeat marks the end of Ottoman expansion and furthers the centuries-long period of Ottoman decline.

1760s

The Wahhabi movement in central Arabia calls for a return to Islam's roots. Wahhabi Islam still prevails in Saudi Arabia and forms the basis for Al Qaeda thought.

WHAT HAPPENED TO THE ARMENIANS?

The final years of the Ottoman Empire saw human misery on an epic scale, but nothing has proved as enduringly controversial as the fate of the Armenians. For millennia, this large but disparate community had lived in eastern Anatolia. In the early 20th century, the Orthodox Christian Armenians made the error of siding with the Russians against the Muslim Turk majority. It was an error for which they paid dearly.

The tale begins with eyewitness accounts, in autumn 1915, of Ottoman army units rounding up Armenian populations and marching them towards the Syrian desert. It ends with an Anatolian hinterland virtually devoid of Armenians. What happened in between remains one of the most controversial episodes in the 20th-century Middle East.

The Armenians maintain, compellingly it must be said, that they were subject to the 20th century's first orchestrated 'genocide'. They claim that more than a million Armenians were summarily executed or killed on death marches and that Ottoman authorities issued a deportation order with the intention of removing the Armenian presence from Anatolia. To this day, Armenians demand an acknowledgement of this 'genocide'. Very few Armenians remain in Turkey, although there are significant Armenian communities in Syria, Iran, and Israel and the Palestinian Territories.

Less compellingly, although with equal conviction, Turkey refutes any claims that such 'genocide' occurred. It does admit that thousands of Armenians died, but claims the Ottoman order had been to 'relocate' Armenians with no intention to eradicate them. The deaths, according to Turkish officials, were the result of disease and starvation, direct consequences of the tumultuous state of affairs during a time of war.

divided the Ottoman Empire into British and French spheres of influence. With a few adjustments, the Sykes-Picot Agreement determined the post-WWI map of the Middle East. Not surprisingly, this remains one of the most reviled 'peace agreements' in 20th-century Middle Eastern history.

European Occupation

In the closing year of the war, the British occupied Palestine, Transjordan, Damascus and Iraq. After the war, France took control of Syria and Lebanon, while Britain retained Egypt in addition to its holdings elsewhere. The Arabs, who'd done so much to free themselves from Ottoman rule, suddenly found themselves under British or French colonial administration, with the prospect of a Jewish state in their midst not far over the horizon thanks to the 1917 Balfour Declaration.

When the newly minted League of Nations initiated its system of mandates in 1922, thereby legitimising the French and British occupations, the sense of betrayal across the region was palpable. As was the colonial way, no one had thought to ask the people of the region what they wanted. As the Europeans set about programs of legal and administrative

1798
Napoleon invades Egypt, ushering in the period of colonial rivalry between France and Britain (who force the French out in 1801) that would ultimately redraw the map of the Middle East.

1839
Mohammed Ali of Egypt, an Albanian Ottoman soldier, establishes de facto control over declining Ottoman Empire from his base in Egypt. The dynasty he founded would rule Egypt until 1952.

1860
The massacre of Christians by the Druze in Lebanon's mountains prompts the French to send troops to restore order. The Ottomans remain nominal sovereigns, but the French never really leave.

1869
Ismail, the grandson of Mohammed Ali and ruler of Egypt, formally opens the landmark engineering feat that is the Suez Canal. Britain is heavily involved in Egyptian affairs.

reform, their occupying forces faced almost continual unrest. The Syrians and Lebanese harried the French, while the predominantly Arab population of Palestine battled the British.

The problems in Palestine were particularly acute. Since taking control of Palestine in 1918, the British had been under pressure to allow unrestricted Jewish immigration to the territory. With tension rising between Palestine's Arab and Jewish residents, they refused to do this and, in the late 1930s, placed strict limits on the number of new Jewish immigrants. It was, of course, a crisis of Britain's own making, having promised to 'view with favour' the establishment of a Jewish state in Palestine in the Balfour Declaration of 1917.

Turkish Independence

As Iraq, Syria, Lebanon and Palestine simmered, Turkey was going its own way, mercifully free of both the Ottoman sultans and their European successors. Stripped of its Arab provinces, the Ottoman monarchy was overthrown and a Turkish republic was declared under the leadership of Mustafa Kemal 'Atatürk', a soldier who became Turkey's first president in 1923.

His drive toward secularism (which he saw as synonymous with the modernisation necessary to drag Turkey into the 20th century) found an echo in Persia, where, in 1923, Reza Khan, the commander of a Cossack brigade who had risen to become war minister, overthrew the decrepit Ghajar dynasty. After changing his name from Khan to the more Persian-sounding Pahlavi (the language spoken in pre-Islamic Persia), he moved to set up a secular republic on the Turkish model. Protests from the country's religious establishment caused a change of heart and he had himself crowned shah instead. In 1934 he changed the country's name from Persia to Iran.

Looking back now at the turbulent years between the two world wars, it's easy to discern the seeds of the major conflicts that would come to define the Middle East in the late 20th and early 21st centuries: the Arab-Israeli conflict, Iran's Islamic Revolution and Turkey's struggle to forge an identity as a modernising Muslim country.

In 1922 there were around 486,000 Palestinian Arabs and 84,000 Jews in Palestine. By 1946 the Palestinian population had doubled to 1.1 million, whereas Jews had increased 550% to around 610,000.

Israel's Independence

For the past 70 years, no issue has divided the Middle East quite like Israeli independence. Four major conflicts, numerous skirmishes and an unrelenting war of words and attrition have cast a long shadow over everything that happens in the region. If a way could be found to forge peace between Israel and the Palestinians, the Middle East would be a very different place.

There is very little on which the two sides agree, although the following historical chronology is *probably* among them: in early 1947 the British announced that they were turning the entire problem over to the newly

1882

Weary of the Egyptian government's alleged financial ineptitude, the British formalise their control over the country, making it their first full-blown colonial possession in the Middle East.

1896

Theodor Herzl publishes *Der Judenstaat* (The Jewish State), in which he makes a call for a Jewish state in Palestine. This book is often described as the moment when Zionism was born.

1914

WWI breaks out. The Ottomans side with Germany, while the Allies persuade the Grand Sherif of Mecca to support them in return for promises of post-war independence for the Arabs.

1915

In the last years of the Ottoman Empire, Turkey's Armenian population is driven from the country. More than a million Armenians are killed in what Armenians claim was a genocide.

ZIONISM: A PRIMER

Contrary to popular belief, Zionism, the largely secular movement to create a Jewish homeland in Palestine, began decades before the Holocaust. In the late 19th century, pogroms against Jews in the Russian Empire and the 1894 Dreyfus Affair (in which a French Jewish officer was wrongly accused of treason) shone uncomfortable light on racism against the Jews in Europe. Two years later, Theodor Herzl, a Hungarian Jew, published *Der Judenstaat* (The Jewish State), which called for the setting up of a Jewish state in Palestine. In 1897 Herzl founded the World Zionist Organization (WZO) at the First Zionist Congress in Basel. At the conclusion of the Congress, Herzl is said to have written in his diary: 'At Basel I founded the Jewish State. If I said this out loud today I would be greeted by universal laughter. In five years perhaps, and certainly in 50 years, everyone will perceive it.' Another leading Zionist, Chaim Weizmann, who would later become the first president of Israel, was instrumental in lobbying the British government for what became the 1917 Balfour Declaration, whose text assured Jews that the British government would 'view with favour' the creation of 'a national home for the Jewish people' in Palestine, provided that 'nothing shall be done which may prejudice the civil and religious rights of existing non-Jewish communities in Palestine'. Over the years that followed, the WZO funded and otherwise supported the emigration of Jews to Palestine under the catch cry 'A land without people for a people without land'. The Jews were indeed a people without land, but the rallying cry ignored the presence in Palestine of hundreds of thousands of Arabs who had lived on the land for generations. The WZO also set up numerous quasi-state institutions that were transplanted to the new Israeli state upon independence.

created UN. The UN voted to partition Palestine, but this was rejected by the Arabs. Britain pulled out and the very next day the Jews declared the founding of the State of Israel. War broke out immediately, with Egypt, Jordan and Syria weighing in on the side of the Palestinian Arabs. Israel won.

Beyond that, the issue has become a forum for claim and counterclaim to the extent that for the casual observer, truth has become as elusive as the peace that all sides claim to want. What follows is our summary of the main bodies of opinion about Israeli independence among Israelis and Palestinians as they stood in 1948.

When Zionist and British policy makers were looking for a homeland for the Jewish people, sites they considered included Uganda, northeastern Australia and the Jebel Akhdar in the Cyrenaica region of Libya.

The Israeli View

For many Israelis in 1948, the founding of the state of Israel represented a homecoming for a persecuted people who had spent almost 2000 years in exile. Coming so soon as it did after the horrors of the Holocaust, in which more than six million Jews were killed, Israel, a state of their own, was the least the world could do after perpetrating the Holocaust or at the very least letting it happen. The Holocaust was the culmination of decades, perhaps even centuries of racism in European countries.

1916–18
TE Lawrence assists in the Arab Revolt against the Ottoman Empire, raising hopes among Arabs that they would be rewarded with independence after World War I.

1916
The French and British conclude the secret Sykes-Picot Agreement, which divides the region between the two European powers in the event of an Allied victory.

1917
The British government's Balfour Declaration promises 'a national home for the Jewish people' in Palestine. The declaration gives unstoppable momentum to the Zionist movement.

1922
The League of Nations grants Syria and Lebanon to the French, and Palestine, Iraq and Transjordan to the British. Egypt becomes independent but Britain remains in control.

In short, the Jewish people had ample reason to believe that their fate should never again be placed in the hands of others.

Although the Jews were offered a range of alternative sites for their state, it could never be anywhere but on the southeastern shores of the Mediterranean. By founding a Jewish state in Palestine, the Jews were returning to a land rich in biblical reference points and promises – one of the most enduring foundations of Judaism is that God promised this land to the Jews. Indeed, it is difficult to overestimate the significance of this land for a people whose traditions and sacred places all lay in Palestine, especially Jerusalem. This may have been the driving force for many observant religious Jews. But the dream of a return had deeper cultural roots, maintained down through the generations during an often difficult exile and shared by many secular Jews. This latter branch of Jewish society hoped to create an enlightened utopia, an egalitarian society in which a strong and just Israel finally took its rightful place among the modern company of nations. It was, according to the popular Zionist song that would become Israel's national anthem, 'the hope of 2000 years'.

Israel was the last country in the region to achieve independence, following in the wake of Egypt (1922), Iraq (1932), Lebanon (1941), Jordan and Syria (both 1946); Iran has never been ruled by a colonial power in the modern era.

The Palestinian View

For many Palestinians in 1948, the founding of the state of Israel was 'Al Naqba' – the Catastrophe. Through no fault of their own, and thanks to decisions made in Europe and elsewhere, and on which they were never consulted, the Palestinians were driven from their land. While the British were promising Palestine to the Jews in 1917, the Palestinians were fighting alongside the British to oust the Ottomans. Later, subject to British occupation, Palestinians suffered at the hands of Jewish extremist groups and found themselves confronted by an influx of Jews who had never before set foot in Palestine but who claimed equal rights over the land. Many Palestinians who had lived on the land for generations could do nothing without international assistance. No one came to their aid. In short, when they were offered half of their ancestral homelands by the UN, they had ample reason to reject the plan out of hand.

As with the Israelis, it is difficult to overestimate the significance of this land for Palestinians, many of whose traditions and sacred places lay in Palestine. Jerusalem (Al Quds) is the third-holiest city for Palestinian Muslims after Mecca and Medina (the Prophet Mohammed is believed to have ascended to heaven from the Al Aqsa Mosque), and the holiest city on earth for Palestinian Christians. But this was never really about religion. Had they not lived alongside the Jews for centuries, many Palestinians asked, considered them equals and given them the respect that their religion deserved? For the Palestinians forced to flee, it was about the right to the homes in which people had lived and to the fields that they had farmed. As they fled into their own exile, they longed for a Palestinian homeland taking its rightful place among the modern company of nations.

1923

Mustafa Kemal Atatürk becomes the first president of Turkey on a mission to modernise the country and create a secular state. Reza Khan seizes power in Iran.

1920s & 1930s

Jewish immigration to Palestine gathers pace. The arrival of the immigrants prompts anger among Palestinian Arabs and the British impose restrictions on the number of arrivals.

1939–45

After decades of anti-Semitism in Europe, more than six million Jews are killed by the Nazis and their allies during WWII, giving fresh urgency to the call for a Jewish state.

1947

Britain hands the issue over to the newly formed UN, which decides to partition Palestine into two states, one Jewish, the other Palestinian. Arabs reject the plan.

ISRAELI INDEPENDENCE: A PRIMER

In addition to following lists of books, *The War for Palestine: Rewriting the History of 1948* (2001), edited by Eugene L Rogan and Avi Shlaim, brings together both Israeli and Palestinian scholars.

History by Israelis

➡ *1948: A History of the First Arab–Israeli War* (Benny Morris; 2008) Israel's most prominent historian has drawn criticism from both sides.

➡ *The Birth of the Palestinian Refugee Problem Revisited* (Benny Morris; 2004) An attempt to explain why 700,000 Palestinians ended up in exile.

➡ *The Arab–Israeli Wars: War and Peace in the Middle East* (Chaim Herzog & Shlomo Gazit; 1982) Although it covers more recent events, Herzog takes a long look at 1948.

➡ *The Ethnic Cleansing of Palestine* (Ilan Pappe; 2006) A controversial text that challenges many of Israel's founding myths.

➡ *The Invention of the Jewish People* (Shlomo Sand; 2008) A polemical book that revisits the question of Jewish identity.

History by Palestinians

➡ *The Question of Palestine* (Edward W Said; 1979) An eloquent, passionate, but fair-minded study of the issue by the late Palestinian intellectual.

➡ *Expulsion of the Palestinians: The Concept of 'Transfer' in Zionist Political Thought, 1882–1948* (Nur Masalha; 1992) Revealing insights from Zionist archives.

➡ *The Iron Cage: The Story of the Palestinian Struggle for Statehood* (Rashid Khalidi; 2006) Looks at 1948 and the decades that preceded it.

Arab Middle East

Arab (Dis)unity

The Arab countries that waged war against Israel were in disarray, even before they went to war. Newly independent themselves, they were governed for the most part by hereditary rulers whose legitimacy was tenuous at best. They ruled over countries whose boundaries had only recently been established and they did so thanks to centuries of foreign rule, ill prepared to tackle the most pressing problems of poverty, illiteracy and the lack of a clear national vision for the future. Although united in the common cause of opposing Israel, they were divided over just about everything else.

The disastrous performance of the combined Arab armies in the 1948 Arab–Israeli War had far-reaching consequences for the region. People across the Middle East blamed their leaders for the defeat, a mood fuelled by the mass arrival of Palestinian refugees in Lebanon, Syria, Egypt and,

1948 The British withdraw from Palestine, Israel declares independence and the Arab armies of neighbouring countries invade. The new State of Israel wins the war and increases its territory.

1951 King Abdullah I, the founder of modern Jordan, is assassinated as recriminations ripple out across the Arab world in the wake of its devastating defeat by Israel.

1952 Gamal Abdel Nasser leads a coup against the monarchy in Egypt and becomes the first Egyptian ruler over Egypt since the days of the pharaohs.

1956 Shortly after becoming Egyptian president, Nasser nationalises the Suez Canal and then stares down Israel, Britain and France, who are forced to retreat. Nasser's popularity soars.

most of all, Jordan, whose population doubled almost overnight. Recriminations over the humiliating defeat and the refugee problem it created laid the groundwork for the 1951 assassination of King Abdullah of Jordan. Syria, which had gained its independence from France in 1946, became the field for a seemingly endless series of military coups.

Rise of Nasser

It was in Egypt, where the army blamed the loss of the war on the country's corrupt and ineffective politicians, that the most interesting developments were taking shape. In July 1952 a group of young officers toppled the monarchy, with the real power residing with one of the coup plotters: Gamal Abdel Nasser. King Farouk, descendant of the Albanian Mohammed Ali, departed from Alexandria harbour on the royal yacht, and Colonel Nasser – the first Egyptian to rule Egypt since the pharaohs – became president in elections held in 1956. His aim of returning some of Egypt's wealth to its much-exploited peasantry struck a chord with Egypt's masses. He became an instant hero across the Arab world.

Nasser's iconic status reached new heights in the year of his inauguration, when he successfully faced down Britain and France in a confrontation over the Suez Canal, which was mostly owned by British and French investors. On 26 July, the fourth anniversary of King Farouk's departure, Nasser announced that he had nationalised the Suez Canal to finance the building of a great dam that would control the flooding of the Nile and boost Egyptian agriculture. A combined British, French and Israeli

WHO ARE THE ARABS?

The question of who the Arabs are exactly is still widely debated. Fourteen centuries ago, only the nomadic tribes wandering between the Euphrates River and the central Arabian Peninsula were considered Arabs, distinguished by their language. However, with the rapid expansion of Islam, the language of the Quran spread to vast areas. Although the Arabs were relatively few in number in most of the countries they conquered, their culture quickly became established through language, religion and intermarriage. In addition to the original nomads, the settled inhabitants of these newly conquered provinces also became known as Arabs. In the 20th century, rising Arab nationalism legitimised the current blanket usage of the term to apply to all the peoples of the Middle East – except the Persians, Kurds, Israelis and Turks.

The most romanticised group of Arabs is no doubt the Bedouin. While not an ethnic group, they are the archetypal Arabs – the camel-herding nomads who roam all over the deserts and semideserts in search of food for their cattle. From among their ranks came the warriors who spread Islam to North Africa and Persia 14 centuries ago. Today, the Bedouin are found mainly in Jordan, Iraq, Egypt's Sinai Peninsula and the Gulf States.

1958–61

Egypt and Syria unite to form the United Arab Republic, a short-lived union that Nasser hopes will spark a pan-Arab megastate that brings together all the Arab countries of the region.

1961

Kurds in northern Iraq launch a short-lived military campaign for an independent Kurdistan. The move fails and will become an important justification for later campaigns against the Kurds.

1964

Against the objections of Jordan and, of course, Israel, the Palestine Liberation Organisation (PLO), an umbrella group of Palestinian resistance groups, is formed.

1967

Israel launches a pre-emptive strike and destroys Egypt's air force. Israel emerges from the resulting Six Day War with much of the West Bank, Sinai, the Golan Heights and the Gaza Strip.

invasion force, which intended to take possession of the canal, was, to great diplomatic embarrassment, forced to make an undignified retreat after the UN and US applied pressure. Nasser emerged from the Suez Canal crisis the most popular Arab leader in history.

Attempts at Unity

Such was Nasser's popularity that the Syrians joined Egypt in what would prove to be an ultimately unworkable union, the United Arab Republic, in 1958. At the time, it seemed as if Nasser's dream of pan-Arab unity was one step closer to reality. But behind the staged photo opportunities in which the region's presidents and monarchs lined up to bask in Nasser's reflected glory, the region was as divided as ever. With the United Arab Republic at Jordan's borders to the north and south, King Hussein feared for his own position and tried a federation of his own with his Hashemite cousins in Iraq; it lasted less than a year before the Iraqi Hashemite monarchy was overthrown, and British troops were sent in to Jordan to protect Hussein. Egypt and Syria went their separate ways in 1961.

There is no finer work in English on the history of the Arabs, from the Prophet Mohammed to modern times, than *A History of the Arab Peoples* (Albert Hourani, 1991) – it's definitive, encyclopedic and highly readable.

Meanwhile, Lebanon was taking an entirely different course, exposing the fault lines that would later tear the country apart. The Western-oriented Maronite Christian government that held sway in Beirut had been, in 1956, the only Arab government to support the US and UK during the Suez Canal crisis, a deeply unpopular decision among Lebanon's Muslim community.

And yet, for all the division and gathering storm clouds, there was a palpable sense of hope across the Arab world. Driven by Nasser's 'victory' over the European powers in the 1956 Suez crisis, there was a growing belief that the Arab world's time was now. While this manifested itself in the hope that the region had acquired the means and self-belief to finally defeat Israel when the time came, it was also to be found on the streets of cities across the region.

Rise of the PLO

All too often, the Arab-Israeli conflict, as with so many other events in the Middle East, has been explained away as a religious war between Jews and Muslims. There has at times indeed been a religious dimension, especially in recent years with the rise of Hamas in the Palestinian Territories and the religious right in Israel. But this has always been fundamentally a conflict over land, as was shown in the years following Israel's independence. Governments – from the Ba'ath parties of Syria and Iraq to Nasser's Egypt – invariably framed their demands in purely secular terms.

This again became clear after the formation in 1964 of the Palestine Liberation Organisation (PLO). Although opposed by Jordan, which was itself keen to carry the banner of Palestinian leadership, the PLO enjoyed the support of the newly formed Arab League. The Palestine National Council (PNC) was established within the PLO as its executive body – the

1968–89

Saddam Hussein emerges as the key powerbroker in Iraq after a coup brings the Ba'ath Party to power. A year later, Yasser Arafat becomes leader of the PLO.

1970

Hafez Al Assad assumes power in Syria after what he called 'The Corrective Revolution'. At the head of the Syrian Ba'ath Party, he ruled Syria until his death in 2000.

1973

Egypt launches a surprise attack on Israel. After initial gains by Egypt, Israel recovers to seize yet more territory. Despite the defeat, the war is hailed as a victory in the Arab world.

1975

After years of tension, war breaks out in Lebanon between Palestinians and Christian militias. The fighting, which draws in other militant groups, lasts until 1990.

closest thing to a Palestinian government in exile. The PLO served as an umbrella organisation for an extraordinary roll call of groups that ranged from purely military wings to communist ideologues. Militant Islamic factions were, at the time, small and drew only limited support.

Just as the PLO was at risk of dissolving into an acrimony born from its singular lack of a united policy, an organisation called the Palestine National Liberation Movement (also known as Al Fatah) was established. One of the stated aims of both the PLO and Al Fatah was to train guerrillas for raids on Israel. Al Fatah emerged from a power struggle as the dominant force within the PLO, and its leader, Yasser Arafat, would become chair of the executive committee of the PLO in 1969 and, later, the PLO's most recognisable face.

At the same time, Islam as a political force *was* starting to stir. Nasser may have been all-powerful, but there was a small group of clerics who saw him, Egyptian or not, as the latest in a long line of godless leaders ruling the country. Sayyid Qutb, an Egyptian radical and intellectual, was the most influential, espousing a return to the purity of grassroots Islam. He also prompted the creation of the Muslim Brotherhood, who would withdraw from society and prepare for violence and martyrdom in pursuit of a universal Muslim society. Qutb was executed by Nasser in 1966, but the genie could not be put back in the bottle, returning to haunt the region, and the rest of the world, decades later.

Arafat (1998) by the Palestinian writer Saïd K Aburish is a highly critical look at one of the Middle East's most intriguing yet flawed personalities. *Arafat: The Biography* (1994) by Tony Walker and Andrew Gowers is also good.

Arab-Israeli Wars

1967 War

With the Arab world growing in confidence, war seemed inevitable. In May 1967 the Egyptian army moved into key points in Sinai and announced a blockade of the Straits of Tiran, effectively closing the southern Israeli port of Eilat. The Egyptian army was mobilised and the country put on a war footing. On 5 June Israel responded with a devastating pre-emptive strike that wiped out virtually the entire Egyptian air force in a single day. The war lasted only six days (hence the 'Six Day War'), and when it was over, Israel controlled the Sinai Peninsula, the Gaza Strip, the West Bank (including Jerusalem's Old City) and the Golan Heights.

After more than a decade of swaggering between Cairo and Damascus, and empty promises to the Palestinians that they would soon be returning home, the Six Day War was viewed as an unmitigated disaster throughout the Arab world and sent shock waves across the region. Not only were leaders such as Nasser no match for the Israelis, despite the posturing, but also tens of thousands more Palestinian refugees were now in exile. The mood across the region was grim. A humiliated Nasser offered to resign, but in a spontaneous outpouring of support, the Egyptian people wouldn't accept the move and he remained in office. In November 1970 the president died of a heart attack, reportedly a broken man.

1977

Egyptian president Anwar Sadat's landmark visit to Jerusalem reverberates around the region. Egypt is expelled from the Arab League, and Sadat is hailed around the world.

1978

Anwar Sadat and Israel's Menachem Begin sign the Camp David peace treaty. Egypt gets Sinai and recognises Israel's right to exist.

1979

After brutal repression of opposition protests, the Shah of Iran, Reza Pahlavi, leaves Iran. The Islamic Revolution brings Āyatollāh Ruhollāh Khomeini to power.

1980

Counting on a weakened Iran in the wake of the Islamic Revolution, Saddam Hussein launches a surprise attack on Iran. The war, in which millions died and neither country gained any territory, lasts until 1988.

1973 War

With Palestinian militancy on the rise, the year 1970 saw the ascension of new leaders in both Egypt (Anwar Sadat) and Syria (Hafez Al Assad). Preparations were also well under way for the next Middle Eastern war, with these radical new leaders under constant pressure from their citizens to reclaim the land lost in 1967. On 6 October 1973, Egyptian troops crossed the Suez Canal, taking Israel (at a standstill, observing the holy day of Yom Kippur) almost entirely by surprise. After advancing a short distance into Sinai, however, the Egyptian army stopped, giving Israel the opportunity to concentrate its forces against the Syrians on the Golan Heights and then turn back towards Egypt. Although the war preserved the military status quo, it was widely portrayed throughout the region as an Arab victory.

Covering Islam (Edward Said; 1981) is a classic, exploring how the Iranian Revolution and Palestinian terrorism forever changed the way we view the Middle East.

When the war ended in late 1973, months of shuttle diplomacy by the US secretary of state, Henry Kissinger, followed. Pressure on the USA to broker a deal was fuelled when the Gulf States embargoed oil supplies to the West 10 days after the war began. The embargo's implications were massive, achieving nothing less than a shift in the balance of power in the Middle East. The oil states, rich but underpopulated and militarily weak, gained at the expense of poorer, more populous countries. Huge shifts of population followed the two oil booms of the 1970s, as millions of Egyptians, Syrians, Jordanians, Palestinians and Yemenis went off to seek their fortunes in the oil states.

Peace & Revolution

By the mid 1970s the Middle East had reached a temporary stalemate. On one side, Israel knew that it had the wherewithal to hold off the armed forces of its neighbours. But Israel also lived in a state of siege and on maximum alert, all the time facing escalating attacks at home and abroad on its citizens from Palestinian terrorist groups aligned to the PLO. On the other side, Arab governments continued with their rhetoric but knew, although none admitted it, that Israel was here to stay. To the north, Lebanon was sliding into a civil war that was threatening to engulf the region. Something had to give.

Shah of Shahs (1982), by journalist Ryszard Kapuściński, is a fast-paced yet perceptive account of Iran in the decade leading up to the revolution, written in a style that draws attention to the absurdities of a deadly serious situation.

Camp David

On 7 November 1977, Egyptian president Anwar Sadat made a dramatic visit to Israel to address the Israeli Knesset with a call for peace. The Arab world was in shock. That the leader of the Arab world's most populous nation, a nation that had produced Gamal Abdel Nasser, could visit Israeli-occupied Jerusalem had hitherto been inconceivable. The shock turned to anger the following year when Sadat and the hardline Israeli prime minister, Menachem Begin, shepherded by US president Jimmy Carter, signed the Camp David Agreement. In return for Egypt's

1981
Anwar Sadat is assassinated in Cairo during a military parade, by a member of his armed forces (and also a secret member of an Islamist group) as the parade passes the presidential box.

1982
Israel invades Lebanon. In September, Israeli forces surround the Palestinian refugee camps, Sabra and Shatila, while Phalangists massacre thousands. Israel withdraws in 1983.

1983
Turkey returns to democratic rule after a succession of coups. The new constitution that forbids prior political participation suggests that the Turkish military remains the real power in the country.

1984
Abdullah Öcalan forms the Kurdistan Workers Party (PKK) and launches a brutal insurgency that paralyses Turkey's southeast. The 'war' lasts until Öcalan is captured in 1999.

long-coveted recognition of Israel's right to exist, Egypt received back the Sinai Peninsula. Egypt did rather well out of the deal, but was widely accused of breaking ranks and betrayal for one simple reason: the Palestinians received nothing. Arab leaders meeting in Baghdad voted to expel Egypt from the Arab League and moved the group's headquarters out of Cairo in protest. The peace treaty won Sadat (and Begin) a Nobel Peace Prize, but it would ultimately cost the Egyptian leader his life: he was assassinated in Cairo on 6 October 1981.

For millennia, Iran was called Persia. However, Reza Shah hated the name and in 1934 changed it to Iran – derived directly from Aryan (meaning 'of noble origin').

Iran's Islamic Revolution

Before his death, and with Sadat basking in the acclaim of the international community, one of the few friends he had left in the region was facing troubles of his own. Discontent with the Shah of Iran's autocratic rule and his personal disregard for the country's Shiite Muslim religious traditions had been simmering for years. Political violence slowly increased throughout 1978. The turning point came in September of that year, when Iranian police fired on anti-shah demonstrators in Tehran, killing at least 300. The momentum of the protests quickly became unstoppable.

On 16 January 1979, the shah left Iran, never to return (he died in Egypt a year later). The interim government set up after his departure was swept aside the following month when the revolution's leader, the hitherto obscure Āyatollāh Ruhollāh Khomeini, returned to Tehran from his exile in France and was greeted by adoring millions. His fiery brew of nationalism and Muslim fundamentalism had been at the forefront of the revolt, and Khomeini achieved his goal of establishing a clergy-dominated Islamic Republic (the first true Islamic state in modern times) with brutal efficiency. Opposition disappeared, executions took place after meaningless trials and minor officials took the law into their own hands.

Although the 1973 war is painted as a victory and reassertion of Arab pride by many historians, by the time it ended, the Israelis actually occupied more land than when it began.

Bloody Aftermath

For decades, the Middle East's reputation for brutal conflict and Islamic extremism owed much to the late 1970s and early 1980s. It was the worst of times in the Middle East, a seemingly relentless succession of bloodletting by all sides. The religious fervour that surrounded Khomeini's Iran and the images of the masses chanting *'Marg bar amrika!'* ('Death to America!') also marked the moment when militant Islam became a political force and announced to the world that the West was in its sights. While this development applied to only a small proportion of the region's Muslims, the reputation has stuck.

The events that flowed from, or otherwise followed, the Iranian Revolution read like a snapshot of a region sliding out of control. In 1979 militants seized the Grand Mosque in Mecca. They were ejected several weeks later only after bloody gun battles inside the mosque itself, leaving more than 250 people dead inside Islam's holiest shrine. In November

1987

A grassroots uprising known as the intifada breaks out in the Palestinian Territories. Although the PLO later tries to claim credit, the intifada is a spontaneous national rebellion.

1990

Saddam Hussein's Iraq invades Kuwait and remains there until the US-led coalition (operating from its bases in Saudi Arabia) drives him out in early 1991. Saddam turns on Iraqi Shiites and Kurds.

1991

Israel and its Arab neighbours sit down for the first time to discuss a comprehensive peace plan in Madrid. Talks dissolve in recrimination, but the fact that they do so face to face is seen as progress.

1993

After a year and a half of secret negotiations between Israel and the Palestinians, Yasser Arafat and Yitzhak Rabin sign the Oslo Accords setting out a framework for future peace.

of that year, student militants in Tehran overran the US embassy, taking the staff hostage. They would be released only after 444 days in captivity. Away to the north, in 1980, Turkey's government was overthrown in a military coup, capping weeks of violence between left- and right-wing extremists. The same year, Saddam Hussein, supported by the US, invaded Khuzestan in southwestern Iran, on the pretext that the oil-rich province was historically part of Iraq. The resulting war lasted until 1988 and claimed millions of lives as trench warfare and poison gas were used for the first time since WWI.

Lebanon Falls Apart

In June 1982 Israel marched into Lebanon, joining Syria, the PLO and a host of Lebanese militias in a vicious regional conflict from which no side emerged with clean hands. The PLO had long been using the anarchy at large in Lebanon to set up a state within a state, from where they launched hundreds of rocket attacks across the Israeli-Lebanese frontier. Led by Defence Minister Ariel Sharon, Israel entered the war claiming self-defence. But these claims lost considerable credibility when, weeks after the PLO leadership had already left Beirut for Tunis, Israeli soldiers surrounded the Palestinian refugee camps of Sabra and Shatila in Beirut and stood by as their Phalangist allies went on a killing rampage. Hundreds, possibly thousands, of civilians were killed. Israel withdrew from most of Lebanon in 1983, but continued to occupy what it called a self-declared security zone in southern Lebanon.

The Lebanese Civil War rumbled on until 1990, but even when peace came, Israel controlled the south and Syria's 30,000 troops in Lebanon had become the kingmakers in the fractured Lebanese polity. In the 15 years of war, more than a million Lebanese are believed to have died.

In 1997 Israeli agents poisoned Hamas activist Khaled Meshaal in Amman. Jordan's King Hussein insisted Israel hand over the antidote. Meshaal later became leader of Hamas. For more on this episode, read *Kill Khalid: The Failed Mossad Assassination of Khalid Mishal and the Rise of Hamas* (2009) by Paul McGeough.

Intifada

Down in the Palestinian Territories, violence flared in 1987 in what became known as the 'First Intifada' (the grass roots Palestinian uprising). Weary of ineffectual Palestinian politicians having achieved nothing of value for their people in the four decades since Israeli independence, ordinary Palestinians took matters into their own hands. Campaigns of civil disobedience, general strikes and stone-throwing youths were the hallmarks of the intifada, which ran until 1993.

War & Peace

While all of this was going on, elsewhere in the region there were a few bright spots. Turkey had returned to democratic rule in 1983, albeit with a new constitution barring from public office anyone who had been involved in politics prior to the 1980 coup. In 1988 Iran and Iraq grudgingly agreed to a ceasefire. A year later Egypt was quietly readmitted to the

1994

Building on the goodwill generated by the Oslo Accords, Jordan under King Hussein becomes the second Arab country (after Egypt in 1979) to sign a peace treaty with Israel.

1995

Israeli prime minister Yitzhak Rabin is assassinated by a Jewish extremist who hoped to end the process Rabin had begun with the Oslo Accords. A year later, the right-wing Benjamin Netanyahu is voted into power.

1999

Jordan's King Hussein dies of cancer, having ruled since 1952. He is seen as one of the architects of peace in the region and more than 50 heads of state attend his funeral.

2000

The second Palestinian intifada breaks out in the Palestinian Territories. In Damascus, Hafez Al Assad dies after 30 years in power and his son, Bashar, becomes president.

Arab League and Jordan held its first elections in more than 20 years. But these important landmarks were overshadowed by events in Lebanon, which had led many people to wonder whether the region would ever be at peace.

Iraq, Kuwait & the West

Just as the region was breathing a collective sigh of relief at the end of the Lebanese Civil War and the cessation of hostilities between Iraq and Iran, Iraq invaded Kuwait in August 1990. The 1990s were, it seemed, destined to repeat the cycle of violence that had so scarred the previous decade.

Fearful that Saddam Hussein had Saudi Arabia in his sights, King Fahd requested help from the US. The result was a US-led coalition whose air and ground offensive drove Iraq out of Kuwait. In the process, Iraqi president Saddam Hussein (previously supported by the West in his war against Iran) became world public enemy number one. When the US-led coalition stopped short of marching on Baghdad, the Iraqi leader used his reprieve to attack the country's Shiite population in the south and the Kurds in the north with levels of brutality remarkable even by his standards. Not willing to wait around for Saddam's response to the Kurds' perceived support for the US-led coalition, hundreds of thousands of Kurds streamed across the border into Turkey in one of the largest refugee exoduses in modern history.

There was another, less immediately obvious consequence of the war. The presence of US troops on Saudi soil enraged many in a country known for its strict (some would say puritanical) adherence to Wahhabi Islamic orthodoxy. To have the uniformed soldiers of what many considered to be Islam's enemy operating freely from the same soil as the holy cities of Mecca and Medina was considered an outrage. From this anger, many respected analysts argue, would come Al Qaeda.

A Modern History of the Kurds (David McDowall; 1958) has been updated to 1996, and it remains an excellent primer on Kurdish social and political history, focusing on Turkey and Iraq. Otherwise try *The Kurds of Iraq* (Mahir A Aziz; 2014) and *The Kurds of Syria* (Harriet Allsopp; 2015).

Israeli-Palestinian Peace

From the ashes of war came an unlikely movement towards peace. While attempting to solicit Arab support for the anti-Iraq coalition, US president George H W Bush promised to make Arab-Israeli peace a priority once the Iraqis were out of Kuwait. Endless shuttling between Middle Eastern capitals culminated in a US-sponsored peace conference in Madrid in October 1991. It achieved little, but by late summer 1993 it was revealed that Israel and the Palestinians had been holding secret talks in Norway for 18 months. The 'Oslo Accords' were cemented with one of the most famous handshakes in history, between Yasser Arafat and Israeli prime minister Yitzhak Rabin on the White House lawn in September 1993.

An unprecedented era of hope for peace in the Middle East seemed on the horizon. Lebanon had just held its first democratic elections for 20 years and the mutually destructive fighting seemed well and truly at

2003

The US and the UK, with a much smaller coalition and less international support than in 1990–91, invade Iraq, winning the war, but Iraq descends into open rebellion.

2004

Evidence of the torture of Iraqi prisoners emerges from the US-controlled Abu Ghraib prison in Baghdad. The United States' reputation in the region sinks to an all-time low.

2005

Yasser Arafat, chairman of the PLO and leader of the Palestinian Authority, dies in Paris and is later buried in Ramallah, ending four eventful decades at the frontline of Middle Eastern politics.

2006

After Hezbollah captures two Israeli soldiers, Israel launches a sustained air attack on Lebanon. The resulting war produces a stalemate and is widely portrayed throughout the region as a victory for Hezbollah.

WHO ARE THE KURDS?

The Kurds, the descendants of the Medes who ruled an empire over much of the Middle East in 600 BC from what is now northwestern Iran, are the Middle East's largest minority group. Kurds (who are predominantly Sunni Muslims) constitute significant minorities in Turkey (18% of the population), Iraq (15% to 20%), Iran (10%) and Syria (7% to 8%). The Kurdish homeland is a largely contiguous area split between southeastern Turkey, northeastern Syria, northern Iraq and northwestern Iran.

Turkey

Turkey's sparsely populated eastern and southeastern regions are home to perhaps seven million Kurds, while seven million more live elsewhere in the country, more or less integrated into mainstream Turkish society; some Kurdish groups estimate that there are 20 million Kurds in Turkey. Relations between Turks and Kurds soured after the formation of the republic, in which Atatürk's reforms left little room for anything other than Turkishness. Until relatively recently the Turkish government refused to even recognise the existence of the Kurds, insisting they be called 'Mountain Turks'.

Since 1984, when Abdullah Öcalan formed the Kurdistan Workers Party (PKK), a separatist conflict raged in Turkey's Kurdish areas, prompting Turkey's government to declare a permanent state of emergency. After 15 years and the deaths of some 30,000 people, Öcalan was captured in 1999. The insurgency died out.

In 2002 the Turkish government finally gave some ground on the issue of Kurdish rights, approving broadcasts in Kurdish and giving the go-ahead for Kurdish to be taught in language schools. Emergency rule was lifted in the southeast. Life for Kurds in the southeast has since become considerably easier, although worrying but periodic fighting and government crackdowns remain a factor of life in the country's southeast.

an end. In 1994 Jordan became the second Arab country to sign a formal peace treaty with Israel.

But, sadly, it was not to last. The peace process was derailed by the November 1995 assassination of Rabin and the subsequent election of hardline candidate Benjamin Netanyahu. A blip of hope re-emerged when Netanyahu lost office to Ehud Barak, a prime minister who pulled his troops out of occupied south Lebanon and promised to open negotiations with the Syrians and the Palestinians. But critical momentum had been lost. When these talks came to nothing at two high-stakes summits at Camp David and in the Egyptian resort of Sharm El Sheikh during the last months of the Clinton presidency, everyone knew that an opportunity had been lost.

In September 2000, after Ariel Sharon, by then the leader of the right-wing Likud Party, visited the Al Aqsa Mosque in Jerusalem, riots broke out among Palestinians. This was the trigger, if not the ultimate cause, for the second Palestinian intifada that has continued in one form or

2006	2008	December 2010	2011
The height of the insurgency against the US military and administrative presence in Iraq. According to the UN, more than 100 civilians die every day, with suicide bombings a near-daily occurrence.	Civil war threatens again in Lebanon after Hezbollah besieges the government. Syria admits to indirect talks with Israel through Turkish mediators.	A young Tunisian man sets himself ablaze in the town of Sidi Bouzid, the trigger for a popular uprising that would lead to the demise of leaders in Tunisia, Libya and Egypt.	Syria descends into civil war, a popular and largely peaceful uprising giving way to an armed insurrection in which army defectors battle government loyalists with civilians caught in between.

Rising Kurdish power in neighbouring Syria and Iraq has caused considerable disquiet in Ankara.

Iraq

Iraq is home to about 4.5 million Kurds, who live in the northern provinces of the country. The 1961 Kurdish campaign to secure independence from Iraq laid the foundations for an uneasy relationship between the Kurds and the Iraqi state. After the 1991 Gulf War, when an estimated two million Kurds fled across the mountains to Turkey and Iran, the Kurdish Autonomous Region was set up in northern Iraq under UN protection and Kurdish Iraq became a model for a future federal Iraqi system.

After the fall of Saddam, the Kurds won 17% of the vote in the 2005 elections and Kurdish leaders restated their commitment to a federal but unified Iraq. In the years since, the leaders of Iraqi Kurdistan have made no secret of their plans to push for independence from Iraq. On 25 September 2017 Iraqi Kurdistan held a referendum on independence, with more 90% of voters voting in favour. However, the vote was not recognised by any of the major international powers and was condemned by the governments of Iraq, Iran and Turkey as a divisive and provocative move.

Iran

An estimated five million to seven million Kurds live in Iran, particularly in the country's northwest which borders Kurdish areas across the borders in Turkey and Iraq. A low-level insurgency against the Islamic Republic by militant Kurdish groups has simmered since the 1979 revolution, although things have quietened considerably in recent years.

another in the years since. The election of that same Ariel Sharon – a politician as reviled by Palestinians as Yasser Arafat was by Israelis – as Israeli prime minister in 2001 was another nail in the coffin of the already much-buried peace process. Although the death of Yasser Arafat in November 2004 offered some signs for hope, the violent occupation of Palestinian land and bloody suicide bombings targeting Israeli citizens continued. By then, the hope that had spread like a wave across the Middle East in the early 1990s had come to seem like a distant memory.

Prelude to the Arab Spring

Some things don't change in the Middle East. Israel and the Palestinians still trade accusations of bad faith and no solution has been found to the Arab-Israeli conflict. Hundreds of thousands of Palestinian refugees (including second- and third-generation exiles) languish in refugee camps, many still holding on to the keys of homes they left in 1948 or 1967. And wars great and small continue to flare around the region.

December 2011

More than eight years after the US-led invasion of Iraq, the last US troops leave the country. Iraqi security forces are now responsible for security and the government is by elected parliament.

2012

The impact of the fighting in Syria ripples across the region with large numbers of Syrian refugees in neighbouring countries, and Turkey accusing Syria of following rebels across the border.

2012

The Muslim Brotherhood emerges from Egypt's first democratic parliamentary elections with 235 of the 508 seats. The biggest surprise is the 121 seats won by the extreme Islamist Salafi party, Nour.

2013

The Brotherhood's Mohammed Morsi is overthrown after only a year as Egyptian president following mass demonstrations across the country.

Iraq War

In 2003 US and UK forces, with support from a small band of allies, invaded Iraq. Their military victory was swift, driving Saddam Hussein from power, but the aftermath has proved to be infinitely more complicated. With large communities of Shiites, Kurds and the hitherto all-powerful Sunnis vying for power, the country descended into a sectarian conflict with strong echoes of Lebanon's civil war. Hundreds of thousands, perhaps millions of Iraqis fled the fighting, placing huge pressure on the resources of neighbouring countries. Iraqis have paid a terrible price for their freedom.

Of the almost 11 million Palestinians worldwide, only five million live in Israel (1.3 million) or the Palestinian Territories (3.7 million). Palestinians comprise around 60% of Jordan's population, with around 400,000 in each of Lebanon and pre-war Syria.

Seeds of Change

In 2006 Israel and Hezbollah fought a bitter month-long war that shattered the Lebanese peace, while fighting broke out between Hezbollah and the Lebanese government in 2008. The power of Hezbollah, and the shifting of Palestinian power from Al Fatah to Hamas in the Palestinian Territories, has confirmed a process that had begun with the PLO in the 1960s: the rise of non-state actors as powerful players in the Middle East.

Governments of Arab countries have singularly failed to meet the aspirations of their people, from bringing about a lasting peace between Israel and the Palestinians to providing the basic services necessary to lift them out of poverty. Little wonder then that many Middle Easterners have turned to organisations such as Hezbollah and Hamas who, in the eyes of many Arabs, have matched their words with actions. Both groups have built up extensive networks of social safety nets and, with limited success, taken on Israel on the battlefield. That these groups are avowedly Islamic in focus and enjoy the support of arch-enemy Iran has only served to widen the gulf between Israel (and the US) and its neighbours.

By 2010 the region had reached something of an impasse, with the issues of the past 60 years frozen into seemingly perpetual division that sometimes spilled over into open warfare, but more often festered like an open wound. The Palestinians still dream of returning home. The Israelis still dream of a world free from fear. In the meantime, the two sides come no closer to a resolution. These are real issues that make life a daily struggle for ordinary people and the sad fact remains that, for many Middle Easterners, life is no easier than it was 60 years ago. If a scrap of consolation can be found amid the ashes of failed peace processes, it is that such a time frame is the mere blink of a historical eye for this part of the world.

A History of the Modern Middle East (William Cleveland and Martin Bunton; 2016), now in its sixth edition, is an excellent primer to modern Middle Eastern history.

The Arab Spring

When a young, unemployed man named Mohammed Bouazizi set fire to himself in the central Tunisian town of Sidi Bouzid in December 2010, few imagined the firestorm of change his desperate suicide would ignite

2013
Isis emerges as the most powerful and brutal of the radical Islamist military forces, and declares a caliphate in the areas of northern Iraq and Syria under its control.

2014
Field Marshal Abdel Fatah Al Sisi is sworn in as Egypt's president after a landslide victory in an election where less than half of the electorate turned out to vote.

2015
Iran reaches a landmark deal with the international community aimed at restricting Iran's nuclear activity in return for a lifting of international economic sanctions.

2015
Russia joins the Syria conflict at the request of Syria's government, turning the tide for a government that had been losing territory.

across the region. Within months the 30-year dictatorship of Egyptian president Hosni Mubarak had been overthrown in a popular uprising. Soon, leaders of similarly long standing had been swept from power in Libya, Tunisia and Yemen. Power had, it seemed, been returned to the people, ushering in a brief interlude of hope in a region desperately in need of good news.

But as Iraqis had long ago learned, getting rid of despotic governments was to prove far easier – except in Syria – than building the open, democratic societies which many of those who had demonstrated for freedom craved. With the dictators gone, most countries faced a profound political vacuum. In the heady days that followed the revolution in Egypt, for example, it became clear that those who had led the push for change did not have the unity, experience nor political program needed to build what came next. The well-organised Muslim Brotherhood swept to power, the army threw the Brotherhood out and seized power for itself. This Egyptian model – idealistic young protesters sidelined by better-organised Islamist groups – was a cautionary tale for those seeking change.

Elsewhere, Jordan seemed to have learned the lesson. For a brief moment in the spring of 2011, it looked as though Jordanians were set to join protesters elsewhere. Comprised largely of young students, and peaceful in their approach, Jordanian protesters argued on the streets of Amman for higher wages and a fuller embracing of democracy. Perhaps fearful of what might follow, the demonstrations soon petered out, however, leaving only weekly gatherings of die-hards after Friday prayers.

Rosewater (2014) dramatises the 2009 Green Movement and its aftermath, by telling the story of an Iranian-Canadian journalist (played by Gael García Bernal) who is detained while on assignment in Iran. It was written, produced and directed by Jon Stewart, formerly the host of *The Daily Show* in the US.

2016
A failed coup attempt in Turkey prompts a government backlash against supporters of exiled opposition figure Fethullah Gulen.

2017
After six years of war in Syria, estimates as to how many people have been killed approach half a million.

2017
Continuing attacks on Egypt's Coptic Christian minority raise the spectre of escalating sectarian violence in the country.

25 September 2017
Voters in Iraqi Kurdistan vote overwhelmingly in favour of independence from Iraq in a referendum denounced by Iraq's government and neighbouring countries.

Religion

The Middle East is where it all began for the three big monotheistic world religions: Judaism, Christianity and Islam. Infusing almost every aspect of daily life in the region, from the five-times-daily call to prayer and cultural norms to architecture and disputes over historical claims to land, these three religions provide an important backstory to your travels in the Middle East.

Islam

Birth of Islam

Abdul Qasim Mohammed Ibn Abdullah Ibn Abd Al Muttalib Ibn Hashim (the Prophet Mohammed) was born in 570 AD. Mohammed's family belonged to the Quraysh tribe, a trading family with links to Syria and Yemen. By the age of six, Mohammed's parents had both died and he came into the care of his grandfather, the custodian of the Kaaba in Mecca.

The flight of Mohammed and his followers from Mecca to Medina (the Hejira) marks the birth of Islam and the first year of the Islamic calendar – 1 AH (AD 622).

At the age of 40, in 610, Mohammed retreated into the desert, and Muslims believe that he began to receive divine revelations from Allah via the voice of the archangel Gabriel; the revelations would continue throughout Mohammed's life. Three years later, Mohammed began imparting Allah's message to Meccans, gathering a significant following in his campaign against idolaters. His movement appealed especially to the poorer, disenfranchised sections of society.

Islam provided a simpler alternative to the established faiths, which had become complicated by hierarchical orders, sects and complex rituals, offering instead a direct relationship with God based only on the believer's submission to God (Islam means 'submission').

By 622, Mecca's powerful ruling families had forced Mohammed and his followers to flee north to Medina where Mohammed's supporters rapidly grew. In 630 Mohammed returned triumphantly to Mecca at the head of a 10,000-strong army to seize control of the city. Many of the surrounding tribes quickly swore allegiance to him and the new faith.

When Mohammed died in 632, the Arab tribes spread quickly across the Middle East, in very little time conquering what now constitutes Jordan, Syria, Iraq, Lebanon, and Israel and the Palestinian Territories. To the east, Persia and India soon found themselves confronted by the new army of believers. To the west, the unrelenting conquest swept across North Africa. By the end of the 7th century, the Muslim armies had reached the Atlantic and marched on Spain in 710, an astonishing achievement given the religion's humble desert roots.

At a time of great uncertainty and inflammatory rhetoric, it is important to remember that Jews, Christians and Muslims once lived alongside each other and at peace. *A History of Muslims, Christians, and Jews in the Middle East* (Heather J Sharkey; 2017) tells that story.

Shiite & Sunni

Despite the Prophet Mohammed's original intentions, Islam did not remain simple. The Prophet died leaving no sons and no instructions as to who should succeed him. Competing for power were Abu Bakr, the father of Mohammed's second wife Aisha, and Ali, Mohammed's cousin and the husband of his daughter Fatima. Initially, power was transferred to Abu Bakr, who became the first caliph, or ruler, with Ali reluctantly agreeing.

Abu Bakr's lineage came to an abrupt halt when his successor was murdered. Ali reasserted his right to power and emerged victorious in the ensuing power struggle, moving his capital to Kufa (later renamed Najaf, in Iraq), only to be assassinated himself in 661. After defeating Ali's successor, Hussein, in 680 at Karbala, the Umayyad dynasty rose to rule the majority of the Muslim world, marking the start of the Sunni sect. Those who continued to support the claims of the descendants of Ali became known as Shiites.

Beyond this early dynastic rivalry, there's little doctrinal difference between Shiite Islam and Sunni Islam, but the division remains to this day. Sunnis comprise some 90% of the world's Muslims, but Shiites are believed to form a majority of the population in Iraq, Lebanon and Iran. There are also Shiite minorities in almost all Arab countries.

The Quran

For Muslims the Quran is the word of God, directly communicated to Mohammed. It comprises 114 suras, or chapters, which govern all aspects of a Muslim's life.

It's not known whether the revelations were written down during Mohammed's lifetime, although Muslims believe the Quran to be the direct word of Allah as told to Mohammed. The third caliph, Uthman (644–56), gathered together everything written by the scribes (parchments, stone tablets, the memories of Mohammed's followers) and gave them to a panel of editors under the caliph's aegis. A Quran printed today is identical to that agreed upon by Uthman's compilers 14 centuries ago.

Another important aspect of the Quran is the language in which it is written. Some Muslims believe that the Quran must be studied in its original classical Arabic form ('an Arabic Quran, wherein there is no crookedness'; sura 39:25) and that translations dilute the holiness of its sacred texts. For Muslims, the language of the Quran is known as *sihr halal* (lawful magic).

The Rise of Islamic State: ISIS and the New Sunni Revolution (Patrick Cockburn; 2015) is the best and most reasoned account of extremist Sunni Islam as it has come to affect the region.

Five Pillars of Islam

To live a devout life, Muslims are expected to observe, as a minimum, the five pillars of Islam.

Shahada This is the profession of faith, Islam's basic tenet: 'There is no god but Allah, and Mohammed is the Prophet of Allah'. This phrase forms an integral part of the call to prayer and is used at all important events in a Muslim's life.

Sala (sura 11:115) This is the obligation of prayer, ideally five times a day: at sunrise, noon, mid-afternoon, sunset and night. It's acceptable to pray at home or elsewhere, except for Friday noon prayers, which are performed at a mosque.

Zakat (sura 107) Muslims must give alms to the poor to the value of one-fortieth of a believer's annual income.

Sawm (sura 2:180–5) Ramadan, the ninth month of the Muslim calendar, commemorates the revelation of the Quran to Mohammed. As Ramadan represents a Muslim's renewal of faith, nothing may pass their lips (food, cigarettes, drinks), and they must refrain from sex from dawn until dusk.

Hajj (sura 2:190–200) Every physically and financially able Muslim should perform the hajj to the holiest of cities, Mecca, at least once in their lifetime. The reward is considerable: the forgiving of all past sins.

The Story of the Qur'an: Its History and Place in Muslim Life (Ingrid Mattson; 2007) is a landmark text that's filled with insights into what it means to be a Muslim in the 21st century.

Call to Prayer

Five times a day, Muslims are called, if not actually to enter a mosque to pray, at least to take the time to do so where they are; the call to prayer is made by the *muezzin*. The midday prayers on Friday, when the imam of the mosque delivers his weekly *khutba*, or sermon, are considered the most important. For Muslims, prayer is less a petition to Allah (in the

Christian sense) than a ritual reaffirmation of Allah's power and a reassertion of the brotherhood and equality of all believers.

The act of praying consists of a series of predefined movements of the body and recitals of prayers and passages of the Quran, all designed to express the believer's absolute humility and Allah's sovereignty.

Karen Armstrong has an impressive portfolio of titles that include *A History of God* (1994), *Islam: A Short History* (2002), *Muhammad: A Prophet for Our Time* (2007) and others. In straightforward prose, she takes a clear-eyed look at the great religions that underpin life in the Middle East.

Islamic Customs

In everyday life, Muslims are prohibited from drinking alcohol (sura 5:90–5) and eating carrion, blood products or pork, which are considered unclean (sura 2:165), the meat of animals not killed in the prescribed manner (sura 5:1–5) and food over which the name of Allah has not been said (sura 6:115). Adultery (sura 18:30–5), theft (sura 5:40–5) and gambling (sura 5:90–5) are also prohibited.

Islam is not just about prohibitions but also marks the important events of a Muslim's life. When a baby is born, the first words uttered to it are the call to prayer. A week later follows a ceremony in which the baby's head is shaved and an animal sacrificed in remembrance of Abraham's willingness to sacrifice his son to Allah. The major event of a boy's childhood is circumcision, which normally takes place between the ages of seven and 12. When a person dies, a burial service is held at the mosque and the body is buried with the feet facing Mecca.

Judaism

Judaism is the first recorded monotheistic faith and one of the oldest religions still practised. Its major tenet is that there is one God who created the universe and remains omnipresent. Judaism's power is held not in a central authority or person, but rather in its teachings and the Holy Scriptures.

Until the foundation of the State of Israel in 1948, Jewish communities lived peacefully alongside their Muslim neighbours in the countries of the Middle East; Iraq was home to a particularly large Jewish community. Tiny Jewish communities remain in some Muslim countries, but most fled or were expelled after 1948.

Foundations of Judaism

The patriarch of the Jewish faith was Abraham who, according to the calculations of the Hebrew Torah, was born 1948 years after Creation and lived to the age of 175. According to Jewish belief he preached the existence of one God and in return God promised him the land of Canaan (the Promised Land in Jewish tradition), but only after his descendants would be exiled and redeemed. Accordingly, his grandson Jacob set off for Egypt, where later generations found themselves bound in slavery. Moses led them out of Egypt and received the Ten Commandments on Mt Sinai.

MUSLIM CALL TO PRAYER

Allahu akbar, Allahu akbar	God is great, God is great
Ashhadu an la Ilah ila Allah	I testify that there is no God but Allah
Ashhadu an Mohammed rasul Allah	I testify that Mohammed is his Prophet
Haya ala as-sala	Hurry towards prayer
Haya ala af-fala	Hurry towards success
Allahu akbar, Allahu akbar	God is great, God is great
La Ilah ila Allah	There is no God but Allah

It was Rambam, the 12th-century Jewish rabbi, who laid out the 13 core principles of Jewish belief. These principles include the belief in one unique God to whom prayer must be directed; the belief that God rewards the good and punishes the wicked; and the belief in the coming of the Messiah and the resurrection of the dead. Having said this, Judaism doesn't focus on abstract cosmological beliefs and rather than a strict adherence to dogmatic ideas, actions such as prayer, study and performing mitzvah, which means adherence to the commandments, are of greater importance.

A Brief Guide to Judaism: Theology, History and Practice (Naftali Brawer; 2008) is one of the better introductions to what is often a complex faith, focusing on major ideas and historical events rather than the minutiae of Jewish doctrine.

The Torah & Talmud

The basis for the Jewish religion is the Torah, the first five books of the Old Testament. The Torah contains the revelation from God via Moses more than 3000 years ago, including, most importantly, God's commandments (613 commandments in total). The Torah is supplemented by the rest of the books of the Old Testament, of which the most important are the prophetic books.

These books are, in turn, complemented by the Talmud, a collection of another 63 books. The Talmud was written largely in exile after the Romans crushed the Jewish state and destroyed the Temple in Jerusalem in AD 70, and within its pages is most of what separates Judaism from other religions. Included are plenty of rabbinical interpretations of the earlier scriptures, with a wealth of instructions and rulings for Jewish daily life.

Jewish Customs

The most obvious Jewish custom you'll experience in Israel is Shabbat, the day of rest. It begins on Friday night with sundown and ends at nightfall on Saturday. No work of any kind is allowed on Shabbat, unless someone's health is at stake. Tasks such as writing or handling money are forbidden. Starting a fire is also prohibited, and in modern terms this means no use of electricity is allowed (lights can be turned on before Shabbat starts but must stay on until it ends). Permitted activities include visiting with friends and family, reading and discussing the Torah, and prayer at a synagogue. Sex is also allowed; in fact, it's a double mitzvah on Shabbat.

God's laws, as recorded in the Torah, govern every facet of an observant Jew's life, including issues like the prohibition of theft, murder and idolatry. There are other commandments to which Jews must adhere, such as eating kosher foods and reciting the shema (affirmation of Judaism) twice daily.

Some Jewish sects are easily recognised by their clothing, although most Jews wear Western street clothes. The most religious Jews, the Hasidim (or *haredim*), are identified by their black hats, long black coats,

The Jews of the Middle East and North Africa in Modern Times (Reeva Simon; 2003) looks at the Jewish presence in the region during the last two centuries, with half of the book taken up with country-by-country sections that include Turkey, Syria, Iraq, Lebanon, Egypt, and Israel and the Palestinian Territories.

SHARED TRADITIONS

As most Muslims will attest, the God invoked in Friday prayers across the Middle East is the same God worshipped in synagogues and churches around the globe. The Quran never attempts to deny the debt it owes to the holy books that came before it. Indeed the Quran itself was revealed to Mohammed by the archangel Gabriel. The suras contain many references to the earlier prophets – Adam, Abraham (Ibrahim), Noah, Moses (Moussa) and Jesus (although Muslims strictly deny his divinity) are all recognised as prophets in a line that ends definitively with the greatest of them all, the Prophet Mohammed. Not surprisingly, given the shared heritage, Muslims traditionally attribute a place of great respect to Christians and Jews as *ahl al kitab* (the people of the book; sura 2:100–15).

collared white shirts, beards and *peyot* (side curls). *Haredi* women, like Muslim women, act and dress modestly, covering up exposed hair and skin (except the hands and face). Many Jews, both secular and orthodox, wear a kippa (skullcap).

Christianity

Christianity is the world's largest religion, with an estimated 2.1 billion followers. Islam comes next with at least 1.7 billion adherents. Judaism has an estimated 14 to 18 million followers.

Jesus preached in what is present-day Israel and the Palestinian Territories, but Christians form only minority groups in all Middle Eastern countries. Lebanon's one million Maronites have followers all over the world, but by far the biggest Christian sect in the region is formed by the Copts of Egypt, who make up most of that country's Christian population. Originally it was the apostle Mark who established Christianity in Egypt, and by the 4th century it was the state religion. The Coptic Church split from the Byzantine Orthodox Church in the 5th century after a dispute about the human nature of Jesus.

Otherwise, the Arab Christians of the Middle East belong to many churches in all main branches of the religion – Orthodox, Catholic and Protestant. The number of Christians in the Middle East is, however, in decline thanks largely to falling birth rates and high rates of emigration among the region's Christians.

Foundations of Christianity

Jesus of Nazareth was born in Bethlehem in what is now the Palestinian Territories in the year zero (or AD 1, depending on who you believe) of the Christian calendar. After baptism by John the Baptist, Jesus was said to have been led by God into the desert, where he remained for 40 days and nights, during which time he refuted the temptations of the Devil. Christians believe that his ministry was marked by numerous miracles, such as healings, walking on water and the resuscitation of the dead (Lazarus). At the age of 33, Jesus was accused of sedition and condemned to death by Jerusalem's Roman governor Pontius Pilate. After being crucified, Christians believe, Jesus was resurrected and ascended to heaven. Christians believe that God's divine nature is expressed in the Trinity: God, Jesus Christ and the Holy Spirit.

From the Holy Mountain: A Journey in the Shadow of Byzantium (William Dalrymple; 1998) takes the reader through the heart of the Middle East and pays homage to the survival of Eastern Christianity.

The followers of Jesus came to be known as Christians (Christ is a Greek-derived title meaning 'Anointed One'), believing him to be the son of God, and the Messiah. Within a few decades of Jesus' death, having interpreted and spread his teachings, his followers had formed a faith distinct from Judaism. A Greek-speaking Christian community emerged in Jerusalem in the mid-2nd century and the Greek Orthodox Church is now the largest denomination in Israel and the Palestinian Territories.

Architecture

Middle Eastern architecture ranges from the sublime to the downright ugly. On one hand, the graceful lines and elaborate tilework of traditional Islamic architecture draw on the rich historical legacy left by the great empires that once ruled the region. On the other, the perennially unfinished cinder-block architecture of grim functionality blights many city outskirts and smaller towns. We prefer to concentrate on the former.

Ancient World

Ancient Egyptian Architecture

The tombs and temples of ancient Egypt rank among the Middle East's most impressive architectural forms. Whereas private homes have disappeared – most were built of sun-dried mud-brick and occurred along now-flooded stretches of the Nile Valley – ancient Egypt's public architecture has stood the test of time, in part because most were built on higher ground than residential areas. In most cases, Pharaonic tombs and temples (including the Pyramids of Giza) were built of locally quarried sandstone and sturdy granite.

The tombs of ancient Egypt were designed at once to impress with their grandeur and to deter tomb raiders from plundering the treasures contained within. As a result, most were almost fortress-like, with thick sloping walls, very few openings and labyrinthine passageways in the interior. Tomb decoration was often elaborate, adorned with hieroglyphics and frescoes, and it is from such imagery that archaeologists have been able to piece together so much of what we know about the period, from religious beliefs and the afterlife to questions of dynastic succession.

Such paintings also adorned the facades of temples, and temple hieroglyphics, once decoded, have also become another rich source of information about historical events and even everyday life. Egyptian temples, each dedicated to one among many Egyptian gods, are most often characterised by the use of flat roofs, massive stone blocks and tightly spaced columns. Most were also aligned with important astronomical occurrences, their measurements and design carefully calculated by royal astronomers and, in some cases, the pharaohs themselves.

Ancient Egyptian Architecture

- *Pyramids of Giza*
- *Temple of Karnak*
- *Great Temple of Abu Simbel*
- *Temple of Hathor*
- *Valley of the Kings*
- *Temple of Horus*
- *Luxor Temple*
- *Temple of Philae*

Greek & Roman Architecture

Although it is Roman architecture that dominates the ruined cities that are such a feature of travelling in the Middle East, the Romans drew heavily on the architecture of the ancient Greeks. Indeed, it was from the Greeks that the Romans acquired their prototypes for temples, theatres, monumental gateways, public squares (agora to the Greeks, forum to the Romans) and colonnaded thoroughfares.

But in the Middle East at least it was the Romans who perfected these forms and it is the Roman version that endures, at once monumental in scale and extremely intricate in detail. The Romans also added their own innovations, many of them to do with water – perhaps the most enduring of these are aqueducts and the concept of richly decorated public baths, the forerunner to the hammam.

AGA KHAN: ISLAMIC ARCHITECTURE'S SAVIOUR

If there's one figure who has been responsible above all others for reviving Islamic architecture worldwide, it's the Aga Khan IV, the imam (religious teacher) of the largest branch of the Ismaili Shiite Muslims since 1957. Through the Aga Khan Development Network (www.akdn.org), one of the largest private development organisations in the world, the Aga Khan funds programs encompassing public health, education, microfinance, rural development and architecture.

One focus of his efforts has been the Historic Cities Program, which aims to rescue, restore and bring back to life public buildings across the Islamic world. Cairo in Egypt and, before the war, Syria's Damascus and Aleppo were the main beneficiaries in the Middle East. Rather than focusing solely on bricks and mortar, the projects prioritise improvements in social infrastructure and living conditions in surrounding areas, thereby transforming architectural restoration into wider projects for social renewal.

In Cairo, a city with one of the lowest ratios of green space to urban population on earth, the first stage of the US$30-million project has involved creating the 30-hectare Al Azhar Park on land reclaimed from what had been a rubbish dump for 500 years. The project also involved restoring 1.5km of the 12th-century Ayyubid Wall, rescuing a number of dilapidated mosques and an integrated plan for improving housing, infrastructure and living conditions in the adjacent Darb Al Ahmar, one of Cairo's poorest districts and home to more than 90,000 people; many of the rooftops were fitted with solar heating systems, water cisterns and vegetable gardens.

A further pillar in the Aga Khan's master plan has been the triennial Aga Khan Award for Architecture (www.akdn.org/architecture), one of the world's most prestigious architecture awards. Winning projects since the award was announced in 1977 have included the restorations of İstanbul's Topkapı Palace, Cairo's Citadel and the rehabilitation of Iran's Tabriz Bazaar. A more recent award winner is the Tabiat Pedestrian Bridge that connects two Tehran parks.

Most of the buildings that survive played critical roles in public Roman life: the temples were the focus of religious devotion, the theatres and amphitheatres were the centrepieces of public entertainment and the monumental arched gateways reinforced the cult that surrounded the emperors of ancient Rome. Private homes, often belonging to wealthy noble families, were often paved in intricate mosaics.

Aside from individual elements of public Roman architecture, the whole was also extremely important and it was in town planning that the Romans really made their mark. In the cities of the ancient Roman Empire, city life revolved around a public square (forum), which was a meeting place (and sometimes a market) and surrounded by imposing temples and administrative buildings. A well-ordered grid of streets, paved with flagstones and sometimes lined with porticoes, surrounded the forum, with two main streets – the north–south *cardo* and the east–west *decumanus*, which usually intersected at the forum providing the main thoroughfares. An outer defensive wall, beyond which lay farmland, usually encircled the core of the city.

Greek & Roman Architecture

- *Ephesus (Efes), Turkey*
- *Baalbek, Lebanon*
- *Caesarea, Israel & the Palestinian Territories*
- *Jerash, Jordan*
- *Temple of Amun, Egypt*

Ancient Persian Architecture

Iran is home to some of the oldest extant structures in the Middle East, among them the remarkable Elamite ziggurat at Choqa Zanbil, which predates the 7th century BC. But the most stirring examples of ancient Persian architecture come from the Achaemenid era (550–330 BC), among them the magnificent ceremonial palace complexes and royal tombs at Pasargadae, Naqsh-e Rostam, Shushtar and awesome Persepolis. These are decorated with bas-reliefs of kings, soldiers, supplicants, animals and the winged figure of the Zoroastrian deity Ahura Mazda.

The Achaemenids typically built with sun-dried brick and stone and there are links with the old ziggurats in both shape and decoration. The Achaemenid style also incorporated features taken from Egyptian and Greek architecture. They built colossal halls supported by stone and wooden columns with typically Persian bull's-head capitals.

Places of Worship

Mosques

Embodying the Islamic faith and representing its most predominant architectural feature throughout the region is the *masjid* (mosque, also called a *jamaa*).

Prayer Hall

The house belonging to the Prophet Mohammed is said to have provided the prototype of the mosque. It had an enclosed oblong courtyard with huts (housing Mohammed's wives) along one wall and a rough portico providing shade. This plan developed with the courtyard becoming the *sahn,* the portico the arcaded *riwaq* and the house the *haram* (prayer hall).

The prayer hall is typically divided into a series of aisles. The central aisle is wider than the rest and leads to a vaulted niche in the wall called the *mihrab*; this indicates the direction of Mecca, towards which Muslims must face when they pray. Also in the prayer hall is usually a *minbar* (a wooden pulpit that stands beside the *mihrab*), from where the imam delivers his *khutba* (sermon) at the main Friday noon prayers.

Before entering the prayer hall and participating in communal worship, Muslims must perform a ritual washing of the hands, forearms, neck and face (by washing themselves before prayer, the believer indicates a willingness to be purified). For this purpose mosques have traditionally had a large ablutions fountain at the centre of the courtyard, often fashioned from marble and worn by centuries of use. These days, modern mosques just have rows of taps.

Rising above the main mosque structure is at least one (but often numerous) minarets, some of which were adapted from former church steeples. In ancient times the minaret was where the muezzin climbed to call the faithful to prayer – these days, a loudspeaker performs a similar function.

Arab & Turkish Styles

When it came to mosque design, each region developed its own local flourishes. The Umayyads of Damascus favoured square minarets, the Abbasid dynasty in Iraq built spiral minarets echoing the ziggurats of the Babylonians, and the Fatimids of Egypt made much use of decorative stucco work. The Mamluks (1250–1517), a military dynasty of former slaves ruling out of Egypt, brought a new level of sophistication to mosque architecture – their buildings are characterised by the banding of different coloured stone (a technique known as *ablaq*) and by the elaborate carvings and patterning around windows and in the recessed portals. The best examples of their patronage are found in Cairo but impressive Mamluk monuments also grace the old city of Jerusalem. Cairo's Mosque of Qaitbey, with its exquisitely carved dome, is perhaps the high point of Mamluk style.

It was the Ottoman Turks who left some of the most recognisable (and, given the reach of the Ottoman Empire, widespread) landmarks. Ottoman mosques were designed on the basic principle of a dome on a square and are instantly recognisable by their slim, pencil-shaped minarets. The Süleymaniye Mosque in İstanbul and the Selimiye Mosque in Edirne, both the work of the Turkish master architect Sinan, represent the apogee of the style.

Islam: Art & Architecture (2013), edited by Markus Hattstein and Peter Delius, is comprehensive, lavishly illustrated and one of those coffee-table books that you'll treasure and dip into time and again.

Good books on Middle Eastern architecture include: *Ornament and Decoration in Islamic Architecture* (Dominique Clévenot and Gérard Degeorge; 2017); *The Illustrated Encyclopedia of Islamic Art and Architecture* (Moya Carey; 2014); *Islamic Architecture in Iran* (Saeid Khaghani; 2017); *The Architecture of the Christian Holy Land* (Kathryn Blair Moore; 2017).

Persian Styles

Even in ancient times, minarets in Persia were far more decorative than practical. Since it was that someone standing atop a minaret could look into the private family areas of nearby houses, Shiite mosques often have a separate hutlike structure on the roof from where the muezzin makes the call to prayer.

The defining aspects of Persian architecture are its monumental simplicity and its lavish use of surface ornamentation and colour. The ground plans of ordinary Persian buildings mix only a few standard elements: a courtyard and arcades, lofty entrance porticoes and four *iwan* (barrel-vaulted halls opening onto the courtyard). These basic features are often so densely covered with decoration that observers are led to imagine the architecture is far more complex than it actually is. The decorations are normally geometric, floral or calligraphic.

The development of the dome was one of the greatest achievements of Persian architecture. The Sassanians (AD 224–642) were the first to discover a satisfactory way of building a dome on top of a square chamber by using two intermediate levels, or squinches – the lower octagonal and the higher 16-sided – on which the dome could rest. Later domes became progressively more sophisticated, incorporating an inner semicircular dome sheathed by an outer conical or even onion-shaped dome. Externally the domes were often encased in tiles, with patterns so elaborate they had to be worked out on models at ground level first.

Under a succession of enlightened and cultivated Safavid rulers (1502–1736), most notably Shah Abbas I, came the final refinement of styles that marked the culmination of the Persian Islamic school of architecture. Its greatest expression was Abbas' royal capital of Esfahan, a supreme example of town planning with one of the most magnificent collections of buildings from one period anywhere in the world – the vast and unforgettable Naqsh-e Jahan (Imam) Sq.

Holy Land Churches

- *Church of the Holy Sepulchre, Jerusalem*
- *Church of the Nativity, Bethlehem*
- *Basilica of the Annunciation, Nazareth*

Churches Beyond the Holy Land

- *St George's Orthodox Cathedral, Beirut*
- *Church of St John the Baptist, Byblos*
- *Kelisa-ye Vank, Esfahan*
- *St George's Church, Madaba*
- *Moses Memorial Church, Mt Nebo*
- *St Katherine's Monastery, Sinai*

Synagogues

Although many synagogues follow a similar style, there is also great variety in their architectural forms. This is partly because Jewish tradition dictates that God can be present wherever there are 10 adults gathered together.

There are, however, some elements common to all synagogues. The first of these is the presence of an ark (in some cases simply a cupboard, or a chest), which contains the scrolls of the Torah. All synagogues also have a table (or in some cases a platform or pulpit) from which the Torah can be read, and from where some services are conducted. In most synagogues, a light is also illuminated at all times to symbolise the menorah (candelabra) in the Temple in Jerusalem. The synagogue, or at the very least its prayer room, should also be aligned to face towards Jerusalem.

There are also a number of Talmudic instructions on the form that synagogues should take – they must have windows and be taller than other buildings in town – although these were often ignored or simply not possible.

Other features of Jewish religious architecture vary from one synagogue to the next – some are simple prayer rooms, others are adorned with inscriptions in Hebrew and otherwise richly decorated. In many cases, there are also separate sections of the synagogue for men and women.

Churches

After the first three centuries of Christianity (during which time the faith was illegal and worshippers most often gathered in private homes), the church evolved from a one-room meeting place to one that contained a space for the congregation and a separate space where the priest could perform the rites of Mass. Over time, church architecture became more sophisticated with aisles (which became necessary as churches grew in size), a steeple (which usually housed the bells), chapels and a baptistery.

Early church architecture, and indeed many of its most enduring forms, owes much to the Romans. It was not the temples that provided the greatest inspiration, because these had little space for the congregation. Rather, inspiration (and indeed the name) came from the Roman basilicas which were not places of worship but places for meetings, markets and administrative functions such as courts. More specifically, many Roman basilicas had a semi-circular apse covered with a half-dome roof, which became an essential element in later church architecture. Roman mausoleums, with their square or circular domed structures, also filtered into Christian architecture – Jerusalem's Church of the Holy Sepulchre is one clear example of this trend.

Another crucial and oft-observed element of church architecture is a floor plan in the shape of a cross. Although the exact shape of this cross may vary depending on the region and date of construction, the two main forms mimic the Latin and Greek crosses – the former has a rectangular form and has a long nave crossed by a shorter transept, while the Greek cross design was usually square with the four 'arms' of equal length.

Mosaics were also a stunning feature of churches, particularly in Byzantine times. The best examples are in Madaba in Jordan.

A Selection of Iran's Unesco Sites

Choqa Zanbil

Pasargadae

Susa

Persepolis

Masjed-e Jameh

Naqsh-e Jahan (Imam) Sqe

Tabriz Bazaar

Golestan Palace

Secular Architecture

Urban Buildings

The Middle East's cities are where the failure of architecture and urban planning to keep pace with burgeoning populations is most distressingly on show. Take Cairo, for example. In 1950, Cairo had a population of around 2.3 million. Now as many as 22 million people live cheek-by-jowl within greater Cairo's ever-expanding boundaries. The result is an undistinguished sprawl of grime-coated, Soviet-style apartment blocks and unplanned shanty towns, often without even the most basic amenities.

Rural Buildings

Architecture in rural areas of the Middle East has always been a highly localised tradition, determined primarily by the dictates of climate. In the oases, particularly the Saharan towns of Egypt's Western Oases, mud-brick was easy to manufacture and ensured cool interiors under the baking desert sun. Although perfectly adapted to ordinary climatic conditions, these homes also proved extremely vulnerable to erosion and rains, which explains why so few examples remain across the region. The best examples are in Siwa (Egypt) and Yazd (Iran).

But the undoubted star when it comes to unique traditional architecture is Cappadocia (Kapadokya), where homes and churches were hewn from the weird and wonderful landscape of caves, rock walls and soft volcanic tuff.

Most forms of vernacular rural architecture face an uncertain future. Rural poverty and unrelenting urbanisation has caused the widespread abandonment of traditional forms of architecture. The simple truth about the future of rural architecture in the Middle East is this: unless places become established as tourist attractions, their traditional architecture will disappear within a generation, if it hasn't done so already.

Turkey's Unesco Sites

Historic areas of İstanbul

City of Safranbolu

Archaeological site of Troy

Selimiye Mosque

Diyarbakır Fortress

Ephesus

Middle Eastern Cuisine

For all the issues that divide the region, an emphatic belief in the importance of good food is one thing on which all people of the Middle East agree. And little wonder given what's on offer. Middle Easterners see eating as a social event to be shared with family and friends, a means of marking the most important moments in life, and a pastime worth spending hours over. Or to put it another way, life revolves around food.

Staples & Specialties

Middle Eastern cooking draws on a range of influences, from sophisticated Ottoman and Persian sensibilities, or the spare improvisation of the desert cooking pot, to a Mediterranean belief in letting fresh ingredients speak for themselves. Where the excitement really lies is in the astonishing variety at large in its feasts of colour and complementary tastes.

A New Book of Middle Eastern Food by Claudia Roden brought the cuisines of the region to the attention of Western cooks when it was first released in 1968. It's still an essential reference, as fascinating for its cultural insights as for its great recipes.

Mezze

Mezze (meze in Turkish) ranks alongside Spanish tapas and Italian antipasto as one of the world's greatest culinary inventions. A collection of appetisers or small plates of food, mezze allows you to sample a variety of often complementary tastes and takes the difficulty out of choosing what to order – choose everything! Mezze mirrors the time-honoured practice of hosts throwing a party, offering up for their guests a banquet of choice. Largely vegetable-based and bursting with colour and flavour, it's the region's most compelling culinary flourish.

Although it's usually perfectly acceptable for diners to construct an entire meal from the mezze list and forgo the mains on offer, there are subtle differences from country to country in just how far you can take this mezze obsession. Mezze is the headline act when it comes to Levantine cuisine, but it's the understudy to kebabs in Turkey and the trusted warm-up to the region's other cuisines.

Breads

For all the variety of the Middle Eastern table, bread *(khobz* or *a'aish,* which means 'life') is the guaranteed constant, considered a gift from God and the essential accompaniment to any Middle Eastern meal. In fact, it's considered such a necessity that few Middle Eastern restaurants dare to charge a cent for it. If you're wandering through the streets of an Arab city in the morning and you see a large queue forming at an otherwise innocuous hole in the wall, you've almost certainly stumbled upon the local bakery.

The staple Middle Eastern bread follows a 2000-year-old recipe. Unleavened and cooked over an open flame, it's used in lieu of cutlery to scoop dips and ripped into pieces to wrap around morsels of meat. Dinner is always served with baskets of bread to mop up mezze, while kebabs are often served with a tasty bread canopy coated in tomato, parsley and spices.

Almost every meal in Iran is accompanied by *nun* (bread). The four main types of *nun* are *barbari* (crisp, salty and often covered with sesame seeds), *lavash* (flat and thin breakfast bread), *sangak* (long and thick and baked on a bed of stones to give it its characteristic dimpled appearance), and *taftun* (crisp with a ribbed surface).

Kebabs & Other Meats

There are more variations on the kebab in this part of the world than you could poke a skewer at. Every country has its specialities – Turkey is understandably proud of its luscious İskender kebap (döner kebap on a bed of pide with a side serving of yogurt) and Lebanon has an unswerving devotion to *shish tawooq* (grilled chicken kebab, often served with a garlic sauce).

In Iran, even in a restaurant with a long menu, most main-dish options will be kabab. These are served either on bread or as *chelo kabab* (on a vast mound of rice), and in contrast with the greasy döner kebabs inhaled after rough nights in the West, Iranian kababs are tasty, healthy and cooked shish-style over hot charcoals. They are usually sprinkled with spicy *sumaq* (sumac) and accompanied by raw onion, grilled tomatoes and, for an extra fee, a bowl of *mast* (yoghurt).

The kebab might be king in most Middle Eastern countries, but when it comes to meat dishes there are courtiers waiting in the wings. Primary among these is *kibbeh,* a strong candidate for the title of Lebanon's national dish. Indeed, these croquettes of ground lamb, cracked wheat, onion and spices are considered the ultimate test of a Lebanese cook's skills. In Beirut, they're served raw like a steak tartare, accompanied with fresh mint leaves, olive oil and spring onions. Raw *kibbeh (kibbeh nayye)* has many variations. In northern Lebanon, you often find mint and fresh chillies mixed through the meat. *Kibbeh saniye* is *kibbeh* flattened out on a tray with a layer of spiced lamb and pine nuts in between.

Arabesque: Modern Middle Eastern Food (Greg & Lucy Malouf, 2013) lists the 42 essential ingredients from the region and offers insights into how they can be used to create authentic dishes.

POPULAR MEZZE SPECIALTIES

Among the seemingly endless candidates, we've narrowed it down to the following dishes (spellings may differ from country to country).

baba ghanoosh – purée of grilled aubergines (eggplants) with tahini and olive oil

basturma – cold, sliced meat cured with fenugreek

borek – pastry stuffed with salty white cheese or spicy minced meat with pine nuts; also known as *sambousek*

fatayer – triangular deep-fried pastries stuffed with spinach, meat or cheese

hummus bi tahina – cooked chickpeas ground into a paste and mixed with tahini, lemon, olive oil and garlic

kibbeh – minced lamb, burghul wheat and pine nuts made into a lemon-shaped patty and deep-fried

labneh – thick yogurt flavoured with garlic and sometimes with mint

loobieh – French bean salad with tomatoes, onions and garlic

mouhamarra – walnut and pomegranate syrup dip

muttabal – purée of aubergine mixed with tahini, yogurt and olive oil; similar to but creamier than baba ghanoosh

shanklish – tangy, eye-wateringly strong goat's cheese served with onions, oil and tomatoes

tahina – paste made of sesame seeds and served as a dip

wara ainab – stuffed vine leaves, served both hot and cold; in Egypt also called *mahshi*

PERSIAN FOOD PHILOSOPHY

Ancient Persians believed good diet was light on fat, red meat, starch and alcohol – these transformed men into selfish brutes. Instead, fruit, vegetables, chicken and fish were encouraged as the food of gentler, more respectable people. In practice, this philosophy was governed by a classification of 'hot' and 'cold' foods, which is still widely used today.

Similar to China's yin and yang, the belief is that 'hot' foods thicken the blood and speed metabolism, while 'cold' foods dilute the blood and slow the metabolism. The philosophy extends to personalities and weather, too. Like foods, people are believed to have 'hot' and 'cold' natures. People with 'hot' natures should eat more 'cold' foods, and vice versa. And on cold days it's best to eat 'hot' foods, and vice versa.

So what's 'hot' and what's not? The classification has nothing to do with temperature, and regional variations exist, but it's generally agreed that animal fat, wheat, sugar, sweets, wine, most dried fruits and nuts, fresh herbs including mint and saffron, and most meats are 'hot' (but not beef). 'Cold' foods include fish, yoghurt and watermelon (all 'very cold'), rice, many fresh vegetables (particularly radishes) and fruits, beef, beer and other non-wine alcohol. Some foods are hotter or colder than others, and some, such as pears, feta and tea, are neutral.

As you travel you'll see the balance in dishes such as *fesenjun* (sauce of pomegranate juice, walnuts, eggplant and cardamom served over roast chicken and rice), where the pomegranate (cold) is balanced by the walnuts (hot). On the table, *mast* (yoghurt), cheese, radishes and greens – all cold – are balanced with 'hot' kebabs, chicken and sweets. Getting the balance right is what is most important. Too much 'cold' food is thought to be particularly unhealthy, so be careful of eating watermelon and *dugh* (churned sour milk or yoghurt mixed with water) with your fish meal, unless the *dugh* comes with chopped herbs to balance it out. 'Hot' foods are apparently not so dangerous: too much 'hot' and you might end up with a cold sore, if you're prone to them.

Another culinary star is kofta (spiced ground meat formed into balls; *köfte* in Turkey), which is served in innumerable ways and is the signature element of the Egyptian favourite *daood basha* (meatballs cooked in a *tagen* pot with pine nuts and tomato sauce).

Rice Dishes

Although not native to the Middle East, rice is a region-wide staple that's ever-present in home cooking but far less common on restaurant menus. Usually cooked with lamb or chicken, a subtle blend of spices and sometimes saffron, its arrival as the centrepiece of an already groaning table is often a high point of the meal. It's also the point at which you wish you hadn't eaten so much mezze.

If your average Middle Easterner loves rice, it's the Bedu who revere it. Easy to store, transport and cook, rice was perfectly suited to the once-nomadic lifestyle of many Bedu. For this hardy desert people, *mensaf* (lamb served on a bed of rice and pine nuts and accompanied by a tangy yogurt sauce) is what it's all about. Such is *mensaf's* popularity that you'll find it on menus in the Palestinian Territories and Jordan.

The Turkish dish *imam bayıldı* ('the imam fainted') is aubergine stuffed with onion and garlic, slow-cooked in olive oil and served cold. Legend has it that an imam fainted with pleasure on first tasting it.

Another regional rice speciality that won't disappoint is *makloubeh* (literally 'upside-down') rice. It's cooked in stock and spices with chickpeas, onions and off-the-bone lamb shanks, and then pressed in a deep bowl and turned upside down to reveal a delicious work of art. The vegetarian version incorporates eggplants with almonds and pine nuts.

Salads

It's inconceivable for most people in the region to eat a meal without salad and it's a zesty, fresh complement to a piping hot kebab. Middle Easterners are loyal to their basic salads and don't mind eating them meal after meal. Elaborations or creative flourishes are rare and simplicity is the key: crunchy fresh ingredients (including herbs), often caressed by a shake of oil and vinegar at the table. Salads are eaten with relish as a mezze or as an accompaniment to a meat or fish main course. Three salads, found throughout the region, form an integral part of the local diet:

fattoush – toasted *khobz*, tomatoes, onions and mint leaves, sometimes served with a smattering of tangy pomegranate syrup

shepherd's salad – colourful mix of chopped tomatoes, cucumber, onion and pepper; extremely popular in Turkey, where it's known as *çoban salatası*

tabbouleh – the region's signature salad combines burghul wheat, parsley and tomato, with a tangy sprinkling of sesame seeds, lemon and garlic

The Complete Middle East Cookbook (Tess Mallos; 1997) is full of easy-to-follow recipes and devotes individual chapters to national cuisines, including those of Turkey, Iraq, Iran, Egypt and Israel. It has been updated a number of times through the years.

Snack Foods

The regional stars of the snack-food line-up are shawarma and falafel, and they're both things of joy when served and eaten fresh. Shawarma is the Arabic equivalent of the Greek *gyros* sandwich or the Turkish döner kebap – strips are sliced from a vertical spit of compressed lamb or chicken, sizzled on a hot plate with chopped tomatoes and garnish, and then stuffed into a pocket of bread. Falafel is mashed chickpeas and spices rolled into balls and deep-fried; a variation known as *ta'amiyya,* made with dried fava beans, is served in Egypt.

In Egypt look out for shops sporting large metal tureens in the window: these specialise in the vegetarian delight *kushari,* a delicate mix of noodles, rice, black lentils and dried onions, served with an accompanying tomato sauce that's sometimes fiery with chilli. An alternative more often seen at Israeli sandwich stands is *sabich,* a falafel alternative with roast aubergine, boiled egg and potato, and salad with a tangy mango dressing, all stuffed into a pita.

In Lebanon, nothing beats grabbing a freshly baked *fatayer bi sbanikh* (spinach pastry) from one of the hole-in-the-wall bakeries that dot city streets. In Turkey, visitors inevitably fall deeply in love with melt-in-the-mouth *su böreği,* a noodle-like pastry oozing cheese and butter.

Variations of the pizza abound, one of the most delicious being Egypt's *fiteer,* featuring a base of thin, filo-style pastry. In Turkey, the best cheap snack is pide, the Turkish version of pizza, a canoe-shaped dough topped with *peynirli* (cheese), *yumurta* (egg) or *kıymalı* (mince). A *karaşık* pide has a mixture of toppings.

The most unassuming of all Middle Eastern fast foods is also one of the most popular. *Fuul* (fava bean paste) is mopped up by bread for breakfast and ladled into a pocket of bread for a snack on the run. You'll find it in Egypt (where it's the national dish), Jordan and Lebanon.

Cooking courses are few and far between in the Middle East, but Petra Kitchen (www.petrakitchen.com) in Jordan has local Bedouin teachers and plenty to learn and sample. In Iran, Persian Food Tours (www.persianfoodtours.com) begins with a morning shopping expedition around Tajrish Bazaar and then moves to its beautiful purpose-built kitchen.

Desserts & Sweets

All Middle Easterners love their sweets but they come closest to worshipping them in Turkey. The prince of the regional desserts is undoubtedly *muhalabiyya* (also known as *mahallabiye*), a blancmange-like concoction made of ground rice, milk, sugar, and rose or orange water, topped with chopped pistachios and almonds. Almost as popular is *ruz bi laban* (rice pudding, known as *fırın sütlaç* in Turkey).

But best of all are the pastries. Although these are sometimes served in restaurants for dessert, they're just as often enjoyed as an any-time-of-the-day snack. Old favourites include *kunafeh,* a vermicelli-like pastry over a vanilla base soaked in syrup; and the famous baklava, made from delicate filo drenched in honey or syrup. Variations on baklava (called *baghlava* in Iran) are flavoured with fresh nuts or stuffed with wickedly rich clotted cream (called *kaymak* in Turkey, *eishta* elsewhere).

VEGETARIAN DISHES

To ask, 'Do you have any vegetarian dishes?' in Egypt say, *'Andak akla nabateeyya?'* In other Arab countries you can ask for dishes that are *'bidoon lahem'* (without meat). In Turkey ask, *'Etsiz yemekler var mı?'* (Is there something to eat that has no meat?), while in Iran, it's *bee gusht va morgh* (no meat) or *giah khaaram* (I am a vegetarian).

Vegetarians & Vegans

Although it's quite normal for the people of the Middle East to eat a vegetarian meal, the concept of vegetarianism is quite foreign. Say you're a vegan and they will either look mystified or assume that you're 'fessing up to some strain of socially aberrant behaviour.

Fortunately, it's not that difficult to find vegetable-based dishes. You'll find yourself eating loads of mezze and salads, *fuul* (fava bean paste), tasty cheese and spinach pastries, the occasional omelette or oven-baked vegetable *tagens* (stews baked in a terracotta pot) featuring okra and aubergine.

Damascus: Tastes of a City (Rafik Schami, 2010) is one of the most engaging books written about Middle Eastern food, introducing you to the kitchens and characters of Old Damascus.

Watch out also for those vegetables that are particular to Middle Eastern cuisine, including *molokhiyya* (aka *moolookhiye* or *melokhia*), a slimy but surprisingly tasty green leafy vegetable known in the West as mallow. In Egypt it's made into an earthy garlic-flavoured soup that has a glutinous texture and inspires an almost religious devotion among the locals. In Lebanon *molokhiyya* is used to make strongly spiced lamb and chicken stews.

The main source of inadvertent meat eating is meat stock, which is often used to make otherwise vegetarian pilafs, soups and vegetable dishes. Your hosts may not even consider such stock to be meat, so may assure you that the dish is vegetarian. Chicken and mutton often lurk in vegetable dishes and mezze.

The best country for vegetarians is Israel, where kosher laws don't permit the mixing of meat and dairy products, resulting in a lot of 'dairy' restaurants where no meat is served.

Drinks

Tea & Coffee

Drinking tea *(shai, chai* or *çay)* is the signature pastime of the region and it is seen as strange and decidedly antisocial not to swig the tannin-laden beverage at regular intervals throughout the day. The tea will either come in the form of a tea bag plonked in a cup or glass of hot water (Lipton is the usual brand) or a strong brew of the local leaves. Sometimes it's served with *na'ana* (mint), and it always comes with sugar. Be warned that you'll risk severe embarrassment if you ask for milk, unless you're in a tourist hotel or restaurant.

Surprisingly, Turkish or Arabic coffee *(qahwa)* is not widely consumed in the region, with instant coffee (always called Nescafé) being far more common. If you do find the real stuff, it's likely to be a thick and powerful Turkish-style brew that's served in small cups and drunk in a couple of short sips. In private homes, a good guest will accept a minimum of three cups, but when you've had enough, gently tilt the cup from side to side (in Arabic, 'dancing' the cup).

Alcoholic Drinks

Though the region is predominantly Muslim and hence abstemious, most countries have a local beer. The best are Turkey's Efes, Egypt's Stella and Sakkara, Lebanon's famous Almaza and Jordan's Amstel, a light brew made under licence from the popular Dutch brewer Amstel. The pick of Israel and the Palestinian Territories' beers are the boutique ale Alexander and the Dancing Camel microbrews from Tel Aviv. The most interesting ale is the preservative-free Taybeh. The product of the Arab world's first microbrewery (p257), in Ramallah, it comes in light and malt-heavy dark varieties.

Wine is growing in popularity in the Middle East, thanks largely to the wines being produced in Lebanon. Lebanon's winemaking, which is based on the 'old-world' style, began with the French winemaker Gaston Hochar, who took over an 18th-century castle, Château Musar in Ghazir, 24km north of Beirut, in 1930. Together with his sons, Hochar created a wine that, despite the civil war, was able to win important awards in France, including the prestigious Winemaker's Award for Excellence. Ninety percent of their produce is exported. The main wine-growing areas are Kefraya and Ksara in the Bekaa Valley, and we particularly recommend the products of Château Musar and Ksara's Reserve du Couvent. Turkey and Israel also have small wine-producing areas.

If there is a regional drink, it would have to be the grape-and-aniseed firewater known as rakı in Turkey and as arak (lion's milk) in the rest of the region. The aniseed taste of these two powerful tipples perfectly complements mezze. You'll find many Middle Easterners for whom mezze without arak (combined with water and served in small glasses) is just not taking your mezze seriously.

The Arab Table: Recipes and Culinary Traditions (May Bsisu; 2005) takes a holistic approach that blends practical recipes with discursive sections on Arab culinary philosophy, with a special focus on celebratory meals.

Other Nonalcoholic Drinks

Juice stalls selling cheap and delicious freshly squeezed *asiir* (juices) are common throughout the region. Popular juices include lemon (which is often blended with sugar syrup and ice, and sometimes with mint), orange, pomegranate, mango, carrot and sugar cane, and you can order combinations of any or all of these. For health reasons, steer clear of stalls that add milk to their drinks.

Other traditional drinks include *aryan,* a refreshing yogurt drink made by whipping yogurt with water and salt to the consistency of pouring cream. Another favourite is the delicious and unusual *sahlab* (*sahlep* in Turkey), a drink made from crushed tapioca-root extract and served with milk, coconut, sugar, raisins, chopped nuts and rosewater. Famed for its aphrodisiacal properties, it is served hot in winter and cold in summer.

In the baking heat of an Egyptian summer, coffee and tea drinkers forgo their regular fix for cooler drinks such as the crimson-hued, iced *karkadai,* a wonderfully refreshing drink boiled up from hibiscus leaves, or *zabaady* (yoghurt beaten with cold water and salt).

Celebrations

Food plays an important part in the religious calendar of the region and holy days usually involve a flurry of baking and hours of preparation in the kitchen.

Food & Rites of Passage

In the Middle East, food is always associated with different milestones in an individual's and a family's life. When a baby is born, Egyptians mark the birth of a son by serving an aromatic rice pudding with aniseed called *meghlie;* in Lebanon it's called *mighlay* and is made of rice flour and cinnamon. The same dish is called *mughly* in the Palestinian Territories, where it is believed to aid lactation.

In Lebanon, chickpeas and tooth-destroying sugar-coated almonds are the celebratory treats when the baby's first tooth pushes through. In Egypt, *ataïf* (pancakes dipped in syrup) are eaten on the day of a betrothal and biscuits known as *kahk bi loz* (almond bracelets) are favourites at wedding parties. Turkish guests at engagement parties and weddings are invariably served baklava.

Mourning carries with it a whole different set of eating rituals. A loved one is always remembered with a banquet. This takes place after the burial in Christian communities, and one week later in Muslim communities. The only beverages offered are water and bitter, unsweetened coffee. In Israel and the Palestinian Territories, Muslims may serve dates as well, while Christians bake *rahmeh,* a type of bun commemorating the soul of the departed. Muted varieties of much-loved sweets, such as *helva* and *lokum* (Turkish delight), are commonly part of the mourning period in Turkey; a bereaved family will make *irmik helvası* (semolina *helva*) for visiting friends and relatives.

The Temporary Bride: A Memoir of Love and Food in Iran (2017), by Jennifer Klinec, is at once a love story and food journey, with the contradictions of modern Iran as a backdrop.

When observant Jews mourn the dead, religious dictates urge them to sit around the deceased for seven days and then have a solemn meal of bread, to signify sustenance, and boiled eggs and lentils, whose circular forms invoke the continuation of life.

Ramadan & Other Islamic Celebrations

The region's most important religious feasts occur during Ramadan (Ramazan in Turkish and Farsi), the Muslim holy month. There are two substantial meals a day during this period. The first, *imsak* (or *sahur*), is a breakfast eaten before daylight. Tea, bread, dates, olives and pastries are scoffed to give energy for the day ahead. *Iftar,* the evening meal prepared to break the fast, is a special feast calling for substantial soups, rice dishes topped with almond-scattered grilled meats and other delicacies. *Iftar* is often enjoyed communally in the street or in large, specially erected tents. In Turkey, a special round flat pide is baked in the afternoon and collected in time for the evening feast.

The end of Ramadan (Eid Al Fitr) is also celebrated in great culinary style. In Turkey, locals mark this important time with Şeker Bayramı (Sugar Festival), a three-day feast in which sweet foods (especially baklava) occupy centre stage.

Jewish Celebrations

The Shabbat (Sabbath) meal is an article of faith for most Jews and central to that weekly celebration is the bread known as *challah* (Sabbath bread), which is baked each week by Jews in Israel and the Palestinian Territories. A slowly cooked heavy stew called *cholent* is another Sabbath tradition widely enjoyed. Fatty meat, beans, grains, potatoes, herbs and spices stewed for hours in a big pot will heartily serve the family as well as their guests.

The Pesah (Jewish Passover) is celebrated even by the nondevout, which comprises the majority of Israelis. Unleavened bread is the best-known ingredient. During Hanukkah, potato pancakes and special jam doughnuts *(soofganiot)* are traditional dishes, while Rosh Hashanah means eating sweet foods like apples, carrots or braided *challah* dipped in honey.

Easter

Easter heralds another round of feasting, with Good Friday's abstinence from meat bringing out dishes such as *m'jaddara* (spiced lentils and rice) or *shoraba zingool* (sour soup with small balls of cracked wheat, flour and split peas) in Lebanon. *Selak,* rolls of silver beet (Swiss chard) stuffed with rice, tomato, chickpeas and spices, are also served. The fast is broken on Easter Sunday with round semolina cakes called *maamoul* stuffed with either walnuts or dates. The Armenian Christmas, the Epiphany (6 January), has the women busy making *owamaut* (small, deep-fried honey balls).

The Arts

The Middle East has an extremely rich artistic heritage, from the modern genre of film-making to literature and music. Under often extremely difficult circumstances, and often from exile, the Middle East's film-makers, writers and musicians of the modern era continue to produce some remarkable work. If you're looking to step beyond the stereotypes and discover new insights into the Middle East's stunning creative diversity, the arts are an ideal place to begin your search.

Cinema

The region's film industries stand at a crossroads. On one level, a small elite company of directors is gaining critical acclaim, picking up awards at international festivals and inching its way into the consciousness of audiences around the world. But many of these live in exile, and the industry as a whole has spent much of the last two decades in crisis, plagued by a critical lack of government funding, straining under the taboos maintained by repressive governments or fundamentalist religious movements, and facing unprecedented competition from Middle Easterners' unfettered access to satellite TV channels. Amid the upheaval of the 2011 revolutions, film-makers have at times been prominent voices for reform, but funding for film-making remains a marginal priority for many of the region's governments.

The way most Middle Eastern directors survive under such conditions is to produce films that either overtly support the government line and stray dangerously close to propaganda, or to focus on the microscopic details of daily life, using individual stories to make veiled commentaries on wider social and political issues. It is in this latter body of work, schooled in subtlety and nuanced references to the daily struggles faced by many in the region, that Middle Eastern film truly shines.

Middle East Film Festivals

Fajr Film Festival, Iran (Febuary)

Antalya Golden Orange Film Festival, Turkey (October)

Beirut International Film Festival, Lebanon (October)

Cairo International Film Festival, Egypt (December)

Egypt: Coming of Age

In its halcyon years of the 1970s, Cairo's film studios turned out more than 100 movies a year, filling cinemas throughout the Arab world. The annual figure dropped to just 20 in 2011, with most of these soap-opera-style genre movies that rely on slapstick humour, usually with a little belly dancing thrown in for (rather mild) spice. Film producers occasionally do the rounds of traveller hostels looking for those willing to fill crowd scenes in such movies. At least one Lonely Planet writer has appeared as an extra as a result of such a sweep...

One Egyptian director who consistently stood apart from the mainstream was Youssef Chahine (1926–2008). He directed more than 35 films, has been called Egypt's Fellini and was honoured at Cannes in 1997 with a lifetime achievement award. His later and more well-known works are 1999's *Al Akhar* (The Other), 1997's *Al Masir* (Destiny) and 1994's *Al Muhagir* (The Emigrant). Others to look out for are *Al Widaa Bonaparte* (Adieu Bonaparte), a historical drama about the French occupation, and *Iskandariyya Ley?* (Alexandria Why?), an autobiographical meditation on the city of Chahine's birth.

MUST-SEE MOVIES

➡ *Lawrence of Arabia* (1962) David Lean's masterpiece captures all the hopes and subsequent frustrations for Arabs in the aftermath of WWI.

➡ *Yol* (The Way; 1982) By Yilmaz Güney and epic in scale, it follows five finely rendered Turkish prisoners on parole around their country.

➡ *A Moment of Innocence* (1996) Semi-autobiographical film by Iran's Mohsen Makhmalbaf about his stabbing of a policeman at a rally as a youth before trying to make amends two decades later.

➡ *West Beirut* (1998) Begins on 13 April 1975, the first day of the Lebanese Civil War, and is Ziad Doueiri's powerful meditation on Lebanon's scars and hopes.

➡ *Paradise Now* (2005) Palestinian director Hany Abu Assad's disturbing but finely rendered study of the last hours of two suicide bombers. It was nominated for the Best Foreign Language Film Oscar in 2005.

➡ *Caramel* (2007) A stunning debut for Lebanese director Nadine Labaki. It follows the lives of five Lebanese women struggling against social taboos in war-ravaged Beirut.

➡ *Once Upon a Time in Anatolia* (2011) Runner-up at the 2011 Cannes Film Festival, this Nuri Bilge Ceylan film broods across the Anatolian steppe.

➡ *A Separation* (2011) Directed by Iranian Ashgar Farhadi and winner of the 2012 Oscar for Best Foreign Language Film, it portrays a couple torn between seeking a better life for their son and staying in Iran to care for an elderly parent with Alzheimer's.

➡ *Omar* (2014) The second Palestinian film to be nominated for the Best Foreign Language Film Oscar, it touches on questions of Palestinian and Israeli revenge and of who can be trusted.

➡ *Queen of the Desert* (2015) Directed by Werner Herzog and starring Nicole Kidman, it focuses on the life of Gertrude Bell and is partially shot in Petra.

➡ *Eshtebak* (Clash; 2016) This intense drama takes place entirely inside a police van during the Arab Spring in Cairo.

Since the 2011 revolution a new wave of film-makers has entered the Egyptian cinema scene and are taking Egyptian cinema into exciting and uncharted territory. In early 2014 Zawya, a new cinema in downtown Cairo, opened, showing art-house movies and work by young Egyptian film-makers. By 2017 the Egyptian movie industry was producing 60 films a year, with the growth as much in quality as in quantity.

More than that, young Egyptian film-makers have become among the principal storytellers and chroniclers of modern Egypt, from box office hits such as romantic comedy *Hepta* (2016), to Mohamed Diab's critically acclaimed *Eshtebak* (Clash; 2016). Other impressive films to emerge under this new wave of directors include *Asmaa* (director Amr Salama; 2011), a searing portrait of an HIV/AIDS patient, and *Nawara* (director Hala Khalil; 2015), which explores the revolution through the eyes of a humble maid.

Arab Film Distribution (www.arabfilm.com) is the Amazon of Arab cinema, with a large portfolio of DVDs that you just won't find on mainstream online sources.

Israel

Film directors from elsewhere in the Middle East must look with envy at the level of government funding and freedom of speech enjoyed by Israeli film-makers. It's a freedom that Israeli directors have used to produce high-quality films that have been praised for their even-handedness by juries and audiences alike at international film festivals.

A readiness to confront uncomfortable truths about Israel's recent history has long been a hallmark of Amos Gitai (b 1950), who has won plaudits for his sensitive and balanced portrayal of half a century of conflict. He became a superstar almost overnight with *Kadosh* (1998), which seriously questioned the role of religion in Israeli society and politics. He followed it up with *Kippur* (1999), a wholly unsentimental portrayal of the 1973 war, and *Kedma* (2001), which caused a stir by questioning many of the country's founding myths through the lens of the 1948 Arab-Israeli War. Avi Mograbi (b 1956) goes a step further than Gitai with no-holds-barred depictions of the difficulties of life for the Palestinians under Israeli occupation.

Beyond the politically charged films that are causing a stir, there's also a feeling within Israel that the country's film industry is entering something of a golden age. Highlighting the sense of excitement, Shira Geffen and Etgar Keret won the Caméra d'Or for best film by debut directors at the 2007 Cannes Film Festival for *Meduzot* (Jellyfish). At the same festival, Eran Kolirin's *The Band's Visit* won the Jury Prize of the International Federation of Film Critics. Joseph Cedar (b 1968) has been nominated twice for an Academy Award for Best Foreign Language Film with *Beaufort* (2007) and *Footnote* (2011).

Recent releases worth watching out for include *The Women's Balcony* (director Emil Ben Shimon; 2016) and *Home Port* (directory Erez Tadmor; 2016), two sensitive portraits of the conflicts between Sephardim and Ashkenazi Jews in modern Israel, while *Norman: The Moderate Rise and Tragic Fall of a New York Fixer* (director Joseph Cedar; 2016) stars Richard Gere.

Israeli films have received more Oscar nominations (10) for Best Foreign Language Film than films from any other Middle Eastern country (including in 2007, 2008, 2009 and 2011), although they've yet to win the prize.

Palestinian Territories

Starved of funding, faced with the barriers erected by Israeli censors and living in occupation or exile, Palestinian film-makers have done it tough, but have nonetheless turned out some extraordinary movies.

One Palestinian director who has made an international impact is the Nazareth-born Michael Khaleifi (b 1950), whose excellent *Images from Rich Memories* (1980), *The Anthem of the Stone* (1990) and *Wedding in Galilee* (1987) were all shot covertly inside the Palestinian Territories. Gaza-born Rasheed Masharawi (b 1962) has been rejected in some Palestinian circles for working with Israeli production companies, but the quality of his work is undeniable. The work of Elia Suleiman (b 1960) is a

YILMAZ GÜNEY: MIRROR TO TURKISH HISTORY

The life of Yilmaz Güney (1937–84) provides a fascinating window onto late-20th-century Turkey. In particular, the life story and films of this Turkish-Kurdish director speak volumes for the often fraught relationship between Turkey's governments and the country's creative talents.

Güney began his professional life as a writer, before becoming a hugely popular young actor who appeared in dozens of films (up to 20 a year according to some reports), before again changing tack to become the country's most successful film director. But behind that seemingly steady rise lies a life that reads like a scarcely believable film plot. Güney was first arrested in 1961 for writing what was condemned as a communist novel and then again in 1972 for sheltering anarchist students. In 1974 he was convicted of killing a public prosecutor. He wrote many of his screenplays behind bars – including the internationally acclaimed *The Herd* (1978). In 1981 he escaped from prison and fled to France.

It was from exile that Güney produced his masterpiece, the Palme d'Or–winning *Yol* (The Way; 1982), which was not initially shown in Turkish cinemas; its portrait of what happens to five prisoners on a week's release was too grim for the authorities to take. His following within Turkey was also never as widespread as his talents deserved, not least because his portrayal of the difficulties faced by Turkey's Kurds alienated many in mainstream Turkish society.

wonderful corpus of quietly angry and intensely powerful films – *Chronicle of a Disappearance* won Best Film Prize at the 1996 Venice Film Festival, while *Divine Intervention* won the Jury Prize at Cannes in 2002.

Lebanese director Ziad Doueiri, whose slick debut *West Beyrouth* (1998) is considered one of the best films about the Lebanese Civil War, was Quentin Tarantino's lead cameraman for *Pulp Fiction* and *Reservoir Dogs*.

Iran

It was in the 1970s that the first 'new wave' of Iranian cinema captured the attention of art-house movie fans around the world: Abbas Kiarostami, Dariush Mehrjui, Bahram Beiza'i, Khosrow Haritash and Bahram Farmanara. The second 'new wave' was made up of post-revolutionary directors such as Mohsen Makhmalbaf, Rakhshan Bani Etemad, Majid Majidi and Jafar Panahi. It helped develop a reputation for Iranian cinema as art house, neorealist and poetic. The newest generation is known as the 'third wave' and its most notable exponents are Asghar Farhadi, Bahman Ghobadi and Mani Haghighi.

Whatever the number, Iranian new wave is consistent in looking at everyday life through a poetic prism that is part fictional feature, part real-life documentary. The strict censorship of the post-revolutionary state has encouraged the use of children, nonprofessional actors and stories that are fixated on the nitty-gritty of life.

Other films worth seeking out include Majid Majidi's film *Children of Heaven*, which was nominated for the Best Foreign Language Film Oscar in 1998. It is a delicate tale focusing on two poor children losing a pair of shoes. *The White Balloon* (1995), written by Abbas Kiarostami and directed by Jafar Panahi, tells the story of a young girl who loses her money while on the way to buy a goldfish. Another fine offering is *A Separation*, the 2012 winner of the Academy Award for Best Foreign Language Film and nominee for Best Original Screenplay. Asghar Farhadi's masterfully told film looks at a Tehran couple's dissolving marriage and how the hiring of a carer for an ill parent complicates matters further. Another Farhadi film to receive recognition with an Oscar nomination for Best Foreign Language Film is *The Salesman* (2016).

Literature

The telling of tales that are both mischievous and reveal the social and political times from which they arise has always occupied centre stage in Middle Eastern life, from the epic tales from the 8th-century Baghdad court of Haroun Ar Rashid, so wonderfully brought to life in *The Thousand and One Nights*, to the wandering storytellers who once entertained crowds in the coffeehouses and theatres of the region. It's a heritage with two tightly interwoven strands: entertainment through suspense and comedy, and thinly veiled commentaries on the issues of the day.

According to one UN estimate, Spain translates more books each year than have been translated into Arabic in the past 1000 years.

But the writers of the region face many challenges, including government repression and the lack of a book-buying culture in Arabic-speaking countries. Storytelling in the Middle East, including poetry, was always a predominantly oral tradition and it was not until the 20th century that the first Arabic-language novels appeared. The audiences never really made the transition from the public performance to the printed page.

Poetry

The Lebanese-born poet Khalil Gibran (1883–1931) is, by some estimates, the third biggest-selling poet in history behind Shakespeare and Lao Tse. Born in Bcharré in Lebanon, he spent most of his working life in the US, but it didn't stop him from becoming a flag bearer for Arabic poetry. His masterpiece, *The Prophet* (1923), which consists of 26 poetic essays, became, after the Bible, America's second-biggest-selling book of the 20th century.

Mahmoud Darwish (1941–2008) has become one of the most eloquent spokesmen for Palestinian rights, his more than 30 volumes of poetry

THE GREAT IRANIAN POETS

Iranians venerate their great poets, who are often credited with preserving the Persian language and culture during times of occupation. Streets, squares, hotels and *chaykhanehs* (teahouses) are named after famous poets, several of whom have large mausoleums that are popular pilgrimage sites.

Ferdosi 940–1020

Hakim Abulqasim Ferdosi, first and foremost of all Iranian poets, was born near Tus outside Mashhad. He developed the *ruba'i* (quatrain) style of 'epic' historic poems and is remembered primarily for the *Shahnamah* (Book of Kings), which took 33 years to write and included almost 60,000 couplets. Ferdosi is seen as the saviour of Farsi, which he wrote in at a time when the language was under threat from Arabic. Without his writings many details of Persian history and culture might also have been lost, and Ferdosi is credited with having done much to help shape the Iranian self-image.

Hafez 1325–1389

Khajeh Shams Ed Din Mohammed, or Hafez (meaning 'One Who Can Recite the Quran from Memory') as he became known, was born in Shiraz. His poetry has a strong mystical quality and regular references to wine, courtship and nightingales have been interpreted in different ways (is wine literal or a metaphor for God?). A copy of his collected works, known as the *Divan-e Hafez*, can be found in almost every home in Iran, and many of his verses are used as proverbs to this day.

Omar Khayyam 1047–1123

Omar Khayyam (Omar the Tentmaker) was born in Neishabur and is probably the best-known Iranian poet in the West because many of his poems, including the famous *Rubaiyat*, were translated into English by Edward Fitzgerald. In Iran he is more famous as a mathematician, historian and astronomer.

Rumi 1207–1273

Born Jalal Ad Din Mohammad Balkhi in Balkh (in present-day Afghanistan), Rumi's family fled west before the Mongol invasions and eventually settled in Konya in present-day Turkey. There his father (and then he) retreated into meditation and a study of the divine. Rumi was inspired by a great dervish, Shams-e Tabrizi, and many of his poems of divine love are addressed to him. He is credited with founding the Maulavi Sufi order – the whirling dervishes – and is also known as Maulana ('the Master').

Sa'di 1207–1291

Like Hafez, Sheikh Mohammed Shams Ed Din (known as Sa'di) lost his father at an early age and was educated by some of the leading teachers of Shiraz. Many of his elegantly phrased verses are still commonly used in conversation. His most famous works, the *Golestan* (Rose Garden) and *Bustan* (Garden of Trees), have been translated into many languages.

reading like a beautifully composed love letter to the lost land of his childhood. At his funeral in August 2008, one mourner told the BBC that he 'symbolises the Palestinian memory'.

Another leading Arab poet and one of the great celebrities of the Arab literary scene is Syria's Nizar Qabbani (1923–98), who was unusual in that he was able to balance closeness to successive Syrian regimes with subject matter (love, eroticism and feminism) that challenged many prevailing opinions within conservative Syrian society. His funeral in Damascus – a city that he described in his will as 'the womb that taught me poetry, taught me creativity and granted me the alphabet of jasmine' – was broadcast live around the Arab world.

MIDDLE EASTERN LITERATURE TOP 10

➡ *The Prophet* (Khalil Gibran; 1923) Somehow expounds in poetic form on the great philosophical questions while speaking to the dilemmas of everyday life.

➡ *The Time Regulation Institute* (Ahmet Hamdi Tanpinar; 1954) This Turkish classic was finally translated into English in 2014 following unforgettable characters and the institute's attempts to set all Turkish clocks to Western time.

➡ *Memed, My Hawk* (Yaşar Kemal; 1955) Deals with near-feudal life in the villages of eastern Turkey and is considered perhaps the greatest Turkish novel of the 20th century.

➡ *The Cairo Trilogy* (Naguib Mahfouz; 1956–57) Egypt's Nobel Laureate brings the streets and cafes of Cairo to life like no-one else can.

➡ *The Black Book* (Orhan Pamuk; 1990) It was with this book that that Pamuk leapt onto the international stage. It follows a man's search for his missing/runaway wife.

➡ *The Map of Love* (Ahdaf Soueif; 1999) The Booker-nominated historical novel by this Anglo-Egyptian writer. *In the Eye of the Sun* (1992) is simply marvellous.

➡ *The Dark Side of Love* (Rafik Schami; 2004) Regarded by many as the first 'Great Arab Novel' of the 21st century, with its follow-up, *The Calligrapher's Secret*,also brilliant; they're written by Syria's master storyteller in exile.

➡ *Taxi* (Khaled Al Khamissi; 2011) Highly original with 58 fictional monologues by the taxi drivers of Cairo.

➡ *Azazeel* (Youssef Ziedan; 2012) A sweeping historical novel set in the 5th century AD and following a Coptic monk's journey through Egypt and the Levant.

➡ *No Knives in the Kitchens of This City* (Khaled Khalifa; 2016) A stunning novel set in war-torn Aleppo, following a family's tragic demise.

In Iran, poetry is overwhelmingly the most important form of writing. Familiarity with famous poets and their works is universal: almost anyone on the street can quote lines from Hafez or Rumi.

Novels

The novel as a literary form may have come late to the Middle East, but that didn't stop the region producing three winners of the Nobel Prize for Literature: Shmuel Yosef Agnon (1966), a Zionist Israeli writer whose works are published in English under the name SY Agnon; Naguib Mahfouz (1988); and Orhan Pamuk (2006).

Maqam (www.maqam.com) claims to be the world's largest distributor and online retailer of Arab music, with a sideline in cinema and musical instruments.

Much of the credit for the maturing of Arabic literature can be given to Naguib Mahfouz (1911–2006), who was unquestionably the single most important writer of fiction in Arabic in the 20th century. A life-long native of Cairo, Mahfouz began writing in the 1930s. From Western-copyist origins he went on to develop a voice that is uniquely of the Arab world and draws its inspiration from storytelling in the coffeehouses and the dialect and slang of the streets. He repeatedly fell foul of Egypt's fundamentalist Islamists, first for his 1959 novel *Children of Gebelawi* (which was banned for blasphemy in Egypt) and later for defending Salman Rushdie; Mahfouz was seriously injured in an assassination attempt in 1994. His best-known works are collectively known as *The Cairo Trilogy*, consisting of *Palace Walk*, *Palace of Desire* and *Sugar Street*.

Orhan Pamuk (b 1952) is Turkey's foremost literary celebrity. His works include an impressive corpus of novels and an acclaimed memoir of İstanbul, *Istanbul: Memories of a City*. His work has been translated into more than 50 languages and, like Mahfouz, Pamuk has never shirked from the difficult issues; in *Snow* (2004), Pamuk unflinchingly explores the fraught relationship between two of the great themes of modern Turkish life: Islamic extremism and the pull of the West. Also like Mahfouz, Pamuk is known as a staunch defender of freedom of speech.

Among the region's other best-known writers are Turkey's Yaşar Kemal (1923–2015) and the Israeli writer Amos Oz (b 1939); Oz's work includes essays and award-winning novels with themes that speak to the pride and angst at the centre of modern Israeli life. Of the native Lebanese writers, the most famous is Hanan Al Shaykh (b 1945), who writes poignant but humorous novels that resonate beyond the bounds of the Middle East. Also worth tracking down are the works of Jordan's Abdelrahman Munif (1933–2004), Egypt's prolific Nawal El Saadawi (b 1931) and Lebanese-born Amin Maalouf (b 1949).

Of the new wave of Middle Eastern writers, the names to watch include Alaa Al Aswany (Egypt, b 1957), Ahdaf Soueif (Egypt, b 1950), Khalid Al Khamisi (Egypt, b 1962), Laila Halaby (Lebanon, b 1966) and Dorit Rabinyan (Israel, b 1972).

Sadeq Hedayat (1903–51) is the best-known Iranian novelist outside Iran, and one whose influence has been most pervasive in shaping modern Persian fiction. *The Blind Owl,* published in 1937, is a dark and powerful portrayal of the decadence of a society failing to achieve its own modernity. Hedayat's uncensored works have been banned in Iran since 2005.

Contemporary Iranian author Shahriar Mandanipour was also banned from publishing between 1992 and 1997 and, after years of struggle against the censor's pen, eventually moved to the US in 2006. In 2009 he published the critically acclaimed *Censoring an Iranian Love Story.*

Naguib Mahfouz: His Life & Times (2008) by Rasheed El Elnany is the first (and, it must be said, long-overdue) English-language biography of the Arab world's most accomplished and prolific novelist.

Music

If you're a music lover, you'll adore the Middle East, which has homegrown music as diverse as the region itself. This is one part of the world where local artists dominate air time and you're far more likely to hear Umm Kolthum, soulful Iraqi oud (Middle Eastern lute) or the latest Lebanese pop sensation.

To learn more about how the stories of *The Thousand and One Nights* came together, read the excellent introduction by Husain Haddawy in *The Arabian Nights* (1990).

Arab

Classical

If one instrument has come to represent the enduring appeal of classical Arabic music, it's the oud, an instrument that has made the transition from backing instrument to musical superstar in its own right. The oud is a pear-shaped, stringed instrument and is distinguished from its successor, the Western lute, by its lack of frets, 11 strings (five pairs and a single

THE THOUSAND & ONE NIGHTS

After the Bible, *The Thousand and One Nights* (in Arabic, *Alf Layla w'Layla,* also known as *The Arabian Nights*) must be one of the best-known, least-read books in the English language.

That few people have read the actual text is unsurprising considering that its most famous English-language edition (translated by the Victorian adventurer Sir Richard Burton) runs to 16 volumes; an old Middle Eastern superstition holds that nobody can read the entire text of *The Thousand and One Nights* without dying.

With origins that range from pre-Islamic Persia, India and Arabia, the stories as we now know them were first gathered together in written form in the 14th century. *The Thousand and One Nights* is a portmanteau title for a mixed bag of colourful and fantastic tales (there are 271 core stories). The stories are mainly set in the semi-fabled Baghdad of Haroun Ar Rashid (r AD 786–809), and in Mamluk-era (1250–1517) Cairo and Damascus.

All versions of *The Thousand and One Nights* begin with the same premise: the misogynist King Shahriyar discovers that his wife has been unfaithful, whereafter he murders her and takes a new wife every night before killing each in turn before sunrise. The wily Sheherezade, the daughter of the king's vizier, insists that she will be next, only to nightly postpone her death with a string of stories that leaves the king in such suspense that he spares her life so as to hear the next instalment.

MIDDLE EASTERN MUSIC – OUR TOP 10 ALBUMS

- *The Lady & the Legend,* Fairouz (Lebanon)
- *Al Atlaal,* Umm Kolthum (Egypt)
- *Awedony,* Amr Diab (Egypt)
- *Le Luth de Baghdad,* Nasseer Shamma (Iraq)
- *Asmar,* Yeir Dalal (Israel)
- *The Idan Raichel Project,* The Idan Raichel Project (Israel)
- *Nar with Secret Tribe,* Mercan Dede (Turkey)
- *Deli Kızın Türküsü,* Sezen Aksu (Turkey)
- *Les Plus Grands Classiques de la Musique Arabe,* various artists
- *Drab Zeen,* Toufic Faroukh (Lebanon)

string) and a neck bent at a 45- to 90-degree angle. Oud players are to be found throughout the region, but its undisputed masters are in Iraq, where the sound of the oud is revered as a reflection of the Iraqi soul.

Even so, Syria produced the Arab world's so-called 'King of the Oud', Farid Al Atrache (1915–74). Sometimes called the 'Arab Sinatra', he was a highly accomplished oud player and composer, who succeeded in updating Arabic music by blending it with Western scales and rhythms and the orchestration of the tango and waltz. His melodic improvisations on the oud and his *mawal* (a vocal improvisation) were the highlights of his live performances, and recordings of these are treasured. By the time of his death, he was considered – and still is by many – to be the premier male Arabic music performer of the 20th century.

The other defining feature of classical Arabic music is the highly complicated melodic system known as *maqam*. The foundation for most traditional music in the Arab world, *maqam* is based on a tonal system of scales and intervals and is wholly different from Western musical traditions. Master *maqam* and you've mastered the centuries-old sound of the region.

Contemporary Arab Music

Seemingly a world away from classical Arabic music, and characterised by a clattering, hand-clapping rhythm overlaid with synthesised twirlings and a catchy, repetitive vocal, the first true Arabic pop came out of Cairo in the 1970s. The blueprint for the new youth sound (which became known as *al jeel,* from the word for generation) was set by Egyptian Ahmed Adawiyya (b 1945), the Arab world's first 'pop star'.

During the 1990s there was a calculated attempt to create a more upmarket sound, with many musicians mimicking Western dance music. Tacky electronics were replaced with moody pianos, Spanish guitars and thunderous drums. Check out the Egyptian singer Amr Diab (b 1961), whose heavily produced songs have made him the best-selling artist ever in the Arab world (achieved with his 1996 album *Nour Al Ain).*

Heading the current crop of megastar singers (the Arabic music scene is totally dominated by solo vocalists, there are no groups) are Majida Al Rumi (b 1956) of Lebanon, Iraqi-born Kazem (Kadim) Al Saher (b 1957) and Iraq's Ilham Al Madfai (b 1942), who founded the Middle East's first rock band back in the 1960s. Syria's prolific Omar Suleyman (b 1966), who emerged from that quintessential Middle Eastern genre of wedding performances, has produced more than 500 albums, appeared at the 2011 Glastonbury Festival and has collaborated with everyone from Björk to Damon Albarn.

Turkish

Traditional Turkish music is enjoying something of a revival with Sufi music, dominated by traditional instrumentation, leading the way. Sufi music's spiritual home is Konya and the sound is bewitchingly hypnotic – a simple repeated melody usually played on the *nai* (reed pipe), accompanied by recitations of Sufi poetry.

Sufi music's growing popularity beyond Turkey's borders owes much to the work of artists such as Mercan Dede (www.mercandede.com; b 1966), whose blend of Sufism with electronica has taken the genre beyond its traditional boundaries and into a mainstream audience. He even doubles as a DJ with the stage name Arkin Allen, spinning hardcore house and techno beats at rave festivals in the US and Canada. Not surprisingly, one Turkish newspaper described him as a 'dervish for the modern world'.

Songlines (www.songlines.co.uk) is the premier world-music magazine. It features interviews with stars, extensive album reviews and a host of other titbits that will broaden your horizons and prompt many additions to your music collection.

But Turkey's most pervasive soundtrack of choice is Turkish pop, with its skittish rhythms and strident vocals, and its stars rank among the country's best-known celebrities. Sezen Aksu (b 1954), known as 'the Queen of Turkish music', launched the country's love affair with the genre with her first single in 1976. Combining Western influences and local folk music to create a thoroughly contemporary sound, she's also an independent spirit not afraid to speak out on environmental issues and Turkey's treatment of its minorities.

Other super-popular pop stars include Tarkan (b 1972), Serdat Ortaç (b 1970) and Mustafa Sandal (b 1970). Notable rock bands include Duman and Mor ve Ötesi. The group maNga create an intriguing mix of metal, rock and Anatolian folk. Their 2012 album *e-akustik* is worth seeking out.

Israeli

In recent decades there has been in Israel a drive to excavate Jewish rhythms from broader European traditions. The result is a deeper, more distinctive Israeli sound.

Perhaps the most successful example of this latter phenomenon is *klezmer*. With its foundations laid by the Jewish communities of Eastern Europe, *klezmer*'s fast-paced, instrumental form was ideally suited to Jewish celebrations and it has sometimes been branded as Jewish jazz, in recognition of its divergence from established musical styles. The modern version has added vocals – almost always in Yiddish.

If *klezmer* takes its inspiration from Jewish diaspora roots in Europe, the Idan Raichel Project (www.idanraichelproject.com), arguably Israel's most popular group, casts its net more widely. Israeli love songs are its forte, but it's the Ethiopian instruments, Jamaican rhythms and Yemeni vocals that mark the group out as something special. Although originally rejected by leading local record labels for being 'too ethnic', the Idan Raichel Project's building of bridges between Israel's now-multicultural musical traditions struck a chord with audiences at home and abroad.

Mizrahi (Oriental or Eastern) music, with its Middle Eastern and Mediterranean scales and rhythms, has its roots in the melodies of North Africa, Iraq and Yemen, and may be Israel's most popular genre. Old-timer Shlomo Bar (www.shlomobar.com), inspired by the traditional Jewish music of Morocco and Iraq respectively, is still performing, joined more recently by superstars Sarit Hadad (www.sarit-hadad.com), who has been described as Israel's Britney Spears, and Amir Benayoun, whose genre-defying concerts mix love songs and medieval Jewish liturgical poems. Moshe Peretz enjoys crossing the line from Mizrahi to mainstream and back again.

Another artist to have adapted ancient musical traditions for a modern audience is Yasmin Levy, who sings in Ladino (the language of Sephardic Jews, who lived in Andalusia for centuries until 1492). The flamenco inflections in her music speak strongly of what she calls 'the musical memories of the old Moorish and Jewish-Spanish world'. Crossing frontiers of a different kind, Yair Dalal is an outstanding Israeli oud player who has collaborated with Palestinian and other Arab musicians.

Landscape & Environment

The Middle East faces some of the most pressing environmental issues of our time and there are few regions of the world where the human impact upon the environment has been quite so devastating. Further, as one of the world's largest oil-producing regions, the Middle East's contribution to the gathering global environmental crisis far outweighs its size. There *are* pockets of good news, but, it must be said, there aren't many.

In the 180-country 2016 Environmental Performance Index (www.epi.yale.edu/country-rankings), Israel ranked highest among Middle Eastern countries at 49th, followed by Jordan (74th), Lebanon (94th), Turkey (99th), Syria (101st), Egypt (104th), Iran (105th) and Iraq (116th).

Land

Wrapping itself around the eastern Mediterranean and with its feet on three continents, the Middle East is home to some suitably epic landforms, from the deserts that engulf much of the region and high mountain ranges of the north to some of history's most important rivers.

Deserts

Deserts consume the countries of the Middle East, covering 93% of Egypt, 77% of Jordanian and Iraqi territory, and 60% of Israel and the Palestinian Territories. Although deserts dominate much of the region, they're rarely home to the sandy landscapes of childhood imaginings. Apart from the Saharan sand seas in parts of Egypt, sand dunes worthy of the name are rare and stony gravel plains are the defining feature. Desert oases – such as Siwa in Egypt – have played an important role in the history of the region, serving as crucial watering points for caravans travelling the Silk Road and the Sahara.

Mountains

More than half of Iran is covered by mountains. The majestic Alborz Mountains skirt the Caspian Sea from the border of Azerbaijan as far as Turkmenistan, and are home to ski fields and the snow-capped Mt Damavand (5671m), the Middle East's tallest mountain. The immense Zagros Mountains stretch about 1500km from Turkey to the Persian Gulf, rising and falling like the ridged back of a great crocodile.

Eastern Turkey is similarly glorious with seriously high mountains rising above 5000m – the 5137m-high Mt Ararat (Ağrı Dağı) is the highest mountain in the country. Southeastern Anatolia offers windswept rolling steppe, jagged outcrops of rock that spill over into far-north Iraq and northwestern Iran. The vast, high plateau of rolling steppe and mountain ranges of Central Anatolia are similarly dramatic.

In Lebanon, the Mt Lebanon Range forms the backbone of the country: the highest peak, Qornet As Sawda (3019m), rises southeast of Tripoli. Other Lebanese ranges include the beautiful Chouf Mountains, the Bekaa Valley, and the Anti-Lebanon Range, a sheer arid massif averaging 2000m in height, which forms a natural border with Syria.

Desert Expeditions

- *Western Oases, Egypt*
- *Sinai Desert, Egypt*
- *Wadi Rum, Jordan*
- *Negev, Israel & the Palestinian Territories*

Rivers

The Nile, which runs for 6695km, 22% of it in Egypt, is the longest river on earth and along its banks flourished the glorious civilisation of ancient Egypt. Other Middle Eastern rivers resonate just as strongly with legends and empires past. According to the Bible, the Euphrates and Tigris are among the four rivers that flowed into the Garden of Eden, and they would later provide the means for the cradle of civilisation in Mesopotamia. The Jordan River, the lowest river on earth, also features prominently in biblical texts. Even today, were it not for the rivers that run through these lands – hence providing a water source and narrow fertile agricultural zones close to the riverbanks – it's difficult to see how these regions could support life at all.

The cedars for which Lebanon is famous are now confined to a few mountain-top sites, most notably at the small grove at the Cedars ski resort and the Chouf Cedar Reserve in the Chouf Mountains.

Wildlife

Animals

Occupying the junction of three natural zones, the Middle East was once a sanctuary for an amazing variety of mammals. Hardly any are left. Worse still, official government policies to protect wildlife are as rare as many of the animals. Casual wildlife sightings are extremely rare in the Middle East, although desert expeditions in Egypt's Sinai or Sahara offer the chance to see gazelles, rock hyraxes, fennec foxes and even the graceful Nubian ibex. Otherwise, if you see anything more exciting than domesticated camels, donkeys and water buffaloes, you'll belong to a very small group of privileged Middle Eastern travellers.

The Middle East is home to 4.5% of the world's population and around half of the world's oil supplies, but only receives 2% of the world's rainfall and possesses just 0.4% of the world's recoverable water supplies.

Iran

Iran is home to 158 species of mammal, about one-fifth of which are endemic. Large cats, including the Persian leopard and Asiatic cheetah, are the standout species. Notable other species include the spectacular Persian wild ass, goitered and Jebeer gazelles, maral, Asian black bear, brown bear and seven species of wild sheep. Most larger mammals are found in the forests of the Alborz Mountains.

Israel

The Israeli initiative known as Hai Bar (literally 'wildlife') is a small beacon of hope amid an otherwise gloomy outlook. Begun in 1960, the Hai Bar program set itself the most ambitious of aims: to reintroduce animals that roamed the Holy Land during biblical times by collecting a small pool of rare animals, breeding them, then reintroducing them to the wild. Consequently, the wild ass, beloved by the Prophet Isaiah, has

SAVING THE ARABIAN ORYX

The endangered Arabian oryx – sometimes said to be the unicorn of historical legend – is a majestic creature that stands about 1m high at the shoulder and has enormous horns that project more than 50cm into the air. Adapted well to their desert environment, wild oryx once had an uncanny ability to sense rain on the wind. One herd is recorded as having travelled up to 155km, led by a dominant female, to rain. In times of drought, oryxes have been known to survive 22 months without water, obtaining moisture from plants and leaves.

Their white coats offered camouflage in the searing heat of the desert, providing a measure of protection from both heat and hunters, but the oryxes and their long, curved horns were highly prized. In 1972 the last wild Arabian oryx was killed by hunters in Oman, which led officials to declare the oryx extinct in the wild. Nine oryxes left in captivity around the world were pooled and taken to the Arizona Zoo for a breeding program. They became known as the 'World Oryx Herd' and eventually grew to more than 200 in number. As a result of programs to reintroduce the Arabian oryx into the wild across the region, an estimated 1000 oryxes are thought to survive in the wild as of 2017, with reintroduced populations in Israel, Oman and Saudi Arabia. There are also between 6000 and 7000 oryxes in captivity around the world.

The most accessible place to see an Arabian oryx (in captivity, but partly free-ranging) is in Jordan's Shaumari Wildlife Reserve.

Top Five Wildlife Experiences

Shaumari Wildlife Reserve

Red Sea Diving

Winter birdwatching, Persian Gulf, Iran

Birdwatching, Al Fayoum Oasis, Egypt

Wild ass and Persian fallow deer, Israel & the Palestinian Territories

turned the corner in Israel, though it's not likely to come off the endangered list any time soon. But the story of the Persian fallow deer is the one that really captured the public imagination. A small flock of the species was secretly flown in from Iran in 1978 on the last El Al flight to leave Tehran before the Islamic revolution. These shy animals have taken hold in the Galilee reserve of Akhziv and around the hills west of Jerusalem.

Jordan

It's in Jordan where you've the best chance of spotting charismatic fauna. Arabian oryx, ostrich, gazelle and Persian onager are all being reared for reintroduction to the wild and are on show at Shaumari Wildlife Reserve in eastern Jordan – safaris to see these and other species rank among the wildlife-watching highlights of the Middle East. Jordan's striking caracal (Persian lynx), a feline with outrageous tufts of black hair on the tips of its outsized, pointy ears, is occasionally seen in Wadi Mujib and Dana Nature Reserves.

Birds

In contrast to the region's dwindling number of high-profile mammals, the variety of bird life in the Middle East is exceptionally rich. As well as being home to numerous indigenous species, the Middle East, despite the critical loss of wetlands in Jordan and Iraq, continues to serve as a way station on migration routes between Asia, Europe and Africa. Twice a year, half a billion birds of every conceivable variety soar along the Syro-African rift, the largest avian flyway in the world, which is compressed into a narrow corridor along the eastern edge of Israel and the Palestinian Territories; indeed, Israel claims to be the world's second-largest flyway (after South America) for migratory birds.

Useful field guides include: *Birds of the Middle East* (Richard Porter & Simon Aspinall; 2010); *A Field Guide to the Mammals of Egypt* (Richard Hoath; 2009); *Carnivores of the World* (Luke Hunter, 2011); and *The Birds of Turkey* (Metehan Ozen and Peter Castell; 2008).

Egypt's Sinai Peninsula and Al Fayoum Oasis, and Wadi Araba in Jordan also receive an enormous and varied amount of ornithological traffic. Egypt alone has recorded sightings of more than 430 different species.

Iran is another exceptional country for birds, boasting almost 500 species, many of which are listed as globally endangered. A growing number of birders are coming to Iran in search of these birds, many of which are hard to find elsewhere, and to enjoy the exceptional birding along the Persian Gulf. In winter in particular, many hundreds of thousands of birds flock to the shallow waters of the Gulf, with the Bandar Abbas-Qeshm areas particularly good. Vast flocks of waders, including crab plovers and terek sandpipers, mingle with various herons, egrets and pelicans and together create one of the most important wintering areas for birds in the Middle East. Birding resources:

Birdlife International (www.birdlife.org/middle-east)

International Birdwatching Center of the Jordan Valley (www.birdwatching.org.il)

Israel Birding Portal (www.birds.org.il)

Royal Society for the Conservation of Nature (www.rscn.org.jo)

Society for the Protection of the Nature of Israel (www.natureisrael.org)

Columbia University's Water in the Middle East (www.library.columbia.edu/locations/global/virtual-libraries/middle_east_studies/water) hosts numerous links to articles on the Middle East's most pressing environmental issue.

Marine Life

The Red Sea teems with more than 1000 species of marine life, an amazing spectacle of colour and form. Fish, sharks, turtles, stingrays, dolphins, corals, sponges, sea cucumbers and molluscs all thrive in these waters. The rare loggerhead turtle nests on some of Turkey's Mediterranean beaches.

Most of the bewildering variety of fish species in the Red Sea – including many that are found nowhere else – are closely associated with the coral reef, and live and breed in the reefs or nearby sea-grass beds. Threats to the coral reefs – from both global warming and more localised causes – therefore threaten a large number of species.

In the Red Sea waters off Hurghada, for example, conservationists estimate that more than 1000 pleasure boats and almost as many fishing boats ply the waters. For decades there was nothing to stop captains from anchoring to the coral, or snorkellers and divers breaking off a colourful chunk to take home. But in 1992 12 of Hurghada's more reputable dive companies formed the Hurghada Environmental Protection & Conservation Association (www.hepca.org). Working with the Egyptian National Parks Office, Hepca works to conserve the Red Sea's reefs through public-awareness campaigns, direct community action and lobbying of the Egyptian government to introduce appropriate laws. Thanks to these efforts, the whole coast south of Suez Governorate is now known as the Red Sea Protectorate.

One of its earliest successes was to establish more than 570 mooring buoys at popular dive sites around Hurghada. In 2009 the NGO also took over responsibility for waste management in the region, implementing door-to-door rubbish collection and recycling in Marsa Alam and Hurghada. Among its current projects are those aimed at sustainable fishing, projects to protect dugongs, turtles and dolphins, and the monitoring of plastic bags, coral and the effects of bleaching and climate change.

In 2014 Egypt had just 20 cu metres of renewable water per capita per year, while Jordan had just 77 cu metres (down from 675 in 1962). Compare this to the UK's 2244. Anything less than 500 cu metres is considered to be a scarcity of water.

National Parks & Wildlife Reserves

Although there are exceptions, most of the Middle East's officially protected areas exist in name only and are poorly patrolled and poorly funded. There are, however, exceptions.

Nearly 25 years ago the Jordanian government established 12 protected areas, totalling about 1200 sq km, amounting, in total, to just 1% of Jordan's territory. Some were abandoned, but the rest survive thanks to the impressive Royal Society for the Conservation of Nature (www.rscn.org.jo), Jordan's major environmental agency.

In recent years, Turkey has stepped up its environmental protection practices. The growing number of protected areas includes 40 national parks, as well as numerous official nature parks and nature reserves. It also includes 112 curiously named 'nature monuments', which are mostly protected trees, some as old as 1500 years. Sometimes the parks' regulations are carefully enforced, but at other times a blind eye is turned to such problems as litter-dropping picnickers. Visitor facilities are rare.

The Middle East's star environmental performer is undoubtedly Israel because of its strong regulation of hunting and a system of nature reserves comprising some 25% of the land. However, the parks are not without their problems. Many are minuscule in size and isolated, providing only limited protection for local species. Moreover, many of the reserves in the south are also used as military firing zones.

Notable National Parks & Reserves

- *Ras Mohammed National Park, Egypt*
- *Chouf Cedar Reserve, Lebanon*
- *Ein Gedi, Israel & the Palestinian Territories*
- *Mount Ararat National Park, Turkey*
- *Golestan National Park, Iran*
- *Lake Orumiyeh National Park, Iran*

DEAD SEA SINKHOLES

In 1990 the Geographical Survey of Israel counted fewer than 100 sinkholes around the shores of the Dead Sea's north555ern basin. By 2017 there were more than 6000, with more than 500 opening up each year. Some are the size of a hot tub while others are 30m deep and 50m across, but together they are creating an environmental crisis.

The sinkholes are the result of the Dead Sea's ever-dropping water level. As the shoreline recedes, underground fresh water dissolves salt deposits located between 5m and 60m below ground, creating cavities that rise to the surface a bit like an air bubble in honey. Eventually, the loosely consolidated land above caves in.

Over the last few years, Ein Gedi Beach, Mineral Beach and a section of Hwy 90 near Ein Gedi have been closed after sections were swallowed up without warning. No one knows where the next gaping crater will suddenly appear, so the only access to the Dead Sea shoreline between the lake's northern tip (Kalya and Biankini Beaches in the West Bank) and Ein Bokek is at Ein Gedi Spa – and even there continued access is far from a sure thing.

For stunning aerial views of the sinkholes, check out the videos on YouTube.

THE NORTHERN BALD IBIS

At least one critically endangered bird species, the northern bald ibis, is still hanging on, although its status in the Middle East remains precarious. Seventy years after the species was declared extinct in Syria, a small breeding colony was found in the Syrian desert, close to Palmyra, in 2002. An intensive conservation program was established to protect the species, although there are fears that recent fighting between Isis and the Syrian government (and the occupation of the area for a time by the former) close to Palmyra may have have finally driven the last northern bald ibises from the region.

Elsewhere, an estimated 500 wild birds survive in southern Morocco, while a semi-wild breeding colony has been established in Turkey (where the species had been driven to local extinction). By mid-2016 the Turkish colony had grown to around 200 birds.

Environmental Issues

Water

It's often said that the next great Middle Eastern war will be fought not over land but over water. Syria and Iraq have protested to Turkey because it is building dams at the headwaters of the Tigris and Euphrates. Egypt has threatened military action against Sudan and Ethiopia or any other upstream country endangering its access to the waters of the Nile. And Jordan and Israel regularly spar over the waters of the shared Jordan River, which has now been reduced to a trickle, half of which is 50% raw sewage and effluent from fish farms.

At the disappearing wetlands of Azraq Wetland Reserve in Jordan, 347,000 birds were present on 2 February 1967. On the same date 33 years later there were just 1200.

One study suggests that Jordan currently uses about 60% more water t han is replenished from natural sources. By some estimates Jordan will simply run out of water within 20 years. Dams on the Yarmouk River, water pipelines, plans to tap underground fossil water and desalination plants are all part of the projected (and extremely expensive) solution.

Desertification

Desertification, which is caused by overgrazing, deforestation, the overuse of off-road vehicles, wind erosion and drought, is a significant problem faced by all Middle Eastern countries, with the possible exception of Lebanon. The seemingly unstoppable encroachment of the desert onto previously fertile, inhabited and environmentally sensitive areas is resulting in millions of hectares of fertile land becoming infertile and, ultimately, uninhabitable. Jordan, Syria, Egypt, Iran and Iraq are on the frontline, but even largely desert-free Turkey is casting a worried eye on the future.

Print environmental resources include: *Water on Sand: Environmental Histories of the Middle East and North Africa* (Alan Mikhail; 2012); *Climate Change – Environment and Civilization in the Middle East* (Arie S Issar and Mattanyah Zohar; 2004); and *Let There Be Water: Israel's Solution for a Water-Starved World* (Seth M Siegel, 2017).

Pollution

Levels of waste have reached critical levels across the region; recycling is almost nonexistent. At one level the impact is devastating for local fishing industries, agricultural output, freshwater supplies and marine environments – Lebanon did not have functioning waste-water treatment plants until the mid-1990s, while up to 75% of Turkey's industrial waste is discharged without any treatment whatsoever. At another level, the great mounds of rubbish and airborne plastic bags provide an aesthetic assault on the senses for traveller and local alike. Plastic bags are also a major issue for marine mammals in the Red Sea, where turtles mistake them for jellyfish; attempts to ban plastic bags in some coastal regions have met with only very limited success.

The related issue of air pollution is also threatening to overwhelm in a region where the motor vehicle is king. In Cairo, for example, airborne smoke, soot, dust and liquid droplets from fuel combustion constantly exceed World Health Organization (WHO) standards, sometimes by as much as 10,000 per cent, leading to skyrocketing instances of emphysema, asthma and cancer among the city's population. Cairo may be an extreme case, but it's a problem facing urban areas everywhere in the Middle East.

Survival Guide

TRAVELLER ETIQUETTE 558

SAFE TRAVEL 560

WOMEN TRAVELLERS........562

DIRECTORY A–Z ... 564

Accommodation........ 564
Customs Regulations ... 565
Discount Cards......... 565
Embassies & Consulates 565
Emergency & Important Numbers..... 565
Gay & Lesbian Travellers............ 565
Insurance............... 566
Internet Acccess........ 566
Legal Matters 566
Money.................. 566
Opening Hours 567
Photography 568
Post.................... 568
Public Holidays......... 568
Telephone 568
Time................... 569
Toilets................. 569
Tourist Information..... 569
Travellers with Disabilities 569
Volunteering 569
Work................... 569

TRANSPORT 571

GETTING THERE & AWAY 571
Entering the Middle East.............571
Air 571
Land 572
Sea 572
Tours....................572
GETTING AROUND......572
Air......................572
Bicycle 573
Boat 573
Bus 573
Car & Motorcycle........574
Hitching.................575
Taxi 575
Train 576

HEALTH 577

BEFORE YOU GO..........577
IN THE MIDDLE EAST.....578

LANGUAGE 582

Traveller Etiquette

Like anywhere else in the world, the people of the Middle East have particular ways of doing things and these customs can seem strange to first-time visitors. While you should always try to follow local customs, most people in the Middle East will be too polite to say anything if you break one of the region's taboos. In most cases, an apology and obvious goodwill will earn instant forgiveness.

EATING ETIQUETTE

Middle Easterners can be a hospitable lot, and it's not unusual for visitors to receive at least one invitation to eat in someone's home while travelling through the region. While each invitation needs to be assessed on its merits, our general advice would be that eating in a family home can be one of your most memorable travel experiences in the Middle East.

Homes

To avoid making your hosts feel uncomfortable, there are a few simple guidelines to follow.

- Bring a small gift of flowers, chocolates, pastries, fruit or honey.
- It's polite to be seen to wash your hands before a meal.
- Always remove your shoes before sitting down on a rug to eat or drink tea.
- Don't sit with your legs stretched out – it's considered rude during a meal.
- Always sit next to a person of the same sex at the dinner table unless your host(ess) suggests otherwise.
- Use only your right hand for eating or accepting food.
- When the meal begins, accept as much food as is offered to you. If you say 'no thanks' continually, it can offend the host.
- It's good manners to leave a little food on your plate at the end of the meal: traditionally, a clean plate was thought to invite famine. It can also suggest to your host that they haven't fed you sufficiently.
- Your host will often lay the tastiest morsels in front of you; it's polite to accept them.
- The best part – such as the meat – is usually saved until last, so don't take it until offered.

Restaurants

There are fewer etiquette rules to observe in restaurants, but it's still worth trying to do so, particularly if you're eating as the guest of a local or sharing a table with locals.

- Picking teeth after a meal is quite acceptable, and toothpicks are often provided.
- Be sure to leave the dining area and go outside or to the toilet before blowing your nose.
- Take food from your side of the table; stretching to the other side is considered impolite.
- It's polite to accept a cup of coffee after a meal and impolite to leave before it's served.

RELIGION

At some point during your travels in the Middle East, the conversation is likely to turn to religion. More specifically, you'll probably be asked, 'What's your religion?' Given that most foreign travellers come from secular Western traditions where religion is a private matter, the level of frankness in some of these discussions can come as a surprise. At the same time, there's no better way of getting under the skin of a nation than talking about the things that matter most in life. So how do you go about answering this question?

It's usually easy to explain that you are Christian or, in some circumstances, Jewish. The overwhelming majority of Muslims won't bat an eyelid and may even welcome the opportunity to talk about the common origins and doctrines that Christianity, Judaism and Islam share. Traditionally, Christians and Jews were respected as 'people of the book' who share the same God. In fact, many a Bedouin encounter begins with a celebration of that fact, with greetings such as 'Your God, my God same – *Salaam* (Peace)!'

The question of religion gets complicated when it comes to atheists. 'I don't believe in God' can call into question the very foundation of a Muslim's existence. If you are concerned your atheism will cause offence, perhaps say, 'I'm a seeker', suggesting you haven't quite made up your mind but may do so in the future. Be aware that Muslims may respond by explaining the merits of Islam to you. If that's not how you planned to spend your afternoon, try saying, 'I'm not religious'. This will likely lead to understanding nods and then, perhaps on subsequent meetings, an earnest attempt at conversion. Phrases like 'You'll find God soon, God-willing' are a measure of someone's affection for you and a reasonable response would be *shukran* (thank you).

GENERAL ETIQUETTE

Tourism has the potential to improve the relationship between the Middle East and the West, but the gradual erosion of traditional life is the flipside of mass tourism. Sexual promiscuity, public drunkenness among tourists and the wearing of unsuitable clothing are all concerns to be aware of.

Try to have minimal impact on your surroundings. Create a positive precedent for those who follow you by keeping in mind the following:

➡ Don't hand out sweets or pens to children on the streets, since it encourages begging. Similarly, doling out medicines can encourage people not to seek proper medical advice and you have no control over whether the medicines are taken appropriately. A donation to a project, health centre or school is a far more constructive way to help.

➡ Buy your snacks, cigarettes, bubble gum etc from the enterprising grannies trying to make ends meet, rather than state-run stores. Also, use locally owned hotels and restaurants and buy locally made products.

➡ Try to give people a balanced perspective of life in the West. Try also to point out the strong points of the local culture, such as strong family ties and comparatively low crime.

➡ Make yourself aware of the human-rights situation, history and current affairs in the countries you travel through.

➡ If you're in a frustrating situation, be patient, friendly and considerate. Never lose your temper as a confrontational attitude won't go down well. For many Arabs, a loss of face is a serious and sensitive issue.

➡ Try to learn some of the standard greetings – it will make a very good first impression.

➡ Always ask before taking photos of people. Don't worry if you don't speak the language – a smile and gesture will be appreciated. Never photograph someone if they don't want you to. If you agree to send someone a photo, make sure you follow through on it.

➡ Be respectful of Islamic traditions and don't wear revealing clothing; loose lightweight clothing is preferable.

➡ Men should shake hands when formally meeting other men, but not women, unless the woman extends her hand first. If you are a woman and uncomfortable with men extending their hand to you (they don't do this with local women), just put your hand over your heart and say hello.

➡ Public displays of physical affection are almost always likely to be misunderstood. Be discreet.

Safe Travel

Don't believe everything you read about the Middle East. Yes, there are regions that are dangerous to visit and you should, of course, always be careful while travelling in the region. But alongside the sometimes disturbing hard facts is more often a vast corpus of exaggeration, stereotyping and downright misrepresentation. We'll try and put this as simply as possible: there's every chance that you'll be safer in many parts of the Middle East than you would be back home.

IS IT SAFE?

Imagine somebody whose image of the USA was built solely on the 9/11 attacks, or who refused to visit Spain, France or the UK as a result of the terrorist attacks in Barcelona, Paris and London in recent years. Just as these countries are rarely considered to be dangerous destinations, so too, day-to-day life in the Middle East very rarely involves shootings or explosions. There are trouble spots where violence is serious and widespread, such as Syria and many regions of Iraq, and there are places where violence flares from time to time, such as in Israel and the Palestinian Territories and Lebanon. But such outbreaks of violence usually receive widespread media coverage, making it relatively easy to avoid these places until things settle down.

Terrorist incidents do occur, and there have been attacks in Israel and the Palestinian Territories and the Red Sea resorts of Egypt's Sinai Peninsula in recent years. While such incidents are clearly major causes for concern, they are the exception rather than the norm. The sad fact about modern terrorism is that you may face similar dangers anywhere in the world and that you're probably no more at risk in much of the Middle East than you may be in your home country. As one holidaymaker was reported saying in the wake of the 2005 Sharm El Sheikh bombings: 'Actually, I live in central London. I don't really want to go home!'

As a foreigner, you may receive the occasional question ('Why does the West support Israel?'), but you'll rarely be held personally accountable for the policies of Western governments. Once in Tehran we stood, obviously Westerners, with cameras and pasty complexions, and watched a crowd march by chanting 'Death to America! Death to Britain!' Several marchers grinned, waved and broke off to come over and ask how we liked Iran.

While most Western governments advise against travel to Gaza, Iraq and Syria, don't let problems in some areas tar your image of the entire region. Keep abreast of current affairs, and if you need to phone your embassy for travel advice, then do so. Otherwise, just go.

COMMON DANGERS

Road Accidents

Perhaps the most widespread threat to your safety comes from travelling on the region's roads. Road conditions vary, but driving standards are often poor and high speeds are common. Tips for minimising the risk of becoming a road statistic:

- Avoid night travel.
- A full-sized bus is usually safer than a minibus.
- If travelling in a shared taxi or minibus, avoid taking the seat next to the driver.

Political Unrest

The Arab Spring uprisings against regimes from Cairo to Damascus have added a layer of uncertainty to travel in the region, although with the exception of Syria and, for a time, Egypt, the enduring impact upon travellers has been minimal. Trouble spots in the region are usually well defined, and as long as you keep track of political developments, you're unlikely to come to any harm. Avoid political demonstrations or large gatherings and always ask the advice of locals if unsure.

Theft & Petty Crime

Crime rates are extremely low in most countries in the Middle East – theft is rarely a problem and robbery (mugging) even less of one. Even so, take the standard precautions. Always keep valuables with you or locked in a safe – never leave them in your room or in a car or bus. Use a money belt, a pouch under your clothes, a leather wallet attached to your belt or internal pockets in your clothing. Keep a separate record of your passport, credit card and travellers cheque numbers; it won't cure problems, but it will make them easier to bear.

GOVERNMENT TRAVEL ADVICE

The following government websites offer travel advisory services and information for travellers:

Australian Department of Foreign Affairs & Trade (www.smartraveller.gov.au)

Canadian Department of Foreign Affairs & International Trade (www.voyage.gc.ca)

French Ministère des Affaires et Étrangères Européennes (www.diplomatie.gouv.fr/fr/conseils-aux-voyageurs)

Italian Ministero degli Affari Esteri (www.viaggiaresicuri.mae.aci.it)

New Zealand Ministry of Foreign Affairs & Trade (www.safetravel.govt.nz)

UK Foreign & Commonwealth Office (www.gov.uk/foreign-travel-advice)

US Department of State (www.travel.state.gov)

COUNTRY BY COUNTRY

Egypt

Egypt remains a relatively safe country to visit, although security has become a concern in some areas in recent years, particularly as it relates to women travellers and/or petty theft. Avoid political demonstrations (especially those in Cairo's Tahrir Sq) and be particularly wary in areas with mixed Muslim-Coptic Christian populations. Check carefully the current travel advisories before travelling to the Sinai Peninsula (the entire northern half is considered unsafe).

Iran

Iran is one of the safest countries of the Middle East in which to travel. Violent crime against foreigners is extremely rare, although the southeast of the country, areas close to the border with Iraq, and within 100km of the border with Afghanistan are considered unsafe. Western embassies advise their nationals to register on arrival.

Iraq

At the time of writing, most foreign governments were advising against travel to most of Iraq, and against all but essential travel to Iraqi Kurdistan and parts of the south.

Israel & the Palestinian Territories

Although the security situation has greatly improved in recent years, travellers should continue to exercise caution in Israel and the Palestinian Territories. Gaza is considered off-limits. Elsewhere, you're unlikely to experience difficulties in most areas. You should always keep your ear to the ground in Jerusalem, Hebron and other potential flashpoints.

Jordan

Jordan has largely escaped the unrest arising from the 2011 revolutions, and it remains one of the safest countries in the region to visit. Foreign governments advise against travel in the immediate vicinity of the Jordan–Syria border.

Lebanon

Although it hasn't happened often and the country remains generally safe to visit, the conflict in Syria has spilled over into Lebanon often enough for us to advise caution. Border areas with Syria and the northern city of Tripoli have been particularly affected, while the Bekaa Valley, including Baalbek, was off-limits at the time of writing. Beyond that, the potential for political unrest and attendant violence remains a constant of Lebanese life, and care should be taken in southern Lebanon and elsewhere.

Syria

Syria is one of the most dangerous countries on earth for travellers to visit. Don't go there – it's as simple as that.

Turkey

Turkey is one of the safest countries in the Middle East for travellers, with a stable political system and well-developed transport infrastructure. Always check the security situation, though, before you travel in areas close to the borders with Syria and Iraq.

Women Travellers

Despite the Middle East's reputation as difficult terrain for women travellers, there's no reason why women can't enjoy the region as much as their male counterparts. In fact, some seasoned women travellers to the Middle East consider their gender to be a help, not a hindrance.

ATTITUDES TOWARDS WOMEN

For many people in the region, both men and women, the role of a woman is specifically defined: she is mother and matron of the household, while the man is the provider. Generalisations can, however, be misleading and the reality is often far more nuanced.

There are thousands of middle- and upper-middle-class professional women in the Arab World and elsewhere who, like their counterparts in the West, juggle work and family responsibilities. Among the working classes or in conservative rural areas where adherence to tradition is strongest, the ideal may be for women to concentrate on home and family, but economic reality means that millions of women are forced to work (but are still responsible for all domestic chores).

Contrary to stereotypes, the treatment of foreign women can be at its best in more conservative societies, providing, of course, you adhere to the prevailing social mores.

The treatment of women can also be a factor of age: older women will find they are greatly respected and may encounter fewer uncomfortable situations than younger women travellers.

LET'S TALK ABOUT SEX

When it comes to sex, the differences between Western and Middle Eastern women become most apparent. Premarital sex (or, indeed, any sex outside marriage) is taboo in most of the region. With occasional exceptions among the upper classes, women are expected to be virgins when they marry, and a family's reputation can rest upon this.

The presence of foreign women presents, in the eyes of some Middle Eastern men, a chance to get around these norms with ease and without consequences, a perception reinforced by distorted impressions gained from Western TV and the behaviour of a small number of women travellers.

PROS & CONS

Advantages

Women travellers are no different from their male counterparts in that meeting local people is a highlight of travelling in the Middle East. And unlike male travellers, they can meet Middle Eastern women without social restrictions, opening up a whole Middle Eastern world that men cannot experience. Local women are as curious about life for women beyond the Middle East as you are about their lives, and they love to chat to women visitors. That said, local women are less likely than men to have had an education that included learning English – you'll find this to be the only major barrier to getting to meet and talk with them.

One other advantage, and one you should exploit to the full, is that in some countries it's often perfectly acceptable for a woman to go straight to the front of a queue or ask to be served first. This is less likely to occur in Lebanon, Turkey, Israel and Iran.

Disadvantages

Sexual harassment is a problem worldwide and the Middle East is no exception. Harassment can come in many forms: from stares, muttered comments and uncomfortably close contact on crowded public transport, to the difficulty of eating in public on your own, where you may receive endless unwanted guests – even the wandering hands of waiters can be a problem. Women also report being followed and hissed at by unwanted male admirers on a fairly regular basis.

That said, although 'mild' harassment can be common in some countries, reports of serious physical harassment are rare. Whether that's because it rarely occurs or because it's rarely reported varies greatly from country to country. Significant social stigma attaches to sexual harassment in many Middle Eastern countries.

TOP TIPS

Your experience of travelling in the region may depend partly on situations beyond your control, but there are some things you can try so as to minimise problems:

- Retain your self-confidence and sense of humour.
- Balance alertness with a certain detachment: ignoring stares and refusing to dignify suggestive remarks with a response generally stops unwanted advances in their tracks.
- Eat in a restaurant's family section, where one exists, or at places more used to tourists.
- If necessary, invent or borrow a husband, wear a wedding ring or even carry a photo of your 'kids'. While this may cause some consternation – what sort of mother/wife are you to have left your family to travel alone? – it will deter many suitors.
- Avoid direct eye contact with local men (dark sunglasses help), although a cold glare can also be an effective riposte if deployed at the right moment.
- Maximise your interaction with local women.
- In taxis, avoid sitting in the front seat unless the driver is female.
- On all forms of public transport, sit next to another woman whenever possible.
- Lost? Try asking a local woman for directions.
- If nothing else works and you can't shake off a hanger-on, go to the nearest public place, such as a hotel lobby. If he persists, asking the receptionist to call the police usually frightens him off.

WHAT TO WEAR

Fair or not, how women travellers dress goes a long way towards determining how they're treated. To you, short pants and a tight top might be an appropriate reaction to the desert temperatures, but to many local men, your dress choice will send an entirely different message, confirming the worst views held of Western women.

The best way to tackle the stereotypes is to visibly debunk them. Do as the locals do, and dress and behave more modestly than you might at home and always err on the side of caution. As with anywhere, take your cues from those around you.

Dressing modestly means covering your upper legs and arms, shoulders and cleavage. A scarf is also useful, both to cover your neckline and to slip over your head when you want to look even more inconspicuous or when the occasion requires it (such as when visiting a mosque).

For all the inconvenience, dressing conservatively means you'll get a much warmer reception from the locals, you'll attract less unwanted attention, and you may feel more comfortable (long baggy clothes will keep you cooler under the fierce Middle Eastern sun).

In Iran, most female travellers will find dress rules to be both an imposition and an inconvenience. Since the revolution of 1979 all women in Iran, including foreigners, have been required by law to wear loose-fitting clothes to disguise their figures and must also cover their hair. This form of dressing is known as *hijab*, a term that refers in general to 'modest' dress, and is also used to refer specifically to the hair-covering.

Signs in public places show officially acceptable versions of *hijab*: the *chador* (literally 'tent' in Farsi), an all-encompassing, head-to-toe black garment held closed with hand or teeth; or a *manteau* (shapeless coat or coat dress) and a *rusari* (scarf) covering the hair and neck.

Directory A–Z

Accommodation

Across the Middle East, Iran and Egypt have the cheapest accommodation, while Turkey, Jordan, Lebanon, and Israel and the Palestinian Territories will cost more.

- **Hotels** Hotels are everywhere. Even in smaller towns, there'll be a hotel, although choice may be limited. There's everything from artfully converted boutique hotels to Mediterranean resorts.
- **Hostels** You'll find a handful of hostels in larger towns and cities wherever tourists tend to congregate.
- **Kibbutz guesthouses** An Israeli speciality, with good locations and atmosphere.
- **Camping** Camping is possible in some countries, but it would be difficult build a trip around solely staying in campgrounds.

Camping

Camping in the Middle East is possible, but stick to officially sanctioned campsites – free camping is fraught with peril and prone to creating misunderstandings: many areas that are military or restricted zones aren't always marked as such, and erecting a tent on an army firing range won't be a highlight of your trip. There are official camping grounds in Egypt, Lebanon, Turkey, and Israel and the Palestinian Territories.

Hostels

There are youth hostels in Egypt, Israel and the Palestinian Territories, and Lebanon. It's not usually necessary to hold a Hostelling International card to stay at these places, but it will often get you a small discount.

Along what's left of the old İstanbul-to-Cairo traveller route, you'll also find non-HI backpacker hostels, especially in Lebanon, Israel and Egypt. These are often dynamic hubs for travellers, with plenty of information on local attractions.

Hotels

BUDGET

In hotels at the bottom end of the price scale, rooms are not always clean. In fact, let's be honest: they can be downright filthy. Very cheap hotels are just dormitories where you're crammed into a room with whoever else fronts up. The cheapest places are rarely suitable for women travelling alone. In Iran, male-dominated *mosafferkhanehs* (literally 'travellers' houses') are basic hotels with dorms; expect shared bathrooms, squat toilets and no spoken English.

That said, elsewhere in the region there are some places that stand out, and while they may have no frills, nor do their shared bathrooms give any indication of the good health or otherwise of previous occupants. Some places treat you like a prince even as you pay the price of a pauper. The happy (and most common) medium is usually a room devoid of character, but containing basic, well-maintained facilities.

MIDRANGE

Midrange rooms have private bathrooms, usually with hot water, fans to stir the air, a bit more space to swing a backpack and (sometimes) TVs promising international satellite channels. These places are found throughout the region, with cities along well-worn traveller routes usually having the widest choice.

TOP END

Hotels at the top end of the range have clean, self-contained rooms with hot showers and toilets that work

BOOK YOUR STAY ONLINE

For more accommodation reviews by Lonely Planet authors, check out http://lonelyplanet.com/hotels/. You'll find independent reviews, as well as recommendations on the best places to stay. Best of all, you can book online.

all the time, not to mention satellite TV, shampoo and regularly washed towels in the bathrooms, air-con to provide refuge from the Middle Eastern sun and a few luxuries to lift the spirits.

An increasing (and entirely welcome) trend is the proliferation of tastefully designed boutique hotels that make a feature of traditional design.

Kibbutz Guesthouses

Capitalising on their beautiful, usually rural locations, quite a few kibbutzim in Israel offer midrange guesthouse accommodation. Often constructed in the socialist era but significantly upgraded since, these establishments allow access to kibbutz facilities (including the swimming pool), have a laid-back vibe and serve deliciously fresh kibbutz-style breakfasts. For details and reservations, check out the Kibbutz Hotels Chain (www.kibbutz.co.il).

Customs Regulations

Customs regulations vary from country to country, but in most cases they aren't that different from what you'd expect in the West – a couple of hundred cigarettes and a couple of bottles of booze.

There was a time when electronics used to arouse interest when entering or leaving Egypt, but it's becoming increasingly rare. If they do pull you up, items such as laptop computers and especially video cameras may be written into your passport to ensure that they leave the country with you and are not sold. If you're carrying printed material that could be interpreted as being critical of the government, be discreet, although customs officials at major entry/departure points rarely search the bags of tourists.

Iran is a notable exception to some of these rules – alcohol is illegal in the Islamic Republic of Iran, and any publications showing (even modestly exposed) female flesh will be confiscated if found.

Discount Cards

An International Student Identity Card (ISIC) can be useful in the Middle East. Egypt, Israel and the Palestinian Territories, and Turkey have various (and often considerable) student discounts for admission to museums, archaeological sites and monuments. In Israel, cardholders also qualify for 10% reductions on some bus fares and 20% on rail tickets. Bear in mind that a student card issued by your own university or college may not be recognised elsewhere; it really should be an ISIC (www.isic.org).

Embassies & Consulates

It's important to realise what your own embassy can and can't do to help you if you get into trouble. Generally speaking, it won't be much help in emergencies if the trouble you're in is remotely your own fault. Remember that you are bound by the laws of the country you're in. Your embassy will not be sympathetic if you end up in jail after committing a crime locally, even if such actions are legal in your own country.

In genuine emergencies, you might get some limited assistance, but only if other channels have been exhausted. For example, if you need to get home urgently, a free ticket home is exceedingly unlikely – the embassy would expect you to have insurance. If all your money and documents are stolen, it might assist with getting a new passport, but a loan for onward travel is out of the question.

Emergency & Important Numbers

Phone number for the police by country:

Egypt	☎ 126
Iran	☎ 110
Israel & the Palestinian Territories	☎ 100
Jordan	☎ 911
Lebanon	☎ 112
Turkey	☎ 155

Gay & Lesbian Travellers

The situation for gay and lesbian travellers in the Middle East is more diverse than you might imagine. Israel is the best place in the region to be gay – homosexuality is legal, and Tel Aviv in particular has a thriving gay and lesbian scene. Elsewhere, especially in conservative Jerusalem, the gay and lesbian scene is well and truly underground. The same doesn't apply to the Palestinian Territories, and hundreds of Palestinian gays have been forced to seek refuge in Israel.

Homosexuality inhabits a legal black hole in Turkey – not illegal nor is it officially legal. On one hand, İstanbul and Ankara are both home to small but thriving gay communities. Turkey is, however, a Muslim country and homophobia is on the rise; the local authorities have from time to time used morality laws to close down gay advocacy groups. As always, discretion is key.

It is slightly more complicated in Egypt and Jordan, where, although the criminal code doesn't expressly forbid homosexual acts, laws regarding public decency have been used to prosecute gays, especially in Egypt; the Jordanian capital Amman nonetheless has a couple of gay-friendly spots.

Homosexuality is illegal in Lebanon, Iran, Syria and Iraq, although Beirut takes a fairly liberal approach with a small but vibrant gay scene. In March 2014 a Lebanese court ruled that same-sex relations are not 'contradicting the laws of nature' and cannot therefore be considered a crime. A number of similar rulings have led some to claim that homosexual acts are effectively legal in the country, but the legal situation remains unclear.

In countries where homosexuality is illegal or ambiguous in a legal sense, penalties include fines and/or imprisonment. That does not mean that there isn't an active gay scene, but it does mean that gay identity is generally expressed only in certain trusted, private spheres.

Useful Resources

Global Gayz – Middle East (www.globalgayz.com/middle-east) An excellent country-by-country rundown on the situation for gays and lesbians in all countries of the Middle East.

Spartacus International Gay Guide (www.spartacusworld.com/gayguide) Good for information on gay-friendly bars and hotels. It also has a Gay Travel Index.

Insurance

Travel insurance covering theft, loss and medical problems is highly recommended. Some policies offer travellers lower and higher medical-expense options; the higher ones are chiefly for countries such as the USA, which have extremely high medical costs. Watch particularly for the small print as some policies specifically exclude 'dangerous activities', which can include scuba diving, motorcycling and even trekking.

Worldwide travel insurance is available at www.lonelyplanet.com/travel-insurance. You can buy, extend and claim online anytime – even if you're already on the road.

Internet Access

Wi-fi access is increasingly the norm in most top-end hotels as well as many in the midrange categories. It's also getting easier to connect in upmarket cafes and restaurants. In some places, like Tel Aviv, there aren't that many places where you *can't* connect.

You're never too far from an internet cafe in all major cities and larger towns across the Middle East, although ones that last the distance are pretty rare. If you need to track one down, ask your hotel reception or head to the university district (if there is one) and ask around.

Given its reputation for political censorship, there are surprisingly few websites that are blocked by governments in the region, although Iran is a significant exception; in the latter everything from BBC news sites to Twitter and Facebook can fall foul of the censors.

Legal Matters

Legals systems differ greatly across the Middle East, with the greatest difference tending to be the extent to which Islamic principles and Sharia law underpins the legal order. The spectrum ranges from the codification of fairly strict Islamic tenets in Iran to more secular laws in Turkey and Israel, with many shades of grey in between.

Despite such differences, as a general rule most of the same activities that are illegal in your country are illegal in the countries of the Middle East, but the penalties are usually much harsher. The penalties for drug or alcohol use and smuggling are harsh. Carrying the smallest amount of hashish can result in a jail sentence; don't expect assistance from your embassy or a comfortable cell. Trafficking heroin or opium carries the death penalty. For most minor crimes foreigners will probably be deported, though this is not an absolute.

Money

ATMs and credit-card use are widespread in the Middle East. US dollars are universally accepted, followed by euros and British pounds. Cash is king in Iran.

ATMs

ATMs are now a way of life in most Middle Eastern countries. This is certainly the case in Turkey, Lebanon, Israel and the Palestinian Territories, Jordan and Egypt, where ATMs are everywhere and they're usually linked to one of the international networks (eg MasterCard, Maestro, Cirrus, Visa, Visa Electron or GlobalAccess systems). ATMs are widespread in Iran, but none accept international cards and are therefore of no use to travellers.

Another thing to consider is whether the convenience of withdrawing money as you go is outweighed by the bank fees you'll be charged for doing so. It's a good idea to check the transaction fees both with your own bank back home and, if possible, with the banks whose machines you'll be using while you travel.

Cash

Although credit cards are increasingly accepted, cash remains the most reliable way to bring your money in the Middle East. And not just any cash. US dollars and, increasingly, euros are the currency of choice in most countries of the Middle East, and not just for changing money – many midrange and top-end hotels prefer their bills to be settled in either currency.

If your funds have run dry and you've no means of withdrawing money, Western Union (www.westernunion.com) has representatives in every country in the region except Iran.

The only danger in relying solely on travelling with cash is that if you lose it, it's lost forever – insurance companies simply won't believe that you had US$1000 in cash.

Credit Cards

Credit cards (especially Visa and MasterCard) are accepted by an ever-growing number of Middle Eastern hotels, top-end restaurants and handicraft shops, but the situation is still a long way from one where you could pay your way solely by flashing the card.

Israel and the Palestinian Territories, Lebanon and Turkey are the most credit-card-friendly countries in the region. You should always be wary of surcharges for paying by card – many Egyptian and Jordanian businesses also sting for commissions over and above the purchase price. Credit cards are useless in Iran.

Tipping

Tipping is expected to varying degrees in all Middle Eastern countries. Called baksheesh, it's more than just a reward for having rendered a service. Salaries and wages are much lower than in Western countries, so baksheesh is often regarded as an essential means of supplementing income. To a cleaner in a one- or two-star hotel, who may earn the equivalent of US$50 per month, the accumulated daily dollar tips given by guests can constitute the mainstay of his or her salary.

For Western travellers who aren't used to continual tipping, demands for baksheesh for doing anything from opening doors to pointing out the obvious in museums can be quite irritating. But it is the accepted way. Don't be intimidated into paying baksheesh when you don't think the service warrants it, but remember that more things warrant baksheesh here than anywhere in the West. One hint: carry lots of small change with you, but keep it separate from bigger bills, so that baksheesh demands don't increase when they see that you can afford more.

Tipping is increasingly expected in midrange and top-end restaurants in Israel and the Palestinian Territories, Lebanon and Turkey. Check your bill closely, however, as many such restaurants include an additional charge for service, in which case a further tip is not necessary. One country where baksheesh or tipping isn't as prevalent is Jordan, where many locals feel irritated when tourists throw their money around, not least because some employers are known to deduct anticipated tips from their employees, resulting in even lower wages!

Other circumstances in which a tip is expected is where you've taken a tour either with a guide or a taxi driver or both. How much to leave depends on the length of the expedition and the helpfulness of the guide.

Opening Hours

With a few exceptions, the working week runs from Sunday to Thursday, so the end-of-week holiday is Friday. In Israel and the Palestinian Territories, it's Saturday (Shabbat), while in Lebanon and Turkey, it's Sunday. In countries where Friday is the holiday, many embassies and offices are also closed on Thursday, although in areas where there are lots of tourists, many private businesses

EXCHANGE RATES

		EGYPT	IRAN	ISRAEL & THE PALESTINIAN TERRITORIES	JORDAN	LEBANON	TURKEY
Australia	A$1	LE14.02	IR26,840	2.86NIS	JD0.57	LL1210	₺2.75
Canada	C$1	LE14.16	IR27,495	2.88NIS	JD0.58	LL1240	₺2.78
Europe	€1	LE20.94	IR40,003	4.26NIS	JD0.84	LL1804	₺4.12
Japan	¥100	LE16.23	IR30,339	3.20NIS	JD0.64	LL1369	₺3.19
New Zealand	NZ$1	LE12.80	IR24,310	2.60NIS	JD0.51	LL1097	₺2.51
UK	UK£1	LE22.72	IR44,304	4.61NIS	JD0.94	LL2000	₺4.46
USA	US$1	LE17.77	IR33,387	3.60NIS	JD0.70	LL1506	₺3.48

For current exchange rates see www.xe.com.

ISLAMIC CALENDAR

All Islamic holidays fall according to the Muslim calendar, while secular activities are planned according to the Christian system.

The Muslim year is based on the lunar cycle and is divided into 12 lunar months, each with 29 or 30 days. Consequently, the Muslim year is 10 or 11 days shorter than the Christian solar year, and the Muslim festivals gradually move around the Gregorian calendar year, completing the cycle in roughly 33 years. Actual dates may occur a day or so later than listed, but probably not earlier, depending on moon sightings.

and shops are open on Thursday and many stores will reopen in the evening on Friday.

It's worth remembering that shops and businesses may have different opening hours for different times of the year – they tend to work shorter hours in winter and open earlier in summer to allow for a longer lunchtime siesta. During Ramadan (the month-long fast for Muslims), almost everything shuts down in the afternoon.

Photography

As a matter of courtesy, never photograph people without first asking their permission. While that's a general rule for photography anywhere, it's especially important in the Middle East. In more conservative areas, including many rural areas, men should never photograph women and in most circumstances should never even ask. In countries where you can photograph women, show them the camera and make it clear that you want to take their picture.

In most Middle Eastern countries, it is forbidden to photograph anything even vaguely military in nature (including bridges, train stations, airports, border crossings and other public works). The definition of what is 'strategic' differs from one country to the next, and signs are not always posted, so err on the side of caution and, if in doubt, ask your friendly neighbourhood police officer for permission.

Photography is usually allowed inside religious and archaeological sites, unless signs indicate otherwise. As a rule, do not photograph inside mosques during a service. Many Middle Easterners are sensitive about the negative aspects of their country, so exercise discretion when taking photos in poorer areas.

Post

Post services are quite reliable in most of the Middle East, although in rural areas the service can range from slow to nonexistent – it definitely pays to send your mail from the main centres.

Letters sent from a major capital take about a week to reach most parts of Europe, and anything between a week and two weeks to reach North America or Australasia. If you're in a hurry, either DHL or Federal Express has offices in almost every capital city in the Middle East.

Public Holidays

All Middle Eastern countries except Israel observe the main Islamic holidays listed here. Countries with a major Shiite population also observe Ashura, the anniversary of the martyrdom of Hussein, the third imam of the Shiites. Most of the countries in the area also observe both the Gregorian and the Islamic New Year holidays. Every country also has its own national days and other public holidays.

Eid Al Adha (Kurban Bayramı in Turkey) This feast marks the time that Muslims make the pilgrimage to Mecca.

Eid Al Fitr (Şeker Bayramı in Turkey) Another feast, this time to herald the end of Ramadan fasting; the celebrations last for three days.

Islamic New Year Also known as Ras As Sana, it literally means 'the head of the year'.

Lailat Al Miraj This is the celebration of the Ascension of the Prophet Mohammed.

Prophet's Birthday This is also known as Moulid An Nabi, 'the feast of the Prophet'.

Ramadan (Ramazan in Turkey and Iran) This is the ninth month of the Muslim calendar, when Muslims fast during daylight hours. Foreigners are not expected to follow suit, but it's considered impolite to smoke, drink or eat in public during Ramadan. As the sun sets each day, the fast is broken with *iftar* (the evening meal prepared to break the fast).

Ashura The anniversary of the martyrdom of Hossein, the third Shiite imam, in battle at Karbala in October AD 680. This is celebrated with religious theatre and sombre parades in Shiite areas, especially in Iran and Lebanon.

Telephone

Wi-fi access is increasingly the norm, so the cheapest way to make international calls is using VoIP operators such as Skype (www.skype.com) from your own device, although Skype is sometimes blocked by Iranian censors.

Internet cafes are usually equipped with webcams, microphones and headsets and can sell you the relevant card (there are usually a number of brands to choose from) and show you how to use it.

Country Codes

Egypt	☎ 20
Iran	☎ 98
Iraq	☎ 964
Israel & the Palestinian Territories	☎ 972
Jordan	☎ 962
Lebanon	☎ 961
Syria	☎ 963
Turkey	☎ 90

Mobile Phones

Mobile networks in Middle Eastern countries all work on the GSM system, and it's rare that your mobile brought from home won't automatically link up with a local operator. That's fine for receiving calls, but roaming charges can make for a nasty surprise back home if you've made a few calls on your trip. If you plan to be in a country for a while, your best option is to buy a local SIM card – an easy process in every country of the region except Turkey, where it can be complex and time-consuming.

Time

Egypt, Israel and the Palestinian Territories, Jordan, Lebanon, Syria and Turkey are two hours ahead of GMT/UTC, Iraq is three hours ahead, and Iran is 3½ hours ahead. All countries operate on daylight-saving hours from around April to September, except for Turkey and Egypt.

Toilets

Outside the midrange and top-end hotels and restaurants (where Western-style toilets are the norm), visitors will encounter their fair share of Arab-style squat toilets (which, incidentally, according to physiologists, encourage a far more natural position than the Western-style invention!).

It's a good idea to carry an emergency stash of toilet paper with you for the times when you're caught short outside the hotel, as most of these toilets have a water hose and bucket for the same purpose.

Tourist Information

Most countries in the region have tourist offices with branches in big towns and at tourist sights. That said, don't expect much. Usually, the most the offices can produce is a free map; help with booking accommodation or any other service is typically beyond the resources of the often-nonetheless-amiable staff. The exceptions to this rule are some of the offices in Israel and the Palestinian Territories, which are very useful. Elsewhere, you'll usually get better results relying on the knowledge and resourcefulness of your hotel reception or a local guide.

Travellers with Disabilities

Generally speaking, scant regard is paid to the needs of disabled travellers in the Middle East. Steps, high kerbs and other assorted obstacles are everywhere, streets are often badly rutted and uneven, roads are made virtually uncrossable by heavy traffic, and many doorways are low and narrow. Ramps and specially equipped lodgings and toilets are extremely rare. The exception is Israel. Elsewhere, you'll have to plan your trip carefully and will probably be obliged to restrict yourself to luxury-level hotels and private, hired transport.

Where Middle Eastern governments have singularly failed to provide the necessary infrastructure, local officials, guides and hotel staff almost invariably do their best to help in any way they can.

Download Lonely Planet's free Accessible Travel guides from http://lptravel.to/AccessibleTravel.

Useful Resources

Accessible Travel & Leisure (www.accessibletravel.co.uk) Claims to be the biggest UK travel agent dealing with travel for the disabled, including some options for Egypt. The company encourages people with disabilities to travel independently.

Society for Accessible Travel and Hospitality (www.sath.org) A good resource that gives advice on how to travel with a wheelchair, kidney disease, sight impairment or deafness.

Tourism for All (www.tourismforall.org.uk) Advice for disabled and less-mobile senior travellers.

Volunteering

There aren't many opportunities for volunteering in the Middle East but some international organisations (including the following) have projects in the region:

Idealist.org (www.idealist.org) Numerous options in the region.

International Volunteer Programs Association (www.volunteerinternational.org) Possibilities in Jordan.

UN Volunteers (www.unv.org) Volunteer with the UN, with occasional opportunities in the region.

Volunteer Abroad (www.goabroad.com/volunteer-abroad) A handful of options in the Middle East.

Work

It's possible to pick up work in the Middle East to extend your stay and eke out your savings – but you have to know where to look and what you're looking for. Realistically, your best options are Egypt, Israel and Turkey, ie the places where other foreigners gather in numbers.

Centres for teaching English – both of the respectable kind and cowboy outfits – can be found throughout the Middle East. Cowboy outfits are often desperate for teachers and will take on people whose only qualification is that their mother tongue is English. Pay is minimal and you'll probably have to stay on a tourist visa, which will be up to you to renew. However, many long-termers finance their stays this way, particularly in Cairo and İstanbul.

Your chances of getting a job are greatly improved if you have a Celta (Certificate in English Language Teaching to Adults). This is what used to be known as TEFL and, basically, it's your passport to work abroad. Qualified teachers should also check www.eslcafe.com for regular job postings.

In Israel and the Palestinian Territories (Jerusalem, Tel Aviv and Eilat) and various places in Turkey (particularly İstanbul, Selçuk, Bodrum, Fethiye and Cappadocia), it's usually possible to pick up work in a hostel, typically cleaning rooms or looking after reception. It doesn't pay much, but it does usually get you a free room, a meal or two a day plus some beer money. The only way to find this kind of work is to ask around.

In all countries of the Middle East, work is not usually permitted on a tourist visa and you will need to obtain a working visa – discuss this with any potential employer before signing any contract.

Transport

GETTING THERE & AWAY

The Middle East is well served by air routes that connect Australasia and Asia with Europe. Overland travel from the west is relatively simple, but routes to/from the region's east were unsafe at the time of writing.

Flights, tours and rail tickets can be booked online at www.lonelyplanet.com/bookings.

Entering the Middle East

Entry requirements vary from country to country. Most border crossings are generally hassle-free, though wait times can be long.

Passport

Note that neither Israeli citizens nor anyone who has an Israeli stamp in their passport will be allowed to enter Iran or Lebanon (or Iraq or Syria when they're considered safe to visit). Israel no longer stamps tourists' passports (though it retains the right to do so). Instead, visitors are given a small loose-leaf entry card.

Air

There are numerous direct flights into the region from Europe and, to a lesser extent, North America. Otherwise, the burgeoning Gulf hubs of Dubai, Abu Dhabi and Doha make convenient waystations en route to the region.

Airports & Airlines

The Middle East's main international airports are as follows. Both Egypt and Turkey have additional airports that receive international flights.

Atatürk International Airport (IST, Atatürk Havalımanı; ☎444 9828; www.ataturkairport.com), İstanbul

Beirut–Rafic Hariri International Airport (☎01 628 000; www.beirutairport.gov.lb)

Ben Gurion International Airport (TLV; www.iaa.gov.il), Tel Aviv

Cairo International Airport (☎flight info from landline 0900 77777, flight info from mobile 27777; www.cairo-airport.com; Wi-Fi)

Imam Khomeini International Airport (IKIA, IKA; www.ikia.airport.ir; Ⓜ Imam Khomeini International Airport), Tehran

Queen Alia International Airport (☎06 401 0250; www.qaiairport.com), Amman

Airlines flying to the Middle East include the following:

Air Arabia (www.airarabia.com)

Arkia (www.arkia.co.il)

EgyptAir (www.egyptair.com.eg)

El Al (www.elal.co.il)

Emirates (www.emirates.com)

Gulf Air (www.gulfair.com)

Iran Air (www.iranair.com)

CLIMATE CHANGE & TRAVEL

Every form of transport that relies on carbon-based fuel generates CO_2, the main cause of human-induced climate change. Modern travel is dependent on aeroplanes, which might use less fuel per kilometre per person than most cars but travel much greater distances. The altitude at which aircraft emit gases (including CO_2) and particles also contributes to their climate change impact. Many websites offer 'carbon calculators' that allow people to estimate the carbon emissions generated by their journey and, for those who wish to do so, to offset the impact of the greenhouse gases emitted with contributions to portfolios of climate-friendly initiatives throughout the world. Lonely Planet offsets the carbon footprint of all staff and author travel.

DEPARTURE TAX

In all countries of the region, departure tax is included in the price of a ticket.

Iraqi Airways (www.iraqiairways.com.iq)

Jazeera Airways (www.jazeeraairways.com)

Middle East Airlines (www.mea.com.lb)

Qatar Airways (www.qatarairways.com)

Royal Jordanian (www.rj.com)

Turkish Airlines (www.turkishairlines.com)

Land

Border crossings in the Middle East can be slow, and it can take hours to pass through immigration and customs formalities, especially if you bring your own car. Showing patience, politeness and good humour *may* speed up the process.

If travelling overland to or from the Middle East, you can approach the region from Africa, the Caucasus, Iran or Europe.

Border Crossings

For information on visas and border crossings, see p38.

Sea

Ferries shuttle reasonably regularly between southern Europe and Turkey. There are other less-frequented routes connecting Egypt with Sudan and Saudi Arabia, though a Saudi visa is near impossible to come by.

Although vehicles can be shipped on most routes, bookings may have to be made some time in advance. The charge usually depends on the length or volume of the vehicle and should be checked with the carrier. As a rule, motorcycles cost almost nothing to ship, while bicycles are free.

You're unlikely to regret taking an adequate supply of food and drink with you on any of these ships; even if it's available on board, you're pretty stuck if it doesn't agree with you or your budget.

Ferry Lines (www.ferrylines.com) is a good place to get started when looking at possible routes into the region.

Cyprus

If you have a multiple-entry visa for Turkey, you should be able to cross over to Northern Cyprus and back again without buying a new one. However, if your visa has expired, you should anticipate long queues at immigration.

Akgünler (www.akgunler.com.tr) heads from Girne (Northern Cyprus) to Taşucu (1½ hours, three weekly) in Turkey.

Greece

Private ferries link Turkey's Aegean coast and the Greek islands. Services are usually daily in summer, several times a week in spring and autumn, and perhaps just once a week in winter.

Car-ferry services operate between Greek ports and several Turkish ports, but not to İstanbul. Among the most important routes are Chios–Çeşme, Kastellorizo–Kaş, Kos–Bodrum, Lesvos–Ayvalık, Rhodes (Rhodos)–Bodrum, Rhodes (Rhodos)–Datça, Rhodes (Rhodos)–Marmaris and Samos–Kuşadası.

Russia & Ukraine

The main routes out of Turkey are Trabzon–Sochi (for Russia) and Istanbul–Illichivsk (for Ukraine). Other seasonal routes may include Samsun–Batumi (Georgia), Samsun–Novorossiysk (Russia) and İstanbul–Sevastopol.

Sari Denizcilik Weekly ferry between Sochi, in Russia, and Trabzon (12 hours).

Stena Sea Line (www.stenasealine.com) Weekly service between İstanbul and Chornomorsk in Ukraine (23 to 25 hours).

UKR Ferry (www.ukrferry.com) Twice-weekly Istanbul–Chornomorsk (23 to 25 hours).

Tours

For a clearing house of sustainable tour options, visit www.responsibletravel.com.

Intrepid (www.intrepidtravel.com) Tours to most Middle Eastern countries.

Passport Travel (www.travelcentre.com.au) Tours to Turkey, Egypt, Iran, Jordan and Israel.

Antichi Splendori Viaggi (www.antichisplendori.it) Experienced Italian operator.

Dabuka Expeditions (www.dabuka.de) German expeditions into the Egyptian Sahara.

Terres d'Aventure (www.terdav.com) French operator that visits most countries in the region.

Zig-Zag (www.zigzag-randonnees.com) Experienced French company that gets off the beaten track.

Ancient World Tours (www.ancient.co.uk) Ancient Egypt specialists.

Andante Travels (www.andantetravels.co.uk) Archaeology tours, including to southeastern Turkey.

Crusader Travel (www.crusadertravel.com) Sinai treks and Red Sea diving.

Bestway Tours & Safaris (www.bestway.com) A huge range of tours to most countries.

Yalla Tours (www.yallatours.com) Middle East specialists.

GETTING AROUND

Air

With no regional rail network to speak of, and distances that make the bus a discomforting test of endurance, flying is certainly the most user-friendly method of transport in the Middle East if your time is tight.

Flying isn't possible between Israel and other Middle Eastern countries, except for Egypt, Jordan and Turkey. But, these exceptions aside, almost every Middle Eastern capital is linked to each of the others.

Airlines

Until recently, most flights were operated by state airlines. Of these, when it comes to service, punctuality and safety, El Al (Israel), Royal Jordanian, Turkish Airlines and Middle East Airlines (Lebanon) are probably the pick of the bunch, with Egypt Air solid and *usually* reliable.

The growth of private (usually low-cost) airlines, especially in Turkey and Israel, means that flying domestic routes within these countries has become a lot more feasible.

Bicycle

Although the numbers doing it are small, cycling round the Middle East is a viable proposition, provided that cyclists are self-sufficient and able to carry litres of extra water.

Most of the people we spoke to reckoned that the most enjoyable cycling was in Turkey. Although hilly, the scenery in Turkey is particularly fine and accommodation is fairly easy to come by, even in the smallest villages. This is definitely not the case elsewhere. In Turkey, if you get tired of pedalling, it's also no problem to have your bike transported in the luggage hold of the big modern buses.

One big plus about cycling through the region is the fact that cyclists are usually given warm welcomes (a trademark of the Middle East in any case) and are showered with food and drinks. There have been, however, reports of kids throwing stones at cyclists along Jordan's King's Highway.

By far the major difficulty cited by all cyclists is the heat, which is at its peak from June to August. May to mid-June and September through October are the best times. Even then, you're advised to make an early morning start and call it a day by early afternoon.

There are bicycle-repair shops in most major towns and the locals are excellent 'bush mechanics', with all but the most modern or sophisticated equipment.

Boat

The most popular boat services are the two ferry services between Nuweiba in Egypt and Aqaba in Jordan. The fast-ferry service takes 45 minutes, while the slow (and cheaper) ferry makes the journey in 2½ to three hours. Vehicles can usually be shipped on these routes, but advance arrangements may have to be made.

Bus

Buses are the workhorses of the Middle East, and in most places they're probably your only option for getting from A to B. Thankfully, most buses are reliable and comfortable.

The cost and comfort of bus travel varies enormously throughout the region. One typical nuisance is bus drivers' fondness (presumably shared by local passengers) for loud videos; sleep is almost always impossible. Another potential source of discomfort is that in most Middle Eastern countries, the concept of a 'non-smoking bus' is not always observed.

Within most cities and towns, a minibus or bus service operates. Fares are very cheap, and services are fast, regular and run on fixed routes with, in some cases, fixed stops. However, unless you're very familiar with the town, they can be difficult to get to grips with (few display their destinations, fewer still do so in English, and they are often very crowded). Unless you can find a local who speaks your language to help you out, your best bet is to stand along the footpath (preferably at a bus stop if one exists) of a major thoroughfare heading in the direction you want to go, and call out the local name (or the name of a landmark close to where you're heading) into the drivers' windows when they slow down.

CYCLING TIPS

- Carry a couple of extra chain links, a chain breaker, spokes, a spoke key, two inner tubes, tyre levers and a repair kit, a flat-head and Phillips-head screwdriver, and Allen keys and spanners to fit all the bolts on your bike.
- Check the bolts daily and carry spares.
- Fit as many water bottles to your bike as you can.
- Confine your panniers to a maximum weight of 15kg.
- Carrying the following equipment in your panniers is recommended: a two-person tent (weighing about 1.8kg) that can also accommodate the bike where security is a concern; a sleeping bag rated to 0°C and an inflatable mattress; a small camping stove; cooking pot; utensils; a water filter (two microns) and a compact torch.

Reservations

It's always advisable to book bus seats in advance at the bus station, which is usually the only ticket outlet and source of reliable information about current services. Reservations are a must over the Muslim weekend (Friday) as well as during major public holidays.

Car & Motorcycle

Driving around the region (whether your own vehicle or a hire care) can be a good way to go, but you'll need to plan your route carefully. Border crossings can be painfully slow and obtaining the necessary documentation can be complicated. Road safety can also be a concern as traffic accidents are common.

Throughout the Middle East, motorcycles are fairly popular as a means of racing around in urban areas, but are little used as long-distance transport. If you do decide to ride a motorcycle through the region, try to take one of the more popular Japanese models if you want to stand any chance of finding spare parts. Even then, make sure your bike is in very good shape before setting out. Motorcycles can be shipped or, often, loaded as luggage onto trains.

Bringing Your Own Vehicle

Bringing your own car to the Middle East will give you a lot more freedom, but it's certainly not for everyone. For all the positives, it's difficult to imagine a route through the Middle East that would justify the expense and hassle of bringing a car and getting it out again.

Anyone planning to take their own vehicle with them needs to check in advance what spare parts and petrol are likely to be available.

A number of documents are also required (if you're unsure what to take, check with the automobile association in your home country):

- **Carnet de passage** Like a passport for your car, and ensures you don't sell your car along the way; can be expensive. Ask your local automobile association for details.
- **Green card** Issued by insurers. Insurance for some countries is only obtainable at the border.
- **International Driving Permit (IDP)** Obtainable from your local automobile association.
- **Vehicle registration documents** In addition to carrying all ownership papers, check with your insurer whether you're covered for the countries you intend to visit and whether third-party cover is included.

Driving Licences

If you plan to drive, get an International Driving Permit (IDP) from your home automobile association. An IDP is compulsory for foreign drivers and motorcyclists in Egypt and Iran (and Iraq and Syria when they are safe to travel to). Most foreign (or national) licences are acceptable in Israel and the Palestinian Territories, Lebanon and Turkey, and for foreign-registered vehicles in Jordan. However, even in these places an IDP is recommended. IDPs are valid for one year only.

Fuel & Spare Parts

Mechanical failure can be a problem as spare parts – at least official ones – are often unobtainable. Fear not, ingenuity often compensates for factory parts; your mechanic back home will either have a heart attack or learn new techniques when you show them what's gone on under your hood in the Middle East.

Generally, spare parts are most likely to be available for Land Rovers, Volkswagens, Range Rovers, Mercedes and Chevrolets, although in recent years Japan has been a particularly vigorous exporter of vehicles to the region. One tip is to ask your vehicle manufacturer for a list of any authorised service centres it has in the countries you plan to visit. The length of this list is likely to be a pretty good reflection of how easy it is to get parts on your travels.

Usually two grades of petrol are available; if in doubt, get the more expensive one. Petrol stations are few and far between on many desert roads. Away from the main towns, it's advisable to fill up whenever you get the chance. Diesel isn't readily available in every Middle Eastern country, nor is unleaded petrol.

Car Hire

International hire companies such as Hertz (www.hertz.com), Avis (www.avis.com) and Europcar (www.europcar.com) are represented in many large towns. Local companies are usually cheaper, but the cars of international companies are often better maintained and come with a better back-up service if problems arise. Local companies sometimes carry the advantage of including a driver for a similar cost to hiring the car alone.

To hire a car, you'll need any or all of the following: a photocopy of your passport and visa; deposit or credit-card imprint; and your driving licence or International Driving Permit. The minimum age varies between 21 and 25 – the latter is most common, particularly with international companies.

Always make sure that insurance is included in the hire price and familiarise yourself with the policy – don't hire a car unless it's insured for every eventuality.

Insurance

Insurance is compulsory in most Middle Eastern countries, not to mention highly advisable. Given the large number of minor accidents, not to mention major ones, fully comprehensive insurance (as opposed to third-party) is strongly advised, both for your own and any hire vehicle.

Make certain you're covered for off-piste travel, as well as travel between Middle Eastern countries (if you're planning cross-border excursions).

In the event of an accident, make sure you submit the accident report as soon as possible to the insurance company or, if hiring, the car hire company, and do so before getting the car repaired.

Road Conditions

Conditions across the Middle East vary enormously, but in almost all cases they'll be worse than you're used to back home. The main roads are generally good, or at least reasonable, but there are plenty of unsurfaced examples, and the international roads are generally narrow and crowded. Turkey, Jordan, and Israel and the Palestinian Territories probably have the best roads, but those in Lebanon and Iran adhere to the following rule: worse than they should be but probably better than you'd expect. Some of Egypt's roads are fine, others are bone-jarringly bad.

Road Hazards

Driving in the Middle East can be appalling by Western norms. Fatalism and high speed rule supreme. Car horns, used at the slightest provocation, take the place of caution and courtesy. Except in well-lit urban areas, try to avoid driving at night, as you may find your vehicle is the only thing on the road with lights.

In desert regions, particularly in Egypt, beware of wind-blown sand and wandering, free-range camels – the latter can be deadly at night.

Road Rules

You're unlikely even to know what the speed limit is on a particular road, let alone be forced to keep to it – the rules exist more in theory than they are enforced in reality.

A warning triangle is required for vehicles (except motorcycles) in most Middle Eastern countries; in Turkey two triangles and a first-aid kit are compulsory.

In all countries, driving is on the right-hand side of the road and the rules of when to give way (at least officially) are those that apply in continental Europe.

Hitching

Although many travellers hitchhike, it's never an entirely safe way of getting around and those who do so should understand that they are taking a small but potentially serious risk. There is no part of the Middle East where hitching can be recommended for unaccompanied women travellers. Just because we explain how hitching works, doesn't mean we recommend you do it.

Hitching as commonly understood in the West hardly exists in the Middle East (except in Israel and the Palestinian Territories). Although in most countries you'll often see people standing by the road hoping for a lift, they will nearly always expect (and be expected) to offer to pay. Hitching in the Middle Eastern sense is not so much an alternative to the public transport system as an extension of it, particularly in areas where there's no regular public transport. The going rate is often roughly the equivalent of the bus or shared taxi fare, but may be more if a driver takes you to an address or place off their route. You may well be offered free lifts from time to time, but you won't get very far if you set out deliberately to avoid paying for transport.

Throughout the Middle East a raised thumb is a vaguely obscene gesture. A common way of signalling that you want a lift is to extend your right hand, palm down.

Taxi

In the West, taxis are usually considered a luxury. In the Middle East they're often unavoidable. Some cities have no other form of urban public transport, while there are also many rural routes that are only feasible in a taxi or private vehicle.

Taxis are seemingly everywhere you look and, if you can't see one, try lingering on the footpath next to a major road and, within no time, plenty of taxis will appear as if from nowhere and will soon toot their horns at you just in case you missed them, even if you're just trying to cross the street.

If you want to save money, it's important to be able to differentiate between the various kinds of taxis.

Regular Taxi

Regular taxis (variously known as 'agency taxis', 'telephone taxis', 'private taxis' or 'special taxis') are found in almost every Middle Eastern town or city. Unlike shared taxis, you pay to have the taxi to yourself, either to take you to a pre-agreed destination or for a specified period of time. They are primarily of use for transport within towns or on short rural trips, but in some countries hiring them for excursions of several hours is still cheap. They are also often the only way of reaching airports or seaports.

Shared Taxi

A compromise between the convenience of a regular taxi and the economy of a bus, the shared taxi picks up and drops off passengers at points along its (generally fixed) route and runs to no

TIPS FOR CATCHING TAXIS

On the whole, taxi drivers in the Middle East are helpful, honest and often humorous. Others – as in countries all over the world – find new arrivals too tempting a target for minor scams or a spot of overcharging. Here are a few tips:

- Not all taxi drivers speak English. Generally, in cities used to international travellers, they will (or know enough to get by), but not otherwise. If you're having trouble, ask a local for help.
- Always negotiate a fare (or insist that the meter is used if it works) before jumping in. If in doubt about local rates, inquire at your point of departure.
- Don't rely on street names (there are often several versions and the driver may not recognise your pronunciation of them). If you're going to a well-known destination (such as a big hotel), find out if it's close to a local landmark and give the driver the local name for the landmark. Even better, get someone to write down the name in the local language.
- Avoid using unlicensed cab drivers at airports or bus stations.
- Note that at the time of writing, travellers to Lebanon were being advised not to use shared taxis because of an increased security risk.

particular schedule. It's known by different names – collect, collective or service taxi in English, *servees* in Arabic, *sherut* in Hebrew, *savari* in Farsi and *dolmuş* in Turkish. Most shared taxis take up to four or five passengers, but some seat up to about 12 and are indistinguishable for most purposes from minibuses.

Shared taxis are much cheaper than private taxis and, once you get the hang of them, can be just as convenient. They are dearer than buses but more frequent and usually faster, because they don't stop so often or for so long. They also tend to operate for longer hours than buses. They can be used for urban, intercity or rural transport.

Fixed-route taxis wait at the point of departure until full or nearly full. Usually they pick up or drop off passengers anywhere en route, but in some places they have fixed halts or stations. Sometimes each service is allocated a number, which may be indicated on the vehicle. Generally, a flat fare applies for each route, but sometimes it's possible to pay a partial fare.

Fares depend largely on time and distance, but can also vary slightly according to demand.

Beware of boarding an empty one, as the driver may assume you want to hire the vehicle for your exclusive use and charge you accordingly. It's advisable to watch what other passengers pay and to hand over your fare in front of them. Passengers are expected to know where they are getting off. 'Thank you' in the local language is the usual cue for the driver to stop. Make it clear to the driver or other passengers if you want to be told when you reach your destination.

Train

There are train networks in Egypt, Israel, Iran and Turkey, and these can represent the best transport option on some routes, such as between Cairo and Luxor in Egypt. Levels of comfort vary from country to country – many of Egypt's trains are badly in need of an overhaul, Iran's are OK, while Israel and Turkey use new trains on some routes.

In general, trains are less frequent and usually slower than buses, while many stations are some distance out of the town centres they serve.

In general, tickets are only sold at the station and reservations are either compulsory or highly recommended.

Health

Prevention is the key to staying healthy while travelling in the Middle East. Infectious diseases can and do occur in the region but are usually associated with poor living conditions and poverty and can be avoided with a few precautions. The most common reason for travellers needing medical help is as a result of accidents – cars are not always well maintained, seatbelts are rare and poorly lit roads are littered with potholes. Medical facilities can be excellent in large cities, but in remote areas may be more basic.

BEFORE YOU GO

Pre-Departure Planning

A little planning before departure can save you a lot of trouble later. See your dentist before a long trip; carry a spare pair of contact lenses and glasses (and take your optical prescription); and carry a first-aid kit with you.

It's tempting to leave it all to the last minute – don't! Many vaccines don't ensure immunity until two weeks after treatment, so visit a doctor four to eight weeks before departure. Ask your doctor for an International Certificate of Vaccination (otherwise known as the yellow booklet), which will list all the vaccinations you've received. This is mandatory for countries that require proof of yellow fever vaccination upon entry (and you'll need this if you're flying in from sub-Saharan Africa), but it's a good idea to carry it wherever you travel.

Travellers can register with the International Association for Medical Advice to Travellers (www.iamat.org). Its website can help travellers to find a doctor with recognised training. Those heading off to very remote areas might like to do a first-aid course (Red Cross and St John Ambulance can help).

Bring medications in their original, clearly labelled containers. A signed and dated letter from your physician describing your medical conditions and medications, including generic names, is also a good idea. If carrying syringes or needles, be sure to have a physician's letter documenting their medical necessity.

Insurance

Find out in advance if your insurance plan will make payments directly to providers or reimburse you later for overseas health expenditures (in many Middle Eastern countries doctors expect payment in cash). It's also worth making sure that your travel insurance will cover repatriation home or to better medical facilities elsewhere. Your insurance company may be able to locate the nearest source of medical help, or you can ask at your hotel. In an emergency, contact your

TRAVEL HEALTH WEBSITES

There is a wealth of travel health advice on the internet. The World Health Organization publishes the helpful *International Travel and Health*, available free at www.who.int/ith. Other useful websites include MD Travel Health (www.redplanet.travel/mdtravelhealth), Travel Doctor (www.traveldoctor.co.uk) and Fit for Travel (www.fitfortravel.scot.nhs.uk).

Official government travel health websites:

Australia www.smartraveller.gov.au/guide/all-travellers/health/Pages/default.aspx

Canada www.hc-sc.gc.ca/index_e.html

UK www.gov.uk/foreign-travel-advice

USA wwwnc.cdc.gov/travel

MEDICAL CHECKLIST

Following is a list of other items you should consider packing in your medical kit.

- acetaminophen/paracetamol (eg Tylenol) or aspirin
- adhesive or paper tape
- antibacterial ointment (eg Bactroban) for cuts and abrasions
- antibiotics (if travelling off the beaten track)
- antidiarrhoeal drugs (eg containing loperamide)
- antihistamines (for hay fever and allergic reactions)
- anti-inflammatory drugs (eg containing ibuprofen)
- bandages, gauze, gauze rolls
- insect repellent that contains DEET (for skin)
- insect spray that contains permethrin (for clothing, tents and bed nets)
- iodine tablets (for water purification)
- oral-rehydration salts
- pocket knife
- scissors, safety pins, tweezers
- steroid cream or cortisone (for allergic rashes)
- sunscreen
- syringes and sterile needles (if travelling to remote areas)
- thermometer

embassy or consulate. Your travel insurance will not usually cover you for anything other than emergency dental treatment. Not all insurance covers emergency aeromedical evacuation home or to a hospital in a major city, which may be the only way to get medical attention for a serious emergency.

Recommended Vaccinations

The World Health Organization (WHO) recommends that all travellers, regardless of the region they are travelling in, should be covered for diphtheria, tetanus, measles, mumps, rubella and polio, as well as hepatitis B. While making preparations to travel, take the opportunity to ensure that all of your routine vaccination cover is complete. The consequences of these diseases can be severe and outbreaks do occur in the Middle East.

IN THE MIDDLE EAST

Availability & Cost of Health Care

The health care systems in the Middle East are varied. Medical care can be excellent in Israel and Turkey, with well-trained doctors and nurses, but can be patchier elsewhere. Reciprocal health arrangements with countries rarely exist and you should be prepared to pay for all medical and dental treatment.

Medical care is not always readily available outside major cities. Medicine, and even sterile dressings or intravenous fluids, may need to be bought from a local pharmacy. Nursing care may be limited or rudimentary as this is something families and friends are expected to provide.

Standards of dental care are variable throughout the region, and there is an increased risk of hepatitis B and HIV transmission via poorly sterilised equipment.

For minor illnesses such as diarrhoea, pharmacists can often provide valuable advice and sell over-the-counter medication. They can also advise as to whether more specialised help is needed.

Infectious Diseases

Diptheria

Diphtheria is spread through close respiratory contact. It causes a high temperature and severe sore throat. Sometimes a membrane forms across the throat requiring a tracheotomy to prevent suffocation. Vaccination is recommended for those likely to be in close contact with the local population in infected areas. The vaccine is given as an injection alone, or with tetanus, and lasts 10 years.

Hepatitis A

Hepatitis A is spread through contaminated food (particularly shellfish) and water. It causes jaundice, and although it is rarely fatal, can cause prolonged lethargy and delayed recovery. Symptoms include dark urine, a yellow colour to the whites of the eyes, fever, and abdominal pain. Hepatitis A vaccine (Avaxim, VAQTA, Havrix) is given as an injection: a single dose will give protection for up to a year, while a booster 12 months later will provide a subsequent 10 years of protection.

Hepatitis B

Infected blood, contaminated needles and sexual intercourse can all transmit hepatitis B. It can cause jaundice, and affects the liver, occasionally causing liver failure. All travellers should make this a routine vaccination. (Many countries now give hepatitis B vaccination as part of routine childhood vaccination.) A course will give protection for at least five years, and can be given over four weeks or six months.

Leishmaniasis

Spread through the bite of an infected sand fly, leishmaniasis can cause a slowly growing skin lump or ulcer. It may develop into a serious life-threatening fever usually accompanied by anaemia and weight loss. Sand fly bites should be avoided whenever possible. Infected dogs are also carriers. Leishmaniasis is present in Iran, Iraq, Israel and the Palestinian Territories, Jordan, Lebanon, Syria and Turkey.

Malaria

The prevalence of malaria varies throughout the Middle East. Many areas are considered to be malaria free, while others have seasonal risks. The risk of malaria is minimal in most cities; however, check with your doctor if you are considering travelling to any rural areas. It is important to take antimalarial tablets if the risk is significant. For up-to-date information about the risk of contracting malaria in a specific country, contact your local travel health clinic.

Middle East Respiratory Syndrome (MERS)

Middle East Respiratory Syndrome (MERS) is present throughout the Middle East and causes serious respiratory problems, with children and the elderly particularly at risk. MERS can be fatal in approximately one-third of cases. The illness can be passed from sick animals (particularly camels) to people – always wash your hands thoroughly and immediately after being in contact with camels – although it is not understood how the virus passes from one person to another. Symptoms include fever, cough, shortness of breath and (sometimes) pneumonia. Other possible symptoms include muscle pain, diarrhoea, vomiting and nausea.

Poliomyelitis

Generally spread through contaminated food and water, polio is present, though rare, throughout the Middle East. It is one of the vaccines given in childhood and should be boosted every 10 years, either orally (a drop on the tongue), or as an injection. Polio may be carried asymptomatically, although it can cause a transient fever and, in rare cases, potentially permanent muscle weakness or paralysis.

Rabies

Spread through bites or licks on broken skin from an infected animal, rabies (present in all countries of the Middle East) is fatal. Animal handlers should be vaccinated, as should those travelling to remote areas where a reliable source of postbite vaccine is not available within 24 hours. Three injections are needed over a month. If you have not been vaccinated you will need a course of five injections starting within 24 hours or as soon as possible after the injury. Vaccination does not provide you with immunity, it merely buys you more time to seek appropriate medical treatment.

Rift Valley Fever

This haemorrhagic fever, which is found in Egypt, is spread through blood or blood products, including those from infected animals. It causes a flu-like illness with fever, joint pains and occasionally more serious complications. Complete recovery is possible.

Schistosomiasis

Otherwise known as bilharzia, this is spread through the freshwater snail. It causes infection of the bowel and bladder, often with bleeding. It is caused by a fluke and is contracted through the skin from water contaminated with human urine or faeces. Paddling or swimming in suspect freshwater lakes or slow-running rivers should be avoided. There may be no symptoms. Possible symptoms include a transient fever and rash, and advanced cases of bilharzia may cause blood in the stool or in the urine. A blood test can detect antibodies if you have been exposed and treatment is then possible in specialist travel or infectious-disease clinics. Be especially careful in Egypt, Iran, Iraq and Syria.

Tuberculosis (TB)

Tuberculosis is spread through close respiratory contact and occasionally through infected milk or milk products. BCG vaccine is recommended for those likely to be mixing closely with the local population. It is more important for those visiting family or planning on a long stay, and those employed as teachers and health-care workers. TB can be asymptomatic, although symptoms can include coughing, weight loss or fever months or even years after exposure. An X-ray is the best way to confirm if you have TB. BCG gives a moderate degree of protection against TB. It causes a small permanent scar at the site of injection, and is usually only given in specialised chest clinics. As it's a live vaccine it should not be given to pregnant women or immunocompromised individuals. The BCG vaccine is not available in all countries.

Typhoid

Typhoid is spread through food or water that has been contaminated by infected human faeces. The first symptom is usually fever or a pink rash on the abdomen. Septicaemia (blood poisoning) may also occur. Typhoid vaccine (typhim Vi, typherix) will give protection for three years. In some countries, the oral vaccine Vivotif is also available.

Yellow Fever

Yellow fever vaccination is not required for any areas of the Middle East. However, the mosquito that spreads yellow fever has been known to be present in some parts of the region. It is important to consult your local travel health clinic as part of your predeparture plans for the latest details. Any travellers from a yellow fever endemic area (eg parts of sub-Saharan Africa) will need to show proof of vaccination against yellow fever before entry.

Environmental Hazards

Heat Illness

Heat exhaustion occurs after heavy sweating and excessive fluid loss with inadequate replacement of fluids and salt. It is particularly common in hot climates when taking unaccustomed exercise before full acclimatisation. Symptoms include headache, dizziness and tiredness. Dehydration is already happening by the time you feel thirsty – aim to drink sufficient water so that you produce pale, diluted urine. The treatment of heat exhaustion consists of fluid replacement with water or fruit juice or both, and cooling by cold water and fans. The treatment of the salt-loss component consists of taking in salty fluids (such as soup or broth), and adding a little more table salt to foods than usual.

Heat stroke is much more serious. This occurs when the heat-regulating mechanism in the body breaks down. An excessive rise in body temperature leads to sweating ceasing, irrational and hyperactive behaviour, and eventually loss of consciousness and death. Rapid cooling by spraying the body with water and fanning is an ideal treatment. Emergency fluid and electrolyte replacement by intravenous drip is usually also required.

Insect Bites & Stings

Mosquitoes may not carry malaria but can cause irritation and infected bites. Using DEET-based insect repellents will prevent bites. Mosquitoes also spread dengue fever.

Bees and wasps only cause real problems to those with a severe allergy (anaphylaxis). If you have a severe allergy to bee or wasp stings you should carry an adrenaline injection or similar.

Scorpions are frequently found in arid or dry climates. They can cause a painful sting, which is rarely life threatening.

Bed bugs are often found in hostels and cheap hotels. They lead to very itchy lumpy bites. Spraying the mattress with an appropriate insect killer will do a good job of getting rid of them.

Scabies are also frequently found in cheap accommodation. These tiny mites live in the skin, particularly between the fingers. They cause an intensely itchy rash. Scabies is easily treated with lotion available from pharmacies.

Snake Bites

Do not walk barefoot or stick your hand into holes or cracks. Half of those bitten by venomous snakes are not actually injected with poison (envenomed). If bitten by a snake, do not panic. Immobilise the bitten limb with a splint (eg a stick) and apply a bandage over the site using firm pressure, similar to a bandage over a sprain. Do not apply a tourniquet, or cut or suck the bite. Get the victim to medical help as soon as possible so that antivenene can be given if necessary.

Traveller's Diarrhoea

To prevent diarrhoea, avoid tap water unless it has been boiled, filtered or chemically disinfected (with iodine tablets). Eat only fresh fruits or vegetables if cooked or if you have peeled them yourself, and avoid dairy products that may contain unpasteurised milk. Buffet meals are risky, as food should be piping hot; meals freshly cooked in front of you in a busy restaurant are more likely to be safe.

If you develop diarrhoea, be sure to drink plenty of fluids, preferably an oral rehydration solution containing salt and sugar. A few loose stools don't require treatment but, if you start having more than four or five stools a day, you should start taking an antibiotic (usually a quinolone drug) and an antidiarrhoeal agent (such as loperamide). If diarrhoea is bloody, persists for more than 72 hours, or is accompanied by fever, shaking chills or severe abdominal pain you should seek medical attention.

TAP WATER

Many locals don't drink the tap water and we recommend that you follow their lead. If you do decide to risk the local water, the safest places to do so are in Israel and Turkey. Don't even *think* of drinking from the tap in Egypt, Iran, the Palestinian Territories or Lebanon. Cheap bottled water is readily available throughout the region.

Travelling with Children

All travellers with children should know how to treat minor ailments and when to seek medical treatment. Make sure children are up to date with the routine vaccinations, and discuss possible travel vaccinations well before departure as some are not suitable for children aged under one year old.

In hot, moist climates any wound or break in the skin may lead to infection. The area should be cleaned and then kept dry and clean. Remember to avoid potentially contaminated food and water. If your child is vomiting or experiencing diarrhoea, lost fluid and salts must be replaced. It may be helpful to take rehydration powders for reconstituting with boiled water. Ask your doctor about this.

Children should be encouraged to avoid dogs or other mammals because of the risk of rabies and other diseases. Any bite, scratch or lick from a warm blooded, furry animal should immediately be thoroughly cleaned. If there is any possibility that the animal is infected with rabies, immediate medical assistance should be sought.

Women's Health

Emotional stress, exhaustion and travelling through different time zones can all contribute to an upset in the menstrual pattern. If using oral contraceptives, remember some antibiotics, diarrhoea and vomiting can stop the pill from working and lead to the risk of pregnancy – it's safest to take other forms of contraception with you.

Emergency contraception is most effective if taken within 24 hours after unprotected sex. The International Planned Parent Federation (www.ippf.org) can advise about the availability of contraception in different countries.

Tampons and sanitary towels are not always available outside of major cities in the Middle East.

Travelling during pregnancy is usually possible, but there are important things to consider. Have a medical check-up before embarking on your trip. The most risky times for travel are during the first 12 weeks of pregnancy, when miscarriage is most likely, and after 30 weeks, when complications such as high blood pressure and premature delivery can occur. Most airlines will not accept a traveller after 28 to 32 weeks of pregnancy, and long-haul flights in the later stages can be very uncomfortable.

Antenatal facilities vary greatly between countries in the Middle East, and you should think carefully before travelling to a country with poor medical facilities or where there are major cultural and language differences compared with home. Taking written records of the pregnancy, including details of your blood group, is likely to be helpful if you need medical attention while away. Ensure your insurance policy covers pregnancy, delivery and postnatal care, but remember insurance policies are only as good as the facilities available.

Language

WANT MORE?

For in-depth language information and handy phrases, check out Lonely Planet's *Middle East Phrasebook*. You'll find it at **shop.lonelyplanet.com**, or you can buy Lonely Planet's iPhone phrasebooks at the Apple App Store.

ARABIC

The following phrases are in MSA (Modern Standard Arabic), which is the official language of the Arab world. There are significant differences between MSA and the colloquial Arabic varieties spoken. Egyptian, Gulf, Levantine and Tunisian Arabic are the most commonly spoken, sometimes mutually unintelligible and with no official written form. Arabic is written from right to left in Arabic script. Read our coloured pronunciation guides as if they were English and you should be understood. Note that a is pronounced as in 'act', aa as the 'a' in 'father', aw as in 'law', ay as in 'say', ee as in 'see', i as in 'hit', oo as in 'zoo', u as in 'put', gh is a throaty sound (like the Parisian French 'r'), r is rolled, dh is pronounced as in 'that', th as in 'thin' and kh as the 'ch' in the Scottish *loch*. The apostrophe (') indicates the glottal stop (like the pause in the middle of 'uh-oh'). The stressed syllables are indicated with italics. Masculine and feminine options are indicated with 'm' and 'f' respectively.

Basics

Hello.	السلام عليكم.	as·sa·*laa*·mu 'a·*lay*·kum
Goodbye.	إلى اللقاء.	'*i*·laa al·li·*kaa'*
Yes.	نعم.	*na*·'am
No.	لا.	laa
Excuse me.	عفواً.	'*af*·wan
Sorry.	آسف. آسفة.	'*aa*·sif (m) '*aa*·si·fa (f)
Please.	لو سمحتَ. لو سمحتِ.	law sa·*mah*·ta (m) law sa·*mah*·ti (f)

Thank you.
شكراً. *shuk*·ran

How are you?
كيف حالكَ؟ *kay*·fa *haa*·lu·ka (m)
كيف حالكِ؟ *kay*·fa *haa*·lu·ki (f)

Fine, thanks. And you?
بخير شكراً.
وانتَ/انتِ؟
bi·*khay*·rin *shuk*·ran
wa·'*an*·ta/wa·'*an*·ti (m/f)

What's your name?
ما اسمكَ؟ maa '*is*·mu·ka (m)
ما اسمكِ؟ maa '*is*·mu·ki (f)

My name is ...
اسمي ... '*is*·mee ...

Do you speak English?
هل تتكلَّمُ/
تتكلَّمِينَ
الإنجليزية؟
hal ta·ta·*kal*·la·mu/
ta·ta·kal·la·*mee*·na
al·'inj·lee·*zee*·ya (m/f)

I don't understand.
أنا لا أفهم. '*a*·naa laa '*af*·ham

Signs – Arabic

Entrance	مدخل
Exit	مخرج
Open	مفتوح
Closed	مغلق
Information	معلومات
Prohibited	ممنوع
Toilets	دوراتُ المياه
Men	الرجال
Women	النساء

Accommodation

Where's a ...?	أين أجدُ ...؟	*'ay*·na *'a*·ji·du ...
guesthouse	بيت للضيوف	bayt li·du·*yoof*
hotel	فندق	*fun*·duk
Do you have a ... room?	هل عِندكم غرفةٌ ...؟	hal *'in*·da·kum *ghur*·fa·tun ...
single	بسريرٍ منفردٍ	bi·sa·*ree*·rin *mun*·fa·rid
double	بسريرٍ مزدوّجٍ	bi·sa·*ree*·rin muz·*daw*·waj
How much is it per ...?	كم ثمنه لِـ ...؟	kam *tha*·ma·nu·hu li ...
night	ليلةٍ واحدة	*lay*·la·tin *waa*·hid

Eating & Drinking

Can you recommend a ...?	هل يمكنكَ أن توصي ...؟	hal yum·*ki*·nu·ka 'an too·*see*·ya ... (m)
	هل يمكنكِ أن توصي ...؟	hal yum·*ki*·nu·ki 'an *too*·see ... (f)
cafe	مقهىً	*mak*·han
restaurant	مطعمً	*mat*·'am

What's the local speciality?
ما الوجبة الخاصّة لهذه المنطقة؟ — maa al·*waj*·ba·tul*khaa*·sa li·*haa*·dhi·hil *man*·ta·ka

Do you have vegetarian food?
هل لديكم طعامٌ نباتيّ؟ — hal la·*day*·ku·mu ta·*'aa*·mun na·*baa*·tee

I'd like the ..., please.	أريد ...، لو سمحتَ.	'u·*ree*·du ... law sa·*mah*·ta
bill	الحساب	hi·*saab*
menu	قائمة الطعام	kaa·*'i*·ma·tu at·ta·*'aam*

Emergencies

Help!	ساعدني!	saa·'id·nee (m)
	ساعديني!	*saa*·'i·dee·nee (f)
Go away!	اتركني!	'it·*ruk*·nee (m)
	اتركيني!	'it·ru·*kee*·nee (f)
Call ...!	اتّصلْ بـ ...!	*'it*·ta·sil bi ... (m)
	اتّصلي بـ ...!	'it·*ta*·si·lee bi ... (f)
a doctor	طبيبٍ	ta·*beeb*
the police	الشرطة	ash·*shur*·ta

I'm lost.
أنا ضائع. — 'a·naa *daa*·'i' (m)
أنا ضائعة. — 'a·naa *daa*·'i·'a (f)

Where are the toilets?
أينَ دورات المياه؟ — *'ay*·na daw·*raa*·tul mee·*yaah*

Numbers – Arabic

1	١	واحد	*waa*·hid
2	٢	اثنان	'ith·*naan*
3	٣	ثلاثة	tha·*laa*·tha
4	٤	أربعة	*'ar*·ba·'a
5	٥	خمسة	*kham*·sa
6	٦	ستة	*sit*·ta
7	٧	سبعة	*sab*·'a
8	٨	ثمانية	tha·*maa*·ni·ya
9	٩	تسعة	*tis*·'a
10	١٠	عشرة	*'a*·sha·ra
100	١٠٠	مائة	*mi*·'a
1000	١٠٠٠	ألف	'alf

Note that Arabic numerals, unlike letters, are written from left to right.

I'm sick. أنا مريض. — 'a·naa ma·*reed*

Shopping & Services

I'm looking for ...
أبحثُ عن ... — *'ab*·ha·thu 'an ...

Can I look at it?
هل يمكنني أن أراه؟ — hal yum·*ki*·nu·nee 'an 'a·*raa*·hu

How much is it?
قديش هيقه؟ — 'ad·*deesh* ha'·'u

Where's an ATM?
أينَ جهاز الصرافة؟ — *'ay*·na ji·*haaz* as·sar·*raa*·fa

Transport & Directions

Is this the ... to (Beirut)?	هل هذا الـ ... إلى (دبي)؟	hal *haa*·dhaa al ... *'i*·laa (Beirut)
boat	سفينة	sa·*fee*·na
bus	باص	baas
plane	طائرة	*taa*·'i·ra
train	قطار	ki·*taar*
What time's the ... bus?	في أيّ ساعةٍ يغادرُ الباص الـ ...؟	fee *'ay*·yee *saa*·'a·tin yu·*ghaa*·di·ru al·*baas* al ...
first	أوّل	*'aw*·wal
last	آخر	*'aa*·khir
One ... ticket, please.	تذكرة ... واحدة، لو سمحت.	*tadh*·ka·ra·tu ... *waa*·hi·da law sa·*mah*·ta
one-way	ذهاب فقط	dha·*haa*·bu *fa*·kat
return	ذهاب وإياب	dha·*haa*·bu wa·'ee·*yaab*

How much is it to ...?
كم الأجرة إلى ...؟ kam al·'uj·ra·ti 'i·laa ...

Please take me to (this address).
أوصلني عند 'aw·sal·nee 'ind
(هذا العنوان) (haa·dhaa al·'un·waan)
لو سمحتْ. law sa·mah·ta

Can you show me (on the map)?
هل يمكنكَ أن hal yum·ki·nu·ka 'an
توضح لي tu·wad·da·ha lee
(على الخريطة)؟ ('a·laa al·kha·ree·ta) (m)
هل يمكنكِ أن hal yum·ki·nu·ki 'an
توضحي لي tu·wad·da·hee lee
(على الخريطة)؟ ('a·laa al·kha·ree·ta) (f)

What's the address?
ما هو العنوان؟ maa hu·wa al·'un·waan

FARSI

The official language of Iran is called Farsi by its native speakers; in the West it's commonly referred to as Persian. Farsi is written and read from right to left in the Perso-Arabic script. If you read our coloured pronunciation guides as if they were English, you'll be understood. Note that a is pronounced as in 'act', aa as the 'a' in 'father', e as in 'bet', ee as in 'see', o as in 'tone' and oo as in 'zoo'. Both gh (like the French 'r') and kh (like the 'ch' in the Scottish *loch*) are guttural sounds, pronounced in the back of the throat, r is rolled and zh is pronounced as the 's' in 'pleasure'. The apostrophe (') indicates the glottal stop (like the pause in the middle of 'uh-oh'). The stressed syllables are indicated with italics.

Basics

Hello.	سلام	sa·*laam*
Goodbye.	خدا حافظ	kho·daa·haa·*fez*
Yes.	بله	ba·*le*
No.	نه	na
Please.	لطفا	lot·*fan*
Thank you.	متشكرم	mo·te·shak·*ke*·ram

Signs – Farsi

Entrance	ورود
Exit	خروج
Open	باز
Closed	بسته
Information	اطلاعات
Toilets	توالت
Men	مردانه
Women	زنانه

Excuse me.	ببخشيد	be·bakh·*sheed*
Sorry.	متاسفم	mo·ta·as·se·fam

How are you?
حالتون چطور هست؟ haa·*le*·toon *che*·to·re

Fine, thanks. And you?
خوبم خیلی ممنون *khoo*·bam khey·*lee* mam·*noon*
شما چطور هستید؟ sho·*maa* *che*·to·reen

What's your name?
اسمتون چی هست؟ es·*me*·toon *chee*·ye

My name is ...
اسم من ... هست es·*me* man ... hast

Do you speak English?
شما انگلیسی حرف sho·*maa* een·gee·lee·*see*
می زنید؟ harf *mee*·za·need

I don't understand.
من نمی فهم man ne·*mee*·fah·mam

Accommodation

Where's a ...? ... كجاست؟ ... *ko*·jaast

guesthouse	مهمان پذير	meh·maan·pa·*zeer*
hotel	هتل	ho·*tel*

Do you have a ... room?	شما اتاق ... دارید؟	sho·*maa* o·taa·*ghe* ... *daa*·reen
single	یک خوابه	yek khaa·*be*
double	دو خوابه	do khaa·*be*
How much is it per ...?	برای هر ... چقدر هست؟	ba·raa·*ye* har ... *che*·ghadr hast
night	شب	shab

Eating & Drinking

Can you recommend a ...?	می توانید یک ... پیشنهاد كنين؟	*mee*·too·neen yek ... peesh·na·*haad* *ko*·neen
cafe	كافه	kaaf·*fe*
restaurant	رستوران	res·too·*raan*

What's the local speciality?
غذای مخصوص gha·zaa·*ye* makh·soo·*se*
محلی چی هست؟ ma·hal·*lee* *chee*·ye

Do you have vegetarian food?
شما غذای sho·*maa* gha·zaa·*ye*
گیاه خواری دارید؟ gee·yaah·khaa·*ree* daa·*reen*

I'd like (the) ..., please.	لطفا من ... را می خواهم	lot·*fan* man ... ro *mee*·khaam
bill	صورت حساب	soo·*rat* he·*saab*
menu	منو	me·*noo*

Emergencies

Help!	کمک!	ko·*mak*
Go away!	برو کنار!	bo·*ro* ke·*naar*
Call ...!	... صدا کنید!	... se·*daa* ko·neen
a doctor	یک دکتر	yek dok·*tor*
the police	پلیس	po·*lees*

I'm lost.
من گم شده ام — man gom sho·*dam*

Where are the toilets?
توالت کجاست؟ — too·vaa·*let* ko·jaast

I'm sick.
من مریض هستم — man ma·*reez* has·*tam*

Shopping & Services

I'm looking for ...
من دنبال ... می گردم — man don·baa·*le* ... *mee*·gar·dam

Can I look at it?
می توانم به آن نگاه کنم؟ — *mee*·too·nam be oon ne·*ghaah* ko·nam

How much is it?
آن چقدر هست؟ — oon *che*·ghadr hast

What's your lowest price?
پایین ترین قیمت تون چند هست؟ — paa·yeen·ta·*reen* ghey·ma·te·*toon* *chan*·de

Where's an ATM?
خود پرداز کجاست؟ — khod·par·*daaz* ko·*jaast*

Transport & Directions

Is this the ... to (Tehran)?	این ... برای (رشت) هست؟	een ... ba·raa·*ye* (Tehran) hast
boat	کشتی	kesh·*tee*
bus	اتوبوس	oo·too·*boos*
plane	هواپیما	ha·vaa·pey·*maa*
train	قطار	gha·*taar*
What time's the ... bus?	اتوبوس ... کی هست؟	oo·too·boo·*se* ... key hast
first	اول	av·*val*
last	آخر	aa·*khar*
One ... ticket, please.	یک بلیط ... لطفا	yek be·*leet* ... lot·*fan*
one-way	یک سره	yek sa·*re*
return	دو سره	do sa·*re*

Numbers – Farsi

1	۱	یک	yek
2	۲	دو	do
3	۳	سه	se
4	٤	چهار	chaa·*haar*
5	٥	پنج	panj
6	٦	شش	shesh
7	۷	هفت	haft
8	۸	هشت	hasht
9	۹	نه	noh
10	۱۰	ده	dah
100	۱۰۰	صد	sad
1000	۱۰۰۰	هزار	he·*zaar*

Arabic numerals, used in Farsi, are written from left to right (unlike script).

How much is it to ...?
برای ... چقدر می شود؟ — ba·raa·*ye* ... *che*·ghadr *mee*·she

Please take me to (this address).
لطفا من را (به این آدرس) ببر — lot·*fan* man ro (be een aad·*res*) *be*·bar

Can you show me (on the map)?
می توانید (در نقشه) به من نشان بدهید؟ — *mee*·too·neen (dar nagh·*she*) be man ne·*shun* *be*·deen

What's the address?
آدرس اش چی هست؟ — aad·*re*·sesh chee hast

HEBREW

Hebrew is the national language of Israel, with seven to eight million speakers worldwide. It's written from right to left in its own alphabet. Most Hebrew sounds have equivalents in English; follow our pronunciation guides and you'll be understood. Note that a is pronounced as 'ah', ai as in 'aisle', e as in 'bet', i as the 'ea' in 'heat', o as 'oh' and u as the 'oo' in 'boot'. Both kh (like the 'ch' in the Scottish *loch*) and r (similar to the French 'r') are throaty sounds, pronounced at the back of the throat. Apostrophes (') indicate the glottal stop (like the pause in the middle of 'uh-oh'). The stressed syllables are indicated with italics. Masculine and feminine options are indicated by 'm' and 'f' respectively.

Basics

Hello.	שלום.	sha·*lom*
Goodbye.	להתראות.	le·hit·ra·*ot*

Yes. כן. ken
No. לא. lo
Please. בבקשה. be·va·ka·*sha*
Thank you. תודה. to·*da*
Excuse me./Sorry. סליחה. sli·*kha*
How are you?
מה נשמע? ma nish·*ma*
Fine, thanks. And you?
טוב, תודה. tov to·*da*
ואתה/ואת? ve·a·*ta*/ve·*at* (m/f)
What's your name?
איך קוראים לך? ekh kor·*im* le·*kha*/lakh (m/f)
My name is ...
שמי ... shmi ...
Do you speak English?
אתה מדבר אנגלית? a·*ta* me·da·*ber* ang·*lit* (m)
את מדברת אנגלית? at me·da·*be*·ret ang·*lit* (f)
I don't understand.
אני לא מבין/מבינה. a·*ni* lo me·*vin*/me·vi·*na* (m/f)

Accommodation

Where's a ...? איפה ...? *e*·fo ...
guesthouse בית ההרחה bet ha·'a·ra·*kha*
hotel בית המלון bet ma·*lon*

Do you have a ... room? יש לך חדר ...? yesh le·*kha*/lakh *khe*·der ... (m/f)
single ליחיד le·ya·*khid*
double זוגי zu·*gi*
How much is it per ...? כמה זה עולה ל...? *ka*·ma ze o·*le* le ...
night לילה *lai*·la

Eating & Drinking

Can you recommend a ...? אתה יכול להמליץ על ...? a·*ta* ya·*khol* le·ham·*lits* al ... (m)
את יכולה להמליץ על ...? at ye·cho·*la* le·ham·*lits* al ... (f)

Signs – Hebrew

Entrance	כניסה
Exit	יציאה
Open	פתוח
Closed	סגור
Information	מודיעין
Prohibited	אסור
Toilets	שירותים
Men	גברים
Women	נשים

cafe בית קפה bet ka·*fe*
restaurant מסעדה mis·a·*da*

What's the local speciality?
מה המאכל המקומי? ma ha·ma·'a·*khal* ha·me·ko·*mi*
Do you have vegetarian food?
יש לכם אוכל צמחוני? yesh la·*khem* o·khel tsim·kho·*ni*

I'd like the ..., please. אני צריך/צריכה את ..., בבקשה. a·*ni* tsa·*rikh*/tsri·*kha* et ... be·va·ka·*sha* (m/f)
bill החשבון ha·khesh·*bon*
menu התפריט ha·taf·*rit*

Emergencies

Help! הצילו! ha·*tsi*·lu
Go away! לך מפה! lekh mi·*po*

Call ...! תתקשר ל ...! tit·ka·*sher* le ...
a doctor רופא ro·*fe*/ro·*fa* (m/f)
the police משטרה mish·ta·*ra*

I'm lost.
אני אבוד. a·*ni* a·*vud* (m)
אני אבודה. a·*ni* a·vu·*da* (f)
Where are the toilets?
איפה השירותים? e·fo ha·she·ru·*tim*
I'm sick.
אני חולה. a·*ni* kho·*le*/kho·*la* (m/f)

Shopping & Services

I'm looking for ...
אני מחפש ... a·*ni* me·kha·*pes* ... (m)
אני מחפשת ... a·*ni* me·kha·*pe*·set ... (f)
Can I look at it?
אפשר להסתכל על זה? ef·*shar* le·his·ta·*kel* al ze
How much is it?
כמה זה עולה? *ka*·ma ze o·*le*
Where's an ATM?
איפה יש כספומט? *e*·fo yesh kas·po·*mat*

Transport & Directions

Is this the ... to (Haifa)? האם זה/זאת ה ... ל (חיפה)? ha·*im* ze/zot ha ... le·(khai·*fa*) (m/f)

boat אוניה o·ni·*ya* (f)
bus אוטובוס o·to·bus (m)
plane מטוס ma·*tos* (m)
train רכבת ra·*ke*·vet (f)

Numbers – Hebrew

1	אחת	a·*khat*
2	שתיים	*shta*·yim
3	שלוש	sha·*losh*
4	ארבע	*ar*·ba
5	חמש	kha·*mesh*
6	שש	shesh
7	שבע	*she*·va
8	שמונה	*shmo*·ne
9	תשע	*te*·sha
10	עשר	*e*·ser
100	מאה	*me*·a
1000	אלף	e·lef

Note that English numerals are used in modern Hebrew text.

What time's the ... bus?	באיזו שעה האוטובוס ה ...?	be·*e*·ze sha·*a* ha·*o*·to·bus ha ...
first	ראשון	ri·*shon*
last	אחרון	a·kha·*ron*

One ... ticket, please.	כרטיס אחד ... בבקשה.	kar·*tis* e·*khad* ... be·va·ka·*sha*
one-way	לכיוון אחד	le·ki·*vun* e·*khad*
return	הלוך ושוב	ha·*lokh* va·*shov*

How much is it to ...?
כמה זה ל ...? *ka*·ma ze le ...

Please take me to (this address).
תיקח/תיקחי אותי (לכתובת הזאת) בבקשה. ti·*kakh*/tik·*khi* o·*ti* (lak·to·*vet* ha·*zot*) be·va·ka·*sha* (m/f)

Can you show me (on the map)?
אתה/את יכול להראות לי (על המפה)? a·*ta*/at ya·*khol*/ye·kho·*la* le·har·*ot* (li al ha·ma·*pa*) (m/f)

What's the address?
מה הכתובת? ma hak·*to*·vet

TURKISH

Turkish is the official language of Turkey and co-official language of Cyprus (alongside Greek). Turkish vowels are generally shorter and slightly harsher than in English. When you see a double vowel in our pronunciation guides, eg sa·*at*, you need to pronounce it twice. Note also that a is pronounced as the 'u' in 'run', ai as in 'aisle', ay as in 'say', e as in 'bet', ee as in 'see', eu as the 'u' in 'nurse', ew as ee with rounded lips, o as in 'pot', oo as in 'zoo', uh as the 'a' in 'ago', zh as the 's' in 'pleasure', r is always rolled and v is softer than in English (pronounced between a 'v' and a 'w'). The stressed syllables are indicated with italics. Polite and informal options are indicated by 'pol' and 'inf' respectively.

Basics

Hello.	*Merhaba.*	*mer*·ha·ba
Goodbye. (when leaving)	*Hoşçakalın.* *Hoşçakal.*	hosh·*cha*·ka·luhn (pol) hosh·*cha*·kal (inf)
Goodbye. (when staying)	*Güle güle.*	gew·*le* gew·*le*
Yes.	*Evet.*	e·*vet*
No.	*Hayır.*	*ha*·yuhr
Please.	*Lütfen.*	*lewt*·fen
Thank you.	*Teşekkür.*	te·shek·*kewr*
Excuse me.	*Bakar mısınız?*	ba·*kar* muh·suh·*nuhz*
Sorry.	*Özür dilerim.*	er·*zewr* dee·*le*·reem

How are you?
Nasılsınız? (pol) — *na*·suhl·suh·nuhz
Nasılsın? (inf) — *na*·suhl·suhn

Fine. And you?
İyiyim. — ee·*yee*·yeem
Ya siz/sen? (pol/inf) — ya seez/sen

What's your name?
Adınız nedir? — a·duh·*nuhz* ne·deer (pol)
Adınız ne? — a·duh·*nuhz* ne (inf)

My name is ...
Benim adım ... — be·*neem* a·*duhm* ...

Do you speak English?
İngilizce konuşuyor musunuz? — een·gee·*leez*·je ko·noo·*shoo*·yor moo·soo·*nooz*

I don't understand.
Anlamıyorum. — an·*la*·muh·yo·room

Accommodation

Where's a ...?	*Buralarda nerede ... var?*	boo·ra·lar·*da* ne·re·de ... var
guesthouse	*misafirhane*	mee·*sa*·feer·ha·ne
hotel	*otel*	o·*tel*

Signs – Turkish

Giriş	Entrance
Çıkış	Exit
Açık	Open
Kapalı	Closed
Danışma	Information
Yasak	Prohibited
Tuvaletler	Toilets
Erkek	Men
Kadın	Women

Numbers – Turkish

1	*bir*	beer
2	*iki*	ee·kee
3	*üç*	ewch
4	*dört*	dert
5	*beş*	besh
6	*altı*	al·*tuh*
7	*yedi*	ye·*dee*
8	*sekiz*	se·*keez*
9	*dokuz*	do·*kooz*
10	*on*	on
100	*yüz*	yewz
1000	*bin*	been

Do you have a ... room?	*... odanız var mı?*	... o·da·*nuhz* var muh
single	*Tek kişilik*	tek kee·shee·*leek*
double	*İki kişilik*	ee·*kee* kee·shee·*leek*
How much is it per ...?	*... ne kadar?*	... ne ka·*dar*
night	*Geceliği*	ge·je·lee·*ee*

Eating & Drinking

Can you recommend a ...?	*İyi bir ... tavsiye edebilir misiniz?*	ee·*yee* beer ... tav·see·*ye* e·*de*·bee·leer mee·see·*neez*
cafe	*kafe*	ka·*fe*
restaurant	*restoran*	res·to·*ran*

What's the local speciality?
Bu yöreye has yiyecekler neler? — boo yeu·re·*ye* has yee·ye·jek·*ler* ne·ler

Do you have vegetarian food?
Vejeteryan yiyecekleriniz var mı? — ve·zhe·ter·*yan* yee·ye·jek·le·ree·*neez* var muh

I'd like the ..., please.	*... istiyorum.*	... ees·*tee*·yo·room
bill	*Hesabı*	he·sa·*buh*
menu	*Menüyü*	me·new·*yew*

Emergencies

Help!	*İmdat!*	eem·*dat*
Go away!	*Git burdan!*	geet boor·*dan*
Call ...!	*... çağırın!*	... cha·*uh*·ruhn
a doctor	*Doktor*	dok·*tor*
the police	*Polis*	po·*lees*

I'm lost.
Kayboldum. — kai·bol·*doom*

Where are the toilets?
Tuvaletler nerede? — too·va·let·*ler* ne·re·de

I'm sick.
Hastayım. — has·*ta*·yuhm

Shopping & Services

I'm looking for ...
... istiyorum. — ... ees·*tee*·yo·room

Can I look at it?
Bakabilir miyim? — ba·*ka*·bee·leer mee·*yeem*

How much is it?
Ne kadar? — ne ka·*dar*

Where's an ATM?
Bankamatik nerede var? — ban·ka·ma·*teek* *ne*·re·de var

Transport & Directions

Is this the ... to (Sirkeci)?	*(Sirkeci'ye) giden ... bu mu?*	(*seer*·ke·jee·ye) gee·*den* ... boo moo
boat	*vapur*	va·*poor*
bus	*otobüs*	o·to·*bews*
plane	*uçak*	oo·*chak*
train	*tren*	tren

What time's the ... bus?	*... otobüs ne zaman?*	... o·to·*bews* ne za·*man*
first	*İlk*	eelk
next	*Sonraki*	son·ra·*kee*

One ... ticket, please.	*..., lütfen.*	... *lewt*·fen
one-way	*Bir gidiş bileti*	beer gee·*deesh* bee·le·*tee*
return	*Gidiş-dönüş bir bilet*	gee·deesh·deu·*newsh* beer bee·*let*

How much is it to ...?
... ne kadar? — ... ne ka·*dar*

Please take me to (this address).
Lütfen beni (bu adrese) götürün. — *lewt*·fen be·*nee* (boo ad·re·*se*) geu·*tew*·rewn

Can you show me (on the map)?
Bana (haritada) gösterebilir misiniz? — ba·*na* (ha·ree·ta·*da*) geus·te·re·bee·leer mee·seen·*neez*

What's the address?
Adresi nedir? — ad·re·*see* ne·*deer*

GLOSSARY

This glossary contains some English, Arabic (Ar), Egyptian (E), Farsi (Far), Hebrew (Heb), Jordanian (J), Lebanese (Leb) and Turkish (T) words and abbreviations you may encounter in this book.

Abbasid dynasty – Baghdad-based successor dynasty to the *Umayyad dynasty*; ruled from AD 750 until the sacking of Baghdad by the Mongols in 1258
abu (Ar) – father or saint
acropolis – high city; hilltop citadel of a classic Hellenic city
agora – open space for commerce and politics in a classic Hellenic city, such as a marketplace or forum
ahwa (E) – see *qahwa*
Ashkenazi – a Jew of German or Eastern European descent
Ayyubid dynasty – Egyptian-based dynasty (AD 1169–1250) founded by *Saladin*

badia (J) – stone or basalt desert
bait – see *beit*
baksheesh – alms or tip
balad (Ar) – land or city
beit (Ar) – house; also *bait*

calèche (E) – horse-drawn carriage
cami(i) (T) – mosque
caravanserai – see *khan*
cardo – road running north–south through a Roman city
carnet de passage – permit allowing entry of a vehicle to a country without incurring taxes
çarşı (T) – market or bazaar
çay (T) – see *shai*
centrale – telephone office
chador (Ar) – black, one-piece, head-to-toe covering garment; worn by many Muslim women

decumanus – road running east–west through a Roman city
deir (Ar) – monastery or convent
dervish – Muslim mystic; see also *Sufi*
diaspora – community in dispersion or exile from its homeland
dolmuş (T) – minibus that sometimes runs to a timetable but more often sets off when it's full

Eid al-Adha – Feast of Sacrifice marking the pilgrimage to Mecca
Eid al-Fitr – Festival of Breaking the Fast celebrated at the end of *Ramadan*
emir – literally 'prince'; Islamic ruler, military commander or governor
evi (T) – house

Fatimid dynasty – Shiite dynasty (AD 908–1171) from North Africa, later based in Cairo, claiming descent from Mohammed's daughter Fatima
felafel – deep-fried balls of chickpea paste with spices; ta'amiyya in Egypt
felucca – traditional wooden sailboat used on the Nile in Egypt
fuul – paste made from fava beans

gebel (E) – see *jebel*
gület (T) – traditional wooden yacht

hajj – annual Muslim pilgrimage to Mecca; one of the five pillars of Islam
hamam (T) – see *hammam*
Hamas – militant Islamic organisation that aims to create an Islamic state in the pre-1948 territory of Palestine; the word is an acronym (in Arabic) for Islamic Resistance Movement
hammam (Ar) – bathhouse; *hamam* in Turkish
haram – anything that is forbidden by Islamic law; also refers to the prayer hall of a mosque
hasid – (plural *hasidim*) member of an ultra-orthodox Jewish sect; also *hared*
Hejira – Mohammed's flight from Mecca to Medina in AD 622; the starting point of the Muslim era and the start of the Islamic calendar
Hezbollah – 'Party of God'; Lebanon-based organ of militant *Shiite* Muslims

imam – prayer leader or Muslim cleric
intifada – Palestinian uprising against Israeli authorities in the West Bank, Gaza and East Jerusalem; literally 'shaking off'

jamaa – see *masjid*
jebel (Ar) – hill, mountain; *gebel* in Egypt
jihad – literally 'striving in the way of the faith'; holy war

keffiyeh (Ar) – chequered scarf worn by Arabs
khan – travellers' inn, usually constructed on main trade routes, with accommodation on the 1st floor and stables and storage on the ground floor; also *caravanserai, han, wikala* in Egypt
kibbutz – (plural kibbutzim) Jewish communal settlement run cooperatively by its members
kilim – woven rug
kippa – skullcap
Knesset – Israeli parliament
Koran – see *Quran*
kosher – food prepared according to Jewish dietary law
Likud – Israeli right-wing political party
lokanta (T) – restaurant

madrassa – Muslim seminary; modern Arabic word for school; *medrese(si)* in Turkey
mahalle(si) (T) – neighbourhood, district of a city
masjid (Ar) – mosque; also *jamaa*
medina – city or town, especially the old quarter of a city
medrese(si) (T) – see *madrassa*
Mesopotamia – ancient name for Iraq from the Greek meaning 'between two rivers'
meydan(ı) – see *midan*
meyhane (T) – (plural meyhaneler) tavern
mezze – a collection of appetisers or small plates of food; *meze* in Turkish
midan (Ar) – town or city square; *meydan(ı)* in Turkish (plural *meydanlar*)
midrahov (Heb) – pedestrian mall
mihrab – niche in a mosque indicating direction of Mecca
minbar – pulpit used for sermons in a mosque
mitzvah (Heb) – adherence to Jewish commandments
muezzin – cantor who sings the call to prayer
mullah – Muslim scholar, teacher or religious leader

nargileh (Ar) – water pipe used to smoke tobacco; *sheesha* in Egypt

obelisk – monolithic stone pillar with square sides tapering to a pyramidal top; used as a monument in ancient Egypt
otogar (T) – bus station

pansiyon – pension, B&B or guesthouse
pasha – Ottoman governor appointed by the sultan in Constantinople
Peshmerga – Kurdish soldiers, literally 'those who face death'
PKK – Kurdistan Workers Party
PLO – Palestine Liberation Organisation
PTT (T) – Posta, Telefon, Telğraf; post, telephone and telegraph office
pylon – monumental gateway at the entrance to a temple

qahwa (Ar) – coffee, coffeehouse; *ahwa* in Egypt
qasr – castle or palace
Quran – the holy book of Islam; also *Koran*

Ramadan – ninth month of the lunar Islamic calendar during which Muslims fast from sunrise to sunset; Ramazan in Turkish
ras (Ar) – cape, headland or head

sahn (Ar) – courtyard of a mosque
Sala – the Muslim obligation of prayer, ideally to be performed five times a day; one of the five pillars of Islam
Saladin – (Salah ad-Din in Arabic) Kurdish warlord who retook Jerusalem from the Crusaders; founder of the *Ayyubid dynasty*
Sawm – the Muslim month of *Ramadan*; one of the five pillars of Islam
servees – shared taxi with a fixed route
settler – term used to describe Israelis who have created new communities on Arab territory, usually land captured from the Arabs during the 1967 war
Shabbat – Jewish Sabbath observed from sundown on Friday to one hour after sundown on Saturday
Shahada – Islam's basic tenet and profession of faith: 'There is no god but Allah, and Mohammed is the Prophet of Allah'; one of the five pillars of Islam
shai (Ar) – tea; *çay* in Turkish
sheesha (E) – see *nargileh*
sheikh – venerated religious scholar; also shaikh
sherut (Heb) – shared taxi with a fixed route
Shiite – one of the two main branches of Islam
shwarma – grilled meat sliced from a spit and served in pita-type bread with salad; also *döner kebap* in Turkish
siq (Ar) – narrow passageway or defile such as the one at Petra
souq – market or bazaar
Sufi – follower of any of the Islamic mystical orders that emphasise dancing, chanting and trances in order to attain unity with God; see also *dervish*
sultan – absolute ruler of a Muslim state
Sunni – one of the two main branches of Islam

ta'amiyya (E) – see *felafel*
Talmud – a collection of 63 Jewish holy books that complement the *Torah*
tell – ancient mound created by centuries of urban rebuilding
Torah – five books of Moses, the first five Old Testament books; also called the Pentateuch

Umayyad dynasty – first great dynasty of Arab Muslim rulers, based in Damascus (AD 661–750); also Omayyad dynasty

wikala (E) – see *khan*
willayat – village

Zakat – the Muslim obligation to give alms to the poor; one of the five pillars of Islam
ziggurat (Far) – rectangular temple tower or tiered mound built in *Mesopotamia* by the Akkadians, Babylonians and Sumerians

Behind the Scenes

SEND US YOUR FEEDBACK

We love to hear from travellers – your comments keep us on our toes and help make our books better. Our well-travelled team reads every word on what you loved or loathed about this book. Although we cannot reply individually to your submissions, we always guarantee that your feedback goes straight to the appropriate authors, in time for the next edition. Each person who sends us information is thanked in the next edition – the most useful submissions are rewarded with a selection of digital PDF chapters.

Visit **lonelyplanet.com/contact** to submit your updates and suggestions or to ask for help. Our award-winning website also features inspirational travel stories, news and discussions.

Note: We may edit, reproduce and incorporate your comments in Lonely Planet products such as guidebooks, websites and digital products, so let us know if you don't want your comments reproduced or your name acknowledged. For a copy of our privacy policy visit lonelyplanet.com/privacy.

OUR READERS

Many thanks to the travellers who used the last edition and wrote to us with helpful hints, useful advice and interesting anecdotes: Alberto Fernandez, Charles Cox, Christian, Enass Isaksson, Harry Machin, James Dahringer, Justin Atcho, Marketa, Mizio Matteucci, Raffaela Brignoni, Stine Kærgaard Nissen

WRITER THANKS

Anthony Ham

Thanks to my editors Helen Elfer and Lauren Keith for the privilege of writing about such an extraordinary corner of the world. Huge thanks to my coauthors who brought such wisdom and expertise to the project; a special mention to Jenny Walker, Andy Symington and Virginia Maxwell for their combined insights over many years. Thanks to Sarah Bailey and Andrea Dobbin for such careful editing.

Paul Clammer

Thanks to Hakim al-Tamimi and Mahmoud Freihat at the Jordan Tourism Board. In Amman, thanks to Muna Haddad, Nabil Tarzi, Daniel Robards, Jon Killpack and Ayman Abd Alkareem. Thanks of course also to Susan Andrew and Soda. Thanks to Odeh Sawalhah and Ammar al-Damseh in Madaba, and to Atallah Dakhilallah in Wadi Rum. Hugs to the brilliant 'Team Feynan' – Kirsten Alana, Jill Robinson, Theresa Jackson, Daniella Van Haltren, Rajesh Oja, Bradley Moss and Tim Neville. Finally, thanks and love above all to Robyn, for everything as always.

Orlando Crowcroft

I would like to thank my friends Nigel Wilson and Mary Pelletier in Ramallah, MC in Jerusalem and Heidi Levine in Tel Aviv. A big shout out to all the staff at Area D Hostel, Ayman at the Cinema Guesthouse in Jenin, Canaan Khoury and family in Taybeh and all those who made me feel welcome during my stay in the Palestinian Territories. I'd also like to thank my editor Lauren Keith and fellow authors Anita Isalska, Daniel Robinson and Dan Savery Raz. And my wife, Helen, for everything.

Mark Elliott

Many, many thanks to gallant guides Shahram and Mojtaba, to Helen, Dylan and Megan for making things possible and to Sally Kingsbury and my unbeatable parents for so much love and support. Thank you also to countless kind Iranians and travellers who were so generous with their time, hospitality and information, notably Vali, Reza and family, Rino, Ahmad, Amir, Jalal, Mohammad and Akbar.

Anita Isalska

Countless chance encounters and conversations enriched my research; thank you to everyone who knowingly or unknowingly guided my travels. I'm especially grateful for the suggestions and insights from Noga Tarnopolsky, Riman Barakat, Linda Gradstein, the Educational Bookshop & Cafe crew, and for Slavica and Einav, who pointed me to some excellent tips. Deep thanks to Anna Heijblok, whose stories of her Jerusalem will stay with me. And, as ever, heartfelt gratitude to Normal Matt for cheerleading from the wings.

Jessica Lee

Among the vast number of people who gave me handy tips, helped with information and dealt with weird and obscure queries, these folk especially deserve a huge *shukran*: Salama Abd Rabbo, Sameh Tawfek, Salah, Asmail, Hisham, Wadia, Ben, Aisha and Mohammed. Also, a big thanks to fellow writer Anthony and to fellow Egypt travellers Chris, Lou and Nat. In Turkey, a big thank you to Celil Ersözoğlu for hilarious stories, Ozan Balkan for wrangling that bit of extra information I needed, Erzurum tourist information office for being Turkey's most astoundingly helpful tourist office, Jodie Redding for cross-checking information updates, Fatih and Faruk Salva for an unexpected southeast Anatolia reunion in Marmaris, and Okba Aldaher for looking after my place while I was on the road.

Virginia Maxwell

Many thanks to Pat Yale, Mehmet Umur, Emel Güntaş, Faruk Boyacı, Tahir Karabaş, Jen Hartin, Eveline Zoutendijk, George Grundy, Ramazan Altuntas, Jess Lee and the many others who assisted me with this update.

Simon Richmond

Many thanks to the following for their assistance in preparation for and during my research in Iran: Andrew Burke, Gabe Kaminski, Laili Sadr, Mathew Scott, Yi-Juan Koh, William Lodder, Navid, Sogand, Matin, Shirin, Ali, Farah, Ramin, Armin, Masoud, Jalal and Berzhad.

Daniel Robinson

Special thanks to (from south to north): Chini Da-Silva, Gili Bat-Sara, Eran Hejams, Jody Sirota and Michael Chen (Eilat); Yair Sela (Samar); Alex Cicelsky, Doria Pinkas and Maya Galimidi (Lotan); Anat Sha'ul (Ne'ot Smadar); David and Ofra Faiman (Sde Boker); Gil Shkedi (Ne'ot HaKikar); David Lew (Masada); Lee, Meitar and Shani (Ein Gedi Field School); Sliman (Ein Gedi Nature Reserve); Eldad Hazan (Ein Feshkha/Einot Tzukim); Nisim Bados (Beit She'an); Nati and Ofer (Banias); Rachel Eshkol (Tzipori); Ido Itai and Amir Aviram (Gamla); Gregory and Hanoch (Yehudiya); Alon Malichi (Katzrin); Omer Feldman and Ya'akov Leiter (Tsfat); Ron Tsvi, Amihai and Tehila (Rosh Pina); HaKupa'it Vera (Tel Hatzor); Mordechai Kohelet Israel (Dalton); Tony (Jish); Inbar Rubin (Agamon HaHuleh); Anat Nissim (Galil Nature Museum); Shadi (Tel Dan); Talal (Mt Hermon); and, most especially, my wife Rachel and my sons Yair and Sasson for their support, understanding and patience.

Anthony Sattin

Many people have helped create this book by providing assistance, information, tips for things to see and even directions when I took a wrong turn. Among them are: H.E. Khaled El-Enani and the staff at the Ministry of Antiquities; Mrs Rasha Azaizi and staff at the Ministry of Tourism; Bahaa Gaber, Cecilia Udden, Mounir Neamatalla, Amr Khalil, Ghada Shahbender, Ahmed Shandawili, Selim Shawer, Wael Abed, Abdallah Baghi, Peter Wirth, Badr Abdalmoghny, Mohsen Abdelmonem, Galal, Zeina Aboukheir, Eleonore Kamir, Enrique Cansino and Mamdouh Sayed Khalifa.

Dan Savery Raz

Thanks to destination editor Lauren Keith for kicking off this project and making it run so smoothly. Also thank you to Maoz Inon (travel entrepreneur and peace warrior), Yoram Hai (for vegan tips) and Bea Hemming (for recommending Bicicletta). Biggest thanks goes to my wife, Shiri, for looking after the kids while I tapped away on my laptop, and my two girls, Hila and Maya, for always making me smile.

Andy Symington

During my trip to Lebanon, I got a big welcome and great advice from so many people that it would be impossible to list them all. But particular thanks for going out of their way to help are to Dana Nasr, Saskia Nout, Joseph Abou Kheir, Pierre Abi Saad, Craig Barker, Walid and Ghayem. Thanks too go to Lauren Keith and the Lonely Planet team for the opportunity to update in this fabulous country.

Jenny Walker

Returning to Jordan is always a pleasure, thanks to the strength of welcome unfailingly received. Over many years of writing and updating the Lonely Planet *Jordan* guide, I have inevitably become indebted to friends in Jordan who have helped shape the information in the general sections of this edition. Alas, there isn't space to do justice to individuals here, but I acknowledge their collective help with gratitude. In Iran, general thanks to all who helped contribute information. Specific thanks to Bijan Nabavi for setting the scene, to Mostafa Ramezanpoor for attention to detail and most especially to Mojtaba Heidari for his extreme efforts in extreme circumstances – not forgetting his signature coffee stops! My biggest thanks, however, are reserved, as ever, to my beloved Sam (Owen) – husband, co-researcher and fellow traveller.

Steve Waters

Thanks to all the beautiful Iranian people who smoothed my way, picked me up when I was miles from nowhere, bought me tea and chocolates, or *chelo kabab*, who taught me lessons in humility, patience and honesty, who told me subversive jokes, made me laugh, shared their food and persevered with my mangled Farsi. And thanks to Rahel, Kaz, Hamish, Megan and Roz for being yourselves.

ACKNOWLEDGEMENTS

Climate map data adapted from Peel MC, Finlayson BL & McMahon TA (2007) 'Updated World Map of the Köppen-Geiger Climate Classification', *Hydrology and Earth System Sciences*, 11, 163344.

Illustrations pp62–3, pp92–3, pp126–7, pp210–11, pp424–5 and pp418–19 by Javier Zarracina; pp322–3 by Michael Weldon.

Cover photograph: Masjed-e Nasir Al Molk, Iran; Alexander Mazurkevich/Shutterstock ©.

THIS BOOK

This 9th edition of Lonely Planet's *Middle East* guidebook was researched and written by Anthony Ham, Paul Clammer, Orlando Crowcroft, Mark Elliott, Anita Isalska, Jessica Lee, Virginia Maxwell, Simon Richmond, Daniel Robinson, Anthony Sattin, Dan Savery Raz, Andy Symington, Jenny Walker and Steve Waters. This guidebook was produced by the following:

Destination Editors Lauren Keith, Tom Stainer

Senior Product Editor Elizabeth Jones

Product Editor Carolyn Boicos

Senior Cartographer Valentina Kremenchutskaya

Book Designer Clara Monitto

Assisting Editors Sarah Bailey, Imogen Bannister, Katie Connolly, Peter Cruttenden, Andrea Dobbin, Emma Gibbs, Carly Hall, Jennifer Hattam, Gabrielle Innes, Ali Lemer, Jodie Martire, Lou McGregor, Rosie Nicholson, Kristin Odijk, Chris Pitts, Gabrielle Stefanos, Ross Taylor, Saralinda Turner, Fionnuala Twomey

Cover Researcher Naomi Parker

Thanks to Stephanie d'Arc Taylor, Kate Chapman, Barbara Delissen, Grace Dobell, Helen Elfer, Sunny Fitzgerald, Shona Gray, Karima Hassan Ragab, Kate James, Andi Jones, Anne Mason, Claire Naylor, Karyn Noble, Jacqui Saunders, Shadi Salehian

Index

ABBREVIATIONS

E Egypt
In Iran
Iq Iraq
IPT Israel & the Palestinian Territories
J Jordan
L Lebanon
S Syria
T Turkey

A

Abu Simbel (E) 106-7
accommodation 136, 564-5, *see also individual locations*
  language 583, 584, 586, 587-8
Acre, *see* Akko
activities 27-30, 42-6, *see also individual activities*
Aegean Coast (T) 436-57, **437**
Afrodisias (T) 453
Agilika Island (E) 106
air travel 571-2, 573
  Egypt 134, 135
  Iran 187-8, 189
  Israel & the Palestinian Territories 281, 282
  Jordan 351, 353
  Lebanon 404
  Turkey 491-2
Ajloun (J) 304
Ajloun Forest Reserve (J) 305
Akko (IPT) 236-7, **237**
Al Haram Ash Sharif (IPT) 208, **210-11**, 210-11
Al Kharga Oasis (E) 107-8
Al Maghtas (J) 307-8
Al Qasr (E) 108
Al Quseir (E) 116
Alamut Valley (In) 155-6
Alanya (T) 468-9
alcohol 540-1
Alexander the Great 500
Alexandria (E) 80-6, **82-3, 84**
Amasra (T) 481
Amman (J) 288-300, **290**, **292-3**, **296**
  accommodation 291-4
  activities 291
  children, travel with 294
  courses 295
  drinking & nightlife 297-8
  emergency services 298
  entertainment 298
  food 294-5
  history 288
  internet access 298
  medical services 298
  money 298-9
  shopping 298
  sights 288-91
  tourist offices 299
  travel to/from 299
  travel within 299-300
ancient cities 23
Ancient Galilee Boat (IPT) 242
Andej (In) 155
Ani (T) 485
animals 26, 311, 327, 553-5
Anıt Kabir (T) 469
Ankara (T) 469-72, **470**
Antalya (T) 463-7, **464**
Anzac Cove (T) 441
Aqaba (J) 337-42, **338**
Arab Spring, the 524-5
Arabic language 582-4
Arabs 515
Aramgah-e Shah-e Cheragh (In) 170-1
Arafat, Yasser 517, 523
archaeological sites 23, *see also* ruins, tombs
  Abu Simbel (E) 106-7
  Afrodisias (T) 453
  Al Bass Archaeological Site (L) 385
  Al Mina Archaeological Site (L) 385
  Alamut Castle (In)
  Ancient Bathhouse (Nazareth; IPT) 238
  Ancient Katzrin Park (IPT) 248
  Ancient Patara (T) 460
  Baalbek Ruins (L) 391
  Beit She'an National Park (IPT) 243
  Bergama Acropolis (T) 443
  Byblos Archaeological Site (L) 373
  Capernaum (IPT) 242
  Catacombs of Kom Ash Shuqqafa (E) 81
  City of David (IPT) 208
  Colossi of Memnon (E) 87
  Dahshur (E) 77
  Deir Al Medina (E) 91
  Gebel Al Mawta (E) 111-12
  Jerash ruins (J) 18, 301, 18
  Jerusalem Archaeological Park & Davidson Centre (IPT) 207
  Kom Al Dikka (E) 81
  Kursi National Park (IPT) 243
  Luxor (E) 15, 86-95, **88-9**, **92-3**, **94-5**, 15, 92-3
  Madaba Archaeological Park I & Virgin Mary Church (J) 314
  Magdala (IPT) 242
  Masada (IPT) 250-1
  Memphis (E) 77
  Necropolis of Al Bagawat (E) 107
  Old Jaffa Visitors Centre (IPT) 224
  Petra (J) 11, 320-6, **322-3**, **324-5**, 10-11, 322-3
  Pyramids of Giza (E) 11, 60-4, **62-3**, **64**, 11, 62-3
  Ruins of Abu (E) 102
  Saqqara (E) 77
  Troy (T) 440
  Unfinished Obelisk (E) 101-2
  Western Wall Tunnels (IPT) 206-7
architecture 225, 531-5
Armenians 510
art galleries, *see* museums & galleries
arts 543-51, *see also individual arts*
Aspendos (T) 466
Aswan (E) 101-6, **102**, **104**
Aswan High Dam (E) 106
Atatürk, Mustafa Kemal 469
ATMs 566
Avanos (T) 478
Aya Sofya (T) 416, 418-19, **418-19**, 418-19
Azraq (J) 311-12

B

Baalbek (L) 390-2
badgir 169
Baghdad (Iq) 502
Baha'i Gardens (Haifa; IPT) 231
Bahariya Oasis (E) 110-11
ballooning 476
Banksy 263
Baraka (J) 22
Basilica Cistern (T) 416
bathrooms 569
Batroun (L) 375-7
Bauhaus architecture 225
bazaars, *see* markets
Bazar-e Bozorg (In) 158-9
Bcharré (L) 380-2

Map Pages **000**
Photo Pages 000

beaches 25
Eilat (IPT) 254
Ein Bokek (IPT) 251
Fethiye (T) 458
Kalkan (T) 461
Patara (T) 460
Tel Aviv (IPT) 224, 227
Beirut (L) 14, 22, 356-72, **358**, **360**, **362**, **14**
accommodation 362-4
activities 359
courses 361
drinking & nightlife 368-70
entertainment 370
festivals & events 362
food 365-8
medical services 371
safe travel 370-1
shopping 370
sights 356-9
tourist offices 371
tours 361-2
travel to/from 371
travel within 371-2
Beirut International Film Festival 30
Beit She'an (IPT) 243-4
Beiteddine Palace (L) 387-8
Bekaa Valley (L) 389-92
belly dancing shows 69
Bergama (T) 443-4
Bethany-Beyond-the-Jordan (Al-Maghtas; J) 307-8
Bethlehem (IPT) 261-4
bicycle travel, *see* cycling
birds 554, 556
Black Desert (E) 110
Black Sea Coast (T) 480-6
Blue Mosque (T) 416
boat travel 572, 573
Egypt 134, 135
Iran 188-9
Jordan 352
Lebanon 404
boat trips 45-6
Alanya (T) 468
Antalya (T) 465
Aswan (T) 106
Bosphorus (T) 416
Fethiye (T) 458-9
Nile (E) 65, 98
Bodrum Town (T) 453-6, **454**
books 494
history 497, 501, 503, 504, 506, 509, 516, 517, 518, 520, 521, 525
Israel & the Palestinian Territories 514
border crossings 40-1, 572
Egypt 40, 134
Iran 40, 188
Israel & the Palestinian Territories 280, 281-2
Jordan 351-2
Lebanon 404
Turkey 41, 491
Bosphorus trips (T) 416
Bursa (T) 442-3
bus travel 573-4
Egypt 135
Iran 188, 189
Israel & the Palestinian Territories 283
Jordan 353
Lebanon 404
Turkey 492
business hours 567-8
Byblos (L) 373-5, **374**
Byzantine Empire 501

C

Caesarea (IPT) 231
Cairo (E) 22, 53-77, **58-9**, **64**, **66-7**, **70**, **72**, **74**
accommodation 64-8
drinking & nightlife 69-71
entertainment 71
food 68-9
history 53
medical services 73
safe travel 73
shopping 71, 73
sights 53-63
tourist offices 74
tours 64
travel to/from 74-5
travel within 75-7
calendars 568
call to prayer 527-8
Çanakkale (T) 436-40
canyoning 314
Capernaum (IPT) 242
Cappadocia (T) 14, 475-80, **475**, **14**
Cappadox Festival 28
car & motorcycle travel 574-5
Egypt 135
Iran 189
Israel & the Palestinian Territories 283-4
Jordan 353
Lebanon 404
safety 560
Turkey 492
Cardo Maximus (IPT) 207
carpets
Iran 184, 187
Jordan 345-6
Turkey 417
Çarşı (T) 472
castles & fortresses 24
Alanya Castle (T) 468
Aljoun Castle (J) 304
Ayasuluk Fortress (T) 447
Bodrum Castle (T) 453
Fortress of Shali (E) 111
Kars Castle (T) 484
Kayseri Castle (T) 480
Marmaris Castle & Museum (T) 456
Nimrod Fortress (IPT) 248
Qasr Al Azraq (J) 311
Qasr Kharana (J) 313
Qusayr Amra (J) 312
cedars 400
Cedars, the (L) 382
cell phones 569
Chak Chak (In) 165
children, travel with 47-8, 581, *see also individual locations*
Chouf Mountains (L) 387-9
Christianity 530
Christmas 30
Christmas (Orthodox) 27, **29**
churches & cathedrals
architecture 534
Basilica of St John (T) 446-7
Basilica of the Annunciation (IPT) 238
Church & Monastery of the Apostles (IPT) 240
Church of All Nations (IPT) 209
Church of Mary Magdalene (IPT) 209
Church of St Sergius & Bacchus (E) 57
Church of the Ascension (IPT) 208
Church of the Holy Sepulchre (IPT) 203
Church of the Nativity (IPT) 261
Church of the Primacy of St Peter (IPT) 242
Greek Orthodox Church of St George (IPT) 266
Greek Orthodox Church of the Annunciation (IPT) 238
Grotto of the Nativity (IPT) 261, **32**
Hanging Church (E) 57
Jacob's Well (IPT) 264
Mount of the Beatitudes (IPT) 242
St Anne's Church (IPT) 203
St Catherine's Church (IPT) 261
St George's Church (J) 313
St James' Cathedral (IPT) 203-4
St Peter's Church (IPT) 240
Çifte Minareli Medrese (T) 482
cinema, *see* film
Çıralı (T) 463
Citadel (IPT) 207
City of David (IPT) 208
climate 20, 27-30, *see also individual locations*
coffee 540
Colossi of Memnon (E) 87, 90
consulates 565, *see also individual locations*
cooking courses 22, 423
Coptic Museum (E) 56-7
country codes 568-9
credit cards 567
crime 561
Crusades, the 503-5
culture 543-51
currencies 20
customs regulations 565
cycling 43, 276, 282-3, 284, 346, 353, 573

D

Dahab (E) 121-5, **122**
Dakhla Oasis (E) 108-9
Dana Biosphere Reserve (J) 318-20
dangers, *see* safe travel
Darakeh (In) 145
Darband (In) 145
Dead Sea (IPT) 249-51, **250**
Dead Sea (J) 17, 308-10, 555, **17**
Dead Sea Scrolls (IPT) 215, 249
Deir Al Qamar (L) 388-9
Dendara (E) 96

Derinkuyu (T) 478
desert castles 311, 312
desert safaris 43-4
desertification 556
deserts 23, 552
Dhiban (J) 317
diarrhoea 580-1
Didyma (T) 452
diptheria 578
disabilities, travellers with 569
diving & snorkelling 25, 44
- Dahab (E) 123
- Eilat (IPT) 253
- Hurghada (E) 114
- Jordan 339
- Kaş (T) 461-2
- Red Sea (E) 17, **17**
- Sharm El Sheikh (E) 119, 120

Doğubayazıt (T) 485-6
Dome of the Rock (IPT) 12, 208, **12**
drinks 376, 540-1
driving, *see* car & motorcycle travel
Dung Gate (IPT) 207

E

Easter 27
Eceabat (T) 440-1
Edfu (E) 101
Egypt 49, 52-135
- accommodation 52, 131
- border crossings 40
- children, travel with 131
- climate & travel seasons 52
- culture 129, 130-1
- electricity 132
- embassies & consulates 131-2
- food 52, 130, 131, 133
- highlights 54, **54-5**
- history 129-30
- internet resources 53
- money 132-3
- safe travel 133
- telephone services 133
- travel to/from 134
- travel within 135
- visas 38-9, 134

Egyptian Museum (E) 53, 56, 57, **56**

Map Pages **000**
Photo Pages **000**

Ein Bokek (IPT) 251
Ein Gedi (IPT) 249-50
Eilat (IPT) 252-6, **253**, **254**
El Alamein 80
El Gouna (E) 113-14
electricity, *see individual countries*
embassies 565, *see also individual locations*
embroidery 346
emergencies 565, *see also individual locations*
- language 583, 585, 586, 588

environmental issues 556
Ephesus (T) 22, 449-51, **450**
Erzurum (T) 482-4, **483**
Esfahan (In) 12, 22, 158-64, **160**
Esna (E) 100-1
etiquette 558-9
Evan Lake (In) 155
events 27-30
exchange rates 567

F

Farsi language 584-5
feluccas 65, 98, 106
festivals 27-30
Fethiye (T) 458-60
film 494, 543-6
food 536-40, *see also individual locations*
- *dizi* 180
- etiquette 558
- kababs 184, 537-8
- language 583, 584-5, 586, 588

fortresses, *see* castles & fortresses

G

Gadara (J) 306-7
Galilee, Lower (IPT) 238-44, **239**
Galilee, Upper (IPT) 244-9, **245**
galleries, *see* museums & galleries
Gallipoli Peninsula (T) 441-2, **442**
Garden of Gethsemane (IPT) 209
Garden Tomb (IPT) 209
gardens, *see individual gardens*
Garmeh (In) 163
gay travellers, see LGBTIQ travellers

Gaza Strip (IPT) 266-7
Gazor Khan (In) 155-6
Gebel Al Ingleez (E) 110
Gelemiş (T) 460
Gelibolu, *see* Gallipoli Peninsula
geography & geology 552-3
Giza pyramids (E) 11, 60-4, **62-3**, **64**, **11**, **62-3**
Golan Heights (IPT) 247-9
Golestan Palace (In) 137
Göreme (T) 476-8
Grand Bazaar İstanbul (T) 417
Grand Bazaar Tehran (In) 137
Güllüdere (Rose) Valley (T) 476

H

Haifa (IPT) 231-6, **232-3**
Hallabat (J) 310-11
hammams 26, 264, 423, 465, 472
Hanukkah 30
Haram-e Razavi (In) 178
health 577-81
heat exhaustion 580
Hebrew language 585-7
Hebron (IPT) 266
hepatitis A 578
hepatitis B 579
Herod's Gate (IPT) 207
Hezbollah 384, 396, 524
High Dam (E) 106
hiking 25, 43, 44-5
- Egypt 22
- Iran 44, 155
- Israel & the Palestinian Territories 44-5, 276
- Jordan 22, 45, 305, 326
- Lebanon 45, 381
- Turkey 45, 460, 462

history 496-525, *see also individual countries*
- 1948 Arab-Israeli War 512
- 1967 Six Day War 517
- 1979 Islamic Revolution 519
- 1991 Iraq War 521
- 2003 Iraq War 524
- Alexander the Great 500
- Arab Spring, the 524-5
- Armenians 510
- Iran-Iraq War 517
- Lebanese Civil War 520
- Phoenician Empire 498
- Sumerian history 496-7

hitching 189, 353, 575
holidays 568
horse riding 45
hot-air ballooning 476
Hurghada (E) 114-16

I

Ihlara Valley (T) 478
insect bites & stings 580
insurance 566, 574-5, 577-8
internet access 566
internet resources 21
Iran 49, 136-89, 494
- accommodation 185
- activities 185
- arts 184-5
- border crossings 40
- calendars 183
- climate 136
- consulates 185-6
- drinking 184
- embassies 185-6
- emergency services 137
- etiquette 186
- exchange rates 137
- food 136, 184
- health 186
- highlights 138, **138-9**
- history 182-3
- insurance 186
- internet access 186
- languages 137
- legal matters 186
- money 137, 182, 186
- opening hours 186
- politics 181-2
- population 523
- safe travel 185
- shopping 187
- telephone services 187
- time 137
- tours 187
- travel to/from 187-9
- travel within 189
- visas 39, 187

Iranian poets 184, 547
Iraq 49, 190-8, 523, **191-8**
Irbid (J) 306
Isis 191-8, 406
Islam 501-2, 526-8
Islamic calendar 568
Israel & the Palestinian Territories 50, 199-284
- accommodation 275-6
- activities 276-7
- arts 273-4
- books 514

border crossings 280, 281-2
checkpoints 258
children, travel with 277
climate 199
embassies & consulates 278
exchange rates 201
food 229, 274, 276
highlights 200, **200**
history 267-71
internet access 278
internet resources 201
itineraries 202
language 274
money 278
opening hours 278-9
politics 271-2
population 271
religion 272-3
safe travel 277, 279
telephone services 279-80
travel to/from 281-2
travel within 282-4
visas 39, 280-1

Israeli passport stamps 39
Israeli settlements 248, 260
Israel's separation wall (IPT) 264
İstanbul (T) 15, 22, 416-36, **420-1**, **426-7**, **430-1**, **434-5**, **15**
accommodation 423, 428-9
courses 423
drinking & nightlife 432
food 429, 432
medical services 433
safe travel 433
sights 416-23
tourist offices 433
tours 423
travel to/from 433
travel within 433, 436

İstanbul Music Festival 28
itineraries 31-7, **31-7**, *see also individual locations*
İzmir (T) 444-6

J

Jaffa (IPT) 224-5, **228**
Jaffa Gate (IPT) 207
Jbail (L) 373-5
Jeita Grotto (L) 372-3
Jenin (IPT) 265-6
Jerash (J) 18, 301-4, **302**, **18**
Jerash Festival 29
Jericho (IPT) 259-61
Jerusalem (IPT) 201-21, **204-5**, **212-13**, **214**
accommodation 215-17
drinking & nightlife 218
entertainment 218-19
food 217-18
history 201-2
internet resources 218
medical services 219
safe travel 219
sights 202-15
tourist offices 219
tours 215
travel to/from 219-20
travel within 220-1

Jolfa (In) 159
Jordan 50, 285-353, 495
accommodation 347
activities 314, 347
arts 345
bathrooms 350
books 344
children, travel with 347
climate 285
consulates 348
culture 345
customs regulations 348
disabilities, travellers with 350
embassies 348
environment 346-7
food & drink 304, 346, 348
highlights 286-7, **286-7**
hiking 305
history 343-4
holidays 350
internet access 348
internet resources 289
itineraries 288, 330
language 289
measures 349
money 289, 347, 348-9
nature reserves 285, 298
newspapers 349
opening hours 349
photography 349
politics 343
postal services 349
public holidays 350
radio 349
safe travel 350
scams 351
smoking 349
telephone services 350
time 350
toilets 350
tourist offices 350
tours 300, 311
travel to/from 351-2
travel within 352-3
TV 349
visas 39, 350
weather 285
weights 349
women travellers 351
work 351

Jordan River (J) 308
Judaism 528-30

K

Kalkan (T) 461
Kaleiçi (T) 463-5
Kandovan (In) 153
Karak (J) 317-18
Karnak (E) 87
Kars (T) 484-5
Kaş (T) 461-2
Kashan (In) 156-8
Katzrin (IPT) 248
Kaymaklı (T) 478
Kayseri (T) 479-80
Khan, Genghis 503
Kharanaq (In) 165
King's Highway (J) 313
Kom Ombo (E) 101
Konya (T) 473-5, **474**
Kurds 522-3
Kuşadası (T) 451-2

L

language 582-8
Arabic 582-4
Farsi 584-5
Hebrew 585-7
Turkish 587-8

Lebanese Civil War 520
Lebanon 50, 354-404
accommodation 354, 401
activities 371
ATMs 402-3
bargaining 401
civil war 396-7
climate 354
embassies 402
emergency services 402-4
environment 400
food & drink 354, 398-9
highlights 355, **355**
history 392-8
holidays 403
internet access 402
language 357
money 357, 402-3
music 400-1
opening hours 403
politics 392
population 357
public holidays 403
religion 399
safe travel 383, 390, 401-2
smoking 403
telephone services 403
travel to/from 404
travel within 404
visas 40, 403
weather 354
women travellers 403-4

legal matters 566
leishmaniasis 579
lesbian travellers, *see* LGBTIQ travellers
LGBTIQ travellers 565-6
Egypt 132
Iran 186
Israel & the Palestinian Territories 278
Jordan 348
Lebanon 402
Turkey 489

Lions' Gate (IPT) 203, 207
literature 546-9, *see also* books
Lone Pine (T) 441
Luxor (E) 15, 86-100, **88-9**, **94-5**, **15**, **92-3**
accommodation 96-7
activities 95-6
drinking & nightlife 98-9
food 97-8
history 86-7
medical services 99
safe travel 99
shopping 99
sights 87-94
tourist offices 99
tours 95-6
travel to/from 99-100
travel within 100

Lycian Way (T) 460

M

Machaerus (J) 316-17
Madaba (J) 313-16
Majdal Shams (IPT) 248-9
malaria 579
markets 23-4
Bazar-e Bozorg (In) 158-9
Carmel Market (IPT) 221

markets *continued*
- Grand Bazaar İstanbul (T) 417
- Grand Bazaar Tehran, (In) 137
- Jaffa Flea Market (IPT) 225
- Kemeraltı Market (T) 444-5
- Khan Al Khalili (E) 57, 60
- Mahane Yehuda Market (IPT) 215
- Spice Bazaar (T) 420-1
- Souq Al Abiad (IPT) 236
- Souq Al Qattanin (IPT) 203
- Tabriz Bazaar (In) 18, 149, **18**
- Trabzon (T) 481

Marmaris (T) 456-7
Marsa Alam (E) 116-17
Masada (IPT) 250-1
Mashhad (In) 178-81, **179**
Masjed-e Jameh (In) 158, 165
Masjed-e Nasir Al Molk (In) 170
Masjed-e Shah (In) 158
medical services 578
Mediterranean Coast
- Egypt 16, 80-6, **16**
- Israel & the Palestinian Territories 221-37
- Turkey 458-69

Memphis (E) 77-80
Mesr (In) 163
Meybod (In) 165
Middle East Respiratory Syndrome (MERS) 579
Miletus (T) 452
Mitzpe Ramon (IPT) 251-2
Mleeta Resistance Tourist Landmark (L) 384
Mo'allem Kalayeh (In) 155
mobile phones 569
monasteries
- Ethiopian Monastery (IPT) 203
- Mar Saba Monastery (IPT) 262
- Monastery of the Qurantul (IPT) 259
- Qadisha Valley (L) 381
- St George's Monastery (IPT) 259
- St Katherine's Monastery (E) 16, 125, **126-7**, **16**, **126-7**
- Sumela Monastery (T) 480-1

money 20, 566-7, *see also individual countries*
Moses 316
mosques 23
- Al Aqsa Mosque (IPT) 208
- Al Azhar Mosque (E) 60
- architecture 533-4
- Aya Sofya (Istanbul; T) 416
- Aya Sofya Mosque & Museum (Trabzon; T) 481
- Blue Mosque (T) 416
- Ibrahimi Mosque/Tomb of the Patriarchs (IPT) 266
- Masjed-e Jameh (In) 158, 165
- Masjed-e Shah (In) 158
- Masjid Jenin Al Kabir (IPT) 265
- Mosque-Madrassa of Sultan Hassan (E) 60
- Rüstem Paşa Mosque (T) 422
- Süleymaniye Mosque (T) 417, 420, **15**
- Ulu Cami (T) 482
- Yeşil Camii (T) 442

Mount of Olives (IPT) 208
Mount of Remembrance (IPT) 215
Mount of Temptation (IPT) 259
mountain biking 43
mountains 552
Mt Ararat (T) 485-6
Mt Gerizim (IPT) 265
Mt Nebo (J) 316, **32**
Mt Sinai (E) 16, 125
Mujib Biosphere Reserve (J) 310
Mukawir (J) 316-17
Muradiye Complex (T) 442
museums & galleries 22
- Alexandria National Museum (E) 81
- Animalia (E) 101
- Antalya Museum (T) 465
- Aya Sofya (Istanbul; T) 416, 418-19, **418-19**, **418-19**
- Aya Sofya Mosque & Museum (Trabzon; T) 481
- Beit Hatfutsot (IPT) 225
- Bergama Archaeology Museum (T) 444
- Bible Lands Museum (IPT) 215
- Bibliotheca Alexandrina (E) 80
- Carpet Museum (T) 417
- Carter's House & the Replica Tomb of Tutankhamun (E) 91
- Clandestine Immigration & Naval Museum (IPT) 232-3
- Darat Al Funun (J) 289
- Egyptian Museum (E) 53, 56, 57, **56**
- Ephesus Museum (T) 446
- Eretz Israel Museum (IPT) 225-6
- Fethiye Museum (T) 458
- Golan Archaeological Museum (IPT) 248
- Golden Mummies Museum (E) 110
- Göreme Open-Air Museum (T) 476
- Haganah Museum (IPT) 221
- Hecht Museum (IPT) 231-2
- Hierapolis (T) 452
- Holocaust History Museum (IPT) 215
- Israel Museum (IPT) 215
- İstanbul Archaeology Museums (T) 417
- İstanbul Modern (T) 422
- İzmir Museum of History & Art (T) 445
- Jordan Museum (J) 291
- Luxor Museum (E) 87
- Manial Palace (E) 57
- Mevlâna Museum (T) 473
- Mit Rahina (E) 77, 80
- Museum of Anatolian Civilisations (T) 469
- Museum of Innocence (T) 422
- Museum of Islamic Art (E) 60
- Museum of Palestinian Heritage (IPT) 262
- Museum of Seljuk Civilisation (T) 479-80
- Museum of Turkish & Islamic Arts (T) 416-17
- Museum of Underwater Archaeology (T) 453
- Museum on the Seam (IPT) 209, 213
- Nubia Museum (E) 101
- Palestinian Heritage Museum (IPT) 209
- Pera Museum (T) 422
- Rockefeller Museum (IPT) 209
- Sa'd Abad Museum Complex (In) 140-1
- Tel Aviv Museum of Art (IPT) 221
- Tile Museum (T) 473
- Treasury of National Jewels (In) 137-40
- Yad Vashem (IPT) 215
- Yakutiye Medresesi (T) 482
- Yasser Arafat Museum (IPT) 256
- Yitzhak Rabin Centre (IPT) 226
- Zelve Open-Air Museum (T) 478

music 549-51

N

Nablus (IPT) 264-5
Na'in (In) 163
Naqsh-e Rajab (In) 177
Naqsh-e Rostam (In) 177
national parks & nature reserves 555
- Ajloun Forest Reserve (J) 305
- Azraq Wetland Reserve (J) 311
- Banias Nature Reserve (IPT) 246
- Caesarea National Park (IPT) 231
- Dana Biosphere Reserve (J) 318-20
- Ein Gedi Nature Reserve (IPT) 249
- En Avdat National Park (IPT) 252
- Hamat Tveriya National Park (IPT) 240
- Hula Nature Reserve (IPT) 246
- Makhtesh Ramon Nature Reserve (IPT) 252
- Ras Mohammed National Park (E) 117
- Shouf Biosphere Reserve (L) 388
- Shaumari Wildlife Reserve (J) 311
- Tel Dan Nature Reserve (IPT) 246
- Travertines (T) 452

Map Pages **000**
Photo Pages **000**

Nazareth (IPT) 238-40
Negev, the (IPT) 251-6
Nevruz (No Ruz) 27
Nile (E) 12, 65, 98, **13**
Nile Valley (E) 86-107
nomads, Iran 162
Nuweiba (E) 125, 128

O
oases 23
Olympos (T) 463
opening hours 567-8
Ordu (T) 481
oryx 22, 553
Ottoman Empire 505-9

P
palaces, *see also* castles & fortresses
  Beiteddine Palace (L) 387-8
  Caesarea (IPT) 231
  Dolmabahçe Palace (T) 422-3
  Golestan Palace (In) 137
  Herodium (IPT) 262
  Hisham's Palace (IPT) 259
  İshak Paşa Palace (T) 486
  Topkapı Palace (T) 417, 424-5, **424-5**, **424-5**
Pamukkale (T) 452-3
paragliding 458
Park HaYarkon (IPT) 226-7
parks, *see individual parks*
Paşabağı (T) 478
Pasargadae (In) 177-8
Passover 28
passports 571
  Israeli stamps 39
Patara (T) 460-1, **45**
Pergamum, *see* Bergama
Perge (T) 466
Persepolis (In) 14, 175-7, **176**, **14**
Petra (J) 11, 320-33, **324-5**, **10-11**, **322-3**
  accommodation 327-30
  activities 326
  ATMs 331
  courses 326-7
  drinking 330
  food 330
  itineraries 330
  money 331
  safe travel 331
  shopping 330
  sights 321-6
  tickets 321
  tourist offices 331
  tours 327, 331
  travel to/from 331-2
  travel within 332-3
Philae (E) 106
Phoenician Empire 498
photography 568
planning, *see also individual countries*
  activities 42-6
  border crossings 40-1
  calendar of events 27-30
  children, travel with 47-8
  countries 49-50
  health 577
  internet resources 21
  itineraries 31-7, **31-7**
  Middle East basics 20-1
  repeat visitors 22
  travel seasons 20, 27-30
  visas 38-40
poetry 546-8
poliomyelitis 579
politics 494-5
pollution 556
population 494-5
postal services 568
Priene (T) 452
public holidays 568
  Egypt 133
  Israel & the Palestinian Territories 279
  Jordan 350
  Lebanon 403
  Turkey 490
Pyramids of Giza (E) 11, 60-4, **62-3**, **64**, **11**, **62-3**

Q
Qadisha Valley (L) 380-2
qanats 170
Qazvin (In) 153-4
Qumran (IPT) 249
Quran, the 527

R
rabies 579
Rabin Square (IPT) 221
rafting 247
Ramadan 28, 542
Ramallah (IPT) 19, 256-9, **19**
Ras Mohammed National Park (E) 117
Red Sea (IPT) 252-6
Red Sea Coast (E) 17, 113-17, **17**
refugees 395, 398
religion 495, 526-30
  etiquette 558-9
religious sites 25, *see also individual sites*, churches & cathedrals, mosques, synagogues
Rift Valley Fever 579
rivers 552-3
Room of the Last Supper (IPT) 204-5
Rosh Hashanah 30
ruins, *see also* archaeological sites, tombs
  Agora (T) 445
  Ani (T) 485
  Asklepion (T) 444
  Aspendos (T) 466
  Ephesus (T) 449-51, **450**
  Kayaköy (Levissi) Abandoned Village (T) 458
  Mausoleum (T) 453
  Monastery of Al Kashef (E) 108
  Olympos (T) 463
  Perge (T) 466
  Persepolis (In) 14, 175-7, **176**, **14**
  Tel Al Sultan (IPT) 259
  Temple of Artemis (T) 447
  Temple of Bacchus (L) 391
  Temples of Apollo & Athena (T) 467-8
  Tyre (L) 19, 385, **386**, **19**, **36**
  Umm Al Jimal Ruins (J) 313

S
Sa'd Abad Museum Complex (In) 140-1
safaris, see desert safaris
safe travel 560-1
  car & motorcycle travel 575
  Egypt 133, 561
  Iran 185, 561
  Iraq 190, 193, 561
  Israel & the Palestinian Territories 277, 279, 561
  Jordan 350, 561
  Lebanon 383, 390, 401-2, 561
  Syria 405, 561
  Turkey 490, 561
  women travellers 87, 562-3
Safranbolu (T) 472-3
Saida (L) 22, 382-4
sailing, *see* boat trips
Saladin 505
Samaritans 265
Saqqara (E) 77
schistosomiasis 579
Sea of Galilee (IPT) 242-3, **239**
Selçuk (T) 446-9, **448**
Shabbat 283, 542
Sharm El Sheikh (E) 117-21
Shaumari Wildlife Reserve (J) 311
Shepherds' Field (IPT) 261
Shiite Muslims 526-7
Shiraz (In) 170-5, **172-3**
Shobak (J) 320
shopping, *see individual locations*
  language 583, 585, 586, 588
Side (T) 467-8
Sidon (L) 382-4
Sinai (E) 117-29, **118-19**
sinkholes 555
Sinop (T) 481
Siwa Oasis (E) 111-13
Six Day War 517
skiing 46, 144, 382
snake bites 580
snorkelling, *see* diving & snorkelling
souqs, *see* markets
Sour (L) 385-7, **386**
South Sinai (E) 117-29
spas 249-50, 309
Sphinx (E) 61
sports, *see individual sports*, water sports
springs
  Ain Gomma (E) 110
  Cleopatra's Spring (E) 112
St Katherine Protectorate (E) 125
St Katherine's Monastery (E) 16, 125, **126-7**, **16**, **126-7**
Sunni Muslims 526-7
Syria 50, 405-12, **407**
synagogues
  architecture 534
  Ashkenazi Ari Synagogue (IPT) 244

synagogues *continued*
- Beit Alpha Synagogue (IPT) 243
- Caro Synagogue (IPT) 244

T

Taba (E) 128
Tabriz (In) 149-53, **150**
Tabriz Bazaar (In) 149
Tafila (J) 318
taxis 575-6
- Egypt 135
- Iran 189
- Israel & the Palestinian Territories 284
- Jordan 353
- Lebanon 404

Taybeh (IPT) 257
tea 540
Tehran (In) 137-49, **140**, **142-3**, **146-7**
- accommodation 141-4
- courses 141
- drinking 145
- food 144-5
- information 146-8
- orientation 146
- shopping 145
- sights 137-41, 145
- tours 141
- travel to/from 148
- travel within 148-9

Tel Aviv-Jaffa (Yafo; IPT) 17, 22, 221-31, **222-3**, **226**, **228**, **17**
- accommodation 227
- activities 226-7
- drinking & nightlife 228-9
- entertainment 229
- food 227-8
- medical services 230
- shopping 229-30
- sights 221-6
- tourist offices 230
- travel to/from 230
- travel within 230-1

telephone services 568-9
Temple Mount (IPT) 208, **210-11**, **210-11**
temples, *see also* archaeological sites, ruins
- Chak Chak (In) 165
- Colossi of Memnon (E) 90
- Deir Al Haggar (E) 108-9
- Karnak (E) 87
- Luxor Temple (E) 87
- Medinat Habu (E) 91
- Memorial Temple of Hatshepsut (E) 91
- Ramesseum (E) 91
- Temple of Horus (E) 101
- Temple of Isis (E) 106
- Temple of Khnum (E) 100-1
- Temple of the Oracle (E) 112
- Temples of Abu Simbel (E) 106-7

textiles 157
Tiberias (IPT) 240-2, **241**
time 569
tipping 567
toilets 569
tombs, *see also* archaeological sites, ruins
- King David's Tomb (IPT) 205-6
- Qarat Al Muzawwaqa (E) 109
- Shrine of the Báb (IPT) 231
- Tomb of Amyntas (T) 458
- Tomb of Rabbi Meir Ba'al Hanes (IPT) 240
- Tomb of the Virgin Mary (IPT) 209
- Tombs of the Nobles (E) 91, 102-3
- Valley of the Kings (E) 90-1
- Valley of the Queens (E) 91, 94

Topkapı Palace (T) 417, 424-5, **424-5**, **424-5**
Torah, the 529
Toudeshk (In) 163
tourist information 569, *see also individual locations*
tours 572
Trablous (L) 377-80
Trabzon (T) 480-1
train travel 576
- Egypt 135
- Iran 188, 189
- Israel & the Palestinian Territories 284
- Turkey 492

travel to/from the Middle East 571-2, *see also individual locations*
travel within the Middle East 572-6, *see also individual locations*
Treasury of National Jewels (In) 137-40
Tripoli (L) 377-80
Troy 440
Tsfat (Safed; IPT) 244-7
tuberculosis 579
Turkey 50, 413-92, 495
- accommodation 413, 488-9
- border crossings 41, 491
- climate 413
- electricity 488
- embassies & consulates 489
- exchange rates 417
- food 413, 488, 490
- highlights 414-15, **414-15**
- history 486-7
- internet resources 417
- money 489-90
- opening hours 490
- politics 486
- population 487, 522-3
- religion 488
- safe travel 490
- telephone services 490
- time 491
- travel to/from 491
- travel within 491-2
- visas 40, 491

Turkish language 587-8
typhoid 580
Tyre (L) 19, 385-7, **386**, **19**, **36**

U

Umm Qais (J) 22
Underwater Observatory Marine Park (IPT) 253
Ünye (T) 481
Ürgüp (T) 478-9

V

vacations 568
vaccinations 578
Valley of the Kings (E) 90-1
vegetarian & vegan travellers 540
Via Dolorosa (IPT) 203
visas 38-40
- Egypt 38-9, 134
- Iran 39
- Israel & the Palestinian Territories 39, 280-1
- Jordan 39
- Lebanon 40
- Turkey 40, 491

volunteering 569

W

Wadi Jadid (J) 315
Wadi Mujib (J) 317
Wadi Musa (J) 327-33, **328**
Wadi Rum (J) 13, 333-7, **13**
Walled Off Hotel (IPT) 263
water, drinking 580
water sports 46, *see also individual sports*
weather 20, 27-30, *see also individual locations*
West Bank (IPT) 256-66
West Bank checkpoints (IPT) 258
Western Wall (IPT) 206
Western Wall Tunnels (IPT) 206-7
whirling dervishes 443, 473
White Desert (E) 110
wildlife 26, 311, 553-5
women travellers 187, 562-3
- health 581

work 569-70

Y

Yad Vashem (IPT) 215
Yazd (In) 19, 164-70, **166**, **19**
yellow fever 580
Yom Kippur 30

Z

Zion Gate (IPT) 207
Zionism 512
Zoroastrianism 168

Map Pages **000**
Photo Pages **000**

Map Legend

Sights

- Beach
- Bird Sanctuary
- Buddhist
- Castle/Palace
- Christian
- Confucian
- Hindu
- Islamic
- Jain
- Jewish
- Monument
- Museum/Gallery/Historic Building
- Ruin
- Shinto
- Sikh
- Taoist
- Winery/Vineyard
- Zoo/Wildlife Sanctuary
- Other Sight

Activities, Courses & Tours

- Bodysurfing
- Diving
- Canoeing/Kayaking
- Course/Tour
- Sento Hot Baths/Onsen
- Skiing
- Snorkelling
- Surfing
- Swimming/Pool
- Walking
- Windsurfing
- Other Activity

Sleeping

- Sleeping
- Camping
- Hut/Shelter

Eating

- Eating

Drinking & Nightlife

- Drinking & Nightlife
- Cafe

Entertainment

- Entertainment

Shopping

- Shopping

Information

- Bank
- Embassy/Consulate
- Hospital/Medical
- Internet
- Police
- Post Office
- Telephone
- Toilet
- Tourist Information
- Other Information

Geographic

- Beach
- Gate
- Hut/Shelter
- Lighthouse
- Lookout
- Mountain/Volcano
- Oasis
- Park
- Pass
- Picnic Area
- Waterfall

Population

- Capital (National)
- Capital (State/Province)
- City/Large Town
- Town/Village

Transport

- Airport
- Border crossing
- Bus
- Cable car/Funicular
- Cycling
- Ferry
- Metro station
- Monorail
- Parking
- Petrol station
- Subway station
- Taxi
- Train station/Railway
- Tram
- Underground station
- Other Transport

Routes

- Tollway
- Freeway
- Primary
- Secondary
- Tertiary
- Lane
- Unsealed road
- Road under construction
- Plaza/Mall
- Steps
- Tunnel
- Pedestrian overpass
- Walking Tour
- Walking Tour detour
- Path/Walking Trail

Boundaries

- International
- State/Province
- Disputed
- Regional/Suburb
- Marine Park
- Cliff
- Wall

Hydrography

- River, Creek
- Intermittent River
- Canal
- Water
- Dry/Salt/Intermittent Lake
- Reef

Areas

- Airport/Runway
- Beach/Desert
- Cemetery (Christian)
- Cemetery (Other)
- Glacier
- Mudflat
- Park/Forest
- Sight (Building)
- Sportsground
- Swamp/Mangrove

Note: Not all symbols displayed above appear on the maps in this book

Dan Savery Raz

Israel & the Palestinian Territories Dan Savery Raz is a journalist and editor from Essex, England. Since 2008, Dan has lived in Tel Aviv with his wife and has co-authored various editions of *Israel & the Palestinian Territories*. He has contributed to numerous Lonely Planet books including *Best in Travel, Happy, Street Food, Global Beer Tour* and *Great Escapes*, and written for BBC.com, *BBC History Magazine, HaAretz, Time Out, EasyJet Traveller* and *The Jerusalem Report*. Back in the UK, Dan was Deputy Editor for *Flybe* magazine and Senior Staff Writer for *A Place in the Sun* in association with Channel 4. For more, see www.danscribe.com.

Andy Symington

Lebanon Andy has written or worked on over 100 books and other updates for Lonely Planet (mostly in Europe and Latin America) and other publishing companies, and has published articles on numerous subjects for a variety of newspapers, magazines and websites. He part-owns and operates a rock bar, has written a novel and is currently working on several fiction and non-fiction projects. Andy, from Australia, moved to Northern Spain many years ago. When he's not off with a backpack in some far-flung corner of the world, he can probably be found watching the tragically poor local football side or tasting local wines after a long walk in the nearby mountains.

Jenny Walker

Iran, Jordan Despite having travelled to over 120 countries, from Mexico to Mongolia and Latvia to Lesotho, Jenny's main interest is in the Middle East, where she has been Associate Dean (PD) of Caledonian College of Engineering in Muscat for the past eight years. Her first involvement with the region was as a student, collecting bugs for her father's book on entomology in Saudi Arabia. She went on to write a dissertation on Doughty and Lawrence (Stirling University), an MPhil thesis on the Arabic Orient in British Literature (Oxford University), and she is currently writing a PhD on the Arabian desert as trope (Nottingham Trent University) in contemporary British literature. Jenny has written extensively on the Middle East for Lonely Planet for more than a decade.

Steve Waters

Iran Travel and adventure have always been a part of Steve's life, and he couldn't imagine a world without them. Steve has been using Lonely Planet guidebooks for more than 30 years in places as diverse as Iran, Central Asia, Kamchatka, Tuva, the Himalaya, Canada, Patagonia, the Australian Outback, Northeast Asia, Myanmar and the Sahara. Little wonder then that he finally got a gig with the company! Steve has contributed to *Iran, Indonesia* and the past four editions of *Western Australia*, and come any September you're likely to find him in a remote gorge somewhere in the Kimberley.

Anita Isalska

Israel & the Palestinian Territories Anita is a travel journalist, editor and copywriter whose work for Lonely Planet has taken her from Greek beach towns to Malaysian jungles, and plenty of places in between. After several merry years as an inhouse editor and writer – with a few of them in Lonely Planet's London office – Anita now works freelance between the UK, Australia and any Balkan guesthouse with a good wi-fi connection. Anita writes about travel, food and culture for a host of websites and magazines. Read her stuff on www.anitaisalska.com.

Jessica Lee

Egypt, Turkey In 2011 Jessica swapped a career as an adventure-tour leader for travel writing and since then her travels for Lonely Planet have taken her across Africa, the Middle East and Asia. She has lived in the Middle East since 2007. Jess has contributed to Lonely Planet's *Egypt*, *Turkey*, *Cyprus*, *Morocco*, *Marrakesh*, *Middle East*, *Europe*, *Africa*, *Cambodia* and *Vietnam* guidebooks and her travel writing has appeared in *Wanderlust* magazine, the *Daily Telegraph*, the *Independent*, *BBC Travel* and lonelyplanet.com. She tweets @jessofarabia.

Virginia Maxwell

Turkey Although based in Australia, Virginia spends at least half of her year updating Lonely Planet destination coverage across the globe. Though the Mediterranean is her major area of interest – she has covered Spain, Italy, Turkey, Syria, Lebanon, Israel, Egypt and Morocco for Lonely Planet guidebooks – Virginia also covers Finland, Armenia, the United States and Australia for Lonely Planet products. Follow her @maxwellvirginia on Instagram and Twitter.

Simon Richmond

Iran Journalist and photographer Simon has specialised as a travel writer since the early 1990s and first worked for Lonely Planet in 1999 on the *Central Asia* guide. He's long since stopped counting the number of guidebooks he's researched and written for the company, but covered countries including Australia, China, India, Iran, Japan, Korea, Malaysia, Mongolia, Myanmar, Russia, Singapore, South Africa and Turkey. For Lonely Planet's website, he's penned features on topics from the world's best swimming pools to the joys of urban sketching.

Daniel Robinson

Israel & the Palestinian Territories Brought up near San Francisco and Chicago, Daniel spent part of his childhood in Jerusalem, a bit of his youth at Kibbutz Lotan and many years in Tel Aviv, where he worked on a PhD in late Ottoman history, covered suicide bombings for the Associated Press, and helped lead the local Critical Mass campaign for bike paths. A Lonely Planet author since 1989, he holds a BA in Near Eastern Studies from Princeton and an MA in Jewish History from Tel Aviv University. His favourite activities in Israel include cycling Tel Aviv's historic avenues, hiking the wadis of Ein Gedi, and birdwatching in the Hula and Arava Valleys.

Anthony Sattin

Egypt Anthony has been travelling around the Middle East for several decades and has lived in Cairo, as well as other cities in the region. His highly acclaimed books include *Lifting the Veil*, *A Winter on the Nile* and *The Gates of Africa*. His latest, *Young Lawrence*, looks at the five years TE Lawrence spent in the Middle East leading up to 1914. He happily spends several months each year along the Nile and is still looking for a plot where he can tread mud-bricks and build himself a house. He tweets about Egypt and travel @anthonysattin.

OUR STORY

A beat-up old car, a few dollars in the pocket and a sense of adventure. In 1972 that's all Tony and Maureen Wheeler needed for the trip of a lifetime – across Europe and Asia overland to Australia. It took several months, and at the end – broke but inspired – they sat at their kitchen table writing and stapling together their first travel guide, *Across Asia on the Cheap*. Within a week they'd sold 1500 copies. Lonely Planet was born.

Today, Lonely Planet has offices in Franklin, London, Melbourne, Oakland, Dublin, Beijing and Delhi, with more than 600 staff and writers. We share Tony's belief that 'a great guidebook should do three things: inform, educate and amuse'.

OUR WRITERS

Anthony Ham

Iran, Iraq, Syria Anthony is a freelance writer and photographer who specialises in Spain, East and Southern Africa, the Arctic and the Middle East. When he's not writing for Lonely Planet, Anthony writes about and photographs Spain, Africa and the Middle East for newspapers and magazines in Australia, the UK and US. Anthony also curated the Plan Your Trip, Understand and Survival Guide chapters.

Paul Clammer

Jordan Paul has worked as a molecular biologist, tour leader and travel writer. Since 2003 he has worked as a guidebook author for Lonely Planet, contributing to over 25 LP titles, covering destination swathes of South and Central Asia, West and North Africa and the Caribbean. In recent years, he has lived in Morocco, Jordan, Haiti and Fiji, as well as his native England. Find him online at paulclammer.com or on Twitter as @paulclammer.

Orlando Crowcroft

Israel & the Palestinian Territories Orlando is a senior editor at *Newsweek*, author and former foreign correspondent who first visited the Palestinian Territories in 2012 to cover a football tournament and has reported from Israel, the West Bank and Gaza regularly ever since. He was based in Tel Aviv as a stringer for the *Guardian* in 2014 when he began writing for Lonely Planet. In 2017 he published his first book, *Rock in a Hard Place: Music and Mayhem in the Middle East*. His passions include sampling local fire-water and road trips (ideally not at the same time) and he has never met a dive bar he didn't like.

Mark Elliott

Iran Mark had already lived and worked on five continents when, in the pre-Internet dark ages, he started writing travel guides. He has since authored (or co-authored) around 60 books including dozens for Lonely Planet. He also acts as a travel consultant, occasional tour leader, video presenter, speaker, interviewer and blues harmonicist.

OVER PAGE MORE WRITERS

Published by Lonely Planet Global Limited
CRN 554153
9th edition – Sep 2018
ISBN 978 1 78657 071 0

10 9 8 7 6 5 4 3
Printed in Singapore